GRANT

JEAN EDWARD SMITH

A TOUCHSTONE BOOK
PUBLISHED BY SIMON & SCHUSTER
NEW YORK   LONDON   TORONTO   SYDNEY   SINGAPORE

TOUCHSTONE
Rockefeller Center
1230 Avenue of the Americas
New York, NY 10020

Copyright © 2001 by Jean Edward Smith
All rights reserved,
including the right of reproduction
in whole or in part in any form.
First Touchstone Edition 2002
TOUCHSTONE and colophon are
registered trademarks of Simon & Schuster, Inc.
For information about special discounts for bulk purchases,
please contact Simon & Schuster Special Sales:
1-800-456-6798 or business@simonandschuster.com
Designed by Edith Fowler
Maps by Jeffery L. Ward
Manufactured in the United States of America

10 9 8 7 6 5 4 3 2 1

Library of Congress Cataloging-in-Publication Data
Smith, Jean Edward.
  Grant / Jean Edward Smith.
    p. cm.
Includes bibliographical references and index.
  1. Grant, Ulysses S. (Ulysses Simpson), 1822–1885.
2. Presidents—United States—Biography.   3. Generals—
United States—Biography.   I. Title.
E672.S627 2001
973.8'2'092—dc21
[B]
00-053794
ISBN 0-684-84926-7
      0-684-84927-5 (PBK)
Frontispiece: Grant in 1863. Photograph by James Bishop,
  courtesy of the Chicago Historical Society.

To John and Elizabeth Drinko,
for their long and continued support
of American education

Contents

List of Maps

He was so pervaded by greatness
that he seemed not to be conscious
that he was great.

RICHMOND DISPATCH
July 26, 1885

Preface

WHEN I WAS TEN OR SO, my father took me and several of my cousins to Shiloh battlefield. We toured the site and as young Southern boys are wont to do, speculated enthusiastically how the Confederates could have won if only they had done this or that. My father, who was not an educated man, listened attentively and then in his soft Mississippi drawl cautioned us about what we were saying. It was bad for us to have lost, he admitted, but it would have been worse if we had won. The United States would not exist if the South had prevailed, and we should thank our lucky stars General Grant was in command that terrible Sunday in 1862. Grant never lost a battle, my father said, and he never ran from a fight. He held his surprised and battered army together at Shiloh, and when the smoke cleared it was the rebels who withdrew, leaving Mississippi open to the Union's advance. Grant saved the United States, my father said, and we should be "damn glad" he did. I had scarcely heard of General Grant before then, but from that day on I was hooked.

Ulysses S. Grant is one of the most complex figures in American history. He is an enigma, a paradox, and the challenge for a biographer is to reconcile the extraordinary disparities in his status and reputation. The story of his life combines abject failure and world fame. He demonstrated superb mastery of the world's most powerful army, and was twice elected president with overwhelming majorities. Yet he was incompetent in personal financial matters, excessively generous toward old friends, and overly loyal to those who had served him. He was a withdrawn, seemingly inarticulate man whose writing sparkled with clarity. "Lee's army will be your objective point," he instructed Meade in the spring of 1864. "Wherever Lee goes, there you will go also." No subordinate ever doubted what Grant intended, and no military action ever miscarried for lack of direction.

In the White House, he dominated the country's political scene for eight years, providing the stability that steadied the nation after years of war and upheaval. Yet his presidency has been denounced by most historians, who rank it marginally above those of James Buchanan and Warren G. Harding. After leaving the White House, he failed miserably, suffering a humiliating bankruptcy when a corrupt business partner brought down the investment firm of Grant & Ward in 1884. Dying of cancer, he rose above the pain of approaching death to write the *Memoirs*,[1] which achieved deserved fame as the greatest military autobiography in the English language. Back and forth, he careened from poverty to riches, from triumph to failure, from humiliation to glorification.

History, as a great historian has observed, is not a science, "for every mind and every age regards it from a different angle."[2] There have been many studies of Grant, including 134 biographies (almost as many as on Washington or Lincoln). Each study reflects the attitudes and predilections of the author, and the time it was written. William Hesseltine, an earlier biographer, attributed the denigration of Grant's presidency to the fact that his enemies wrote better than his friends. "Consciously or unconsciously, they stuffed the ballot boxes of history against Grant."[3] Modern historians followed along. Grant did not look like a president any more than he looked like a general. Seedy, careworn, always slightly rumpled and reeking of cigar smoke, he was easy to put down. Those who saw Grant for the first time during the Civil War often made the same mistake. But it was difficult to dismiss Donelson, Vicksburg, and Appomattox. Presidential accomplishment is more ambiguous, and there is always room to disagree about what constitutes political success.

David Herbert Donald, Pulitzer Prize–winning biographer of Lincoln, called Grant the most underrated American in history. Not because of his generalship, but because of his political skill as president. "It is easy to see why Grant is often belittled," wrote Donald. "He was not well educated, was not articulate in arguments, was not flashy, had no connection with the Eastern world of intellect and power." Yet "he was the only president between Abraham Lincoln and Woodrow Wilson to be elected to two consecutive terms of office. His enemies ridiculed him and belittled him, but he survived them all."[4]

It was not just Grant's appearance, or his manner, or the fact that his enemies wrote better than his friends. Grant was condemned because of what he stood for. As president, he fought for black equality long after his countrymen had tired of "the Negro question." He defended the rights of African-Americans in the South with the same tenacity that held the Union line at Shiloh. For Grant, Reconstruction meant a new order, with the freedmen integrated into the social and political fabric of the South. By the late 1870s that view was no longer fashionable. And for almost a hundred years, mainstream historians, unsympathetic to black equality, brutalized Grant's presidency.

Similarly, biographies written by academic historians who stressed the inhumanity of war during the Vietnam era denigrated Grant's role in saving the Union.[5] His victories were attributed to a simple willingness to sacrifice troops in battle. That view, off and on, has permeated Civil War historiography, despite the fact that Grant's casualty ratio was considerably lower than Lee's, and his strategic mastery of the Confederate army was unique among Union generals.[6]

Grant made victory look easy. The clarity of his conception and the simplicity of his execution imparted a new dimension to military strategy. Grant ignored Southern cities, rail junctions, and other strategic points and concentrated on destroying the enemy army. His systematic deployment of overwhelming force not only led to victory in 1865, but established the strategic doctrine that became the basis for American triumphs in two world wars and more recently in the Persian Gulf. Grant's personal contribution demands recognition. Sheridan maintained "he was the steadfast center about and on which everything else turned."[7] Sherman said, "Grant is the greatest soldier of our time if not all time. He fixes in his mind what is the true objective and abandons all minor ones. If his plan goes wrong he is never disconcerted but promptly devises a new one and is sure to win in the end."[8] Longstreet wrote simply, "He eclipsed us all."[9]

It has been customary for biographers to divide Grant's career at Appomattox almost as if he were two different men: the successful military commander and the failed politician. This biography emphasizes the continuity in Grant's life. The common thread is strength of character—an indomitable will that never flagged in the face of adversity. Sherman, who knew him as well as anyone, once remarked that he did not understand Grant and did not believe Grant understood himself. There was something mysterious about him—a deep, primal force that sustained him through defeat and humiliation. Every setback seemed to enhance his inner strength. Grant was not brilliant, his appearance was not striking, his personality did not shine. He was not visited by the flashes of inspiration that animated Stonewall Jackson. He did not have Lee's Olympian presence. His mind lacked the subtleties of Lincoln's thought. Sometimes he blundered badly; often he oversimplified; yet he saw his goals clearly and moved toward them relentlessly. "The art of war is simple enough," he said. "Find out where your enemy is. Get at him as soon as you can. Strike him as hard as you can and as often as you can and keep moving on."[10]

Grant was the most unlikely of heroes: a great captain who disliked the military academy and rejected the peacetime army. "If I could have escaped West Point without bringing myself into disgrace at home, I would have done so. . . . A military life had no charms for me, and I had not the faintest idea of staying in the army even if I should be graduated, which I did not expect." If Grant had his way he would have become "a professor of mathematics in some college," but the Mexican War intervened.[11] Grant loved Mexico and developed an abiding affection for the Mexican people. He thought the American cause unjust and repeatedly condemned war in general as the most destructive and unsavory activity of mankind. After the war Grant served in a succession of frontier postings, grew stale on garrison routine, despaired for his absent wife and children, and took to drinking heavily. He resigned from the army on April 11, 1854. During the next seven years he tried and failed at several occupations — farmer, real estate salesman, rent collector, and businessman. Poverty stared him in the face. In December 1857 he pawned his gold pocket watch to provide his family with presents for Christmas. Later he was reduced to peddling firewood on a St. Louis street corner in a faded army overcoat.

When Beauregard fired on Fort Sumter in 1861, the thirty-eight-year-old Grant was working as a clerk in an Illinois leather goods store run by his two younger brothers. He immediately volunteered but was denied a place in the regular army. Instead, he was commissioned a colonel in the Illinois militia. In July he led his newly formed regiment into northeastern Missouri to attack Confederate forces assembling there. "My sensations as we approached what I supposed might be 'a field of battle' were anything but agreeable. I had been in all the engagements in Mexico that it was possible for one person to be in; but not in command. If someone else had been colonel and I had been lieutenant-colonel I do not think I would have felt any trepidation. . . . As we approached the brow of the hill from which it was expected we would see the enemy . . . my heart kept getting higher and higher until it felt as though it was in my throat. I would have given anything to have been back in Illinois, but I had not the moral courage to halt and consider what to do; I kept right on. When we reached a point from which the valley below was in full view I halted. The place where the Confederates had been encamped was still there but the troops were gone. My heart resumed its place. It occurred to me at once that [Colonel Thomas] Harris had been as much afraid of me as I had been of him. This was a view of the question I had never taken before; but it was one I never forgot afterwards."[12]

Grant was promoted to brigadier general and given command of Union troops on the Mississippi. He moved south, and in February 1862 captured a Confederate army of 15,000 men at Fort Donelson, the first important Union victory of the war. "No terms except complete and unconditional surrender can be accepted," he informed his old friend from West Point, General Simon Bolivar Buckner. The following year Grant cleared the Mississippi of Southern resistance and captured another Confederate army at Vicksburg. Once again the terms were unconditional surrender. In victory, Grant was magnanimous. At both Donelson and Vicksburg, Confederate officers were permitted to retain their side arms and the troops their personal baggage. After Donelson, Buckner told his men that if the fortune of war turned, he hoped they would show Grant's forces the same generosity. Grant described the scene at Vicksburg. "The prisoners were allowed to occupy their old camps behind the entrenchments. No restraint was put upon them except by their own commanders. They were rationed about as our own men, and from our supplies. The men of the two armies fraternized as if they had been fighting for the same cause. When they passed out of the works they had so long and so gallantly defended, between the lines of their late antagonists, not a cheer went up, not a remark was made that would give pain. Really, I believe there was a feeling of sadness just then in the breasts of most of the Union soldiers at seeing the dejection of their late antagonists."[13] Grant hated vindictiveness. He had known humiliation before the war and would not inflict it upon others.

Appomattox was Grant's greatest triumph. For the third and final time he took the surrender of a Confederate army. The scene provided dramatic contrast: Lee, the exemplar of Virginia's slaveholding aristocracy, resplendent in dress uniform, wearing embroidered gauntlets and carrying a burnished sword; Grant, fresh from the field, his boots spattered with mud, wearing the flannel blouse of an army private with no indication of rank save the shoulder straps. The terms were simple. Grant demanded unconditional surrender. Lee acquiesced. As at Vicksburg, the Confederates were paroled and sent home. This time they were allowed to keep their horses. "I said further [to General Lee] I took it that most of the men in the ranks were small farmers. The whole country had been so raided by the two armies that it was doubtful whether they would be able to put in a crop to carry themselves and their families through the next winter without the aid of the horses they were then riding. The United States did not want them and I would, therefore, instruct the officers I left behind to receive the paroles of his troops to let every man in the Confederate army who claimed to own a horse or mule take the animal to his home."[14]

Grant wrote the terms in longhand. Of his own accord he concluded with a sentence that took a massive step toward bringing the nation together. The officers and men who turned in their weapons and returned home were "not to be disturbed by United States authority so long as they observe their paroles and the laws in force where they reside." With those words Grant pardoned the Army of Northern Virginia and undercut the vengeance festering in Union circles to hang the Confederate leaders for treason. In the bitter days of reprisal following Lincoln's assassination it was Grant's word alone that stood between Lee and the gallows.* And if General Lee could not be hanged, no one could be.

In 1868 Grant reluctantly ran for president. It was a tumultuous time. Reconstruction, foreign affairs, the Panic of 1873, and successive waves of corruption engulfed the nation. During Reconstruction, confronted with massive Southern resistance, Grant deployed the army to ensure that the verdict of Appomattox was not frittered away. No other president carried on such a determined struggle, against such hopeless odds, to protect the freedmen in the exercise of their constitutional rights. In foreign affairs, after a wrongheaded attempt to annex Santo Domingo, he avoided war with Spain over Cuba, restored cordial relations with Great Britain (ruptured during the Civil War), and directed the United States onto the world stage. In the West, he halted white efforts to annihilate the Plains Indians and pioneered the peace policy that provided for the eventual assimilation of Native Americans. In Washington, he initiated civil service reform, pressed the investigation against the miscreants in the Whiskey Ring, and broke the efforts of Jay Gould and Jim Fisk to corner the gold market on Black Friday. When financial disaster struck in 1873, he withstood both Wall Street and Congress to veto an inflationary expansion of the nation's money supply: a veto that paved the way for the resumption of specie payment, reestablished a sound currency, and provided the basis for the orderly growth of the American economy.

Grant was less successful dealing with corrupt adventurers who flocked to his administration. " 'No' to him was the most difficult word in the English language," said his longtime friend General Edward Beale.[15] Yet in times of crisis he was superb. When the nation almost came unglued following the Hayes-Tilden election in 1876, Grant's evenhanded mediation of the crisis preserved the peace and paved the way for a successful presidential transition.

Under Grant's leadership the wounds of war eventually began to heal. His funeral in 1885 was a testament to national reconciliation. Major General Winfield Scott Hancock, accompanied by former Confederate generals John B. Gordon and Fitzhugh Lee, led a parade of 60,000 mourners up Broadway to Riverside Park. The *New York Times* reported a record one and a half million spectators lined the route as veterans of the Stonewall

---

* In May 1865 a federal grand jury in Norfolk indicted General Lee for treason. Lee contacted Grant, and Grant took the case immediately to President Johnson. When Johnson insisted Lee be tried, Grant said he would resign. "When can these men be tried?" asked the president. "Never," replied Grant, "unless they violate their paroles." Johnson realized his administration would be helpless without Grant's support, and backed down. On June 20 Attorney General James Speed instructed the United States attorney in Norfolk to drop the proceedings. Grant thereupon wrote Lee, assuring him there would be no prosecution. Grant to Lee, June 20, 1865, 15 *The Papers of Ulysses S. Grant* 210–211, John Y. Simon, ed. (Carbondale: Southern Illinois University Press, 1967).

Brigade marched in somber unison with the Grand Army of the Republic.[16] At Grant's request, the pallbearers included an equal number of Southern and Union generals. Sherman and Sheridan marched alongside Joseph E. Johnston and Simon Bolivar Buckner in a final tribute to their fallen comrade. They were followed by President Cleveland, ex-presidents Hayes and Arthur, and the entire cabinet. Grant's tomb was not complete, but the words from his first election campaign would be emblazoned above the portal facing south: *Let Us Have Peace.*

CHAPTER ONE

THE EARLY YEARS

No man since Washington has better illustrated the genius of American institutions or the temper of Americans as a people.

MONTGOMERY (ALA.) ADVERTIZER
July 25, 1885

ULYSSES GRANT was born at Point Pleasant, Ohio, April 27, 1822. This was the period in American history known as the "Era of Good Feelings." James Monroe was in the White House, political partisanship was on the wane, and the Supreme Court under Chief Justice John Marshall was hammering together the constitutional underpinnings for the expansion of federal power. Slavery loomed as a source of trouble for the Union, but the Missouri Compromise of 1820 papered over the conflict, maintaining, for a while at least, the balance between slave states and free.

It was also a time of national expansion as America's rivals for the continent fell off one by one. Commodore Oliver Hazard Perry had dispatched Great Britain's freshwater fleet to the bottom of Lake Erie and with it all British hopes to control the Northwest Territory. William Henry Harrison broke Indian resistance at Tippecanoe. France had ceded the Louisiana Territory to the United States, opening the vast area west of the Mississippi for settlement. In the Southeast, the United States supplanted Spain in the Floridas, and in the Southwest, a feeble Mexican republic retained a tenuous hold on Texas and California.

Grant's family was part of the nation's westward migration. His paternal ancestor, Matthew Grant, landed in Massachusetts Bay Colony in 1630. Successive generations inched their way across the country—first to the Connecticut River, then to the rocky uplands beyond, eventually to Pennsylvania, Kentucky, and Ohio. Grant represented the eighth generation in this American pilgrimage. His great-grandfather, Captain Noah

Grant, was killed in action during the French and Indian War. His grandfather fought at Bunker Hill.[1] His father, Jesse Root Grant, operated a tannery at Point Pleasant, a village of less than a dozen dwellings on the north bank of the Ohio River, twenty-five miles east of Cincinnati.

Grant's mother, Hannah, came from a family of Scottish Protestants by the name of Simpson. Her grandfather landed in Philadelphia in 1762, established a flourishing farm on the outskirts of the city, and fought with Washington during the Revolutionary War. His son, Hannah's father, sold the homestead in 1817 and moved the family to Ohio where he bought a large farm in the fertile alluvial lands north of the Ohio River, not far from Grant's home in Point Pleasant. Hannah was twenty-two when she and Jesse met; he was twenty-seven. Friends at the time described her as slim, above medium height, handsome but not pretty, serious, steadfast, and supremely reserved. ("I never saw my mother cry," Grant confessed to a friend many years later.[2]) The couple married June 24, 1821, and Grant was born the following year. Those who knew Jesse and Hannah said the general inherited his equable disposition and endurance from his mother. Some claimed he also got his good sense from her.[3]

Grant, a big, strapping baby, weighed ten and three-quarters pounds at birth, and was immediately christened Hiram Ulysses. His father favored Hiram; his maternal grandparents suggested Ulysses. (Mrs. Simpson was enthralled with the prowess of the Grecian hero whose exploits she had followed in Fénelon's epic *Telemachus*). Hannah, a dyed-in-the-wool Democrat,[4] wanted to name the baby Albert Gallatin in honor of Jefferson's able secretary of the treasury, but the rest of the family did not share her partisan devotion. In the end, everyone agreed upon Hiram Ulysses.

One year after Grant's birth, Jesse sold the Point Pleasant tannery and moved the family and his business twenty miles east to Georgetown, Ohio, the seat of Brown County. Georgetown was no larger than Point Pleasant, but from a business standpoint it had several advantages. The town was situated on the White Oak River, a fast-flowing tributary of the Ohio, and was surrounded by towering hardwood forests. Fresh water and tanbark, preferably stripped from oak trees, are essential in the tanning process. By transferring his operations to Georgetown, Jesse insured ready access to both.

The move proved successful and the family remained in Georgetown for the whole of Grant's childhood. In time, Grant was joined by five siblings: three sisters and two brothers. The general wrote that his boyhood was uneventful.[5] Certainly, his schooling was unremarkable. Initially he attended a one-room school in Georgetown. Later he was sent to board for a year in Maysville, Kentucky, and then for a year in Ripley, Ohio. At no time did Grant stand out as a scholar. "I was not studious in habit, and probably did not make progress enough to compensate for the outlay for board and tuition. At all events, both winters were spent in going over the same old arithmetic and repeating: 'A noun is the name of a thing' . . . until I had come to believe it." [6]

While he did not take naturally to school, Grant, from an early age, developed an enduring affinity with horses. As a toddler, he often played beneath the bellies of customers' teams hitched at the tannery gate, sometimes swinging on a horse's tail. Horrified neighbors would rush to warn Hannah, but she never seemed concerned. "Horses seem to understand Ulysses," she would say. [7] By the age of eight Grant was able to handle the wagon team that hauled wood for the tannery. "I could not load it on the wagons . . . but I could drive, and the choppers would load, and some one at the house would unload." At eleven, he was plowing the family's fields. "From that age until seventeen I did all the work with horses. For this I was compensated by the fact that there was never any scolding or punishing by my parents; no objections to rational enjoyments, such as fishing, going to the creek to swim in summer, taking a horse and visiting my grandparents in the adjoining county, fifteen miles off." [8]

In addition to earning him his parents' gratitude, Grant's horsemanship soon became well known in the larger community. Indeed, he became a local celebrity while still in his teens. Farmers brought spirited colts to the Georgetown tannery for him to train, and more often than not an admiring crowd would gather in the village square to watch him work. Grant rarely raised his voice, relying instead on a gentle firmness that won the horse's confidence. As Pulitzer Prize–winning biographer Hamlin Garland wrote, there was something mysterious about Grant's ability to communicate to a horse his wishes. "He could train a horse to trot, rack, or pace, apparently at will." [9]

When Grant turned seventeen his father told him he was sending him to West Point. Several young men from southern Ohio had gone to the military academy, and Jesse Grant was eager to secure a professional education for his son at the government's expense. West Point trained its cadets as civil engineers, one of only two schools in the United States to do so at the time, and as the nation moved westward the demand for engineers grew steadily. For that reason, few of the young men who went to West Point did so with the intention of making the army a career. It was no disgrace to resign from the service to take a better civilian position, and of the 1,058 cadets who had graduated from the academy between its inception in 1802 and 1839, only 395 remained on active duty. Albert Sidney Johnston, Joseph E. Johnston, and Jefferson Davis stayed in the military just long enough to establish professional reputations. Lieutenants George Meade and Jubal Early resigned after completing their one-year obligated tour. Those whose fathers enjoyed political influence often left the army sooner. Leonidas Polk, son of a leading North Carolina banker, quit after five months; Lloyd Tilghman, son of a Maryland congressman, left after two; Henry Clay's son, who finished second in the class of 1831, resigned after four months.[10]

Despite the advantages a West Point education offered, Grant was less than pleased at the prospect and initially said he would not go. But a brief discussion with Jesse resolved the matter. "He said he thought I would, *and I thought so too, if he did.*"[11] Grant's appointment came at the hand of Democratic congressman Thomas Hamer, who at one time had been a close friend of Jesse's. The two had parted company with some bitterness as a result of political differences in the early 1830s. Both men regretted the rupture, and when Jesse swallowed his pride and wrote to Hamer requesting the appointment, the congressman responded with alacrity. "I received your letter and have asked for the appointment of your son, which will doubtless be made. Why didn't you apply to me sooner?"[12] In his haste to send Grant's name to the War Department, Hamer made a slip of the pen. Instead of writing Hiram Ulysses Grant, he wrote "Ulysses S. Grant." Knowing Hannah was a Simpson, Hamer carelessly assumed that to be Grant's middle name.[13] The name Ulysses S. Grant was duly recorded on the roll of incoming cadets, and despite Grant's protests to the contrary, Ulysses S. Grant it remained.[14]

Grant went to the academy without enthusiasm. The one bright spot he saw was the opportunity to travel. "I had been east to Wheeling, and north to the Western Reserve, west to Louisville, and south to Bourbon County, Kentucky, besides having driven or ridden pretty much over the whole country within fifty miles of home. Going to West Point would give me the opportunity of visiting the two great cities of the continent, Philadelphia and New York. This was enough. When those places were visited I would have been glad to have had a steamboat or railroad collision, or any other accident happen, by which I might have received a temporary injury sufficient to make me ineligible . . . to enter the Academy. Nothing of the kind occurred, and I had to face the music."[15]

The military rigmarole of West Point has changed little over the years. The harsh plebe summer, the rigid discipline, the spit and polish, the painstaking attention to detail, meld a corps of cadets conditioned to adversity. "I slept for two months upon one single pair of blankets," Grant wrote to his cousin after plebe summer. "This sounds romantic and you may think it is very easy. But I tell you what coz, it is *tremendous hard.*"[16] Grant adjusted to the rigor of West Point, but had little love for the trappings of army life. "My pants sit as tight to my skin as bark to a tree and if I don't walk *military,* that is if I bend over quickly or run, they are apt to crack with a report as loud as a pistol. When I come home [on furlough] in two years, if I live, the way I shall astonish you *natives* will be *curious*. I hope you won't take me for a Babboon." [17]

In May 1839 the corps of cadets numbered 250 men divided into four classes: most in the fourth (plebe) class, least in the first, attrition taking a heavy toll. Among the first classmen when Grant entered were William Tecumseh Sherman and George H. Thomas. Sherman was the wit of the senior class: iconoclastic, erratic, volatile, a volcano waiting to erupt. Thomas was the opposite. Grave, ponderous, statuesque, nicknamed "George Washington" by his classmates, he already displayed the rocklike qualities that would hold the Union line at Chickamauga.[18] The sarcastic Richard Ewell of Virginia was there along with Ohio's William Rosecrans and Mississippi's fiery renegade, Earl Van Dorn. In the class ahead of Grant were John Pope and James Longstreet. Behind him came Simon Bolivar Buckner of Kentucky and Winfield Scott Hancock of Pennsylvania. When Grant was a senior, the entering class included fifteen-year-old George B. McClellan, considered a prodigy for having attended the University of Pennsylvania for two years. At the opposite end of the academic spectrum was Thomas J. Jackson from the hills of western Virginia, raised initially by his indigent mother, with little schooling, but nevertheless fiercely determined to graduate.

Sharing a common plight, cadets acquired reputations and nicknames that followed them into the service. Rosecrans inevitably became "Rosey"; Longstreet, for reasons long forgotten, was "Pete"; Sherman was "Cump"; and Grant became "Sam." "I remember Grant's first appearance among us," said Sherman. "I was three years ahead of him. I remember seeing his name on the bulletin board, where all the names of the newcomers were posted. I ran my eye down the columns, and there saw 'U.S. Grant.' A lot of us began to make up names to fit the initials. One said, 'United States Grant.' Another 'Uncle Sam Grant.' A third said 'Sam Grant.' That name stuck to him." [19]

It is often suggested that the friendships and acquaintances made at West Point contribute to the effectiveness of the officer corps in time of war: that they enable officers who serve together to know more about each other; to have more, or less, confidence in each other, as the case may be. The benefit is more apparent than real. As a reflective general officer once noted, "Of course you know whether you like them or not. But the later development of some of the members of my own class did not indicate that my judgment was any too accurate. I just don't think you have enough maturity of judgment for that to have much value." [20]

Grant's friends at the academy are a case in point. Everyone assumed that Rosey Rosecrans and Nathaniel Lyon, a born disciplinarian, would go on to brilliant careers.[21] By contrast, Longstreet and Jackson, who stood near the bottom of their respective classes, were not given much of a chance. In fact, Lyon and Rosecrans took early exits, while Longstreet and Jackson became Civil War legends. Curiously, Grant hit it off best with Longstreet.[22] The two made an unlikely pair. Grant, small for his age, with a slight stoop and noticeably unmilitary bearing, the son of an Ohio tanner, was reserved, sensitive, and serious. The hulking Longstreet, one of the largest men to attend the military academy in the nineteenth century, a scion of coastal Georgia's aristocracy, was boisterous, exuberant, and carefree. He enjoyed rough-and-tumble athletics, military exercises, bayonet drill, and swordsmanship—all of which Grant detested. And yet, despite these differences the two men were, in some respects at least, remarkably similar. Longstreet was a natural hell-raiser, and his open disregard for academy regulations held a vicarious appeal for Grant. Longstreet, for his part, considered Grant "fragile" and believed his "delicate frame" kept him out of sports. Grant's distinguishing trait, said Longstreet, "was a girlish modesty; a hesitancy in presenting his own claims; a taciturnity born of his modesty; but a thoroughness in the accomplishment of whatever task was assigned to him. We became fast friends at our first meeting. [He had] a noble, generous heart, a loveable character, and a sense of honor which was so perfect . . . that in the numerous cabals which were often formed his name was never mentioned."[23]

Another cadet remembered that although Grant was a small fellow, he was active and muscular. "His hair was reddish brown and his eyes grey-blue. We all liked him. He had no bad habits. He couldn't, or wouldn't, dance. He had no facility in conversation with the ladies, a total absence of elegance, and naturally showed off badly in contrast with the young Southern men, who prided themselves on being finished in the ways of the world."[24]

Grant had mixed feelings about the course of study at the academy. "I did not take hold of my studies with avidity," he wrote. "In fact, I rarely read over a lesson the second time. I could not sit in my room doing nothing. There is a fine library connected with the Academy from which cadets can get books to read in their quarters. I devoted more time to these than to books relating to the course of studies. Much of the time, I am sorry to say, was devoted to novels. I read all of the works of Bulwer's then published, Cooper's, Marryat's, Scott's, Washington Irving's works, Lever's, and many others that I do not now remember."[25] These contemporary authors offered Grant an escape from the confines of cadet life. Reading novels that were not part of the school curriculum also gave him a way of expressing his skepticism of the routine memorization that masqueraded for learning in many courses, and there is no doubt it sharpened his appreciation for linguistic precision.[26]

In addition to reading fiction, Grant sought relief from military routine in the drawing courses offered by Robert Walter Weir, one of the most gifted teachers ever to grace a college faculty. Weir was a painter of exceptional ability,[27] and his studio was a haven for cadets whose interests went beyond the cut-and-dried requirements of daily recitation. The ostensible purpose of the drawing course was to teach future officers to sketch terrain features. Weir, however, encouraged his charges to express their imagination. Grant was one of a number of cadets who drew well. Another who profited from Weir's tutelage was James McNeill Whistler. "If silicon had been a gas, I would have been a major general,"[28] the artist said later, referring to his dismissal from the academy for failing chemistry.

Nine of Grant's artworks have survived. Four are skillful pen-and-ink drawings of Italian cityscapes rendered with considerable clarity and attention to detail—probably based on lithographs after Samuel Proutt or another recent artist, and presumably intended to teach the principles of perspective. Three are watercolors of European scenes, brave and fluid attempts to deal with the larger effects of light and shade in a demanding medium. Grant did two oil paintings of subjects nearer home: a marvelous, whimsical painting of a draft horse with its nose in a feedbag, and a gentle depiction of an Indian family trading with an itinerant merchant—the latter painting possibly inspired by an artist of the 1830s such as George Catlin or Paul Kane. Grant continued to draw in Mexico, but he made no mention of his artistic bent in his *Memoirs,* and there is no indication that he drew seriously in his later years.

Art courses aside, Grant viewed the academy as a necessary evil. He had no intention of making the army a career. West Point was merely a means to acquire professional standing.[29] When Congress considered abolishing the academy in 1839, Grant supported the move. "I saw this as an honorable way to obtain a discharge, and read the debate with much interest."[30] He learned to tolerate military life, but never embraced it. During his sophomore year he was promoted to cadet corporal, and to sergeant the next. "The promotion was too much for me," he wrote. Demerits proved his undoing, and he was busted back to the ranks. Grant was one of the few first classmen who served out his senior year as a buck private in the corps of cadets.

Academically, Grant finished 21st among the thirty-nine men who made up the graduating class of 1843. His fourth-year marks placed him 16th in engineering, 28th in ethics, 25th in artillery tactics, 28th in infantry tactics, and 17th in geology. In conduct he stood in the bottom half: number 156 in a corps of 233. Only in horsemanship did he excel. To the consternation of his plantation-reared classmates from below the Mason-Dixon line, no cadet could rival Grant's ability in the saddle. During graduation exercises in June 1843, he was the center of attention. When the first classmen completed their mounted drill, the riders formed their horses into a single line down the middle of the riding hall. Sergeant Herschberger, the academy's Prussian-trained riding master, moved to the jumping bar, lifted it higher than his head, fixed it in place, and then, facing the class, called out, "Cadet Grant."

According to a plebe who witnessed the scene, "A clean-faced, slender young fellow, weighing about one hundred and twenty pounds, dashed from the ranks on a powerfully built chestnut-sorrel horse, and galloped down the opposite side of the hall."[31] Grant was on York—a massive animal infamous for his intractability. Only Grant and one other cadet could ride him, and only Grant could ride him well.[32] At the far end of the hall, Grant turned York, and the two came thundering down toward the bar. As the plebe recalled, "The horse increased his pace, and measured his strides for the great leap before him, bounded into the air, and cleared the bar, carrying his rider as if man and beast were welded together. The spectators were breathless."[33] Grant's jump on York set an academy record that held for twenty-five years.[34] Whenever reminded of the feat, Grant would invariably smile and defer to his mount. "York was a wonderful horse. I could feel him gathering under me for the effort as he approached the bar."[35]*

Assignments after West Point were based on class standing. Those at the top of the class were brevetted to the engineers, while the combat arms took the remainder. Grant requested the cavalry, but with only one regiment on active duty there were no vacancies. His second choice, the 4th Infantry at Jefferson Barracks, Missouri, was approved. Before reporting to their initial assignments, the graduates were given three months' leave. Grant returned to Ohio and spent the summer recuperating from a debilitating cough he contracted at West Point. Doctors called it "Tyler's Grip." Painfully thin, Grant weighed 117 pounds, exactly the weight at which he

---

* Grant never outgrew his love for spirited horses. Captain Alfred M. Fuller of the 2nd Cavalry reported seeing Grant in Milan in 1878, during his world tour. Grant was scheduled to review the famous flying Bersaglieri regiment of the Italian army, and some young officers arranged for him to ride a blooded bay horse of immense proportions. "A more restless, wicked appearing animal I have seldom seen," said Captain Fuller. "I was in mortal fear that our general would be speedily thrown and crushed to death by the cruel hoofs. From the sly winks and nudges that passed between these dandyish officers it looked to me very much as if they had assigned to the general a young, untamable horse that had never been ridden. My fears were somewhat removed when I saw General Grant's eyes light up with admiration as he gazed upon the horse." The elderly ex-president mounted the horse with some difficulty, but as soon as he was seated his horsemanship so impressed the crowd they broke into spontaneous applause. "The horse, after a few futile plunges, discovered that he had his master, and started off in a gentle trot. From that time on horse and rider were as one being." "Grant's Horsemanship," 8 *McClure's Magazine* 501 (1897).

had entered the academy although he had grown six inches in the interim.[36] That summer Grant recognized, perhaps for the first time, what the army meant to him. West Point had made more of an impression than he anticipated. When his tailored infantry uniform arrived, he immediately tried it on. "I was impatient to see how it looked, and probably wanted my old school-mates, particularly the girls, to see me in it."[37]

That day Grant learned a lesson he never forgot. Riding into Cincinnati in his new regimentals with his sword dangling at his side, imagining everyone was looking at him with awe and admiration, he was jeered as a no-account tin soldier. "A little urchin, bareheaded, barefooted, with dirty and ragged pants and a shirt that had not seen a wash-tub for weeks, turned to me and cried: 'Soldier! Will you work? No sir-ee; I'll sell my shirt first!' " When he returned home that evening, Grant found a drunken stable attendant parading the streets in a homemade imitation of his uniform, sending the townspeople into gales of laughter. According to Grant, the joke was on him. The two humiliations gave him a permanent distaste for military uniforms. Throughout the remainder of his career he would go to great lengths to avoid wearing full service dress, and never wore a sword unless ordered.[38]

Grant reported to Jefferson Barracks on the last day of September 1843. The post occupied a seventeen-hundred-acre reservation on the banks of the Mississippi ten miles south of St. Louis, and was the largest military cantonment in the country, garrisoned by the 3rd and 4th infantry regiments. It was America's principal bastion on the Western frontier, the prime protector of settlers heading across the Great Plains, and the site of the infantry's School of Practice, a nascent postgraduate institution where junior officers were taught tactics. The commanding officer was Colonel Stephen Watts Kearny, one of the ablest officers in the army.[39] Kearny kept discipline tight, but never harassed the men with unnecessary requirements. "Every drill and roll call had to be attended, but in the intervals officers were permitted to enjoy themselves, leaving the garrison, and going where they pleased . . . so long as they were back for their next duty."[40]

Grant admired Kearny's style of leadership. Like Kearny, he believed in sensible discipline and was contemptuous of commanders who nitpicked excessively. "It did seem to me, in my early army days, that too many of the older officers, when they came to command posts, made it a study to think what orders they could publish to annoy their subordinates and render them uncomfortable. I noticed, however, a few years later, when the Mexican war broke out, that most of this class of officers discovered they were possessed of disabilities which entirely incapacitated them for active field service."[41]

The 4th Infantry numbered twenty-one officers and 449 enlisted men, divided into eight companies. Grant was assigned to I Company, commanded by First Lieutenant Benjamin Alvord, a scholarly Vermonter who had graduated from West Point ten years earlier. James Longstreet and Richard Ewell had joined the regiment the year before; Grant's class-mate Robert Hazlitt reported when Grant did. Grant learned the trade of a company officer at Jefferson Barracks. His salary was $779 a year, which was more than adequate to cover his expenses, yet he looked forward to a teaching career at a private college as soon as he could find a suitable posi-tion. To prepare himself, Grant wrote to the head of the mathematics de-partment at West Point requesting assignment to the academy as an assistant professor. His offer was accepted and Grant was told he would be called back when the next vacancy occurred. That might come within one year, two at the most. "Accordingly, I laid out for myself a course of studies to be pursued in garrison. I reviewed my West Point course of mathemat-ics, and read many valuable historical works, besides an occasional novel."[42]

In addition to company duties and getting ready for his West Point assignment, Grant occupied himself with trips into the Missouri country-side. The family of Fred Dent, his academy roommate, lived only five miles from Jefferson Barracks. Dent had been assigned to Fort Towson, a frontier post on the Red River in Indian Territory,[43] and Grant was urged to accept the family's hospitality in Dent's absence. That autumn Grant rode over to get acquainted. Longstreet, whose mother was related to the Dents, accompanied him.[44]

The Dent estate was known as White Haven—925 acres of lush Mis-souri bottomland on the Gravois road that led southwest from St. Louis toward Springfield and Joplin. The Dents were originally from Maryland and the name White Haven was chosen to commemorate the family's tide-water estate.[45] Colonel Dent was a heavyset man of large frame and irasci-ble temperament. Originally trained as a lawyer and businessman, he became a plantation grandee: supervising his slaves, watching his crops grow, and belligerently defending the Southern way of life to all who would listen. Dent had no previous military experience; the designation "Colonel" went with the lifestyle. Mrs. Dent, who was in her late forties, was small and slender, with sparkling gray eyes and an engaging manner. She was as gentle as her husband was gruff, and together they had eight children, four of whom, two boys and two girls, were still at home.

Grant visited the Dents often that winter, sometimes accompanied by Longstreet, but more frequently going alone. Both men appreciated White Haven as a home away from home, and the Dents, who took their social obligations seriously, enjoyed entertaining the young officers. Soon, however, Longstreet's trips to the estate became less frequent as he found himself drawn to the daughter of his commanding officer.[46] Grant, on the other hand, struck up a lively rapport with the Dent family. He and Colonel Dent enjoyed talking politics, and Mrs. Dent's initial liking for her son's roommate ripened into admiration. As one of the Dents' younger daughters noted, "I think the rare common sense he displayed, his quiet, even tones, free from gestures and without affectation, especially attracted her. On many occasions after he had ridden away, I've heard her say, 'That young man will be heard from some day. He has a good deal in him. He'll make his mark.' "[47]

In February, White Haven became even more attractive to Grant. Instead of going for dinner once or twice a week he visited four and five times. Julia, the Dents' oldest, fairest daughter, had returned from spending the season in St. Louis. Seventeen, almost eighteen, she had recently completed studies at Miss Mauro's fashionable finishing school,[48] and her first season in St. Louis society had been a decided success. Already it was rumored she had had several affairs of the heart.[49] To observers Julia appeared well-informed for her age, intelligent, striking if not beautiful, and marvelously self-assured. Neither tall nor short, with long brown hair and expressive brown eyes, she had a rosy, outdoor complexion and a firm, athletic figure.

Grant quickly became Julia's regular escort. Once, when he was on duty, she attended a ball at the post without him. "Where is that small man with the large epaulets?" Lieutenant Charles Hoskins, adjutant of the 4th Infantry, jokingly asked her.[50] Julia found Grant's sense of humor attractive. When her pet canary died, Grant made a miniature coffin for the bird, painted it yellow, and presided at a mock funeral attended by eight fellow officers in solemn dress.[51] As the weather improved that spring, she and Grant rode daily along the woodland roads near White Haven. Julia was a talented rider and, like Grant, a good judge of horseflesh. Her mount, Psyche, was part Arabian and one of the few horses that could keep up with her escort's spirited animal. "Such rides!" Julia wrote later.[52]

At the end of April, Grant received leave to visit his parents. Before departing he went to see Julia and spent the day with her. "As we sat on the piazza alone, he took his class ring from his finger and asked me if I would not wear it?" Julia declined. Her mother, she said, would not approve of her accepting a gift from a gentleman. Grant seemed put out by her reply and left shortly afterward, lingering just long enough to ask if she would miss him. "I, child that I was, never for a moment thought of him as a lover. But, Oh! How lonely I was without him."[53]

Four days after Grant departed for Ohio, the 4th Infantry was ordered to the field. It was to occupy a position in Louisiana near the Texas border. Texas had declared its independence from Mexico and following

Sam Houston's resounding victory on the San Jacinto, the Lone Star Republic had become a reality. Annexation, which had long loomed on the horizon, appeared imminent, and the United States was flexing its muscle. The ostensible reason for sending the army to Louisiana was to prevent filibustering by American adventurers. The real purpose was to menace Mexico and deter any possible Mexican intervention in Texas.

A messenger from the regiment was sent after Grant, but failed to intercept him. Grant did not learn of his unit's deployment until he was back with his parents in Ohio. "A day or two after my arrival I received a letter from a classmate and fellow lieutenant in the 4th [Robert Hazlitt] informing me, and advising me not to open any letter postmarked St. Louis or Jefferson Barracks until the expiration of my leave, and saying that he would pack up my things and take them along for me. His advice was not necessary, for no other letter was sent to me." [54]

Grant observed the terms of his leave and reported back to Jefferson Barracks on May 20. He knew the regiment had departed, and was in no hurry to join it. He was, however, eager to see Julia. "If the 4th Infantry had remained at Jefferson Barracks it is possible, even probable, that life might have continued for some years without my finding out that there was anything serious the matter with me." [55] With the regiment in the field, life had changed and Grant realized he was in love.

The officer on duty in St. Louis when Grant reported back was Lieutenant Richard Ewell, who had been left behind to clear up matters when the regiment departed. Ewell was highly regarded in the regular army for his common sense. Grant explained his desire to go to White Haven and asked that his leave be extended for several days, and Ewell readily agreed. There was nothing of any immediate consequence Grant could do in Louisiana and if he had personal business to attend to, Ewell said he should take care of it. [56]

Grant left for White Haven forthwith. The Gravois Creek was out of its banks and he almost drowned trying to ford it. His uniform was soaked, but he pressed on. Grant had a superstitious aversion to turning back and never retraced his steps. He arrived at White Haven wet and disheveled. Then, in Grant's words, "I mustered up courage to make known, in the most awkward manner imaginable, the discovery I had made on learning that the 4th Infantry had been ordered away from Jefferson Barracks." [57]

Julia's recollection of their meeting is more romantic. "He declared his love and told me that without me life would be insupportable. When he spoke of marriage, I simply told him I thought it would be charming to be engaged, but to be married—no! I would rather be engaged. I do not think he liked this arrangement, but . . . he let the matter rest." [58]

Julia and Grant became secretly engaged. He gave her his ring and she gave him a lock of her hair.[59] Grant and Julia said nothing to her family, and the two spent the remainder of the week taking long rides and walks through the countryside. On May 27, 1844, Brevet Second Lieutenant Grant departed Jefferson Barracks to join his regiment in Louisiana.

CHAPTER TWO

MEXICO

*Poor Mexico! So far from God
and so close to the United States.*

GENERAL PORFIRIO DÍAZ

IN THE 1830S AMERICA'S WESTWARD EXPANSION accelerated. In the Northwest, a seemingly endless column of pioneers snaked its way along the Oregon Trail to the Pacific Coast. Another column spread across the plains of Kansas to the headwaters of the South Platte River and to the Rockies beyond. A third band moved into Mexican territory in the Southwest. Texas, New Mexico (including Arizona), and California appeared ripe for the picking. Explored by the Spanish in the sixteenth century, thinly colonized, with only an occasional mission dotting the countryside, these frontier provinces were attached to the Mexican republic by the weakest of ties.

California was virgin territory. The local Mexican population numbered less than 5,000, and what Americans knew of the region derived largely from literary descriptions provided by Richard Henry Dana's *Two Years Before the Mast* and the tales of other New England seafarers.[1] Santa Fe, the capital and only town in New Mexico, was the end point for an annual caravan of traders from Independence, Missouri. These intrepid merchants, following an ancient Indian trail (soon to be famous as the Santa Fe Trail), returned to the heartland each year with wondrous tales of a land of enchantment. Texas, however, was the principal prize the settlers sought. Seven hundred and fifty miles wide from the Sabine River to El Paso, and of equal distance from north to south, it was larger than France and its natural riches would prove as great.

American settlement of the province commenced in the early 1820s.

The Mexican government initially encouraged emigration from the United States but did not anticipate the size of the response.[2] By 1834, barely a decade after the first arrivals, American colonists outnumbered native Mexicans four to one. Concentrated in the fertile areas of East Texas where the deep soil was ideal for growing cotton, the settlers, mainly from the lower Mississippi valley, introduced slavery (despite Mexico's law to the contrary) and soon became restive under the rule of a Spanish-speaking government. In 1835, when Mexican president Antonio López de Santa Anna introduced a unified national constitution that would have extinguished local autonomy, the American settlers revolted, proclaimed an independent Republic of Texas, legalized slavery, and expelled the local garrison. Santa Anna's effort to reconquer the province ended ignominiously on the banks of the San Jacinto River on April 21, 1836, when Texas cavalry put his army to rout. The Mexican leader was taken prisoner and under duress signed the Treaty of Velasco recognizing Texas's independence. Although the Mexican government subsequently repudiated the treaty, it made no attempt to reassert its authority over the region. Great Britain and France quickly recognized the Lone Star Republic, and on March 3, 1837, the last day of President Andrew Jackson's term, the United States followed suit.

From the beginning most Texans preferred annexation by the United States to independence, but the proposal to add Texas to the Union bogged down in the dispute over slavery. Southern states favored admission; the Northern states resisted. So explosive was the issue that for almost a decade the matter lay fallow. Finally, in the spring of 1844, President John Tyler, a proud, slaveholding Virginian eager to make his mark as president, revived the question. At Tyler's direction, Secretary of State John C. Calhoun began negotiations with Texas president Sam Houston for a treaty of annexation. To make the offer credible, and to ensure that Mexico did not intervene, the United States army was ordered to the Texas border.

Grant was a very junior second lieutenant at the time, yet he followed the events closely. In his *Memoirs* he said most army officers were indifferent to annexation. "For myself, I was bitterly opposed to the measure, and to this day regard the war [that followed] as one of the most unjust ever waged by a stronger against a weaker nation."[3] In Grant's view, the conquest of Mexico was a sordid episode in which the United States was "following the bad example of European monarchies in not considering justice in their desire to acquire additional territory." Throughout his life he believed that the settlement of Texas, its separation from Mexico, and its ultimate annexation were part of a conspiracy to acquire additional slave states for the Union. "Even if the annexation itself could be justified, the manner in which the subsequent war was forced upon Mexico cannot."[4] Grant also believed that the South's attempt to secede from the Union in 1861 was an outgrowth of the Mexican War; that the Southern states were encouraged by the addition of new territory in which slavery was permitted; and that once Texas joined the Union the Civil War became inevitable. "Nations, like individuals, are punished for their transgressions. We got our punishment in the most sanguinary and expensive war of modern times."[5]

Grant was a good soldier. He kept his political views to himself and performed his duty as required. Today the Mexican War is largely forgotten in American history. Yet the percentage of soldiers killed was the highest of any war fought by the United States. Of the 78,718 men who served during the conflict, 13,283 perished: a casualty ratio slightly higher than Union losses in the Civil War, seven times greater than that of World War II, and twenty-four times that of Vietnam.[6]

The 4th Infantry did not go into action immediately. It moved leisurely in a flotilla of steamboats down the Mississippi to its confluence with the Red River, and then up the Red some 150 miles to Natchitoches, the oldest town in Louisiana. Instructed to await further orders, the regiment went into bivouac in the piney woods on a high sandy ridge thirty miles from the Texas border. Grant reported to the regiment on June 3, and by then a rough campsite had been laid out. Called Camp Salubrity by the soldiers, it was home to the 4th Infantry for the next year. "The great elevation of our situation and the fact that one of the best springs of water in the state puts out here are the only recommendations this place has," Grant wrote shortly after arriving. "I have a small tent that the rain runs through as it would through a sieve. The swamps are full of alligators, and the wood full of red bugs and ticks. So much for Camp Salubrity."[7]

With action pending, Grant recognized his appointment to the faculty at West Point was unlikely. He stopped studying mathematics, bought a horse, and, as he had done at Jefferson Barracks, undertook to explore the Louisiana countryside. "I stayed out of doors most of the time, and entirely recovered from the cough which I had carried from West Point. I have often thought that my life was saved, and my health restored, by exercise and exposure, enforced by an administrative act, and a war, both of which I disapproved of."[8]

On June 8, 1844, the Senate defeated the Texas annexation treaty that Secretary of State Calhoun had negotiated, and the prospect of American intervention temporarily subsided. The Tyler administration hunkered down but did not give up the fight. The 4th Infantry, joined by the 3rd Infantry regiment, was designated the "corps of observation" with a mandate to keep a watchful eye on the border. Brevet Brigadier General

Zachary Taylor, "Old Rough and Ready," was dispatched to take command, and throughout the summer the size of the corps was slowly augmented.

America's expansionist appetite had been whetted, and the annexation of Texas figured prominently in the 1844 presidential election. James K. Polk of Tennessee, the dark horse nominee of the Democrats, campaigned on a platform pledging the "Re-annexation of Texas" and the "Re-occupation of Oregon," although Oregon played only a small role in the election. Henry Clay, seeking the presidency for a third time on behalf of his beloved Whigs, supported annexation only if it could be achieved "without war, and with the common consent of the Union," which, given the vehement opposition of anti-slavery forces in the North, effectively meant no annexation. All of this converted the election into a plebiscite on Texas with the outcome too close to call.

As the weeks dragged into months at Camp Salubrity, Grant and his fellow officers sought relief from the boredom of camp life in frequent visits to the homes of the Red River's plantation aristocracy, impromptu athletic events, makeshift horse races, and endless games of brag—an early form of poker especially popular in the army.[9] Grant excelled at racing, but brag did not come naturally to him. It was a game of bluff and he was too guileless to be a good bluffer. "We instructed Grant in the mysteries of brag," said Longstreet, "but he made a poor player. The man who lost seventy-five cents in one day was esteemed a peculiarly unfortunate person," and Grant often lost the limit.[10] Grant's longing for Julia intensified that summer. He wrote frequently, but her replies were few and far between. "Does Mrs. Dent know of the engagement between us?" he asked plaintively at the end of July.[11] When Julia's first letter arrived in August, he was ecstatic. She assured him of her love, and Grant for the umpteenth time pledged his in return. "Find some name beginning with 'S' for me," he pleaded. "You know I have an 'S' in my name and don't know what it stands for."[12]

The presidential election in November was one of the closest on record. Polk received 1,339,494 popular votes to Clay's 1,300,004. It was even closer in the electoral college where the outcome turned on the results from New York—which went to Polk by 5,000 votes, anti-slavery Whigs having deserted Clay to vote for abolitionist James G. Birney.[13] After Polk's victory, the lame-duck Tyler administration resumed its effort to annex the Lone Star Republic. Rather than risk the defeat of another treaty, the president asked that Texas be admitted by a joint resolution of the House and Senate. A joint resolution required only a simple majority, not a two-thirds vote. The House of Representatives, controlled by the Democrats, quickly complied, and on February 27, 1845, the Senate, by a vote of 27–25, agreed to make Texas the twenty-eighth state of the Union.[14] President Tyler signed the measure on March 3, 1845, his last day in office, and immediately dispatched a courier to the Texas capital, Washington-on-the-Brazos, with the news. Mexico promptly broke diplomatic relations with the United States, placed its army on a war footing, and offered to recognize Texas if it would remain independent.

At Camp Salubrity the corps of observation anticipated that action would be forthcoming. But the Texas Congress delayed its response to Tyler's offer, and on April 1 Grant requested leave to return to St. Louis.[15] The Dent family was still unaware of his engagement to Julia, and he planned to seek their permission for marriage. When Grant returned to White Haven and broached the idea, Mrs. Dent and Julia's siblings sided with the young couple immediately. Colonel Dent proved noticeably cool. He did not object to Grant personally, he said, but to the fact Grant was in the army. An officer's family lived a transient life, the pay was low, and promotions in peacetime painfully slow. Julia's younger sister Emmy, who eavesdropped on the conversation between Grant and her father, said Grant replied "with the air of a man not to be put aside by anything in the world," and it was his directness that won her father's consent. "But after all, it was nonsense for father to be pretending that he had anything to say about it. Julia, having once said Yes, had made his decision for him."[16]

Grant returned to Camp Salubrity with his betrothal settled. But marriage had to wait. On June 26, 1845, the Texas Congress, given the choice between recognition as an independent nation by Mexico and annexation by the United States, voted unanimously for statehood. Three days later General Taylor received orders from acting Secretary of War George Bancroft to move into Texas and take up a position "on or near the Rio Grande del Norte" that would be "best adapted to repel invasion."[17] The corps of observation was rechristened the Army of Occupation, reinforcements were dispatched from the northern and western frontiers, a four-gun field battery under Lieutenant Braxton Bragg was added to provide artillery support, and Taylor was given authority to call upon the state governors for additional troops.

Taylor interpreted his orders liberally. Rather than attempt an arduous march overland, he elected to move his infantry by water. And instead of taking up a position on the Rio Grande, he chose a site at the mouth of the Nueces River near the fishing village of Corpus Christi, 200 miles to the north. The arid region between the Nueces and the Rio Grande belonged to the Mexican state of Tamaulipas. It was claimed by Texas but had never been incorporated into the Lone Star Republic. For all practical purposes it was Mexican soil. Taylor decided his force was too small to risk in the disputed area, and he did not want to create a casus belli unnecessarily.[18]

On July 2 the 4th Infantry boarded riverboats at Natchitoches for the trip downstream to New Orleans; the 3rd Infantry followed several days later. From New Orleans the regiments moved in a convoy of sailing ships and steamers, arriving off Nueces Bay in early August. The passage was uneventful, except that Grant almost drowned going ashore. "I thought I had learned enough of the working of the double and single pulley, by which passengers were let down, and determined to let myself down without assistance. Just as I did so someone called out 'hold on.' It was too late. I tried to hold on with all my might, but my heels went up, and my head went down so rapidly that my hold broke, and I plunged head foremost into the water some twenty-five feet below. When I came to the surface again, being a fair swimmer, and not having lost my presence of mind, I swam around until a bucket was lowered for me. I do not believe there was a man on board who sympathized with me in the least when they found me uninjured."[19]

At Corpus Christi, Taylor's force made ready for action. Reinforcements poured in, and by the end of October almost 4,000 men were in camp. This was the bulk of America's military establishment. Taylor now commanded five of the nation's eight infantry regiments, one of the two cavalry regiments, and all of the country's field artillery.[20] Each unit was composed entirely of regulars: tough, disciplined, reliable in a fight, accustomed to hardship and privation. More than half of the enlisted men were foreign-born, 42 percent German or Irish. The company officers were mostly West Pointers: artillerymen like Bragg, George H. Thomas, and Joe Hooker; infantry stalwarts such as Grant, Edmund Kirby Smith, Longstreet, Winfield Scott Hancock, Simon Bolivar Buckner, and Earl Van Dorn; and cavalrymen in the mold of Albert Sidney Johnston and Philip Kearny. Taylor's engineer was Lieutenant George G. Meade, back on active duty after a stint in civil life.[21] Grant said later, "A better army, man for man, probably never faced an enemy than the one commanded by General Taylor."[22]

Taylor was a gifted commander. Recommended to Polk by Andrew Jackson, Old Rough and Ready focused on battlefield results, not garrison routine. Firm and fit at the age of sixty-one, he was a proven veteran of every war and Indian skirmish fought by the United States since 1812. His dislike of military formality was legendary. Instead of a general's uniform he habitually wore blue denim pants, a long linen duster, and a big palmetto hat. "He dressed entirely for comfort," wrote Grant, "rarely wearing anything in the field to indicate his rank, or even that he was an officer."[23] Taylor believed it was important to see things through his own eyes, not those of his staff. He would saunter through his command daily, talking casually about the crops on his Louisiana plantation or the price of cotton.

His easy, disarming manner helped him forge a strong personal bond with his troops. He knew the name of every officer in the Army of Occupation and that of many enlisted men as well. In the field, when reviewing troops or watching maneuvers, he would usually sit sideways in the saddle, both feet dangling on one side, chewing tobacco—looking like a man watching field hands harvesting a crop.

Grant admired Taylor's style. "General Taylor was not an officer to trouble the administration much with his demands, but was inclined to do the best he could with the means given him. If he had thought that he was sent to perform an impossibility, he would probably have informed the authorities and left them to determine what should be done. If the judgment was against him he would have gone on and done the best he could . . . without parading his grievance before the public."[24] Grant also appreciated the general's lean way with words. "He knew how to express what he wanted to say in the fewest well-chosen words, and would not sacrifice meaning to the construction of high-sounding sentences."[25] Above all, Grant respected Taylor's sangfroid. "No soldier could face either danger or responsibility more calmly than he. These qualities are more rarely found than genius or physical courage."[26]

Veterans of the Mexican War who served with Grant in the Civil War recognized that Taylor was his role model. In the spring of 1864, General George G. Meade, who had not seen Grant for almost twenty years, was struck by the parallel. "He puts me in the mind of old Taylor," Meade told his wife, "and sometimes I fancy he models himself on old Zack."[27] Taylor, for his part, seemed to recognize his own good qualities in the young Grant. One day at Corpus Christi Taylor rode down to the beach and saw Grant trying to get his detail of men to clear some underwater obstacles. Failing to make himself understood, he jumped into the water, which was up to his waist, to work with his men. From the bank "some dandy officers," as Taylor called them, made fun of Grant, whereupon Old Zack intervened. "I wish I had more officers like Grant who would stand ready to set a personal example when needed."[28] Shortly thereafter Grant was promoted from temporary second lieutenant to full second lieutenant in the regular army.[29]

Taylor trained the Army of Occupation relentlessly, and throughout the summer the army's morale remained high. Many of the officers knew one another, either from prior service or from West Point, and a family atmosphere developed quickly. Lieutenant Edmund Kirby Smith, commanding a company in the 5th Infantry, described arriving in camp and being greeted "by cordial welcomes from the well-known voices of old companions, whom I had not met for many years."[30] Lieutenant Meade told his wife he met nearly two thirds of the officers in the American army, "and you would be surprised how many highly educated and refined gentlemen there are among them. I do not believe any army in the world can compare with them in this respect, and I have been most gratified to find such a high-toned gentlemanly feeling, so much intelligence and refinement, among a body of men the larger proportion of whom have been in the western wilds for years."[31]

Grant filled his off-duty hours exploring the countryside and was astonished by the widespread use of tobacco among Mexicans in the region. "Almost every Mexican above the age of ten, and many much younger, smoked the cigarette. Nearly every Mexican carried a pouch of leaf tobacco, powdered by rolling in the hands, and a roll of corn husks to make the wrappers." The Mexican government maintained a tight hold on the sale of tobacco, and in Grant's view that helped to explain the popularity of smoking. "I know from my own experience at West Point, the fact that tobacco was prohibited, and the mere possession of the weed severely punished, made the majority of cadets, myself included, try to acquire the habit of using it."[32]

Sometimes Grant rode escort with supply wagons bound for outlying detachments in San Antonio and Austin. On one such occasion he and his friend, Lieutenant Calvin Benjamin of the 4th Artillery, heard the howling of wolves nearby. "To my ear it appeared that there must have been enough of them to devour our party, horses and all, in a single meal." Benjamin, wise to the ways of the frontier, pressed on, and Grant, "lacking the moral courage to turn back," followed along. Finally, Benjamin broke the silence. "Grant, how many wolves do you think there are in that pack?"

"Suspecting that he thought I would overestimate the numbers, I determined to show my acquaintance with the animal by putting the estimate below what possibly could be correct, and answered, 'Oh, about twenty,' very indifferently. He smiled and rode on. In a minute we were close upon them, and before they saw us. There were just *two* of them. Seated on their haunches, with their mouths close together, they had made all the noise we had been hearing for the past ten minutes."[33]

Grant's affection for horses continued unabated. He wrote with awe of the vast herd of mustangs ranging between the Nueces and the Rio Grande. Like buffalo, the horses moved in a solid mass. "The country was rolling prairie, and from the higher ground the vision was obstructed only by the earth's curvature. As far as the eye could reach, the herd extended. There was no estimating the number of animals in it; I have no idea that they could have been corralled in the State of Rhode Island, or Delaware, at one time. If they had been, they would have been so thick that the pasturage would have given out the first day."[34] Grant said the Mexicans captured the horses in large numbers to sell to the army. "The horses were very strong, formed much like the Norman horse, and with very heavy manes and tails. A picked animal could be purchased at from eight to twelve dollars, but taken wholesale they could be bought for thirty-six dollars a dozen." [35]

Many officers acquired horses for their own use. When broken, they proved reliable mounts far better adapted to the terrain than horses from the East. Longstreet recalled Grant paying a record price of $12 for a particularly spirited stallion. Everyone except Grant was afraid of the animal. "He had the horse blindfolded, bridled, and saddled, and when firmly in the saddle he threw off the blind, sank his spurs into the horse's flanks, and was soon out of sight. For three hours he rode the animal over all kinds of ground, through field and stream, and when the horse and rider returned to camp the horse was thoroughly tamed. For years afterward the story of Grant's ride was related at every campfire in the country." [36]

Grant wrote Julia regularly. He assured her the climate on the Texas coast was superb and the possibility of war remote. "We are so numerous here now that we are in no fear of an attack upon our present ground." [37] But the separation gnawed at him and he was impatient to be married. "Don't you think it time for us to begin to settle upon some plan for consummating what we believe is our mutual happiness? After an engagement of sixteen or seventeen months ought we not to think of bringing that engagement to an end, in the way that all true and constant lovers should?" If Julia's parents objected, he offered to resign. "Your Pa asks what I could do out of the Army? I can tell you: I have at this time the offer of a professorship of mathematics in a tolerably well endowed college in Hillsboro, Ohio, a large and flourishing town, where my salary would probably equal or exceed my present pay." Grant said his father approved the idea and had given him until next spring to decide. [38]

In February 1846 the Army of Occupation was still encamped at Corpus Christi. Grant wrote Julia that orders had been received to move into the disputed territory near the Rio Grande, but the date had not been set. *

---

* On February 3, 1846, Taylor received orders from Washington "to advance and occupy . . . positions on or near the east Bank of the Rio [Grande] del Norte as soon as it can be conveniently done with reference to the Season and the routes by which your movement must be made." Taylor was instructed not to treat Mexico as an enemy, "but should she assume that character by a declaration of war, or any open act of hostility toward us, you will not act merely on the defensive." The general was given discretion as to the placement of his forces on the Rio Grande, but the evidence appears conclusive that President Polk, frustrated in seeking a peaceful settlement, sought to provoke Mexico into war, partially to settle the Texas boundary question, but more importantly to loosen the republic's hold on California and New Mexico. See Secretary of War William Marcy to Taylor, January 13, 1846, U.S. Congress, House, Executive Document No. 60, 30th Cong., 1st sess., *Messages of the President of the United States with the Correspondence Therewith Communicated, Between the Secretary of War and Other Officers of Government on the Subject of the Mexican War* 91 (Washington, D.C.: Wendell and Van Benthuysen, 1848).

"In all probability this movement to the Rio Grande will hasten the settlement of the boundary question, either by treaty or the sword, and in either case we may hope for early peace and a more settled life in the army."[39] As for resigning, Grant told Julia it "would not be right in the present state of affairs and I shall not think of it again for the present."[40]

It required over a month for the Army of Occupation to move forward. Taylor divided his infantry into three echelons, one day's march apart, with the 4th Infantry in the rear. The army's supply train consisted of 307 wagons, eighty-four of them pulled by oxen. Grant wrote Julia that they were going into position on the Rio Grande opposite Matamoros, "a town of considerable importance in Mexico, and as we are informed, occupied by several thousand troops who it is believed by many will make us fight for our ground before we will be allowed to occupy it. But fight or no fight everyone rejoices at the idea of leaving Corpus Christi."[41]

Before setting out, Taylor instructed his troops to avoid plundering and "to observe, with the most scrupulous regard, the rights of all persons who may be found in the peaceful pursuit of their respective avocations. No person, under any pretense whatsoever, will interfere in any manner with the civil rights or religious privileges of the people, but will pay the utmost respect to both."[42] Grant, whose admiration of Taylor grew daily, retained a copy of the order in his knapsack. He reported that the general undoubtedly "looked upon the enemy as the aggrieved party and was not willing to injure them further than his instructions from Washington demanded."[43]

On March 11 the 4th Infantry commenced its march to the Rio Grande. The route measured 196 miles across desolate prairie offering no settlements and little water. Meade called the region "the most miserable desert that I ever saw described, and perfectly unfit for the habitation of man."[44] Grant wanted to walk with his unit but his company commander provided him with a newly purchased mustang for the journey. "I was sorry to take him because I really felt that belonging to a foot regiment it was my duty to march with the men. But I saw the Captain's earnestness in the matter, and accepted the horse for the trip. The day we started was the first time the horse had ever been under saddle. I had little difficulty breaking him, though there were frequent disagreements between us as to which way we should go, and sometimes whether we should go at all. At no time during the day could I choose exactly the part of the column I would march with; but after that I had as tractable a horse as any with the army."[45]

On March 19 the advance guard of the Army of Occupation reached the Arroyo Colorado, thirty miles north of Matamoros, well within the range of Mexican cavalry patrols. Swollen by spring rains, the river posed a major obstacle and Taylor concentrated his forces for a full-scale assault rather than cross piecemeal. As his brigades assembled, Mexican horsemen appeared on the opposite bank. "Buglers, concealed from our view by the brush, sounded the 'assembly' and other military calls. Like the wolves they gave the impression that there was a large number of them and that, if the troops were in proportion to the noise, they were sufficient to devour General Taylor and his army."[46] Grant told Julia that Taylor met with the Mexican commander, who indicated that an attempt to force passage of the Colorado would be resisted. "General Taylor replied that he was going over and that he would allow them fifteen minutes to withdraw; if any one of them should show his head after he had started over, that he would fire upon them."[47]

As soon as Taylor positioned his artillery to support the crossing, four companies of red-legged infantry* led by Captain Charles Ferguson Smith marched into the waist-deep water. Lieutenant Edmund Kirby Smith, no relation, called it "one of the most exciting moments of my life. We watched them in breathless silence as they deepened in the water, expecting that at every step they would receive a withering fire."[48] But the attack never came. Once Taylor's intention to advance became clear, the Mexicans withdrew. When the American column reached the opposite bank, the troops waiting to cross cheered and the regimental bands broke into "Yankee Doodle." Thus, wrote Kirby Smith, "the great battle of Arroyo Colorado was terminated."[49] Taylor's determination carried the day. The tactical situation clearly favored defenders. Crossing a river under hostile fire is a hazardous undertaking, but Taylor's determination was decisive. It was Grant's good fortune to observe Taylor assert his authority.

His army assembled, Taylor marched the last thirty miles with three infantry brigades abreast—a magnificent spectacle on the open prairie. As the force neared the Rio Grande the regiments' marching colors were unfurled and the bands struck up a medley of patriotic airs. Across the river the tiled roofs of Matamoros reflected the morning sun. The tricolor of the Mexican republic flew from every conceivable location. The town was ablaze with color, red roses climbing on white walls, the verdant valley contrasting starkly with the parched countryside the troops had just marched through. On the opposite bank a picket line of sentries watched the army's arrival. The atmosphere was uncertain, not hostile. The rival armies faced each other, but the two nations were formally at peace.

The standoff continued for three weeks. Taylor entrenched his forces on the north bank, constructed a powerful redoubt (immediately desig-

---

* The term applies to artillery soldiers serving as infantrymen. The uniform of the artillery was distinguished by a red trouser stripe.

nated Fort Texas), and emplaced his heavy artillery to resist attack.[50] For provisions and resupply, the army depended on shipments from New Orleans, and Taylor promptly established a depot at Point Isabel, a tiny port below South Padre Island, twenty-seven miles northeast of Matamoros. As the American units refitted, reinforcements poured into Mexico's Army of the North. By mid-April, Taylor's present for duty strength at Fort Texas numbered close to 3,000; the Mexican force opposite was twice that size.[51]

On April 12, 1846, the lull was broken when General Pedro de Ampudia, commander of the Matamoros garrison, delivered an ultimatum to Taylor. Unless the American army broke camp and returned to the Nueces within twenty-four hours, a state of war would exist. "If you insist on remaining upon the soil of the Department of Tamaulipas, it will certainly result that arms, and arms alone, must decide the question."[52] Taylor responded politely. He said he had been ordered to the Rio Grande by his government and had no authority to withdraw by his own accord. "I regret the alternative which you offer; but, at the same time, wish it understood that I shall by no means avoid such alternative."[53]

The following week Mexican cavalry crossed the Rio Grande upstream from the American position. Taylor dispatched two squadrons of dragoons to investigate, but they rode into an ambush. Sixteen were killed or wounded, and the remainder taken prisoner. Taylor immediately informed Washington that "hostilities may now be considered as commenced."[54] President Polk received Taylor's dispatch Saturday evening, May 9. At noon on Monday he asked Congress to recognize that "a state of war exists between the Government of the Republic of Mexico and the United States."[55] After a thirty-minute debate the House of Representatives voted for war, 173–14. The Senate agreed the following day, 40–2.

Meanwhile, Taylor found his hands full. His supply line to the coast was vulnerable, and on May 1 he learned the Mexican army had crossed the Rio Grande in strength, somewhere between Matamoros and the sea. Taylor assumed they were heading for his base at Point Isabel. He left 550 men from the 7th Infantry to defend Fort Texas and immediately moved to protect his supplies. "Our march was as severe as could be made," wrote Grant. "Until 3 o'clock at night we scarcely halted. Then we laid down in the grass and took a little sleep and marched the balance of the way the next morning. Our march was mostly through grass up to the waist with a wet and uneven bottom yet we made 30 miles in much less than a day." Grant said it was equivalent to walking sixty miles in one day "on good roads and unencumbered with troops."[56]

Taylor's forced march allowed him to reach Point Isabel before the Mexicans. He ordered his supply wagons loaded with food and ammunition, and made arrangements for defending the depot. As the work pro-

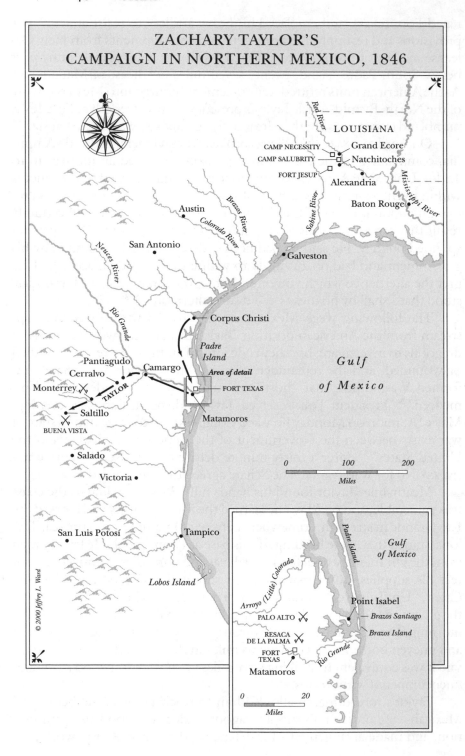

ZACHARY TAYLOR'S
CAMPAIGN IN NORTHERN MEXICO, 1846

ceeded the rumbling of artillery could be heard in the distance. The Mexican army had slipped between Taylor and Matamoros and was apparently attacking Fort Texas. Grant wrote that it was not possible to know what was happening but it had to be unfavorable. "What General Taylor's feelings were during this suspense I do not know; but for myself, a young second lieutenant who had never heard a hostile gun before, I felt sorry that I had enlisted. . . . The war had begun." [57]

If Taylor felt any anxiety, he did not show it. He continued loading the wagons and laying out a perimeter defense for Point Isabel, which he christened Fort Polk. On May 7, when the work was complete, Taylor put the army in motion once more. He was confident the 7th Infantry could hold out, but told his troops they would probably have to cut their way through the Mexican lines to reach them. "The commanding general has every confidence in his officers and men. If his orders and instructions are carried out, he has no doubt of the result, let the enemy meet him in what numbers he may." [58]

At noon the following day, May 8, after marching eleven miles from Point Isabel, Taylor struck the main body of the Mexican army on the plain of Palo Alto. Drawn up in line of battle astride the road to Matamoros, 7,000 men awaited the American advance. [59] Grant noted the formidable impression made by the rows of bayonets and lances glistening in the noonday sun. [60] Taylor halted his column and formed his own line of battle. The 3rd, 4th, 5th, and 8th infantry regiments moved abreast of one another, each regiment separated by a flying battery of howitzers. The heavy artillery went into position on the road. At the same time, the massive wagon train closed in the rear, protected by a battalion of dragoons. By 2 P.M. the American battle line was ready. Few of the men had faced an enemy before, and for some the tension was growing unbearable. Taylor rode to the front of his line, turned, and abruptly ordered one platoon from each company to stack arms, collect the canteens from the other platoons, and fill them in a nearby waterhole.

> *When it comes to slaughter,*
> *You will do your work on water,*
> *An' you'll lick the bloomin' boots*
> *of 'im that's got it.* [61]

As the men quenched their thirst, Taylor nonchalantly pushed back his floppy palmetto hat, lifted his leg across the pommel, and sat sideways on Old Whitey, a massive wad of tobacco in his cheek. The tension eased. When the men were back in their places, Taylor gave the order to advance. There was no saber rattling; no grand exhortations. Taylor simply ordered the line forward and trusted his officers to do their jobs. As Grant marched ahead with his unit he looked down the long line of blue and contemplated the loneliness of command. "I thought what a fearful responsibility General Taylor must feel, commanding such a host and so far away from friends."[62]

When the distance between the two armies narrowed to a thousand yards, the Mexican artillery began its barrage. The guns, all 12-pounders, fired solid brass shot: superb for battering fortifications at close range but ineffective against distant lines of advancing infantry. Grant wrote "the balls would strike the ground long before they reached our line, and ricocheted through the tall grass so slowly that the men would see them and open ranks and let them pass."[63] At 500 yards Taylor halted the advance and ordered his own howitzers into position a few paces in front of the line of infantry. Old Rough and Ready was about to give the army a lesson in the art of war perfected by Napoleon. When the artillery was in place, Taylor ordered them to commence firing. "Canister and grape, Major Ringgold.[64] Canister and grape."*

The American artillery assault got underway at 3 P.M. Grant said the infantry stood at order arms, watching the shells spray upon the enemy. "Every moment we could see the charges from our pieces cut a way through their ranks making a perfect road, but they would close up the interval without showing signs of retreat. Their officers made an attempt to charge upon us but the havoc had been so great that their soldiers could not be made to advance. Some of the prisoners that we have taken say that their officers cut and slashed among them with their sabers at a dreadful rate to make them advance but it was no use."[65] Grant wrote Julia he had not felt a sensation of fear until near the end of the firing. "A ball struck close by me killing one man instantly. It knocked Captain Page's jaw off, and knocked Lt. Wallen and one sergeant down besides, but they were not much hurt. Captain Page is still alive."[66]

Late in the afternoon Mexican cavalry moved around Taylor's left to strike the wagon park. Once more the artillery intervened. Noting the Mexican maneuver, Captain James Duncan hitched up his howitzers, dashed to the flank, and poured a withering fire into the horsemen. At dusk the fighting subsided. The infantry had not closed with each other, and both armies bedded down on their own ground. "We supposed that

---

* Canister shot were small iron balls packed in a tin cylinder fitting the bore of the howitzer from which it was fired. Grape shot were somewhat larger projectiles, fitted in shells of three layers. Canister shot covered a wider area; grape had a more devastating effect. Both were examples of the case shot used so effectively by Napoleon. The tactic required that the artillery be highly mobile, because the guns galloped into position well in front of the infantry. Then, with case shot fire, they annihilated a portion of the enemy line, permitting the infantry to reach the gap unmolested.

the loss of the enemy had not been much greater than our own," wrote Grant, "and expected of course that the fight would be renewed in the morning. During that night I believed all slept as soundly on the ground at Palo Alto as if they had been in a palace. For my own part I don't think I ever dreamed of battles."[67]

When dawn broke the Mexican rear guard could be seen riding away in the direction of Matamoros. As the Americans moved forward, they discovered that Mexican losses were much greater than originally estimated. Grant told Julia "it was terrible to go over the ground the next day and see the amount of life that had been destroyed. The ground was literally strewed with the bodies of dead men and horses. The loss of the enemy is variously estimated from about 300 to 500. Our loss was comparatively small. About 12 or 15 of our men were killed and probably 50 wounded."[68]

The victory at Palo Alto belonged to the horse-drawn field artillery. The battle marked its first effective deployment in North America, and the fire it had laid down was devastating.[69] In the span of four hours it utterly destroyed the will to fight of Mexico's Army of the North. Meade, who was at Taylor's side, wrote afterward, "Our fire was so galling, the enemy deserted by battalions, and were only restrained by their officers shooting them from running *en masse*. If we had charged them just at the close, we should have routed them *in toto*. But the smoke . . . prevented us from seeing the impression our artillery was making and deterred the General from ordering the charge."[70]

Throughout the battle Taylor had been concerned about the safety of his supply train. Accordingly, on the morning of the 9th he decided to move forward without it. He left an additional 300 men and the heavy artillery to protect the wagon park, and set out with the remainder of his force in pursuit of the Mexican army. Shortly after 2 P.M. scouts reported the enemy was entrenched behind a strong defensive position blocking the Matamoros road at Resaca de la Palma, a banana-shaped, brush-encrusted ravine that was once the channel of the Rio Grande. The forward bank of the resaca provided a natural breastwork that the Mexicans strengthened by piling up dead trees in their front. The ground on either side was covered with thick, thorny shrubs that the Texans called chaparral, impenetrable except for a few trails and, as Grant wrote, "so dense that you may be within five feet of a person and not know it."[71]

The Mexican force had been reinforced during the night with troops from the Matamoros garrison. Meade estimated its number at 6,000. Taylor brought 1,700 men to the battle.[72] But the Mexican line was strung out over a mile in an attempt to defend the entire resaca. By contrast, Taylor concentrated his forces in a small area adjacent to the Matamoros road, and as a result achieved numerical superiority at the point of impact. Once more he galloped his howitzers to the front. This time, however, the high chaparral obscured the gunners' view and the artillery fire was ineffective. Old Rough and Ready then ordered the infantry forward, and the entire American line, flushed with the previous day's victory, attacked the Mexican center.

"I was with the right wing," wrote Grant, "and led my company through the thicket wherever a penetrable place could be found, taking advantage of any clear spot that would carry me towards the enemy. At last I got pretty close without knowing it. The balls commenced to whistle very thick overhead. We could not see the enemy, so I ordered my men to lie down, an order that did not have to be enforced."[73] The Mexicans fought courageously for well over an hour, but when the 4th Infantry penetrated their left, and the 8th Infantry broke through on the right, the embattled troops gave way. Grant charged with his company, only to find another American unit was already there. "This left no doubt in my mind but that the battle of Resaca de la Palma would have been won, just as it was, if I had not been there."[74]

When the center of their line collapsed, the Mexican troops panicked. Frightened soldiers threw down their weapons, rushed to the Rio Grande, and attempted to swim across—only to drown in the treacherous currents. Meade reported enemy losses at 1,200 killed and wounded, 300 drowned, and almost 2,000 deserters. "We captured seven pieces of artillery, all their pack mules, all their ammunition, and all their baggage."[75] Taylor reported his own losses at 34 killed and 113 wounded.[76]

After the battle Grant wrote to Julia, using a captured drum as a desk. "The victory for us has been a very great one. No doubt you will see accounts enough of it in the papers. There is no great sport in having bullets flying about one in every direction but I find they have less horror when among them than when in anticipation."[77] Grant was more candid to John Lowe, a family friend in Ohio. "You want to know what my feelings were on the field of battle! I do not know that I felt any peculiar sensation. War seems much less horrible to persons engaged in it than to those who read of the battles."[78]

The following week the remnants of the Mexican army evacuated Matamoros. Taylor crossed the Rio Grande on May 18, established his headquarters under a tree outside the town, instructed his surgeons to look after the Mexican wounded, and waited for reinforcements.[79] Observing life in Matamoros, Grant wrote it was General Taylor's policy to prohibit the taking of private property without satisfactory compensation. As a result the people of the town enjoyed the best market they had ever known. As for the social system, Grant said "the people of Mexico are a very different race of people from ours. The better class are very proud and tyrannize over the lower and much more numerous class as much as a hard master does over his negroes, and they submit to it quite as humbly."[80]

It took Taylor four months to accumulate the necessary men and equipment to continue his pursuit of the Mexican army. Volunteers arrived in droves, but they were raw and undisciplined. Meade considered troops from Texas equivalent to Italian banditti "without their amenity of manners." Those from the deep South were so accustomed to slaves that they were unable to cut their own wood or draw their own water. "I fear the mortality will be terrible among them, from their utter ignorance of the proper mode of taking care of themselves."[81] To whip the volunteers into shape was a time-consuming process. The logistical problem Taylor faced was even greater. The United States had never mounted an extended expeditionary effort into enemy territory and simply did not have the transportation to sustain an army in the field. Meade described the situation to his wife. His letter is one of the most powerful arguments for military professionalism ever written:

> Loud complaints are being made against General Taylor by the Texans and other volunteers, vociferously demanding to be led forward, and criticizing his slow movements, calling them scientific, saying it is all nonsense to take such a quantity of supplies, [and that] they never carried wagons and such things.
>
> True enough, but what was the result? Why, when [the Texans] met the enemy, one hour's fight *exhausted* all their *ammunition,* and they had to retire, and when they retired, they abandoned their sick and wounded on the field. And if a man was taken sick on a march he was left, to join them if he could get well, if not, to die alone in the midst of the prairie; and after they took a place, they had to abandon it in a few days, because they had no means of holding it. This is not our plan. When we advance it is for some object, and we shall have the means of holding every advantage we gain, of taking care of our people en route, and being able to fight several battles before our ammunition gives out. But to do this preparations must be made, and preparations require time in every country, but most particularly in this.[82]

It was not until August that Taylor was ready to move. He had lost contact with the Mexican army and so set his sights on Monterrey, the principal city in northern Mexico, 250 miles southwest of Matamoros. Located astride a major pass through the eastern Sierra Madre, Monterrey was the gateway to Mexico's central valley. In Taylor's view its strategic importance could scarcely be overestimated: Whoever held Monterrey held northern Mexico.

Once again Old Rough and Ready chose to move by water. The bulk of his army, swelled to almost 12,000 men with the influx of volunteers, moved in a shuttle of rickety riverboats 100 miles up the Rio Grande to the head of navigation at Camargo. The boats were not the sturdiest craft afloat. Of such steamers Abraham Lincoln once said, "When they moved they couldn't whistle, and when they whistled they couldn't move."[83] Grant's unit, the 4th Infantry, along with the artillery and cavalry, marched overland, moving at night to avoid the scorching heat of the Rio Grande valley in mid-August.

At Camargo, Taylor, still strapped for transportation, pared his expeditionary force to 6,500 men. Taking his regulars and 3,000 volunteers he set out for Monterrey.[84] To insure the army's resupply, Taylor reorganized the commissary system. He ordered the purchase of 1,900 pack mules to supplement his wagon train, and required each regiment to designate an officer as regimental quartermaster responsible for the unit's logistics.[85] Because of his skill with figures and his way with animals (it was assumed his ability with horses made him well suited to manage a mule train), Grant was appointed quartermaster and commissary officer of the 4th Infantry. He protested immediately and wrote his commanding officer that he did not want any position "which removes me from sharing in the dangers and honors of service with my company at the front." His request prompted the following response:

> Lieutenant Grant is respectfully informed that his protest cannot be considered. Lieutenant Grant was assigned to duty as Quartermaster and Commissary because of his observed ability, skill, and persistency in the line of duty. The commanding officer is confident that Lieutenant Grant can best serve his country in present emergencies under this assignment.
> LT. COL. [JOHN] GARLAND, *4th Inft. Comdg. Brigade.*[86]

Although Grant bitterly regretted his posting, it ultimately proved beneficial because it taught him the intricacies of military logistics from the bottom up. For a man who would go on to command large armies, no training could have been more valuable. During the Civil War Grant's armies might occasionally have straggled, discipline might sometimes have been lax, but food and ammunition trains were always expertly handled. While Grant's military fame deservedly rests on his battlefield victories, those victories depended in no small measure on his skill as a quartermaster. Unlike many Union armies, the forces he led never wanted for the tools of war.

Grant's biggest problem as regimental quartermaster in Mexico was his intractable pack mules. As he saw it, there were not enough men in the entire army to manage the mule train without the assistance of Mexican handlers. On its march to Monterrey the army moved out early each day. "After they had started, the tents and cooking utensils had to be made into packages, so that they could be lashed to the backs of the mules. Iron kettles, tent-poles, and mess chests were inconvenient articles to transport in that way. It took several hours to start each morning, and by the time we were ready some of the mules first loaded would be tired of standing so long with loads on their backs. Sometimes one would start to run, kicking up until he scattered his load; others would lie down and roll over; others with tent-poles for part of their loads would manage to run a tent-pole on one side of a sapling while they would take the other. I am not aware of ever having used a profane expletive in my life; but I would have the charity to excuse those who may have done so, if they were in charge of a train of Mexican pack mules at the time." [87] Despite the frustrations, Grant learned to handle the animals well enough that his supplies were never late arriving in camp. A fellow lieutenant in the 4th Infantry said admiringly, "There was no road so obstructed . . . but that Grant, in some mysterious way, would work his train through and have it in the camp of his brigade before the campfires were lighted." [88]

Taylor's force reached the outskirts of Monterrey on September 19, only to find the city heavily defended. General Ampudia had consolidated his army, brought in reinforcements from as far away as Guadalajara, and fortified every possible vantage point. The northern approach to the city was guarded by a massive citadel built on the stone foundations of an unfinished cathedral. Dubbed the Black Fort by Taylor's troops, its guns commanded the plain that lay between the American army and the city. To the south, Monterrey was protected by the Santa Catarina River and the Sierra Madre. The eastern approach was covered by a series of smaller redoubts, and the west by the heavily gunned Bishop's Palace and Fort Soldado. These latter installations, sited on high ridges, controlled the road to Saltillo, which was Ampudia's supply line. Altogether, Ampudia could call on the services of 7,000 regulars, 3,000 rancheros, plus the able-bodied men of the city, who pitched in to help the defenders. Taylor's force, which had been augmented by two regiments of Texas cavalry, totaled 7,230. [89]

The military rule-of-thumb when attacking a fortified position is that the attacking force should outnumber the defenders at least three to one. But Taylor, having taken the measure of his opponents at Palo Alto and Resaca de la Palma, was undeterred. His regulars, now hardened veterans, would lead the assault, supported by the volunteers.

In laying out his plan of attack, Taylor recognized that the powerful armament of the Black Fort precluded an assault from the north. Since the river protected Monterrey on the south, that left only the east and the west. Once again Old Zack confounded military orthodoxy. Gambling that Ampudia would not forsake his defensive position to attack, Taylor chose to divide his force and strike the city from east and west simultaneously. It was an audacious decision because the two wings of the army would operate independently and would be too far apart to provide mutual support.* The major effort was entrusted to Brigadier General William J. Worth, who was to lead his division of regulars, cut the Saltillo road, and strike the city from the west.[90] The remaining regulars, led by Grant's brigade commander, Colonel John Garland, would mount a secondary attack along the eastern approaches, while Taylor would hold the volunteers in reserve.

Worth initially encountered little difficulty. His advancing forces easily deflected a Mexican cavalry charge, and by the morning of September 21 had taken possession of the Saltillo road, severing Ampudia's sole link with the outside world. Fort Soldado, which proved to be weakly defended, fell later that day, and the Bishop's Palace the day after. Worth's losses were light: less than thirty casualties after two days' fighting. By contrast, Garland's attack from the east met heavy resistance. The approach brought his men under the fire of the Black Fort as well as the guns to their front. The 3rd and 4th infantry were subjected to a blistering cross fire. Grant, who, as quartermaster, had been left in charge of the brigade's base camp, heard the guns in the distance. "My curiosity got the better of my judgment, and I mounted a horse and rode to the front to see what was going on. I had been there but a short time when an order to charge was given, and lacking the moral courage to return to camp—where I had been ordered to stay—I charged with the regiment."[91] The Mexican fire was devastating. Within five minutes one-third of the 4th Infantry lay dead or wounded. The order to retreat was given and Grant noticed the regimental adjutant, Lieutenant Charles Hoskins, exhausted and limping badly. "I offered him my horse and he accepted the offer."[92] The retreat was a pell-mell affair and Hoskins was killed. Grant was named acting adjutant and carried the regimental colors to safety.

---

* It is a tenet of military thought that a commander does not divide his force in the face of a powerful enemy, since each element becomes vulnerable to attack and defeat sequentially. Yet the novelty and risk of the maneuver often carries the day. General Sir William Howe's stunning defeat of George Washington on the Brandywine in the Revolutionary War is a prime example. Howe bet that Washington would not stir from his defensive position behind the river. The British general split his army, hit the unsuspecting Washington in the flank, and rolled up the American line.

Writing about the attack years later, Grant said the charge was ill-conceived and poorly executed. If Garland had moved to his left he could have avoided the deadly fire from the Black Fort, and would have found substantial cover from the guns to his front as well.[93] That, in fact, is how Taylor salvaged the situation. When the general saw Garland's predicament, he turned to the volunteers. Brigadier General John A. Quitman, veteran commander of the Mississippi militia, was ordered to deploy his brigade on the left flank and storm the Mexican batteries. Shielded initially from enemy fire, the Mississippi Rifles and the 1st Tennessee regiment dashed forward. Both suffered heavy casualties when their cover ran out, but they made it to the foot of the Mexican defenses, swarmed over the parapets, seized the guns and turned them against the defenders. Legend has it Colonel Jefferson Davis, commanding the Mississipians, was the second man over the works.[94]

With the Mexican guns east of the city silenced, Taylor once more ordered Garland's brigade forward, supported now by the 1st Ohio volunteers. The units reached the outlying streets of Monterrey only to encounter even more stubborn resistance. Canister shot at close range killed ten officers instantly and wounded ten more. "It was as if bushels of hickory nuts were hurled at us," one survivor remembered.[95] When the regulars faltered, Colonel Albert Sidney Johnston, then with the Texas volunteers, came forward to steady the line. Captain Joseph Hooker wrote that Johnston saved the day. "The coolness and magnificent presence he displayed . . . left an impression on my mind that I have never forgotten."[96] Hooker later commanded the Army of the Potomac; Johnston, the Confederacy's Department of the West.

As dusk gathered, Taylor realized the attack had lost its momentum. Monterrey was invested, but the carnage in the streets was unforgiving. After insuring Quitman's brigade could hold the captured Mexican fortifications, Taylor ordered a general withdrawal. It had not been a good day. Meade wrote that the 3rd and 4th infantry "were literally cut to pieces, and were obliged to retire, leaving their dead and wounded on the ground."[97] American casualties totaled 394—over 10 percent of those engaged. Mexican losses were half that. Taylor for once had lost perspective. He allowed Garland's secondary effort to evolve into a major attack, committed his forces piecemeal, and in the end gave up much of the ground taken.

That night Grant returned to the battlefield. Lieutenant Calvin Benjamin of the 4th Artillery, riding from the city on a gun carriage, saw a figure in the shadows, lifting the head of a wounded man, "giving him water from a canteen and wiping his face with a moistened handkerchief." Benjamin said "it was my dear friend Grant," who, remembering where

Hoskins had fallen, came out "alone in the dark on the awful battlefield" to identify the body, and then discovered a wounded man close by.[98]

The following day, Tuesday, September 22, Taylor regrouped. Ampudia also reassessed his position. His men had fought gallantly, but the American advance was relentless. Garland might be stalled on the east, but Worth appeared unstoppable on the west. The Saltillo road was cut, Monterrey was besieged, and except for the Black Fort, most of the outlying fortifications had fallen. That evening Ampudia withdrew his forces to the heart of the city. The Mexican general calculated that his defensive perimeter would be shortened, and hence manned more easily. But the effect of the withdrawal on his troops' morale was devastating. In their eyes, just when it seemed the Americans might be defeated, the Army of the North was ordered to pull back.

When dawn broke on Wednesday, American pickets noticed the streets before them were empty. Taylor sent Meade forward on reconnaissance. "I ascertained that the enemy had abandoned all that portion of the town in our direction, and had retired to the vicinity of the central plaza, where they were barricaded, and all the houses occupied by their infantry."[99] Taylor cautiously ordered the army back into the city. Fighting was house-to-house and casualties were heavy. Once more Garland's brigade, now down to ten companies, was in the thick of it. When American mortar shells began to fall on the central plaza, Ampudia requested a cease-fire so women and children could be evacuated. Taylor declined. The city was surrounded and he knew Ampudia's supplies would run out more rapidly if there were women and children to feed. Only surrender would ease their plight, said Taylor.

Heavy fighting continued throughout the afternoon. Grant, acting as adjutant, was back with his regiment. Late in the day ammunition ran low. The brigade urgently needed to be resupplied, but sending a messenger back to division headquarters would be hazardous. Mexican musket fire raked every intersection and the air was filled with grape shot. Colonel Garland called for a volunteer. Grant said he would go. Like a trick rider in a rodeo, he hooked one foot around the cantle of his saddle, one arm around the neck of his horse, Nelly, and with his body clinging to the sheltered side, galloped away at full speed. "It was only at street crossings that my horse came under fire, but these I crossed at such a flying rate that generally I was past and under cover of the next block of houses before the enemy fired." Grant and Nelly reached headquarters safely and delivered the message.[100] As friends noted later, Grant "appeared to look upon Nelly's conduct as more courageous than his own."[101]

At nightfall Taylor called a halt and the army rested in place. They were one block from the central plaza on all sides, and victory the next day seemed certain. Just before daybreak an emissary from General Ampudia approached the American lines under a white flag. On behalf of the Mexican commander, the messenger asked for an armistice. Taylor agreed and immediately extended the cease-fire. He and Ampudia met twice that day. Negotiations lasted through the night and terms were fixed before dawn on Friday. The Mexican army would evacuate Monterrey, surrender the Black Fort, and retire to a line below the Rinconada Pass, sixty miles to the south. Fighting would halt for eight weeks. The Army of the North would march out of the city under its own officers, a division at a time. The soldiers would be permitted to take their muskets and the cavalry their horses. Ampudia would be allowed six pieces of light artillery, but all other public property was to be left behind. At noon the Black Fort struck its colors. The garrison fired a final salute and filed out behind drums and bugles, their weapons carried at the trail. As the Stars and Stripes were hoisted above the fort's dark walls, American artillery boomed its own salute: twenty-eight guns—one for each state in the Union.

Armchair strategists condemned Taylor's generosity. Polk was indignant. Taylor, he claimed, had violated his orders.[102] The enemy was "in his power" and Old Zack should have made prisoners of them all, stripped them of their arms, and pushed on further into Mexican territory.[103] Meade offered a more sober assessment. The enemy was dug in around the central plaza with 3,000 troops and twenty pieces of artillery. The Black Fort, with 2,500 men and eight pieces of artillery, was untouched. Both could have been subdued, but the cost would have been immense.[104] Meade said there "was no *military necessity* that induced General Taylor to grant such liberal terms, but a higher and nobler motive. First, to grant an opportunity to the two governments to negotiate for peace. Second, to stop the unnecessary effusion of blood, not only of soldiers, but of women and children who were crowded in with the troops. Third, as a tribute of respect to the gallantry of the Mexicans, who had defended their place as long as it was in their power."[105] Like Meade, Grant saw nothing to criticize in the Monterrey armistice. Twenty years later at Appomattox he would pay unspoken tribute to Taylor, offering virtually identical surrender terms to the Confederate army. In Grant's words, writing about Monterrey, "The prisoners were paroled and permitted to take their horses and personal property with them."[106]

The American victory was costly. In three days of fighting, Taylor lost 122 men killed and 368 wounded. Twenty-seven of the dead were officers, and of those, twenty-three were regulars—primarily from the 3rd and 4th infantry.[107] The following week Grant wrote Julia describing the battle. "We found all their streets barricaded and the whole place well defended with artillery, and taking together the strength of the place and the means the Mexicans had of defending it, it is almost incredible that the American army now are in possession here." He told her of the friends they lost— Hoskins, Hazlitt, and a half-dozen others from Jefferson Barracks—and said he wished this would be his last battle. "I hope it may be so for fighting is no longer a pleasure." [108]

Even so, Grant was captivated by the beauty of Monterrey. "If it was an American city I have no doubt it would be considered the handsomest one in the Union." He told Julia it was heavily treed, built entirely of stone, and virtually surrounded by mountains. "Monterrey is so full of orange, lime, and pomegranate trees that the houses can scarcely be seen." Julia's letters to Grant have been lost, but it seems she teased him about other suitors. His response was predictable. "What made you ask me the question, Dearest Julia, 'if I thought absence could conquer love?' I can only answer for myself, that Julia is as *dear* to me today as she was . . . two years ago, when I first told her of my love. From that day to this I have loved you constantly." Separation intensified Grant's longing for Julia. "You have not told me for a long time Julia that you still love me, but I never thought to doubt it." [109]

In Washington, Taylor's string of victories triggered a Whig revival. In November the party won control of both houses of Congress and Old Rough and Ready was boomed for president. That was too much for Polk. In a scheme worthy of the Borgias, the president decided to bypass Taylor, reduce his force, and entrust the final victory in Mexico to General Winfield Scott, the army's commanding general. Like Taylor, Scott was a Whig who also had presidential ambitions, but he lacked the grassroots appeal of Old Zack, and consequently posed less of a political threat. Polk could also count on the fact that as the senior officer on active duty, Scott's authority to command the army in the field would go unquestioned. Finally, Scott had always opposed the invasion of Mexico from the Rio Grande and advocated striking directly at Mexico City from Veracruz—the invasion route of Hernando Cortés three centuries earlier. In desperation, Polk turned to Scott and put Taylor on the shelf. Or so he thought.

Winfield Scott's ability was unquestioned. At fifty-nine (two years younger than Taylor), he had spent more than half his life as a general officer, having been made a major general during the War of 1812. He commanded American forces during the Seminole War, faced down South Carolina during the nullification crisis, executed President Jackson's controversial order to relocate the Cherokees, and had been the army's general in chief since 1841. In style and manner, he and Taylor were polar opposites. Known as Old Fuss and Feathers by his troops, Scott, in Grant's words, "wore all the uniform the law allowed." [110] Whenever inspecting his lines he appeared in full regalia, accompanied by a large staff similarly attired. Unlike Taylor, Scott did not mingle. His orders were always in writing and prepared with meticulous care, written, it seemed, as much for future historians as for those immediately affected. Scott's verbal style was rhetorical, colored with classical metaphors, and he often referred to himself in the third person. Yet despite their obvious differences, both he and Taylor were gifted commanders.* Grant said "both were pleasant to serve under—Taylor was pleasant to serve with."[111]

In what was either an incredible oversight or a deliberate snub, the administration neglected to inform Taylor of Scott's appointment, and the general arrived unannounced in Point Isabel two days after Christmas, 1846. Taylor was in the field south of Monterrey and the two did not meet. Scott assumed command of the renamed Army of Invasion, informed Taylor by letter that he was taking all of Old Rough and Ready's veterans for an attack on Veracruz, and instructed him to go on the defensive, pulling back to the Rio Grande if necessary. "Providence may defeat me," wrote the supremely confident Scott, "but I do not believe the Mexicans can."[112]

Taylor, although furious that his troops were being transferred without his consent, made the best of the situation. He was left with three batteries of field artillery, 200 dragoons, the Mississippi Rifles, and a promise of 5,000 new volunteers. As his veteran regiments departed, Old Zack went to say farewell. One soldier afterward wrote of Taylor: "He is a very pleasant old man and very sociable not only to officers but to buck privates also. He is not a proud man at all. When he came to see us he rode a mule and looked like an old man a going to mill. He left us and bid goodbye as though he had always been acquainted with us and told us to be good boys and fight like men if needs be and then left."[113]

Mexican president Santa Anna, who intercepted a copy of Scott's message to Taylor, knew it would take Scott a month or more to assemble his army for a landing at Veracruz, and decided to attack Taylor's depleted force in the meantime. The defeat of Old Rough and Ready would give a powerful boost to the nation's morale, restore his army's confidence prior

---

* A handy way of looking at the differences between Taylor and Scott is to remember Eisenhower and MacArthur. The former shared Taylor's down-to-earth style; the latter gloried in the pomp and ceremony that Scott so loved. Like their predecessors, both men were brilliant exemplars of the military profession and both were eminently successful in battle. It may also be true, as Bruce Catton has suggested, that if Grant emulated Taylor, General Lee was inspired by Scott. "The business of living and looking the part of a great soldier, with splendor worn as a familiar cloak about starred shoulders; the battle technique of bringing troops to the scene of action and then relying on subordinates to run things; the willingness to rely on sheer audacity in the face of superior numbers—all of these, characteristic of Lee in Virginia, were equally characteristic of Scott in Mexico." *U.S. Grant and the American Military Tradition* 38 (Boston: Little, Brown, 1954). Also see Douglas Southall Freeman, 1 *R.E. Lee* 294–98 (New York: Charles Scribner's Sons, 1934).

to meeting Scott, and liberate northern Mexico. Accordingly, in late January Santa Anna set out with an army of 20,000 men to destroy Taylor. "Great anxiety is felt for our old and much loved commander," Meade wrote to his wife on February 17, 1847. "Should anything happen to General Taylor, the country will demand the reason for his being left in the most exposed point, with so insufficient a force." [114]

The Mexican army hit Taylor on the windswept plateau of Buena Vista, February 22, 1847. The battle raged two days, with the Americans outnumbered almost four to one. It was touch and go, but Taylor managed to hold his battered line of green volunteers together. He shuffled his artillery from point to point to deflect repeated Mexican assaults and used the red-shirted Mississippi Rifles to steady his infantry. [115] Late in the afternoon of February 23, the fire from Braxton Bragg's guns broke Santa Anna's final charge and the Mexicans retreated in disorder. [116] Taylor lost 673 men; Santa Anna about 4,000. The Mississippi Rifles and the American artillery performed brilliantly. Bragg's battery fired 250 rounds per gun, a sustained rate of fire unmatched in the history of muzzle-loading cannon. But the victory belonged wholly to Taylor. Sitting nonchalantly on the battlefield astride Old Whitey, a conspicuous target for Mexican artillery, he inspired his men with confidence. "He did more than engineer success," wrote one historian, "he created it." [117] In an instance of poetic justice, Taylor's victory at Buena Vista with an army composed almost entirely of volunteers made his election as the twelfth president of the United States inevitable.*

Meanwhile, Scott assembled the Army of Invasion at Point Isabel. Grant's regiment was reassigned to the division commanded by Brigadier General William Worth. Worth was a superb battlefield commander, but when not under fire he was erratic and impatient, constantly shifting his men with little rhyme or reason. "Some commanders can move troops without fatigue," wrote Grant. "Others can wear them out in a few days without accomplishing much. General Worth belonged to this latter class." [118] As the troops made ready to sail for Veracruz, reinforcements from the United States poured in. Joining Worth's division were two of Grant's acquaintances from West Point—Lieutenant D. H. Hill from North Carolina, and Lieutenant Thomas J. Jackson from Virginia. Brothers-in-law, Hill and Jackson shared a devotion to the Presbyterian Church that bordered on fanaticism, and both eagerly sought combat. [119] Army

---

* The victory at Buena Vista also catapulted Colonel Jefferson Davis, the commander of the Mississippi Rifles, into the United States Senate. Severely wounded early in the battle, Davis continued to lead his regiment until the Mexicans withdrew. The unit was subsequently referred to as "the only regiment never to turn its back to the enemy." Davis was appointed to fill a Mississippi vacancy in the United States Senate later that year. He was elected to a full term in 1850, and appointed secretary of war in 1853 by President Franklin Pierce.

headquarters also fleshed out. Scott was more dependent on staff support than Taylor, and marshaled an imposing array of talent. Meade was joined in the engineering department by Captain Robert E. Lee, already the beau ideal of many academy graduates; Captain Joseph E. Johnston, fresh from a tour as the army's assistant adjutant general; and Lieutenant Pierre Gustave Toutant Beauregard, a swashbuckling New Orleans aristocrat who graduated second in the West Point class of 1838. Altogether, Scott's force numbered approximately 12,000 men, of whom the vast majority were combat veterans.

After two unpleasant weeks at sea the army arrived off Veracruz on March 7, 1847. Scott personally reconnoitered possible landing sites, selected a beach three miles south of the city, and sent his troops ashore at sunset on March 9. For some reason the Mexican garrison did not contest the landing and by March 14 the city was surrounded. Here, Grant learned another valuable lesson. Rather than assault the fortified walls of the city as Taylor did at Monterrey, Scott settled into a siege. The aqueducts carrying Veracruz's water supply were cut, siege guns and heavy mortars were emplaced, and on March 22 the bombardment began. For three straight days American artillery pounded the city. On the 25th, the consuls of Great Britain, France, and Prussia requested the shelling be halted so women and children could be evacuated. Scott refused. The next day Veracruz capitulated. In victory, Scott, like Taylor, was magnanimous. The 5,000-man garrison was allowed to march out with full military honors, stack their muskets, and return to their homes. American forces were instructed to conduct themselves with dignity; private and religious property was to be scrupulously protected; and the priests and hierarchy of the Roman Catholic Church were to be rendered every honor. Scott himself, resplendent in full-dress uniform, attended a special service at the Veracruz cathedral commemorating the victory.[120] The battle cost seventeen American dead and sixty wounded. The Mexicans lost over 1,100 killed and wounded, 400 pieces of artillery, vast quantities of ammunition, and control of Mexico's principal seaport.

As soon as Veracruz was secured, Scott moved inland with 8,500 men to take Mexico City. The capital was 250 miles away—along the old National Road, portions of which had been constructed by Cortés in 1519. The route wound its way upward through the foothills and steep mountain passes of the Sierra Madre to the great central plateau of Mexico. Grant called the road "one of the best in the world."[121] Because of the sudden zigzags, abrupt precipices, and narrow defiles it was also easily defended. Sixty miles west of Veracruz, Scott encountered Santa Anna with an army of 12,000 men dug in behind a virtually impregnable position at a place called Cerro Gordo. Grant likened the challenge to Napoleon crossing the Alps: "Cerro Gordo is a long narrow pass, the mountains towering far above the road on either side. Some five of the peaks were fortified and armed with artillery and infantry. At the outlet of the mountain gorge a strong breastwork was thrown up and five [howitzers] placed in embrasure sweeping the road so that it would have been impossible for any force in the world to have advanced." [122]

Scott, parsimonious with his soldiers' lives, decided a frontal assault was out of the question and ordered his engineers to find a route around the emplacements. It was Lee who discovered a little-used mountain trail that skirted the Mexican left, returning to the main road well behind Santa Anna's position. The engineers worked for two days to make the route passable, and on April 17, 1847, Scott dispatched his main force along the trail to envelop the enemy. Miraculously, the movement went undetected. At dawn on the 18th the assault began. The Mexicans were taken completely by surprise and by 10 A.M. the battle was over. Santa Anna lost between 1,000 and 1,200 killed and wounded, 43 pieces of artillery, and 5,000 muskets. An additional 3,000 men were taken prisoner. Scott's losses totaled 63 killed and 368 wounded. [123] Grant commented that Taylor's earlier victory at Buena Vista contributed significantly to Scott's triumph at Cerro Gordo. "If Santa Anna had been successful at Buena Vista, his troops would no doubt have made a more stubborn resistance at Cerro Gordo." [124] Grant saw Scott in a new light. Despite the pomp and ceremony, the general in chief was a complete professional. His planning for the battle had been meticulous. Grant wrote that the attack at Cerro Gordo "was made as ordered, and perhaps there was not a battle in the Mexican war, or of any other, where orders issued before an engagement were nearer being a complete report of what afterwards took place." [125]

With the road to Mexico City open, Scott moved his force quickly through the mountains. The Mexican army offered no resistance. By early May the Army of Invasion reached the city of Puebla, an important market town and religious center on the central plateau, seventy-five miles east of Mexico City. Here Scott halted. The enlistments of most of his volunteers were about to expire and rather than push on, he elected to wait for reinforcements. He sent the volunteer regiments back to Veracruz, severed his communications with the port city, and went on the defensive. With 5,500 regulars, Scott settled into Puebla, where the devout Catholic population welcomed the Americans as a preferable alternative to the secular government of Santa Anna in Mexico City. [126] The general in chief was determined to subsist off the land until a new contingent of volunteers arrived. It was another bold decision and military observers were not optimistic. "Scott is lost," the Duke of Wellington declared. "He cannot capture Mexico City and he cannot fall back on his base." [127]

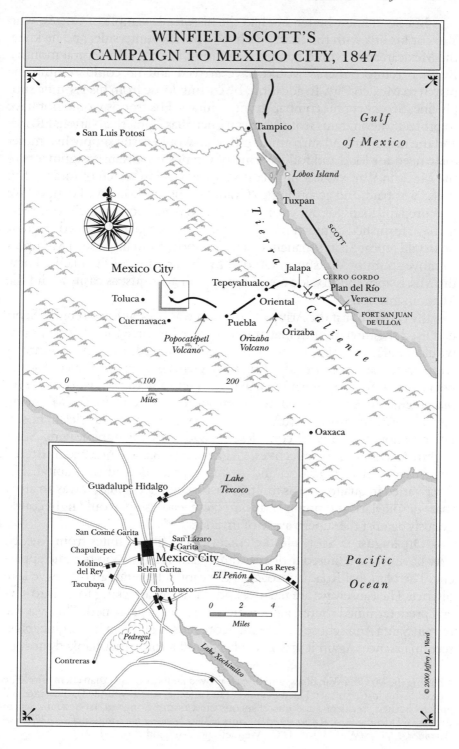

WINFIELD SCOTT'S
CAMPAIGN TO MEXICO CITY, 1847

Gulf of Mexico

San Luis Potosí

Tampico

Lobos Island

Tuxpan

Tierra

SCOTT

Mexico City

Jalapa

Tepeyahualco

CERRO GORDO

Plan del Río

Veracruz

Toluca

Oriental

FORT SAN JUAN DE ULLOA

Caliente

Cuernavaca

Puebla

Orizaba

Popocatépetl Volcano

Orizaba Volcano

0   100   200

Miles

Oaxaca

Guadalupe Hidalgo

Lake Texcoco

San Cosmé Garita

San Lázaro Garita

Chapultepec

Mexico City

Molino del Rey

Belén Garita

Los Reyes

Pacific

Tacubaya

El Peñón

Ocean

Churubusco

0   2   4

Miles

Pedregal

Contreras

Lake Xochimilco

© 2000 Jeffrey L. Ward

But Scott knew better. He had the historical example of Cortés, who also cut his link with the coast and lived off the countryside, and he knew the Mexican army would be in no condition to attack for several months. By then reinforcements would have arrived and he could resume the march to Mexico City. In addition, by cutting loose from his 175-mile supply line, Scott kept his combat strength intact. His troops would not have to protect wagon trains from Mexican guerrillas along the National Road, and the lush farmland surrounding Puebla would easily supply his immediate need for food and fodder. One of Grant's important assignments in the Mexican War was leading Scott's supply train in search of forage. Top dollar was paid, and according to Grant "we never thought of danger. We procured full loads for our entire train at two plantations, which could easily have furnished as much more." [128] Grant watched and learned. In 1863 he would repeat Scott's maneuver, cutting loose from his base in Memphis to move south of Vicksburg. Guided by the example of Puebla, he knew the Mississippi countryside could support an army just as easily as did the Mexican interior.

By early August the Army of Invasion was back at full strength. Scott had used the three-month hiatus to organize his force for what he hoped would be its final campaign. As his regulars rested, the new volunteers were drilled and made ready. Brigadier General Franklin Pierce, former governor of New Hampshire, arrived in Puebla with the last body of replacements on August 6 and Scott set out for Mexico City the following day. The army numbered 14,000 men, but of those, 2,500 lay sick in hospital and another 600 were convalescing and unfit for duty, leaving Scott slightly less than 11,000 effectives.* Against this, Santa Anna had mustered an army of between 30,000 and 35,000 men to defend the capital. His force varied in quality, but as military historians have noted, it was an army that "despite lack of training and competent leadership, would fight courageously against the superb army of invaders." [129]

On August 12 Scott's lead elements were fifteen miles from Mexico City having encountered little resistance. The reason soon became apparent. The National Road approaches the capital through an extensive lake district. The causeways are narrow and funnel an attacking force into several predetermined routes, all of which were heavily fortified. This was the terrain Santa Anna chose to defend. Scott paused and sent his engineers on reconnaissance. Again it was Lee who found a route that flanked most of

---

* During the Mexican War, illness and disease proved far more deadly than enemy fire. The United States lost 1,721 men killed in action (and another 4,102 wounded), but 11,562 fell prey to sickness, accidents, and miscellaneous causes. 30th Congress, 1st Session, Senate Executive Document 36, *Report of the Secretary of War Showing the Number of ... Killed and Wounded. ...* 6–7 (Washington, D.C.: Wendell and Van Benthuysen, 1848).

the Mexican defenses and approached the city from the south. Accordingly, Scott shifted the army south. Santa Anna responded by moving south as well, and on August 20 battle was joined.

The American attack was two-pronged. The initial assault, launched against the towns of Contreras and San Gerónimo, broke the outer chain of Mexican defenses, and the follow-up, at Churubusco, penetrated the inner chain. Grant, with Garland's brigade, took part in the assault on Churubusco. The fighting along both approaches was often hand-to-hand and the casualties were heavy. Scott lost 1,053 men at Contreras and Churubusco,[130] but Mexican losses were much greater: 4,297 killed or wounded, 2,637 prisoners (including eight generals), and perhaps 3,000 missing.[131] Vast quantities of small arms and ammunition also fell into American hands. In one day's fighting Santa Anna lost one third of his army. His outer and inner defenses were pierced, and the Army of Invasion stood at the gates of Mexico City. Scott wrote characteristically, "I doubt whether a more brilliant victory—taking into view the ground, artificial defenses, batteries and the extreme disparity of numbers, without cavalry or artillery on our side—is to be found on record."[132] Grant, who was amused at Scott's self-aggrandizement, nevertheless recognized his good fortune in serving under another gifted commander. "Both the strategy and tactics displayed by General Scott in those various engagements of the 20th of August, 1847, were faultless. The enemy outside the city outnumbered our soldiers quite three to one, but they had become so demoralized by the succession of defeats this day that the City of Mexico could have been entered without much bloodshed."[133]

Instead of moving into the city, Scott agreed to a truce to allow peace negotiations to commence. The United States was represented by Nicholas P. Trist, President Polk's special emissary; the Republic of Mexico by Santa Anna. Scott believed it was important to secure peace without humiliating Mexico and he trusted Trist to do this.[134] But Trist's instructions from Polk left little room to negotiate, and on September 2 he informed Santa Anna of America's terms: the Texas boundary was to be set at the Rio Grande; New Mexico and California were to be ceded to the United States for a sum to be determined subsequently; and the United States was to acquire transit rights across the Isthmus of Tehauntepec, one of the proposed interocean canal routes. Grant wrote, "I do not suppose Mr. Trist had any discretion whatever in regard to boundaries. The war was one of conquest, in the interest of an institution [i.e., slavery], and the probabilities are that private instructions were for the acquisition of territory out of which new States might be carved."[135]

Traditional American accounts suggest Santa Anna was stalling and that the possibility of an agreement was nil from the beginning.[136] Grant was more charitable. The Mexicans, he said, "felt so outraged at the terms proposed that they commenced preparations for defense, without giving notice of the termination of the armistice."[137] Whatever Santa Anna's intent, when Scott learned of the renewed Mexican preparations he broke off the truce and set out to resume his attack. Relying once again on his engineers to plot an approach, the general in chief elected to attack the city from the west, moving along two broad causeways that led, respectively, to the *garitas* (gates) of Belén and San Cosmé.

Scott now made the one miscalculation of his campaign. The approaches he selected came under the guns of the Castle of Chapultepec and were partially blocked by Molino del Rey (the king's mill), a sprawling pile of stone buildings 200 yards long. Scott assumed the mill was lightly defended and on September 8 dispatched Worth's division to subdue it. The result was a bloodbath. The mill was taken, but in two hours of fighting Worth's division lost 25 percent of its strength: 116 dead, 671 wounded, and 22 missing. The casualties included 58 officers. The total was more than Taylor had lost in three days at Monterrey.

Garland's brigade was in the thick of the fighting. Grant was one of the first to enter the mill and assisted in disarming the garrison.[138] The losses were staggering. "A few more such victories and this army would be destroyed," said Colonel Ethan Allen Hitchcock, commanding the 3rd Infantry.[139] Lieutenant John Sedgwick, who would be killed leading his corps at Spotsylvania, wrote his father that some of the men who had fought most gallantly soon deserted, "so desperate they thought our situation."[140] Grant did not criticize the assault at the time, but he later wrote that the San Cosmé and Belén *garitas* could have been reached by alternate routes, making the attack on the mill unnecessary.[141]

With Molino del Rey occupied, Scott decided to take the fortress of Chapultepec before assaulting the city itself. Situated high on a rocky hill, with a commanding field of fire in all directions, the castle was home to Mexico's military academy (Colegio Militar), a symbol of national honor. It was defended by 1,000 regular army soldiers, the cadets—all of whom voted to remain—and another 4,000 infantrymen close by.[142] Scott could not afford a defeat at this stage and deployed three of his four divisions in the assault. The artillery preparation began at 5 A.M. on September 12 and continued throughout the day. The effect was devastating. The walls of the castle were formidable, but the roof was tile and provided little protection from the barrage Scott's guns let loose. At dawn on the 13th the shelling resumed and continued until 8 A.M. As the fire lifted, six brigades of infantry charged up the steep slopes to the castle wall. Joseph E. Johnston's Voltiguer regiment was the first over the battlements, followed by the South Carolina Palmetto Regiment and the 8th Infantry. When Longstreet, who was carrying the colors of the 8th, fell to the ground with a musket ball in his thigh, he handed the banner to George Pickett, who carried it over the wall. By 9:30 the fortress had fallen. As Old Glory was hoisted above the ramparts, Santa Anna, watching from a distance, said to his assembled officers, "If we were to plant our batteries in Hell, the damned Yankees would take them from us." Ampudia replied sullenly, "God is a Yankee." [143]

Once Chapultepec was in American hands, Worth's division moved to take the causeway leading to San Cosmé *garita*. General Quitman led a second column against Belén *garita*. With the assaults channeled along the narrow causeways, Mexican defenders were able to concentrate their fire against the onrushing troops and for a time Worth's division found it impossible to advance. But Garland's brigade worked its way forward, shielded by the giant arches carrying the city's aqueduct along the causeway. Grant led a detachment that outflanked several Mexican artillery pieces and in the late afternoon he hauled a light, mountain howitzer atop the belfry of San Cosmé church, the fire from which broke the final Mexican resistance. Reflecting on the episode years later, Grant wrote that when he knocked for admission to the church, the priest was extremely polite but "declined to admit us."

> With the little Spanish then at my command, I explained to him that . . . I intended to go whether he consented or not. He began to see his duty in the same light as I did, and opened the door, though he did not look as if it gave him special pleasure to do so. The gun was carried to the belfry and put together. We were not more than two or three hundred yards from San Cosmé. The shots from our little gun dropped in upon the enemy and created great confusion. Why they did not send out a small party and capture us, I do not know. [144]

General Worth, who was directing his division's assault, saw the effect the gun was having and sent his aide, Lieutenant John C. Pemberton, to bring Grant to him.* Worth congratulated Grant and instructed him to take along another gun and its officer and crew. "I could not tell the General that there was not room enough in the steeple for another gun, because he probably would have looked upon such a statement as a contradiction from a second lieutenant. I took the captain with me, but did not use his gun." [145]

By sundown on September 13 both the San Cosmé and Belén *garitas* were in American hands. Altogether, Scott's casualties that day totaled 130 killed, 703 wounded, and 29 missing. Mexican losses were estimated at

* Pemberton defended Vicksburg against Grant in 1863.

three to four times that.[146] Worth's and Quitman's divisions were inside the city although Santa Anna still had about 10,000 troops at his disposal and a bitter house-to-house struggle lay in the offing.[147] But that night the battle ended. At 2 A.M., yielding to the pleas of city officials, Santa Anna withdrew the remnants of his army to Guadalupe Hidalgo. For all practical purposes the war was over. The following day General Scott, preceded by the divisions of Quitman and Worth, rode triumphantly into Mexico City's Grand Plaza. The commanding general slept that evening in the Halls of the Montezumas, guarded by a company of United States marines.

Grant gave Scott and Taylor full credit for the American victories. Taylor, he said, "considered the administration accountable for the war, and felt no responsibility resting on himself other than the faithful performance of his duties."[148] Grant said General Scott may have been more concerned about his reputation than Taylor, but acknowledged that "his successes are the answer to all criticism. He invaded a populous country, penetrated two hundred and sixty miles into the interior, with a force at no time equal to one-half of that opposed to him; he was without a base; the enemy was always entrenched, always on the defensive; yet he won every battle, he captured the capital, and conquered the government."[149]

In Grant's view, two additional factors contributed to America's success: the professional quality of the United States army, and the lack of professionalism of its Mexican counterpart:

> At the battles of Palo Alto and Resaca de la Palma, General Taylor had a small army, but it was composed exclusively of regular troops, under the best of drill and discipline. Every officer, from the highest to the lowest, was educated for his profession, not at West Point necessarily, but in the camp, in garrison, and many of them in Indian wars. The rank and file were probably inferior to the volunteers that participated in the later battles of the war; but they were brave men, and drill and discipline brought out all there was in them. . . . The volunteers who followed were of better material, but without drill or discipline at the start. They were associated with so many disciplined men and professionally educated officers, that when they went into engagements it was with a confidence they would not have felt otherwise. They became soldiers themselves almost at once.

Grant thought the problem with the Mexican army was not with the men but with the officers. Despite the fact the soldiers were "poorly clothed, worse fed, and seldom paid," they fought bravely. In virtually every battle the Mexicans performed well initially. "The trouble seemed to be a lack of experience among the officers, which led them after a certain time simply to quit, without being particularly whipped, but because they had fought enough." [150]

With the fighting over, Grant wrote immediately to Julia. "Since my last letter four of the hardest fought battles that the world ever witnessed have taken place, and the most astonishing victories have crowned the American arms. But dearly have they paid for it. The loss of officers and men killed and wounded is frightful." Grant told Julia, "out of all the officers that left Jefferson Barracks with the 4th Infantry, only three besides myself now remain with us." Of the twenty-one officers originally assigned to the regiment, only four had survived. [151]

CHAPTER THREE

RESIGNATION

And there shall arise . . . seven years of famine; and all the plenty shall be forgotten in the land of Egypt. . . .

GENESIS 41:30

THE MEXICAN WAR ENDED with the capture of Mexico City. The American army remained another ten months because there was no government in Mexico capable of concluding a peace treaty. In late September, after a desultory attempt to besiege Scott's base at Puebla, Santa Anna resigned and went into hiding. A provisional government was not elected until November, and negotiations did not get underway until December. In the meantime Nicholas Trist had been recalled by Polk, who held him responsible for the failure of the earlier armistice. Instead of obeying his instructions, Trist stayed, and at Scott's urging successfully negotiated the Treaty of Guadalupe Hidalgo, signed on February 2, 1848.[1] Under the terms of the treaty, Mexico ceded all of the land north of the Rio Grande, New Mexico (including Arizona), and Upper California. The United States, for its part, relinquished its demand for the Baja Peninsula (Lower California) and agreed to pay the claims of various American citizens against Mexico. It also agreed to provide $15 million directly to the Mexican government. Polk embraced the treaty, faced down Democratic efforts to annex northern Mexico, and then petulantly relieved both Scott and Trist. The Senate gave its consent to the treaty on March 10, 1848, and the Mexican National Congress followed suit on May 30.[2]

For Grant, the ten months of peacetime service in Mexico were among the happiest of his life. Although he longed for Julia, he developed a deep affection for Mexico and the Mexican people. "No country was ever so blessed by nature," Grant wrote his betrothed. "There is no fruit nor grain that can't be raised here nor no temperature that can't be found at any season. You have only to choose the degree of elevation to find perpetual snow or the hottest summer."[3] Later, as his impressions deepened and his knowledge of Spanish improved, Grant wrote that he pitied Mexico. Despite fertile soil and a wonderful climate, "She has more poor and starving subjects who are willing and able to work than any country in the world. The rich keep down the poor with a hardness of heart that is incredible."[4]

The day the fighting stopped, September 14, 1847, Grant was still a second lieutenant. "I had gone into the Battle of Palo Alto a second lieutenant and I entered Mexico City sixteen months later with the same rank, after having been in all the engagements possible for any one man, in a regiment that lost more officers during the war than it ever had present at any one engagement."[5] With peace established, retroactive promotions came quickly. On September 16 Grant was advanced to the permanent rank of first lieutenant in the regular army, and given two temporary promotions for bravery under fire: to first lieutenant with date of rank as of September 8, 1847, "for gallant and meritorious conduct in the Battle of Molino del Rey"; and to captain with date of rank September 13, for his role at the San Cosmé *garita*. The temporary promotions allowed Grant to wear the insignia and assume the duties of a captain, although he was paid as a first lieutenant and would revert to that rank when the army returned to the United States.

Grant's belated promotions allowed him to join the eight men in his class who had already become captains. Sixteen classmates received one temporary promotion and were first lieutenants, and ten, most of whom did not see action in Mexico, remained second lieutenants. Four men in Grant's class were killed in action. That was a relatively low ratio. Between 1802 and 1847 West Point graduated 1,365 officers. Over one third left the army for civil life, but of those remaining, 286 perished in Mexico.[6] For the survivors, the Mexican War had been an opportunity to practice their trade under grueling conditions. It was a proving ground that established the value of military professionalism and gave firsthand experience to a generation of American officers. It also revealed the distinction between the theory of battle as taught at West Point and the practice of war in the field. Cadets who thrived on the aphorisms of Napoleon, men such as Henry W. Halleck and George B. McClellan, found the reality of conflict unsettling.[7] On the other hand many of Grant's friends, men like Thomas J. Jackson and D. H. Hill, discovered their calling. Jackson graduated well down in the class of 1846—three years after Grant—yet was now a major in the field artillery. Wounded twice, he had won three brevets for gallantry. Hill, who was sometimes called "the bravest man in the army,"[8] was also a major. So too was Longstreet. Braxton Bragg advanced three ranks, moving from first lieutenant to lieutenant colonel, as did Joseph E. Johnston, another officer Grant admired. Robert E. Lee and Joseph Hooker, who began the war as captains, were now colonels. P. G. T. Beauregard, George H. Thomas, and Don Carlos Buell jumped two ranks, from first lieutenant to major. Meade and Buckner, like Grant, advanced two grades and were captains, as was William Tecumseh Sherman, who served in the relatively bloodless conquest of California. Hooker said that as practical soldiers, Buell, Thomas, and Bragg stood highest in the estimation of the army.[9] Sherman shared that assessment.[10] Grant noted he had served with more than fifty officers "who afterwards became generals on one side or the other in the rebellion, many of them holding high commands."

> The acquaintance thus formed was of immense service to me. . . . I do not pretend that all movements, or even many of them, were made with special reference to the characteristics of the commander against whom they were directed. But my apprecia-tion of my enemies was certainly affected by this knowledge. The natural disposition of most people is to clothe a commander of a large army with superhuman abilities. A large part of the Na-tional army, for instance, and most of the press of the country, clothed General Lee with such qualities. But I had known him personally, and knew that he was mortal; and it was just as well that I felt this.[11]

During the occupation of Mexico, Grant's regiment was stationed at Tacubaya, a small village four miles southwest of the capital that, because of its higher elevation, was healthier and more accommodating. As regi-mental quartermaster, Grant found himself busier than most officers in garrison. Initially the problem was clothing. Scott's army had not been re-supplied and uniforms were torn and threadbare. It was Grant's task to contract with Mexican seamstresses for replacements. That awakened an entrepreneurial impulse, perhaps inherited from his father. In order to raise money for the regimental fund, Grant entered the bakery business. "In two months I made more money for the fund than my pay amounted to for the entire war."[12] Grant was already unlucky with money, however. Thieves broke in and stole the chest in which he kept $1,000 in cash for the fund.[13]

With his fellow officers Grant explored the Mexican countryside: climbing almost to the rim of Popocatépetl's volcano; spelunking the great limestone caves at Cuernavaca; attending the racetrack, the theater, and once, a bullfight. Grant left the arena early, sickened by the tormenting of the bulls. "I could not see how human beings could enjoy the sufferings of beasts, and often of men, as they seem to do on these occasions."[14]

Grant missed Julia enormously. Regularly each month, as the mail wagon left for Veracruz, he wrote tenderly of his despair.[15] When Longstreet, who had been wounded at Chapultepec, departed in January to marry Louise Garland in St. Louis, Grant was more despondent than ever. He asked for leave to return home but was refused.[16] In February he pleaded with Julia to send her daguerrotype. "How very much I would like to have it to look at since I must be deprived of seeing the original." [17] In March he speculated about her joining him in Mexico. "How happy I should be if such a thing was possible. If you were here I should never wish to leave Mexico, but as it is I am nearly crazy to get away." [18] Time grew heavy. "There is a great deal of talk of peace here now," Grant wrote in early May. "It is too bad, ain't it? Just think we have been engaged almost four years and have met but once in that time, that was three years ago." [19]

When the Mexican National Congress accepted the Treaty of Guadalupe Hidalgo on May 30, 1848, Grant knew his separation from Julia was nearly over. In June the army began to withdraw, division by division, back to the coast for passage home. General Worth's division was the last to leave. Worth, who placed great faith in military symbols, claimed to have been the first man across the Arroyo Colorado, the first into Monterrey, Veracruz, Puebla, and Mexico City. He insisted on being the last to ride out.[20] On July 16, after an uneventful march to the sea, the 4th Infantry boarded transports bound for the United States. One week later Grant landed in Pascagoula, Mississippi, and immediately received a two-month leave of absence.[21] Booking passage on the first available steamer heading upriver from New Orleans, he arrived in St. Louis on July 28. The Dents were not at White Haven that year; they were spending the summer in the city. Julia, awaiting Grant's arrival, was surprised when the bronzed captain of infantry strode up to the house on Fourth Street. Grant had changed noticeably in three years; Julia less so. Although Julia was the only woman he ever loved, Sam Grant had become a man of the world: self-assured, secure in his profession, accustomed to command. The Dents noticed he was "sturdier and more reserved in manner." [22] He no longer thought of resigning from the army and becoming a professor, and did not renew his application to teach at West Point. Although he was eager to marry Julia, Grant had decided to remain on active duty. His first lieutenant's salary, almost $1,000 a year, including rations for his family and fodder for his horses, would provide a secure livelihood.

Julia set the wedding for August 22. St. Louis society took on a decidedly martial tone with the return of the army to Jefferson Barracks, and the family's comfortable town house overflowed with Southern belles and officers in full dress. Longstreet, who was Julia's cousin, was Grant's best man; his messmate, Cadmus Wilcox, and Bernard Pratte of St. Louis served as ushers. All three would surrender to Grant at Appomattox. At 8 P.M. the knot was tied. "My wedding cake was a marvel of beauty," wrote Julia. "We had music, and I think two of my bridesmaids took a turn around the room."[23] The following day, the couple left for the home of Grant's parents, sailing down the Mississippi to its confluence with the Ohio, and then upstream to Louisville and Cincinnati. Julia marveled at the steamboat on which they traveled. "It seemed to me almost human in its breathing, panting, and obedience to man's will. Then I enjoyed sitting alone with Ulys. He asked me to sing to him, something low and sweet, and I did as he requested."[24]

Following its return to the United States, the 4th Infantry was assigned to frontier duty on the Canadian border. Regimental headquarters was established at Detroit and the various companies were dispatched to a string of small posts from Sault Ste. Marie in Michigan to Plattsburgh and Sackets Harbor in New York. This was the peacetime army. Officers were reduced to their permanent rank, a parsimonious Congress pared the active-duty strength of the military establishment to 8,000 men, and command of the 4th Infantry reverted to Colonel William Whistler, an elderly relic whom Taylor had relieved at Matamoros and sent home. After an extended honeymoon, Grant, with his new bride, reported for duty November 17, 1848. He recognized that this was a different army from the one he had known in Mexico. Instead of assigning him to Detroit, where his duties as quartermaster required his presence, Whistler ordered Grant to join the two rifle companies at Sackets Harbor. Whistler's decision reflected ignorance, not spite. Not having served in the Mexican campaign he was unfamiliar with the post of regimental quartermaster Taylor had created and simply assumed it had expired at war's end. To him, Grant was another lieutenant available for troop duty.[25]

Grant objected to the posting as soon as he was informed. This was a different Grant from the young plebe who obligingly changed his name to suit the military academy's bureaucracy. Two years of combat duty had hardened him. Perhaps Grant took himself too seriously, but he understood his prerogatives as an officer and knew he was still regimental quartermaster. He may also have wanted to remain with Julia in Detroit, rather than subject her to the rigors of an outlying detachment. "I will, of course, obey your orders, Colonel Whistler, but you must know that I will make a remonstrance at once to Washington."[26]

Because it was late in the year and the lakes were closed to navigation, Grant and Julia made the overland trek to Sackets Harbor, a remote village on the east shore of Lake Ontario, arriving on December 2.[27] The post, designated Madison Barracks in honor of the fourth president, had been established after the War of 1812. It was twenty-five miles below Fort Frontenac, the main British base on the Canadian border, and was an important link in America's northern defense chain.[28] When Grant arrived he discussed his assignment with the garrison commander, an old friend from Mexico, Colonel Francis Lee. (It was Lee who recommended Grant be decorated for gallantry at the San Cosmé *garita*.)[29] Despite the fact he was short of officers at Madison Barracks, Lee agreed that Grant's proper place was in Detroit. Accordingly, with Lee's approval, Grant wrote to Major General John E. Wool, commander of the Eastern Department, requesting orders be cut returning him to regimental headquarters. "In no way, either by resignation or removal, have I vacated the office of Regimental Quarter-Master, neither has the Colonel Commanding ever considered that I have."[30] Lee endorsed the request ("Lieutenant Grant has unquestionably been hardly and wrongly done by"),[31] and General Wool concurred. On March 2, 1849, Grant received orders transferring him back to Detroit.[32]

Because of the mistaken assignment, Grant and Julia spent the winter of their first year of marriage at Madison Barracks. Ironically, it proved a delightful sojourn. Grant's duties were not arduous, and he and his new bride enjoyed their quiet time together. They set up housekeeping, Grant gave Julia a monthly allowance (which she usually exceeded), and they settled into the comfortable routine of garrison life on the northern frontier. Servants were plentiful, Julia enjoyed entertaining (though she seldom cooked), and the Grant household became a model of domesticity. "Grant, you look so happy, so comfortable here, that we are all almost tempted to get married ourselves," Julia quoted several bachelor officers as saying.[33]

In the spring of 1849, when the lakes thawed, Grant returned to Detroit. Julia took advantage of the transfer to visit her parents at White Haven, stopping to see Grant's parents en route. Grant adapted easily to the routine at regimental headquarters, and rented a five-room frame house that he furnished and had ready for Julia when she arrived in July. Duty in Detroit was, if anything, less demanding than at Sackets Harbor. Grant filled his leisure hours tending his horses, racing them occasionally down Jefferson Avenue, while Julia occupied herself with the house parties and entertaining incumbent upon an officer's wife.[34] In the spring of the following year, the Grants' first child was born, named Frederick Dent Grant in honor of Julia's father.

As the months passed, duty at regimental headquarters lost its attraction for Grant. He had relished being quartermaster in Mexico, where added responsibilities heightened the excitement of service in the field. In Detroit, he discovered that peacetime paperwork offered little challenge. "I was no clerk, nor had I any capacity to become one. The only place I ever found in my life to put a piece of paper so as to find it again was either a side coat-pocket or in the hands of a clerk more careful than myself." [35] A brother officer noted Grant "read little, smoked a pipe incessantly, [and] was regarded as a restless, energetic man, who must have occupation, and plenty of it, for his own good." [36]

Grant received a respite from his ennui in the spring of 1851 when the War Department reduced the size of its installation in Detroit, moving the headquarters of the 4th Infantry to the field. Colonel Whistler was given the choice of Fort Niagara or Madison Barracks, and to Grant's delight he chose the latter. Grant wrote Julia (who was visiting her parents) that he was glad the colonel's wife was out of town when the order arrived from Washington. "The old lady disliked Sackets Harbor very much. You know . . . that if she had been here the Col. would never have dared make the change." [37] As quartermaster, Grant supervised the move, and he and Julia were pleased to be back among old friends at Madison Barracks. [38] That spring brought another pleasant surprise when Grant was restored to the temporary rank of captain. [39] The War Department, under General Scott's direction, was sorting out the officer corps and many of the brevet ranks awarded in Mexico were reactivated.

Grant's second assignment to Sackets Harbor was short-lived. The discovery of gold in California triggered a tidal wave of prospectors and settlers to the state, and in the spring of 1852 the 4th Infantry was ordered to reinforce the slender American garrison on the West Coast. For Grant it was a mixed blessing. On the one hand he relished the adventure of going to California, but on the other, Julia was eight months pregnant with their second child and in no condition to face the perils of such a trip. As quartermaster, Grant energetically undertook arrangements to assemble the regiment on Governors Island in New York harbor preparatory to sailing, and did his utmost to insure that dependents accompanying the unit were accommodated. When Julia insisted on going despite her condition, Grant's better judgment prevailed. "You know how loath I am to leave you, but crossing Panama is an undertaking for one in robust health." [40] It was agreed that Julia would go first to Grant's parents in Ohio, and then on to White Haven. He would send for her and the children as soon as it was possible. [41]

The California posting marked a watershed in Grant's life. He was instinctively a loner, but after four years of marriage he and Julia had become inseparable. She filled a void he had never known existed, and he depended upon her more than he realized. Separation would prove more than he could bear. In the spring of 1852 neither Grant nor Julia anticipated they would be separated for a long period of time. And while he was involved in organizing the regiment's move, Grant did not feel her absence keenly. But when he said farewell to Julia on June 15, 1852, a new phase of his life began: a phase characterized by misery, misfortune, and failure.

Grant arrived at Governors Island with the rifle companies from up-state New York on June 19. It would take a week or more for the detachments from Michigan to arrive, and a sailing date had not been set. "All preparation for starting devolves on me," he wrote Julia, "so that I am the only one who cannot get a leave of absence."[42] Grant did manage a brief trip to Washington, his first visit to the capital, where he unsuccessfully attempted to settle the matter of the $1,000 stolen from the regimental fund in Mexico. A military board of inquiry had found Grant was not to blame, and the War Department lost interest after that.[43] But federal statutes prevented government auditors from writing off the loss, and so the deficit was carried forward from year to year on the books of the 4th Infantry.[44] This gnawed at Grant. He considered it a point of honor to have the record cleared, and since only Congress could provide relief, he decided to lay his case before the Military Affairs Committee of the House of Representatives.[45] It was a quixotic effort. When he arrived in Washington, Congress was in recess mourning the death of Henry Clay, and Grant returned to Governors Island empty-handed.*

On July 5, 1852, the 4th Infantry sailed from New York on the steamship *Ohio*. Moving a complete infantry regiment with its equipment and dependents to the Pacific Coast was a daunting undertaking in the 1850s. The army had never attempted such an enterprise by sea and the quartermaster general's office, which made the arrangements, had been lulled into false optimism by the Mexican War. Scott and Taylor had moved their armies from the Gulf Coast to Mexico and back with little difficulty, and staff planners simply extrapolated. As the War Department saw it, the 4th Infantry's move divided into three phases: a steamer from New York to Panama; an overland trek across the isthmus; and then another steamer to San Francisco. Simple on paper, but fraught with danger for a unit exceeding 700 men, women, and children with no base of support along the way. "How little did we realize what awaited us," recalled Delia Sheffield, the wife of a sergeant in Company H. "Had we known a tithe of the perils of the trip and that nearly one-half of the brave fellows who took ship with us, with such pleasant anticipations and high hopes, would not live to reach their journey's end, we should have shrunk in horror for the embarkation."[46]

The 4th Infantry's travail began when it boarded the *Ohio*. The 3,000-ton side-wheeler, one of the newest plying the New York–Panama route, was designed to carry 330 passengers in comfortable cabins on three rela-

* On June 17, 1862, two months after the battle of Shiloh, a grateful Congress enacted legislation settling Grant's account as quartermaster of the 4th Infantry and appropriating $1,000 for that purpose. *Public Laws,* Thirty-seventh Congress, 2d sess., 1862, chapter 56.

tively spacious decks.[47] But these facilities were completely booked when the War Department decided to send the 4th Infantry. As a result, the regiment spent ten days on open decks, eleven hundred persons sharing accommodations designed for one third that number.[48] The combination of overcrowding and exposure took its toll. Despite calm seas, seasickness was rampant and the troops disembarked considerably weakened by the voyage.

The discomfort aboard ship was merely a prelude to the chaos that met the regiment when it went ashore. It was the rainy season in Panama. A cholera epidemic was raging and the local transportation arranged by the War Department failed to materialize. Grant, who was responsible for the regiment's logistics, confronted the crisis with the calm determination that would become his hallmark. He discharged the local contractor, sent the able-bodied men ahead, used his knowledge of Spanish to rent pack animals on the open market—regulations to the contrary notwithstanding—and then organized a mule train of dependents and baggage that he led single file across the mountains.[49] Meanwhile, cholera worked its will. "Men were dying every hour," wrote Grant. Delia Sheffield said, "The ravages of the disease were dreadful. We did not know who would be the next victim, and it grew to be a common sight to see strong men be taken with cramps and die in a short time." She credited Grant and the surgeons with great presence of mind and tireless energy in checking the spread of the disease. "It was not an easy task to control almost seven hundred men during a siege of cholera, for they grew nervous and panic-stricken and Captain Grant had not only the sick ones to contend with but also the well."[50]

When the regiment reached Panama City on the Pacific Coast, the disease was raging even more virulently. Grant established a field hospital on nearby Flamingo Island and moved the worst cases to an old barge anchored a mile off shore. When orderlies balked at tending the sick, Grant undertook the nursing himself. "He was like a ministering angel to us all," said one survivor. Another called Grant a "man of iron, so far as endurance went, seldom sleeping, and then only two or three hours at a time." Captain Henry Wallen, who served with Grant throughout the Mexican War, recalled that when cholera struck, Grant was one of the few who kept his head. "He was the coolest man I ever saw."[51] Grant survived the epidemic unscathed, but would often reflect upon the suffering he saw. "The horrors are beyond description," he wrote Julia.[52] "Every child of Fred's age or younger, and there were twenty of them, either died on the crossing or shortly thereafter."[53] Those who knew Grant in later years said he talked more about Panama than any of his battles.[54] Certainly his recollection of crossing the isthmus remained vivid. In his first presidential message to Congress, December 6, 1869, he recommended construction of a canal linking the two oceans, and instructed the navy to explore various Central American alternatives.[55]*

By early August 1852 the cholera epidemic had run its course. After three weeks on the isthmus, 450 survivors of the regiment boarded the steamship *Golden Gate* for passage to San Francisco. According to shipping figures, about 35,000 passengers made the journey across Panama that year, but none suffered more severely than the 4th Infantry.[56] The *Panama Herald* wrote, "There is great fault somewhere and just censure should be meted out . . . the whole business reflects great discredit upon the United States."[57] Military authorities in California blamed the War Department, recommending that in the future troops be sent by ship around Cape Horn. "Recent experience has shown that, unless in a case of emergency, the Isthmus is a very trying route, causing much sickness, and a great loss in public property, besides doubling the expense, compared with the other route. The 4th Infantry, which recently arrived, show the impractibility as their loss has been great, while those who have arrived are broken down by disease, the seeds of which were engendered in the Isthmus."[58] Grant wrote Julia, "There is great accountability somewhere for the loss which we have sustained," but he declined to point his finger at anyone.[59]

After two uneventful weeks at sea, the *Golden Gate* tied up at San Francisco's long wharf the evening of August 17, 1852. The gold rush was at its height. California, which was admitted to the Union in 1850, and whose population barely totaled 20,000 in 1848, now numbered 225,000 with more than 50,000 persons arriving annually.[60] San Francisco, a simple fishing village in 1849, boasted almost a fifth of the total. Eggs sold for $10 a dozen and a shot of whiskey cost a pinch of gold. Grant called the city "the wonder of the world. It has been burned down three times and rebuilt each time better than before."[61] In his words: "Steamers plied daily between San Francisco and both Stockton and Sacramento. Passengers and gold from the southern mines came by the Stockton boat; from the northern mines by Sacramento. In the evening when those boats arrived, Long Wharf was alive with people crowding to meet the miners as they came down to sell their 'dust' and to 'have a time.' "[62]

Grant was caught up in the excitement. His first evening ashore he won $40 at faro and treated himself to a splendid dinner.[63] Three days later

---

* David McCullough, principal historian of the Panama Canal, reports that "Grant, despite his subsequent reputation as a President of little vision or initiative, was more keenly interested in an isthmian canal than any of his predecessors had been. He was indeed the first President to address himself seriously to the subject. If there was to be a water corridor, he wanted it in the proper place — as determined by civil engineers and naval authorities — and he wanted it under American control." *The Path Between the Seas* 26 (New York: Simon & Schuster, 1977).

he wrote Julia he had "seen enough of California to know that it is different from anything that a person in the states could imagine in their wildest dreams. There is no reason why an active, energetic person should not make a fortune a year." Already officers such as Henry Halleck and Joseph Hooker were amassing money moonlighting (Halleck as a lawyer, Hooker speculating in land), and Grant raised the possibility of leaving the army. In one year, he told Julia, he could make enough money "to make us comfortable" for the rest of our lives. "Of course I do not contemplate doing anything of the sort, because what I have is a certainty, and what I might expect to do, might prove a dream."[64] Nevertheless, the lure of easy money beckoned. Having miraculously avoided infection by cholera in Panama, Grant was bitten by the gold bug as soon as he landed in California. Years later, matured by his own unhappy experience, he wrote with wry understatement that "those early days in California brought out character."[65]

The 4th Infantry remained in the San Francisco area four weeks. Grant spent the time visiting Julia's two brothers, who had struck it rich operating a hotel and ferry service on the Stanislaus River—midway between San Francisco and the diggings. Grant's envy was manifest. He told Julia "there are three stages per day, each way, crossing at the ferry, and generally come loaded with eight to twelve passengers each. All of these stop at the hotel and dine." Dinner cost $1 and the ferry $2. The brothers also ran a livery service and a cattle ranch—"all worth about tribble what they would be in the Atlantic States. . . . [A]s to profits they are clearing about fifty to one hundred dollars daily."[66]

In mid-September the 4th Infantry boarded ship for passage to its final destination, Fort Vancouver on the Columbia River. The regiment was ordered to spread its force over northern California and the Oregon Territory to protect the incoming settlers. Regimental headquarters would be at Fort Vancouver, the former headquarters of Great Britain's Hudson's Bay Company, about six miles down the Columbia from Portland in what is now the state of Washington. At the beginning of the nineteenth century the Hudson's Bay Company enjoyed a monopoly of the fur trade on the Pacific Coast and was a leading force in the settlement of the region. A territorial dispute between the United States and Great Britain riled relations between the two nations for decades, but in 1846 the Polk administration concluded a treaty with the government of Lord Aberdeen fixing the boundary at the 49th parallel. The treaty was a compromise between the American demand expressed in the slogan "Fifty-four Forty or Fight" and the British desire to set the boundary at the north bank of the Columbia River. The final outcome left Fort Vancouver in American hands. The Hudson's Bay Company moved its headquarters northward to Victoria Island in British Columbia, but continued to do business in the region until the Civil War.[67]

Grant settled easily into the routine at Fort Vancouver. Unfortunately, without Julia, he was soon adrift on a sea of financial speculation. "Living is expensive," he wrote his wife in early October, "but I have made fifteen hundred dollars since I have been here and I have every confidence that I shall make more than five thousand within the year."[68] The profit was illusory, and the first in a long string of financial misadventures had begun. Grant seldom met a man he did not trust, and all too often his trust was misplaced. In this case the man was Elijah Camp, a merchant from Sackets Harbor who accompanied the 4th Infantry to San Francisco. Camp persuaded Grant to go into partnership in a sutler's store: Grant to provide the capital, Camp to run the store. The enterprise prospered initially, and after a month Camp offered to buy Grant out for $1,500. Rather than paying cash, however, he gave Grant an unsecured note for that amount. In the spring of 1853 Camp tired of California, sold out, and returned to Sackets Harbor still owing Grant for his original investment. Afterward, Julia chided her husband for his credulity. "Compared to you, the Vicar of Wakefield's Moses was a financier."[69]*

Grant's ill-fated deal with Camp was just the beginning. In the autumn of 1852 he began buying cattle and hogs to sell in the spring. Captain Henry Wallen threw in with him and took the animals to market. "We continued that business until both of us lost all the money we had," said Wallen.[70] Later that winter Grant, Wallen, and Grant's West Point classmate Rufus Ingalls, who was also stationed at Fort Vancouver, heard ice was selling for an outrageous price in San Francisco. They cut and loaded 100 tons aboard a sailing schooner bound for the metropolis and waited for their windfall. The windfall came, but it was a headwind blowing offshore that retarded the vessel's progress by two weeks. The ice melted and their investment was lost.[71]

Then, in the spring of 1853, Grant, Wallen, and two fellow officers decided they could make money farming. They leased 100 acres from the Hudson's Bay Company, bought horses, a wagon, harness, farming implements, seed stock, and hired enlisted men to clear the underbrush. The costs were substantial. "Seed potatoes cost $2 a bushel," Grant wrote Julia, "and I shall put in 200 bushels."[72] In early March, prospects looked good. "By the end of the coming week myself and partners will have planted twenty acres of potatoes and an acre of onions. In a week or two more we will plant a few acres of corn."[73] Grant said he was farming in earnest. "All the ploughing and furrowing I do myself. I was surprised to find that I could run as straight a furrow now as I could fifteen years ago and work all

* The reference is to Moses Primrose, second son of the Vicar of Wakefield, who, in Oliver Goldsmith's novel, was "designed for business" but easily swindled.

day quite as well. I never worked before with so much pleasure either, because now I feel sure that every day will bring a large reward." [74]

Grant also bought an enormous quantity of timber, which he had cut and stacked to sell to incoming steamboats. "I will get $2.50 per cord more than it cost me to get it cut," he wrote Julia. [75] But disaster struck. In late spring the snow on the Cascade range melted, the Columbia River flooded, and the officers' vegetable crop was destroyed. The potatoes and onions rotted in the ground, the grain was washed away, and the wood had to be removed and restacked, wiping out the profit Grant anticipated. [76]

Desperate to recoup their investment, Grant and Wallen entered the chicken business. They bought up all the chickens within twenty miles of Fort Vancouver, chartered a vessel, and shipped them off to San Francisco. Once again the vessel was delayed, the chickens died, and they lost the money they put into the effort. [77] The would-be moguls turned next to the entertainment business. Remembering their experience at the Aztec Club in Mexico City—a social club established by American officers after the armistice—they leased space in the Union Hotel in San Francisco and hired an agent to operate it as a social club and billiard room. San Francisco was full of unattached males and the idea looked foolproof. However, the agent they hired absconded with the officers' funds. Yet another project had miscarried. [78] Wallen expressed the problem succinctly. "Neither Grant nor myself had the slightest suggestion of business talent. He was the perfect soul of honor and truth, and believed everyone as artless as himself." [79]

Grant longed for Julia. Her first letter did not arrive until December 1852, and by then he was desperate for news of her and the children. Whether she had given birth successfully, whether it was a boy or a girl, whether they were well and properly cared for—all of this he had yet to hear. "Just think, our youngest is at this moment probably over three months of age, and yet I have never heard a word from it," he wrote that fall. [80] On December 3 the mail drought ended and the steamer brought four long-delayed letters from Julia. Grant was beside himself. "When I got these letters I jumped with joy. You have no idea how happy it made me feel." [81] But the mail steamer came to Fort Vancouver only twice a month, and even when it did bring a letter from Julia, it was a poor substitute for the companionship Grant needed. By year's end he was more dispirited than ever. "I would prefer sacrificing my commission and try something [else] to continuing this separation. If I could see Fred and hear him talk, and see little Ulys [his second son, Ulysses S. Grant, Jr., born July 22, 1852], I could then be contented provided their mother was with them." [82]

As Grant's financial situation deteriorated his letters became more melancholy. Repeatedly he asked about the children. "Does Fred know his letters yet?"[83] "What does the S stand for in Ulys's name? In mine you know it does not stand for anything."[84] "Does Ulys walk yet?"[85] Julia's letters to Grant have been lost, but from his replies it is apparent she encouraged him to resign and go into business with his father. Grant was not convinced. "I have heard nothing of the proposition to resign that you spoke of. I shall weigh the matter carefully before I act."[86]

Separated from his wife and children, and in despair over his failure to earn the money that might enable them to join him on the West Coast, Grant began to drink more than was good for him. The army was a hard-drinking outfit in those years, especially on the frontier where officers were without family. Virtually everyone drank, and drank quite a lot, but in Grant's case a little liquor went a long way.[87] His slight frame (Grant stood five feet seven inches and weighed 135 pounds) would have limited his capacity in any event, but his metabolism was such that every drink showed. A couple of swallows slurred his speech, and a drink or two made him drunk.[88] Lieutenant Henry Hodges, a close friend of Grant's who served with him at Fort Vancouver, said the future commanding general recognized his problem and usually abstained. "He would perhaps go on two or three sprees a year, but was always open to reason, and when spoken to on the subject would own up and promise to stop drinking, which he did."[89]

In 1853 Grant's "sprees" became more frequent and for the first time began to affect his performance. One of Grant's responsibilities as quartermaster was to outfit the numerous survey parties dispatched by the War Department to map the Oregon Territory. One such party, headed by Captain George B. McClellan, arrived at Fort Vancouver in July, intent on exploring the Cascade range and locating, if possible, a pass for the Northern Pacific Railroad. McClellan and Grant were acquainted from the Mexican War, and Little Mac had recently acquired professional prominence in the Corps of Engineers for his surveys of the Red River and the Texas coast. Grant worked diligently to assemble the horses and supplies McClellan needed.[90] Before the task was finished, however, Grant began drinking and as Hodges recalled, "got on one of his little sprees, which annoyed and offended McClellan exceedingly, and in my opinion he never quite forgave Grant for it, notwithstanding the necessary transportation was soon in readiness."[91]

Grant, who had held the temporary rank of captain since the spring of 1851, was now the ranking first lieutenant on the permanent roll of the 4th Infantry. The next vacancy among the regiment's regular army captains would bring a permanent promotion and with it a new assignment and an increase in pay.* In anticipation, Grant resigned as regimental quartermaster at the end of August 1853 and wrote the War Department requesting a return to Washington to settle his accounts. "I am particularly anxious to be present in Washington for the reason that I had public funds stolen from me during the Mexican War, and for which I have been petitioning Congress ever since."[92] Grant's request was a cry for help. He missed Julia and the children terribly, and believed that if he returned to Washington he could retrieve them and bring them to California.[93] Traveling under military orders would defray the costs. That was Grant's rationale, and his commanding officer at Fort Vancouver, Lieutenant Colonel Benjamin Bonneville, endorsed the request.[94] But the War Department turned Grant down. "There is no necessity for your presence at Washington to settle your accounts," wrote the quartermaster general. "You have only to forward them and they will be properly settled."[95] Grant, in his brooding loneliness, had exaggerated his importance and convinced himself the War Department would order his return. Army regulations were specific as to how quartermaster accounts should be settled, however, and the refusal he received was routine.

Two weeks after writing to Washington, Grant received notification of his promotion to captain in the regular army.[96] With the promotion he became an officer of the line and a company commander. Secretary of War Jefferson Davis instructed him to "proceed, without delay, to join your company (F) at Fort Humboldt, California."[97] Located on a high bluff above Humboldt Bay, 250 miles north of San Francisco, the post to which Grant was assigned had been established by the 4th Infantry shortly after its arrival on the Pacific Coast. It was remote and largely inaccessible except by water, but its idyllic location amidst the towering redwood forests of northern California made it a desirable posting and many of Grant's contemporaries considered it preferable to Fort Vancouver.[98] The garrison consisted of two companies—B and F—and the commanding officer was Brevet Lieutenant Colonel Robert C. Buchanan, a West Point graduate of the class of 1830 who, like Grant, had spent his entire military career in the 4th Infantry. Buchanan was "old army"—a phrase used by soldiers to describe a commanding officer more punctilious than the situation required. Lieutenant Hodges considered him "a very good soldier but a martinet."[99] Breveted twice for gallantry in the Mexican War—it was said he forced the doors of Molino del Rey with his bare hands[100]—Buchanan was the senior

---

* Permanent rank (and pay) in the pre–Civil War army was determined on a regimental basis. Each regiment had a permanent roster of officers, many of whom were detached to serve elsewhere, but who nevertheless were carried on the regiment's roll. Advancement from one rank to the next was based strictly on seniority whenever a vacancy occurred.

captain in the regular army in 1853 and there is no question he ran a tight ship. The inspector general rated Fort Humboldt highly. "The discipline is good, arms and equipment in good serviceable order, and attention paid to the comforts of the men." [101]

Grant was dubious about his new assignment. There were no family quarters at Fort Humboldt and mail delivery was even more irregular than at Fort Vancouver. On the other hand, Buchanan was due for permanent promotion to major and as Grant told Julia, "I should [then] have command of the post, with double rations and two companies." [102] Nevertheless, Grant was in no rush to join his new command. He took three months to settle his accounts at Fort Vancouver, and did not arrive until January 5, 1854. Two weeks later Grant wrote Julia that his feelings about Fort Humboldt were mixed. The remoteness was unbearable. "Imagine a place . . . closed in by a bay that can be entered only with certain winds." [103] But F Company was better than he expected. "All the men are old soldiers and very neat in their appearance. The contrast between them and the other company here is very great." Grant's company was only at one third of its authorized strength, however, and aside from garrison routine there was little to keep him busy. By early February the tedium got to him. Grant was suffering from the military equivalent of cabin fever. "You do not know how forsaken I feel here," he wrote Julia. "I do nothing but sit in my room and read and occasionally take a short ride on one of the public horses." [104]

A contractor who supplied the garrison with beef saw what was happening to Grant:

> The line captain's duties were fewer and less onerous than the quartermaster's had been and the discipline was far more rigid and irksome. No greater misfortune could have happened to him than this enforced idleness. He had little work, no family with him, took no pleasure in the amusements of his fellow officers—dancing, billiards, hunting, fishing, and the like. The result was a common one. He took to liquor. Not in enormous quantities, for he drank far less than other officers. . . . [But] like Cassio, he had a poor brain for drinking.* The weakness did not belong to his character, for in all other respects he was a man of unusual self-control. [105]

---

* The reference is to Michael Cassio, Othello's lieutenant in Shakespeare's play, an abstemious soldier whom Iago plies with strong drink and then discredits. "Reputation, reputation, I have lost my reputation! I have lost the immortal part, sir, of myself, and what remains is bestial." Act II, scene 3, lines 254–57. Cassio survived, and at the end of the play is given command of Cyprus, thereby loosely fitting Shakespeare's formula of a man who suffers in order to be cleansed.

As each day passed Grant's loneliness increased. By mid-February he had not received a single letter and was not yet aware the War Department had denied his request to return to Washington. "The state of suspense I am in is scarcely bearable," he wrote Julia. "I think I have been from my family quite long enough and sometimes I feel as though I could almost go home *'nolens volens.'** I presume, under ordinary circumstances, Humboldt would be a good enough place but the suspense I am in would make paradise form a bad picture." Grant consoled himself with the thought that many were in a worse fix than he. "Misery loves company, and some have been separated much longer from their families than I have been." [106]

The separation began to take a physical toll on Grant. For the first time in years he became ill—first with a tooth that had to be extracted, then with chills and fever. Fort Humboldt post returns list him as "sick" for the month of February.[107] In March, utterly despondent, he wrote Julia he was "so anxious to see you, and our little boys, that I am almost tempted to resign and trust to Providence, and my own exertions for a living where I can have you and them with me. . . . Whenever I get to thinking upon the subject however *poverty, poverty,* begins to stare me in the face and then I think what would I do if you and our little ones should want for the necessities of life." [108] In the summer he planned an excursion out to the gold mines, and in the fall he would take a trip along the immigrant trail. "This will help pass off much of the time." [109]

Despite the morose tone of his letters to Julia, there is no indication Grant planned to leave the army. To the contrary. On April 3 he wrote that he feared Fort Humboldt would be shut down and he would be transferred to a less desirable post in the interior. "The best we can hope for is Fort Jones [located on the Scott River in the mountains of northern California] where the buildings . . . are just rough log pens, covered over, with places for a door and windows but left without these luxuries as well as without floors." Grant told Julia his health had improved and repeated his plans to spend a month on the trail.[110]

The following week, Grant resigned abruptly. Addressing a one-sentence letter to the adjutant general, he wrote:

> I very respectfully tender my resignation of my commission as an officer of the Army, and request that it may take effect from the 31st of July next.
>
> Very Respectfully,
> Yr. Obt. Svt.
> U.S. GRANT, *Captain 4th Inf.*[111]

---

* Usually translated as "whether willing or not," or "willy-nilly," but in the military vernacular the phrase was used to mean going absent without leave (AWOL).

That was it. No reason. No explanation. Only a simple declarative state-ment. Army gossip holds that Colonel Buchanan forced Grant's resigna-tion after discovering him inebriated during pay call. Because of Grant's distinguished service in Mexico, Buchanan allegedly offered him the choice of resigning or being court-martialed, and Grant chose to resign. Lieutenant Hodges summarized the episode: "It seems that one day while his company was being paid off, Captain Grant was at the pay table, slightly under the influence of liquor. This came to the knowledge of Colonel Buchanan; he gave Grant the option of resigning or having charges preferred against him. Grant resigned at once." Hodges said the regiment thought Colonel Buchanan "was unnecessarily harsh and se-vere," and perhaps should have overlooked "this first small offence at his post."[112]

Rufus Ingalls, who roomed with Grant plebe year at West Point and who remained his lifelong friend, corroborated the account. According to Ingalls:

> Grant, finding himself in dreary surroundings, without his family, and with but little to occupy his attention, fell into dissi-pated habits, and was found one day, too much under the influ-ence of liquor to properly perform his duties. For this offense Colonel Buchanan demanded that he should resign, or stand trial. Grant's friends at the time urged him to stand trial, and were confident of his acquittal; but, actuated by a noble spirit, he said he would not for all the world have his wife know that he had been tried on such a charge. He therefore resigned his com-mission, and returned to civil life.[113]

The story rings true. Grant, in his letters to Julia, flirted with the idea of resigning but always backed off: *"poverty, poverty,* begins to stare me in the face." The week before his resignation he wrote he was in good health and planned to spend a month in the mountains. He even seemed to ap-preciate Fort Humboldt's attractions. There is no doubt he missed his family, had too little to do, and was drinking too much, but there is no ev-idence that he was seriously contemplating leaving the army. His resigna-tion was too abrupt to have been a calculated move. And whatever one may say about Grant, precipitate action was not characteristic of his be-havior.

Neither Grant nor Buchanan made any public comment about the episode—which lends further authenticity to the tale. If Buchanan were giving Grant an honorable way out, honor would dictate nothing more be said. Grant's official explanation was that he resigned because he could not support his wife and children on the Pacific Coast on his army salary.[114] Years later, however, he told educator John Eaton "the vice of intemperance had not a little to do with my decision to resign."[115] Buchanan said nothing until the Civil War, when he was pressed for details by one of his regimental commanders, at which point he confirmed that he had given Grant the choice of resigning or standing trial.[116]*

Julia's reaction is difficult to determine. In her *Memoirs* she wrote simply, "After an absence of over two years, Captain Grant, to my great delight, resigned his commission in the U.S. Army and returned to me, his loving little wife."[117] The record, however, indicates Grant was sufficiently concerned as to what Julia's response might be that he did not write her until May 2, the day after he was relieved of command, and even then did not mention he had resigned. The letter is curt, almost abrasive:

> Dear Wife: I do not propose writing you but a few lines. I have not yet received a letter from you and as I have a "leave of absence" and will be away from here in a few days do not expect to. After receiving this you may discontinue writing because before I could get a reply I shall be on my way home. You might write directing [the letter] to the City of New York.[118]

Grant's father was stunned when he heard the news. Grant had not written to him either. In early June, Jesse was informed by Congressman

---

* Buchanan was the quintessential professional soldier. His troops from the 4th Infantry put down the Rogue River Indian uprising in 1856, and he led the U.S. forces that reasserted federal authority in Utah during the Mormon War of 1857–1858. When the Civil War came, he was given command of the Regular Brigade of the Army of the Potomac—the closest American equivalent to Napoleon's Old Guard. Brevetted twice more for gallantry, his troops fought with distinction at Gaines Mill, Malvern Hill, Antietam, Fredericksburg, and the second battle of Bull Run. When McClellan broke off his attack on Richmond in 1862 and retreated to Harrison's Landing, it was the Regular Brigade that covered his withdrawal. *The Dictionary of American Biography* states Buchanan "was affectionately known to Civil War soldiers as 'Old Buck,' and his brigade of regular soldiers proved always a dependable reserve in many of the earlier battles of the war. That such was the case was largely due to his wide experience, fine attainments, and high sense of duty and discipline." 3 DAB 217–18.

Promoted to major general on Grant's recommendation in 1865, Buchanan served as assistant commissioner of the Freedmen's Bureau until 1867 when he was tapped to assume command of the military occupation of Louisiana, which had encountered great difficulty. General Sheridan, the first commander, had been too rigid, and Winfield Scott Hancock, his successor, had been too lenient. To restore order, Grant turned to Buchanan, who proved once more he was a complete professional. He followed Grant's instructions to the letter (volume 18 of the *Grant Papers* is replete with telegrams between Grant and Buchanan), deferred to the commanding general's judgment on political issues, and successfully terminated the occupation following the state's ratification of the Fourteenth Amendment. John Rose Ficklen, *History of Reconstruction in Louisiana* 201 (Baltimore: Johns Hopkins University Press, 1910).

Andrew Ellison that the War Department had announced Grant's resignation, effective July 31, 1854.[119] Jesse intervened immediately. He was not aware of the circumstances but felt instinctively his son was making a mistake. Jesse urged Congressman Ellison to have the War Department order Grant home on recruiting duty, and if that were not possible, then to allow him a six-month leave of absence. Ellison, who was an old friend of the Grant family, transmitted Jesse's request to Secretary of War Jefferson Davis, but to no avail.[120] On June 7, 1854, Davis confirmed Grant had resigned, and that his resignation had been accepted. It is doubtful if Davis knew of the situation at Fort Humboldt, but the army had a surplus of officers after the Mexican War and only by death or resignation could that surplus be reduced.[121] When Ellison informed Jesse of the secretary's reply, Grant's father wrote to Davis on his son's behalf:

> If it is consistent with your powers and the good of the service, I would be much gratified if you would reconsider and withdraw the acceptance of his resignation and grant him a six month leave, that he may come home and see his family.
>
> I never wished him to leave the service. I think after spending so many years in the service, he will be poorly qualified for the pursuits of private life.[122]

Jesse told Davis that Grant had fought in all of the battles of the Mexican War except Buena Vista, and had a two-year-old son whom he had never seen. "Would it then be asking too much for him to have a leave that he may come home and make arrangements for taking his family to his post?" Davis replied that Grant had given no reasons as to why he wanted to leave the service and his motives were unknown. "He only asked that his resignation should take effect on the 31st July next and it was accepted accordingly. The acceptance is, therefore, complete, and cannot be reconsidered."[123]

Grant arrived in New York on June 25, 1854, dejected and virtually penniless.[124] His passage from the West Coast had been arranged by Major Robert Allen, the chief quartermaster of the Pacific Division, an old friend from southern Ohio who did his utmost to assist.[125] No letter from Julia was waiting for him when he arrived and Grant was uncertain whether he could return home.* Simon Bolivar Buckner, who was on commissary duty in New York, recalled Grant coming to his office for help. "He had

---

* In her *Memoirs,* Julia quotes Grant as saying, "You know I had to wait in New York until I heard from you." The implication is that Grant did not know whether he would be welcome at White Haven. *The Personal Memoirs of Julia Dent Grant* 72, John Y. Simon, ed. (New York: G. P. Putnam's Sons, 1975).

been staying at the old Astor House and his money was gone. He asked for a loan in order to pay his bills at the hotel, and reach his father in southern Ohio."[126] Buckner took charge of Grant, guaranteed his bills at the Astor House, and urged him to write his father for money. For Grant that had been unthinkable—a humiliation he could not face. Reluctantly, he accepted Buckner's advice. Jesse sent the money promptly, whereupon Grant paid his New York bills and bought a train ticket to Cincinnati. Buckner noted that when their positions were reversed after the surrender of Fort Donelson and "I became his prisoner, Grant tendered me the use of his purse. It showed his appreciation of my aid to him years before, which was really very little."[127]

Grant did not leave New York immediately. He still had not heard from Julia and so decided to go to Sackets Harbor to collect the money Elijah Camp owed him. Grant wrote Camp he was coming, Camp left town, and Grant returned to New York so much the poorer for the trip.[128] His only satisfaction was that Julia's letter was waiting for him. Laying to rest his worst fears, it welcomed him home with open arms.[129]

Grant's odyssey in the wilderness was just beginning. For the next seven years he would struggle to support his family, without capital, occasionally destitute, working with his hands to make ends meet. It was one of the lowest periods in Grant's life. It was also a time of testing. As he and Julia faced hardship together, they rekindled a love that tided them through the worst times. He did not drink and he seldom lost hope. In 1862 he would defend the Union's overrun position at Shiloh with the same stoicism and resolve. Grant recalled those lean years in Missouri with clarity:

> In the late summer of 1854 I rejoined my family, to find a son I had never seen. I was now to commence, at the age of thirty-two, a new struggle for our support. My wife had a farm near St. Louis, to which we went, but I had no means to stock it. A house had to be built also. I worked very hard, never losing a day because of bad weather, and accomplished the object in a moderate way. If nothing else could be done I would load a cord of wood on a wagon and take it to the city for sale. I managed to keep along fairly well until 1858, when I was attacked by fever and ague. It lasted over a year, and, while it did not keep me in the house, it did interfere greatly with the amount of work I was able to perform. In 1858 I sold out my stock, crops and farming utensils at auction and gave up farming.[130]

The farm to which Grant referred consisted of sixty acres of uncleared land given to Julia by her father as a wedding present. Grant spent the first year clearing the land and the second building a house—a squared-off log structure with hand hewn timbers and the rough appearance of a pioneer dwelling. "It was so crude and so homely I did not like it at all," wrote Julia. "It looked so unattractive that we facetiously decided to call it Hardscrabble."[131] Strapped for operating expenses, Grant did the best he could. He had only one team of horses and one field hand, and was often unable to buy seed.[132] "I wanted to plant sixty or seventy bushels of potatoes," he wrote his father at the close of 1856, "but had not the money to buy them." The same was true of the cabbages and cucumbers he wanted to plant.[133] Grant swallowed his pride and asked for a loan. "It is always usual for parents to give their children assistance in beginning life (and I am only beginning, though nearly thirty-five years of age) and what I ask is not much. I do not ask you to give me anything. But what I do ask is that you lend, or borrow for, me five hundred dollars, for two years, with interest at 10 percent payable annually, and with this if I do not go on prosperously I shall ask no more from you."[134] Jesse did not reply and the money was not forthcoming.

Whatever income Grant derived—and it rarely exceeded $50 a month—came from selling firewood in St. Louis. Grant would load his wagon, hitch his team, and drive to the city, where he would pull up at a busy street corner and peddle the wood to passers-by. Occasionally he would meet former comrades. "Great God, Grant, what are you doing?" asked one officer who had not seen him since Mexico.

"I am solving the problem of poverty," Grant replied.[135]

Lieutenant William W. Averell of the 3rd Infantry, off on an expedition to New Mexico, had progressed fourteen miles west of St. Louis when he saw "a horseman in a faded blue overcoat, a hat broken and worn, and a stubby, sandy beard" overtake the column and engage the commissary officer, Lieutenant William Craig, in conversation. After a time the man rode away and Craig said, "That's old Ulysses S. Grant of the 4th Infantry. He wanted a job as a commissary clerk to drive beef cattle and issue rations as we were crossing the plains. I couldn't employ him."[136]

Brigadier General Edward F. Beale won Grant's undying loyalty one day when, arriving from California, he saw a man outside the Planters' Hotel wearing old army clothing from which the insignia had been removed. The general recognized Grant instantly and invited him to dinner.

"I'm not dressed for company," said Grant.

"Oh, that doesn't matter, come in!"

Grant talked easily with the officers accompanying Beale but his conversation, they noted, was about old friends—where they were now and what they were doing.[137]

Officers from Jefferson Barracks who regularly saw Grant reported he did not drink. Don Carlos Buell, then with the adjutant general's department, said Grant "drank nothing but water." Major Joseph J. Reynolds, a classmate of Grant's who was resigning to become an engineering professor at Washington University in St. Louis, confirmed Buell's assessment. "He will go into the bar with you," said Reynolds, "but he will not touch anything." [138]

One day in late 1857 Grant met another down-and-out West Pointer on the streets of St. Louis. William Tecumseh Sherman had resigned from the army in 1853 to become a banker, only to lose everything in the financial panic that struck the United States in August 1857. The two ex-soldiers had not seen each other in sixteen years and they briefly compared notes on their parallel careers. Sherman considered himself "a dead cock in the Pit"; Grant told of his farming misadventure. Both agreed that "West Point and the Regular Army were not good schools for farmers, bankers, merchants, and mechanics." [139]

Grant too lost heavily in the Panic of 1857. Just when it seemed he might make it, commodity prices collapsed. "My oats were good, and the corn . . . the best I ever raised." [140] The potatoes, cabbages, and melons also produced bumper crops. But Grant was stuck with them. With no market, most of his produce had to be given away. On December 23, 1857, he pawned his gold watch—his last valuable possession—so his family might have money to celebrate Christmas. [141]

When the nation's economic distress eased in the spring of 1858, a new glimmer of hope appeared for Grant. Colonel Dent, now a widower, decided to leave White Haven and move to the city. He rented the farm to Grant and Julia, and the two anticipated a bright future. They moved into the big house, leased Hardscrabble, and began planting. Grant optimistically wrote his sister Mary, "I have now three Negro men, two hired by the year and one of Mr. Dent's, which, with my own help, I think, will enable me to do my farming pretty well. I shall have about 20 acres of potatoes, 20 of corn, 25 of oats, 50 of wheat, 25 of meadow, some clover and other smaller products." [142] But even this was not to be. As with his farming venture in California, it was the weather that proved Grant's undoing. A cold spring destroyed most of the crops and a record freeze on June 5 killed what remained. Grant was reduced once more to peddling firewood on St. Louis street corners.

Major James Longstreet, returning that summer from an assignment in Texas, stopped briefly at the Planters' Hotel where he met several old friends from Jefferson Barracks. According to Longstreet, "It was soon proposed to have an old-time game of brag." Finding themselves one short, Captain Edmund Holloway, also in from Texas, said he would find someone. "In a few minutes he returned with a man poorly dressed in citizen's clothes and in whom we recognized our old friend Grant." It was a happy reunion but Longstreet was saddened because he saw "Grant had been unfortunate, and he was really in needy circumstances."

> The next day I was walking in front of the Planters', when I found myself face to face again with Grant who, placing in the palm of my hand a five dollar gold piece, insisted that I should take it in payment of a debt of honor over fifteen years old. I peremptorily declined to take it, alleging that he was out of the service and more in need of it than I.
>
> "You must take it," said he. "I cannot live with anything in my possession which is not mine." Seeing the determination in the man's face, and in order to save him mortification, I took the money, and shaking hands we parted.

Longstreet said, "The next time we met was at Appomattox, and the first thing that General Grant said to me when we stepped aside, placing his arm in mine, was: 'Pete, let's have another game of brag, to recall the old days which were so pleasant to us all.' His whole greeting and conduct was as though nothing had ever happened to mar our pleasant relations." [143]

By autumn 1858 Grant had had enough. The chills and fever that crippled him as a youth had returned, and he decided to sell out and seek employment in St. Louis.[144] Grant found no job at first, and walked the streets looking for work.[145] Eventually Colonel Dent secured a place for him in the real estate business of his nephew Harry Boggs. The firm was restyled "Boggs & Grant," and they advertised themselves as general agents who collected rents, negotiated loans, and bought and sold real estate. Grant's task was to keep the records, push the properties listed with the firm, and collect rents for various landlords. He hoped to trade Hardscrabble for a house in the city as soon as possible and move his family into town. In the meantime, he stayed with Harry and Louisa Boggs at 209 South Fifteenth Street. "We gave him an unfurnished back room and told him to fit it up as he pleased," recalled Mrs. Boggs. "It contained very little during the winter he lived there. He had a bed, and a bowl and a pitcher on a chair; and, as he had no stove, he used to sit at our fire almost every evening." On Saturdays Grant walked the twelve miles to White Haven, and on Sundays he walked the twelve miles back. Louisa Boggs thought Grant was "a very domestic man and extremely homelike in his ways," but always seemed depressed. "He would smile at times, but I never heard him laugh out loud. He was a sad man. I don't believe he had any ambition other than to educate his children and take care of his family." [146]

Grant's unfitness for commercial life soon became apparent. He was too tenderhearted to be a rent collector and too candid to sell real estate. Property values were soaring in St. Louis (between 1856 and 1858 the assessed valuation of the city's real estate climbed from $60 million to $82 million[147]) and demand was brisk. Nevertheless, the firm of Boggs & Grant languished. A lawyer who worked with Grant said, "He just doesn't seem to be calculated for business, but a more honest, more generous man never lived. I don't believe that he knows what dishonesty is."[148]

Grant was so trusting that even the sale of Hardscrabble miscarried. In the spring of 1859 he traded the property for a house of lesser value in St. Louis and took a $3,000 note to cover the difference. The city house was mortgaged, however, and the seller undertook to discharge the mortgage as part of the transaction. This he failed to do. Grant did not get clear title to the house until he paid the mortgage himself. The $3,000 note Grant held on Hardscrabble also was not paid and he was forced to sue. The litigation was interrupted by the war, and Grant did not regain possession of the farm until 1867.[149]

The circumstances are not clear, but sometime during his last year at White Haven he acquired possession of the young slave Colonel Dent left behind, a thirty-five-year-old man named William Jones. Grant's views on slavery were ambivalent and Jones was the only slave he ever owned. When he moved to St. Louis, Grant was initially tempted to rent the man out, but soon decided against it. On March 29, 1859, he went to circuit court and filed the manumission papers to emancipate Jones.[150] Grant never discussed his motives, but the action speaks for itself. Able-bodied slaves sold for a thousand dollars or more, and Grant surely could have used the money. Instead, he set Jones free.

By the summer of 1859 it was apparent the firm of Boggs & Grant could not survive. Grant withdrew from the partnership and resumed his search for employment. In August, when the position of county engineer became vacant, he applied for the job. His application was supported by a number of prominent St. Louis citizens, including the former president of the American Medical Association and the publisher of the *Missouri Democrat*. Professor Joseph Reynolds, Grant's classmate, wrote a strong personal endorsement as did Daniel Frost, another West Pointer in business in St. Louis.[151] Grant failed to secure the position, but the decision of the five-man county council was primarily political. It did not reflect upon Grant's qualifications for the job. The two Democratic members of the council voted for him; the three Free-Soilers voted against. Grant was disappointed but not surprised. He wrote his father that because of his relationship with the Dents he was tagged as a Democrat, although he had never voted the Democratic ticket.[152] Grant said he had supported James Buchanan for president in 1856, but that was only to defeat former general

John C. Frémont, who was running as a Republican.[153] In later years Grant quipped he voted for Buchanan because he didn't know him, and voted against Frémont because he did.[154]

That winter Grant found employment as a clerk in the United States customshouse. The pay was $1,200 a year and the income was steady. His ill luck, however, continued. Within a month the collector of customs died and the new Democratic appointee let Grant go.[155] High and dry once more, he looked desperately for work. He was behind in his rent, could not meet the family's daily living expenses, and was going deeply into debt to maintain the semblance of a normal lifestyle. A friend who met him on the street said Grant was disconsolate. "I had never before seen him so depressed. He was shabbily dressed, his beard was unshorn, his face anxious, the whole exterior of the man denoting a profound discouragement at the result of his experiment to maintain himself in St. Louis. 'I must leave,' he said. 'I can't make a go of it here.'"[156]

Grant faced up to the inevitable. With no place to turn, and with Julia's encouragement,[157] he asked his father for a job. As a boy, Grant had sworn he would never work in the family's tannery.[158] Now, the leather business was his last hope. In April, he would be thirty-eight. The older he got the more rapidly failure seemed to strike. Four years at West Point; eleven years as an officer in the regular army—including two years of combat in Mexico; four years farming; two years collecting rents and hunting for jobs. After twenty-one years his prospects were nil. It was a wrenching experience for Grant to admit he had failed. When he visited his father he suffered a severe migraine, yet he stated his case directly.[159] He needed work. Jesse responded sympathetically. He had declined to help Grant so long as he remained in Missouri but now, realizing his son's desperation, Jesse offered him a place in the Galena, Illinois, headquarters of the business. It was no more than a clerkship initially, the salary was $600 a year, and Grant would be working under his two younger brothers. But it was a job, it would secure his future, and Grant promptly accepted.

The worst was over. Years later, when he was living in the White House, Grant entertained an old acquaintance from St. Louis who happened to be passing through Washington. During his Missouri years Grant often delivered cord wood to the man's home, piling it on the woodpile at the rear of the house, and going to the door afterward to get his money. Nostalgia colored Grant's recollection. "There were happy days," the president told his guest. "I was doing the best I could to support my family."[160]

Grant departed for Galena in May 1860. Jesse's leather business had prospered over the years and now employed upward of fifty people. In addition to the tannery, the firm operated a half dozen retail outlets in the upper Mississippi valley with the nerve center located in Galena. Situated in the northwest corner of Illinois on a navigable tributary of the Mississippi, Galena was a bustling commercial and lead mining town of 14,000 people and, until the railroads bypassed it, the principal trading center for settlers heading west. The 200-room DeSoto Hotel, pride of the Northwest, hosted scores of Yankee merchants, steamboat gamblers, and Southern lawyers. More than fifty saloons slaked the thirst of Welsh miners and Irish deckhands, while German, Swiss, and Scandinavian immigrants thronged the land offices, seeking to establish themselves on the virgin farmlands nearby. The Grant firm was one of the most active in the region, and at 145 Main Street, it was located in what many regarded as the best business building in town, the Milwaukee Block.[161] Grant established his family in a small brick house a short distance from the store and set about learning the leather business.

Grant's addition to the firm caused little stir. W. T. Burke, a cousin who was also employed as a clerk, said it was really a family partnership. "Nominally we were to get $600 per year, but as a matter of fact, we were all working for a common fund, and we had what we needed. We were not really upon salaries in the ordinary sense. Captain Grant came into the firm on the same terms. There was no 'bossing' by Simpson or Orvil [Grant's younger brothers]. There was no feeling against Ulysses coming in, no looking down on him as a failure. We all looked up to him as an older man and a soldier. He knew much more than we in matters of the world, and we recognized it."[162]

Grant became the firm's billing clerk and collection agent, but he also sold goods, bought hides, and handled the paperwork. Whether he had his heart in his work is open to doubt. Jesse Grant was satisfied with his son's progress, but others were skeptical.[163] John E. Smith, who owned a jewelry shop nearby, thought Grant made a poor businessman. He made little effort to ingratiate himself with the townspeople and didn't like to wait on customers. "If a customer called in the absence of the sales clerks, he would tell them to wait a few minutes till one of the clerks returned. If [the customer] couldn't wait, he would go behind the counter, very reluctantly, and drag down whatever was wanted; but he hardly ever knew the price of it, and, in nine cases out of ten, he charged either too much or too little."[164]

Because Grant insisted on paying back all of the money he had borrowed in St. Louis—personal loans, back rent, various small grocery bills, and the like—he initially found it difficult to make ends meet. But the firm advanced him additional money, and by the end of the year he was solvent. "I have become pretty conversant in my new employment," Grant wrote to a friend in December 1860. "I hope to be a partner soon, and am sanguine that a competency at least can be made out of the business."[165] As in Missouri, Grant avoided liquor. Friends in Galena noted that while he smoked to excess, "he totally abstained from drink." John M. Shaw, whose law office was adjacent to the Grant store, and who saw Ulysses daily, said "there was not the slightest lapse from sobriety." The bartender at the DeSoto Hotel remembered when Eastern salesmen "treated" Grant, he took a cigar, not a drink. A tavern keeper in Wisconsin with whom Grant often stayed while on business said he usually took one drink after the evening meal, but none at other times.[166] Grant was a perfect family man. Had peace prevailed he would have lived out his days as a slightly rumpled shopkeeper in the upper Mississippi valley, indistinguishable from his friends and neighbors.

But that was not to be. On December 20, 1860, following confirmation of Abraham Lincoln's election as president, South Carolina announced its decision to secede from the Union. In Washington the outgoing administration of James Buchanan dithered, and the dreadful chain of events was set in motion. Mississippi followed South Carolina's lead on January 9, Florida acted the next day, and Alabama the day after. On January 19 Georgia joined the secessionists, as did Louisiana on the 26th, and Texas on February 1. Lincoln took office five weeks later, March 4, 1861, determined to preserve the Union. After renewing his pledge to respect slavery where it existed and to enforce the fugitive slave law, the president advised the Southern states that the Union was perpetual and indissoluble. "I shall take care, as the Constitution expressly enjoins me, that the laws of the Union be faithfully executed in all of the States. . . . In your hands, my dissatisfied fellow-countrymen, and not in mine, is the momentous issue of civil war." [167]

Undeterred by the president's words, the Congress of the newly organized Confederate States of America voted immediately to raise an army of 100,000 volunteers. Federal property in the seceded states was ordered seized, and by the beginning of April only Fort Sumter in Charleston harbor, and Fort Pickens at Pensacola, remained in Union hands. On April 11, Brigadier General Pierre G. T. Beauregard, who had resigned as superintendent of the United States Military Academy to assume command of Confederate forces in Charleston, demanded the surrender of Fort Sumter. Beauregard's demand was cloaked in the genteel civility common among officers in the old army.[168] Fort Sumter's commander, fifty-six-year-old Major Robert Anderson, who had been Beauregard's artillery instructor at West Point, and who was himself a former slave owner from Kentucky, declined with equal politeness.[169] Anderson's sympathies lay with the South, but he declined to forsake his duty to the Union. With Anderson's reply, the requirements of military etiquette had been satisfied. At 4:30 the following morning, April 12, 1861, Beauregard's guns opened fire. The Civil War had begun.[170]

WAR

He usually wore a plain blue blouse coat, and an ordinary black felt hat, and never had about him a single mark to distinguish his rank.

James L. Crane
Chaplain, 21st Illinois

PRESIDENT LINCOLN'S PATIENCE during his first six weeks in office bore fruit. Intent on mobilizing public support to preserve the Union, he left it to the South to fire the first shot.[1] It was Jefferson Davis and the Confederate cabinet who ordered the attack on Fort Sumter,[2] and the flamboyant Beauregard, living in "an ecstasy of glory and rhetoric," who happily complied.[3] To most in the North, the Confederate leadership bore unmistakable responsibility for the war. "They attacked Sumter—it fell, and thus did more service than it otherwise could," said Lincoln to a friend from Illinois.[4]

Ironically, the fall of Fort Sumter unified North and South alike. In the North, abolitionists from New England were euphoric, confident the Union with its vast superiority in manpower and matériel would quickly prevail. "The heather is on fire," wrote Harvard professor George Ticknor. "The whole population, men, women, and children, seem to be in the streets with Union favors and flags."[5] The *New York Times* predicted victory in thirty days.[6] Horace Greeley's *New York Tribune* assured its readers "Jeff. Davis & Co. will be swinging from the battlements at Washington . . . by the 4th of July."[7] The *Chicago Tribune* anticipated success "within two or three months at furthest," because "Illinois can whip the South by herself."[8] Lincoln's 1860 Democratic opponent, Stephen A. Douglas, captured the mood when he told a huge crowd in Chicago, "There are only two sides to the question. Every man must be for the United States or against it. There can be no neutrals in this war, *only patriots—or traitors.*"[9]

In the South, the demonstrations were equally exuberant. After hearing of Sumter's surrender, Jefferson Davis telegraphed Beauregard, "All honor to the gallant sons of Carolina, and thanks to God for their preservation."[10] Leroy Pope Walter, the Confederate secretary of war, assured a gathering in Montgomery, "The flag which now flaunts the breeze here will float over the dome of the old Capitol at Washington before the first of May."[11] John B. Gordon, leading a band of Georgia volunteers to the new Confederate capital, found the line of march an unbroken celebration: fires lighted the hilltops; fife-and-drum corps shrilled and thumped; cannons exploded their welcome.[12] In Virginia, which had not yet joined the seven states of the Cotton Kingdom, a jubilant throng lowered the American flag from the state capitol and ran up the Confederate Stars and Bars. The Richmond Artillery Company fired a hundred-gun salute "in honor of the victory" in Charleston.[13] In North Carolina, which also teetered on the brink of secession, the correspondent of the London *Times* watched "an excited mob" with "flushed faces, wild eyes, screaming mouths, hurrahing for 'Jeff Davis' and 'the Southern Confederacy.' "[14]

On April 15, 1861, the day after Fort Sumter surrendered, Lincoln issued a call for 75,000 volunteers to put down "combinations too powerful to be suppressed by the ordinary course of judicial proceedings."[15] The president's call for troops precipitated the upper South into the Confederacy. Virginia seceded on April 17, followed quickly by Arkansas, Tennessee, and North Carolina.[16] Four border states hung in the balance. Delaware tilted toward the Union; Kentucky toward Dixie; and Maryland and Missouri divided down the middle. Should the latter three defect to the Confederacy, seccession could well triumph.

North of the Mason-Dixon line Lincoln's proclamation loosed a tidal wave of patriotic enthusiasm. Eager volunteers flocked to the colors. Illinois was assigned a quota of six regiments which was oversubscribed by week's end. A mass meeting in Galena (over which Grant was asked to preside) voted to organize a rifle company immediately.* As the only military veteran in town, Grant was suddenly the center of attention. "I never went

---

* A Civil War rifle company, commanded by a captain, consisted of 100 men. There were ten companies in an infantry regiment (commanded by a colonel), and four regiments in a brigade (commanded by a brigadier general). Three, sometimes four, brigades constituted a division, commanded by either a brigadier or a major general. Two or more divisions formed a corps, commanded by a major general. Armies, such as the Army of the Potomac or the Army of the Ohio, consisted of several corps, and were also commanded by major generals. Theoretically, the full strength of a regiment was 1,000 men; a brigade 4,000; a division 12,000; and a corps 24,000 or more; but throughout the war most Union units were at half-strength or less. Confederate divisions and corps (the latter commanded by lieutenant generals) tended to be larger than their Union counterparts because a Southern division frequently contained four brigades and a corps four divisions. James M. McPherson, *Battle Cry of Freedom* 330 note 23 (New York: Oxford University Press, 1988).

into our leather store after that meeting, to put up a package or do other business."[17] The day after the meeting, Grant wrote his father-in-law in St. Louis, urging him to remain faithful to the Union.

> I know it is hard for men to apparently work with the Republi-can party but now all party distinctions should be lost sight of and every true patriot be for maintaining the integrity of the old *Stars and Stripes,* the Constitution and the Union. The North is responding to the President's call in such a manner that the rebels may truly quake. I tell you there is no mistaking the feel-ings of the people. The Government can call into the field not only 75,000 troops but ten or twenty times 75,000 if it should be necessary.[18]

Grant told Colonel Dent it would be a mistake to assume Northern-ers were too sensitive about their pocketbooks to fight. "In times like the present no people are more ready to give of their own time or their abun-dant means." Grant said the South was the aggressor and the Lincoln ad-ministration had remained on the defensive: "more on the defensive than she would dared to have done but for her consciousness of strength and the certainty of right prevailing in the end."

> The news today is that Virginia has gone out of the Union. . . . Her position, or rather that of Eastern Virginia, has been more reprehensible from the beginning than that of South Carolina.* She should be made to bear a heavy portion of the burden of the War for her guilt. —In all of this I can see but the doom of slav-ery. The North do not want, nor will they want, to interfere with the institution. But they will refuse for all time to give it protec-tion unless the South shall return soon to their allegiance.[19]

Grant was offered the captaincy of the Galena company but he de-clined. "I think I can serve the State better at Springfield,"[20] he said frankly. Grant was a poor businessman but he recognized the value of his military experience. He told friends that after eleven years in the regular army he

---

* Grant clarified this view in a letter ten days later to his sister Mary. "Great allowance should be made for South Carolinians," he wrote. "For the last generation have been edu-cated, from their infancy, to look upon their government as oppressive and tyrannical and only to be endured til such time as they might have sufficient strength to strike it down. Virginia, and other border states, have no such excuses and are therefore traitors at heart as well as in act." Grant to Mary Grant, April 29, 1861, 2 *The Papers of Ulysses S. Grant* 13–14, John Y. Simon, ed. (Carbondale: Southern Illinois University Press, 1969).

was fitted to command a regiment.[21] Nevertheless, he said he would do everything he could to prepare the Galena company for service.

From that moment on, Grant was constantly busy. He selected the cloth and superintended the making of the company's uniforms.[22] He drilled the men, taught the manual of arms, and instructed the company officers. Townsmen began to find in him qualities they had not previously noted. On April 21 Grant found time to write his father. "Whatever may have been my opinions before, I have but one sentiment now. That is we have a Government, and laws and a flag and they must all be sustained." Taking his cue from Stephen Douglas, he continued: "There are but two parties now, Traitors and Patriots and I want hereafter to be ranked with the latter." Grant felt obliged to his father for rescuing him from penury and he feared his absence from the store would put Jesse in an awkward position. Accordingly, Grant asked for approval to return to the army. He also worried about his father's safety in Covington, Kentucky, given Jesse's outspoken Republican views. "My advice would be to leave where you are if you are not safe with the views you entertain. I would never stultify my opinions for the sake of a little security."[23]

In a week the town's rifle company was ready to proceed to Spring-field. Its departure unleashed another celebration. A brass band, the local fire company, the Masonic society, the Order of Odd Fellows, the mayor, and various civic officials escorted the unit to the train. As the procession moved through the streets, Grant watched it pass. An observer recalled that when the last rank passed, a small man dressed in shabby civilian clothes and carrying a battered carpetbag, "fell in left and rear of the company and marched with it to the station."[24]

Illinois's preparations for war placed a heavy burden on the railroads. Locomotives were in short supply and the Galena company did not arrive in Springfield until the following evening. Grant wrote Julia, "Our trip was a perfect ovation. At every station the whole population seemed to be out to greet the troops. There is such a feeling aroused through the country now as has not been seen since the Revolution."[25] At the mustering site, named Camp Yates in honor of Governor Richard Yates, Grant was greeted by an old friend from the regular army, Captain John Pope. Pope had been with Grant for three years at West Point, graduated in 1842 with Rosecrans and Longstreet, and served on General Taylor's staff in Mexico. Physically imposing, with a temperament to match, Pope had been detailed by the army to serve as the mustering officer for Illinois volunteers. He expected to be elected a brigadier general as soon as a brigade was formed.[26] The two men reflected on the fate of some of their old acquaintances.

Friends from the deep South like Longstreet, Kirby Smith, and Earl

Van Dorn had already embraced the Confederate cause.[27] Five days after Virginia seceded, Colonel Robert E. Lee departed to assume command of that state's forces. Richard Ewell, Ambrose P. Hill, and Thomas J. Jackson entered Confederate service shortly thereafter. Samuel Cooper, the army's adjutant general, went to Richmond to assume a similar position. Joseph E. Johnston, serving as United States quartermaster general, agonized more than most before he, too, cast his lot with the Confederacy.[28] John Pemberton of Pennsylvania, married to a Virginian, also went south.[29] A sprinkling of Virginians remained loyal, notably General Winfield Scott and George H. Thomas, commanding the 2nd Cavalry at Carlisle Barracks. When Virginia seceded, Thomas presented himself before a local magistrate and reaffirmed his oath "to preserve, protect, and defend the Constitution."[30] Brigadier General Albert Sidney Johnston, commanding the army's Pacific Division from Alcatraz Island, became the nation's highest ranking officer to leave the service when his resignation was accepted on May 6. He hoped to remain on the sidelines during the war but eventually was drawn into Confederate service. As Johnston told his wife, "It seems like fate that Texas has made me a Rebel twice."[31]

In the North, Sherman, Joseph Hooker, and George B. McClellan were back on active duty. Sherman, taken to the White House by his brother John, the junior senator from Ohio, turned down Lincoln's offer of a brigadier general's commission and was a colonel commanding a regiment in Washington.[32] Hooker, who had commanded the California militia since 1859, was a brigadier general of volunteers.[33] McClellan, the highest paid railroad executive in the country, resigned his position as superintendent of the Illinois Central and was a major general commanding the Ohio department with headquarters in Cincinnati.[34] Henry W. Halleck, considered by many to be America's foremost military strategist,* gave up his prosperous law practice in San Francisco and at General Scott's urging was en route to Washington, perhaps to succeed Scott as general in chief.[35]

In the border states the choice was not as simple. Major General Simon Bolivar Buckner, commanding the Kentucky State Guard, labored desperately to keep the state neutral. When war came, he joined the South reluctantly.[36] Grant's friend George Crittenden fought for the Confederacy, his brother Thomas for the Union. Three grandsons of Henry

---

* Known as "Old Brains" in the regular army, Halleck had written one of the principal American texts on the art of war, *Elements of Military Art and Science,* published in 1846. The work relied heavily on the writings of Baron Henri Jomini, the Swiss military historian, especially in its treatment of war as a rational activity. Halleck emphasized fortifications, interior lines of operations, a strong supply base, and the occupation of territory (a war of position) rather than the destruction of enemy armies. For a summary of Jomini's views, see Lt. Col. J. D. Hittle, *Jomini and His Summary of the Art of War* (Harrisburg, Pa.: Military Service Publishing, 1947).

Clay fought for the North; four for the South. In Maryland, Robert C. Buchanan, Grant's former commander, sided with the Union. His half-brother, Captain Franklin Buchanan, the first superintendent of the United States Naval Academy, became the leading admiral of the Confederacy.[37] In Missouri, Professor Joseph Reynolds, formerly of Washington University, was now a colonel of volunteers stationed in Indianapolis. Daniel Frost, another of Grant's classmates, commanded the anti-Lincoln militia in Missouri and was preparing to move on Federal forces in St. Louis, which were commanded, in turn, by another of Grant's friends from West Point, red-haired Nathaniel Lyon, a dedicated abolitionist from Connecticut. Altogether, of the 1,108 officers on active duty in 1861, 313 resigned their commissions to join the Confederacy. Virtually none of the 15,000 enlisted men in the regular army did so. Among West Point graduates in civil life, 393 accepted commissions in various state militias, while 115 reentered Federal service.[38]

John Pope urged Grant to return to the army as soon as possible, and offered to use his influence among Illinois politicians to help him secure a commission. Pope came from a prominent Illinois family, was a longtime friend of Governor Yates's, and had accompanied Lincoln on his inaugural train to Washington in February 1861.[39] His prestige in Springfield was enormous and there is no doubt a recommendation from him would have carried great weight. Grant was grateful for Pope's offer, but demurred. As he expressed it, "I declined to receive endorsement for permission to fight for my country."[40]

Grant's disinclination to accept political support almost kept him out of the war. Springfield crawled with would-be colonels and brigadiers exploiting whatever political leverage they could muster. A man of Grant's modesty was easily overlooked. "I might have got the Colonelcy of a Regiment," he wrote his father, "but I was perfectly sickened at the political wire pulling and would not engage in it."[41] At the last minute, Grant's luck changed. The Galena company had been mustered into state service, and he was preparing to return to home, still without a position. On the eve of his departure, Congressman Elihu Washburne paid him a visit and urged him to stay in Springfield a few days longer.[42] Washburne had represented Galena in Washington since 1852. He was the longest serving Republican in the House of Representatives, chairman of the Commerce Committee, and had been a close friend of Abraham Lincoln's for more than twenty years.[43] An admiring newspaper correspondent described Washburne as a "broad-shouldered, good-bellied man, eastern in his appearance but western in his thinking."[44] He told Grant to have patience. "Everything can't be done in a moment."[45] Washburne volunteered to speak to Governor Yates and said he was certain things would work out.

Why Washburne sought to help Grant remains a matter of conjecture, since the two men never discussed the matter afterward.[46] Washburne was a hard-core Republican, an ardent abolitionist, and a devout Christian who never drank or smoked, and who disapproved of the theater. Grant was none of those things, and in politics he was generally regarded as a Douglas Democrat. They were barely acquainted in Galena. Their sole common ground was support for the Union. The most plausible explanation is that Washburne, dedicated to the war effort, wanted to do what he could for his hometown and at that point Grant was the only Galenian qualified for higher rank. Nearly every member of Congress had pet officers to advance; Washburne latched on to Grant.[47]

Why Grant accepted Washburne's assistance after spurning Pope's is equally unclear. It may be that he was more optimistic about his chances when he spoke with Pope and now realized he needed help.[48] More likely is that the manner in which the aid was proffered was more palatable to Grant. Washburne did not ask Grant's approval (as Pope had done), but simply informed him of what he intended to do. This required no acknowledgment or commitment on Grant's part. He could stand aside and let matters develop, secure in the belief he had not sought political assistance.

That evening, as Grant stood at the front door of his hotel, ready to walk to the station to take the train to Galena, Governor Yates approached him. Yates was staying at the same hotel, but the two men had not spoken previously.

"Captain," said the governor, addressing Grant by his old army rank. "I understand you are planning to leave the city." Grant replied he was, whereupon Yates asked him to stay overnight and call at the executive office the next morning. Grant did as the governor requested, and the following morning Yates asked him to go down the hall to the state adjutant general's office and help out as best he could.[49]

The appointment was only temporary, but Grant could scarcely believe his good fortune. On April 29 he wrote his sister Mary saying he had intended to leave for Galena "last evening," but the governor detained him "and I presume will want me to remain with him until all the troops called into service are fully mustered and completely organized."[50] The state of Illinois desperately needed someone to sort out the chaos of mobilization and Grant filled the bill. The adjutant general's office was in shambles. The peacetime duties of the Illinois adjutant general were honorific, and the incumbent, Thomas S. Mather, a successful insurance agent, had little knowledge of military regulations and procedure.[51] Grant was still dressed in the shabby suit he had worn from Galena, but he found an unused table in an anteroom and sat down, a supply of cigars at the ready, and began transcribing orders. He inventoried the weapons in the arsenal,[52] brought the state's paperwork up to date, and answered questions about army regulations. In Grant's own quiet way he became military adviser to the mobilization effort. It was soon bruited about that anyone could ask him a question and receive a clear, concise, and definite answer.[53] On May 4, when John Pope failed to be elected brigadier general of the Illinois volunteers and left Springfield in a huff, Grant was appointed to succeed him as commandant of Camp Yates.[54] Four days later he was appointed "mustering officer and aide" to the governor at a salary of $4 a day.[55]

Grant's duties as mustering officer took him to Mattoon, Belleville, and Anna to swear in the regiments from the seventh, eighth, and ninth congressional districts.[56] At Mattoon, eighty miles east of Springfield, he spent two days with the new regiment, the 21st Illinois.[57] "He made a strong impression on us," said Lieutenant Joseph Vance. "Part of this was due to the fact that he was the first officer to come to us clothed with authority from the State. But we also saw that he knew his business, for everything he did was done without hesitation. He was a little bit stooped at the time, and wore a cheap suit of clothes and a soft black hat. Anyone who looked beyond that recognized that he was a professional soldier."[58]

After mustering in the 21st, Grant returned to Springfield where he drew his pay, amounting to $130.[59] This was the first money he had received and he desperately needed it. Thus far, Grant had been living on advances provided by his brother Orvil, occasionally skipping dinner to save fifty cents.[60] But after receiving his pay there was nothing further for him to do. The regiments had been mustered in, the government clerks were growing accustomed to military usages, and rumors of Grant's past bouts with the bottle (which began to circulate in Springfield) made officials leery of entrusting him with additional responsibility. An officer who knew Grant at the time said most politicians considered him "a military deadbeat" and many citizens saw him simply as "another decayed soldier."[61]

Charles Lanphier, editor of the *Springfield Register,* remembered meeting Grant in the lobby of the Chenery Hotel, looking "fagged out, lonesome, poor, and dejected."

"What are you doing, Captain?" asked Lanphier.

"Nothing. Waiting," Grant replied.[62]

On May 23, with Governor Yates's permission, Grant took leave to visit his family in Galena. The following day, convinced his prospects in Springfield were all but exhausted, Grant wrote to an old acquaintance from Mexico, Brevet Brigadier General Lorenzo Thomas, who had succeeded Samuel Cooper as the army's adjutant general. Because of the circumstances surrounding his resignation from the 4th Infantry, Grant had held off writing to Washington. Now it seemed his only hope.

Sir:

   Having served for fifteen years in the regular army, including four years at West Point, and feeling it the duty of every one
who has been educated at the Government expense to offer
their services for the support of that Government, I have the
honor, very respectfully, to tender my services, until the close of
the War, in such capacity as may be offered. I would say that in
view of my present age, and length of service, I feel myself competent to command a regiment if the President, in his judgment, should see fit to entrust one to me.[63]

General Thomas did not reply. Rather than refuse an old friend he simply
tucked Grant's letter in his desk and forgot about it.* Grant recognized
that his chances of returning to the regular army were virtually nil and after
six days in Galena returned to Springfield.[64] He moped around the Chenery Hotel for another week "blue as a whetstone," and then on June 9 took
the train to Cincinnati, ostensibly to visit his parents in nearby Covington.[65] In reality, he wanted to call on another old acquaintance, George B.
McClellan, who had already made a name for himself organizing what
later became the Army of the Ohio. Little Mac was a major general and
Grant hoped to secure a position on his staff.[66] On the morning of the
10th, he called at McClellan's headquarters and was received by another
old friend, Major Seth Williams, who was serving as McClellan's adjutant.
As Grant recalled the episode:

   I was told that [McClellan] had just gone out, and was
asked to take a seat. Everybody was so busy that they could not
say a word. I waited a couple of hours. I never saw such a busy
crowd—so many men at an army headquarters with quills behind their ears. But I suppose it was all right, and was much encouraged by their industry. It was a great comfort to see the men
so busy with the quills.

   Finally, after a long wait, I told an officer that I would come
in again next day, and requested him to tell General McClellan
that I had called. Next day I came in. The same story. The General had just gone out, might be in at any moment.

* Grant's letter was not filed among the War Department's incoming correspondence and
was not recovered until December 1876, when General Edward D. Townsend, who replaced Lorenzo Thomas as adjutant general, stumbled across it while cleaning out his office
preparatory to moving with army headquarters to St. Louis. 1 *Personal Memoirs of U.S.
Grant* 240 (New York: Charles L. Webster, 1885).

Would I wait? I sat and waited for two hours, watching officers with their quills, and left.

McClellan never acknowledged my call, and, of course,
after he knew I had been at his headquarters I was bound to
await his acknowledgment. I was older, had ranked him in the
army, and could not hang around his headquarters watching
men with quills behind their ears.

Still, I should like to have joined McClellan. I thought he
was the man to pilot us through and I wanted to be on his staff.[67]

McClellan's slight hit Grant hard. The ill luck that dogged him for the
past seven years seemed to have returned. He poured out his troubles to
Chilton White, a boyhood chum from Georgetown who had served with
him in Mexico and who was now a member of the Ohio legislature. "I've
tried to reenter service in vain. I must live, and my family must live. Perhaps I could serve the army by providing good bread for them. You remember my success at baking bread in Mexico."[68]

At the end of the week Grant left for Springfield, telling his father he
planned to stop for a day or two to visit a favorite classmate, Joe Reynolds,
at Camp Morton in Indianapolis. Having failed in three attempts to secure
a post, Grant hoped Reynolds, soon to be a brigadier general, would be
able to find a place for him among the Indiana volunteers.[69]

Providence now took a hand in Grant's future. No sooner had he departed from Covington than a telegram arrived from Governor Yates offering him command of the 21st Illinois infantry regiment, the unit he
mustered in at Mattoon. The colonel originally elected had proved unable
to maintain discipline. The men had become unruly, rioting over bad food
and burning the guardhouse. Some foraged wantonly about the countryside, stealing pigs and chickens, while others caroused drunkenly through
the streets of Mattoon. Ordered by Yates to proceed to Springfield, the
regiment disrupted the train during the journey, and upon arrival in the
capital the officers unanimously requested a new colonel be appointed,
"preferably Captain Grant."[70] Yates was still unsure about giving Grant a
command and turned to his aides for advice. State auditor Jesse Dubois,
who was from Mattoon, and John S. Loomis, an assistant in the adjutant
general's office, had both worked with Grant during mobilization and
strongly endorsed his appointment.[71] Yates, for whom the regiment had
become an embarrassment, dispatched a telegram to Covington offering
Grant the position. Jesse relayed the message to Indianapolis, and Grant
telegraphed his acceptance on June 14, 1861. The following day Governor
Yates signed an executive order appointing him to command the 21st Illinois.[72] As with Washburne's earlier intervention, Yates's offer arrived unex-

pectedly. Grant, who had been considering baking bread for the army, was now a colonel of Illinois volunteers.

Grant arrived in Springfield on June 17 and assumed command of the regiment the next day.[73] John Smith, a Galena merchant who happened to be in Springfield, rode out with him to Camp Yates on the horse trolley. According to Smith, Grant "was dressed very clumsily, in citizen's clothes—an old coat, worn out at the elbows, and a badly dinged plug hat." A few of the soldiers began to make fun of him whereupon Grant "looked at them just for an instant, and in that instant they saw they had a man of nerve to deal with."[74]

The 21st Illinois was a regiment that would have tested the mettle of any colonel. Drawn from the prosperous, strongly Republican counties in the east-central part of the state, its members were "vigorous, hardy boys unused to any kind of restraint, every man inclined to think and act for himself."[75] They had deposed one colonel, and the second-in-command noted despairingly that company commanders had "entirely lost sight of the rules of discipline."[76] The unit's chaplain recalled the regiment being in chaos and confusion, "each man having as much authority as another. It was a disorderly mass, a hodge-podge of entanglements, an unsystematic, unarranged hurly-burly of officers and privates."[77]

Grant quickly sized up the situation. The men were not the problem. It was a lack of leadership. And so as Old Rough and Ready might have done, he walked casually into the adjutant's tent, said he "guessed he'd take command," and sat down to write out his first order of the war.

> The undersigned, having been duly appointed Colonel of the 7th Congressional District Regt. of Illinois Volunteers by order of Govr. Richard Yates, hereby assumes command.
>
> In accepting this command, your Commander will require the cooperation of all the commissioned and non-commissioned Officers in instructing the command, and in maintaining discipline, and hopes to receive also the hearty support of every enlisted man.[78]

The phraseology is vintage Grant. The cooperation of officers and noncommissioned officers was *required;* the support of the enlisted men was something to be *hoped for.* That distinction became a hallmark of Grant's leadership. No West Point–trained officer understood the nature of the Union's volunteer army better than Grant. Having survived a number of years on the bottom rung in civil life, he had developed an instinctive feel for how civilians behaved. He recognized that volunteer soldiers were not regulars and never tried to impose the spartan discipline of the old army. Instead, Grant saw the recruits of the 21st Illinois as men who thought for themselves and who could be reasoned with. They could be led, but not driven.

By focusing on his officers and NCOs, Grant was also establishing a framework for the regiment. Any colonel who hoped to train and discipline his men had to start with the company officers, simply because it was their deficiencies that made discipline so lax. Taking command of a regiment in which rowdiness had become the rule, Grant would have made little progress if he had simply invoked the harsh punishments provided for in the Articles of War. He had to begin with the junior officers and the senior enlisted men: Teach the cadre their responsibilities and the troops would fall into line.[79]

For the next several days Grant meandered through Camp Yates in rumpled civilian clothes and observed what was going on. If a veteran of the Mexican War had been present, he would have recognized Old Zack's mannerisms immediately. "We called him 'the quiet man,' " one soldier remembered, "and in a few days he reduced matters in camp to perfect order."[80]

Grant's first official act was to replace the arbitrary rules imposed by the previous commander with a system based on common sense. Expanding on the principle he learned from Colonel Stephen Watts Kearny at Jefferson Barracks in 1843, Grant said enlisted men as well as officers were free to come and go as they pleased during the day provided they were present for roll calls and drill. "In extending this privilege to the men of this command the Colonel Commanding hopes that this leniency will not be so abused as to make it necessary to restrict it. All men when out of Camp should reflect that they are Gentlemen—in camp, soldiers; and the Commanding Officer hopes that all of his command will sustain these two characters with fidelity."[81] Long after the war a veteran of the 21st said "the effect of that order was wonderful. The men responded enthusiastically, and discipline ceased to be a problem."[82]

Grant applied the same logic to the regiment's training. Recognizing that constant drilling was counterproductive, he set squad drill from 6 to 7 A.M., with company drill running from 10 to 11 A.M., and again from 5 to 6 P.M.—avoiding the hottest hours of the day. Officers were required to be present at drill and assume responsibility for their unit's instruction.[83]

After a week Grant was satisfied the 21st had settled down and he arranged a hasty trip to Galena to raise money to buy a uniform, a horse, and what soldiers called "horse furniture"—bridle, saddle, blanket, and other equine accoutrements. Grant decided he needed a uniform as a regimental commander, but as the chaplain of the 21st recalled, the only time he wore it was on dress parade.[84]

As it turned out, raising money for his purchases was not as easy as Grant anticipated. Specie was in short supply that summer and most merchants, fearing paper money would soon be worthless, insisted on payment in gold. Like many others, Grant's brother Orvil was unable to provide any funds, Jesse was similarly strapped, and Grant ended up asking E. A. Collins, his father's former business partner, to endorse his note at the bank for $500.[85]

When Grant returned to Springfield, the regiment had backslid. Officers were on the town each night, their attendance at drill was spotty, and on the evening of June 25 several members of the guard detail deserted their posts. Grant responded with articulated firmness. He came down hard on the officers. Henceforth they would not be permitted off post in the evening without his express approval and he explicitly required their presence at all formations. "All officers not reported sick, or otherwise excused by competent authority, will attend all Drills and Parades. They will give strict attention that the men of their respective commands receive proper instruction."[86]

Grant took a more lenient approach with the enlisted men. They needed guidance, and he was determined to win their cooperation. In an order distributed throughout the regiment, Grant said he learned with regret that a number of the men had deserted their guard posts last night.

> This is an offence against all military rule and law, which no punishment can be prescribed for by a commanding officer at his discretion, but must be the subject for a General Court Martial. It cannot, in time of peace, be accompanied with a punishment less than the forfeiture of $10 from the pay of the soldier, together with corporal punishment such as confinement for thirty days with ball and chain at hard labor. In time of war, the punishment is death.

Grant said he believed the men now in the brig were unaware of the magnitude of their offense. Accordingly, he was "not disposed to visit them with the full vigor of the law, but would admonish them, and the whole command, against a repetition of the offence, as it will not be excused again in this regiment."[87] In his *Memoirs*, Grant wrote it was hard work to bring the men into subordination, but after a week or so "all were reduced to as good discipline as one could ask."[88] Lieutenant Vance remembered Grant as a strict disciplinarian, although he was never vindictive. "If he punished a man, he did it in a quiet way, and in a spirit that did not enrage the one punished."[89] James Crane, chaplain of the 21st, commented on Grant's "unostentatious vigor and vigilance. He would correct every infraction on the spot, but in as cool and unruffled a manner as you would give directions to your gardener before breakfast."[90]

Grant's low-key leadership was exactly what the 21st needed. At the end of June, when the men's original enlistments expired and they were called upon to volunteer for three years of Federal service, they signed up almost to a man.[91] One veteran said the regiment had become proud of Grant. "We knew we had the best commander and the best regiment in the State."[92]

No sooner were the men mustered into Federal service than Grant received orders to take the regiment to Quincy, Illinois, on the Mississippi River. The move was preparatory to reinforcing Union forces in Missouri, where secessionist elements were on the verge of making the state the twelfth to join the Confederacy. Quincy lies 116 miles west of Springfield, and Grant, to the consternation of state officials, chose to march the distance rather than travel by rail. "This is an infantry regiment," he told Governor Yates. "The men are going to do a lot of marching before the war is over and I prefer to train them in friendly country, not in the enemy's."[93]

Grant's experience managing the supply trains for Taylor and Scott during the Mexican War was much in evidence. Colonel John Williams, the Illinois commissary general, told Yates that Grant was the only regimental commander who knew exactly what he needed. "Colonel Grant's requisition on me for supplies seemed to be complete in every detail, for nothing was added to or omitted from the requisition. He selected his horses, wagons and camp equipage, and superintended the loading of the same into the wagons. He seemed to have just the right number of wagons, and the necessary amount of supplies to fill them."[94]

The 21st Illinois marched out of Springfield on July 3, 1861—two years to the day before Grant would meet with John Pemberton under a stunted oak tree on a parched Mississippi hillside to arrange the surrender of Vicksburg. The first day out the regiment marched eight miles. Grant ordered the march to be resumed at six the next morning. Morning came, and at 6 A.M. no one was ready. Grant waited, and after an hour or so, everyone had eaten and packed up, and the regiment got underway. That night he repeated his order that the march would resume at 6 A.M. At six the next morning, just as before, no one was ready. Grant ordered the march to begin regardless. Half the men were left behind, scurrying to strike tents and pack gear, and the remainder went off half dressed and hungry, carrying their clothing and boots. After a couple of miles Grant called a halt so the men could finish dressing and the laggards could catch up. That evening, he announced a six o'clock start the next morning. This time the company commanders got the message. At 6 A.M. the regiment was fed, dressed, packed up, in formation, and ready to go. Late that day they reached the Illinois River.[95]

On Sunday the regiment rested by the river and Grant wrote to Julia. The farmland the regiment passed through, he said, was some of the most beautiful in the world and the entire population turned out to greet them. "At Jacksonville, one of the prettiest towns that I ever saw, the ladies were all out waving their handkerchiefs, and one of them (I know she must be pretty) made up a bouquet and sent it to me with her name." Grant said the regiment had not been issued all its equipment. It would be another two weeks before it would be ready for action and a month before the men would be ready for serious combat. "It was in a terribly disorganized state when I took over but a very great change has taken place. I don't believe there is a more orderly set of troops now in the volunteer service. I have been very strict with them and the men seem to like it. They appreciate that it is all for their own benefit."[96]

Grant crossed the Illinois on Monday, expecting to be in Quincy two days later. But at noon he received a dispatch directing him to return to the river and await steamboat transportation to take the regiment to St. Louis. From there it was to proceed by rail to join the command of Brigadier General Nathaniel Lyon facing rebels in southwest Missouri.[97] Grant immediately put the men into camp and, with combat approaching, ordered his officers to check the men's equipment.[98] Later that day he distributed a hortatory broadside to the troops—an unthinkable act in the regular army, but a fitting tribute to the volunteers he led.

> The Colonel commanding this Regiment deems it his duty at this period in the march to return his thanks to the Officers and men composing the command on their general Obedience and Military discipline. Having for a period of years been accustomed to strict military duties and discipline he deems it not inappropriate at this time to make a most favorable comparison of this command with that of veteran troops in point of Soldierly bearing, general good order, and cheerful execution of commands.[99]

Believing they were on the eve of battle, Grant did his utmost to reinforce the regiment's esteem. This time, however, combat was delayed. The river steamer en route to pick up the 21st ran aground on a sandbar, and the following evening Grant received new orders directing him to proceed to Quincy, cross the Mississippi, and deploy the regiment to protect the Hannibal & St. Joseph Railroad from rebel marauders.[100] For the next month the 21st remained on constabulary duty in northern Missouri. Grant was occupying what was putatively enemy territory, yet he insured that citizens were not molested and that private property was protected.[101]

Later, Grant wrote his father "the majority in this part of the State are se-cessionists, but deplore the present state of affairs. They would make al-most any sacrifice to have the Union restored, but regard it as dissolved and nothing is left for them but to choose between two evils." Grant said the newspapers were full of reports of Federal troops being annihilated, al-though no engagements had taken place. "My Regiment has been re-ported cut to pieces, whilst a gun has not been fired at us. These reports go uncontradicted here and give confirmation to the conviction already en-tertained that one Southron is equal to five Northerners."[102]

Grant continued to train the regiment. The men became proficient at squad and company drill, but had not yet attempted to move in battalion formation. At West Point, Grant had been uninterested in infantry tactics, and during the Mexican War, as quartermaster, he had not attended battal-ion drill. And so like any freshly minted colonel he procured a copy of the army's latest drill manual and studied the first lesson, "intending to con-fine the exercise of the first day to the commands I had thus learned."

"We were encamped just outside of town on the common, among scattering suburban houses with enclosed gardens, and when I got my reg-iment in line and rode to the front I soon saw that if I attempted to follow the lesson I had studied I would have to clear away some of the houses and garden fences to make room." Rather than follow the text, Grant impro-vised. "I found no trouble in giving commands that would take my regi-ment where I wanted it to go and carry it around all obstacles. I do not believe that the officers of the regiment ever discovered that I had never studied the tactics that I used."[103]

While Grant was stationed in northern Missouri, and well before he entered combat, he was promoted to brigadier general. Once again, the appointment was unexpected. Chaplain Crane, sitting in the shade of his tent perusing the latest issue of the *Missouri Daily Democrat,* stumbled across Grant's name among a list of brigadiers confirmed by the Senate. "Well, sir," said Grant, "I had no suspicion of it. . . . That's some of Wash-burne's work."[104]

And indeed it was. During the emergency session of Congress that summer, Lincoln had been authorized to appoint thirty-four brigadier generals of volunteers.[105] The president parceled out the appointments by states. Illinois was awarded six—two more than any other state (not sur-prising, given Lincoln's background)—and the congressional delegation huddled to prepare a slate of nominees. Washburne urged that Grant's name be included, his colleagues acquiesced, and Lincoln agreed. Grant's commission was backdated to May 17, 1861, making him eighteenth on the list of the army's new brigadier generals and thirty-fifth in the overall chain of command headed by Winfield Scott.[106]

Grant's promotion coincided with the arrival in St. Louis of Major General John C. Frémont, assigned by Lincoln to command the Western theater of operations.[107] Widely known as the Pathfinder of the West, Frémont played a major role in detaching California from Mexico.* He was one of the state's first two senators, and the Republican party's first nominee for president, losing to Buchanan in 1856. Frémont was in France at the outbreak of the war, but came straight to Washington, where Lincoln made him a major general and gave him carte blanche in the West.[108] To many Americans, Frémont was a national hero and Lincoln relied on him, a trifle optimistically, to keep Missouri in the Union.

Initially, the conflict in Missouri was confined to guerrilla warfare, hit-and-run raids by Confederate insurgents, and occasional instances of ambush and arson. But the fighting quickly escalated. In May, Nathaniel Lyon, who commanded Federal forces in St. Louis, foiled a rebel attempt to seize the United States arsenal in the city, and in mid-June he peremptorily dismissed an offer from Southern leaders for the state's neutrality. "Rather than concede to the State of Missouri the right to dictate to my Government, I would see . . . every man, woman, and child in the State dead and buried."[109] Believing he could nip secession in its infancy, Lyon dispatched Colonel Franz Sigel and his regiment of German volunteers to occupy southwestern Missouri, while Lyon himself marched to take possession of the state capital at Jefferson City. The Confederates responded energetically. On July 5 a pickup force of rebel riflemen repulsed Sigel in a skirmish near Carthage, and the Missouri militia, commanded by ex-governor Sterling Price, mobilized in the Ozarks. Reinforced by several thousand Confederate troops from Arkansas, Louisiana, and Texas, Price's force numbered about 12,000 when Frémont arrived. Meanwhile, Confederate general Leonidas Polk was moving up the Mississippi from Memphis with another 12,000 men. Midway between Price in the southwest and Polk in the southeast, General William J. Hardee was advancing with 3,000 cavalrymen along the route of the St. Francis River.

All three Southern generals were formidable opponents. Price had won distinction commanding a regiment of volunteers during the Mexican War and enjoyed immense popularity in Missouri. Known to his troops as "Pap," he was always where the fighting was thickest. Polk, a tall

---

* An officer for eleven years in the army's Corps of Topographical Engineers, Frémont had mapped the Oregon Trail, discovered Lake Tahoe, scaled the Sierra in midwinter, and given the Golden Gate its name. In 1841 he married Jessie Benton, the accomplished, ambitious, and vivacious daughter of Missouri senator Thomas Hart Benton, thereby establishing a political alliance with one of the most powerful families in the Middle West—a fact Lincoln had very much in mind when he sent Frémont to St. Louis. Allan Nevins, 2 *Frémont: The West's Greatest Adventurer* 531–36 (New York: Harper and Brothers, 1928).

man with an imposing soldierlike bearing, had been a West Point class-mate of Jefferson Davis's. He had resigned from the army in 1826 to enter the ministry and had risen to become Episcopal bishop of Louisiana. When war began, Davis commissioned him a major general and assigned him to command Confederate forces in the Mississippi valley. Polk consid-ered his military duties temporary and to the delight of many Southerners did not resign his bishopric. He felt, he said, "like a man who has dropped his business when his house is on fire, to put it out." [110] Hardee, the junior of the three, had been commandant of cadets at West Point and was the au-thor of the army's *Rifle and Light Infantry Tactics,* the manual Grant pur-chased while commanding the 21st. [111]

In contrast to the efficiency with which the Confederates were mov-ing, Frémont found his own forces dispersed and disorganized. Brigadier General John Pope (whom Lincoln had promoted six weeks before Grant [112]) commanded the scattered formations north of the Missouri River, where the men were engaged primarily in protecting the railroads from Southern raiding parties. Lyon was at Springfield with 6,000 men, including Sigel's defeated troops, while Brigadier General Benjamin Pren-tiss, a volunteer officer in the Mexican War, commanded a weak detach-ment on the Mississippi River at Cairo, Illinois.

Frémont responded to the crisis as best he could. He raised volun-teer regiments wherever possible, purchased weapons and equipment on the open market, sent his wife, Jessie, to Washington to plead with Lin-coln for reinforcements, and began to concentrate his troops on the Mis-sissippi. Lyon was ordered to fall back, Prentiss was reinforced, and Grant, the new brigadier general in the command, was sent to the rail-head at Ironton to hold the center against Hardee's anticipated advance. On August 8, 1861, Grant assumed command of 3,000 untrained and "badly Scart" troops and quietly began to make ready. [113] His first task was to impose discipline. Grant ordered the saloons in Ironton and nearby Pilot Knob closed, and instructed company officers to read the Articles of War to their commands "at least twice within the next four days." [114] Grant told Frémont he did not believe an attack was imminent. "It is for-tunate too if this is the case for many of the officers seem to have so little command over their men, and military duty seems to be done so loosely, that I feel at present our resistance would be in inverse ratio to the num-ber of troops to resist with." [115]

Two days after Grant arrived in Ironton, disaster struck Federal forces in Missouri. Rather than withdraw as ordered, General Lyon, pugnacious, headstrong, and overconfident, chose to attack Sterling Price's much larger force on the high ground opposite Wilson's Creek, ten miles south of Springfield. As Lyon saw it, if he did not attack Price, Price would attack

him, and he thought he could deliver a knockout blow while the Confederates slept in bivouac. Lyon divided his command and sent Sigel on a wide
sweep to attack the rear of the rebel camp while he launched the main assault
at Price's front. Unfortunately for Lyon, neither jaw of his pincer was powerful enough to prevail against the Confederate mass. Federal troops benefited initially from surprise, but the Confederates steadied themselves and
counterattacked quickly. As Lyon rallied his men, a bullet struck him in the
heart and he went down instantly. The Union lines broke, green soldiers
dropped their weapons and fled, leaving their dead and wounded on the
battlefield. It was Bull Run all over again. These were the first two significant battles of the war, Bull Run in the East, Wilson's Creek in the West, and
the South won both.[116] Price was unable to get his weary men into column
to pursue, but western Missouri was now open to the Confederate advance.

The week after the defeat at Wilson's Creek, Frémont sent General
Prentiss to take command at Ironton and Grant returned to St. Louis.* He
hoped to secure leave to visit Galena, but was instructed by Frémont to proceed immediately to Jefferson City and take command of the troops assembled there.[117] Sterling Price was moving against the state capital, and
Frémont wanted Grant to defend it. Once again, as at Ironton, Grant found
things in disarray. "Most of the troops are without clothing and equipment,
ammunition is down to about ten rounds [per man] and for the artillery
none is left." Grant said the quartermaster and commissary departments
were in deplorable condition and there were no rations to issue. "From reports received here the whole of this country is in a state of ferment."[118]

Within a week Grant had the situation under control. Supplies were
replenished and various regiments were deployed on the outskirts of the
city to guard the approaches. Despite orders to the contrary, Grant told
headquarters he was not constructing fortifications. He said he had a personal aversion to gaining a reputation "for a branch of the service that I have
forgotten all about. . . . Drill and discipline are more necessary for the men
than fortifications."[119] This was a prejudice Grant retained throughout the
war. Fortifications reflected a defensive mentality alien to his nature.

On August 26 Grant wrote Julia that the expected attack on Jefferson
City was unlikely to materialize. The Confederate troops from Arkansas

---

* Frémont's headquarters evidently assumed Prentiss was senior to Grant. Both held their
brigadier general commissions with date of rank May 17, 1861, and Prentiss had been serving
in that rank six weeks longer than Grant. But because of Grant's prior service as a captain in
the regular army, he was actually the senior of the two. As the secretary of war advised Frémont, "When two commissions, as in this instance, have the same date, reference must be
had to former commissions, and by that rule Genl. Grant should rank." Grant, who was unwilling to serve under an officer junior to him, briefed Prentiss on the situation at Ironton
and took the next train back to St. Louis to report to Frémont. Simon Cameron to Frémont,
September 19, 1861, 2 *Grant Papers* 177 note. Also see *Grant,* 1 Memoirs 257.

and Louisiana were badly battered at Wilson's Creek and had returned home to refit. Price's Missouri volunteers had melted away to bring in the autumn harvest. Grant told his wife he was busier than ever and was in excellent health. "All my old friends in the Army seem to heartily congratulate me." He reassured Julia that Frémont had promised him leave to visit Galena, "but if a forward movement is to take place I fear I shall not."[120]

With the threat of an advance by Price on Jefferson City diminished, at least until after harvest season, Frémont elected to take the offensive. The key to victory in the West was the Mississippi. It was like a giant tree: Whoever controlled the trunk controlled the upper branches. Leonidas Polk was already moving to take possession of the river, and Frémont decided to meet him head-on. Southern Missouri and downstate Illinois were vulnerable; and Kentucky was ripe for the picking. Beyond Kentucky lay Tennessee and the Mississippi delta. Capture Memphis, lop off Vicksburg and New Orleans, and the Confederacy would wither. The plan would require a combined offensive by Federal forces and a field commander who could be relied upon. On August 27 Frémont sent for Grant.[121]

Frémont's selection of Grant to command the Union advance is a benchmark in American history akin to FDR's selection of Eisenhower to lead the Normandy invasion. It was the right choice at the right time. John Pope was the senior brigadier general in the Western Department and might have been selected; so, too, might Prentiss. But Frémont passed them over in favor of Grant.[122] At the time, Frémont had met Grant only twice. The general from Galena was still dressed in the shabby civilian suit he had brought with him, and his appearance was anything but prepossessing.[123] Frémont later said he selected Grant because he discerned his unusual qualities. "I believed him to be a man of great activity and promptness in obeying orders without question or hesitation. For that reason I gave General Grant this important command at this critical period. I did not consider him then a great general, for the qualities that led him to success had not had the opportunity for their development. I selected him for qualities I could not then find combined in any other officer, for General Grant was a man of unassuming character, not given to self-elation, of dogged persistence, and of iron will."[124] Frémont said some of his staff had been opposed "for reasons that were well known," but that Grant's bearing and demeanor removed whatever doubts he might have had.[125] He ordered Grant to take command of all Union forces in southeastern Missouri and southern Illinois, secure his position on the Mississippi, and "occupy Columbus in Kentucky as soon as possible." The purpose, he said, was "to establish a base for operations against Memphis and Nashville."[126] Frémont also suggested Grant should get a uniform.[127]

On August 30, 1861, Grant assumed command of the Union army on the Mississippi.[128] He was at Cape Girardeau, 120 miles below St. Louis, on the west bank of the river looking south. Suddenly, uncharacteristically, Grant was awed by his responsibility. "You should be cheerful and try to encourage me," he wrote Julia. "I have a task before me of no trifling moment and want all the encouragement possible. The safety of the country, to some extent, and my reputation and that of our children, greatly depends upon my acts."[129] To Jesse, Grant noted he had been "sent to Ironton when the place was weak and threatened with a superior force and as soon as it was rendered secure I was ordered to Jefferson City, another point threatened. I was left there but a week when orders were sent ordering me to this point and putting me in command of all the forces in S.E. Mo. and South Ill. and everything that can operate here. All I fear is that too much may be expected of me."[130]

Grant mastered his doubts quickly. He assembled his forces at Cairo, Illinois—where the Ohio River joins the Mississippi—preparatory to moving into Kentucky and seizing Columbus, only to learn on September 4 that the Confederates had beaten him to it. Located on the Mississippi River eighteen miles below Cairo, Columbus was the northern terminus of what Southerners called the "M an' O," the Mobile & Ohio Railroad, the principal overland link between the Gulf Coast and America's midsection. The town was surrounded by high bluffs that dominated the river. Artillery positioned there could block passage in either direction. In effect, whoever held Columbus held the Mississippi gateway to the South, and Polk was determined not to let it fall into Union hands. The town's pro-Southern citizens had petitioned the Confederates to march to their defense,[131] and on Tuesday, September 3, 1861, the Louisiana bishop, disregarding Kentucky's declared neutrality, ordered his troops to cross the state line and take possession of the town. Grant was lucky once again. By moving first, Polk secured Columbus for the South. But in so doing he lost Kentucky to the Union. Because they had violated the state's neutrality, the Confederates were seen as the aggressors. The American flag was hoisted over the state capitol at Frankfort and the legislators, most of whom had been sitting on the fence, voted by a three-to-one margin that Kentucky had been "invaded by the forces of the so-called Confederate States. . . . Therefore, Be it resolved that the invaders must be expelled."[132]

Grant responded to the loss of Columbus without batting an eye. He calmly telegraphed Frémont the news, saying the Confederates were marching overland from Columbus to seize Paducah, at the mouth of the Tennessee River, and unless instructed otherwise he intended to get there first.[133] Strategically, Paducah was as important as Columbus. Located at the confluence of the Tennessee and the Ohio, forty-five miles upstream from Cairo, it provided an alternative water entrance to the interior of the Confederacy as the majestic Tennessee River dipped down into northern Mississippi and Alabama before returning to the state of Tennessee near Chattanooga. Grant, who was alert to the political ramifications of moving into Kentucky, sought to cushion the impact by sending a telegram to the speaker of the state legislature informing him of the Confederate invasion. Grant did not say he intended to respond, but the message was implicit.[134] Late that afternoon Grant dispatched a second telegram to Frémont: "I am getting ready to go to Paducah. Will start at 6½ o'clock."[135]

Grant loaded the 9th and 12th Illinois onto river steamers, added a battery of artillery, picked up two gunboats for fire support, and headed up the Ohio. It was an easy overnight trip and he reached Paducah at 8:30 on the morning of September 6.[136] The troops went ashore promptly, battle flags aloft, stepping smartly to the beat of the two regimental bands. Paducah's citizens, anticipating the arrival of Polk's Confederates later that morning, were taken by surprise. "I never saw such consternation on the faces of the people," Grant wrote. "Men, women and children came out of their doors looking pale and frightened."[137] Grant told Frémont numerous secession flags were flying over the city when the troops arrived, but they quickly disappeared.[138]

Within two hours Paducah was under Union control. Not a shot had been fired. Grant deployed his troops "so as best to command the city and least annoy peaceable citizens," seized a large number of rations earmarked for the Confederate army, and took possession of the railroad. General Polk's oncoming troops were estimated to number 3,800. Less than sixteen miles away, they evidently were not prepared to do battle. When they discovered that Union troops had occupied Paducah, they hightailed it back to Columbus. Grant laid out a defensive perimeter and returned to Cairo late that afternoon. Before leaving he issued a brief proclamation to reassure the townspeople of the Union's benign intent.* He also ordered General Eleazer Paine, whom he left in charge, "to take special care and precaution that no harm is done to inoffensive citizens. . . . [S]oldiers

---

* Proclamation,
to the Citizens of
Paducah!

I have come among you, not as an enemy, but as your friend and fellow-citizen, not to injure or annoy you, but to respect the rights, and to defend and enforce the rights of all loyal citizens. An enemy, in rebellion against our common Government, has taken possession of, and planted its guns upon the soil of Kentucky and fired upon our flag. Hickman and Columbus are in his hands. He is moving upon your city. I am here to defend you against this enemy and to assert and maintain the authority and sovereignty of your Government and mine. I have nothing to do with opinions. I shall deal only with armed rebellion and its aiders and abetors. You can pursue your usual avocations without fear or hindrance. The strong arm of the Government is here to protect its friends, and to punish only its enemies. Whenever it is manifest that you are able to defend yourselves, to maintain the authority of your Government and protect the rights of all its loyal citizens, I shall withdraw the forces under my command from your city. 2 *Grant Papers* 194–95.

shall not enter any private dwelling nor make any private searches unless by your orders. Exercise the strictest discipline against any soldier who shall insult citizens, or engage in plundering private property." [139]

Contemporary historiography has portrayed Grant as a political bumbler insensitive to the nuances of power. Yet operating in the field for the first time on his own authority, with no adviser to turn to, he laid the groundwork with the Kentucky legislature for the Union's move into the state, addressed the concerns of the civilian population of Paducah, set a standard for the protection of private property, and with a timely show of force seized control of the mouth of the Tennessee, bluffing a larger Confederate force into retreating.

When Grant returned to Cairo he found a telegram from Frémont authorizing him to take Paducah "if you feel strong enough." [140] He also received a message from the Pathfinder's headquarters rapping his knuckles for writing directly to the speaker of the Kentucky House. All such matters, Grant was told, should be left "to the Major General Commanding the Department." [141] That evening Frémont telegraphed Grant that he wished him to exercise personal command of the movement down the Mississippi, and that he was sending the legendary Charles Ferguson Smith to take command at Paducah. [142]

Brigadier General Charles Ferguson Smith was a soldier's soldier, and with the possible exception of Winfield Scott, there was no one in the regular army whom Grant admired more. Smith had been commandant at West Point when Grant was a cadet and he was regarded throughout the army as the embodiment of military professionalism. [143] Later Grant would write, "His personal courage was unquestioned, his judgment and professional acquirements were unsurpassed, and he had the confidence of those he commanded as well as those over him." [144] Smith's distinguished service stretched over forty years.* Now, by quirk of fate (and Elihu Wash-

---

* Charles Ferguson Smith entered West Point in 1821—the year before Grant's birth. He was commissioned initially in the artillery but returned to the academy in 1829 as an instructor of infantry tactics. In 1831 he became adjutant, and in 1838 was named commandant. During the Mexican War he commanded a battalion of artillery serving as infantry; and it was his red-legged soldiers who led Zachary Taylor's army across the Colorado River in the face of Mexican cavalry. Smith was brevetted for gallantry at Palo Alto and Resaca de la Palma, again at Monterrey, and for a third time at Contreras, ending the war as a colonel. In 1856 he led an expedition to the Red River of the North, participated in the Mormon expedition in 1857, and commanded the Utah Department for a time. At the outbreak of the Civil War he was on temporary duty in Washington, and late in August Frémont secured his assignment to the Western theater. He had been nominated for brigadier general, but had not yet been confirmed by the Senate. Tall and physically imposing with a proclivity for profanity, Smith cut a handsome military figure, sporting a white walrus mustache that extended well below his chin. One observer wrote he was the only general officer at the beginning of the war who "could ride along a line of volunteers in the regulation uniform of a brigadier general—plume, chapeau, epaulets and all, without exciting laughter."

burne's intervention), Grant was the senior of the two. Out of respect for Smith's age and experience, Frémont established an independent command for him at Paducah, but the arrangement worked poorly. The only way St. Louis could communicate with Smith was through Grant's headquarters at Cairo, and Smith depended upon Grant for his supplies. After several months the arrangement was scrapped and Smith was placed under Grant's command. And in the curious way of the old army, there was never any friction. Grant considered Smith his model and mentor. "It does not seem quite right for me to give General Smith orders," he told his staff. Whenever it was necessary to do so, Grant's instructions were written with extraordinary deference.[145] Smith, for his part, showed no resentment and was frankly proud of his former pupil. "I am now a subordinate," he said simply. "I know a soldier's duty. I hope you will feel no awkwardness about our new relations."[146]

The harmonious relationship between Grant and Smith was one of the high points of the Union campaign on the Mississippi. Grant watched Smith closely, studied his manner, and generally assigned him the toughest tasks. The two shared a common outlook. Grant's instinct was to carry the fight to the enemy. Smith put it more eloquently. "Battle is the ultimate to which the whole life's labor of an officer should be directed. He may live to the age of retirement without seeing a battle; still, he must always be getting ready for it exactly as if he knew the hour of the day it is to break upon him. And then, whether it come late or early, he must be willing to fight—he *must* fight."[147]

Ten days after arriving in Paducah, Smith reached out to occupy the nearby village of Smithland, at the juncture of the Cumberland River and the Ohio. The Cumberland was the gateway to Nashville and the highlands of central Tennessee. Its mouth, along with that of the Tennessee, was now in Federal hands. The day after Smith moved, Grant asked Frémont for permission to attack Columbus. "All the forces show great alacrity in preparing for any movement that looks to meeting the enemy. . . . If it was discretionary with me, with a little addition to my present force I would take Columbus."[148] Grant said he thought that a feint from Paducah, supported by a movement from Cairo, would force the Confederates to abandon the city. "I submit this for your consideration and will hold myself in readiness to execute this or any plan you may adopt."[149]

Frémont turned cautious. He authorized Grant and Smith to move forward "should the enemy expose a weak point . . . but at present I am not in favor of incurring any hazard of defeat."[150] The fact is, the Pathfinder's attention was diverted elsewhere. Shortly after Grant left Jefferson City his successor sent a force of 3,500 men 125 miles up the

Missouri River to occupy the trading center of Lexington—the largest town between St. Louis and Kansas City. The isolated Federal garrison made a tempting target, and with the harvest gathered, Sterling Price, with 18,000 men, surrounded the town and laid siege. Union efforts to come to the aid of Lexington were halfhearted and ineffective. On September 20, after eight days of spirited resistance, the garrison surrendered and Frémont's prestige plummeted. Half of Missouri was now in rebel hands. Lincoln told the Pathfinder he expected him "to repair the disaster at Lexington without loss of time."[151] Frémont had already incurred Lincoln's ill will,* and unless the setback were reversed, his days in command of the Western Department would be numbered. Accordingly, he decided to take the field himself and was hastily putting together an army to pursue Price. "Keep me informed minutely" of the situation at Cairo, he told Grant, but for the time being an offensive on the Mississippi would have to wait.[152]

Frémont rarely did anything by half measures. By early October he had assembled a force of 38,000 men, eighty-six pieces of artillery, several thousand supply wagons, three million rations, and was on the march toward the Ozarks. It was the first deliberate Union offensive in the West, and except for Grant's troops on the Mississippi, the entire department had been put in motion. On October 16 Lexington was retaken, and by the end of the month the Union army, organized into five divisions, was deployed at Springfield in line of battle. But the rebels slipped away. The Missouri Confederates lacked the men and equipment for a sustained campaign, and Sterling Price withdrew sixty miles further south. As he reported to Jefferson Davis, his men were "half-fed, half-clothed, and half-supplied," and "could not cope with the Unionists in numbers."[153] For Frémont, time had run out. Before he could catch up with Price, he was relieved of command. Lincoln's order was delivered on November 2, 1861, thus ending the Fed-

---

* Frémont took Lincoln's carte blanche literally, and on August 30, 1861, without consulting Washington, he declared martial law throughout Missouri, announced the death penalty for guerrillas caught behind Union lines, and confiscated the property and freed the slaves of all Confederate activists. Lincoln asked Frémont to rescind the measures, and when he declined, the president ordered him to do so. Lincoln was concerned above all to keep Kentucky in the Union ("to lose Kentucky is nearly the same as to lose the whole game"), and feared Frémont's premature emancipation attempt "would alarm our Southern Union friends, and turn them against us—perhaps ruin our rather fair prospect for Kentucky." The president also told Frémont that if he shot guerrillas indiscriminately, "the Confederates would very certainly shoot our best men in their hands, and so on, man for man, indefinitely." Frémont's proclamation of August 30, 1861, is in 3 *The War of the Rebellion: A Compilation of the Official Records of the Union and Confederate Armies,* Series I, 466–67 (Washington, D.C.: Government Printing Office, 1880). For Lincoln's response, see 4 *The Collected Works of Abraham Lincoln* 531–32, Roy P. Basler, Marion Delores Pratt, and Lloyd A. Dunlap, eds. (New Brunswick, N.J.: Rutgers University Press, 1954).

eral drive into southwestern Missouri.* Frémont was succeeded temporarily by Major General David Hunter, an old soldier who had fought with distinction at Bull Run, and then on November 19 by Henry W. Halleck.

Grant spent the month of October readying his command for combat. Reinforcements poured in and by November 1 his present for duty strength totaled more than 15,000 men, distributed among a half dozen subposts along the Mississippi. Leonidas Polk's forces increased proportionately. Confederate strength between New Madrid and Memphis numbered over 20,000 with another 13,000 to 15,000 dug in at Columbus.[154] Grant reported that rumors of a rebel offensive were swirling but he discounted them. "My own impression is that they are fortifying strongly and preparing to resist a formidable attack but have little idea of risking anything upon a forward movement."[155]

Grant occupied his time turning civilians into soldiers. The men he commanded were volunteers. Many had never been away from home before, and most were innocent of the realities of camp sanitation and hygiene. Sickness was so prevalent in the 2nd Iowa that the regiment had to be returned to St. Louis so the men could recover.[156] Morale among the citizen-soldiers was another serious concern, especially after the initial patriotic fervor wore off and the everyday drudgery of soldiering set in. One matter Grant attended to personally was the mail. No one knew better than he how important a letter from home could be and he did his utmost to insure the mail was delivered promptly. At Grant's request, a special agent of the Post Office Department visited Cairo and worked out a system whereby letters between camp and home were given a high priority. Even when the troops were on the march, mail wagons trailed after them. Grant said later, "The officers and men were in constant communication with kindred and friends at home and with as much regularity as the most favored in the large cities of the Union."[157]

The lack of equipment created additional problems. By the autumn of 1861 there was no shortage of volunteers (the War Department was actu-

---

* In early October Lincoln dispatched Secretary of War Simon Cameron and Adjutant General Lorenzo Thomas to investigate matters in the Western Department. Both were highly critical of Frémont, and on October 24, Lincoln, convinced the Pathfinder had become a loose cannon, wrote out the order relieving him. The president entrusted the message to Brigadier General Samuel Ryan Curtis to deliver. Curtis was told the order should not be handed to Frémont if "he shall then have, in personal command, fought and won a battle, or shall then be in the immediate presence of the enemy in expectation of a battle." Since neither of those conditions prevailed, the order was delivered and Frémont was removed. For the drama surrounding Frémont's relief, see Nevins, 2 *Frémont* 616–26. For Lincoln's instructions, see 4 *Collected Works of Lincoln* 562. General Curtis's appreciation of the situation is found in "With Frémont in Missouri in 1861: Letters of Samuel Ryan Curtis," Kenneth E. Colton, ed., 24 *Annals of Iowa*, 3rd Series, 153–54 (1942).

ally turning away regiments), but there was a dreadful scarcity of weapons and clothing. "My cavalry are not armed nor my artillery equipped. The infantry is not well armed and transportation is entirely inadequate to any forward movement," Grant reported on October 27.[158] "The clothing received has been almost universally of inferior quality and deficient in quantity. The quartermaster department has been carried on with so little funds that Government credit has become exhausted." Grant's previous experience as quartermaster of the 4th Infantry proved invaluable as he battled with headquarters in St. Louis for the necessary supplies—a task made somewhat easier when an old army friend from Ohio, Major Robert Allen, was appointed chief quartermaster of the Western Department.* Once Allen was on board, funds were provided and the Cairo district was permitted to do much of its own purchasing. As a result, many of the shortages of which Grant had complained soon disappeared.[159]

When a congressional committee investigating government contracting arrived in Cairo at the end of October, Grant was called to testify. He answered the committee's questions knowledgeably and convinced them that whatever contracting problems the War Department had encountered were not attributable to mismanagement in Cairo.[160] Elihu Washburne, who was a member of the committee, wasted no time extolling Grant's virtues to Washington. "General Grant, who is in command of this whole section, is one of the best officers in the army," he wrote to Salmon P. Chase, his former congressional colleague who was now secretary of the treasury. Grant, said Washburne, "is doing wonders in bringing order out of chaos. He is as incorruptible as he is brave"—praise destined for the president's ear given Lincoln's concern for the situation in Kentucky.[161]

Washburne's accolade was useful to have on record, especially with action approaching. On November 1, one day before he was relieved of command, Frémont ordered Grant to have his entire command prepared for battle and ready to move at an hour's notice. Grant was also instructed to "make demonstrations with your troops" along both sides of the Mississippi in the direction of Columbus, "and keep your columns constantly moving back and forward . . . without however, attacking the enemy."[162] Frémont believed his own set piece battle with Sterling Price was imminent and he wanted Grant to threaten Polk sufficiently to prevent him from sending reinforcements to the Ozarks.

Before Grant could take action, he received additional instructions

---

* Robert Allen, from Georgetown, Ohio, graduated from West Point in 1836 and was chief quartermaster of the Pacific Division when Grant was stationed in California. After Grant resigned from the army, it was Allen who provided him with money to buy a steamship ticket to New York. Lloyd Lewis, *Captain Sam Grant* 336–37 (Boston: Little, Brown, 1950).

from Frémont directing him to send a force to find and fix the rebel cavalry of Jeff Thompson, estimated at 2,500 troopers, then raising havoc along the St. Francis River some sixty miles to the west. A gifted leader of irregular forces, Thompson constantly harassed Union supply lines, and Grant was told to assist Federal troops in the region "in driving him back to Arkansas."[163] Grant seized the opportunity. On November 3 he ordered Colonel Richard Oglesby, commanding the 8th Illinois, to take three infantry regiments, plus artillery and cavalry support, and set out for the St. Francis in pursuit of Thompson. Colonel Joseph Plummer, commanding at Cape Girardeau, was instructed to take his brigade and reinforce Oglesby.[164] "The object of the expedition is to destroy this force, and the manner of doing it is left largely at your discretion."[165] Grant's rephrasing of his instructions provides a textbook example of his attitude toward war. Frémont's headquarters ordered Thompson's force driven back to Arkansas; Grant wanted it destroyed.

Grant reinterpreted his orders to conduct demonstrations in front of Columbus even more egregiously. On November 5 he notified Smith at Paducah that he was "fitting out an expedition to menace Belmont and will take all the force proper to spare from here. If you can make a demonstration toward Columbus at the same time with a portion of your command, it would probably keep the enemy from throwing over the river much more force than they now have there, and might enable me *to drive those they have there out of Missouri*."[166] Belmont was the steamboat landing on the Missouri side of the Mississippi River opposite Columbus. It was lightly garrisoned—not much more than an infantry regiment—and Grant saw it as a target of opportunity. Frémont had explicitly instructed Grant not to attack the enemy; despite those orders, he was going for Belmont.

After informing Smith of his plans, Grant organized his assault. "A reconnaissance in force will be made starting probably tomorrow evening," he informed his brigade commanders. Grant did not disclose his destination, but the officers were told to hold their troops in readiness "with two days rations in their Haversacks, and forty rounds of ammunition."[167] On the morning of the 6th, the soldiers of Grant's command began feverish preparations for departure.[168] At 2 P.M. General Smith dispatched two brigades (about 3,000 men) overland toward Columbus from Paducah.[169] An additional two regiments (about 1,600 men) marched south from Fort Holt, Grant's outpost on the Kentucky shore opposite Cairo.[170] Both columns were ordered to make a show of force to distract Polk, but were under strict instructions not to engage the enemy.

Back at Cairo, four regiments of Illinois volunteers, the 7th Iowa, two troops of cavalry, and the Chicago Light Battery, assembled at the levee. Grant put together a fleet of six steamers, supported by the gunboats *Tyler* and *Lexington,* and began embarking his men in the middle of the after-noon. The loading was hasty and the vessels inadequate. Surgeon John Brin-ton complained he could not get on board "one ambulance or spring wagon of any description."[171] Grant sent fresh orders to Colonel Oglesby to turn his column toward New Madrid on the Mississippi "and communicate with me at Belmont."[172] Colonel William H. L. Wallace was ordered to take his regi-ment, the 11th Illinois, join Oglesby, and orally inform him to turn his col-umn toward Belmont.[173] "I move tonight with all my available force, about four thousand," Grant telegraphed Smith. "If necessary, I can . . . add nearly five thousand more"—a reference to the men under Oglesby's command.[174]

Why Grant disregarded his instructions not to attack Polk can only be surmised, but the record makes clear it was not done capriciously. His im-patience to move south had been manifest for some time. In September he wrote Julia, "I would like to have the honor of commanding the Army that makes the advance down the river, but unless I am able to do it soon can-not expect it. There are too many Generals who rank me that have com-mands inferior to mine for me to retain it."[175] Ambition therefore played a part. There was also the prospect of quick success. He had taken Paducah without a fight, Smith had occupied Smithland, and Belmont looked like another easy target. Finally, the troops had to be considered. They were as eager as Grant to meet the enemy. Unlike many senior officers—McClel-lan particularly—Grant did not believe in waiting until the men were drilled to perfection. "The enemy organizes and improves as rapidly as yourself, and all the advantages of prompt movement are lost."[176]

Grant had long considered the possibility of assaulting Belmont. On October 13, he discussed the possibility with Commander William D. ("Dirty Bill") Porter, captain of the gunboat *New Era.* Porter had just completed a re-connaissance of Confederate positions downriver and he urged Grant to at-tack quickly before Polk had a chance to reinforce the garrison.[177] Ten days later Commodore Andrew H. Foote, who commanded the Union gunboat flotilla on the Mississippi, visited Cairo and sat down with Grant to plan the opera-tion. Foote suggested it would require two gunboats and 4,000 men, and of-fered to come down from St. Louis and take out the gunboats himself.[178]

Aside from his discussions with Porter and Foote, Grant kept his own counsel. The more he thought about the plan, however, the better he liked it. At the end of October he went to consult Smith in Paducah. Grant ar-rived late in the afternoon and was billeted in the quarters of Colonel Lew Wallace.* After dinner General Smith called and took Grant for a walk.

---

* Lew Wallace, who gained fame after the war as the author of *Ben-Hur,* commanded the 11th Indiana Volunteer Infantry Regiment. He is not to be confused with Colonel William H. L. Wallace, who commanded the 11th Illinois, and who was killed at Shiloh.

They were gone for two hours. There is no record of what they said to each other, although Wallace wrote that in the days afterward Smith's face often lit up and he spoke enthusiastically about "Opportunities—opportunities—opportunities."[179] In Wallace's opinion Grant came to Paducah to discuss his plan for Belmont, and it stands to reason he may have wanted his mentor's advice before embarking on the scheme.[180]

When Frémont ordered Grant to conduct demonstrations along both banks of the Mississippi, "opportunity" beckoned. But the Pathfinder's instructions carried an explicit admonition not to attack, and Grant could not violate the express command of his superior. Only after Frémont was relieved did Grant put his plan to seize Belmont in motion. When he issued his alert order on November 5, word of the Pathfinder's dismissal had already circulated through the department. That gave Grant the opportunity he needed.[181] If he was victorious all would be forgiven. If he failed. . . . Well, Grant rarely thought in those terms.

At 9 P.M. on November 6 Grant's task force slipped anchor, eased out into the main channel, and dropped down the Mississippi, the gunboats *Tyler* and *Lexington* leading the way. Nine miles below Cairo the convoy pulled close in to the Kentucky shore and tied up for the night. Grant chose the Kentucky shore hoping Polk would assume his target was Columbus. Smith's approach from Paducah, plus the two regiments marching from Fort Holt, would make the ruse even more convincing. Grant continued to maintain operational secrecy. Only C. F. Smith knew Belmont was his objective, and it was not until 2 A.M. on the 7th that Grant issued orders to his brigade commanders announcing the landing would be on the Missouri side of the river.[182]

At first light on the 7th, the ships of Grant's little convoy cast off their moorings and steamed south, *Tyler* and *Lexington* still leading the way. Three miles above Belmont, the transports veered toward the Missouri shore and tied up at Hunter's Point, a little-used steamboat landing shielded by a skirt of timber from the heavy Confederate guns on the bluffs surrounding Columbus. While the gunboats continued downstream to engage the rebel batteries, the Union infantry swarmed ashore and by 8:30 the landing was complete. "The early autumnal morning was delightful," wrote Dr. John Brinton. "The air fresh and invigorating, without being cold."[183]

Grant formed his regiments into march column and moved south toward Belmont. Presently the advance guard came under heavy musket fire from their immediate front. Grant sent a battalion of infantry to protect the landing site, and then deployed his troops in line of battle. As Taylor had done at Palo Alto, he ordered his five regiments abreast, divided his six howitzers among them to provide direct support, and dispatched the cavalry to protect his right flank.

The Confederates meanwhile were busy reinforcing the garrison at Belmont. Polk learned of the landing at Hunter's Point shortly after 7 A.M. He considered it a feint to divert attention from what he believed would be the main Union thrust against Columbus. Nevertheless, it had to be met. The Tennessee division of Brigadier General Gideon Pillow was already in formation under arms and Polk ordered it ferried across the river to contain the situation. The Confederates were just as eager to do battle as the Union soldiers, and it was Pillow's line of skirmishers that Grant's lead elements encountered. Pillow formed his men into his own line of battle, five regiments facing Grant's five, the center of the Southern line exposed among the stalks of a recently harvested cornfield. Grant's line, by contrast, lay protected by a growth of heavy timber, affording considerable cover from Southern sharpshooters.

At ten o'clock Grant ordered two companies in each regiment to deploy as skirmishers, push through the woods, and test the enemy position. Within minutes the two battle lines were engaged and, as he wrote, "the *Ball* may be said to have fairly opened."[184] When Grant discovered Pillow's center was exposed in the cornfield, he massed his six howitzers and loosed a barrage of grape and canister. The 21st and 22nd Tennessee regiments wavered, then broke, and the center of the Confederate line collapsed.[185] The rebel retreat began in good order but dissolved into a rout as panic set in. By 2 P.M. the fighting appeared to be over. Union forces swept through the Southern encampment, while demoralized Confederates ran to the river and huddled behind the high banks for protection.

But the tide of battle turned quickly. Grant's volunteers became as disorganized in victory as the Southerners were in defeat. Union soldiers laid down their weapons and ran uncontrolled through the Confederate camp, looting and celebrating with abandon. The Stars and Stripes was hoisted to the top of the rebel flagpole, regimental bands circled around and commenced a medley of patriotic tunes. Those soldiers who were not rummaging for trophies "joined in singing with boundless exuberance." A carnival spirit prevailed. Grant wrote afterward that some of his senior officers "were little better than the privates. They galloped about from one cluster of men to another and at every halt delivered a short eulogy upon the Union and the achievements of the command." Grant said the Confederates crouched under the riverbank were ready to surrender if anyone had approached them, but no one did.[186]

From the other side of the river General Polk watched the proceedings. He still anticipated the main Union attack would be directed at Columbus, but when he saw Pillow's men flung back to the landing he ordered Brigadier General Benjamin Cheatham to cross the river with five more regiments. Three went to rally Pillow's men on the riverbank, while

Grant's parents, Jesse and Hannah. Jesse was a successful businessman, Hannah a lifelong Democrat who refused to visit her son in the White House.

Grant's birthplace at Point Pleasant, Ohio, twenty miles east of Cincinnati on the Ohio River. When Grant was one year old the family moved to nearby Georgetown, where he grew up.

Jesse R. Grant
Hannah Grant

FATHER & MOTHER OF GENERAL U.S. GRANT

1

2

3

Cadet artillery drill on the Plain at West Point, where Grant studied from 1839 to 1843. Considered one of the best equestrians ever to attend the academy, he nevertheless graduated a buck private in the corps of cadets.

Grant had remarkable artistic ability and a powerful pictorial imagination. This charcoal drawing of a bridge in Monterrey is typical of many he did during the Mexican War.

4

Major General Zachary Taylor, "Old Rough and Ready," who commanded the American advance into northern Mexico. A no-nonsense commander who rarely appeared in uniform, Taylor was Grant's military role model. "No soldier could face either danger or responsibility more calmly than he."

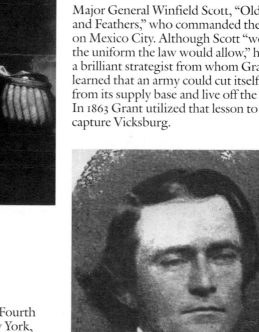

Major General Winfield Scott, "Old Fuss and Feathers," who commanded the drive on Mexico City. Although Scott "wore all the uniform the law would allow," he was a brilliant strategist from whom Grant learned that an army could cut itself off from its supply base and live off the land. In 1863 Grant utilized that lesson to capture Vicksburg.

Grant as a first lieutenant in the Fourth Infantry at Sackets Harbor, New York, 1849. Grant was stationed at Sackets Harbor for three years, an idyllic posting where he and Julia set up housekeeping in commodious quarters at Madison Barracks.

8

Fort Vancouver on the Columbia River, Grant's first duty station on the Pacific coast. Grant longed for his absent family, began to drink heavily, and resigned his commission in 1854.

"Hardscrabble," the rough-hewn house Grant constructed for Julia and the children during his ill-fated attempt at farming in the 1850s. When crops failed and money ran short, Grant peddled firewood on St. Louis street corners to support his family.

9

10

Galena, Illinois, 1860. Unable to find employment elsewhere, Grant was working in Galena as a clerk in his father's leather-goods store when the Civil War began.

Elihu Washburne, Galena's long-time Republican congressman, who was a close friend of Lincoln and Grant's political patron. Throughout the war Washburne looked out for Grant's interests. When Grant became president he appointed Washburne minister to Paris, a post he served with distinction for eight years.

II

12

Grant was a muddy-boots general who liked to see things for himself. He is depicted here reconnoitering the Confederate position at Spotsylvania.

Major General Simon Bolivar Buckner, a close friend of Grant who assisted him financially after he resigned from the army in 1854. It fell to Buckner to surrender Fort Donelson to Grant eight years later.

13

14

General Pierre Gustave Toutant
Beauregard. When Albert Sidney
Johnston was killed at Shiloh,
Beauregard took command and
conducted a brilliant retreat from
Corinth to Tupelo. In 1864 his
masterly defense of Petersburg
held Grant at bay until Lee's
veterans could arrive.

Grant as commander of the
Army of the Tennessee, Oxford,
Mississippi, 1862. The battles of
Donelson and Shiloh were
behind him, Vicksburg was
ahead.

15

16

An artist's rendition of Union
gunboats running the Confederate
gauntlet at Vicksburg, April 16,
1863. Admiral Porter considered
the painting so authentic that he
hung a reproduction of it over the
mantel in his library.

Admiral David D. Porter
commanded the Union fleet at
Vicksburg. Porter and Grant
worked so effectively together that
when Grant went east as general in
chief, Porter was reassigned to
support him.

17

19

Above right: Lieutenant General John C. Pemberton, one of the few Northerners to fight for the Confederacy. A master of defensive tactics, he held Grant at Vicksburg for eight months until forced to surrender on July 4, 1863.

Above left: Commodore Andrew H. Foote, first commander of the Navy's gunboat flotilla on the Mississippi. A hard-bitten sailor of forty years' experience, he shared Grant's view of taking the fight to the enemy.

Admiral David G. Farragut, commander of the Union blockade fleet in the Gulf of Mexico. His victory at Mobile Bay in August 1864 contributed significantly to Lincoln's reelection.

Above right: Admiral Daniel Ammen, a boyhood friend from Georgetown, Ohio, who remained close to Grant throughout his life. When Grant was in the White House, Ammen and his wife had a standing invitation for Sunday dinner.

Above left: Major General George H. Thomas, commander of the Army of the Cumberland. A native Virginian who fought to save the Union, Thomas was without peer when fighting on the defensive. Grant thought he was too slow to attack, but Thomas's methodical style proved itself at the Battle of Nashville in 1864.

Edwin M. Stanton, Secretary of War, 1862–1868. Strong-willed and irascible, Stanton ran the War Department with an iron hand. His dismissal by Andrew Johnson in 1868 led to Johnson's impeachment trial.

After fighting Lee to a draw in the Wilderness, Grant ordered the Army of the Potomac to move south. The army's response (shown here cheering Grant as he rode past) was enthusiastic. Sherman called Grant's decision "the supreme moment of his life."

General William Tecumseh Sherman, who succeeded Grant as Union commander in the West. "Our strategy was simple enough," said Sherman. "I was to go after Joe Johnston, and Grant was to go after Lee."

26

Major General Philip H. Sheridan, commander of the Army of the Shenandoah. At five foot five and 120 pounds, the diminutive Sheridan was the most aggressive general in the Union Army. After the war Grant sent him to the Mexican border to assist the patriotic movement of Benito Juárez, then to Louisiana to enforce Reconstruction.

Below left: Major General Henry W. Halleck, "Old Brains." A desk soldier par excellence, Halleck became general in chief in 1862. When Grant succeeded him, Halleck remained in Washington as chief of staff.

Below right: Major General George G. Meade, commander of the Army of the Potomac. Meade was in the awkward position of having Grant, the general in chief, make his headquarters with the Army of the Potomac.

27

29

Lieutenant General James Longstreet. Known affectionately as Old Pete, Longstreet was Grant's closest friend in the peacetime army. A superb tactician, he came within an eyelash of rolling up Grant's flank in the Wilderness until he was wounded at a critical moment.

Below left: General Robert E. Lee, Army of Northern Virginia. Grant knew Lee from Mexico and did not share the sentiment that he was invincible. "I am heartily tired of hearing about what Lee is going to do," Grant told a distraught brigadier at the Wilderness.

Below right: General Joseph E. Johnston, Army of the Carolinas. Grant considered Johnston the most able Confederate general. Parsimonious with his men's lives, Johnston preferred to give ground until he could fight a battle on his own terms. In 1881, as a member of Congress, he introduced legislation to restore Grant's rank as general of the army.

30

31

Grant had a photographic memory for topography. He is shown here at his headquarters in northern Virginia studying a map with his aide, Colonel Theodore S. Bowers, and his adjutant, Brigadier General John A. Rawlins.

Above left: When the struggle in Virginia became one of static trench warfare in late 1864, Grant was joined at his City Point headquarters by Julia and their youngest son, Jesse. A devoted family man, Grant was at his best when Julia was near.

Above right: This powerful photograph by H. F. Warren, taken in the field, March 15, 1865, depicts Grant's determination to end the war quickly.

Lithograph of Lee's surrender at Appomattox. Grant wrote the terms in longhand and of his own accord pardoned the officers and men of the Army of Northern Virginia "so long as they observe their paroles and the laws in force where they reside."

Grand review of the Army of the Potomac, May 23, 1865. Sherman's troops from the West marched the following day. The photo shows Horatio Wright's Sixth Corps near the intersection of Twelfth Street and Pennsylvania Avenue.

Thomas Nast cartoon depicting Emperor Andrew Johnson watching the massacre of African-American innocents in New Orleans, July 30, 1866. Grant, lower left, restrains Sheridan from using his sword. Stanton sits above Grant; Seward leans over Johnson.

the other two landed between Grant and Hunter's Point, cutting off his withdrawal.[187] Once he was convinced Columbus was not endangered, Polk himself led the last contingent across the river.

Grant was caught by surprise. He failed to notice that *Tyler* and *Lexington,* no match for the Confederate artillery on the bluffs above Columbus, had withdrawn upstream, leaving his flank on the Mississippi unprotected.[188] With the Union gunboats gone, Polk was able to ferry his reinforcements across the river unmolested. Grant attempted to rally his own artillery to fire at the boats ("gray with soldiers from boiler-deck to roof"), but his cannoneers were too busy celebrating to respond.[189] "Here the volunteer spirit showed itself," wrote Dr. Brinton. "The men had done their day's work and did not care much about further fighting."[190] Grant's effort to restore order proved futile. In desperation he commanded his staff to torch the rebel tents, hoping this would bring the men to their senses. The immediate effect of the flames was to attract the fire of the Confederate artillery across the river, and it was the rebel shells exploding among them that finally enabled Grant to bring his troops under some semblance of discipline. He ordered a quick retreat to Hunter's Point, but it was more of a rout than a retreat.

"We were demoralized," reported Lieutenant Pat White. "Officers would call to their men to fall in but the men would pay no attention. Every man was trying to save himself, some would throw down their arms and part of a regiment would take one route and the other part start another way."[191] When the troops discovered a solid line of Confederates between them and their transports, panic set in. Men began to cry "Surrounded, surrounded," and inexperienced officers concluded there was nothing to do but surrender. Grant was in his element. "We cut our way in and we can cut our way out," he told his regimental commanders.[192] He called up the Chicago Light Battery, which was now back in action, ordered the gunners to double-shot their tubes with canister, and once again the rebel line was split open.[193] Colonel John "Black Jack" Logan, a former member of Congress who now commanded the 31st Illinois, spearheaded the breakout. "Follow the flag and myself," he ordered, as the Confederates gave way.[194] Grant's troops funneled through the opening behind Logan, and straggled back to the landing site. "It was a second 'Manassas,' " wrote one Southern officer. "The road was strewn with overcoats, blankets, haversacks, guns, cartridge boxes, coats, caps, etc. . . . Every fence corner had a knapsack or a gun in it; the cornfields were covered with them."[195] The Union army left over a thousand rifles in the field. Dr. Brinton lost his matched set of French-made surgical instruments; Grant lost his mess chest.[196]

As the troops neared the boats, Grant acted as his own rear guard.

Dressed in the blouse of an army private—which had become his standard duty uniform—he watched over the evacuation of the wounded and was the last man to leave the shore. "There is a Yankee. You may try your marksmanship on him if you wish," Polk told his staff, but no one did.[197]

According to Grant's account, "the captain of a boat that had just pushed out but had not started, recognized me and ordered the engineer not to start the engine; he then had a plank run out for me. My horse seemed to take in the situation. . . . [He] put his fore feet over the bank without hesitation or urging, and with his hind feet well under him, slid down the bank and trotted aboard the boat, twelve or fifteen feet away, over a single plank."[198]

Belmont was scarcely the victory Grant sought. The battle followed the general pattern of the major battles of 1861—Bull Run, Ball's Bluff, and Wilson's Creek: the Union attackers achieving initial success, the Confederates giving way to early panic, rallying suddenly and driving the Yankees from the field. Casualties were heavy and about equal. Polk lost 642 killed, wounded, and captured; Grant, 607. That was roughly 19 percent of the Union troops engaged, the 7th Iowa and the 22nd Illinois bearing the brunt of the losses.[199] On the trip upriver, Grant was solemn. Officers crowded into the main cabin of the *Belle Memphis* and talked glibly of the battle. Grant, deep in thought, sat alone and spoke to no one. "We thought he was hard-hearted, cold, and indifferent," said one veteran, "but it was only the difference between a *real* soldier and amateur soldiers."[200]

Grant had taken a risk and now faced the consequences. Upon reaching Cairo he immediately dispatched a messenger to Colonel Oglesby, countermanding his orders to march to Belmont. With Grant's task force repulsed, Oglesby's command would be in grave danger if it continued on alone.[201] The second message Grant sent was to C. F. Smith at Paducah. "They had eleven regiments against our 3000 men," and he left it to Smith to draw the inference.[202] Grant's third message was a cryptic report to department headquarters in St. Louis. It was less than candid: "We met the rebels about nine o'clock this morning two and a half miles from Belmont, drove them step by step into their camp and across the river. We burned their tents and started on our return with all their artillery. . . . The rebels recrossed the river and followed in our rear to place of embarkation. Loss heavy on both sides."[203]

Throughout his life Grant was sensitive to criticism of his generalship at Belmont. In 1864, shortly after he was appointed general in chief, he had his staff prepare a revised report of the battle (backdated November 17, 1861)[204] in which it was asserted that the purpose of the raid was to deter Polk from dispatching reinforcements to Sterling Price, and to prevent Colonel Oglesby's column from being cut off by the Confederates.[205] Rather than accept responsibility for moving independently against Belmont, Grant sought protective cover.[206] Not until the last year of his life, when writing his memoirs, did Grant acknowledge that he had attacked without orders.[207]

During his seven years of civilian life, Grant could do nothing right. Now, he could do nothing wrong. The 19 percent casualty rate at Belmont made it one of the more sanguinary battles of the war. But after some initial carping, the nation's press hailed it as a victory.[208] The *Cincinnati Gazette* called the attack entirely successful. "The undertaking seems to have been creditable to the enterprise of our Generals in command of the expedition, and highly honorable to the courage and conduct of the troops."[209] The *Chicago Journal,* reporting from Cairo, said Grant's men fought like veterans. "Every regiment suffered severely . . . but the general opinion prevails that the rebels suffered far greater losses than we."[210] The *National Intelligencer* in Washington and the *Philadelphia Daily Ledger* quoted Grant approvingly that "our victory at Belmont was complete."[211] The *New York Times* noted, "Under all the circumstances the late battle at Belmont, Mo., is considered in high degree creditable to all our troops concerned in it, and the success of the brilliant movement is due to Gen. Grant."[212] The *St. Louis Republican* praised Grant for being "present where the balls flew thickest, directing every movement as calmly as if on parade."[213] The *New York Herald* proclaimed Belmont a victory "as clear as ever warriors gained."[214] Even the *Chicago Tribune,* which at first severely criticized the raid, shifted its editorial stance and asserted the battle was a victory. According to the *Tribune,* the impact of Grant's attack was such that Belmont had now been abandoned by the rebels.[215]

Grant was making his own luck. As a commanding general he had been as green as his raw Illinois and Iowa volunteers. Yet he led them to victory in a stand-up fight against an entrenched Confederate force of equal size, and extracted them from defeat when they were outnumbered. He braved the same dangers as his men and won their respect on the battlefield. Veterans of Belmont were henceforth "Grant's men," the core of what would soon become the Army of the Tennessee.

The initial success at Belmont stemmed from the boldness of Grant's conception and the audacity with which he deployed his regiments in combat. The defeat resulted from his failure to pursue Pillow's beaten force, his inability to coordinate his naval support, and his underestimation of the enemy's ability to counterattack. Grant always thought more about what he was going to do to the enemy than what the enemy might do to him, and he rarely credited his Confederate opponents with either the capability or the inclination to attack. This caused the reversal at Belmont. It would get him into trouble again at Donelson, and would almost bring his defeat at Shiloh.

After talking to the Illinois troops who took part in the battle, Elihu Washburne (who had remained in Cairo with his investigating committee) hustled back to Washington "to drop a flea" in the president's ear about Grant's role at Belmont.[216] Lincoln did not know it yet, but here was the general he had been looking for.[217]

CHAPTER FIVE

"UNCONDITIONAL SURRENDER"

There is not a sufficiency of Union sentiment left in this portion of the state to save Sodom.

GRANT to Halleck
November 22, 1861

GRANT STUMBLED AT BELMONT, but recovered quickly. He had carried the battle to the enemy, confirmed his view that the rebels could be whipped, and was soon ready to try again. Downriver, the effect of the battle was just the opposite. Initially the Confederates celebrated Belmont and believed they had won a decisive victory. Polk jubilantly telegraphed Jefferson Davis that the Union force numbered 8,000 and had been completely routed. Grant, he said, was reported killed.[1] In his official report three days later Polk said "the battle was fought against great odds," and while he could not state the enemy loss precisely, "I am satisfied it cannot fall short of 1500."[2] Poems and songs, including "The Belmont Quick Step," were written to lionize the rebel soldiers,[3] and in Richmond the Confederate congress voted a resolution to commemorate "a triumphant victory" against an enemy force "greatly superior in numbers and appointments."[4] When boatloads of Confederate dead and wounded arrived in Memphis, however, the grim reality of war dawned in the cotton South.* And when it was learned Grant's force numbered 3,000, not 8,000, celebrations turned glum. Rather than being outnumbered, the Confederates had enjoyed a two-to-one advantage at Belmont. Polk called in his out-

---

* Three of Polk's regiments, the 2nd Tennessee, the 21st, and the 154th, were Memphis regiments. The *Nashville Banner* reported "Memphis today is like Rachel mourning for her children." Schools closed and men and women lined the riverbank waiting for the incoming boats. *Nashville Banner,* November 10, 1861. Also see the *Memphis Appeal,* November 9, 10, 11, 1861.

lying detachments, hastened work on the fortifications surrounding Columbus, and hunkered down to await a renewed Union onslaught. In retrospect, the fruits of Belmont seem clear. Grant gathered momentum, while the Confederates settled into a defensive posture.

The battle of Belmont coincided with the appointment of Henry W. Halleck to command the Western theater of operations.[5] After six months of war, the Union command structure had sorted itself out. In the east, thirty-four-year-old George B. McClellan had been given command of the Army of the Potomac, and on November 1 he succeeded the loyal but aged Winfield Scott as general in chief, holding both posts simultaneously. The central theater was entrusted to another of Grant's prewar acquaintances, Don Carlos Buell, who commanded the Army of the Ohio with headquarters at Louisville.[6] Reporting to Buell was Brigadier General George H. Thomas, who commanded Union troops in the mountainous regions of eastern Kentucky and Tennessee. These troops formed the nucleus of what later became the Army of the Cumberland. Halleck's principal subordinates in the West were Grant at Cairo, C. F. Smith at Paducah, John Pope on the Missouri, and Samuel Curtis, who fell heir to the troops Frémont had assembled in western Missouri.

The Confederate chain of command was simpler, but the task more difficult. Earlier in the fall Albert Sidney Johnston, fresh from California, assumed command of all rebel forces west of the Appalachians. Headquartered in Nashville, Johnston's line stretched from the barrens of eastern Kentucky, through the bluegrass region, on across the Mississippi to the Ozarks and Indian Territory beyond. Johnston had no difficulty asserting his authority (Jefferson Davis called him "the greatest soldier, the ablest man, civil or military, Confederate or Federal, then living"[7]); his problem was that his line extended in a crazy-quilt pattern for over 500 miles. To defend it with the 75,000 men the Confederacy provided was impossible unless he could mass his forces at the point of Union attack.

Johnston met the challenge as best he could. He dispatched Earl Van Dorn, his most energetic subordinate, to take command of the 20,000 troops beyond the Mississippi, and left him to devise his own strategy. Johnston anchored the east end of his line in the vicinity of the Cumberland Gap, one of the few terrain features that worked to his advantage. Believing his flanks protected, Johnston concentrated on the critical 150-mile sector between Nashville and Columbus, which became the pivot of his defense. The Confederates were outnumbered, but the Memphis & Ohio Railroad ran laterally within the southern perimeter, affording a means of shifting troops rapidly from one point to another. At Columbus, Polk had 18,000 men facing Grant and Smith, whose combined force totaled more than 20,000. Polk's fortified position—the "Gibraltar of the West"—was

virtually impregnable; the disadvantage was that he lacked freedom to maneuver. The center of the Confederate line formed up in the vicinity of
Bowling Green, Kentucky, an important railroad junction sixty-one miles
north of Nashville where Major General William Hardee's 30,000-man
Army of Central Kentucky faced 50,000 men under Buell. On his right
flank, Johnston deployed 5,000 men under former Tennessee congressman Felix Zollicoffer against an equivalent Federal force under George
Thomas. Another 4,000 Confederates were constructing fortifications on
the Cumberland and the Tennessee rivers, while a cavalry force under
hard-fighting Nathan Bedford Forrest was somewhere out in front of
rebel lines, preying on Yankee communications. Altogether, Johnston
could field slightly more than 55,000 combat effectives east of the Mississippi versus 75,000 Union troops.

Johnston's position was further complicated by the two great rivers,
the Tennessee and the Cumberland, which pierced the center of his line: "a
double-barreled shotgun leveled at his heart," in the words of one historian.[8] C. F. Smith's forces sat astride the mouths of both rivers, and despite
their northerly flow, they offered easy access for steam-powered Union
gunboats into the vital center of the Confederacy and the supply base of
Johnston's army. Even worse, the railroads Johnston depended upon to
shuttle his forces spanned both rivers only a few miles from Union lines.
Gunboats could destroy the railroad bridges and the trestles leading to
them in a matter of hours. To counter that threat, Johnston's predecessors
had begun construction of two forts, Fort Henry on the right bank of the
Tennessee, and Fort Donelson on the left bank of the Cumberland. The
forts were located twelve miles apart: close enough to reinforce each other,
but not so close as to provide mutual support. Johnston ordered both forts
completed as quickly as possible.

The one advantage Johnston possessed—almost the only one—was
unity of command. The Confederate army had a single head. Whether the
Union's Halleck and Buell could coordinate their efforts was not clear.
Both reported directly to McClellan, and they were darkly suspicious of
each other.[9] Their commands divided at the Cumberland River, which
may have looked like a tidy demarcation line to the War Department, but
in reality was the focal point of rebel resistance. Johnston sagely placed his
center of gravity in the seam between the two Union armies and initially
enjoyed substantial success. Overstating the size of his force by a factor of
two, sometimes three, his threats to move on Lexington, Louisville, and
Cincinnati were trumpeted widely by the press in both North and South.
As a result, both Buell and Halleck misjudged Confederate strength and
were reluctant to attack. Indeed, when Buell suggested a joint advance
against Nashville, Halleck dismissed it as "madness."[10]

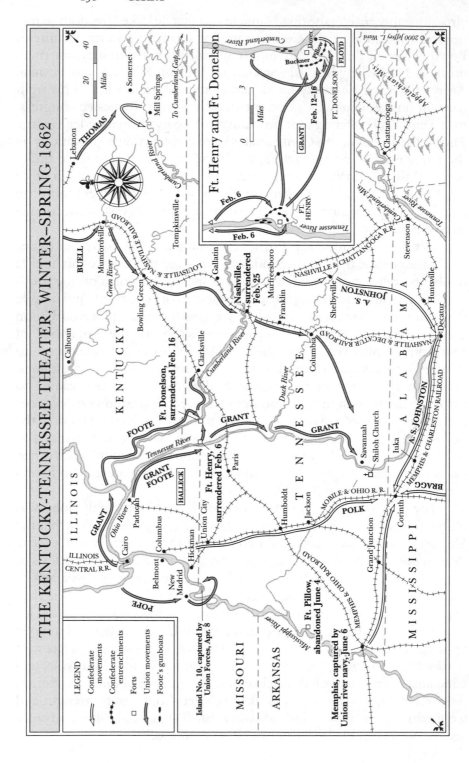

THE KENTUCKY-TENNESSEE THEATER, WINTER–SPRING 1862

Ft. Henry and Ft. Donelson

© 2000 Jeffrey L. Ward

LEGEND
Confederate movements
Confederate entrenchments
Forts
Union movements
Foote's gunboats

Island No. 10, captured by
Union Forces, Apr. 8

Ft. Pillow,
abandoned June 4

Memphis, captured by
Union river navy, June 6

Johnston's bluff flummoxed Halleck and Buell, but Grant and Smith did not buy it, nor did George Thomas. Imperturbable and phlegmatic—"Old Slow Trot" he had been called in the 2nd Cavalry—Thomas was moving steadily against Zollicoffer and on January 19, 1862, at Mill Springs, Kentucky, he met and routed the Confederate force, totally destroying its combat effectiveness. Johnston's right flank collapsed. Thomas's troops poured through the Cumberland Gap and would have taken Knoxville had their supplies not given out.[11]

At the same time Thomas was rolling over Johnston's right, Grant and Smith were probing the Confederate left. Halleck was dragging his feet launching an offensive to support Buell—"To operate on exterior lines against an enemy occupying a central position will fail, as it has always failed, in 99 cases out of 100," he wrote the president[12]—but after continued prodding from Lincoln and McClellan[13] he eventually ordered Grant to conduct a demonstration in the direction of Columbus to prevent Polk from sending reinforcements to Bowling Green. "Make a great fuss," Halleck told Grant, "and by all means avoid a serious engagement."[14]

Grant needed no prodding. Halleck's instructions were virtually identical to those he had received from Frémont two months earlier, yet this time Grant stayed within the letter of the order. On January 14, 1862, he moved with 9,000 men down the left bank of the Mississippi, supported by a flotilla of gunboats under Commodore Foote. Simultaneously, Smith moved up the Tennessee from Paducah, buttressed by two additional gunboats. Grant's cavalry engaged rebel pickets three miles from Columbus, while he and Foote took the naval vessels under the guns of the citadel. After making a personal thirty-five-mile survey on horseback of the roads leading to the Confederate stronghold ("sloppy, miserable, and virtually impassable at this time of year"), he returned to Cairo on January 20.[15]

Grant had a field soldier's contempt for making an empty show of force, but in his report to Halleck he put on a good face. "The expedition, if it had no other effect, served as a fine reconnaissance."[16] To his staff he was more candid. "This sloshing about in mud, rain, sleet and snow for a week without striking the enemy, only exposing the men to great hardships and suffering in mid-winter, is not war."[17]

Smith returned to Paducah the following day and filed a glowing report about the prospect of quick success. Grant had come to consider Smith, who was sixteen years his senior, a personal tutor in the art of war. Smith said his troops had approached within two and a half miles of Fort Henry, and the defensive layout corresponded to the sketch he and Grant had reviewed. The garrison consisted of 2,000 to 3,000 men, but the works were incomplete and because the Tennessee River was at flood stage, many of the gun emplacements were underwater. "I think two iron-clad gunboats would make short work of Fort Henry." [18]

Grant was delighted. Fort Henry and Fort Donelson were the key to Johnston's position. Their capture would not only open the Tennessee and the Cumberland to Federal gunboats, but would drive a wedge between the Confederate forces at Columbus and those at Bowling Green. Polk's fortress on the Mississippi would be outflanked and Hardee's Army of Central Kentucky would be dangerously exposed. A rebel withdrawal would become inevitable; the state of Kentucky would be back in Union hands, and it would be doubtful if Johnston could hold central Tennessee. Grant immediately transmitted Smith's report to Halleck, and requested permission to visit St. Louis headquarters. [19]

Grant's request landed on Halleck's desk just as he received word of General Thomas's victory at Mill Springs. The rivalry between Halleck and Buell now worked to Grant's advantage. Unless Thomas's victory could be offset, Buell could easily emerge as the overall Union commander west of the Appalachians. Halleck told Grant to report to St. Louis immediately. [20]

Grant believed the opportunity to move south was at hand. On the eve of his departure for St. Louis he shared his enthusiasm with his sister Mary. "I now have a larger force than General Scott commanded" in Mexico, he wrote. "I do hope it will be my good fortune to retain so important a command for at least one battle. I believe there is no portion of our whole army better prepared to contest a battle than there is within my district." [21]

But Grant's meeting with Halleck went poorly. The commanding general and his Cairo subordinate had not served together previously and had little more than a nodding acquaintance. [22] Halleck graduated from West Point in 1839—the spring before Grant entered—and during the Mexican War he was with General Kearny in California. He was practicing law in San Francisco when Grant was stationed at Fort Humboldt and was privy to the gossip surrounding his resignation. When Halleck assumed command of the Missouri Department in November he had been skeptical of Grant's ability, [23] and was still not sure what to make of him. An inspection team dispatched to Cairo in December reported favorably on Grant's command—one of the few bright spots in the department [24]—and Grant's promptness in carrying out orders recommended itself. He rarely complained, never asked for reinforcements, and went ahead and did the job with whatever resources were available. Accordingly, on December 20, 1861, Halleck had enlarged Grant's Cairo command to include the troops under C. F. Smith at Paducah. [25] This was a logical move given the lines of communication from St. Louis. [26] Nevertheless, Halleck remained uncomfortable with Grant. To some extent, it was the inevitable tension between a man of words and a man of action. Halleck was a superb administrator, but he did his best soldiering at army headquarters. He was cautious and out of place in the field, while Grant was just the opposite.

On his part, Grant was awed by Halleck's reputation as a military thinker. Old Brains was considered a powerful intellect and Grant rarely traveled in such company.[27] Consequently, both men were awkward and ill at ease when they met. The initial awkwardness between Grant and Halleck was something the two men never overcame. For the next three and a half years they would work together in a one-two relationship, one man's strength complementing the other's weakness. Almost in spite of themselves, they made an effective combination: Grant in the field; Halleck at headquarters. Old Brains was the senior of the two until March 1864 when Grant was appointed general in chief and became Halleck's superior. But regardless of who was in command, the relationship—beneficial though it was for the Union—was never an easy one.

Grant wrote later that at his initial meeting with Halleck he was "received with so little cordiality that I perhaps stated the object of my visit with less clearness than I might have done, and I had not uttered many sentences before I was cut short as if my plan [to capture Fort Henry] was preposterous. I returned to Cairo very much crestfallen."[28]

Grant did not remain crestfallen for long. On January 27 President Lincoln, thoroughly frustrated at the failure of Union commanders to assume the offensive, took the unprecedented step of issuing the "President's General War Order No. 1." It ordered a general advance of the land and naval forces of the United States within the month and threatened to hold all commanders strictly accountable for carrying out the order. Lincoln did not announce a specific plan of battle, but called explicitly for advances by the Army of the Potomac, Buell's forces in Kentucky, the naval units on the Gulf Coast, and "the Army and Flotilla at Cairo."[29] His purpose, he told a friend from Illinois, was to give a jolt to the military, a warning they must act.[30]

Grant recognized opportunity when he saw it. He perceived the leverage the president's order provided and, with characteristic persistence, immediately resumed his effort to move south. "With permission I will take Fort Henry on the Tennessee and hold and establish a large camp there," he telegraphed Halleck on January 28.[31] Since Lincoln mentioned the navy contingent at Cairo in his order, Grant roped in Flag Officer Andrew Foote to support the plan. "Grant and myself are of the opinion that Fort Henry on the Tennessee can be carried with four Iron-clad Gunboats," the commodore cabled Halleck. "Have we your authority to move for that purpose?"[32]

Grant pressed the issue hard—scarcely what a dutiful subordinate turned down so abruptly less than a week earlier would have done, except that the president was on record demanding action. The next day he filed a more extensive request with Halleck.

> In view of the large force now concentrating in this District and the present feasibility of the plan I would respectfully suggest the propriety of subduing Fort Henry, near the Kentucky and Tennessee line, and holding the position. If this is not done soon there is but little doubt that the defenses on both the Tennessee and Cumberland rivers will be materially strengthened. From Fort Henry it will be easy to operate either on the Cumberland, Memphis, or Columbus. It will besides have a moral effect upon our troops to advance them toward the rebel states.[33]

Grant dropped his customary deference and spoke in army lingo Halleck could appreciate. "The advantages of this move are as perceptible to the General Commanding the Department as to myself therefore further statements are unnecessary."[34]

With the president's directive hanging over him, Halleck could not help but see Grant's plan in a new light. Earlier he had told McClellan it would require at least 60,000 men to move up the Cumberland.[35] Grant had barely one third that number. But if Grant, Foote, and C. F. Smith were unanimously recommending action, Halleck decided it was a risk he must take. "Make your preparations to take and hold Fort Henry," he telegraphed Grant on January 30. "I will send you written instructions by mail."[36]

Halleck's follow-up letter was brief and to the point. Grant was told to move by steamer up the Tennessee as far as possible and, because of the weather, to rely on the roads no more than he had to. "Fort Henry should be taken and held at all hazards." The railroad bridges upstream were to be rendered impassable but not destroyed. Halleck said he was informed by Washington that General P. G. T. Beauregard, the hero of Fort Sumter and Bull Run, was on his way from Virginia with fifteen regiments to reinforce Johnston. Accordingly, "you will move with the least possible delay."[37]

Telling Grant to move with the least possible delay was like lighting a short fuse to a charge of dynamite. "Will be off up the Tennessee at six o'clock," he wired Halleck from Paducah on the morning of February 3. "Command twenty-three regiments in all."[38] That was it. Grant had a talent for understatement. The great Union offensive in the West was launched with a telegram of fourteen words. In three days Grant organized his command for battle, issued rations and ammunition, provided for resupply, procured river transportation, and coordinated the movement of seven Union gunboats, four of which were ironclads.[39]

The army Grant led against Fort Henry numbered approximately 15,000 men, all of whom (except for C. F. Smith) were volunteers, primarily from Illinois, Indiana, and Iowa.[40] Grant divided it into two divisions, the first commanded by Brigadier General John A. McClernand, a former congressman from Illinois who had served as deputy commander at Belmont, and the second by Smith. McClernand shared date of rank with Grant, had practiced law alongside Lincoln in Springfield, and had a sharp eye for personal advancement. Brave but unaccustomed to the military way of doing things, his political ambition lurked dangerously close to the surface—a fact of which Grant was acutely aware.

McClernand required watching, but Grant was more concerned about Halleck. As the troop convoy cast off from the dock, Grant's staff noticed he seemed tense and kept looking back at the wharf boat, as if he feared a last-minute recall might arrive from St. Louis. When the flagship finally turned upstream and Paducah fell from sight, Grant became a new man. He clapped John Rawlins, his aide from Galena, on the shoulder—a surprising act, to Rawlins, for Grant habitually showed no emotion—and said: "Now we seem to be safe, beyond recall. . . . We will succeed, Rawlins; we must succeed."[41]

Grant's concern about Halleck was not misplaced. The commanding general had never participated in a major offensive and, according to his principal biographer, as soon as Grant moved out Halleck was gripped with panic.[42] He anxiously asked Buell to launch a diversion toward Bowling Green and then wired McClellan for reinforcements.[43] In the space of two days, Halleck, Buell, and McClellan exchanged twenty-two telegrams with respect to Fort Henry. The result was that Buell eventually dispatched a green brigade to Grant, though it arrived too late to be of use.

Halleck's nervousness worked in Grant's favor. Concerned though he was, Halleck was too experienced to second-guess his deputy in the field. He believed "a general in command of an army is the best judge of existing conditions" and that it would be disastrous for him to dictate to his field commander on the basis of incomplete information.[44] Accordingly, he set about to do everything he could to insure Grant's success. The unthinking teamwork between the two men sprang into place. Halleck stripped the immediate St. Louis area to rush four more regiments to Cairo and he ordered Pope and Curtis to have additional reinforcements ready. He also sent his chief of staff, Brigadier General George W. Cullum, to Cairo to expedite the movement of men and supplies. Cullum was authorized to issue orders in Halleck's name to make certain Grant got what he needed. "Time now is everything to us," Halleck told Cullum. "Don't delay one instant."[45]

Along with Cullum, Halleck dispatched Lieutenant Colonel James B. McPherson to serve as Grant's chief engineer, and William Tecumseh Sherman to command Grant's rear area. Sherman had come a cropper while he briefly commanded Union forces in Kentucky, suffered what appeared to be a nervous breakdown, and had been relegated to a training command at Benton Barracks in St. Louis. Halleck, who in 1846 had been a wardroom companion of Sherman on the six-month voyage of the frigate *Lexington* from New York to San Francisco, was one of the few military men who retained confidence in his old friend. By sending Sherman to Grant, Halleck was giving him a second chance. McPherson, who graduated first in his class at West Point in 1853, was regarded as "a very clever young officer" with a brilliant career ahead of him.[46] In addition to his duties as chief engineer, Halleck instructed McPherson to observe conditions downriver closely and to keep a special eye on Grant. Rumors concerning his drinking were prevalent in St. Louis and Halleck wanted a firsthand report.[47]

Already Grant's momentum was attracting the resources of the Union. But for the time being he made do with what he had. Grant's fleet of nine passenger steamers was insufficient to transport his entire army, and so he moved by echelon from Paducah, McClernand's division going first. The vessels traveled upstream at night, their running lights dimmed, escorted by the ironclads *Essex* and *St. Louis*. At 4:30 A.M. on February 4 the convoy hove to on the east bank of the Tennessee at Itra Landing and the troops went ashore. This was sixty-five miles above Paducah and eight miles from Fort Henry. Thus far Grant had maintained tactical surprise. The dark wintry night cloaked his movement and, almost miraculously, Confederate spies in Cairo and Paducah flashed no warning to Fort Henry.[48] The transports returned to Paducah for Smith's division, and Grant boarded the *Essex* for a reconnaissance upriver.

Grant's task was to find a landing site as close to Fort Henry as possible, but beyond the range of its heavy guns. This was complicated by the fact that Panther Creek, a tributary of the Tennessee two and a half miles north of the fort, was hopelessly swollen because of heavy rains. Grant wanted to avoid having his infantry ford the deep, swirling waters of the creek, but landing between it and Fort Henry might bring the transports under Confederate artillery fire with resulting havoc and probably disaster. Grant decided to test the range of the guns at Fort Henry himself. He told Captain William Porter to take the *Essex* close in to the Confederate stronghold and draw its fire. The vessel steamed past Panther Creek, the guns of the fort opened up, and the initial volleys fell far short. Just as Grant was about to return to the bivouac area, confident his troops could land south of Panther Creek, a heavy six-inch rifled gun swung into action.

The first shell landed well beyond the creek and the second hit the *Essex* squarely, passing uncomfortably close to where Grant and Porter were standing.[49] Grant had the information he wanted. *Essex* limped back to Itra Landing, and Grant began preparations for the troops to debark at Bailey's Ferry, a mile or so north of Panther Creek.

Unlike the Confederate citadel at Columbus, Fort Henry was a target waiting to be taken. The main position consisted of a series of earth-work revetments covering about ten acres. It was sited on low ground, dominated by the heights across the river, and subject to flooding when the Tennessee rose above its banks. In February 1862 the water was so high the decks of the Union gunboats actually rode above the level of the fort, allowing the gunners to pour a plunging fire into the rebel post. The decision to construct the fort had been taken hastily after Tennessee seceded from the Union in April 1861.[50] The principal consideration was to locate it as close as possible to a corresponding fort to be constructed on the Cumberland (Fort Donelson). Unlike the Cumberland site, how-ever, the land adjacent to the Tennessee River was flat bottomland on an al-luvial floodplain. Engineers who surveyed the area concluded that no suitable location could be found for a fort on the right bank of the Tennessee, and the one they came up with was the best they could do.* Brigadier General Lloyd Tilghman, a West Point classmate of Longstreet's and John Pope's who became responsible for the completion of Fort Henry, said later "the history of military engineering records no parallel to this case."[51]

Aside from the unwisdom of its location, Fort Henry was under-gunned and undermanned. Its armament consisted of seventeen pieces of heavy artillery (all but one of which were smoothbore), which were col-lected piecemeal from various depots and foundries throughout the South. Two were so poorly cast they exploded during an initial test firing and several others had to be condemned, leaving only eleven guns facing the river, of which only nine were equipped with shot and shell of the ap-propriate caliber. The garrison comprised six raw infantry regiments, two batteries of light artillery, and some irregular cavalry—a total of about 3,400 men. The best equipped unit, the 10th Tennessee, was armed with old flintlock "Tower of London" muskets that had seen service in the War of 1812. Other units made do with their men's personal squirrel guns and

---

* Military historians have often suggested the Confederates would have done better to construct their fortifications at the Birmingham Narrows in Kentucky where the twin rivers are only three miles apart. In the spring of 1861, however, this was not possible, since Kentucky had not seceded and was jealously guarding its neutrality. For greater detail on the siting of Fort Henry, see Benjamin Franklin Cooling, *Forts Henry and Donelson: The Key to the Confederate Heartland* 46–48 (Knoxville: University of Tennessee Press, 1987).

fowling pieces.[52] Confederate intelligence was so poor that Tilghman did not learn of the Union army's approach until mid-morning on February 4 when Grant's fleet appeared downriver and transports began disgorging their troops at Bailey's Ferry. "Far as the eye could see," wrote one Confederate survivor, "the course of the river could be traced by the dense volumes of smoke issuing from the flotilla—indicating that the long-threatened attempt to break our lines was to be made in earnest."[53]

Grant's intelligence was equally faulty. He had no way of knowing the size of the garrison, or whether Tilghman had been reinforced by troops coming overland from Fort Donelson, or by rail from Bowling Green and Memphis. But if Fort Henry could be taken by 15,000 men and seven gunboats, he intended to do so.[54] His battle plan was simple enough. Incorporating the lessons he learned from Belmont, Grant instructed C. F. Smith to take his division and seize the high ground on the west bank of the Tennessee opposite Fort Henry. McClernand's 1st Division would move forward simultaneously, angle its way around the head of Panther Creek, cut the road to Fort Donelson, and wait "in readiness to charge and take Fort Henry, by storm, promptly, upon the receipt of orders."[55] At the same time, Commodore Foote would engage the enemy with his gunboats. The combined movement was to commence at 11 A.M. on February 6. Grant hoped the late hour would give the saturated countryside additional time to dry.

Throughout Wednesday, February 5, Smith's 2nd Division shuttled across the river in full view of the Confederate garrison at Fort Henry. "All day long the flood-tide of arriving and the ebb of returning transports continued ceaselessly," wrote Captain Jesse Taylor, a graduate of the United States Naval Academy who commanded the fort's heavy artillery.[56] That evening Grant wrote Julia, "the sight of our camp fires on either side of the river is beautiful and no doubt inspires the enemy with the idea that we have full 40,000 men. Tomorrow will come the tug of war. One side or the other must tomorrow night rest in quiet possession of Fort Henry."[57]

The key to Grant's attack was the firepower of Foote's flotilla. Commodore Andrew H. Foote was a hard-bitten, sock-it-to-'em naval officer of forty years' experience. His father, Samuel A. Foote, had been governor of Connecticut, and in 1822—the year of Grant's birth—Foote was appointed a midshipman in the United States Navy.[58] He served for years on the China station, chased slavers in the South Atlantic, and, puritanically religious, conducted a Bible school for his crew every Sunday from his quarterdeck. Foote was a man of pronounced opinions, especially on three subjects: alcohol, slavery, and how to fight. He considered it his calling to eliminate drunkenness at sea, and in 1845 his ship *Cumberland* became the first temperance vessel in the navy. His crusade against slavery was legendary, and his zeal commanding the *Perry* off the African coast from 1848 to 1850 effectively dried up the slave trade for almost two years. But fighting was Foote's first love. In 1856 while evacuating the American garrison from Canton, his relief boat came under fire from Chinese barrier forts guarding the harbor's entrance. Foote considered that an act of aggression. Without hesitating he brought his squadron to bear on the outermost of the forts, loosed a devastating broadside, and then led the storming party ashore to subdue the fortress. There were four barrier forts in all, and in two days Foote stormed all of them, capturing 176 pieces of heavy artillery and opening Canton to American trade.[59] Grant had mixed feelings about slavery and had his own problem with alcohol, but his view of war coincided with Foote's. They made a unique team, rising above service rivalry, and together pioneered the art of combined operations. The army and the navy, said Foote, "were like blades of shears—united, invincible; separated, almost useless."[60]

As an example of what he meant, the gunboats Foote commanded were not of navy design but owed their construction to John C. Frémont, who envisaged them as mobile artillery to spearhead his drive down the Mississippi. They were built on army contract by St. Louis industrialist James B. Eads, who put 4,000 men to work around the clock and completed eight boats in 100 days. Designed for river warfare, they were 175 feet long and 50 feet across, with two-and-a-half-inch armor plate sloped at a 35 degree angle to deflect incoming artillery fire. They mounted thirteen guns apiece, and despite their weight were remarkably maneuverable. They drew only six feet of water, which meant they could go almost anywhere along the Mississippi and its tributaries. The boats were crewed mostly by volunteers from Grant's command who had river experience, and the navy, which had been skeptical of the project at first, provided some of its best officers to command them. Except for the skirmish at Belmont—in which no ironclads participated—the ability of the gunboats to support ground troops was untested, and Foote planned to make an example of Fort Henry.

The Confederates meanwhile were getting ready. Tilghman chose not to contest Grant's landing at Bailey's Ferry, or the transfer of Smith's division to the west bank of the Tennessee, but to consolidate his forces within Fort Henry's trench line. Rather than hit the Union forces when they were most vulnerable, he would rely on the strength of his fortifications. Despite the lesson that should have been drawn from General Winfield Scott's victory at Veracruz, it was the type of position warfare most West Pointers embraced, and against Grant and Foote it would prove to be a mistake. Tilghman withdrew the two regiments occupying the high ground across the river, sent his infantry to man the rifle pits, and braced to receive the Union attack. "If you can re-enforce [us] strongly and quickly," Tilghman wired Johnston at Bowling Green, "we have a glorious chance to overwhelm the enemy."[61]

It was not to be. No reinforcements were forthcoming and Grant launched his attack on schedule. Promptly at 11 A.M. on February 6, C. F. Smith's 2nd Division set out to occupy the heights opposite Fort Henry. At the same time McClernand's 1st Division moved to cut the Donelson road and invest the Confederate garrison. Smith encountered virtually no opposition and within the hour his cavalry patrols were resting on the high ground. The 1st Division did not have it so easy. It was not a matter of rebel resistance—the crossing of Panther Creek was uncontested—but the floodplain surrounding Fort Henry had turned into a waxy gumbo. The distance to be covered by McClernand's men was less than five miles, but his lead elements were making less than one mile an hour, mired in deep Tennessee mud.

Foote, who was confident his gunboats would arrive first at Fort Henry, waited for an hour and then at precisely twelve noon hoisted his signal pennant to prepare for battle. The four ironclads—*Carondelet, Cincinnati* (Foote's flagship), *Essex,* and *St. Louis*—came abreast to form a line of battle, followed in the second rank by the wooden vessels *Tyler, Conestoga,* and *Lexington,* each mounting twelve guns. At 12:30 the gunboat flotilla was one mile north of Fort Henry. Foote turned to the captain of the *Cincinnati* and ordered him to commence firing.* The other vessels joined in and the heavy guns of Fort Henry belched in reply. Captain Taylor called the Confederate volley "as pretty and simultaneous a 'broadside' as I ever saw flash from the sides of a frigate."[62] Initially the rebel gunners held the advantage. Their guns had been sited with care, and the ranges were predetermined, whereas on the Union side only the bow guns of the approaching vessels could be brought to bear on the fort. But Foote closed the distance rapidly. "It must be victory or death," he told his captains that morning.[63] At 600 yards the line of ironclads slanted diagonally to bring their full armament to bear. *Cincinnati* moved to within 400 yards of Fort Henry, while the three wooden gunboats took up a supporting position near the west bank of the river. For the next thirty minutes the firing was intense, and as one defender remembered, "as accurate as the heart could wish."[64] *Cincinnati* took the brunt of the rebel fire, sustaining thirty-two hits, her stacks, boats, and after cabin riddled with incoming rounds. *Carondelet* suffered almost as many hits, *St. Louis* somewhat less, and the luckless *Essex* received a

---

* "Have the gunners mind their aim," said Foote with Yankee thriftiness. "Every charge you fire costs the government eight dollars." *Boston Journal,* n.d., quoted in Cooling, *Forts Henry and Donelson* 100.

shot to her boiler that rendered her powerless, and left thirty-eight men including Captain Porter scalded in the blast. Out of control, the ship swung broadside in the current and drifted downstream out of the fight.

Nevertheless, the fifty-nine Union guns Foote leveled against Fort Henry proved overwhelming. One by one the Confederate cannons were disabled or destroyed, or malfunctioned. By 1:30 P.M. only four of Fort Henry's guns were still firing, while Foote's barrage continued unabated, the three remaining ironclads now at point-blank range. Recognizing that further resistance was useless, Tilghman hoisted a white flag and the firing ended. The navy took Fort Henry while McClernand's 1st Division was still struggling against Mother Nature in the Tennessee countryside, unable to move forward quickly enough to block the Donelson road, much less join in the battle.

Grant, who positioned himself with McClernand's division, arrived at the fort at 3 P.M. "Fort Henry is ours," he wired Halleck. "The Gun-boats silenced the batteries before the investment was completed." Grant was euphoric. "I shall take and destroy Fort Donelson on the eighth and return to Fort Henry,"[65] he told Halleck. This time Grant did not ask permission. That night he wrote Julia "Fort Henry is taken and I am not hurt. This is news enough for tonight. I have been writing until my fingers are tired and therefore you must excuse haste and a bad pen. Kiss the children for me. Ulys."[66]

What of the 3,400-man garrison at Fort Henry? Traditional Civil War historiography has accepted the revised rebel version that Tilghman ordered the men to Fort Donelson before the Union attack began. In reality, the troops were in the trenches when Foote launched his barrage and panicked at the destructive force of the incoming artillery. Discipline collapsed, and the men deserted their posts, desperate to reach the safety of Fort Donelson. The South could scarcely admit that after ten months of preparation its principal bastion on the Tennessee surrendered after only one hour, or that the garrison ran away; thus the story was concocted that Tilghman ordered the withdrawal and simply maintained a covering fire from the fort to let the garrison escape.[67] Grant was perfectly happy to accept the revised version because he was embarrassed that the 1st Division had not moved quickly enough to cut the Donelson road.[68] If the troops at Fort Henry had already departed, it freed him of blame for their escape. In effect, one hand washed the other. Grant trimmed the truth in his account of the battle of Belmont. At Fort Henry, he assisted Tilghman in doing so.

Grant's demeanor in victory was captured by Captain Taylor, who represented Tilghman when the Union troops arrived. "Here I saw General Grant, who impressed me as a modest, amiable, kind-hearted but resolute man," he wrote.

While we were at headquarters an officer came in to report that he had not as yet found any papers giving information about our forces, and, to save him further looking, I informed him that I had destroyed all the papers bearing on the subject, at which he seemed very wroth, fussily demanding, "By what authority?" Did I not know that I laid myself open to punishment, etc., etc. Before I could reply fully, General Grant quietly broke in with, "I would be very much surprised and mortified if one of my subordinate officers should allow information which he could destroy to fall into the hands of the enemy." [69]

Grant billeted the captured Confederate officers on his headquarters steamer *Tigress,* and they took their meals with his staff. According to Taylor, Grant treated them with every courtesy.

The fall of Fort Henry galvanized public opinion in the North. Coming just two weeks after Thomas's victory at Mill Springs, it provided hope that the tide was turning in favor of the Union. In St. Louis, Halleck was the first to take credit. He issued a statement to the press: "Fort Henry is ours! The flag of the Union is re-established on the soil of Tennessee. It will never be removed." [70] On Capitol Hill, Representative Charles Sedgwick read Commodore Foote's official dispatch of the battle to the House, where it was received with tumultuous applause. [71] The *New York Times* reported, "Talk of peace and a restoration of the Union has revived with the taking of Fort Henry." [72] Horace Greeley's *New York Tribune* crowed, "A few more events such as the capture of Fort Henry, and the war will be substantially at an end." [73]

In the South, Fort Henry's surrender plunged Johnston's headquarters into despair. The center of the Confederate line had been breached and the mighty Tennessee was now open to the Union advance. On February 7 Grant destroyed the railroad bridge linking Memphis and Bowling Green. Polk's army at Columbus was now separated from that of Hardee. To add insult to injury, Commodore Foote, in a naval show of force, sent his three wooden gunboats 150 miles up the Tennessee to the head of navigation at Muscle Shoals, Alabama. For the gunboats it was a victory lap. They destroyed or captured six Confederate vessels, revived scattered Union sentiment along the way, and sowed fear in the heart of Dixie. [74]

On the afternoon of the 7th, Johnston met with Beauregard and Hardee at Bowling Green to fashion a response. As Halleck warned Grant, Beauregard had arrived from Richmond three days earlier, but instead of fifteen regiments he brought only a handful of staff officers with him. Now the trio of generals faced a dilemma. Johnston could make a stand in southern Kentucky or he could withdraw, save his army, and strike back at a time and place of his own choosing. Whatever they decided would be crucial to the Confederacy. Beauregard, flush with his victories in South Carolina and Virginia, was the most aggressive. He urged Johnston to leave a small force at Columbus and Bowling Green, concentrate both wings of his army at Fort Donelson, destroy Grant, and then turn on the slow-moving Buell and drive him back across the Ohio. It was a Napoleonic tactic the New Orleans Creole could not resist.[75]

Johnston and Hardee, instinctively more cautious than Beauregard, were not convinced. The risk of being trapped between Grant and Buell was too great. Johnston had already advised Richmond that Fort Donelson was "not long tenable."[76] He decided to leave a token force there to delay Grant and withdraw the bulk of his troops to a line anchored on Memphis. For the time being the two elements of the Confederate army would operate independently. Beauregard would take command at Columbus and pull back to Grand Junction, Tennessee, located on the main railroad line between Memphis and Charleston, South Carolina. Hardee would retire from Bowling Green to Nashville, and then to Decatur, Alabama— also on the Memphis–Charleston line. Johnston assumed Grant would continue to move south away from Buell. By using the Memphis– Charleston railroad Johnston could bring the two wings of his army together and crush Grant in southern Tennessee before meeting Buell. It meant surrendering Kentucky and most of Tennessee—with a deleterious effect on Confederate morale—but in a strategic sense it afforded Johnston the opportunity to mass his army near his base of supply, draw Grant away from his, and deliver a crippling defeat sufficient perhaps to end the war.

Certainly it was a viable option. Indeed, it was almost as daring as Beauregard's proposal.[77] But for reasons never adequately explained, Johnston began to temporize.[78] Instead of defending Fort Donelson with all the resources of his command, or sacrificing the position in order to fight later, Johnston abruptly chose to reinforce the garrison and take on Grant with only a portion of his troops. With the advantage of hindsight, it is clear this was an error of catastrophic proportions. General J. F. C. Fuller, the British military analyst, attributed Johnston's move to his shock at the fall of Fort Henry. The loss "was so unexpected that it completely bewildered him."[79] Whatever the reason, Johnston was compromising his plan to fight a decisive battle on his own terms far to the south. Between February 8 and February 12 he moved three of Hardee's most effective brigades—commanded respectively by Generals John B. Floyd, Gideon Pillow, and Simon Bolivar Buckner—to assist in the defense of Fort Donelson. By dawn on February 13 the garrison numbered 17,000 men, slightly more than Grant was bringing against it.* Johnston later wrote Jefferson Davis, "I determined to fight for Nashville at Donelson, and gave the best part of my army to do it."[80]

In fairness to Johnston, his response was not as harebrained as it appears in retrospect. Donelson, unlike Fort Henry, was a formidable installation. Dominating the Cumberland from a bluff that rose abruptly 100 to 150 feet above the river, the fort embraced almost 100 acres. On the east, or water side, three tiers of heavy guns were emplaced, the lower one near the water, the second fifty feet above, and the third fifty feet above that. The guns were protected by earthen parapets sixteen feet thick and were sited with precision to control the river approaches—the Cumberland being far narrower and the current much swifter than that of the Tennessee.

The north side of the fort was protected by Hickman Creek, a tributary of the Cumberland that was deep and wide, flooded with backwater from the river. To the south, Indian Creek, another tributary clogged with backwater, protected the approach. On the west, running between Hickman and Indian creeks, a continuous line of rifle pits had been constructed, running generally in an arc along a crest of high ground for about three miles. If Fort Donelson was to be assaulted by land, the attack would have to be mounted against this western perimeter and it would not be easy. The ground was broken and wooded, the trees outside the rifle pits had been cut down for a considerable distance to provide a clear field of fire for the defenders, and an extensive abatis had been constructed in front of the entire line. A deep ravine, running north and south well beyond the trench line, completed the position. Troops attacking the fort would have to charge up the side of the ravine to reach the rebel rifle pits. Johnston may well have decided that Donelson, properly reinforced, was invulnerable. He now provided twenty-eight infantry regiments to defend it, along with Nathan Bedford Forrest's cavalry and six batteries of field artillery. With 17,000 men under arms at Donelson there was every reason to believe the garrison could hold its own.

---

* The size of garrison at Fort Donelson cannot be stated precisely. Grant estimated there were 21,000 Confederates in the fort on February 15 (1 *Memoirs* 315). Adam Badeau, in his *Military History of Ulysses S. Grant,* which was written from official sources, put the number at 21,123 (I, 51 note–52 note) (New York: D. Appleton, 1881). General Albert Sidney Johnston estimated 17,000 men were present on February 13 (7 *War of the Rebellion* 283, 922). A list of the regiments at Donelson is provided in 1 *Battles and Leaders of the Civil War* 429, Robert Underwood Johnson and Clarence Clough Buel, eds. (New York: Century, 1887). After analysis, Thomas L. Livermore accepted Grant's estimate of 21,000 (*Numbers and Losses in the Civil War in America: 1861–1865* 78–79 [Bloomington: Indiana University Press, 1957]). Benjamin Franklin Cooling, in his 1987 study of the battle, simply notes between 15,000 and 21,000 were present and lets it go at that. *Forts Henry and Donelson* 149. Shelby Foote uses the figure 17,500. 1 *The Civil War* 195 (New York: Random House, 1958). To avoid overstating the size of the garrison I have adopted Johnston's number.

Grant meanwhile was delayed. On the 7th he issued warning orders to McClernand and Smith to have their divisions ready to move against Fort Donelson the following morning.[81] But first the weather intervened, making movement impossible, and then Foote's gunboats disappeared. The three timberclads were chasing rebels on the upper Tennessee, while the ironclads returned to Cairo for refit. Grant dispatched cavalry patrols each day to reconnoiter the approaches to Donelson, and on February 9 he joined them, but it was not until the next afternoon that he called his officers together and instructed them to move forward. Foote's gunboat flotilla was not yet reassembled, but Grant anticipated it would join him on the Cumberland. In any event he was tired of waiting. "I intend to keep the ball moving as lively as possible," he wrote his sister Mary. "By the time you receive this you will hear, by telegraph, of Fort Donelson being attacked."[82]

In St. Louis, Halleck became increasingly concerned. Unlike Grant, Old Brains was consumed with worrying what the Confederates might do. According to classic military theory, Grant's army between the two rivers was dangerously exposed. The approved solution was to dig in, solidify your base, and wait for reinforcements. Rather than building on the momentum that had developed, Halleck thought defensively. "Hold on to Fort Henry at all hazards," he telegraphed Grant on February 8. "It is of vital importance to strengthen your position. Impress slaves of secessionists in vicinity to work on fortifications. Shovels and picks will be sent you." Grant was told to mount his artillery on the land side of Fort Henry to resist a rebel attack. "Keep me informed of all you do, as often as you can."[83]

Halleck was not alone in his concern. A generation of American officers had been schooled to believe the art of generalship required rigid adherence to certain textbook theorems. Buell thought Grant would either be forced out of Fort Henry or his army would be captured.[84] McClellan was so worried he wired Halleck that either he (Halleck) or Buell should go immediately to Fort Henry and take command.[85] Assistant Secretary of War Thomas A. Scott, who was inspecting installations along the Mississippi, told Washington that Grant was "in extreme danger of being cut off by Beauregard."[86]

Halleck began working both sides of the street. He continued to rush reinforcements to Grant, but maneuvered feverishly to replace him. First he requested Secretary of War Edwin M. Stanton to recall Major General Ethan Allen Hitchcock, an elderly figure from the Mexican War, to active duty to take command of Grant's forces.[87] Then Halleck offered the post to Sherman.[88] Finally, he dangled the opportunity before Buell. "Why not come down and take the immediate command of the Cumberland column yourself? If so, I will transfer Sherman and Grant."[89] Hitchcock, who was then sixty-four, declined. Sherman said he preferred serving under Grant, even though he ranked him,* and Buell made no reply.[90]

Grant paid no attention. He had no knowledge of Halleck's efforts to replace him, and if the commanding general wanted to send picks and shovels to the front that was fine. But organizing a defensive position would have to wait. "There are no Negros in this part of the Country to work on Fortifications," he reported on February 11. Otherwise, Grant made no response.[91] Instead, he issued marching orders to McClernand and Smith. The division commanders were instructed to move out along separate roads in the direction of Fort Donelson as rapidly as possible and to take up a position two miles from the fort, forming a continuous line facing the enemy. Grant said reports of rebel strength varied so greatly "it is impossible to give exact details of attack but the necessary orders will be given on the field."[92] Grant wanted his troops on the move and presumably out of reach of headquarters in St. Louis. He would sort things out once his forces were in place.

The nature of Grant's greatness has been a riddle to many observers. The evidence begins with the assault on Fort Donelson. Grant did not hedge his bets but on his own authority moved immediately against an enemy occupying a powerful fortified position. In so doing he disregarded explicit instructions to entrench at Fort Henry, ignored Halleck's order to prepare to receive a Confederate attack, and took virtually all of his command with him. Grant was in the heart of enemy country, facing a hostile force at least as large as his own, with nothing to fall back on in case of disaster. He was violating every maxim held dear by the military profession. But the fact is, Grant was adding a new dimension to Civil War generalship: the ability to learn from the battlefield. He wrote later that he never recalled having read Jomini,[93] and at West Point he finished near the bottom of his class in tactics. But Grant had served with distinction in Mexico, and had seen how Taylor and Scott carried the fight to the enemy in similar circumstances. Unlike many of his contemporaries, Grant learned from Mexico—not just small-unit tactics and battlefield bravery, but the essence of strategic warfare. He developed great respect for the Mexican army, and never sold their soldiers short. Yet he saw how time and again Zachary Taylor and Winfield Scott moved against a numerically superior foe occupying a fortified position, and how important it was to maintain the momentum of the attack. Grant put the matter succinctly. "I was very im-

---

* "Command me in any way," Sherman wrote Grant from Paducah. "I feel anxious about you as I know the great facilities [the Confederates] have of concentration by means of the river and railroad, but [I] have faith in you." February 15, 1862. National Archives, Record Group 393, District of West Tennessee, Letters Received.

patient to get to Fort Donelson because I knew the importance of the place to the enemy and supposed he would reinforce it rapidly. I felt that 15,000 men on the 8th would be more effective than 50,000 a month later."[94] One of the tests of military greatness is the ability to recognize and respond to opportunities presented. By moving quickly against Fort Donelson, Grant was demonstrating just that.

By the afternoon of February 12 Grant's army was arrayed before the Confederate stronghold. A holiday mood gripped the marching columns as troops made their way up from the Tennessee lowlands. Regimental bands tooted the songs of an army on the move, and Grant was caught up in the festive spirit. When Surgeon John Brinton's powerful black stallion pressed ahead of the rest, Grant joked, "Doctor, I believe I command this army, and I think I'll go first."[95] Throughout the march discipline was lax. As the sun rose higher and the terrain got steeper, young soldiers shed what they could spare. The telegraph road between Henry and Donelson was littered with discarded blankets and overcoats not needed on a warm winter day in Dixie.

As the march column approached Fort Donelson, Grant deployed McClernand's division to the right toward Indian Creek, and Smith's division to the left toward Hickman Creek. Both divisions took up strong positions along the crests of ridges. The rebel fortress was invested, but the Union line was stretched thin. Grant actually had fewer men surrounding Fort Donelson than were present for duty inside. That night the troops slept on the ground in sight of the Confederate trench line. Grant had an aversion to digging in, and waited for the arrival of Foote's gunboats to repeat the magic of Fort Henry. In retrospect, it seems curious that the rebel commanders at Fort Donelson made no effort to impede Grant's deployment. Like Tilghman at Henry, they buttoned up inside the fort and waited for the Union attack.

Grant spent Thursday, February 13, filling the gaps in his line. He ordered the last 2,500 troops up from Fort Henry, while McClernand and Smith launched probing attacks against what they thought were weak spots in the Confederate line. Both were repulsed with heavy losses. A cold front came in that evening and the balmy February weather turned raw. Freezing rain turned to snow, and the temperature dropped to 12 degrees Fahrenheit. The exposed Union troops—many now without overcoats or blankets—endured as best they could. "There was much discomfort and absolute suffering," wrote Grant.[96] Newsmen covering the war were as miserable as the troops. "Writing is something accomplished with great difficulty," said the correspondent of the *New York Tribune*. "Our hands are often so cold that we cannot move our fingers to form legible characters. Campaigning in winter in this portion of Dixie is as gloomy as Pluto."[97]

St. Valentine's Day dawned gray and overcast. Foote came up early in the morning with four ironclads and the wooden gunboats *Tyler* and *Conestoga*. Accompanying him was a convoy of twelve transports carrying a brigade of Nebraska infantry—troops Halleck rushed forward from St. Louis. Grant put them into line between Smith and McClernand, added the reinforcements from Fort Henry, and created a 3rd Division under the command of Brigadier General Lew Wallace. By noon the troops were in position and Grant requested Foote to commence his bombardment. The plan was for the three Union divisions (Grant now enjoyed slight numerical superiority) to hold the rebels in place and prevent their escape while the gunboats closed in and blew Fort Donelson apart.

Confident of an easy victory, Grant positioned himself on the bluff overlooking the river to watch the battle.[98] The gunboats *Cincinnati* and *Essex,* heavily damaged at Fort Henry, had been replaced by their sister ships *Louisville* and *Pittsburgh.* The timberclad *Lexington* leaked so badly it could not move upriver, leaving only two wooden gunboats to provide fire support. Foote would have preferred more time to prepare, but with Grant urging an immediate assault he put his ships into line of battle. At 3 P.M. the flotilla moved to the attack. It came on as it did at Henry, the four ironclads out in front, *Tyler* and *Conestoga* 1,000 yards astern. At a mile and a half the big guns of the fort opened fire. Foote closed more slowly this time, the swift current of the Cumberland retarding the flotilla's progress. The narrow channel also kept the gunboats bunched, and the rebels enjoyed the height advantage. From the battlements at Donelson they poured a plunging fire into the ironclads, "tearing off the side armor as lightning tears the bark from a tree."[99] Nevertheless, the gunboats came on confidently. At a mile's distance Foote's flagship, *St. Louis,* opened with its bow guns, the other vessels following suit. At a quarter of a mile Foote thought he saw signs of panic among the gun crews on the bluff. The fire from the fort slackened, and in fifteen minutes, the commodore wrote, Donelson would have fallen.[100]

Foote was denied those fifteen minutes. A solid shot ripped through the pilothouse of the *St. Louis* mortally wounding the pilot and catching Foote in the ankle. The flag officer seized the wheel and made a game effort to guide the craft when additional incoming rounds blew away the steering mechanism.[101] *St. Louis* faltered, unable to maintain its course against the current. It drifted downstream out of the fight. *Louisville* was next to go, its tiller ropes shot away by rebel gunners. *Pittsburgh,* hit repeatedly between wind and water and in danger of sinking, broke off the engagement because its crew could not serve pumps and guns at the same time. That left only the *Carondelet,* commanded by Captain Henry Walke. Hit repeatedly along the waterline, it too dropped downriver, firing as it withdrew.[102] Union losses were heavy. Aside from damage to the vessels

(*St. Louis* had taken fifty-nine hits, the others almost as many), fifty-four sailors were killed or wounded. Confederate losses were minimal. There was some damage to the fort's earthen parapets and gun portals, but not one man had been killed or one gun disabled.

The repulse of Foote's flotilla was a bitter pill for Grant. Fort Henry showed what the gunboats could do; Fort Donelson showed what they could not.[103] Grant did not inform Halleck of the defeat, and filed only a minimal report with Cullum in Cairo. "Matters here look favorable in one sense. We have the works of the enemy well invested and they do not seem inclined to come out."[104] That evening he wrote Julia, "The taking of Fort Donelson bids fair to be a long job. The rebels are strongly fortified and are in very heavy force. When this is to end is hard to surmise but I feel confident of ultimate success."[105]

Despite the defeat on the 14th Grant held an intangible advantage over the defenders of Donelson: He knew what he wanted. Inside the fort, the rebel command was racked with indecision. Thus far the garrison had done well. They had driven back the probes of McClernand and Smith, and routed the Union gunboats. But already the elation over the afternoon's success had turned to despair. The fort was besieged, Grant was believed to have something over 40,000 men—with additional reinforcements arriving daily, and the Union navy, setback or no, retained control of the river. There were two alternatives: wait and hope for a relief column, or fight their way out and rejoin the Confederate army at Nashville. Albert Sidney Johnston provided little guidance. Informed of the victory over Foote, he replied enigmatically, "If you lose the fort, bring your troops to Nashville if possible."[106] No instructions, no orders, an implicit suggestion to hold out, but an acknowledgment that it might not be possible.

Johnston's message placed the decision in the hands of the trio of brigadiers in command at Donelson. For the Confederacy, it was an ill-chosen triumvirate. John B. Floyd, the ranking officer, a veteran Virginia politician who had served as James Buchanan's secretary of war (and who, during his last days in office, attempted to transfer federal ordnance to arsenals in the South), lacked military experience and was out of his depth. A patronage appointee of the governor of Virginia, his seniority came by accident. Gideon Pillow, second in date of rank, had made a fool of himself in the Mexican War by building a parapet with the ditch on the wrong side, and was one of the few general officers, North or South, for whom Grant openly expressed contempt.* Like Floyd, Pillow was a planter and

---

* Grant subsequently told Buckner that if he had captured Pillow at Donelson, "I would have turned him loose. I would rather have him in command of you fellows than as a prisoner." John R. Proctor, "A Blue and Gray Friendship," 31 *Century Magazine* 944 (1897).

politician by profession. But he had served for years in the Tennessee militia and considered himself an expert at leading men in battle. He was, however, one of the few who held that view. Third in seniority was Simon Bolivar Buckner, the only trained soldier among the three. Buckner was a reluctant rebel—he had hoped his native Kentucky could remain neutral—and like Grant, he despised Pillow for his martial pretensions. The bad blood between the two dated back to the Mexican War and, if anything, their relationship had deteriorated further during the intervening years. When Pillow sought election to the United States Senate in 1857, Buckner wrote a series of scathing letters to the *Nashville Republican Banner* belittling his service in Mexico and mocking his claims of valor. Pillow lost the election and held Buckner partially responsible.[107]

Unsure what to do, Floyd called a council of war the evening of February 14 to ask his subordinates' advice. Pillow, who commanded the Confederate left (opposite McClernand), advocated a breakout led by the troops under his command to open the route to Nashville. Buckner questioned its possibility for success but agreed it was the best alternative. His division (opposite C. F. Smith), would slip left behind Pillow and hold the shoulder of the breakout while the remainder of the garrison was evacuated. The meeting broke up at 1 A.M. with the attack set for dawn—meaning the men would get little or no rest that night as they moved into position. No one discussed what would happen if the breakout succeeded. Pillow assumed the attack would be so successful, and the defeat of Grant's army so complete, the troops could return to the fort to retrieve their possessions and whatever equipment was left behind. Buckner believed no one would return after the battle and instructed his men to take everything with them. Floyd, his inexperience showing, made no provision one way or the other and thus sowed the seeds for the Confederate undoing.[108]

At about the time the rebel war council was breaking up, Commodore Foote dispatched a note to Grant requesting he come to the flotilla anchorage four miles north of Donelson to discuss their next move. Foote said he ordinarily would have called on Grant, but his wounds prevented him from leaving his flagship. "I at once made my preparation for starting," wrote Grant. "I directed my adjutant-general to notify each of the division commanders of my absence and instruct them not to bring on an engagement until they received further orders, but to hold their positions." Grant said later he had "no idea that there would be any engagement on land unless I brought it on myself."[109]

Shortly before dawn on February 15 Grant, accompanied by a single orderly, rode out over the icy roads for the steamboat landing where the battered Union gunboats bobbed at anchor. Three miles to the south of Grant's headquarters, Pillow continued to mass his division for the assault on the Union right. Altogether it was seven miles from where Foote's flotilla lay to the point the rebels would attack, but as Grant said, he did not anticipate that the Confederates would come out of their entrenchments. At first light, and with Grant riding in the opposite direction, skirmishers from the 26th Mississippi made contact with Union outposts along the river road leading to Nashville. The weight of Pillow's division, some 8,000 to 10,000 strong, then fell on the Union right. By 8 A.M. McClernand's division was in trouble. By late morning the Confederates had rolled up the Union flank and the road to Nashville lay open. "On the honor of a soldier, the day is ours," Pillow wired Johnston.[110]

Grant was unaware a battle was taking place. A strong north wind blew the sound of the fighting away and kept him ignorant of what was happening at the far end of the Union line. Sitting in the wardroom of the *St. Louis,* Foote told Grant the ironclads were no longer seaworthy and he wanted to take the entire flotilla back to Cairo for repairs. That would take about two weeks, said Foote, and he urged Grant to entrench and await his return.[111] Grant recognized the vessels needed repair, but suggested Foote remain a few days longer while the army tried its hand against Donelson. Eventually a compromise was reached. Foote would take the two worst-damaged vessels to Cairo, leaving the rest to support the ground forces as best they could. Grant agreed to entrench partially, and ordered the picks and shovels Halleck had sent to be unloaded from their transports and shipped forward.[112] At noon the conference ended and Grant was rowed ashore. As he stepped from the boat an ashen-faced aide rode up bringing word the Confederates had come out from their lines in force and attacked McClernand's division, which was in full retreat.

Grant was riding his favorite stallion, Jack, that day. Though not a large horse, Jack was reliable and surefooted. He would gladly do whatever Grant asked and the two set out at a gallop over the frozen, treacherous roads of mid-February. General Philip H. Sheridan's 1864 ride to Winchester became a Civil War legend, immortalized in the poem of Thomas B. Read. But it was Grant's seven-mile dash to the fighting at Donelson that changed the course of the war. It can be argued that Grant should not have left the field to meet with Foote, that he should have anticipated a Confederate breakout, and that he should have left his division commanders with crisper instructions. All of that may be true. But confronted with disaster on the Union right, Grant hastened to the front to take command.

It was close to one o'clock when Grant reached Smith's division at the north end of the Union line. Everything appeared quiet. Grant told his old mentor what had been reported and instructed him to prepare for action. Next in line was Lew Wallace's division. Grant found it too was quiet and in place. Wallace, on his own authority, had sent his Nebraska brigade to support McClernand, and it was holding firm when Grant arrived. With McClernand's division it was a different matter. The Confederate attack had subsided and a lull had settled over the battlefield. But the 1st Division was in disarray. Troops had run out of ammunition, unit cohesion had evaporated, and casualties were heavy: over 1,500 killed, wounded, or missing. Worse still, the Union position blocking the Nashville road had been lost. Grant found men standing in clusters, talking excitedly, with no idea what to do. "No officer seemed to be giving any directions."[113]

Grant rode on. He discovered tons of ammunition lying about in boxes; the problem was that inexperienced brigade and regimental commanders had not recognized the need to keep their men resupplied. He heard men say the rebels had attacked with their haversacks filled with rations. "They seemed to think this indicated a determination to stay out and fight as long as the provisions held out." Grant drew a different conclusion. The rebels were attempting to break out from Donelson but had been unsuccessful and had fallen back. They must be at least as demoralized as McClernand's men, he told his staff. "The one who attacks first now will be victorious, and the enemy will have to be in a hurry if he gets ahead of me." Grant's presence had a tonic effect. Riding alongside the knots of stragglers he told McClernand's men, "Fill your cartridge boxes, quick, and get into line. The enemy is trying to escape and he must not be permitted to do so." Grant wrote later, "This worked like a charm. The men only wanted someone to give them a command."[114]

Grant found McClernand and Wallace sitting on horseback discussing the situation. After receiving their report, he told McClernand to re-form his division behind Wallace's line, and told Wallace to muster all of the troops he could and prepare to attack. Wallace remembered Grant was in total control. He wasted no words. "Gentlemen, the position on the right must be retaken."[115] With that, Grant turned and galloped off toward the other end of the Union line where C. F. Smith was waiting. Somewhere along the way Grant dispatched a message to Flag Officer Foote requesting that whatever gunboats were available put in an immediate appearance and lob a few shells from long range. Grant said he did not expect the boats to go into battle, but the sound of naval gunfire would have a salutary effect. "A terrible conflict ensued in my absence, which has demoralized a portion of my command. I think the enemy is much more so."[116]

The lull in the fighting Grant observed was attributable to incredible Confederate misjudgment. At 1:30 P.M., just as Grant was approaching McClernand's division, Pillow ordered his troops to break off contact and return to Fort Donelson. Rather than pursue the defeated enemy, the

Confederate soldiers were instructed to consolidate, pack their gear, load the supply wagons, retrieve the fort's heavy artillery, and prepare for an orderly departure for Nashville. Pillow had been swept away by the stunning victory that morning. He believed the Union army was in full retreat and that his troops could depart the fort at their leisure.[117] When Buckner protested and urged that the army march immediately to Nashville, Floyd overruled him. The road out of Donelson was relinquished, and the Confederate troops returned to the lines they held before the battle began.

To give Pillow his due, a Union commander less dogged than Grant might not have exploited the situation. It would have been tempting to fall back and regroup, and perhaps Pillow should not be blamed for assuming that is what the Union army would do. Certainly it would have done so if Halleck or McClellan (or even Sherman at that stage of the war) had been in command. It was Pillow's ill luck to be facing Grant, and he had no reason to anticipate what happened next.

Brigadier General Charles Ferguson Smith sat under a tree, talking casually to an aide when Grant rode up. Smith had already reconnoitered the ground to his front, and for the past hour he had been moving his regiments into position. With the patience of an old soldier he waited for Grant's orders, knowing he would be called on.[118]

"General Smith," said Grant, "all has failed to our right. You must take Fort Donelson."

It was as if C. F. Smith had been waiting for such an order all his life. "I will do it, General," he replied, and rode off to start work. Smith was hard on his volunteers, but he had turned them into soldiers. They were brave men, he thought, and if properly led would storm the Gates of Hell. "Take the firing caps off your guns and fix bayonets," he commanded. "No firing until inside the enemy's works." Smith was going to take Fort Donelson with a bayonet charge. It was something no other division commander would have attempted in the early days of 1862, and that few could have accomplished at any time.

Smith placed his favorite regiment, the 2nd Iowa, in the lead; four more regiments massed in column behind it. He rode across the Iowans' front, pointed toward the high ground where the Confederates were entrenched, and said, "Second Iowa, you must take the fort. I will lead you." Sitting high on his horse, "like a Marshal of France," a brother officer recalled, Smith led the Iowans off the ridge top and toward Buckner's works. Down the steep side of the ravine, through underbrush "too thick for a rabbit to get through," across a small stream at the bottom, and up the opposite slope into the rebel abatis. They went on, through the fallen timber and up the ridge, enemy fire intensifying at every step. The Iowans wavered. "No flinching now, my lads, this is the way. Come on," shouted

Smith. Erect as if on parade, his sword aloft, he rode on, timing the gait of his horse to the movement of his colors.[119] He was a conspicuous target and the air around him whistled with minié-balls, but he never flinched. "I was nearly scared to death," a young soldier said afterward, "but I saw the Old Man's white mustache over his shoulder, and I went on."[120] The rebel defenders were no match for Smith's division. Union troops swarmed over the Confederate trench line and would have taken the fort itself if Buckner had not arrived with reinforcements. By 4 P.M. the fighting was over. Smith had cracked Fort Donelson's outer defenses without firing a shot.[121] Thirty minutes later Wallace's division retook possession of the road to Nashville. Night came quickly in February and the Union army slept once again on the snow-covered ground, ready to assault Donelson's inner works at daybreak.

Riding back to his farmhouse headquarters, Grant passed numerous dead and wounded from both armies. He saw a Union officer and a Confederate soldier, both severely wounded, lying side by side. The officer was trying, without much success, to give the Confederate a drink from his canteen. Grant dismounted and asked his staff officers if anyone had a flask. One was produced and Grant gave each man a swallow of brandy. "Send for stretchers," he called to Captain Rawlins. "Send for stretchers at once for these two men." As the aidmen came up, Grant remounted, only to notice the stretcher bearers ignored the Southern soldier. "Take the Confederate too," he ordered, "the war is over between them."[122]

The men were borne away and Grant rode off with his staff. There were so many dead and wounded near the roadside that the horses shied repeatedly. Finally, Grant turned to his chief of staff, Colonel Joseph D. Webster: "Let's get away from this dreadful place. I suppose this work is part of the devil that is left in us all." Under his breath, barely audible, Grant recited the words of Robert Burns:

> *Man's inhumanity to man*
> *Makes countless thousands mourn.*[123]

That evening Floyd convened another council of war. Mutual recriminations hung heavy in the air.[124] Confederate losses were substantial: about 2,000 killed, wounded, or captured. Grant, it was believed, had received another 10,000 reinforcements, sent forward by General Cullum from Cairo.[125] According to Floyd's bloated estimate, that brought the Union force to eighty regiments—well over twice what was actually on hand. Gloom settled in quickly. Not only had the Nashville road been abandoned, but C. F. Smith's artillery was now emplaced on the ridge dominating the rebel redoubt. At dawn the shelling would begin and it was simply a matter of time until the fort would be taken. The discussion was acrimonious, but the will to fight was lacking. It was agreed Donelson should be evacuated. Orders were issued for the garrison to march out before dawn and the meeting broke up to make ready.

The Confederate assumption was that the road to Nashville, though abandoned by Pillow's division, was still open. Rebel pickets soon brought back news to the contrary. Not only was the ground reoccupied, but the Union army was there in greater numbers than before. A second meeting was called—one of the most bizarre in American military history—and the trio of brigadiers concluded they had no alternative but to surrender. Buckner said it would cost three quarters of their command if the army tried to fight its way out, and no general "had the right to make such a sacrifice of human life." [126]

Donelson had to be surrendered, but no one wanted to take responsibility for doing so. Floyd, who should have done so, wanted to avoid being taken prisoner. He had been indicted in Washington for malfeasance as secretary of war and although the charge was nol-prossed, he feared it might be reopened. For personal reasons never completely explained, Pillow also wanted to avoid capture. [127] That left Buckner. Trained at West Point, he recognized charges of treason were the likely penalty for rebellion but he believed a general should remain with his men and share their fate.

The author of a comic opera would have been hard pressed to construct such a scene:

"I turn the command over, sir," Floyd told Pillow.

"I pass it," Pillow told Buckner.

"I assume it," said Buckner. "Give me pen, ink, and paper, and send for a bugler." [128]

Floyd commandeered two steamboats and fled upriver with 1,500 men from his Virginia brigade. Pillow made his escape across the Cumberland on a small flatboat procured by his chief of staff. Colonel Nathan Bedford Forrest, the fourth participant at the meeting, made no effort to conceal his disgust. He vowed he would never surrender and, with Buckner's permission, led his cavalrymen out of Fort Donelson across an icy stream too deep for infantrymen to ford and escaped with the 700 troopers of his command.

Buckner would be the first Confederate general to surrender, and he remembered the generous terms Beauregard extended to Major Anderson at Fort Sumter. The garrison had been permitted to march out under arms, while the victors rendered a salute. Buckner also knew Grant was not a vindictive man. He may even have reflected on their last meeting in New York, eight years earlier, when he had guaranteed Grant's hotel bill and helped him secure a railroad ticket home. He took pen and wrote: "In consideration of all circumstances governing the present situation of affairs at this station, I propose to the commanding officers of the Federal forces the appointment of commissioners to agree upon terms of capitulation of the forces and post under my command, and in that view suggest an armistice until 12 o'clock today." [129]

It was shortly after 4 A.M. when a Confederate staff officer under a flag of truce approached Smith's lines with Buckner's message. Smith was sleeping on the snow with the 2nd Iowa that night, his head resting on his saddle. "I'll make no terms with rebels with arms in their hands," the old warrior told his staff when he read the message. "My terms are immediate and unconditional surrender." [130] But Smith knew it was not his decision to make. An orderly saddled Smith's horse and he immediately rode to Grant's headquarters, the Confederate officer in tow.

Grant was stretched out on a mattress on the kitchen floor of his farmhouse headquarters when Smith arrived. "There's something for you to read," said Smith, handing Grant the letter. Surgeon John Brinton, who was present, said Smith asked for something to drink. "My flask was handed to him and he helped himself in a soldier-like manner. The exposure of these nights must have told on him severely. I can almost see him now, erect, manly, every inch a soldier, standing in front of the fire, twisting his long white mustache and wiping his lips." [131]

Grant read the message and looked up, surprised it came from his old friend Buckner and not Floyd or Pillow. "What answer shall I send to this, General Smith?"

"No terms with the damned rebels," Smith replied.

Grant chuckled and began to write—one of the most famous dispatches in the history of warfare. When he finished he read it aloud.

> Sir: Yours of this date proposing Armistice and appointment of Commissioners to settle terms of Capitulation is just received. No terms except complete and unconditional surrender can be accepted. I propose to move immediately upon your works. I am sir, very respectfully
>
> > Your obt. svt.
> > U.S. GRANT
> > *Brig. Gen.* [132]

Smith grunted, thought a moment, and said, "It's the same thing in smoother words." He took the letter, stalked out to deliver it to the waiting Confederate officer, then returned to his command. It was time to prepare. Grant's threat "to move immediately upon your works" was not a bluff. Long before Buckner's letter arrived, Smith had been instructed to renew his assault at daybreak, and McClernand and Wallace had been ordered to attack as soon as they heard Smith's guns open up. Grant was going to take Donelson in the morning—one way or another.

Buckner was stunned when he read Grant's reply. Aside from the personal friendship between the two men, the Civil War thus far had been waged beneath a facade of romantic chivalry. The myth of the gentleman warrior figured prominently in the mental makeup of the senior officers in both armies. Grant was changing the rules. A man who hated war and who could not bear to see the wounded suffer was driving the consequences of rebellion home to the South. Complete and unconditional surrender. The sentiment was that of Grant's elderly role model, C. F. Smith, but it was Grant who put the thought into words for the nation to hear.

Buckner recognized he had no choice but to submit. Nevertheless, he was peeved Grant had treated him so brusquely. "The overwhelming force under your command, compels me, notwithstanding the brilliant success of the Confederate armies yesterday, to accept the ungenerous and unchivalrous terms which you propose."[133]* It was sunup when Grant received Buckner's reply. The divisions of Smith and Wallace were ordered to march in and take possession of Donelson, while Grant rode forward to accept the surrender.

Buckner and his staff were eating a breakfast of cornbread and coffee when Grant arrived. Their resentment faded quickly. Buckner reported that due to the departure of various troops with Floyd, Pillow, and Forrest, he could not tell with any degree of accuracy the number of men remaining at Donelson, but it was somewhere between 12,000 and 15,000. Grant did his best to put Buckner at ease. Soon they were bantering. Buckner said if he had been in command from the beginning, Grant would not have been able to get up to Donelson as easily as he did. Grant replied if Buckner had been in command, "I should not have tried in the way I did."[134] Buckner requested permission to send burial parties onto the battlefield and Grant agreed. The two commanders discussed the short rations the Confederates were on. Grant said the Union commissary would provide whatever additional food was necessary. Southern officers were al-

---

* Years later Buckner told his family lawyer he deliberately used the words "ungenerous and unchivalrous" knowing the public would not understand what he meant but Grant would. On his part, Grant, on his deathbed, confided to Buckner he thought Pillow was in command and that Buckner was simply writing as his agent. He told Buckner if he had realized Buckner was commanding "the articles of surrender would have been different." Mrs. Delia C. Buckner to H.A. Watkins, May 25, 1929, in Arndt Stickles, *Simon Bolivar Buckner: Borderland Knight* 168, 172 (Chapel Hill: University of North Carolina Press, 1940).

lowed to retain their sidearms and personal servants, and the enlisted ranks their clothing and blankets.[135]

The actual surrender was accomplished without formality. Dr. Brinton asked Grant when the official ceremony would be held? When would the rebels be paraded, their weapons stacked, and their standard lowered? "There will be nothing of the kind," said Grant. "The surrender is now a fact. We have the fort, the men, the guns. Why should we go through vain forms and mortify and injure the spirit of brave men, who, after all, are our own countrymen."[136]

Later that morning, February 16, 1862, Grant telegraphed Halleck that Fort Donelson had fallen. In addition to the garrison, Grant said the Union army captured "twenty thousand stand of arms, forty-eight pieces of artillery, seventeen heavy guns, and from two to four thousand horses."[137] In his handwritten dispatch to Cullum at Cairo, Grant gave credit where credit was due. The charge of General Smith's division, he said, had been decisive. "It was most brilliantly executed and gave to our arms full assurance of victory."[138]

In St. Louis and other Northern cities there was dancing in the streets. Church bells rang and cannons fired repeated salutes to celebrate the victory at Donelson. A newspaper editorial announced "any person found sober after nine o'clock in the evening would be arrested as a secessionist." Halleck, never bashful when it came to embracing success, told a cheering crowd, "I promised when I came here that with your aid I would drive the enemies of our flag from your state. This has been done, and they are virtually out of Kentucky and will soon be out of Tennessee."[139] The following day he wired McClellan, "Make Buell, Grant, and Pope major generals of volunteers and give me command of the West. I ask this in return for Forts Henry and Donelson."[140]

In Washington, McClellan also basked in reflected glory.[141] Guns boomed all day long, and General Cullum's dispatch from Cairo announcing Donelson's capture was read verbatim to the House and the Senate. On Monday, Secretary of War Stanton recommended Grant (and only Grant) be promoted to major general. Lincoln happily complied. The fact Grant entered service from Illinois gave the president special pleasure. He did not feel competent to speak about the fighting qualities of Eastern men, Lincoln observed as he signed Grant's commission, but the gallant behavior of Illinois troops at Donelson showed that "if the Southerners think that man for man they are better than our . . . western men, they will discover themselves in a grievous mistake."[142]

Back at Donelson, Grant wrestled with the aftermath of victory. Not since Yorktown had an American general taken the surrender of a whole army in the field. Grant wrote Julia he believed it was the largest capture ever made on the continent.[143]* To deal with so many prisoners was more than Grant's battlefield staff could handle. The severe February weather made it essential to move the men quickly lest they die of exposure, and when Buckner volunteered the use of his staff to assist, Grant accepted without hesitation. He wrote out an order authorizing the prisoners be collected at the nearby village of Dover "under their respective company and regimental commanders, or in such manner as may be deemed best by General S.B. Buckner."[144] In effect, the Confederate officers handled their own internment, and by late Monday most of the men had been loaded onto steamers bound for Cairo. Grant told Cullum that in the future he would suggest paroling all prisoners rather than keeping them in custody. Most would honor their paroles, he thought, and it required too much effort for an army in the field to handle them. The taste of victory was sweet, and Grant evidently decided it was a good time to replenish the overcoats and blankets his men threw away on the march from Fort Henry. "Send me 5000 blankets and 1000 overcoats as soon as possible," he wrote Cullum. "Many were lost on the battlefield and the men are now without."[145] When Buckner and his staff boarded the last of the transports on Tuesday, Grant went to say farewell. Before leaving he drew Buckner aside. "You are separated from your people," said Grant, "and perhaps you need funds. My purse is at your disposal." Buckner thanked him for his thoughtfulness but declined. Later Buckner said Grant always recognized a favor extended to him, and the offer of money "was a recognition of the kindness which I had done him."[146]

Grant came into his own. The lightning victories at Fort Henry and Fort Donelson captured the public's imagination. Within ten days the center of Albert Sidney Johnston's line had been breached, Kentucky secured, and the deep South opened to invasion. Grant lost 3,000 men at Donelson, roughly 11 percent of those engaged. Southern losses were much greater. Aside from battlefield casualties and the 14,000 men who went into captivity, a Confederate army with all of its horses, equipment, and weapons was taken out of the war. The effect on morale in Dixie was devastating. Tennessee, one of the most populous states in the nation, was denied to the South. Said differently, the rebel army was deprived of at least 50,000 potential recruits between the ages of eighteen and forty-five.[147] Equally important, Grant's victory at Donelson resonated strongly throughout Europe. The first significant Union triumph in the war, it slowed the movement to recognize the Confederacy and helped insure the war would be seen as an American domestic affair.[148]

Overnight Grant became famous. His initials were taken to mean

* The Union commissary general subsequently reported rations were issued to 14,623 prisoners from Donelson at Cairo. Grant, 1 *Memoirs* 314.

"Unconditional Surrender" and schoolchildren throughout the North memorized his message to Buckner. Newspaper accounts were unremitting in praise of his cool direction of the battle. When readers learned he smoked a cigar throughout the 2nd Division's attack, gifts of cigars flooded in. Grant gave up smoking a pipe, if for no other reason than there were dozens of boxes of cigars lying around headquarters and it seemed a shame to let them go to waste.[149] Reporters had a field day making the most ordinary of men appear extraordinary. Grant's features were described as "carved from mahogany," his eyes clear blue, his jaw "squarely set, but not sensual." One writer saw three expressions in his face: "deep thought, extreme determination, and great calmness." Readers were told that on horseback Grant sat firmly in the saddle, eyes straight ahead, "as if only intent on getting to some particular point." The words "square" and "straight" and "firm" were the ones used most often, and people liked them.[150]

The whole campaign against Henry and Donelson seemed a marvel of generalship, a superb combination of simplicity and determination—in stark contrast to the dilatory maneuvering of the forces under Buell or the Army of the Potomac under McClellan. The public's perception was not far off the mark. Grant, like few American generals before or since, understood the momentum of warfare. He had a quickness of mind that allowed him to make on-the-spot adjustments. His battles were not elegant set-piece operations—as Scott's textbook victory at Cerro Gordo had been—but unfolded unpredictably as opportunities developed. At the root of Grant's success was his army. Properly trained and supplied it was an instrument to be deployed against the enemy as circumstances dictated. Donelson was typical. On Thursday, Grant's probes were repulsed with heavy losses. On Friday, Foote's flotilla was routed. On Saturday, disaster struck the Union right and by noon the road to Nashville lay open. Undeterred, Grant counterattacked. C. F. Smith's intrepid leadership carried his division over Donelson's revetments; Wallace retook the Nashville road; and McClernand put his battered division back together. Grant was the author of the Union's deliverance, and the next morning he accepted Donelson's surrender.

From Cairo, General Cullum sent his congratulations. "I, in common with the whole country, warmly congratulate you upon this remarkable achievement which has broken the enemy's center, dispersed the rebels, and given the death blow to secession." The 5,000 blankets and 1,000 overcoats Grant requested would of course be sent forward immediately. Cullum, who made no attempt to conceal his satisfaction, said the victory was attributable entirely to "your brilliant leadership."[151] In St. Louis, Halleck made no comment. He did not acknowledge Grant's telegram announcing the capture of Fort Donelson, and sent no congratulations whatever.[152]

CHAPTER SIX

SHILOH

Over the field where April rain
Solaced the parched ones stretched in pain
Through the pause of night
That followed Sunday's fight
Around the church of Shiloh

"Shiloh"
Herman Melville, 1862

THE FALL OF FORT DONELSON threw Johnston's forces into disarray. On February 16 the disheartened remnants of Hardee's Army of Central Kentucky filed through Nashville on their way south. Reduced by straggling and sickness to fewer than 14,000 men, their morale was sapped and their supplies abandoned. In the Mississippi valley, Beauregard began the withdrawal from Columbus. He reinforced the garrisons at New Madrid and Island No. 10, and ordered the bulk of Polk's force—some 10,000 men—to Humboldt, Tennessee, at the juncture of the Memphis, Clarksville & Louisville and the Mobile & Ohio railroads.

Grant was alert to the opportunity. The two wings of the Confederate army were vulnerable. He wanted to move quickly against Johnston and Hardee before turning on Beauregard and Polk. On February 18, barely forty-eight hours after taking Donelson, he dispatched Flag Officer Foote and the gunboats *Conestoga* and *Cairo* to reconnoiter Confederate strength at Clarksville, Tennessee—an important rail center halfway up the Cumberland toward Nashville. Foote found the town evacuated, the rebel troops having decamped to join Johnston's retreat. The next day Grant informed General Cullum he was sending C. F. Smith's division to take possession of Clarksville. Grant said if Halleck wished him to do so he could take Nashville the following Saturday. "Please inform me as soon as possible of the Commanding General's desires."[1]

On Thursday Grant made his own reconnaissance of Clarksville and was informed by Sherman of another 12,000 reinforcements on their way to him.[2] That brought the size of his command to 36,000 men, two thirds of whom were battle-hardened veterans. Grant reorganized his army into four divisions, and resumed his effort to move against Johnston.[3] "I am now in possession of Clarksville," he wrote Cullum on February 21. "It is my impression that by following up our success Nashville would be an easy conquest."[4]

But it was not to be. Before Grant could take action he received a telegram from Halleck instructing him not to proceed further upstream than Clarksville.[5] Grant and Foote were stunned. Foote, who was outside the army's chain of command, launched a broadside at Cullum in Cairo. "Genl Grant and myself consider this a good time to move on Nashville. We were about moving for this purpose, when Genl Grant, to my astonishment, received a telegram from Genl Halleck not to let the gunboats go higher than Clarksville. The Cumberland is in a good stage of water, and Genl Grant and I believe that we can take Nashville—Please ask Genl Halleck if we should do it."[6]

Halleck was not interested, at least not then, and the evidence suggests he was more concerned with advancing his career than advancing against the Confederate army. Rightly or wrongly he believed that he, not Grant, had been the victor at Fort Henry and Fort Donelson, and before setting out in pursuit of Johnston he wanted to secure overall command of Union forces west of the Appalachians.[7] "I must have top command of the armies [in this theater]," he wired McClellan on February 20. "Hesitation and delay are losing us the golden opportunity. Lay this before the President and Secretary of War. May I assume command? Answer quickly."[8] In effect, Grant and Foote were hostage to Halleck's ambition. Old Brains instructed Cullum to inform them he was awaiting instructions from the War Department and until then everything should remain *"in status quo."*[9]

McClellan, who had not replied to Halleck's earlier request for supreme command,[10] answered quickly—and the answer was an unequivocal no. McClellan said General Buell in Bowling Green was a better judge of the situation than Halleck in St. Louis, and he declined to present Halleck's request to Stanton and Lincoln. It was another example of the rivalries bedeviling the Union army in the early years of the war; Little Mac simply was unwilling to advance Halleck's prospects.* Commodore

---

*After McClellan rejected his request, Halleck circumvented the chain of command and approached Secretary of War Stanton directly. "One whole week has been lost already by hesitation and delay. There was, and I think there still is, a golden opportunity to strike a fatal blow, but I can't do it unless I can control Buell's army. . . . There is not a moment to be lost. Give me the authority, and I will be responsible for the results." To Assistant Secretary of War Thomas A. Scott, who was then in Louisville, Halleck sent a similar message, asking him to come to the Cumberland "and divide the responsibility with me. I am tired of waiting for action in Wash-

Foote, a forty-year veteran of dealing with angleworms in the navy, recognized the problem immediately. "I am disgusted that we were kept from going up and taking Nashville," he wrote his wife. "It was jealousy on the part of McClellan and Halleck. . . . I shall report McClellan and Halleck to the [Navy] Department, and soon there will be a row."[11]

Grant was more tolerant. He had little experience with infighting at upper echelons and he put the best face on the delay he could. "I want to push on as rapidly as possible to save hard fighting," he wrote Julia on February 24. "Gen. Halleck is clearly the same way of thinking and with his clear head I think the Congressional Committee for investigating the Conduct of the War will have nothing to enquire about in the West."[12] Throughout his life Grant believed that if he had been permitted to pursue Johnston and destroy the Confederate army piecemeal after the fall of Fort Donelson, the war in the West would have ended in 1862. In his view, Chattanooga, Corinth, Memphis, and Vicksburg were all within reach that spring. Their occupation would have split the South, denied the men and resources of the Mississippi and Tennessee valleys to the Confederacy, and avoided the carnage that followed. "Providence ruled differently," Grant wrote in his *Memoirs*. "Time was given the enemy to collect armies and fortify his new positions, and twice afterwards he came near forcing his north-western front up to the Ohio River."[13]

Halleck's orders prevented Grant from moving on Nashville, but it was clear the city—with its vast supply depot—was ready for capture. On February 23 a group of Nashville surgeons came downriver to Donelson to treat the Confederate wounded. They told Grant that Johnston had evacuated the city and retreated forty miles southeast to Murfreesboro. Nashville, they said, was rent with violence and they urged Grant to push forward "and restore confidence to the people."[14] Grant assumed the doctors wanted the Union army to protect private property. Nevertheless, he was champing at the bit.[15] The following day he found deliverance when Brigadier General William "Bull" Nelson arrived at Fort Donelson at the head of a division of Buell's army that had been sent down the Ohio and up the Cumberland to reinforce Grant if Grant needed reinforcing. The fight-

---

ington. They will not understand the case. It is as plain as daylight to me." Halleck to Stanton, February 21, 1862, 7 *War of the Rebellion* 655; Halleck to Scott, February 21, 1862, ibid. 648.

The most generous interpretation of Halleck's action is that he overestimated the fighting capacity of Johnston's force and believed Grant's army alone was insufficient to defeat it. Since Grant had almost three times as many men as Johnston, and since his army, unlike the Confederate, was riding the momentum of victory, it is a difficult argument to sustain. In any event, Stanton, like McClellan, turned Halleck down flatly. "The President does not think any change in the organization of the army or the military departments at present advisable." Stanton to Halleck, February 22, 1862, ibid. 652.

ing at Donelson had been over for a week and there was no need for another division. Grant ordered Nelson not to debark his troops from their transports but to continue upriver to Nashville. The gunboat *Carondelet* was attached as escort, and Grant told Nelson to wait in Nashville until Buell arrived. If Grant could not take the Tennessee capital with his own troops, he would take it with Buell's.[16]

Bull Nelson was the man for the job. Six foot five and pushing 300 pounds, the foul-mouthed, hard-driving brigadier shared the fighting spirit of Foote and C. F. Smith. A native of Maysville, Kentucky, he had been appointed a midshipman in the United States Navy in 1840. When the Civil War broke out he was on duty at the Navy Yard in Washington, D.C., and had been sent by Lincoln to Kentucky to distribute rifles to the state's loyalists. Nelson proved so effective he was commissioned a brigadier general of volunteers and given command of the 4th Division of Buell's army. No fight was too big for Nelson and he admired the audacity of Grant's plan. Told that ammunition for two of his brigades had been sent mistakenly to Cairo, Nelson said not to worry. "I will endeavor to find the enemy with the bayonets of my division."[17] Since Johnston's army had evacuated Nashville that proved unnecessary and Nelson took possession of the city late that evening.*

Buell meanwhile was making his way cautiously toward the Tennessee capital from Bowling Green, encumbered by a massive wagon train, a desire to repair the railroad as he went, and a Jominian determination to secure all avenues of approach before advancing. As a sympathetic historian has written, Buell preferred preparation to execution and it was not until the morning of February 25 that the lead elements of the Army of the Ohio reached the north bank of the Cumberland opposite Nashville.[18] By then Bull Nelson had already secured the city and raised the Stars and Stripes. Buell was furious, humiliated, and panic-stricken. He believed Johnston had upward of 30,000 men ready to pounce on Nelson, while his own troops were still strung out on the march. Thinking a Confederate attack imminent, Buell sent Nelson's transports downriver to Clarksville

* Nelson's fighting career ended abruptly September 29, 1862, when he was shot and killed by Indiana brigadier Jefferson C. Davis in the corridor of Galt House in Louisville, Kentucky. Nelson had insulted Davis the week before. When Davis demanded satisfaction, Nelson slapped him in the face with the back of his hand. Davis procured a pistol from a bystander and shot Nelson. General Philip H. Sheridan said "the ball entered Nelson's breast just above the heart, but his great strength enabled him to ascend the stairway notwithstanding the mortal character of the wound, and he did not fall till he reached the corridor on the second floor. He died about half an hour later." 1 *Personal Memoirs of P. H. Sheridan* 188 (New York: Charles L. Webster, 1888); Kirk C. Jenkins, "A Shooting at the Galt House: The Death of General William Nelson," 43 *Civil War History* 101–118 (1997). Also see Howard H. Peckham, "I Have Been Basely Murdered," 14 *American Heritage* 88–92 (1963).

with orders for C. F. Smith's division to rush to Nashville. Buell said Nelson had occupied the city contrary to his wishes, his division was dangerously exposed, and he needed reinforcements immediately.[19] Smith contemptuously told Grant that Buell's order "is nonsense," but "of course I must obey."[20]

Don Carlos Buell was two years ahead of Grant at West Point and had been brevetted three times for gallantry during the Mexican War. There he acquired a reputation as an effective combat commander and a strict disciplinarian. But for the past thirteen years he had served in the adjutant general's department. In that assignment Buell became a friend of detail. He grew less daring and the fire in his soul was extinguished.[21] A close personal friend of McClellan's for many years, he came to share Little Mac's view that war involved maneuver, not bloodshed. "The object is not to fight great battles," Buell wrote in December 1861, "but by demonstrations and maneuvering to prevent the enemy from concentrating his forces."[22] Lincoln once said McClellan suffered from "the slows." Of Buell it could be said that he suffered from the *very slows*.[23] With no opposition facing him, he took nine days to move sixty miles from Bowling Green to Nashville. The Confederate army escaped, and Johnston, rather than preparing to attack Nelson, was hanging on for dear life in Murfreesboro, grateful for the opportunity to replenish his supplies and rekindle the spirit of his demoralized troops.[24]

With Nelson's division already in Nashville and Smith's on the way, Grant decided it was time to confer with Buell. Once again, he was pushing the limits of his authority. "I shall go to Nashville immediately after the arrival of the next Mail, should there be no orders to prevent it," he informed Cullum on February 25.[25] Grant waited a day, heard nothing from headquarters, and on the evening of the 26th wrote Julia he was off to Nashville. "Gen. Buell is there, or at least a portion of his command is, and I want to have an interview with the commanding officer and learn what I can of the movements of the enemy."[26] Grant traveled aboard his headquarters steamer, the *W. H. Brown,* accompanied by his staff, General McClernand, Colonel William H. L. Wallace of the 11th Illinois, and Colonel Jacob Lauman of the 7th Iowa—men who had served together from the time before Belmont. They arrived in Nashville at dawn on the 27th. Grant and his party went ashore only to find that Buell "for security reasons" was still on the north bank of the Cumberland and had not yet entered the city.[27] After meeting with Bull Nelson, Grant visited the wounded, paid a courtesy call on the widow of President Polk (a staunch secessionist), and, to the delight of newsmen who enjoyed contrasting him to Buell, moved freely about the city protected only by his adjutant, Captain Rawlins.[28]

Late in the afternoon, as Grant was returning to the *W. H. Brown* for the journey back to Fort Donelson, Buell crossed the river to meet him. The encounter was frosty. Buell was annoyed at Grant's uninvited presence in his department, while Grant, now the tenth-ranking general in the army, was strutting his newly won stars at Buell's expense.[29] Grant noted cuttingly that the only Union troops in Nashville were those he had sent, while the bulk of the Army of the Ohio was still north of the Cumberland. Repeating what he had learned from Nelson, he told Buell that Johnston was retreating as quickly as he could toward the Alabama line. Buell disagreed. There was fighting just ten miles away, he said, and Nashville was in imminent danger of Confederate attack. Grant said the Confederates "were trying to get away from Nashville and not return to it."[30] Buell insisted he was correct and disaster threatened Union forces on the left bank. Grant pointed out that the troops of C. F. Smith's division were debarking in Nashville at that moment. If Buell found after a day or two he did not need them, would he please send them back.[31] Grant, after his lightning victories at Henry and Donelson, was uncharacteristically full of himself in his meeting with Buell. Given Grant's seven years in the wilderness, his euphoria is understandable. But Buell, who was still commander of the Department of the Ohio, thought he was trying to take charge. Grant was correct concerning Johnston's withdrawal south, but he strained his relationship with Buell to the point that working together afterward became difficult.

Grant's trip to Nashville served no useful purpose. Halleck, when he learned of the visit, was furious. "I have had no communication with General Grant for more than a week," he wired McClellan on March 3. "He left his command without my authority and went to Nashville. His army seems to be as much demoralized by the victory of Fort Donelson as was that of the Potomac by the defeat of Bull Run. It is hard to censure a successful general immediately after a victory, but I think he richly deserves it." Halleck, deskbound in St. Louis and desperate for information, told McClellan that he could get no reports and no returns from Grant: "Satisfied with his victory, he sits down and enjoys it without any regard to the future. I am worn-out and tired with this neglect and inefficiency. C. F. Smith is almost the only officer equal to the emergency."[32]

Halleck was testing the ground with Washington. In his opinion Grant had gotten too big for his britches. But Grant was a national hero and Old Brains was cautious not to take disciplinary action unless he was certain of McClellan's support. Fortunately for Halleck, Grant's past had not been forgotten. McClellan still had him pegged as the drunken captain he knew at Fort Vancouver, and he was unforgiving: "The future success of our cause demands that proceedings such as Grant's should at once be checked. Generals must observe discipline as well as private soldiers. Do not hesitate to arrest him at once if the good of the service requires it, and place C. F. Smith in command. You are at liberty to regard this as a positive order if it will smooth your way." [33] Like Halleck, McClellan recognized he was playing with dynamite and he too wanted to be covered. Before transmitting his reply to St. Louis the general in chief showed the message to Secretary of War Stanton, and retained a file copy with the word "Approved" written in the secretary's hand.

With the War Department in his corner, Halleck thought it best to bolster Little Mac's suspicions. The following day he wrote McClellan, "A rumor has just reached me that since the taking of Fort Donelson General Grant has resumed his former bad habits. If so, it will account for his neglect of my oft-repeated orders. I do not deem it advisable to arrest him at present, but I have placed General Smith in command of the expedition up the Tennessee." [34] There was no substance to the rumor Halleck reported. Lieutenant Colonel James McPherson, who had recently returned to St. Louis for medical treatment after serving on Grant's staff at Donelson, told Halleck just the opposite. [35] Grant was on the wagon and Old Brains knew it. Nevertheless, gossip about Grant's drinking was commonplace in St. Louis and Halleck apparently assumed it would buttress his position if he passed some of it along.

In part the trouble between Grant and Halleck was due to the inevitable friction that accompanies troop movements in wartime. After Donelson's surrender, the two men lost contact. For over a week they lost communication without realizing it. On February 25 Halleck instructed Grant to assemble his army at Fort Henry preparatory to moving up the Tennessee. [36] Grant did not receive the message and continued to focus on the Cumberland. Halleck thought Nelson's division was at Clarksville and Smith's at Fort Henry. Grant, unaware of Halleck's instructions, sent Nelson to Nashville and acquiesced when Buell called for Smith.

On his part, Grant reported regularly on the status of his command to Cullum in Cairo but the messages were not forwarded to St. Louis. Repeatedly Grant cautioned headquarters about the need for fresh beef and potatoes to curb the dysentery ("the Tennessee quickstep") that had become prevalent among his troops, and he reported the Nashville deployment of Nelson and Smith as soon as it occurred. [37] Halleck was not informed. In effect, both men were operating in the dark. Halleck did not realize Grant had not received his instructions, and Grant, with no orders from St. Louis, was operating as he usually did in such circumstances, seeking out the enemy army and edging toward it.

Much of the difficulty lay with the military telegraph system, which was run by civilian operators outside the jurisdiction of local commanders. The operators reported directly to the superintendent of military tele-

graphs in Washington, who was answerable only to the secretary of war.*
In his *Memoirs* Grant wrote that the telegraph operator at Paducah proved
to be a Confederate sympathizer who deliberately did not relay Halleck's
messages. Grant claimed the operator deserted his post, taking the messages with him.[38] Whatever the reason, there can be no doubt the system
was so unreliable that Grant and Halleck simply lost contact.

On March 4, armed with the support of McClellan and Stanton, Halleck wired Grant to place C. F. Smith in command of the expedition up the
Tennessee. The object was to destroy Confederate rail and telegraph communications in the vicinity of Eastport and Corinth, Mississippi, and then
withdraw. Grant was told to avoid a full-scale engagement. "It will be better to retreat than to risk a general battle."[39] Meanwhile, Grant was to
remain at Fort Henry. He was not relieved of command—Halleck scrupulously sent his instructions to Smith through Grant—but he was prevented from leading the troops himself. It was a slap on the wrist. "Why do
you not obey my orders to report the strength and positions of your command?" asked Halleck.[40]

For Grant, Halleck's telegram was a lightning bolt.[41] Until then, he
was unaware he had incurred his commander's displeasure. After returning from Nashville, he had written Julia he considered Halleck "one of the
greatest men of the age. There are not two men in the United States who I
would prefer serving under to McClellan and Halleck."[42] Pulled up short,
Grant told Halleck the expedition would be sent under the command of
General Smith "as directed."

Grant had been reprimanded, but remained as aggressive as ever. Halleck envisaged the Tennessee River operation as a hit-and-run raid against
rebel communications. Grant converted it into a major offensive. "Information received this morning [indicates that] the force going to Eastport
and Corinth must go prepared to meet a force of 20,000 men," he advised
Halleck. "This will take all my available troops."[43] Critics who have
doubted Grant's subtlety should study carefully his message of March 5,
1862. Ordered to move south with a small task force, he managed to send
his entire command. He also deflected Halleck's criticism. "I am not aware
of ever having disobeyed any order from Headquarters—certainly never
intended any such thing. I have reported almost daily the condition of my
command and reported every position occupied. . . . My reports have
nearly all been made to General Cullum, chief of staff, and it may be that

* The independence of the military telegraph service was a problem for Union commanders throughout the war. Its shortcomings are detailed with great exactitude by Dean
Roscoe Pound of the Harvard Law School (a Civil War buff), in "The Military Telegraph in
the Civil War," 66 *Proceedings of the Massachusetts Historical Society* 185–203 (1938).

many of them were not thought of sufficient importance to forward." For Halleck's benefit Grant summarized his army's strength: forty-six infantry regiments, three cavalry regiments, and ten batteries of artillery. "In conclusion, I will say that you may rely on my carrying out your instructions, in every particular, to the very best of my ability."[44]

Grant had no qualms about entrusting the expedition to C. F. Smith—if that was Halleck's preference.* Looking back on the incident years later, Grant said the general opinion probably was that "Smith's long services in the army and distinguished deeds rendered him the more proper person for such command. Indeed I was rather inclined to this opinion myself at that time."[45] On the evening before the expedition sailed, Grant and Smith walked the deck of the *W. H. Brown* for several hours. Grant revered Smith, although Dr. Brinton, who observed the scene, thought the admiration was mutual. "I could not help noticing that there was an unconscious deference on the part of Smith to Grant as a soldier. It was apart from rank; it seemed indescribable; but it was there, it was the recognition of the master."[46] Grant expressed their relationship best when he said he "would have served as faithfully under Smith as he had done under me."[47]

At this point Halleck should have let matters rest. But there was a hectoring streak in the department commander. Sherman wrote that Halleck was "working himself into a passion [about Grant], but was too far from the seat of war to make due allowance for the actual state of facts."[48] On March 6, after receiving Grant's reply, Old Brains fired another volley, disingenuously invoking the authority of the War Department:

> General McClellan directs that you report daily the number and positions of the forces under your command. Your neglect of repeated orders to report the strength of your command has created great dissatisfaction and seriously interfered with military plans. Your going to Nashville without authority, and when your presence with your troops was of utmost importance, was a matter of very serious complaint at Washington, so much so that I was advised to arrest you on your return.[49]

It was a letter that Halleck, having vented his frustration, should have torn up after writing. Grant's disappointment turned to anger. Choosing

---

* Smith was as eager as Grant to close with Johnston. Writing to a friend shortly after moving upriver, Smith said: "My orders are to accomplish a certain purpose without bringing on a general engagement; to retire rather than doing so. Now if my men were soldiers in the proper acceptation of the term, this piece of strategy might do very well, but as they are not soldiers I mean to fight my way through if necessary. And when I get them into a fight it shall be no child's play." Addressee unknown, March 9, 1862. C. F. Smith Papers, Glenbrook, Connecticut.

his words carefully he told Halleck he had done everything possible to keep him informed. "I have averaged writing more than once a day, since leaving Cairo, to keep you informed of my position; and it is no fault of mine, if you have not received my letters." As for his going to Nashville, Grant said the trip "was strictly intended for the good of the service, not to gratify any desire of my own." Then he raised the ante. "If my course is not satisfactory remove me at once." Grant said he thought there must be enemies "between you and myself who are trying to impair my usefulness," and he closed by asking to be relieved from further duty in the department.[50] Whether Grant did so himself; whether it was Captain Rawlins acting on Grant's instructions; or whether it was Rawlins acting alone, is not clear, but copies of Halleck's message of March 6 and Grant's reply were forwarded immediately to Congressman Elihu Washburne in Washington.[51]

The contretemps continued. On March 8 Halleck told Grant "There is no enemy between you and me." The problem was he and McClellan were still waiting for a status report after Fort Donelson and they were running out of patience. "What is the number and position of your command? Answer by telegraph in general terms."[52]

Grant did not realize the various returns he had filed with General Cullum had not arrived in St. Louis, and he was perplexed why Halleck was hounding him. He replied testily that Halleck was better placed to know the size of his command during the fighting at Donelson than he was. "Troops were reporting daily, by your order, and immediately assigned to brigades. There were no orders received from you until the 28th of February to make out returns, and I made every effort to get them in as early as possible. . . . I renew my application to be relieved of further duty."[53]

In a separate telegram on March 9 Grant provided Halleck with a summary report. His present for duty strength included 35,147 infantry, 3,169 cavalry, and 12 batteries of field artillery, aggregating 54 pieces and 1,231 men. Of the total, 25,206 were embarked with Smith, and 5,740 were at the landing above Fort Henry awaiting transportation. The remainder were garrisoned at Clarksville and Fort Donelson. Grant said the figures included 7,829 men in a newly organized 5th Division under General William Tecumseh Sherman.[54]

That seemed to end the matter. The lengthy status report Grant mailed from Paducah on March 6 arrived in St. Louis, and Halleck replied soothingly. He told Grant that he may have been partially at fault because he had not enforced discipline sufficiently. "I really felt embarrassed to telegraph back to Washington time and again that I was unable to give the strength of your command." It was not an apology; as a rule, generals don't apologize. But it was close to it. Halleck then got down to business. General Samuel Curtis had just routed the Confederate army of Earl Van Dorn at Pea Ridge, Arkansas, and the pressure on Union troops west of the Mississippi had eased. Grant was told reinforcements intended for Curtis were being redirected his way. Halleck said they should be sent up the Tennessee as rapidly as possible. "As soon as these things are arranged you will hold yourself in readiness to take command. There will probably be some desperate fighting . . . and *we* should be prepared."[55]

Grant was off the shelf. Or almost off. On March 11 he wrote Smith that reinforcements from Arkansas were on the way and when they arrived Halleck expected him to take the field. "I think it exceedingly doubtful whether I shall accept; certainly not until the object of the expedition is accomplished."[56] Grant thought Smith was entitled to finish what he had begun, and he was reluctant to supersede his old mentor. Smith on the other hand was delighted. "I wrote you yesterday to say how glad I was to find that you were to resume your old command from which you were so unceremoniously and (as I think) improperly stricken down." To reassure Grant, Smith said he would likely have to relinquish command in any event because he had become immobile. "I cannot mount a horse. In jumping into a yawl two days ago I miscalculated the distance and the seat scraped my leg and shin in a rude manner—hurting the bone. I hope for the best but it is with great difficulty that I limp thro' the cabin from one chair to another."[57]

The affection between Grant and Smith—similar to that between Grant and Sherman in the later years of the war—contrasts sharply with the backbiting that afflicted less accomplished commanders. It was a relationship that epitomized the military profession at its best. Smith captured the spirit in a letter to a friend, March 17, 1862:

> The public are all astray about General Grant. His habits (drink) are unexceptionable. His absence during the [Donelson] engagement to see Flag Officer Foote was explained to the satisfaction of General Halleck, and his going to Nashville was perfectly proper if he thought fit to go. The reason why both McClellan and Halleck were down upon him was they had no information for two weeks, although he always wrote once and sometimes twice or thrice a day and sent daily reports of the strength of his force. Why these reports were not received is not known, but the moment Halleck had Grant's explanation he was restored to command.
>
> Grant is a very modest person. From awe of me—he was one of my pupils from 1838 to 1842 (I think)—he dislikes to give

me an order and says I ought to be in his place. Fancy his surprise when he received no communication from the General for two weeks after the fall of Donelson, and then a telegram of bitterest rebuke! He showed it to me in utter amazement, wondering at the cause, as well he might.[58]

Halleck's timely reinstatement of Grant preceded by one day the bombshell that landed on his desk from the adjutant general in Washington. Elihu Washburne had not been idle. As soon as he got word of the fracas between Halleck and Grant he made a beeline to the White House. Grant was Washburne's man and he was not going to let him be pushed aside. Lincoln needed no convincing. Desperate to find a general who would fight, the president had developed a quick affection for the man who demanded "unconditional surrender." A year earlier, Lincoln would have let matters in the military take their course. Now, he intervened immediately. "By direction of the President," General Lorenzo Thomas wired Halleck, "the Secretary of War desires you to ascertain and report whether General Grant left his command at any time without proper authority, and if so, for how long; whether he has made to you proper reports and returns of his force; whether he had committed any acts which were unauthorized or not in accordance with military subordination or propriety, and, if so, what."[59]

Halleck ran for cover. Grant, he told Thomas, explained everything satisfactorily. He had gone to Nashville with "good intentions" and acted "from a praiseworthy although mistaken zeal for the public service. I respectfully recommend that no further notice be taken of it." Halleck said Grant made all of the required reports; he simply had not received them. And "there never has been any want of military subordination on the part of Genl Grant." Whatever irregularities there might have been in his command "have now been remedied."[60]

That ought to have ended it. But on March 13 Grant received a belated letter of harsh criticism Halleck had written during his funk the previous week.[61] Grant wired back heatedly asking for a third time "to be relieved from further duty."[62] Halleck, who recognized the mail had been delayed and that the letter to which Grant was responding was out of date, was unruffled. "You cannot be relieved from your command," he wired back. "There is no good reason for it. I am certain that all which the authorities in Washington ask, is, that you enforce discipline and punish the disorderly. The power is in your hands; use it, and you will be sustained by all above you. Instead of relieving you, I wish you, as soon as your new army is in the field, to assume the immediate command and lead it on to new victories."[63]

The pieces were back in place. Grant told Halleck he would resume command "and give every effort to the success of our cause."[64] Over the years that followed, Grant grew increasingly bitter about his treatment after Donelson. In his *Memoirs* he wrote he was "virtually in arrest and without a command."[65] That was not true. And the fact is Grant benefited from the experience. He immediately reorganized his staff and assigned each member specific duties to insure the reports required by higher head-quarters were filed on time.[66] He personally undertook to write the essential dispatches from the field, which became markedly crisper and more businesslike. And he learned to weather criticism. Grant was always ready to meet the enemy in his front; the post-Donelson period taught him to withstand attacks from his rear. Even more important, he was brought back to earth. Grant's brief bout with obscurity was a happy accident. The two weeks' punishment Halleck administered restored his perspective.

On March 16 Grant headed upriver to rejoin his command. "What you may look for is hard to say," he wrote Julia. "Possibly a big fight. I have already been in so many that it begins to feel like home to me."[67] Halleck, who had finally realized his dream of commanding all Union forces in the West,* may have trembled at the thought of unleashing his action-prone subordinate. Before sending him off, he warned Grant against anything rash. "As the enemy is evidently in strong force, my instructions not to advance so as to bring on an engagement must be strictly obeyed." Halleck said Buell was coming to join forces and that 10,000 to 15,000 additional reinforcements would soon be en route from Missouri. "We must strike no blow till we are strong enough to admit no doubt of the result."[68]

After an overnight boat trip Grant arrived at C. F. Smith's headquarters in Savannah, Tennessee—a small village on the east bank of the Tennessee River, 100 miles above Fort Henry and twenty-eight miles from the all-important rail junction of Corinth, Mississippi: the point at which the north–south Mobile & Ohio Railroad intersected with the east–west Memphis & Charleston line. These were the two principal railroads in the Mississippi Valley. Grant found Smith eager to see him but hobbling badly on his injured leg. His condition was worsening, exacerbated by a recurrence of the erysipelas he had contracted in Mexico fourteen years earlier. Nevertheless, Smith's ardor was intact. "I occasionally send out a few

---

* On March 11, 1862, President Lincoln, fretting over McClellan's inaction, reorganized the Union high command. Little Mac was relieved as general in chief although allowed to remain as commander of the Army of the Potomac. John C. Frémont was recalled and entrusted with command of Union forces in western Virginia, and Halleck was made commander of a newly created Department of the Mississippi, merging the old departments of the Missouri and the Ohio. For the interim there would be no general in chief and Lincoln would direct the armies through Stanton. President's General War Order Number 3, March 11, 1862, 8 *War of the Rebellion* 596.

thousand men to look at the enemy in the direction of Corinth and wake them up," he told Grant.[69] "By God, I ask nothing better than to have the rebels come out and attack us! We can whip them to hell."[70]

Grant's army, soon to be known as the Army of the Tennessee, consisted of five divisions. The 1st and 2nd divisions, veteran units commanded by McClernand and Smith, were encamped near Savannah, Tennessee. Lew Wallace's 3rd Division, another veteran force, was across the river at Crump's Landing, six miles upstream. Also on the west bank, nine miles upstream at Pittsburg Landing, were the army's two newest divisions, the 4th under Brigadier General Stephen A. Hurlbut, and the 5th under Sherman. Neither had fought at Donelson, yet Smith, trusting to Sherman's experience, placed them closest to the enemy at Corinth. Recognizing the faulty deployment of his army—half on one side of the Tennessee, half on the other—Grant ordered the 1st and 2nd divisions to Pittsburg Landing.[71]

The site had been selected by Sherman the week before. "The ground itself admits of easy defense by a small command, and yet affords admirable camping ground for a hundred-thousand men."[72] Grant took Sherman's word for it. Pittsburg Landing was no more than a good day's march from Corinth, and landing sites on the west bank of the Tennessee were few and far between. The landing was narrow—no more than five vessels could dock at the same time—but it offered easy access up a steep bluff to a broad plateau covered with old-growth hardwood timber, interrupted by scattered clearings cut by farmers for orchards and crops. Some fields were as large as seventy or eighty acres, some no larger than three or four.[73] Numerous paths and wagon trails crisscrossed the area, and the flanks were protected by Lick Creek and Owl Creek, each of which emptied into the Tennessee.[74] The creeks were roughly three miles apart and ran parallel to each other for about five miles. Both were swollen with spring rains and impassable. The area between the creeks, a rough quadrilateral, sloped gently away from the bluff at the river's edge. Any rebel attack would have to be made uphill through the three-mile gap between the creeks. The Union encampment was a natural fortification: hard to assail, easy to defend. When Grant saw it, he hastened the movement of the 1st and 2nd divisions from Savannah, and, with reinforcements arriving daily, created a 6th Division under Brigadier General Benjamin Prentiss, which he told Sherman to deploy as he deemed best.

On March 18 Grant thought he discovered an opening that would allow him to take the offensive. Halleck telegraphed from St. Louis that the Confederates had moved away from Corinth, intending to cut Grant's supply line somewhere between Savannah and Fort Henry. "If so, Genl Smith should immediately destroy R.R. connexion at Corinth."[75] Grant knew the Confederates were not attempting any such thing. But Halleck's instructions to destroy the rail junction at Corinth sounded like an authorization to attack. Grant ordered Smith to prepare the command at Pittsburg Landing to march at a moment's notice, "three days rations in Haversacks, and seven in wagons."[76] Then he wired Halleck: "Immediate preparations will be made to execute your perfectly feasible order. I will go in person, leaving General McClernand in command here."[77]

Halleck saw through Grant's gambit. "Keep your forces together until you connect with Buell," he shot back. "Don't let the enemy draw you into an engagement now. Wait until you are properly reinforced and you receive orders."[78] Even without Halleck's admonition, Grant's effort to move against Corinth in mid-March would have been difficult. Spring rains rendered the roads impassable for his artillery, and Confederate troop trains were arriving daily with reinforcements. Grant estimated the rebel force at 30,000. He told Halleck "this would indicate that Corinth cannot be taken without a general engagement, which from your instructions is to be avoided." Grant said he would sit tight at Pittsburg Landing until he received further orders.[79] "The temper of the rebel troops is such that there is little doubt but that Corinth will fall much more easily than Donelson did, when we do move. All accounts agree in saying that the great mass of the Rank and file are heartily tired."[80] Writing to Smith two days later Grant expressed his impatience at the restrictions Halleck imposed. "I do not hear one word from St. Louis," he complained. "I am clearly of the opinion that the enemy are gathering strength at Corinth quite as rapidly as we are here, and the sooner we attack the easier will be the task of taking the place."[81] Grant saw opportunity slipping away. While Halleck cautiously waited for the even more cautious Buell to reach Pittsburg Landing, Johnston was massing his army at Corinth.

When Fort Donelson fell on February 16 the Confederate position was desperate. Hardee's bedraggled force was moving retrograde from Bowling Green and Nashville toward Decatur, Alabama, hoping to reach the Memphis–Charleston railroad before the Union army overtook them. Two hundred miles to the west, Beauregard was retreating with another 10,000 men. Both Grant and Buell were between the two Confederate armies, and both were closer to Corinth than either Beauregard or Hardee. But the advantage was wasted. Halleck hesitated while the South, confronted with disaster, moved quickly. Major General Braxton Bragg, with 10,000 troops scattered along the Gulf Coast between Pass Christian and Pensacola, was ordered north to Corinth forthwith. So was Brigadier General Daniel Ruggles with 5,000 men from New Orleans. Across the Mississippi, Van Dorn was instructed to march the survivors of Pea Ridge to Memphis, where boxcars were waiting to rush them to Corinth. Added to the forces of Beauregard and Hardee, the Confederates planned to assemble almost 60,000 men at Corinth—less than Grant and Buell combined, but substantially more than either on their own. It was a race against time. If Johnston could concentrate his force before Buell reached the Tennessee, he would attack Grant, destroy his six divisions, and then move against Buell. Grant had the opportunity to defeat the separate wings of the Confederate army after Donelson but was restrained from doing so. Now Johnston was about to turn the tables. In six weeks he had nudged the Confederacy from the rim of certain defeat to the threshold of victory.

While the Confederates were converging on Corinth, Buell was inching his way across central Tennessee. Lead elements of the Army of the Ohio departed Nashville on March 16, and although Halleck had instructed Buell to link up with Grant "as rapidly as possible,"[82] ten days later the army was still on the outskirts of the state capital. Part of the problem was Buell's inbred caution, plus a grudging reluctance to speed to Grant's support. A more formidable obstacle was the rain-swollen Duck River at Columbia, forty-two miles south. Retreating Confederates had burned the only bridge and Buell, who had prepared for almost every contingency, ironically neglected bridging equipment.[83] For more than a week 37,000 troops idled their time while inexperienced engineers wrestled with the task of bridging the river.[84] Buell insisted on building a permanent replacement, and on March 27 he wired Halleck the project was more complicated than anticipated. The bridge probably would not be finished until March 31.[85] Neither Buell nor Halleck seemed concerned, nor for that matter was Grant.[86] It was also on the afternoon of March 27 that Buell learned Grant was no longer at Savannah but had moved his army across the Tennessee and was encamped at Pittsburg Landing. Buell was surprised, but once again he was not concerned.[87] The fact is neither he, nor Halleck, nor Grant, nor any of Grant's division commanders believed they were in the slightest danger from Johnston's army at Corinth. As Grant subsequently noted, "I regarded the campaign we were engaged in as an offensive one and had no idea that the enemy would leave strong entrenchments to take the initiative when he knew he would be attacked where he was if he remained."[88]

Bull Nelson was an exception to the prevailing Union consensus. The not-so-genial giant was sitting on the north bank of the Duck River on the afternoon of March 27 watching the bridge-building efforts when he learned that the Tennessee no longer stood between Johnston and Grant. "By God," he exclaimed to a startled staff officer, "we must cross that river at once [pointing to the Duck] or Grant will be whipped."[89] Nelson galloped off to Buell's headquarters and eventually obtained permission for his division to ford the unbridged stream. That night Nelson assembled his brigade commanders. They would cross at dawn on the morning of the 29th, he told them.

"Will the bridge be completed?" asked Colonel Jacob Ammen, an old soldier (West Point 1831) commanding the 10th Brigade.

"No," said Nelson.

"Are there boats?" Ammen inquired.

"No," Nelson responded, "but the river is falling, and damn you, get over for we must lead the advance and get the glory."[90]

The Duck was a sprawling flood 200 yards wide, and at dawn on the 29th the men of Nelson's 4th Division stripped to their underdrawers and waded into the waist-deep water.* Miraculously they made it across without the loss of a single man or wagon. The remainder of the army followed. Savannah was eighty-two miles away and the roads were wretched, but Nelson's division set a fast pace. On his own authority Nelson sent his cavalry ahead to secure every remaining bridge between Columbia and Savannah, determined to link up with Grant before Johnston could attack. After a series of forced marches, the 4th Division cleared Waynesboro on April 3. The Tennessee River was thirty miles away. Nelson wired Grant he would reach Savannah on Saturday morning, April 5. Grant said not to hurry. Boats would not be available to ferry Buell's army across the river until the 8th. Nelson ignored the message and continued to press full speed ahead.[91]

It was also on April 3—with Nelson thirty miles from Savannah—that Albert Sidney Johnston put his army in motion toward Pittsburg Landing. Van Dorn's legion had not arrived, but the Army of the Mississippi, as

---

* Nelson personally wrote the division's order of the day, which was read to the troops at dress parade on the 28th.

"Reveille will be sounded tomorrow at 4 A.M. At 6 A.M., the Tenth Brigade will move with one day's rations in haversacks. . . . The wagons will be carefully loaded with reference to fording Duck River—tents and other articles not liable to injury from water at the bottom, and ammunition on top.

"On reaching the ford, the men will strip off their pantaloons, secure their cartridge boxes about their necks, and load knapsacks on the wagons; bayonets will be fixed, and the pantaloons, in a neat roll, will be carried on the point of the bayonet. A halt will be ordered on the other side of the ford, to allow the men to take off their drawers, wring them dry, and resume their clothing and knapsacks.

"Strong parties will be detailed to accompany the wagons, to assist them cross the ford. The rear-guard of each regiment will consist of one company under charge of field [grade] officer, whose particular province it will be to assist the passage of the [supply] train over the ford."

E. Hannaford, *The Story of a Regiment: A History of the Campaigns and Associations in the Field of the Sixth Regiment Ohio Volunteer Infantry* 232–33 (Cincinnati: Hannaford, 1868).

Johnston's force was called, numbered 43,968 men present for duty (out of about 56,000 on the muster rolls). This was the largest Confederate concentration thus far, and about 6,000 more combatants than Grant commanded.* Numbers were not everything, however. Half of Grant's men were victorious veterans of Fort Donelson and Fort Henry; whereas only a sprinkling of the Southerners had seen combat, either at Belmont or with Forrest's cavalry regiment. The Union army was better armed, better clothed, and better fed. Artillery was distributed more or less equally, each army boasting about 110 pieces, but the Federal tubes were professionally cast by experienced munition makers, while most of Johnston's cannons were homemade.[92] Only in spirit had the Confederates regained an edge. "You can but march to a decisive victory over the agrarian mercenaries sent to subjugate and despoil you of your liberties, property, and honor," Johnston exhorted the army as it moved out. "Remember the dependence of your mothers, your wives, your sisters, and your children on the result; remember the fair, broad, abounding land, the happy homes and the ties that would be desolated by your defeat. The eyes and hopes of eight millions of people rest upon you."[93]

The key to Johnston's strategy was surprise: to hit Grant before he knew what was coming. To accomplish that Johnston divided his army into four corps: 10,000 men under Major General Leonidas Polk, still on leave from the Army of the Lord; 16,000 under Bragg; 9,000 under Hardee; and 7,000 under Brigadier General John C. Breckinridge, who had served as Buchanan's vice president from 1857 to 1861, and who was the Southern Democrats' nominee for president in 1860. Beauregard would serve as deputy army commander, Bragg as chief of staff. Johnston planned to move quickly from Corinth along two separate roads on April 3, converge southwest of Pittsburg Landing at dusk, and attack the Union camp at dawn on the 4th. His intention was to turn Grant's left flank, drive him away from the Tennessee, cut off his retreat, and pin him against Owl Creek, where he would be obliged to surrender.[94]

Nothing went as planned. Polk's lead corps did not get underway until noon on the third. Hardee, jammed up behind, was twelve hours late leaving and Bragg was even later. By noon of the 4th his corps was only halfway from Corinth to the rendezvous point. Breckinridge's corps did not even clear Corinth until dawn on the 4th. Recognizing that his forces would not be in place in time, Johnston postponed the attack for a day. But

---

* The five Union divisions at Pittsburg Landing totaled 37,500 men present for duty, plus another 7,500 noncombatants—cooks, medics, teamsters, and the like. Lew Wallace's 3rd Division, six miles away at Crump's Landing, numbered 7,300. That brought Grant's combat strength to roughly the same as Johnston's, although Wallace's division was not present when the Confederate attack began.

on the evening of the 4th it began to rain, a Mississippi torrential rain. Roads washed out and troop columns were unable to move. Once more Johnston postponed the attack. Not until sundown on the 5th was the Army of the Mississippi in position to attack.

Having conquered the elements, Johnston faced a crisis among his subordinates. With the army poised to assault, Beauregard decided the approach had taken too long. "There is no chance for surprise. They will be entrenched to their eyes." [95] Beauregard thought the offensive should be canceled and the entire army returned to Corinth. Bragg initially agreed. Provisions were low and he too thought the element of surprise had been lost. Johnston listened courteously, then said he still hoped to find the enemy unprepared. "Gentlemen, we shall attack at daylight tomorrow." [96] It was a momentous decision—the type commanding generals are expected to make. Beauregard and Bragg were soldiers of proven ability and high moral courage. Yet Johnston was confident of victory. "Tomorrow at twelve o'clock we will water our horses in the Tennessee River." [97]

Grant was caught napping. At Belmont he had not anticipated a rebel counterattack. At Donelson he had been absent with Foote when the Confederates came out of their lines. Again at Shiloh he was not ready. Grant's experience in Mexico served him poorly on these occasions, for he never credited the enemy with a capacity to take the offensive. C. F. Smith shared that prejudice. He thought they would have to march to Corinth and "root the badger out of his hole." [98] Sherman, whose division fronted the Federal position, agreed. On April 5 he reported "All is quiet along my lines. I have no doubt that nothing will occur today. . . . I do not apprehend anything like an attack on our position." [99] When a colonel of volunteers nervously reported Confederate infantry massing in the woods, Sherman contemptuously told him to "Take your damn regiment back to Ohio. Beauregard is not such a fool as to leave his base of operations and attack us in ours." [100] That evening Grant wired Halleck, "I have scarcely the faintest idea of an attack (general one) being made upon us, but will be prepared should such a thing take place." [101] Unbeknownst to Grant, the Army of the Mississippi had advanced undetected twenty-three miles from Corinth. It had been three days on the road with all of its accoutrements and impedimenta, its march discipline lax, its inexperience evident, yet it was drawn up in line of battle two miles from the Union encampment. Rebel pickets were so close that evening they could hear Sherman's drums beat the tattoo. In the distance, a Yankee band sounded the melancholy strains of "Home Sweet Home." [102]

The five divisions of Grant's army at Pittsburg Landing were drawn up like the five spot in a set of dominoes. It was not a tactical arrangement designed for mutual support but rather for comfort and convenience, the various division camps selected because of the availability of fresh water and open fields for drilling. Sherman and Prentiss occupied the front between Owl and Lick creeks, McClernand's 1st Division was in the middle, and the 2nd and 4th divisions held the rear. Smith's health had deteriorated to the point he could no longer take the field and command of the 2nd Division was entrusted to Brigadier General William H. L. Wallace.

The magnitude of the Union encampment awed recruits and veterans alike. "There is no end to the tents," a Michigan soldier wrote his parents. "We can see them scattered in all directions as far as we can see."[103] An Iowa volunteer thought the camp had the appearance of "a gigantic picnic."[104] An Illinois infantryman concurred. "The scene reminds one of a camp meeting, only on a very large scale. No doubt a 'looker-on' would be led to think war 'a glorious thing.' "[105] A holiday atmosphere prevailed. Spring had arrived, a light foliage covered the trees, and peach orchards turned pink with blossoms. Drill was light and men lulled themselves playing cards and dice, pitching horseshoes, writing letters, reading old newspapers, and browsing about numerous peddler wagons that attended the camp.[106] Overconfidence was pervasive. "I think the rebellion is getting nearly played out, and I expect we will be home soon," an Ohio soldier wrote his brother and sister on March 27.[107] Smith had chosen not to dig in or fortify the encampment. "Our men have come here to fight, and if we begin to spade it will make them think we fear the enemy."[108] Sherman said the purpose was to move forward, "not to fortify our camps against attack. Such a course would have made our raw men timid."[109] When Grant arrived he directed Colonel James McPherson, the senior engineer officer, to lay out a line of entrenchments. But when McPherson reported the best location was to the rear of the campsite, Grant dismissed the matter.[110]

Grant retained his headquarters at Savannah but spent each day at Pittsburg Landing. In his *Memoirs* he acknowledged he should have moved his operations forward sooner, but was waiting for Buell and believed Savannah, which had become the major Union supply point on the upper Tennessee, was the best place to meet. On the night of April 4, during the same heavy rainstorm that delayed Johnston, Grant was inspecting his perimeter when his horse lost its footing and fell, pinning him beneath it. "The extreme softness of the ground, from the excessive rains, no doubt saved me from a severe injury. As it was, my ankle was very much injured, so much so that my boot had to be cut off. For two or three days after I was unable to walk except with crutches."[111]

Because of his injury Grant remained in Savannah Saturday morning, April 5. Nelson reported at noon, requesting permission to march on and establish his division at Pittsburg Landing. "Not immediately," Grant replied. "Encamp for the present at Savannah." Nelson was churning like a riverboat and asked Grant if he was not concerned about Johnston attacking. "The wonder to me is that he has not done so before." Grant replied casually that he had more men at Pittsburg Landing than at Fort Donelson and they could hold their own. Smith, who was sitting nearby, reassured Nelson the rebels were still in Corinth and unlikely to come out.[112] When Colonel Ammen, commanding Nelson's lead brigade, volunteered that his men were not tired and could easily push on, Grant told them to relax. Ammen, like Grant, hailed from Georgetown, Ohio. He had taught Grant mathematics at West Point and later approved his appointment as an instructor. They were well acquainted and spoke freely. Grant told Ammen, "You cannot march through the swamps [from Savannah to Pittsburg Landing]. Make the troops comfortable. I will send boats for you Monday or Tuesday, or sometime early in the week. There will be no fight at Pittsburg Landing. We will have to go to Corinth, where the rebels are fortified."[113]

So much for Union awareness. Johnston's luck was holding. Just before first light on Sunday, April 6, the Confederate picket line moved forward. Johnston delegated to Beauregard the task of drawing the attack plan and that may have been his first mistake. Known as Special Orders No. 8, it was modeled on Napoleon's blueprint for the battle of Waterloo.[114] Common sense suggests Beauregard should have recalled what happened to Napoleon at Waterloo, but like most West Pointers he was mesmerized by the military reputation of the emperor. (Curiously, the stodgy tenacity of the Duke of Wellington never excited much respect at West Point, although it was exactly this trait in Grant that prevailed at Shiloh.) Like Napoleon, Beauregard aligned the four Confederate corps in echelon rather than side by side. Normally, three corps would have been abreast with the fourth in reserve. In Beauregard's view such an alignment would have diminished the shock of the attack, and, with Johnston's approval, he stacked the corps one behind the other. This would permit the Confederate attack to come in successive waves as each corps advanced. Beauregard spoke euphorically of "an Alpine avalanche."

Aside from its romanticism, the plan posed two major problems. First, each corps would be operating over the same area. Units would become intermingled, rendering command and control difficult. Second, the tandem deployment of the corps minimized the amount of artillery that initially could be brought to bear on the enemy. Each corps moved with its own guns, and when the first wave went forward only the guns of that corps were available. By contrast, a side-by-side deployment would have allowed all 110 Confederate guns to open on the Union position simultaneously.

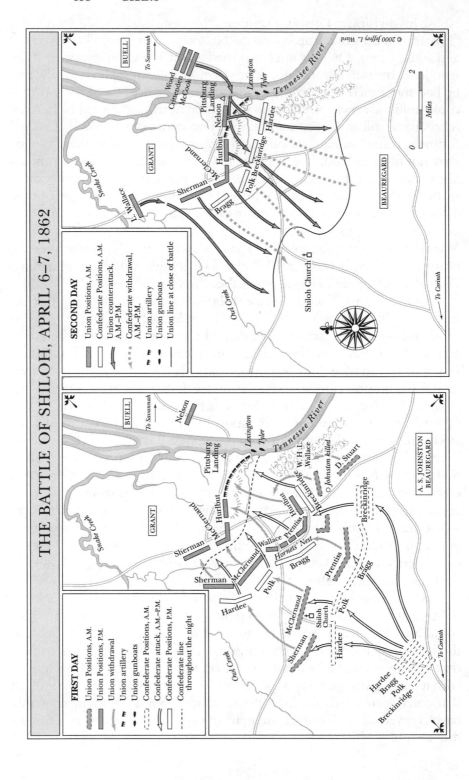

THE BATTLE OF SHILOH, APRIL 6–7, 1862

Pride of place in the Confederate attack was given to Hardee's veterans from the old Army of Central Kentucky. Strung out in line of battle, the 9,000 men of the 3rd Corps moved forward at 6:30 A.M. A quarter of a mile behind Hardee, Bragg's corps, also in line of battle, followed the front. After Bragg was Polk's corps, formed in columns of brigades along the Corinth road, and after Polk came Breckinridge, also deployed in brigade column. From the line of skirmishers out in front to the tail of Breckinridge's corps, the Confederate formation stretched nearly two miles.[115] Johnston ordered the attack for sunrise (6 A.M.). But it took an additional thirty minutes to get the sluggish battle line moving, and another hour until it closed on the Union camp. The loss of those precious ninety minutes of daylight would return to haunt the Confederates; the immediate effect was to squander the element of surprise. Prentiss's division, though not dug in, had been alerted by the movement to its front and was deployed to receive the rebel attack, while a half mile to the west Sherman's troops were being put into line.

At about 7:30 Hardee's battle line struck Prentiss. Thirty minutes later the Confederate left hit Sherman. "We were dumbfounded by seeing an enormous force marching directly toward us," wrote Private Charles Morton of the 25th Missouri.[116] Another Missourian said it was a "sublime but awful scene as they advanced slowly, steadily and silently until within about 125 yards."[117] Beauregard was right in one respect: The initial impact of the Confederate assault was overwhelming. Once Hardee's line was fully engaged, Johnston ordered Bragg's corps forward, and then the leading brigade of Polk's. Within the hour, eight of sixteen brigades of the Army of the Mississippi were deployed against Prentiss. Both Prentiss and Sherman called for reinforcements from the Union divisions to their rear, but the momentum of the Confederate attack swept through Prentiss's camp before help could arrive. By 9 A.M., for all practical purposes the 6th Division of Grant's army ceased to exist. Of the 5,400 troops who answered roll call that morning, over a thousand had been killed, wounded, or captured. Another 2,000 or so—not much more than a brigade—remained in the field under arms. The rest of the division melted away, fleeing northward to Pittsburg Landing. Union ambulance and wagon drivers whipped their teams to the rear as well, adding to the general panic.[118]

Sherman fared better. His troops had served together longer than Prentiss's and the division occupied more favorable terrain. Protected from the initial rebel onslaught by a boggy branch bottom that slowed the attack, the division was drawn up in order of battle on the high ground beyond. Sherman's line centered on a little country church called Shiloh—

named by early Methodist settlers for the Israelite shrine established by Joshua after the conquest of the land of Canaan.* Until reinforcements could arrive, Sherman's left was in the air, but his right was anchored by impassable Owl Creek—the western boundary of the Union position. With few exceptions, Sherman's raw infantrymen held their ground like veterans and his artillery took a heavy toll of advancing Confederates. The 6th Mississippi, mostly farmers from the north-central woodlands of the state—an area where slavery was not significant—lost 300 of 425 men (a staggering 70.5 percent) in three suicidal attempts to storm Sherman's line.

Grant arrived on the field about 8:30—too late to help Prentiss, but in time to stitch together the Union defense. He was at breakfast in Savannah when the low rumble of artillery sounded in the distance. It was not clear whether the firing came from Pittsburg Landing or from the isolated 3rd Division at Crump's Landing. Grant sat motionless for a moment and then stood up. "Gentlemen," he told his staff, "the ball is in motion. Let's be off." [119] Within fifteen minutes the command group of the Army of the Tennessee—staff, clerks, orderlies, and horses—were aboard the mail packet *Tigress* steaming upriver. Grant paused only long enough to send three hasty dispatches. The first was a brief message to Bull Nelson instructing him to march his division overland "to the river opposite Pittsburg." [120] The second went to Brigadier General Thomas J. Wood, who commanded the 6th Division of Buell's army. Wood was directed to move immediately to Savannah "where steamboats will be in waiting to transport you to Pittsburg." [121] Grant wrote a longer message to Buell: "Heavy firing heard up the river, indicating plainly that an attack has been made upon our most advanced positions. . . . This necessitates my joining the forces up the river instead of meeting you today as I had contemplated." [122] Grant did not know it, but Buell was already in Savannah, having spent the night at Nelson's headquarters. Because of their chilled relationship, Buell chose not to call on Grant when he arrived and as a consequence Grant assumed the commander of the Army of the Ohio was still en route.

When Grant reached Crump's Landing—it was shortly after 8 A.M.—he found Lew Wallace waiting on the deck of his own headquarters boat. From the sound of guns in the distance it was clear the attack was at Pittsburg Landing. Without stopping, Grant called out to Wallace, "General, get your troops under arms and have them ready to move at a moment's

---

* *Joshua* 18:1. Shiloh, in the province of Ephraim, was the custodial site for the ark of the covenant under the priesthood of the house of Eli. It was leveled by the victorious Philistines after the battle of Ebenezer in 1050 B.C. 1 *Samuel* 4:1–22. The excavated site is nineteen miles north of Jerusalem. 24 *Encyclopaedia Britannica* (11th ed.) 860.

notice." Wallace shouted back he had done so, Grant nodded, and *Tigress* eased back into the main channel.[123]

Little *Tigress* was one of the fastest boats on the river and as it hammered its way upstream at forced draft the din of battle grew louder. At Pittsburg Landing the roar was incredible. Even more incredible was the scene that greeted Grant: several thousand stragglers and deserters cowering under the bluff—untrained officers and men from Prentiss's division who had discarded their weapons and run to the rear for safety. Grant was assisted onto his horse and rode into battle, a crutch strapped to his saddle like a carbine. His first task was to reestablish order at the landing site. Finding two Iowa regiments recently arrived and drawn up on the bluff awaiting orders, he formed a straggler line and added a battery of artillery with its guns trained on the road leading out of the uproar.

Riding forward on the Corinth road Grant met General William Wallace, who told him what he knew of the situation. "Prentiss is attacked and falling back on Hurlbut, who has formed in line. Sherman is falling back; McClernand is supporting him. I have been posted here on your orders, issued by [Colonel] McPherson, as a central reserve to be used to fill in the gaps between our center and right or left. McPherson is up now posting my First brigade, but ought to be back soon and can tell you how things are."[124]

Grant could see for himself things looked grim, yet he remained supremely composed. Colonel McPherson, the senior staff officer on the spot, had assumed command of the Union center awaiting Grant's arrival and appeared to be on top of the situation. It was also clear Johnston's main force was engaged in the attack and Crump's Landing was not endangered. Grant calmly turned to his adjutant, Captain Rawlins, and said, "Send [Captain Algernon S.] Baxter in the *Tigress* to tell [Lew] Wallace to march up at once."[125] Then he ordered his quartermaster officers to start the ammunition wagons forward. Resupply had been a problem at Donelson and Grant wanted to avoid his earlier mistake. Before riding on he wrote another message to Bull Nelson: "You will hurry up your command as fast as possible. The boats will be in readiness to transport all troops of your command across the river. All looks well, but it is necessary for you to push forward as fast as possible."[126]

With ammunition and reinforcements provided for, Grant continued along the Corinth road. Up to now Johnston had things very much his way. When the troops of Hardee and Bragg stormed Prentiss's camp, victory seemed within reach. The rebels paused to celebrate. Many had not eaten since Corinth, and the bountiful Sunday breakfast bubbling on Union cooking fires was a temptation few could resist.[127] "The Yankees . . . left everything they had," wrote Liberty Nixon of the 26th Alabama.

"Corn, oats, pants, vests, drawers, shirts, shoes, and a great many other things of the finest quality."[128] For a moment the victorious Confederate phalanx dissolved into a disorganized rabble intent on plundering Prentiss's camp. An hour ticked by while brigade and regimental commanders scurried about desperately trying to reestablish control. The delay was crucial because it allowed the Union center to re-form behind the sprawling tent city. As order was restored, Johnston heard sounds of a savage fight to the west. The six brigades of the Confederate left wing were driving on Sherman's line at Shiloh church. It was axiomatic among military men in the nineteenth century to march toward the sound of the guns, and Johnston gave orders for the troops occupying Prentiss's camp to veer northwest and assist the attack in progress. By ten o'clock five additional brigades joined the assault. The redirection of the main Confederate attack from northeast to northwest was Johnston's second mistake—and a serious one. The original plan had been to turn Grant's left and separate him from the Tennessee. Now the Confederate impetus was directed at Grant's right, forcing him back on Pittsburg Landing and the Tennessee.

Grant arrived at Sherman's position with the attack in progress. Cool and steady under fire, Sherman was magnificent in battle, shoring up his raw troops, inspiring them to hurl back the initial Confederate assaults, even instructing them how to cut the fuses for their artillery shells.[129] Already he had been wounded twice, first in the hand, then by a spent minié ball that bruised his shoulder. Three horses would be shot from under him, and before dusk a bullet would pass through the crown of his hat. Grant told Sherman what he would repeat to each of his division commanders: Lew Wallace's division would soon be up, Nelson was marching overland to the river, and the rest of Buell's army was closing on Savannah. Sherman said one of his brigades disintegrated under fire but the others were holding firm. He worried that his men would run out of ammunition. Grant complimented the division's performance and said ammunition wagons were rolling forward. Satisfied Sherman could hold his own, Grant rode eastward along the front.[130] "I never deemed it important to stay long with Sherman," he said later.[131]

Next to Sherman, Grant found McClernand's 1st Division. The gap in the Union front had been closed and McClernand's lines were stable. In the center, the veteran troops of William Wallace's 2nd Division were now in place, joined by remnants of Prentiss's depleted force. Here the Union line was sited along an eroded wagon trial, a sunken road one to three feet deep that ran along the front, forming a natural trench for the defenders. To the south of the road was a large open field across which the Confederates must advance; to the rear was a dense thicket that provided cover. Seven thousand men and twenty-five pieces of artillery were deployed along this half-mile segment of the front. Grant was pleased with the position and instructed Prentiss to "maintain it at all hazards." [132]

On Prentiss's left was Hurlbut's 4th Division. Grant visited it next. Iowa soldiers who saw him ride up said his face "wore an anxious look, yet bore no evidence of excitement or trepidation." Another soldier said Grant was smoking a cigar, seemingly as cool as if he were making a routine inspection. The sight reassured the men, who felt the worst must be over. [133] Beyond Hurlbut a single brigade was posted on the Union left flank. Commanded by former Michigan congressman David Stuart, the 2,300 troops of the 2nd Brigade (detached from Sherman's division) were positioned on favorable terrain behind Lick Creek but the line was stretched painfully thin. Fortunately for Grant, all was quiet in Stuart's sector.

As Grant inspected his line, the fighting rose to a crescendo along that portion of the front held by Sherman and McClernand. Virtually all of Johnston's army except Breckinridge's corps was engaged in the assault—a tidal wave of gray rolling forward. Sherman sent an aide to locate Grant with a request for reinforcements, "if there are any." If none were available, Sherman said he would fight with what he had. "We are holding them pretty well just now—but it's hot as hell." [134] Shortly after ten o'clock the impact of three Confederate corps proved unstoppable. Sherman ordered his men to fall back and McClernand followed suit. The rebels took possession of two more Union camps. Once again precious minutes were wasted foraging through abandoned tents, liberating what the Yankees left behind. Three of five Union camps were in Confederate possession, but it was evident Beauregard's attack plan had come unglued. The front was now almost three miles wide, Grant's line had not cracked, and the troops of Hardee, Polk, and Bragg—initially deployed in echelon—had become hopelessly commingled. Acting on their own initiative, the three Confederate generals divided the front into sectors. Regardless of original corps designations, Hardee took command of the troops on the left, Polk the left-center, and Bragg the right-center. On the right, Johnston retained personal control, waiting the arrival of Breckinridge's corps for what he assumed would be the final attack to drive the Union army from the field.

Changing the order of battle in midstream was anything but simple and additional time was lost as corps commanders sought to rework their chains of command and provide new supply channels to keep the offensive moving. By eleven o'clock units were in place and the attack on Sherman and McClernand resumed full force. Within thirty minutes the Union right was driven back another thousand yards. Sherman and McClernand struggled to stabilize their line and the Confederates paused to regroup, yet by 11:30 Grant's right flank had been all but turned. Sherman and McClernand were no longer anchored on Owl Creek and were being slowly pushed back on Pittsburg Landing and the river. This was exactly opposite to what Johnston intended, although in the heat of battle no one noticed.[135]

After checking the front and consulting with each division commander, Grant rode back to the center of the Union line. McClernand was asking for reinforcements and Grant ordered the two Iowa regiments manning the straggler line to move forward. That left no straggler line and no central reserve but Lew Wallace was expected anytime and Nelson was on the way. It was now close to noon. Grant dispatched an aide to check on Wallace's progress and then returned to the landing to look for Nelson. The right bank of the Tennessee offered an abundance of weed stalks and bushes, with a young cornfield in the distance, but no trace of the 4th Division of Buell's army. Grant sent another message upriver, this time more anguished—not unlike the one he wrote to Foote at Donelson: "The appearance of fresh troops would have a powerful effect, both by inspiring our men and disheartening the enemy. If you will get upon the field, leaving all your baggage on the east bank of the river, it will be more to our advantage, and possibly save the day for us." Grant said rebel forces numbered over 100,000 men, leaving it to Nelson to draw his own conclusion.[136]

The battle was just beginning. Grant wrote later that Shiloh was a case of "Southern dash against Northern pluck and endurance."[137] Wellington could have said something similar in 1815. On the Union right, Sherman and McClernand took advantage of the pause in the Confederate offensive to launch a counterattack. Twenty-two battered regiments moved forward, catching the rebels unprepared and driving them back almost a half mile with heavy losses. In the center, Breckinridge's corps had come up and Johnston hurled it against the Union position along the sunken road. On Grant's left, Confederate cavalry were probing the weak Federal flank and the all-important link to the Tennessee.

Fighting was heavy all along the front, but the growing fury in the center was unprecedented. Johnston ordered Bragg's corps to join Breckinridge in the assault, and by early afternoon upward of 18,000 men were pressing forward along a half-mile segment. Union troops on the sunken road and its flanks—the combined forces of William Wallace, Prentiss, and Hurlbut—held their ground and fired relentlessly at the advancing Confederates. "It's a hornets' nest in there," rebel soldiers cried,[138] recoiling from charge after charge at what appeared to be an impregnable position.

It was about this time that General Buell and his staff arrived by steamer at Pittsburg Landing. The scene was more chaotic than when Grant arrived earlier that morning. With no straggler line to arrest deserters, the number of malingerers on the riverbank had multiplied. Buell estimated a quarter of Grant's army was huddled under the bluff. Disaster, he thought, was imminent. His meeting with Grant was brief. Judging from Buell's report of the encounter he was not entirely unhappy with Grant's predicament.[139] Germans have a word for it: *Schadenfreude* — to take pleasure in the misfortune of others. Grant explained the situation, indicating the battle had reached a critical stage. "What preparations have you made for retreating?" asked Buell. None, said Grant. "I haven't despaired of whipping them yet."[140]

While Grant was meeting with Buell, Johnston was rallying Breckinridge's corps for another assault on Hurlbut's line, slightly east of the sunken road. A peach orchard and a large open field separated the Union and Confederate troops. Three times the Southerners charged and three times they were repulsed with heavy losses. Breckinridge told Johnston one of his brigades was unwilling to attack again. Johnston said he would help. Riding among the reluctant troops, he spoke gently and tapped their bayonets with a little tin cup he had taken from Prentiss's camp. "Men, they are stubborn. We must use the bayonet." When the brigade was formed, 300 yards south of the orchard, Johnston rode to the center of the line. "Follow me, I will lead you." The men surged forward and this time the charge was not repulsed. With five Confederate brigades joining the assault, the peach orchard fell and Hurlbut retreated to the woods beyond. For Johnston, victory was in the offing. Grant's left, which had stalled the Confederate advance four hours, finally yielded. As Johnston watched his men celebrate he suddenly reeled in the saddle and went pale.

"General — are you hurt?" an officer asked.

"Yes, and I fear seriously," Johnston replied.[141]

Toward the end of the attack, Johnston had been hit in the calf of his right leg with a minié ball, severing an artery. He apparently did not feel the shot and no effort was made to stop the bleeding.* He died from an acute loss of blood at 2:45 P.M. — the highest ranking officer of either army killed during the war.

Johnston's loss was tragic, but the blow did not doom the Confederate cause. Throughout the battle Johnston had exposed himself recklessly, leading regiments and exhorting brigades to close with the enemy. His leadership was inspirational. But his command of the battlefield had been nominal. Despite his seniority Johnston had never commanded more than a regiment in combat, and at Shiloh he acted as a regimental commander. Because of his unfamiliarity with handling large formations he left the at-

---

* In a duel fought in Texas in 1837, Johnston was struck in the right hip by a pistol ball that cut the sciatic nerve. From that time onward, his leg had been numb to pain, heat, and cold, and it is likely he was unaware he was shot until he fell in the saddle.

tack plan to Beauregard; after Prentiss's camp was taken he instinctively but mistakenly shifted the Confederate thrust northwest instead of northeast, undermining his goal of separating Grant from the Tennessee; and he did not sort out the confusion caused by the intermingling of assault waves, leaving it to corps commanders to make their own adjustments. Grant, by contrast, seized control of the Union side of the battlefield the moment he arrived. He had learned progressively in the hard school of experience how to command ever-larger formations in battle. In central Missouri a year earlier he commanded a regiment; at Belmont in the autumn, a brigade; two divisions at Fort Henry, and three at Donelson. At Belmont and Donelson he faced an enemy under almost equal conditions. He learned the importance of ammunition resupply, of seeing the front as a whole, and providing general direction for his division commanders. Grant handled the Army of the Tennessee by handling his division commanders and relying on them to fight the troops under their control.

One of Grant's most serious problems the first afternoon at Shiloh was that one of his division commanders was missing. Lew Wallace's 3rd Division, which should have been on the field by noon, was nowhere in sight. Shortly after leaving Buell, Grant dispatched Colonel McPherson and Rawlins to find the errant division and bring it onto line, reinforcing the Union center. Although the reasons remain cloaked in controversy, Lew Wallace never understood the urgency of the situation. His troops ate a leisurely Sunday dinner, did not get underway until twelve o'clock, and then took the wrong road. McPherson and Rawlins found them marching west from Crump's Landing, not south. Wallace wrote later he intended to come around behind the front and hit the Confederates in the rear.[142] But that is not where Grant needed him.[143] When Grant's messengers peremptorily ordered him to reverse direction and march to Pittsburg Landing, Wallace led the front of the column back through the formation (instead of about facing) and continued at what Rawlins described as a "cool and leisurely pace."[144] Despite McPherson's urgings to move rapidly, Wallace's advance guard did not arrive until 7:15 P.M. and the day's fighting was over. It had taken ten hours instead of the usual two to march six miles from Crump's Landing. Wallace spent the rest of his life trying to live down his mistake, and the episode is one of the few instances in which Grant was unforgiving. Later he said that if Morgan L. Smith, the senior colonel, had been in command, the 3rd Division would have been on the field by noon.[145]

When Hurlbut was forced to withdraw from the peach orchard, Grant recognized that without Lew Wallace's division the center could not hold indefinitely. He turned to his chief of staff, Colonel Joseph Webster, and informed him he was now the army's chief of artillery. Webster was instructed to assemble every gun he could lay his hands on for a last-ditch stand at the landing. Grant then redeployed his cavalry (which was of little use in the broken terrain) as a new straggler line, after which he rode to the front. He found Hurlbut had re-formed on the left-center and Prentiss was holding firm. Grant said Prentiss "was as cool as if expecting victory." [146] William Wallace's troops on the right-center were under heavy attack and were also standing fast. On the far right, Sherman and McClernand could not hold the ground they recaptured and had fallen back under heavy pressure. Stung by the Union counterattack, Beauregard committed the last Southern reserves and by mid-afternoon the lines were back more or less where they were at noon. Once again the Confederates paused to regroup while Sherman and McClernand, doubtful they could hold their line without reinforcements, retreated to high ground less than a mile from Pittsburg Landing. The noose around the Union position was tightening, but Grant's line had not broken.

By three o'clock Beauregard knew Johnston was dead. He also knew Sherman and McClernand had fallen back and that there was heavy fighting in the vicinity of the hornets' nest, where the Confederate drive had come to a standstill in front of Prentiss's position. At this point Beauregard did what should have been done earlier and redeployed the bulk of the rebel forces from the left to the right. Hardee would continue to peck at Sherman's line, but for the remainder of the day the heaviest fighting would be done on the eastern half of the battlefield. Eventually fourteen of the sixteen Confederate brigades on the field would move against the hornets' nest. [147]

Late in the afternoon, confronted with overwhelming odds, Hurlbut gave way on the left side of Prentiss and retreated on Pittsburg Landing. The fourth Union camp fell into Confederate hands. To the right of Prentiss, William Wallace's flank was exposed when McClernand pulled back. Prentiss and Wallace bent their lines back and continued to hold their ground, but there was nothing on either side of them except Confederates. The hornets' nest became an isolated salient resembling a mule shoe. Twelve separate assaults were launched against the Union position and all twelve were repulsed. Grant wrote the ground was "so covered with dead that it would have been possible to walk across, in any direction, stepping on dead bodies, without a foot touching the ground." [148]

Rather than bypass the Prentiss-Wallace salient and strike Grant's depleted force at the landing, Beauregard insisted the pocket be taken. The Confederates massed their artillery and at 4:30 fifty-three guns—the largest battlefield concentration of field artillery on the North American continent to date—opened an intense bombardment of the hornets' nest. Incoming rounds hit with the force of a hurricane. At five o'clock Wallace

ordered the remnants of his division to withdraw. Confederate troops converged on the salient and Wallace was mortally wounded as his men pulled
back. Prentiss's line on the sunken road continued to hold. At 5:30, after six
hours of continuous fighting, the back door to the hornets' nest was
slammed shut when Confederate forces comprising the right and left
wings of the army came together in Prentiss's rear, sealing him off from the
Union line at Pittsburg Landing. Further resistance was futile. White flags
went up and bugles sounded cease-fire. The 2,250 survivors of the hornets'
nest surrendered. Grant had ordered Prentiss to hold the position at all
hazards, and he did so literally. As one historian wrote, Prentiss lost everything except honor: men, guns, colors, and finally the position itself.[149]
But his resistance saved the Union army. It was almost 6 P.M., dusk was settling over the battlefield, and Ammen's brigade of Nelson's division had
crossed the Tennessee and come on line. Beauregard, miscalculating
Grant's resilience, frittered away the opportunity to hit him at the landing
when he was weakest.

At five o'clock, as Confederate artillery pounded the hornets' nest,
Bull Nelson arrived at the riverbank opposite Pittsburg Landing. Despite
Grant's order to march to the Tennessee, Buell had kept the 4th Division at
Savannah until 1:30 waiting for the situation to clarify. When Buell and his
staff departed to meet Grant, Nelson put his division in motion overland.
Five hours had been lost, but the former naval officer pressed through the
black-mud swamp at what seafarers called flank speed. "The roar of cannon
continues, and volleys of musketry can be distinguished," Colonel Ammen
noted in his diary. "The men appear cool yet march at a good rate through
the mud, anxious to meet the foe."[150] Nelson, mounted on an enormous
Kentucky stallion and attired in battle regalia General Winfield Scott
might envy, led the troops ashore through the mass of deserters cowering
along the bank. "Draw your sabers, gentlemen, and trample these bastards
in the mud."[151] With regimental bands sounding the strains of "Hail, Columbia," the 10th Brigade marched up the bluff where Grant and Buell
were waiting. One of Grant's soldiers wrote he could never forget the new
hope that came to him when he heard Nelson's bands, and he said the men
all around him cheered "till the whole woods fairly shook for joy."[152]

Nelson arrived just in time. Colonel Webster had worked frantically
all afternoon to piece together a defense line at Pittsburg Landing. Known
by historians as Grant's last line, the Union position stretched from the
river, up the slope, and along the high ground for about 2,000 yards.
Along this ridge Webster emplaced almost seventy cannon, including a
battery of enormous siege guns. The gunboats *Tyler* and *Lexington*, Grant's
old friends from Belmont and Fort Henry, anchored the left of the line,
while Sherman and McClernand held the right. Hurlbut, plus the sur-

vivors of William Wallace's division, took position next to McClernand. Altogether about 18,000 Union infantry formed up in front of the artillery. But there was a quarter-mile gap on the left end of the line between Hurlbut and the river with no troops whatever. The guns were exposed without infantry support. Grant posted Nelson at that end of the line. Ammen's brigade moved quickly and was in position when the Confederates began their final assault.

It had taken Beauregard some time to reorganize his forces after the hornets' nest fell, but as the sun sank toward the horizon he launched a final go-for-broke attack to separate Grant from the Tennessee. The men were exhausted, the terrain was difficult, and Grant was ready. Nevertheless 8,000 troops moved forward under Bragg's command to challenge the Union left. "One more charge, my men, and we shall capture them all." [153] There was irony in Bragg's exhortation. At Buena Vista his battery broke the final Mexican charge for Zachary Taylor. Now he was on the other side of the muzzle. When the rebel assault wave came into view, Webster's guns erupted with an intensity that surpassed the Confederate cannonade at the hornets' nest: Grape and canister from the field artillery, shot and shell from the siege guns and gunboats. Less than half of Bragg's 8,000 men advanced far enough to close with the Union infantry and they were repulsed easily. Bragg was ready to try again when Beauregard called him off. "The victory is sufficiently complete; it is needless to expose our men to the fire of the gunboats." [154] Like Pillow at Donelson, Beauregard believed the battle had been won. He ordered his troops to pull back and spend the night in the captured Union camps. Bragg was less sanguine. For a moment he considered disobeying Beauregard's order, then he saw Polk and Breckinridge falling back. "My God, my God, it is too late." [155]

Mounted among his smoking cannon, Grant watched the Confederate attack fade away. For a moment he was alone with his thoughts. An aide heard him mutter under his breath and to no one in particular, "Not beaten yet. Not by a damn sight." [156] Then Grant turned his horse and went about the business of preparing for tomorrow. Union losses were enormous. At least 7,000 men had been killed or wounded, and as many as 3,000 captured. Another 5,000 to 10,000 milled along the riverbank, too frightened to be of service. Two divisions—the 2nd and the 6th—no longer existed. General William Wallace was missing and Prentiss a prisoner. Forty pieces of artillery had been lost or destroyed, and four of five division camps had been captured by the Confederates. Tons of supplies, ammunition, and foodstuffs had fallen into rebel hands. Grant was holding little more than a beachhead. The front was two miles behind where it had been that morning, junior officers commanded the remnants of shattered regiments, and Lew Wallace's 3rd Division had yet to make an appearance. Whether Buell would commit more than Nelson's division had not been settled.*

"General, things are going decidedly against us," said an Illinois surgeon standing by.

"Not at all, sir," said Grant. "We're whipping them now." The doctor said afterward that no other man in the army would have responded as Grant did.[157] A newsman who heard the conversation asked Grant what he meant. "The enemy has done all he can do today. They can't break our lines tonight—it is too late. Tomorrow we shall attack them with fresh troops and drive them, of course."[158]

It was in that frame of mind that Grant visited each of his division commanders. "So confident was I that the next day would bring victory if we could only take the initiative that I directed them to throw out heavy lines of skirmishers in the morning as soon as they could see, and push them forward until they found the enemy, following with their entire division, and to engage the enemy as soon as found."[159] Grant told Sherman the situation was similar to that at Fort Donelson: "both sides seemed defeated, and whoever assumed the offensive was sure to win."[160] The instructions Grant gave his division commanders illustrate his control of the battlefield. He made the decision to attack at dawn and left it to them to put their troops in motion.

About 10 P.M. a slow drizzle began to fall. Grant was sitting with his staff around a smoldering fire when Colonel McPherson rode up, having inspected the preparations for tomorrow. "Well, Mac, how is it?" asked Grant. McPherson said he was pessimistic—a third of the army was out of action and the rest downcast and disheartened. When Grant made no reply, McPherson asked, "General Grant, under this condition of affairs, what do you propose to do, sir? Shall I make preparations for retreat?"

"Retreat?" Grant asked incredulously. "No. I propose to attack at daylight and whip them."[161]

Later, sometime after midnight, raining harder now, Sherman went looking for Grant. He had worked five hours to prepare his division to attack, but it seemed hopeless. His men had been thoroughly beaten and Sherman—who would have been the last to say so—thought it important "to put the river between us and the enemy." This is why he sought Grant, to see when and how the retreat could be arranged. The rain was coming down in buckets, punctuated by heavy thunder and lightning in the background. In this surreal setting Sherman found Grant standing alone under

---

* "Buell seemed to mistrust us," wrote Sherman, "and repeatedly said he did not like the looks of things, especially about the boat landing, and I really feared he would not cross over his army that night, lest he become involved in a general disaster." William Tecumseh Sherman, 1 *Memoirs of General William T. Sherman* 266 (New York: Library of America, 1990). (Reprint.)

a large oak tree, dripping wet, hat slouched down over his face, coat collar up around his ears, a dimly glowing lantern in his hand, cigar clenched between his teeth. Sherman looked at him for a moment from a distance. Then, "moved" as he put it later, "by some wise and sudden instinct not to mention retreat," Sherman approached and said, "Well, Grant, we've had the devil's own day, haven't we?"

"Yes," answered Grant, puffing hard on his cigar. "Yes. Lick 'em tomorrow though." [162]

The second day at Shiloh was a reflection of Grant's determination. As Sherman's comment suggests, a general imparts attitude to an army. It is not simply a matter of issuing orders, but infusing spirit and initiative. An inchoate bond develops between a successful commander and the army. His will becomes theirs. Grant's relationship with the Army of the Tennessee at Shiloh exemplified that bond. Lee established it with the Army of Northern Virginia. Washington did it with the Continental Army. The men fought because they knew Grant expected them to, and they trusted his judgment that they could do so.

Beauregard was equally confident. "I thought I had Grant just where I wanted him." [163] That evening he wired Richmond: "We this morning attacked the enemy in strong position in front of Pittsburg, and after a severe battle of ten hours, thanks be to the Almighty, gained a complete victory, driving the enemy from every position." [164]

The Southern army, officers and men alike, shared Beauregard's assessment. All believed a great victory had been won. If the defeated Union army remained in the field, which most doubted, they would make short work of it in the morning. As for Buell, Beauregard received a dispatch that evening from the Confederate command in Alabama stating the Army of the Ohio had been diverted to Decatur and would not link up with Grant after all. [165] At the very time Beauregard was reading the dispatch, Thomas L. Crittenden's division of Buell's army was debarking at Pittsburg Landing, to be followed by Alexander McCook's in the early morning hours. The indefatigable Nathan Bedford Forrest, who alone among Confederate commanders had not withdrawn his cavalry patrols, noted the increased river traffic, investigated, and reported to Hardee that Grant was receiving reinforcements by the thousands. "If this army does not move and attack them between now and daylight, it will be whipped like hell before ten o'clock tomorrow." [166] Hardee evidently assumed the movement Forrest observed was the Union army evacuating. He told the Memphis cavalryman to maintain a strong picket line and then went back to sleep, not bothering to pass Forrest's report up the chain of command. [167]

Hardee's error was critical but understandable. What few recognized was that thanks in part to Beauregard's initial attack plan, the Confederate army was far more disorganized at this point than Grant's. The Army of the Tennessee had lost two divisions. But the cohesion of the remaining four and the army's command structure remained intact. Man for man, Union and Confederate losses were similar. But rebel troop units were hopelessly intermingled and discipline had all but collapsed, compromised by the delirious looting of Federal camps that continued through the night. Five to ten thousand Union soldiers might be cowering on the riverbank, but at least as many Southerners were out of action in search of plunder.[168] On paper the Confederate army numbered perhaps 33,000 present for duty Sunday evening. The reality was closer to 23,000. The corps commanders—Hardee, Polk, Bragg, and Breckinridge—agreed with Beauregard that the best thing to do was to wait until daylight to sort things out. No front was established, few officers undertook to resupply their men with ammunition—though millions of cartridges were lying about in Union camps—and no attempt was made to entrench. While Grant readied his attack, Beauregard and Bragg spent the night in Sherman's tent, relishing Southern victory.

The celebration was short-lived. First off the mark Monday morning was Bull Nelson. At 3 A.M. he roused his staff and at five o'clock his picket line moved forward. Nelson's division occupied the far left of the Union position, its flank anchored on the Tennessee. Next to Nelson was Critten-den, then McCook. Grant's four divisions constituted the right wing of the army: Hurlbut, McClernand, and Sherman, with Lew Wallace's 3rd Division on the flank. Altogether the Union attack force numbered close to 40,000 men, more than half of whom were fresh troops eager to take on the enemy. Grant was with Lew Wallace when the report of artillery sounded from Nelson's front. "Move out that way," said Grant, pointing southwest in the direction of the Confederate left flank. Wallace acknowl-edged the order and asked if he was to adopt any particular formation. "I leave that to your discretion," said Grant. With those few words the attack on the Union right began. Grant never burdened his division commanders with excessive detail. No elaborate staff conferences, no written orders prescribing deployment or combat objectives. Grant said nothing to Wal-lace about yesterday's fight, Buell's arrival, or who would be supporting him. He wanted Wallace to move in a particular direction and left it at that. The genius of Grant's command style lay in its simplicity. Better than any Civil War general, Grant recognized the battlefield was in flux. By not specifying movements in detail, he left his subordinate commanders free to exploit whatever opportunities developed.[169]

Monday's fight was a repeat of Sunday, in reverse. The massive Union assault caught the Southerners off guard, and the most advanced Confed-erate units succumbed quickly. "At daybreak our pickets came rushing in under a murderous fire," said Joseph Thompson of the 38th Tennessee. "The first thing we knew we were almost surrounded by six or seven regiments of Yankees."[170] Hardee and Bragg held their ground, counterattacked, yet were eventually overwhelmed. The Confederate line yielded grudgingly, but like Grant's the day before, it did not crack. Once again, fighting was heavy all along the front. "The rebels fall back slowly, stubbornly, but they are losing ground," Colonel Ammen recorded.[171] By early afternoon the outcome was no longer in doubt. Southern morale deteriorated as exhausted troops battled against ever lengthening odds.

Shortly after two o'clock, Beauregard's adjutant, Colonel Thomas Jordan, asked if it would not be prudent to break off the fight and withdraw. "General, do you not think our troops in the condition of a lump of sugar thoroughly soaked with water, but yet preserving its original shape, though ready to dissolve."[172] Beauregard agreed. Corps commanders were instructed to pull back, saving as much ordnance as possible. At 3 P.M. the retreat began, effectively covered by Breckinridge's corps, which steadfastly held the Corinth road below Shiloh church as the army withdrew. The retrograde movement, one of the most difficult maneuvers to undertake in the heat of battle, was executed smoothly. Bragg, Hardee, and Polk led their corps a mile or so south and camped where they had slept two nights earlier on the eve of battle. Breckinridge remained in position to discourage pursuit. But there was no pursuit. After two days of the fiercest fighting ever seen in North America, the Union army was content to regain possession of the battlefield.

Grant watched the enemy retire. "I wanted to pursue, but had not the heart to order the men who had fought desperately for two days, lying in the mud and rain whenever not fighting, and I did not feel disposed to positively order Buell, or any part of his command to pursue."[173] In his *Memoirs* Grant wrote, "Shiloh was the severest battle fought at the West during the war, and but few in the East equalled it for hard determined fighting." Until then, Grant said he thought the Confederate government would collapse quickly if the Union could win a decisive victory. But the audacity the rebels displayed in assuming the offensive, and the gallantry with which they fought at Shiloh, convinced him that the Union could not be saved except by total victory.

Up to that time it had been the policy of our army, certainly of that portion commanded by me, to protect the property of citizens whose territory was invaded, without regard to sentiments, whether Union or Secession. After this, I regarded it as humane to both sides to protect the persons of those found at their homes, but to consume everything that could be used to support or supply armies. . . . I continued this policy to the close of the war.[174]

Shiloh was a watershed, not only for Grant, but for North and South alike. The losses were stupefying, and about equal. The difference was the Union could replenish its men and equipment, the Confederacy could not. Of the 100,000 men who fought at Shiloh, 23,746 were killed, wounded, or captured. Combined Union and Confederate casualties were nearly double the losses at Bull Run, Wilson's Creek, Fort Donelson, and Pea Ridge added together. In two days of bitter fighting more casualties were inflicted than in all of America's previous wars (Revolution, 1812, Mexico) combined. Grant lost 1,754 killed, 8,408 wounded, and 2,885 missing, for a total of 13,047. Beauregard reported 1,728 killed, 8,012 wounded, and 959 missing, a total of 10,699.

Grant's victory at Shiloh, bloody and bitter though it was, doomed the Confederate cause in the Mississippi valley. In the East, fighting had just begun. But in the West a great turning point had been reached and passed. The chances of Confederate victory, long to begin with, had become immeasurably longer.

The battle, as Wellington said of Waterloo, was "a near run thing."[175]* If Johnston could have hit Prentiss with his main battle line at dawn, the extra ninety minutes of daylight might have furnished the margin of victory. If Johnston had concentrated on driving Grant back from the Tennessee and had not been diverted to reinforce the attack on Sherman, victory might have come early. If rebel soldiers had not stopped to loot Union camps, Grant's center might not have had time to re-form. If Beauregard had bypassed the hornets' nest and hit Grant at the landing before Nelson arrived, the outcome might have been different. If anyone other than Grant had been in command Sunday night, the Union army certainly would have retreated. Battles often hinge on *ifs,* and at Shiloh the *ifs* were on the Union side.

In Washington, news of the victory in "the bloodiest battle of modern times," triggered massive rejoicing.[176] Congress suspended business and President Lincoln declared a national day of worship. The *New York Times*

---

* The parallel between Shiloh and Waterloo is striking. Not only were the French and Confederate battle plans similar, but so were the British and Union responses. All day Wellington withstood whatever Napoleon threw against him. The British line bent but never broke. So too with Grant. Late in the afternoon, the final charge of the French Old Guard collapsed before the compact squares of the Union and Household brigades. The final Confederate assault was broken at dusk by the massed artillery of Grant's last line. At the tail end of the battle, Blücher came to Wellington's support just as Buell came to Grant's. Of the 100,000 men who fought at Shiloh, one out of every four was killed, wounded, or captured. Casualties were 24 percent, the same as at Waterloo.

and the *New York Herald* celebrated Grant as a national hero.[177] But when fearful casualty lists appeared and rumors of Union unpreparedness made their rounds, a harsh reaction set in. Old stories of Grant's intoxication resurfaced and the clamor for his removal engulfed the White House. Lincoln listened attentively one evening to old friends and advisers who urged that Grant be sacked. At length the president rose from his chair and spoke in an earnest tone that ended the conversation: "I can't spare this man; he fights."[178]

CHAPTER SEVEN

VICKSBURG

General Grant is a great general. I know him well. He stood by me when I was crazy and I stood by him when he was drunk.

WILLIAM TECUMSEH SHERMAN

AT SHILOH, AS AT DONELSON, Grant turned defeat into Union victory. Unlike Donelson, however, the triumph was incomplete. Rather than pursue Beauregard's battered army, Grant was ordered to hold his position. "Avoid another battle, if you can, until reinforcements arrive," Halleck telegraphed on April 9. Old Brains said he was en route to Pittsburg Landing to assume command and that John Pope's Army of the Mississippi, having finally taken New Madrid and Island No. 10, would be joining Buell and Grant. That would increase Union strength to 120,000 men — the largest Federal force yet to take the field. Grant was told that once the army was assembled, "We shall be able to beat them without fail." [1]

Despite the opportunity to deliver a knockout blow, caution prevailed. The Confederates were broken, the rail junction at Corinth was within easy reach, and Beauregard would have been hard pressed to withstand a concerted Union attack. [2] "Our condition is horrible," Bragg wrote on April 8. "Troops utterly disorganized and demoralized. Road almost impassable. No provisions and no forage." [3] Breckinridge, whose corps constituted the rebel rear guard, said: "My troops are worn out. I don't think they can be relied on after the first volley." [4] Starved horses died by the roadside, guns were abandoned, and thousands deserted. An observer who rode alongside the retreating columns wrote that he saw more human agony and despair than he thought possible. [5] Despite its hopeless condition, the Confederate army withdrew to Corinth unmolested.

Halleck arrived at Pittsburg Landing on April 11. The department commander had never fought a pitched battle or seen a major battlefield and Shiloh was a dismal lesson in the destructiveness of war. Halleck was shocked by the waste and disorder. Accustomed to lacquered garrison routine, he was equally unprepared for the untidiness of soldiers in the field.* "This army is undisciplined and very much disorganized," he wrote his wife upon arrival.[6] Grant's Army of the Tennessee, which suffered most, aroused Halleck's particular displeasure. "Immediate and active measures must be taken to put your command in condition to resist another attack by the enemy," he instructed Grant.[7] Halleck said Grant and Buell would retain command of their respective armies, but his detailed order of the day made clear that Grant's loose style of leadership would not be tolerated.[8] "The Major General Commanding desires that you will again call the attention of your officers to the necessity of forwarding official communications through the proper military channel. *Letters should relate to one matter only, and be properly folded.*"[9]

Sherman thought Halleck had been prejudiced against Grant by rumors of Union unreadiness at Shiloh.[10] That may be true. But it is equally true that Halleck and Grant were reading from different pages in the military hymnal. Grant believed war meant fighting, and the object of the present fighting was to destroy Beauregard's army. Once it was whipped and the troops dispersed, the Mississippi valley would fall to the Union by default. Halleck, as America's leading disciple of Jomini, subscribed to the places theory of war. In his view the Confederacy could not stand without Corinth, Vicksburg, New Orleans, Atlanta, Richmond, and so forth. Capture the key places by maneuver and fighting would prove unnecessary. In his *Elements of Military Art and Science,* Halleck wrote: "General battles are not to be fought" except under compelling circumstances.[11] Once he took command at Pittsburg Landing, Union sights were fixed on Corinth. Beauregard's army ceased to be a target.[12] The result was that Corinth eventually fell, the Confederate army escaped, and the war in the West was prolonged another eighteen months.

The conceptual differences between Grant and Halleck went unarticulated in the spring of 1862. Halleck underrated Grant, but so did almost everyone else. Nevertheless, he recognized Grant's usefulness. When Secretary Stanton, acknowledging public clamor, wired to inquire whether "any neglect or misconduct of General Grant . . . contributed to the sad casualties that befell our forces" at Shiloh,[13] Old Brains declined to make

---

* Captain Philip H. Sheridan, who was delegated to be Halleck's mess officer, thought he was a fish out of water. "General Halleck did not know much about taking care of himself in the field. His camp arrangements were wholly inadequate, and in consequence he and all the officers about him were subjected to much unnecessary discomfort." 1 *Personal Memoirs of P. H. Sheridan* 137 (New York: Charles L. Webster, 1888).

Grant a scapegoat. "A Great Battle cannot be fought or a victory gained without many casualties, and in this instance the enemy suffered more than we did."[14] Despite their conceptual differences, Grant, for his part, continued to view Halleck as "one of the greatest men of the age."[15]

For Grant the curtain came down on Shiloh. John Pope's Army of the Mississippi arrived by convoy on April 21 and went into position on the Union left. Four days later Charles Ferguson Smith succumbed to the infection that had set in after his leg was injured. Everyone in the army would miss him, but no one more than Grant.[16] In a letter to Mrs. Smith, Grant said, "The nation has lost one of its most gallant and able defenders." Putting his loss in personal terms, Grant wrote: "It was my fortune to have gone through West Point with the General (then captain and commandant of cadets) and to have served with him in all his battles in Mexico and in this rebellion, and I can bear honest testimony to his great worth as a soldier and friend. Where an entire nation condoles with you in your bereavement, no one can do so with more heartfelt grief than myself."[17] Sherman was equally affected. Years later he wrote that if Smith had lived, "no one would have ever heard of Grant or myself."[18] Halleck ordered a salute fired at every post and aboard every warship in the department,[19] and in Washington Secretary Stanton publicly noted Smith's passing.[20] The *Philadelphia Inquirer* said it best: "There was no better soldier in the army than General Smith."[21]

By the end of April, Halleck was ready to move against Corinth. Grant's army occupied the position on the Union right, Buell the center, and Pope the left.[22] The advance began April 29 and the following day Halleck fine-tuned his command structure. Grant was designated to be second in command—similar to the post Beauregard held under Johnston—and the army's right wing was entrusted to George Thomas.[23] The change made sense. Halleck lacked combat experience and needed Grant to remedy that deficiency. Grant was also the ranking major general after Halleck, and Thomas was an able field commander who could handle the army's right wing. The problem was that Grant was not Beauregard, nor was Halleck Johnston. Unlike the suave aristocrat from New Orleans, Grant was temperamentally incapable of being second in command and had never served in that capacity. As quartermaster with the 4th Infantry in Mexico he commanded the unit's supply train, and when he returned to the service in 1861 he commanded a regiment. He had never filled the role of backstage adviser and general courtier, humoring his chief and pointing out tactfully the reasons why the chief should do this and not that. Even the vocabulary was alien. Grant was a man of action. Command decisions came naturally. He moved on intuition, which he often could not explain or justify to someone else.[24]

Halleck was equally ill suited to the arrangement. Unlike Albert Sidney Johnston, Old Brains was a one-man show. He considered himself a strategist of the highest order with the formal rules of warfare at his fingertips. He did not need Grant unless the fighting became serious, and if Halleck planned carefully there would be no fighting. Grant was an insurance policy: Use only in case of catastrophe. Finally, there was the chemistry. The relationship between Johnston and Beauregard was lubricated with the genteel civility of the Old South. Grant and Halleck were products of a colder environment. Their dealings were formal, sometimes abrupt, always businesslike, and never reached a level of familiarity. Grant quickly came to resent the arrangement although there is no evidence Halleck meant any injustice.

The advance on Corinth consumed the month of May. The rebel rail junction was twenty miles away but the Union army inched forward like a glacier, plowing up the countryside as it went. Halleck, who feared that Beauregard would attack any moment, insisted the entire front entrench after each day's march. Four hours digging; six hours sleep. Grant said "the movement was a siege from the start to the close."[25] Sherman called it "a magnificent drill."[26] Black Jack Logan, commanding an Illinois brigade, contemptuously told observers, "My men will never dig another ditch for Halleck except to bury him."[27]

As the siege tightened, Grant became morose. He was hypersensitive to the fact he was no longer in command and could not adjust to his new responsibilities. The bitterness seeped into his letters to Julia. After assuring her he was "sober as a deacon no matter what was said to the contrary," Grant wrote he was thinking of returning home after Corinth was taken. "I have been so shockingly abused [by the press] that I sometimes think it almost time to defend myself." If the war continued, Grant told Julia he preferred to serve elsewhere. "I have probably done more hard work than any other General officer and . . . although I will shrink from no duty, I am perfectly willing that others should have every opportunity for distinguishing themselves."[28]

On May 11 Grant sent his complaint to Halleck. Their tents were 200 yards apart yet Grant put his hurt in writing. He told Halleck the removal from an active command in the face of the enemy implied censure and he considered his present job demeaning. "I believe it is generally understood through this army that my present position differs little from that of one in arrest." Grant said he wished to be restored to command of the Union right or relieved from further duty.[29]

Halleck was genuinely unaware of Grant's discomfort. As a desk soldier who disliked field duty, he could not understand Grant's complaint. "Your position as second in command of the entire force here in the field rendered it proper that you should be relieved from direct charge of the right wing. I am very much surprised, General, that you should find any cause of complaint in the recent assignment of commands. You have precisely the position to which your rank entitles you." Halleck said he had not intended to injure Grant's feelings or reputation. "For the last three months I have done everything in my power to ward off the attacks which were made upon you. If you believe me your friend, you will not require explanation; if not, explanation on my part would be of little avail."[30]

Grant felt reassured. The tone of his letters to Julia immediately improved. "We are moving slowly but in a way to insure success," he wrote on May 16. Grant said he was in excellent health "and am capable of enduring any amount of fatigue."[31] Grant's health was a tip-off to his mental state because, like Sherman, he was not immune to psychosomatic ailments. The following week he was more upbeat. "When the great battle will come off is hard to predict. No pains will be spared to make our success certain and there is scarcely a man in our army who doubts the result."[32] Grant reached a modus vivendi with Halleck's command structure. "My duties are much lighter than they have been heretofore. Gen. Halleck being present relieves me of great responsibility and Rawlins has become thoroughly acquainted with the routine of office and takes off my hands the examination of most papers." As Grant did frequently, he instructed Julia about their finances. "Get yourself everything of the very best, and the same for the children, but avoid extravagance. A few thousand saved now will be of great benefit after a while."[33]

By May 28 Halleck's ponderous war machine was within cannon shot of Beauregard's works. Corinth was surrounded on three sides. Union troops outnumbered the Confederates two to one, yet Old Brains continued to worry about a rebel attack. When Grant suggested that Pope's troops swing around the Union right and block Beauregard's retreat, Halleck indignantly dismissed the idea. The goal was to force Beauregard to withdraw from Corinth, not destroy him.[34] It was an axiom of the classic military thought to which Halleck subscribed that an avenue of retreat be left open. "I was silenced so quickly," said Grant, "I felt that possibly I had suggested an unmilitary movement."[35]

Seeking to avoid a general engagement, Halleck settled in for a lengthy wait. The wait ended before it began. Shortly after midnight on May 30 John Pope informed Halleck that Beauregard was being heavily reinforced. Trains were coming and going constantly on the Mobile & Ohio tracks leading into Corinth from the south. "I have no doubt, from all appearances, that I shall be attacked in heavy force at daylight," warned Pope.[36] Halleck's fears seemed to have come true. Ten minutes after receiving Pope's report, Old Brains alerted Buell: "There is every appearance that Pope will be attacked this morning. Be prepared to reinforce him, if necessary." A similar message went to Thomas on the Union right.[37] In reality, the trains Pope heard were carrying Beauregard's army out of Corinth to Tupelo, fifty miles south. When Union pickets moved forward at first light they found the Confederate works deserted. Beauregard had slipped his army out of harm's way. Even rebel civilians were scarce, all but two of the local families having departed with the troops. Corinth was a ghost town. Dummy soldiers, some with grins painted on, greeted Pope's advance guard. "These premises to let; inquire of P. G. T. Beauregard."[38] According to Grant: "There was not a sick or wounded man left by the Confederates, nor stores of any kind. The trophies of war were a few Quaker guns—logs about the diameter of ordinary cannon, mounted on wheels of wagons and pointed in the most threatening manner towards us."[39] Lew Wallace said, "Corinth was not captured; it was abandoned to us."[40]

Reviews were mixed. Sherman called the taking of Corinth "a victory as brilliant and important as any recorded in history."[41] On the other hand an officer in the 3rd Iowa wrote that he and his comrades had "an indescribable feeling of mortification that the enemy with all his stores and ordnance had escaped."[42] The *Chicago Tribune* said, "General Halleck . . . has achieved one of the most barren triumphs of the war." The *Cincinnati Commercial* thought Beauregard, by his timely withdrawal, "achieved another triumph."[43] Halleck, sensitive to criticism the Confederates slipped away, put the best face on the capture he could. "Beauregard evidently distrusts his army," he wired Stanton, "otherwise he would have fought."[44]

In his *Memoirs* Grant placed the capture of Corinth in perspective, focusing implicitly on the difference between Halleck and himself. The officers and men, he wrote, "could not see how the mere occupation of places was to close the war while large and effective rebel armies existed. They believed that a well-directed attack would at least have partially destroyed the army defending Corinth. For myself, I am satisfied that Corinth could have been captured in a two days' campaign commenced promptly on the arrival of reinforcements after the battle of Shiloh."[45]

True to form, Halleck began to fortify Corinth as if the final battle of the war would be fought there. The little momentum the army had acquired quickly eroded. In Tupelo meanwhile Beauregard refitted and reorganized, taking full advantage of the Union army's failure to pursue. As the northern gateway to the lush black belt of eastern Mississippi, Tupelo and its environs offered a congenial setting for the rebels to gather reinforcements, their morale boosted by the ease with which they extricated themselves from almost certain defeat. As the Union troops dug in and the Confederates regrouped, Grant grew despondent. Second in command of the vast army at Corinth, his position carried enormous prestige—not unlike the vice president of the United States. And like the vice president, Grant had little or nothing to do. Three days after Corinth fell, Sherman discovered him packing to leave. "As I rode up, [Grant's staff] were standing in front of his headquarters, and piled up near them were the usual office and camp chests, all ready for a start in the morning.

"I inquired for the general, and was shown to his tent, where I found him seated on a camp stool with papers on a rude camp table. He seemed to be employed in sorting letters and tying them up with red tape into convenient bundles." After exchanging pleasantries, Sherman asked Grant if he were going away.

"Yes," said Grant. "Sherman, you know. You know that I am in the way here. I have stood it as long as I can, and can endure it no longer."

"Where are you going?" asked Sherman.

"St. Louis."

"Have any business there?"

"Not a bit," Grant replied.

Sherman was touched. On the field at Shiloh, when the Union cause looked hopeless, he developed enormous respect for the rumpled little man who said "lick 'em tomorrow." Like C. F. Smith, Sherman recognized Grant's unique gift for warfare and understood the loss the Union would suffer if he departed. In his hard-bitten way, Sherman had formed an affection for Grant, who suffered even more than he in the 1850s. He pleaded with Grant not to leave, buttressing the argument with his own example. "Before the battle of Shiloh, I was cast down by a mere newspaper assertion of 'crazy,' but that single battle gave me new life, and I am now in high feather." Sherman told Grant that if he went away, events would move along and he would be left out. If he remained, "some happy accident might restore him to favor and his true place."[46]

Grant was struck by Sherman's candor.[47] As at Fort Humboldt in 1854, perhaps he was taking himself too seriously. He promised Sherman to think about what he said.[48] That evening Grant wrote Julia he would not be coming home after all. "Necessity changes my plans, or the public service does, and I must yield."[49] The next day he wrote Sherman to tell him he would stay. Sherman rejoiced. "You could not be quiet at home for a week when armies were moving."[50] Casual conversations occasionally constitute critical turning points in history. The few words exchanged by Sherman and Grant changed the course of Grant's life and perhaps the Civil War.[51] Grant had rallied Sherman at Shiloh; Sherman came to Grant's rescue at Corinth.

Halleck's decision not to attack Beauregard or pursue him to Tupelo was a near-fatal mistake. The opportunity to deliver a knockout blow was missed and the rebels regained the initiative by default. Four days after taking Corinth, Halleck put the Union army on the defensive. As Old Brains saw it, this was a time to consolidate. "There is no point in bringing on a battle," he informed his wing commanders, "if the object can be obtained without one. I think that by showing a bold front for a day or two the enemy will continue his retreat, which is all that I desire." The Union army would become an army of occupation. "The repair of the railroads is now the great object to be attended to," said Halleck.[52] The early pattern of the war in the West was repeating itself. After Donelson, Union delay allowed Johnston to regroup and consolidate. After Shiloh, Beauregard's defeated army was not pursued, and it was the same story after Corinth. Union commanders were imbued with the importance of consolidating gains, holding territory, and operating on interior lines of communication. Grant was the exception. His instinctive recognition that victory lay in relentlessly hounding a defeated army into surrender had yet to gain a place in Union strategy.

On June 10 Halleck dispersed the army for occupation duty. Buell, with four divisions from the Army of the Ohio, was dispatched along the tracks of the Memphis & Charleston railroad 200 miles east to Chattanooga, instructed to repair the line as he went. Pope's Army of the Mississippi was deployed in front of Corinth to defend the vital rail junction,* while Grant, restored to command of the Army of the Tennessee, was sent west to Memphis, his troops strung out across half a dozen railheads along the Mississippi-Tennessee border.[53] Halleck acknowledged to Stanton that the disposition had a flaw, but did not grasp how serious that flaw might be. "This plan is based on the supposition that the enemy will not attempt an active campaign during the summer months. Should he do so . . . the present dispositions must be varied to suit the change of circumstances."[54]

Grant set out for Memphis on June 21 accompanied by his staff and a dozen troopers for escort. Grant, the best equestrian in the army, preferred to travel the hundred miles on horseback rather than by train, and he arrived two days later, narrowly avoiding capture by Confederate cavalry who had been alerted he was coming.[55] Grant found Memphis "in rather bad order, secessionists governing much in their own way."[56] The population remained adamant in their attachment to the Confederacy. Aside from the problems this created for civil government, local clergymen per-

---

* On June 17, 1862, General Pope was ordered to Washington to replace Frémont in western Virginia. He was succeeded at Corinth by William S. Rosecrans.

sisted in offering prayers each Sunday for the president of the Confederacy. Union officers ordered all references to Jefferson Davis deleted from church services and required that prayers be said for President Lincoln instead. Grant was unwilling to go that far. The day after his arrival his assistant adjutant general announced: "I am directed by Major General Grant to say that you can compel all Clergymen within your lines to omit from their church services any portion you may deem *treasonable,* but you will not compel the insertion or substitution of anything."[57]

Grant was gratified to have his army back, although his relations with Halleck remained awkward. Not strained, not hostile, just awkward. The two men were so unlike it was difficult to communicate. Halleck was sarcastic and Grant unduly sensitive. By the end of June they were trading ripostes. Halleck fired first: "You say thirty thousand rebels are at Shelbyville to attack La Grange or Memphis. Where is Shelbyville? I can't find it on a map. Don't believe a word about an attack in large force on La Grange or Memphis. Why not send out a strong reconnaissance and ascertain the facts. It looks like a mere stampede. Floating rumors are never to be received as facts."[58]

Grant returned the shot. "I did not say 30,000 troops at Shelbyville but at Abbeyville, which is south of Holly Springs, on the road to Grenada. I heed as little of floating rumors as anyone. . . . Stampeding is not my weakness—on the contrary I will always execute any order to the best of my ability with the means at hand."[59]

Halleck let the matter rest. He had not intended to offend Grant, although his words had had that effect. Four days later he apologized. "I made no insinuation that there had been the slightest neglect on *your* part. Nor did I suppose for a moment that *you* were *stampeded,* for I know it is not in your nature." Halleck soothed Grant's ruffled feathers. "I must confess that I was very much surprised at the tone of your dispatch, and the ill feeling manifested in it, so contrary to your usual style, and especially towards one who has so often befriended you when you were attacked by others."[60] The brief set-to reflected no ill will between Grant and Halleck. It was merely a failure to communicate, exacerbated by Grant's fragile self-esteem and Halleck's patronizing manner.[61]

Grant's assignment to Memphis coincided with a shake-up in the Confederate high command. Jefferson Davis, like Halleck, was a places strategist and the loss of Corinth set poorly in Richmond. Failing to recognize that Beauregard's army at Tupelo, reinforced by the recent arrival of Van Dorn's legion from the trans-Mississippi, was ideally positioned to strike the fragmented Union command and roll it up, Davis relieved the Creole commander on June 17 and replaced him with Braxton Bragg. Bragg lacked Beauregard's flair, but he was a thorough professional, a strict disciplinarian,* and was considered a fearsome opponent. The rate of fire of his battery at Buena Vista still stood as a record for muzzle-loading artillery, and at Shiloh he led the final assault on Grant's last line. The Confederate defeat, he wrote, taught a valuable lesson: "Never, on a battlefield, lose a moment's time, but leaving the killed, wounded, and spoils to those whose special business it is to care for them, press on with every available man, giving a panic-stricken and retreating foe no time to rally."[62] Like Grant, Bragg was a fighter, and within a month he was ready to take the offensive.

Meanwhile in the East, the long-awaited Union offensive against Richmond had miscarried. McClellan battled Joseph E. Johnston to a draw at Seven Pines in early June, but on June 25 the Army of Northern Virginia, fighting under Lee for the first time,[†] ripped into Federal forces on the banks of the Chickahominy River. In a series of hard-fought engagements known as the Seven Days' battles (June 25–July 1, 1862), the Confederates forced the Army of the Potomac to retreat down the Virginia peninsula to Harrison's Landing, where Union troops took refuge under the protection of Navy gunboats. McClellan was whipped, Richmond was saved, and Lincoln—at the urging of John Pope, who served as the president's informal military adviser during the crisis—ordered Halleck to Washington to assume the responsibilities of general in chief.[63]

Lincoln's telegram arrived in Corinth July 11. "Your orders are received," Halleck wired the president. "General Grant, next in command, is at Memphis. I have telegraphed to him to immediately repair to this place. I will start for Washington the moment I can have a personal interview with General Grant."[64] Halleck's message to Grant was cryptic. "You will immediately repair to this place [and] report to these headquarters."[65]

Grant had no inkling what was in store. "Am I to bring my staff?" he asked.[66]

"This place will be your headquarters," Halleck replied. "You can judge for yourself."[67]

In his *Memoirs,* Grant was critical of Halleck's failure to inform him why he was being summoned to Corinth.[68] Halleck's abruptness was well established, however, and chattiness was not his command style. More important, the telegraph line from Corinth to Memphis ran for more than a hundred miles through rebel-infested territory. Unlike the command link

---

* Bragg enjoyed the distinction of being the only American officer fragged during the Mexican War, when a disgruntled cannoneer exploded a 12-pound shell under his cot. When the smoke cleared the cot was reduced to kindling, but Bragg emerged without a scratch. Grady McWhiney, 1 *Braxton Bragg and Confederate Defeat* 95–96 (New York: Columbia University Press, 1969).
† Joseph E. Johnston, commanding the Army of Northern Virginia, was seriously wounded during the first day's fighting at Seven Pines and was succeeded by Robert E. Lee, Jefferson Davis's personal military adviser, on June 1, 1862.

to Washington, it was scarcely secure. As Halleck saw it, there was no reason to inform the Confederates of the changeover until it was made.[69]

Grant arrived in Corinth on July 15. The following day Halleck issued Special Field Orders No. 161, which gave Grant the military department embracing north Mississippi, west Tennessee, and Kentucky west of the Cumberland, as well as command of two armies—his own and Pope's old force, now under Rosecrans, "heretofore known as the Army of the Mississippi."[70] Buell's Army of the Ohio, moving laboriously toward Chattanooga, became a separate command. Both Buell and Grant reported directly to Halleck as general in chief. In retrospect this was another serious error on Halleck's part. He may have felt that because of the tension between Grant and Buell it was best for them to operate independently, or (more likely) he may have wanted to keep control of the Western theater in his own hands.[71] But the effect was to divide the army he had assembled into separate commands, deprive it of numerical dominance at a single point of concentration, and allow Bragg to strike each element at times and places of his own choosing. The troops Grant inherited—approximately 80,000 men organized into ten divisions—were dispersed from hell to breakfast in north Mississippi and west Tennessee, incapable of offensive action and barely able to keep the most important rail lines free from rebel marauders. Grant wrote later that "the most anxious period of the war" was during the summer of 1862 when "the Army of the Tennessee was guarding the territory acquired by the fall of Corinth and Memphis and before I was sufficiently reinforced to take the offensive."[72]

Bragg was quick to take advantage of the situation. The question was whether to hit Grant or Buell, and Bragg chose Buell. His plan was to beat the slow-moving Army of the Ohio to Chattanooga, link up with Edmund Kirby Smith, who commanded a Confederate force of 18,000 troops in eastern Tennessee, crush Buell, liberate Nashville, and then move north into Kentucky and menace Cincinnati. "*De l'audace, encore l'audace, et toujours de l'audace*," said Beauregard approvingly when informed of the plan.[73] Bragg left Sterling Price at Tupelo with 16,000 men to protect north Mississippi, sent Van Dorn to Vicksburg with another 16,000, and on July 23 loaded his Shiloh veterans onto cars of the Mobile & Ohio for a circuitous 776-mile rail journey to Chattanooga via Mobile, Montgomery, and Atlanta. The trip involved six separate railroads, some of different gauge, and a ferry ride across Mobile Bay. Nevertheless, lead elements of Bragg's command chugged around Lookout Mountain into Chattanooga on July 29 while Buell was still picking his way through north Alabama, a hundred miles away. Bragg had moved men farther, faster than troops had ever moved before. He had united two Confederate armies, his own and Smith's, and stood poised to reverse the direction of the war.

Grant meanwhile scrambled to concentrate his forces. On July 30 he wired Halleck that Bragg's army was in Chattanooga and that Sterling Price had formed up at Holly Springs, an important commercial center on the Mississippi Central railroad forty miles southwest of Corinth. Grant requested permission to drive Price south.[74] Halleck cut Grant slack with one hand, but reined him in with the other: "You must judge for yourself the best use to be made of your troops [but] be ready to reinforce Buell if necessary."[75] Grant, delighted to be in command once more, did not quibble. He understood what Halleck meant. "We will have to draw in our horns a little," he wrote Rosecrans, "and spread again when we can."[76] This was a more mature Grant than the one who stretched his orders at Belmont and Donelson.

Knowing Halleck as he did, Grant recognized what was in store. George Thomas's division was transferred immediately to Buell, two more divisions were shifted in mid-August, and on September 2 a fourth division was ordered to Louisville. That reduced Grant's strength to 46,000 men—enough to defeat Price and Van Dorn, or Bragg for that matter, but not enough to defend hundreds of miles of railroad, pacify western Tennessee, and thwart rebel guerrillas, particularly with Nathan Bedford Forrest on the loose. Grant, against his instincts, was forced on the defensive.

Bragg, unopposed, moved north from Chattanooga on August 28. At the same time, Kirby Smith left Knoxville, skirted the Cumberland Gap, and marched directly on Lexington, Kentucky. In the East, Lee delivered a knockout blow to John Pope's Federal Army of Virginia at Second Manassas, and on September 4 the Gray Fox crossed the Potomac heading north. Smith took Lexington on September 2, and on September 6 Stonewall Jackson, leading the 2nd Corps of the Army of Northern Virginia, occupied Frederick, Maryland. The following week Jackson's corps captured the United States arsenal at Harpers Ferry, taking 12,000 prisoners and liberating a vast storehouse of Federal equipment. It was ebb tide for the Union. Buell, marching parallel to Bragg's army, had already fallen back to Nashville and was heading retrograde toward Louisville. In effect, central Tennessee had been retaken by the Confederates without firing a shot. At this point Bragg ordered Price to join the advance. "Sherman and Rosecrans we leave to you and Van Dorn, satisfied that you can dispose of them, and we shall confidently expect to meet you on the Ohio."[77]

As was often the case the Confederates counted their chickens too soon. Grant was yet to be reckoned with. In compliance with his orders from Bragg, Sterling Price moved north on September 7 and struck the eastern anchor of Grant's line at Iuka, Mississippi, on September 13. Twenty-odd miles east of Corinth on the Memphis & Charleston line, Iuka was a shipping point for hill country cotton. Price planned to dispose of the small Union garrison, replenish his supplies, and march on to join Bragg in Kentucky. It was a strategic miscalculation of the first magnitude. If Price had moved due east along the Holly Springs–Tupelo axis into Alabama before heading north, he would have avoided Grant's troops and reached Bragg unmolested. Instead, he ran into the left flank of a Union army waiting to pounce. "If Price would remain in Iuka until we could get there, his annihilation was inevitable," said Grant.[78]

Grant wasted no time. He ordered Rosecrans to move from Corinth with two divisions and hit Price from the south. Major General Edward Ord, as able a Union commander as the war produced, was instructed to swing north with another two divisions and assault Iuka from that direction. Rosecrans would attack first and divert Price, at which point Ord would fall on the unprotected rebel rear and render the coup de grâce. The plan was too ambitious. Later in the war Union troops might have accomplished such a maneuver, but not in 1862. Rosecrans was late getting into position, an acoustic shadow (similar to what Grant experienced at Donelson) prevented Ord from hearing the fighting when it began, and Price—a wily old peckerwood—stole away after dark on a road south that Rosecrans neglected to block. Grant had reversed Price's thrust northward and prevented him from joining Bragg, but the Confederates escaped with their forces intact. So ended the battle of Iuka. Rosecrans lost 790 men; Price 535.

Van Dorn meanwhile had come north from Vicksburg and was encamped at Holly Springs. Headstrong, wily, and ambitious, "Coon" Van Dorn was itching to join the Confederate advance. Ordering Price to join him at the north Mississippi hamlet of Ripley, he proposed to press north along the Hatchie River until they reached the Memphis & Charleston at Pocahontas, turn east and strike Rosecrans at Corinth before help could arrive. The plan was as daring as Bragg's move into Kentucky or Lee's crossing the Potomac. Corinth was the centerpiece of Grant's position. Once cracked, the Union army would be vulnerable to defeat in detail. Rosecrans had four divisions defending the rail junction, roughly 20,000 men. Between them, Van Dorn and Price had 22,000. "No army ever marched to battle with prouder steps, more hopeful countenance, or with more courage," said Van Dorn as his troops moved out.[79]

On October 3 the Confederates struck Corinth with full fury. Rosecrans, who had spent four years at West Point with Van Dorn, was ready and waiting, his troops dug in behind a formidable double line of entrenchments. Considering the relatively small size of the forces engaged, the battle of Corinth was one of the fiercest of the war. By mid-afternoon the Southerners had penetrated two miles but were bogged down before Rosecrans's inner defense line. Federal artillery took a deadly toll, while the unseasonable 94 degree heat wilted defenders and attackers alike. The next morning Van Dorn renewed his assault into the face of the Union guns. "Our lines melted under their fire like snow in a thaw," a rebel officer recalled.[80] Rosecrans counterattacked at noon and the exhausted Confederates gave way. By one o'clock Van Dorn was in full retreat. Southern losses were staggering. Of the 22,000 rebel troops engaged, 5,000 were killed, wounded, or missing. Rosecrans lost 2,000. Price wept as he watched his thinned ranks withdraw, the men desperately aware they had suffered a crushing defeat.

Grant ordered Rosecrans to pursue the retreating Confederates and sent Ord and McPherson to assist. Ord blocked Van Dorn on the Hatchie, but Rosecrans was once again slow off the mark and the Southerners made good their escape after losing another 600 men. Although Grant failed to destroy the rebel army, the Corinth campaign proved to be the last Confederate offensive in the Mississippi theater. Van Dorn and Price had been thwarted in their attempt to move north, and with reinforcements arriving daily, the initiative reverted to Grant.

The tide turned elsewhere as well. On September 17, 1862, Lee's veteran soldiers slammed into McClellan's vastly expanded Army of the Potomac along Antietam Creek near the sleepy Maryland village of Sharpsburg. Outnumbered two to one, the Confederates fought the enemy to a standstill in one of the bloodiest battles of the war.* But the rebel invasion of the Northern heartland was defeated. Lee withdrew his battered army and recrossed the Potomac heading south, relieving the threat to Harrisburg, Baltimore, and Washington.

In Kentucky, Don Carlos Buell, prodded into action by Lincoln and Halleck, met Bragg sixty miles southeast of Louisville along a ridgeline near Perryville. Buell brought eight seasoned divisions to the encounter; Bragg, who had divided his army, could muster only three. Yet the North Carolinian concentrated his troops, attacked boldly, and almost carried the day. Later Bragg wrote that "for the time engaged, it was the severest and most desperately contested engagement within my knowledge."[81] But like Lee's thrust into Maryland, the Confederate invasion of Kentucky had run out of steam. What had been heralded as a full-scale offensive to establish the northern border of the Confederacy along the Ohio River petered out as Bragg (to the consternation of his subordinates) ordered his army back to Tennessee.[82]

---

* Exact figures are elusive. Most estimates suggest McClellan brought approximately 75,000 men to the field, of whom 13,000 were killed, wounded, or captured. Lee's force numbered approximately 40,000 and suffered about 10,500 casualties. Combined losses at Antietam were four times greater than those suffered by American troops on the beaches of Normandy on D-Day. James M. McPherson, *Battle Cry of Freedom* 544 (New York: Oxford University Press, 1988).

Lincoln, who now despaired of bringing the South back into the Union short of total victory, seized on McClellan's limited success at Antietam to issue a preliminary emancipation proclamation, utilizing his war powers as commander in chief to announce the freedom, effective January 1, 1863, of "all persons held as slaves within any State or designated part of a State, the people whereof shall then be in rebellion against the United States."[83] The president emphasized that reunion, not abolition, was still the object of the war. Loyal slave owners would be compensated for their loss, and the rebels had three months to make up their minds. Two days later, September 24, 1862, Lincoln suspended the writ of habeas corpus throughout the United States—a draconian war measure that he believed essential to the preservation of the Union. The president acted pursuant to congressional authorization, but it was clear that civil liberties, like emancipation, took a back seat to saving the Union.* "Are all the laws, *but one* [the right to habeas corpus], to go unexecuted, and the government itself go to pieces, lest that one be violated?" Lincoln asked.[84]

Grant took heart from the victories of Buell and McClellan and immediately laid plans to capture Vicksburg. Two weeks after Corinth, he wired Halleck that in the absence of any instructions from Washington he proposed to abandon the railheads he occupied, concentrate his forces in northern Mississippi, and assume the offensive. Grant said that with a few reinforcements from Memphis, "I think I would be able to move down the Mississippi Central [Rail]road and cause the evacuation of Vicksburg and be able to capture or destroy all the boats in the Yazoo River."[85] After waiting a week, during which time Halleck made no reply, Grant put his plan

* Article I, Section 9, of the Constitution provides that "The privilege of the Writ of Habeas Corpus shall not be suspended, unless when in Cases of Rebellion or Invasion the public Safety may require it." But the clause fails to specify who, or which branch of government, shall make that decision. Chief Justice Marshall, speaking for the Supreme Court in *Ex parte Bollman,* 4 Cranch 75, 101 (1807), asserted by way of dictum that the responsibility lay with Congress, but the text of the Constitution is ambiguous. Accordingly, on April 27, 1861, President Lincoln, confronted with disorder along the Philadelphia–Washington corridor, acted unilaterally to suspend the writ in that area, thus permitting military authorities to make summary arrests of persons believed to be aiding the Confederacy. The measure was of limited scope, but led to the finding of Chief Justice Taney (on circuit) in *Ex parte Merryman,* 17 Fed. Cas. 144 (No. 9487) (C.C.D. Md. 1861), that the president's action was invalid. Lincoln ignored Taney's ruling, but public reaction was such that the president, in his message to Congress of July 4, 1861, asked for specific authorization to suspend the writ. Congress complied almost instantly (12 Stat. 755), and on September 24, 1862, Lincoln acted, providing for military trial of "all Rebels and Insurgents, their aiders and abettors within the United States, and all persons discouraging volunteer enlistments, resisting militia drafts, or guilty of any disloyal practice, affording comfort to the Rebels against the authority of the United States." See *Ex parte Vallandigham,* 1 Wallace 243 (1863), cf. *Ex parte Milligan,* 4 Wallace 2 (1866). Also see George Clarke Sellery, "Lincoln's Suspension of *Habeas Corpus* as Viewed by Congress." 1 *Bulletin of the University of Wisconsin* 213 (1907).

in motion. On November 2, 1862, he informed the War Department that he was moving against Grand Junction—the intersection of the Memphis & Charleston and the Mississippi Central lines—with five divisions. "Will leave here [Jackson, Tennessee] tomorrow evening and take command in person." Grant said he then planned to attack the rebel base at Holly Springs and push on to Grenada, Mississippi.[86] For Washington, it was a pleasant surprise. Halleck had not anticipated that Grant would act so swiftly, but once it became clear that the Army of the Tennessee was on the move, he not only wired his support but said that reinforcements would be immediately forthcoming. "I hope for an active campaign on the Mississippi this fall."[87]

Grant's alacrity in moving against the enemy in the autumn of 1862 contrasts sharply with the caution displayed by McClellan and Buell following their victories at Antietam and Perryville. It took McClellan six weeks to cross the Potomac at Sharpsburg, and by then Lee was safely back in front of Richmond. In Kentucky, Buell showed no inclination to pursue Bragg's retreating army and insisted instead on returning to Nashville. After repeated warnings from Halleck to take action or else, Buell was relieved of command of the Army of the Ohio (redesignated the Army of the Cumberland) on October 24 and replaced by Rosecrans. McClellan, who was equally obdurate to entreaties to attack, was removed on November 7. As one historian has written, "The guillotine had fallen on two of the foremost exponents of limited, cautious, gentlemanly warfare."[88] Of the three Union commanders who had stemmed the rebel tide in 1862, only Grant remained. And Grant, who now enjoyed the confidence of the War Department, could scarcely be described as a devotee of limited warfare.

The Vicksburg campaign opened auspiciously. Grant took Holly Springs against token resistance on November 13, and by early December he had occupied Oxford, Mississippi, accumulated a mountain of supplies, and was ready to begin his advance. With 40,000 men, Grant planned to move southward along the Mississippi Central Railroad, take the capital city of Jackson, sever Vicksburg's rail link with the eastern Confederacy, and then turn west and assault the river bastion. Sherman, with another 33,000 men, would descend the Mississippi River from Memphis and join the assault.[89] Confronting Grant, Lieutenant General John C. Pemberton was entrenched with an army of 25,000 men along the Yalobusha River at Grenada, an important rail junction on the Mississippi Central, 100 miles north of Jackson and Vicksburg. Another 25,000 Confederates manned the battlements at Vicksburg and the downriver fortress of Port Hudson.

The forty-eight-year-old Pemberton, a native of Philadelphia married to a Virginian, was one of the few Northern-born regular army officers to side with the South. Grant, who knew Pemberton from Mexico, once sympathetically described him as "a northern man who had got into bad company." [90] Promoted rapidly by the Confederacy, Pemberton had been recently assigned by Jefferson Davis—to the consternation of most Mississippians—to defend Vicksburg, superseding Van Dorn and Price, who remained under his command. A classmate of Bragg's at West Point, Pemberton's abrasive self-assurance had already made him persona non grata in Charleston, his previous assignment, but Davis hoped that it was precisely that combination of certitude and inflexibility that could hold Vicksburg against Grant's onslaught.

Grant, for his part, was energized by rumors, soon confirmed, that the second-ranking officer in his command, Major General John McClernand, was back in Illinois raising volunteers for an independent assault on Vicksburg. In one of the more bizarre episodes of the Civil War, McClernand, a prominent Illinois lawyer, Democratic member of Congress, and close friend of Lincoln's, took leave of Grant in early autumn and journeyed to Washington to see the president and another old friend, Secretary of War Edwin Stanton. Fueled by dreams of military glory and critical of Grant's ability to command, the politically ambitious McClernand persuaded Lincoln that he could rekindle the patriotism of Democrats in the old Northwest Territory if given the opportunity to raise a new army of volunteers, descend the Mississippi, capture Vicksburg, and "open navigation to New Orleans." [91] Without informing Grant, Lincoln approved the scheme. McClernand left Washington in late October armed with a confidential order dictated by the president authorizing him to proceed to the Middle West and raise a separate force to capture Vicksburg. Halleck protested the arrangement and at the last minute convinced Lincoln to insert language in McClernand's instructions that made whatever troops he raised subject to the general in chief's orders "according to such exigencies as the service . . . may require." [92]

Halleck was not about to have an independent command operating in Grant's department. [93] As Halleck saw it, it was not merely a matter of correct military organization. Grant was a professional soldier who could be relied upon. McClernand was a political loose cannon. Accordingly, Halleck set about to cut his troops from under him. As soon as McClernand raised a new regiment, Halleck ordered it to Memphis, where it reported to Grant. Historians have stressed the tension between Halleck and Grant, but in this instance they worked together seamlessly. Halleck played his cards close to his chest. Without mentioning McClernand, he told Grant in early November that Memphis would be the depot for a joint army and navy expedition against Vicksburg. [94] Grant was equally circumspect. He had heard rumors of what McClernand was up to and asked Halleck whether he was to go ahead with his plans to move south, or should he wait until the new expedition was fitted out. Specifically, Grant asked if Sherman, at Memphis, was still under his command or "reserved for some special service."[95] Halleck's response was probably more than Grant hoped for: "You have command of all troops sent to your Department, and have permission to fight the enemy when you please."[96]

That was all Grant needed. His immediate problem was that McClernand ranked Sherman. If Grant delayed moving south, McClernand would return to Memphis and take command of the river expedition regardless.[97] Grant moved quickly. On December 8 he ordered Sherman to take charge of all troops on the Mississippi. "Move with them as soon as possible down the river to the vicinity of Vicksburg, and with the cooperation of the gunboat fleet under command of Flag-officer [David D.] Porter [the brother of "Dirty Bill" Porter], proceed to the reduction of that place in such manner as circumstances, and your own judgment, may dictate."[98] The following day Grant wired Halleck that he had received a letter from McClernand stating that he would be leaving Illinois for Memphis shortly. "Sherman has already gone," said Grant.[99]

It is impossible to know what Grant and Halleck felt at that moment. Halleck's biographer notes that the general in chief "had taken the responsibility of meeting intrigue with intrigue and may have enjoyed the resulting farce."[100] Grant said at the time that McClernand was "unmanageable and incompetent."[101] Later he wrote, "I had good reason to believe that by forestalling him I was by no means giving offence to those whose authority to command was above both him and me."[102] The point was that Grant and Sherman were on their way to Vicksburg.

It was not clear sailing. On December 10 Nathan Bedford Forrest, the most dangerous of Confederate cavalrymen, rode westward from central Tennessee with 1,800 troopers to wreak havoc in Grant's rear areas. Picking up recruits along the way, Forrest, in a three-week campaign, outmaneuvered, outfought, and outwitted a Union force ten times his size. He severed Grant's principal supply line north of Jackson, Tennessee; destroyed fifty miles of Mobile & Ohio track so effectively that that portion of the road was out of commission for the rest of the war; cut telegraph lines with such abandon that Grant was unable to communicate with much of his command for over a week; and captured or destroyed vast quantities of Federal food and equipment, including 10,000 rifles and over a million rounds of ammunition. When he withdrew on New Year's Day, Forrest had inflicted 2,500 Union casualties and established a reputation for daring that never waned. Forrest, in fact, became the one Confederate horse soldier Grant dreaded because, as an aide remarked, "he was amenable to no known rules of procedure, was a law unto himself for all military acts, and was constantly doing the unexpected at all times and places."[103]

While Forrest was tearing up western Tennessee, Earl Van Dorn was striking Grant's midsection. With another 3,500 cavalrymen, Van Dorn rode northeast from Grenada on December 18, circled around the Union left, slipped past a force sent to intercept him, and fell upon Grant's Holly Springs depot at dawn on the 20th. Although the post commander had been warned of Van Dorn's approach, no preparations were made to receive him and the Union garrison was taken by surprise. Holly Springs was the field equivalent of the Federal arsenal at Harpers Ferry—a massive supply base stacked with food, forage, and ammunition to sustain Grant's advance. Van Dorn's troopers had a field day burning what could not be carried off, and taking 1,500 prisoners.[104] Moving north from Holly Springs, Van Dorn tore up several sections of the Memphis & Charleston Railroad before returning safely to Grenada the following week. Grant, who believed the garrison at Holly Springs had been more than adequate to defend the base, was mortified. His plans to move overland against Vicksburg had gone up in smoke. Pemberton was pulling back from the Yalobusha, but Grant saw no possibility of pursuing him. Van Dorn had destroyed the supplies he had stockpiled, and Forrest had made it impossible for him to bring up more. Grant called off his overland move against Vicksburg and ordered a withdrawal, sending his main body back to Grand Junction, Tennessee. Deprived of resupply, the army lived off the countryside. "I was amazed at the quantity of supplies the country afforded," Grant said later. "We could have subsisted off the country for two months instead of two weeks. . . . This taught me a lesson."[105] Grant would apply that lesson with spectacular results shortly, but just now his retreat left Sherman's river expedition against Vicksburg dangerously exposed.

When Grant pulled back, Sherman was already downriver. He planned to arrive at Vicksburg by Christmas and quickly overrun what he thought would be the city's lightly manned defenses.[106] That was based on the assumption that Grant would keep the bulk of Pemberton's army pinned on the Yalobusha. Thanks to Van Dorn and Forrest, however, the telegraph lines were down and Sherman was unaware Grant had withdrawn. As a result, the river expedition ran into more than they bargained for. Pemberton rushed troops from Grenada to man the battlements at Vicksburg, and when Sherman's troops went ashore the Confederates were ready and waiting. On the morning of December 29 Sherman launched four divisions in a frontal assault against rebel defenses on the Chickasaw Bluffs north of the city and the carnage was severe. Within two hours Sherman lost 1,800 men. At noon he called it quits. "Our loss has been heavy," he wrote later, "and we accomplished nothing."[107] The second prong of Grant's winter offensive against Vicksburg had been repulsed.

Sherman reembarked his task force on the boats that had brought them and headed back upriver.

December 1862 was the low point of Grant's Civil War career. In addition to his own and Sherman's aborted attempts to take Vicksburg, on December 17 Grant issued an order that would stain his reputation forever. In one of the most blatant examples of state-sponsored anti-Semitism in American history, Grant expelled all members of the Jewish faith from the Department of the Tennessee.[108] The order was rooted in the illicit cotton trade along the Mississippi, which Grant had been unsuccessful in stamping out. Cut off from foreign markets by the Union blockade, Southern producers found ready purchasers for their cotton in the legion of Yankee speculators who followed the army. Often these speculators worked surreptitiously with Grant's troops, creating a serious disciplinary problem. As a War Department agent reported to Washington, "Every colonel, captain, or quartermaster is in secret partnership with some operator in cotton; every soldier dreams of adding a bale of cotton to his monthly pay."[109] To complicate matters further, Grant received contradictory instructions as to how to handle the cotton trade. The Treasury Department wanted to restore business with occupied areas to win back the inhabitants' loyalty. But the War Department worried that Southern profits from cotton sales might reach Confederate hands and prolong the war. As a compromise, trade was permitted so long as the traders held permits, did not cross into enemy territory, and did not trade in gold.[110] Grant found the rules impossible to enforce, and so as he moved south he attempted to prevent cotton traders from moving with the army.

Although most of the traders were not Jewish, several of the most visible were.[111] Grant gave vent to his displeasure November 9, instructing General Hurlbut to refuse all permits to cotton merchants who sought to go south of Jackson, Tennessee. "The Israelites especially should be kept out."[112] The next day he told Colonel Joseph D. Webster, who commanded the railroads: "Give orders to all the conductors on the road that no Jews are to be permitted to travel on the railroad south from any point. They may go north and be encouraged in it; but they are such an intolerable nuisance that the department must be purged of them."[113] Still frustrated by his inability to control the illicit trade, Grant wrote Sherman that "in consequence of the total disregard and evasion of orders by the Jews my policy is to exclude them so far as practicable from the Department."[114] On December 17 he made the policy official. General Orders No. 11, published for the guidance of the whole department, read as follows:

> The Jews, as a class, violating every regulation of trade established by the Treasury Department, and also Department orders, are hereby expelled from the Department.

Within twenty-four hours from the receipt of this order by Post Commanders, they will see that all of this class of people are furnished with passes and required to leave, and anyone remaining after such notification, will be arrested and held in confinement until an opportunity occurs of sending them out as prisoners unless furnished with permits from these headquarters.[115]

Apologists for Grant have suggested that the order was issued by staff officers without Grant's knowledge;[116] that it was issued pursuant to instructions from Washington;[117] or that the word "Jew" was used in a shorthand way of describing anyone considered shrewd, acquisitive, aggressive, and possibly dishonest.[118]

None of this is true. Grant's adjutant, Colonel John Rawlins, argued strenuously against the order. The record suggests that it was dictated personally by Grant and issued over Rawlins's protest. "They can countermand this from Washington if they like," Grant is reported to have said.[119] There is also no record in the extensive files of the War Department of any instructions authorizing or encouraging General Orders No. 11.[120] It is conceivable that Grant may have been using the terms "Jew" and "cotton trader" interchangeably, but that too is unlikely. Grant understood nuanced distinctions and he used the English language as precisely as any military commander before or since. More important, however, the sentiment expressed in General Orders No. 11 is consistent with a streak of nativism that ran deep in Grant.[121] Xenophobia and anti-Semitism were prevalent throughout the United States in the 1860s, particularly in the army, and Grant shared the prevailing prejudices.[122]

In any case, General Orders No. 11 had a short life. Newspapers throughout the country were quick in their condemnation. The *New York Times,* which normally supported Grant, led the way. "It is a humiliating reflection," said the *Times,* "that after the progress of liberal ideas even in the most despotic countries has restored the Jews to civil and social rights . . . it remained for the freest Government on earth to witness a momentary revival of the spirit of the medieval age."[123] Lincoln, when informed of the order, insisted upon its immediate revocation.* Halleck notified Grant

---

* General Orders No. 11 was brought to the president's attention by Cesar J. Kaskel of Paducah, Kentucky, who led a special delegation to Washington for that purpose. After explaining the matter, Kaskel reports the dialogue as follows:

LINCOLN: And so the children of Israel were driven from the happy land of Canaan?

KASKEL: Yes, and that is why we have come unto Father Abraham's bosom, asking protection.

LINCOLN: And this protection they shall have at once.

Bertram Wallace Korn, *American Jewry and the Civil War* 125 (Philadelphia: Jewish Publication Society of America, 1951).

of the president's decision, but he did so with respect bordering on deference: "A paper *purporting* to be General Orders No. 11, issued by you December 17, has been presented here. By its terms, it expels all Jews from your department. *If such an order has been issued,* it will be immediately revoked."[124] Whether Halleck was handling Grant with kid gloves, or whether he may have agreed with the order is unclear. Later he wrote Grant a sympathetic letter giving him the benefit of the doubt. "The President," said Halleck, "has no objection to your expelling traders and Jew pedlars, *which I suppose was the object of your order,* but [because] it prescribed an entire class, some of whom are fighting in our ranks, the President deemed it necessary to revoke it."[125] Reaction in Congress divided along party lines. Democratic efforts to censure Grant failed by the narrowest of margins in the House, 53–56, but by a lopsided 7–30 in the Republican-dominated Senate.[126] Grant revoked the order on January 6, 1863, but he mustered little grace in doing so and made it clear that he was complying with instructions from Washington.[127]

To add to Grant's problems in the winter of 1862, McClernand returned from his recruiting expedition, went downriver, and assumed command of Sherman's force steaming back from Vicksburg. McClernand was still under the impression that he had been empowered by the president to command an independent Mississippi River offensive. He restyled Sherman's four-division task force the Army of the Mississippi, designated Sherman to be one of two corps commanders, and undertook to "reinspire" the troops by leading them against the small Confederate garrison at Arkansas Post, some forty miles up the Arkansas River. "General McClernand has fallen back to White River, and gone on a wild-goose chase to the Post of Arkansas," Grant wired Halleck on January 11.[128] "I am ready to reinforce, but must await further information before I know what to do." Halleck replied promptly. "You are hereby authorized to relieve General McClernand from command of the expedition against Vicksburg, giving it to the next in rank or taking it yourself."[129]

For Grant, Halleck's telegram was a godsend. Because of the close relationship between Lincoln and McClernand, and because McClernand carried a personal letter of authorization from the president, Grant had been uncertain how to handle him. Halleck's message cleared the air. The following day Grant informed McPherson, whose corps was back in Tennessee after the retreat from the Yalobusha, that he intended to take command of the expedition down the river in person.[130] The assault on Vicksburg would consist of a single thrust. The overland drive down the Mississippi Central would be abandoned. In this instance personnel considerations dictated Union strategy. Grant doubted McClernand's ability and distrusted his ambition. So did Sherman and Admiral Porter.[131] Grant said later that he "would have been glad to have put Sherman in command of an independent drive down the Mississippi," but since he was junior to McClernand, there was no alternative but to assume command himself.[132]

Having made his decision, Grant hastened to Young's Point, Louisiana, where the river force was assembled. On January 30, 1863, he issued General Orders No. 13 assuming command. As he would do throughout the war, Grant said department headquarters "will hereafter be with the expedition."[133] The commanding general would be in the field. More important, McClernand had been superseded. Obviously stunned by Grant's presence, he filed an immediate reclama, recounting how he had been invested "by special order of the President . . . with the command of all forces operating on the Mississippi river." McClernand demanded the question be referred to Washington immediately, "and one or the other, or both of us, relieved. One thing is certain, two generals cannot command this army"[134]

Grant's reply was blunt. He told McClernand that he was taking direct command of the expedition against Vicksburg, "which necessarily limits your command to the 13th Army Corps." Grant said he was not aware of any order from Washington "to prevent my taking immediate command in the field." To the contrary, Grant said he had received specific instructions from Halleck to do so if he believed it necessary.[135] Once again McClernand insisted the issue be referred to Lincoln,[136] and Grant willingly complied. In forwarding McClernand's complaint to Washington, he told Halleck that if the president ruled in McClernand's favor, "I will cheerfully submit . . . and give a hearty support."[137] Grant assumed, however, that he had Lincoln's backing and he was not disappointed. If given the choice between supporting his fellow townsman or the one Union general who would fight, the president clearly preferred the latter. "Don't engage in an open war" with the army high command, Lincoln cautioned McClernand. The president said he already had "too many FAMILY controversies" to enter another. McClernand was told to devote his attention to winning the war in whatever position he might be assigned by the War Department.[138]

After displacing McClernand, Grant confronted the task of taking Vicksburg. Union morale was sagging, anti-war Democrats had gained in the midterm elections, and without a quick victory the days of the Lincoln administration appeared numbered. Recruiting had already dried up, the army depended on the draft for replacements, and desertions were approaching an all-time high.[139] Grant's headquarters at Young's Point was less than ten miles in a direct line from Vicksburg. Yet as he surveyed the swampy morass that led to the Chickasaw Bluffs, much of which would be underwater for months to come, he recognized that he had abandoned the high ground along the Mississippi Central too quickly. He could not, however, retrace his steps to the Yalobusha. Grant said that to move back from Vicksburg and start over "would be interpreted as a defeat. There was nothing left to be done but go forward." [140] Since Sherman had already proved that a head-on attack up the face of the bluffs could not succeed, the question for Grant was how to get beyond Vicksburg and assault the rebel position from the high ground south and east of the city.

For the next ten weeks Grant busied himself with a variety of halfbaked schemes to divert the Mississippi from its main channel and provide an alternate water route to flank Vicksburg's defenses. In his *Memoirs,* Grant called the measures a series of experiments designed to consume time, divert the attention of the enemy, keep the troops busy until the ground hardened in spring, and convince the Northern public that the army was moving forward. [141] Grant said he "never felt great confidence" that any of the experiments would succeed, but he had always been ready "to take advantage of them if they did." First, Sherman's corps was set to digging a canal across the base of a tongue of land in front of Vicksburg to allow union vessels to move south of the city without coming under fire from Confederate artillery on the bluffs. Lincoln, who was familiar with the Mississippi from his youth, was enthusiastic about the project, but it was hopeless from the beginning. "If the river rises 8 feet more we will have to take to the trees," said Sherman, and it soon did just that. [142] A second project involved creating a ship channel from Lake Providence, fifty miles above Vicksburg, through a series of Louisiana swamps and bayous to the Black River, the Red River, and back to the Mississippi 150 miles below Vicksburg. McPherson's corps was harnessed to the task, but the project was too ambitious and Grant lacked enough shallow-draft boats to move his army even if a channel had been reamed through. "I let the work go on," Grant wrote, "believing employment was better than idleness for the men." [143]

Grant's third experiment involved blowing the levee at Yazoo Pass, Mississippi, 200 miles north of Vicksburg. The resulting flood, it was anticipated, would raise the level of delta rivers sufficiently to allow gunboats and transports to proceed down the Tallahatchie to the Yazoo and hit Vicksburg from behind. The rivers indeed flooded, and in early March a naval flotilla headed down the Tallahatchie into the heart of rebel territory. The Confederates blocked the channel with a sunken steamer, constructed a hasty fort near Greenwood, Mississippi, and entrusted the defense of the fort to Brigadier General Lloyd Tilghman, who was determined to restore his reputation, having surrendered Fort Henry to Grant the year before. Outnumbered and outgunned, Tilghman handled his artillery masterfully. The Union ironclads backed off, the flotilla commander collapsed with a nervous breakdown, and another "experiment" went for naught.

Grant's fourth effort to turn the Confederate position flowed literally from the third. The cut in the levee at Yazoo Pass had flooded the delta to such an extent that Admiral Porter believed he could navigate the swamps and bayous around Vicksburg with his ironclads and convey Grant's troops inland unopposed. After cruising the area with Porter, Grant ordered Sherman to embark a division for what became known as the Steel Bayou expedition. It too failed miserably. Porter found his iron monsters surrounded by rebel riflemen in the narrow bayous, sent an urgent message to Sherman for help, and quickly called off the exercise. "I never knew how helpless an ironclad could be steaming around through the woods without an army to back it up," said Porter.[144]

It was now late March and Grant was no closer to taking Vicksburg than when he assumed command in January. Casting about for another ploy, he put McClernand's corps to digging a second canal, departing from the Mississippi at Duckport, just above Young's Point. When completed, the cut would give light-draft vessels access to Roundabout Bayou, which flowed back into the Mississippi at New Carthage, thirty-five miles downstream from Vicksburg. The project depended on continued high water, whereupon the Mississippi, perverse to the ways of man, began to fall, leaving Grant with another failed experiment.

Counting his own and Sherman's unsuccessful efforts to take Vicksburg in December, Grant had made seven attempts to dislodge Pemberton, who was now more firmly entrenched than ever. To add to Grant's winter misery, he lost his teeth in mid-February and had to go without dentures for almost a month. Grant wrote Julia that contrary to his usual habit he had taken his teeth out when he went to bed, put them in a washbasin and covered them with water. "The servant who attends my stateroom [on Grant's headquarters vessel, the *Magnolia*] came in about daylight and finding water in the basin threw it out into the river teeth and all."[145]

Public opinion also turned against Grant, abetted by grumbling from the occasional officer with too much time on his hands. Brigadier General Cadwallader Washburn, an officer in McPherson's corps, wrote to his brother Elihu,* who was Grant's chief congressional supporter, that the Vicksburg campaign was being badly managed. "All Grant's schemes have failed. He is frittering away time and strength to no purpose. The truth must be told even if it hurts. You cannot make a silk purse out of a sow's ear."[146] The perennially gloomy *New York World* remarked archly that "we have the best of reasons for believing that neither the generals in command of our land forces there nor their superiors at Washington expect or hope

---

* Elihu added an "e" to his last name. His brothers spelled their last names without an "e."

to take Vicksburg this year."[147] Joseph Medill, editor of the *Chicago Tribune,* thought an armistice was inevitable. "If Vicksburg cannot be conquered, the South has won the war."[148] Marat Halstead, editor of the *Cincinnati Commercial,* expressed his concern to an Ohio friend, Salmon P. Chase, secretary of the treasury. Grant, wrote Halstead, was "a jackass in the original package. He is a poor drunken imbecile. He is a poor stick sober, and he is most of the time more than half drunk, and much of the time idiotically drunk."[149] Chase passed the letter to Lincoln, noting that "Reports concerning General Grant similar to the statements made by Mr. Halstead are too common to be safely or even prudently disregarded." The president was unimpressed. "I think Grant has hardly a friend left, except myself," said Lincoln. "What I want, and what the people want, is generals who will fight battles and win victories. Grant has done this and I propose to stand by him."[150]

Chaplain John Eaton, who supervised the resettlement of freed slaves for Grant, saw Lincoln a short time later. Eaton reported that the president told him that a delegation of congressmen had come to the White House recently to urge that Grant be relieved because he drank too much. According to Eaton, Lincoln said: "I then began to ask them if they knew what he drank, what brand of whiskey he used, telling them seriously that I wished they could find out. They conferred with each other and concluded they could not tell what brand he used. I urged them to ascertain and let me know, for if it made fighting generals like Grant, I should like to get some of it for distribution."[151]

Did Grant drink? Had he revisited old habits? The evidence is overwhelming that during the Vicksburg campaign he occasionally fell off the wagon.[152] Grant was a binge drinker. In a clinical sense, he may have been an alcoholic.[153] He could go for months without a drink, but once he started it was difficult for him to stop. Assistant Secretary of War Charles Dana, who was sent by Stanton to keep an eye on Grant, said "General Grant's seasons of intoxication were not only infrequent, occurring once in three or four months, but he always chose a time when the gratification of his appetite for drink would not interfere with any important movement that had to be directed or attended to by him." Grant's favorite device was to commandeer a steamer for an overnight excursion. On one such occasion Dana reports Grant "getting as stupidly drunk as the immortal nature of man would allow; but the next day he came out fresh as a rose, without any trace or indication of the spree he had passed through."[154]

For the most part Grant remained sober, protected from alcohol by his adjutant, Colonel John Rawlins, and especially by Julia. "If she is with him all will be well and I can be spared," said Rawlins.[155] During the Civil War, senior officers were often accompanied by their wives during the lulls between battles, and Julia had joined Grant briefly after Belmont. She returned again when he was in Oxford and Holly Springs, but was not present during the dreary winter months before Vicksburg. As a result, Rawlins had his hands full. Rawlins's father was an alcoholic, and he saw in Grant another potential victim whom he must save. He did not pull his punches. Writing to Grant after one debauch, Rawlins said: "The great solicitude I feel for the safety of this army leads me to mention what I had hoped never again to do—the subject of your drinking. . . . I have heard that Dr. McMillan, at General Sherman's a few days ago, induced you . . . to take a glass of wine, and today, I found a case of wine in front of your tent, and tonight, when you should have been in bed, I find you where the wine bottle has just been emptied, in company of those who drink and urge you to do likewise. [The] lack of your usual promptness of decision and clearness in expressing yourself in writing tend to confirm my suspicions." Rawlins told Grant that unless he ceased drinking immediately, "no matter by whom asked or under what circumstances, let my immediate relief from duty in this department be the result."[156] Rawlins remained with Grant throughout the war, and followed him to Washington, where he served faithfully until his death from tuberculosis in 1869. Grant periodically backslid and went on a bender, but thanks to Rawlins's vigilance such episodes were few and far between. As a journalist who covered Grant's campaigns wrote: "It can be safely asserted that no officer or civilian ever saw any open drinking at General Grant's headquarters from Cairo to Appomattox. This was wholly and solely the result of Rawlins' uncompromising attitude, and Grant's acquiescence in what he knew to be for his own good."[157]

Stymied in the shadow of Vicksburg, Grant had critics aplenty although the troops he commanded were not among them. A reporter for the *New York World* wrote that despite the repeated setbacks, "General Grant still retains his hold upon the affections of his men." They admire "his energy and disposition to do something." There are "no Napoleonic displays, no ostentation, no speed, no superfluous flummery."[158] An Illinois private put it best when he said the army trusted Grant. "Everything that Grant directs is right. His soldiers believe in him. In our private talk among ourselves I have never heard a single soldier speak in doubt of Grant."[159] Above all, the troops appreciated Grant's unassuming manner. Most generals went about attended by a retinue of immaculately tailored staff officers. Grant usually rode alone, except for an orderly or two to carry messages if the need arose. Another soldier said the men looked on Grant "as a friendly partner, not an arbitrary commander." Instead of cheering as he rode by, they would "greet him as they would address one of their neighbors at home. 'Good morning, General,' 'Pleasant day, General'. . . . There was no nonsense, no sentiment; only a plain businessman of the republic, there for the one single purpose of getting that command over the river in the shortest time possible."[160]

A doctor on McPherson's staff wrote that Grant was "plain as an old shoe," and said it was hard to make new recruits believe that this man in a common soldier's blouse with old cavalry pants stuffed in muddy boots was really the commanding general.[161] Grant's style reflected conscious choice, not lassitude. Sherman commented on his casual intensity. Grant, he said, was a man who let nothing slip by. "He remembered the most minute details and watched every point."[162] An enlisted man noted that Grant knew every regiment "and in fact every cannon. He will ride along the long line of the army, apparently an indifferent observer, yet he sees and notices everything."[163] A veteran of the Mexican War, had one been present, would have recognized Zachary Taylor's mannerisms immediately. Grant even took to wearing a Tayloresque linen duster and a battered civilian hat over his uniform.[164] And like Old Zack, his conversation with aides and associates revolved around horses and farming rather than the business at hand.[165]

Charles Dana's capsule sketch of Grant captures the essence of the little man from Galena who moved so effortlessly among his troops. Grant, he wrote, was "the most modest, the most disinterested and the most honest man" he ever knew. He had a temperament "nothing could disturb and a judgment that was judicial in its comprehensiveness and wisdom. Not an original or brilliant man, but sincere, thoughtful, deep and gifted with a courage that never faltered. When the time came to risk all, he went in like a simple-hearted, unaffected, unpretending hero, whom no ill omens could deject and no triumph unduly exalt."[166]

Grant's moral courage—his willingness to choose a path from which there could be no return—set him apart from most commanders. Lee, of course, shared this attribute, and both men were uniquely willing to take full responsibility for their actions. Writing years later, Grant explained his attitude toward command. With wry modesty he allowed as how he would have given anything to command a brigade of cavalry in the Army of the Potomac. But the president chose the nation's commanders, and Grant believed that one served where he was assigned, "without application or the use of influence to change his position." Having been selected to command the Army of the Tennessee, Grant said his responsibility ended with doing the best he knew how:

> If I had sought the place, or obtained it through personal or political influence, my belief is that I would have feared to undertake any plan of my own conception, and would probably have

awaited direct orders from my distant superiors. Persons obtaining important commands by application or political influence are apt to keep a written record of complaints and predictions of defeat, which are shown in case of disaster. Somebody must be responsible for their failures.[167]

Paradoxically, with the press and the public demanding action, Grant's relations with Halleck improved. Grant was stalled at Vicksburg but not for lack of trying. The general in chief, sweating the war from Washington, found Grant to be the one general who could be relied on to take the fight to the enemy. Ambrose Burnside, who had succeeded McClellan, vacillated at Fredricksburg in December and suffered a resounding defeat. He was replaced by "Fighting Joe" Hooker, who, despite his sobriquet, proved equally hesitant on the battlefield. In Tennessee, Rosecrans turned out to be as obstinate as Buell, and seemed more concerned with his date of rank than moving against Bragg or Edmund Kirby Smith.[168] Grant was the exception. The McClernand charade had unquestionably brought Halleck and Grant closer together, and their correspondence became so cordial that one might have assumed they were the best of friends. "The eyes and hopes of the whole country are now directed to your army," Halleck wrote on March 20. "In my opinion the opening of the Mississippi River will be to us of more advantage than the capture of forty Richmonds. We shall omit nothing which we can do to assist you."[169]

Grant needed no prodding. On April 1, accompanied by Admiral Porter and Sherman he steamed abreast of the Vicksburg bluffs on a waterborne reconnaissance. The river was still high, there was little ground on which the troops could land, and the Confederate emplacements high above looked more imposing than ever. Grant told Porter an attack on the bluffs would be immensely costly and would likely fail.[170] Sherman concurred. The following day Grant wired Halleck that the Confederate position was impregnable.[171] It could not be turned from upriver, so he proposed to attack it from below.

Grant's decision to move south of the Confederate citadel, cut himself off from his supply base at Memphis, march east into Mississippi toward Jackson, turn 180 degrees and strike Vicksburg from the side on which it was vulnerable, ranks as one of the great strategic gambits in modern warfare. Unlike his desperate midwinter experiments to get behind Vicksburg, the plan was neither harebrained nor devised on the spur of the moment. As early as January 18 Grant advised Halleck he thought "our troops must get below the city to be effective."[172] As January dragged into February, and February into March, and as one experiment after another failed, Grant brooded over getting his army downstream past the sixteen-mile gauntlet of rebel artillery on the bluffs. Night after night he sat alone at a mahogany table in what had been the ladies' salon of the *Magnolia,* poring over charts and maps and keeping his own counsel. Gradually through the haze of cigar smoke the plan emerged, and during the final week of March Grant stayed up late each evening applying the final brush strokes. Once, in the early morning hours, McPherson ventured into the smoke-filled room and invited Grant to join him for a drink. "Throw this burden off your mind," urged McPherson. Grant said whiskey wouldn't help. What he really wanted was to be left alone—"and a dozen more cigars."[173]

Grant's plan was breathtakingly simple but fraught with peril at every step. McClernand's corps, still at work on the Duckworth canal, was ordered to stop digging and to repair the road that paralleled the ditch to New Carthage. The ground was mushy, four bridges were out, the levee was broken in several places, and the bayou currents ran rapid with floodwaters. Whether the route could be made serviceable was doubtful, yet McClernand's men, buoyed by the prospect of seeing action, rose to the occasion. One week after getting underway, the first division of Grant's army, including its artillery, arrived at New Carthage without the loss of a single man or gun.

Convinced now that the army could move down the west bank, Grant informed Halleck of his plan on April 4. The army would assemble near New Carthage, cross the mile-wide Mississippi with the aid of Porter's gunboats, move against the Confederate garrison downriver at Grand Gulf, then on to Vicksburg. "This is the only move I now see as practicable, and hope it will meet your approval. I will keep my army together and see to it that I am not cut off from my supplies or beat in any other way than a fair fight."[174] What Grant did not say was that all of his generals except McClernand thought the plan too risky. Admiral Porter was equally skeptical, and it was far from clear that the gunboats and steamers essential to the river crossing could pass safely downstream beneath Vicksburg's heavy guns.

As soon as he learned of the move, Sherman was so concerned that he called on Grant to register his objections. "I was seated on the piazza engaged in conversation with my staff when Sherman came up," wrote Grant. "After a few moments' conversation he said that he would like to see me alone. We passed into the house and shut the door after us. Sherman then expressed his alarm . . . saying that I was putting myself in a position which an enemy would be glad to maneuver a year to get me in. I was going into the enemy's country, with a large river behind me and the enemy holding points strongly fortified above and below. He said that it was an axiom in war that when any great body of troops moved against an enemy they should do so from a base of supplies, which they would guard as they would the apple of the eye." Sherman told Grant the proper military thing to do was to return to Memphis, establish a base, and then retrace their steps to Grenada.[175] Grant heard Sherman out. Then he told him that he had no intention of changing his plans. The Union needed a victory, so they had to go forward. "You will be ready to move at ten o'clock tomorrow morning."[176] Sherman loyally ordered his corps forward, but not before putting his views in writing and once again asking Grant to reconsider.[177] Grant read the letter but did not reply. Insofar as he was concerned, the die was cast. Later Grant wrote that Sherman "gave the same energy to make the campaign a success that he would have done if it had been ordered by himself. . . . I did not regard either the conversation between us or the letter as protests, but simply friendly advice which the relations between us fully justified."[178]

Halleck, grateful that Grant was moving forward, evidently did not share Sherman's concern. After advising Grant to live off the land as much as possible and to give "but little attention to the occupation of the country," Halleck restated his trust in the commander of the Army of the Tennessee. "I am confident you will do everything possible to open the Mississippi river. In my opinion this is the most important operation of the war, and nothing must be neglected to ensure success."[179] Halleck did not explicitly approve or disapprove of Grant's plan. It was Grant's call, and the campaign was his to win or to lose.

On the moonless night of April 16, Admiral Porter commenced his hazardous descent downriver. With the flagship *Benton* leading the way, the Union flotilla of seven ironclads and three transports slipped anchor and drifted silently with the current toward the imposing batteries of the latest "Gibraltar of the West." Porter had banked his furnaces hoping the vessels could slip past unnoticed, and for a while it looked as though the ruse would succeed. Suddenly all hell broke loose. From the opposite bank rebel lookouts lit massive bonfires of tar barrels and pine logs, illuminating the sky as though it were high noon and silhouetting the fleet for artillerymen on the bluff. The guns of Vicksburg opened a devastating barrage, which Porter's ironclads answered. So ferocious was the firing that people sixty miles away heard the cannonade.[180] It required one and a half hours for the ships to pass, and the Confederate big guns spat shot and shell as rapidly as their crews could serve them. All told, rebel gunners fired 525 rounds, scored sixty-eight hits, but sank only one of the transports and none of the seven gunboats. Grant, who witnessed the passage of the fleet from the deck of the *Magnolia*, called the sight "magnificent, but terrible."[181] Pemberton, who five days earlier had informed Richmond triumphantly that "most of Grant's forces are withdrawing to Memphis,"[182] failed to recognize what was in store. He acknowledged that Porter's presence downstream blocked Confederate navigation of the lower Mississippi, but did not link passage of the fleet to the possibility that Grant might cross the river below Vicksburg.[183] The Confederate high command in Richmond also missed the point. When asked for his opinion, Robert E. Lee assured Jefferson Davis that the Union "can derive no material benefit" from Porter's run, and predicted that the arrival of additional artillery in Vicksburg would prevent any repeat performance.[184]

Encouraged by the passage of Porter's flotilla, Grant prepared to make another run of the Vicksburg gauntlet, this time with additional transports and barges needed for the river crossing. On April 22 the vessels got underway, drifting at night with the current. This was an all-army show. When the civilian crews balked at taking the unarmed ships under the guns on the bluff, they were replaced by infantry volunteers from Black Jack Logan's division: men who had served with Grant since Belmont. "I want no faltering," Logan told his troops before embarking. "If any man leaves his post, I want him shot on the spot."[185]

Once again luck was on Grant's side. The Confederate batteries fired 391 rounds that night, but managed to sink only one vessel and disable a few barges. The next day Grant moved his headquarters downriver to New Carthage. By the end of the month he had two of his three corps thirty miles south of Vicksburg and had assembled a motley fleet of vessels to assist the crossing. "If I do not underestimate the enemy," he wired Halleck, "my force is abundant with a foothold once obtained to do the work."[186] Porter was less confident. After a tugboat reconnaissance of the river with Grant, he informed Navy Secretary Gideon Welles that he saw "no certainty of a successful landing of our army on the Mississippi side."[187]

Grant planned to force a crossing at Grand Gulf, storm the Confederate fortress located there, and overrun the defenders. Porter, who believed an assault crossing would prove too costly, preferred to run past the rebel works at Grand Gulf and cross the army below.[188] When Grant insisted, Porter dutifully responded. At 8 A.M. on April 29 his squadron of gunboats launched a preparatory bombardment. The entrenched Confederate artillery replied with ferocious counterfire. Toe-to-toe, the gunners slugged it out for five hours. Losses aboard the fleet were staggering. *Benton* was struck forty-seven times and its sister ship, the *Tuscumbia,* eighty-one. Nevertheless, Federal firepower proved overwhelming. By 1 P.M. Porter's tubes had fired 1,729 rounds (almost twice what Japanese battleships launched against Guadalcanal in 1942),[189] and the Confederate guns fell silent. Porter told Grant it was safe to cross. Now it was Grant's turn to have second thoughts. Southern firepower had been impressive, and he worried that there might be additional batteries that had not been silenced. These could wreak havoc upon his infantry, exposed during the crossing on unarmored transports and open barges. Porter's original advice looked sound. Demonstrating the flexibility that had become his hallmark, Grant decided not to force a crossing at Grand Gulf. Instead, he ordered the troops to march downstream to the vicinity of Port Gibson, where they could embark safely out of range of any lingering rebel artillery. "A landing will be effected [on] the east bank of the river tomorrow," Grant wrote Halleck on April 29. "I feel that the battle is now more than half won." [190]

As the troops slogged southward, Grant took up a position at the near end of a narrow bridge they must cross. Sitting his horse at roadside, he encouraged the men to hurry over. "Push right along," he gently urged the marchers, speaking in a simple conversational tone. The soldiers' spirits were lifted by Grant's presence, but an officer noted that their only response was to "hurry over." They did not cheer as they passed; they merely did as Grant directed. "It was as if, in the course of the long winter of repeated failure, they had caught his quality of quiet confidence." [191]

Shortly after dawn on April 30, the first division of McClernand's corps cast off from the Louisiana shore. The greatest amphibious operation in American history to date was underway. Like Caesar's descent on Britain, Grant was risking the future of his army on the crossing, and Porter mobilized his fleet to assist. Troops crammed aboard gunboats, river steamers, coal barges, and the occasional bayou flatboat. Even the *Benton*, Porter's flagship, served as a ferry. The mass of shipping allowed Grant to cross a division at a time, and, fortuitously, the landing was unopposed. By dusk McClernand's corps had completed the mile-wide crossing, as had a division of McPherson's corps. Grant had 23,000 men across the river and was marching on Port Gibson. In his *Memoirs* he wrote that he felt "a degree of relief scarcely ever equalled since. . . . I was now in the enemy's country, with a vast river and the stronghold of Vicksburg between me and my base of supplies. *But I was on dry ground on the same side of the river with the enemy.* All the campaigns, labors, hardships and exposures . . . that had been made and endured were for the accomplishment of this one object." [192]

To keep Pemberton off balance, and to prevent him from disrupting the crossing, Grant had earlier suggested to Sherman that he launch a diversionary attack against the bluffs at Vicksburg. "I am loath to order it," said Grant, because "it would be hard to make our troops understand . . . and our people at home would characterize it as a repulse." [193] Sherman still harbored doubts about Grant's strategy, but he had no qualms about complying with his commander's request.* "You are engaged in a hazardous enterprize," he wrote Grant, "and for good reason wish to divert attention. That is sufficient to me and it shall be done."[194]

On April 30, as McClernand's troops began their crossing, a task force under Sherman's command entered the Yazoo River steaming upstream toward the Chickasaw Bluffs and Vicksburg's front door. Intent on making the greatest show of strength, Sherman spread his troops across the decks of the transports with orders for "every man to look as numerous as possible."[195] The following morning the troops went ashore near the site of their December repulse. Under Sherman's watchful eye they marched and countermarched as if Grant's entire army would soon follow. Meanwhile, the remnants of Porter's squadron (several woodclad gunboats that did not attempt to run the Vicksburg gauntlet) shelled the bluffs with calculated abandon. At noon Sherman wrote Grant all was well. "Our diversion has been a perfect success, great activity seen in Vicksburg, and troops pushing this way." Sherman said he would reopen his cannonade at 3 P.M. and prolong the effort until after dark. Then he would hurry south.[196]

Another diversion, designed to sow confusion in its own right, involved a daring raid by Union cavalry to disrupt Confederate communications in Mississippi. Tired of being victimized by the dashing exploits of Forrest and Van Dorn, Grant sent his cavalry brigade deep into rebel territory to destroy Pemberton's supply line and divert attention from his own move south. Led by Colonel Benjamin Grierson, a former music teacher who loathed horses, Grant's troopers rode 600 miles in sixteen days, marauding through central Mississippi. They tore up fifty miles of three different rail lines, burned rolling stock and depots, and lured most of Pemberton's cavalry plus a full infantry division on a wild-goose chase during the last two weeks of April. Sherman called Grierson's raid "the most brilliant expedition of the war."[197] Grant, reporting to Halleck, said "Grierson has knocked the heart out of the State," which was not far off the mark.[198]

Pemberton was flummoxed. For almost five months he had held Grant at bay, and he was cosseted by rosy optimism. On May 1, as McPherson's corps completed its crossing of the Mississippi and Sherman knocked at Vicksburg's outer gate, a local newspaper boasted that the city was safer than at any time since the fall of Fort Donelson. "Let any man

* The day prior to receiving Grant's request, Sherman wrote his brother, Senator John Sherman of Ohio, that he had "less confidence" in Grant's Vicksburg strategy "than in any similar undertaking of the war." Despite his doubts, General Sherman's prompt compliance with Grant's request bespeaks a loyalty that typifies the military service at its best. That Grant inspired such loyalty speaks for itself. William T. Sherman to John Sherman, April 26, 1863, in Rachel Sherman Thorndike, ed., *The Sherman Letters* 201 (New York: Charles Scribner's Sons, 1894).

who questions the ability of General Pemberton only think for a moment on the condition of this department when he arrived. No general has evinced a more sleepless vigilance in the discharge of his duty, or accomplished more solid and gratifying results."[199] Pemberton was not led astray by his good press. But like any West Point–trained general he had difficulty comprehending what Grant was up to. The idea of uprooting an entire army from its base of supply did not seem credible. Not until May 2 when Grant marched into Port Gibson did Pemberton realize that the Army of the Tennessee had slipped past, crossed the river, and was ensconced on his vulnerable southern flank.

The battle of Port Gibson was sharp but brief. Brigadier General John Bowen, a friend and former neighbor of Grant's from his hardscrabble days in Missouri, evacuated his entrenchments at Grand Gulf and boldly set out with the 6,000-man garrison, placing himself between the Union army and the beautiful neoclassic village of Port Gibson. Outnumbered four to one, Bowen took up a strong defensive position along two ridgelines and checked Grant for twelve hours until the weight of the Federal advance overwhelmed him. Casualties were about equal: 832 Confederates and 875 Union troops were killed, wounded, or missing. Grant told Halleck that Bowen's defense "was a very bold one and well carried out. My force however was too heavy." Grant said the Mississippi countryside would supply abundant beef and forage, but ammunition and other supplies would have to be transported overland down the west bank from Milliken's Bend. "This is a long and precarious route but I have every confidence in succeeding in doing it."[200]

Part of Grant's confidence rested on Sherman, who was now en route. On the same day he wrote to Halleck, Grant told his most trusted lieutenant to organize a 120-wagon supply train and fill it with rations: "*one hundred thousand* pounds of bacon, the balance coffee, sugar, salt, and hard bread. For your own use on the march you will draw three days rations and see they last *five days*. It's unnecessary for me to remind you of the overwhelming importance of celerity. . . . The enemy is badly beaten and greatly demoralized. The road to Vicksburg is open."[201]

Grant's enthusiasm was contagious, but it scarcely reflected the situation. After the clash at Port Gibson, Bowen returned with his force to the powerful defensive works at Grand Gulf. Pemberton, with 26,000 men—almost as many as Grant's two corps—was poised at Vicksburg; another 10,000 rebel troops were scattered at detachments along the Yazoo; and a hundred miles to the south 12,000 Confederate effectives manned the battlements at Port Hudson. In addition, General Joseph E. Johnston, recovered from his wounds at Seven Pines, was collecting an army in eastern Mississippi and Alabama and heading toward Jackson. Grant was surrounded in enemy territory and his supply line was uncertain. On the other hand, his forces were massed, while the enemy was scattered. Above all, Grant had seized the initiative. Better than almost any general before or since, Grant recognized the value of momentum. His troops were on the move and the rebels had been thrown off balance.

Wasting no time, Grant decided to bypass the garrison at Grand Gulf and head north. His objective was Hankinson's Ferry, a hamlet six miles away where the main road to Vicksburg crossed the Big Black River, the last natural obstacle between his army and its goal. Grant wanted to establish a bridgehead on the other side of the river before the Confederates could regroup. The term *blitzkrieg* had yet to be coined, but those were the tactics Grant employed. Within the next two weeks his army would cut loose from its supply line, march 180 miles, change direction twice, fight five major engagements against an enemy whose combined strength exceeded his own, inflict over 7,000 casualties while suffering half of that, and pin Pemberton's demoralized troops against the ropes at Vicksburg.

The dash to the Big Black was the stuff of which legends are made. McPherson's 17th Corps was in the lead, Logan's division in the van. "Push right along. Close up fast," the troops heard Grant say as they passed him standing in the dust at roadside.[202] Nearing the Hankinson's Ferry bridge, Logan's lead regiment double-timed ahead, only to find a Confederate demolition team preparing to blow the span. The troops stormed the bridge before the charges could be detonated and gave Grant the toehold on the opposite bank he hoped for.[203]

By moving north quickly and crossing the Big Black, Grant turned the Confederate position at Grand Gulf. Bowen had no choice but to withdraw quickly toward Vicksburg or risk being cut off. The evacuation was completed before dawn on May 3. The mighty river fortress fell to Grant without a fight. Porter said later the rebel works were impregnable. "No fleet could have taken them."[204] Grant left it to McPherson to complete the lodgment on the Big Black and rushed to Grand Gulf with a small cavalry escort. Like his army, Grant had been traveling light. His headquarters had been in the saddle, and he rode a borrowed horse at that. He had been without his baggage and mess since leaving New Carthage a week ago. "Consequently, [I] had had no change of underclothing, no meal except such as I could pick up sometimes at other headquarters, and no tent to cover me. The first thing I did was to get a bath, borrow some fresh underclothing from one of the naval officers and get a good meal on the flagship."[205] Grant then turned to his correspondence. He told Halleck the army was in fine spirits and that he would not pause to occupy Grand Gulf "but immediately follow the enemy and . . . not stop until Vicksburg

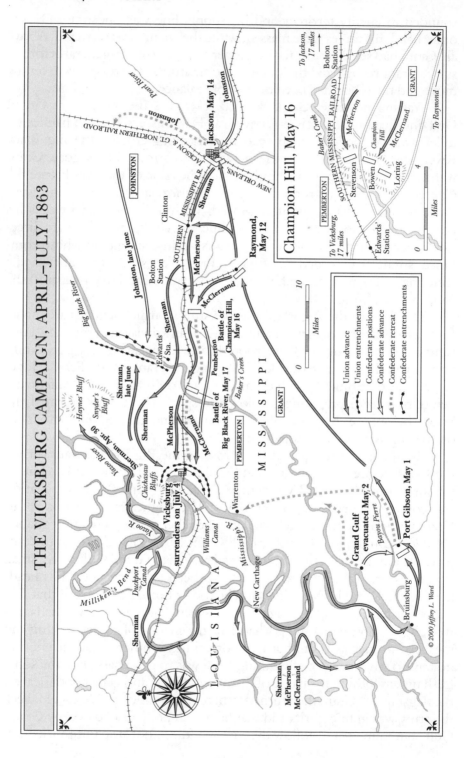

THE VICKSBURG CAMPAIGN, APRIL–JULY 1863

Champion Hill, May 16

© 2000 Jeffrey L. Ward

is in our possession." [206] To Julia he wrote that the bloodless capture of Grand Gulf represented an important victory. "Management I think has saved us an immense loss of life and gained all the results of a hard fight. I feel proud of the army at my command. They have marched day and night without tents and with irregular rations without a murmur of complaint." [207]

At Grand Gulf on May 3 Grant made the crucial decision of the campaign. His instructions from Washington emphasized the importance of subduing the Confederate base at Port Hudson, 100 miles downriver, before assaulting Vicksburg. Major General Nathaniel P. Banks, commanding at New Orleans, was to push north and assist, after which the two armies would tackle Pemberton.

Shortly after he arrived at Grand Gulf, Grant received a letter from Banks, written on the Red River three weeks before, informing him that developments in western Louisiana would prevent any move northward by his troops until at least May 10. Grant had assumed the attack on Port Hudson could begin immediately and that Banks could deploy 30,000 troops for the effort. Instead, Banks numbered his strength at half that. Grant, who was determined to maintain the momentum of his advance, decided he would be better off without Banks. "To wait for his co-operation would have detained me at least a month," he wrote later. "The enemy would have strengthened his position and been reinforced by more men than Banks could have brought. I therefore determined to move independently of Banks, cut loose from my base, destroy the rebel force in the rear of Vicksburg and invest or capture the city." [208]

For the next four days Grant acted as the quartermaster he had been in the Mexican War, firing off logistical instructions to subordinates, stockpiling ammunition, and dispatching foraging parties into the countryside. Rolling stock for the army's train was in particularly short supply, but scavenger teams returned from their raids with an abundant array of farm vehicles, ranging from long-tongued wagons designed for hauling cotton bales, to elegant plantation carriages, upholstered phaetons, and surreys. The vehicles were drawn by an equally odd assortment of horses, mules, and oxen—probably the most unmilitary military train ever assembled. But the pickings were bountiful. "We live fat," wrote Private Isaac Jackson of the 83rd Ohio Infantry. "Plenty of the best beef and mutton," to say nothing of the bags of sweet potatoes, sacks of corn, honey, and fresh strawberries. If the South was starving, there was no evidence of it in central Mississippi. [209]

From his position on the Big Black, Grant could have moved due north against Vicksburg. But the broken terrain was easily defended and access roads few and far between. "This part of Mississippi stands on edge," Grant wrote later. "The hillsides are covered with timber and the ravines with vines and canebreakes. This makes it easy for an inferior force to delay, if not defeat, a superior one."[210] Instead of attempting to crash through, Grant shifted the axis of his advance 90 degrees and moved east toward Jackson. His aim was to place his army between Pemberton and Johnston, defeat each in turn, and then assault Vicksburg from the east. With Jackson in Union hands, Vicksburg's rail link to the eastern Confederacy would be severed. The Mississippi River fortress could then be taken by storm, or besieged until it surrendered.

On May 6 Grant asked Halleck whether Rosecrans might be stirred into action to prevent Bragg from rushing reinforcements to Vicksburg.[211] Otherwise he kept Washington in the dark. By noon on the 6th, Sherman's corps had completed its crossing of the Mississippi. That brought Grant's total strength to about 40,000. The advance on Jackson commenced the following day: McClernand on the left, Sherman in the center, McPherson on the right. Sherman, who eighteen months later would march through Georgia and the Carolinas with no supply line whatever, was still the orthodox West Pointer in 1863, and he continued to worry about Grant's logistics. From his vantage point near Grand Gulf he could see the confusion caused by too few vehicles making too many shuttles on too few roads. "Stop all troops until your army is partially supplied with wagons," he wrote Grant in considerable agitation on May 9.[212]

Grant, who had not yet informed his corps commanders of his plans, was keeping his own counsel. If his principal subordinates did not know his intentions, then it was safe to assume that Pemberton did not either. Grant tipped his hand slightly. "I do not calculate upon the possibility of supplying the Army with full rations from Grand Gulf. What I do expect however is to get up what rations of hard bread, coffee & salt we can and make the country furnish the balance." Grant told Sherman that to wait for wagons would "give the enemy time to reinforce and fortify." He hoped to be in Vicksburg in seven days and the rations on hand would last until then.[213] Grant fretted about his lack of cavalry[214] and took care to insure that plenty of ammunition was on hand,[215] but he knew the army could feed itself.

With Grant pressing his corps commanders, the Army of the Tennessee moved quickly. The four dreary months encamped in the mud across the river from Vicksburg had forged the army into a well-oiled machine. Like Washington at Valley Forge, or Zachary Taylor in more salubrious climes, Grant had used the time to perfect the army's discipline and responsiveness. By May 11 lead elements were within twenty miles of Jackson and had yet to encounter serious opposition. A young soldier in McPherson's corps was moved by the march: "O, what a grand army this is. I shall never forget the scene today, while looking back upon a mile of solid columns, marching with their old tattered flags streaming in the summer breeze, and harkening to the firm tramp of their broad brogans keeping step to the pealing fife and drum, or the regimental bands discoursing 'Yankee Doodle' or 'The Girl I Left Behind Me.' "[216]

That evening Grant wrote Halleck that he had advanced as far as he could without bringing on a general engagement. Belatedly he informed the general in chief that he was cutting loose. "I shall communicate with Grand Gulf no more except it becomes necessary to send a train with heavy escort. *You may not hear from me again for several days.*"[217] Grant did not inform Halleck of his plans and once again he did not ask for approval. In fact, his message did not reach Washington until the following week. As he noted in his *Memoirs,* "I knew well that Halleck's caution would lead him to disapprove this course; but it was the only one that gave any chance of success. The time it would take to communicate with Washington and get a reply would be so great that I could not be interfered with until it was demonstrated whether my plan was practicable."[218] Like Lord Nelson at the battle of Copenhagen, who put the telescope to his blind eye so as not to see the flagship's signal to withdraw, Grant was pressing ahead on his own.

After writing to Halleck, Grant put his army in motion. McClernand was instructed to move cautiously but rapidly at first light "so that your entire corps will arrive at Fourteen mile creek simultaneously and in compact line."[219] Sherman was ordered to arrive there at the same time. McPherson was also told to push ahead, seize the village of Raymond, and take possession of whatever commissary stores might be located there. "We must fight the enemy before our rations fail, and we are equally bound to make our rations last as long as possible."[220]

As Grant's troops moved out on the morning of May 12 they were uncertain what to expect. The Mississippi capital of Jackson lay dead ahead, yet there was no way of judging what Pemberton had deployed to defend it. In reality, very little, because the Confederate commander was convinced that Grant intended to strike north from the Big Black and assault Vicksburg directly, and that the Union push toward Jackson was a feint. Consequently, Pemberton arrayed his troops, some fifteen brigades, in defensive echelon behind the Big Black. The Confederate force was roughly the same size as Grant's, and Pemberton was ready for a replay of the autumn confrontation on the Yalobusha. The only rebel troops between Grant and Jackson were a single brigade commanded by Texas brigadier John Gregg, bivouacked in the vicinity of Raymond. Pemberton believed that once battle was joined at Vicksburg, Gregg would be operating behind Grant's lines. Thus Gregg was instructed to fall on the Union flank or rear if the opportunity presented itself.[221] He was not informed that the entire Army of the Tennessee was bearing down upon him.

At mid-morning on the 12th Gregg received word that an undisclosed number of Union troops were approaching. It was Logan's division, out in front of McPherson's corps. Believing he was facing a small rear guard, Gregg readied his brigade to attack. He and his troops had surrendered to Grant at Donelson, and they were thirsting for revenge. The result was a sharp and surprisingly hot encounter in which seven Confederate regiments took on a whole Union corps. Gregg stood his ground for two hours but eventually gave way, losing one man in every six. McPherson entered Raymond late in the afternoon and halted for the night.

Grant was with Sherman when he learned of the fighting at Raymond. With the enemy in the field in front of him, he decided to press ahead at full throttle to take Jackson as soon as possible. Based on past performance, Grant judged that Pemberton would not venture from his position on the Big Black to attack, but the window of opportunity might close quickly. Accordingly, Grant ordered Sherman and McClernand to close on Raymond at daylight.[222]

On May 13 Grant's army converged. McPherson was now in the lead, with Jackson six miles away. Sherman was deployed to the right with orders to move abreast of McPherson, while McClernand was instructed to face west to guard against an attack by Pemberton, and to be ready to lead the advance on Vicksburg once Jackson had fallen.

By mid-morning on Thursday, May 14, the troops of McPherson and Sherman, sloshing through a torrential rainstorm, reached the outskirts of Jackson. Grant felt sufficiently secure at this point to inform Halleck of the situation, knowing it would be several days before the message arrived in Washington. "McPherson took [Raymond] on the twelfth after a brisk fight," wrote Grant. "McPherson is now at Clinton, Sherman on the main Jackson road, and General McClernand bringing up the rear. I will attack the State Capital today."[223]

The attack proved to be a ritual exercise. General Joseph E. Johnston, who had arrived in Jackson the day before, recognized the futility of attempting to defend the city with the 6,000 troops that were available. Rather than lose them he ordered the city evacuated, leaving a small rear guard to slow Grant's advance. Johnston informed the Confederate government in Richmond that the Union army was between him and Pemberton, and that he had arrived in Jackson "too late."[224] He sent a second message to Pemberton stating that he expected another 12,000 or 13,000 troops from the East. When they arrived the two armies should link up and make a combined effort to defeat Grant. "Can he supply himself from the Mississippi?" asked Johnston. "Can you cut him off from it, and above all, should he be compelled to fall back for want of supplies, beat him?"[225] Johnston was as effective a commander as the South produced, yet even he could not appreciate that Grant had cut loose from the Mississippi River and was supplying himself from the countryside. Indeed, with the capture of the rebel larder at Jackson, Grant's immediate logistical problems were all but over.

McPherson and Sherman disposed of Johnston's rear guard early on May 14 and swept into Jackson virtually unopposed—the third Confederate capital (after Nashville and Baton Rouge) to fall to the Union. Grant's advance had been so sudden that many of the city's residents did not realize what had taken place. That afternoon he and Sherman went on an inspection tour, in the course of which they came upon a factory where the mostly female employees were busy weaving tent cloth for the Confederate army. No one seemed to notice the two generals, who watched for some time in amused admiration. "Finally," said Grant, "I told Sherman I thought they had done work enough. The operatives were told they could leave and take with them what cloth they could carry."[226] Once the workers were gone, Grant ordered the factory burned, a task that fitted Sherman to a tee.

Grant established his headquarters in the Bowman House, Jackson's best hotel. From the lobby he had a clear view of the state capitol, where six months earlier Jefferson Davis had predicted that his fellow Mississippians would "hurl back these worse than vandal hordes."[227] Grant slept on a mattress for the first time in two weeks. General Johnston, he was told, had occupied the same room the night before.[228] The respite was brief. That evening Grant received an intercept of a letter from Johnston to Pemberton, ordering the Vicksburg commander to cross the Big Black and join forces with him at Clinton, some ten miles west of Jackson on the main rail line. Johnston believed that once combined, the Confederate forces could break Grant's supply line and deliver a crippling blow to his army that would relieve the threat to Vicksburg once and for all. Since Grant had no supply line he did not worry about Johnston disrupting it. But he was determined not to allow his adversaries to link up. Before retiring for the night he ordered McClernand to intercept Pemberton before he could reach Clinton. "Turn all your forces toward Bolton Station and make all dispatch in getting there," said Grant.[229] McPherson was told to move out of Jackson at dawn and join McClernand "with all possible dispatch."[230] Sherman was to remain in the city an additional day, wrecking railroad facilities and destroying foundries, arsenals, factories, machine shops, and anything else that might be of use to the Confederacy—a dress rehearsal that foreshadowed the Army of the Tennessee's March to the Sea. Then he too would move west. At first light Grant rode toward Clinton, with McPherson's 17th Corps following briskly.

Taking their cue from their commander, Grant's army marched out of Jackson imbued with a sense of victory. For Pemberton's troops it was just the opposite. A wary commander inspires little enthusiasm. Unlike Johnston, who was comfortable in fluid situations, Pemberton was a defensive practitioner par excellence. He preferred to meet Grant from a fortified position behind the Big Black and was uncomfortable maneuvering in open country. That attitude was amplified down the chain of command. As a result, Pemberton's strike force, roughly 23,000 men, moved in fits and starts, crisscrossing and doubling back on itself, never sure of its route and vainly searching for Grant's nonexistent supply line. It spent the night of May 15 huddled in march column, unaware that Grant was closing on it with 30,000 men deployed for battle.

By contrast to the confusion in the Confederate ranks, Grant's approach march went off without a hitch. Staff officers and route guides marked the way and by dusk on the 15th he had concentrated seven divisions, ready to move at dawn against Pemberton. Johnston, who evidently assumed Grant would linger in Jackson, was still retreating northeast with his 6,000 infantry, moving further away from Pemberton with each step. When he learned the Union army was heading west, he inexplicably continued marching northeast.[231] The following morning when Grant struck, the two Confederate forces were thirty miles apart.

Sunrise on May 16 saw three Union columns converging on Pemberton. The troops were from McClernand's 13th Corps and were under orders to move cautiously with skirmishers out in front to feel for the enemy.[232] McPherson followed closely on the Union right, while Sherman marched post haste from Jackson with another two divisions. Shortly before 7 A.M. Union pickets encountered Pemberton's cavalry screen on the left. McClernand's center column came under sharpshooter fire shortly afterward, as did Brigadier General Alvin Hovey's division on the right. Grant had instructed McClernand not to bring on a general engagement until the rest of the army was in position.[233] Accordingly, McClernand formed his troops in line of battle along all three approaches, loosed his artillery, but refrained from moving forward pending Grant's arrival. McClernand's unaccustomed caution gave Pemberton time to deploy to meet the Union onslaught. The sound of artillery to his front meant that Grant, not Johnston, was at hand and that he could either run or fight. Pemberton chose to fight. Demonstrating his natural bent for defense, he deployed his force along a wooded ridgeline dominated by a seventy-foot elevation known as Champion Hill, the highest point in the region. Grant wrote somewhat sarcastically that whether taken "by accident or design," the position Pemberton chose was unquestionably well selected.[234] The Confederate force was divided into nine infantry brigades, two cavalry regiments, and fifteen batteries of artillery. The troops were organized for battle in three divisions, commanded (from left to right) by major generals Carter Stevenson, Grant's friend John Bowen, and William Loring. If given time to prepare, Pemberton possessed the strength to defend the position, which the topography rendered formidable.[235]

Grant recognized that immediately. Riding forward with McPherson, he arrived in front of Hovey's division around 10 A.M. Hovey was taking a pounding from rebel artillery mounted high above on Champion Hill, and was eagerly waiting for the order to attack. By 10:30 two of McPherson's divisions (Logan and Marcellus Crocker) had come up and Grant decided he had sufficient force to begin the assault. Hovey was unleashed up the steep incline of Champion Hill, while Logan moved right to extend the Union flank. Crocker brought up the rear. Within the hour Union skirmishers reached the main Confederate battle line, at which point Grant told McPherson to storm the hill. At the same time he ordered McClernand to move forward on the left. McPherson responded aggressively. Supported by Union artillery, twenty-one infantry regiments, 10,000 men in all, swept forward along a mile-and-a-half front. McClernand, for reasons never adequately explained, sat tight. His artillery boomed, but his infantry exerted no pressure whatever on Pemberton's line. Twice more that afternoon Grant sent word to McClernand to attack, yet he failed to do so. As a result, the battle of Champion Hill was waged exclusively by the three divisions on the Union right.

By half past one Hovey's division had taken the crest of the hill, capturing the eleven pieces of rebel artillery that had been pounding them. Logan meanwhile had worked around the Confederate left, blocking any retreat in that direction. Pemberton responded quickly. To his front, McClernand was inert. Gambling that he would continue to be, Pemberton ordered Bowen, who held the Confederate center, to sidle left, counterattack, and retake the ridge. At 2:30, as Union troops celebrated their victory, Bowen's division of hard-fighting veterans swept forward from a fringe of woods and not only retook the lost ground, but surged down the forward slope of Champion Hill with irresistible force. The tide of battle changed ominously. Hovey said later his division "seemed to be melting under the intense Mississippi sun."[236] Grant's right was in peril. McClernand still did not move and Sherman was six miles away. Confronted with impending disaster, Grant massed whatever artillery he could lay his hands on for another last stand. Then he turned to Crocker, whose second and third brigades were just now coming on line. "Hovey's division are good troops," said Grant. "If the enemy has driven them, he is not in good plight himself. If we can go in again here and make a little showing I think he will give way."[237] This was the Grant of Fort Donelson and Shiloh, focusing on the enemy's weakness rather than his own. A soldier standing nearby said Grant was smoking the stump of a cigar. "I was close enough to see his features. Earnest they were, but signs of inward movement there were none."[238]

Raked by Union artillery, Bowen's drive ground to a halt. Crocker's troops were emboldened by the heavy barrage and moved to the attack. Two regiments, the 17th Iowa and the 10th Missouri, 500 men in all, charged the butternut line. Bowen's troops were fought out and, as Grant anticipated, the charge by fresh troops broke their spirit. They fell back in good order, but the battle's momentum shifted irrevocably. Union soldiers watching the charge rallied for another attack. What was left of Hovey's division joined in and Logan's men moved left in the final assault. By 4 P.M. Champion Hill was back in Union hands and the Confederates were in headlong retreat. So complete was the victory that Pemberton's rightmost division, fearing it would be cut off, marched to join Johnston, never to see Vicksburg again. In addition to the loss of an entire division, the Confederates suffered 3,840 men killed, wounded, or missing, along with the capture of twenty-seven irreplaceable field pieces. Grant lost 2,441 men, half of whom were from Hovey's division. In his official report, Hovey said, "I cannot think of the bloody hill without sadness and pride. Sadness for the great loss of my true and gallant men; pride for the heroic bravery they displayed."[239]

The battle of Champion Hill sealed the fate of Vicksburg. What appears so stark in retrospect is that the battle turned on a dime. On May 16, 1863, almost one million men were serving in the Union and Confederate armies. In a fight that some historians have called the decisive battle of the war, it came down to a struggle of less than 30,000 men—the Southern soldiers belonging to Stevenson and Bowen, the Northern troops in the divisions of Hovey, Logan, and Crocker.[240] Grant believed that Vicksburg could have been taken immediately if McClernand had attacked the Confederate right and then cut off the enemy's retreat. "Had McClernand come up with reasonable promptness," Grant wrote later, "I do not see how Pemberton could have escaped with any organized force."[241] He also believed that Pemberton should have marched to join Johnston. "This would have given up Vicksburg," said Grant, but "it would have been his proper move, and the one Johnston would have made had he been in Pemberton's place."[242]

With his remaining force, Pemberton retreated to the Big Black, ten miles west. This was the position he had previously prepared and where he wanted to meet Grant in the first place. Replete with rifle pits, cotton bale parapets, and prepositioned artillery, it provided the defenders with exceptional fields of fire against any enemy approach. Grant arrived in front of

Pemberton's position early on the 17th, took one look at the works, and decided that a frontal assault was out of the question. He deployed McClernand's corps in line of battle opposite, but hunkered down to wait for Sherman, whom he had ordered to cross the Big Black five miles to the north. McClernand would hold Pemberton in place while Sherman came down on his flank.

While Grant was waiting, a hard-riding courier from General Banks's staff at Baton Rouge rode up with a letter for him. It was from General Halleck, dated May 11, and had been sent by way of New Orleans. Halleck ordered Grant to return to Grand Gulf and cooperate with Banks against Port Hudson before moving on Vicksburg. The officer bearing the message insisted that Grant comply immediately. Grant replied that the order had come too late: that if General Halleck knew the present situation, he would never have issued it.[243] At that point the conversation was interrupted by an enormous shout along the right of the Union line. McClernand's troops, embarrassed by their poor showing the day before, were spontaneously charging the Confederate works. Led by sword-waving Brigadier General Michael Lawler, a massive Irishman from Illinois, four regiments from Eugene Carr's division were moving forward on the double. Grant rode off in the direction of the charge and soon the entire Union line was surging ahead. In three minutes the rebel works had been stormed and the charge was over. A veteran reporter called it "the most perilous and ludicrous charge I witnessed during the war."[244] Pemberton's troops, unnerved by the defeat at Champion Hill, retreated in disorder. Lawler lost 200 men killed and wounded; the Confederates 1,751, along with eighteen more pieces of artillery.

At noon the remnants of Pemberton's force straggled back into Vicksburg. It was a Sunday, and parishioners returning from service were shocked by the exhausted appearance of the soldiers who streamed by. "I shall never forget the woeful sight of a beaten, demoralized army—humanity in the last stage of endurance. Wan, hollow-eyed, ragged, footsore, bloody, the men limped along unarmed, followed by siege guns, ambulances, gun carriages and wagons in aimless confusion."[245]

Pemberton was the most distressed of all. His men had abandoned a fortified position of considerable strength. If they would not stand fast on the Big Black, where would they stand? Thirty hours before, his mobile force totaled 23,000 men. Less than a third that number tumbled back into Vicksburg. Despondently, he told an aide that his military career had begun on this day thirty years ago. "Today it is ended in disaster and disgrace."[246]

Grant spent Sunday getting his men across the Big Black. Sherman, on the Union right, was ordered to march northwest, seize the high ground, and interpose himself between Vicksburg and the Yazoo. McPherson's 17th Corps, in the center, was to push due west along the Jackson–Vicksburg corridor, while McClernand moved southwest to strike the Mississippi below Vicksburg. Porter's gunboat flotilla controlled the river on the west. By nightfall on May 18 the city was invested. Grant rode with Sherman that day, somewhat in advance of the army, impatient to reach the bluffs that had eluded capture in December. The rebel works were deserted when they arrived, the heavy guns spiked, and the garrison withdrawn. Sherman looked down on Chickasaw Bayou where his corps lay helpless five months earlier. After several minutes he turned to Grant to express his admiration: "Until this moment I never thought your expedition a success. I could never see the end clearly until now. But this is a campaign. This is a success if we never take the town."[247] As news of Vicksburg's investment filtered back to Washington, President Lincoln added his concurrence. "Whether General Grant shall or shall not consummate the capture of Vicksburg, his campaign from the beginning of this month . . . is one of the most brilliant in the world."[248]

Grant hoped to take Vicksburg while the defenders were still in shock. On May 19 he ordered an attack all along the front. "Corps commanders will push forward carefully, and gain as close position as possible to the enemy's works, until 2 P.M.; at which hour they will fire three volleys of artillery from all the pieces in position. This will be the signal for a general charge of all army corps along the whole line."[249] At the appointed hour the Union line sprang forward. They were met by a hail of rebel bullets that broke up the assault almost before it began. Ensconced behind the most formidable defensive works of the war, Pemberton's troops had taken heart. Grant lost almost a thousand men, but still thought the Confederate position could be taken by storm.

On May 22 he tried again. At dawn 220 field pieces supported by 100 guns on Porter's ironclads launched the biggest artillery barrage yet seen. Four hours later the men of all three corps rushed forward, only to be met by even more furious rebel fire. "For about two hours we had a severe and bloody battle," wrote Sherman, "but at every point we were repulsed."[250] At several places the Union troops actually effected shallow penetrations, but they were quickly expelled by Confederate counterattacks. For the second time in four days Pemberton's troops held firm. This time Grant suffered more than 3,000 casualties. Total Union losses in the two days of fighting at Vicksburg amounted to almost as many as Grant had experienced during the previous three weeks' campaign that had brought him to the city's doorstep. Grant did not regret the assaults; he only regretted that they had failed.[251] "The enemy are now undoubtedly in our grasp," he wrote Halleck. "The fall of Vicksburg, and the capture of most of the garrison, can only be a question of time." [252] Later, in self-justification, Grant wrote that the troops thought they could carry the Confederate works, "and would not have worked so patiently in the trenches if they had not been allowed to try." [253]

Convinced now that Vicksburg could not be taken by storm, Grant settled into a siege. He had seen General Winfield Scott effect one at Veracruz, where the defenses were at least the equal of Vicksburg's, and he decided it was not worth incurring additional casualties. Pemberton saw the handwriting on the wall. "I will hold Vicksburg as long as possible," he informed Johnston in a message smuggled through Union lines. "I still conceive it to be the most important point in the Confederacy." [254] But Pemberton realized that unless Johnston came to his relief, Vicksburg was doomed. Grant was receiving reinforcements from Memphis daily: not individual men, but whole divisions. Union strength would soon exceed 70,000 whereas his own garrison numbered less than half that. Grant had 220 field pieces, plus another hundred on Porter's vessels. Pemberton had half that. Grant's supply of ammunition was limitless; Pemberton's was dwindling fast. Grant's logistics were anchored once more on the Mississippi. As a consequence, his troops did not want for food, clothing, or the thousands of items upon which an army in the field depends. Pemberton was limited to the supplies on hand and those stocks were rapidly being depleted. In brief, Grant and Pemberton both knew that unless Johnston could break the siege, Vicksburg's surrender was inevitable.

Initially, Vicksburg's defenders were of stout heart, confident the Confederacy would not forsake them. "The undaunted Johnston is at hand," proclaimed the *Vicksburg Daily Citizen* in early June. "We may look at any hour for his approach. . . . Hold out a few days longer and our lines will be open." [255] The *Whig,* shrunk to tiny tabloid size and printed on wallpaper, was even more optimistic, reaffirming that once Johnston arrived, Grant would be defeated and his army destroyed. [256] As the days turned into weeks and Johnston did not come, spirits sagged. The army was reduced to half rations, then to a quarter, finally to one biscuit and a mouthful of bacon each day. By the end of June, half of Pemberton's army was on the sick list, suffering from malnutrition and scurvy. It was no longer "Johnston is coming," but "Where is Johnston?" [257]

Joseph E. Johnston did not share the Southern sentiment that Vicksburg should be held at all costs. Like Grant, he focused on the enemy army, and he believed his primary effort should be to link up with Pemberton, after which the two could fall on the Union army and, if they could not destroy it, at least render it incapable of further offensive action. But first, Johnston needed reinforcements. On May 29 he told Pemberton, "I am too weak to save Vicksburg. Can do no more than attempt to save you and your garrison. It will be impossible to extricate you unless you co-operate."[258] Johnston's message was not delivered until June 13—so tight was the Union cordon. Pemberton replied two days later that the shelling of Vicksburg had become continuous. His troops were greatly fatigued but could hold out for another twenty days. "What aid am I to expect from you?"[259] Johnston did not belabor the point. He now had 30,000 men but virtually no artillery and precious little transport. Grant's army had grown to almost 80,000. To make matters worse, Grant had posted Sherman in his rear with six divisions to arrest any move toward Vicksburg Johnston might make.[260] On June 22 Johnston told Pemberton the roads were blocked and that as a consequence he could do nothing to relieve the city. "Rather than surrender the garrison," Johnston suggested that Pemberton attempt to escape across the river and go west—a pipe dream given the presence of Porter's ironclads in the river.[261]

Toward the end of June, after being prodded incessantly by Richmond to take action, Johnston probed feebly toward Vicksburg but the effort lacked conviction, and in any event was too little and too late. "I think Johnston wisely abstained from making an assault on us," Grant wrote later, "because it would simply have inflicted loss on both sides without accomplishing any result."[262] Johnston said much the same. "The defeat of this little army," he told Richmond, "would at once open Mississippi and Alabama to Grant."[263] Later he wrote, "I did not indulge in the sentiment that it was better for me to waste the lives and blood of brave soldiers, 'than, through prudence even,' to spare them."[264]

Pemberton faced the inevitable. On July 3, with one day of limited rations remaining and his men too weak to attempt a breakout, he asked for terms. At 10 A.M. white flags were broken out along a portion of the rebel works. The Union cannonade ceased and two Confederate officers, Major General John Bowen and Pemberton's aide-de-camp, rode toward Grant's lines. Bowen was selected because he had befriended Grant in Missouri. He carried a letter from his commander requesting an armistice "with a view to arranging terms for the capitulation of Vicksburg."[265] Grant replied there was no reason to discuss terms because the only term he would consider was unconditional surrender. "Men who have shown so much endurance and courage as those now in Vicksburg, will always challenge the respect of an adversary, and I can assure you will always be treated with all the respect due to prisoners of war." Grant softened the message by telling Bowen that if Pemberton wished, he would be happy to meet him between the lines in front of McPherson's corps at three o'clock.[266]

Promptly at three o'clock Pemberton, Bowen, and several aides rode to meet Grant, whom they found standing on a hillside between the lines, a few hundred feet from the rebel breastworks. McPherson, Logan, and Ord* were there, together with several members of Grant's staff. The introductions were cordial. "Pemberton and I had served in the same division in the Mexican War," wrote Grant, "and I greeted him as an old acquaintance."[267] But when Pemberton asked what terms Grant proposed, the conversation turned sour. Grant said he had no terms to offer, other than unconditional surrender.

Pemberton, obviously under great pressure, became irritable. "If this is all you have to offer, the conference might as well end," and he turned as if to mount his horse.

"Very well," said Grant, apparently content to let it go at that. Both men were playing showdown poker, and neither could afford to appear weak or conciliatory.

At this point General Bowen intervened, suggesting that he and one of Grant's subordinates discuss certain technical matters while the commanding generals withdrew. It was a face-saving gesture that both Pemberton and Grant could embrace. The two retired to the meager shade of a stunted oak tree nearby while Bowen and McPherson discussed terms. In point of fact, by allowing Bowen and McPherson to talk, Grant was bending on unconditional surrender, and on his part, Pemberton was anticipating better conditions than had been offered initially. After thirty minutes it was clear that Bowen and McPherson could not reach agreement, but the informal chat under the oak tree between Grant and Pemberton broke the ice. Before adjourning, Grant agreed to announce his final terms by 10 P.M.

The sticking point was whether the Vicksburg garrison would be taken prisoner or paroled under their own recognizance. Prodded by his corps and division commanders, Grant yielded and informed Pemberton that he would accept parole rather than transport the men to Union prison camps.† "As soon as the rolls can be made out, and paroles be signed by officers and men, you will be allowed to march out of our lines, the officers taking with them their side-arms and clothing. The rank and file will be allowed all their clothing, but no other property."[268]

Sometime after midnight Pemberton replied. In general, the terms were acceptable. His troops would march out at 10 A.M., stack their

---

* On June 18, 1863, after McClernand overstepped by issuing a dispatch exaggerating his role in the fighting of May 22, Grant relieved him of command of the 13th Corps and replaced him with Major General Edward O. C. Ord. Special Orders No. 164, 8 *Grant Papers* 385 note.

† In his *Memoirs* Grant indicated that the meeting of corps and division commanders that he called ("the nearest approach to a 'council of war' I ever held") was almost unanimous against paroling the Vicksburg garrison and that he overruled them. Grant's memory apparently deserted him, because the fact is the roles were reversed. After meeting with Pemberton on July 3, Grant wrote Sherman, "Pemberton wants conditions to march out paroled, etc. The conditions are such as I cannot give." 8 *Grant Papers* 461. Cf. Grant, 1 *Memoirs* 560–61.

weapons and colors in front of their lines, and turn the city over to Grant. But he suggested two additional provisions: first, the officers were to retain their personal property; and second, "the rights and property of citizens" was to be respected. Grant suspected that "property" used in that context meant slaves, and he promptly rejected the proposals. Pemberton acquiesced, and after holding out for forty-seven days Vicksburg surrendered.

July 4, 1863, was a memorable day for the Union. At ten o'clock, Pemberton ordered the Stars and Stripes hoisted over the principal Vicksburg battlement. White flags were then broken out along the eight-mile trench line, and regiment after regiment marched out in perfect order, their colors flying, their bands playing.[269] So close were the battle lines in some places that Confederate troops stacked their arms on Union parapets. For their part, Federal soldiers watched with undisguised respect. There was little cheering, no triumphant exaltation. An almost reverential silence hung over the battlefield. A day earlier, twelve hundred miles away in Pennsylvania, the Army of the Potomac dealt Lee a resounding defeat at Gettysburg. The high tide of the Confederacy receded.

John Logan's division was selected by Grant to lead the occupation, and it marched in about eleven. Shortly afterward the Stars and Stripes were hoisted over the Vicksburg courthouse for the first time in two and a half years. A Vicksburg woman who watched Logan's troops captured the essence of the campaign. "What a contrast to the suffering creatures we had seen so long were these stalwart, well-fed men, so splendidly set up and accoutered. Sleek horses, polished arms, bright plumes—this was the pride and panoply of war. Civilization, discipline, and order seemed to enter with the measured tramp of these marching feet."[270] The good behavior of the Union troops mitigated the bitterness of defeat. Rations were shared, and the stores of speculators who had been hoarding food were broken open and their contents distributed.[271]

Grant rode in about noon to meet Admiral Porter at the levee. Porter's new flagship, the *Black Hawk,* was ablaze with color, banners aloft and the crew nattily attired in white pants and blue jackets. Porter opened his wine locker to toast the victory. Grant joined in briefly but then moved away from the celebrants and sat alone, his thoughts to himself. Years later Porter recalled that, "No one, to see him sitting there with that calm exterior amid all the jollity . . . would ever have taken him for the great general who had accomplished one of the most stupendous military feats on record."[272]

Grant was rewarded for the victory at Vicksburg by promotion to major general in the regular army, the highest rank the nation could bestow. The most notable accolade, however, came from President Lincoln:

My Dear General:

I do not remember that you and I ever met personally. I write this now as a grateful acknowledgment for the almost inestimable service you have done the country. I wish to say a word further. When you first reached the vicinity of Vicksburg, I thought you should do, what you finally did—march the troops across the neck, run the batteries with the transports, and thus go below; and I never had any faith, except in a general hope that you knew better than I, that the Yazoo Pass expedition, and the like, could succeed. When you got below and took Port Gibson, Grand Gulf and vicinity, I thought you should go down the river and join Gen. Banks; and when you turned Northward East of the Big Black, I feared it was a mistake. I now wish to make the personal acknowledgement that you were right, and I was wrong.

Yours very truly,
A. Lincoln[273]

CHAPTER EIGHT

CHATTANOOGA

*Loss of hope is worse than loss of men and land. It was the moral ef-
fect, above all, which made Vicksburg the great turning point of
the war.*

LIDDELL HART

GRANT WASTED LITTLE TIME before following up his victory at Vicksburg.
No sooner had the celebration died down the afternoon of July 4 than the
13th Corps, now under Edward Ord, was sent marching to join Sherman.
General Joseph E. Johnston, with an army that now exceeded 30,000
men, was coiled somewhere between Vicksburg and Jackson, and Grant
wanted to dispose of him before he could strike. "Drive him out in your
own way," Grant told Sherman, "and inflict on the enemy all the punishment you can." [1] This was a new style of warfare. The days of measured
combat were past; Grant was unleashing Sherman to do his damnedest.

At the same time, two additional divisions were dispatched southward to assist Banks at Port Hudson. That effort proved unnecessary.
When the Confederate garrison downriver learned that Vicksburg had
fallen, they surrendered unconditionally on July 9. The following week the
steamboat *Imperial* tied up at the wharf in New Orleans, arriving direct
from St. Louis after an undisturbed trip down the Mississippi. "The Father of Waters again goes unvexed to the sea," President Lincoln announced. [2] The South had been split in two.

West of the Mississipi—now virtually an autonomous region—a
badly outnumbered Confederate force commanded by Edmund Kirby
Smith kept the Union at bay in Arkansas and Texas, while Richard Taylor
rode roughshod over Yankee forces in western Louisiana. But despite
Confederate success, the trans-Mississippi was a sideshow. The principal

fight would be waged in the East, where Lee's Army of Northern Virginia was ensconced once more below the Rapidan, Bragg's formidable Army of Tennessee stood between Union forces and Chattanooga, and Joseph E. Johnston, with a newly raised Army of the Mississippi, was poised less than fifty miles east of Vicksburg.

While Grant was contemplating his next move, Sherman made quick work of Johnston, who pulled back to Jackson as soon as he got word of Vicksburg's surrender. Sherman's forces enjoyed a two-to-one numerical advantage and by July 11 Union troops had invested the Mississippi capital on three sides and severed the city's rail links with the outside world. A brief frontal attack on July 12 proved costly—Johnston was dangerous when cornered—and Sherman settled in for a siege, moving slowly and deliberately to cut the rebels' avenue of retreat eastward. Johnston, who had hoped to lure Sherman into another frontal attack, realized the game was up and during the night of July 16 stole away across the Pearl River in a withdrawal that for its effectiveness rivaled Beauregard's departure from Corinth a year earlier. Unlike Pemberton, Johnston saved his army with all of its artillery and heavy equipment. The price was the abandonment of central Mississippi to the Union army. During the brief siege of Jackson the Confederates lost 604 men, Sherman twice that many. Yet as one historian has written, Johnston's retreat from Jackson came as icing on the cake of Grant's Vicksburg campaign.[3] "Grant is my man," the president declared, "and I am his the rest of the war."[4]

The emergence of Grant was a godsend for Lincoln. "He is a copious worker, and fighter," the president confided to another officer, "but a very meagre writer, or telegrapher."[5] That was a new experience for Lincoln. The president said that unlike other generals, Grant "doesn't worry and bother me. He isn't shrieking for reinforcements all the time. He takes what troops we can safely give him . . . and does the best he can with what he has got."[6] Lincoln's description was accurate enough. What few recognized was that Grant's attitude had been nurtured fifteen years earlier in Mexico watching the way Zachary Taylor operated. In fact, the words used by Lincoln to describe Grant are virtually identical to those chosen by Grant to depict Taylor.[7] Perhaps the best example of Grant's attitude involved his unquestioning acceptance of Lincoln's policies on emancipation and the recruitment of Negro troops. Unlike McClellan and Buell, Grant dismissed whatever personal doubts he may have had and pitched in wholeheartedly. When Halleck instructed him to assist Lorenzo Thomas, the adjutant general, in enlisting freed slaves, Grant said frankly, "I never was an abolitionist, nor even what could be called anti-slavery. [However,] you may rely upon it I will give him all the aid in my power. I would do this whether arming the negro seemed to me a wise policy or not, because it is an order that I am bound to obey and I do not feel that in my position I have a right to question any policy of the government."[8]

Grant's forthright approach endeared him to Lincoln. The result was that shortly after Vicksburg the president toyed with the idea of bringing him east to command the Army of the Potomac. George Meade had held the line magnificently at Gettysburg, but in the aftermath of battle he allowed Lee's army to escape. Lincoln was grateful for the victory but despondent there had been no pursuit.[9] Grant seemed to be the answer. Assistant Secretary of War Charles Dana, back in Washington after Vicksburg, wrote Grant in late July to apprise him of what was afoot. Halleck likewise sounded Grant out, although the general in chief had already advised Lincoln he was certain Grant would prefer to remain in the West. On August 5, 1863, Grant made it official. Writing to Dana, Grant said, "General Halleck and yourself were both very right in supposing it would cause me more sadness than satisfaction to be ordered to the command of the Army of the Potomac. Here I know the officers and men and what each general is capable of. . . . There I would have all to learn. Here I know the geography of the country and its resources. There it would be a new study. Besides, more or less dissatisfaction would necessarily be produced by importing a general to command an army already well supplied with those who have grown up, and been promoted, within it." Grant said if ordered he would comply. But he hoped it would not come to that.[10]

Grant's reluctance to go east carried the day. But for the time being he was without a mission. In late July he suggested to the War Department that the next target should be Mobile, Alabama—the last deepwater port available to the Confederacy on the Gulf Coast east of the Mississippi—and he offered to send Sherman or McPherson to command the operation. Once Mobile was taken the army could move north against Bragg.[11] The suggestion made sense militarily, but by this time President Lincoln had become preoccupied with the worsening situation in Mexico.

When the Civil War began, Benito Juárez, newly elected head of the Mexican government, had declared a two-year moratorium on the payment of foreign debt. Britain, Spain, and France intervened militarily and obtained satisfaction, whereupon Britain and Spain withdrew their troops but France did not. Attracted by the wealth of Mexico, Napoleon III (whose sympathies lay with the Confederacy) chose to pursue the course of empire, confident the United States would be powerless to intervene. French occupation forces swelled to 35,000, and in the spring of 1863 the emperor's army set off from the coast to Mexico City as Winfield Scott had done in 1847. In June the Mexican capital fell to the French, and Napoleon installed Austrian Archduke Maximilian as emperor of Mexico. Aside from the obvious violation of the Monroe Doctrine, Lincoln was concerned about the establishment of a pro-Confederate French satellite on America's southern flank. Napoleon III had been quietly advocating European intervention in the Civil War for the past two years, and the president wanted to defend the Rio Grande boundary should France decide to move north. As a result, the expedition against Mobile was stillborn.

On August 6 Halleck wired Grant, "There are important reasons why our flag should be restored to some part of Texas without delay. . . . On this matter we have no choice, but must carry out the views of the Government."[12] Ord's 13th Corps was ordered downriver to New Orleans, and Banks was told to secure the border with Mexico as quickly as possible.[13] Grant was disappointed, but Lincoln took it upon himself to pull the sting. "I see by a dispatch of yours that you incline quite strongly toward an expedition against Mobile. That would appear tempting to me also were it not that, in view of recent events in Mexico, I am greatly impressed with the importance of reestablishing national authority in western Texas as soon as possible."[14]

Grant spent the remainder of the summer marking time. In July, Halleck asked both him and Sherman for their opinion concerning civil government in the occupied South. "Write me your views," urged the general in chief, "I may wish to use them with the President."[15] Characteristically, Sherman took a hard line. "I would not coax them, or even meet them halfway, but make them so sick of war that generations would pass before they would again appeal to it."[16]

By contrast, Grant inclined toward reconciliation. Like Lincoln, he understood the need to bring the defeated states back into the Union. "The people of these states," he wrote, "are beginning to see how much they need the protection of Federal laws and institutions. They have experienced the misfortune of being without them, and are now in a most happy condition to appreciate the blessings."[17] Grant said he agreed with Sherman that they should destroy the rebel armies, but "I think we should do it with terms held out that by accepting they could receive the protection of our laws."[18]

Grant's sympathetic approach helped to turn the tide of public opinion in Memphis, a city that had been among the most devoted to the Confederacy. On August 25 the board of trade hosted a dinner in his honor, and on the next night the mayor and city council followed suit. Grant was presented to the 200 guests with the toast, "Your Grant and my Grant," in which his reopening of the Mississippi to commerce was compared to the exploits of two other local heroes, Hernando de Soto and Robert Fulton. Grant declined to speak on both occasions, but at the second banquet General Stephen Hurlbut, the Memphis commander, read a brief statement Grant had written thanking the citizens for their kindness and expressing his pleasure at the public exhibition of loyalty to the United States. "The stability of this Government and the unity of this nation depend solely on the cordial support and the earnest loyalty of the people. . . . I am profoundly gratified at this public recognition, in the city of Memphis, of the power and authority of the Government of the United States." When Hurlbut concluded, the audience gave Grant a prolonged standing ovation.[19]

From Memphis Grant went downriver to New Orleans, where he arrived on September 2. Two days later General Banks staged a massive review in his honor, Ord's 13th Corps and the Gulf Department's 19th Corps marching past. As Ord's veterans went by, moving with that loose, easy stride that marked the Army of the Tennessee, Grant was deeply affected. Ordinarily he cared little for military pageantry, but as each set of regimental colors passed, adorned with the names of recent upriver victories, he lifted his hat in heartfelt tribute, his eyes moist with feeling.[20] Riding back to his hotel afterward, Grant's borrowed mount shied when an approaching locomotive sounded a piercing whistle. The horse lost its footing and fell, knocking Grant unconscious and severely injuring his left side and leg. General Lorenzo Thomas, who was present, wrote in his diary that Grant's horse "threw him over with great violence. The General who is a splendid rider maintained his seat in the saddle, and the horse fell upon him."[21] Almost immediately word spread that Grant was inebriated and had fallen from his horse in a drunken stupor. It was even said the fall occurred during the review. Grant knew nothing of this at the time, and was carried to the nearby St. Charles Hotel, where he regained consciousness somewhat later to find several doctors hovering over him.[22] "My knee was swollen from the leg to the thigh, and the swelling, almost to the point of bursting, extended along the body up to the armpit. The pain was almost beyond endurance. I lay in the hotel something over a week without being able to turn myself in bed."[23]

While Grant was confined to bed, first in New Orleans and then back in Vicksburg, disaster visited Union forces in Tennessee. Throughout the spring of 1863 Washington had pressed Rosecrans to take the offensive against Bragg. Finally on August 4 Halleck peremptorily ordered him to advance "without further delay," and to report daily on the progress he had made. Thus prompted, Rosecrans moved adroitly in late August to force the Confederates back on Chattanooga. Bragg chose to withdraw rather than give battle, and on September 9 Rosecrans entered the Lookout City at the head of 60,000 men without having fired a shot. Encouraged by this initial success, Rosecrans plunged ahead and by September 18 had advanced fifteen miles through the mountainous terrain south of Chattanooga to the vicinity of Chickamauga Creek. The commander of the

Army of the Cumberland assumed Bragg was in headlong retreat and that the road to Atlanta lay open. Union troops were strung out along a loosely organized front thirty miles wide with little heed paid to Confederate movements. In effect, the usually cautious Rosecrans was overextending himself. Unbeknownst to Union intelligence, Bragg had been heavily reinforced during the past two weeks with veteran troops from throughout the South, including two divisions of Longstreet's splendid corps from the Army of Northern Virginia.[24] Rather than retreating toward Atlanta, Bragg stood poised with 65,000 battle-hardened troops itching to attack the disjointed Union position and cut Rosecrans to pieces.

On September 18 the Confederate counterattack commenced. For three days the desperately bloody battle of Chickamauga raged on, total losses on both sides approaching the staggering figure of 38,000. On September 18 and 19, the fighting was bitterly contested all along the front with neither side gaining an advantage. But on the 20th, Longstreet, with five rebel divisions in tow, broke through the Union line in front of him and split Rosecrans's army in two. Panic set in on the Union right as troops fled the battlefield in demoralized confusion. Rosecrans was overcome by the catastrophe and, believing his army destroyed, joined the retreat to Chattanooga hoping to salvage what was possible. The disaster would have been complete had not George Thomas, commanding the Union left, stood his ground tenaciously, beating back assault after assault until nightfall. With skill and determination Thomas held his corps in place, resisting the combined efforts of both Confederate wings to sweep the field. "This army does not retreat," said the imperturbable Virginian, earning him the name by which he would be known thereafter: "The Rock of Chickamauga."[25] In a tribute to Thomas's gallant stand, Lincoln said that it was doubtful "whether his heroism and skill . . . has ever been surpassed."[26]

The defeat on Chickamauga Creek, coming on the heels of Union victories at Vicksburg and Gettysburg, caused immediate consternation in Washington. Rumors that Rosecrans was preparing to evacuate Chattanooga swirled menacingly, and the momentum of the war seemed perilously close to shifting once more in favor of the Confederacy. To all but a handful of friends and partisans, it was clear that Rosecrans was unequal to the crisis. Dana, who witnessed the debacle, reported to Stanton that he had never seen a talented officer "with less steadiness in difficulty and greater practical incapacity than General Rosecrans."[27] Lincoln told his secretary that Rosecrans seemed confused and stunned, behaving "like a duck hit on the head."[28] A quick fix was needed urgently, and it was equally obvious that a shakeup in the Union command structure was overdue. Halleck ordered Grant to provide reinforcements for the Army of the

Cumberland as quickly as possible, and Stanton prevailed upon Lincoln to transfer two additional corps from the Army of the Potomac. Grant was still confined to bed when the instructions from Washington arrived, but he immediately dispatched Sherman with five divisions to move by rail from Memphis to Chattanooga, repairing the line as he went. By the end of September almost 40,000 reinforcements were rushing to Rosecrans, half from Grant's Army of the Tennessee under Sherman, half from Meade's Army of the Potomac under Joe Hooker.

With the situation at Chattanooga hanging in the balance, Halleck told Grant to repair to Cairo as soon as he was able to travel and to report by telegraph to the War Department.[29] Grant received the message on October 10, and although he was still laid up, went immediately upriver to the closest telegraph post, arriving on the 16th.[30] The following morning Grant received a message from Halleck directing him to proceed at once to Galt House in Louisville, where he would receive further instructions from "an officer of the War Department." Grant was told to take his staff with him "for immediate operations in the field."[31] He promptly boarded a train for Louisville, by way of Indianapolis. That afternoon, as the train was about to pull out of the Indianapolis depot, a messenger scrambled across the tracks to flag it down. Behind him came a well-dressed gentleman whom Grant had never met. It was Edwin M. Stanton, the secretary of war, whose special train had just arrived, and who was en route to Louisville to meet Grant. Learning that the general's train was still in the station, Stanton chose to ride the rest of the way with him.[32] Grant was still unaware of what was in store, but as the train rocked toward Louisville, Stanton explained the situation at Chattanooga and handed Grant two versions of a War Department order dated October 16. Both versions had the identical first paragraph: "By direction of the President of the United States, the Departments of the Ohio, of the Cumberland, and of the Tennessee, will constitute the Military Division of the Mississippi. Major General U. S. Grant, United States Army, is placed in command of the Military Division of the Mississippi, with his headquarters in the field."[33]

Lincoln was reorganizing the Union chain of command between the Appalachians and the Mississippi. Henceforth, the three armies in the region, the Tennessee, the Cumberland, and the Ohio, would report to Grant, whose headquarters would be "in the field"—a clear indication that the president wanted action. That was the first version of the order. The second version contained an additional paragraph that relieved Rosecrans as commander of the Army of the Cumberland and replaced him with George Thomas. Grant was told by Stanton that he could choose whichever version he preferred. "I accepted the latter," Grant noted laconically.[34] Sherman would succeed Grant as commander of the Army of the

Tennessee, and Ambrose Burnside would continue to head the Army of the Ohio, at least for the present.

When Grant arrived in Louisville, reports of an impending Union withdrawal from Chattanooga were flooding in. Accordingly, he quickly wrote out an order assuming command of the Military Division of the Mississippi, and then dispatched two orders of his own: the first to Rose-crans informing him that he was relieved of command,[35] the second to Thomas instructing him to "hold Chattanooga at all hazards." Grant said he would be there as soon as possible and he asked how long the army's provisions would last.[36] Thomas replied that he had five days' rations on hand, with two additional days' rations expected momentarily. But as if to say not to worry, Thomas added: "We will hold the town till we starve."[37] Grant appreciated the force of Thomas's reply, but he recognized that the situation was critical. Unless the Army of the Cumberland could be resup-plied quickly, its surrender was inevitable.[38]

The problem was that in its hasty retreat from Chickamauga, the Union army had given up the high ground around Chattanooga to the Confederates. Bragg held Lookout Mountain, Raccoon Mountain, and Missionary Ridge. Artillery mounted on the heights commanded all of the routes into the city except for a torturous wagon road over the mountains to the north, and rebel cavalry had made that route hazardous as well. For-age for Union horses was exhausted, there was no timber within Federal lines for fuel, worn-out shoes and tattered clothing could not be replaced, and, despite Thomas's vow, the troops were already down to half-rations.

Grant was unable to walk without assistance. Nevertheless, he set out by rail for Chattanooga the next morning. A fellow passenger wrote to his wife that the general "was seated entirely alone on the side of the car next to me. He had on an old blue overcoat, and wore a common white wool [cap] drawn down over his eyes, and looked so much like a private soldier, that but for the resemblance to the photographs . . . it would have been impossible to recognize him."[39] At Stevenson, Alabama, Grant met Rose-crans, who was on his way north. "He was very cheerful, and seemed as though a great weight had been lifted off his mind," said Grant.[40] "He came into my car and we held a brief interview in which he described very clearly the situation at Chattanooga, and made excellent suggestions as to what should be done. My wonder was that he had not carried them out."[41]

From Stevenson the train proceeded to Bridgeport, Alabama, near the Tennessee border, where, thanks to Confederate raiding parties, rail-road transportation ended. Grant made the last sixty miles on horseback, his crutches strapped to his saddle. Fall rains had turned low-lying por-tions of the road into a quagmire, while other stretches were completely washed out. Grant had to be lifted from his saddle and carried across the roughest places, which were not safe to traverse on horseback. This road was Chattanooga's lifeline and it offered a grim preview of what lay ahead. The route was strewn with discarded military equipment and the debris of shattered wagons, while the carcasses of thousands of starved mules and horses littered the roadside, their decaying bodies putrefying the atmosphere. Rawlins called the road "the roughest and steepest ever crossed by army wagons and pack mules."[42] At one time 500 wagon teams were hung up in the mud, unable to move in either direction. Grant's party, traveling light, required two full days, pelted by wind and rain, to make the sixty-mile journey. At dusk on October 23, a bone-weary Grant was assisted from his horse and hobbled into the small frame house that served as Thomas's headquarters. "Wet, dirty, and well," as Lincoln learned the next day, the commanding general of the Division of the Mississippi had arrived in Chattanooga.[43]

Emotionally, Grant and Thomas were cut from the same cloth. Both were tight-lipped stoics who prided themselves on never showing the slightest feeling. Yet under that shell both were warm and sensitive, Thomas affectionately known as "Old Pap" by his troops. The two men greeted each other formally and Grant was served a warm meal, after which they sat together by the fireside, neither saying a word.[44] Members of Grant's staff, quick to take offense, thought they sensed hostility in Thomas's reserve. Grant knew better. And so did Thomas. The two old soldiers were simply enjoying a rare moment of solitude, bonding with one another in the quiet by the hearth. Grant, for his part, was well aware that the Army of the Cumberland could not have been in better hands, and Thomas, like C. F. Smith in front of Fort Donelson, was patiently waiting for his commander to express his wishes. Both Smith and Thomas had ranked Grant in the old army, but their new relationship was not a problem. "Tell Grant to have no hesitancy about giving me orders," Thomas had told General Joseph Reynolds, his chief of staff, who was one of Grant's oldest friends. "I will be ready to obey his every wish."[45] Eventually a member of Thomas's staff called his attention to the fact that Grant's clothes were soaked and that he might like to change. Thomas was mortified that he had overlooked something so obvious. His old-time Virginia hospitality was aroused and he begged Grant to step into a nearby bedroom and change his clothes. Grant politely declined, lit another cigar, and pulled his chair closer to the fire. Both Thomas and Grant were more or less oblivious to creature comforts, and in their silent way each was inwardly focusing on the military situation at hand.

For Grant, the initial task was to reestablish a viable supply route for the Army of the Cumberland—what he called "a cracker line." It would do no good to bring Sherman's and Hooker's troops to Chattanooga if they could not be fed. But that was merely the first step. Bragg had the city besieged and the trap had to be sprung. As the evening progressed, it became clear that Grant's thoughts were about how to resume the Union offensive as quickly as possible. General Thomas had arranged for his staff to call after supper, and for the next several hours Thomas and his chief engineer, General William F. "Baldy" Smith, briefed Grant on the situation. Smith had been at West Point with Grant and he had commanded a corps in the Army of the Potomac, but his differences with Burnside and Hooker caused him to be transferred to Chattanooga. Here he found his calling. Grant wrote later that Smith "explained the situation of the two armies and the topography of the country so plainly that I could see it without inspection."[46] Grant was greatly taken with Smith, particularly when Baldy laid out in detail a plan to regain possession of the Tennessee River and reestablish easy contact with the army's supply depot at Bridgeport.

According to a participant at the conference, Grant sat "immovable as a rock and as silent as the sphinx" as he listened to Thomas and Smith. When they finished, he became animated and fired question after question at the pair. "So intelligent were his inquiries, and so pertinent his suggestions, that he made a profound impression upon everyone by the quickness of his perception and the knowledge which he had already acquired. . . . Coming to us with the laurels he had gained in Vicksburg, we naturally expected to meet a well-equipped soldier, but hardly anyone was prepared to find one who had the grasp, the promptness of decision, and the general administrative capacity which he displayed at the very start."[47]

Early the following morning, Grant, Thomas, and Smith set out on a personal inspection of the Union lines. At several points the three dismounted and approached the riverbank on foot. Grant wrote afterward that they were within easy range of Confederate pickets on the opposite shore but were never fired upon. "I suppose they looked upon the garrison of Chattanooga as prisoners of war, feeding or starving themselves, and thought it would be inhuman to kill any of them except in self-defense."[48]

That night Grant approved Smith's plan to reopen the route to Bridgeport. Thomas's troops would secure both banks of the Tennessee and move downriver while Hooker would march overland from Bridgeport, retake the railroad, and link up with Thomas at Brown's Ferry, about halfway between. Because of his familiarity with the topography, Grant placed Smith in command of the operation, despite the fact that he was then a staff officer and not with troops. It was a felicitous decision. Smith's planning and supervision left little to be desired and by October 29, five days after Grant arrived, the Confederate blockade had been broken and the cracker line to Bridgeport established.*

Within a week the Army of the Cumberland was receiving full rations. "It is hard for anyone not an eye-witness to realize the relief this brought," Grant wrote later. "The men were soon reclothed and also well fed; an abundance of ammunition was brought up, and a cheerfulness prevailed not before enjoyed in many weeks."[49] Grant wired Halleck that the supply question "may now be regarded as settled." He said the danger of losing Chattanooga had passed, and that he was preparing for offensive operations.[50] Grant gave credit to Thomas and Smith, making it clear that "the plan had been set on foot before my arrival."[51] Nevertheless, it was inevitable that Grant would garner most of the praise simply because reopening the line to Bridgeport happened a few days after his arrival. A junior Union officer spoke for most when he said that when Grant came on the scene "we began to see things move. We felt that everything came from a plan."[52]

The burst of activity did wonders for Grant's injured leg. Three days after arriving in Chattanooga he wrote Julia that he was almost well. "The very hard ride over here and necessary exercise since to gain full knowledge of the location, instead of making my injury worse has almost entirely cured me. I now walk without the use of a crutch or cane, and mount my horse from the ground without difficulty."[53]

One of the best descriptions of Grant was provided by a member

---

* For the first and only time in military history, the Union advance was aided by a charge of unattended pack mules. During the fighting the night of October 28, Hooker's teamsters became frightened and deserted their tethered mules. The animals broke loose from their fastenings and stampeded directly toward Longstreet's troops, who in turn became frightened, believing that a brigade of Union cavalry was coming down on them. They too stampeded, leaving it to an Ohio infantryman to immortalize the episode as Tennyson had done for the Light Brigade in the Crimea.

> Half a mile, half a mile,
>   Half a mile onward,
> Right toward the Georgia troops
>   Broke the two hundred,
> "Forward, the Mule Brigade;
>   Charge for the rebs!" they neighed.
>
> When can their glory fade?
> O the wild charge they made!
>   All the world wondered.
> Honor the charge they made;
> Honor the mule brigade,
>   Long-eared two hundred.

Shelby Foote, 2 *The Civil War* 810–11 (New York: Random House, 1963).

of Thomas's staff, who was struck by his modesty and gentleness of manner:

> Many of us were not a little surprised to find him a man of slim figure, slightly stooped, five feet eight in height, weighing only 135 pounds. His eyes were dark-gray, and were the most expressive of his features. His hair and beard were of a chestnut brown color. The beard was worn full, no part of the face being shaved, but, like the hair, was always kept closely and neatly trimmed. His face was not perfectly symmetrical, the left eye being lower than the right. His voice was exceedingly musical, and one of the clearest in sound and most distinct in utterance that I have ever heard. It had a singular power of penetration, and sentences spoken by him in an ordinary tone could be heard at a distance which was surprising. His gait of walking [was] decidedly unmilitary. He never carried his body erect, and having no ear for music or rhythm, he never kept step to the airs played by the bands, no matter how vigorously the bass drums emphasized the accent. . . . When not pressed by any matter of importance he was often slow in his movements, but when roused to activity he was quick in every motion, and worked with marvelous rapidity. He was civil to all who came in contact with him, and never attempted to snub anyone, or treat anybody with less consideration on account of his inferiority in rank.[54]

Another officer wrote that Grant could pass for a "slouchy little subaltern," yet "he is a man of the most exquisite judgment and tact. He handles those around him so quietly and well, he so evidently has the faculty of disposing of work and managing men, he is cool and quiet, almost stolid and as if stupid, in danger, and in a crisis he is one against whom all around, whether few in numbers or a great army as here, would instinctively lean."[55]

Chattanooga, which, in the Cherokee language means "the hawk's nest,"[56] lies on the south bank of the Tennessee River, at a point where the Cumberland mountains crowd together. Standing at Thomas's headquarters and looking south, Grant saw on his left the long spine of Missionary Ridge, 300 feet high, seven miles long, and swarming with Confederates who had had a month to dig in.[57] Dead ahead, Lookout Mountain rose twelve hundred feet above the city and the river, its upper third a vertical reach of sheer rock. Through his glasses Grant could see rebel cannoneers lounging about in various stages of repose, as if to emphasize the advantage they enjoyed over the Union troops below. Beyond Lookout Mountain to Grant's right lay Raccoon Mountain; not as high, broader at its base and more gently sloping, it too was covered from top to bottom with Southern soldiers. Not only did the Confederates hold the high ground, but for one of the few times in the Civil War they enjoyed a significant numerical advantage. Bragg had deployed almost 70,000 men on the heights surrounding Chattanooga, while Thomas had no more than 45,000 effectives present for duty. Hooker, it is true, was standing by at Bridgeport with 18,000 men, and Sherman was coming east with another 20,000 from the Army of the Tennessee. But they had not yet arrived.

Grant saw his work cut out for him. Once the cracker line was opened, he undertook a personal inspection of the picket lines, riding from west to east. As he often did he rode alone, except for a bugler who trailed at a respectful distance. When he reached Chattanooga Creek, a tributary of the Tennessee that drained the area between Missionary Ridge and Lookout Mountain, he found the picket lines of the two armies set on either side, separated by little more than a stone's throw. As Grant approached, the Union sentinel called, "Turn out the guard for the commanding general." Across the creek, the Confederate sentry responded: "Turn out the guard for the commanding general, General Grant." The rebel line formed swiftly, front-faced north, and came to the salute, which Grant returned. It was, as Grant occasionally remarked, a war between countrymen, and at Chattanooga friendly relations existed between the pickets of the two armies. As Grant continued his ride he noticed a tree that had fallen across the creek, which was used by the soldiers of both armies in drawing water for their camps. The Confederates manning the line were from Longstreet's corps and in Grant's words, "wore blue in a different shade from our uniform. Seeing a soldier in blue on this log, I rode up to him, commenced conversing with him, and asked whose corps he belonged to. He was very polite, and, touching his cap to me, said he belonged to General Longstreet's corps. I asked him a few questions—not with a view of gaining any particular information—all of which he answered, and I rode off."[58]

While Grant planned his attack, the Confederate army opposite fell to bickering. Bragg was never easy to get along with, and, in the aftermath of Chickamauga, Southern generals vied with one another castigating him for his failure to destroy Rosecrans when he had the chance. Bragg, for his part, blamed his corps commanders for the tardiness and lassitude that allowed the Army of the Cumberland to escape. Polk, D. H. Hill, and Buckner petitioned Jefferson Davis to remove Bragg, and Longstreet sent a personal note to the Confederate secretary of war, James A. Seddon, asserting that "nothing but the hand of God can save us or help us as long as we have our present commander." Davis decided he had no alternative but to visit Bragg's headquarters and straighten out the mess. The Confederate president, who had never forgotten how Bragg saved the day (and his own Mississippi Rifles) at Buena Vista, had a warm spot in his heart for the brittle North Carolinian, and he was reluctant to relieve the one general who had gained an advantage over the Yankees. When the four corps commanders repeated their view that Bragg must go, Davis procrastinated. Longstreet did not want the job, Beauregard was still in Davis's black book for surrendering Corinth, and Joseph E. Johnston, who would have been ideal, was blamed by the president for the loss of Vicksburg. Bragg would stay, the corps commanders would go. Polk and D. H. Hill were relieved, Buckner was transferred, and Davis urged Bragg to detach Longstreet's corps for an independent campaign against Burnside at Knoxville. The Confederate chieftain believed that the Army of the Cumberland, then beaten and starving, must inevitably surrender, and there was no reason to keep Southern troops idle. Burnside's hold on Knoxville was as tenuous as the Union position at Chattanooga, and Davis assumed Longstreet would make quick work of the Army of the Ohio.

Confederate strategy proved fatally flawed, but it was not necessarily so. Burnside's position at Knoxville was vulnerable, and a logical Union response would have been to send men from Chattanooga to reinforce him. Indeed, that is precisely what Halleck and Lincoln urged when they learned Longstreet had moved north. What Southern strategy failed to take into account was that Grant was in command. As he saw it, the departure of Longstreet's corps from Chattanooga meant the Confederates no longer enjoyed numerical superiority. When Grant discovered on November 5 that Bragg had diminished his force by one quarter, he wanted to attack immediately. In his view, the most effective way to help Burnside was to defeat Bragg at Chattanooga. That would open the road to Atlanta, compel Longstreet to fall back, and place the Confederates on the defensive. Sherman and Hooker were not yet up, but on November 7 Grant ordered Thomas to move between Longstreet and Bragg, turn Bragg's right flank, and dislodge the Confederates from Missionary Ridge.

Thomas agreed it was important to attack Bragg, but he told Grant that he was not ready. Thomas pointed out that he did not have enough draft horses to move his artillery out of the gun park, much less put the guns into battery to support the infantry. Grant once said that "Old Tom" was too brave to run away, but too slow to move forward,[59] yet in this instance Thomas was right. The cracker line had been open for a week and the troops were back on full rations, but no replacements had yet arrived for the artillery horses that had starved to death. Without artillery support, any attack was bound to fail. Grant suggested that Thomas hitch mules to the guns, or use officers' mounts to tow them, but Thomas, an old artilleryman, patiently explained to Grant why that would not work. Unlike horses, the mules were undependable under fire, and the officers' horses had not been broken to work in traces and were too light for heavy pulling in any event. It is understandable that Grant was eager to attack, but he was acting impetuously. Thomas's rocklike refusal to move prematurely saved the Union army from disaster. Two weeks later, when the attack was finally mounted, Federal troops were fought to a standstill in the area that Grant had wanted Thomas to assault, and without artillery they would have been slaughtered. Neither Thomas nor Grant was happy about the situation, but it was clear the artillery could not move. Eventually, Grant was convinced. "Nothing was left to be done," he wrote, "but to answer Washington dispatches as best I could; urge Sherman forward, although he was making every effort to get forward, and encourage Burnside to hold on, assuring him that in a short time he should be relieved." [60]

Grant was frustrated. The opportunity to attack Bragg's diminished force was too good to be true. "I have never felt such restlessness before as I have at the fixed and immovable condition of the Army of the Cumberland," he wired Halleck. [61] By sending Longstreet's corps away, Bragg had prepared the way for his own defeat. Grant knew it, yet he found himself unable to strike, at least until Sherman came up and Thomas's draft horses were replaced. The best he could do was to hurry things along. "Twenty days hence," he wrote Julia, Union forces will be "in a more favorable position . . . than they have been in since the beginning of the rebellion." [62]

On November 13 Sherman reached Bridgeport—sixty miles away. The bulk of his corps was two days behind, but he hurried on to Chattanooga to see Grant. The following evening as he rode up to Thomas's headquarters, he found Grant waiting for him. The exuberant Sherman bounded up the stairs into a remarkable welcome. Sherman and Thomas had been classmates at West Point and were the closest friends, while Grant treasured Sherman above all others.

"Take the chair of honor, Sherman," said Grant, motioning toward a rocking chair by the fire.

"Take the chair of *honor*? Oh no—that belongs to you, General."

"Never mind that," Grant replied. "I always give precedence to age."

"Well, if you put it on that ground I must accept," said Sherman, as he sat down in the most comfortable chair and lit a cigar. [63] The three general officers sat by the fire enjoying their smokes, bantering easily, and then turned to the business at hand. The informality startled observers unaccustomed to Grant's ways. General Oliver Otis Howard, fresh from the Army of the Potomac, wrote later that he'd never witnessed a strategy conference so relaxed. Grant, Thomas, and Sherman simply talked things out. Sherman bubbled with ideas, Thomas waded in with stubborn facts, describing the roads, the rivers, and the mountains in the area, and Grant mostly listened. Howard thought it was like being in a courtroom. Sherman was the flamboyant lawyer, Thomas the stern judge, and Grant the jury whose verdict would settle everything.[64]

The next morning the three generals rode out to inspect the terrain, Grant pointing out how he envisaged the battle unfolding. Sherman was amazed as he looked out at the Confederate entrenchments on Missionary Ridge. Rebel sentinels, in a continuous chain, were walking their posts in plain view, not a thousand yards off. "Why, General Grant, you are besieged," the red-haired Sherman exclaimed, not altogether in jest.

"It's too true," Grant nodded, and then proceeded to tell Sherman and Thomas what he had in mind.[65] A frontal assault was out of the question. Vicksburg had taught Grant that it was hazardous to attack a heavily fortified position and the Confederates were not only well entrenched, but held a mass of high ground that appeared impregnable. Instead, Grant proposed to turn Bragg's flanks, force him out of his breastworks, and deny him the advantage of topography. It would be a double envelopment. Thomas's Army of the Cumberland, located in the center, would maintain its position facing Missionary Ridge and hold Bragg in place while Hooker and Sherman rolled up the Confederate left and right respectively. If Bragg shifted troops from the center to reinforce his flanks, then Thomas could storm forward and carry Missionary Ridge against a depleted Confederate force. Grant had worked on the plan since his arrival in Chattanooga and was confident of its success. He also liked the flexibility. He could reinforce the attack on whichever flank was successful, or he could advance Thomas to render the coup de main.

Grant placed primary emphasis on turning Bragg's right and moving down the long axis of Missionary Ridge from the north—the direction Bragg least expected. This he assigned to Sherman and his corps from the Army of the Tennessee. These were Grant's troops and he was relying on them to carry the principal attack. With his four divisions still on their approach from the west, Sherman was instructed to leapfrog Hooker, slip northeast behind Thomas, and take up a position on the Union left. Hooker, on the right, would prepare to move against Lookout Mountain with his veterans from the Army of the Potomac and attack Bragg from that direction. Grant had less confidence in the Army of the Cumberland. It had been mauled at Chickamauga and almost starved afterward. He did not believe the men could spearhead the attack, but if Sherman and Hooker could turn Bragg's flanks, Grant counted on Thomas to finish the job by moving against the Confederate center. Given the weather and the condition of the roads, Grant allowed five days for Sherman's troops to reach their position. Accordingly, he set the attack for November 21. The final order of battle assigned four divisions to Sherman, four to Thomas, three to Hooker, with two in reserve under General Howard—a total of 75,000 men. For the second time in the Civil War, troops from three Union armies would fight shoulder to shoulder. At the capture of Corinth in 1862, Halleck commanded the armies of Buell, Pope, and Grant. At Chattanooga, Grant commanded men from the Army of the Cumberland, the Army of the Potomac, and the Army of the Tennessee.

Sherman was late getting into position, mainly because of the weather. It rained steadily for two days and the roads, which were already bad, became impassable. A pontoon bridge across the Tennessee washed away and another threatened to do so. As a result, Sherman's men did not arrive at their jump-off point until late in the day on November 23. By this time Grant was worried that Bragg might slip away. Already two Confederate divisions had been dispatched to assist Longstreet, and rumors were flying that Bragg was about to pull out toward Atlanta. Grant could not bear to see his covey escape. He was also under increasing pressure from Washington to assist Burnside. Accordingly, at 11 A.M. on November 23, with Sherman still on the march, Grant instructed Thomas to extend his lines toward Missionary Ridge and gauge Bragg's response. It was another example of Grant's battlefield flexibility. If Sherman wasn't ready, he'd use Thomas. Thomas's lines were separated from the base of Missionary Ridge by a rolling, open plain roughly two miles wide. Grant wanted Thomas to probe Bragg's front, drive in his skirmish line, and move closer to the base of the ridge. That would provide Thomas with a better takeoff point should he be required to assault the main Confederate battle line. It would also capture Bragg's attention and prevent him from running.

Thomas outdid himself. The Army of the Cumberland was smarting because of the secondary role they had been assigned, and from Thomas down the troops wanted to dispel the image of defeat at Chickamauga. In addition, Thomas's normally placid manner had been set on edge. Several days earlier Thomas, with utmost courtesy, had sent through the lines a personal letter addressed to a Confederate officer from his kinfolks. Thomas attached a note to Bragg, requesting his former battery commander to pass it along. The letter was promptly returned with Bragg's endorsement: "Respectfully returned to General Thomas. General Bragg declines to have any intercourse with a man who has betrayed his State." Thomas was furious. Sherman, who had known Thomas for almost thirty years, said that he had never seen him so angry.[66] Old Pap was itching to get even.

Ninety minutes after receiving Grant's order, Thomas had three divisions on line, with a fourth massed in reserve, all ready to move out. Rather than merely feel Bragg's position, Old Pap was readying a sledgehammer. On the open plain, in clear view of the Confederates high on Missionary Ridge, the Army of the Cumberland ostentatiously dressed their ranks for almost an hour. A staff officer recalled the inspiring sight. "Flags were flying; the quick, earnest steps of thousands beat equal time. The sharp commands of hundreds of company officers, the sound of drums, the ringing notes of the bugles, companies wheeling and countermarching and regiments getting into line . . . all looked like preparations for a peacetime pageant, rather than for the bloody work of death."[67] Rebel soldiers, watching from above, concluded the Yankees were going to hold a parade. They stood on their parapets and called to one another to watch the men in blue pass in review. About 1:30 Thomas's artillery roared into action and the drums and bugles changed tempo. The regiments wheeled to face the enemy and Thomas sent the troops charging forward, the divisions of Wood and Sheridan in the van. The attack was in full force before the Confederates realized it. The massive blue tide flooded the plain between the lines, swept over the rebel outposts, and drove the defenders back to Bragg's main battle line. Thomas's men took over the rebel trenches, reversed the parapets to face the other way, and settled down for the night, one mile in advance of where they were in the morning. Casualties were light. Thomas lost less than 200 men; Confederate figures were similar.[68]

The assault by the Army of the Cumberland was executed flawlessly. In Grant's eyes, Thomas's men had redeemed themselves. They also proved that Bragg was not retreating. That too pleased Grant. "The advantage was greatly on our side now," he wrote, "and if I could only have been assured that Burnside could hold out ten days longer I should have rested more easily."[69] A Southern newsman, watching the fight from the top of Missionary Ridge, agreed that the initiative had shifted to the Union. "General Grant has made an important move that is likely to exert an important influence on military operations," he wrote, and predicted that Bragg would have to weaken his line on Lookout Mountain to reinforce the troops on Missionary Ridge that now seemed menaced by Thomas's advance.[70]

November 24 dawned with a cold drizzle. Thomas's men continued to strengthen their position, while on the left and the right Sherman and Hooker moved to turn Bragg's flanks. Sherman encountered heavy opposition. Poor reconnaissance and bad map reading placed his corps not on the north end of Missionary Ridge but on a detached spur separated by a deep ravine from the main spine. Traversing the unexpected obstacle was proving more difficult than either Grant or Sherman anticipated.

On the right, Hooker moved ahead quickly. Bragg had indeed shifted two divisions from Lookout Mountain and as a result the Confederate line was lightly held. Troops from three Union divisions scrambled up the mountain over boulders and fallen logs through an intermittent fog that in later years was romanticized as the "battle above the clouds." Grant was with Thomas in the center of the Union line, sitting their horses at Thomas's command post, and straining to catch a glimpse of the fighting on the right. "The day was hazy," Grant wrote later, "so that Hooker's operations were not visible to us except at moments when the clouds would rise. But the sound of his artillery and musketry was heard incessantly."[71] Suddenly, in mid-afternoon, the sun came out and the fog drifted away. From Grant's vantage point the entire battle could be seen. The Confederates were in full retreat and around the mountain wall came rank after rank of Union troops, regimental flags aloft, rifle barrels glinting in the sunlight, victory in plain view of both armies below. Thomas's troops cheered wildly and regimental bands spontaneously broke into tune, until the celebration engulfed the entire Federal line. Just as suddenly, clouds moved in front of the sun and hid the battle from view. Hooker's troops had not reached the summit, but there was no doubt Lookout Mountain had fallen.

At 6 P.M. Grant passed the word to Halleck. "The fight today progressed favorably. Sherman carried the end of Missionary Ridge . . . and troops from Lookout Valley carried the point of the Mountain and now hold the eastern slope and a point high up. Our loss is not heavy. Hooker reports 2000 prisoners taken besides which a small number have fallen into our hands from Missionary Ridge."[72]

The relief in Washington was palpable. President Lincoln wired his personal congratulations to Grant: "Well done. Many thanks to all. Remember Burnside."[73] Halleck was equally pleased. "I congratulate you on the success," said the general in chief. "Burnside is hard pressed and any further delay may prove fatal. I know that you will do all in your power to relieve him."[74]

Grant was thinking less about Burnside than about destroying Bragg's army the next day. Shortly after midnight he ordered Sherman to move forward "at early dawn" and attack the north end of Missionary Ridge.[75] Hooker was instructed to move eastward from Lookout Mountain, cross the Chattanooga valley, and assault the Confederate position on the southern end of the ridge.[76] Thomas was told to be prepared to assist Sherman, but to await Grant's order before moving. "Your command will either carry the rifle pits and ridge directly in front of them, or move to the left as the presence of the enemy may require."[77]

November 25 opened clear and bright. And for the next eight hours that was the best Grant could say about it. Nothing went as planned. During the night Bragg had reinforced his right with a hard-fighting division commanded by one of the most able combat commanders in the Confederate army, Major General Patrick Cleburne—a Texas original. Sherman went forward at dawn, found Cleburne's division in his path, and was stopped cold. By eleven o'clock Sherman had yet to make a dent in the Confederate line and Grant sent Howard's two divisions to assist. It was six divisions against one but the rebels, defending a narrow stretch of high ground, held their position against everything Sherman could throw at them. By early afternoon, after six hours of solid fighting and almost 2,000 casualties, it was clear that the principal Union assault had bogged down. Sherman signaled Grant that he was facing heavy opposition and was stuck. "Attack again," Grant replied, but he realized that the effort to turn the north end of Bragg's line had come to naught.[78]

It was no better at the south end of Missionary Ridge. Hooker's advance through the Chattanooga valley required him to cross Chattanooga Creek, which was more of an obstacle than the word "creek" implied. Retreating Confederates had burned the only bridge, and it required four hours for Union engineers to construct another one. The result was that it was almost 3 P.M. before any of Hooker's men were in position to attack Bragg's left. Grant's plan for a double envelopment had come unhinged. With Sherman stuck and Hooker late, he turned to Thomas. Grant had spent the entire day with the Army of the Cumberland, and now he asked Old Pap to carry the attack. Grant had hesitated to order Thomas forward because of the imposing strength of the main Confederate battle line. He was also concerned that the rebel flanks had not been turned, which meant that Bragg could devote his entire attention to repelling Thomas's attack. What Grant did not know was that his original plan had worked better than he realized. Bragg had already thinned his ranks on Missionary Ridge to support his flanks, and he was on the verge of sending more men to resist Sherman—although Cleburne didn't need them. General William Hardee, who commanded the troops on the ridge, acknowledged to a nervous staff officer that the Confederate line was thinly held, but he saw no reason to worry. The natural strength of the position was so formidable, said Hardee, that the Yankees probably would not attack it at all.[79]

It was close to 3:30 when Grant ordered Thomas forward. Old Pap was instructed to carry the rifle pits at the base of the ridge preparatory to assaulting the summit itself.[80] For a while nothing happened and Grant grew impatient. It took time for orders to filter down and the remaining hours of daylight were slipping away. Suddenly the signal guns went off and from behind a rise the soldiers appeared, three double-ranks deep, a grand panorama of massed infantry along a front that stretched for more than a mile from flank to flank. Thomas, wielding a sledgehammer again, placed all four divisions of the Army of the Cumberland on line: Sheridan and Wood in the center, Absalom Baird on the left, Richard Johnson on the right. At Old Pap's command, almost 24,000 men—sixty regiments of infantry—began their dash across a mile of open plain toward the first line of rebel entrenchments. It was Pickett's charge at Gettysburg revisited with a vengeance: Thomas deployed twice as many men as Lee had used, and the Confederate position on Missionary Ridge was far more imposing than the line Meade had held in Pennsylvania.

As soon as the blue phalanx moved forward, rebel artillery on the ridge opened a devastating barrage. Bragg had 112 guns, and as one Union soldier recalled, "A crash like a thousand thunderclaps greeted us."[81] Philip H. Sheridan rode in front of his division, and as the projectiles burst over and among the advancing troops the men broke into a run. Sheridan looked back and said the line suddenly became a crowd, all glittering with bayonets, a "terrible sight" for the rebels who had to look at it.[82] Brigadier General Montgomery Meigs, the army's quartermaster general, who was in Chattanooga to confer with Grant, wrote afterward that, "Every gun on Missionary Ridge broke out with shell and shrapnell upon the heads of our gallant troops, who never halted until they reached the [enemy] breastworks."[83]

As the men drew near Bragg's battle line they saw unmistakable signs of panic setting in. Here and there defenders began to waver, flinching at the sight of the oncoming mass, deserting their posts and running up the ridge. As Thomas anticipated, the immense weight of the charging infantry simply rolled over the rebel defenses and swamped them. Grant wrote, "Our men drove the troops in front of the lower line of rifle pits so rapidly, and followed them so closely, that rebel and Union troops went over the first line of works almost at the same time."[84]

Having taken their first objective, the soldiers of the Army of the Cumberland now performed a magnificent act of insubordination. Rather than dig in and regroup as their officers commanded, the men kept going. The fact is, it was too hot to stay where they were. A murderous, plunging fire from the Confederate second line, midway up the slope, made their position untenable. They were sitting ducks for rebel gunners and the only practical solution was to continue the charge. At first by squads and platoons, then by companies and regiments, the blue mass swarmed up the steep slope of Missionary Ridge, aligning their ragged lines as best they could, caught up in the exhilaration of the moment. "Chickamauga! Chickamauga!" soldiers yelled with sweet revenge as the stunned rebels panicked, broke, and fled.[85] Soon sixty regimental flags appeared to be racing each other to the summit.

Back at Thomas's command post, Grant watched the unexpected development—first with bewilderment, then with growing alarm. Bragg had a well-deserved reputation as a counterpuncher, and if his troops re-

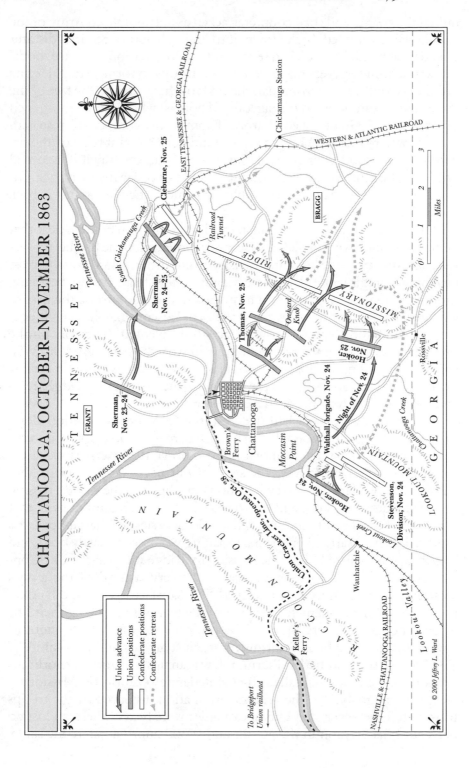

CHATTANOOGA, OCTOBER–NOVEMBER 1863

Union advance
Union positions
Confederate positions
Confederate retreat

Miles
0 1 2 3

TENNESSEE

GEORGIA

Tennessee River

South Chickamauga Creek

Tennessee River

Tennessee River

EAST TENNESSEE & GEORGIA RAILROAD

WESTERN & ATLANTIC RAILROAD

Chickamauga Station

Cleburne, Nov. 25

Railroad Tunnel

BRAGG

Sherman, Nov. 24–25

GRANT

Sherman, Nov. 23–24

Thomas, Nov. 25

Orchard Knob

MISSIONARY RIDGE

Hooker, Nov. 25

Rossville

Brown's Ferry

Chattanooga

Moccasin Point

Walthall, brigade, Nov. 24

Night of Nov. 24

Hooker, Nov. 24

Stevenson, Division, Nov. 24

LOOKOUT MOUNTAIN

Lookout Creek

Chattanooga Creek

Lookout Valley

Wauhatchie

Union Cracker Line opened Oct. 28

R A C C O O N   M O U N T A I N

Kelley's Ferry

To Bridgeport
Union railhead

NASHVILLE & CHATTANOOGA RAILROAD

© 2000 Jeffrey L. Ward

pulsed the charge and then counterattacked as a demoralized Army of the Cumberland tumbled back down into the valley, a first-class disaster would be at hand. Thomas had sent all four of his divisions forward, nothing was kept in reserve, and there were no troops to form a straggler line on which to rally. Aside from that, the odds of charging into the face of the Confederate guns seemed outrageous. "Thomas, who ordered those men up the ridge?" Grant asked sharply. Thomas, his composure restored, replied matter-of-factly, "I don't know. I did not." [86] Grant realized the situation was beyond their control. Someone would catch hell if it turned out badly, he muttered, but he said he would not order the men back. Instead, he clamped his teeth on his unlit cigar and turned his attention back to the ridge.

It was now almost 5 P.M. And in the distance it soon became clear that Grant need not have worried. The second Confederate line had been overrun, and the men of Sheridan's division were driving hard for the crest beyond. Six regimental flags were plainly visible from below, bobbing, drooping, disappearing momentarily, each unit seeking to be the first to gain the heights. The honor went to the 24th Wisconsin, whose eighteen-year-old adjutant, Captain Arthur MacArthur, planted the colors on the precipice after leading the regiment upward with the battle cry "On, Wisconsin." According to his son Douglas, MacArthur was embraced by Sheridan: "Take care of him," the jubilant general told the Badger regiment, "he has just won the Medal of Honor." [87]

As unit after unit reached the crest, the Confederate position along Missionary Ridge unraveled. Bragg himself barely escaped capture as rebel soldiers threw away their weapons and fled down the reverse slope, seeking safety in the rear. It was "the sight of our lives," one Union soldier wrote. "Gray clad men rushed wildly down the hill into the woods, tossing away knapsacks, muskets, and blankets as they ran. In ten minutes all that remained of the defiant rebel army that so long besieged Chattanooga was captured guns, disarmed prisoners, moaning wounded, ghastly dead, and scattered, demoralized fugitives. Missionary Ridge was ours." [88] The Confederates abandoned forty-one pieces of artillery, a third of the army's total, and left 7,000 muskets in the field. "No satisfactory excuse can possibly be given for the shameful conduct of the troops in allowing their line to be penetrated," wrote Bragg. "The position was one which ought to have been held by a line of skirmishers against any assaulting column." [89] The Army of the Cumberland's triumph was an upset victory of enormous proportions. Grant later called the Confederate position on Missionary Ridge "impregnable." [90] The grim determination displayed by the troops took its toll, however, and Union casualties were heavy. Sheridan lost 20 percent of his division in the assault and Wood approximately the same.

An Indiana regiment began its ascent with 337 men and lost 202 of them, or nearly 60 percent. Overall, Union losses totaled 5,475 killed and wounded; the Confederates lost less than half that. But the number of men captured or missing told a different story. Grant lost 349; Bragg 4,146.

Grant attributed the victory in part to Bragg's faulty deployment of his army. Too many men were placed on the plain in front of what was an otherwise easily defended position.[91] When they fell back, the troops behind them panicked. Despite their smashing victory at Chickamauga, despite the enormous advantage of terrain and artillery support, despite the powerful resistance that Cleburne's division put up against Sherman, the brute strength of Thomas's charge was too great to withstand. The shock action of sixty infantry regiments descending en masse on the main Confederate battle line disconcerted the defenders. After the first rifle pits were overrun, Union attackers followed the retreating rebels so closely that it became impossible for Bragg's troops to make a stand. Momentum carried the day. And morale. Thomas had done a superb job reorganizing the Army of the Cumberland after Rosecrans's departure, and Grant's presence had a tonic effect. The men knew what was expected of them and gave all they had. By contrast, the bickering among Confederate generals seeped downward through the ranks. Once the corps commanders lost confidence in Bragg, it was inevitable that the dissatisfaction would spread through the army.

The battle of Chattanooga was won by the soldiers of the Army of the Cumberland. Credit Grant for effectively deploying the troops from three separate armies, devising a battle plan that fit the situation, and relying on his subordinates to carry through. Sherman's performance was disappointing, but Thomas made up for it. Jefferson Davis deserves some credit for the Union victory as well. The decision to detach Longstreet's corps altered the balance of forces at Chattanooga and gave Grant the opportunity he needed. Writing about the battle years later, Grant said, "Mr. Davis had an exalted opinion of his own military genius," and on more than one occasion during the war "came to the relief of the Union army."[92]

There was no formal surrender ceremony at Chattanooga, but Grant's compassion for his defeated adversaries was again on display. A Confederate soldier who was taken prisoner recorded that as he and other prisoners were being taken to the rear, they were halted to allow a group of Union generals and their staffs to pass by. The officers rode past the Confederates smugly without any sign of recognition except by one. "When General Grant reached the line of ragged, filthy, bloody, despairing prisoners strung out on each side of the bridge, he lifted his hat and held it over his head until he passed the last man of that living funeral cortege. He was the only officer in that whole train who recognized us as being on the face of the earth."[93]

Another portrait of Grant was provided by Major General David Hunter, the senior general on active duty, who spent most of November in Chattanooga. Writing to Secretary of War Stanton, Hunter said that Grant had received him with great kindness. "He gave me his bed, shared with me his room, gave me to ride his favorite warhorse, read to me his dispatches, accompanied me on my reviews, and I accompanied him during the three days of the battle. In fact, I saw him almost every moment, except when sleeping, of the three weeks I spent in Chattanooga. He is a hard worker, writes his own dispatches and orders, and does his own thinking. He is modest, quiet, never swears, and seldom drinks, as he only took two drinks during the three weeks I was with him. He listens quietly to the opinions of others and then judges promptly for himself, and he is very prompt to avail himself in the field of all the errors of the enemy."[94]

Vicksburg was Grant's great victory in the West and the turning point of the war. But as one historian has noted, the triumph at Chattanooga proclaimed Grant's military genius.[95] As at Fort Donelson and Shiloh, he converted certain defeat into a smashing Union victory. Had he not been dispatched by Washington to take command, it is fair to surmise that the Army of the Cumberland would have perished. Burnside at Knoxville would have been forced to surrender, eastern Tennessee would have fallen to the Confederacy, rebel momentum would have accelerated, and the survival of the Union would have been imperiled. As it was, the remnants of Bragg's army were in headlong retreat toward Atlanta. Grant continued the pursuit for two days, but then halted to march to Burnside's assistance—a situation that took care of itself before Sherman's relief column could arrive. After learning of Bragg's defeat, Longstreet decided that the soundest course would be to attack Burnside, dispose of the Army of the Ohio, and regain the initiative. "There is neither safety nor honor in any other course," Longstreet told his skeptical subordinates.[96] Accordingly, on November 29, four days after the battle of Chattanooga, Confederate troops attempted to storm the Union lines at Knoxville and were repulsed with heavy losses. Against the odds, Burnside had held out. Longstreet broke off the battle and on December 3 withdrew northward. The siege of Knoxville was lifted and both sides settled down for the winter.

Grant was unhappy about going into winter quarters. He saw no reason to keep the army idle, and the pause would give the rebels time to reorganize.[97] Accordingly, he wrote Halleck on December 7 suggesting that the operation against Mobile be reactivated. "I would hope to secure that place, or its investment, by the last of January." If the enemy mounted a stubborn resistance, Grant proposed to isolate the city and move with the bulk of his army into central Alabama and possibly Georgia. "It seems to me this move would secure the entire states of Alabama & Mississippi, and a part of Georgia." Grant said that if he did so it would force Lee to abandon Virginia and come south, because "without his force the enemy have not got army enough to resist the army I can take."[98]

Officials in Washington were less sanguine than Grant and gave little credence to the impact of an offensive in the South on Lee's Army of Northern Virginia. Halleck eventually approved the operation against Mobile, provided Tennessee was liberated first. In particular, both Lincoln and Halleck wanted Longstreet ejected from east Tennessee before tackling the Gulf Coast city.[99] Grant did not disagree, but the severity of the winter in the mountainous country north of Knoxville made any advance against Longstreet impractical until spring. Accordingly, he improvised. Rather than wait for spring, he sent Sherman to Vicksburg with instructions to launch a massive raid east through Mississippi, seize the rail junction at Meridian, and destroy the track, rolling stock, and whatever else might be of use to the Confederacy. This was truly a prelude to Sherman's March to the Sea, and Uncle Billy performed the task with enthusiasm.* Thomas was ordered to cooperate with Sherman's movement by making a show of advancing from Chattanooga toward Atlanta, while the Army of the Ohio was to block any attempt by Longstreet to move south. Simply put, Grant was stirring the pot in the Division of the Mississippi and keeping the rebels off balance while waiting to take the offensive in spring.

The deliverance of Chattanooga and Knoxville was celebrated throughout the North with thanksgiving and reverence. President Lincoln coupled his announcement of the victories with a recommendation that people gather in their churches to thank the Lord "for this great advancement of the national cause." He then sent a personal message to Grant:

> Understanding that your lodgement at Chattanooga and Knoxville is now secure, I wish to tender you, and all under your command, my more than thanks, my profoundest gratitude, for the skill, courage and perseverance with which you, and they, over so great difficulties, have effected that important object. God bless you all![100]
>
> A. LINCOLN

---

* "My movement to Meridian stampeded all Alabama," Sherman wrote. The Confederates "retreated across the Tombigbee and left me to smash things at pleasure. . . . We broke absolutely and effectively a full hundred miles of railroad and made a swath of desolation fifty miles broad across the State of Mississippi which the present generation will not forget." Foote, 2 *Civil War* 934.

CHAPTER NINE

GENERAL IN CHIEF

The great thing about Grant is his perfect coolness and persistency of purpose . . . he is not easily excited . . . and he has the grit of a bulldog.

ABRAHAM LINCOLN

HONORS DESCENDED ON GRANT. The citizens of Galena and Jo Daviess County subscribed for a diamond-hilted sword with a gold scabbard listing the battles he had fought. Congress, not to be outdone, passed a joint resolution thanking Grant and his troops for their gallantry at Vicksburg and Chattanooga, further providing that "a gold medal be struck . . . to be presented to Major General Grant in the name of the people of the United States."[1] Inevitably legislation was introduced to revive the rank of lieutenant general, last held by George Washington in 1798. The bill was sponsored by Elihu Washburne in the House and James Doolittle of Wisconsin in the Senate, and the purpose was to ensure that Grant, for whom the rank was intended, would assume command of the Union military effort.[2]* According to Senator Doolittle, Grant had won seventeen battles, captured 100,000 prisoners, and taken 500 pieces of artillery. "He has organized victory from the beginning, and I want him in a position where he can organize *final* victory and bring it to our armies and put an end to the rebellion."[3]

Debate on the bill, which consumed the month of February 1864, took place before the backdrop of a boomlet pushing Grant for president. Lincoln's renomination and reelection were by no means assured. Despite

---

* The bill reviving the position of lieutenant general made it explicit that the person holding that rank would "under the direction of the President, *command the armies of the United States.*" (Emphasis in original.)

arguments for not switching horses in the middle of the stream, the one term principle seemed firmly fixed in the mind of the electorate. No incumbent president had been renominated since 1840, and none had been reelected since Andrew Jackson won a second term in 1832. Already rival candidates, including Secretary of the Treasury Salmon P. Chase, were waiting in the wings preparing to contest the Republican convention at Baltimore in June. Grant, a potential wild card, was wooed by prominent members of both parties. "The next president must be a military man," wrote James Gordon Bennett, publisher of the *New York Herald*. "General Grant celebrated Independence Day of 1863 by marching into Vicksburg, and on Thanksgiving Day he coolly gave Bragg a tanning and a thrashing. Perhaps he has something in store for Christmas, and he may give the rebels a call on New Year's Day in Atlanta. On the fourth of March 1865 [Inauguration Day], he will be in Washington."[4]

Even before Bennett began to beat the drum, Grant received a letter from the chairman of the Democratic party in Ohio requesting that he permit his name to be placed in nomination.[5] "The question astonishes me," Grant replied. "I do not know of anything I have ever done or said which would indicate that I could be a candidate for any office whatever." Grant said he would continue to do his duty to suppress the rebellion, and would support whatever administration was in power. Recognizing that even a denial on his part might lead to further speculation, Grant asked the Ohio chairman to keep the correspondence private. "But wherever you hear my name mentioned, say that you know from me direct that I am not 'in the field.'"[6]

Other inquiries were turned aside firmly. Old friends were given the message politely.[7] Grant's father, pressing the issue from Covington, Kentucky, was told to stand down somewhat more abruptly. "Nothing personal could ever induce me to accept a political office," wrote Grant.[8] The most extensive reply went to Congressman Isaac N. Morris of Illinois, a determined foe of Lincoln:

> In your letter you say I have it in my power to be the next President. This is the last thing in the world I desire. I would regard such a consummation as being highly unfortunate for myself, if not for the country. Through Providence I have attained to more than I had ever hoped and . . . infinitely prefer my present position to that of any civil office within the gift of the people.[9]

Lincoln, who wanted to turn the war over to Grant, was nevertheless concerned about creating another rival standing between him and reelection. "When the presidential grub once gets into a man, it can gnaw deeply," he told a visitor, and Lincoln wondered whether it was gnawing at Grant. To find out, the president asked his old friend from Illinois, Elihu Washburne. "About all I know of Grant I have got from you," said Lincoln. "I have never seen him. Who else besides you knows anything about Grant?"[10]

Washburne said the man to talk to was the United States marshal in Chicago, J. Russell Jones, formerly of Galena, who had kept in touch with Grant throughout the war. Jones, said Washburne, knew Grant as well as anyone. Off to Jones went an urgent message from the White House: Come to Washington immediately, the president wishes to see you.[11]

Jones was aware of the efforts to create a presidential bandwagon for Grant, and he had written a friendly note urging the general to ignore them. Grant wrote back that he had received a great deal of mail asking him to run, and that he invariably threw it into the wastebasket. "I already have a pretty big job on my hands, and . . . nothing could induce me to think of being a presidential candidate, particularly so long as there is a possibility of having Mr. Lincoln re-elected."[12]

Grant's letter was delivered to Jones the day before he left Chicago for Washington. When he called at the White House, Lincoln asked point-blank if Grant wanted to be president and Jones gave him the letter. "My son, you will never know how gratifying this is to me," said the president.[13] Later, Jones concluded that the letter "established a perfect understanding" between Lincoln and Grant.[14]

With Grant's position clarified, Lincoln added his support to the bill to revive the rank of lieutenant general. The measure was passed by the House (117–19) on February 1, by the Senate (31–6) on February 26, and signed into law by the president on Leap Year Day, February 29, 1864.[15] The following day Lincoln sent Grant's name to the Senate. He was confirmed March 2, and on March 3 Halleck wired Nashville instructing him to "report in person to the War Department as soon as practicable."[16] Halleck said Grant's commission as lieutenant general had been signed by the president and would be delivered to him when he arrived. "I sincerely congratulate you on this recognition of your distinguished and meritorious service."[17]

Grant's promotion to lieutenant general meant that he would supersede Halleck as general in chief. Halleck had come to Washington from Corinth in the summer of 1862, but had failed to live up to his early promise. Lincoln told John Hay that he had sent for Halleck when McClellan proved incompetent. Halleck, he said, had stipulated that he should be given full power and responsibility as general in chief. "He ran it on that basis till Pope's defeat [at Second Manassas]; but ever since that event he has shrunk from responsibility whenever it was possible."[18]

The fault was not entirely Halleck's. Except for Grant, the Union's field commanders in 1863–1864 were either unwilling or unable to take the fight to the enemy. McClellan, Burnside, Hooker, and even Meade were reluctant to move against the Army of Northern Virginia, while Banks at New Orleans and Frémont in West Virginia were uninspiring at best when confronting the enemy. Topside, Halleck's task was also not easy. Despite Lincoln's pledge to give the general in chief full control, both he and Secretary of War Stanton continually intervened to determine military strategy. As Halleck wrote Sherman, "I am simply a military adviser of the Secretary of War and the President, and must obey and carry out what they decide upon, whether I concur in their decisions or not. As a good soldier I obey the orders of my superiors. If I disagree with them I say so, but when they decide, it is my duty faithfully to carry out their decision." [19]

What went unnoticed by Halleck's critics was his exceptional capacity to organize and equip the army while deflecting political meddling by Congress. The army he was about to turn over, if not a well-oiled machine, was at least superbly supplied and positioned to respond to Grant's direction. And in the way of the old army, Halleck did not begrudge Grant's promotion. "General Grant is my personal friend," the general in chief wrote to an old associate, "and I heartily rejoice at his promotion." Halleck said that by law Grant would become the army's commander and that it was a situation into which individual feelings could not enter. "Undoubtedly it will be said that I throw up my office in dudgeon because General Grant has been promoted over my head. There is no possible ground for such an accusation. The honor was fully due to him, and with the honor he must take the responsibilities which belong to the office." [20]

Grant departed Nashville for Washington on March 4. When he left, it was with the firm intention of returning to Tennessee and, while he retained control of all the armies, of personally commanding the drive from Chattanooga to Atlanta to the sea. "I am ordered to Washington," Grant wired Sherman on March 4, but "I expect in the course of ten or twelve days to return to this command." [21]

In a lengthy personal letter, hand-carried to Sherman by one of Grant's aides, he told his most trusted associate what was in store: "Dear Sherman: The bill reviving the grade of lieutenant general has become law, and my name has been sent to the Senate for the place. I now receive orders to report to Washington immediately in person, which indicates either a confirmation or a likelihood of confirmation." Grant told Sherman that he would not accept the appointment if it required him to remain at a desk in Washington, and proceeded to thank him and McPherson "as the men to whom, above all others, I feel indebted for whatever I have had of success. How far your advice and suggestions have been of assistance, you know. How far your execution of whatever has been given you to do entitled you to the reward I am receiving, you cannot know as well as me."[22]

Sherman read the letter with mixed emotions. He was delighted that his friend had received the promotion he deserved, but he worried that Grant would be overwhelmed by the political responsibilities of general in chief, especially if he were cut off from active campaigning in the field. After mulling the matter for two days, he sent Grant a heartfelt reply.

> You do yourself injustice, and us too much honor, in assigning to us too large a share of the merits which have led to your advancement. . . . At Belmont you manifested your traits—neither of us being near. At Donelson, also, you illustrated your whole character. I was not near, and McPherson in too subordinate a capacity to influence you. Until you had won Donelson, I confess I was almost cowed by the terrible array of anarchical elements that presented themselves at every point; but that victory admitted a ray of light I have followed since. . . . The chief characteristic of your nature is the simple faith in success you have always manifested, which I can liken to nothing else than the faith a Christian has in the Savior. This faith gave you victory at Shiloh and Vicksburg. When you have completed your preparations, you go into battle without hesitation, as at Chattanooga—no doubts—no reserve; and I tell you that it was this that made us act with confidence. I knew wherever I was that you thought of me, and if I got into a tight place you would help me out, if alive. My only points of doubt was in your knowledge of grand strategy and of books of science and history, but I confess your common-sense seems to have supplied this.

Sherman recognized that if Grant remained in Washington overall command in the West would likely fall to him. And though he wanted the job, he did not want it at his friend's expense. "Don't stay in Washington," he urged Grant. "Halleck is better qualified than you to stand the buffets of intrigue and policy. Come West. For God's sake and your country's sake, come out of Washington! I foretold General Halleck, before he left Corinth, the inevitable result to him, and now I exhort you to come out West. Here lies the seat of coming empire. When our work is done, we will make short work of Charleston and Richmond."[23]

Grant arrived in Washington with typical understatement. The White House had designated a welcoming committee to meet the train and escort him to his hotel, but the arrangements fell through and no one was on hand when he arrived the afternoon of March 8, accompanied by his thirteen-year-old son, Fred. Inconspicuous and unrecognized, a travel-stained linen duster hiding most of his uniform, he made his way to the Willard Hotel, two blocks down Pennsylvania Avenue from the White House. Grant had stayed at the old Willard twelve years earlier when he had sought to clear the army's books of the missing $1,000 in quartermaster funds from Mexico. A bored desk clerk, accustomed to dealing with the capital's most distinguished guests, looked at him, saw no one in particular, and allowed as how there might be a small room on the top floor, if that would do. Grant said it would be fine and signed the register. The clerk twirled the book around to write a room number after the name, and saw: "U. S. Grant and son, Galena, Illinois." Suddenly, everything changed. The stunned clerk, recognizing his error, became the soul of Washington hospitality. Forgotten now was the top-floor room Grant had modestly accepted. Instead, the clerk suggested Parlor 6, the best suite in the hotel, where Lincoln had stayed the week preceding his inauguration. Grant accepted the change without comment. As he saw it, any room would do and he certainly did not want to call attention to himself.

Word of Grant's presence in the hotel spread quickly. When he returned downstairs with Fred for dinner, people at nearby tables gawked and craned their necks to see the nation's hero. Presently one of the diners, unable to contain his enthusiasm, mounted his chair and led the guests in "three cheers for Lieutenant General Grant." These were given "in the most tremendous manner," followed by a pounding on tabletops that made the glasses and silverware tinkle.[24] Grant stood up, fumbled with his napkin, bowed impersonally in all directions, and resumed his seat. He tried to go on with his meal but left shortly afterward to another standing ovation.

When Grant returned to Parlor 6 a message was waiting for him from the White House. The president's weekly reception was in progress, and Mr. Lincoln asked if he would care to come by. Grant had not yet changed from his well-worn traveling uniform, but after seeing that Fred was put to bed, he headed over to the executive mansion. There he found himself ushered through the foyer, down the great corridor, and into the brightly lit East Room, where the reception was in full swing. As Grant entered, the crowd fell silent, then parted before him like the waters of the Red Sea to disclose at the far end of the room the tall, gaunt figure of the president of the United States. As Grant walked toward him, Lincoln extended his hand and smiled broadly. "Why, here is General Grant! Well, this is a great pleasure, I assure you." The handshaking over, the two stood together for a moment, Lincoln beaming down with vast good humor, Grant looking up at him, his right hand grasping the lapel of his uniform.[25] There was a smattering of applause, the crowd resumed its buzz, and Lincoln turned

Grant over to Secretary of State William H. Seward for presentation to Mrs. Lincoln. Mrs. Lincoln told Grant how pleased she was to meet him, and she and the general chatted pleasantly for a few minutes. The guests had by this time become so curious that they surged forward for a closer look and perhaps an exchange of greetings. A White House official recalled that Grant "blushed like a schoolgirl," sweating heavily from embarrassment and the task of shaking hands with those nearest. Cries arose of "Grant, Grant, Grant," followed by cheer after cheer. Seward, after some persuasion, induced Grant to stand on a sofa, thinking the guests would be satisfied with a view of him, but it only made the frenzy worse.[26] "It was the only real mob I ever saw in the White House," a newsman wrote. "People were caught up and whirled in the torrent which swept through the great East Room. . . . For once at least the President of the United States was not the chief figure of the picture. The little, scared-looking man who stood on the crimson-covered sofa was the idol of the hour."[27]

At last Seward managed to extricate Grant and take him to the Blue Room where Lincoln and Secretary of War Stanton were waiting. The president told Grant he would be given his commission as lieutenant general at a White House ceremony the next day. Lincoln said he would speak briefly and Grant would be expected to make a short reply. So that Grant would know what was in store, the president gave him a copy of his remarks, suggesting that the general say something to obviate any jealousy that might arise in the army, especially in the Army of the Potomac.

Grant returned to the Willard and, using Lincoln's text as a guide, wrote out his reply in pencil. The remarks were appropriate and attained the eloquence that brevity permitted. "Mr. President, I accept this commission with gratitude for the high honor conferred. With the aid of the noble armies that have fought on so many fields for our common country, it will be my earnest endeavor not to disappoint your expectations. I feel the full weight of the responsibilities devolving on me and know that if they are met it will be due to those armies, and above all to the favor of that Providence which leads both nations and men."[28]

After the ceremony Lincoln took Grant upstairs for a short talk. The president told the new general in chief that he was not a military man, did not know how campaigns should be conducted, and had never wanted to interfere in them. But the procrastination of previous commanders and the pressure from Congress had forced him into issuing a series of presidential military orders. As Grant recalled, Lincoln said, "He did not know but they were all wrong, and did know that some of them were. All he wanted or had ever wanted was someone who would take the responsibility and act, and call on him for all of the assistance needed, pledging himself to use all the power of the government in rendering such assistance.

Assuring him that I would do the best I could with the means at hand, and avoid annoying him or the War Department, our first interview ended."[29]

Both men were delighted. Grant spent the remainder of the day inspecting Washington's fortifications, and dined with Secretary Seward that evening. Lincoln, who had dealt with Napoleonic figures like Frémont and McClellan, blustery show-offs like Hooker and Pope, and academic strategists like Halleck, was relieved to find a plain, direct, unassuming commander who eschewed the trappings of command, who never raised his voice, and who shared his view that the quickest way to end the war was to defeat the Confederate army. A British journalist, covering the war from Washington, noted that unlike his predecessors, Grant was unmoved by flattery. "I never met a man with so much simplicity, shyness, and decision. . . . He is a soldier to the core, a genuine commoner, commander of a democratic army from a democratic people. From what I learn of him, he is no more afraid to take responsibility of a million men than of a single company."[30]

The next morning the general in chief set out to confer with General Meade at the headquarters of the Army of the Potomac, located in the Virginia hamlet of Brandy Station, some sixty miles southwest of Washington. The failure of the Army of the Potomac—the Union's largest and best equipped army—to move aggressively against Lee was perhaps the major problem Grant faced, and he wanted to examine the situation firsthand. Was Meade the problem, or did the trouble lie deeper? Had the Army of the Potomac been trained and conditioned to a life of caution and inertia? Was the army's lack of initiative a problem of command, or had it been bred into the bone? Grant came east inclined to believe that the removal of Meade was a prerequisite to correcting the problem,[31] but he had to see for himself to be sure.

Grant knew Meade only slightly. The latter was eight years ahead of Grant at West Point, and the two men had served together as lieutenants with Zachary Taylor in Mexico. However, they had not met since then. Both had won stunning victories the previous summer, but Meade's failure to pursue Lee after Gettysburg had brought him into bad odor, and his reluctance to launch an offensive in northern Virginia in the autumn of 1863 had accelerated talk of his replacement. "Nothing is to be hoped for from [the Army of the Potomac] so long as it remains under its present commander," Assistant Secretary of War Charles Dana wrote Grant in December.[32] Radical Republicans in Congress had already lined up to restore Fighting Joe Hooker to the post. An unseemly scramble for Meade's job among his subordinates further weakened his position. Grant's appointment to succeed Halleck made a change appear imminent. Meade understood that. On the day Grant arrived in Washington, Meade wrote his wife that the new general in chief "may desire to have his own man in command, particularly as I understand he is indoctrinated with the notion of the superiority of the western armies and that the failure of the Army of the Potomac to accomplish anything is due to their commanders." [33]

It was raining heavily on Thursday, March 10, when Grant's train pulled into Brandy Station. Rain or no rain, a regiment of Zouaves, brightly attired in red fezzes and baggy trousers, were drawn up to render the salute while an army band, unaware that Grant was tone-deaf (he once remarked that he knew only two tunes: "One was Yankee Doodle. The other wasn't." [34]) rolled out "The General's March" to welcome the new commander. Meade and his staff stood stiffly to attention during the downpour, waiting for Grant to emerge from the general in chief's special car. Tall and dour, professorial in appearance, with a hair-trigger temper that kept his staff on edge, George Meade waited patiently for his head to be handed to him.

Nothing of the kind happened. Grant was already revising his plan to shift commanders when he stepped down from his car, and to the surprise of almost everyone, he and Meade hit it off immediately. "I had a great fondness for Meade," Grant told *New York Herald* reporter John Russell Young after the war,[35] and Meade, a few days after the meeting, told Mrs. Meade that he was "much pleased with Grant. You may rest assured that he is not an ordinary man." [36] What impressed Grant about Meade, aside from his professionalism, was his selflessness. Meade opened the conversation by suggesting that Grant might want to replace him with a Western officer with whom he was familiar: someone like Sherman, perhaps. If so, he begged Grant not to hold back. As Grant remembered, Meade said "the work before us was of such vast importance to the whole nation that the feeling or wishes of no one person should stand in the way of selecting the right men for all positions. For himself, he would serve to the best of his ability wherever placed." Grant was taken with Meade's candor. The offer, he said, "gave me even a more favorable opinion of Meade than did his great victory at Gettysburg, and I assured him that I had no thought of substituting anyone for him." [37]

There were additional reasons why Grant chose not to replace Meade. His talks with Lincoln and Stanton convinced him that neither wanted to remove the Pennsylvanian, although they were ready to do so if Grant requested it. Neither the president nor the secretary of war blamed Meade for the inaction of the Army of the Potomac, since Meade was simply following Halleck's cautious lead. With a more audacious general in chief, both men thought Meade would be fine.[38] Meade himself agreed with that assessment. After several weeks he told his wife that Grant "is so much more active than his predecessor, and agrees so with me in his views, I cannot but rejoice at his arrival, because I believe success to be the more probable from the above facts." [39]

An even more urgent consideration was Grant's recognition that as general in chief he would have to remain near Washington. Despite his desire to command the cross-Georgia march to the sea, two days in the nation's capital convinced him that the commanding general could not afford to be elsewhere. "No one else," said Grant, "could resist the pressure that would be brought to bear upon him to desist from his own plans and pursue others." That evening Grant put the pieces together. His meeting with Meade had gone better than he had anticipated, and he knew they could work in harmony. Grant also saw that the Army of the Potomac was in superb condition and that Meade handled it efficiently. Meade knew the officers and their capabilities, and he knew the terrain and the enemy. What he needed was direction and encouragement to move aggressively, and to be freed from second-guessing in Washington. In the West, Grant knew that Sherman was fully capable of commanding the army he had left behind, that McPherson could do Sherman's old job, and that Black Jack Logan could replace McPherson. With the clarity of conception that had become his military hallmark, Grant arrived at a solution that was simple, logical, original, and most likely to be effective. First, the general in chief, taking full advantage of the Union's telegraph network, would maintain his headquarters in the field. That was Grant's command style and he was comfortable with it. Only this time his headquarters would be with the Army of the Potomac. Second, Meade would retain command of the army, simplifying Grant's administrative responsibility and allowing him to utilize the command structure already in place. Third, Sherman would assume command in the West, also under Grant's direction; and fourth, Halleck would remain at his desk in Washington where his organizational talent and accumulated knowledge of the political ways of the capital would free Grant to concentrate on fighting Lee.

Of the changes, Grant was most concerned about Meade. "He was commanding an army and, for nearly a year previous to my taking command of all the armies, was in supreme command of the Army of the Potomac. All other general officers occupying similar positions were independent in their commands so far as any one present with them was concerned." Grant wrote later that the situation "proved embarrassing to me if not to him. I tried to make General Meade's position as nearly as possible what it would have been if I had been in Washington or any other place away from his command. I therefore gave all orders for the movements of the Army of the Potomac to Meade to have them executed." [40]

Grant established his headquarters near Meade's, and only when required to do so by extreme necessity did he give a direct order to any of Meade's subordinates.

Grant returned to Washington on Friday, March 11. The day afterward, the War Department issued orders formalizing the changes he desired, taking special care to let Halleck down gently. The orders specified that Halleck had been relieved as general in chief "at his own request," and that Grant was succeeding him. Halleck would continue to serve in Washington as chief of staff, "under the direction of the Secretary of War and the lieutenant general commanding."[41] Grant met with Lincoln that afternoon and informed the president that he was leaving for Nashville immediately to close out his headquarters and turn the command over to Sherman. The president invited Grant to stay for a banquet planned in his honor, and the general in chief politely but firmly declined. "I appreciate the honor, but time is very important now, and I have had enough of this show business." The past three days, he told an appreciative Lincoln, had been "rather the warmest campaign I have witnessed during the war."[42]

Thus far Grant had not taken a false step. Horace Greeley's *New York Tribune* reported that "he hardly slept on his long journey East, yet he went to work at once. Senators state with joy that he is not going to hire a house in Washington and make war ridiculous by attempting to manoeuver battles from an arm-chair." His refusal to dine at the White House was commented on with equal approval. The *New York Herald* said, "We have found our hero."[43]

Grant's modesty captured the nation's imagination. An acquaintance described him at the time as "a man who could remain silent in several languages."[44] Meade noted that he was "very reticent and somewhat ill at ease among strangers; hence a first impression is never favorable. At the same time, he has natural qualities of a high order, and is a man whom, the more you see and know him, the better you like him."[45] A staff officer who worked with Grant said "the whole man was a marvel of simplicity, a powerful nature veiled in the plainest possible exterior."[46] Despite his rank, Grant retained what one historian called "the odd quality of unintentionally vanishing from view in any crowd."[47] Stopping in Cincinnati on his way back to Nashville, Grant planned to visit his parents in nearby Covington. Jesse knew when the train was arriving, and sent a driver and carriage to meet him. Several hours later, Jesse and Hannah saw Grant coming up to the house on foot, carpetbag in hand, his well-worn travel duster over his uniform. The driver, it developed, had gone to the station but had been unable to find him.[48]

On March 17 Grant met Sherman in Nashville. Sherman had brought with him four men whom Grant wished to see as well: McPherson,

Logan, Sheridan, and Grenville Dodge, an infantry division commander who had achieved remarkable success rebuilding the railroads in Mississippi and Tennessee. These were men Grant knew and trusted. He could relax among them. And for the next two days he discussed his plans with casual informality, listening intently to what was said by longtime colleagues in a way that would not have been possible in the East. Adam Badeau, a former newsman who had become Grant's military secretary, captured the scene, noting the contrast between Grant's measured ways and Sherman's intensity:

> Sherman was tall, angular, and spare, as if his superabundant energy had consumed his flesh. His words were distinct, his ideas clear and rapid, coming, indeed, almost too fast for utterance, in dramatic, brilliant form. No one could be with him half an hour and doubt his greatness.
>
> Grant was calmer in manner a hundred fold. The habitual expression on his face was so quiet as to be almost incomprehensible. His manner, plain, placid, almost meek, in great moments disclosed to those who knew him well immense, but still suppressed, intensity. In utterance he was slow and sometimes embarrassed, but the words were well-chosen, never leaving the remotest doubt of what he intended to convey.
>
> Not a sign about him suggested rank or reputation or power. He discussed the most ordinary themes with apparent interest, and turned from them in the same quiet tones, and without a shade of difference in his manner, to decisions that involved the fate of armies, as if great things and small were to him of equal moment. In battle, the sphinx awoke. The outward calm was even then not entirely broken; but the utterance was prompt, the ideas were rapid, the judgment was decisive, the words were those of command. The whole man became intense, as it were, with a white heat.[49]

While closing out his headquarters and turning matters over to Sherman, Grant took advantage of the opportunity to unbutton. One evening the officers went to see a local production of *Hamlet;* on another, Grant led them on a quest for fresh oysters, one of the few foods he relished.[50] Sherman recalled that the mayor of Galena had come to Nashville to present Grant with the jeweled sword his fellow townsmen had subscribed for. The mayor made a dignified speech and read a resolution the city council had adopted to mark the event. According to Sherman, Grant listened attentively and then began to fumble in his pockets for his reply.

"First his breast-coat pocket, then his pants, vest, etc., and after consider-able delay he pulled out a crumbled piece of common yellow cartridge-paper which he handed to the mayor. His whole manner was awkward in the extreme. . . . I could not help laughing at the scene so characteristic of the man who then stood prominent before the country, and to whom all had turned as the only one qualified to guide the nation in a war that had become painfully critical."[51]

Grant left Nashville for Cincinnati on March 19, accompanied by Sherman and Dodge. On the train, he discussed his plans in greater detail, and then in Cincinnati Grant and Sherman checked into a hotel for pri-vacy, spread their maps, and worked out a preliminary draft of the coming campaign. Dodge recalled that Grant wanted every Union army to move in a coordinated manner against the enemy, so that Lee and Johnston (who had succeeded Bragg) could not detach any troops to reinforce one another. "He also informed us of the necessity of closing the war with this campaign."[52] Years later, Sherman summarized the strategy: "He was to go for Lee and I was to go for Joe Johnston. That was the plan."[53]

The following week Grant was back in Washington. With the senior command in place and the basic strategy set, Grant confronted organiza-tional and structural problems the solution to which had eluded Halleck and every commanding general since George Washington. Among the most serious was the statutory independence of various army staff sections such as quartermaster, commissary, ordnance, and the adjutant general. Over the years a jealous Congress, fearful of a military strongman, had provided that the heads of these departments report directly to the secre-tary of war, not the commanding general. By tradition and practice they were outside the army chain of command and were prone to ignore orders not only from field commanders but also from the general in chief. Grant insisted that the branches be subordinated to the chain of command, and he took the matter to the president. Lincoln told Grant that although he could not legally give him command of the staff departments, "there is no one but myself that can interfere with your orders, and you can rest as-sured that I will not."[54]

A second problem was the size of the army's logistical tail. Virtually half of the soldiers in Federal service were holding down rear-area jobs, guarding supply lines, providing garrisons for cities and forts in occupied areas, and were not available for battlefield duty. George Thomas, for ex-ample, had almost 120,000 soldiers in the Department of the Cumberland but could muster no more than 60,000 men for front-line service. Grant instructed Halleck to forward all new recruits to the field immediately, and to strip each department "to the lowest number of men necessary for the duty to be performed."[55] By summer, Grant had cleaned out the rear areas and had reduced the ratio of garrison to combat troops by half, an accomplishment no previous general in chief had considered possible.[56]

Grant's determination to increase the combat strength of the army brought on his first clash with Secretary Stanton, who complained that too many men were being withdrawn from Washington's defenses.

"I think I rank you in this matter, Mr. Secretary," said Grant.

"We shall have to see Mr. Lincoln about that," Stanton replied.

Off to the White House they went, the secretary of war and the general in chief, where Stanton laid the matter before the president. Lincoln heard the secretary out, but did not bother to ask Grant to explain. Smiling good-naturedly he said simply, "You and I, Mr. Stanton, have been trying to boss this job, and we have not succeeded very well with it. We have sent across the mountains for Mr. Grant, as Mrs. Grant calls him, to relieve us, and I think we had better leave him alone to do as he pleases."[57]

The most difficult problem Grant faced was concentrating Union efforts against Lee and Johnston. Previous generals in chief, bowing partially to congressional pressure, had taken a fly-swatter approach to the Confederacy, dispersing troops against a plethora of targets, few of which were vital to final victory. When Grant assumed command, Union forces were scattered about the country in nineteen separate military departments, plus the Army of the Potomac. Federal forces in these departments acted independently and without concert, enabling the South to exploit its interior lines of communication and shift troops from one sector to another as the need arose. In several instances that ability proved decisive. Bragg's victory at Chickamauga, for example, was in large measure attributable to the timely arrival of Longstreet's corps from the Army of Northern Virginia.

"I was determined to stop this," said Grant. "My general plan was to concentrate all the force possible against the main Confederate armies in the field [Lee and Johnston] . . . and to arrange a simultaneous movement all along the line."[58] As a preliminary step, Union forces deployed piecemeal along the Atlantic Coast in Florida, Georgia, and the Carolinas, inching forward against isolated objectives, were ordered north to Virginia and consolidated with the army on the James River. In the West, Grant shook out the garrisons protecting navigation on the Mississippi, and did his utmost to curtail the slow-moving offensive on the Red River, instructing General Banks to return to New Orleans and prepare to support Sherman's drive on Atlanta. To reduce the number of troops deployed in the northern heartland, Grant proposed to abolish superfluous commands, merge a number of military departments, and retire or dismiss a hundred or more general officers who were manifestly unfit for further service. This last request was ticklish business in an election year, and little came of it. Lincoln, mindful of the danger of making political enemies, let go only a fraction of those Grant recommended.[59] Finally, officers and soldiers on furlough, of whom there were thousands, were ordered back to their units. "Concentration was the order of the day," Grant wrote, and it was necessary to accomplish it "in time to advance at the earliest moment the roads would permit."[60]

The centerpiece of Grant's strategy was a combined offensive by Meade's Army of the Potomac against Lee, and Sherman's Division of the Mississippi against Johnston. "Lee's army will be your objective point," Grant instructed Meade on April 9. "Wherever Lee goes, there you will go also."[61] Sherman was told to move against Johnston's army, "break it up and get into the interior of the enemy's country as far as you can, inflicting all the damage you can against their resources."[62] Sherman's force, representing the combined armies of the Tennessee, the Cumberland, and the Ohio, numbered about 120,000—which was about twice what Johnston could muster. Meade boasted a similar advantage over Lee. On April 1, 1864, the Army of the Potomac's present for duty strength was slightly less than 100,000. But Grant held an independent corps under Ambrose Burnside in reserve, which, when deployed, would raise the total to slightly above 120,000. Lee's Army of Northern Virginia numbered 61,025 effectives, with additional troops in the Shenandoah valley, North Carolina, and a standing garrison of 6,000 in Richmond.[63]

Grant sought to improve the odds by ordering coordinated attacks by Union armies adjacent to the main thrusts. In the West, Banks was instructed to drive on Mobile with a force of 30,000 men, and to work in tandem with the Gulf squadron of Rear Admiral David G. Farragut. In Grant's view, a move against Mobile would draw off whatever reserves Johnston might have in Mississippi and Alabama, and would prevent their use against Sherman. Once Mobile was taken, Banks could head north and fall on Johnston's rear. As Grant told Sherman, "It will be impossible for him to commence too early."[64]

In the East, Grant planned a variant of his tactics at Chattanooga. Meade's Army of the Potomac would engage Lee frontally, as Thomas had done with Bragg. On the left flank, General Benjamin Butler, former Democratic congressman from Massachusetts, was ordered to move up the James River from Fortress Monroe with 35,000 men, seize City Point, cut the railroad between Petersburg and Richmond, and threaten the Confederate capital from the south. "His movement will be simultaneous with yours," Grant told Meade.[65]

On the right flank Grant planned a two-pronged attack. Major General Franz Sigel, the prominent German immigrant whose prompt support for the Union in 1861 helped prevent Missouri from seceding, was ordered to move up the Shenandoah Valley, pin down its defenders, cut Lee's communication with that region, and strike Richmond from the west if the opportunity presented itself. A second column of Sigel's command, led by Brigadier General George Crook, would move east from Charleston, West Virginia, against the Virginia & Tennessee Railroad, take Lynchburg, and sever the Confederate lifeline to the southwest. Grant said he did not "calculate on very great results" from the West Virginia contingent, but it would keep the enemy occupied and prevent Lee from drawing reinforcements from the region.[66] A crucial difference between Grant's strategy in the spring of 1864 and that at Chattanooga, aside from the vast distances involved, was that at Chattanooga he was dealing with three military professionals: Sherman, George Thomas, and Joe Hooker. Grant's flank men in Virginia were political generals with little practical experience in the field. Sigel had been commissioned to attract German-speaking patriots to the colors, and Butler had been made a general officer to prove to Democrats that the war was not exclusively a Republican affair.[67] So too in the South. Nathaniel P. Banks, commanding the Gulf Department on Sherman's flank, was a former Republican congressman from Massachusetts who had been speaker of the House of Representatives. Like Sigel and Butler, his political influence far exceeded his military capacity.

Grant made one final organizational change before leaving Washington to join Meade at the front. After suffering the stings of Nathan Bedford Forrest and Earl Van Dorn in Mississippi, Grant expressed to Lincoln and Halleck his dissatisfaction with Union cavalry operations and suggested that if properly led the cavalry was capable of accomplishing much more than it had done. "I said I wanted the very best man in the army for that command."

"Would Sheridan do?" asked Halleck.

"The very man I want," said Grant.

Lincoln told Grant he could have anyone he wished, and Sheridan, then commanding an infantry division under George Thomas, was immediately ordered to Virginia to assume command of the cavalry corps of the Army of the Potomac.[68] Sheridan had just turned thirty-three, and was one of the few officers in the army who was smaller than Grant, standing five feet five inches tall and weighing 115 pounds. "The officer you brought on from the West is rather a little fellow to handle your cavalry," someone at headquarters remarked to Grant shortly after Sheridan reported for duty. "You'll find him big enough before we get through," Grant replied, and then took another pull on his cigar.[69]

Grant's last call in Washington was on President Lincoln. He felt duty-bound to inform the president what was afoot, but had been warned by Halleck that the commander in chief could not keep a secret. The interview had scarcely begun when Lincoln gave Grant the same warning. "He said he did not want to know my plans, for everybody he met was trying to find out from him something about the contemplated movements, and there was always a temptation to 'leak'."[70] As a consequence, Grant confined his report to general principles. He told the president that he intended to bring "the greatest number of troops practicable" against the enemy, and that he would "employ all the force of all the armies continually and concurrently, so that there should be no recuperation on the part of the rebels, no rest from attack."[71] When Grant explained how all the armies could contribute to victory simply by advancing even if they won no battles, Lincoln remarked, in all apparent innocence: "Oh yes! I see that. As we say out West, if a man can't skin he must hold a leg while someone else does."[72] Grant, the son of a tanner, relished the remark so much that he passed it along to Sherman the following week in a letter explaining Sigel's role in the Virginia campaign. "If Sigel can't skin himself he can hold a leg while someone else does."[73]

Lincoln was perhaps even more pleased than Grant with the interview. His secretary, John Hay, recorded that the president was "powerfully reminded" of his "old suggestion so constantly made and as constantly neglected, to Buell, Halleck, et al., to move at once upon the enemy's whole line so as to bring into action our great superiority in numbers."[74]

Grant by this time had become the center of attention in the East. New England Yankees, curious about his military success, were initially puzzled. Some were dismayed to find no trace of breeding or gentility. An observer seeing Grant for the first time noted only an "ordinary, scrubby-looking man, with a slightly seedy look, as if he was out of office on half-pay." Another saw someone with "the look of a man who did, or once did, take a little too much to drink." Once it was revealed that this "short, round-shouldered man" was the general in chief, second assessments followed. The pale eye became "a clear blue eye," the slightly dissipated face took on "a look of resolution, as if he could not be trifled with." The answer to the riddle of Grant's success, it was decided, lay in his unpretentious but resolute demeanor, his shy but manly bearing. "He habitually wears an expression as if he had determined to drive his head through a brick wall, and was about to do it." A critical New Yorker who had watched a half-dozen generals come and go because "they did not know how to march through Virginia to Richmond" believed that "Grant may have the talisman."[75]

Grant would be the seventh Union commander to try to smash the Confederacy in Virginia. In 1861, Irvin McDowell came to grief at Manassas. In 1862, McClellan turned tail on the peninsula, John Pope was routed at Second Manassas, and Burnside met his master at Fredericksburg. In

1863, Joe Hooker stumbled at Chancellorsville and Meade called off a hopeless attack at Mine Run and pulled back to avoid destruction. Six Union generals, six Southern triumphs, the last three in the region where the Army of the Potomac was now deployed, and the last five at the hands of Robert E. Lee, the Confederacy's finest soldier. For many in the South, Grant was simply the seventh name to be added to the list of failed Yankee generals. "If I mistake not," a young officer on Lee's staff wrote home after hearing of the arrival of the new Union commander, "Grant will shortly come to grief if he attempts to repeat the tactics in Virginia which proved so successful in Mississippi."[76]

Longstreet was one of the few who dissented from the rebel consensus. "Do you know Grant?" Longstreet asked the buoyant Virginians. None did. "Well, I do," Old Pete replied. "I was with him for three years at West Point, I was present at his wedding, I served in the same army with him in Mexico, I have observed his methods of warfare in the West, and I believe I know him through and through. And I tell you we cannot afford to underrate him and the army he now commands. We must make up our minds to get into line of battle and stay there, for that man will fight us every day and every hour till the end of this war. In order to whip him we must outmaneuver him, and husband our strength as best we can."[77]

Grant differed from his predecessors in many ways. As general in chief he commanded 533,000 troops "present for duty, equipped," organized for battle in twenty-one corps of two to four divisions each.[78] This was one of the largest military commands in history, and Grant, whose supreme authority was unchallenged, chose to run it from the field. That insured he would be on the scene in Virginia, where the principal struggle would take place. It also freed him from being distracted by administrative details in Washington and from being drawn into the swirling political currents of the capital. Finally, it permitted him the luxury of entrusting the conduct of campaigns elsewhere to proven commanders such as Sherman, subject only to the broad direction of the general in chief at the far end of a telegraph line. Grant set himself up in such a way so as not to be distracted from the major task facing the commanding general: defeating the Army of Northern Virginia and Robert E. Lee.

On March 24, 1864, Grant left Washington for Culpeper, Virginia, six miles beyond Meade's headquarters at Brandy Station, about midway between the two important rivers of the region, the Rappahannock and the Rapidan. He traveled light. His staff as general in chief consisted of fourteen officers, two of whom were left behind in Washington.* Initially,

* Incredible as it may seem, Grant commanded the Army of the United States from the field with a staff of twelve: Brig. Gen. John Rawlins, chief of staff; Lt. Col. Theodore S. Bowers,

headquarters was established in a small brick house on the outskirts of Culpeper. In the field, the headquarters of the Army of the United States consisted of three tents: a large hospital tent where the mess was housed, a slightly smaller one for business, and a very small one where Grant slept. Its only furniture consisted of a portable cot made of canvas stretched over a light wooden frame, a tin washbasin that stood on an iron tripod, two folding camp chairs, and a plain pine table. The general's baggage consisted of a single trunk, which contained underclothing, toilet articles, a suit of clothes, and an extra pair of boots. According to an aide, meals were casual and informal. Officers sat where they wished at the table, coming and going as their duties required, and the conversation "was as familiar as that which occurs in the household of any private family."[79]

Grant ate less and talked less than anyone. He breakfasted frequently on a cup of coffee and a sliced cucumber doused with vinegar. If he ate meat it had to be roasted black, and he never ate fowl. ("I could never eat anything that goes on two legs.") His favorite fare was old army standbys: pork and beans, and buckwheat cakes.[80] But if Grant ate lightly, he smoked heavily. When he started his rounds each morning he loaded his pockets with two dozen cigars—a day's supply—and carried a small silver tinderbox containing a flint and steel with which to strike a spark, and a coil of fuse that was easily ignited and not affected by the wind.[81]

The one luxury Grant permitted himself was his choice of horses. At forty-two, Grant remained one of the best equestrians in the United States, and his legendary jump on York at West Point in 1843 was the prelude to a string of marvelous mounts that carried him through the Civil War. Jack, the cream-colored stallion that rushed Grant from Commodore Foote's flagship to Donelson, was high-spirited and intelligent, "a noble animal in every way." In 1864 Grant donated him to the Sanitary Fair in Chicago, where he was raffled off, bringing $4,000 to the Sanitary Commission.[82] Grant's second warhorse was Fox, a powerful roan gelding of great endurance who accidentally fell with Grant in the saddle the night

---

Ass't. Adj. Gen.; Lt. Col. Cyrus B. Comstock, senior aide-de-camp; Lt. Col. Orville E. Babcock, aide-de-camp; Lt. Col. Frederick T. Dent, aide-de-camp; Lt. Col. Horace Porter, aide-de-camp; Lt. Col. W. L. Duff, Inspector General; Lt. Col. William R. Rowley, secretary; Lt. Col. Adam Badeau, secretary; Capt. Ely S. Parker, Ass't Adj. Gen.; Capt. Peter T. Hudson, aide-de-camp; 1st Lt. William M. Dunn, acting aide-de-camp. Two additional officers, Capts. George W. Leck and H. W. Janes, were left to handle details in Washington. Four men were regular army officers and graduates of West Point (Comstock, Porter, Babcock, and Dent), and Dent, who was Grant's roommate at the academy, was also his brother-in-law. The other officers were volunteers, Rawlins, Rowley, and Parker, a full-blooded Indian, hailing from Galena. Two officers, Adam Badeau and Theodore Bowers, had been newsmen in civil life. See Grant to Halleck, April 6, 1864, 10 *The Papers of Ulysses S. Grant* 221–22, John Y. Simon, ed. (Carbondale: Southern Illinois University Press, 1982).

before Shiloh. It was at Shiloh that Grant acquired Kangaroo, a Thoroughbred found wandering on the battlefield, wasted and in need of care. After a short period of rest and feeding he proved to be such a magnificent mount that Grant used him during the Vicksburg campaign. The fourth horse Grant rode was Jeff Davis, a pony of a horse, liberated by a scouting party from the plantation of Jo Davis, brother of the Confederate president. Although Jeff Davis was much smaller than the horses he usually rode, Grant enjoyed the horse's easy gait and always used him when traveling a long distance. Grant's most famous charger was Cincinnati, an enormous animal, seventeen and a half hands high, acquired after the battle of Chattanooga from a well-wisher in St. Louis. The son of Lexington, the fastest four-mile Thoroughbred in the United States (7.195 minutes), Cincinnati was the apple of Grant's eye. Grant rarely permitted anyone to ride the horse, the exception being Lincoln, whom Grant considered an excellent horseman, and who rode Cincinnati whenever he visited the front.[83]* In 1865, Grant refused an offer of $10,000 for the horse.

Grant spent April poring over maps at Culpeper and working out his plans for the spring offensive. As he had done a year before in the ladies' salon of the *Magnolia,* where he planned the campaign that took Vicksburg, the general in chief darkened the air with cigar smoke and kept his own counsel. Whatever orders he issued were logistical, designed to bring the greatest number of troops and their equipment to the scene, but providing no tip-off as to the direction of the coming Union assault.

"Lee's army will be your objective point," Grant had told Meade, and he counted on the Confederacy's need to defend Richmond to fix Lee's position. Richmond was not only the capital of the South, loaded with the prestige of government, but Lee's supply base and the principal railroad hub of the Confederacy. Aim at Richmond, and the Army of Northern Virginia would spring to its defense. Richmond, however, was not Grant's target but merely a means to an end. His object was not to capture the Confederate capital but to destroy the rebel army. Richmond was to be at-

---

* The horses of Civil War generals were often as recognizable to the troops as the generals themselves. Lee's iron gray Traveller and Stonewall Jackson's Little Sorrel became Confederate legends. Meade's battle-scarred mount Baldy was wounded twice at Bull Run, left on the field for dead at Antietam, shot between the ribs at Gettysburg, yet survived his owner by ten years. Philip H. Sheridan's spirited Morgan Rienzi (renamed Winchester) stood seventeen hands and carried Sheridan on his famous ride to the battle of Cedar Creek in October 1864. Many who saw Rienzi considered him the strongest horse in the country. George Thomas rode a heavy-bodied bay named Billy (after Thomas's friend Sherman), a horse, like its owner, that was deliberate in its movements and not easily disturbed by the turmoil of battle. Sherman rode a half-Thoroughbred, Sam, a horse of great speed and endurance who lived on in retirement until 1884. Theo. F. Radenbough, "War Horses," in 4 *Photographic History of the Civil War* 289–316, Francis T. Miller, ed. (New York: Review of Reviews, 1911).

tacked because it was defended by Lee, not Lee because he defended Richmond. In fact, Grant preferred to fight his way to Richmond rather than arrive at its gates unmolested, because he hoped to annihilate Lee's army on the way.[84]

When Grant arrived in Culpeper, the Army of the Potomac, organized into three infantry and one cavalry corps, was entrenched in the vicinity of Brandy Station, a railhead on the Orange & Alexandria Railroad, fifteen miles north of the Rapidan. Below the Rapidan, deployed along a front of nearly twenty miles, was the Army of Northern Virginia, secure in entrenchments they had spent the last six months improving. A frontal attack across the river into the face of the rebel fortifications was out of the question. The problem for Grant was how to get around Lee, flank him out of his earthworks, and meet him in open country. Should he move left or move right, east or west, around that twenty-mile line of entrenchments?

To move right, toward the Blue Ridge Mountains, offered considerable tactical advantage. The countryside was open, and the advance, along the Orange & Alexandria and the Virginia Central railroads, would take Grant to Lynchburg, perhaps let him get behind Lee and invest Richmond as he had done at Vicksburg. Thinking about the possibility years later, Grant said, "I thought of massing the Army of the Potomac in movable columns, giving the men twelve days rations, and throwing myself between Lee and his communications. If I had made this movement successfully—if I had been as fortunate as I was when I threw my army between Pemberton and Joe Johnston—the war would have been over a year sooner. I am not sure that it was not the best thing to have done; it certainly was the plan I should have preferred."[85]

What deterred Grant was that he was unfamiliar with the Army of the Potomac. "If it had been six months later, when I had the army in hand, and knew what a splendid army it was, and if I could have had Sherman and McPherson to assist in the movement, I would not have hesitated for a moment."

The problem, however, was that the downside risk was too great. Just as the defense of Richmond limited Lee's options, the need to protect Washington curtailed Grant's mobility. To move right would uncover the capital and give Lee the opportunity to launch a lighting strike at the seat of the national government. "I did not dare take the risk," said Grant.[86] A second drawback was logistical. Unlike the lush Mississippi delta, northern Virginia had been devastated by three years of war, and there was no possibility of living off the land. To move right would make Grant entirely dependent on the railroad for resupply. To guard the line against rebel raiders would entail a crippling redeployment of men from the front, and even then it was not clear that the single-track railroad would be sufficient to supply food and ammunition for an army of 120,000 men, fodder for 56,000 horses and mules, plus everything else an army in the field required. Finally, there was an important strategic consideration. To move right would draw Grant away from Butler and the Army of the James, impairing the concentration of force on which the offensive against Lee depended.

The answer seemed clear. The Army of the Potomac would move left. That would keep it between Lee and Washington, the linkup with Butler would be facilitated, the distance would be shorter, and the supply problem would be solved by using the navigable rivers flowing into the Chesapeake, allowing rapid all-weather connection with well-stocked coastal depots protected by the United States Navy's control of the waterways. Evacuation of the wounded was an additional consideration, the transportation of injured men by ship presenting far less of a hardship than doing so overland.

There was, however, a drawback, and it was serious. Once the Rapidan was crossed, the route to the left would take the army through a desolate reach of pine barrens and scrub oak known as the Wilderness, a vast forbidding region, with few roads, and a dense undergrowth, making maneuver impossible and nullifying the Union's preponderance in men and artillery. It was a doom-struck area familiar to every veteran of the Army of the Potomac. Joe Hooker had come to grief here the year before, and this is where Meade withdrew without a fight in November, considering himself lucky to have extricated the army without disaster. This is where units fell apart, where military cohesion dissolved in claustrophobic thickets so impenetrable that friend and foe could not be told apart, where artillery fired blind if it could fire at all, where men panicked sometimes for no reason, and the outcome of battle was always uncertain. As a military obstacle, the Wilderness ranked high on anyone's list: Lee treasured it; Grant believed he could minimize its danger by moving quickly. Once the fords across the Rapidan were secure, if the army marched fast enough it could get through the Wilderness and gain the open country beyond it before Lee had time to react.[87]

To enhance the army's mobility, Grant ordered Meade to reduce the baggage that accompanied the troops as sharply as possible: two wagons for a 500-man regiment, one wagon for a brigade or division headquarters, two for corps headquarters. Playing his cards close to his chest—just as he had done before the Vicksburg campaign—he told Meade to prepare to move either by the left or by the right. If the army moved right, it would require at least 500 rounds of ammunition per man. This should be on hand and ready to use. To cover the possibility of a move to the left, Meade should have supplies stockpiled at the Union logistics depot on the Pamunkey River. "Your estimates for this contingency should be made at once."[88]

For the most part, Grant confined his planning to the evening hours.

During the day he took the measure of the Army of the Potomac—and he liked what he saw. On April 19 he told Sherman everything was well and morale was high.[89] The following week he wrote Brigadier General John E. Smith, an old friend from Galena: "The Army of the Potomac is in splendid condition and evidently feel like whipping somebody. I feel much better with this command than I did before seeing it. There seems to be the best of feeling existing."[90]

The army sized up Grant as well. Initially, skepticism was the order of the day. A brittle artillery colonel from the old army wrote home that he found the general in chief "stumpy, unmilitary, slouchy, and western-looking; very ordinary, in fact."[91] An officer in 2nd Corps said, "There is no enthusiasm in the army for General Grant. On the other hand there is no prejudice against him. We are prepared to throw up our hats for him when he shows himself the great soldier here in Virginia against Lee and the best troops of the rebels."[92] Many found him an enigma. Lieutenant Morris Schaff of Meade's staff marveled at the "fascinating mystery in his greatness," and said that at headquarters Grant was "the center of a pervasive quiet."[93]

Enlisted men sorted it out more quickly. They liked Grant's reticence, his disregard for pomp and ceremony, his eye for the essential. A Wisconsin veteran said, "He looks as if he means it."[94] An enlisted diarist from New Jersey wrote that the troops "look with awe at Grant's silent figure."[95] A New England soldier noted simply, "We all felt at last that *the boss* had arrived."[96] One source of satisfaction among the troops was Grant's relentless effort to strip soldiers from cushy assignments in rear areas and add them to the fighting force. In April alone he extracted thousands of heavy artillerists manning unnecessary fortifications and turned them into straight-leg infantry. This was taken as a good omen by soldiers who had spent the war at the front.

One story that made the rounds quickly was Grant's encounter with Brigadier General Rufus Ingalls, chief quartermaster of the Army of the Potomac. Ingalls had been his first-year roommate at West Point, and the two had not met since Grant resigned from the army in 1854. Ingalls needed to confer with him about the supplies that would be required for the coming campaign. In the East, an interview with the commanding general was a formal occasion, and Ingalls put on his dress uniform with full regalia and rode over in the finest quartermaster wagon drawn by a matched set of four carefully groomed horses attended by four equally well turned out orderlies.

On the road near Culpeper, Ingalls saw Grant riding toward him and asked the driver to halt. The two men shook hands warmly, and Ingalls said he had some business to discuss. Grant said: "Very well—we can talk about it here." He dismounted and Ingalls got down from the wagon and they started walking up and down the road together. There was a slight drizzle, the road was muddy, and every time a horse or wagon went by the generals were spattered. An hour later the conversation was finished and Grant said, "That's all—goodbye, General," remounted Jeff Davis and rode away. Ingalls returned to the headquarters of the Army of the Potomac muddy and bedraggled, and immediately sought out Meade. "I tell you, General," said Ingalls, "Grant means business."[97]

Back in Washington, Lincoln had a pretty clear picture of what was happening. William O. Stoddard, the president's third secretary, who had been ill when Grant arrived in Washington, was back on duty at the White House and asked what sort of man Grant was. Lincoln said he was "the quietest little fellow you ever saw," and remarked that several times Grant had been in the room for a minute or so before the president knew he was there. "The only evidence you have that he's any place is that he makes things git! Wherever he is things move."

Stoddard asked about Grant's military ability. "Stoddard," said the president, "Grant is the first general I've had. He's a general." When Stoddard paused, Lincoln replied: "I'll tell you what I mean. You know how it's been with all the rest. As soon as I put a man in command of the army he'd come to me with a plan of campaign and about as much as say, 'Now, I don't believe I can do it, but if you say so I'll try it on,' and so put the responsibility of success or failure on me. They all wanted me to be the general. It isn't so with Grant. He hasn't told me what his plans are. I don't know, and I don't want to know. I'm glad to find a man who can go ahead without me."

Lincoln told Stoddard that all the previous commanders would "pick out some one thing they were short of and that they knew I couldn't give them and then tell me that they couldn't win unless they had it; and it was generally cavalry.

"When Grant took hold I was waiting to see what his pet impossibility would be, and I reckoned it would be cavalry, for we hadn't horses enough to mount even what men we had. There were fifteen thousand or thereabouts up near Harper's Ferry, and no horses to put them on. Well, the other day, just as I expected, Grant sent to me about those very men. But what he wanted to know was whether he should disband them or turn 'em into infantry.

"He doesn't ask me to do impossibilities for him, and he's the first general I've had that didn't."[98]

Under Grant's overall command, the Army of the Potomac prepared for battle. In the South, Sherman made ready to move through Georgia; Butler appeared to have things in hand on the James; and Sigel, after a brief wrangle pertaining to the proper command channels he should use, looked as though he was ready to advance up the valley. But one of Grant's flank men was already in trouble. On April 8 a Confederate force under Major General Richard Taylor, the feisty son of Old Rough and Ready, fell on Nathaniel Banks's Army of the Gulf while it was in march column at Sabine Crossroads, Louisiana, thirty-five miles south of the Union objective of Shreveport. In the resultant rout, Banks lost 2,235 men, twenty guns, and 200 wagons. A stream of anguished telegrams from Banks convinced Grant that the Red River expedition was in deep trouble and whatever help Sherman might have expected from the Gulf command was becoming increasingly unlikely. He ordered Banks to return to New Orleans, and sent the army's senior trouble-shooter, Major General David Hunter, to Louisiana to investigate. Hunter's report was devastating. "The Department of the Gulf is one great mass of corruption. Cotton and politics, instead of the war, appear to have engrossed the army. The vital interests of the contest are laid aside . . . and the lives of our men are sacrificed in the interests of cotton speculators." Hunter said Banks had lost the confidence of the army and that if he were not replaced quickly "we shall lose the navigation of the Mississippi." [99]

Grant needed no convincing. The disaster in Louisiana, he told Halleck, was unmistakably attributable to Banks's incompetence. "His failure has absorbed ten thousand veteran troops that should now be with General Sherman, and thirty thousand of his own that should have been moving towards Mobile." [100] The immediate consequence of the debacle was that Joseph E. Johnston received 15,000 reinforcements from Alabama whom Banks might otherwise have engaged, Sherman got no help whatever, and Grant's efforts to have Banks relieved foundered in the political quicksand of an election year. Grant, who was sympathetic to Lincoln's plight, acquiesced gracefully, and on April 29 urged Halleck "to go in person and take charge of the trans-Mississippi" until the situation could be sorted out. Old Brains showed little interest in Grant's suggestion, but eventually the Department of the Gulf was carved up, leaving Banks responsible for Louisiana's civil administration and placing military matters in the hands of Major General Edward Canby, a reliable professional officer. [101]

Across the Rapidan, Lee readied the Army of Northern Virginia for the coming onslaught. "All the information that reaches me goes to strengthen the belief that General Grant is preparing to move against Richmond," he wrote Jefferson Davis on April 5. [102] Lee was blessed with a multitude of reliable scouts in northern Virginia, and as additional reports trickled in he refined his prognosis. Three days later he informed Richmond: "The general impression [is] that the great battle will take place on the Rapidan, and that the Federal army will advance as soon as the weather is settled." [103] The following week, with schooled insight bordering on clairvoyance, Lee told Davis he anticipated three separate Union attacks to be delivered simultaneously from three directions. The main assault would come more or less against his front from across the river. A second attack would come up the James and menace Richmond from the east, and a third, largely diversionary effort, would be made in the Shenandoah valley. Lee said, "If Richmond could be held secure against the attack from the east," he intended to fall on the flank of the main Union effort. Rather than wait for Grant to attack him, he intended to attack Grant when he was least prepared for it. "Should God give us a crowning victory, all their plans would be dissipated," and the Union would be forced on the defensive.[104]

On April 18 Lee ordered all surplus baggage sent to the rear and prepared his army to move out of its entrenchments as soon as Grant's line of march became clear. Lee deployed two corps forward, Richard S. Ewell on the right, Ambrose P. Hill on the left, with Longstreet's veterans, recently returned from Tennessee, in reserve. He could move either right or left, depending on which direction Grant chose. By April 30 the clash appeared imminent. The Army of the Potomac had not yet struck its tents, but Lee informed Davis that "engineer troops, pontoon bridges, and all of the cavalry of Meade's army" had been advanced to the vicinity of the Rapidan. "Everything indicates a concentrated attack on this front."[105]

Grant spent the last days of April adding the final brushstrokes to his attack plan. Ambrose Burnside, who commanded the 9th Corps, Grant's four-division reserve, was ordered forward from his staging area near Annapolis and instructed to assume the responsibility for protecting the Army of the Potomac's supply line south of Washington, freeing Meade's troops for combat. "You can give orders to your troops to move to the front as soon as relieved," Grant told Meade on April 27.[106] Because Burnside had once commanded the Army of the Potomac and still ranked Meade on the army's list of major generals, Grant believed it would spare both men embarrassment if the 9th Corps remained independent, at least for the moment. Accordingly, Grant addressed separate orders directly to Burnside, and kept Meade informed of what was happening. It was an awkward arrangement, but Grant had a warm spot in his heart for Burnside after his spirited defense of Knoxville.[107]

April 27 was Grant's forty-second birthday. On that day a year before, looking eastward from the Louisiana shore of the Mississippi, he had marshaled the Army of the Tennessee for crossing the mighty river and opening the final stages of the Vicksburg campaign. As one historian has observed, it was therefore a fitting day to fix the date for the commencement of the spring offensive that Grant hoped would bring the war to a close.[108] It was a Wednesday. Believing that it would take a week to put the Army of the Potomac in motion, he set the date for Wednesday next: May

4, 1864. Grant visited Meade that afternoon and gave his instructions orally. The direction of march was not disclosed, merely that the army would be crossing the Rapidan. Whether he intended to move west and turn Lee's left, or east through the Wilderness, Grant kept to himself. The following day, he passed the word to Sherman, Butler, and Sigel. "Get your forces up so as to move by the fifth of May," Grant instructed his deputy in Georgia.[109] He ordered Butler to "Start your forces the night of the 4th so as to be as far up the James River as you can by daylight the morning of the 5th."[110] Sigel was told to begin his move up the valley on May 2, "unless you hear orders from me to the contrary."[111]

On April 29 Grant informed Halleck of the jump-off date, but continued to keep his plans under his hat. "Our advance will commence on the 4th of May. General Butler will operate on the south side of the James River, Richmond being his objective point. I will move against Lee's Army attempting to turn him by one flank or the other. . . . My own notions about our line of march are entirely made up. But, as circumstances beyond my control may change them, I will only state that my efforts will be to bring Butler's and Meade's forces together."[112]

Whether Halleck informed Lincoln of Grant's message is unclear, but it seems likely because the following day the president wrote Grant a personal message of encouragement.

> Lieutanant General Grant: Not expecting to see you again before the spring campaign opens, I wish to express, in this way, my entire satisfaction with what you have done up to this time, so far as I understand it. The particulars of your plans I neither know, or seek to know. You are vigilant and self-reliant; and, pleased with this, I wish not to obtrude any constraints or restraints upon you. While I am very anxious that any great disaster, or the capture of our men in great numbers, shall be avoided, I know these points are less likely to escape your attention than they would be mine. If there is anything wanting, which is within my power to give, do not fail to let me know it. And now, with a brave Army, and a just cause, may God sustain you.
>
> Yours very truly,
> LINCOLN[113]

Grant replied the next day. After thanking Lincoln for his support, he took full responsibility for the coming campaign. Grant told the president that since he had become general in chief, he had been "astonished at the readiness with which everything asked for has been yielded without even an explanation being asked. Should my success be less than I desire, and expect, the least I can say is, the fault is not with you." There would be no alibi for failure.[114]

At 3 P.M. on May 2, Grant put the armies in motion. "Move at the time indicated in my instructions," he wired Sherman. "All will strike together."[115] Butler was told, "Start on the date given in my letter. There will be no delay with this army."[116] Meade, with whom Grant was in continuous contact, was instructed orally to take the Army of the Potomac across the Rapidan, using the lower fords, i.e., the fords to the left (Lee's right). Whether Meade anticipated moving left is unclear, but his orders to the army were prepared with textbook precision. Sheridan's cavalry would seize the Germanna and Ely fords at midnight on May 3 and hold them until the infantry arrived. Germanna Ford was ten miles below Lee's right, Ely was six miles below that. Both had been used by Meade when he crossed the Rapidan in November, and the topography was familiar to the army. Two infantry corps, commanded respectively by Gouverneur Kemble Warren and John Sedgwick, would cross at Germanna Ford and move quickly toward Wilderness Tavern, five miles south. Winfield Scott Hancock's 2nd Corps, the bulk of the artillery, and the army's train would cross at Ely Ford and move in a parallel direction toward Chancellorsville. In a separate communication, Grant ordered Burnside to bring his corps forward as soon as Meade crossed the river. "Your line of march, after crossing the Rapidan, will be in the rear of the right flank of the Army of the Potomac."[117] At noon on May 3 Grant told Halleck, "This Army moves tomorrow morning." The direction would be to the left.[118] Grant counted on taking Lee by surprise. With a series of forced marches, he planned to have the army through the Wilderness before battle was joined.

In the West, Grant had capitalized on Southern errors. At Donelson, Gideon Pillow's decision to return to the fort after opening the Nashville road allowed Grant to invest the garrison and storm the revetments. At Shiloh, Beauregard's order to reduce the hornets' nest before pressing on permitted Grant to re-form his line for a successful last stand before sunset. At Vicksburg, the failure of Pemberton and Johnston to join forces enabled Grant to slip between them and defeat each in turn. And at Chattanooga, the dispatch of Longstreet's corps to Knoxville and Bragg's faulty deployment of his infantry rendered an impregnable position vulnerable.

Robert E. Lee was not prone to mistakes. If he made one, he rectified it quickly. At noon on May 2, as Grant ordered the Union armies forward, the fifty-seven-year-old Confederate icon was meeting with his corps and division commanders near the crest of Clark's Mountain, ten miles in a direct line from Grant's headquarters at Culpeper. From the ridge, some 700 feet above the Rapidan floodplain, a panoramic view unfolded, a living map of the future battlefield. Like Grant, Lee gave his lieutenants enormous leeway in battle, and he wanted them to digest the geographic features of the land over which they would be fighting. For the past two months, the rebel chief had studied Grant's options, placing himself in the shoes of the Union commander. Gleaning what he could from an assortment of intelligence sources, and studying the same maps Grant was using, he had arrived at what he thought was the answer. Pointing downstream, well below the right anchor of his own line, he announced simply, "Grant will cross by one of these fords." Lee said he expected Grant to throw the Army of the Potomac across either the Germanna or the Ely ford, and he let it go at that. The evidence was not all in, the tents of Meade's army had not been struck, and at this point his conclusion was merely an educated guess.

Whether it was a guess or not, Lee's plan, according to his most assiduous biographer, was already set. He would not defend the Rapidan or attack Grant while he was crossing. Instead, he would wait until the entire Army of the Potomac had crossed to the south bank of the river, and then, when they and their immense trains were entangled in the Wilderness, fall upon their right flank with everything he had. In Lee's view, the Wilderness was a great equalizer. He would take advantage of it to whip Grant as thoroughly as possible, as quickly as possible, and send the Yankees reeling back across the Rapidan.[119]

On Tuesday, May 3, rebel lookouts on Clark's Mountain reported heavy activity in Union encampments. As the day progressed, the activity heightened, into the evening hours. Near midnight, signalmen flashed the word to Lee's headquarters. Long columns of troops were passing in front of campfires, marching toward the Rapidan. Back came the response: Were the troops moving upstream toward the Blue Ridge, or downstream toward the fords? The signalmen could not tell. It was too dark. But the Union army was in motion. It was now after midnight. May 4 would dawn in a few hours. Lee gambled. Prepare your troops to move right, he instructed his corps commanders.[120]

The Army of the Potomac crossed the Rapidan without incident. Grant, who for the rest of his life believed he had taken Lee by surprise,[121] wired the good news to Halleck 1 P.M. on May 4. "The crossing of the Rapidan effected. Forty-eight hours now will demonstrate whether the enemy intends giving battle this side of Richmond."[122] The answer came sooner than Grant anticipated.

CHAPTER TEN

THE WILDERNESS

The foe that held his guarded hills
Must speed to woods afar;
For the scheme that was nursed by the Culpepper hearth
With the slowly smoked cigar—
The scheme that smoldered through winter long
Now bursts into act—into war—
The resolute scheme of a heart as calm
As the Cyclone's core.

HERMAN MELVILLE
"The Armies of the Wilderness"

SOUTHERNERS RARELY TIRED of pointing out that Grant had never faced "Bobby Lee." By the same token, Lee had never faced Grant. And the fact is, just as Grant's principal victories capitalized on Confederate miscues, Lee's triumphs over McClellan during the Seven Days, Pope at Second Manassas, Burnside at Fredericksburg, and Hooker at Chancellorsville, rested to some degree upon Union ineptitude. Both generals were superb at exploiting an adversary's weakness, both were prime practitioners of taking the fight to the enemy, and both recognized that the fate of their country was in their hands. Grant enjoyed significant numerical superiority. His artillery was abundant, his equipment matchless, his supply line unending. Yet as a recent arrival from the West, he was fighting on unfamiliar ground and had not yet gained his army's confidence. Lee was outmanned, outgunned, and perennially short of food, forage, and ammunition. Yet he had the love and trust of his soldiers, and he knew the terrain like the back of his hand. He could ask the impossible from his men, and they often accomplished it. On this note the battle of the Wilderness was joined.

The Wilderness is traversed by four principal roads. Two run south from the Rapidan, two run east from Orange, Virginia, to Fredericksburg. The Army of the Potomac was marching on the roads running south. Lee would soon put the Army of Northern Virginia in motion using the roads heading east. Both sets of roads intersect in the vicinity of Wilderness Tavern, a ramshackle stage-house five miles below the Rapidan. This would be the scene where the final battle for the Union would commence. From May 1864 until April the following year, the armies of Lee and Grant would be locked in a continuous struggle from which only one could emerge victorious.

Grant rode out from Culpeper toward Germanna Ford at 8 A.M., Wednesday, May 4. He was mounted on his massive bay horse, Cincinnati, sitting the same worn saddle he'd used in every campaign since Donelson. Unlike earlier campaigns, Grant wore his dress uniform—an unbuttoned uniform frock coat over a blue vest, pants neatly tucked into new knee-length boots, a gold cord added to his customary black slouch hat, a general's sash about the waist and a sword at his side.[1] Grant almost never wore a sword, and in the field he rarely wore anything other than the uniform of a private soldier, with stars attached. Adam Badeau believed that he dressed in full regalia that day because "he seemed to consider the occasion one of peculiar dignity."[2]

It was a perfect spring day. A member of Meade's staff wrote, "As far as you could see in every direction, corps, divisions, brigades were moving on in a waving sea of blue."[3] *New York Herald* correspondent Sylvanus Cadwallader wrote glowingly of the "dense columns of troops on the march, with the shimmer of their bright bayonets resembling the glitter of frost on hedgerows in winter." In Cadwallader's view, "Never since its organization had the Army of the Potomac been in better spirits, or more eager to meet the enemy. And never did an army seem in better condition for marching and fighting."[4] Charles Page of the *New York Times* noted he had "never seen the army move with more exact order, with a less number of stragglers, and with so little apparent fatigue to the men."[5] Brigadier General Rufus Ingalls, the army's quartermaster, observed with pride that "Probably no army on earth ever before was in better condition in every respect than was the Army of the Potomac."[6]*

Shortly before noon Grant crossed the Rapidan using one of the pontoon bridges laid early that morning. The four divisions of Warren's 5th Corps had already crossed; John Sedgwick's three 6th Corps divisions were following. Grant rode to the top of the bluff overlooking the crossing, dismounted, and established temporary headquarters in an abandoned farmhouse. The general in chief sat pensively on the porch for a

---

* Each Union soldier, in addition to his kit, carried fifty rounds of ammunition, full rations for three days, and partial rations for three more. Ingalls's supply train of 4,300 wagons hauled an additional ten days of food, fodder, and ammunition. "Had these wagons been placed in a single line, at the intervals required on the march, they would have reached from the Rapidan to Petersburg, and probably beyond." Sylvanus Cadwallader, *Three Years with Grant* 175 (Lincoln: University of Nebraska Press, 1996). Reprint.

while, watching Sedgwick's corps pass over the bridge. Presently news was brought that Winfield Scott Hancock's 2nd Corps had cleared Ely Ford. "Everything is across," Hancock reported. Grant was relieved. "It removed from my mind the most serious apprehensions I had entertained, that of crossing the river in the face of an active, large, well-appointed and ably commanded army." Grant said Lee should be aware by now that the Army of the Potomac was in motion, but he doubted if Lee realized the full extent of the movement. "We shall probably soon get some indication as to what he intends to do."[7]

Grant did not wait long. Shortly after 1 P.M. Meade sent word that intercepts of rebel signals indicated that Lee had left his entrenchments and was moving east with at least one corps. "That gives just the information I wanted," Grant told Colonel Horace Porter. "It shows Lee is drawing out from his position, and is pushing across to meet us."[8] Grant asked for his dispatch book and quickly scribbled a message to Burnside. "Make force marches until you reach this place," he told the 9th Corps commander. "Start your troops now in the rear the moment they can be got off, and require them to make a night march."[9]

Grant was marshaling his forces. That afternoon he and Meade made a critical decision that shaped the nature of the upcoming battle. Meade's original plan called for the infantry to march at a sustained pace throughout the day. They had started just after midnight, and a forced march would bring them through the Wilderness before sunset.[10] Meade's timetable assumed Lee would be taken by surprise, would react slowly, and that the initiative would remain with the Army of the Potomac. With Lee on the move, those calculations were upset. The problem was the massive wagon train of the army. The infantry might clear the Wilderness by nightfall, but it would be impossible for Ingalls's wagons to do so. They would be strung out from hell to eternity and make ripe picking for Lee's cavalry. Accordingly, and with Grant's approval, Meade halted the march in the early afternoon to allow the wagons to catch up. Preoccupied with protecting the army's supplies, Grant and Meade gave Lee the opportunity to bring on a battle in the Wilderness, where odds favoring the Confederates were greatest.

Had Grant become overconfident? The lesson of Shiloh, where he failed to anticipate the Confederate attack, appears to have been forgotten. One of Grant's strengths was his ability to focus on what he intended to do to the enemy without worrying about what the enemy might do to him. Sometimes that strength got him into trouble. Indeed, Grant would soon learn that he must anticipate Lee's moves, and that it was dangerous to underestimate his opponent's capacity to do the unexpected.[11]

As soon as it became clear that the Army of the Potomac was heading south through the Wilderness, Lee moved with breathtaking speed. At 9 A.M. Ewell's 2nd Corps, Stonewall Jackson's old command, was ordered east along the Orange turnpike. At the same time, A. P. Hill's 3rd Corps was directed to move east along the Orange plank road, parallel to the turnpike and about two miles south. The two corps were within easy supporting distance of each other, and less than eighteen miles from the Germanna Ford road the Union army was using. Lee planned to make his approach march on May 4 and strike Grant at dawn on the 5th. Longstreet, in reserve at Gordonsville, was ordered to move east behind Hill, and add the weight of 1st Corps to the attack once battle was joined. That evening, rebel troops bivouacked less than five miles from the Army of the Potomac. Ewell and Hill were instructed to move as early as possible the next morning. Lee wished "to bring [the enemy] to battle as soon now as possible." [12]

Lee planned to fight the final battle of the war. He didn't intend simply to defeat the Army of the Potomac, he wanted to destroy it. At first light on Thursday, May 5, he would assault the exposed right flank of Meade's march column with the 2nd and 3rd corps, fix the Union army in place, and hold it in the Wilderness. Ewell and Hill would continue their assault Friday, setting up Longstreet—whose corps would be up by then—to fall on the left of Grant's line, roll it up, and send the Army of the Potomac reeling back across the Rapidan in panicked disorder. The odds were long, but the risk was justified. A Confederate victory would snuff yet another Union general's invasion of northern Virginia, undercut Lincoln's effort to be renominated, encourage anti-war sentiment in the North, and set the stage for a negotiated peace. Lee's principal worry was that the 40,000 men Ewell and Hill could deploy would be gobbled up by the much greater force Meade could bring against them. But as Lee anticipated the Wilderness was an equalizer. Lee's troops had never lost an encounter there, and it was a fact of life that country boys from the South were far more adept at fighting amid the eerie undergrowth than their Northern counterparts.

Lee's upbeat mood was matched by that of the troops of the 2nd and 3rd corps. Like the men in blue trooping south from Germanna Ford, the rebel columns marched with an air of exaltation. "The morning is bright and pleasant," wrote a member of the Stonewall Brigade. "All nature seems smiling on this spring morning. What a grand sight is the army in motion. The whole brigade is all life—seems as though they are never conquered." [13] Another commented on the obvious disparity in numbers between the opposing armies. "And yet, knowing all this, these lunatics were sweeping along to that appallingly unequal fight, cracking jokes, laughing, and with not the least idea in the world of anything else but victory. I did

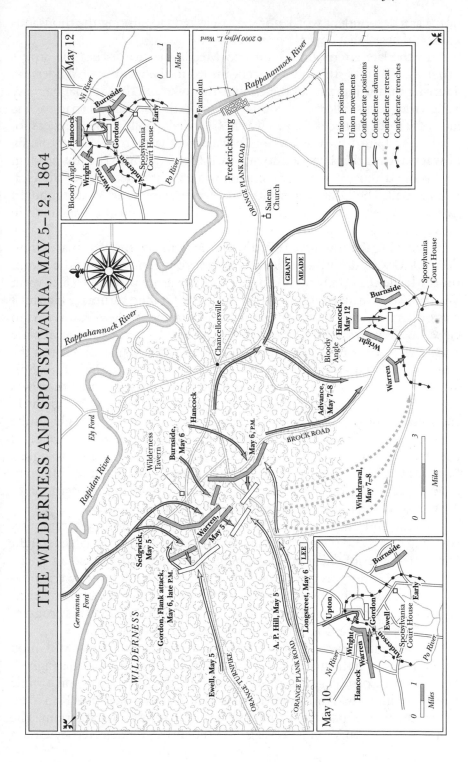

THE WILDERNESS AND SPOTSYLVANIA, MAY 5–12, 1864

© 2000 Jeffrey L. Ward

not hear a despondent word, nor see a dejected face among the thousands I saw and heard that day." [14]

In the late afternoon, Grant and Meade met to discuss the army's progress. Warren's 5th Corps was encamped in the vicinity of Wilderness Tavern, near the juncture of the Orange turnpike and the Germanna road. Sedgwick's corps followed, bedding down on the Germanna road back as far as the ford. Hancock's corps was in Chancellorsville, nine miles east of Warren, and Burnside was coming forward posthaste from Warrenton. By now it was clear that Lee was moving east. Meade assumed he was heading for his old defensive line at Mine Run, some eight miles west of the Germanna road. The Mine Run position was formidable, and Meade thought Lee would halt there and wait to be attacked—just as he had done in November.

Believing the initiative rested with the Army of the Potomac, Grant decided to wait until Burnside arrived before pressing on. In the meantime, Meade could tidy up his formation. The army pivoted to face west, Warren was instructed to move out along the Orange turnpike, Hancock was ordered to take a position to the left of Warren, Sedgwick was told to close on Warren's right, and Burnside received instructions to replace Sedgwick at the ford—the extreme right of the Union line. To protect the supply train from a possible raid by Confederate cavalry under J. E. B. Stuart, Sheridan was ordered east toward Fredericksburg (where Stuart was last seen) with two cavalry divisions, leaving but one to screen the army on the west.[15] The decision by Grant and Meade to spend the night in the Wilderness, combined with insufficient cavalry cover to the west, gave Lee the opening he was looking for. Neither Union general intended to fight a battle in the Wilderness, but rather to use the woods as a jump-off point from which to attack Lee.[16] Their troop dispositions on the afternoon of May 4, however, invited the Confederates to strike first.

Grant and Meade spent the evening sitting before the campfire, smoking cigars and reviewing plans for the next day. As they talked, Grant received a series of telegrams informing him that Sherman had advanced in Georgia, Butler was ascending the James, and Sigel's forces were moving up the Shenandoah valley. Meade retired to his headquarters soon afterward, and Grant turned in a little before midnight, satisfied his program to keep the enemy engaged on all fronts was off to a good start.[17]

First light comes early in springtime Virginia, and by 5 A.M. Union columns were on the march to take up the positions Meade had assigned. Warren's 5th Corps began to move west along the Orange turnpike while Union engineers laid three additional bridges across Wilderness Run to facilitate the troops' passage through some of the forest's worst terrain. The Army of Northern Virginia was also on the move. Undetected by Union cavalry, Ewell's 2nd Corps was already deployed in line of battle on either side of the turnpike, less than two miles from Warren's approaching column. Three miles south, A. P. Hill's 3rd Corps, with Lee riding at its head, was advancing on the Orange plank road, also undetected. Lee instructed Ewell to coordinate his moves with that of the 3rd Corps, to make contact with the enemy with his skirmish line, but not to bring on a general engagement. With only eight thin divisions against Grant's fifteen, Lee had reconsidered his plan to attack quickly. It would be prudent, he now decided, to wait until Longstreet arrived before opening his assault. He would hold the Army of the Potomac in the Wilderness with his skirmishers, but put off a pitched battle until the following day.[18]

Shortly after 6 A.M., Warren's troops sighted Ewell's men dug in astride the turnpike. A shock wave rippled through the 5th Corps. Lee was supposed to be entrenched on Mine Run, yet here was the Army of Northern Virginia ready and waiting in line of battle. Warren immediately ordered his lead division to feel out and determine the enemy strength, and then dispatched a warning to Meade that Confederate infantry held the turnpike in front of him.[19] Meade, who was in the process of moving his headquarters from Germanna Ford to Wilderness Tavern, quickly caught up with Warren and instructed him to hit the enemy with everything he had. "If there is to be any fighting this side of Mine Run, let us do it right off."[20] Meade still assumed that Lee's main body was ensconced along Mine Run, and that Warren had encountered a small detachment sent out to delay the Union advance. Nevertheless, he issued new instructions to Hancock and Sedgwick to close quickly on Warren, and then notified Grant, who was waiting for Burnside back at Germanna Ford: "The enemy have appeared in force on the Orange pike, and are now reported forming in line of battle. . . . I have directed General Warren to attack them at once with his whole force. . . . I think the enemy is trying to delay our movement and will not give battle, but of this we shall soon see."[21]

At this point it was Lee's turn to be surprised. The option of joining battle today or waiting for tomorrow was no longer his. Grant was ready to fight. "If any opportunity presents itself for pitching into a part of Lee's army, do so without giving time for disposition," he told Meade.[22] Grant said Burnside's advance guard was already crossing the Rapidan, and that as soon as Burnside himself arrived, he would ride forward. "It was my plan then, as it was on all other occasions, to take the initiative whenever the enemy could be drawn from his entrenchments if we were not entrenched ourselves."[23]

Thirty minutes later Grant received a second message from Meade. Warren was getting ready to attack and Sedgwick was coming up in support. Meade said he still thought Lee was merely making a demonstration to gain time, but "if he is disposed to fight this side of Mine Run, he shall be accommodated." [24]

It was now nine o'clock. Burnside had yet to arrive, and Grant concluded it was best not to wait. Meade's message had an urgent quality about it. If an attack was getting underway, Grant wanted to be there. After leaving word for Burnside to close on Sedgwick as soon as possible, the general in chief rode to the front. The business of war was at hand, and Grant wore his work clothes: plain black hat, private's uniform, no braid, no sword, and mounted comfortably on little Jeff Davis. Colonel Joseph W. Keifer, commanding a regiment in Sedgwick's corps, saw Grant ride by and commented on the contrast between Grant and his "gaily dressed and equipped staff. He saluted and spoke pleasantly, but did not check his horse from its rather rapid gait." [25]

Grant arrived at Wilderness Tavern about ten o'clock and found the situation unraveling. A. P. Hill's corps had been discovered advancing along the Orange plank road threatening Meade's left, Confederate cavalry were reported slipping around the Union right menacing the army's supply line, and Ewell was entrenched in front of Warren, waiting for battle. It was apparent this was not a rearguard action by Lee, and Meade was disconcerted. He had not anticipated that Lee would fight in the Wilderness, and he seemed unsure how to react. Sedgwick had not yet closed on Warren, Hancock was not up, and Warren's corps was reluctant to attack. Grant sensed the Army of the Potomac was slipping into a defensive posture. The bravado of the morning had vanished and Meade seemed more concerned about protecting his flanks than seizing the initiative. [26]

Grant calmly took charge. He suggested that he and Meade establish a joint headquarters on a nearby knoll, and then began to sort things out. If Lee wanted to fight in the Wilderness, "that is all right," he reassured Meade. [27] Grant then issued a series of brief orders to regain control of the battlefield. Sedgwick and Warren were told to move ahead in the turnpike sector and engage the enemy immediately. Hancock was directed to hurry right and attack A. P. Hill's approaching column. Pending Hancock's arrival, Grant deployed Meade's reserve division, commanded by George Getty of Sedgwick's corps, to hold the vital crossroads where the Orange plank road met the road from Germanna Ford (Brock road). That done, Grant took a seat on a nearby stump, lit a cigar, took a penknife from his pocket and began to whittle a stick, seemingly unperturbed by the action around him. [28]

The most critical situation was on the Orange plank road. [29] If Hill captured the Brock road intersection, the Army of the Potomac would be divided: Hancock's 2nd Corps would be cut off, and Hill would be free to move against Warren's exposed left flank. Getty's job was to hold the intersection against Hill's corps until Hancock arrived. Fortunately for Grant and Meade, George Getty was one of the best, if not the best, division commander in the Army of the Potomac. A classmate of Sherman's and Thomas's at West Point, Getty was known as an officer equal to any emergency.[30] He double-timed his division of New York and Vermont volunteers to the intersection, arrived moments before Hill's advance, planted his flag in the center of the crossroads, and held on tenaciously against everything Hill could throw against him until Hancock arrived near two o'clock. "We must hold this point at any risk," Getty told his men, and they did so.[31]

Grant was less fortunate with Warren and the 5th Corps. Meade had ordered his youngest corps commander to move against Ewell at 7 A.M. It was now close to noon and Warren's troops had not budged. Brigade and regimental commanders were reluctant to assault what by now had become a formidable line of rebel entrenchments, and division commanders declined to order their troops forward until their flanks were aligned with supporting units—a virtual impossibility given the terrain and undergrowth.[32] At noon Grant rode forward with Warren to inspect the ground over which the attack would be launched, recognized the hazards, but saw no reason to delay. He told Warren to move out immediately and then returned to his stump in the headquarters clearing.

By one o'clock Warren had not moved and Grant's patience was wearing thin. When Warren appeared to ask Meade for an additional delay, Grant observed that the Army of the Potomac seemed reluctant to start a fight. Meade was stung to the quick. The courage of his army had been questioned, and not without reason. He turned to Warren and said sharply, "We are waiting for you."[33] As a result of the 5th Corps's delay, Ewell had been given an additional six hours to prepare his position. Warren, who would eventually be relieved, rode to the front and very reluctantly ordered the advance to begin. The rebels were ready and waiting.

Grant's insistence that the Army of the Potomac attack quickly was well founded. Although Meade worried about his flanks and was having difficulty getting his corps aligned, Lee was in much worse trouble. He had just realized there was a mile-wide gap in his line between Ewell and Hill. The turnpike and the Orange plank road, originally two miles apart, were now more than three miles distant. Ewell's corps was entrenched on the turnpike; Hill's troops were engaged on the plank road, and there was nothing between them. Had Warren moved forward promptly, the 5th Corps would have torn through Lee's undefended middle and driven a wedge between the two wings of the Confederate army. By not moving until early afternoon, Warren allowed Lee time to plug the hole and forestall what would have been almost certain defeat. Even with the gap filled

Lee faced the uncomfortable fact that Ewell and Hill were too far apart to provide mutual support. If the Army of the Potomac should throw its entire weight against either, a Confederate collapse would be unavoidable.[34]

The difficulties Lee and Grant confronted that first day in the Wilderness illustrate the friction involved in going into battle. Grant saw the Confederate army in the tangled underbrush and wanted to get at it as quickly as possible. By the same token, Lee wanted his troops to avoid a general engagement. Neither succeeded. Once Grant decided to bring on the battle there was nothing Lee could do to prevent it. But the inbred caution of the Army of the Potomac prevented the hammer blows Grant wanted from being delivered promptly, and the time lag worked to Lee's advantage.

It was well after one o'clock when Warren gave the command for the 5th Corps to move forward. By then Ewell's position, which extended one mile to either side of the turnpike, was close to impregnable. Confederate riflemen, protected by substantial breastworks, laid down a hail of lead that stopped the assault in its tracks. Union divisions became disoriented in the forest, units went into action piecemeal, brigades and regiments fought isolated encounters, and casualties were enormous. As one historian observed, Warren's attack was "a study in the failure of division and corps command."[35] By 2:30 the Union offensive had petered out. The 5th Corps hobbled back to its starting point, dug in, and despite orders to attack once more, made no further effort to move beyond its trench line.[36] On the Confederate side, Ewell had done everything Lee asked of him. He held his position effectively, beat back a major Union assault, and above all, avoided getting sucked into a general engagement. As dusk approached, fighting in the turnpike sector subsided into an exchange of sporadic rifle fire between half-hidden lines of infantry.

The failure of the 5th Corps to respond aggressively to Grant's direction on May 5 was not simply a failure of corps and divisional command. Looking back on the episode, a member of Meade's staff attributed the problem to an inherent shortcoming of the Army of the Potomac: "the lack of springy formation, and audacious, self-reliant initiative. This organic weakness was entirely due to not having had in its youth skillfully aggressive leadership. Its early commanders had dissipated war's best elixir by training it into a life of caution, and the evil of that schooling [was] unmistakable."[37]

To the south on the Orange plank road, the major battle of the day was shaping up. Lee and Grant both recognized the importance of the Brock road intersection and Lee, who was with Hill's corps, urged his combative lieutenant to take it if he could "without bringing on a general engagement."[38] Hill tried for several hours to do so, but Getty's men proved immovable. Lee was forced to weaken his thrust along the road to shift troops left to fill the gap between Hill and Ewell, and by mid-afternoon Union reinforcements were on the field. Whatever opportunity there might have been had slipped past. Hancock arrived shortly after 2 P.M., riding at the head of his powerful four-division corps, and by three o'clock he had two divisions on line on either side of Getty. Although Grant and Meade pressed for an immediate attack, Hancock preferred to wait until all of his troops were up. Nevertheless, at 4 P.M., when he and Getty received peremptory orders from Meade to advance, the Federal line moved forward.

Hancock, who had been badly wounded at Gettysburg, was in Grant's estimation the Union's finest corps commander,[39] and on the afternoon of May 5 he lived up to his reputation. Despite the unfriendly terrain and the disadvantage of assaulting an enemy that was well concealed, Hancock launched four separate attacks at the rebel line, each more vigorous than the last. Never had the Army of the Potomac been engaged under more adverse conditions. Cavalry was of no use, there were no fields of fire for the artillery, and it was impossible for the infantry to see where they were going because of the dense undergrowth. Yet the rifle fire was never more intense. Advancing Union troops delivered blind volleys of musketry that lopped the saplings and clipped the branches at breast height, while prone Confederate soldiers, lying flat beneath the incoming sheets of lead, responded with even more deadly fire.

As the afternoon wore away, the weight of the Union assault made itself felt. By six o'clock Hancock had all four of his divisions in the attack and outnumbered Hill's men three to one. Grant threw an additional division in on Hancock's right and Lee brought back the troops that had attempted to link up with Ewell. As dusk settled over the battlefield, Hill found himself facing more than a third of Meade's army. At this point Lee had exhausted his reserves and had darkness not intervened, the Army of Northern Virginia would have faced catastrophic defeat.

Hancock paid heavily. Union officers, with their gold braid and bright uniforms, were especially hard hit. Thomas McParlin, the army's medical director, reported that in proportion to enlisted men, more officers were shot the afternoon of May 5 than in any battle he could remember.[40] One of the casualties was Brigadier General Alexander Hays, a lifelong friend of Grant, shot in the head while leading his brigade forward. Colonel Horace Porter, Grant's aide, was with Hancock at the time and carried the news of Hays's death back to headquarters. "General Grant was by no means a demonstrative man," Porter wrote, "but he was visibly affected. He was seated upon the ground with his back against a tree, still whittling pine sticks. He sat for a time without uttering a word, and then, speaking in a low voice, and pausing between sentences, said: "Hays and I were cadets for three years. We served for a time in the same regiment in the Mexican war. He was a noble man and a gallant officer. I am not surprised that he met his death at the head of his troops; it was just like him. He was a man who would never follow, but would always lead in battle."[41]

That night the wounded lay in an inferno of a no-man's-land, trapped by fires that sprang up and spread rapidly when the night breeze fanned wayward sparks into flames amid the undergrowth. "Throughout the night," a Pennsylvania soldier wrote, "as the fires, which had blazed since early afternoon, drew nearer and nearer to the poor unfortunates who lay between the lines, their shrieks, cries, and groans rent the air until death relieved the sufferers, or the battle of musketry drowned all the other sounds in its dominating roar."[42] Cries of wounded men went unheeded as rescue parties shrank from entering the desolate space between picket lines for fear of setting off rifle broadsides from troops made panicky by fear of a night attack at close quarters.

The fighting on May 5 had been as intense as anyone connected with the Army of the Potomac could remember. Journalists accompanying the army instinctively reported that Meade was so overwhelmed he wanted to withdraw across the Rapidan under cover of darkness and make a fresh start somewhere else. The report was false, and in any event Grant would have none of it.[43] For him the battle was a prelude. Discussing the day with his staff that evening, he pointed out that neither Burnside's corps nor Longstreet's had been engaged, and most of the day had been spent fighting for position. "Today's work has not been much of a test of strength," he told his listeners.[44]

The Army of the Potomac was under new management. Grant had pushed the troops to their limit, and the grinding attacks that he ordered on the Orange plank road had no precedent in the East.[45] Darkness had come before the fruits of those attacks could be realized—General Humphreys, Meade's chief of staff, thought one more hour of daylight would have brought victory[46]—but overall Grant said he was "pretty well satisfied with the engagement." Lee, he noted, had tried to hit the army in the flank "before it could be put into line of battle," and he had failed.[47] Unlike Meade, Grant looked at Lee's weakness, not his own. As he saw it, the Army of Northern Virginia was now vulnerable. He told Meade to resume the attack at first light. Victory was in the offing.

Grant's plan for May 6 was simple enough. Warren and Sedgwick would renew their attack against the Confederate 2nd Corps, hold Ewell in place, and prevent any reinforcements from being sent to Hill. Hancock, meanwhile, reinforced with everything Meade could lay his hands on, would deliver the principal Union attack along the Orange plank road and annihilate Hill before Longstreet arrived. In addition to the four divisions of the 2nd Corps, Hancock was assigned one division from each of the other three corps—a total of seven, half of Meade's army. At the same time, Burnside, with the remaining divisions of the 9th Corps, would take up a position on Hancock's right, plunge between the two wings of Lee's army, and then shift south to roll up Hill's flank. Grant set the attack for first light, 4:30 A.M., which he thought would allow time to complete the destruction of Lee's right before Longstreet could intervene.

Late that evening, Meade discussed the plan with his corps commanders. All expressed concern that Burnside, "who had a genius for slowness," would not be in position by 4:30.[48] The added weight of the 9th Corps was critical to thrashing Hill, and so Meade, as diplomatically as possible, and without mentioning Burnside by name, suggested to Grant that the attack be postponed until six o'clock.[49] Grant, who by now had taken Lee's measure, gave Meade an additional thirty minutes. The attack was set for 5 A.M. To wait later, said Grant, would give Lee time to mount his own attack, which he "especially wanted to avoid."[50]

Grant's concern was justified. Lee, who was determined to retain the initiative, set his own offensive for daybreak. It was a mirror image of Grant's plan. Ewell would send his skirmish line forward to hold Warren and Sedgwick in place, Hill would sidle left and close the gap with Ewell, and Longstreet would come up behind Hill, replace the 3rd Corps on the plank road, and assault the Union left. Lee believed that Longstreet's corps could repeat the magic of Chickamauga and crumple Grant's flank, at which point Ewell and Hill would join the attack against the Federals to their front and fling the Army of the Potomac back across the Rapidan. Like Grant, Lee counted on momentum: getting his assault underway before the lines of blue formed against him. The difficulty, which was not appreciated until well after midnight, was that Longstreet was not up. The march from Gordonsville had taken longer than expected. The 1st Corps had marched thirty-two miles in twenty-four hours but still had ten to go. It would not reach the battlefield until dawn at the earliest. Until Longstreet's men could get into position, Hill's battered corps would have to bear the brunt of the juggernaut Grant was sending forward. For both Lee and Grant, Longstreet was the key. Grant intended to destroy the rebel right before Longstreet arrived; Lee needed to hold the line on plank road until Old Pete could make his presence felt.

For Lee, betting on Longstreet's arrival was a gamble. The signal gun for the Union advance sounded at 5 A.M. with Old Pete still five miles away. That was not Longstreet's fault. He had doubled up his divisions into tighter formations for more efficient marching, taken every shortcut possible, and pressed his men to the utmost. "Every man stripped himself for the fight and I have never seen so much yellow corn meal thrown away in my life," a South Carolinian wrote.[51] But the road was difficult, and Longstreet was still well over the horizon when Hancock's troops moved forward. Lee had staked everything on the 1st Corps's appearance and luck had turned against him.

Hancock's assault was overwhelming. Overnight Meade had stripped his rear area of every available man. When the 2nd Corps moved forward it was virtually at full strength, with the casualties of May 5 replaced with engineers, cannoneers, and support troops of every description. Up the Orange plank road the Federals came, two divisions deployed on either side, a fifth slanting in from the right. Hill's corps wilted under the onslaught. "The pressure was irresistible," a Confederate officer recalled. "There was no panic and no great haste. The men seemed to fall back [out of] a deliberate conviction that it was impossible to hold the ground and foolish to attempt it. It was mortifying, but it was only what every veteran has experienced."[52]

On the Union side a soldier wrote that "sometimes our advance was very slow and every inch hotly contested, and then again we progressed for some distance in a short time, but all the while fighting an almost unseen enemy in thick woods." Another called it "bushwhacking with the enemy on a grand scale." Jubilant at his early success, Hancock shouted to a staff officer on the scene, "We are driving them beautifully. Tell Meade we are driving them *most beautifully*."[53]

In the turnpike sector, it was much the same as the day before. Troops battled between breastworks with neither side willing to risk a frontal assault against entrenchments that had become virtually impregnable. In a sense, Warren and Sedgwick were doing what Grant asked by tying Ewell down and preventing him from shifting troops south. In similar fashion, Ewell was complying with Lee's wishes by keeping two Union corps engaged.

The missing piece in Grant's attack plan was Burnside, who literally had gone missing. Grant was employing the 9th Corps as an independent maneuver element under his personal control and it proved to be a serious mistake. Burnside had been ordered to fill the gap between Warren and Hancock and drive on Hill's flank, but when the attack began he was nowhere in sight. Moving under its own command, the 9th Corps was hopelessly lost somewhere behind the front, wandering in circles as the battle raged. When told of Burnside's absence, Hancock was furious. "Just what I expected," he told a member of Meade's staff. "If he could attack now we would smash A. P. Hill all to pieces."[54] With 12,000 troops, Burnside would have added significant weight to Hancock's attack and could have hastened Hill's defeat. As it was, the 2nd Corps seemed to be doing well enough without Burnside's help, although the tangled undergrowth slowed its advance. All along the line Hill's men were giving way. As one observer recalled, it was a scene "such as we had never witnessed before in Lee's army."[55]

As dispirited Confederate troops streamed toward the rear, Lee worked feverishly to stiffen what little was left of Hill's resistance. Having risked all, he stood to lose all—the battle, the army, the war—unless Longstreet appeared. "Go bring him up," he shouted to General Cadmus Wilcox, whose division was rapidly disintegrating. Anticipating the worst, Lee ordered the army's supply train to prepare for withdrawal. The Confederacy hung by a thread. All that stood between the Army of Northern Virginia and defeat were the guns of the 3rd Corps's artillery, Lee's last line, sited along a rise slightly behind the battle with a clear field of fire covering the Orange plank road. The gunners could slow Hancock's advance; they could not stop it. Each minute, however, brought Longstreet closer. "It was the most anxious moment of the war," wrote a member of Hill's staff. "Everything looked like disaster."[56] A. P. Hill, an old artilleryman, had dismounted and was helping to serve one of the pieces. Lee remained mounted among the guns, his presence inspiring the cannoneers to a final effort. Without infantry support the guns would soon be overrun, but for a moment the Union advance was held at bay. One Southern historian judged the artillery's stand to be the bravest of the war. "This single incident brought more honor . . . than most soldiers attain in a lifetime."[57]

In the midst of the smoke and chaos, Lee caught a rearward glimpse of a tightly bunched mass of troops marching forward. They wore blue, not the deep federal blue of the Union army, but the lighter blue of the Confederate 1st Corps. They packed the Orange plank road, eight abreast, and as they approached the guns, they broke to double-time. "Like a fine lady at a party, Longstreet was often late in his arrival at the ball," wrote Private William Dame of the Richmond Howitzers. "But he always made a sensation when he got in, with the grand old First Corps sweeping behind him as his train."[58]

Pushing Hill's beaten men aside, Longstreet's troops came on "in perfect order, ranks well closed, and no stragglers," remembered Alabama general Evander Law.[59] As the lead brigade hurdled past the blazing guns of the 3rd Corps's artillery, Lee was overcome with emotion. "Which brigade is this?" he asked hard-fighting Brigadier General John Gregg, who was new to the Army of Northern Virginia.

"The Texas brigade, sir."

"Hurrah for Texas," Lee shouted, as he raised high in his stirrups, took off his wide-brimmed hat and waved it. Texans in the front ranks responded with a rebel yell that could be heard for miles around.[60] Spared what appeared to be certain defeat, Lee could not contain his excitement. The Texans continued forward, 800 strong, straight toward Hancock's lines, when they noticed that riding among them, his face flushed with emotion, was Lee himself. He had spurred Traveller to join them, intent on leading the charge himself. The Texans slowed to a walk. "Lee to the rear." "General Lee, go back. Go back," echoed across the front. Lee seemed not to hear. The brigade sergeant major grabbed Traveller's bridle, Gregg remonstrated, and finally an aide pointed out Longstreet and urged Lee to join him. Lee looked to the far end of the field, and for the first time since Gregg's Texans appeared, realized his responsibility as commanding general. He turned Traveller's head and rode off to meet the man who had saved the day.

Years later Longstreet recalled the incident. Lee was "off his balance," said Old Pete. When he rode up, "I told him in a jocular manner that his line would be recovered in an hour if he would permit me to handle the troops, but if my services were not needed I would like to ride to some place of safety, as it was not quite comfortable where we were."[61] Lee took the point and retired westward a short distance, content to leave matters to his War Horse.

Longstreet was one of the finest tacticians the Civil War produced. He recognized instantly that his two divisions, even with the remnants of Hill's corps, would be no match for the mass Hancock had assembled if they were spread thinly across the front. Perhaps remembering Zachary Taylor's tactics at Resaca de la Palma, he massed his corps in brigade columns on either side of the plank road, gained numerical superiority at the point of contact, punched a hole in Hancock's line, and forced the Federals to pull back lest their formation be cut in half. For over an hour the fighting was intense. Of the 800 men of the Texas brigade, only 250 survived unharmed. By nine o'clock the Confederate line was back to where it stood originally. Longstreet's counterattack had spent its force and the two armies settled down to the grim work of slugging it out at close quarters. Neither side was capable of breaking through the other, and neither was willing to retreat. Hancock's early morning assault, which came so close to victory, had gone for naught. Grant's second-day offensive had been brought to a standstill. Moxley Sorrel, of Longstreet's staff, wrote afterward: "I always thought that in its entire splendid history the simple act of forming the line in that dense undergrowth, under heavy fire, amid the routed men of A. P. Hill, and driving the enemy under these circumstances was perhaps [the 1st Corps's] greatest performance."[62]

At ten o'clock a lull settled over the battlefield. A Confederate regimental commander called it "the ominous silence that precedes the tornado."[63] Reconnaissance parties scouted the opposing lines, and it rapidly became clear that Grant was in far worse shape than Lee. Burnside, like Lew Wallace at Shiloh, was still AWOL; there was a gap in the Union line between Warren and Hancock, and both flanks were uncovered. Never had a Union army faced Lee in such circumstances without paying heavily for it.

At Union headquarters the early morning's elation had given way to apprehension and concern. Meade fretted over the inability of Warren and Sedgwick to dent Ewell's line, and his famous temper rose to the boiling point over Burnside's inexplicable absence. Longstreet's arrival on the rebel right was greeted with dismay, and the shredding of Hancock's offensive with consternation. When stragglers from several Union divisions began streaming through the headquarters clearing, a genuine alarm set in.

Grant remained unperturbed. Throughout the day, regardless of the news from the front, he expressed no impatience and manifested no excitement. When a decision was required, he made it instantly. As one observer noted, "He never exhibited to better advantage his peculiar ability in moving troops with unparalleled speed to critical points on the line of battle, or, as it was sometimes called, 'feeding a fight'."[64] At one point late in the morning rebel artillery found the range of the Union command post and a few shells exploded nearby. Grant rose briefly from his stump, surveyed the scene, puffed thoughtfully on his cigar, and then resumed his seat, content to let events take their course. When a nervous staff officer, fearful the position was about to be overrun, suggested it would be prudent to move the headquarters rearward, Grant stopped whittling and looked up. "It strikes me," he said very quietly, "it would be better to order up some artillery and defend the present location."[65] The guns were duly limbered forward, a few rounds of counterbattery fire were discharged, and the shelling ceased.

The situation on the south end of the Union line was not so easily corrected. Shortly after 10 A.M. Confederate reconnaissance parties reported to Longstreet that Hancock's left was in the air and wide open to attack. A Union division was posted a mile or so further south ostensibly to protect the flank, but there was a gaping hole between it and Hancock's main battle line. Not only that, an unfinished railroad cut afforded a concealed approach perpendicular to the unguarded flank. Troops could form along the roadbed without being detected. Longstreet recognized the opportunity. For the last day and a half the two armies had hammered each other in a series of frontal assaults all of which ground down without issue. By using the abandoned railroad cut, Old Pete would hit the unsuspecting Hancock in the flank, roll up the Union line, and break the battle open. As Lee's aide recalled, the maneuver was superb. "Longstreet, always grand in battle, never shone as he did here."[66] Longstreet, who now commanded the entire rebel right, deployed four brigades, roughly 5,000 men, in the flanking force. He kept his remaining eleven brigades in position on either side of the plank road, facing Hancock head-on and ready to move forward at the appropriate moment. It required almost an hour to get the flankers in place. "Hit hard when you start," cautioned Longstreet, "but don't start until everything is ready."[67] At eleven o'clock the attack exploded on the Union left and began to roll northward. Longstreet then ordered his main body forward to exploit the panic that engulfed Hancock's ranks.[68] "Our lines broke and ran like sheep," a Union soldier recorded in his diary. Another said, "It was a regular skedaddle."[69] Two Union divisions melted under the impact of the unexpected rebel assault, and Hancock worked frantically to re-form his line lest the entire Federal position collapse. Almost instantly the momentum of battle shifted. The question was no longer how to attack Lee, but how to save the Army of the Potomac. Years later, with undisguised admiration, Hancock told Longstreet, "You rolled me up like a blanket."[70]

As the flank attack gained momentum, charging Confederates clattered across the front of Longstreet's main battle line. In the heat of the moment, with lead flying everywhere, it was impossible to distinguish friend from foe. Inevitably the flankers came under friendly fire. Longstreet, who was on the scene, rode forward immediately to stop the firing and was hit solidly by a bullet that passed through his neck and lodged in his right shoulder. As one historian has noted, Confederate exaltation turned to dismay as word spread that Old Pete was down.[71] The steam went out of the rebel attack. Less than a year before, Stonewall Jackson had been mortally wounded by friendly fire in these same woods, not more than four miles from where Longstreet was hit. It too came at the climax of a successful flanking attack. Longstreet remained conscious long enough to instruct his successor to continue the assault, but with the front now at right angles it took precious hours to adjust the rebel lines. As Old Pete was transported to the rear, many in the 1st Corps wept openly. Lee was among the most distraught. "I shall not soon forget the sadness in his face, and the almost despairing movement of his hands, when he was told that Longstreet had fallen," wrote one observer.[72]

With Longstreet out of action, Lee took over direction of the Confederate right. By 4 P.M. the 1st Corps' lines had been straightened out, and Lee, who was determined to drive Grant back across the Rapidan, prepared to resume the attack. The four-hour hiatus, however, gave Hancock time to recover. He shored up his exposed left flank, brought up reinforcements, strengthened his breastworks, and established a secondary line in support of the first. Equally important, Burnside, whose 9th Corps had been lost to the Federal war effort for ten hours, arrived on the scene and went into position on Hancock's right. The gap in the center of Grant's line was plugged and the right flank of the United States 2nd Corps was covered for the first time since the battle began.

At 4:15 the Confederate battle line moved forward. This time there was no effort to envelop the Union flank. The 1st Corps, supported by the remnants of A. P. Hill's command, advanced straight up the Orange plank road. As at Gettysburg ten months earlier, Lee sought to redeem the battle with a frontal assault against the Union center. As at Gettysburg, Hancock's 2nd Corps was once again ready and waiting. Lee's attack was another gamble—an attempt to overwhelm the Federal line by brute force and achieve the breakthrough that thus far had eluded him. The rebels came on with unquenchable aggressiveness. A Massachusetts soldier called the attack "the most desperate of the day." *New York Times* correspondent Charles Page called Lee's charge the "most wicked assault thus far encountered—brief in duration, but terrific in power and superhuman momentum."[73]

As it had done at Gettysburg, Hancock's corps held firm. Here and there Confederate troops achieved momentary penetrations, but in each instance the breakthrough was snuffed out by Federal artillery. By 5:15 Lee's attack had run its course. "The enemy has been finally and completely repulsed," Hancock reported to Meade.[74] That afternoon's charge by the 1st Corps along the Orange plank road would be the last major offensive thrust by the Army of Northern Virginia. Its audacity was breathtaking. Yet as Longstreet's artillery commander, Brigadier General Porter Alexander, wrote, it "ought never, never to have been made. It was sending a boy on a man's errand. It was wasting good soldiers whom we could not spare."[75]

When the attack on the Orange plank road sputtered out, Lee rode to the north end of the Confederate line to consult with Ewell. Could the Confederate 2nd Corps launch an attack on Grant's right? "Cannot something be done on this flank?" asked Lee.[76] Ewell replied that the Union entrenchments facing him were so formidable that an attack would be pointless, and in this he was supported by Jubal Early, whose division had been up against Sedgwick for the past two days. Brigadier General John B. Gordon, whose Georgia brigade held the left end of the Confederate line, happened to be with Ewell and Early when Lee rode up. Gordon had reconnoitered the area beyond his position and discovered that Sedgwick's right flank was uncovered. All afternoon he had been urging that he be allowed to attack, and had been repeatedly turned down. Ewell and Early were convinced that Burnside was posted in Sedgwick's rear and that Gordon would walk into more than he could handle. "With as much earnestness as was consistent with the position of junior officer," Gordon recalled,

"I recounted the facts to General Lee." [77] Lee needed no convincing. He knew Burnside had moved next to Hancock, and readily accepted Gordon's account. The attack was ordered immediately.

At 6 P.M., with little more than two hours of daylight remaining, Gordon led three brigades against the exposed Union position. Sedgwick's flank was not only in the air, but the line was lightly held, several brigades having been shifted earlier to reinforce Warren and Hancock. Taken by surprise, the Federal right disintegrated. A soldier from the 61st Georgia recalled coming upon the Yankees "all resting, cooking and eating; with their guns stacked, their blankets spread. . . . We fired one volley at them, raised a yell, and charged them. They fled at once, leaving their guns, blankets, knapsacks, tents, and, in fact, everything they had." [78] As Gordon's troops rolled forward, two Union brigades collapsed, netting over 600 prisoners, including two general officers. By seven o'clock Sedgwick had lost a tenth of his command. "Uncle John," Meade's oldest and least excitable corps commander, worked steadily to re-form his line. Reinforcements were shifted from left to right, and shortly after nightfall the 6th Corps had stopped Gordon dead in his tracks. The Union flank had been rolled up for about a mile, but the rebels were unable to hold that position. Under cover of darkness the Confederates pulled back to Ewell's entrenchments.

Throughout Gordon's foray, reports of disaster flooded back to Union headquarters. Courier after courier brought news that another unit had folded under the onslaught. Excited aides concluded that the 6th Corps had broken, that the army's wagon train would soon be in rebel hands, and that the enemy was advancing southward along the Germanna Ford road. Meade was steady as a rock. If anyone could handle the crisis he knew that Sedgwick could, and he refused to be stampeded. "Nonsense!" he told nervous staffers. "If they have broken our lines, they can do no more tonight." [79]

Grant provided unshakable reassurance. He quietly interrogated the officers who brought the reports, sifted the truth from fanciful exaggerations, and gave concise directions to meet the crisis. After instructing Meade to reinforce Sedgwick, he lit another cigar and settled back to his whittling. At the height of the alarm, a lathered Union brigadier rode back to headquarters to personally bring the warning of impending calamity. "General Grant," he said excitedly, "this is a crisis that cannot be looked upon too seriously. I know Lee's methods well by past experience; he will throw his whole army between us and the Rapidan, and cut us off completely from our communications." Grant got up from his stump, pulled the cigar from his mouth, and let fly: "Oh, I am heartily tired of hearing about what Lee is going to do. Some of you always seem to think he is suddenly going to turn a double somersault and land in our rear and on both flanks at the same time. Go back to your command, General, and try to think what we are going to do ourselves, instead of what Lee is going to do." [80]

The incident was as close as Grant came to losing his composure. Several times during the day he and Meade rode out to critical points along the battle line, but on each occasion the situation seemed to be in hand and there was nothing they could do but offer a few words of encouragement. Like Meade, Grant fretted about Burnside's tardiness, but he realized it was out of his hands. "The only time I ever feel impatient," Grant told Horace Porter, "is when I give an order for an important movement of troops in the presence of the enemy, and am waiting for them to reach their destination. Then the minutes seem like hours." [81]

Once, during a lull in the fighting, Grant strolled down to the Germanna Ford road. While he was standing there a herd of beef cattle were driven past. One of the animals strayed in Grant's direction and a drover yelled out: "I say, stranger, head off that critter for me, will you?" For a moment, the general in chief was back on his hardscrabble farm in Missouri. Without changing his expression he stepped forward, threw up his hands, and shouted to the animal. It stopped, took a look, and ambled back to join the herd. The drover had not recognized Grant, dressed as he was in his unadorned government-issued uniform, and Grant seemed to think the episode to have been perfectly natural. [82]

At about 8 P.M. Hancock rode into headquarters to brief Grant and Meade on the day's fighting. He was exhausted, but as one witness reported, "there was still plenty of fight left in him." Grant felt in his pocket to proffer a cigar and found he had only one left—which he jokingly gave Hancock. Deducting the number he had given away from the supply he started with that morning, Grant had smoked about twenty during the day, all very large and very strong. It is true it had been a particularly long and trying day, but as an aide noted, Grant "never afterward equaled that record in the use of tobacco." [83]

With the repulse of Gordon's attack on the Union right, the battle of the Wilderness came to a close. As night settled over the battlefield, both sides took stock. After two days of the most ferocious fighting yet seen in North America, Grant had lost 17,666 men—roughly 18 percent of his command: 2,246 killed, 12,037 wounded, 3,383 captured or missing. [84] Lee's losses were similar. Of the 60,000 troops of the Army of Northern Virginia who took part ("muskets for duty"), approximately 11,000 became casualties—roughly 18 percent.* The previous spring at Chancel-

---

* Confederate numbers are difficult to come by. The figure 11,000 is from Gordon C. Rhea, *The Battle of the Wilderness,* May 5–6, 1864 440 (Baton Rouge: Louisiana State Uni-

lorsville, Joe Hooker, with fewer losses than Grant had sustained, threw in the sponge and pulled back across the Rapidan. Grant was not Hooker. "At present we can claim no victory," he wrote Halleck. "[N]either have they gained a single advantage." [85]

At this point, the intensity of the battle was known only to the participants. When the Army of the Potomac crossed the Rapidan, Grant issued orders forbidding newsmen from using the telegraph. The only way they could file a story was to send it back by messenger, or return with it themselves. Even Lincoln and the War Department were at a loss as to what was happening. Grant's laconic message to Halleck was his first dispatch from the front. What Grant intended to do next was even more of a mystery. Grant preferred it that way. If his friends didn't know his plans, it was safe to assume that the enemy did not either.

Grant may have worried about that, at least insofar as President Lincoln was concerned. That evening he took what for him was an unprecedented step. He used an informal back channel to keep the president informed. About nine o'clock Henry Wing, a young reporter for the *New York Tribune,* approached Grant as he sat with his staff by the fire and said he would be leaving for Washington the next morning. Did the general in chief have anything he wanted to say?

"Yes," said Grant. "You may tell the people that things are going swimmingly down here."

Wing could scarcely believe what he heard, but he dutifully wrote it down. As he walked away he sensed someone coming up behind him. It was Grant. Speaking quietly so no one would hear, he asked, "Do you expect to get through to Washington?" Wing said he did. "Well, if you see the President, tell him from me that whatever happens, there will be no turning back." [86]*

---

versity Press, 1994). Based on an examination of independent sources, Rhea puts Hill's losses at 7,000, Longstreet's at 3,000, and Ewell's at 1,250. There are no morning reports to corroborate. Cf. Edward Porter Alexander, *Military Memoirs of a Confederate* 508–9 (Bloomington: Indiana University Press, 1962). Reprint.

* Wing was the youngest of four reporters from the *Tribune* with the Army of the Potomac. Because he was the youngest, he was selected to make the hazardous journey through the hostile Virginia countryside to Washington. After a day and a half of dodging rebel guerrillas, he arrived safely in the capital during the early morning hours of Saturday, May 7, and was taken immediately to the White House, where Lincoln and the cabinet were waiting. In Wing's words: "A half hour or more was spent in description of the movements of the troops, and in explanation, from a large map on the wall, of the situation at the time when I left. Then, as the company was dispersing, I turned to Mr. Lincoln, and said: 'Mr. President, I have a personal word for you.'

"He took a short, quick step toward me, and, stooping to bring his eyes level with mine, whispered, in tones of intense, impatient interest, 'What is it?'

"I was so moved I could hardly stammer: 'General Grant told me to tell you, from him, that, whatever happens, there is to be no turning back.'

As Grant saw it, the fighting had been a success. He told his staff that while the battle might appear to have been a draw, "we remain in possession of the field," and "the Confederates have withdrawn into a defensive position. We cannot call the engagement a positive victory, but the enemy have only twice actually reached our lines in their many attacks, and on both occasions they were repulsed." Grant was sitting on the ground, looking at a map, his legs tucked under him like a tailor. He said there was no point in continuing to fight in the Wilderness. "I can certainly drive Lee back into his works, but I shall not assault him there. He would have all the advantages in such a fight." Grant told his listeners that if Lee pulled back and entrenched, "my notion is to move promptly toward the left." That would force Lee "to throw himself between us and Richmond, and in such a movement I hope to be able to attack him in a more open country, and outside of his breastworks."[87]

As at Shiloh after the first day of battle, Grant may have been the only one in the Union army who saw the battle of the Wilderness in a positive light. Twice victory had been within reach: on May 5 when darkness prevented Hancock from completing the destruction of Hill's 3rd Corps, and on the morning of the 6th before Longstreet came up to counter Hancock's dawn attack along the Orange plank road. But on two other occasions defeat stared the Army of the Potomac in the face. Longstreet's assault on Hancock's flank threatened to roll up the entire Union line and might well have done so had not Old Pete been struck down while the fighting was at its height. Gordon's evening attack on the Union right was eventually contained by Sedgwick's 6th Corps, but had it been mounted earlier in the day, and with greater strength, it too could have spelled disaster.

What the battle revealed was that the Union command structure left much to be desired. Grant's attempt to coordinate Meade and Burnside had been a failure. Meade's handling of his own generals was uninspiring. Warren proved to be overcautious, while Sedgwick and Hancock, who were perfectly willing to take the fight to the enemy, neglected to secure their flanks and thus placed the entire army in jeopardy. The massive wagon train of the Army of the Potomac had proven to be a tactical embarrassment, and Sheridan, with three divisions of cavalry, had been no help whatever—due more to the terrain and the need to protect the army's trains than to Little Phil's inability.

Late that evening Grant sat by a smoldering campfire, alone except

---

"Mr. Lincoln put his great, strong arms about me and, carried away in the exuberance of his gladness, imprinted a kiss upon my forehead." Henry E. Wing, *When Lincoln Kissed Me* 37–39 (New York: Abingdon, 1913).

for Sylvanus Cadwallader of the *New York Herald*. They were the last in the headquarters compound still awake. Cadwallader had been with Grant for almost two years and for the first time, as he wrote afterward, he began "to question . . . my faith in him. We had waged two days of murderous battle, and had but little to show for it. Judged by comparative losses, it had been disastrous for the Union cause. We had been compelled by General Lee to fight him on a field of his own choosing, with the certainty of losing at least two men for his one, until he could be dislodged and driven from his battle ground. We had scarcely gained a rod of the battlefield at the close of a two days' contest." Cadwallader wondered whether he had followed Grant from the Tallahatchie, to Vicksburg, to Chattanooga, only "to record his defeat . . . in the dark and tangled thickets of the Wilderness." Cadwallader looked over at Grant. "His hat was drawn down over his face, the high collar of an old blue army overcoat turned up above his ears, one leg crossed over the other knee, eyes on the ashes in front." He assumed Grant's thoughts were as gloomy as his own.

When Grant saw he was not alone, he began what Cadwallader called "a pleasant chatty conversation upon indifferent subjects," none of which had anything to do with the past two days' fighting. As he got up to go to bed, Grant spoke briefly of "the sharp work General Lee had been giving us for the past two days," and then entered his tent. That was all. Once Cadwallader realized that Grant did not share his gloomy thoughts, everything looked different. "It was the greatest sunburst of my life. I had suddenly emerged from the slough of despond, to the solid bed-rock of unwavering faith."[88] Grant's quiet self-confidence affected Cadwallader much as it had Sherman that terrible Sunday night at Shiloh. Grant did not say "Lick 'em tomorrow," but he might well have done so.

For Lee, the battle of the Wilderness was the beginning of the end. Confronted with an enemy twice his size, with an almost unlimited capacity to make good its losses, he had chosen to attack. He gambled on being able to wield a decisive blow that would send Grant reeling back across the Rapidan. And he nearly succeeded. Had Longstreet not been wounded at a critical moment, Hancock's corps might have collapsed and the entire Union line could have been rolled up. But the fact that success or failure hung on such a whim of fate illustrated the shakiness of Lee's gamble. His desperate decision to send the 1st Corps forward against Hancock's well-prepared Brock road position Friday afternoon—like sending Pickett forward the third day at Gettysburg—was the act of a high-stakes gambler behind on the night. The odds were stacked against him, and the result was more casualties than he could afford.

Having gambled and lost, Lee faced the inevitable. Despite the advantage of fighting on friendly soil, and the élan of his soldiers, the Army of Northern Virginia was incapable of mounting another attack in the Wilderness against a foe as numerous and as well dug in as the Army of the Potomac. Previous Union commanders, confronted with the losses Grant had sustained, would likely have withdrawn to lick their wounds. Lee knew that Grant, given his reputation, was unlikely to do that. As Lee saw it, the best alternative, indeed, the only alternative, was to entrench, hunker down, and hope that Grant might attack once more. That might lead to his repulse, and another repulse, if decisive enough, could tip the balance.[89] It would mean going on the defensive and waiting for Grant to make a mistake. This did not come easily to Lee, because it meant surrendering the initiative.

Lee's soldiers considered the battle of the Wilderness a success. The latest Union drive on Richmond had been thwarted, and Grant had been fought to a standstill. A North Carolina soldier wrote his family: "The enemy are evidently much worsted and their plans frustrated. Our army is in splendid condition, confident of success and victory, trusting in God and General Lee."[90] Brigadier General William Pendleton, Lee's chief of artillery, informed his wife that "the Yankees have been seriously beaten."[91] Was it whistling in the dark? Or were the Confederates so confident of victory they could not contemplate defeat? Napoleon is said to have observed that in battle the morale is to the physical as three to one. Were that to be the case, the unshakable morale of Lee's army goes a long way toward explaining how so few held so many for so long.

Saturday, May 7, 1864, dawned cloudy and overcast. A slow drizzle moved in and an uneasy quiet settled over the battlefield. Union reconnaissance parties, making their way between the lines, found that Lee had pulled his skirmish line back half a mile and that the rebels were buttoned up in their breastworks, content to sit tight. The Union lines were likewise quiet. For this the troops were grateful, especially those who had taken a close-up look at the rebel entrenchments. They were also puzzled. Unlike his Confederate counterpart, the average Union soldier thought his side had been whipped. "Most of us thought it was another Chancellorsville," a Massachusetts veteran recalled.[92] "Two days of deadly encounter," wrote another. "Every man who could bear a musket was put in. Hancock and Warren repulsed, Sedgwick routed; the cavalry drawn back; the trains seeking safety behind the river; thousands and thousands killed and wounded . . . and the air pervaded with a lurking feeling of being face-to-face with disaster."[93] Almost to a man the troops assumed the next order they received would be to withdraw and recross the Rapidan, probably to undergo yet another reorganization under yet another commander who would eventually lead them into another battle that would end in another retreat. That was the all-too-familiar pattern of the Army of the Potomac when it faced Robert E. Lee in Virginia.[94]

That afternoon when the artillery limbered up and moved out, the troops believed their suspicions had been confirmed. The army was pulling back and the artillery was moving first. Sure enough, soon after dark the march order came down. Warren and Sedgwick were to lead the way, while Hancock's troops held their position lest Lee attack. The men dutifully slung their packs and fell into line. To their astonishment the columns headed south. They were not marching back across the Rapidan but toward Richmond and the tiny hamlet of Spotsylvania Court House, an important road intersection twelve miles southeast of the Wilderness, in open country and directly athwart Lee's line of communications. Once again Grant had played his cards close to his chest. He wanted to reach Spotsylvania before Lee, and surprise was essential. At 6:30 that morning he issued written instructions to Meade to move south.[95] Yet he told Meade not to pass the order along until three o'clock. That would still allow the artillery and the army's trains time to clear the roads before nightfall, at which point the infantry would move, the direction of march hopefully cloaked by darkness.

For the troops of the Army of the Potomac, the realization they were moving south was a tonic like no other. Packs became lighter, the pace quickened, and a buzz of excitement spread down the marching columns. "Our spirits rose. We marched free, and the men began to sing," wrote a Pennsylvania soldier.[96] About nine o'clock a group of riders rode slowly past the columns, also heading south. "Give way to the right. Give way to the right," echoed through the night. Then the recognition. It was Grant on his massive bay, Cincinnati, Meade on the indestructible Baldy, and their staffs. "Wild cheers echoed through the forest," wrote Colonel Horace Porter. "Men swung their hats, tossed up their arms, and pressed forward to within touch of their chief, clapping their hands, and speaking to him with the familiarity of comrades. Pine-knots and leaves were set on fire, and lighted the scene with their weird flickering glare. The night march had become a triumphal procession."[97] The Army of the Potomac was marching south and it was showing its appreciation. Regimental bands did their share. As Grant passed, one after another broke into the Sunday spiritual, "Ain't I Glad to Get Out of the Wilderness."

Looked at tactically, the battle of the Wilderness was a draw. Grant may even have lost. Yet in a strategic sense, it was an important victory. Within forty-eight hours after crossing the Rapidan, Grant had forced Lee on the defensive. His decision to move south was the final turning point of the war. Sherman called it the supreme moment in Grant's life: "Undismayed, with a full comprehension of the importance of the work in which he was engaged, feeling as keen a sympathy for his dead and wounded as anyone, and without stopping to count his numbers, he gave his orders calmly, specifically, and absolutely—'Forward to Spotsylvania.' "[98]

Grant took a more modest view. Speaking to his staff, he said, "All things are relative. While we were engaged in the Wilderness I could not help thinking of the first fight I ever saw—the battle of Palo Alto. As I looked at the long line of battle, consisting of three thousand men, I felt that General Taylor had such a fearful responsibility resting upon him and I wondered how he ever had the nerve to assume it. And when, after the fight, the casualties were reported, and the losses ascertained to be nearly sixty . . . the engagement assumed a magnitude in my eyes which was positively startling. . . . Now, such an affair would scarcely be deemed important enough to report to headquarters."[99]

CHAPTER ELEVEN

GRANT AND LEE

I propose to fight it out on this line if it takes all summer.

ULYSSES S. GRANT

With the blessing of God, I trust we shall be able to prevent General Grant from reaching Richmond.

ROBERT E. LEE

NO TWO MEN better exemplified the cause for which they fought than Robert E. Lee and Ulysses Grant. Slaveholder, patrician, scion of the First Families of Virginia, the fifty-seven-year-old Lee personified the romantic virtues of the Old South. His father was Light-Horse Harry Lee, Washington's larger-than-life cavalry commander, governor of Virginia, spendthrift, womanizer, and ultimately a fugitive from debtor's prison who spent his last years in self-imposed exile in the West Indies. His mother was Ann Carter, daughter of the Tidewater Carters, the most prominent of James River planters, and once reputed to be the wealthiest family in America.[1] Eager to emulate his father's soldierly example, and equally desirous of sparing his mother the cost of a civilian education, Lee entered West Point in 1825 and rarely looked back.[2] Brevetted to the engineers, he served with distinction on the staff of General Winfield Scott during the Mexican War, became the ninth superintendent of the military academy in 1852, and three years later assumed temporary command of the 2nd Cavalry, his first troop duty in twenty-six years of active service.[3] In 1859 Lee commanded the detachment that captured John Brown at Harpers Ferry, and on March 16, 1861, he was promoted to full colonel and assigned to command the 1st Cavalry regiment. The following month, when Virginia seceded, Lee promptly resigned his commission and headed south. "I cannot raise my hand against my birthplace, my home, my children," he wrote a Northern friend.[4]

Lee's decision to join the Confederacy was not easily taken. The very day he learned Virginia had left the Union, he was offered the field command of the United States Army by the War Department. "I declined the offer," Lee wrote later, "stating as candidly and as courteously as I could, that though opposed to secession and deprecating war, I could take no part in an invasion of the Southern States."[5] Five days later, April 23, 1861, Lee assumed command of Virginia's military forces. Three weeks after that, with the formation of the Confederate States of America, he became a brigadier general in the Confederate army, and on August 31, 1861, was confirmed in the rank of full general.*

Lee was a strikingly handsome man, above medium height and well proportioned. He had a massive torso, and sitting on a horse, his shoulders and neck made him appear larger than he actually was. According to his principal biographer, he preferred the company of women, especially pretty women, to that of men, although there was never a suggestion of scandal. Deeply religious, Lee's belief in God was personal, not denominational. He read his Bible and prayer book daily, and spent much time on his knees seeking solace and support. He did not use tobacco, hated whiskey, and rarely drank even the smallest amount of wine.[6] Like Grant, he was blessed with great powers of endurance and a strong nervous system. Despite his innate dignity, he met people easily and had a well-developed memory for names. His mind was mathematical, directed toward problem solving rather than abstraction. He was an accomplished linguist, his reading encompassed a broader range than that of most officers, and, like many gifted commanders, he was bored by office routine. He viewed his father as a Revolutionary War hero, not a tragic bankrupt, and George Washington was his idol. Douglas Southall Freeman wrote that by 1861 Lee "had come to view duty as Washington did, to act as he thought Washington would, and even, perhaps, to emulate the grave, self-contained courtesy of the great American rebel."[7]

During the first year of the war, Lee's star was eclipsed. His initial assignment was to reclaim western Virginia for the Confederacy—an effort that ended in failure, in part because of Lee's timidity. Like Grant at Belmont, he was still learning the art of command. Lee reluctantly ordered an autumn pullback from the Kanawha, and was castigated by the bellicose Richmond press as "Granny Lee," a theoretical desk soldier who would not fight. Lee's second assignment was to improve coastal defenses in the Carolinas and Georgia—an assignment that placed him at loggerheads with the cream of Southern soldiery. At that point in the war, it was be-

---

* Lee ranked third among the original five full generals of the Confederate army: after Samuel Cooper, the adjutant general, and Albert Sidney Johnston; ahead of Joseph E. Johnston and P. G. T. Beauregard.

neath the dignity of a white man to dig fortifications, besides which a brave man would not hide behind earthworks in the first place. This unwelcome duty earned Lee a second sobriquet, "King of Spades."[8] He returned to Richmond in early 1862 to become Jefferson Davis's military secretary and adviser, an inauspicious posting that promised an abundance of desk work and little future. "Granny Lee." "King of Spades." The war, it seemed, had passed him by.

Opportunity appeared by accident. In May 1862, McClellan had pushed to within six miles of Richmond. Confederate forces under Joseph E. Johnston held the line on the Chickahominy, and on May 31 counterattacked at Seven Pines. At the climax of the battle, Johnston was seriously wounded, and Davis turned to Lee. It was an inspired choice and also a brave one. The fact that Lee was the ranking Confederate general available scarcely offset the disappointing reputation he had acquired. More troublesome was that in thirteen months of war, Lee had not taken part in a general engagement. Justified or not, Lee was viewed as a military theoretician who was out of place in the field. Most of Johnston's subordinates expressed discomfort at being placed under "a staff officer like Lee," and Union reaction was joyous. "I prefer Lee to Johnston," McClellan wrote Lincoln. "The former is too cautious and weak under grave responsibility. Personally brave and energetic to a fault, he is yet wanting in moral firmness when pressed by heavy responsibility, and is likely to be timid and irresolute in action."[9]

Union celebrations were short lived. Despite his unpromising start, Lee proved to be, as his friend Major General Henry Heth observed, "the most belligerent man in the Confederate army."[10] Within a month McClellan was on the run, outmaneuvered and outfought at Mechanicsville, Gaines' Mill, White Oak Swamp, and Malvern Hill. In August, Lee routed Pope at Second Manassas. Twice within the next year he crossed the Potomac to carry the fight to the North, hoping to sap Yankee sentiment to continue the war and coming perilously close, both at Antietam and Gettysburg, to smashing the Union line. Twice again he defeated the Army of the Potomac in Virginia: Burnside at Fredericksburg in 1862, Hooker at Chancellorsville in 1863. The battle of the Wilderness saw Lee on the attack once more. Whether Lee's aggressiveness aided or hurt the Confederacy is an argument recently renewed by historians,[11] but for Grant and Meade in 1864 the answer was scarcely debatable.

Ulysses Grant, the son of an Ohio tanner, a man indistinguishable in a crowd even in uniform, personified the egalitarian values of a modernizing, democratic society. Modest, rumpled, sometimes a bit seedy, Grant was an ordinary man gifted with an extraordinary talent for making war. His simple exterior cloaked a formidable intellect and a rock-solid self-confidence that was equal to any crisis on the battlefield. He had a topographer's feel for landscape, a photographic memory when it came to maps, and a command of the English language at its incisive best. "There is one striking feature of Grant's orders," said Meade's chief of staff, Major General A. A. Humphreys. "No matter how hurriedly he may write them in the field, no one ever had the slightest doubt as to their meaning, or even has to read over them a second time to understand them."[12]

Grant had an eye for the main chance. He focused on the enemy's weakness, not his own. No matter how badly things were going, he instinctively assumed they were worse for his opponent. After three years of war, he had become a master at maneuvering large bodies of troops on the battlefield. The battle of the Wilderness was not the best example. The working relationship between him and Meade had yet to be refined, and Grant had been unfamiliar with the capacities and shortcomings of the Army of the Potomac. Nevertheless, for the first time since the war began, a Union army was moving south after fighting Lee in Virginia. With the tenacity that had become his hallmark, Grant had captured the initiative. The democratic general of a democratic fighting force, he was determined to bring the Army of Northern Virginia to its knees.

Grant's object in moving on Spotsylvania was to force Lee out of his works in the Wilderness and bring him to battle in open country. Twelve miles southeast of Wilderness Tavern, Spotsylvania was situated on a direct line between Lee and Richmond. The town itself was of little importance except that it provided an easy approach to the two rail lines of central Virginia that were vital to the supply of Lee's army. By moving quickly, Grant planned to insert the Army of the Potomac between Lee and Richmond, take up a strong defensive position, and compel the Confederates to attack on terrain of his choosing.

The key to Grant's plan was to reach Spotsylvania before Lee. Once again, however, the Army of the Potomac proved sluggish and unresponsive. Despite the fact that it had a considerable head start, a better road, and a shorter distance to travel, the Union vanguard did not reach Spotsylvania until mid-morning of May 8. By then the Confederate 1st Corps was there and waiting. Lee anticipated Grant's move, and Longstreet's veterans—commanded now by Major General Richard Anderson—had marched briskly through the night, sliced ahead of Meade's forces, and secured the town before the Federals arrived. For Grant, the result was disappointing. Rather than standing between Lee and Richmond, he once again confronted the rebel army dug in and holding the high ground. Piecemeal attacks by Union infantry failed to dislodge the Confederates, and for the rest of the day Grant and Lee brought up reinforcements and deployed their armies in line of battle.

The town of Spotsylvania lies on a ridge between the Po and Ni rivers, two of the four northern Virginia streams (the Mat, the Ta, the Po, and the Ni) that join to form the Mattaponi River. At Spotsylvania, the ridge is about three miles wide and affords a strong defensive position. Neither the Po nor the Ni is especially wide, but the streams are deep, with steep banks, and bordered by heavily wooded bottom land.[13] Crossing them is difficult, and Lee utilized the rivers to secure his flanks. To the front, elaborate rebel breastworks stretching between the rivers dominated the ridgeline. Taking full advantage of the natural features of the terrain, the Confederates laid out their fortifications in the shape of a huge inverted U, or "hog's snout," a configuration that would also enable Lee to shift troops internally from one side to the other as the need arose. Rebel artillery was sited to be mutually supporting, and wherever practicable, an abatis of fallen timber was put in place.

Lee's eye for taking advantage of the topography had been sharpened under Scott in Mexico, and at Spotsylvania he more than demonstrated his proficiency. The man who had been ridiculed in 1862 as "King of Spades" had discovered a means of countering Grant's numerical superiority. The era of trench warfare, which had been slowly developing, came to fruition at Spotsylvania. Interlocking timber-and-dirt barriers blocked the way forward, deep traverses zigzagged to provide cover against Union artillery fire, and head logs, chocked a few inches above hard-packed soil from the trenches, afforded rebel riflemen a protected slit through which they could take deliberate aim at an approaching enemy. As Meade's chief of staff noted, Lee's fortifications during the last year of the war multiplied his defensive strength fourfold. And if the works were manned properly, "there is scarcely any measure by which to gauge the increased strength thereby gained."[14]

On May 9, 1864, with his troops dug in and his flanks snug between the rivers, Lee waited confidently to smash the inevitable Union attack. "With the blessing of God," he wrote Jefferson Davis, "I trust we shall be able to prevent General Grant from reaching Richmond."[15]

By late afternoon on May 8 most of Grant's troops were in place. The Union line faced south and was laid out in a rough semicircle paralleling the Confederate works. Hancock's 2nd Corps was deployed on the right, Warren and Sedgwick in the center, and Burnside on the left. From a tactical point of view, Grant was in no better position than in the Wilderness. He had moved south because he saw no advantage in assaulting the works Lee's men had thrown up in the forest, yet the Confederate fortifications at Spotsylvania were even more formidable, laid out on dominant terrain between unfordable rivers.[16] If Grant was perturbed, he did not show it. He wanted to bring on a battle, unwelcome as the setting might be, and proceeded accordingly.

The one bright spot that afternoon was Sheridan. Thus far the Union cavalry had rendered little assistance. Meade held to the view that horse soldiers could best be used screening the army's advance and protecting slow-moving wagon trains. Sheridan wanted to mass the troopers into a compact hard-hitting body, take off deep into the Confederate rear, lure Jeb Stuart into battle, and whip the socks off him. The dispute broke into the open on May 8. Both Meade and Sheridan were endowed with fiery tempers, and as the recriminations ("highly spiced with expletives") escalated, Meade decided to take the matter to Grant.[17] He stalked over to Grant's tent and related the conversation he had had with his cavalry commander. When he got to Sheridan's claim that he would destroy Stuart if Meade would only let him, Grant perked up. "Did Sheridan say that?" he asked, more amused than angered by the cavalryman's insubordination. Meade nodded. "Well, he generally knows what he is talking about. Let him start right out and do it."[18]

Meade took this with good grace, although by traditional standards of military discipline Grant was wrong. Rather than support the commander of the Army of the Potomac in a dispute with a subordinate, he winked at Sheridan's infraction. By now Grant was thoroughly frustrated with the Eastern army's caution, and if the obstreperous cavalry commander believed he could beat Stuart, Grant wanted him to go to it.[19]

Early the next morning Sheridan set out with his three cavalry divisions in the direction of Richmond. Riding four abreast, the column of troopers stretched thirteen miles in length and moved at a walk—a deliberate provocation to entice Stuart to attack. Sheridan's first target was Lee's advance supply base at Beaver Dam Station, fifteen miles south. Stuart nipped at Sheridan's heels, but was unable to prevent the destruction of three weeks' rations for the Army of Northern Virginia, twenty miles of railroad track, a hundred freight cars, and half the locomotives of the Virginia Central line. After wreaking havoc in Lee's rear, Sheridan continued south. Stuart stayed abreast of the Union column but did not make a stand until the Federals reached Yellow Tavern, a point six miles north of Richmond where the rebel leader hoped to receive reinforcements from the city's garrison. The reinforcements failed to arrive, and Stuart's cavalry proved no match for Sheridan's troopers, who outnumbered them two to one and who were armed with rapid-fire carbines instead of the South's standard-issue muzzle loaders. Stuart was mortally wounded in the fighting—a devastating blow to the Southern cause—and the once invincible Confederate cavalry was routed. Sheridan pushed on, easily rode through Richmond's outer defenses, but paused before plunging into the city itself. "I could have gone in and burned and killed right and left," Sheridan wrote later, but it would have been for no permanent advantage.[20] Tempted though he was, Little Phil led his troopers into Butler's lines on the James, rested his mounts, refitted, and rejoined the Army of the Potomac on May 24.

While Sheridan was crossing swords with the Confederate cavalry near Richmond, Grant and Lee were engaged in a titanic struggle at Spotsylvania. May 9 was a day of preparation. Lee's troops continued to improve their position, and Grant, after probing the Confederate center, dispatched Hancock to turn the rebel left. Grant was looking for a weak spot. Rather than assault the formidable Confederate works head-on, he would first try to slip the 2nd Corps around the entrenchments for a sudden descent on Lee's rear. Unfortunately, the maneuver required Hancock to cross the Po River twice, and by the time the troops were ready to attack on May 10, Lee had shifted two divisions under Jubal Early to counter the threat. Early's men had industriously dug themselves in, and with the element of surprise gone, Hancock reluctantly informed Grant that an attack would be futile.[21]

A greater disappointment for Grant was the death of John Sedgwick. After meeting with Grant the morning of May 9, the 6th Corps commander had gone forward to the center of his line, found the troops were nervous because of scattered fire from Confederate sharpshooters, and tried to reassure them. The rebel marksmen were a good 800 yards away and Sedgwick mocked: "They couldn't hit an elephant at this distance." The next crack of the rifle sent a bullet that struck Sedgwick in the head, killing him instantly. Uncle John, the best loved general in the Army of the Potomac, was gone. Meade wept, Lee was saddened by the death of his old friend, and Grant was incredulous. "Is he really dead?" he asked Horace Porter. "His loss to this army is greater than the loss of a whole division."[22]

The good news on May 9 was that the war elsewhere was going as Grant hoped. A package of dispatches from Washington revealed that Sherman was moving swiftly through northwest Georgia and that Joseph E. Johnston had yet to make a stand. A report from Butler stated he had landed at City Point and was preparing to move on Petersburg. Butler said he anticipated hard fighting and asked for reinforcements. General Sigel reported from the Shenandoah valley that he had not yet encountered the enemy and would soon be moving on the railhead at Staunton, an important supply point for Lee's army. Grant had already instructed Halleck to provide reinforcements for Butler,[23] and after digesting the messages from the field, he telegraphed Washington a brief report on the situation at Spotsylvania. "Enemy hold our front in very strong force and evince strong determination to interpose between us and Richmond to the last."

As if to reassure the capital, Grant added, "I shall take no backward step." He asked Halleck to rush another five million rounds of small arms ammunition to the front and "all the infantry you can rake and scrape. . . . We can maintain ourselves and in the end beat Lee's army, I believe."[24]

Since Lee had withdrawn two of Early's divisions from his line to meet the threat Hancock presented on his left, Grant concluded (wrongly as it turned out*) that he must have weakened his center. Still seeking a soft spot, the general in chief ordered a frontal attack for 5 P.M. on May 10, the principal thrust directed at the tip of the hog's snout—or "mule shoe," as it came to be called. As was too often the case with the Army of the Potomac, the attack was poorly coordinated. Warren's 5th Corps moved out an hour early, Hancock's corps, which had to make a forced march back from the Po, was an hour late, and instead of a weakened Confederate center, Union troops ran directly into the massed firepower of the Confederate 1st and 2nd corps. Losses were heavy all along the line, except among Burnside's troops, who once again barely got into action.[25] At no point was the rebel line breached, except briefly in front of the 6th Corps where Colonel Emory Upton led an elite force of twelve regiments and demonstrated that Lee's line was not impregnable providing the attackers moved quickly.

A brash twenty-four-year-old West Pointer from New York who took soldiering seriously and himself even more so, Upton had no patience with incompetent brother officers or tactics that proved manifestly outdated. Strong on theory and eager to test it in the field, Upton argued that the way to breach a fortified position was to attack it on a narrow front and on a dead run, not stopping to fire or reload until the troops were over the parapets and inside the enemy's works. So persuasive was Upton that Grant decided to give his plan a try. Martin McMahon, the hard-bitten 6th Corps chief of staff, handpicked twelve regiments for the task. "Upton," said McMahon, "you are to lead those men upon the enemy works this afternoon, and if you don't carry them, you are not expected to come back." Upton replied predictably that he intended to carry the position, and then set about to organize his attack.[26]

The point selected for Upton's assault was about midway down the west face of the mule shoe. Confederate artillery was thickest there, but Upton planned to overrun the guns before they had a chance to do much damage. He deployed his regiments three abreast, four lines deep. The

---

* Rather than denude his center, Lee had taken advantage of his hog's snout configuration to move two divisions (Mahone's and Heth's) from his extreme right to his extreme left. The rebel line was weakened, but it was weakened facing Burnside, whom Lee concluded would pose less of a threat than Meade. Gordon C. Rhea, *The Battles for Spotsylvania Court House and Yellow Tavern, May 7–12, 1864* 187 (Baton Rouge: Louisiana State University Press, 1997).

first line was to charge across no-man's-land without pausing, breach the ramparts, and fan out left and right to widen the gap. The second line would plunge straight ahead to deepen the penetration, while the third and fourth lines would follow on to provide support wherever needed. The troops were instructed to cover the distance as rapidly as possible: no firing, no loading, and no pausing to give aid or succor to wounded comrades.

Grant rode out to observe the attack, found a suitable knoll, dismounted, and sat down on a fallen tree to write a dispatch. No sooner had he started writing than a shell exploded directly in front of him. Grant looked up briefly and then resumed writing. A group of wounded from the 5th Wisconsin were being carried past at the time, and one remarked: "Ulysses don't scare worth a damn."[27]

At ten past six, Upton gave the signal to advance. Rebel gunners opened a deadly barrage but in less than four minutes men of the three leading regiments were swarming over the Confederate parapets and fighting hand-to-hand in the trenches. The second wave followed and quickly overwhelmed the defenders. The first Federal line fanned out, the second line continued forward, and the third and fourth waves came on to round up a thousand or so dazed defenders. So far, everything had worked as Upton said it would. Lee's line had been punctured and the road to Richmond seemed open. At this point, Union follow-through failed to materialize. Lee, on the spot as always, rushed reinforcements to contain the breakthrough, rebel artillery boomed all along the front, and the division assigned to support Upton crept forward cautiously and crawled back ignominiously as soon as it came under fire. Deprived of support, Upton's twelve regiments were unable to withstand the withering counterattack Lee mounted. The breakthrough had gone for naught. The men of the 6th Corps fell back to the main Union battle line, leaving a thousand or more casualties. Southern losses were similar. That evening a Confederate band assembled near the site of Upton's breakthrough and mournfully intoned "Nearer My God to Thee." A Union band responded with the "Dead March" from *Saul*. The rebel musicians followed with "Home Sweet Home," and in the words of an enlisted man from Georgia, "A united yell went up in concert from the men on both sides, such a one as was never heard among the hills of Spotsylvania county before or since."[28]

Grant was annoyed that the Army of the Potomac had failed to exploit Upton's breakthrough, but the tactics of the young West Pointer had proved promising. (Upton, who had been wounded, received an on-the-spot promotion to brigadier general.[29]) Grant decided to repeat the maneuver using a whole corps instead of simply a brigade. He would employ Hancock's 2nd Corps and hit Lee on the snout—the apex of the rebel salient, traditionally believed to be a weak point in such a formation because not as many guns could be brought to bear. Meade was instructed to slip the 2nd Corps behind Warren and Wright (who had succeeded Sedgwick) to the center of the Union line, and set the attack for 4 A.M., May 12.[30] Burnside was to move forward simultaneously on Hancock's left, while Wright and Warren kept up the pressure on the right and far right. Grant believed the one-day delay would allow the troops time to get in place, and give Hancock an opportunity to make a thorough reconnaissance of the avenue of attack. The downside was it afforded Lee an additional day to prepare.

Wednesday, May 11, dawned cold and wet, a seasonal spring rain breaking the heat that had set in two weeks earlier. As Grant sat drinking his breakfast coffee he was joined by Congressman Elihu Washburne, who had accompanied the army since crossing the Rapidan. Washburne was returning to Washington that day, and asked Grant if he could give him a statement for President Lincoln and Mr. Stanton. "I know they would be greatly gratified if I could carry a message from you giving what encouragement you can as to the situation."[31]

Grant hesitated. He knew any statement he sent would be released to the press, and he did not want to engender false hopes of an early victory. He also did not want to disappoint Washburne, to whom he owed just about everything. Rather than send a message to the president, Grant said he would write a letter to Halleck. "I generally communicate through him, giving the general situation, and you can take it with you."[32]

Grant stepped inside his tent, sat down at his writing table, and jotted a brief message, cigar firmly clinched between his teeth. "We have now ended the sixth day of very heavy fighting. The result to this time is much in our favor. But our losses have been heavy as well as those of the enemy." Grant estimated his casualties at 20,000. He said Lee's army was "very shaky," and that it entrenched at every opportunity in order to protect itself. He closed with a flourish, soon to be splashed across the front pages of Northern newspapers in large headlines: "I propose to fight it out on this line if it takes all summer."[33]

It was on May 11 that Lee made one of his rare tactical errors. In the afternoon rebel scouts reported massive Federal wagon trains moving northeast toward Fredericksburg. Grant was sending his empty vehicles back for a fresh supply of food and ammunition, but Lee, after studying the reports, concluded that his opponent was going to break off the fight at Spotsylvania and pull back behind the Rappahannock to regroup. If the Union army was withdrawing, Lee wanted to take advantage of it. "We must attack those people if they retreat," he told Henry Heth. "This army cannot stand a siege. We must end this business on the battlefield, not in a fortified place."[34] Lee thereupon ordered the artillery deployed in the mule shoe to be limbered up and withdrawn, ready to set out in pursuit of the Federals when their retreat got underway. Lee had completely misread Grant's intentions. Rather than retreating, the general in chief was deploying his forces to launch the most powerful attack thus far in the campaign. Hancock's 2nd Corps would hit Lee's line exactly at the point from which the guns were being withdrawn.

It rained incessantly throughout the night of May 11. Hancock's troops, drenched to the bone, sloshed through ankle-deep Virginia mud to their rendezvous area, a thousand yards from the flattened apex of the Confederate salient. The soldiers were dead tired, some units having marched for seven hours, but by 2 A.M. 2nd Corps was in place. Grant's plan to storm the mule shoe head-on had yet to be communicated to the rank and file, but the troops sensed that something out of the ordinary was in the offing. "Great events have a power of self-proclamation," wrote a soldier from Massachusetts. "The feeling ran through the ranks that they were near to momentous happenings."[35]

Hancock deployed his corps two divisions abreast, two deep. Each division was tightly massed, five paces between regiments, ten between brigades. A member of Hancock's staff described the corps as a "solid rectangular mass of nearly 20,000 men to hurl upon the enemy's works as soon as it should be sufficiently light for our purpose."[36] Some of the men dozed in the mud, most stood in ranks, swaying restlessly, wiping the rain from their face, straining to hear the command to advance.[37] Orders were to rush forward silently, with no firing until the rebel line was breached. Surprise was the watchword.

The appointed jump-off time of 4 A.M. came and went. It was still pitch black and Hancock wanted at least a glimmer of daylight. At 4:35, when the first hint of dawn appeared, the order to advance was given and the troops moved forward—almost as many as Thomas mustered for the charge up Missionary Ridge at Chattanooga, twice as many as Pickett led at Gettysburg. "It did not require anyone to tell us what to do," an infantryman from Pennsylvania remembered. "Everyone seemed to catch the inspiration that his safety depended on getting to those works."[38] Another wrote, "All line and formation was now lost, and the great mass of men, with a rush like a cyclone, sprang upon the entrenchments and swarmed over."[39] Sergeant Albert Marsh of the 64th New York noted, "It was a brilliant charge, with the bayonet, hardly a gun being fired."[40]

The Confederate defenders were not taken entirely by surprise, but they were not exactly ready for the blow either. Powder was damp, muskets misfired, and the awesome weight of the Federal mass struck fear into even the most intrepid rebel rifleman. "As far as the eye could reach," an officer from Louisiana wrote, "the field was covered with the serried ranks of the enemy, advancing in close columns to the attack."[41] The most serious problem for the Confederates was the lack of artillery, the two dozen guns that anchored the salient having been withdrawn during the night under Lee's instructions. Major General Edward Johnson, whose division held the forward edge of the salient, became apprehensive that evening with his gun pits standing empty and urged that his cannons be returned lest Grant not be retreating. Johnson, known affectionately as "Old Allegheny," the oldest (at forty-eight) of Lee's division commanders, had no hard evidence to go on other than the distant rumble of troops on the march. Yet a sixth sense warned him of impending calamity. Lee, who continued to believe Grant was heading toward Fredericksburg, was puzzled by Johnson's request but acquiesced, ordering that the guns be returned to the salient by daylight.[42] They arrived just as the blue tide surged over the rebel ramparts, too late to be of service, too far forward to be withdrawn. All but two of the pieces fell into Union hands, along with most of Johnson's division, which melted under the onslaught.

Grant was up well before daylight that morning, his ear cocked for sounds of Hancock's attack. The salient was more than a mile away, but soon the distant roar of cheers and the rattle of musketry drifted back. Shortly after 5 A.M. a staff officer galloped in with a report from Hancock. "Our men have the works with some hundred prisoners. Impossible to say how many; whole line moving up."[43] On the first rider's heels came another: "Prisoners come in rapidly. Probably over 2000."[44] Fifteen minutes later Hancock reported capturing two general officers, Edward Johnson and George H. Stuart of Maryland. Grant's aides began to celebrate Lee's defeat, Meade's staff was dubious, and Grant remained seated on a camp stool near the fire stoically digesting the reports, the cape of an old army overcoat shrouding his reaction.[45] Eventually he allowed that "Hancock is doing well," and sent instructions to Burnside to "push on with all vigor." The 9th Corps had moved against the east face of the salient simultaneously with Hancock, and was encountering stiff resistance.[46]

Meade was sitting with Grant that morning when a prisoner rode into the compound wearing the uniform of a Confederate major general. It was Edward Johnson, an old friend of Hancock's who had been in the Corps of Cadets with Meade and served in Mexico with Grant. Hancock had given him a horse and told him to report to Union headquarters. Johnson's uniform was torn and he was covered with mud, but he dismounted with dignity and saluted his captors. Meade rose instantly, took Johnson's hand, and introduced him to Grant.

"It's been a long time since last we met," said Grant.

"Yes," replied Johnson, "it is a great many years, and I had not expected to meet you under such circumstances."

"It is one of the many sad fortunes of war," Grant acknowledged, as he offered Johnson a cigar, picked up a camp chair and placed it near the fire. "Be seated, and we will do all in our power to make you as comfortable as possible."

The three generals commenced an animated conversation, reminiscing about the past, when another message arrived from Hancock. "I have finished up Johnson," it said, "and am now going after Early." Out of consideration for Johnson's feelings, Grant handed the dispatch around rather than reading it aloud as he usually did.[47] Arrangements were then made to have Johnson transported to the rear in a Union ambulance. No sooner had Johnson departed than a message arrived from Burnside reporting that his right wing had lost contact with Hancock. "Push the enemy with all your might," replied Grant. "That is the way to connect."[48]

Lee had been taken by surprise. Hancock's corps had ripped a half-mile hole in his line and was on the verge of splitting the Army of Northern Virginia in two. The shoulders on either side of the breakthrough were holding, which meant that the breach was laterally contained, but the reserve division of General John B. Gordon,* positioned at the base of the salient, was all that held the two wings of Lee's army together. Unless Gordon could seal the fissure, Grant would pour through the opening, turn left and right, and defeat the Confederate army in detail.

Fortune now smiled on Lee. As one historian has written, no Southerner was better fitted for the bloody work ahead than John B. Gordon, whose lack of formal military training was more than made up for by an instinctive grasp of tactics and a temperament of unadorned aggressiveness.[49] With the first report of Hancock's attack, Gordon had formed his brigades into line of battle across the neck of the salient. When the breakthrough was confirmed, he ordered his troops forward. Lee arrived on the scene just as Gordon's men moved out. "The picture he made, as the grand old man sat there on his horse, with his noble head bare . . . can never be forgotten by a man that stood there," wrote a soldier of the 52nd Virginia.[50] Lee rode to the center of Gordon's line where he turned Traveller toward the oncoming Federals, obviously intent on leading the charge as he had tried to do six days earlier in the Wilderness. When Gordon saw Lee he was horrified, and once again the shouts echoed across the rebel front, "Go back, General Lee." "Lee to the rear." "Lee to the rear." Gordon wheeled his

---

* On May 8, 1864, Ambrose P. Hill became critically ill and was replaced as commander of the Confederate 3rd Corps by Jubal Early. Gordon, as a result of the initiative he displayed in the Wilderness, was promoted by Lee to command what had been Early's division.

horse and confronted Lee. "These men are Georgians and Virginians," said the young brigadier. "They have never failed you and will not fail you here." When Lee showed no sign of turning back, a tall Virginia sergeant grabbed Traveller's rein, jerked his head around, and led him to the rear through ranks of cheering infantrymen.[51]

The charge of Gordon's division at Spotsylvania, like that of Longstreet's corps on the Orange plank road a week earlier, stopped the Union drive in its tracks. Inspired by Lee and led by Gordon, the men in gray advanced headlong into the Federal mass, the sheer audacity of the effort taking Hancock's troops by surprise. It was three brigades against four of the finest divisions in the Union army, but the impetus of the Confederate counterattack was overwhelming. "Onward they swept," wrote Gordon, "pouring their rapid volleys into Hancock's confused ranks, and swelling the deafening din of battle with their piercing shouts."[52] The massive blue tide wavered and then lurched back. Hancock's troops were already in disarray when Gordon hit, the overextended victims of their initial success. The breakthrough was so rapid that the Federal line had become hopelessly jumbled. Close to 20,000 men had charged into the salient and were now wedged shoulder to shoulder in an area not much larger than two football fields. Union troops were packed so tightly that some men could not lift their arms to use their weapons. Subjected to the withering fire that Gordon's advancing troops laid down, Hancock's men broke and tumbled back to the toe of the mule shoe, seeking shelter in the entrenchments they had captured on their way in.

It was close to 6 A.M. when Hancock fell back to the mule shoe perimeter, and at that point Grant hurled Wright's 6th Corps against the west angle of the salient, the infamous Bloody Angle in Civil War historiography. The 6th Corps had been held back initially to avoid hitting Hancock's troops with friendly fire. The two corps were adjacent and attacking at right angles. Both could not safely go forward at the same time. Once Hancock pulled back, the way was open for Wright. And so at six o'clock another 15,000 men slammed into the west face of the mule shoe, 200 yards from where Hancock hit. "The enemy seemed to have concentrated the whole engine of war at this point," a Mississippian remembered. "Shells of every kind and shape from field pieces raked the approaches, while a forest of muskets played with awful fury over the ground itself."[53] To a South Carolinian it seemed as if "Grant ha[d] all the hosts of hell in assault upon us."[54]

For the next eighteen hours North and South grappled hand-to-hand in the most horrendous fighting of the war thus far. "The flags of both armies waved at the same moment over the same breastwork," wrote a 6th Corps survivor.[55] "It was a literal saturnalia of blood," wrote another. "Nothing but the piled up logs of breastworks separated the combatants.

Our men would reach over the logs and fire into the faces of the enemy, would stab over with their bayonets. Many were shot and stabbed through the crevices and holes between the logs. Men mounted the works and with muskets rapidly handed to them kept up a continuous fire until they were shot down, when others would take their places."[56]

The slaughter was unrelenting. So too was the rain, turning trench floors into an oozy muck where the dead and wounded were trampled out of sight by men fighting for their lives. Close-in fighting like this usually ended quickly when one side broke and ran, but at Spotsylvania neither line broke. As a Confederate officer wrote, "There was one continuous roll of musketry from dawn until midnight."[57] In places the dead were sprawled eight or ten bodies deep. So intense was the firing that an oak tree, two feet in diameter, was cut down by the chipping bullets. "I never expect to be fully believed when I tell what I saw of the horrors of Spotsylvania," one of Wright's officers wrote, "because I should be loath to believe it myself were the case reversed."[58]

All day long and well into the night Grant and Lee continued to throw reinforcements into the angle. Grant was determined to achieve a breakthrough; Lee was equally determined to hold his line until Confederate engineers completed a new set of works across the base of the salient. For each, strategic considerations dictated the tactics, and those considerations were remarkably similar. In Grant's case, he wanted to destroy the Army of Northern Virginia, and every casualty Lee suffered was a step in that direction. Lee, on the other hand, wanted to wear down the Northern will to fight. The longer he held out, and the more casualties he inflicted, the more likely it was that Union enthusiasm for the war would erode. For better or worse, both were engaged in a war of attrition. As Lee saw it, the glass was half full. He could win the war by not losing it. For Grant, the glass was half empty. He had to destroy Lee before anti-war sentiment in the North took control.

It was close to midnight when Lee gave the order to withdraw. The weary rebel troops disengaged unit by unit, and stealthily fell back a half mile to where a new and even more formidable line had been dug. Equally tired Federal troops let them go, content to take possession of the trenches they had fought over for the last eighteen hours. Exhausted, out of contact at last, rebels and Yanks slept on their arms in the mud where they lay, oblivious to the pelting rain. Daybreak revealed the damage. Grant had lost almost 7,000 men in the day-long assault on the mule shoe; Lee's losses were similar: nearly 3,000 veteran troops captured, and a somewhat larger number killed and wounded.[59] Since crossing the Rapidan on May 5, the Army of the Potomac had lost 32,000 men killed, wounded, and missing—more than for all Union armies combined in any previous week of the war.[60] Lee's casualties, though less, had been proportionately as great: about 18,000 of the 60,000 troops engaged. Far more serious, however, the Army of Northern Virginia had lost twenty of fifty-seven corps, division, and brigade commanders—the leadership cadre of the army. Grant had lost but ten.

At this point in the war, reinforcements were still available, though the Southern supply was dwindling fast. Within the week each army had made good at least half of its losses. Six brigades from Richmond and two from the Shenandoah joined Lee; Grant continued to draw from the store of artillerymen assigned to defense duty in the rear. A more worrisome problem for the general in chief was that the three-year enlistments of many regiments would expire in the next six weeks. Unless the men reenlisted, the drain on Union manpower would be substantial.

Grant was able to witness more of the fighting at Spotsylvania than in the Wilderness because the terrain was more open. During the afternoon he ordered his reliable pony Jeff Davis saddled and rode out to several points where he could observe Hancock's troops fighting at the tip of the mule shoe and Wright's assault on the west angle. On balance, Grant thought things were going well. Back at headquarters that evening, he wired Halleck: "The eighth day of battle closes, leaving between three and four thousand prisoners in our hands and thirty pieces of artillery." Grant said the enemy was obstinate and "seemed to have found the last ditch." But he remained optimistic. The Army of the Potomac had not lost a single unit, while the enemy had surrendered an entire division and a full brigade.[61] Later he wrote Julia that he was well and full of hope. "The world has never seen so bloody or so protracted a battle as the one being fought and I hope never will again. The enemy were really whipped yesterday but their situation is desperate beyond anything heretofore known. To lose this battle they lose their cause. As bad as it is they have fought for it with a gallantry worthy of a better." [62]

The following day, as the rain continued and the armies regrouped, Grant wrote Stanton to recommend the promotion of Meade and Sherman to major general in the regular army, traditionally the highest rank the nation could bestow. Meade, said Grant, "has more than met my most sanguine expectations. He and Sherman are the fittest officers for large commands I have come in contact with." Conscious of his need to maintain a balance between the Eastern and Western theaters, Grant cautioned Stanton that he "would not like to see one of these promotions without seeing both." [63]*

---

* On May 23, Halleck wrote Grant that there were in fact two vacancies as major general in the regular army. Meade and Sherman had been recommended, he said, but a number of

Since crossing the Rapidan, Grant and Meade had worked hand in hand to throw the weight of the Army of the Potomac against Lee. Meade, the older man, was instinctively more cautious, yet Grant was pleased with the Pennsylvanian's coolness under pressure and his ability to administer the nation's largest army. Nevertheless, the dual command arrangement was cumbersome. Meade's chief of staff, writing after the war, took the traditional view: "There were two officers commanding the same army. Such a mixed command was not calculated to produce the best results that either singly was capable of bringing about." [64]

Grant's staff took a similar position. After the fighting at the Bloody Angle, Rawlins and others strenuously urged Grant to bypass Meade and issue his orders directly to the corps and division commanders of the Army of the Potomac. Their contention was that too much time was lost under the present system; that Grant's incisive orders lost force and vigor when filtered through Meade's headquarters; and that Meade had an irascible temper that often irritated officers in contact with him. According to Colonel Horace Porter, the discussion became heated and undoubtedly reflected the tension that had developed between two general staffs that operated side by side with their respective fields imperfectly defined. [65]

Grant listened, but dismissed the suggestion. He told his staff he was aware of the problems, but it could not be otherwise. "I am commanding all the armies, and I cannot neglect others by giving my time exclusively to the Army of the Potomac." Grant said that to take over from Meade would involve him in the detailed duties of an army commander, "enforcing discipline, reviewing court martial proceedings, and so on." In addition, Meade knew the Army of the Potomac thoroughly, and had led it to a memorable victory at Gettysburg. "I have just come from the West, and if I removed a deserving Eastern man from the position of army commander, my motives might be misunderstood." Grant said that he and Meade worked together easily. "He is capable and perfectly subordinate, and by attending to the details he relieves me of much unnecessary work." [66]

For his part, Meade accepted the situation with good spirit. Writing to his wife during the battle of Spotsylvania, he noted that journalists

---

Washington politicians were urging that Bejamin Butler and Daniel Sickles be appointed instead to "break down 'West Point influence.' This is *entre nous*." Grant evidently contacted Elihu Washburne, who called on Lincoln June 15 and expressed Grant's concern that the promotions go to Meade and Sherman, not Butler and Sickles. Later that day Secretary Stanton wrote Grant that Meade and Sherman would indeed be appointed, but that the government wanted to wait until Sherman reached Atlanta and Meade reached Richmond. Grant replied on June 19 that he had "no objection to deferring their promotions to the end of the Campaign as you propose." 10 *Papers of Ulysses S. Grant* 471 note, John Y. Simon, ed. (Carbondale: Southern Illinois University Press, 1982).

seemed puzzled at the command relationship and had apparently decided that "Grant does the grand strategy, and I do the grand tactics. Coopée in his *Army Magazine* says, 'the Army of the Potomac, directed by Grant, commanded by Meade, and led by Hancock, Sedgwick and Warren,' which is quite a good distinction, and about hits the nail on the head." [67]

The problem with the Army of the Potomac was not with Meade but with its corps commanders. When he was in the West, Grant could rely on Sherman and McPherson, and at Chattanooga, George Thomas and Joe Hooker. Each general was as eager as Grant to take the fight to the enemy. But in the Wilderness and at Spotsylvania, only Hancock proved up to snuff. Horatio Wright at this point was an uncertain replacement for Sedgwick, while Warren and Burnside simply lacked the fighting instinct. Burnside had been tardy in the Wilderness, and at Spotsylvania he again failed to get his divisions on line in sufficient time to support Hancock's assault on the mule shoe. He was the senior major general south of the Rapidan, but his lapses were a serious embarrassment for Grant.[68]*

Warren was a different problem. Talented, youthful, intelligent, Gouverneur Kemble Warren was cut in the mode of McClellan, Buell, and Halleck. He firmly believed war was a rational exercise, to be conducted by carefully planned maneuvers that flanked the enemy out of position without the necessity for fighting set-piece battles. He was uncomfortable with Grant's head-on style, and found it difficult to launch his men against a prepared enemy position. "An excess of caution, a delay in assuming the offensive, even when ordered, an indisposition to take tactical risks," is how Grant's secretary, Adam Badeau, described Warren.[69] Meade simply thought Warren had lost his nerve.[70] Grant, who at one time had considered Warren a possible replacement for Meade as commander of the Army of the Potomac, despaired at his timidity. "He could see every danger at a glance before he had encountered it." [71] On the morning of May 12, when Warren was late once more in getting his attack organized, Grant told Meade to relieve him and replace him with the army's chief of staff, Major General A. A. Humphreys, if he did not move forward immediately.[72] Warren's troops eventually got into action and acquitted themselves well, but had they moved sooner Lee would have been hard pressed to hold the

---

* On May 24, Grant terminated the independent status of the 9th Corps and folded it into the Army of the Potomac, making Burnside subordinate to Meade. Burnside, to his credit, took the change in stride. The following day, when Grant rode past the 9th Corps headquarters, Burnside came out, shook Grant's hand, and said: "I have received the instructions assigning my command to the Army of the Potomac. That order is excellent. It is a military necessity, and I am glad it has been issued." Grant was favorably impressed. According to Colonel Horace Porter, he and Burnside remained close friends for the remainder of their lives. Horace Porter, *Campaigning with Grant* 144–45, 269 (New York: Century, 1897).

salient. "Burnside is a d——d Humbug, and Warren is a ditto," wrote Captain Oliver Wendell Holmes, Jr., a 6th Corps staff officer.[73] Emory Upton said it equally pungently: "Some of our corps commanders are not fit to be corporals. Lazy and indolent, they will not even ride along their lines."[74]

Grant was not ready to call it quits at Spotsylvania. Although it rained steadily for the next two days and into a third, the general in chief continued to probe Lee's line for a weak spot. On Saturday the 14th, the 5th and 6th corps attempted to move around the Confederate right but bogged down on the road and the attack had to be called off.[75] On the 18th, believing that Lee was falling back, Grant sent Hancock and Wright against what he assumed was the thinned-out rebel line at the base of the mule shoe. Lee was not falling back, the line was defended more robustly than ever, and after two hours of fruitless assault the Union attack fizzled out. "We found the enemy so strongly entrenched," Meade wrote his wife, "that even Grant thought it useless to knock our heads against a brick wall, and directed a suspension."[76] After six days of effort, Grant recognized that Lee's position at Spotsylvania could not be stormed by frontal assault and could not be turned by short-range flanking maneuvers. He decided to swing wide to his left, move once more between Lee and Richmond, and force his opponent away from his Spotsylvania entrenchments and into the open country. As his immediate objective, Grant chose Hanover Junction, just beyond the North Anna River, twenty-five miles south. The two rail lines on which Lee depended, one from the Shenandoah valley, the other from Richmond, intersected there and Grant assumed Lee would rush to defend it. Once more the premium was on getting to Hanover Junction first, the North Anna representing a serious natural obstacle and dangerous to cross in the face of an enemy as powerful as the Army of Northern Virginia.

As Meade prepared the marching orders, Grant received another series of communications from the field. The good news was that in Georgia, Sherman had taken Dalton, and outflanked Johnston at Resaca. As a result, the Confederates were falling back toward Atlanta. The bad news involved Union forces in the Shenandoah and on the James. In the valley, Sigel had not only failed to capture Lee's base at Staunton, but was in headlong retreat toward Winchester, the victim of a resounding defeat delivered by General John C. Breckinridge at New Market. Breckinridge, former vice president of the United States, and the electoral college runner-up to Lincoln in 1860, had come north to join Lee after the battle of Chattanooga. Leading a pickup rebel force of 5,000, including 247 cadets from the Virginia Military Institute, he laced into Sigel just after dawn on May 15 and routed him. Grant, who was counting on the Shenandoah offensive to pin Lee down, was furious, but Halleck was not surprised. "If you expect anything from Sigel you will be mistaken," he wired Grant. "He will do nothing but run. He never did anything else."[77] The upshot was that Lee continued to draw supplies from the Shenandoah unmolested, and Breckinridge's troops entrained to join the Army of Northern Virginia near Hanover Junction. Grant solved the Sigel problem by prevailing upon Lincoln to relieve him, but the Shenandoah remained firmly fixed in rebel hands.

On the James, Benjamin Butler, another leg holder, had also run into trouble. After landing midway between Petersburg and Richmond with 30,000 men on May 5, the former Massachusetts legislator did not move against the Confederate capital until a week later. By then General P. G. T. Beauregard, back on active duty in southside Virginia, had amassed a force almost as large and on May 16 lashed into the Federals at Drewry's Bluff, eight miles south of Richmond. After an all-day battle, with heavy losses on both sides, Butler pulled back to his trench line across the neck between the Appomattox and James rivers. Beauregard entrenched a line immediately opposite Butler's, and the two armies settled into a stalemate. Beauregard could not advance past Butler's works, but Butler could not advance either. Grant told Halleck that Butler's Army of the James was "shut off from further operations as if it had been in a bottle strongly corked."[78] Both the Confederate line and the Union line could be held with relatively few troops. As a consequence, 6,000 of Beauregard's troops were sent to reinforce Lee, while Grant ordered the 18th Corps under Major General William F. "Baldy" Smith to join him on the North Anna.[79]

On May 21 Grant put the Army of the Potomac in motion toward Hanover Junction. "We were now to operate in a very different country from any we had before seen in Virginia. The roads were wide and good, and the country well cultivated." Grant said there were no maps, but "our course was south, and we took all roads leading in that direction which would not separate the army too widely."[80]

Lee, who moved along interior lines, kept his army between Grant and Richmond and arrived on the North Anna well ahead of the Union vanguard. He took up a defensive position on the south bank of the river, entrenched behind a formidable series of earthworks, and waited for Grant to attack. "If I can get one more pull at him, I will defeat him," Lee confided to his staff surgeon.[81]

As soon as Grant had his troops arrayed in order of battle, he probed the center of the Confederate line and then briefly attempted a double envelopment. But Lee's works were too strong. Grant thereupon called off the assault in favor of another crablike sidle to the left to force his opponent into open country. As he told Halleck, "Lee's right rests on a swamp, his center rests on the North Anna, and his left on Little river. . . . To make a direct attack would cause a slaughter of our men that even success would not justify." As a consequence, Grant said he would try to turn the rebel right by breaking off contact and moving twenty miles downriver. Like Lee, Grant was sanguine about victory. As he informed Washington:

"Lee's army is really whipped. The prisoners we now take show it, and the actions of his Army show it unmistakably. A battle with them outside of entrenchments cannot be had. I may be mistaken but I feel that our success over Lee's army is already insured." [82]

Four days later, with the Army of the Potomac on the move, Grant instructed Halleck to round up all the pontoon bridging the Union possessed and send it posthaste to Fortress Monroe at the mouth of the James River. [83] He did not explain why he wanted it, but his intention was obvious. As he had done at Vicksburg, Grant was thinking about crossing another mighty river, taking the enemy by surprise, outflanking Lee's army once and for all, and approaching Richmond from the south. It had worked on the Mississippi in 1863; Grant believed it might work again.

By nightfall on May 29 the Army of the Potomac had reached Totopotomy Creek, nine miles northeast of Richmond,* only to find the Army of Northern Virginia drawn up in line of battle, artillery emplaced, and all three corps dug in and waiting. Since crossing the Rapidan on May 5, Grant had pressed forward relentlessly and was now at the outskirts of the Confederate capital. Wishful thinking aside, however, the rebel army remained as formidable as ever. Grant had captured the initiative, but Lee had countered every assault, trading space for time in an equally relentless effort to wear down Union morale and perhaps even defeat Grant should he let his guard down. "The grand object," Lee told Major General Richard Anderson, "is the destruction of the enemy." [84] Indeed, the Confederate retreat from the Rapidan was not without its blessings. Lee was now close to his principal base of supply, his lines of communication were considerably shortened, and in a pinch he could call on the 6,000 troops in the Richmond garrison for support.

Just as on the North Anna, Grant probed Lee's defenses on Totopo-

---

* The rivers of northern Virginia flow generally in a southeasterly direction, rising in the Appalachians and draining into Chesapeake Bay. In 1864, most were navigable up to the fall line. Since the waterways were firmly controlled by the United States Navy, the rivers provided Grant with a reliable means of resupply. But they also constituted significant barriers against an overland advance, which worked to Lee's advantage. The Rapidan, which Grant crossed May 5, flows into the Rappahannock near Chancellorsville, some dozen miles above Fredericksburg. As already noted, the Ma, Ta, Po, and Ni join to form the Mataponi. The North Anna and the South Anna unite five miles below Hanover Junction to become the Pamunkey. Forty miles below that the Pamunkey and the Mataponi join to form the York. Totopotomy Creek is a tributary of the Pamunkey. The next water barrier for an army moving south was the Chickahominy River, which flows into the James well below Richmond.

tomy Creek and decided he did not like what he found. After two days of skirmishing he sidled to the left once again, moving southward to take the vital road intersection of Cold Harbor, halfway between Totopotomy Creek and the Chickahominy. There is no anchorage at Cold Harbor. The misleading name is of British lineage signifying an inn that offered overnight lodging without hot food. It was adopted here because the settlement's main feature was a frame tavern set in a grove of trees at the juncture of five roads coming in from all sides.[85] Lee shifted right to stay between Grant and Richmond, counterattacked briefly on May 31 hoping to catch the Union army strung out on the march, but was quickly repulsed. During the night of June 1–2 the remainder of both armies arrived and began to entrench facing each other for the seven miles between the Totopotomy and the Chickahominy.

Grant put his forces on line and made ready to attack. With the arrival of Smith's 18th Corps from the James, the Army of the Potomac now numbered approximately 110,000 men. Lee could count on the services of almost 60,000. Both armies had built themselves back up almost to their numbers at the start of the campaign four weeks earlier.[86] Those weeks had been without precedent. Grant's casualties totaled some 44,000; Lee's losses were proportional, roughly 25,000. Never before had the two armies been continuously engaged for so long, and the hammering was having its effect. "Many a man," wrote Captain Oliver Wendell Holmes, Jr., "has gone crazy since the campaign began from the terrible pressure on mind and body."[87]

By now Grant was well aware of how costly it was to attack Lee once the Confederates had dug in. On the North Anna and at Totopotomy Creek he confronted virtually impregnable rebel positions and passed up an assault in order to maneuver Lee out of those positions. Cold Harbor looked like the opportunity he was waiting for. The country was open and rolling, and he had finally beaten Lee to the battlefield. Grant's plan was to move forward as early as possible on June 2 before the rebel works were completed. All five corps of the Army of the Potomac were on line: Hancock on the left, Burnside on the right, with Wright, Smith, and Warren in the center. Once again, however, the Union response was sluggish. Hancock's corps, which had the furthest to march, was late getting into position, and Smith's corps, fresh from the James, was having difficulty sorting itself out. Rather than go forward piecemeal, Grant instructed Meade to postpone the attack until first light the next morning, Friday, June 3, 1864. The twenty-four-hour delay proved fatal. Lee was given more than enough time to prepare a defensive line of interlocking trenches supported by artillery, sometimes out in front of the infantry, so that it could lay down a killing crossfire on all avenues of approach along the entire seven-mile front. Having disposed his army to meet the attack, he was content to leave the rest to the defensive skill of his troops, which was formidable.[88]

Late in the afternoon of June 2 an opportunity flickered briefly on the right of the Union line but it disappeared just as quickly. As Burnside and Warren were adjusting their lines, they were attacked by the Confederate troops opposite. After some hard fighting the attacks were repulsed, and Burnside and Warren were content to let it go at that. Grant was not informed of the attack until several hours later, and he was angry that neither corps commander had taken advantage of the opportunity to attack the rebels outside their breastworks. The object of the whole campaign since crossing the Rapidan had been to catch the Confederate army in the open, and Burnside and Warren had been oblivious to the possibility. Grant directed Meade to instruct each corps commander to attack immediately whenever the enemy came out of his works and to follow up the attack vigorously. As Grant saw it, the Army of the Potomac, with the exception of Hancock's corps, had become content with repelling rebel attacks and was slow to take advantage of the enemy's lapses.[89]

Having waited a day, Grant ordered the attack for 4:30 A.M. on June 3. Hancock, Wright, and Smith were to carry the burden of the Union assault, while Warren and Burnside, on the right and far right, were to move forward at the same time and, if possible, turn Lee's flank. The rebel and Union lines hugged one another between the Totopotomy and the Chickahominy and all day long the men in blue could see the Confederate earthworks grow and become more formidable. As the troops made ready that evening, Colonel Horace Porter passed through the Union lines on foot with last-minute orders. Porter noticed that in one regiment many of the soldiers had taken off their coats and seemed to be engaged in mending them. He thought that strange, and when he looked closer he found that the men "were calmly writing their names and home addresses on slips of paper, and pinning them on their coats, so that their dead bodies might be recognized and their fate made known to their families." Porter noted that the troops were veteran soldiers, and were simply preparing for the desperate work ahead with a courage he thought to be sublime.[90]

At the appointed hour, more than 60,000 closely packed troops belonging to 2nd, 6th, and 18th corps dashed forward, striking for three points along the center and right-center of the rebel line. Up ahead, the Confederate trenches erupted with a hail of screaming lead. "It seemed more like a volcanic blast than a battle," a Federal survivor recalled. Another said, "It had the fury of the Wilderness musketry with the thunder of the Gettysburg artillery superadded." Never before, in this or any other

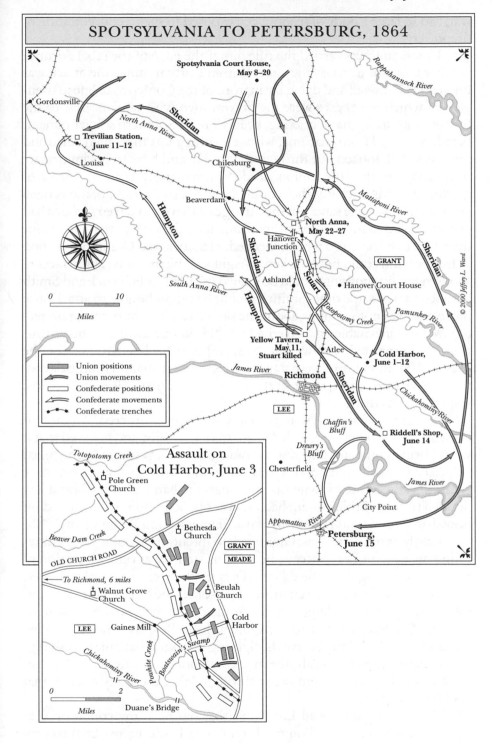

SPOTSYLVANIA TO PETERSBURG, 1864

Rappahannock River

Spotsylvania Court House,
May 8–20

Gordonsville

Sheridan

North Anna River

Trevilian Station,
June 11–12

Louisa

Chilesburg

Mattaponi River

Beaverdam

Hampton

North Anna,
May 22–27

Hanover
Junction

Sheridan

Sheridan

GRANT

South Anna River

Ashland

Stuart

Hanover Court House

Hampton

Totopotomy Creek

Pamunkey River

0   10
Miles

Yellow Tavern,
May 11,
Stuart killed

Atlee

Cold Harbor,
June 1–12

James River

Richmond

Sheridan

Chickahominy River

Union positions
Union movements
Confederate positions
Confederate movements
Confederate trenches

LEE

Chaffin's
Bluff

Riddell's Shop,
June 14

Drewry's
Bluff

Chesterfield

James River

Totopotomy Creek

Assault on
Cold Harbor, June 3

Pole Green
Church

City Point

Appomattox River

Petersburg,
June 15

Beaver Dam Creek

Bethesda
Church

OLD CHURCH ROAD

GRANT

MEADE

To Richmond, 6 miles

Walnut Grove
Church

Beulah
Church

LEE   Gaines Mill

Cold
Harbor

Powhite Creek

Boatswain's Swamp

0   2

Chickahominy River

Miles   Duane's Bridge

© 2000 Jeffrey L. Ward

war, had so large a body of troops been exposed to such a concentration of firepower.[91]

Union attackers carried the rifle pits at the edge of the rebel skirmish line but that was as far as they got. Within thirty minutes the attack was broken.[92] "The dead and dying lay in front of the Confederate line in triangles, of which the apexes were the bravest men who came nearest to the breastworks under that withering, deadly fire," a Southern soldier remembered. A colonel from Alabama, whose regiment lost three men killed and five wounded, looked out through the smoke and haze to his immediate front and saw that the Union dead "covered more than five acres of ground about as thickly as they could be laid."[93] To the right of the Federal line the effect was the same but the carnage less severe. Warren's troops had not attempted to move forward and Burnside's did little better. Orders for the attack to be renewed went unheeded. Hancock told Grant the position in front of him could not be taken. Wright said he might be able to secure a lodgment, but nothing would be gained by it unless Hancock and Smith advanced at the same time. Smith thought he might be able to attack once more, but was not sanguine about the prospects. At that point Grant recognized the inevitable and called a halt. "Hold our most advanced position," he instructed Meade, but "suspend any further advance for the present."[94] Union losses were staggering. Grant's casualties for the day totaled more than 7,000, most of them during the first half hour. Lee lost something less than 1,500.

"I regret this assault more than any I have ever ordered," Grant told his staff that evening. "I regarded it as a stern necessity, and believed that it would bring compensating results; but no advantages have been gained sufficient to justify the heavy losses suffered."[95] Meade, somewhat more circumspectly, wrote his wife that although the battle ended without any decided results, "I think Grant had his eyes opened, and is willing to admit now that Virginia and Lee's army is not Tennessee and Bragg's army."[96]

Costly as the battle was, Grant had no intention of pulling back or relaxing his grip on Lee. Success, he told his staff, "was only a question of time."[97] Lee recognized the danger. Despite the victory at Cold Harbor, his army was exhausted. Even more worrisome, the lack of efficient commissary support was taking its toll. "Some of the men now have scurvy," Lee told Confederate Postmaster General John Reagan, who had ridden out from Richmond to observe the fighting. Lee said that unless fresh vegetables were supplied quickly, the men could not go on. Reagan asked Lee what would happen if Grant broke through. Were there any reserves that could be called on?

"Not a regiment," said Lee. "And that has been my condition ever since fighting commenced on the Rapidan. If I shorten my lines to provide a reserve, Grant will turn me; if I weaken my lines to provide a reserve, he will break them."[98]

Grant had no detailed knowledge of Lee's predicament nor was he privy to the Confederate commissary problem, but he knew instinctively that sooner or later the Army of Northern Virginia would collapse under the hammering he was administering. Colonel Adam Badeau, who was with Grant at Cold Harbor, wrote afterward that the general in chief was in no way deterred by the setback:

> Neither the skill of his opponent, nor the splendid fighting of the rebel army; neither the disappointment when he saw his immediate plans frustrated; nor his chagrin when his troops found the hostile works impregnable; neither the unavoidable losses which his army sustained, and which no man appreciated more acutely or deplored more profoundly than he; neither the increasing responsibilities nor the settling gloom of this terrible and seemingly endless campaign—depressed or discouraged, so far as those nearest him could discover, this imperturbable man. He believed, all through these anxious days and weary nights, that if he had not accomplished a positive victory, he was yet advancing, not only toward Richmond, but toward the goal he had proposed to himself, the destruction of Lee and of the rebellion.[99]

Despite the incredible carnage during the initial minutes of the Union assault on June 3, Grant's casualties during the fighting at Cold Harbor were significantly less than the Army of the Potomac suffered in the Wilderness and at Spotsylvania.* The morale of the army remained

---

* According to official War Department figures, Grant's losses since crossing the Rapidan were as follows:

	Killed	Wounded	Missing	Total
Wilderness, May 5–7	2,261	8,785	2,902	13,948
Spotsylvania, May 8–21	2,271	9,360	1,970	13,601
North Anna, May 23–27	186	792	165	1,143
Totopotomy, May 27–31	99	358	52	509
Cold Harbor, May 31-June 12	1,769	6,752	1,537	10,058
	6,586	26,047	6,626	39,259

Precise Confederate figures are difficult to come by. Lee's principal biographer, after comparing morning reports, estimates Southern losses at 25,000, a figure proportional to Union losses and somewhat surprising since most of the time Lee fought from behind breastworks. Douglas Southall Freeman, 3 *R. E. Lee* 446 note (New York: Charles Scribner's Sons, 1934). Ulysses S. Grant, 2 *Personal Memoirs of U.S. Grant* 290 (New York: Charles L. Webster 1886).

high, although there was a growing reluctance to attack heavily fortified positions frontally. A Union staff officer wrote his wife that McClellan would not like what the troops were saying now: "They all say if he had not retreated with them, but stood and let them fight it out as Grant is doing, they would have been in Richmond two years sooner." [100] Charles Francis Adams, Jr., a captain in the 1st Massachusetts Cavalry, wrote to a friend that "so far Grant has out-generalled Lee and he has, in spite of his inability to start Lee one inch out of his fortifications, maneuvered himself close to the gates of Richmond." [101] A soldier in Baldy Smith's corps, which suffered heavily at Cold Harbor, wrote, "We have the gray backs in a pretty close corner at present and intend to keep them so. There is no fall back with U. S. Grant." [102] Another soldier assured his parents, "Grant has been successful in all his movements during the campaign and his men feel sanguine of success, although it will no doubt take time to do it." [103]

In the North, the heavy casualties sustained by the Army of the Potomac had diminished public support for Grant but did not affect delegates to the Republican National Convention, which met in Baltimore the week following Cold Harbor. Lincoln was renominated without opposition and the convention adopted a platform that recommended a constitutional amendment to prohibit slavery in the United States. Lincoln too was worried about the casualties in Virginia but he did not budge in his support for Grant. When the Ohio delegation serenaded him with a brass band after his renomination, he responded: "What we want, still more than Baltimore conventions or presidential elections, is success under General Grant," and he urged his listeners to do everything possible to support "the brave officers and soldiers in the field." In public meeting after public meeting the president expressed his gratitude to the soldiers, to the officers, and especially to "that brave and loyal man, the modest general at the head of our armies, General Grant." [104]

When the fighting ended on June 3 Grant faced a critical decision. He could not smash Lee's line with a frontal assault, and if he sidled left once more it would put the Army of the Potomac in the swampy bottoms of the Chickahominy. Even if he cleared that hurdle, the army would confront the permanent defenses of Richmond, which, after three years of war, had become far more formidable than the improvised entrenchments Lee had thrown up at Spotsylvania and Cold Harbor. Looking at the situation from the map room in the War Department, Halleck urged Grant to lay siege to Richmond from his present position, draw his supplies from the Fredericksburg railroad, stay between Lee and Washington, and move on the Confederate capital in slow, methodical stages: in effect, a repeat of Halleck's tactics at Corinth. It was the conservative way to wage war, and if anyone was reluctant to take risks it was Halleck.

Grant thought otherwise. To creep forward against Richmond from the north would play into Lee's hands. It would allow the Confederacy to make maximum use of its fortified position and would turn the fighting into a lengthy war of attrition. As Grant saw it that would fan anti-war sentiment in the North, encourage those who wanted to make peace, and imperil President Lincoln's reelection.

Instead, Grant sought a breakthrough: to get the drop on Lee by doing what he least expected. For the past two weeks Grant had been mulling over his strategy at Vicksburg. On May 25 he had instructed Halleck to ship every pontoon he could lay his hands on to Fortress Monroe. It was now time to put that plan into effect. He would disengage at Cold Harbor, swiftly take the Army of the Potomac across the James, seize Petersburg and its hub of railroads linking Richmond with the South, strike Richmond from its soft underbelly, and force Lee into the open. The risks were enormous. What Grant contemplated involved breaking off contact with a powerful opponent along a seven-mile trench line, with rebel revetments sometimes no more than forty yards away; stealthily withdrawing across the Chickahominy swamps to a crossing site on the James during which time the army would be vulnerable to attack; and crossing a powerful tidal river half again the width of the Mississippi below Vicksburg, during which the army would be even more vulnerable. Grant has often been credited with little imagination. Yet his decision to cross the James ranks with his crossing of the Mississippi as a tactical breakthrough. Crossing the Mississippi paved the way for victory in the West; crossing the James set the stage for Lee's ultimate defeat.

On June 5 Grant informed Washington of what he intended. He told Halleck it was not practical to hold a line north of Richmond and rely on the Fredericksburg railroad for support. "To do so would give us a long vulnerable line of road to protect, exhausting much of our strength in guarding it, and would leave open to the enemy all of his lines of communication on the south side of the James. My idea, from the start, has been to beat Lee's army north of Richmond. . . . I now find that after more than thirty days of trial that the enemy deems it of the first importance to run no risks with the Armies they now have. They act purely on the defensive, behind breastworks, or feebly on the offensive immediately in front of them and where, in case of repulse, they can instantly retire behind them." Grant said he could not prevail in the present setting "Without a greater sacrifice of human life" than he was willing to make.

"I have therefore resolved upon the following plan. I will continue to hold the ground now occupied by the Army of the Potomac, taking advantage of any favorable opportunity that may present itself, until the cavalry can be sent to destroy the Virginia Central railroad. When this is effected I will move the Army to the south side of the James river." Once across the James he would cut Lee's supply line, and prepare for a final showdown.

For Grant, Cold Harbor had been a setback, not a defeat. He concluded his message to Washington on a high note. "The feeling of the two Armies now seems to be that the rebels can protect themselves only by strong entrenchments, whilst our Army is not only confident of protecting itself, without entrenchments, but that it can beat and drive the enemy whenever and wherever he can be found without this protection."[105] For the Army of the Potomac, this was a new experience.

CHAPTER TWELVE

APPOMATTOX

As billows upon billows roll,
*   On victory victory breaks;*
Ere yet seven days from Richmond's fall
*   And crowing triumph wakes*
The loud joy-gun, whose thunders run
*   By sea-shore, streams, and lakes.*
The hope and great event agree
*   In the sword that Grant received from Lee.*

HERMAN MELVILLE, 1865
"The Surrender at Appomattox"

IN DECEMBER 1944, during the Battle of the Bulge, General George Patton broke contact with the enemy to his front, wheeled 90 degrees north, and took the Third Army on a forced march parallel to the line of battle to extricate the 101st Airborne at Bastogne. It was a perilous maneuver and an incredible tactical achievement,[1] and it in no way diminishes Patton's accomplishment to say that it pales alongside Grant's withdrawal from Cold Harbor and his crossing of the James in June 1864.

The week after his costly assault Grant laid plans and made ready. As at Vicksburg he kept his plans to himself. Various staff officers were assigned discreet tasks and engineers were kept busy, but no one, not even Meade, was told initially what was in store. The Chickahominy was bridged and the roads through the swampy bottoms were improved and corduroyed—all of which could have suggested that Grant planned another sidle to his left. A flotilla of ferryboats was assembled well out of sight on the lower James, and the navy assumed a position upstream to guard against rebel raiders, but that too could have been considered routine. An out-of-the-way crossing point thirty miles downriver was selected but no work was undertaken to improve it. Grant ordered the government's pontoons moved up from Fortress Monroe and a large supply of bridging lumber laid in but this also could have been interpreted as preparatory to a move against Richmond along the Chickahominy.[2] To further mask his intention, Grant ordered Sheridan to take two cavalry divisions and ride west, destroying the Virginia Central Railroad as he went. That, he assumed, would draw the Confederate cavalry in pursuit and deprive Lee of his eyes and ears. So well were Grant's plans concealed that on June 12 when he gave the order to move, the Confederate army was still tightly buttoned up in its Cold Harbor entrenchments girding for another Union onslaught.

Under cover of darkness, Baldy Smith's 18th Corps slipped away first, marching eastward to White House Landing on the Pamunkey, where ships were waiting to rush the troops down the York and up the James to rejoin Butler at Bermuda Hundred. Smith's corps was familiar with the terrain on the south side of the James and Grant wanted it in position first. As Smith's men moved out, the Union cavalry division not with Sheridan crossed the Chickahominy in a feint toward Richmond that would mask Grant's move from rebel scouts. Warren's 5th Corps followed behind the cavalry to add heft to the maneuver and also to protect the exposed Union flank if Lee should not be taken in. Burnside's 9th Corps, which had the longest distance to march, moved next, and then at midnight, with the Confederate line still quiet, Hancock and Wright pulled back. Not until dawn the next morning did rebel troops discover that the long Union trench line in front of Cold Harbor was empty. Grant was gone. The Army of the Potomac—115,000 men—had marched away so quietly that Confederate pickets had not observed its departure.

For the first time since Grant crossed the Rapidan, the two armies had lost contact. Lee responded as best he could. With his cavalry off chasing Sheridan, however, he had no way of fixing the Union army's location. It was possible that Grant might be crossing the James. But the most immediate threat was to Richmond, eight miles away, and the most likely scenario was that Grant was making another of his patented sidles to the left and would descend on the capital as McClellan had done, in the stretch of land south of the Chickahominy. Uncertain where Grant was, Lee decided to meet the most immediate threat. He threw the Army of Northern Virginia across the Chickahominy to cover the approaches to Richmond. Overnight the situation had changed abruptly. Grant was dealing a new hand. In a tactical sense, whether he was on the north side of the James or the south side made little difference. Several weeks earlier Lee had said to Jubal Early: "We must destroy this army of Grant's before it gets to the James River. If he gets there it will become a siege, and then it will be a mere question of time." [3]

For Grant, the march to the James went like clockwork. The Union advance guard reached Wilcox Landing in the late afternoon of June 13, coming down to it past the plantation once owned by ex-president John Tyler. The next day Hancock's corps, which Grant wanted to cross first, began boarding ferries that shuttled all night to put the troops on the

MOVEMENT TO THE JAMES RIVER,
JUNE 12–16, 1864

Union positions
Union movements
Confederate positions
Confederate movements

Ashland Station

Early

Burnside

Pamunkey River

Mechanicsville

W. F. Smith

Wright

Gaines's Mill

Old Cold Harbor

White House

New Bridge

Hancock

Richmond

Warren

RICHMOND & YORK RIVER RAILROAD

Fair Oaks Station

Seven Pines

A. P. Hill

Anderson

Warren

Malvern Hill

James River

Beauregard

Butler

James River

Wilcox Landing

Harrison's Landing

Charles City C.H.

City Point

Jordan's Point

W. E. Smith

James River

Windmill Point

Appomattox River

Petersburg

© 2000 Jeffrey L. Ward

0   5   10

Miles

south side by dawn of the 15th. While Hancock crossed, engineers commenced construction of the pontoon bridge Grant ordered: thirteen feet wide, 2,100 feet in length, and, for stability, tied to a small fleet of ocean-going schooners anchored upstream. Work on the bridge began at 9 A.M. on June 14 and was finished by eleven o'clock that night. When finished this was the longest pontoon bridge in military history.

Grant was in his element. He had recovered the mobility that had been lacking in the campaign and had run a risk few would have dared. He had exposed the Army of the Potomac to piecemeal destruction while on the march and had arrived at his embarkation point safe and sound. "Our forces will commence crossing the James today," he wired Halleck. "The enemy show no sign of having brought troops to the south side of Richmond. I will have Petersburg secured, if possible, before they get there in much force. Our movement from Cold Harbor to the James River has been made with great celerity and so far without loss or accident."[4]

Halleck, who continued to worry that Grant was leaving Washington uncovered by moving south of the James, did not reply.[5] But at 7 A.M. on June 15 President Lincoln responded:

> I have just received your dispatch of 1 p.m. yesterday. — I begin to see it. You will succeed. — God bless you all.
>
> A. LINCOLN[6]

Attempting to cross the broad expanse of the James below Richmond was an enormous gamble. The river was eighty feet deep, the current at midstream was fearsome, and there was a four-foot tidal surge to contend with. No one knew whether a slender pontoon bridge could withstand such conditions. No army had ever built a floating bridge longer than 1,000 feet, and scarcely ever in tidal waters. There was also the weather to worry about. A sudden storm blowing in from the Chesapeake could destroy the bridge in minutes. Another danger was the Confederate flotilla at Richmond, which included three ironclads mounted with heavy-caliber guns. If not intercepted, they could shell the crossing to pieces. Even fire-boats floated downstream could wreck the structure. Worst of all, Lee might scent what was up, break through the thin covering force Grant deployed, wait until the Union army was partially across the river, and then fall on the Federals stranded on the north bank with victory assured. Such a win would redeem every Confederate failure, defeat whatever thrust Grant might make toward Richmond, and place Lincoln's reelection in jeopardy. As Grant saw it, the chances of failure were high, but like Eisenhower on D-Day, he took the risk. "No man ought to win a victory," he said years later, "who is not willing to run the risk of defeat."[7] Grant was betting that Lee would not stir from his entrenchments at Cold Harbor to pursue him, or that if he did he would move south to cover the approach to Richmond along the Chickahominy. The tides and the weather would be left to chance.

On Wednesday morning, June 15, Grant stood upon a bluff on the north bank of the James watching the spectacle spread out before him. The Army of the Potomac was crossing the river, flags unfurled to the wind, guns reflecting in the sunlight, an endless column of marching men, horse-drawn artillery, and resplendent wagon trains, white canvas tightly tacked against the breeze. Once before, on a hill near Chattanooga, when he watched the Army of the Cumberland stretch out across the plain toward Bragg's lines on Missionary Ridge, he had witnessed the terrible beauty of the massed might of an army in motion. Now Grant was watching a larger army trying a greater thing. He stood alone, his hands clasped behind his back, his cigar thrown away, looking down at the sparkling river with its amazing bridge and the long blue lines going across.

The approaches to the river on both banks were covered with troops moving briskly to their new positions or waiting patiently to cross. Warships cruised upstream while a fleet of steamboats shuttled back and forth with scheduled precision, carrying men for whom the bridge had no room. On the north shore, regimental bands blared out stirring marches (although the men on the bridge were not allowed to keep in step), and here and there a plume of white steam punctuated the crossing when some vessel sounded its whistle. The bizarre mixed with the sublime as the army's cattle herd of 3,500 animals waited its turn to cross. It was a matchless pageant, and the man who conceived it stood watching in profound silence. Grant was on his way to Petersburg, a city the Confederacy could not lose, and Lee had been left behind. Not one man, one animal, or one vehicle would be lost in the crossing.

At noon Grant boarded a steamer and headed upriver to City Point, a small boat landing on the south bank of the Appomattox at the point where that river flowed into the James. Grant established his headquarters there on a high bluff overlooking the water and issued a brace of orders to move the army forward. Never had the Army of the Potomac been in a better strategic position. Having crossed the James successfully it was squarely in the rear of Lee's army, which remained dug in south of the Chickahominy, ready to defend Richmond from an attack that would not happen. Grant had outfoxed Lee and stood poised to take Petersburg, the lightly defended southern gateway to the Confederate capital.[8] Time, however, was running out. Grant had to strike before Lee could recover. Baldy Smith's 18th Corps, which arrived by ship the evening of June 14, was to lead the Union advance. The Confederate trench line at Petersburg was six miles away. Smith's force numbered 18,000 men. Beauregard, who was in command of rebel units southside, had deployed most of his troops facing Butler at Bermuda Hundred and could muster only a mixed assortment of 2,500 irregulars, home guard, and convalescents to man the city's battlements.

Grant instructed Smith to move forward under cover of darkness and storm the Confederate works at dawn.[9] The general in chief had a high opinion of Smith, particularly after his performance at Chattanooga, and entrusted the crucial role in the offensive to him. In this instance, Grant's confidence was misplaced. Smith dawdled the night away, moved forward aimlessly the next morning, and did not have his troops in place until noon. At that point he hesitated to attack.[10] Still shaken by the carnage at Cold Harbor, Smith insisted on making a lengthy personal reconnaissance of rebel defenses before advancing. This consumed an additional four hours after which he readjusted his lines for another two, and it was not until just before sundown that the attack got underway. Union forces swept forward and easily overran the Confederate position, taking more than two miles of earthworks and fifteen pieces of artillery. Beauregard wrote later that "Petersburg was clearly at the mercy of the Federal commander, who had all but captured it."[11] Smith, however, failed to exploit his advantage. Overcome once again by caution, and fearing that Confederate reinforcements were arriving by the trainload, he declined to push ahead during the evening hours and the 18th Corps settled down for the night. An observer on the spot noted that Smith's failure to continue forward on June 15 was "the greatest mistake of the campaign."[12] Grant said later, "I believed then, and still believe, that Petersburg could have been easily captured at that time."[13] If Smith had done so, it would have been almost impossible for Lee to make a stand in front of Richmond and the war might have ended eight months sooner.

Thursday, June 16, was another day of missed opportunity. Hancock's corps had come up during the night bringing Union strength close to 35,000. Beauregard received an infusion of veterans from nearby units but still could not muster more than 7,000 when dawn broke. Inexplicably, Smith still did not attack, preferring to wait until yet more Union reinforcements arrived. Beauregard took full advantage of the delay. Recognizing that it was essential to hold Petersburg at all costs, the flamboyant Creole stripped his line corking Butler at Bermuda Hundred and rushed every available man to the city's trenches. Grant, who was becoming increasingly impatient at the Union delay, instructed Burnside to bring his corps forward as quickly as possible and then ordered Meade to launch a full-scale attack on the Confederate position at 6 P.M. By then it was too late. Beauregard had deployed his troops with consummate skill and was ready and waiting when the attack came. Once again the Union assault was uneven and loosely coordinated. Hancock and Burnside went forward aggressively but Smith hung back, still obsessed with the failure at Cold Harbor. The 2nd Corps captured an additional stretch of Petersburg's outer defenses, Burnside's men took an important redan, but at no point was a breakthrough achieved.

That evening, to shorten his line, Beauregard pulled back to the outskirts of Petersburg itself. On the Union side, Warren came up to occupy a position on the Federal left, and Meade ordered another attack for dawn on June 17. It was the same old story of inadequate coordination and insufficient follow-through. Burnside moved forward on time, but Hancock was two hours late and Warren and Smith failed to move at all. Beauregard said if Warren had advanced from his position on the flank, "I would have been compelled to evacuate Petersburg without much resistance."[14]

By June 18 the Union's opportunity had slipped past. Meade ordered an attack all along the line at noon. Noon came, each corps commander waited for his neighbor to go first, no concerted attack was made, and by then Lee had caught up. Hard-marching veterans from the Army of Northern Virginia began to file into the trenches before Petersburg and the odds against Beauregard shrank to manageable proportions. Disjointed Union attacks continued through the afternoon, costly in Federal lives but completely ineffective, and by night it was all over. The rebel trenches were held in full strength and a successful frontal assault was out of the question. Meade called off the assault, and Grant concurred.[15]

In the four days since crossing the James, Union losses totaled 11,386 killed, wounded, and missing.[16] Petersburg was invested on the east, but the city, with its vital rail lines, remained in rebel hands. The problem was not with Grant's plan but with its faulty execution. As one historian has written, the Army of the Potomac remained a little out of control at Petersburg. "The reflexes of the corps commanders continued to be sluggish and there was always a gap between the will and the act. Orders were executed late, often half-heartedly, and now and then they were reinterpreted on the spot so that what was ordered was not done at all."[17] Also give credit to Beauregard, who may have had his finest hour. General J. F. C. Fuller, the British military analyst, wrote that the Confederate general "was worth 10,000 reinforcements," and if it had not been for him Petersburg would have fallen.[18]

If Grant was disappointed he did not show it. This was not the first time he had anticipated a quick victory only to have his opponent rally and turn the tables. At Donelson he had watched confidently as Commodore Foote's ironclads steamed up the Cumberland to lay waste the fort and saw them tumble back in defeat and disarray. At Pittsburg Landing he had ea-

gerly laid plans to dig the rebels out of Corinth only to have Albert Sidney
Johnston surprise him at Shiloh and come within an inch of victory. In
both instances Grant simply picked up the pieces and continued forward.
And so it would be at Petersburg. Unable to seize the city by surprise or to
take it by storm, he settled into a siege. And like Lee, he realized it was
merely a question of time—provided the Northern heartland remained
behind the war and Mr. Lincoln was reelected.

Neither was assured. The high casualty rate of the Army of the Potomac threatened to erode public support for the war. Since crossing the
Rapidan on May 4, Grant had lost close to 65,000 men and there seemed
to be no letup in sight. Lee, whose army was half as large, had lost half as
many (35,000). With an election pending, Lincoln could have turned on
Grant and made him a scapegoat. Yet he declined to do so. He had found
his general and would stick by him. Taking the long view, Lincoln recognized that Lee's casualties had been proportional, and that the South
would have far more difficulty finding replacements than the North.
Bloody as it was, the war was moving along satisfactorily. Grant had
driven the Army of Northern Virginia eighty miles south, partially inter-
dicted Lee's communication with the rest of the Confederacy, and pinned
him down in defense of Petersburg and Richmond.[19] Speaking to a large
public meeting in Philadelphia on June 16 the president took a hard line.
"We accepted this war for the worthy object of restoring the national authority over the whole national domain, and the war will end when that
object is attained. Speaking of the present campaign, General Grant is reported to have said, 'I am going through on this line if it takes all summer.'
I say we are going through on this line if it takes three years more."[20]

The partnership between Lincoln and Grant would prove to be the
key to Union success. It provided the North with a common outlook on
the conduct of the war and a unity of command the South could only envy.
Three days after returning from Philadelphia, the president decided to pay
a visit to City Point, consult with the general in chief, and take a firsthand
look at the war on the James. Unheralded and accompanied only by his
son, Tad, Lincoln arrived by steamer on the afternoon of June 20 looking,
as one of Grant's aides wrote, very much like a boss undertaker in his black
suit and stovepipe hat. After shaking hands all around, the president told
Grant, "I just thought I would jump aboard a boat and come down and
see you. I don't expect I can do any good, and in fact I may do harm but I'll
put myself under your orders and if you find me doing anything wrong
just send me [off] right away."[21] Lincoln stayed at City Point for the next
two days, visited the troops at the front, and spent much of the time riding
Cincinnati, the general in chief's massive charger, while Grant accompanied him on little Jeff Davis. The president regaled Grant and his staff with

his endless fund of stories, and seemed more intent on measuring the atmosphere and the attitude at headquarters than in discussing future plans or military strategy. Grant nevertheless took the occasion to reassure Lincoln that the present course would ultimately lead to victory. "You will never hear of me farther from Richmond than right now. I am just as sure of going into Richmond as I am of any future event. It may take a long summer day, as they say in the rebel papers, but I will do it."[22]

The president beamed his approval. "I cannot pretend to advise," he replied, "but I do sincerely hope that it all may be accomplished with as little bloodshed as possible." That was as close as Lincoln came to expressing an attitude on the fighting, and Grant did not consider it a rebuke. The fact is, both men were revived by the president's visit. Grant felt their acquaintanceship had ripened into a genuine friendship.[23] Lincoln, tanned and sunburned, returned to the White House on June 23, and, as one cabinet officer remarked, the trip had "done him good, physically, and strengthened him mentally."[24]

At Petersburg, Grant tightened his siege lines. It was reminiscent of Vicksburg, but on a larger scale.* And Lee was a far more dangerous opponent than Pemberton. Twice during the latter days of June, Grant attempted to sever the rail lines running south and west from the city, and did manage to break them temporarily, but Lee eventually beat back the assaulting columns, inflicting heavy losses. July brought a flurry of excitement when Jubal Early, having routed Union forces in the Shenandoah, continued down the valley, crossed the Potomac, and descended on Washington. On July 9, with 15,000 seasoned troops, Early easily defeated a pieced-together Union force commanded by Major General Lew Wallace at the Monocacy River east of Frederick, Maryland. This was the last Federal force between Early and the nation's capital. Grant responded by rushing the 6th Corps under Horatio Wright to Washington and redeploying the 19th Corps, which was arriving by boat from New Orleans.

It was another race against time. Early reached the Washington suburb of Rockville on July 10. At 2 P.M. Lincoln telegraphed Grant informing him that for all practical purposes the capital was undefended. The president thought Grant should shift onto the defensive at Petersburg and

---

* After the war, General Porter Alexander, artillery commander of the Confederate 1st Corps, wrote that Lee's army did not "fully comprehend" the strength of Grant's position initially. "But already the character of the operations removed all risks of serious future catastrophe. However bold we might be, however desperately we might fight, we were sure in the end to be worn out. It was only a question of a few months, more or less. We were unable to see it at once. But there soon began to spring up a chain of permanent works, the first of which were built upon our original lines captured by the skirmishers the first afternoon, and these works, impregnable to assault, finally decided our fate when, on the next March 25, we put them to the test." Edward Porter Alexander, *Military Memoirs of a Confederate* 557–558 (New York: Charles Scribner's Sons, 1910).

come to Washington immediately with whatever troops he could shake loose. "This is what I think . . . and is not an order."[25] Grant, who was eager to see Early's force destroyed, briefly considered returning but then decided Wright could handle the task alone. At 10:30 that evening he wired the president that he had dispatched "a whole Corps commanded by an excellent officer" who would be able to meet any threat Early might pose. "I think on reflection it would have a bad effect for me to leave here." Grant said he had complete faith in Wright and that Early would be hard pressed to make good his retreat to the Shenandoah.

As Early approached, the panic in Washington intensified. Halleck telegraphed Grant the morning of July 11 that the enemy had reached Silver Spring, six miles from the White House, and that Wright had arrived but his troops were not yet up. "Militia ordered from New York delayed by the Governor for some reason not explained. Pennsylvania will do nothing to help us."[26] Lincoln, less panicky, wired that Longstreet's corps was rumored headed for Washington but he did not repeat his request that Grant return and take charge.[27] Meanwhile, Quartermaster General Montgomery Meigs, who was acting on his own authority, moved out to the trenches around Washington at the head of 1,500 armed employees of the Quartermaster Department. If the capital was going to be attacked, Meigs was going to defend it. Later that day Assistant Secretary of War Charles Dana informed Grant that "Washington and Baltimore are in a state of great excitement. Both cities are filled with country people fleeing from the enemy. The damage to private property done by the invaders is almost beyond calculation." Help, he implied, was urgently needed.[28]

Grant refused to be stampeded. The fortifications surrounding the capital were strong, and by the evening of the 11th Wright's troops were marching into the works. Confederate skirmishers moved forward at dawn the next day, found the trenches manned by hard-fighting veterans of the 6th Corps, and pulled back without making a full-scale assault. Early decided his luck had run out and it was time to return to Virginia.[29] That evening the rebels recrossed the Potomac and headed for Leesburg. Whatever pursuit Wright was able to organize was too little and too late.

Early's foray shook confidence on the Northern home front. Grant was at the gates of Richmond but the Confederates had been able to move on Washington more or less unmolested. Public perception that the Union was winning the war declined noticeably. "The Confederacy is more formidable than ever," commented the London *Times*.[30] On foreign markets the U.S. dollar dropped to 37 cents, its lowest level of the war. "I see no bright spot anywhere," wrote New York diarist George Templeton Strong. "The blood and treasure spent on this summer's campaign have done little for the country."[31]

Grant was on the spot, and like Lincoln, his steadfastness served the Union well. The public might wonder about the progress of the war but the general in chief had no doubt. He had Lee by the throat and Sherman was closing on Atlanta. Grant was not about to relax the pressure. But he agreed that something had to be done about Early's corps in the valley. For three years Union forces in the Shenandoah had been humiliated. They had been beaten repeatedly, and beaten badly. First by Jackson, then Ewell, then Breckinridge, now Early. Grant believed it was a problem of command, and to put the right man in charge he met the president at Fortress Monroe the last day of July. Neither Grant nor Lincoln ever said much about their July 31 meeting, but the next day, with the president's concurrence, Grant wired Halleck: "I want Sheridan put in command of all the troops in the field with instructions to put himself south of the enemy and follow him to the death."[32] Grant was reaching down the army seniority list to select one of the most junior major generals, assign to him the defense of Washington, and give him three infantry corps and two cavalry divisions, a total of 48,000 men, to do the job.

Back in Washington, Lincoln saw the order two days later, and though he had already approved Sheridan's assignment, he was so taken with the ring of Grant's message that he wired his congratulations— together with a warning. "This, I think, is exactly right as to how our forces should move, but please look over the dispatches you may have received from here, ever since you made that order, and discover if you can, whether there is any idea in the head of anyone here, of 'putting our army *South* of the enemy' or of 'following him to the death' in any direction. I repeat to you it will neither be done or attempted unless you watch it every day, and hour, and force it."[33]

The partnership between Lincoln and Grant was never more apparent. The president was alerting Grant to the opposition in the War Department to Sheridan's appointment as well as to the tactics the general in chief prescribed. Both Halleck and Stanton thought Sheridan (at thirty-three) too young for so important an assignment, and both trembled at the thought of leaving Washington uncovered to pursue Early.[34] Lincoln knew they would do their best to undercut Sheridan. If Grant wanted Little Phil to fight an aggressive war in the valley, he was going to have to ride shotgun for him.

Grant was grateful for the warning. As soon as he read the president's message he ordered a dispatch boat to get up steam for a quick voyage up the bay. Grant had not believed it was necessary for him to leave Petersburg when Early was driving on Washington. But if his authority as general in chief was going to be questioned, it required an immediate response. He was on his way to the upper Potomac within the hour. In

Washington the next morning Grant visited neither the White House nor the War Department, but went straight to the railway station and caught a train to Monocacy Junction, headquarters for Union forces from the Shenandoah.

Sheridan arrived the next day. Grant told him he wanted Early driven from the valley and the Shenandoah made so desolate that the enemy would have no desire to return. "Eat out Virginia clear and clean . . . so that crows flying over it . . . will have to carry their provender with them."[35] To insure that his orders would not be countermanded, Grant told Sheridan that he was to report directly to him, not to Halleck or the War Department.[36] Grant said he had every confidence in Sheridan's judgment, and would not embarrass him with detailed instructions.[37]

The meeting was brief. Inside of two hours Little Phil was on his way to the front and Grant was heading back to City Point. On his return he stopped briefly in Washington and brought the War Department to heel. Meeting first with Halleck and then with Stanton, he snuffed out potential interference with his orders and reasserted his control of military affairs — which is exactly what Lincoln wanted him to do.[38] Grant's aide Colonel Theodore S. Bowers, who accompanied the general in chief, wrote afterward that "Grant now runs the whole machine independently of the Washington directory. Halleck has no control over troops except as Grant delegates it. He can give no orders and exercise no discretion."[39]

Grant seemed satisfied. On August 7 he wrote Sherman that he had just come from the Monocacy "after having put all our forces in motion after the enemy and after having put Sheridan in command who I know will push the enemy to the very death."[40] Back on the James, he wrote Julia in a similar vein, and appeared more concerned with having her come east with the children and finding a convenient place for them to live. Princeton, he thought, would be a nice place, and if they could not find a house there, then perhaps Philadelphia.[41]

Back at Petersburg another effort to break Lee's lines ended in frustrating failure. This was the Crater fiasco. A section of Burnside's front, not more than 150 yards from rebel entrenchments, was held by the 48th Regiment of Pennsylvania volunteers, many of whom were coal miners. The regiment was commanded by Colonel Henry Pleasants, a mining engineer before the war, and together they proposed tunneling under the Confederate works, stacking the colliery with explosives, and blowing the rebel line to Kingdom Come. Meade, an old army engineer, had no faith in the enterprise, but the Pennsylvanians succeeded in excavating a tunnel 511 feet long, with lateral galleries in which they stacked four tons of gunpowder. Once the explosives were detonated, Burnside's corps was to charge through the opening, with the 18th Corps following behind. Burnside designated a fresh division to lead the assault, an all-black unit commanded by Brigadier General Edward Ferrero. Ferrero's division had crossed the Rapidan with the 9th Corps on May 5 but had not seen combat, being deployed primarily to guard rear-area supply lines. At the time, white officers in the East doubted the fighting capacity of black troops, but Burnside was an exception. The African-American soldiers received special training for the task and were ready to go before dawn on July 30 when the mine was scheduled to explode. At the last minute Meade ordered Burnside to send a white division in first.* Burnside, who was stunned, tried unsuccessfully to get Meade to reconsider, and then apparently lost interest in the project. The commander of the division designated to lead the assault (chosen by drawing straws) was a notorious alcoholic who was dead drunk when the explosion went off.

The blast blew a crater 170 feet long, sixty feet wide, and thirty feet deep, burying an entire rebel regiment in the debris, along with a four-gun battery of artillery. The Confederates were momentarily helpless, yet the opportunity was not exploited. With no preparation and little leadership the Union troops attacked in disordered fashion and were quickly repulsed. As one historian has written, the plan was flawless but the execution was wretched.[42] Within the hour the breach in the rebel line had been mended, and by mid-morning the Confederates were counterattacking. Union casualties were heavy: some 4,000 against fewer than half as many for the enemy. Grant, sorely disappointed at another missed opportunity, told Halleck, "It was the saddest affair I have ever witnessed in this war. Such an opportunity for carrying fortifications I have never seen and do not expect again to have."[43]

The Crater fiasco set the tone for the summer of 1864. The Army of the Potomac was stalled in front of Petersburg, Sherman had failed to take Atlanta, and Sheridan was making little progress in the valley. Except for Lincoln and Grant, pessimism prevailed in Northern circles. In mid-August Halleck wrote to warn of possible draft riots in New York and Pennsylvania, as well as in Indiana and Kentucky. If that occurred, Old Brains thought it would be necessary to withdraw combat troops from Meade to put down the riots and maintain order. "Are not the appearances such that we ought to take in sail and prepare the ship for a storm?"[44]

---

* Despite the fact that they had been carefully rehearsed for the assignment, Meade had no confidence in Ferrero's troops. Grant felt differently, but provided cover for Meade in later testimony before the congressional Committee on the Conduct of the War. "If we put the colored troops in front and [the attack] should prove a failure, it would then be said . . . that we were shoving these people ahead to get killed because we did not care anything about them." William H. Powell, "The Battle of the Petersburg Crater," 4 *Battles and Leaders of the Civil War* 548, Clarence C. Buel and Robert U. Johnson, eds. (New York: Century, 1888).

Grant thought not. His reply was uncompromising. Such police work should be left to the state governors and the various state militias. "If we are to draw troops from the field to keep the loyal states in the harness it will prove difficult to suppress the rebellion in the disloyal states." Grant said if he took troops from Petersburg, Lee would be able to send soldiers to defend Atlanta, just as he had reinforced Bragg at Chickamauga the year before, and that "would insure the defeat of Sherman." In short, Grant had no intention of relaxing his efforts on the James.[45]

Lincoln read Grant's reply on August 17 and immediately telegraphed his approval. "I have seen your dispatch expressing your unwillingness to break your hold where you are. Neither am I willing. Hold on with a bull-dog grip, and chew and choke as much as possible."[46]

Looking over the president's message at his City Point headquarters, Grant laughed aloud—something he seldom did—and when staffers came over to see what amused him, he showed them the president's telegram. "The president has more nerve than any of his advisers," he chuckled.[47]

Grant's views at this time were expressed in a lengthy letter to Elihu Washburne. His concern was not with Lee but the Union home front. "The rebels are down to their last man," he wrote. "A man lost by them cannot be replaced. They have robbed the cradle and the grave equally to get their present force. Besides what they lose in frequent skirmishes and battles they are now losing from desertions and other causes at least one regiment a day. With this drain upon them the end is visible if we will be true to ourselves." Grant said the enemy wanted to hold out until after the presidential election. "They hope for a counter revolution. They hope for the election of the peace candidate. In fact, like McCawber, they hope for *something* to turn up."[48]*

Writing to his boyhood chum from Georgetown, Ohio, Commodore Daniel Ammen, Grant restated his view that the end was in sight. After briefly describing events at Petersburg, he criticized those in the North who sought peace at any price. "It would be but the beginning of the war. The demands of the South would know no limits. They would demand indemnity for expenses incurred in carrying on the war. They would demand return of all their slaves . . . and they would keep on demanding until it would be better dead than submit longer."[49] Grant thought the war must be carried through to complete victory; there could be no compromise peace, no matter how ardently people wanted one, because the Union and slavery could no longer coexist.

---

* The reference is to Wilkins Micawber, a character in Charles Dickens's *David Copperfield*, who lived in poverty while waiting for "something to turn up," a Dickensian phrase indicating unrealistic optimism.

Grant had no party affiliation and had never been an anti-slavery man. His view of the war had evolved over time, and by the summer of 1864 he defined it in the same terms as Republicans like Lincoln. Indeed, there was a growing, almost symbiotic relationship between these two sons of the Ohio valley. Instinctively, Lincoln took his military cues from Grant, while Grant, for his part, adopted the same stance as the president in political matters. Neither Grant nor Lincoln worried any longer about the outcome of the war provided the Union held the course; both worried intently whether it would do that, and about the upcoming election.*

Anticipating victory in the fall, the Democratic convention met in Chicago on August 29 and on the first ballot acclaimed George McClellan as the party's nominee. His running mate was Congressman George H. Pendleton of Ohio, long an advocate of a negotiated peace. The party platform demanded "immediate efforts be made for a cessation of hostilities, with a view to an ultimate convention of the States, or other peaceable means, to the end that at the earliest practicable moment peace may be restored on the basis of the Federal Union of the States." Emancipation of Southern slaves went by the boards, and the Copperhead view of the war dominated the convention.[50]

The Democrats adjourned on August 31 in a mood of campaign euphoria. Two days later the bubble burst. On September 2 Major General Henry Slocum, commanding the 20th Corps in the Army of the Tennessee, wired the War Department: "GENERAL SHERMAN HAS TAKEN ATLANTA." The next day Sherman sent his own message: "So Atlanta is ours, and fairly won."[51] Church bells rang across the land as they had not rung since Grant took Vicksburg. Lincoln proclaimed a day of thanksgiving and prayer, and at Petersburg the general in chief ordered a hundred-gun salute fired from every battery that bore on the rebel works. As the rumble of Union artillery celebrated Atlanta's fall, Grant poured out his heart to Sherman: "I feel you have accomplished the most gigantic un-

---

* On August 23 Lincoln wrote a personal memorandum acknowledging the probability of his defeat, and at the cabinet meeting that day he asked each member to sign the back, sight unseen, pledging the administration's acceptance of the people's verdict and its support for the president elect. Lincoln's memorandum stated:

> This morning, as for some days past, it seems exceedingly probable that this Administration will not be reëlected. Then it will be my duty to coöperate with the President-elect as to save the Union between the election and the inauguration; as he will have secured his election on such ground that he cannot possibly save it afterwards.
>
> A. Lincoln

7 *The Collected Works of Abraham Lincoln* 514, Roy P. Basler, et al., eds. (New Brunswick: Rutgers University Press, 1955).

dertaking given to any general in this war, and with a skill and ability that will be acknowledged in history as not surpassed, if not unequalled. It gives me as much pleasure to record this in your favor as it would in favor of any living man, myself included." [52]

Public opinion rallied to the president. The *St. Paul Dispatch* headlined the news:

VICTORY

Is the War a Failure?

Old Abe's Reply to the Chicago Convention
Consternation and Despair Among the Copperheads. [53]

Grant's relentless effort to turn the Confederate position at Petersburg was also having its effect. Already the rebel line was stretched to the breaking point. "Unless some measure can be devised to replace our losses, the consequences may be disastrous," Lee warned Confederate Secretary of War James Seddon. [54] "Grant," he said, "could move his troops to the left or the right without our knowledge until he has reached the point at which he aims, and we are then compelled to hurry our men to meet him, incurring the risk of being too late to check his progress." [55] Lee told Seddon that without more troops "I cannot see how we are to escape the natural military consequences of the enemy's numerical superiority." [56]

The Union regained momentum. Flush with Sherman's success, Lincoln and Grant began to apply pressure on Sheridan in the Shenandoah. In late August Grant had informed Little Phil of Lee's losses at Petersburg—which he estimated at 10,000 killed and wounded in the past two weeks—and instructed him to push Early "with all vigor. Give the enemy no rest. Do all the damage to railroads and crops you can. Carry off stock of all descriptions and negroes so as to prevent further planting. If the War is to last another year we want the Shenandoah valley to remain a barren waste." [57] Sheridan, with his first independent command, seemed unsure how to proceed, and on September 12 Lincoln suggested that Grant urge his protégé forward. "Sheridan and Early are facing each other at a deadlock," wrote the president. "Could we not pick up a regiment here and there, to the number of say ten thousand, and quietly but suddenly concentrate them at Sheridan's camp and enable him to make a quick strike? This is but a suggestion." [58]

For Grant, a suggestion was enough. He replied the next day that he had been planning to visit Sheridan for some time and "arrange what was necessary to enable him to start Early out of the Valley." [59] Grant set out the following day, his second trip up the Potomac in six weeks, and reached

Charles Town, West Virginia, on Friday September 16, where Sheridan joined him.*

"That's Grant," a sergeant in Wright's 6th Corps told a comrade, pointing him out. "I hate to see that old cuss around. When that old cuss is around there's sure to be a big fight on hand."[60]

The meeting was brief. Grant had taken with him a plan to drive Early away from Winchester. Sheridan had his own plan, not merely to drive Early from Winchester, but to annihilate him. Grant heard Little Phil out, and found him to be "so clear and so positive in his views, and so confident of success," that he accepted Sheridan's proposal and kept his own plan in his pocket. "Can you be ready to move by Tuesday?" asked Grant. Sheridan said he would be off before daylight on Monday. "That's fine," said Grant. "Go in."[61]

Sheridan was as good as his word. He hit Early on Opequon Creek at dawn on Monday, September 19, and after an all-day battle sent him whirling back through Winchester with heavy losses. Grant ordered another hundred-gun salute at Petersburg, recommended Sheridan for promotion to brigadier general in the regular army (which was promptly conferred), and instructed him to follow up the victory as quickly as possible. "Make all you can of it," said Grant.[62] This time Sheridan needed no prompting. On September 22 he fell upon Early at Fisher's Hill, two miles south of Strasburg, and routed him, sending what was left of the Confederate 2nd Corps stumbling up the valley toward Harrisonburg and Staunton. "May your good work continue," Grant telegraphed. "Your great victory wipes out much of the stain upon our arms by previous disasters in [the valley]."[63]

Eight weeks earlier, Confederate troops had been knocking at the door to the nation's capital. Now they were a hundred miles south of the Potomac and unlikely to return, given Sheridan's two smashing victories. Grant briefly considered having Sheridan march on Richmond from the Shenandoah, but gave up the idea when Little Phil demurred because of lack of transportation. "I think the best policy will be to let the burning of the crops in the Valley be the end of this campaign," he told Grant.[64] Union horsemen swept down the valley like a plague of locusts. On October 6 Sheridan reported that his troops had "destroyed over 2000 barns filled

---

* In his *Memoirs* Grant said he realized that he had to see Sheridan personally if he wanted action. "I knew it was impossible for me to get orders through Washington to Sheridan to make a move, because they would be stopped there and such orders as Halleck's caution (and that of the Secretary of War) would suggest would be given instead, and would, no doubt, be contradictory to mine." (Stanton exercised absolute control over the military telegraph lines and all messages from Grant to commanders in the field passed through his hands. Delays and alterations of the text were not unheard of.) 2 *Personal Memoirs of U.S. Grant* 327 (New York: Charles L. Webster 1886).

with wheat, hay and farming implements; over 70 mills filled with flour and wheat. . . . Tomorrow I will continue the destruction down to Fisher's Hill. When this is completed the Valley, from Winchester up to Staunton, 92 miles, will have but little in it for man or beast."[65]

One last battle remained in the Shenandoah. As Sheridan withdrew down the valley, Lee decided to exploit whatever opportunity that provided for a counterattack. Early was reinforced, and at dawn on the morning of October 19 he struck the unsuspecting Union army in bivouac on Cedar Creek, fifteen miles south of Winchester. Outnumbered three to two, Old Jube had the advantage of surprise and by ten o'clock he had smashed the Federal left and appeared on the verge of a major victory. Sheridan, who had gone to Washington to confer with Halleck, was in Winchester when the attack began and hurried to the scene, spurring his powerful Mississippi Morgan, Rienzi, in the breakneck ride immortalized by Thomas B. Read as "Sheridan's Ride":

> *Hurrah! hurrah for Sheridan!*
> *Hurrah for the horse and man!*
> *And when their statues are placed on high,*
> *Under the dome of the Union sky,*
> *Be it said in letters both bold and bright:*
> *"Here is the steed that saved the day*
> *By carrying Sheridan into the fight,*
> *From Winchester—twenty miles away!"**

When Sheridan arrived on the scene, he found that Wright's corps, though beaten back, was holding firm in the Union center. Little Phil rallied the remainder of his army and late in the afternoon led the troops forward in a dazzling counterattack that swept the rebels from the field. Early's army was demolished. Routed for the third time in thirty days, it would never again offer serious resistance in the valley. Sheridan was the hero of the hour. Single-handedly he had converted certain Union defeat into a tumultuous victory. "Such a scene as his presence and such emotion as it awoke cannot be realized but once in a century," a Vermont veteran in the 6th Corps recalled.[66]

Grant ordered another hundred-gun salute in honor of Little Phil's

---

* Read added eight miles to the distance Sheridan traveled, although subsequent historians estimate that Rienzi covered seventy-five miles that day, mostly at a gallop, carrying Sheridan along the Union lines. The jet black gelding was aided by the fact that Sheridan weighed no more than 120 pounds, boots and spurs included. Three days after the battle, Sheridan renamed his mount *Winchester* to commemorate the exploit. Samuel Eliot Morison, *The Oxford History of the American People* 694 note (New York: Oxford University Press, 1965).

victory, Lincoln wired his congratulations, and Meade, who had never been an admirer of Sheridan, called his victory at Cedar Creek "one of the most brilliant feats of the war."[67] To follow up, Grant ordered Meade to hit both ends of Lee's line at Petersburg. The assaults were unsuccessful, but Lee was forced to lengthen his defenses further, so that they now stretched thirty-five miles from Deep Bottom east of Richmond to the Weldon Railroad southwest of Petersburg. The Confederate line had become so extended that Lee informed Jefferson Davis that unless he received immediate reinforcements, "I fear a great calamity will befall us."[68] Lee briefly attempted to find his own replacements by suggesting to Grant an informal "man for man" exchange of prisoners on the Petersburg front. Grant agreed, provided that black soldiers fighting for the Union be exchanged on the same basis as white. Lee declined. "Negroes belonging to our Citizens are not Considered Subjects of exchange and were not included in my proposition," he wrote. Grant then ended the correspondence by stating that the United States government insisted all soldiers be treated equally. Lee's refusal to grant such rights to former slaves "induces me to decline making the exchange you ask."[69]

Sheridan's triumph in the valley, combined with Sherman's capture of Atlanta and the August victory of Admiral Farragut in Mobile Bay ("Damn the torpedoes. Full speed ahead!"), paved the way for Lincoln's landslide reelection. Having won by a mere plurality over a divided field in 1860, this time the president garnered 55 percent of the popular vote and swept the electoral college 212–21. The soldier vote, which some had assumed would swing to McClellan in protest against the war, went to Lincoln three to one, leaving Little Mac only the states of Delaware, New Jersey, and Kentucky.* "Congratulate the President for me," Grant wired Stanton. "The election having passed off quietly, no bloodshed or riot throughout the land, is a double victory, worth more to the country than a battle won."[70] Writing several days later to his friend J. Russell Jones in Chicago, Grant said, "I suppose you and [Elihu] Washburne are as happy over the result of the election as 'Clams in high tide.' The immense majority which Mr. Lincoln has received is worth more to us than a victory in the field, both in its effect on the rebels, and in its foreign influence."[71] To Julia he wrote that he hoped the results would be quietly accepted. "If there was less [dissension] in the North the rebellion would be much sooner put down."[72]

With Lincoln confirmed in office, Grant prepared for the final push

---

* The popular vote divided 2,203,831 for Lincoln, 1,797,019 for McClellan. The military vote that was counted separately went 119,754 for the president, 34,291 for the challenger. State by state the results were closer than the aggregate figures suggest. Lincoln carried Connecticut by a mere 2,000 votes and New York by less than 7,000.

to topple the Confederacy. First on his agenda was Sherman. Uncle Billy had taken Atlanta, but John Bell Hood's Army of Tennessee* was still in the field, depleted but eager for revenge. After the battle of Atlanta, Hood moved west, planning to circle around Sherman, cut his rail connection with Chattanooga, and pounce at leisure on the starving fragments of the isolated 120,000-man Union army. Jefferson Davis boasted that Sherman had no escape. "The fate that befell the army of the French Empire in its retreat from Moscow will be re-enacted," to which Grant retorted: "Who is to furnish the snow?"[73]

Sherman met the challenge by dividing his army. With Grant's approval he sent George Thomas west toward Tennessee to contain Hood, while he took the remaining 60,000 eastward to the sea. Sherman told Grant that by moving on Savannah he could divide the Confederacy in two. "If you can whip Lee, and I can march to the Atlantic, I think Uncle Abe will give us a 20 days leave to see the young folks."[74] At first, Grant was skeptical of the plan, but Sherman quickly convinced him. "We cannot remain here on the defensive," he told Grant. "But I can make the march and make Georgia howl."[75]

Grant relied on Sherman's judgment.[†] The march to the sea was entirely Sherman's idea, but as general in chief Grant accepted final responsibility. "On reflection I think better of your proposition," he wired Sherman. "You will no doubt clear the country where you go of railroad tracks and supplies. I would also move every wagon, horse, mule and hoof of stock as well as Negroes."[76] Grant then took it upon himself to convince Stanton and Lincoln, who were initially opposed to the plan.[77] "Sherman's proposition is the best that can be adopted," Grant wired Stanton. "With a long railroad in rear of Atlanta Sherman cannot maintain his position. If he cuts loose . . . he leaves a wide and destitute country for the rebels to

---

* On July 17, 1864, Jefferson Davis, dissatisfied with the way the war was going in Georgia, relieved Joseph E. Johnston as commander of the Army of Tennessee and replaced him with thirty-three-year-old John Bell Hood. Johnston had conducted a cautious campaign, delaying Sherman but avoiding pitched battles as much as possible. Hood, pugnacious and impetuous, took on the Union army and was whipped decisively at Peachtree Creek, Ezra Church, Jonesborough, and on the outskirts of Atlanta. All lion and no fox, said Lee dismissively, when he learned of Hood's appointment. *The Wartime Papers of R. E. Lee* 821–22, Clifford Dowdey, ed. (Boston: Little, Brown, 1961).

† When Sherman initially suggested his plan, some of Grant's staff urged the general in chief to instruct him to hold a council of war with his commanders and discuss the alternatives. "No," said Grant. "I will not direct anyone to do what I would not do myself. I never held what might be called councils of war and I do not believe in them. They create divided responsibility, and at times prevent that unity of action so necessary in the field. Some officers will in all likelihood oppose any plan that is adopted; and when it is put into execution, such officers may, by their arguments in opposition, have so far convinced themselves that the movement will fail that they cannot enter upon it with enthusiasm. . . . I believe it is better for a commander to consult his generals informally, get their views and opinions, and then make up his mind what action to take, and act accordingly." Horace Porter, *Campaigning with Grant* 316 (New York: Century, 1897).

pass over. . . . Such an army as Sherman has, (and with such a commander) is hard to corner or capture."[78] Given the go-ahead by Grant, Sherman moved out on November 16, cut a swath of destruction sixty miles wide from Atlanta to the sea, and on December 22 telegraphed the president: "I beg to present you, as a Christmas gift, the city of Savannah, with 150 heavy guns and about 25,000 bales of cotton."[79]

Except for 3,500 rebel cavalry commanded by Joseph Wheeler and a scattering of home guard militia, Sherman's 285-mile march to Savannah was uncontested. George Thomas did not have it so easy. Hood was determined to avenge the fall of Atlanta and aggressively followed the Federals into Tennessee. Thomas husbanded his forces, withdrew to Nashville, and hunkered down to meet Hood's attack. That was not Grant's style. Concerned that Hood might bypass Nashville and head north into Kentucky, the general in chief peppered Thomas with orders to attack. As at Chattanooga, Old Tom would not be hurried. He patiently assembled his forces and readied a knockout blow to destroy Hood once and for all. Watching Thomas's methodical style was like watching paint dry. Grant grew impatient, then exasperated. On December 8 he instructed Halleck to relieve Thomas if he did not attack immediately. "There is no better man to repel an attack than Thomas," said Grant, "but I fear he is too cautious ever to take the initiative."[80] Thomas stood his ground. Subordinate but immovable, he wired Grant, "I have done all in my power to prepare. If you should deem it necessary to relieve me I shall submit without a murmur."[81] Grant backed off. "I have as much confidence in your conducting a battle rightly as I have in any other officer," he told Thomas, "but it has seemed to me that you have been slow, and I have had no explanation of affairs to convince me otherwise."[82]

Ready at last, the Rock of Chickamauga ordered an attack for dawn on December 10 only to have an ice storm intervene. Movement became impossible and Thomas waited for the storm to abate. Grant fumed helplessly. "Delay no longer for weather or reinforcements," he telegraphed on December 11. "Will obey the order as promptly as possible however much I may regret it," Thomas shot back. "The whole country is covered with a perfect sheet of ice and sleet."[83] Frustration now got the better of Grant. Never having experienced the conditions Thomas confronted, he ordered Major General John Logan, who was visiting City Point on leave from Sherman's army, to proceed immediately to Nashville and take command if Thomas had not moved by the time he arrived. Uncharacteristically, Grant made the decision in a moment of pique, and he soon became uncomfortable with it. He fidgeted for a day at City Point and then took the dispatch boat to Washington. If Thomas was to be relieved, Grant decided he owed it to Old Tom to do the job himself.

On the night of December 14, 1864, as Grant approached Washington, a thaw set in along the Cumberland. The ice melted and the next morning Thomas attacked all along the line. It was a typical George Thomas sledgehammer blow, similar to the assault of the Army of the Cumberland at Missionary Ridge. Hood reeled back, Thomas advanced aggressively, and after two days of intense fighting the Confederate Army of Tennessee was smashed beyond recognition. Hood limped back to Tupelo, Mississippi, with barely half of the 40,000 men he had led northward seven weeks earlier, a bedraggled and dispirited band that soon melted away.[84] Grant and Lincoln wired their congratulations to Thomas, another hundred-gun salute battered Lee's line at Petersburg, and Logan returned to join his command with Sherman.

It was the beginning of the end. With Hood's army dismantled, the Confederacy now consisted of little more than the Carolinas and the southern third of Virginia. Sherman was heading north through the former while Meade and Sheridan tightened their grip on Lee in the latter. On foreign exchanges, the Confederate dollar slipped to 2 percent of its 1861 value, and in Richmond—deprived of its breadbasket in the Shenandoah—food became scarce and meat virtually nonexistent. "The deep waters are closing over us," wrote Civil War diarist Mary Chesnut on December 19.[85]

Of more immediate military import, desertions from the Army of Northern Virginia now reached epidemic proportion. In January the army lost 8 percent of its strength and another 8 percent in February. "Hundreds of men are deserting nightly," Lee informed Jefferson Davis. "Unless it can be changed, it will bring us calamity."[86] But no change was in sight. Instead, Grant stepped up the pressure. Union armies fanned out throughout the South, snuffing what little resistance remained, while Sherman moved inexorably north from Georgia through South Carolina. At Petersburg, Meade continued to extend his lines, forcing Lee to do likewise. By mid-February the last road into town from the south was cut and the last railroad taken under fire.

Nevertheless, the lack of visible progress in Virginia caused some in Congress to become restive. Rumors swirled that legislation would soon be introduced to elevate Sherman to a second lieutenant generalcy and that he might supersede Grant. In Savannah, Sherman heard the rumors and asked his brother, Senator John Sherman of Ohio, to scupper the bill. "It would be mischievous," he wrote Grant, "for there are enough rascals who would try to sow differences between us. I would rather have you in command than anyone else [and] I should emphatically decline any commission calculated to bring us into rivalry."[87]

Grant was unruffled. He wrote Sherman a warm reply that reflected his attachment. "No one would be more pleased at your advancement than I, and if you should be placed in my position and I put subordinate it would not change our relations in the least. I would make the same exertion to support you that you have ever done to support me and I would do all in my power to make our cause win." [88] Whatever schemes were being hatched died stillborn. Grant continued to tighten the noose around Petersburg while Sherman moved on Columbia, South Carolina.

Already Confederate peace feelers were in the air. A brief conference between President Lincoln and rebel leaders at Hampton Roads in early February ended without results, and at the end of February Major General Edward Ord, who had succeeded Benjamin Butler as commander of the Army of the James, had a chance meeting with General Longstreet under a flag of truce to arrange an exchange of political prisoners. The two were old friends and after their business was completed began to talk about the chance for peace. Perhaps, Ord suggested, a meeting between Grant and Lee might pave the way. Longstreet took the suggestion back to Confederate headquarters and on March 3 — the day before Lincoln's second inaugural — Grant received the following letter from General Lee:

> Lieutenant General Longstreet has informed me that in a recent conversation between himself and Major General Ord as to the possibility of arriving at a satisfactory adjustment of the present unhappy difficulties by means of a military convention, General Ord stated that if I desired to have an interview with you on the subject you would not decline, provided I had authority to act. Sincerely desiring to leave nothing untried which may put an end to the calamities of war, I propose to meet you at such convenient time and place as you may designate, with the hope that upon an interchange of views it might be found practicable to submit the subjects of controversy between belligerents to a convention of the kind mentioned. [89]

Grant had been handed a hot potato. He immediately forwarded the message to Washington and asked for instructions. Lincoln was on Capitol Hill when Grant's telegram arrived, signing bills that had been passed during the last day of the session. After consulting Stanton and Secretary of State Seward, Lincoln wrote out a carefully worded reply, which was signed by Stanton and forwarded to Grant.

> The President directs me to say that he wishes you to have no conference with General Lee unless it be for the capitulation of Gen. Lee's army, or on some minor or purely military matter. He

instructs me to say that you are not to decide, discuss or confer upon any political question. Such questions the President holds in his own hands; and will submit them to no military conferences or convention. Meanwhile you are to press to the utmost your military advantages.[90]

Pressing his military advantages was precisely what Grant intended. Already he had instructed Sheridan to move out from the valley, destroy the rail junction at Lynchburg, then turn eastward toward Danville and an eventual linkup with Sherman approaching from the south.[91] Grant was worried that after eight months of siege at Petersburg, Lee might imitate his own maneuver at Cold Harbor, silently steal away some moonless night, and march south to join the Carolina army of Joseph E. Johnston, the only other effective Confederate force still in the field.

Those last days of winter, Grant wrote later, were one of the most anxious periods of the war. "I was afraid, every morning, that I would awake from my sleep to hear that Lee had gone, and that nothing was left but his picket line. I knew he could move much more lightly and more rapidly than I, and that, if he got the start, he would leave me behind so that we would have the same army to fight again further south—and the war might be prolonged another year."[92] Sheridan's job was to slam the door on Lee's escape route. On March 2 Little Phil fell on the remnant of Early's Shenandoah command at Rockfish Gap near Waynesboro, and annihilated it. At that point Sheridan found the road to Lynchburg impassable and headed east with two divisions of cavalry to join Grant on the James. With Sheridan's arrival, Grant's forces on the Richmond front totaled slightly more than 120,000 men: the Army of the Potomac under Meade, the Army of the James under Ord, and the mounted troops from the Army of the Shenandoah under Sheridan.

Lee, with his Army of Northern Virginia now down to 50,000 men, of whom only 35,000 were fit for duty, was stunned by Early's defeat.[93] To wait for Grant to attack would be to court disaster. The thinly held Confederate line could be easily overrun by the mass of the Federal army, or encircled by Sheridan's fast-moving troopers. Aggressive to the end, Lee decided to strike a surprise blow at the weakest point in Grant's line, lock the Union army in place, and then under cover of the fighting withdraw quickly to the south. That would mean abandoning Richmond, but the alternative, as Lee saw it, was to lose the army. It was a desperate gamble, and to accomplish the task, Lee turned to his scrappiest subordinate, Lieutenant General John B. Gordon, now commanding Stonewall Jackson's old corps. Gordon was instructed to hit Fort Stedman, a run-down Federal installation midway between the Crater and the Appomattox, at dawn on Saturday, March 25, puncture Grant's line, and exploit whatever opportunity presented itself. Gordon moved forward aggressively and tore a three-quarter-mile hole in the Union front, but was quickly contained by the 9th Corps, Burnside's old command, now ably led by thirty-six-year-old John G. Parke. A prompt Northern counterattack retook the ground, plus the forward trenches of the Confederate line as well, trapping many of Gordon's men and forcing them to surrender. Lee lost 5,000 men, almost 15 percent of his combat effectives, against fewer than 1,500 Union casualties. The attack had never been more than a forlorn hope, and Lee now faced the inevitable Federal onslaught considerably worse off than before.

The attack on Fort Stedman, Lee's last offensive gambit, had been so feeble that Grant scarcely took notice. At the time of the assault he was meeting with President Lincoln at City Point. Shortly after the inauguration, Grant had invited the president to come down from Washington ("I think the rest would do you good."[94]), and Lincoln had accepted with alacrity, arriving on the steamer *River Queen* at 9 P.M. the night before. Grant called Gordon's foray "a little rumpus up the line," and told the president it was a measure of Lee's desperation and a likely signal that he was planning to withdraw.[95] As he usually did, Lincoln enjoyed his visit to headquarters enormously, reviewed the troops of Warren's 5th Corps just hours after Gordon's attack, and visited the wounded in an army field hospital, where he made a point of shaking hands with the wounded Confederates.[96]

The president stayed busy for the next several days attending reviews and various inspections Grant arranged, and then on the morning of March 28 met with Grant, Sherman, and Admiral David Porter aboard the *River Queen* to discuss the progress of the war. Strictly speaking it was not a council of war, given Grant's aversion to such meetings, but the four men roamed at length over the military situation, Sherman having come up from North Carolina especially for the meeting. Lincoln said his greatest worry was that his generals might let victory slip through their hands, permitting Lee and Johnston to escape and continue the fight for months to come. Grant and Sherman made it clear that would not happen, and then Sherman asked the president, "What is to be done with the rebel armies when defeated?" Lincoln replied at length, emphasizing his desire for reconciliation. He wanted to offer the most generous terms, he said, in order to "get the men comprising the Confederate armies back to their homes, at work on their farms and in their shops." Warming to his subject, Lincoln observed that once the men surrendered and reached their homes, "they won't take up arms again. Let them go, officers and all. I want submission and no more bloodshed. . . . I want no one punished; treat them liberally all round. We want those people to return to their allegiance to the Union and submit to the laws."[97]

Did that include Jefferson Davis and the Confederacy's political leadership? the officers asked. Lincoln responded by telling the story of a teetotaler who was asked if he wanted his lemonade spiked with whiskey. The man replied that if he didn't know it, he supposed it would be all right, from which Grant and Sherman concluded that if Davis and his colleagues quietly escaped abroad, the president wouldn't mind.

When the meeting concluded, Lincoln, with a twinkle in his eyes, turned to Sherman. "Sherman," he asked, "do you know why I took a shine to Grant and you?"

"I don't know, Mr. Lincoln. You have been extremely kind to me, far more than I deserve."

"Well," said Lincoln, "you never found fault with me." [98]

Sherman left immediately after the meeting to rejoin his command. He never saw Lincoln again. Reflecting on the meeting years later, he wrote: "Of all the men I have met, he seemed to possess more of the elements of greatness, combined with goodness, than any other." [99]

The day after the conference with the president, Grant assumed the offensive. It was another sidle to the left. Sheridan, supported by the 5th Corps, was ordered to turn Lee's right ten miles southwest of Petersburg. Meade followed laterally, the 2nd Corps in the van, while Ord's army crossed the James and took up the positions the Army of the Potomac vacated. Sheridan was aiming for Five Forks, a critical road intersection vital to Lee's withdrawal south. Lee responded by sending George Pickett with two reinforced infantry divisions and the remaining Confederate cavalry, about 12,000 men, to hold the crossing. A drenching downpour slowed Sheridan's troopers, but by nightfall on the 29th he was at Dinwiddie Court House, five miles from his objective.

With Sheridan leading the way ("the left-hand man of Grant the left-handed," wrote one reporter [100]), Grant had remedied the lack of aggressiveness that had bedeviled the Army of the Potomac. That evening he turned Little Phil loose: "I feel like ending the matter," he wired Sheridan. "In the morning push around the enemy, if you can, and get onto his right rear. We will all act together as one army until it is seen what can be done." [101] Grant was no longer trying to cut Lee's line of retreat. Instead, he was preparing a knockout punch, looking for a final victory. Later, he wrote, "My hope was that Sheridan would be able to carry Five Forks, get on the enemy's right flank and rear, and force them to weaken their center to protect their right so that an assault in the center might be successfully made." [102]

For two days the rain continued. Pickett held Sheridan at Dinwiddie Court House on March 31, but late the next afternoon, with the ground drying, Little Phil broke through, personally leading the final infantry charge that shattered Pickett's line. Lee's right flank was in shambles. Pickett lost more than 5,000 men, most of whom had been encircled and surrendered, at a cost of 634 for Sheridan. It was the most one-sided Union victory of the war. When the news reached Grant that evening, he ordered an attack all along the line at four the next morning, April 2, 1865.

Lee's losses at Five Forks, combined with those a week earlier at Fort Stedman, had cost him a good fourth of his army. With his line now stretched beyond the breaking point, it was scarcely a contest when the Union troops went forward at dawn. Sheridan captured the last rail line into Petersburg from the south, while the 2nd, 6th, and 9th Corps punched through the main Confederate battle line. The first bank of rebel entrenchments fell under the onslaught, then the second, as the embattled Army of North Virginia fell back to Petersburg's inner defenses. "I see no prospect of doing more than holding our position here till night," Lee informed Jefferson Davis. "I am not certain that I can do that. If I can I shall withdraw tonight north of the Appomattox. . . . I advise that all preparations be made for leaving Richmond tonight."[103]

Richmond fell and the war became a footrace. Just before midnight, the Confederate army pulled back from the Petersburg defenses they had held with such fortitude for the past 293 days. Lee's objective was Amelia Court House, forty miles to the west, a shipping point astride the Richmond & Danville Railroad, the last rail link to North Carolina and the forces of Joseph E. Johnston, a hundred or so miles to the south. For Grant, time was crucial. Lee had an eight-hour head start, but Grant had Sheridan's fast-moving cavalry and five infantry corps closing in on the kill. "We never endured such marching before," a footsore enlisted man wrote afterward.[104] Rather than pursue Lee ("A stern chase is a long one," Sherman once said[105]), Grant moved to block his route south by cutting the Danville–Richmond line ten miles below Amelia Court House. With Sheridan in the lead, the Union army raced westward alongside the Confederates, hell-bent for the railroad.

Reduced to little over 30,000 men, Lee took two days to assemble his army at Amelia Court House. The troops had withdrawn successfully from their entrenchments and moved by three separate columns toward their destination, but with none of the élan or enthusiasm of past campaigns. "We moved on in disorder," wrote a captain from North Carolina, "keeping no regular column, no regular pace. When a soldier became weary he fell out, ate his scanty rations—if, indeed, he had any to eat—rested, rose, and resumed the march when his inclination dictated. There were not many words spoken. An indescribable sadness weighed upon us."[106]

At Amelia Court House the collapse of the Confederacy became apparent. The rations Lee had ordered for his hungry army failed to arrive. Instead, the waiting boxcars, the last to leave Richmond, were crammed

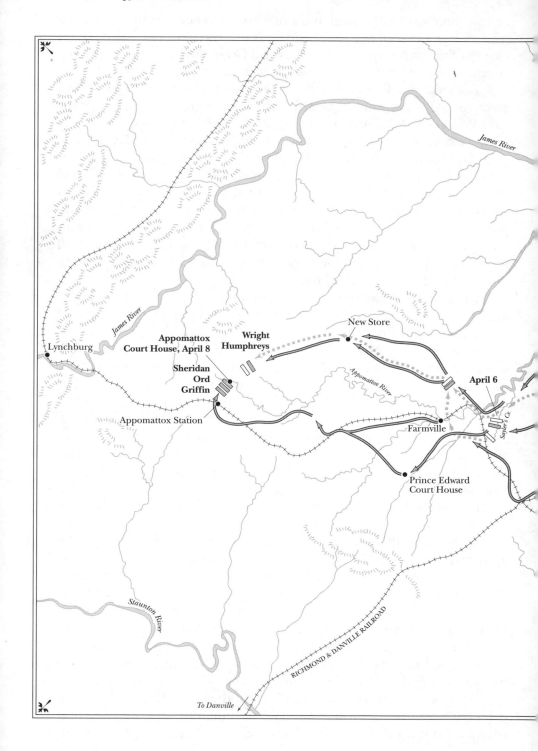

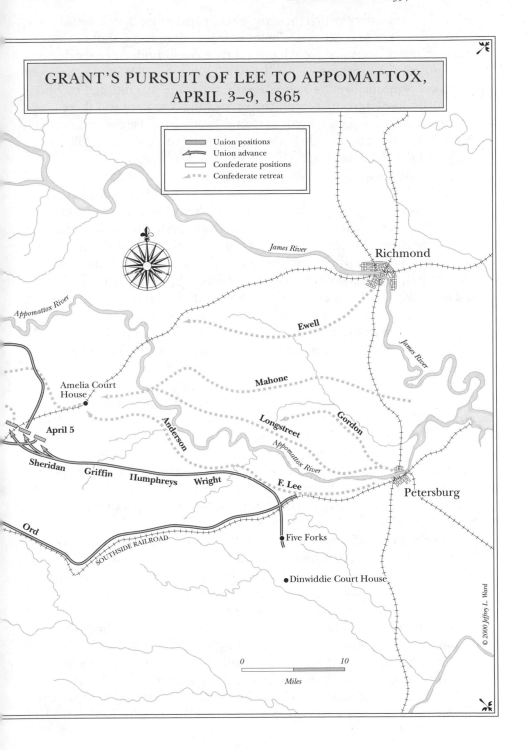

GRANT'S PURSUIT OF LEE TO APPOMATTOX,
APRIL 3–9, 1865

Union positions
Union advance
Confederate positions
Confederate retreat

James River

Richmond

Appomattox River

Ewell

Mahone

Amelia Court
House

April 5

Anderson

Longstreet

Gordon

Appomattox River

James River

Sheridan   Griffin   Humphreys   Wright

F. Lee

Petersburg

Ord

SOUTHSIDE RAILROAD

Five Forks

Dinwiddie Court House

0   10

Miles

© 2000 Jeffrey L. Ward

with ammunition, of which the army already had more than it could carry. Lee's only recourse was to call a halt while his commissary staff scrounged through the countryside for what food they could find. Another day was lost and on the morning of April 5 when what was left of the Army of Northern Virginia began to move south, the route was blocked by Sheridan's dismounted troopers with their repeating Spencers and three corps of Union infantry. Lee veered west and headed for Farmville, eighteen miles away on the Southside Railroad, where he could draw supplies from Lynchburg, before continuing his effort to join Johnston.

Sheridan was first off the mark. "I wish you were here," he wired Grant, who was with Ord's troops fifteen miles back but coming up fast. "I feel confident of capturing the Army of Northern Virginia if we exert ourselves. I see no escape for Lee." [107] Grant was apparently waiting just for such a summons. He immediately set out across the hostile Virginia countryside with four staff officers and a squad of cavalry for escort. Shortly after 10 P.M. he rode up to Sheridan's pickets, who were astonished to see the general in chief ride in out of nowhere at that hour of the night.

Encouraged by Grant to press on, Sheridan fell upon Lee's retreating column the next afternoon at Sayler's Creek, half a dozen miles from Farmville. It was, as historians have written, the "Black Thursday of the Confederacy." [108] Sheridan dismounted his troopers and led them along with two divisions from Wright's 6th Corps straight at the distended rebel line, inflicting more than 2,000 casualties while taking 6,000 prisoners and most of Lee's wagon train. "I attacked . . . and routed them handsomely," he informed Grant. "If the thing is pressed I think Lee will surrender." [109] Late that night Grant passed Sheridan's message along to Lincoln, who was waiting for news back at City Point. The president's reaction can be judged by his response. On the morning of April 7 he telegraphed Grant: "Gen. Sheridan says, 'If the thing is pressed I think Lee will surrender.' Let the thing be pressed." [110]

Lee won the race to Farmville, but his army was melting away. Reduced by straggling, desertion, and battle casualties to fewer than 15,000 men, the troops barely had time to regroup from the defeat at Sayler's Creek before pressing on toward Appomattox Junction, a rail stop twenty miles west on the Southside line where trains loaded with food and forage were waiting. The Union army was close behind. Grant reached Farmville Friday afternoon, April 7, on the heels of the rebel rear guard. He had left all of his baggage behind on that night ride to Sheridan and was still wearing the mud-spattered uniform in which he started out. He sat on the porch of the village hotel, watching the men of Wright's 6th Corps march through town, when a messenger from Sheridan rode in. Little Phil had learned that rations for Lee were waiting at Appomattox Junction and he was hurrying on, confident he could get there first and take possession.

As Grant read the message, Generals Ord and Gibbon came up to ask for instructions.* Without batting an eye, Grant sent them hurrying after Sheridan, intent on heading off Lee while Meade continued the chase. Gibbon remembered that Grant then paused for a moment and, "in his quiet way," unexpectedly said: "I have a great mind to summon Lee to surrender."[111] He seemed as surprised as his listeners by the thought, but immediately called for his dispatch book—a bound book of flimsy yellow paper with black sheets of carbon between the pages—and began to write, dating the message at Farmville, April 7, 1865.

General R. E. Lee
Commanding C. S. Army

General: The results of the last week must convince you of the hopelessness of further resistance on the part of the Army of Northern Virginia in this struggle. I feel it is so, and regard it as my duty to shift from myself the responsibility of any further effusion of blood by asking of you the surrender of that portion of the Confederate States army known as the Army of Northern Virginia.

Very respectfully, your obedient servant,

U. S. GRANT, Lieutenant General
Commanding Armies of the United States[112]

Brigadier General Seth Williams, who had been Lee's adjutant at West Point and who was now Grant's inspector general, was entrusted to deliver the message and Grant settled down to wait. As night fell and the men of the 6th Corps continued to march up the street, they spotted Grant on the veranda, his cigar glowing in the shadows. As in the Wilderness, when he had ordered the army to move south, the troops broke into cheers as they passed, spontaneously saluting the man who had brought them to the eve of victory.

---

* By April 1865, Grant had quietly replaced all of the senior commanders in Virginia except for Meade. As has been mentioned, Ord succeeded Butler commanding the Army of the James; Charles Griffin replaced Warren leading the 5th Corps (Warren was relieved by Sheridan at Five Forks); Hancock, disabled by his Gettysburg wounds, was superseded by Meade's chief of staff, A. A. Humphreys, at the 2nd Corps; Wright had taken the place of Sedgwick with the 6th Corps; Parke replaced Burnside with the 9th Corps; and John Gibbon took Baldy Smith's place commanding the 24th Corps. Those changes, plus the advent of Sheridan, went a long way toward remedying the leadership deficiencies under which the Union army struggled in the spring of 1864.

Lee received Grant's message about 10 P.M. Longstreet was with him at the time. Lee opened the envelope himself, read the letter silently, and then passed it to his lieutenant. "Not yet," said Old Pete. Lee made no reply, but took up a single sheet of ruled note paper and began to write.

7th Apl. '65

Genl

I have received your note of this date. Though not entertaining the opinion you express of the hopelessness of further resistance on the part of the Army of N. Va.—reciprocate your desire to avoid the useless effusion of blood, and therefore before considering your proposition, ask the terms you will offer on condition of its surrender.[113]

Lee was not ready to surrender, but he did not want to break off negotiations. It was well after midnight when Seth Williams returned to Farmville with Lee's reply. Grant was awakened, read the message, and decided there was nothing to be done until morning. He rose early, however, and rode forward so that further correspondence with Lee could go through the lines with the least delay. Like his Confederate counterpart Grant wanted to keep the ball rolling. His answer was conciliatory. "Peace being my great desire," he wrote, "there is but one condition I would insist upon—namely, the men and officers surrendered shall be disqualified for taking up arms against the Government of the United States until properly exchanged." This was a far cry from the unconditional surrender Grant demanded at Donelson and Vicksburg. Now he was saying that once the Confederates laid down their arms they would be free to go, as Lincoln wished, back to their homes and farms with the war behind them. The terms were as generous as Grant could make them, and he went out of his way to spare Lee embarrassment, adding considerately: "I will meet you, or will designate officers to meet any officers you may name for the same purpose, at any point agreeable to you, for the purpose of arranging definitely the terms upon which the surrender of the Army of Northern Virginia will be received."[114]

Lee did not receive Grant's message until late in the afternoon of the 8th. There was no fighting to speak of that day, and the remnants of Lee's exhausted army went into bivouac that evening near Appomattox Court House, just five miles from the trains laden with supplies waiting at the junction. The next day Lee planned to reprovision his forces and, if possible, move south to complete the linkup with Johnston, and if not, continue westward along the rail line to Lynchburg. It was in that frame of mind that he replied to Grant's letter. Denying that he had proposed surrender in his previous response, or that his army was in such dire peril, Lee said only that he would be willing to meet between the lines for a general discussion that might "tend to a restoration of peace."[115]

Grant, who was sometimes beset by psychosomatic ailments in the hours leading up to major events, was suffering from a severe migraine and had gone to bed when Lee's message was delivered. He studied the document and once again decided to answer it the next morning. "It looks like Lee means to fight," he said, more saddened than angered by what he read.[116] What Grant knew, and Lee did not, was that Sheridan had reached Appomattox Junction just before dusk, capturing four freight trains loaded with Confederate rations and driving off three more. Sheridan said he had taken a gun park crammed with reserve artillery and a considerable number of prisoners, and that he was dug in athwart the Lynchburg road, blocking Lee's escape. Ord's Army of the James and Griffin's 5th Corps were following close behind Sheridan. "If they can get up tonight we will perhaps finish the job in the morning," said Little Phil.[117]

Palm Sunday, April 9, 1865, dawned bright and sunny. Grant rose early, took his morning coffee at Meade's headquarters, and then framed his reply to Lee. Knowing that his quarry had been driven to ground, Grant once again held out an olive branch. He declined to meet Lee between the lines for a general discussion, an area Lincoln had warned him not to enter, but renewed his plea for an end to the fighting. By laying down their arms now, he said, the South could have peace. There were no further conditions. "Seriously hoping that all our difficulties may be settled without the loss of another life, I subscribe myself, etc. *U. S. Grant*, Lieutenant General."[118] As best he could, Grant was keeping the door ajar, allowing Lee time to adjust to the situation created by Sheridan's arrival at Appomattox Junction.

For Lee, Palm Sunday was a day of increasing disappointment. Reduced to little more than 12,000 combat effectives, with only sixty-one guns remaining, his only hope was to punch through Sheridan's line and escape. Again, it was John B. Gordon to whom he turned, believing that if anyone could lead a breakout it was the hard-fighting general from Georgia. Gordon did his best. He hit Sheridan's dismounted troopers at dawn and sent them reeling. But then, as he watched the cavalrymen scamper to safety reality stared him in the face. There in the rear of the gap his troops had torn in Sheridan's line stood long rows of Union infantry, rank upon rank, braced and waiting. It was Ord and Griffin, with close to 15,000 men apiece. They had arrived in the early morning hours and were ready to repel any attack. Gordon saw the situation was hopeless. At 7:30 he pulled back and informed Lee that he could do nothing further.

Lee received the message calmly. If a general like Gordon could not break through, the fight was over. "There is nothing left for me to do but go and see General Grant," Lee told his staff, "and I would rather die a thousand deaths."[119] A subordinate suggested an alternative. The men would take to the woods and fight as guerrillas. "No," said Lee. "We must consider the effect on the country as a whole. Already it is demoralized by four years of war. If I took your advice, the men would be without rations and under no control of officers. They would be compelled to rob and steal in order to live. They would become mere bands of marauders, and the enemy's cavalry would pursue them and overrun many sections they may never have occasion to visit. We would bring on a state of affairs it would take the country years to recover from."[120]

Lee headed out to meet Grant shortly before nine. He was accompanied by an orderly bearing a flag of truce—a soiled white handkerchief, tied to a stick—and his military secretary, Lieutenant Colonel Charles Marshall, grandson of the great chief justice. The three horsemen had gone little more than half a mile when they met a Union officer, also under a flag of truce, bearing the message Grant had written that morning. Lee, who had assumed the meeting he had requested the previous evening was still in place, was startled by Grant's reply and initially feared that the general in chief, now that he had the Confederate army virtually surrounded, intended to impose harsher conditions. Lee's misgivings were heightened when the rumble of artillery, marking Meade's advance, sounded from the front. Yet he had no alternative. He dictated the following message to Marshall:

April 9th, 1865

General,

I received your note this morning on the picket line, whither I had come to meet you and ascertain definitely what terms were embraced in your proposal of yesterday with reference to the surrender of this army. I now ask an interview in accordance with the offer contained in your letter of yesterday for that purpose.[121]

Lee signed the letter in a large, bold hand, and sent Marshall forward to arrange a cease-fire while the message was being delivered. That proved easier said than done. Both Meade and Sheridan were moving forward for what they knew would be the final assault of the war and neither wanted to back off, lest the rebel army escape. Accordingly, Lee wrote out a second message to Grant requesting a suspension of hostilities until the terms of surrender could be established.[122] Marshall gave the letter to Meade, who reluctantly ordered an informal cease-fire until Lee could get in touch with Grant, and at five minutes after eleven on Palm Sunday the Union guns went silent.

Grant was riding toward Sheridan when Lee's first message was delivered. It was then close to noon. Grant dismounted and read the letter, sitting on a grassy knoll by the roadside. Later he wrote that the migraine from which he was suffering disappeared immediately.[123] Grant asked for his dispatch book and dashed off a quick reply. He told Lee where he was and said he would "push forward to the front for the purpose of meeting you." The message was entrusted to Grant's aide Lieutenant Colonel Orville Babcock, who was told to escort Lee to whatever site he chose.[124]

It took Babcock thirty minutes to reach Lee. When he rode up, he found him sitting on a blanket-covered pile of fence rails, talking to Longstreet. Lee was concerned, Longstreet later reported, that Grant might demand stiffer terms. Old Pete did not think so. He told Lee that he had known Grant intimately before the war, and he believed he would impose only such terms as Lee himself would if the roles were reversed.[125]

Lee sat up when Babcock dismounted, and then rose to greet him.* After digesting the contents of Grant's note, he sent Marshall ahead to select a suitable meeting place. Then he set out with Babcock alongside and his orderly, Sergeant George Tucker, ahead. At a stream, Lee paused to let Traveller drink, and then rode on to the little village of Appomattox Court House, where Colonel Marshall had found a first-floor parlor room in the house of Wilmer McLean, on the south side of the road to Lynchburg. In a curious quirk of fate, McLean had owned a farm near Manassas in 1861 and a shell had come crashing through one of his windows during the opening skirmish of the war. He promptly sold the farm and moved to Appomattox, a remote hamlet in southern Virginia, which he assumed was of no military value to either side. The war he fled was now about to end on his doorstep; in fact, in his front room, where Lee, Marshall, and Babcock now awaited Grant's arrival.

Half an hour passed. Colonel Marshall recalled that "we talked in the most friendly and affable way."[126] About 1:30 there was a clatter of hoofbeats in the road, and a minute or so later Babcock saw Grant coming up the steps to the porch, followed by Ord, Sheridan, Rawlins, and assorted staff officers. Grant came in alone. He was wearing the same mud-spattered uniform he wore on the ride to see Sheridan two nights before: a

---

* Babcock was struck by the fact that Lee was in full dress, wearing a new gray uniform, his boots highly polished, a red silk sash gathered about his waist, over which he had buckled a splendid sword with an ornate hilt and scabbard. Though he was always immaculately turned out, this was not Lee's customary field attire. Babcock did not inquire, but when a rebel staffer had commented earlier on his finery, Lee replied: "I have probably to be General Grant's prisoner, and thought I must make my best appearance." Babcock manuscript, "Lee's Surrender," Orville Babcock Papers, Chicago Historical Society; Douglas Southall Freeman, 4 *R. E. Lee: A Biography* 118 (New York: Charles Scribner's Sons, 1934).

government-issue flannel shirt with trousers tucked into muddy boots, no side arms, not even spurs, the only sign of rank being the tarnished shoulder straps pinned to his blouse. Colonel Marshall thought "he looked as though he had had a pretty hard time." Colonel Amos Webster of Grant's staff put it less charitably, recalling that "Grant, covered with mud in an old faded uniform, looked like a fly on a shoulder of beef." [127]

The generals greeted each other cordially. Grant took a chair in the middle of the room and Lee resumed his seat by an unlit fire, while Marshall remained standing beside him. "What General Lee's feelings were I do not know," Grant said later. "As he was a man of much dignity, with an impassive face, it was impossible to say whether he felt inwardly glad that the end had finally come, or felt sad over the result, and was too manly to show it. Whatever his feelings, they were entirely concealed from my observation; but my own feelings, which had been quite jubilant on the receipt of his letter, were sad and depressed. I felt like anything rather than rejoicing at the downfall of a foe who had fought so long and valiantly." [128] The two men chatted easily for a few minutes, recalling the time they met in Mexico, after which Babcock ushered in Sheridan, Ord, and Rawlins, as well as a number of other Union officers. The newcomers arranged themselves behind Grant as quietly as swords and spurs would permit. Grant made no reference to their coming. Lee showed no resentment at their presence. [129]

Presently, Lee brought the conversation around to the subject they had been avoiding. "I suppose, General Grant, that the object of our present meeting is fully understood. I asked to see you to ascertain upon what terms you would receive the surrender of my army." Grant responded quietly, with no visible change of expression. "The terms I propose are those stated substantially in my letter of yesterday,—that is, the officers and men who are surrendered are to be paroled and disqualified from taking up arms again until properly exchanged, and all arms, ammunition, and supplies to be delivered up as captured property."

Like Grant, Lee continued to mask his feelings, but inwardly he certainly breathed a sigh of relief: Longstreet had been right and his own fears had been groundless. He told Grant the conditions were more or less what he expected. The conversation then drifted into unrelated matters until Lee once again returned to the subject at hand. Speaking with the understated courtesy of a man fifteen years Grant's senior, he asked that the terms be written out "so that they may be formally acted upon." Grant immediately agreed and called for his dispatch book, which he opened flat on the small round marble-topped table in front of him. He lit his cigar, puffed furiously for a minute or so, waved the smoke aside and began to write. "When I put my pen to paper I did not know the first word I should make use of in writing the terms," Grant said later. "I only knew what was in my mind, and I wished to express it clearly so there could be no mistaking it." He did just that. Writing rapidly, he brought the war in Virginia to a close with less than 200 well-chosen words, reflecting the charity that Lincoln desired and his own innate generosity. Officers were to give their individual paroles not to take up arms against the government of the United States until properly exchanged, and were to sign paroles for the men of their commands. Artillery and small arms were to be parked and stacked, "and turned over to the officers appointed by me to receive them. This will not embrace the side arms of the officers, nor their private horses or baggage. This done, each officer and man will be allowed to return to their homes, not to be disturbed by United States authority so long as they observe their paroles and the laws in force where they reside." By adding the final two sentences, Grant was taking a massive step toward reconciliation. Not only was the military dignity of his opponents being respected, but there would be no imprisonment or captivity. More important, there would be no trials or witch hunts. Strictly speaking, the rebels had committed treason. But Grant's last sentence, written on his own initiative, effectively pardoned all who surrendered. It was a general amnesty, which, he hoped, would free the country from reprisals and vengeance.

When he was finished, Grant walked over to Lee and handed him the dispatch book. "General, is that satisfactory?" Lee read the document carefully. His expression did not change until he reached the closing sentence. He looked up and said warmly, "This will have a very happy effect upon my army." Grant asked if he wished to make any changes before an official copy was prepared for signing. Lee hesitated. Then he said the Confederate cavalrymen and artillery soldiers owned their horses. Would they be permitted to retain them? This came as a surprise to Grant. He told Lee that as written, the terms did not permit it. Only the officers were allowed to take their private property. Lee read the document again. "No, I see the terms do not allow it; that is clear."

Grant responded sympathetically. He knew what Lee wanted, and he would not humiliate him by forcing him to ask for a modification of terms that were already generous. "I did not know that any private soldiers owned their own animals, but I think this will be the last battle of the war—I sincerely hope so—and I take it that most of the men in the ranks are small farmers, and as the country has been so raided by the two armies, it is doubtful whether they will be able to put in a crop to carry themselves and their families through the next winter without the aid of the horses they are now riding. I will arrange it this way: I will not change the terms as now written, but I will instruct the officers I shall appoint to receive the paroles to let all the men who claim to own a horse or mule to take the animals home with them to work their little farms."

Lee was appreciative. "This will have the best possible effect upon the men. It will be very gratifying and will do much toward conciliating our people." Waiting for the final documents to be prepared, Lee told Grant that his army was without rations and had been living on parched corn for the past few days. Grant said he would supply whatever food Lee needed. "Suppose I send over 25,000 rations, do you think that will be a sufficient supply?" Lee agreed that it would. "And it will be a great relief, I assure you."

It was close to four o'clock when the documents were completed. Lee rose, shook hands with Grant once more, and went out onto the porch where several Federal officers sprang to their feet and saluted. He put on his hat to return their salutes, walked down the steps and waited for Traveller to be brought up. Lee mounted slowly and with an audible sigh. At that moment Grant came down the steps on his way to where Jeff Davis was tethered. Stopping suddenly, he removed his hat in salute, as did the officers with him. Silently, Lee raised his own hat in return, and passed out through the gate and down the road.[130]

Grant did not pause to celebrate, and he halted the firing of victory salutes. "The war is over," he told his staff. "The rebels are our countrymen again."[131] He then wrote out a telegram to Secretary Stanton:

> General Lee surrendered the Army of Northern Virginia this afternoon on terms proposed by myself. The accompanying additional correspondence will show the conditions fully.
>
> U.S. GRANT, LIEUTENANT GENERAL [132]

The next day Grant met Lee between the lines for an informal conversation. Sitting on their horses, in sight of the two armies, the two generals conversed for more than an hour. Grant suggested among other things that Lee go to Washington and meet President Lincoln to help restore peace. Lee respectfully declined,* and Grant departed that afternoon for City Point and the capital.

The surrender ceremony took place two days later, when the Army of Northern Virginia formed up for the last time to stack their weapons, furl

---

* Colonel Marshall, to whom Lee spoke after meeting with Grant, quotes Lee as saying: "General Grant, you know that I am a soldier of the Confederate army, and cannot meet Mr. Lincoln." Marshall added that in his view, "I have always thought that if General Lee and Mr. Lincoln could have met as General Grant proposed, we could have had immediate restoration of peace and brotherhood among the people of these States." Colonel Charles Marshall, *An Aide-de-Camp of Lee* 275 (Boston: Little, Brown, 1927).

their flags, and leave for home. The Union officer in charge was Major General Joshua L. Chamberlain, former colonel of the 20th Maine, a twice-wounded veteran who had won the Medal of Honor for his tenacious defense of the Federal flank at Little Round Top at Gettysburg. Two Union brigades were drawn up in double ranks facing each other on opposite sides of the street, leaving space for the Southerners to pass between. The long blue lines were dressed and straight, the troops in full kit, bayonets fixed, and standing at attention. The Confederate column was led by Lieutenant General John B. Gordon of Georgia, Lee's most resolute corps commander, "riding with heavy spirit and downcast face." First in line of march behind him was the Stonewall Brigade, five regiments containing 210 ragged survivors of four years of war. As Gordon approached, Chamberlain gave a brief order and a bugle sounded. Instantly the Union line from right to left, regiment by regiment in succession, shifted from order arms to carry arms, the marching salute. Hearing the familiar snap and rattle of the muskets, Gordon looked up in surprise, caught the meaning, and wheeled to face Chamberlain, "making himself and his horse one uplifted figure, with profound salutation as he dropped the point of his sword to his boot toe."[133] Gordon then turned and ordered each Confederate brigade to march past the Union troops at carry arms, honor answering honor, a soldier's mutual salutation and farewell. In perfect order, the men stacked arms and cartridge boxes and laid down their flags. General Gordon, his eyes moist, addressed the men from horseback, urging them to depart in peace, to obey the laws and work for the future of the united nation.*

* John B. Gordon returned to Georgia and was elected three times to the United States Senate and served two terms as governor. Chamberlain returned to Maine, served four successive terms as governor, and was president of Bowdoin College from 1871 to 1883. They never met again.

CHAPTER THIRTEEN

RECONSTRUCTION

With malice toward none; with charity for all; with firmness in the right, as God gives us to see the right, let us strive . . . to bind up the nation's wounds.

ABRAHAM LINCOLN
Second Inaugural, March 4, 1865

THE TERMS GRANT OFFERED LEE came as a pleasant surprise to most Confederates. His personal undertaking to allow soldiers to keep their horses was especially well received. General Porter Alexander, Longstreet's artillery commander—whose men were directly affected by the promise—thought the tone Grant set bespoke "a great & broad & generous mind." It was fortunate for the entire country, said Alexander, "that of all the Federal generals it fell to Grant to receive the surrender of Lee."[1] John B. Gordon, who met Grant at Appomattox, commented on his modest demeanor. "There was nothing in the expression of his face or in his language or general bearing which indicated exaltation at the great victory he had won."[2] No one knew that better than Longstreet. When Grant spied his old friend on the steps of the McLean house, he walked over, grabbed both of his hands and embraced him. Having just won the greatest victory imaginable, Grant's thoughts were on those hard-luck days in St. Louis when he was peddling firewood and Longstreet had befriended him. "Pete, let us have another game of brag, to recall the old days which were so pleasant to us all."[3]

Like Lincoln, Grant believed it was important to heal the wounds of war quickly. When the president was serenaded at the White House on the evening following Lee's surrender, he had asked the band to play "Dixie," "one of the best tunes I have ever heard."[4] In a similar manner, and with the nation's press focused upon him, Grant declined to visit Richmond on his way back to Washington, arguing that his presence "might lead to demonstrations which would only wound the feelings of the residents, and we ought not do anything at such a time which would add to their sorrow."[5] As one diehard Confederate happily noted, Grant "spared everything that might wound the feelings or imply the humiliation of a vanquished foe."[6] Grant recognized that magnanimity had its critics, especially among those in the North who sought retribution. But as he told Adam Badeau, "Mr. Lincoln is certain to be on my side."[7]

After an all-night passage from City Point, Grant arrived in Washington Thursday morning, April 13, 1865. True to form, he slipped into the Willard Hotel unnoticed, and then walked over to army headquarters to begin the process of winding down the war—which was costing the nation $4 million a day. He instructed Quartermaster General Montgomery Meigs to suspend the purchase of additional supplies, ordered the immediate discharge of convalescent soldiers, canceled the charter of unnecessary vessels, and halted all drafting and recruiting as of that day. In the evening, there was a "grand illumination" of the public buildings in Washington to celebrate Lee's surrender. Grant accompanied President Lincoln on a whirlwind tour of the city, where they were cheered at every street corner.

April 14 was Good Friday. At the president's invitation, Grant attended a cabinet meeting at eleven, very much the hero of the hour, and afterward accepted an invitation for him and Julia to accompany the Lincolns to the theater that evening. It was the final performance of a raucous farce, *Our American Cousin,* and Mary Lincoln wanted especially to see Laura Keene, the actress in the starring role. Before Grant left the White House a messenger arrived with a note from Julia. She wanted to leave Washington at once to return to their temporary home in Burlington, New Jersey, and see the children. "Some incident of a trifling nature had made her resolve to leave that day," Grant said later, and so he made his excuses to the president and left to rejoin Julia at the Willard.[8]

That evening the Grants boarded the private car of railroad magnate John W. Garrett, bound for Philadelphia. At Havre de Grace, Maryland, where the train paused before crossing the Susquehanna, an unidentified man tried to force entry into the car but was rebuffed by the train crew.* The Grants arrived at Broad Street station about midnight and went directly to Bloodgood's Hotel, where a telegraph messenger was waiting. A dispatch was handed to Grant, who read it silently and then passed it to Julia. It was from the War Department:

* It may well be that Grant was a target for assassination. The following day he and Julia received an anonymous letter that read: "General Grant, thank God, as I do, that you still live. It was your life that fell to my lot, and I followed you on the train. Your car door was locked and thus you escaped me, thank God." Julia Dent Grant, *The Personal Memoirs of Julia Dent Grant* 156–57, John Y. Simon, ed. (New York: G. P. Putnam's Sons, 1975).

THE PRESIDENT WAS ASSASSINATED AT FORD'S THEATER AT 10:30 TONIGHT AND CANNOT LIVE. THE WOUND WAS A PISTOL SHOT THROUGH THE HEAD. SECRETARY SEWARD AND HIS SON FREDERICK WERE ALSO ASSASSINATED AT THEIR RESIDENCE AND ARE IN A DANGEROUS CONDITION. THE SEC-RETARY OF WAR DESIRES THAT YOU RETURN TO WASHINGTON IMMEDIATELY.[9]

"It was the darkest day of my life," Grant told newsman John Russell Young. "I did not know what it meant. Here was the Rebellion put down in the field, and starting up in the gutters. We had fought it as war, now we had to fight it as assassination."[10]

Grant told Julia he was filled with apprehension. But it was for another reason. "The President was inclined to be kind and magnanimous, and his death at this time is an irreparable loss to the South." When Julia asked if Andrew Johnson would become president, Grant said yes, and he was not sure why, but "for some reason I dread the change."[11] For one thing, Grant had established a close working relationship with Lincoln. The two men had become friends and they thought alike on most issues. Grant knew Johnson only slightly from his days as military governor of Tennessee, and the remembrance was, at best, mixed. What Grant did not know, but what he sensed, was that Johnson was vindictive where Lincoln was not. That very afternoon, in fact, Johnson had met with the president in the White House—their first meeting since inauguration day—and had complained about the terms Grant gave Lee at Appomattox. "I felt that reconstruction had been set back, no telling how far," Grant recalled.[12]

Grant always regretted not having gone to Ford's Theatre with the president. He was certain that if he had been there he would have heard Booth enter the box and would have been able to protect Lincoln. His admiration for the president added to his sense of loss and kept alive his feeling of guilt for many years.[13]

Grant escorted Julia across the Delaware River to Burlington and then returned to Washington without escort or bodyguard. In the capital, a momentary panic raged. Lincoln's assassination was seen as a rebel plot to subvert the government, and Grant, overcome by grief, was briefly caught up in the hysteria. Not knowing the extent of the conspiracy, he fired off a telegram to General Ord in Richmond instructing him to incarcerate any member of the old Confederate city council who had not taken the oath of allegiance to the United States. "Also arrest all paroled officers and surgeons until they can be sent beyond our lines, unless they take the oath of allegiance. Extreme rigor will have to be observed whilst assassination remains the order of the day with the Rebels."[14]

Ord kept his head. He admired the general in chief but he realized Grant was overreacting. There was no complicity in Richmond, and Ord said so. "Lee and his staff are in town among the paroled prisoners. Should I arrest them?" Ord said to do so would reopen war. "I will risk my life that the present paroles will be kept." Ord told Grant the Richmond leadership was ignorant of the assassination, and asked that he be allowed to use his own judgment. "Please answer."[15]

Ord's message hit Grant like a splash of cold water. "On reflection I withdraw my dispatch," he wired back. Ord was told to handle the situation as he thought best.[16] The exchange between Grant and Ord reflected the old army at its best. Momentarily swept away, Grant had given a rash order. Ord had the moral courage to say it was rash, and when it was called to his attention, Grant had enough humility to admit he was wrong. The next day he wrote Julia that the assassination plot had blown itself out and there was nothing more to fear. Grant said he would sleep in the office a few nights and go out only for meals, but things were returning to normal.[17]

A letter from his old friend Richard Ewell, confined with other Confederate generals at Fort Warren, Massachusetts, helped to restore Grant's perspective. Ewell said that "of all the misfortunes which could befall the Southern people," the worst would be to be accused of complicity in the assassination of the president. "No language can adequately express the shock produced upon myself, in common with all the other general officers confined here, by the occurrence of this appalling crime. Need we say that we are not assassins, nor the allies of assassins, and . . . we would be ashamed of our own people were we not assured that they will reprobate this crime."[18]

For the next two days Grant busied himself with arrangements for Lincoln's funeral. He ordered an African-American regiment back from Richmond to serve as honor guard and organized the official ceremony in the East Room of the White House on April 19. The president's casket, draped in black, rested on a raised platform under a domed black canopy. President Johnson, the Supreme Court, members of the cabinet and the diplomatic corps, congressmen and senators, were seated in the room. At the foot of the catafalque were chairs for the president's family, represented only by young Robert Lincoln. Mrs. Lincoln felt unable to attend. At the head of the catafalque, standing alone throughout the ceremony, was Grant—the living symbol of the cause for which the president had given his life. Correspondent Noah Brooks reported that the general "was often moved to tears."[19] Years later Grant said he would always remember that

Mr. Lincoln had spent most of his final days with him at City Point. "He was incontestably the greatest man I have ever known." [20]

Following the funeral Grant returned to his office to organize the final mop-up of Confederate resistance. Union forces had already marched into Montgomery, Alabama, the first capital of the Confederacy; John Mosby's cavalry irregulars had been disbanded in lower Virginia; and west of the Mississippi John Pope was preparing to take the surrender of the forces commanded by Kirby Smith on the same terms as those offered to Lee. Grant's concern was North Carolina, where Joseph E. Johnston's army was still in the field. Soon a telegram from Sherman arrived, dated April 17. Uncle Billy told Grant that Johnston was prepared to surrender, and they would meet the next day to work out the details. "He evidently seeks to make terms for Jeff Davis and his Cabinet." Sherman said that unless peace was made quickly, "there is great danger that the Confederate armies will dissolve and fill the whole land with robbers and assassins — and I think this is one of the difficulties that Johnston labors under." [21]

Gratified the war was coming to a close, Grant did not pick up on Sherman's reference to Jefferson Davis and the Confederate cabinet. Two days before, Cump had alerted Grant that the end of the fighting was near, and had assured him that he would offer Johnston the same terms Grant gave Lee "and be careful not to complicate any points of civil policy." [22] Grant trusted Sherman's judgment and had always delegated broad authority to him. Given Sherman's previous message, he saw no reason to intervene now. [23]

Grant quickly came to realize that he had been mistaken. On April 21, Major Henry Hitchcock, Sherman's aide, arrived at Grant's office with a copy of the agreement Sherman had made with Johnston. "If approved by the President," wrote Sherman, it "will produce Peace from the Potomac to the Rio Grande." [24] Despite his earlier disclaimer, Sherman had proposed a general peace settlement. Rather than surrender in the field, Confederate troops were to march to their respective state capitals, deposit their weapons in state arsenals, and disband. Rebel state officials and legislators would take the oath of allegiance, whereupon the existing state governments would be restored to the Union with full authority. Courts would be reopened, and all Southerners would regain full political and property rights "as defined by the Constitution and the states, respectively." This provision, it could be argued, would have provided for the perpetuation of slavery. [25]

Grant read the document with increasing concern. Sherman had overstepped and had to be pulled back. Grant hoped to do so without offending his old friend and the sooner it was done the better. He quickly dashed off a note to Stanton (who was at home eating dinner), telling him that the text of Sherman's agreement with Johnston had arrived and that it should be referred to the president and the cabinet immediately. "I would respectfully suggest . . . the meeting take place tonight."[26]

By eight o'clock the cabinet was assembled. Grant read Sherman's memorandum aloud, and not one person, himself included, thought the document should be approved. President Johnson and Stanton were especially bitter in their condemnation, impugning Sherman's motives and suggesting that his action smacked of treason. Grant bristled at the ad hominem and defended Sherman's motives vigorously. But he agreed the document had to be repudiated, and he volunteered to go to North Carolina and notify Sherman personally.[27] Grant wanted to tamp down the crisis. His presence would keep Sherman in line, and he could bring his most trusted subordinate up-to-date on the shifting political climate in Washington.

After the meeting Grant returned to army headquarters and wrote to Julia. It was II P.M., and he said he would be leaving for North Carolina within the hour. It was obvious a crisis had arisen, but Grant did not explain it. Instead, he became reflective. He was clearly bothered by recent events, and turned to his wife for solace. "I find my duties, anxieties, and the necessity for having all my wits about me, increasing instead of decreasing. I have a Herculean task to perform and shall endeavor to do it, not to please anyone, but for the interests of our great country."[28]

Grant, who always traveled unobtrusively, was especially careful this time to avoid attracting notice. He wanted to keep his mission to North Carolina secret because he did not want to embarrass Sherman any more than he had to. He arrived unannounced at Uncle Billy's Raleigh headquarters the morning of April 24, informed his friend why the agreement with Johnston would not do, and told him to negotiate a new accord based on the terms Lee received at Appomattox. Sherman was not surprised. He had been following Northern press reaction to President Lincoln's assassination and had already informed Johnston that their agreement was unlikely to be approved.[29] Grant stayed in the background; Sherman met again with Johnston, and on April 26 concluded a new agreement identical to the terms Grant had given Lee.[30]*

* Like Lee and Grant, Sherman and Johnston conducted the proceedings with mutual respect. Sherman provided ten days' rations for Johnston's troops to facilitate their return to their homes. Johnston observed that the "enlarged patriotism" reflected in the generous terms Sherman offered "reconciles me to what I previously regarded as the misfortune of my life—that of having had you to encounter in the field." Twenty-six years later Johnston, after standing bareheaded on a frosty February day at Sherman's New York funeral, contracted pneumonia and died. "General, please put on your hat," a spectator had urged. Johnston refused. "If I were in his place and he were standing here in mine, he would not put on his hat." Gilbert Govan and James Livingwood, *General Joseph E. Johnston, C.S.A.: A Different Valor* 373, 397 (New York: Smithmark, 1995). Reprint.

While Grant was waiting for Sherman to finish matters, he again poured his heart out to Julia. In his view, it was a time for compassion. "The suffering that must exist in the South the next year, even with the war ending now, will be beyond conception. People who talk now of further retaliation and punishment . . . either do not conceive of the suffering endured already or they are heartless and unfeeling and wish to stay at home, out of danger, whilst the punishment is being inflicted." [31]

For Grant, getting Sherman and Johnston to sign a new accord was the easy part. The more complicated problem was handling the fallout from the episode. While Grant was en route to North Carolina, Stanton had gone public with a virulent outburst against Sherman, suggesting to newsmen that the Union commander had sold out to the rebels and might even be complicit in facilitating Jefferson Davis's escape. Halleck, whom Grant had sent to Richmond, compounded matters by suggesting that Sherman's troop movements would allow Davis to escape capture and flee to Europe with the gold from the Confederate treasury.* Grant was personally outraged at the comments, which he considered "infamous," but the general in chief's reaction was pale beside that of Sherman. [32] The victor of Atlanta fired back at Stanton, and in a flurry of public letters let loose his pent-up feelings about the secretary of war. "It is true that noncombatants, men who sleep in comfort and security while we watch on distant lines, are better able to judge than we poor soldiers, who rarely see a newspaper, hardly hear from our families, or stop long enough to draw our pay. I envy not the task of 'reconstruction,' and am delighted that the Secretary of War has relieved me of it." [33]

With the revised agreement between Sherman and Johnston in his pocket, Grant headed back to Washington to continue the work of winding down the army.† The high point before the men were mustered out

---

* Davis and a shadow Confederate government had fled Richmond with Lee's retreating troops and then traveled south to join Johnston. When Johnston surrendered, Davis continued south and was apprehended at Irwinville, Georgia, on May 10. He was imprisoned at Fortress Monroe, off Hampton Roads, Virginia, where he remained for two years until released without trial.
† One of Grant's responsibilities as general in chief was to keep watch over the officer corps as the army decreased in size, retaining those senior officers who had proved capable, separating those who were less so. By and large, Grant leaned toward retaining regulars rather than volunteers. A volunteer general, he wrote Sherman, would be more likely to "introduce hostilities where a milder course would be much more efficient. An officer whose rank is permanent has a personal interest in preserving quiet." One officer Grant did not overlook when it came time for retention was "Old Buck" Buchanan, his former commanding officer in the 4th Infantry at Fort Humboldt. At the age of fifty-five, Buchanan was still a regular's regular, and though he had forced Grant's resignation from the army in 1854, the general in chief bore no resentment. "I have the honor to recommend that Brevet Major General R. C. Buchanan be brevetted Colonel [in the regular army] for his service at the battle of Gaines Mills, June 27, 1862," Grant wrote Stanton on October 18. Grant said that such a promotion would be "just to him and would

was a mammoth parade set for May 23 and 24, when the massed armies of Meade and Sherman would march down Pennsylvania Avenue and pass in review before Grant, Stanton, and the new president. First, however, there was some unfinished business on the Rio Grande. Mexico was still under the heel of the Emperor Maximilian, supported by a French army of occupation. Grant, with President Johnson's blessing, wanted to topple the regime and restore Benito Juárez, the duly elected president. As Grant saw it, Napoleon III's effort to establish a colonial empire in Mexico was a deliberate attempt to subvert the United States. Maximilian's Mexico had given aid and comfort to the Confederacy, and the victory of the Union would not be complete until the French army was forced to withdraw. Those were the policy reasons. But Grant's motives were also personal. Like many who had fought in the Mexican War, Grant had developed an abiding affection for the land and the people. He always felt guilty about the war and believed the American cause was unjust. The United States, he thought, had an obligation to Mexico, and by helping to liberate it some of that debt would be paid.[34]

As general in chief of what was still the most powerful army in the world, Grant had the means to do so. In late April he assembled a force of 50,000 men in south Texas, ostensibly to ensure the area's speedy return to the Union. Then on May 3 he sent for Sheridan. Little Phil's written instructions were to assume command in Texas and Louisiana and take the surrender of all remaining Confederate troops in the region. Off the record, Grant told him to assist Juárez in any way possible, and to be ready to intervene if the opportunity presented itself. Grant thought that possibility was small—Secretary of State Seward adamantly opposed any action that might precipitate war with France—but he was confident that with 50,000 troops camped along the Rio Grande under the Union's most aggressive commander, Maximilian's days would be numbered. Once again, Sheridan did not disappoint. He established contact with Juárez, surreptitiously supplied him with 60,000 rifles, and breathed new life into the republican cause. By the summer of 1866, Juárez's forces controlled all of northern Mexico down to San Luis Potosí. At that point Napoleon III cut his losses, withdrew the French army, and Maximilian's empire collapsed.[35]

The grand review of the Army of the United States was a military spectacle that has never been equaled. For two days the troops marched past—200,000 men in glorious unison—a final celebration and a fitting close. The war was over, the badges of mourning for Lincoln's death had

---

place his relative rank among brother officers" who had received similar promotions. Grant to Sherman, March 3, 1866; Grant to Stanton, October 18, 1866, 16 *Grant Papers* 92–93, 337.

been removed from the buildings in Washington, and for the first time since April 15 the White House flag was back at full staff.

May 23 began hazy and overcast, but the clouds burned away quickly. Promptly at 9 A.M. a distant signal gun sounded and the Army of the Potomac stepped out on the three-mile line of march from the Capitol to the White House. At the head of the column rode Meade on Old Baldy, followed by Sheridan's cavalry, seven miles in length, and four corps of infantry. For nearly eight hours the procession continued, the troops in perfect alignment, muskets glimmering, bands playing, bullet-riddled battle flags proudly carried aloft.

The next day was Sherman's turn. At nine o'clock another signal gun and the Army of the Tennessee began its march. These were the men of Shiloh, Vicksburg, and Atlanta, a leathery, hard-looking bunch. Most of them had marched 3,000 miles; some were said to have gone 7,000. The rank and file were not so well dressed as the Army of the Potomac. They marched with the long, loping step of light infantry, contemptuous of regulation drill, eager to arrive at their destination. As Sherman approached the White House reviewing stand a band broke into "Marching Through Georgia," which the troops picked up with full-throated enthusiasm. Sherman dismounted, took his place in the reviewing stand, shook hands warmly with President Johnson, and, with calculated offense, refused the outstretched hand of Secretary of War Stanton, turning instead to embrace Grant. At 3:30 the last artillery caisson passed and the review concluded. By November 1865, the Union's million-man army would be reduced to 183,000, and by the end of 1866 to about 25,000—a number that remained constant for the next thirty years.

Reconstruction was now front and center. Five days after the review President Johnson, acting pursuant to his constitutional authority to grant pardons and reprieves, issued an amnesty proclamation to restore civil rights to most Southerners upon taking an oath of allegiance. There were a number of exceptions: Confederate generals, West Point graduates who had resigned their commission to join the Confederacy, and individuals possessing more than $20,000 in taxable property. When shown a draft of the proclamation, Grant had objected to the exclusions, but overall he supported the measure, believing it was a step in the right direction.[36] There was also an escape clause. Individuals in the excluded categories could petition the president directly for a pardon, with the assurance that "clemency will be liberally extended."[37]

Grant hoped Lee would take advantage of that provision. As he wrote Halleck, although a pardon for Lee would be opposed by many in the North, "I think it would have the best possible effect towards restoring good feelings and peace in the South. . . . All the people there except a few political leaders will accept whatever he does as right and will be guided by his example." [38]

Lee, who was well aware of his hold on Southern opinion, had come to the same conclusion. He would petition for a pardon. As he informed Beauregard, "True patriotism sometimes requires of men to act exactly contrary, at one point to that which it does at another, and the motive which impels them—the desire to do right—is precisely the same. The circumstances which govern their actions change; and their conduct must conform to the new order of things." [39]

While Grant and Lee were taking the high road to reconciliation, the seeds of vengeance were sprouting in the North. Led by the *New York Times,* much of the nation's press began a crusade to try Lee for treason. Benjamin Butler, back in Washington after his lackluster leadership of the Army of the James, told Johnson that Grant "had no authority to grant amnesty" at Appomattox, and Attorney General James Speed, acting at the president's behest, provided a legal opinion that "the terms of capitulation were strictly military," implying that they provided no shield against subsequent civil action. [40] This was the context when, on June 7, 1865, a federal grand jury sitting in Norfolk indicted Lee, Johnston, Longstreet, and a host of other Confederate generals for treason.

According to his most distinguished biographer, Lee was not worried about standing trial, but he questioned whether such proceedings were permissible under the terms of the Appomattox agreement. [41] Lee believed he should write to Grant, the officer who had taken his parole, but he was not certain what the general in chief's reaction would be, and he did not want to embarrass either Grant or himself by asking for clemency and being turned down. Accordingly, Lee contacted an old friend, Senator Reverdy Johnson of Maryland, to determine how Grant felt. Senator Johnson communicated Lee's concern to Adam Badeau, Grant's military secretary, and the following day was informed by Badeau that Grant stood by his agreement and would endorse Lee's application favorably. [42]

On June 13 Lee wrote Grant enclosing his petition for clemency, and asking whether the terms of surrender did not preclude actions such as that taken by the Norfolk grand jury. [43] Grant immediately forwarded Lee's request to Secretary of War Stanton with a vigorous endorsement: "In my opinion the officers and men paroled at Appomattox and since . . . cannot be tried for treason so long as they observe the terms of their parole. This is my understanding. Good faith as well as true policy dictates that we should observe the conditions of that convention."

Grant reminded Stanton that the terms he imposed at Appomattox "met with the hearty approval of the President at the time, and of the country generally." He said that the action by the grand jury in Norfolk "has already had an injurious effect, and I would ask that [presiding judge John C. Underwood] be ordered to quash all indictments found against paroled prisoners of war, and to desist from further prosecution of them."[44] Stanton, who was less enthusiastic than Grant about clemency for Lee, dutifully carried Lee's request to a cabinet meeting the next day but did not press the issue and the matter was postponed.[45] Grant then took it upon himself to raise the matter with the president.

When Grant went to the White House, he found Johnson unyielding. The president said he wanted "to make treason odious," stating that Lee and other rebel leaders had to face punishment. Grant objected. He told Johnson he could do as he pleased "about civil rights, confiscation of property, and so on," but the terms of Appomattox had to be honored.

"When can these men be tried?" asked Johnson.

"Never," replied Grant. "Never, unless they violate their parole."

Johnson persisted, demanding by what right "a military commander interferes to protect an arch-traitor from the laws."

Grant, who rarely lost his temper, was livid. He told the president that as the responsible commander in the field he had an obligation to destroy Lee's army. "I have made certain terms with Lee, the best and only terms. If I had told him and his army that their liberty would be invaded, that they would be open to arrest, trial, and execution for treason, Lee would have never surrendered, and we should have lost many lives in destroying him. My terms of surrender were according to military law, and so long as General Lee observes his parole, I will never consent to his arrest. *I will resign the command of the army rather than execute any order to arrest Lee or any of his commanders so long as they obey the law.*"[46]

Andrew Johnson was a stubborn man, but he knew when he was overmatched. He realized that without Grant's support his administration would be in serious trouble. He did not doubt Grant meant what he said, and so he backed down. On June 20 Attorney General Speed instructed the United States attorney in Norfolk to drop the proceedings. Grant then wrote to Lee, enclosed a copy of his endorsement of Lee's request for clemency, and, without mentioning his discussion with Johnson, said simply that the government had accepted his interpretation.[47] In effect, the general in chief would defend the Appomattox agreement, Lee would not be prosecuted, and the nation was spared a reopening of old wounds. If Appomattox was Grant's finest hour, his determination to protect those who surrendered there ranks a close second.

Grant eased off during the summer of 1865. After four arduous years at the front, living much the same as the troops he commanded, the general in chief welcomed the opportunity to relax and unwind. Basking in the nation's adoration, he visited New York and received a hero's welcome.

His last visit had been in 1854 when he arrived penniless and despondent, discharged from the army and without employment. In his own quiet way he completed the circle, staying at the Astor House, the hotel where Simon Buckner saved him from eviction ten years before. From New York he traveled to West Point, where he called on General Winfield Scott, the grand old man of the American army, then living in retirement at the military academy. Scott, seventy-nine, received Grant in full regalia. His memoirs had recently been published* and Scott had inscribed a copy for Grant, "From the Oldest to the Greatest General." Scott had been an early hero of Grant's, and as a prominent Virginian who remained loyal to the Union, his star was never brighter. Grant stood in awe before his old commander, who took him by the arm and escorted him to lunch overlooking the Hudson.

From West Point, Grant went to Chicago to attend a fair organized to benefit disabled soldiers and sailors. His Chicago welcome, if anything, surpassed his reception in New York. Mounted on old Jack, the clay-bank warhorse who faithfully bore him along the icy roads to the field at Donelson, Grant led a procession through the Windy City that was witnessed by half a million people. After Chicago, Grant returned briefly to Washington before leaving on an extended tour of the Northeast and Canada, arriving in Galena on August 18. There he was greeted by another gala reception, welcoming speeches by Congressman Washburne and the town dignitaries, and the gift of a substantial summer home, given to the Grants to use whenever they had the opportunity. From Galena, the Grants went to Covington, Kentucky, to visit Jesse and Hannah, and were back in Washington on October 6. "Do you see that pile of baggage," Grant said to a friend when a grossly overloaded railway baggage cart was pulled past. "Well, that is the Grant baggage. Do you see that little black valise way up on top? That's mine."[48]

Grant had hoped to live in Philadelphia and commute each week to Washington. Learning the general's preference, the Union League promptly purchased an elegant town house for him at 2009 Chestnut Street, which they proceeded to furnish in elaborate fashion.[49] Julia loved the house, but Grant soon found that his responsibilities as general in chief required his constant presence in Washington. In late October he purchased a large, four-story, Federal-style dwelling at 205 I Street, NW, moved most of the furniture that had been given to him from Philadelphia, and rented out the house on Chestnut Street for $1,600 a year.[50] Grant put no cash into the Washington property. It was bought for him by a family friend from Missouri, Abel Rathbone Corbin, who later married

* *Memoirs of Lieut.-General Scott* (New York: Sheldon, 1864).

Grant's sister Virginia (Jennie). Corbin, former editor of the *Missouri Republican,* had made a fortune in the stock market, and frequently acted as an agent for New York speculators Jay Gould and James Fisk. Corbin paid $30,000 for the I Street property, transferred title to Grant, and took back a mortgage for the entire amount, which Grant agreed to amortize over ten years. "I suppose a man out of debt would be unhappy," the general in chief wrote Charles Ford, an old friend in St. Louis. "I never tried the experiment myself, however." [51]

Grant did not stay in debt long. In fact, he made no payment on the mortgage. In February 1866, Major General Daniel Butterfield, a volunteer officer with deep roots in the New York financial world, presented the general in chief with a testimonial check for $105,000. Butterfield recognized that Grant's social obligations in postwar Washington would probably exceed his income, and for the past several months he had been busy raising money from his Wall Street friends on Grant's behalf. [52] A third of the amount Butterfield raised went to pay off the mortgage on the I Street property, $55,000 was put into government bonds, and the general in chief took the remainder in cash. [53]

Grant accepted the largess without question. As he saw it, the houses in Philadelphia and Galena, as well as the one in Washington, were gifts from a grateful nation for a job well done. [54] No laws were infringed, the gifts (at least in Philadelphia and Galena) were public and aboveboard, and there was no assumption of a future quid pro quo. The Washington transaction and the New York testimonial were not so disinterested. By February 1866 Grant was being touted as the next president by knowledgeable handicappers, and Butterfield and his associates were quite aware of that. To ingratiate themselves with the odds-on favorite could certainly do them no harm. Grant was also not free from blame. As soon as wealth came his way, his good sense deserted him. The gold bug that bit him in California had never died, and Grant was already, albeit unknowingly, shading the line between right and wrong. As in California, he instinctively trusted those he should have questioned. Corbin and Butterfield were experienced operators from the dog-eat-dog financial world, and Grant should have been on guard. [55]

Grant's relations with President Johnson warmed during the summer and autumn of 1865. To some extent, each man needed the other. Johnson, who was moving toward leniency for the South, saw the general in chief as a bedrock of support, which was an accurate reading of Grant's position. Grant, for his part, not only found himself in broad agreement with Johnson's goals, at least as he understood them at the time, but also brought an instinctive deference to their relationship. Andrew Johnson was commander in chief, and Grant was his subordinate. The line of command was clear, and Grant respected that. But Grant also had his own priorities and he needed Johnson's support. The general in chief was determined to topple Maximilian in Mexico, and he depended upon Johnson to give him a free hand.* He also needed the president as a counter to Secretary of War Stanton, whose officiousness was increasingly burdensome. Finally, Grant believed that Congress would make the ultimate decision about how to deal with the South, and until Congress acted, the president was in charge.

The alliance between Grant and Johnson reached its zenith at the close of 1865. In November, the president asked the general in chief to undertake a fact-finding tour of the South and report on the conditions he found. Grant departed Washington on November 27, visited Virginia, the Carolinas, Georgia, and Tennessee, and returned to the capital on December 11. He told Johnson that time was required to bring the South back into the Union, but reconciliation was making headway. "I am satisfied that the mass of thinking men in the South accept the present situation of affairs in good faith."

Nonetheless, the army would have to remain on occupation duty for some time. Grant noted that a habit of lawlessness had crept into Southern society during the war, and it had not yet been eradicated. "I did not meet anyone . . . who thinks it is practicable to withdraw the Military from the South at present. The white and the black mutually require the protection of the general government."

To Johnson's dismay, Grant said the Freedmen's Bureau, which was established during the last days of the war to administer the affairs of freedmen in the South, would also have to remain. In his view, it was "an absolute necessity until civil law is established and enforced securing to the freedmen their rights and full protection." Grant acknowledged there were occasional rogue agents, but the head of the bureau, Major General Oliver O. Howard, was doing a superb job and should be given additional support.[56]

When the 39th Congress convened in December, the question of how to treat the South moved to the top of the nation's agenda. President Johnson, aside from an early desire to punish the leading Confederates for treason, took the position that the Southern states had never left the Union

---

* During late 1865 Grant watched the Rio Grande like a hawk, not only prodding Sheridan to step up his assistance to Juárez, but countermanding efforts by local commanders along the California border to curtail the shipment of arms to the republican forces. "It should not be our policy to prevent the liberals of Mexico from getting all they need from us," he wired Halleck on November 13. "We do not want to give a more liberal construction of the meaning of neutrality than was given by the French Government when we were in trouble." 15 *The Papers of Ulysses S. Grant* 416, John Y. Simon, ed. (Carbondale: Southern Illinois University Press, 1988).

and that their recently elected representatives should be seated immediately in Congress.* Johnson was a Jacksonian Democrat. He had been co-opted onto the Republican ticket in 1864 as a gesture toward national unity, and he looked on Reconstruction as a means of breaking the ascendancy of the South's slaveholding aristocracy and replacing it with a rising white working class of small farmers and village artisans. But his vision of a new South made no provision for the civil or political equality of the freed slave, whom the president viewed as only slightly less pernicious than his former master. "This country is for white men," Johnson told Governor Thomas E. Fletcher of Missouri, "and by God, as long as I am President, it shall be governed by white men." [57] †

During the last six months of 1865, under Johnson's direction, representatives of the South's white yeomanry assembled in their various state capitals, repealed ordinances of secession, rewrote state constitutions, and enacted legislation (known as Black Codes) that systematically stripped African-Americans of the political and social benefits of emancipation. This first phase of Reconstruction, labeled Presidential Reconstruction by historians, sought to bring the white South back into the Union at the expense of Negro rights.

The Republican Congress saw matters differently. Most members were shocked at the treatment of the freedmen by the post-Appomattox state governments in the South, and were unwilling to write off the nation's black population in order to achieve reconciliation. Accordingly, when the House of Representatives convened, the names of the newly elected Southern congressmen (which included sixteen former Confederate officeholders, four generals, and five colonels) were omitted from the roll. Instead, a Joint Committee on Reconstruction was established to investigate conditions in the South and report on whether any states were entitled to representation.

In February, acting partly on Grant's recommendation, the new Congress passed legislation to extend the life of the Freedmen's Bureau. That was followed in March by passage of a civil rights bill to ensure the legal equality of the freed slaves and to protect them from discriminatory state

* Johnson's position that the Southern states had never left the Union was partially endorsed by the Supreme Court in *Texas v. White*, 7 Wallace 700 (1869). Asserting that the Constitution created "an indestructible Union, composed of indestructible States" [at 725], Chief Justice Salmon P. Chase held that secession was illegal and that Texas had never left the Union. But Chase went on to hold that during the Civil War, Texas did not have a lawful government, and that under the "Guarantee Clause" of the Constitution (Article Four, Section 4), Congress had the authority to reestablish a new state government. Overall, the decision endorsed the Republican position that Reconstruction was a political problem that lay within the scope of congressional powers.

† During this period the *Jackson News,* Mississippi, carried as its masthead: "This is a white man's country—President Johnson."

legislation. At this point Johnson threw down the gauntlet. Rather than seek a compromise with Congress he vetoed both measures. His rejection of the Freedmen's Bureau bill was sustained by two votes in the House, but his veto of the civil rights legislation was easily overridden, the first time in American history that Congress passed a major piece of legislation over a presidential veto.

Congress now had the bit in its teeth. It followed up its override of Johnson's civil rights veto with passage of the Fourteenth Amendment to the Constitution, and then on July 16 passed (over another presidential veto) a revised measure extending the life of the Freedmen's Bureau for an additional two years. The Fourteenth Amendment, adopted by the requisite two-thirds majority in both Houses, reflected Republican desire to secure constitutional equality for the freedmen, and to insure that Reconstruction remained in the hands of the Congress. Taken as a whole, the amendment enshrined the view of Washington, Lincoln, and Chief Justice John Marshall that the Union derived from the people, not the states, and that the people had made it supreme. Section 1 of the amendment granted citizenship to *"all persons* born or naturalized in the United States," and made every person a citizen of the state in which he resided—thus preventing Southern states from denying citizenship to blacks.* It also prohibited the states from abridging the "privileges and immunities" of citizenship, depriving any person of life, liberty, or property "without due process of law," or denying to any person "the equal protection of the laws." The amendment did not mandate Negro suffrage, but it provided for a proportional reduction in congressional representation for any state that denied the right to vote to any portion of its male citizens.[58] The amendment also barred from office any previous federal or state officeholder who had taken an oath to defend the Constitution and had subsequently supported the Confederacy; it prohibited payment of the Confederate war debt; and it gave Congress the power to enforce the amendment through appropriate legislation.

Johnson fought the amendment. In his view, its passage was illegal, since the Southern states were not represented, and he did not believe a majority of white voters would support equality for blacks. He urged the states not to ratify the amendment and chose to make it the centerpiece of upcoming congressional elections. Grant was caught in the middle. As the nation's top soldier he was obliged to comply with the orders of his commander in chief, yet he firmly believed the ultimate responsibility

* Emphasis added. The intention was to nullify the holding of the Supreme Court in *Dred Scott v. Sandford,* 19 Howard (60 U.S.) 393 (1857), in which Chief Justice Roger Brooke Taney, speaking for the Court, held that African-Americans were ineligible for United States citizenship, even if descended from free persons in a free state. Id at 404–6, 417–18, 419–20.

for making policy rested with Congress. Like Johnson, Grant sought reconciliation with the South, but not at the expense of equal rights for the freedmen.

Throughout the spring of 1866 Grant did his utmost to minimize the conflict between the president and Congress. On April 6, the day the Senate overrode Johnson's veto of the civil rights bill, he and Julia hosted a gala reception at their I Street home, the final event of the Washington social season. "General Grant's reception tonight . . . is a grand affair," wrote a reporter from the *New York Times.* "The capacious drawing rooms and library are literally packed with guests. It is rumored that the ladies are, if possible, more elegantly and richly attired this evening than at any reception this season."[59]

President Johnson, who normally did not attend evening functions outside the White House, came early with his two daughters and remained for an hour or two, standing by Grant's side to receive the guests as they entered.[60] The Radical Republicans, flush with victory on the Senate floor, were equally eager to claim Grant's support. They arrived in a celebratory mood and were stunned at Johnson's presence, but not nearly so much as when they saw Georgia's Alexander Stephens, former vice president of the Confederacy. It was Grant's way of demonstrating that the war was over, and, in fact, Stephens proved to be the hero of the evening. Radical Republican leader Thaddeus Stevens "shook hands cordially with Andy [Stephens]," wrote Ohio Congressman Rutherford B. Hayes. "It was the happiest gathering I have seen."[61] For Grant and Julia the evening was a triumph. Working against the odds, they had created a moment of national reunion amidst the discord of Reconstruction.[62]

The moment was short-lived, shattered by an outbreak of racial violence in the South. On May 1, 1866, a minor traffic dispute in Memphis escalated into three days of rioting and pillage. White mobs, led by numerous off-duty policemen, rampaged through black sections of the city, killed at least forty-six people (eight of whom were discharged Union soldiers), injured scores more, and burned hundreds of homes, schools, and churches.[63] Memphis officials stood by and did nothing. The army eventually put down the disorder, but Grant was appalled. The incident, he told Stanton, "stamps a lasting disgrace upon the civil authorities of Memphis." Grant recommended that the leaders of the riot be taken into custody by the military and held until local officials agreed to press charges.[64] Stanton passed Grant's recommendation along to Attorney General Speed, but to no avail. The Johnson administration was unwilling to intervene. Local law enforcement was a matter for the state of Tennessee, said Speed. "The military stationed at Memphis performed their duty in acting to suppress mob violence. Having done that, they can have nothing to do with the redress of private grievances, or prosecution for public wrongs."[65] Grant's hands were tied. But it was increasingly apparent to him that the Johnson administration had little interest in protecting the freedmen from white terrorism in the South.

For Grant, it seemed as though Union victory was slipping away. On May 26 he told the *New York Times* that those sections of the South that had not felt the war directly "are much less disposed to accept the situation in good faith than those portions which have been literally overrun by fire and sword." Whites in the deep South, he said, had become more defiant. "A year ago they were willing to do anything; now they regard themselves as masters of the situation."[66]

Grant stepped into the void as best he could. In early July, following another rash of violence against freedmen, this time in north Mississippi, Grant dispatched four companies of cavalry to the region. "The object to be obtained," Grant told area commander George Thomas, "is to suppress violence that is now being committed by outlawry in North Mississippi. If the Civil Authorities fail to make arrests for the past violence let the troops make them and hold the parties in confinement until they, the Civil Authorities, give satisfactory evidence that justice will be done."[67] That same day Grant issued General Orders No. 44 instructing all army commanders in the South to arrest civilians for crimes whenever civil authorities failed to act, and to detain them until they could be brought to trial.[68]

Despite Grant's efforts it was impossible to stem the tide of racial violence. In New Orleans on July 30, a white mob supported by city police assaulted delegates to a black suffrage convention, and killed forty people before federal troops arrived to restore order. Sheridan, who was out of town at the time, pulled no punches when he reported the incident to Grant. "The more information I obtain of the affair . . . the more revolting it becomes. It was no riot, it was an absolute massacre by the police. . . . It was a murder which the mayor and police of this [city] perpetrated without the shadow of a necessity. Furthermore, I believe it was premeditated, and every indication points to this."[69] Grant insisted that Sheridan's report from New Orleans be published in full, and then authorized Little Phil to maintain martial law so long as necessary. "Persevere exactly in the course your own good judgment dictates," wrote Grant. "It has never led you astray."[70]

In August, Andrew Johnson took his fight against the Fourteenth Amendment to the country. Traveling to Chicago to dedicate the tomb of the late Stephen A. Douglas, the president converted the trip into a "swing around the circle," an unprecedented speaking tour in which he lambasted the Republicans for refusing to readmit Southern representatives to Con-

gress, and derided the amendment as a threat to white supremacy.*
Johnson's party included all the members of the cabinet, save Stanton, as
well as Grant and Admiral David Farragut. Grant was reluctant to join the
tour, but when Johnson insisted, he acquiesced—doing his utmost for the
next two weeks to avoid being drawn into the controversy.[71]

For Grant, the high point of the tour occurred in New York City the
second day out, when the president's party traveled from lower Manhattan, up Fifth Avenue, and through Central Park on their way to board the
River Queen for a quick trip up the Hudson to West Point. President Johnson, Secretary Seward, Mayor John T. Hoffman, and assorted local dignitaries rode in the first coach, an elegant six-horse rig owned and driven by
industrialist Abram S. Hewitt. In the second coach, driven by financier
Leonard Jerome (whose daughter Jennie would soon marry Lord Randolph Churchill), rode Grant, Meade, Butterfield, George Custer, and Admiral Farragut. Jerome's team was a four-in-hand, a matched set of four
superb animals "the very sight of which would warm the coldest cockles of
a horseman's heart," reported the *New York Times*.[72] Midway through Central Park, Grant, who was sitting on the box beside Jerome, took the reins,
pulled alongside the president's coach, and, "with a twinkle in his eye,"
challenged Hewitt to race to the top of the park. After checking with the
president, Hewitt accepted and the two coaches took off at breakneck
speed. Grant quickly pulled ahead. Jerome's team moved so fast that the
Times reported "the nondriving gentlemen in Mr. Grant's coach began to
consider with some anxiety the probability of a safe arrival." Grant won
hands down, and Johnson was reported to have been exhilarated by the
race. Grant was also pleased. "It was the first time I ever drove a four-in-
hand," he told an incredulous reporter for the *New York Herald*.[73]

Politically, Johnson's swing around the circle was a disaster, although
the trip began well enough. Throngs of well-wishers flocked to see the
president, and state officials turned out in droves. But Johnson's intemper-
ate, often vulgar, occasionally inebriated stump style soon alienated his au-
diences. He allowed himself to be drawn into shouting contests with
hecklers, bandied insults with hostile crowds, and ranted about Republican obstructionism. His message seldom varied: the South was loyal, the
real traitors were the Radical Republicans who refused to readmit South-

---

* Prior to undertaking the trip, Johnson was visited in the White House by a delegation of
African-Americans headed by Frederick Douglass, urging Negro suffrage as a condition of Reconstruction. "Those damned sons of bitches thought they had me in a trap," Johnson told his
secretary. "I know that damned Douglass; he's just like any nigger, and he would sooner cut a
white man's throat than not." Hans L. Trefousse, *Andrew Johnson: A Biography* 242 (New York:
W. W. Norton, 1989). For the transcript of the Johnson-Douglass meeting, see 10 *The Papers of
Andrew Johnson* 41–48, Paul H. Bergeron, ed. (Knoxville: University of Tennessee Press, 1992).

ern representatives, and he, Andrew Johnson, was the one man in Washington who understood that. In St. Louis on September 8 he launched a muddled tirade against his opponents, accusing the Radicals in Congress of plotting the New Orleans riot and blaming them for the bloodshed. Johnson expressed no regret concerning the incident. "Why hang Jeff Davis?" he asked rhetorically. "Why don't you hang Thad Stevens and [abolitionist leader] Wendell Phillips? A traitor at one end of the line is as bad as a traitor at the other."[74]

It was too much for Grant. Despite shouts of "Grant, Grant, Grant" wherever the presidential party appeared, the general in chief had done his best to say nothing and remain in the background: silent window dressing for a tour that had become increasingly partisan. Johnson's remarks in St. Louis ended Grant's reticence. The next day he wrote Julia: "I have never been so tired of anything before as I have been with the political stump speeches of Mr. Johnson. I look upon them as a National disgrace."[75] Three days later, pleading illness, he left the presidential party and returned to Washington alone.[76] The next week when a former aide, speaking in Indiana, mentioned that Grant supported Johnson's campaign, the general in chief sent a sharp rebuke. "No man is authorized to speak for me in political matters, and I ask you to desist."[77]

Back in Washington, Johnson decided that Grant was more than he could handle. It was apparent that the general in chief opposed his policy in the South, yet it was equally clear, especially after the swing around the circle, that he was too popular to remove. Johnson settled on a plan reminiscent of James K. Polk's 1846 attempt to sidetrack Zachary Taylor. He would call Sherman to Washington, send Grant on a diplomatic mission to Mexico, then insert the victor of Atlanta as general in chief ad interim. Alternatively, he could dismiss Stanton as secretary of war and appoint Sherman in his place. Either way Grant's authority would be diminished. But the scheme collapsed before it could be set in motion. Sherman wouldn't bite and Grant wouldn't budge. "This is some plan to get Grant out of the way, and to get me here, but I will be a party to no such move," Sherman wrote his wife in October.[78] When Johnson dangled Stanton's job in front of him, Uncle Billy declined.

Grant was equally adamant about not leaving Washington. Among other things, he feared Johnson might be planning a coup d'état to prevent a Republican victory in November, and he did not want to make it easy. Johnson had already asked Attorney General Henry Stanbery, a prominent Ohio lawyer who had replaced James Speed on July 24, 1866, for an opinion as to the legitimacy of the 39th Congress.[79] Rumors swirled that the president contemplated recognizing a new Congress made up of Southern representatives and cooperative Northern Democrats. In fact, he posed such a possibility to Grant to gauge his reaction. The general in chief did not mince words. "The army will support the Congress as it now is and disperse the other."[80]

Grant was sufficiently concerned about Johnson's plans that he quietly ordered the removal of weapons and ammunition from federal arsenals in the South.[81] He then wrote Sheridan warning him to be on guard. The president, said Grant, had become increasingly agitated about his opponents. "I much fear that we are fast approaching the point where he will want to declare [Congress] itself illegal, unconstitutional and revolutionary. Commanders in the Southern states will have to take great care to see, if a crisis does come, that no armed headway can be made against the *Union*."[82]

By mid-October Grant was so worried that he canceled plans to attend the Galena wedding of his aide Colonel Orville Babcock. "I cannot fully explain to you the reason," he wrote Congressman Elihu Washburne, "but it will not do for me to leave Washington before the elections. This is a matter of great regret to me, but you will appreciate my staying."[83]

The crisis came to a head at a cabinet meeting on October 23. Grant had been invited to attend. As the first order of business, Johnson asked Secretary Seward whether Grant's instructions for the mission to Mexico had been prepared. Seward replied that they had, and began to read them. Grant interrupted to remind the president that he did not wish to go.[84] Johnson lost his temper. Turning to Stanbery, he asked, "Mr. Attorney General, is there any reason why General Grant should not obey my orders?"[85]

Grant was on his feet before Stanbery could reply. As an officer in the military, Grant fumed, he was obliged to carry out the president's military orders. "But this is a purely diplomatic duty." Grant said he would obey any legal military order from the president but this was not one of those. "No power on earth can compel me to it." Grant uttered those words looking directly at the president. Johnson remained silent. When no one else spoke, Grant turned and left the meeting. He returned to his office, gave Badeau a blow-by-blow description of what happened, and then arranged for Sherman to take his place on the Mexican mission.[86]*

Grant's fear of a presidential coup was not unfounded. With two weeks remaining before the election, Johnson was pressing to deploy federal troops in Maryland to support the white supremacist state govern-

---

* After the cabinet session, Johnson continued to fret about Grant's refusal. On October 26 he wrote Stanton, instructing him to "request General Grant to proceed" to Mexico. Stanton passed the request along to Grant, who replied in writing the next day, once more declining to go. The matter ended on October 30 when Johnson wrote Stanton to prepare orders for Sherman instead. The correspondence is reprinted in 16 *Grant Papers* 357–359.

ment against Unionist forces in Baltimore.[87] The issue involved adding ex-rebels to the voting lists, many of whom did not qualify. City registrars were opposed to adding the names and the governor was threatening to replace the officials with men more sympathetic. When Johnson asked the army to intervene on the governor's side to prevent violence, Grant dug in his heels. The use of troops, he advised the president, "would produce the very result intended to be averted." Grant said military intervention before an election "would be interpreted as giving aid to one of the factions no matter how pure the intentions or how guarded and just the instruction." If the president wanted to order troops to Baltimore, that was his prerogative. But Grant made it clear that Johnson would bear personal responsibility. To drive that point home, the general in chief said he hoped he would never be called upon "to send troops into a state *in full relations with the General Government,* on the eve of an election, to preserve the peace." Grant told Johnson that if an insurrection occurred, the law specified the method for ordering troops to the scene. "No such condition seems to exist now."[88]

From their different perspectives, Grant and Johnson continued to monitor the situation in Baltimore. Grant, wearing civilian clothes, visited the city twice in the next ten days to mediate the dispute, and the president rumbled about declaring martial law, but the troops were never ordered out. In the end, the election came and went peacefully. The Democrats claimed victory, Johnson rejoiced, and Grant was hailed as a peacemaker by both parties.[89]

The Democratic victory in Maryland was the exception in 1866. Elsewhere Johnson's supporters were swept away in a Republican landslide. Thanks partly to Johnson's swing around the circle, the election turned into a referendum on the Fourteenth Amendment, and Northern voters came down squarely on the side of the Radicals. The Republicans elected 128 members to the House, against thirty-three Democrats, and retained their three-to-one edge in the Senate. In every state where a governorship was contested, the Republicans won; in every state other than Maryland where the legislature was up, the Republicans carried it.[90] Seldom has an election been so decisive.

With the election results in, Grant called on the president to urge compromise and conciliation. Those who had fought to preserve the Union, he told Johnson, had spoken decisively in favor of the Fourteenth Amendment, and it was time for the president to pull back. In Grant's view, a failure by the Southern states to ratify the amendment (a course that Johnson continued to encourage) would bring down the wrath of the new Congress. On the other hand, ratification would bring immediate readmission with all the attendant rights and privileges.[91] His argument fell on deaf ears. "I told him my views candidly," Grant wrote former Confederate general Richard Taylor. "It elicited nothing satisfactory from him, but did bring out the strong objection he sometimes shows to views not agreeing with his own."[92] At the close of 1866 Grant was not yet in the camp of the Radicals. But Johnson was pushing him inexorably in that direction.

Did Grant have presidential ambitions? Johnson certainly thought so. Newspaper reports on election eve relate that the president had become so concerned about the possibility that he promised Grant "any favors in my power to bestow" if he would promise not to run. Grant's response scarcely gave Johnson solace. He said he was not a candidate, "But suppose the people insist on making me one, what can I do? And besides, Mrs. Grant has been recently looking at the White House, and she thinks she can run that establishment quite as well as it is run now. And you know, Mr. President, that these women will do pretty much as they please. And Mrs. Grant would decidedly object to my giving any such promise."[93] The exchange is most likely apocryphal. But it was widely reported, which in itself must have given Johnson restless nights.

CHAPTER FOURTEEN

LET US HAVE PEACE

So boys! a final bumper
While we all in chorus chant—
"For next president we nominate
Our own Ulysses Grant!"

MIKE O'REILLY
1868

THE LAME DUCK 39TH CONGRESS reassembled in Washington on December 3, 1866. Its term would expire March 3, and ordinarily the newly elected 40th Congress would not meet until the next December. But the Republicans were unwilling to allow so long an interval, lest President Johnson use the hiatus to undo their plans for Reconstruction. Almost as its first order of business the outgoing Congress broke precedent and enacted legislation calling the 40th Congress into session on March 4, 1867.* That would ensure continuous legislative oversight of Reconstruction and limit President Johnson's ability to act independently. Congress then passed a District of Columbia bill enfranchising freedmen in the nation's capital, a tenure-of-office measure designed to shield Republican appointees from the president's removal power, and the first of three Reconstruction Acts placing the South under military government. All three measures became law over Johnson's veto. Finally, the president's power as commander in chief was curtailed through a rider attached to the military appropriations bill for 1867–1868. Henceforth, any orders Johnson might have for the army would have to be issued through Grant as general in

---

* Article I, Section 4 of the Constitution specified that Congress should convene each year on the first Monday in December "unless they shall by Law appoint a different Day." The action by the 39th Congress marked the first time a new Congress did not convene initially in December. The constitutional requirement to meet in December was repealed by the Twentieth ["Lame Duck"] Amendment, adopted in 1933, which provides that the new Congress meet on January 3 immediately following the election.

chief, who, the rider specified, could not be removed without the Senate's consent. Johnson signed the appropriations bill lest the army's funds expire, but he was furious at the diminution of his constitutional authority.[1]

The three measures Johnson vetoed went to the heart of the president's worsening relationship with Congress: black suffrage, political patronage, and readmission of Southern states to the Union. Johnson opposed black suffrage in principle, but in the District of Columbia, where freedmen constituted one fourth of the population, he found it particularly objectionable.[2] The Tenure of Office Act was pure politics. During the last six months of 1866 Johnson had replaced almost seventeen hundred postmasters, three quarters for political reasons.[3] Postmasterships were the heart of the nation's patronage system and the Republicans responded with alarm. The act prohibited the president from dismissing any appointee who had been confirmed by the Senate unless the Senate concurred. The measure protected the grassroots patronage dear to each congressman. The president's cabinet was afforded less protection. The act stated they should hold office "for and during the term of the President by whom they were appointed . . . subject to removal by and with the advice and consent of the Senate." Whether that applied to Lincoln's appointees (Seward, Stanton, and Welles) was debatable.[4]

The Military Reconstruction Act of 1867, usually designated the First Reconstruction Act, was the most far-reaching of the three measures. The South was divided into five military districts, the existing state governments were declared provisional, and each district commander was vested with plenary authority. In effect, the South was placed under military rule. The act specified that the various state governments would be recognized and their representatives readmitted to Congress as soon as they called new constitutional conventions, provided for black suffrage, and ratified the Fourteenth Amendment. As one historian has observed, the measure was "an unprecedented experiment in interracial democracy."[5]

Grant and Stanton took an active interest in the legislation. The rider to the military appropriations bill was Stanton's handiwork.[6] The Reconstruction Act reflected Grant's view that more effort was required to protect Southern blacks. Military government seemed the only solution. It was deplorable to consider such a possibility, he told Stanton, but the failure of local authorities in the South to investigate and punish crimes against the freedmen "constitutes what is practically a state of insurrection." Grant said military rule would provide relative security "to all classes of citizens without regard to race, color, or political opinions, and could be continued until society was capable of protecting itself."[7]

When the Reconstruction bill went into conference committee to reconcile the House and Senate versions, Grant worked closely with

Sherman's brother, sponsor of the bill in the Senate, to fashion a measure that would provide for black suffrage and at the same time indicate to Southern states how the military occupation could be ended.[8] Grant's role was widely reported. The *New York Independent* noted, "For once, at least, there is no doubt whatever of the General's position. He has spoken in all places, where he could do so with propriety, in support of the bill."[9]

What was most surprising was Grant's endorsement of black suffrage. Throughout 1865 and 1866 he had been skeptical about enfranchising the freedmen, at least immediately. But continued resistance on the part of white Southerners to granting legal equality to African-Americans, combined with the increasing violence in the South, convinced him that black suffrage was essential. Only by weaving the freedmen into the political fabric of the nation could past injustices be corrected and the current wave of violence be brought under control. "The General is getting more and more Radical," Grant's aide Colonel Cyrus Comstock noted in his diary on March 1.[10]

Grant's support for the Reconstruction Act opened a new phase in his relationship with Andrew Johnson. He was no longer simply a military subordinate but a political figure in his own right. Caught in the conflict between the president and Congress, Grant found Congress to be a valuable ally. If Johnson wanted to emasculate Reconstruction, the Radicals on Capitol Hill could be counted on to prevent him. Johnson, for his part, could no longer ignore Grant's wishes. Aside from the fact that Congress had guaranteed his position, the general in chief's popularity ensured that the president could not afford an open break. It was preferable to keep Grant in the administration, where he would at least be subject to the president's direct military orders. In the frontier phraseology that Johnson favored, it was better to have Grant inside the tent pissing out, than outside the tent pissing in. An English visitor to Washington put it more elegantly: "At the present time, when the President and Congress are defying one another, and are at open rupture . . . the General in Chief becomes a very interesting person."[11]

When Congress overrode Johnson's veto of the Reconstruction Act, Grant was delighted. The legislation, he wrote Washburne, would provide a solution to problems in the South "unless the President proves an obstruction." Grant added that Johnson's veto message, redolent with racism, was "one of the most ridiculous that ever emanated from any President."[12]

Elihu Washburne, Grant's longtime sponsor, was one of the few men with whom the general in chief spoke frankly. Sherman was another. Apologizing to Uncle Billy for his tardiness in writing, Grant said he deferred sending a letter "while you were in Mexico because I did not know how to address you except through the Secretary of State and I have nothing to do with that functionary when it can be avoided." Grant warned Sherman about the growing conflict between the president and Congress, and said he wanted to travel abroad for a year or so, "but to leave now would be like throwing up a command in the face of the enemy."[13]

Sherman replied that Grant should not leave Washington under any circumstances. As for himself, he wanted no part of it. The army had enough problems to deal with, and in Sherman's view, "We ought to be allowed to confine ourselves to our pure Military business."[14] As the second-ranking officer in the army,* Sherman commanded United States forces on the frontier, where problems of Reconstruction were compounded with the need to protect settlers crossing the Great Plains. Cump warned Grant of the danger of a race war developing in Arkansas. "The Whites and Blacks are nearly balanced in numbers, and a general War between them would be an ugly case for us." On the other hand, said Sherman, if such a war broke out, it would be like the bear fight in which "the woman said she did not care much whether the bear or the husband whipped."

The situation on the Plains was equally urgent. In December 1866, 3,000 Sioux warriors under Chief Red Cloud ambushed the cavalry patrol of Captain William J. Fetterman near Fort Phil Kearny in the Wyoming Territory. All ninety-four troopers were killed, and the public was crying for vengeance.[15] Both Grant and Sherman were sympathetic to the plight of the Indians, who were fighting to preserve their hunting grounds, and neither wanted to undertake a winter campaign or launch a general war. Sherman's solution was to restrict the Sioux henceforth to the area north of the Platte and west of the Missouri, and to keep the other tribes south of the Arkansas. That would leave a broad band for settlement between the Platte and the Arkansas rivers that Sherman believed could be protected.

Grant agreed. On January 15, 1867, he urged Stanton's approval of Sherman's proposal "provided it does not conflict with our treaty obligations with the Indians now between the Platte and the Arkansas."[16] The general in chief told Sherman that unless he heard otherwise he could consider the plan accepted.[17] Grant continued to watch the situation on the frontier closely. He was soon convinced that many of the Indian agents appointed by the government to trade with the tribes were major contributors to the problems the army faced. They plied the Indians with liquor, ignored their true needs, and sold them repeating rifles despite orders to the contrary. Grant told Stanton, not entirely in jest, that if the system was not reformed, the only course left open would be "to carry on formidable

---

* On July 25, 1866, Grant was confirmed by the Senate as general of the army, an unprecedented four-star rank. Upon Grant's promotion, Sherman was elevated to the lieutenant generalcy.

hostilities until all the Indians or all the Whites upon the great plains are exterminated."[18] Grant resisted public pressure to take military action and left it to Sherman to sort things out. On March 9 he informed Stanton, "Present preparations look more to preventing further massacres than to hostile action toward the Indians on the plains."[19]

Passage of the Reconstruction Act was a massive step toward racial equality in the South. But it was scarcely the panacea Grant expected it to be. The act spelled out how the Southern states could regain representation in Congress, but it failed to specify how the process was to begin. This was a serious omission. With no compulsion to act, white Southerners did nothing, content to remain under military rule rather than cooperate in adopting new constitutions with black suffrage. The 40th Congress met the challenge by passing a Second Military Reconstruction Act (over another Johnson veto), placing responsibility for action on each district commander. The generals were instructed to register eligible voters, establish a timetable for holding constitutional conventions, and set up machinery for ratification.

Grant was optimistic. The day after enactment of the Second Reconstruction Act, he wrote to Charles Ford, his old friend in St. Louis, that he was "looking forward with a good deal of confidence" to a final settlement in the South.[20] In a similar vein he told former Congressman Isaac Morris, another old friend, that Reconstruction was "now in a fair way of being finally and favorably consummated."[21] As he had done so often during the war, Grant was looking on the bright side. He was confident of the force he could bring to bear in the South, but as at Shiloh and in the Wilderness, he underestimated the capacity of the enemy to resist. Above all, he failed to take into account Andrew Johnson's determination to circumvent the will of Congress.

As during the last year of the war, Grant was again at the head of military efforts in the South. Technically, responsibility for the occupation was vested in each district commander. But when in doubt, each looked exclusively to Grant for direction. The difference this time was that Grant no longer had the support of the commander in chief. To the contrary, he was Congress's man, carrying out Congress's policy, which the president strongly opposed. Grant found solace in the fact that in constitutional terms the policy of Congress was the law of the land. His duty was to uphold the law, not to kowtow to the president—and in this instance he firmly believed Congress's policy was correct.

It is a tribute to Grant's diplomatic skill—a trait with which he is seldom credited—that he was able to push Reconstruction and at the same time maintain amicable relations with the president. He gave Johnson all the deference due his office, and by so doing was able to postpone a final break between the Executive and Congress. In a curious way, Grant's equanimity, his ability to move forward without getting flustered, was as important for Reconstruction as it was during combat. His calm demeanor reassured both sides. As his secretary, Adam Badeau, expressed it, Grant felt it was important not to inflame passion.

> He was careful not to exasperate North or South. A word from him would have excited Congress beyond its own control; an appeal to the North might have precipitated another war. He cautioned his subordinates; he strove to hold in check the hotheads in Congress. He felt extreme reluctance to use arbitrary power in the South. But he felt that the emancipated millions must be protected and that the recently hostile population must be held in check.[22]

At first things moved smoothly. "Everything is getting on well here under the Congressional Reconstruction Bill," Grant wrote Washburne in early April. "All will be well if Administration and Copperhead influence do not defeat the objects of that measure." Grant said there had been no interference thus far with the actions of the five district commanders, "all of whom are carrying out the measures of Congress according to the spirit of the acts."[23]

When a mob of white demonstrators in Mobile attacked Republican Congressman William D. "Pig Iron" Kelley of Pennsylvania, John Pope, heading the Third Military District, removed the mayor and chief of police.[24] Kelley was part of a congressional delegation touring the South to organize the Republican party. After the outbreak, Grant instructed other commanders to take precautionary measures to prevent future violence. In New Orleans, Sheridan ordered the desegregation of streetcars and the admission of blacks to jury duty. In the Carolinas, General Daniel Sickles issued orders revising the civil and criminal codes to remove discriminatory provisions that denied the freedmen equal justice. General John Schofield, commanding in Virginia, offered military protection "in cases where the civil authorities fail to give such protection."[25]

Grant provided constant support. He could not issue orders in civil matters, he told Pope, but "I can give my views, for what they are worth." Grant said the district commanders were responsible for the faithful execution of the Reconstruction Act, and that Pope's actions showed prudence and good judgment. "Rest assured that all you have done meets with the approval of all who wish to see the Act of Congress executed in good faith."[26]

Resistance to Reconstruction was most pronounced in New Orleans, and Sheridan moved to take matters in hand. Officeholders who impeded reorganization would be promptly removed, he announced, and on March 27 he discharged the mayor of New Orleans, the state attorney general, and a district judge, all of whom had been implicated in plotting the riot the previous July. Later he removed the white supremacist governor. Grant wired his immediate support. "It is just the thing," he told Little Phil. "I approve what you have done. I have no doubt it will also meet with the approval from the *reconstructed*."[27]

Sheridan's action did not sit well at the White House. Congress had stripped Johnson of responsibility for administering the Reconstruction Act, but as commander in chief he retained the power to appoint and remove the district commanders. If Sheridan insisted on forcing Reconstruction, Johnson planned to remove him and install someone more lenient. On April 5 Grant warned Sheridan to be on guard. Grant said the attorney general was preparing an opinion pertaining to the authority of the district commanders, and he urged Sheridan to make no more removals until it was issued. "Then make up your own mind as to the proper course to pursue, and pursue it, without fear, and take the consequences. No officer is going to be hurt by a faithful performance of his duty."[28]

Attorney General Stanbery's opinion, issued June 12, 1867, interpreted the Reconstruction Acts in the narrowest possible fashion.[29] Despite clear congressional intent to the contrary, he held that the army's control of civil government was restricted to police duties; that district commanders could not remove civilian officials; and that voting registrars must accept without question a prospective voter's oath that he had not participated in the rebellion. Grant was appalled; the district commanders even more so. Sheridan complained that Stanbery's ruling opened "a broad macadamized road for perjury and fraud to travel on."[30] Grant and Stanton protested the opinion, and Johnson was sufficiently shaken by the vehemence of their objections that he chose not to issue the attorney general's finding as an executive order.[31] Instead, it was transmitted to the district commanders "for their information." Grant interpreted that to mean it was not binding.

Grant now became the focus of the Reconstruction Act's enforcement. Until Congress could reconvene, he took personal responsibility. When Edward Ord, commanding in Arkansas and Mississippi, said that pursuant to Stanbery's ruling he intended to register everyone who took the required oath, whether he perjured himself or not, Grant pulled him up short. The attorney general's opinion was merely his own personal view, said Grant. "My opinion is that it is the duty of the Board of Registration to see that no unauthorized person is allowed to register."[32] To Pope and Sheridan, he was even more direct. "Enforce your own construc-

tion of the Military Bill until ordered to do otherwise," he told Pope in Atlanta. "The opinion of the attorney general has not been distributed to district commanders in language or manner entitling it to the force of an
order." [33] To Sheridan he said simply that the attorney general's views were
not controlling unless the argument was convincing. [34] In effect, Grant was
doing everything he could to limit the effect of Stanbery's ruling. As Adam
Badeau noted, "the situation was approaching mutiny on one side, or else
treason on the other." [35]

Congress did not leave Grant out on a limb for long. Confronted
with Johnson's intransigence, the House and Senate met in special session
in July to plug the loopholes opened by Stanbery's ruling. On July 13 Congress passed the Third Military Reconstruction Act, officially setting aside
the attorney general's opinion. Johnson vetoed the measure July 19, and
Congress overrode the president that same day. [36] Under the act, the
Southern state governments were made subordinate to the military district commanders—who were given explicit authority to remove civil officials and appoint replacements. Voter registration boards were authorized
to reject potential voters believed to have perjured themselves concerning
their prior allegiance; future opinions of the attorney general were declared nonbinding; and Grant was given oversight responsibility to insure
that the Reconstruction Acts were faithfully enforced. "The responsibility,
the fidelity, the sagacity of General Grant," said the *New York Times*, "constitute the only guarantee vouchsafed to us for the adequate enforcement
of the conditions dictated by Congress in the spirit in which they were
conceived." [37]

In its haste to escape the sweltering heat of a Washington summer,
Congress failed to heed Grant's advice that the district commanders be
protected by statute from the president's removal power. The commander
in chief's authority to appoint officers in the military was the last weapon
in Johnson's arsenal, and, as Grant feared, when Congress adjourned the
president unlimbered it. His first target was Sheridan. Little Phil was
proving as aggressive in reconstructing Texas and Louisiana as he had been
in the Shenandoah. On July 30, with Grant's approval, he deposed the
governor of Texas, holding him responsible for the upsurge of violence in
the state. Then, in quick succession he removed a majority of the New Orleans city council, the city treasurer, and the chief of police. This was too
much for Johnson. On August 1 he summoned Grant to the White House
and informed him that he intended to relieve Sheridan. Not only that, but
with Congress in recess he planned to remove Stanton as well. Would
Grant take over Stanton's duties as secretary of war ad interim? he asked. [38]

Grant was taken by surprise. Rumors of Sheridan's removal had been
swirling for weeks, and it was an open secret that Johnson wanted to rid

himself of Stanton, the only member of the cabinet who supported the Reconstruction Acts. Yet Grant did not believe the president would move so quickly. Confronted with Johnson's determination, he protested vigorously. Then he returned to his office and put his objections in writing. Stanton, he said, had earned the confidence of the country, and was protected by the spirit if not the letter of the Tenure of Office Act. Sheridan had proved himself to be a brilliant commander during the war and was the most effective military administrator in the South. "He has had difficulties to contend with which no other District Commander has encountered." To remove the two men would send shock waves through the country, said Grant. He warned Johnson that the people of the North would be outraged. "I would not have taken the liberty of addressing the Executive of the United States thus but from a sense of duty feeling that I know I am right in this matter." [39]

Johnson evidently believed that by convincing Grant to replace Stanton he would deflect much of the criticism. He also recognized that Grant's acceptance of the post would tarnish his appeal to the Republicans and make it less likely that he would be the party's presidential nominee. Johnson might be willful and sometimes out of control, but he was also cunning. He was counting on Grant's popularity to shield the administration, while at the same time he was undermining the general's base of support. Whether Johnson assumed Grant would make a difference in the cabinet is less clear. Grant and Stanton were not close, and there was a history of friction between them.[40] But on Reconstruction the two saw eye to eye. Most historians have assumed that Johnson considered Grant a political neophyte who, with Stanton out of the way, could be manipulated to suit the president's purpose.[41]

Johnson had not anticipated that Grant would refuse the post. The president delayed several days and then on August 5 wrote Stanton asking for his resignation.[42] Stanton declined. "Public considerations of a high order . . . constrain me not to resign the office of Secretary of War before the next meeting of Congress," he told the president.[43] Stanton was determined to sit tight. But if the president persisted, Stanton advised Grant to take his position. That would prevent Johnson from appointing someone more objectionable, and it would mitigate the danger that Reconstruction would be scuttled.[44]

Johnson also discussed the matter with Grant. On August 11 he informed the general in chief that he definitely intended to remove Stanton, and he asked once more if Grant would take the post. This time Grant did not refuse. Was there any substantial point of disagreement between them? the president asked. "Nothing personal," Grant replied, but he said they disagreed on the Fourteenth Amendment and the Reconstruction

Acts. This came as no surprise to Johnson. He accepted Grant on that basis and instructed his secretary to deliver his letter of dismissal to Stanton.[45]

Johnson's letter, dated August 12, was in strict conformity to the Tenure of Office Act. Stanton was "suspended" until Congress reconvened, and was instructed to transfer his files and records "to General U. S. Grant, who has this day been authorized and empowered to act as Secretary of War *ad interim*."[46] Stanton denied the president's authority to suspend him without the Senate's consent, but yielded "under protest."[47] Grant thereupon walked across the street from army headquarters to the War Department* and took over Stanton's office on a temporary basis.* Both Grant and Stanton recognized the move was necessary, but it was awkward nevertheless. Stanton was bitter that the change had actually come to pass. Grant tried to pull the sting. "In notifying you of my acceptance," he wrote, "I cannot let the opportunity pass without expressing my appreciation of the zeal, patriotism, firmness, and ability with which you have ever discharged the duty of Secretary of War."[48]

As Johnson anticipated, Grant's acceptance of Stanton's post sent tremors through the Republican party. The *New York Independent* lamented that the general in chief "appears to have become a cat's paw for the President."[49] St. Louis journalist Carl Schurz, writing to his wife, said Grant had taken "the only step which could prevent him from becoming President."[50] Henry D. Cooke, brother of financier Jay Cooke, made a special trip to Washington to sound Grant out. Afterward he wrote Senator John Sherman that the general's motives were pure. "I have no doubt that Grant's object was to prevent a *general sweep* of the military Reconstruction District Commanders, and the substitution of *obstructionists*."[51]

That was certainly one of Grant's concerns and not without reason. On August 17 Johnson prepared orders relieving Sheridan and replacing him with George Thomas, then commanding the Department of the Cumberland.[52] Removing Sheridan and substituting Thomas was a calculated

---

* Army headquarters was located in the Winder Building on the west side of 17th Street opposite the White House. The War Department was on the east side of 17th, backing onto the grounds of the executive mansion. Grant did his best to keep his two positions distinct. He visited both offices daily, going first to the War Department, then to army headquarters. His staff did not accompany him to the War Department and he made no changes in department routine. Letters to the secretary of war went one place, those to the commanding general to another. Adam Badeau reports that when he was required to see Grant in his office as secretary of war, "I thought he received me with more formality than at other times; but on his return to his headquarters later in the day he threw aside the manner of a Cabinet Minister and was a soldier with his staff, as intimate and unrestrained as ever." Badeau said he thought whenever anything came before Grant as secretary of war, he decided the matter as he thought Stanton would have done, whether he felt that way or not. Adam Badeau, *Grant In Peace* 109–10 (Hartford, Conn.: Scranton, 1887).

move by the president. In peace as in war, Old Slow Trot was solid and dependable. His military reputation was unblemished and his seniority placed him near the top of major generals on active duty. He could be counted on to do his duty, but unlike Sheridan he would not press his adversaries relentlessly. And he was a Virginian. Even more important, however, the removal of Sheridan would send an important message through the South.

Before transmitting the orders, Johnson asked Grant for his opinion. Once again Grant told the president that to replace Sheridan would be a mistake. "General Sheridan has performed his civil duties faithfully and intelligently. His removal will only be regarded as an effort to defeat the laws of Congress. It will be interpreted by the unreconstructed element in the South as a triumph. It will embolden them to renewed opposition, believing they have the Executive with them." [53]

Johnson was visibly annoyed. Sheridan's rule in Louisiana and Texas, the president replied, "has been one of absolute tyranny. He has rendered himself exceedingly obnoxious by the manner in which he has exercised the powers conferred by Congress, and still more by a resort to authority not granted by law." Grant was instructed to transmit the order placing Thomas in command without further delay. [54]

As it turned out, Thomas wanted no part of the arrangement. He was suffering from a liver ailment and was undergoing treatment in White Sulphur Springs, West Virginia. When he learned of his assignment, he fired off an immediate protest to Grant. Sheridan, he said, could do a far better job in Louisiana and Texas than he could. "Knowing my sentiments, I fear the reconstruction of those states will be very much retarded, if it does not fail altogether, by appointing me to that Command." Thomas said the interests of the service would be "eminently more advanced by permitting me to remain in my present command . . . than to place me where I could be of no use whatever." [55]

Grant did not pass Thomas's protest on to Johnson. Instead, he gave the president a telegram from the medical director of the Department of the Cumberland noting Thomas's ill health and asserting that it would be a great risk for him to go to New Orleans. [56] Johnson reluctantly agreed, but he did not back away from his determination to relieve Sheridan. The following week he told Grant to send Winfield Scott Hancock to Louisiana and have Sheridan replace Hancock at Fort Leavenworth. Hancock, like Thomas, had impeccable Civil War credentials. He was also a lifelong Democrat and less likely than either Sheridan or Thomas to press Reconstruction vigorously.

With Sheridan out of the way, Johnson turned to the Carolinas. General Daniel Sickles had also offended Southern whites with his vigorous enforcement of the Reconstruction Acts, and Johnson decided that he too must go. Grant was ordered to replace him with Major General Edward R. S. Canby, a capable professional officer but a cautious commander unlikely to rile the Carolina establishment.[57]

Again Grant protested. This time he challenged the president directly. The Third Reconstruction Act, he said, gave him the responsibility to see that the laws of Congress were enforced in the South. Grant agreed that as commander in chief it was the president's prerogative to name the district commanders. But he insisted upon his right to be consulted "as to the Agents who are to aid me." Furthermore, he said, "I emphatically decline yielding any of the powers given the General of the Army by the laws of Congress."

In Grant's surprisingly harsh words, the relief of Sheridan and Sickles could only be interpreted as an attempt by the president to "defeat the laws of Congress for restoring peace, Union and representation to the ten States now not represented." That was deplorable, he said, because the people "had come to look upon the reconstruction policy of the country as settled whether it pleased them or not."[58]

Grant subsequently withdrew the letter, but he and Johnson were on a collision course. On August 29, acting under the authority vested in him by the Third Reconstruction Act, Grant issued Special Orders No. 429 forbidding the new district commanders from restoring civilian officials deposed by their predecessors.[59] The following day his staff released to the press Grant's letter of August 17 protesting Sheridan's removal. "Every word is golden," proclaimed the *Army and Navy Journal*. The *Philadelphia North American* noted that the letter placed "Grant before the country in his true light as the earnest and reliable adherent of the Congressional policy of Reconstruction and as the determined opponent of the reactionary policy upon which Johnson has been bent." The *Hartford Courant* said approvingly, "Grant is a Radical all over."[60]

Just to be sure the president got the message, Grant distanced himself from Johnson's cabinet. He was a soldier, not a politician, he told the president, and he was uncomfortable when partisan issues were discussed. Besides, he had not been confirmed by the Senate and was only holding office until Congress reassembled. Most important, Grant did not want to be linked to decisions with which he disagreed. He attended the cabinet meetings to which he was summoned, submitted the papers that required the concurrence of his colleagues or the approval of the president, but he retired as soon as his business was completed. As plainly as he could, Grant was indicating that he was not in accord with the administration and did not wish to be identified with it.[61]

The principal issue that separated Grant from Johnson was the treatment of the South. Grant's determination to see that the Reconstruction

Acts were enforced was colored by his desire to bring the Southern states back into the Union as quickly as possible. At the same time he wished to ensure that the rights of the freedmen were protected. He was also concerned about the army's prolonged involvement in civil affairs. "The best way to secure a speedy termination of Military rule," he wrote Ord in Vicksburg, "is to execute all the laws of Congress in the spirit in which they were conceived, firmly but without passion. Politicians should be perfectly satisfied with the temperate manner in which the Military have used authority thus far, but if there is a necessity for continuing too long there is great danger of a reaction against the Army." [62]

Johnson's opposition to Reconstruction was in part constitutional and in part political, buttressed by virulent racial prejudice. In constitutional terms, Johnson believed the Southern states had never left the Union and that with the surrender of the Confederate government they were entitled to immediate admission to Congress, with its attendant rights and privileges. Politically, he recognized that the Democrats could not retain the presidency or capture Congress without the votes of the South.

Above all, however, Johnson was dedicated to white supremacy. In his mind, his task as president was to rescue the Southern states from "Negro rule." His third annual message to Congress left little doubt that Johnson saw Reconstruction primarily in racial terms.[63] "The subjugation of the States to negro domination would be worse than the military despotism under which they are now suffering." Not only were blacks "utterly ignorant of public affairs," but "negroes have shown less capacity for government than any other race of people." If they were given the right to vote, the Southern states would sink into barbarism: "All order will be subverted, all industry cease, and the fertile fields of the South [will] grow up into a wilderness." Johnson said that of all the dangers the United States had yet encountered, "none are equal to those which must result from the success of the effort now making to Africanize the half of our country." [64]

By autumn Johnson recognized that Grant would not yield on Reconstruction. Once again the president decided to send for Sherman. Perhaps he could convince the scourge of Atlanta to take over the War Department.[65] Johnson, who had never served in the military, attributed to Sherman the same motives of ambition and self-seeking that he encountered daily in politics. He failed to understand the loyalty that soldiers often share, and he totally misread the special bond between Sherman and Grant. When Sherman received Johnson's order to report to Washington, the first thing he did was to alert Grant.[66] When he arrived in Washington, he went directly to Grant's office. He stayed in the capital as Grant's houseguest, took his meals with the family, and was thoroughly briefed on the political situation by the time he called on the president. As Sherman anticipated, Johnson indicated that he would like him to supersede Grant as acting secretary of war. The discussions carried over for several days. Johnson did his best to convince Sherman, but Cump made it plain that he wasn't interested in a cabinet post and would certainly not be used against Grant.[67] The problem, Sherman wrote his wife afterward, was that "the president don't comprehend Grant." There was not yet an open breach between the two, but "it is manifest there is not a cordial understanding."[68]

Congress reconvened in early December with Johnson on the defensive. Impeachment proceedings had begun in the House charging Johnson with failure to enforce the Reconstruction acts, and Thaddeus Stevens had introduced legislation to suspend the president pending a trial. Johnson was determined to resist. Where did the army stand? More precisely, where did the general in chief stand? To find out, Johnson called on Grant at the War Department. By now, Grant had come to detest Johnson, but his duty was clear. He told the president he would resist any effort to depose or arrest him prior to the conclusion of an impeachment trial. The constitutional process would be protected. Grant then took it upon himself to inform congressional Republicans of his view and at that point the Stevens bill faded into obscurity.[69]

The most critical issue facing the president was Stanton's removal as secretary of war. Under the Tenure of Office Act, Johnson was required to submit to the Senate his reasons for the suspension within twenty days of the meeting of Congress. If the Senate concurred, that ended the matter. But if it failed to do so, "such officer so suspended shall forthwith resume the functions of his office."[70]

On December 12, 1867, Johnson dutifully complied with the statute. Drafted by Stanbery, the White House message put Stanton's removal in the best possible light. It stressed the president's responsibility as chief executive, his need for advisers in whom he had confidence, and (ironically) Grant's able performance as secretary of war ad interim.[71] Johnson's case was a strong one, and initially his message was well received. Once again, however, the president proved to be his own worst enemy. Rather than strike a conciliatory stance, Johnson resumed his offensive against Reconstruction in the South.

The situation on the Gulf Coast drew the president's attention first. When Hancock assumed command in New Orleans, he initially issued orders nullifying many of Sheridan's policies and declaring the state's civil authority paramount.[72] Grant immediately reversed him, but Johnson sent a special message to Congress tacitly censuring Grant and urging that Hancock be given a vote of thanks.[73] The lawmakers greeted the message with astonishment. Congressman John Covode of Pennsylvania asked if it were a hoax; Washburne offered an amendment to condemn Johnson for removing Sheridan; and the *Washington Daily Chronicle* called the president's message a "direct taunt in the face of Congress."[74]

The following week Johnson replaced two more military district commanders with more conservative generals whom he thought would follow Hancock's example. In the Georgia-Alabama-Florida district, Pope was removed to make way for George Meade, and in Mississippi and Arkansas, Ord was replaced by Alvan C. Gillem, a personal friend of the president's.[75] "The removal of the District Commanders must embarrass reconstruction very much, if it does not defeat it under the Congressional plan," a Republican editor wrote Congressman James A. Garfield.[76] A member of the Georgia constitutional convention informed Charles Sumner that the removal of Pope doomed Reconstruction "because of the persistent opposition of A. Johnson and the encouragement of Rebels to oppose the letter and spirit of the Acts themselves." Georgia Republican Foster Blodgett wrote Senator William P. Fessenden of Maine that the rebels were rejoicing at the removal of Pope. Another Southern Unionist wrote, "It is pitiful to see Congress floundering along, from one expedient to another, vainly endeavoring to tie the hands which they should have chopped off years ago."[77]

Stung by the reaction in the South, Senate Republicans recognized that Johnson, by deft use of his appointing authority, was on the verge of overturning Reconstruction. Conservative senators who had been willing to give the president the benefit of the doubt on the removal of his secretary of war began to have second thoughts. Senate leaders also came to realize that if Stanton were not reinstated, Johnson would be free to ask Grant to step down and could then replace him with a critic of Reconstruction.[78] The mood in the Senate shifted against the president. On January 10, 1868, to the capital's surprise, the Committee on Military Affairs issued a report vindicating Stanton and recommending his reinstatement.[79]

The administration was stunned by the committee report. What had been a remote possibility began to look inevitable. Rather than sustain the president in his choice of advisers, the Senate was moving to reinstate Stanton. That evening Grant reread the Tenure of Office Act. To his astonishment he learned that if the Senate should fail to concur with the secretary's removal, Stanton would be immediately restored to office. If Grant failed to vacate the position, he was subject to a $10,000 fine and a five-year jail term.* The next morning, Saturday, January 11, Grant closeted

---

* Section 5 of the Tenure of Office Act provided: "That if any person shall, contrary to the provisions of this Act, accept any appointment to or employment in any office, or shall hold or exercise any such office or employment, he shall be deemed, and is hereby declared to be, guilty of a high misdemeanor, and upon trial and conviction thereof, he shall be punished therefor by a fine not exceeding ten thousand dollars or by imprisonment not exceeding five years, or both said punishments, in the discretion of the court."

himself with his staff to discuss the implications. Sherman, who was back in Washington—this time at Grant's request to chair a board revising the Articles of War—also attended. Grant said he had intended to hold the office of secretary of war until Johnson had time to find a suitable replacement, but the provisions of the act made that impossible. If the president wished to violate the law, that was his privilege. But he, Grant, did not intend to do so. If the Senate ordered Stanton reinstated, he would immediately step down. Sherman inquired whether Grant had informed Johnson of his decision. Grant said he had not, but would go to the White House that afternoon and do so.[80]

At 4 P.M. Grant entered the president's office. Johnson received him cordially, and for the next hour the two discussed the situation. Their recollections of the conversation differ substantially. Grant said he told the president that if the Senate refused to concur with Stanton's suspension, he could no longer serve as secretary of war ad interim. "I went to the President for the sole purpose of making this decision known and did so make it known." Later Grant wrote that "a doubt never entered my mind about the President fully understanding my position."[81] Johnson, who tried to argue Grant out of leaving, maintained that no decision was reached and that the two men agreed to meet again to discuss the issue.[82] The chances are that both Grant and Johnson correctly reported their understanding of the discussion. Grant, in the quiet, crisp manner that was his military hallmark, had spoken with the clarity of command. Insofar as he was concerned, that ended the matter. Johnson, with a lifetime in politics, thought in more subtle shades. He heard what Grant said, but assumed that the decision was not final and that he could convince the general to remain.[83]

The next afternoon, Sunday, January 12, Sherman called on Grant at his I Street home. Sitting in the library before a blazing fire, the two men discussed the situation once again. Grant repeated his determination not to remain in office. Neither man was enthusiastic about Stanton returning and Sherman suggested that Johnson be urged to appoint Governor Jacob D. Cox of Ohio as secretary of war. Cox was a moderate Republican and a former major general of volunteers with a superb war record.* He had not been critical of Johnson in the past, and his term as governor was about to expire. Sherman had already canvassed a number of senators and reported

---

* Born in Montreal and educated at Oberlin, Jacob D. Cox was one of the leading lawyers in Ohio when the Civil War began. He was also a brigadier general in the militia, and led the first troops who volunteered across the Ohio and up the Kanawha against Lee in 1861. Subsequently a division commander under Sherman, McPherson, and Thomas, he fought with distinction in Georgia and Tennessee, rising to become commander of the 23rd Corps in the Army of the Ohio during the battle for Atlanta. His spirited stand at the battle of Franklin, November 30, 1864, paved the way for Thomas's smashing victory over Hood at Nashville two weeks later.

that Cox would be easily confirmed. Grant was enthusiastic. He knew Cox from the war, thought he would be acceptable to the army, and although he had opposed Negro suffrage, believed they could work together on Reconstruction. Most important, it would extricate Grant from an untenable position and would provide Johnson with a means of replacing Stanton with the Senate's concurrence.

The generals spent the rest of the day drumming up support for Cox.[84] Sherman's father-in-law, former senator Thomas Ewing, Sr., lent a hand, telling the president that if he nominated Cox, his choice was certain to be ratified. Senator Reverdy Johnson of Maryland delivered a similar message. The president told both that he had a high opinion of Cox, but gave no intimation that he intended to act on their advice.

Early Monday morning Grant and Sherman met once again. Sherman reported that Johnson was apparently not going to send Cox's name forward. Grant, disappointed, asked Cump to go at once to the White House and repeat the proposal, saying that Grant not only approved, but was enthusiastic about the possibility. Sherman dutifully walked across to the executive mansion and was admitted to see the president shortly after eleven. When he mentioned Cox, Johnson indicated that he did not intend to appoint him. Sherman told Grant afterward that since the president had obviously thought about it, "I did not deem it proper for me further to urge the matter, only stating that I thought General Cox in every way qualified, and that I knew from you personally that his appointment would be most acceptable."[85]

Why Johnson declined to nominate Cox is unclear. Presidential biographers have suggested that stubbornness played a part: Johnson balked at having a cabinet choice dictated to him.[86] Others have suggested that the president wanted to test the Tenure of Office Act in the courts and to do so he needed Stanton in the picture. A third possibility is that Johnson was deliberately seeking a showdown with the Senate, believing public opinion was on his side. Or it may be that Johnson didn't fully appreciate what Grant had said on Saturday and simply assumed he would stay on.[87]

Grant did not see the president Monday. Late in the afternoon the Senate broke a halfhearted Democratic filibuster and voted 33–6 to approve the committee report and reinstate Stanton. To Grant the statute was clear: his term as secretary of war ad interim expired with the Senate vote.

That evening there was a levee at the White House. Grant did not plan to attend, but Julia, with a number of houseguests in tow, insisted on going and finally coaxed the general into accompanying them. When they arrived, Johnson grasped Grant's hand cordially and the two men spoke amiably for a few minutes. Neither mentioned the action on the Senate floor or Grant's decision to vacate the War Office. Afterward, Grant told Julia he "really felt embarrassed" because the president had been so cordial.[88]

The next morning Grant went to the War Department at his usual time. He went directly to the secretary's office, bolted one door from the inside, locked the other from the outside, and turned the key over to the army's adjutant general, whose office was down the corridor. "I am to be found at my office at army headquarters," said Grant.[89] He then wrote immediately to the president, enclosing an official copy of the Senate's resolution reinstating Stanton. "My functions as Secretary of War, *ad interim,* ceased from the moment of the receipt of the within notice," said Grant.[90]

What happened next took everyone by surprise. Grant had assumed that Stanton would contact him before returning to his office—permitting the general to gather his papers and close out business, just as he had done for Stanton when the secretary was suspended in August.[91] That would still give Johnson time to find a replacement, allowing Grant to comply with the law while assisting the president to dump Stanton with the Senate's concurrence. Unfortunately, Stanton made a bizarre rush into the breach. Upon receiving notice of the Senate's action, he laid plans for a swift return to the War Department. Within minutes of the time Grant turned over the key, Stanton was back in his office, doing business as usual. First off, he peremptorily ordered Grant to report and be informed that he was back. Upset by this unexpected turn of events, Grant made his way across the street to the War Department, only to be further upset by the secretary's brusque manner of receiving him. Whatever doubts Grant may have had about Stanton's suitability as secretary of war came rushing back with a vengeance. As one scholar has noted, if Grant had known what Stanton intended, he probably would not have turned over the keys in the first place.[92]

Grant's surprise that Stanton was back was nothing compared to the shock Johnson suffered. Summoning Grant to a meeting of the cabinet that afternoon, he asked for an explanation. Addressing the general as "Mr. Secretary," the president peppered him with questions. Grant stood to reply. Firmly but politely he told the president that he was no longer the acting secretary of war and was present only because he had been invited. He reminded Johnson of their previous conversation. Grant said he had made it clear on Saturday that if the Senate voted to reinstate Stanton, he would step down. When the Senate acted, he did so. He was surprised that Stanton had moved so quickly to reoccupy the office, but he had nothing to do with that. Finally, Grant pointed out that both Sherman and Reverdy Johnson had called on the president to suggest that Governor

Cox be nominated for the post. If Johnson had wanted to head Stanton off, he should have sent Cox's name forward.[93]

Johnson was excited and indignant. He asserted that the Tenure of Office Act was unconstitutional and that Grant was under no obligation to obey it. If he was convicted for violating it, Johnson grandly announced that he would personally pay the fine and serve the jail sentence.[94] The president then accused Grant of duplicity, suggesting that he had gone back on an earlier promise to hold the office until a suitable replacement could be found. Grant replied that he had given the president due notice that he did not intend to violate the statute. The discussion ended. Grant asked to be excused and walked out.[95]

The next morning the *National Intelligencer,* a Washington daily sympathetic to the administration, carried an account of the exchange between Johnson and Grant. Obviously primed by the White House, the article alleged that Grant had deceived the president and was working in collusion with Stanton. When Grant read the article, he was furious. Taking Sherman with him, he went to the White House to demand a correction. "The President received us promptly and kindly," Sherman wrote afterward. "We were all seated. Nobody in the room but the President, [Grant], and myself."[96] When Grant called the president's attention to the article, Johnson claimed he had not read it. "Well," the general replied, "the idea is given there that I have not kept faith with you." Grant restated his efforts to give Johnson time to make another appointment, noting once again that it was Stanton's unexpected return that had upset everything. Sherman noted that the president seemed "gratified and pleased" by Grant's explanation. At the conclusion of the conversation, Grant observed that just because Stanton was back in his old office, it did not automatically make him secretary of war, any more than if he were at home in his private library. Grant suggested that the president issue an order stating that "we of the Army are not bound to obey the orders of Mr. Stanton as Secretary of War." Sherman reported that Johnson liked the idea and agreed to do so. Sherman also liked the idea. "I thought that your explanation, that Mr. Stanton's being in a particular room did not make him lawful secretary of war, was conclusive," he told Grant.[97]

At this point Johnson could have repaired the rift with Grant, worked around Stanton until he found a replacement acceptable to the Senate, and retained control of the situation. Instead, he chose to challenge Grant's credibility. It was a fight he could not win. As the *New York Tribune* observed, "In a question of veracity between a soldier whose honor is as untarnished as the sun, and a President who has betrayed every friend, and broken every promise, the country will not hesitate."[98]

For the next two weeks the press was filled with the quarrel. Leaks from the White House cascaded across the nation's front pages. Democratic journals declared that Grant had "acted a part inconsistent with his honor as a gentleman." False allegations resurfaced that Grant was drinking heavily; the *New York Times* outlandishly reported a capital rumor that Johnson had become so enraged that he broke a chair over Grant's head.[99] Stung by the president's campaign, Grant decided it was time to protect himself. He was perfectly willing to circumvent Stanton if the president directed it, but given Johnson's recent behavior the general thought it prudent to have those instructions on paper. "I have the honor, very respectfully, to request to have, in writing, the order which the President gave me verbally . . . to disregard the orders of the Hon. E. M. Stanton," Grant wrote on January 24.[100] Johnson procrastinated. Rather than go on record, the president turned once again to Sherman. Hope sprang eternal in Johnson's breast, but Grant's old comrade offered no succor. As decorously as he could, Sherman deflected the president's overture and said that what he really wanted to do was return to St. Louis and settle down. For the past ten years, Cump told Johnson, he had not been at home more than thirty days out of every three hundred and sixty-five.[101]

On January 28 Grant, who was fast losing his patience, repeated his request for written instructions. His anger was evident. "I am compelled to ask these instructions in writing, in consequence of the many and grave misrepresentations, affecting my personal honor, circulated through the press for the last fortnight, purporting to come from you, the President, of conversations which occurred either with the President privately, or in Cabinet meeting . . . What is written admits of no misunderstanding," Grant told the president.[102]

Taking that as his cue, the general proceeded to set down his own version of recent events. Grant was not yet ready to break with the president, but he was laying down an artillery barrage just in case. He reminded Johnson of their January 11 meeting, of his clearly expressed determination to step aside if the Senate voted to reinstate Stanton, and of the suggestion that Governor Cox be nominated in Stanton's place. He concluded with a restatement of what had occurred at the cabinet meeting on January 13, and explicitly rejected the press reports inspired by the White House.

Sherman added his voice to Grant's. Uncle Billy was still in Washington putting the final touches on his report revising the Articles of War, and on January 30 he called on Johnson in a last-ditch effort to smooth things over. The president, he found, was not interested. Johnson again offered Sherman the War Department and, failing that, suggested the creation of a new military command for him in the East with headquarters in Washington. Cump wouldn't bite. He told Johnson that if the political atmosphere in Washington could ruffle the equanimity of someone so guarded and so prudent as Grant, "what will be the result with one so careless, so outspoken as I am. Washington, never." [103]

By writing forcefully to the president, Grant hoped to lure Johnson to put his position on record. The president rose to the bait. On January 31, the White House delivered Johnson's response to Grant's letter. "My recollection of what transpired is diametrically the reverse of your narration," wrote the president. Johnson then gave his own version of events, suggesting that Grant had collaborated with Stanton to allow the secretary to regain his office, and again accusing Grant of duplicity. [104] With Johnson's letter, the battle was joined.

Grant replied on February 3 recounting his dealings with Stanton and for all practical purposes calling the president a liar. "I here reassert the correctness of my statements in [my letter to you of January 28], anything in yours in reply to the contrary notwithstanding." Grant's prose was sharp. "The course you would have it understood I agreed to pursue," he told Johnson, "was in violation of the law. The course I did pursue, and which I never doubted you fully understood, was in accordance with the law." Having made clear that he was not going to cooperate with the president in evading the will of Congress, Grant counterattacked: "And now, Mr. President, where my honor as a soldier and integrity as a man have been so violently assailed, pardon me for saying that I can but regard this whole matter, from the beginning to the end, as an attempt to involve me in the resistance to the law, for which you hesitated to assume the responsibility in orders, and thus to destroy my character before the country." [105]

The exchange between Grant and Johnson quickly became public knowledge. Congress asked for the correspondence, and Grant won the nation's support hands down. "General Grant has driven his pen through the President like a spear," the *New York Independent* reported. Another New York daily, calling the affair "a paltry personal wrangle," noted that Grant's reputation had not been damaged in any way. "It simply adds another to the proofs his whole career has afforded, that he obeys the law and is content with doing his duty." [106] Radical Republicans were beside themselves. When Thaddeus Stevens saw Grant's letter, he rejoiced. "He is a bolder man than I thought him," declared the High Priest of Radicalism. [107] A Midwestern Republican told Washburne that the exchange "has imparted a ground *swell* to the tide of [Grant's] popularity." The abolitionist *National Anti-Slavery Standard,* not always in Grant's corner, praised the general effusively: "The correspondence is altogether creditable to the great soldier. It will relieve the anxieties of the American people as to his real status." When the dust settled, it remained for the *New York Times* to sum up the episode: "General Grant's heavy guns have almost completely silenced the small artillery of his traducers." [108]

The letters that passed between Grant and Johnson ended any possibility of reconciliation. Before the exchange, Grant had sought to preserve an outward appearance of harmonious subordination to the president. When the publication of their correspondence tore away that facade, the two men became implacable enemies. Aside from the most formal communications, contact between them ceased. Grant was not yet a candidate for president. But as Adam Badeau observed, the general's letter of February 3 was "a stroke of political genius; it made any candidate other than Grant impossible for the Republicans. Of course, Grant might and probably would have been President had the correspondence never occurred; but the letter made his nomination and election certain." [109]

With Stanton hanging on and Grant estranged, Johnson was now isolated from the army. Yet again he turned to Sherman. Advisers close to the president warned him that Uncle Billy would not take a position that placed him at odds with Grant, but Johnson persisted, created a new military division,* ordered Sherman to it, and sent his brevet nomination for four-star general to the Senate. Sherman was appalled. "I never felt so troubled in my life," he wrote Grant. "Were it an order to go to Sitka, to the Devil, to do battle with rebels or Indians, you would not hear a whimper from me. But it comes in such a questionable form that, like Hamlet's Ghost, it curdles my blood." [110] Sherman immediately wired his brother to fight his promotion on the Senate floor, loosed a blizzard of letters to friends in Washington asking them to intervene, and then wrote Johnson to decline the post. Sherman told the president that he had no desire to be placed in a position opposed to Grant. "Our relations have always been most confidential and friendly, and if unhappily any cloud of difficulty should arise between us, my sense of personal dignity and duty would leave me no alternative but resignation." [111]

Confronted with Sherman's opposition, Johnson had no alternative but to abandon his plans and retract his orders. Before doing so, however, he made a final, desperate effort to entice George Thomas to take the post. On February 22, and without informing Thomas, Johnson sent his name to the Senate with a recommendation that he be promoted to brevet lieutenant general and brevet general. Like Sherman, Thomas had no desire to go to Washington. "Whilst sincerely thanking you for the proposed compliment," he wired the president, "I earnestly request you to recall the

* On February 12, 1868, Johnson instructed Grant to create a new military division, "to be called the Division of the Atlantic, to be composed of the Department of the Lakes, the Department of the East, and the Department of Washington, and to be commanded by Lieutenant General William T. Sherman, with his headquarters at Washington." 13 *Johnson Papers* 556.

nomination. I have done no service since the war to deserve so high a compliment, and it is now too late to be regarded as a compliment if confirmed for services during the war."[112]

Johnson had run out of options. He could not whip Grant in the court of public opinion, he could not outflank him with Sherman and Thomas, and he could not remove him without violating an act of Congress. At this point the president turned his attention back to Stanton. If he were going to have any influence on the army, it would have to be through a new secretary of war. This is where Johnson made the mistake that almost brought him down. Rather than replace Stanton with a new appointee acceptable to the Senate, he tried to bull his way through, defy the Tenure of Office Act, and confront Congress with a fait accompli.

Johnson first tapped the chief clerk of the War Department, John Potts, to succeed Stanton, but Potts wanted nothing to do with the scheme. The president then turned to a longtime fixture in Washington society, the aging and garrulous Major General Lorenzo Thomas, former adjutant general of army. Thomas was well past his prime but he detested Stanton (the feeling was mutual), and he agreed to throw in with the president. On February 21, Johnson provided Thomas with written orders relieving Stanton and appointing him to be the new secretary of war.[113] Neither the cabinet nor Johnson's Democratic supporters in Congress were informed beforehand.[114]

That afternoon Thomas delivered the president's letter to Stanton. Grant was with the secretary at the time, and Stanton, in Grant's presence, asked Thomas for time to consider whether he would obey. Thomas left the room briefly, Grant urged Stanton to stick to his post, and the secretary, fortified by the general in chief's presence, subsequently advised Thomas that he would not yield. News of the encounter flashed through Washington like wildfire. Republicans in Congress rushed to the War Department to urge Stanton to resist. Charles Sumner sent his famous one-word telegram, "Stick," and Grant took the necessary measures to secure the War Department against all comers. Late that afternoon the Senate went into executive session and shortly before 9 P.M. passed a resolution reaffirming that the president had no right to relieve Stanton.[115] In the House, Representative John Covode offered a motion to impeach Johnson for high crimes and misdemeanors. The House adjourned before action could be taken, but on Monday February 24, it voted 128–47 to approve the resolution. Then the House appointed a committee to draw up specific charges.[116]*

---

* On Sunday, February 23, the president called the commander of the military district of Washington, Major General William H. Emory, to the White House to inquire about

During most of Johnson's impeachment trial Grant remained a passive observer. He was summoned to give testimony about his conversation with the president, and did so without any show of animosity.[117] Many of Grant's supporters were initially reluctant to support impeachment for fear it might jeopardize the general's chances for election. Should Johnson be removed, and since the office of vice president was vacant, Benjamin Wade of Ohio, a fire-eating Radical who was president pro tempore of the Senate, would become president. Some worried that once in the White House he might be able to corral the necessary convention support to deny Grant the nomination. The general was unconcerned. "Impeachment seems to grow in popularity," he wrote Sheridan at the end of March, "and indications are that the trial will not be protracted."[118]

Grant supported conviction because (among other things) he thought Johnson created too much turbulence in his wake. Writing to his old friend Charles Ford, the general allowed as how he thought the president's removal would "give peace to the country."[119] Newspapers put Grant's position in stark terms of policy. The *New York Tribune* quoted him as saying "the acquittal of Mr. Johnson would threaten the country, especially the South, with revolution and bloodshed."[120] But it was Senator John B. Henderson of Missouri to whom Grant may have confided his deepest reason. Riding alongside Henderson on a streetcar shortly before the vote, Grant said, "I would impeach him because he is such an infernal liar."[121]

Johnson survived impeachment by one vote. Thirty-five senators voted to convict and nineteen to acquit: one short of the constitutional two thirds required to remove the president from office. Seven Republicans joined the Senate's twelve Democrats in voting to dismiss the charges. In an ironic twist of fate, Grant played a pivotal role in securing Johnson's acquittal. The moderate Republicans who voted no were all "Grant men."* They were reluctant to make Wade president, yet they were also determined that if Johnson remained in office he not interfere with Reconstruction. It was James Grimes of Iowa who struck the deal with the president whereby Johnson pledged that if acquitted he would abide by the statutes and take no rash action. Convinced of Johnson's sincerity, Grimes passed

---

troop dispositions in the capital. Emory replied that no great changes had taken place, but that under the Military Appropriations Act any orders the president might have would have to come through General Grant. Johnson said the act was unconstitutional; Emory said that might be so, but he was bound by it. *Trial of Andrew Johnson* 233–36 (Washington, D.C.: Government Printing Office, 1868).

* William Pitt Fessenden of Maine; Joseph F. Fowler, Tennessee; James W. Grimes, Iowa; John B. Henderson, Missouri; Edmund F. Ross, Kansas; Lyman Trumbull, Illinois; and Peter G. Van Winkle of West Virginia.

the word to his colleagues that they could vote for acquittal without fear of the consequences.[122] Grimes also suggested that Johnson appoint a new secretary of war acceptable to the Senate. After some additional prodding the president settled on Major General John Schofield, a protégé of Grant who headed the military district of Virginia. Schofield was the last of the original five military commanders in the South. He had just replaced the governor of Virginia and was fresh from the state convention that had adopted a new constitution.[123]

Schofield was approached by William Evarts, Johnson's principal defense lawyer, the afternoon of April 21 at the Willard Hotel. Schofield said he would have to ask Grant, with whom he was having dinner that evening. The general in chief made it clear that he favored Johnson's impeachment, but said he had no objection to Schofield accepting the post. Schofield saw Evarts again that evening, then Grant again, and finally accepted, on condition that Johnson commit himself to the enforcement of the Reconstruction Acts. Johnson agreed, and Schofield's name was sent to the Senate on April 25, 1868. By concurring in Schofield's appointment, Grant helped to provide the moderate Republican votes that acquitted Johnson.[124]*

On May 20, four days after Johnson's acquittal, the Republican convention convened in Chicago. Eight thousand people jammed Crosby's Opera House to watch the Grand Old Party nominate Grant. Bishop Matthew Simpson, Radical leader of the Methodist Church, opened with a prayer. Carl Schurz of Missouri gave the keynote address, a ringing appeal for justice to the Union men and freedmen of the South. A platform embodying those demands was quickly adopted. Then Major General John "Black Jack" Logan, back in Congress from his old district in Illinois, but now as a Republican, rose to place Grant's name in nomination. No

* Johnson's trial in the Senate, like that of Justice Samuel Chase in 1805, provides compelling parallels to more recent proceedings. In both the Johnson and Chase trials, the House managers were partisan politicians who proved no match for the seasoned legal professionals deployed by the defense. President Johnson's counsel—William Evarts, Benjamin R. Curtis, Henry Stanbery, and William S. Groesbeck—were men of outstanding character and ability who demonstrated effectively how little protection the Tenure of Office Act afforded Lincoln's appointees. Evarts and Curtis were especially devastating in their arguments. Evarts subsequently served as secretary of state under Hayes; Curtis had been an associate justice of the Supreme Court (1851–1857) and played an important role in shaping the constitutional law of the era. (He dissented in *Dred Scott.*)

The House managers, Thaddeus Stevens, George Boutwell, Benjamin Butler, John Logan, Thomas Williams, James Wilson, and John Bingham, were shrill, unfocused, and too careless with the fine points of the law. As *The Nation,* which favored conviction, noted afterward, "The Managers were overmastered throughout in learning and ability. There is no way now in passing this over without notice. The contrast was patent to everybody throughout the trial and was a constant subject of comment." 6 *The Nation* 404 (May 21, 1868).

other candidate was offered, and the convention unanimously made Grant its nominee. For vice president, the delegates picked House Speaker Schuyler Colfax on the fifth ballot, passing over Benjamin Wade and a host of favorite sons.

In Washington Grant went quietly about his duties. Up to the hour of the convention he had given no indication of any interest in the nomination.[125] While he was being acclaimed in Chicago, he was working at his desk at army headquarters. Across the street in the War Department, Stanton sat by the telegraph awaiting news. As soon as Grant's nomination was confirmed, the secretary rushed over to the general's office. "I had never seen Stanton there before," wrote Badeau, "but this time he did not send for Grant."

"General," Stanton exclaimed, "I have come to tell you that you have been nominated by the Republican party for President of the United States." Grant received the news in silence and stolidly accepted Stanton's congratulations. "There was no shade of exaltation or agitation on his face, not a flush on his cheek, nor a flash in his eye," Badeau remembered. "I doubt whether he felt elated, even in those recesses where he concealed his innermost thoughts."[126]

That night there was celebration throughout the country. Senator John Sherman caught the mood: "Your nomination," he told Grant, "was not made by our party but by the people, and in obedience to the universal demand that our candidate should be so independent of party politics as to be a guarantee of peace and quiet."[127]

The following evening, a great procession formed on Pennsylvania Avenue, headed by the marine band, and marched to serenade the nominee. Congressman George Boutwell of Massachusetts introduced Grant as "the next president of the United States." The general responded with his first political speech.

> Gentlemen, being entirely unaccustomed to public speaking and without the desire to cultivate the power, it is impossible for me to find appropriate language to thank you for the demonstration. All I can say is, that to whatever position I may be called by your will, I shall endeavor to discharge its duties with fidelity and honesty of purpose. Of my rectitude in the performance of public duties you will have to judge for yourselves by the record before you.[128]

The week after the convention, General Joseph R. Hawley, its presiding officer, led a delegation to Washington to make a formal tender of the nomination to Grant and Colfax. The two candidates, their wives, and more than a hundred friends and supporters received the delegates in Grant's I Street home. Dressed in black, the general stood while Hawley spoke, and then replied briefly expressing his thanks. In a formal letter written the next day, Grant accepted the nomination, endorsed the platform, and promised to administer the laws in accordance with the popular will. He closed with elegant simplicity: "Let us have peace."[129]

CHAPTER FIFTEEN

GRANT IN THE WHITE HOUSE

Our eight years in the Executive Mansion were delightful, but there were some dark clouds in the bright sky. There was that dreadful Black Friday.

JULIA DENT GRANT

THE ELECTION OF 1868 provided little excitement and few surprises. The Democrats were in disarray and Grant settled back to await the inevitable. Unlike the Republicans, the party of Jefferson and Jackson was deeply divided by the war. The dominant faction, out of touch with much of the Northern electorate, sought to turn back the clock on Reconstruction and pushed through a platform pledged to restore white supremacy and terminate "carpet-bag government" in the South.[1] Former Confederate generals Wade Hampton and Nathan Bedford Forrest played prominent roles at the convention and set the tone of the gathering.

As their candidate, the Democrats (after twenty-one exhausting ballots) chose the frail and colorless Horatio Seymour, ex-governor of New York, a last-minute, Tammany-inspired compromise who posed little threat to Grant. Seymour's conduct as wartime governor of the Empire State (where he addressed New York City draft rioters as "my friends") surrendered the loyalty issue to the Republicans, and his close ties to Wall Street precluded any hope of appealing to Western populists.[2] The racist campaign waged by the party further alienated many war Democrats, who deserted the party in droves. When the votes were counted, Grant carried twenty-six of the thirty-four states and smothered Seymour in the electoral college, 214–80. The Republicans also retained their two-thirds majority in the Senate, and won four fifths of the House of Representatives.

Grant conducted no campaign as such. His words "Let us have peace" were his last campaign utterance. The phrase contrasted starkly with the

Democratic appeal to counterrevolution, and struck a responsive chord in an electorate weary from four years of war and nearly four more years of political discord over Reconstruction. In a curious reversal of roles, Grant, who had overturned the ancien régime in the South, stood as the candidate of order and stability, while the Democrats seemed to promise little except renewed conflict and continued unrest.

Grant waged a calculated noncampaign as deliberate as any military action he ever commanded. Fully aware that he was a poor public speaker and that whatever active role he might play could backfire, Grant did what he did best. He remained at his post as general in chief, stayed in Washington until Congress adjourned, and then, with Sherman and Sheridan at his side, went west to inspect the forts on the frontier. A gaggle of newsmen followed, reported his every move, and filled the nation's press with homey accounts of the simple soldier whom the people were calling to the White House. "This will probably be the last chance I will ever have to visit the plains, and I thought I would avail myself of the opportunity to see them," Grant wrote Julia from Fort Leavenworth.[3] After stopping in Denver and briefly visiting the gold mines nearby, he returned to Galena and remained there until after the election.

Grant's sojourn in Galena was devoid of politics: another deliberate effort to present himself as the candidate of the people, standing above partisanship.[4] It was also a long-needed vacation in the bosom of his family after the turmoil of the Johnson years. In Washington, chief of staff John Rawlins handled the duties at army headquarters, acting in Grant's name whenever the situation demanded and serving as informal liaison with Republican leaders. Adam Badeau was instructed to handle whatever correspondence came in. "Such as are on official business refer to Rawlins. All others do with as your judgment dictates, only do not send any to me except such as you think absolutely require my attention and will not keep 'till my return."[5]

The one matter that required Grant's attention that summer was an outcry over wartime General Orders No. 11, issued at Oxford, Mississippi, in December 1862, expelling all members of the Jewish faith from his department. Democrats seized on the issue and Jewish leaders throughout the country directed anguished letters to Grant seeking an explanation. Badeau did his best to contain the outcry,[6] but by mid-September Grant felt it necessary to respond. His old friend Isaac Morris had written enclosing a letter from a former captain in the Confederate army, Adolph Moses, inquiring about Grant's views.* This was one of several hundred

---

* On September 3, 1868, Moses wrote Morris enclosing a letter to Grant concerning General Orders No. 11. "It will hardly surprise you that we, as a people, already over-sensitive

letters Grant received on the subject. Using Morris's letter as a vehicle of reply, Grant set forth his position in some detail.

"I do not pretend to sustain the order," he wrote. "The order was made and sent out, without any reflection, and without thinking of the Jews as a sect or race to themselves, but simply as the persons who had successfully violated an order [involving trading with the enemy], which violation inured greatly to the help of the rebels."

Grant instructed Morris to "give Mr. Moses assurances that I have no prejudice against sect or race but want each individual to be judged by his own merit. Order No. 11 does not sustain this statement, I admit, but then I do not sustain that order. It never would have been issued if it had not been telegraphed the moment penned, without one moment's reflection." [7]

Grant's days in Galena were spent in artful repose. There was a Republican rally in town but he did not attend. His mornings were spent reading the daily press and answering the few letters that would not wait, and in the afternoons he visited old friends, sat in their offices and stores, and took tea with their families in turn. [8] "My time passes very pleasantly and quietly here," he wrote Washburne in late September. "A person would not know there was a stirring canvass going on if it were not for the accounts we read in the papers of great gatherings all over the country." [9] Two days later he wrote Secretary of War John Schofield that he did not plan to return to Washington until after the election. The letter hinted at Grant's ambivalent feelings about government. The general said he was pleased that the War Department "has fallen where it has" and was now administered in the interest of the nation. "It is a rare thing that Government Departments are so administered. They are generally administered in the interest of a political party and not to serve the public interest." [10]

As the campaign entered its final month, Grant hoped Sherman would shed his contempt for politics and make a public statement pledging his support. A word from Sherman would carry great weight among veterans of the Army of the Tennessee. Alternatively, his silence could be interpreted negatively. But the two men did not discuss the matter explicitly. Grant, who in many ways shared Sherman's principles, respected his

---

through former oppression and contumely, should lament the issuance of that order, whatever the immediate causes might have dictated. I am assured by high authority, some of which I might call Jewish, that you regret the sweeping effect of the order. . . . I regret that our people who love to enjoy the quiet retreat of private life should be so prominently paraded in this campaign; but the instinct of self-defense presses utterance, however unwelcome the task. Our demands are simply to be judged like other people, and not to have the vices and shortcomings of our bad men illuminated at the expense of the many virtues and excellent qualities of our good men." 19 *The Papers of Ulysses S. Grant* 38 note, John Y. Simon, ed. (Carbondale: Southern Illinois University Press, 1995).

friend's independence; and Sherman was reluctant to raise the matter. Yet as old friends often do, they worked out an implicit compromise. In early October, Grant paid a visit to his farm outside St. Louis, and Sherman, whose headquarters was in the Gateway City, arranged for the general in chief to stay at his home throughout the visit. Sherman's hospitality spoke for itself. There was no question whom he supported, yet he avoided making a public statement. Sherman hated politics and politicians, and to endorse Grant would be to participate in a process he despised.[11]

On election day Grant accompanied his neighbors to the polls, where he voted Washburne for Congress and the entire Republican ticket, but deliberately refrained from casting a ballot in the presidential election.[12] At ten that evening he walked to Washburne's home, where telegraph machinery had been installed, to receive the election returns. A dozen or so friends and neighbors were assembled when Grant arrived, and for the next several hours they waited as the results trickled in. The general's demeanor was predictably placid. Grant at times appeared more interested in a card game in progress than the voting returns from distant states. By 2 A.M. the results were sufficient to declare victory. The Lead Mine Band appeared from nowhere to serenade the winner, and Grant walked back to his house to inform Julia of the outcome.[13] Standing on the doorstep, the president-elect addressed a group of fifty to a hundred townspeople who had gathered to wish him well. As at Appomattox, Grant exhibited no elation. His words were concise: "The responsibilities of the position I feel, but I accept them without fear."[14]

Across the nation, Grant's victory was greeted with relief. Democrats and Republicans alike hailed the results as a triumph for conservative principles: sound money, government economy, and the restoration of the South under Reconstruction. The country had spoken clearly, and hitherto recalcitrant rebel leaders such as Tennessee's Nathan Bedford Forrest accepted the result "cordially and heartily." That was true on the Western frontier as well. Sherman wrote Grant that "everything has settled down as quiet as a New England village. All people are figuring on four years of peace."[15]

Two days after the election Grant left Galena by train for Washington. He was accompanied by his family and three military aides. Before the election, Grant had received several assassination threats, but took no special note of them. His route was known in advance and he made no alterations. Badeau reported that the aides were armed, but this was without Grant's knowledge.[16]* The president-elect arrived in the capital shortly

---

* Aside from the possible attempt on his life at the time of Lincoln's assassination, Grant had already escaped two postwar plots to kill him. The first occurred in North Carolina on his return from the surrender of Johnston to Sherman, when the train on which he was traveling was derailed. Grant's coach was the only car on the train, and there was little doubt

after noon on November 7. It was a typical, inconspicuous Grant entrance. There was no welcoming party to meet him and the general hired a public hack to take him and Julia to their I Street residence. Not until the next day, when newsmen observed Grant walking on 17th Street near army headquarters, did the public learn that he was back in Washington.

Inauguration day was four months away, and to the dismay of Republican politicians Grant put his plans on hold and turned his attention to the army. He was still general in chief, and military business, which had been neglected for several months, required his immediate attention. Most important, Grant wanted to provide for his succession. Sherman would follow him as general in chief and inherit four stars. The problem was who would succeed Sherman as the army's sole lieutenant general. Since the war, the lieutenant general had commanded U.S. forces on the frontier. This was the army's only active command, and carried with it the responsibility for taming the West. Hostile Indians continued to threaten settlers crossing the Great Plains and there was always the danger of a general uprising.

Grant had a choice of five major generals on active duty: Halleck, Meade, Sheridan, Thomas, and Hancock. Halleck was too old and Hancock too junior, besides which Grant did not care to promote either. That left Meade, Sheridan, and Thomas. Meade was senior, Sheridan was physically and temperamentally better suited to the rigors of Western campaigning, and Thomas, who would be hurt if not chosen, was the junior candidate. Sherman suggested that Congress provide for the promotion of all three officers to lieutenant general, but in a time of retrenchment that was a forlorn hope.[17] Grant settled on Sheridan. Meade, profoundly disappointed, was given command of the Atlantic Division with headquarters in his hometown of Philadelphia, and Thomas was awarded the Pacific Division, based in San Francisco. For secretary of war, Grant preferred to stick with Schofield, but that would have to await more formal decisions pertaining to the structure of the cabinet.

Grant was gratified that Sherman was coming to Washington. For the past three years he had struggled to maintain the army's integrity, and with Sherman in town he could be certain the task would continue in good hands. The changeover also provided Grant with an opportunity to transfer his Washington residence to Sherman at a substantial profit to both. Grant's financial failures in the 1850s undoubtedly colored his judgment,

---

what had been intended. A second attempt was made in southern Indiana in late 1865 when once again his single-car train was derailed as it approached a bridge over a stream eighty feet below. Grant escaped injury on both occasions and insisted on keeping the incidents secret. As he told his staff, crime was contagious, and to announce one attempt was likely to beget another. Adam Badeau, *Grant in Peace* 150–51 (Hartford, Conn.: Scranton, 1887).

and he was acutely interested in putting away a nest egg for future years. When New York department store magnate Alexander Stewart, reputed to be one of the richest men in America, suggested that he and others purchase the I Street residence for $65,000 and donate it to Sherman, Grant leapt at the opportunity to double his money.[18]* Sherman, who knew better than to look a gift horse in the mouth, accepted, although he later wrote his brother that he would not have paid $65,000 for the property.[19]

Two other items of unfinished business awaited the president-elect. The first was personal. As a calculated affront to Grant, Andrew Johnson had recently appointed General William Rosecrans minister to Mexico. The animosity between Grant and Rosecrans dated from the latter's failure to move effectively against Sterling Price at Iuka in September 1862, and time had not diminished the enmity. Using Badeau as an intermediary, Grant informed his friends in the Mexican government how distasteful he found Rosecrans's appointment. It would have been discourteous of Johnson to have made a major diplomatic appointment on the eve of a new administration without consultation, but to select someone openly hostile to the incoming president was in Grant's view unforgivable.[20] The Juárez government, deeply indebted to the president-elect, responded with alacrity. Grant was assured that Mexico City would conduct no business with Johnson's minister. The Mexican government, wrote Foreign Minister Matías Romero, was already suspicious of Rosecrans because of his intense Catholicism, and given Grant's views, it would have no intercourse with him. "If he is a man of sense, he will not come to Mexico," wrote Romero.[21]

The second matter that concerned Grant pertained to negotiations undertaken by the Johnson administration to settle difficulties with Great Britain arising out of the *Alabama* claims from the Civil War.[22] These related to the damage done to Union shipping by the cruisers C.S.S. *Alabama, Florida,* and *Shenandoah.* The vessels had been constructed in English shipyards, and the United States held the British government responsible for their depredations. In point of fact, relations with Great Britain was the most serious item on the nation's foreign policy agenda,

---

* Grant had previously agreed to sell the house to Sayles J. Bowen, mayor of Washington, D.C., for $40,000. On January 30, 1869, Grant wrote Bowen that he had reconsidered. Bowen protested in a letter to Grant the following day, but Grant declined to reopen the matter. Later, Julia asserted that she had blocked the sale to Bowen, although the evidence for that is sketchy. When Grant stood for reelection in 1872, Bowen threatened to bring suit for $25,000 damages, but the matter was eventually dropped. 19 *Grant Papers* 118–19, 124–25; *The Personal Memoirs of Julia Dent Grant* 173, John Y. Simon, ed. (Carbondale: Southern Illinois University Press, 1975); *New York Times,* July 29, 30, 1872; *New York Tribune,* July 4, August 27, 1872.

and Grant bridled at Secretary Seward's determination to resolve the issue without consultation.

Grant made his objections known both to Seward and to the British minister in Washington, Sir Edward Thornton.[23] Nevertheless, Seward persisted and that winter fashioned an accord with Great Britain that provided for the settlement of the claims of individual Americans but ignored the general damage done by the Confederate cruisers to the Union war effort.* In addition to being an unwarranted intrusion into his own approaching prerogatives, Grant considered the agreement prejudicial to United States interests. His objections resonated powerfully on Capitol Hill. When the Johnson administration submitted the accord to the Senate for approval, the senators voted to reject it, 54–1.[24]

Aside from these two episodes, Grant kept his own counsel. Not since George Washington had a president been elected who was so little beholden to the political powers of the day. And not since Monroe had a president-elect been more closely involved with the major issues confronting the nation. After Lincoln's death, Grant had carried the burden of Reconstruction. He had demobilized the world's largest army, maintained order in the West, assisted in the overthrow of the Archduke Maximilian in Mexico, and ushered the freedmen of the South into a new era. He had steered adroitly between an obstructionist president and the Radical firebrands in Congress, and when Johnson chose to do battle, Grant had routed him as thoroughly as he had Bragg at Chattanooga. Grant was not an instinctive politician, but his familiarity with the ways of Washington had been finely honed by three years of vicious infighting. Those days, he thought, were behind him. In November 1868 Grant stood poised to shepherd the nation into a period of growth and tranquillity. The young Henry Adams, writing about himself in the third person, captured the mood of the country:

> At least four-fifths of the American people—Adams among them—had united in the election of General Grant to the Presidency, and probably had been more or less affected in their choice by the parallel they felt between Grant and Washington. Nothing could be more obvious. Grant represented order. He was a great soldier, and the soldier always represented order. He might be as partisan as he pleased, but a general who had organized and commanded half a million or a million men in the field, must know how to administer. Even Washington, who

---

* The agreement, negotiated in London under precise instructions from Seward by U. S. minister Reverdy Johnson (former United States senator from Maryland), was known as the Johnson-Clarendon Convention, Lord Clarendon being foreign secretary in the Gladstone government.

was, in education and experience, a mere cave-dweller, had known how to organize government.

    ... No doubt the confusion, especially in the old slave States and in the currency, was considerable, but the general disposition was good, and everyone had echoed the famous phrase: "Let us have peace."[25]

More seasoned observers shared Adams's view. James Russell Lowell noted that Grant had always chosen able lieutenants. "My own opinion is that the extreme Republicans will be woefully disappointed in Grant. If he should throw away his opportunity to be an independent President, he is not the man I take him to be."[26] Oliver Wendell Holmes, after meeting Grant for the first time, wrote that he had never felt such an impression of power combined with modesty.[27] Henry Ward Beecher predicted that Grant would be known "even more favorably for the wisdom of his civil administration" than for his military success.[28] E. L. Godkin of *The Nation* shared that view. He told readers of his weekly column that Grant had taken up arms against the cheap politicians; that he was about to cleanse the government of unprincipled adventurers; and that he would remodel the administrative machinery "and make it really democratic."[29]

    Grant prepared for the advent of his administration in the same methodical way as when he made ready to move south of Vicksburg or cross the James. And with the same secrecy. He had taken no one into his confidence when he planned the strategy that led to those victories, and he saw no reason to depart from that formula. Grant told no one of his plans, not even Rawlins or Washburne, and he kept the press at arm's length. When Henry J. Raymond, publisher of the *New York Times* and a longtime supporter, wrote to obtain a hint of Grant's intentions so that he might be prepared to advocate them, he received no reply. Horace Greeley of the *Tribune,* a recent adherent to the Grant bandwagon, was also left in the dark. Even Julia was kept guessing. Grant joked that he had to wake up several times each night and examine the pockets of his vest—hidden beneath his pillow—lest Mrs. Grant discover the list of his cabinet appointees.[30]

    Traditional interpretations of the Grant administration assert that the president-elect erred in not consulting broadly among the nation's political leaders before selecting his cabinet. Yet for the previous seven years—in Washington and in the field—Grant had relied exclusively on his own judgment. He confided his plans to no one, and then moved with frightening energy to carry them into effect. It is not surprising that he adopted the same pattern when entering civil life. He was accustomed to appointing commanders without consulting their wishes, and he was no doubt influenced by the belief that his decisions had proven correct. The adulation he received upon returning to the capital in the autumn of 1868 may also have affected him. Everyone was assuring Grant that the people placed full confidence in him, that he was the sole arbiter of the nation's policy, the judge of last resort. Finally, by playing his cards close to his chest and not divulging his cabinet appointees, Grant kept the country's attention focused on himself. Only he was in the spotlight. At forty-six, Grant was the youngest man ever elected to the presidency, and youthful exuberance may also have played a role. He alone was to be president, and he alone would bear the responsibility. Yet as Badeau observed, Grant's determination not to consult or seek advice "betrayed a confidence in himself almost unprecedented."[31]

Inauguration day, March 4, 1869, dawned cold and rainy in Washington. The rain gradually subsided, but the clouds did not burn off until midday. At half-past nine Grant walked out from his I Street home, stepped into Julia's newest carriage, and was whisked by a matched set of impeccable bays to army headquarters, where his staff was waiting. Joined by Vice President–Elect Schuyler Colfax, the presidential party set out at 10:40 for the short journey up Pennsylvania Avenue to Capitol Hill. At the White House gate the cavalcade paused briefly, only to be told that President Johnson was too busy to get away. Whether Grant rebuffed Johnson by declining to invite him earlier, or whether Johnson snubbed Grant by refusing to attend remains in dispute. But for the third and last time in American history an outgoing president did not accompany his successor on the ceremonial trip to take the oath of office.*

At seventeen minutes after twelve the marine band sounded the "President's March," and Grant, wearing a finely tailored black suit, strode down the steps of the portico on the east front of the Capitol, escorted by Chief Justice Salmon P. Chase and the members of the Supreme Court. The diplomatic corps, serried ranks of generals and admirals in full dress, congressmen and senators, and a record crowd of spectators stood at attention as the 5th Field Artillery thundered the traditional twenty-one-gun salute. After taking the oath, Grant stepped to the improvised podium to deliver his brief inaugural address. At twelve hundred words, it was not so short as Lincoln's second inaugural, but was still one of the briefest on record. Like Lincoln, Grant had written it himself, and though it lacked the majesty of the Great Emancipator's prose, there was an elegant simplicity to his remarks.

---

* In 1801 President John Adams left Washington at dawn on inauguration day to avoid seeing Thomas Jefferson sworn in, and in 1829 his son, John Quincy Adams, refused to attend Andrew Jackson's inauguration.

"I will always express my views to Congress, and when I think it advisable, will exercise the constitutional privilege of interposing a veto. But all laws will be faithfully executed whether they meet my approval or not." Grant pledged himself to protect citizens, their property, and their political opinions "in every part of our common country, without regard to local prejudice." Fully half of the speech was devoted to fiscal issues: prompt payment of the national debt, faithful collection of revenue, and "the greatest practicable retrenchment in government expenditures." In foreign relations Grant promised to protect all citizens, at home and abroad, and to deal with other nations on the basis of fairness and equity. The most heartfelt passages in the speech concerned the nation's minorities: Indians and African-Americans. No president before him had taken up the cause of the country's original inhabitants, and Grant was keenly aware that the public mood was decidedly hostile. Nevertheless, he said his administration would pursue any course that would assist the integration of native peoples into American society and that would lead to their ultimate citizenship. As for the freedmen, the president made it clear that he favored unrestricted black suffrage. "It seems to me very desirable that the question should be settled now, and I entertain the hope and express the desire that it may be by ratification of the Fifteenth Amendment to the Constitution."[32]*

Press reports were overwhelmingly favorable. The *New York Times* ranked Grant's speech with Lincoln's second inaugural, "which is now regarded as one of the gems of the language." According to the *Times*, "General Grant had something to say, and he has said it strongly and well."[33] *The Nation* said the speech had "the merit of being a plain, sensible, practical document. It has been received with the greatest satisfaction by the press of all parties."[34] *Harper's Weekly,* which also compared Grant's effort to Lincoln's 1865 address, called the speech "brief, pointed, decisive, and admirable. Let any man reflect upon the kind of person that was made President in the latter days of Democratic ascendancy, and he will comprehend the immense progress marked by the mere presence of a man such as GRANT in the White House."[35] The South also greeted the speech approvingly. One editor pointed out that it read "like the bulletin of a great

* The Fifteenth Amendment, designed to give African-Americans the right to vote throughout the nation (not just in the South), was drafted in the interim between Grant's election and his inauguration on March 4, 1869. It passed Congress by the required two-thirds vote February 26, 1869, and had been submitted to the states for ratification when Grant spoke. Ratification followed party lines: Republicans were in favor, Democrats against. The battle was closely fought, but on March 30, 1870, the requisite three-quarters of the states having assented, the amendment became part of the Constitution. Since blacks were already voting in the South under military Reconstruction, the practical effect of the amendment was to open the ballot to African-Americans in seventeen Northern and border states.

general." Another remarked that the document "manifested a most catholic and winning spirit toward the whole country."[36] Praise poured in from abroad. Chancellor Bismarck of Prussia was among the first to cable his congratulations, while the head of the Berlin stock exchange informed Grant that the exchange closed briefly so that the members might give three cheers for the new president.[37]

Grant did his utmost to convince the capital's organizing committee to dispense with the traditional inaugural ball, but to no avail.[38] That evening, in the newly completed Treasury Building, 6,000 guests paid $10 a ticket to attend what the press called "a ball such as Washington has never seen before."[39] After eight years of tension and tragedy the city cut loose with a display of pomp to rival any European court. At eleven o'clock President Grant entered the hall, followed by Mrs. Grant (escorted by General George Thomas) and Vice President and Mrs. Colfax.[40] The guests were packed too tightly to do much dancing (Grant did not venture near the dance floor), but society reporters, always eager to chronicle difficulties, had nothing but praise for the event.[41]

On March 5 Grant advised the Senate of his cabinet nominees. The selections were a surprise. Grant had based his decisions on personal chemistry, not the political clout a particular individual might bring to the administration. In the context of 1869 that was understandable. Grant, a trifle optimistic no doubt, felt he did not need additional support. He also wanted to avoid the personal friction and petty animosities he had witnessed in the cabinets of the past two administrations. What he sought was a group of men he would be comfortable with: subordinates who could manage their departments and who at the same time would do his bidding cheerfully and effectively. For a city built on political influence, where hardened politicians were accustomed to cutting deals with equally hardened politicians, those criteria were astonishing.

For secretary of state Grant chose his old friend and former mentor, Elihu Washburne. For the Treasury, New York City's Alexander Stewart, the nation's most successful retailer. Stewart was another personal friend, though of more recent vintage, and had led the group that purchased Grant's I Street home for Sherman. For the Navy, Grant turned to Adolph E. Borie of Philadelphia. Like Stewart, Borie had no previous political experience. He also had no discernible qualifications to be secretary of the navy. A wealthy retired merchant who had prospered in the East India trade, Borie had been one of the founders of the Union League Club in Philadelphia and had been prominent among those who gave Grant the house on Chestnut Street. Borie had entertained Grant several times at his fine estate on the Delaware, and the general enjoyed his company. Advised that he should have someone in his cabinet from Pennsylvania, Grant settled on Borie.

Interior and the Post Office were placed in more reliable hands. As secretary of the interior, Grant chose former Ohio governor Jacob D. Cox. Cox had been Grant's candidate to succeed Stanton at the War Department in 1868, and a better choice for Interior would have been difficult to come by. A professor of law at the University of Cincinnati, with a brilliant war record behind him, Cox was a man of studious habits with a flair for the crisp dispatch of whatever business came his way.[42] For postmaster general and primary custodian of the nation's political patronage, Grant turned to the gifted and debonair John A. J. Creswell of Maryland. A former Democrat turned Radical, Creswell had served in the House of Representatives during the war, represented Maryland in the Senate from 1865 to 1867, and had organized the Old Line State's delegation to the 1868 Republican convention behind Grant. Creswell would prove to be one of the most effective postmaster generals in the country's history. He improved mail service, reduced postage rates, introduced the penny postal card, codified the laws relating to the post office department, and distributed patronage so effectively that he became virtually indispensable.[43]

As attorney general, Grant selected Judge Ebenezer Rockwood Hoar of Massachusetts. A genial New Englander, Hoar was a social and literary delight. He was also a close friend of Senator Charles Sumner's and a member of Harvard University's board of overseers. Hoar brought a world of erudition and learning to the cabinet.[44] For nearly ten years he had been an associate justice on the Supreme Judicial Court of Massachusetts, and as a lawyer he had few superiors. As the principal legal adviser to the president, Hoar, like Cox and Creswell, was a superb appointment. Grant did not submit a nomination for the War Department. He had promised the post to Rawlins, but felt obliged to Schofield for standing between him and Johnson during the past year. As a sign of his appreciation Grant did not replace him immediately.

After the initial shock subsided, the Senate acted swiftly. Moving into executive session, it took less than two hours to confirm Grant's nominees unanimously. Party regulars were disappointed, but the president's prestige was such that not even token opposition was offered. Throughout the country Grant's selections were greeted with applause. People rejoiced that the new president had "cut himself loose from the party hacks" who had dominated government in the past.[45] The New York Times took up the cry. "General Grant will have for his chief assistants only those who are untainted with the trickery and corruption which are the bane of contemporary politics."[46] The Tribune proclaimed that "the new Cabinet means business emphatically."[47] *Harper's Weekly* noted the "able and harmonious" nature of Grant's selections.[48]

Public applause notwithstanding, Grant immediately ran into trouble. The 1789 statute drafted by Alexander Hamilton that established the Department of the Treasury provided that "no person . . . concerned or interested in carrying on the business of trade or commerce" could head the department.[49] Under the terms of the statute, Stewart clearly was barred. Ordinarily that could have been ironed out if Grant had prepared the way beforehand, but he had not done so. And the Senate, its feelings ruffled from not having been consulted about the cabinet, decided to teach him a lesson.

When Grant was informed of the statutory barrier on March 6, he wrote immediately to the Senate requesting that Stewart be exempted.[50] That afternoon Senator John Sherman asked unanimous consent to introduce a resolution to that effect. At that point two Senate titans intervened. First, Charles Sumner objected and demanded the matter be referred to committee. Then Roscoe Conkling, the senior senator from New York, waded in. Conkling had worked hard to secure Grant's election and he was aggrieved that he had not been consulted about a cabinet appointee from his own state, especially since he and Stewart had been on opposite sides of the political fence for years. Seeing an opportunity to settle old scores, Conkling offered a number of additional statutory impediments to Stewart's appointment.[51] Conkling's opposition settled the matter. Grant recognized that senatorial courtesy was so deeply ingrained that it was unlikely a majority of the New Yorker's colleagues would vote against him. Rather than fight a long, drawn-out battle, Grant accepted Stewart's offer to step down.

Stewart's abrupt departure disappointed those who thought Grant meant to encourage business.[52] The sudden resignation of Elihu Washburne later in the week struck observers as simply bizarre. When Grant initially named Washburne to be secretary of state it was widely assumed the president wanted his surefooted friend nearby. Washburne had no particular talent for foreign affairs, but neither had Seward when Lincoln appointed him. It quickly turned out that Grant had no intention of retaining Washburne at State. There is no paper trail, but Badeau (who was privy to Grant's thinking) reports that shortly before inauguration Grant offered the Interior Department to Washburne. The congressman said he preferred Treasury, but Grant was already committed to Stewart. Washburne then asked for State, but Grant was reluctant. At that point Washburne (whose wife was French) asked to be appointed minister to France. As a personal favor, however, he requested that he be allowed to hold the post of secretary of state for a few days before going to Paris. Strange as the request was, Grant felt he could not refuse. He knew Washburne had expected more than he was receiving, and he did not want to disappoint the man to whom he owed so much. Without tipping his hand, Grant sent Washburne's name forward with the original appointees.[53] The secretary submitted his resignation on March 10 citing ill health, and Grant named him minister to France the following day.[54]*

The War Department was another special case. Grant had originally planned to give Rawlins command of the military Department of Arizona and send him west for his health. The general's chief of staff had been stricken with tuberculosis and Grant believed the hot, dry climate of Arizona would help him recover. When informed of the plan, Rawlins objected. He said what he really wanted was to be secretary of war. Grant agreed instantly: another example of his loyalty to those who had befriended and assisted him. Grant did not have the heart to deny Rawlins what he desired, even though he sensed it was a terminal request.[55]

At the end of his first week in office, Grant's cabinet was only half full. Seasoned political observers clucked at the inauspicious beginning, the false starts and near misses, but Grant was unruffled. Donelson and Vicksburg had started that way and Shiloh had been much worse. It was not the first time he had been rebuffed, and Grant continued to be supremely confident of his ability to cope with the situation.[56] At noon on March 11, acting once again without consultation, he filled the vacancies at State, Treasury, and the War Department with exemplary appointments. For secretary of state, Grant chose Hamilton Fish of New York. The Treasury went to Congressman George S. Boutwell of Massachusetts, and Rawlins's name was sent forward to succeed Schofield.[57] Once again the nominees were confirmed unanimously. The press waxed eloquent about Grant's choices. Fish was hailed as an eminent elder statesman who would add experience to the cab-

---

* Washburne served as United States minister to France for eight and a half years, a record for an American envoy, and he did an outstanding job. He remained at his post in Paris throughout the Franco-Prussian War, endearing himself to the French for his steadfastness during the siege of Paris, while at the same time protecting German property in the city. During the Commune, Washburne was the only head of mission who did not flee Paris, and the American legation became a refuge for citizens of all nationalities. At one time, Washburne was feeding over 4,000 people in the U.S. compound. Acting without instructions from Washington, Washburne interceded on behalf of the archbishop of Paris, Georges Darboy, when he was arrested, but he was unable to save the prelate's life when the Commune fell. Bismarck proposed awarding Washburne the highest decoration Germany could bestow on a foreigner but the minister declined to accept the honor. Nevertheless, when Washburne's tour in Paris ended, the emperor sat for an oil portrait which was then presented to him. "You will please receive the same," wrote William I, "as a remembrance of the eventful times during which you have been in a position to render beneficial and efficient services to my government, and at the same time as a sign of my regard and kind wishes." Gaillard Hunt, *Israel, Elihu, and Cadwallader Washburn: A Chapter in American Biography* 258–62 (New York: Macmillan, 1925).

inet. The *New York Times* said Boutwell's appointment "gives great satisfaction to all. The confidence of the people in his integrity is so great that there will unquestionably be a hearty response in all quarters."[58] The *New York Tribune* noted that it was a "strong and safe cabinet. There is not a man in it who sought his position, nor one who has not accepted cheerfully."[59]

Along with the names of his final three cabinet appointees, Grant transmitted several additional nominations to the Senate. The most prominent was that of his old comrade, former Confederate general James Longstreet, to be surveyor of customs of the port of New Orleans. This was one of the most lucrative appointments the president could bestow. Longstreet's nomination, coming in the first week of Grant's term, and again without consultation, stunned the nation. Southern Republicans were dismayed but elsewhere, once the news was digested, the response was warm and genuine. Grant had taken another important step toward bringing the nation together. "Our new president has done many acts for which his country will hold him in grateful remembrance," wrote Horace Greeley, "but he never did a wiser or nobler act than his nomination yesterday of General James Longstreet."[60] The fact that Longstreet, virtually alone among the South's former military commanders, had spoken out forcefully for compliance with the Reconstruction Acts, made the appointment doubly satisfying. The *New York Times* called it a "gesture of reconciliation which will work a very great change in the temper of the Southern people."[61] James Gordon Bennett's *New York Herald,* after reminding readers that Longstreet had come within an eyelash of rolling up Grant's flank in the Wilderness, called the appointment "a new and important moment in Southern reconstruction."[62]

In early April Grant stunned the nation once again when he appointed his longtime aide, Brigadier General Ely S. Parker, commissioner of Indian affairs.* In his inaugural, Grant had spoken in heartfelt terms about the plight of Native Americans and the appointment of Parker

---

* After the embarrassment caused by Stewart's appointment, Grant wanted to be certain that Parker was eligible. No Indian had ever served as commissioner, and because Indians were not citizens, Grant thought it best to inquire before sending Parker's name forward. Although the Fourteenth Amendment granted citizenship to "all persons born or naturalized in the United States," it was qualified by the phrase "and subject to the jurisdiction thereof," and the Civil Rights Act of 1866 specificallly excluded "Indians not taxed" from citizenship. Presumably that applied to those living on reservations and not to individuals like Parker. To be certain, Grant asked Attorney General Hoar for an opinion. Hoar replied on April 12, 1869 that "on the facts presented, I do not perceive that he is disqualified from holding such office under the Constitution and laws of the United States." Hoar did not provide reasons or rationale, but his opinion was sufficient for Grant. The following day he nominated Parker, who was confirmed (36–12) by the Senate on April 14, 1869. 19 *Grant Papers* 197 note. Also see William H. Armstrong, *Warrior in Two Camps: Ely S. Parker, Union General and Seneca Chief* 135–36 (Syracuse, N.Y.: Syracuse University Press, 1978).

underlined his concern. As general in chief, Grant had employed his Seneca aide as his eyes and ears with respect to the tribes in the West, and as president-elect he had used him to explore with the Society of Friends the possibility of employing Quakers as Indian agents.[63] Because of the resistance in Congress, Grant had given up the idea of transferring the Bureau of Indian Affairs to the War Department. But he continued to believe that the bureau, and the agents selected by it, were a major cause of unrest on the frontier.[64] By appointing Parker and enlisting the Quakers he was moving briskly to put in place what would soon be known as "Grant's Peace Policy" toward the Plains Indians.

Unlike most of his immediate predecessors, Grant's transition to the presidency was remarkably easy. In a sense, he was merely moving across the street from being general in chief (and the second most important figure in Washington) to being commander in chief. Nevertheless, it was not until two weeks after the inauguration that he and Julia moved into the White House. Julia insisted the move be delayed so that she might refurbish the mansion and make it more livable. Mary Todd Lincoln had redecorated with a fury when she moved in, but within six weeks the nation was at war. Then came Lincoln's assassination and the Johnson interregnum, with the new president's wife an invalid. For almost eight years little had been done. The carpets were worn, the paint dingy, the furniture scratched and shabby.

Julia tackled the task with gusto. The mansion was cleaned and repainted, the furniture refinished and rearranged, new draperies were installed and the carpets replaced. Most important for daily living, the staff was spruced up and a professional chef engaged. The social calendar became Julia's responsibility. Twice a week the Grants received visitors, once in the afternoon when ladies could call on Julia, the other on Wednesday evening for people to see the president. Washington society was delighted. As one biographer has written, Julia became the most popular first lady since Dolley Madison.[65] She not only turned the White House into a comfortable place to live, but made it once again the focus of the capital's social life.

The Grant household at this time consisted of the president and first lady, their two youngest children, Nellie and Jess, plus Julia's eighty-three-year-old father, whom time had not mellowed. An unreconstructed Democrat, Colonel Dent offered his antediluvian views to anyone who would listen, prompting Julia to ensure that he was always seated next to her at the dinner table so that she might restrain him. In addition to the family, two of Grant's former aides, Horace Porter and Orville Babcock, now serving as secretaries to the president, also took up residence at the White House. The two oldest Grant children were away at school, or soon would be. Fred, age nineteen, was at West Point, and Ulysses Jr., two years younger, would go to Harvard.

The family rooms were on the second floor of the mansion. So too were the president's office and the cabinet room. The library did double duty as the Grants' parlor. The grand salons on the first floor were used for official functions: weekly receptions in the Blue Room, larger affairs in the elegant East Room, formal dinners in the State Dining Room. In the evenings the Grants received personal guests in the Red Room and normally had their meals in the Green Room, overlooking the South Lawn and the still unfinished Washington Monument. The table was always set so that half a dozen unexpected guests might be accommodated.[66]

As a rule, presidents did not dine out, attend private parties, or pay social calls. Grant, perhaps because of his relative youth or his familiarity with Washington, set a different tone. He regularly accepted invitations from the members of his cabinet and old friends from the military, who were free to drop in to see the president whenever they wished. On Sundays, Grant's childhood friend Daniel Ammen, now Rear Admiral Daniel Ammen, had a standing invitation for lunch.[67]

Following Lincoln's assassination Congress had created the Secret Service, and when Grant moved into the White House there were guards stationed throughout the mansion. Grant dismissed them. For the next eight years he was as unprotected as presidents traditionally had been. He no longer rode the streetcar, but he often walked the streets alone, just as he had when general in chief.[68]

Most days Grant woke at seven and read the Washington and New York newspapers before escorting Julia to breakfast at 8:30. Breakfast at 8:30 was a ritual, and the entire family was expected to attend. After breakfast Grant went for a stroll around the neighborhood and was back at his office at ten. For the next five hours he dealt with the business that came across his desk and whatever appointments might have been scheduled. The cabinet met at 2 P.M. on Tuesdays, and the meetings usually lasted two hours. In the late afternoon Grant would either go for a drive in an open carriage, or take another stroll, sometimes dropping in on friends unexpectedly. If boys were playing ball in the park, he would often stop to watch, smoking a cigar. On Sundays, if the weather was good, he liked to take a six-mile walk around Georgetown.[69]

Grant reorganized the presidential office. Accustomed to crisp staff efficiency, he installed his former aides as presidential secretaries. Nominally they remained on Sherman's staff, but their place of duty was at the White House. Porter and Babcock handled the paperwork, while Colonel Frederick Dent, Grant's brother-in-law, was made appointments secretary and put in charge of the reception room. Visitors had to convince Dent that their business warranted a meeting with the president.[70] Adam Badeau, who would soon be appointed deputy chief of mission in London, was given a room near the president's office where he would be able to work on his history of Grant's military campaigns and be available for whatever special assignments might be necessary.[71]

Badeau lived in the same Washington boarding house as Henry Adams, and several weeks after the inauguration he took his young friend to a reception at the White House. Adams's description of Grant, not unlike that of Richard Henry Dana upon seeing the general in chief for the first time in 1864 (see Chapter 9), captured the essential force of the president while dwelling on what a privileged Bostonian might consider his lack of breeding and refinement. Writing about himself in the third person, Adams compared Grant to Garibaldi.

> Of the two, Garibaldi seemed a trifle the more intellectual, but, in both, the intellect counted for nothing; only energy counted. The type was pre-intellectual, archaic, and would have seemed so even to the cave dwellers. Adam, according to legend, was such a man.
>
> Adams did not feel Grant as a hostile force . . . he saw only an uncertain one. When in action he was superb and safe to follow; only when torpid he was dangerous. To deal with him one must stand near, like a Rawlins, and practice more or less sympathetic habits. Simple-minded beyond the experience of Wall Street or State Street, he resorted . . . to commonplaces when at a loss for expression. . . . Robert E. Lee betrayed the same intellectual commonplace, in a Virginia form, not to the same degree, but quite distinctly enough for one who knew the American. What worried Adams was not the commonplace; it was, as usual, his own education. Grant fretted and irritated him, like the *Terebratula* as a defiance of first principles.* He had no right to exist. He should have been extinct for ages. The idea that, as society grew older, it grew one-sided, upset evolution, and made of education a fraud. That, two thousand years after Alexander the Great and Julius Caesar, a man like Grant should be called— and should actually and truly be—the highest product of the most advanced evolution, made evolution seem ludicrous. One must be as commonplace as Grant's own commonplaces to maintain such an absurdity. The progress of evolution from President Washington to President Grant, was alone evidence enough to upset Darwin.[72]

---

* The *Terebratula* was a shellfish that Adams had been told appeared to be identical from the beginning to the end of geological time.

Adams's portrait, often quoted, reflected the bitterness of a self-indulgent and overly genteel young man who had gone to Washington confident of securing a position with the Grant administration and not found one. Adams had missed the Civil War, serving in England as secretary to his father, Charles Francis Adams, who was Lincoln's minister to the Court of St. James. When he returned to the United States in 1868 it was a much different country from the one he had left, and the impressionable Adams, having acquired a veneer of European sophistication, was not certain it was a better one.

Adams's portrayal of Grant should be read alongside the sketch penned by his older brother, Charles Francis Adams, Jr., after the battle of the Wilderness. Both brothers saw the same man, both recognized Grant's force of character, but Charles Francis, a captain in the 1st Massachusetts Cavalry, then on staff duty, saw something more. "Grant is certainly a very extraordinary man," he wrote his father.

> He does not look it. Neither do I know that he shows it in conversation, for he never spoke to me and doesn't seem to be a very talkative man anyhow. The truth is, he is in appearance a very ordinary looking man, one who would attract attention neither in one way or the other.
>
> In figure Grant is comical. He sits a horse well, but in walking he leans forward and toddles. Such being his appearance, however, I do not think that any intelligent person could watch him, even from such a distance as mine, without concluding that he is a remarkable man. He handles those around him so quietly and well, he so evidently has the faculty of disposing of work and managing men, he is cool and quiet, almost stolid. He is a man of the most exquisite judgment and tact. See how he has handled this Army. The materials were all ready for an explosion at the first mistake Grant made. All this has passed away. . . . He has effected this simply by the exercise of tact and good taste. The result is that even from the most jealously disposed and the most indiscreet of Meade's staff, not a word is heard against Grant. The result is of inestimable importance. The army has a head and confidence in that head.[73]

Grant in peace was the same man as Grant in war. Charles Francis Adams, Jr., saw beneath the surface; Henry Adams did not.

For Grant, being president was scarcely more difficult than being general in chief. His new adversaries, such as Senator Charles Sumner, were formidable. But Robert E. Lee had been just as formidable a foe, if not more so. The principal difference, as Grant soon learned, was that the army chain of command was explicit. Things did not always go according to plan; indeed, Grant's strength as a commander lay in his ability to improvise when things went awry. But there was always a denouement. A battle was won or lost, and after that one moved on. In the White House problems lingered. The president could not command, and most issues required trimming and compromise. Alliances were transitory. Criticism, second-guessing, and backbiting were continuous. Occasionally one had to choose between friends. Those who lost out could be unforgiving. But as Grant saw it, responsibility for making decisions went with the office.

The first issue in which Grant found himself between a rock and a hard place involved the organization of the War Department. During his tenure as general in chief Grant chafed because bureau chiefs such as the adjutant general and the quartermaster general were responsible to the secretary of war, not the commanding general.* Grant assured Sherman he would correct the problem.[74] One of his first acts as president was to instruct Schofield to issue an order making the seven bureau heads subordinate to the general in chief.† General Schofield, who viewed the matter as a line officer, agreed that such an order was long overdue and on March 5, 1869, the day after Grant's inauguration, sent down a general order placing the staff sections under Sherman "by direction of the President."[75]

Grant was pleased with the change, Schofield was enthusiastic, and

---

* Friction between the secretary of war and the general in chief traced to legislation enacted during the Madison administration that established independent staff bureaus and made them responsible to the secretary of war. The purpose was to assist the secretary in fulfilling his legal obligation to manage the War Department but it removed the bureaus from the military chain of command. John C. Calhoun, who was secretary throughout the eight years of Monroe's presidency, utilized the statute to consolidate civilian authority and effectively controlled the War Department, besting General Andrew Jackson in the process. Thirty years later Jefferson Davis as secretary of war used his statutory authority to ride roughshod over General Winfield Scott. [The antagonism between Davis and Scott was exacerbated by strong personal dislike, Davis being the son-in-law of Zachary Taylor. Davis admired Taylor, played a key role helping Old Rough and Ready win the battle of Buena Vista, and was resentful of the treatment Taylor received at the hands of Scott during the Mexican War.] Grant complained about the relationship to Lincoln in 1864 and secured Lincoln's acquiescence to issue orders to the bureau chiefs, but it was an ad hoc arrangement. The Union command structure worked during the war because Grant and Stanton made it work, but Grant always resented the secretary's ultimate authority over the bureaus. For background, see L. D. Ingersoll, *A History of the War Department of the United States* 114–28 (Washington, D.C.: Francis D. Mahun, 1880); William H. Carter, *Creation of the American General Staff*, 68th Congress, 1st sess., 2 *Senate Documents* (Serial 8254), no. 119; Russell F. Weigley, *History of the United States Army* 134–43, 284–87 (New York: Macmillan, 1967).
† Each of the seven staff bureaus was headed by a general officer: A. A. Humphreys, chief of engineers; Edmund D. Townsend, adjutant general; Montgomery C. Meigs, quartermaster general; William G. Marcy, inspector general; Joseph K. Barnes, surgeon general; Joseph Holt, judge advocate general; and Albert J. Meyer, the chief signal officer. All were friends of Grant and Sherman, yet their institutional loyalties ran to their branches.

Sherman was delighted, but the bureau chiefs, almost to a man, resented the loss of their independence and promptly took their complaints to Congress. The Senate Military Affairs Committee took up their cause. Charles Sumner called the order "an act of revolution exalting the military power above the civil."[76] Grant was informally advised by friends on Capitol Hill that Schofield's order contravened the statutes that established the bureaus.

Grant was shaken. Having stubbed his toe against a statute when Stewart was appointed, he was not eager to do so again. On top of that, Rawlins was offended. As chief of staff to Grant, Rawlins had shared the view that the bureau chiefs belonged in the military chain of command. But as secretary of war he saw the matter differently. Schofield's order, he told Grant, made him a mere figurehead, and he begged the president to rescind it.[77]

Grant faced a disagreeable choice. Sherman was his dearest friend and closest ally. He had given Cump a commitment, and the order to that effect had been issued. In addition, Grant genuinely believed that the staff bureaus should be subordinate to the general in chief. To reverse himself would make the administration look clumsy and indecisive, it would certainly offend Sherman, and insofar as the army was concerned it would not be the right answer.

On the other hand, Grant felt a deep obligation to Rawlins. For eight years the chiseled-featured lawyer from Galena had been his confidant and alter ego. He had stood by Grant in every crisis, and, on the few occasions when it was required, had kept the general in chief on the straight and narrow. He was the one man who would talk frankly to Grant, and one of the few men to whom Grant listened. Rawlins had earned the right to be secretary of war. He was terminally ill, and the president could not bear to disappoint him.

No matter what Grant decided, one or the other of his closest friends was going to be disappointed. The clincher was the statute. Once again Grant had erred in not reconnoitering the legal ground before acting. Just as with Stewart's nomination, he could have avoided the problem if he had asked Judge Hoar for an opinion beforehand. As chief executive, Grant's duty was to see that the laws be faithfully executed. The Constitution required it, and in his inaugural address Grant pledged himself to do so. That left no alternative. At a White House dinner on March 25 the president broke the news to Sherman. Drawing his friend aside, Grant said, "I guess we have to revoke that order of Schofield's." Sherman was stunned. Grant mentioned the statute, and then said that Rawlins felt bad about the order. "I don't like to give him pain now."

Sherman reminded Grant that Schofield's order had been the president's idea and that it reflected his thinking as to how the army should be organized. "It's your order," said Sherman, "how will it look if you rescind it?"

"Well, if it's my own order, I can rescind it, can't I?" Grant replied.

"Yes, Mr. President," said Sherman, terminating the conversation. The military chain of command reasserted itself.[78] Neither man was happy about the exchange and the following morning Sherman sent Grant an additional reclama, just as he had done before embarking on the Vicksburg campaign. "Please do not revoke your order of March 5 without further reflection," wrote Sherman. "It would put me in a most unpleasant dilemma because the Army and country would infer your want of confidence."[79] It was too late. Rawlins's order restoring the status quo ante had already been issued.[80] Grant paid heavily for his mistake. He and Sherman remained friends, but the warmth was no longer there. "He is a mystery to me," Sherman wrote later. "And I believe he is a mystery to himself."[81]

Grant's first clash with Congress occurred over repeal of the Tenure of Office Act. Eighteen sixty-nine was a time of legislative supremacy in the United States, and America's solons were reluctant to surrender the power they had wrested from the executive. The Republicans had used the act to thwart Johnson's power to remove subordinates and it was now a matter of senatorial prerogative. When Grant indicated that he wanted the statute repealed, the Senate leadership circled the wagons. On March 2, the next-to-the-last day of Johnson's term, the upper house voted down a bill to repeal the act, 35–15. Two thirds of the Senate served notice it had no intention of yielding its authority. "I wish to leave the President-elect free to the full and useful exercise of the good judgment and good qualities which we all ascribe to him," said New York's Roscoe Conkling. "At the same time, I wish . . . to preserve the position which the Senate has maintained in the last and most dire emergency known in our jurisprudence."[82]

When the new Congress convened following Grant's inauguration, another effort was made to repeal the statute. Led by Congressman Benjamin Butler of Massachusetts, now one of Grant's staunchest supporters, the House voted overwhelmingly in early March to overturn the act. Once again the Senate balked. Grant responded by announcing that until the law was repealed he would enforce it vigorously. He would not remove any of Johnson's appointees and would only fill offices that were vacant. The effect of the president's announcement was to deny Congress the spoils it was expecting. There would be no new postmasters, pension clerks, or customs collectors until the Senate acted. Grant was scarcely the political babe in the woods sometimes depicted. By halting patronage appointments the president was using the one weapon the senators understood. Even Roscoe Conkling now suggested compromise.[83] Within three weeks a bill emerged that permitted the president to remove executive appointees either with the consent of the Senate or by the appointment of a successor whom the Senate would accept. More important, the president was given complete control over removals from his cabinet. Grant was satisfied. Rather than fight a protracted struggle for total repeal of the Tenure of Office Act, he signed the new measure on April 6.*

One of the most serious problems Grant confronted was the economy. Wartime financing had put the credit of the United States at risk. The national debt, which in 1860 stood at $64 million, had ballooned to $2.8 billion, most of it in the form of bonds bearing 6 percent interest. In addition, there was $356 million in unredeemable greenbacks circulating. These had driven gold coins out of circulation, and $160 million in fractional paper currency had replaced silver coins.[84] European bankers discounted dollars heavily and fears of a default on government bonds abounded, exacerbated by populist clamor in the United States to repudiate the national debt. The Republicans viewed the matter differently and so did Grant. Echoing Alexander Hamilton at the nation's founding, the new chief executive stood squarely for payment of the country's debt in full. "The payment of this *principal* and *interest,* as well as the return to a specie basis [gold or silver], as soon as it can be accomplished without material detriment to the debtor class, must be provided for," said Grant in his inaugural. As he saw it, more than national honor was at stake. The economy hinged on the credit of the central government and that credit must be protected.[85]

Congress responded to the president's leadership with the Act to Strengthen the Public Credit, which Grant signed on March 18—the first law of his administration. The act pledged the United States to pay all bondholders in "gold or its equivalent," and to redeem paper money "at the earliest practicable period."[86] As soon as Grant signed the bill, gold on the New York exchange fell to $130 an ounce, the lowest point since the suspension of specie payment in 1862.[87]

George Boutwell, Grant's secretary of the treasury, became the point man in the administration's effort to bolster the dollar. A fifty-one-year-old former governor of Massachusetts and overseer of Harvard, he had been appointed the first commissioner of the Internal Revenue Service in 1862 and had organized the bureau efficiently. Elected to Congress later in the

---

* The authority of the Senate to approve the removal of lesser executive appointees remained on the statute books until declared unconstitutional by Chief Justice Taft, speaking for the Supreme Court in *Myers v. United States,* 272 U.S. 52 (1926). In Taft's view, the removal power was vested exclusively in the president. *Myers* remains the primary case relied on by those seeking to interpret presidential power broadly. Compare *Humphrey's Executor v. United States,* 295 U.S. 602 (1935). Also compare Taft's earlier view expressed in his book, *Our Chief Magistrate and His Powers* 139–40 (New York: Columbia University Press, 1916).

Inauguration Day, March 4, 1869. Grant, who did not campaign, carried twenty-six of thirty-four states and at the age of forty-six became the youngest president ever elected.

Julia as first lady. Four years younger than Grant, she presided over social life in the capital with grace and charm.

Hamilton Fish, Grant's secretary of state for eight years, is ranked by diplomatic historians as one of America's greatest.

Judge Ebenezer Rockwood Hoar of Massachusetts served with distinction as Grant's attorney general. Appointed by Grant to the Supreme Court, he failed Senate confirmation.

John A. Rawlins, Grant's
wartime adjutant, served as
secretary of war until his death
from tuberculosis in 1869.

George Boutwell, Grant's first
secretary of the treasury, restored
United States credit abroad and
defeated the efforts of Jay Gould
and Jim Fisk to corner the gold
market on Black Friday.

Amos T. Akerman of Georgia, Hoar's successor as attorney general, spearheaded the Grant administration's efforts to suppress the Ku Klux Klan.

Benjamin H. Bristow, solicitor general (1870–1872) and secretary of the treasury (1874–1876), led the investigation that broke the Whiskey Ring.

Frederick Douglass, the most articulate spokesman of African Americans, consistently supported Grant and urged black voters to do the same. "We will not find a candidate equal to General Grant."

"Visit of the Ku Klux" by Frank Bellew, depicting the Klan's reign of terror. Grant intervened personally to secure passage of the Ku Klux Klan bill in 1871, and under it more than 3,000 indictments were returned, effectively breaking the power of the Klan.

Grant's peace policy struck a responsive chord among the Sioux. Red Cloud *(top right)* and Spotted Tail *(bottom right)* led the delegation that visited the White House at the president's invitation in 1872.

Roscoe Conkling of New York, Grant's principal supporter in the Senate and one of the great constitutional lawyers of the era. Ambitious for higher elective office, he declined appointment as Chief Justice of the United States.

Grant took great interest in architecture and sprinkled federal buildings across the country to consolidate the Union. The massive State, War, and Navy Building in Washington is the best example of what art historians call "General Grant style."

Thomas Nast admired Grant and often depicted him as a lion. He is shown here triumphant over the asses in Congress with his veto of the inflation bill in 1874.

One of the last photographs of Grant shows him sitting on the porch of his cottage at Mount McGregor working on the manuscript for his *Memoirs*. Dying of cancer, Grant completed the task one day before his death.

Grant's *Memoirs* were a phenomenal success. Mark Twain, who published them, presented Julia with a $200,000 royalty check—at the time the largest ever written.

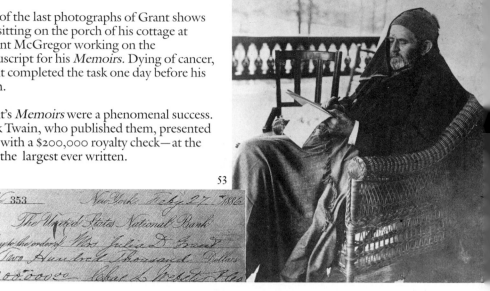

Grant's funeral cortege at Broadway and Thirteenth Street in New York. *The New York Times* reported 1.5 million spectators lined the route as veterans of the Stonewall Brigade marched in somber unison with the Grand Army of the Republic.

war, he became a leader of the Radical Republicans. He had been an early abolitionist, an advocate of Negro suffrage, a member of the Committee on Reconstruction, and, as chairman of the House Judiciary Committee, was one of the principal architects of the Thirteenth, Fourteenth, and Fifteenth amendments. Long known as an advocate of conservative financial reform, Boutwell, of all the cabinet, stood closest to the business interests of the country. With the exception of Rawlins, he was also the closest to Grant. In 1867 he had introduced the rider to the army appropriations bill that guaranteed Grant his position as general in chief, and throughout the Johnson years he had been a frequent guest at the Grants' I Street residence.

Boutwell's first order of business was to put the Treasury Department in order. He discharged redundant employees, initiated sweeping changes in the Bureau of Printing and Engraving to safeguard the currency from counterfeiters, and revitalized tax collections to hasten the gathering of revenue. So effective were Boutwell's efforts that the Treasury was soon showing a monthly surplus.

Grant treated Boutwell as he would have treated a proven army commander like Sherman or Sheridan, and gave him abundant latitude. With the president's approval, Boutwell developed his own policy and was soon selling the government's growing gold surplus at weekly auctions for greenbacks and buying back wartime bonds with the currency. The result was to reduce the national debt without shrinking the money supply, while at the same time keeping the gold surplus in the Treasury at a minimum and the price of the precious metal low. By the end of May, Boutwell had reduced the debt by $12 million. At the beginning of September, after six months in office, the secretary could boast that the nation's indebtedness was $50 million lower than when the administration took power. Public approval was quick in coming. "We don't object to buying up bonds with Greenbacks," said the *New York Tribune,* "we only insist on buying still more of them." The *New York Times* concluded there was "no reason to fear that the new administration will not fully meet the expectations of the country." [88]

Grant was more than satisfied. Setting out on a late summer vacation the president wrote Badeau that everything was well. "Public affairs look to be progressing very favorably. The revenues of the country are being collected as they have not been before, and expenditures are looked after more carefully. The first thing it seems to me is to establish the credit of the country. This is policy enough for the present." [89]

The gold market in New York was thin—probably not more than $15 million circulating at any given time—and by September the government's weekly auctions had become sufficient to fix the market price. The more gold the government sold, the lower the price, and vice versa. For Wall Street speculators, that made for an unpredictable market. Rather than financial conditions it was the government's decisions that determined the weekly value of gold. And Boutwell was inscrutable. The cabinet was deliberately not informed beforehand of the amount of gold to be disposed of and the secretary placed all of his sell orders through the United States assistant treasurer in New York, former general Daniel Butterfield. To minimize any chance for foul play, Boutwell announced his orders publicly through the Associated Press at the same time he telegraphed them to Butterfield.[90]

If a speculator could discern the government's intentions beforehand, he could make a killing. Better yet, if he could manipulate government policy, an even larger profit could be turned. Among Wall Street speculators, none were more daring than the pair of financial buccaneers who controlled the Erie Railway, Jay Gould and "Jubilee Jim" Fisk. And none recognized opportunity more quickly. If they could limit Boutwell's sales, or at least give the impression they could do so, they could corner the gold market, drive up the price, and then sell their holdings for an inflated amount before the price collapsed.

Gould and Fisk were unlikely partners. Both had escaped from a childhood of rural poverty in upstate New York and both shared a voracious acquisitiveness, but there the similarity ended. Gould, at thirty-three, was already a legend on Wall Street, having taken on and bested Commodore Cornelius Vanderbilt for ownership of the Erie Railway. Silent, introverted, and fidgety, Gould possessed a calculating shrewdness in business that amounted to financial genius. A devoted husband and father, he drank milk, not liquor, and cloaked his rapaciousness in a Victorian respectability.

Fisk, by contrast, was everything Gould was not. A newcomer to Wall Street, one year older than Gould, he was an extroverted, hard-living salesman with a talent for showmanship. His audacity was breathtaking. During the Civil War he distinguished himself smuggling contraband cotton through Union lines and accumulated a fortune, which he spent freely on women, diamond stickpins, and good times. A rogue of the financial world, Fisk had himself elected colonel of a militia regiment and strutted in his uniform until he acquired a packet of river steamers and conferred the title of "admiral" upon himself. Utterly unscrupulous, he joined with Gould in a loosely structured partnership that centered on railways but whose far-flung operations dipped into every field where easy profits might be made. While Gould took the lead in concocting ever new schemes for amassing wealth, seducing politicians, watering stock, and defrauding competitors, Fisk amused himself by parading his immorality.[91]

To corner the gold market required access to administration policy, so

Gould and Fisk cast about for allies. The first they snared was the sixty-one-year-old Abel Rathbone Corbin, the president's brother-in-law. A former editor, bureaucrat, lobbyist, and real estate speculator (it was Corbin who sold the house at 205 I Street to Grant for no money down in 1865), Corbin was a fringe player on Wall Street who lived discreetly but well in a five-story, high-stooped brownstone on West 27th Street. His asset, insofar as Gould and Fisk were concerned, was his recently acquired kinsman. Grant and Corbin had known each other since the president's bad days in Missouri in the 1850s. Grant liked him and trusted him. The fact is, Grant rarely met a businessman he did not trust. During the inaugural festivities in Washington, Corbin (whose wife had died the previous April) met, flirted with, and won the affection of Miss Virginia Paine Grant, the president's favorite sibling. Jennie, who was blond, attractive, and well spoken, was nevertheless at thirty-seven still unmarried and living with her parents in Covington, Kentucky. She was swept off her feet. After a whirlwind engagement the couple were married in May (Grant gave the bride away), and Jennie took up residence on West 27th Street. Grant was delighted that his sister had found so agreeable a partner. Henceforth, during his visits to New York, which were frequent in the summer of 1869, he made a point of staying with the newlyweds in the Corbin town house.

Gould took Corbin into his confidence, but only partially. He laid out a cockamamie theory about the benefits that would accrue to the American economy (and the Grant administration) if the price of gold went up, indicated his desire to contribute to that, and suggested that Corbin might like to participate. Corbin was hooked, but it could not be said that he was a knowing conspirator.[92]

The same was true of Daniel Butterfield. With Corbin on board, the conspirators turned their attention to the assistant treasurer in New York who handled the gold sales. This was the same Daniel Butterfield who had raised a $105,000 testimonial for Grant in 1866, and who was a family friend of Corbin's. Whether Butterfield would provide the Gold Ring with inside information was unclear, but Gould believed it was worth a try. Introduced by Corbin, the president of the Erie Railway promptly gave Butterfield a personal check for $10,000 "to cover expenses," no questions asked. That was the way Gould did business. Butterfield, whose annual government salary was $8,000, pocketed the money, but subsequently declined Gould's invitation to join the ring.* Nevertheless, his friendship and perhaps some degree of cooperation could reasonably be expected.[93]

* In testimony before the House Committee investigating the gold conspiracy, Butterfield maintained that the money from Gould was a real estate loan, albeit interest-free with no documentation or repayment date. *Gold Panic Investigation* 317–19, U.S. House of Representatives, Report No. 31, 41st Cong., 2nd sess., March 1, 1870.

Gould also tried to bribe General Horace Porter, Grant's personal secretary, offering to purchase $500,000 in gold in Porter's name. Porter promptly declined.[94] Gould, who had rarely encountered a public servant who turned down free money, took Porter's no for a yes and proceeded to open a brokerage account in the general's name and buy a half million dollars' worth of gold for him. When informed of the transaction, Porter turned that down too, this time in writing.[95] Corbin went Gould one better and attempted to entice Mrs. Grant. During the summer he offered her half-interest in $250,000 in bonds that he had purchased for his wife. Julia also declined, though she later said she appreciated the gesture.[96]

To gain leverage for the gold scam, Gould purchased the Tenth National Bank in New York, using funds supplied by his friends and longtime associates, the Tweed ring.[97] The Tenth National was a Wall Street brokers' bank, and Gould wanted it as a ready source for the certified checks he would need when trading in the Gold Room neared a climax. (The Tenth National enjoyed a reputation for sweetheart arrangements with favored customers, and as the bank's new owner Gould had every reason to believe those arrangements would continue.)[98] But the key to cornering the gold market was Grant. If he could be convinced to order Boutwell to suspend or reduce sales, the road would be open for the conspirators.

Through Corbin the Erie buccaneers now had access to the president. Whenever Grant visited New York, Corbin brought them together. Dinner at the Corbin mansion, the theater in Gould's box, a trip to Boston on Fisk's steamer, *Providence,* a journey to upstate New York on a private railroad car provided by the Erie. On each of these occasions Gould and Fisk laid out in great detail for the president the alleged advantages that would accrue to the United States if the price of gold went up. Grant listened but was noncommittal. Reticent by nature, he had perfected the art of hearing the opinions of others without giving the slightest indication of whether he agreed or disagreed. Gould mistook Grant's silence for acquiescence. But he should have been warned. When Gould inquired at one point if the president would share "a little intimation" of his gold policy, Grant pointedly declined. Giving private tips "would not be fair," he said, and any change in the government's plans would be announced by Secretary Boutwell "through the newspapers as usual, so that everybody might, at the same time, know what it was, thus excluding any possible charge of favoritism."[99] Grant was not averse to accepting the hospitality of rich men, and that may have been a personal failing, but he was not about to give them an unfair advantage as a result. Nevertheless, the fact that Grant was often seen in the company of Gould and Fisk during the summer of 1869 legitimized the pair and lent credence to the belief that the government supported their economic views.[100] That in itself gave them enormous clout on Wall Street and to that extent Grant was culpable. He should have been more careful of appearances, but that was not his way. The most trusting of men, he was totally unaware he was being used.

Believing that at the very least Grant was not opposed to rising gold prices, the conspirators set their plan in motion. Gould's first step was to reward his unwitting collaborators, Corbin and Butterfield: "an anchor thrown to the windward," he later told congressional investigators.[101] On September 1 he instructed his brokers to purchase $1.5 million in gold for Corbin's account, and another $1.5 million for Butterfield. For every dollar increase in the price of gold, each man would net a $15,000 profit. Butterfield and Corbin were Gould's early warning network. If the government planned to change policy, it was now in their interest to let him know. With the insurance in place, Gould and Fisk began buying gold aggressively. By Monday, September 6, the price had climbed to $137—a $4.50 jump in less than a week. For the next several days the price hovered between $135 and $137 as the bears fought back.

At this point Grant may have inadvertently encouraged Gould and his associates. On September 12, before leaving New York for a final week in the mountains of western Pennsylvania, Grant wrote a brief letter to Boutwell, who was due in the city shortly. The president entrusted the sealed envelope to Corbin to give to Butterfield to hold for Boutwell's arrival. The wish being father to the thought, Corbin assumed it was an order for Boutwell to suspend gold sales and allow the price to rise. He passed the word to Gould, and the ring's buying intensified.

In fact, Grant was instructing Boutwell to stay the course. After warning the secretary that the bulls and the bears were out in force on Wall Street, he told him to remain neutral. "A desperate struggle is now taking place, and each party want the government to help them out. I think, from the lights before me [an old railroading expression], I would move on, without change, until the present struggle is over."[102] Boutwell needed no prodding. After two days in New York, during which time he conferred with the nation's leading bankers, he was convinced that the government was being used by the speculators. To withhold gold from the market would guarantee Gould and the Gold Room bulls a huge windfall, the consequences of which would be to dry up the collection of customs duties (paid in gold), send the value of government bonds plunging, devalue the greenback, and erode American credit abroad. He returned to Washington determined, if anything, to step up the sale of gold to maintain the market's equilibrium.

Boutwell's visit to New York alarmed Corbin and he transmitted his concern to Gould. The secretary had given Corbin the brush-off when he called at Boutwell's hotel, and Corbin sniffed a hardening of government policy against any further rise in gold. Gould cringed at the prospect. If

Boutwell was running with the bears, the only recourse was for Grant to rein him in. At Gould's insistence, Corbin wrote his brother-in-law urging him to stay the secretary's hand. The letter ran page after page, Gould later recalled, intermingling arguments about the gold market with bits of family news and political gossip.[103] To ensure that Boutwell did not reach the president first, Gould had the letter hand-carried directly to Grant at his isolated Pennsylvania retreat. When the messenger arrived a day and a half later, the president and General Porter were engaged in a blistering round of cottage country croquet, totally unaware of the excitement in the Gold Room. The agent waited until the game was over, handed the message to Grant, and asked if there was a reply. "No, nothing," said the president, and the courier hurried to the nearest telegraph office to inform Gould. When he arrived at the station several hours later, the courier scribbled a hasty wire to New York: "Letter delivered all right." In transmission, the message was transposed to read: "Letter delivered. All right." Knowing what Corbin had written, Gould and Fisk interpreted this as a cryptic signal from Grant. Instantly they redoubled their efforts, assured, they believed, of the government's support.[104]

Grant, for his part, was put on edge by Corbin's letter. The fact that a purely personal message was hand-carried by an Erie employee on a non-stop journey from New York made no sense. What had Corbin found so urgent? When Porter told the president of Gould's attempt to buy him a $500,000 stake in the gold market, Grant put two and two together. Corbin and Gould were in collusion to corner the gold market and were counting on him, the president of the United States, to cover their investment. "I blame myself for not checking this," Grant told Porter. "I fear he [Corbin] may be ruined—and my poor sister."[105]

Rarely did Grant reveal his emotions, and almost never did he explode at Julia. But this was an exception. He barged into her room and demanded to know, "Whom are you writing to?"

"Your sister."

"Then write this," said Grant, and he proceeded to dictate the following: "The general says, if you have any influence with your husband, tell him to have nothing to do with Jay Gould and Jim Fisk. If he does, he will be ruined, for come what may, he (your brother) will do his duty to the country and the trusts in his keeping." Grant told Julia to seal the letter and send it by the first mail.[106] Other than informing his sister that Corbin should cease speculating in gold, Grant took no further action. He was content to leave policy in Boutwell's hands, and remained at his idyllic Pennsylvania retreat until Wednesday, September 22, arriving back in the capital the next day.

In New York meanwhile the scene in the Gold Room approached

bedlam. Buoyed by the telegram from Gould's emissary, the conspirators pressed ahead. Gould even opened an account at his brokerage called the National Gold Account to give the illusion of government support.[107] On Monday and Tuesday, September 20 and 21, the price of gold crept upward under the pressure of relentless buying by the conspirators. On Wednesday gold closed at $141, up almost $4 on the day. Gould and Fisk together owned $50 to $60 million in gold, about triple the public supply in New York. The price rise on that day alone generated a profit of over $1.75 million for the ring.[108]

Wednesday evening Gould called once again on Corbin. Julia's letter had just arrived, and the president's brother-in-law was distraught. Sitting in the dimmed library he read the relevant passages to Gould. "I must get out instantly—instantly," said Corbin. Gould took the message in stride. If nothing else, his early warning system was flashing the signal to be cautious. He urged Corbin not to dump his holdings, offered to buy him out for $100,000 profit, and then left to prepare for the next day's trading, forewarned that a break in the market could come at any moment.[109]

Gould did not pass Corbin's information on to Fisk. On Thursday, his agents began quietly to reduce his holdings, while at the same time buying publicly to maintain a bullish stance. Fisk led the buying charge that day, and after another round of riotous trading, gold closed at $144.50, up another $3.50. The two weeks' struggle in the Gold Room had devastated commerce across the country. The sudden demand for gold on Wall Street made it virtually impossible to find sufficient specie for foreign exchange. Imports and exports ground to a halt. Prices for wheat, cotton, and corn on the produce exchange all slumped. "The foreign trade of the United States [has come] to a dead stop," said the *New York Tribune*. "Goods offered for export cannot be sold; goods ready for shipment cannot be shipped; vessels half laden could receive no more cargo. . . . The whole army of working men occupied by our export trade [are] compelled to be idle."[110]

Boutwell followed developments closely from his desk in Washington. Linked by telegraph with the principal banking institutions in New York, and with a stream of emissaries moving back and forth, the treasury secretary recognized that the gold crisis was approaching a climax. A stock panic or a major bankruptcy could come at any moment, perhaps triggering a national depression. It had happened before. The devastating Panic of 1857 (which had destroyed Sherman's banking career and left Grant with no market for his crops) had been sparked by the collapse of the Ohio Life and Trust Company, a large Eastern bank. Publicly, Boutwell gave every appearance of indifference to the ruckus in the Gold Room. He answered no messages from New York, and made no comment to the press. Like a general preparing a counterattack, he let the enemy deploy.

Grant had returned to the capital Thursday morning. His day was spent catching up with his presidential workload. Each cabinet officer needed to see him, as did numerous senators and congressmen whose requests had been put on hold while the president vacationed. "A large crowd of visitors were present [at the White House]," the *New York Times* reported, "but were unable to see the President because of important business with prominent officials here."[111] Boutwell bided his time. Rather than press into the crowded White House schedule he waited until evening. Then he would have the president's undivided attention, and the day's activity in the Gold Room would be concluded. Already, however, the secretary had put his small army of regulators in motion. Alerted that the Tenth National Bank was certifying checks for Gould and Fisk far in excess of their assets, Boutwell ordered the comptroller of the currency to send a platoon of bank inspectors to New York to seize the Tenth National before it opened for business Friday morning and shut down any illegal cash flow.[112]

Face-to-face Thursday evening, Boutwell gave the president a crisp rundown of the situation on Wall Street. Grant agreed that a gold price of $144 was "unnatural." As Boutwell later explained, "We thought the business of the country was endangered." Grant was in full command of the situation. His orders were quick, decisive, and complete. If the price of gold advanced materially in Friday's trading, he instructed Boutwell to sell gold "to save the country from a panic."[113] The secretary had his marching orders. He left the White House and rode off into the Washington night armed with the president's directive to crush the Gold Room bulls the next day. The surprise would be complete.

Friday, September 24, 1869, Black Friday in the annals of American finance, was bright and sunny, the temperature unseasonably warm. By now the conspirators had accumulated calls for over $100 million in gold and held the New York financial community by the throat. The *New York Times* reported that the financial district brimmed with a carnival atmosphere as crowds flocked in to see Fisk and Gould complete their corner and render the coup de grâce to the banks of the old order. "Representatives of almost every class were there," wrote a *Times* reporter. "The great merchant stood side-by-side with the *sans culotte*—the gutter snipe of society; the man of law compared notes with the Wall Street 'goat,' an individual known only to brokers."[114]

Fisk was the center of attention on Friday, barking orders to his minions on the exchange floor. "We have it in our power to put gold up to $200, and we mean to do it," he told one newsman.[115] By 9:30 the price was at $150, with the ring buying every offering in sight. "This is the day," Fisk shouted to Henry Benedict, chairman of the gold exchange, a nervous onlooker at the carnage.[116] By eleven o'clock the price had crept up to $155 and was edging toward $160, with Fisk still buying. Washington was deluged with urgent telegraph messages from frantic bankers urging the government to intervene. "Immediate interference in this gold market is imperative," wired Harris Fahnestock of Jay Cooke and Company. "Exchange of four millions gold for bonds immediately done would change current at once. Otherwise advance [in gold price] is indefinite."[117] Moses Grinnell, the United States surveyor of customs in New York, telegraphed both Grant and Boutwell, telling them that unless the government acted a large proportion of the city's reliable merchants and bankers would have to close their doors permanently by three o'clock.[118]

Boutwell had been following the market intently. Shortly after eleven he walked briskly from the Treasury to the White House, a sheaf of telegrams in his hand. Grant had been expecting him. "We had very little conversation," Boutwell recalled. The secretary suggested that the government sell $3 million in gold from the New York subtreasury to break the corner. "I think you had better make it five million," said Grant.[119] The meeting was brief. Boutwell hurried back to the Treasury and dictated a telegram to Butterfield. He split the difference:

SELL FOUR MILLION ($4,000,000) GOLD TOMORROW, AND BUY FOUR MILLION ($4,000,000) BONDS.

> GEO. S.
> BOUTWELL
> SECRETARY
> TREASURY[120]

The uncoded message was transmitted immediately over the open lines of Western Union and the Franklin Telegraph Company. The news hit the Gold Room like an avalanche. Gold, which had been hovering between $160 and $162, plummeted to $133 within minutes. The Gold Ring had been broken. Grant's role was decisive. As on numerous Civil War battlefields he had given the crucial order. Launching Boutwell against the Gold Ring on Friday was not much different. Grant acted without remorse, without emotion, and without second thoughts.

Sunday, September 26, was family day at the White House. The president, Julia, all four of the children, Colonel Dent, Horace Porter, along with Admiral Ammen and his wife, sat down to the midday meal. They were joined by Jennie and Abel Corbin, who had come down especially from New York. Grant had made no public comment about the events of Black Friday, and he chose not to mention it now. Corbin eventually led into the topic, describing how his friends had suffered in the panic and how the government could help both bulls and bears if it rescinded its order to sell. Grant listened politely, puffed on his cigar, and then rose from his chair, cutting his brother-in-law off in mid-sentence. "This matter has been concluded," the president said. "I cannot open up or consider the subject."[121] The United States, for the first time, had intervened massively to bring order to the marketplace. It was a watershed in the history of the American economy.

The gold crash devastated the United States economy for months. From September 24 to October 1, aggregate stock prices on Wall Street dropped 20 percent and trading dried up. Only four million shares changed hands between January and September 1870, less than half the volume of the year before. Dozens of brokerages went bankrupt, and many traders who sold paper gold to Fisk during the run-up to Black Friday were left holding the bag when he refused to pay. Farmers, who constituted more than 50 percent of the American workforce, suffered worst of all. Wheat plummeted on the Chicago exchange from $1.40 to 77 cents a bushel. Corn fell from 95 to 68 cents, and rye, oats, and barley suffered similar losses. Battered by tight money and dwindling markets, American agriculture went into a steep decline from which it did not recover for years.

Jay Gould and Jim Fisk survived Black Friday unscathed. Defended by the best legal talent money could buy, including the renowned David Dudley Field, and with an array of Tweed Ring judges at their beck and call, including Judge Albert Cardozo, the pair easily defeated charges against them.[122] Gould remained a force on Wall Street for the next twenty-three years and commanded major segments of the nation's communications and transportation networks. He died in December 1892 and left a fortune probated at more than $70 million. Like Gould, Fisk prospered for the next few years, living outrageously and laughing off the slurs of respectable New Yorkers. His joie de vivre did him in, however. He was shot and killed by the jealous rival for a lady's affections on January 6, 1872. For his part, George Boutwell served in an exemplary manner as Grant's secretary of the treasury until 1873 when he resigned to become United States senator from Massachusetts. He served in the Senate until 1877, after which he returned to private life.

CHAPTER SIXTEEN

DIPLOMACY

The hostility of England to the United States during our rebellion
was not so much real as it was apparent.

ULYSSES S. GRANT

WHEN GRANT TOOK OFFICE, two foreign policy issues stood front and center: a fierce, ongoing insurrection against Spanish rule in Cuba, and the *Alabama* claims against Great Britain. These fell within the bailiwick of Hamilton Fish and the Department of State, and Grant relied on Fish to oversee them, just as he relied on Boutwell to manage the administration's economic policy. A former governor, congressman, and United States senator from New York, Fish, at the age of sixty, had been out of public service twelve years when Grant chose him to be secretary of state. Descended from one of America's richest families, Fish was cultured, traveled, learned (he spoke four languages), and possessed a broad international outlook. "Yours will be the rare happiness of restoring to the national character as represented by the State Department the high-toned dignity and noble principle which marked the diplomacy of the Revolution," a fellow New Yorker gushed at the time of his appointment.[1]

That perception of Fish was widespread. When the press wrote about him, the words character, grace, judgment, and experience were frequently employed. His long absence from politics had allowed him to escape the rancor of the Johnson years, and of all the members of the cabinet he rose above partisanship most easily. Fish would remain with Grant for the entire eight years of his presidency and would prove to be one of the most able secretaries of state in the nation's history.

The relationship between Grant and Fish was complex: not unlike the ties that bound Eisenhower and Dulles, or Truman and Acheson. Despite dissimilar backgrounds, the two men shared a common outlook about America's role in the world and about their respective responsibilities as president and secretary of state. Grant considered Fish the most able member of the cabinet, and Fish gave Grant his unstinting support. And curious as it may seem, they possessed certain traits in common. As Badeau observed, both exhibited "a natural plainness, almost ruggedness of character, in Fish's case doubtless inherited from his Dutch ancestors." Both were incredibly stubborn and shared an unforgiving temperament when affronts became personal. "But more than all, there was in each an unwillingness, if not an inability, to express in manner or words the warm regard that lay beneath an undemonstrative exterior; this gave them an undefined fellowship of feeling, and yet threw a certain constraint about their intimacy. They knew and liked each other better, I believe, than either ever said to the other."[2]

For Grant and Fish, the Cuban insurrection presented a vexing problem. Americans instinctively regarded Spanish rule in the Western Hemisphere as an anachronism. When rebellion broke out on the eastern reaches of the island in 1868, an immediate clamor arose demanding intervention. Manifest Destiny beckoned. Some Americans sought annexation, others advocated independence, but there was no question that Cuba's effort to throw off the Spanish yoke quickly won public support. It was not simply a matter of Old World oppression. Well over half a million Africans were still held in bondage on Cuban plantations and a clandestine slave trade persisted there despite the efforts of the United States and Great Britain to suppress it. This added moral force to the revolutionary cause. The fighting had raged with savage intensity for almost six months when the Grant administration took office, and public pressure to take action was increasing daily.

Fish hesitated. The United States had just fought the bloodiest and most expensive war in history. The last thing the country needed was a costly foreign adventure. There was also the situation vis-à-vis Great Britain. If the United States recognized a rebel Cuban government, or even acknowledged a state of belligerency, it would undermine the administration's efforts to collect damages from Britain for its aid to the Confederacy. Washington could scarcely pursue the *Alabama* claims if it was actively supporting a rebellion against Spanish rule in Cuba. International law also had to be taken into account. Under established practices there was no precedent for recognition of Cuban belligerency, much less independence. The rebels had no government, no stable military force, and they held no territory. At this point the rebellion was merely a guerrilla movement, albeit a powerful one. Finally, Fish was skeptical of the Cuban exile committee in New York. It was an energetic source of propaganda, but the secretary doubted their capacity to govern. They seemed prepared only "to meet the hated Spaniard in Union Square, with a tailor on one flank, a washerwoman on the other, and Delmonico's in the rear."[3]

Grant was of two minds. Like most Americans he sympathized with the Cuban rebels, but he was heedful of Fish's reservations. In the cabinet, Boutwell, Attorney General Hoar, and Navy secretary Borie supported Fish, while Rawlins, Cox, and Creswell urged Grant to take immediate action to support the insurrection. The lines were tightly drawn. In his diary, Fish recorded the discussion in cabinet on April 6: "President introduced subject of the recognition of Cuba, saying that strict justice would justify us in not delaying action on this subject, but too early action might prejudice our case with Great Britain in support of our claims. I thought it too soon to consider the question. . . . Rawlins inclined to more speedy action. Hoar strongly opposed. The President decided not to entertain it at present."[4]

Rawlins, who always had Grant's ear, did everything possible to promote the Cuban cause. Readily accessible to the press, he laid down a steady barrage in favor of recognition and was evidently prepared to risk war with Spain if necessary.[5] Rawlins's motives may have been pure,* but in this instance his influence on the president was pernicious. The first member of the Grant administration to succumb to temptation, the secretary of war was the potential beneficiary of $28,000 in Cuban bonds given to him by the Cuban exile committee in New York. The bonds were worthless when Rawlins accepted them, but intervention and recognition would have awarded him their face value. This was a maneuver used brazenly by the Confederacy to gain support among European politicians during the Civil War, and Rawlins should have been forewarned. Instead, he took the bonds, assuming their existence would not be discovered, and advocated the Cuban cause with growing intensity until he succumbed to tuberculosis later that summer. Grant, who was the executor of Rawlins's estate, ordered the bonds destroyed but apparently no one was willing to do so and the certificates kept turning up like a proverbial bad penny.[6]

Throughout the spring and summer of 1869 the infighting within the Grant administration over Cuba continued. Congress also put in an oar and on April 10 the House passed a resolution of sympathy with the rebels, pledging its support for the president if he accorded them belligerent status. Interventionist meetings were held throughout the country, and the Grand Army of the Republic, that greatest of veterans organizations, announced its readiness to take up weapons to support the Cuban cause.[7]

---

* In 1867, well prior to the revolt in Cuba, Rawlins delivered a highly publicized speech in Galena in which he advocated the extinction of all European authority in the New World, and said he looked forward to "the departure of the last foreign power from this continent." That could have been a reference to British presence in Canada, but it also fit Spain. James Harrison Wilson, *The Life of John A. Rawlins* 500–501 (New York: Neale, 1916).

The situation was further complicated by the growing number of private filibustering expeditions launched from American shores on the rebels' behalf. At Fish's urging, Grant issued an executive order on July 14 prohibiting the mounting of such endeavors, and Attorney General Hoar and Secretary Boutwell stepped up enforcement efforts with some success. Nevertheless, American relations with Spain deteriorated markedly. Objectively seen, the Spanish were equally at fault. Finding it difficult to distinguish legitimate merchantmen from filibustering vessels bound for Cuba, ships of the Spanish high seas fleet intercepted all American ships they encountered. This sometimes led to the arrest and imprisonment of United States citizens, and on several occasions to the execution of the men detained. Grant, who considered the protection of citizens abroad a constitutional obligation, was incensed. He ordered the West Indian squadron reinforced, several warships were called back from the Pacific, Admiral Porter directed two first-class ironclads to proceed at once to Key West, and the heavily gunned frigates *Lancaster* and *Sabine* were fitted out for service. By early summer a flotilla of American warships was in Cuban waters. Admiral Henry K. Hoff, the squadron commander, was instructed to resist the capture of any American vessel unless she were found actually landing armed men or contraband of war on the coast of Cuba. Since Spain had more than fifty warships on the Cuba station, including the ironclads *Victoria* and *Saragoza,* a clash seemed likely. If Spanish warships continued sending shots across the bows of American steamers, Hoff's vessels would inevitably respond.

Once again fate intervened on Grant's behalf. As the two nations drifted toward war, Washington received unexpected word that Spain might be prepared to relinquish Cuba in return for a large cash payment guaranteed by the United States. The news was brought to the White House by Paul S. Forbes, an American businessman with close ties to the ruling junta in Madrid. The Bourbon-Hapsburg monarchy had recently been overthrown, and the new government was staring at a bankrupt treasury. The sale of Cuba would enable Spain to meet its debts and help extricate the country from financial chaos. Napoleon, to ease the financial burden on France, had sold Louisiana to the United States for 75 million francs; Russia, in need of money, had sold Alaska; why should not Spain do the same? Forbes was an old friend of Adam Badeau's, and through Badeau he gained quick access to Grant. The president summoned Fish, and the two listened attentively to Forbes's report. The discussion was conducted in complete secrecy.[8] Two days later, June 4, 1869, Fish placed before the cabinet a pencil-written memorandum summarizing the proposal: Spain would grant independence to Cuba; Cuba would pay Madrid an indemnity, the amount to be determined through negotiations; slavery was to be abolished; an armistice declared while discussions went forward; and the United States would serve as mediator. Money for the indemnity would be raised through the sale of Cuban bonds that the United States would guarantee. In return for that guarantee, all discriminatory duties against American products would be abolished and the United States would be given the authority to approve or disapprove all other Cuban duties.[9]

The cabinet was enthusiastic. Rawlins voiced skepticism, but did not object to the plan. Grant entrusted the negotiations to General Daniel Sickles, the minister-designate to Spain, who sailed for Madrid on July 1.* The stage was set for a diplomatic triumph. War would be averted, Cuba would gain its independence, slavery would end, Spain would depart, and the United States would gain undisputed control of the Caribbean. All of this accomplished without the loss of an American life or the expenditure of a single dollar, the Cuban financial guarantee offset by a lien against Havana's customs revenue. Grant agreed to preside over a Washington conference between Spain and the rebel leadership, and Cuban peace, it seemed, was in the offing.

That rosy scenario evaporated quickly. Sickles reported in late July that the Madrid junta had not reached a decision on sale of the island,[10] and a new round of violence in eastern Cuba, including the execution of two Americans by Spanish authorities, caused the president to consider whether the United States should not simply accept that a state of belligerency existed, in effect granting tacit recognition to the rebels.

On the other hand, Grant did not want to take precipitate action if a negotiated settlement were possible. He drafted a neutrality proclamation that recognized Cuban belligerency but instead of issuing it, he left it with

* Grant initially nominated Henry S. Sanford as minister to Spain but withdrew the nomination after receiving unfavorable reports of Sanford's wartime business dealings. Sickles had been slated to go to Mexico City and was elevated to the post in Madrid. Sickles never served directly under Grant during the war, but the general in chief had a high opinion of him, particularly after his stint as military governor of the Carolinas, where he proved himself second only to Sheridan in enforcing the Reconstruction Acts.

Sickles was not a professional soldier, but a Tammany-trained war Democrat whom Lincoln appointed a general officer in 1861. A flamboyant character in an age littered with larger-than-life figures, Sickles, in 1859, as a congressman from New York, had shot and killed a prominent Washington attorney, Philip Barton Key, son of the author of "The Star Spangled Banner," after discovering Key and his own wife in flagrante delicto. Defended by Edwin Stanton and Reverdy Johnson, Sickles was acquitted based on the then-novel defense of temporary insanity. An effective wartime officer, he commanded the Union 3rd Corps at Gettysburg and lost a leg leading his troops in the spirited defense of Devil's Den and the peach orchard on the second day of the battle. A living symbol of wartime sacrifice, Sickles campaigned enthusiastically for Grant in 1868 and played a vital role keeping New Hampshire in the Republican column. Nat Brandt, *The Congressman Who Got Away with Murder* (Syracuse, N.Y.: Syracuse University Press, 1991). Also see Joseph A. Fry, *Henry S. Sanford: Diplomacy and Business in Nineteenth-Century America* 54–56, 84–85 (Reno: University of Nevada Press, 1982).

Fish while he and his family went to the seaside on vacation. When press reports in early August indicated the fighting in Cuba was intensifying, Grant wrote Fish on August 14 and instructed him to issue the proclamation unless Sickles had received "an entirely satisfactory reply" from Madrid.[11] Improbable as it may seem, Grant's letter to Fish was delivered simultaneously with an encouraging message from Sickles stating that the Spanish government had bitten the bullet and was prepared to accept United States mediation. The conditions set by Madrid (including a demand that the rebels first lay down their arms) were unacceptable,[12] but the secretary decided that sufficient progress had been made to allow him to hold up Grant's proclamation, at least for the present. Two days later, Fish met the president in New York, suggested that the Spanish terms could be improved upon, and asked that Sickles be given more time. Grant agreed. On August 20 Horace Porter wrote Fish that "the President's views in regard to Cuba coincide exactly with your own."[13]

When the cabinet convened on August 31 (its first meeting since early July*), Cuba was at the top of the agenda. Sickles had not reported back, fighting had intensified on the island, and the interventionist press was shouting for action, ripping into Grant for his timidity. Charles Dana, now publisher of the *New York Sun,* who as assistant secretary of war (1862–1865) had been one of Grant's most eloquent supporters, wrote that it was America's duty "at once to interfere in Cuba" and put a stop to the atrocities committed by the Spanish. "But this is a duty which we cannot hope to see performed by an Administration so barren of great ideas, and so deficient in character."[14]

Grant, who had spent the last several days at Fish's Hudson valley estate, refused to be stampeded. Fish believed a diplomatic solution was possible, and Grant was ready to take the gamble. But first there was a cabinet wrangle with Rawlins. The secretary of war, cadaverous and near death, had risen from his sickbed to make a final plea for the Cuban cause. Trembling with emotion, he lambasted Fish for letting the Spanish hoodwink

---

* Summers in Washington before air conditioning were no treat, and the summer of 1869 was particularly unpleasant. The temperature in Fish's State Department office, supposedly the coolest room in the building, hovered in the mid-90s throughout August. Rockwood Hoar wrote his wife that Washington "is hot! hotter!! hottest!!! hottentot! hottentotter! hottentottest! more hottentotter! most hottentottest!!!!!!!! The daily bill of fare is as follows: For breakfast, Attorney General broiled; for dinner, Attorney General roasted; For supper, Attorney General boiled, and the same dish kept hot in an oven, and served at any hour of the night." On July 16, 1869, the official temperature reached 106 degrees, and downtown at the National Hotel, 110 degrees. It is scarcely surprising that government virtually shut down during July and August, and that those who could, beat hasty retreats to the seashore or to the mountains. Moorfield Storey and Edward W. Emerson, *Ebenezer Rockwood Hoar: A Memoir* 215–16 (Boston: Houghton Mifflin, 1911).

him and demanded that the United States immediately recognize that a state of war existed in Cuba. It was an able and impassioned argument—as able as Grant had ever heard—and when it was finished Rawlins sat back exhausted. He then apologized to Grant for his vehemence: "I have been your adjutant, and I think you will excuse me for being earnest."[15]

It was evident that Rawlins was dying and this would be his last battle. Grant consoled him. "You are still my adjutant," said the president, choked with emotion, as he turned to Fish for a response. The secretary of state, like the others present, was moved by Rawlins's presentation. Yet he kept his head and calmly reviewed the reasons it was important to delay. As Fish spoke, Grant began to write, hunched over the table, seemingly oblivious to the secretary's remarks. This was Grant of the battlefield, calmly writing out an order as the shells whistled overhead. When he finished he pushed the paper toward Fish. "There is my decision," he said. Fish took the paper and read it aloud:

> The United States are willing to mediate between Spain and Cuba, on following terms: Immediate armistice. Cuba to recompense Spain for public property. All Spaniards to be protected in their persons and property if they wish to remain on the island, or to withdraw from it, at their option. The United States not to guarantee except with the approval of Congress. These conditions to be accepted by Sept. 25 (or Oct 1), or the United States to be regarded as having withdrawn all offer to mediate.[16]

Grant's decision meant that the United States would not intervene. With the president standing firm, public interest in Cuba temporarily subsided. The danger of war diminished. Rawlins died the next week and no one within the administration took up the rebel cause, at least not with the same intensity.[17] Nothing came of negotiations in Madrid. Spanish pride prevented the junta from relinquishing the island, and guerrilla fighting continued unabated. Washington took a wait-and-see attitude, pressuring the Spanish government to relax its grip, but staying well out of the line of fire. In his annual message to Congress in December 1869, Grant recounted American efforts to mediate the struggle, criticized Spain for its conduct, and repeated his view that it would be inappropriate to intervene: "The people and government of the United States entertain the same warm feelings and sympathies for the people of Cuba in their pending struggle, that they manifested throughout previous struggles between Spain and her former colonies, in behalf of the latter. But the contest has at no time assumed the conditions which amount to a war in the sense of International law. [For that reason] I have not felt justified in recognizing belligerency." Grant said he hoped that in due time "Spain, as well as other European powers" would find it in their interest to liberate their New World colonies, but the United States would not enforce its views without invitation.[18]

In June 1870 the issue of intervention in Cuba resurfaced. Congressional war hawks, energized by the continuing drumbeat in James Gordon Bennett's *New York Herald* and Dana's *Sun,* passed a joint resolution to recognize Cuban belligerency. Aside from serious questions pertaining to its constitutionality,* the resolution, if passed, would be a blow to the administration's foreign policy and a direct slap at the president himself. Grant fought back. At 4 P.M. on June 13, minutes before debate on the resolution was to begin, he sent Congress a message that diplomatic historians rank among his most effective.[19] Referring to his December address to Congress, Grant said there had been no change in the situation in Cuba that would justify recognition of the rebels. "The insurgents hold no town or city, have no established seat of government; they have no prize courts; no organization for receiving and collecting revenues." Grant deplored the brutality of the conflict, but castigated the efforts of rebel sympathizers to involve the United States in hostilities with Spain. Raising the issue of corruption to public notice, he deprecated the distribution of large sums in Cuban bonds by the exile committee in New York, and announced once more his determination to keep the United States out of war.[20]

The message created a sensation. On the floor of the House, Benjamin Butler, who had fallen into line behind Grant, held up a fistful of Cuban bonds to emphasize congressional culpability. General John "Black Jack" Logan, the floor leader of the war hawks, lit into his former comrade in arms, accusing Butler of "a contemptible trick, worthy only of a police-court lawyer."[21] The debate raged for two days. Late on June 16 the decisive vote was taken on Logan's resolution to grant belligerent rights to the Cubans. Grant's intervention proved decisive. The motion lost, seventy votes in favor, 100 against. The House then passed a substitute motion authorizing the president to protest the barbarities practiced by both sides, and to cooperate with other governments, if he thought it proper, in mitigating the severity of the war in Cuba. Grant's victory was complete. "It is the greatest triumph the Administration has yet achieved," gloated Rockwood Hoar. Secretary Fish, who had been in the vortex of the struggle,

* Article II of the Constitution entrusts the power of recognition to the president. Legal scholars call this "textual commitment," and it is well settled that the authority to recognize a foreign power, or the existence of a state of belligerency, belongs exclusively to the president. See John Bassett Moore, 1 *International Law Digest* 243–44 (Washington, D.C.: Government Printing Office, 1906).

took a more measured view. The House vote, he wrote in his diary, "had shown that the representatives of the country can rise above the temporary and fervent appeals of momentary excitement of popular sympathy in support of the obligations of national duties, and in the line and direction of honesty and right, even when opposed by clamor and by appeals to passion."[22]

In retrospect, it is clear that Grant's timely message arrested the interventionist momentum that was building in Congress and averted a possible war with Spain over Cuba. One month after the House vote he wrote Fish, noting his appreciation for the secretary's steadfastness. "You almost forced me to sign that message to Congress," said Grant. "The measure was right and the country acquiesced in it. I desire most sincerely to thank you."[23]

The Cuban issue moved in tandem with a more dubious Caribbean endeavor, the effort by the Grant administration to annex Santo Domingo (the Dominican Republic). American interest in the island republic had been aroused by naval exigencies during the Civil War. Santo Domingo, the Virgin Islands, and Puerto Rico control the principal passages from the Atlantic into the Caribbean—the Windward Passage and the Mona Passage—and the Lincoln administration became convinced of the necessity for naval bases in the region, not only to prevent hostile intrusions, but also to cover transit across the isthmus of Panama and burgeoning East Coast trade with the Pacific.[24]

Secretary Seward, who was the prime mover, proposed to the Danish government the purchase of the Virgin Islands in January 1865, and was equally interested in acquiring the harbor at Samaná Bay in the Dominican Republic. Negotiations for both went forward simultaneously, and on October 24, 1867, Seward signed a treaty with Denmark for the purchase of the islands of St. Thomas and St. John for $7.5 million. The Dominican government, harassed by internal dissent and the threat of invasion from the Francophone republic of Haiti, offered to lease Samaná, even to sell it outright, or to accept protectorate status under an American guarantee. But the estrangement between President Johnson and Congress, plus growing opposition to the purchase of Alaska, doomed the Danish treaty and caused Seward to hesitate before accepting Samaná Bay.[25]

At that point the Dominican government urged the United States to take over the republic outright; they even offered to declare themselves annexed, content with being an American protectorate until the details of annexation could be worked out by Washington. Seward noted that annexation was a matter for Congress, and in his last annual message Andrew Johnson recommended the annexation not just of the Dominican Republic but of Haiti as well.[26] The House of Representatives took up the matter, and on January 13, 1869, decisively defeated (36–126) a resolution introduced by Congressman Nathaniel P. Banks of Massachusetts authorizing the president to extend a protectorate over the Dominican Republic and Haiti. Two weeks later, the House defeated (63–110) a resolution proposing the annexation of the Dominican Republic and its incorporation into the union.

The Grant administration inherited the problem. The issue was first broached in April 1869 when Joseph Warren Fabens, an expatriate New Englander with a shady reputation and a fortune amassed from wheeling and dealing in the Dominican Republic, called on Secretary of State Fish and presented him with a memorandum from the island government proposing annexation to the United States with full "entrance into the American Union as a free and independent state."[27] Fish was unenthusiastic. Congress had already expressed its opposition to assuming responsibility for the Dominican Republic and he saw no reason to reopen the matter. The following day, April 6, 1869, he dutifully reported the offer to the cabinet but suggested there was no reason to discuss the issue further. No member objected. As the secretary recorded in his diary, "the subject was passed by, mainly for want of time before the close of the session [of Congress]."[28]

The Dominican story might have ended at that point had not the navy cherished the thought of a base in the Caribbean. Admiral Porter, the acting secretary of the navy, had longed for a coaling station at Samaná Bay since he first inspected the site for Secretary of State John C. Calhoun in the 1840s, and Admiral Daniel Ammen was his ready disciple. Both were close friends of Grant's, Ammen especially, and the two lost no opportunity to tout the advantages of the Dominican Republic.[29] Grant, who like Fish was initially skeptical, cut the admirals some slack. On May 17 he instructed the navy to send a warship to the Dominican Republic to bring back information on the finances, agriculture, commerce, political situation, and the attitude of the people concerning annexation by the United States. Having opposed the war with Mexico, Grant did not want to undertake territorial expansion without the overwhelming support of the local population.[30] The gunboat *Nipsic*, Commander Thomas O. Selfridge, Jr., sailed shortly thereafter but developed boiler trouble and returned to Hampton Roads in mid-July with little information.

Grant also asked Fish to undertake an inquiry. On June 2 the secretary appointed Benjamin P. Hunt of Baltimore as a diplomatic special agent to the Dominican Republic with detailed instructions to ascertain the extent of the country's national debt and determine whether the Dominican people were really in favor of annexation by the United States.[31] Hunt unfortunately took ill before he could depart. Grant then turned to his White House secretary, Brevet Brigadier General Orville Babcock. As the president advised the cabinet in early July, "The Navy people seemed so anxious to have the Bay of Samaná as a coaling station that he thought he would send General Babcock down to examine it and report upon it as an engineer."[32] Like Badeau and Horace Porter, Orville Babcock had become a member of Grant's personal family as well as his official one. The president had few close friends. Daniel Ammen was one, and perhaps Sherman and Sheridan, although the chain of command prevented intimacy. And so his immediate associates, the men who had served with him through the war, became substitutes for a circle of companions and Grant treated them accordingly.

A native Vermonter, Babcock had graduated from West Point in 1861, was commissioned in the Engineers, served ably at the front, and came to Grant's attention during the Chattanooga campaign, largely as a result of his construction skills. Bright, agreeable, and ambitious, he was added to the staff in 1864 when Grant became general in chief. Most people thought well of him. Sherman did, so did Fish, and Grant often used him on confidential assignments where trust and discretion were essential.[33] He was the aide who stood just behind Grant when Lee surrendered at Appomattox, and he had been at Grant's side ever since.

Babcock was not given diplomatic authority, although Grant gave him a personal letter of introduction to Buenaventura Báez, president of the Dominican Republic. Addressing Báez as his "Great and Good Friend," Grant said he was sending Babcock as a special agent to obtain information. "Having been one of my aides-de-camp while I commanded the armies of the United States, and having since been intrusted by me with confidential business of importance, I have entire confidence in his integrity and intelligence, and I commend him to your excellency accordingly." The president signed himself, "Your good friend, U. S. Grant."[34]

Babcock returned to Washington in September with a draft protocol providing alternatively for the annexation of Santo Domingo or, failing that, the sale of Samaná Bay to the United States for $2 million—the price proposed by Seward in 1867. Grant instructed Fish to prepare a formal treaty of annexation based on Babcock's draft, and it was presented to the cabinet on October 19, 1869.[35] At this point the negotiations were closely held. Little effort was made to cultivate public opinion and the Senate was kept in the dark. That was Grant's error. Reflecting his experience at Vicksburg and crossing the James, he preferred to keep his plans secret until he could spring a fait accompli. It worked in war, but the tactic often led him astray in politics.

Babcock returned to the island in November, secured Dominican approval for the treaty, and was back in Washington in mid-December. Under the terms of the document the United States would provide a flat payment of $1.5 million to be applied to the Dominican national debt, no further indebtedness was to be incurred pending ratification, and ultimately Santo Domingo would become an American state. As part of the agreement, the United States would acquire base rights at Samaná Bay for fifty years at an annual rental of $150,000. Taking a page from the book of John Tyler, who in 1844 guaranteed Texas against foreign intervention while the treaty of annexation was pending, Grant made a similar commitment to Santo Domingo.[36]

As soon as the Christmas holidays ended, Grant set about to secure the treaty's adoption. The evening of January 2, 1870, he walked resolutely across Lafayette Park to call unannounced on Senator Charles Sumner, the powerful chairman of the Foreign Relations Committee. For Grant, the trek across the park represented an act of political groveling reminiscent of the bad old days in St. Louis when the future president, hat in hand, would call on prospective employers, invariably without success. Grant instinctively disliked the senior senator from Massachusetts, and Sumner felt the same about Grant.

For the president, Charles Sumner personified Puritan elitism at its worst: narrow-minded, sanctimonious, ever ready to transform mundane practicalities into precious issues of principle. In Sumner's case those characteristics were exacerbated by a waspish tongue and an effete manner that were difficult to digest for a soldier like Grant. Above all, however, it was Sumner's intellectual arrogance that annoyed the president. When Boutwell asked one day whether he had ever heard Sumner converse, Grant, a twinkle in his eye, observed that he had never had the privilege, though he had "often heard him lecture."[37] Like Massachusetts's Elbridge Gerry, the quintessential loose cannon of the early republic, Sumner treated politics as the pursuit of perfection. When Grant was told that Sumner did not believe in the Bible, he was not surprised. "Well, he didn't write it," said the president.[38] Years later Grant noted sadly that, "Sumner is the only man I was ever anything but my real self to; the only man I ever tried to conciliate by artificial means."[39]

Sumner's opinion of Grant was much like the disdainful view of Henry Adams. Whereas men of the world like Fish, Boutwell, and Hoar recognized the silent strength Grant brought to the presidency, Sumner saw only a simple soldier: untried, untrained, and reeking of tobacco smoke. Sumner believed Grant was not a true Republican, had little understanding of politics, and no capacity for statesmanship. Bitter that he had not been chosen secretary of state, the Massachusetts senator was eager to assert his authority to the administration's discomfiture.[40]

Grant was aware of Sumner's hostility. In fact, he had it much in mind when he rang the doorbell that evening. By calling unannounced, Grant was appealing to the senator's vanity. He was humbling himself to gain the treaty's approval. As Assistant Secretary of State Bancroft Davis remarked, Grant was doing what "no other President ever did before under such circumstances."[41]

Sumner, who was at dinner with two well-known Washington journalists, was taken aback by Grant's sudden appearance, but he welcomed him courteously. Seating the president at the table, he offered a glass of sherry, which Grant declined. The journalists, sensing that something important was in the wind, asked to be excused, but Grant insisted they remain. Briefly he explained the purpose of his visit: to secure Sumner's support for the treaty Babcock had negotiated. Grant described the agreement in general terms and spoke of the benefits that would accrue to the United States. His description was concise. Boutwell stopped in as Grant concluded his presentation, and the president rose to leave. "I'll send the documents over to you in the morning by General Babcock," he told Sumner.[42] Asked by one of the journalists if he would support the treaty, Sumner replied: "Well, Mr. President, I am a Republican and an Administration man, and I will do all I can to make your Administration a success. I will give the subject my best thought, and I will do all I can rightly and consistently to aid you."[43]* Grant departed, confident of the Massachusetts senator's support. As Sumner's principal biographer has written, the president doubtless "chuckled quietly to himself at how little sugar it took to make the medicine go down. He had come to disarm Sumner's suspicions of a treaty that had been negotiated without his knowledge and to secure for it a prompt and fair hearing; he returned with a pledge of the Senate leader's support."[44]

Once again, Grant was too optimistic. As at Donelson, he assumed victory prematurely. Sumner's statement that he was an "Administration man" and would aid Grant as best he could after he studied the treaty would, in the mouth of almost any other senior Washington politician, be

---

* Sumner's exact words have long been in dispute. Sumner maintained he was noncommittal and merely assured the president that he would consider the matter carefully. The two journalists, Ben: Perley Poole and John W. Forney, remember Sumner telling Grant that "he would cheerfully support the treaty." Boutwell retained a vivid recollection of Sumner's words: "I expect Mr. President to support the measures of your administration." Whatever the case, Sumner evidently did not feel bound by his reply, and Grant, for his part, later had reason to feel that the Massachusetts senator had double-crossed him. Compare Charles Sumner, 13 *The Works of Charles Sumner* 126 (Boston: Lee and Shepard, 1875); Forney to Babcock, June 6, 1870, 20 *The Papers of Ulysses S. Grant* 164 note, John Y. Simon, ed. (Carbondale: Southern Illinois University Press, 1995); Ben: Perley Poole to the *Boston Journal,* October 21, 1877; George S. Boutwell, "Memorandum," November 12, 1877, Fish Papers.

construed as a pledge of support. In Sumner's case it meant simply that he would approach the issue as he did any other proposed by the president. That did not bode well for Grant. During the past nine months, all the while claiming to be an administration man, Sumner had defeated Grant's effort to repeal the Tenure of Office Act, blocked the nomination of Alexander Stewart as secretary of the treasury, held up numerous diplomatic nominations in his committee, and conducted his own foreign policy toward Great Britain and the *Alabama* claims, Secretary Fish notwithstanding. Sumner was not deliberately deceitful in his pledge to Grant; he was simply speaking with a subtlety the soldier-president did not comprehend. And he believed that the policy of the Republican party was set in the United States Senate, not the White House.

On January 10, 1870, Grant sent the Dominican treaty to Capitol Hill. The Senate proved to be in no hurry to take action. The Foreign Relations Committee did not commence hearings until mid-February, and Babcock was not called to testify until March 11. As Fish shrewdly observed, "the Senate has been for two or three years accustomed to originate measures and to resist what the Executive originated. The habit of criticism, if not opposition, became somewhat fixed, and on the accession of a friend to the Executive Chair, the habit could not entirely and at once subside—it is difficult to voluntarily relinquish power."[45]

Initially, Sumner kept his own counsel. "Not for weeks," wrote Senator Carl Schurz of Missouri, "did the other members of the committee get the least hint that Sumner would oppose the treaty."[46] On March 15 the blow fell. Reporting to the Senate in secret session, Sumner announced that the Committee on Foreign Relations opposed the treaty, 5–2. Nine days later, again in closed session, he spoke for four hours against the accord and for an additional hour and a half the next day. Sumner's opposition, aside from a large dollop of personal enmity, reflected his fear that the annexation of Santo Domingo would be prohibitively expensive, that it would launch the United States on a vast program of Caribbean expansion, and would inevitably entail the incorporation of an alien culture. He also feared American annexation of Santo Domingo would threaten the independence of Haiti, the only independent black republic in the hemisphere. "To the African belongs the equatorial belt, and he should enjoy it undisturbed."[47] Sumner's address was masterly, and it foreshadowed the treaty's defeat.

Grant rallied as best he could. Casting precedent aside he went to Capitol Hill, established his command post in the President's Room near the Senate chamber (normally used only during the last day of session to expedite the signing of last-minute legislation), met with as many senators as possible, and placed the administration's prestige on the line.[48] The votes were not forthcoming. A careful poll of the Senate in mid-May indicated the president was still eight votes short of the necessary two thirds.* When Senate supporters suggested a compromise that would have made Santo Domingo a protectorate but deferred the question of statehood, Grant refused. Rather than accept half a loaf, he held out for total victory.[49] This time his tenacity did him in. When the final vote was taken on June 30, the treaty failed 28–28, with sixteen senators absent, paired, or not voting. The core of the party stayed with Grant, but eighteen Republicans joined Sumner in opposition.

Grant did not give up. He devoted a major portion of his annual message in December 1870 to the Dominican Republic, deplored the Senate's rejection of the treaty, and urged Congress to authorize the appointment of a special commission to explore the situation on the island and report back. "So convinced am I of the advantages to flow from the acquisition of Santo Domingo, and of the great disadvantages—I might say calamities—to flow from non-acquisition, that I believe the subject has only to be investigated to be approved."[50] This time Grant was able to marshal the votes. Despite Sumner's vigorous opposition, the Senate, after an all-night debate, adopted a resolution introduced by Senator Oliver P. Morton of Indiana authorizing the commission, and the House followed suit.[51]

Grant had recaptured the initiative. His appointments to the commission were inspired: former senator and president pro-tempore of the Senate Benjamin Wade of Ohio, a darling of the Radical Republicans; Andrew D. White, founding president of Cornell University, an eminent scholar and respected publicist; and Dr. Samuel Gridley Howe of Massachusetts, a lifelong reformer and friend of Sumner's who received his M.D. from Harvard in 1824 and spent the next six years fighting for Greek independence.[52] As secretary to the commission Grant appointed Frederick Douglass, perhaps the most articulate spokesman for African-Americans, another friend of Sumner's, but who, like Grant, considered Santo Domingo a possible refuge for the freedmen. The military adviser was General Franz Sigel, another adroit appointment designed to undercut Carl Schurz among Missouri's German-American population. The commission's staff included a full panoply of geologists, mineralogists, and other scientists.

The commission spent almost three months in the Dominican Republic. It issued a final report on April 5, 1871, that fully sustained Grant's claims concerning the productivity of the island, the unanimity of the people for annexation by the United States, and the potential for future devel-

---

* The Senate in 1870 numbered seventy-two: eleven Democrats and sixty-one Republicans. If all senators were present and voting, Grant needed forty-nine votes for the treaty's approval. Separate polls taken by Missouri's Carl Schurz and William M. Stewart of Nevada on May 14 indicated forty-one senators would vote in favor, thirty-one against. Allan Nevins, 1 *Hamilton Fish: The Inner History of the Grant Administration* 325–26 (New York: Frederick Ungar, 1957).

opment.[53]* But Grant's efforts were too late. By the time the commission reported, public opinion had crystallized against annexation and the document made little impression. Recognizing the inevitable, the president transmitted the report to Congress without recommendation. "And now my task is finished, and with it ends all personal solicitation. My duty being done, yours begins; I gladly hand over the whole matter to the judgment of the American people and of their representatives in Congress assembled."[54] Much to Grant's disappointment that judgment was negative, and the subject of Santo Domingo faded from the nation's agenda.

It was while Grant was engaged with Cuba and the Dominican Republic that he got his first opportunity to affect the composition of the Supreme Court. During the Civil War, to insure a pro-Union majority on the Court, Congress had increased the number of justices from nine to ten.[55] Three years later—July 23, 1866—another act was passed reducing the size of the Court to seven, the change to be effected by the death or retirement of the justices then sitting.[56] The purpose of the 1866 act was to prevent Andrew Johnson from making any appointment to the Court.[57] When Grant took office there were eight justices on the bench.[58] Encouraged by the fact that there was now a Republican in the White House, Congress passed a new statute raising the number of justices to nine and authorizing the president to make a new appointment when the Senate reconvened in December.[59] Grant was delighted. On December 14, 1869, he sent the name of Rockwood Hoar forward, confident his attorney general would be confirmed. The following day, seventy-five-year-old Justice Robert Cooper Grier resigned, giving the president a second vacancy to fill. Grant did not hesitate. Taking the country by surprise, he called on his old chief, former Secretary of War Edwin Stanton, offered the position to him, and sent his name to the Senate on December 20.

Grant's nominees presented a striking contrast. Hoar, with ten years experience on the Supreme Judicial Court of Massachusetts, was widely commended by the public and the press as a paragon of judicial virtue. "His distinguished abilities are conceded and his elevation to the Supreme

---

* At Grant's request the commission undertook to investigate whether there was any evidence that he or any other American official had received any concessions or favors from the Dominican government. (Such accusations had been bandied about by Sumner and others.) The commission stated explicitly that it found nothing to substantiate such charges. "No pains were spared to ascertain the exact truth on this subject. After this investigation the commission can declare, without hesitation, that there was no particle or color of evidence for these charges." Years later, Andrew White addressed the topic in his *Autobiography* and reaffirmed that "the closest examination of men and documents relative to titles and concessions on the island failed to reveal any personal interest of his [Grant's] whatsoever." *Report of the Commission of Inquiry to Santo Domingo* 31, Senate Ex. Doc. No. 9, 42 Cong., 1st sess. (1874); 1 *Autobiography of Andrew Dickson White* 487–88 (New York: Century, 1905).

Bench is received with profound satisfaction by all," wrote the *New York Times*.[60] Stanton on the other hand was a partisan's partisan. Republicans were delighted. The *Washington Chronicle* called his choice "the equivalent of a Constitutional Amendment." The Democrats were appalled. "No one could be more out of place than such a hasty, violent, imperious zealot," lamented the *New York World*. Objective observers, while questioning Stanton's temperament and arbitrary manner, hailed his legal acumen and hoped for the best. Many noted Grant's generosity in elevating a man with whom he had often been at odds.[61]

Neither of Grant's appointees made it to the Court. Stanton was confirmed immediately (46–11) by the Senate's Republican majority, but succumbed to a fatal heart attack three days later. Hoar encountered a minefield of hostility on the Senate floor. As attorney general he had been rigorous in vetting appointments to the federal bench, insisting on the highest judicial standards, and senators whose nominees had been turned down now took their revenge. Others were negative on personal grounds. Hoar did not suffer fools gladly and his brusque Massachusetts manner grated the sensibilities of less erudite politicians. Finally, senators from the South, Democrats and Republicans alike, thought Grant should have gone below the Mason-Dixon line for his first appointee, given the fact there was no Southerner on the Court. The result was that the Senate voted on December 22 to table Hoar's nomination. Rather than withdraw the attorney general's name, Grant stood by his nominee and lobbied for confirmation, but to no avail. In an up-or-down vote on February 3, 1870, the Senate rejected Hoar 24–33.[62]

As a consequence, Grant still had two vacancies to fill. At the recommendation of Hoar, and following a lengthy discussion in cabinet, the president turned to two leaders of the American bar, William Strong of Pennsylvania and Joseph P. Bradley of New Jersey. Strong, at sixty-two, had for the past eleven years been a judge of the Pennsylvania Supreme Court, and Bradley, fifty-seven, was a prominent New Jersey practitioner who enjoyed the support of Democrats and Republicans alike. At noon on February 7, 1870, Grant sent the nominations to the Senate. One hour later, the Supreme Court, in a surprise 4–3 decision, held the Legal Tender Act of 1862 unconstitutional.* The act had been passed during the Civil War when Congress found itself unable to raise sufficient money to pay the soldiers in the field. The Treasury had been authorized to issue notes (greenbacks) that, though not redeemable in specie, were made legal tender in the payment of private debts. In *Hepburn,* the Court held that debts incurred before the passage of the act must be paid in gold.

---

* *Hepburn v. Griswold,* 8 Wallace 603 (1870).

The banks and most creditors were delighted with the decision, but the bulk of the business community was dismayed. The greenbacks had done good service during the war, the country still needed them, and their legal-tender quality should not be impaired. Businessmen feared the decision would shrink the nation's money supply and would be disastrous for the economy. Grant shared this view, as did every member of his cabinet. Attorney General Hoar believed the decision was neither good law, good reason, nor safe doctrine for a country that might again need to issue paper currency in an emergency.[63] Accordingly, on March 31, 1870, Hoar went before the Supreme Court and asked for a rehearing. One year later the Court reversed itself 5–4, Justices Bradley and Strong voting with the new majority.* Grant was accused of packing the Court, but he had had no knowledge of the *Hepburn* decision when the nominations of Bradley and Strong went forward.[64]

The defeat of the Dominican treaty was a bitter pill for Grant. Yet in a strange way it facilitated settlement of the *Alabama* claims and a host of other issues that had poisoned relations between the United States and Great Britain. These included the contentious problem of North Atlantic fisheries, free navigation of the St. Lawrence River, Fenian raids into Canada, and the Northwest water boundary between the Washington Territory and British Columbia, which involved ownership of the San Juan Islands southwest of Vancouver in the Strait of Juan de Fuca.

Grant had taken office in 1869 riding a tide of Anglophobia. The Senate had killed the Johnson-Clarendon accord,† Hibernian patriots were conducting a hit-and-run border war along the Canadian frontier, and clashes between rival fishermen along the Atlantic shelf made monthly headlines. The undisputed leader of anti-British sentiment in the United States was Charles Sumner. As longtime chairman of the Foreign Relations Committee, Sumner exerted his vast influence to arouse public opinion against Great Britain, and he pursued the *Alabama* claims relentlessly. In a widely heralded speech to the Senate on April 13, 1869, he had set the tone of American policy by asserting that British aid to the Confederacy had cost American taxpayers $2 billion, and suggesting that Canada be ceded to the United States as a down payment.[65] At the time, Grant agreed with Sumner. He had read and approved the senator's speech before it was delivered, and against the advice of Secretary Fish, appointed a Sumner acolyte, Harvard history professor John Lothrop Motley, United States minister to the Court of St. James.[66]

---

* *Legal Tender Cases* (Knox v. Lee), 12 Wallace 457 (1871).
† This was an agreement negotiated in London by the United States minister, Reverdy Johnson, and the British foreign secretary, Lord Clarendon, that provided a means for settling the *Alabama* claims. Public opinion considered the terms unfavorable to the United States. See Chapter 15.

Gradually, Grant changed his mind. Under Fish's subtle tutelage he came to realize the importance of restoring peaceful relations with Great Britain, while Boutwell helped him to see the role London banks played in underwriting the Treasury's debt. By the end of the year, Grant had reversed himself. In his annual message to Congress in December, the president suggested it might be propitious to reopen negotiations on the *Alabama* claims "with the determination not only to remove the causes of complaint in the past, but to lay the foundation of a broad principle of public laws which will prevent future differences and [promote] continued peace and friendship."[67]

In late 1870 the opportunity arrived. Gladstone's Liberals had ousted the Tory government of Benjamin Disraeli and appeared ready to restore amicable relations with the United States. In point of fact, the British had reason to reconsider the wisdom of their Civil War policy of fitting out ships for the Confederacy. Russia had just renounced the Treaty of Paris neutralizing the Black Sea, and the possibility of a renewal of the Crimean conflict loomed on the horizon. That, plus the Franco-Prussian War, convinced the Gladstone government it was time to mend its fences. The last thing Britain needed was for her adversaries to build naval cruisers in neutral American shipyards. The seas would swarm with new *Alabama*s and British shipping would be devastated. The change in British attitude coincided with the defeat of the Dominican treaty, which, in turn, precipitated a shift in American policy. Grant held Sumner responsible for the loss and he broke irrevocably with the Massachusetts senator. Motley was replaced as United States minister in London, and when the 42nd Congress convened the following March, Sumner, at Fish's insistence, was deposed as chairman of the Foreign Relations Committee.[68]* Both Motley and Sumner had been obstacles to bettering relations with Great Britain, and both were now cast aside.

With the decks clear, the British took the initiative. Gladstone cut through diplomatic caution and proposed wrapping all outstanding issues into a single package. "If we could sweeten the *Alabama* question for the United States by bringing in Canada, perhaps we might also sweeten the fisheries question for Canada by paying her compensation for the Fenian

---

* The vote in the Senate Republican caucus to remove Sumner was 26–21. Fish worked assiduously to replace the Massachusetts senator, and on the eve of the vote, he explained why to Elihu Washburne: "Sumner is bitterly vindictive and hostile, he is determined to oppose and if possible to defeat everything that the President proposes or wishes or does. He is at work in advance, endeavoring to prevent any settlement of the British questions. I am convinced he is crazy; vanity, conceit, ambition have disturbed the equilibrium of his mind; he is irrational and illogical, and raves and rants. No mad bull ever dashed more violently at a red flag than he does at anything that he thinks the President is interested in." February 20, 1871. Reprinted in Nevins, 2 *Hamilton Fish* 461.

raids," he instructed the Foreign Office.[69] Prodded by the prime minister, British diplomats tailored a package calling for the establishment of a Joint High Commission that would arbitrate the *Alabama* claims, revise the rules of international law pertaining to maritime neutrality, fix North American fishing boundaries, settle the San Juan boundary dispute, and assign compensation to Canada for the Fenian raids. To make the preliminary overture to the United States, the Foreign Office called on Sir John Rose, the unofficial Canadian representative in London. Rose was well known in Washington, and the British government preferred to proceed informally outside official diplomatic channels until the American response was known.

Rose arrived in Washington, January 9, 1871. He dined with Fish that evening, and the two conversed through the night. Agreement did not come easily. Taking his cue from Grant, Fish insisted that whatever deal was struck would have to pass Senate muster. That meant Britain would have to apologize for the damage done by the *Alabama* and her sister cruisers. Rose demurred. Britain wanted to settle all outstanding issues but with no risk of humiliation. No ministry could survive if it apologized, and the Liberals were in no mood to commit political suicide. By dawn the two men had thrashed out an understanding as to procedure. The British government would officially propose a Joint Commission to settle Canadian questions; the United States would then propose to include the *Alabama* claims, and England would agree. Once the commission met, a draft treaty wrapping up all issues would be forthcoming. Fish and Rose agreed that the time was ripe for settlement.[70]

The following day Fish laid the proposal before Grant, suggesting that the commission meet in Washington, not London. Grant was doubtful. He thought British concessions would be more likely if the commissioners had ready access to their government, but Fish convinced him otherwise. The Gladstone ministry, said the secretary, was distracted. It had too much on its plate to give the commission much attention, and his conversation with Rose had reassured him the British delegates would come to Washington empowered to settle all issues. What Fish did not say, and what may have been even more important, was that the secretary could control negotiations in Washington directly, rather that relying on diplomatic proxies and laborious telegraph communications.

Grant reviewed the matter with his cabinet on January 17. Each member expressed himself in favor, provided Britain "admit her liability for the losses sustained by the acts of the *Alabama*." This demand would have torpedoed the conference if Grant had insisted on it. Instead, he instructed Fish to submit the *Alabama* claims to arbitration, asking only that Britain issue a statement expressing regret. As for the Senate, Fish worked diligently to line up support. Sumner was bypassed, and it soon became evident that the Republican leadership—men like Morton, Conkling, and Simon Cameron, the new chairman of Foreign Relations—was as eager for a treaty as Grant or Fish. Refinancing the country's massive debt at a more favorable interest rate was at the top of the party's agenda, and to do so required peace with Great Britain.

For the remainder of January, Fish and Rose sparred over details. Eventually it was agreed that Grant and Queen Victoria would each appoint five commissioners to meet in Washington and resolve the differences between the two countries. On February 2, 1871, the British government officially informed Washington that it was prepared to send the proposed mission, and on February 9 Grant sent the nominations of the American commissioners to the Senate. In addition to Fish, who would serve as chairman, the nominees were Rockwood Hoar; Senator George H. Williams of Oregon; General Robert C. Schenck, a former congressman from Ohio who was Motley's successor as American minister to London; and Justice Samuel Nelson of the Supreme Court. Justice Nelson was a Democrat from New York whom Tyler had appointed to the bench, and who possessed an extensive knowledge of international law.[71] The British commissioners were equally distinguished. The Earl of Ripon, a prominent member of Gladstone's cabinet, was chairman.* He was supported by Sir Stafford Northcote, an equally prominent Conservative member of Parliament; Professor Mountague Bernard, Chichele Professor of International Law at All Souls College, Oxford; and Sir John A. Macdonald, prime minister of Canada, considered by some the ablest statesman of the era.[72] Sir Edward Thornton, the British minister in Washington, would serve as secretary to the delegation.

The British commissioners arrived in Washington, Friday, February 24, 1871, and were received with great cordiality. *Harper's Weekly* said the Joint Commission offered a "simple and satisfactory" road to peace. *The Nation* called it "a triumph of civilization." James Gordon Bennett's *New York Herald* predicted the word "Alabama" would revert to its aboriginal meaning, "Here we rest." Grant and Julia hosted a gala reception for the commissioners Saturday evening, and on Monday the work began. Protocol to the contrary, the commission met on American home turf in the State Department library. The sessions began at noon, and lasted until four or five in the afternoon. The atmosphere was businesslike but not abrasive.

---

* The Earl of Ripon, George Fredrick Samuel Robinson, who sometimes was referred to as the Earl de Grey. Because of possible confusion with Earl Grey of Fallodon, who was British foreign secretary, 1905–1916, I have used Ripon throughout. In 1880, Lord Ripon succeeded Lord Lytton as viceroy of India, later served as first lord of the Admiralty (1892–1895) and colonial secretary (1895–1898). From 1905 to 1908 he was Liberal leader for the House of Lords.

Fish and Ripon developed an immediate liking for each other, and the most important work of the commission was done by the two meeting informally, either at Fish's home in the evening, or in the elegant town house Ripon had rented. Fish kept Grant minutely informed. Almost daily he would call at the White House, or the president, cigar in hand, would stroll across Lafayette Square to see how things were going. Both men were at their best. The plainspoken president, comfortable with accepting final responsibility, was content to leave day-to-day tactics in the hands of his foreign policy subordinate. And Fish, a master of diplomatic nuance, played his negotiating cards deftly, encouraged by the knowledge of Grant's trust and support.[73]

Considering the complexity of the issues, the negotiations proceeded with remarkable smoothness. In two months, with a total of thirty-seven meetings, the task was finished. On Monday, May 8, the Treaty of Washington was signed with pomp and ceremony at the State Department, the last signature affixed at twelve minutes past eleven. "This is the proudest day of my life," Ripon told Fish. "I congratulate you, and myself, and my two countries [Britain and Canada] and I thank you most cordially for what you have done." Fish returned the compliment. Afterward, he confided to his diary that he felt much as he did in college when he had taken an examination for which he had studied hard, and was waiting for the results: "A feeling of want of something to do, and of the absence of the excitement under which the labor had been sustained."[74]

The Treaty of Washington is a landmark of international conciliation. Forty-three articles long, it provided for the settlement of all disputes then existing between the United States and Great Britain. The *Alabama* claims were referred to binding arbitration. This was a precedent-setting breakthrough in adjusting international differences. A five-person arbitral tribunal was to be established in Geneva, one member each to be appointed by President Grant, Queen Victoria, the king of Italy, the emperor of Brazil, and the president of the Swiss Confederation. Great Britain also expressed regret "for the escape, under whatever circumstances, of the *Alabama* and other vessels from British ports, and for the depredations committed by those vessels." Most important, perhaps, the treaty promulgated new guidelines governing the obligations of neutral nations. While Her Majesty's Government noted explicitly that these rules were not international law at the time the Confederate cruisers escaped from British ports, it agreed that they should provide the basis of the arbitral decision.

The rules governing maritime neutrality laid out in the Treaty of Washington became the basis for international law on the subject, and were formally adopted by all nations at the second Hague Conference in 1907.[75] A nation was to "use due diligence" to prevent the outfitting of any vessel that it had reasonable grounds to believe was intended to make war against another nation. It was also bound to prevent any belligerent from making use of its ports as a base of naval operations, and it must exercise "due diligence" in its ports and waters and over all persons within its jurisdiction to prevent any violation of these obligations.[76]

Given the overarching interest of the United States and Great Britain in reaching a settlement, the issues pertaining to the *Alabama* claims and maritime neutrality fell into place easily. It was Canadian matters that proved most difficult, and almost two thirds of the commission's meetings were devoted to Atlantic fisheries, reciprocal trade, navigation, and the intractable San Juan boundary dispute.[77] Sir John A. Macdonald, who was looking after Dominion interests, drove a hard bargain, and the treaty reflected his skillful negotiating and occasional intransigence. American fisherman were given access to Canadian territorial waters for a period of ten years, Canadian fishermen were given reciprocal privileges in American waters, and both nations were permitted to ship fish and fish products to the other duty-free. As Sir Stafford Northcote wrote Macdonald, Canada might have found it beneficial to trade the fishing rights for access to the American market, "even if you got nothing to boot."[78] Finally, to ensure that dominion interests were fully protected, an international commission was to meet at Halifax and determine what additional compensation the United States should pay for the privilege of fishing in Canadian waters.

Issues of trade and navigation were compromised more easily. The St. Lawrence was thrown open to Americans in perpetuity, while the same principle was applied on behalf of Canada to the rivers (Yukon, Porcupine, and Stikine) that flowed through Alaska to the sea. Both nations were given access to the canals connecting the Great Lakes–St. Lawrence system, and Canadians were given free navigation of Lake Michigan for ten years. Various small border issues were settled amicably, and the Gladstone government assumed responsibility for compensating Canada for the Fenian raids.

The final question of importance, the international boundary through the Strait of Juan de Fuca, proved the most difficult. The islands in question were neither large nor valuable, but the issue had generated so much excitement on the Pacific Coast that neither side felt it could give way. In desperation the commission resorted once more to arbitration, and referred the dispute to Emperor William I of Germany for settlement. The choice of the emperor as arbitrator reflected the prestige Germany had acquired after its victory in the Franco-Prussian War, and the trust both the United States and Great Britain had in the Berlin government. The British were bound by kinship—Queen Victoria's daughter Vicky was married to William's eldest son, the crown prince—while the Americans, ably represented at the Prussian court by George Bancroft, knew that Bismarck would have a say in the final judgment and no European statesman was more pro-American.[79]*

Grant had little trouble with the Senate. Fish had kept key senators informed throughout the negotiations and it was manifest that the United States benefited enormously from the treaty. Public reaction was overwhelmingly positive. The *New York Times* and the *New York Tribune* waxed enthusiastic. The *New York World,* normally Democratic, found "nearly all the concessions were made on the British side." *The Nation* concluded that the United States had obtained all that a self-respecting nation could ask, or a self-respecting nation could give. On May 24, 1871, the Senate gave its consent, 50–12. Three Republicans voted no, two Democrats crossed the aisle and voted yes.[80] Sumner, after announcing initially that he intended to offer amendments, did not do so and voted with the majority. The treaty, he said generously, would be "hailed with joy by the thinking men of Great Britain and the United States."[81] In England, the only important opposition came from Lord Russell, but his speech condemning "British surrender" found little resonance.

The Treaty of Washington was a watershed in Anglo-American relations. Never again would the two nations be seriously at odds. The goodwill engendered by the document inaugurated a new relationship. Observers noted with feeling that the Senate's action was taken on Queen Victoria's birthday. Formal ratifications were exchanged in London on Bunker Hill Day, June 17, and Grant proclaimed the treaty, placing it in effect, on July 4, 1871. The following year, the Geneva arbitration commission awarded the United States an indemnity of $15.5 million for the damages wrought by the *Alabama* and her sister ships. Fish was delighted. "We are quite content with the Geneva award," he wrote Washburne. "It decides that 'Great Britain was culpable.' The amount awarded [is] a secondary consideration."[82]

It remained for Grant to write finis to the episode. "The relations of the United States with foreign powers continues to be friendly," he told Congress in his annual message. "The year has been an eventful one in wit-

---

* The issue in dispute concerning the San Juan Islands traced to the ambiguous wording of the 1846 treaty between the United States and Great Britain, which stipulated that the international boundary should proceed from the point at which the 49th parallel reached the coast, thence "along the middle of the channel which separates the continent from Vancouver Island." The question was whether that channel was the Canal de Haro, claimed by the United States, or the Strait of Rosario, claimed by Great Britain. The former would place the San Juan Islands in the United States, the latter would put the islands in Canada. The San Juan Islands command the entrance to Puget Sound, as well as access to Vancouver and the mouth of the Fraser River. William I issued his finding October 21, 1872, holding that the Haro Channel was the main channel, thus placing the entire San Juan archipelago in possession of the United States.

nessing two great nations, speaking one language and having one lineage, settling by peaceful arbitration a dispute of long standing and one liable at any time to bring these nations into bloody and costly conflict. An example has thus been set which . . . may be followed by other civilized nations and finally be the means of returning to productive industry millions of men now maintained to settle the disputes of nations by the bayonet and the broadside." [83]

The Treaty of Washington was an unprecedented accomplishment. Not only did it pull the United States and Great Britain back from the brink of war, but it provided one of the most striking triumphs for arbitral methods that the world had yet witnessed. It dispelled every serious cloud darkening Anglo-American relations. John Bassett Moore, among the most learned of international law scholars, said the Treaty of Washington "occupies a place in the annals of American diplomatic history second only to the Treaty of Paris," which ended the Revolutionary War. [84]

Grant's role in American diplomacy was not unlike that of Eisenhower almost a century later. Both enjoyed enormous international stature, and both provided firm yet understated guidance to United States foreign policy. Reflecting their background as supreme commanders, both delegated day-to-day operations to their secretary of state. Yet both made the final decisions and set the course. By avoiding details, they maintained perspective and provided a constancy that American foreign policy has not always enjoyed. Grant kept the United States out of war with Spain, made peace with Great Britian, settled the *Alabama* claims, and established a precedent for the arbitration of international disputes. Under his leadership the United States crept onto the world stage, almost unnoticed.

CHAPTER SEVENTEEN

GREAT WHITE FATHER

The only good Indian is a dead Indian.

PHILIP H. SHERIDAN, 1869

We took away their country and their means of support, broke up their mode of living, their habits of life, introduced disease and decay among them, and it was for this and against this they made war. Could any one expect less?

PHILIP H. SHERIDAN, 1878

THE AMERICAN DRIVE to expand westward under the banner of Manifest Destiny was not without cost, and most of the cost was borne by Native Americans. The history of their treatment by the United States is a sordid tale, marred by greed, brutality, duplicity, corruption, and, at times, extermination. Brief intervals of government enlightenment buffered the spread of European civilization westward, and the eight years of the Grant administration were more enlightened than most. Grant felt a romantic kinship with the nation's first inhabitants. He sympathized with their plight, regretted their degradation, and was determined to shepherd them into full membership in American society.[1] His peace policy was exactly that: an attempt to substitute kindness for bloodshed. It marked a fundamental shift in official attitude and laid the foundation for the program by which the Plains Indians were eventually accommodated.[2]

Early North American settlers claimed title to Indian land by discovery and conquest.* Treaties of cession were concluded with tribal chiefs

---

* In the leading case of *Johnson v. McIntosh*, 8 Wheaton 543 (1823), Chief Justice Marshall expressed skepticism concerning the "original justice" of the nation's claim to Indian land. Nevertheless, he held it was a political matter beyond the Court's jurisdiction. In Marshall's words: "However extravagant the pretension of converting discovery of an inhabited country into conquest may appear; if the principle has been converted in the first instance, and afterwards sustained; if a country has been acquired and held under it; if the property

when possible, and it quickly became colonial policy to establish boundary lines demarcating Indian territory.[3] In 1763, to further minimize friction, George III prohibited settlement west of the Appalachians. The colonies were forbidden to grant titles to land beyond the headwaters of the rivers that flowed into the Atlantic.[4] The ban on settlement helped keep the peace. But it was sorely resented by Americans living along the frontier.

With independence from Britain, the westward surge of pioneers resumed. Land was wealth, and Indian land seemed to be there for the taking. In 1803 Thomas Jefferson suggested relocating the Indians west of the Mississippi.[5] Monroe expanded the idea, recommending that the tribes be invited to remove to the region "between the present States and Territories and the Rocky Mountains."[6] Congress responded in 1830 with passage of the Indian Removal Act, appropriated half a million dollars for the purpose, and authorized the president to grant lands in the unoccupied portion of the Louisiana Purchase in exchange for those relinquished in the East.[7]

Some tribes went peaceably, others did not. President Jackson assumed responsibility for relocating four Indian nations of the Southeast Confederacy: the Creek, Cherokee, Choctaw, and Chickasaw.[8] The Seminoles of Florida resisted relocation until 1842. Their removal eventually cost the United States some $20 million and the lives of 1,500 soldiers and settlers. By the end of John Tyler's term in 1845, the Indian problem appeared to have been solved. Most tribes had been moved west. A new demarcation line running from Lake Superior to the Red River on the Texas border separated tribal land from white settlement. Behind this boundary the Indians were guaranteed possession "as long as grass grows and water flows."[9]

But the march of pioneers was relentless. The discovery of gold in California and later in Colorado precipitated the great migrations of the late 1840s and 1850s. Prospectors, cattlemen, and farmers swarmed onto the Great Plains with complete disregard for Indian rights.[10] New railroads brought thousands of additional settlers, disrupted traditional migration patterns, and placed a great strain on wildlife, particularly the buffalo, which were essential to the survival of the Plains Indians.

---

of the great mass of the community originates in it, it becomes the law of the land, and cannot be questioned. So too with the concomitant principle, that the Indian inhabitants are to be considered merely as occupants, to be protected, indeed, while in peace, in the possession of these lands, but to be deemed incapable of transferring absolute title to others."

Marshall went on to hold that although the Indians (in this instance, the Piankesaw tribe in Illinois) did not own tribal land in fee simple, they were entitled to continued possession of it. Marshall's recognition of the right of native possession established the basic rule of North American jurisprudence. As the Supreme Court of Canada observed, the chief justice's opinion in *Johnson* is "the locus classicus of the principles governing aboriginal title." *Calder v. Attorney-General of British Columbia,* [1973] S.C.R. 313, 380.

Indian resentment rose as their lands were overrun. The Sioux of Minnesota went on the warpath in 1862.[11] Two years later the Cheyenne, following a series of incidents in eastern Colorado, took up weapons against encroaching white settlers. Aided by the Arapahos, Kiowas, and Comanches they virtually isolated the territory by midsummer. Mail and stage service was disrupted, and a general Indian uprising appeared imminent. In the autumn, tribal elders drew back. Led by Black Kettle and six other chiefs, the Cheyenne sought to make peace. In early November they surrendered their weapons and went into winter encampment on Sand Creek, forty miles northeast of Fort Lyon, near the Kansas border. Here, on the morning of November 29, they were attacked without warning by Colorado militia, and the butchery that followed is unparalleled in the annals of Plains warfare.[12] Black Kettle hoisted first an American flag, then a white flag, but the slaughter continued unabated. Defenseless men, women, and children were shot and sabered, their bodies scalped and mutilated. Of some 700 Cheyenne encamped on Sand Creek, 500 were reported slain.[13] Black Kettle and others escaped, but the massacre set the Plains aflame from Mexico to the Canadian border.

Sand Creek became a cause célèbre.* Three formal investigations were launched, each of which sharply condemned the nation's mistreatment of the Plains Indians.[14] Most of the clashes that had occurred were attributed to "the aggressions of lawless white men."[15] The reports fixed on the loss of tribal hunting grounds as a major source of unrest and urged a series of reforms within the Bureau of Indian Affairs to ensure the Indians got a fair shake. But the reforms were stillborn.[16]

Sporadic fighting continued along the frontier for the next two years. In 1867 Congress responded by establishing a Peace Commission to carry an olive branch to restive tribes. Composed of four distinguished civilians and three army officers, including Sherman, the commission toured the West, conducted hearings, and met with tribal leaders.[17] In January 1868 it released its report, recommending that the Indians be resettled on protected reservations where they could be taught the white man's ways. English was to be introduced, schools established, and resident farmers provided to teach the nomadic tribesmen agricultural techniques. "Let the women be taught to weave, to sew and to knit. Let polygamy be punished. Encourage the building of dwellings, and the gathering there of those

---

* Grant was facing Lee before Petersburg when the Sand Creek massacre occurred, but he took time out to tell Governor John Evans of Colorado that the affair was not a battle but "a murder of Indians who were supposed to be under the protection of the Federal Government." Samuel F. Tappan, "Autobiography," Samuel F. Tappen Papers, Kansas State Historical Society, in Robert Winston Mardock, *The Reformers and the American Indian* 49 (Columbia: University of Missouri Press, 1971).

comforts which will endear the home." [18] Two large reservations were designated, one on the southern Plains that took in the present state of Oklahoma; one in the north encompassing most of the present state of South Dakota. The commission then concluded a series of treaties, first with the southern tribes (Cheyenne, Arapaho, Kiowa, and Comanche), then with those in the north (principally the Sioux), to put the recommendations into effect. The Indians agreed to move to the areas assigned, and the government undertook to provide food, clothing, and other supplies to ease the transition. In addition, three military posts located on what was designated as tribal land were razed.

Peace appeared in the offing. But that hope faded quickly. The House and Senate fell to feuding over the financial terms of treaties, the requisite funds were not appropriated, some of the treaties were not ratified, and the Indians became destitute waiting for succor. [19] In the autumn of 1868 the truce was shattered on the southern Plains. Raiding parties of Cheyenne and Arapaho, desperate because promised supplies were not forthcoming, launched a series of attacks on white settlers in central and western Kansas. Sherman, who was in overall command on the frontier, resolved to punish the raiders and push the tribes onto the designated reservations. Sheridan was given tactical command, instructed to mount a rare winter campaign, and to show no mercy. "I want you to go ahead, kill and punish the hostiles, capture and destroy the ponies, lances, carbines, etc., etc., of the Cheyennes, Arapahoes, and Kiowas," said Sherman. [20] As he wrote his brother, "The more [Indians] we can kill this year, the less we will have to kill next year." [21] The result was the Cheyenne War of 1868. Sheridan, back in the saddle, pressed his troopers relentlessly. In late November, Lieutenant Colonel George Armstrong Custer, at the head of the 7th Cavalry, came upon the Cheyenne encampment on the banks of the Washita. Attacking at first light, Custer routed the Indians and inflicted heavy losses. Whether the attack was necessary is debatable. Critics maintained the Cheyenne had gone into winter quarters and were actually on the reservation when Custer struck. "I cannot but feel that innocent parties have been made to suffer for the crimes of others," the superintendent of Indian affairs told Congress. [22] Sheridan disputed the charge, claimed only the guilty had been punished, and commended Custer for his conduct. [23]

The defeat on the Washita was a serious blow to the Cheyenne. But it scarcely settled matters. When Grant took office in March 1869, the Plains seethed with unrest. Congress still had not appropriated the requisite funds, the tribes were becoming increasingly militant, settlers were clamoring for protection, and the army was girding for battle. A president less confident of his military judgment, or who stood more in awe of wartime heroes, would likely have given Sherman and Sheridan their head. The result would have been total war. The Indian tribes would have been driven mercilessly. Tens of thousands would have perished, and ethnic cleansing would have been the order of the day. Instead, Grant abruptly changed direction. Rather than fight, he chose to make peace with the Plains Indians. This was a surprise. As one historian has written, "Suddenly and inexplicably, the nation's preeminent warrior seemed to have gone over to the enemy."[24]

The situation is analogous to that in 1952. Voters cast their ballots for Eisenhower, believing the former Allied commander would bring quick victory in Korea. Instead, Ike sized up the situation, concluded the war could not be won, and halted the fighting on the best terms he could get. With Grant it was much the same. He carried the frontier states easily in 1868.[25] Voters believed that as president the general in chief would make fast work of the recalcitrant tribes who were blocking westward expansion. But like Eisenhower, Grant recognized the costs would be prohibitive. Even more important, he thought the Indians deserved better treatment. Curious as it may seem, the two soldier-presidents drew on their military experience to lead the nation out of war.

Unlike Sherman and Sheridan, Grant believed most of the problems on the frontier were attributable to the settlers. This was a view of long standing. As a junior officer with the 4th Infantry in California, he wrote Julia: "You charge me to be cautious riding out lest the Indians get me. Those about here are the most harmless people you ever saw. It really is my opinion that the whole race would be harmless and peaceable if they were not put upon by whites."[26] The intervening years had not changed Grant's mind. Peace with the Indians was preferable to war, he wrote Sherman in 1868, but "our white people seem never to be satisfied without hostilities with them."[27] Grant firmly believed that errant warriors should be punished. But he carefully distinguished those renegades who were at war with the United States from the Indian people. Grant also believed Indian affairs had been consistently mishandled. "Indian wars have grown out of mismanagement of the Bureau [of Indian Affairs]," he wrote Sheridan in disgust on Christmas Eve, 1868. "If the men who have to do the fighting could have the management in time of peace, they would most likely preserve peace, for their own comfort if for no other reason."[28] Above all, Grant believed Indians should be treated as individuals, not on a tribal basis, and that they should be afforded the opportunity to become citizens as quickly as possible.[29]

Grant's conciliatory approach to Indian affairs was shocking to many Americans, especially Sherman and Sheridan.[30] It also raised important constitutional issues. In 1831 the Supreme Court, speaking through Chief Justice Marshall, held the Indian tribes were "domestic dependent nations. . . . They are in a state of pupilage. Their relation to the United States resembles that of a ward to his guardian. They look to our government for protection; rely upon its kindness and its power; appeal to it for relief of their wants." Marshall went on to hold that under the umbrella of federal protection, the tribes were distinct political societies capable of governing themselves.[31] That did not preclude citizenship, but it implied that an Indian's primary allegiance was to the tribe.*

More to the point, the Fourteenth Amendment, which defined citizenship and granted equality to African-Americans, was written in such a way to exclude Indians from its provisions. According to the text, "All persons born or naturalized in the United States, and subject to the jurisdiction thereof, are citizens of the United States and of the State wherein they reside." The phrase "and subject to the jurisdiction thereof" was held to exclude those Indians who were subject to tribal law.[32] This is not conclusive. The Constitution gives Congress authority to enact legislation pertaining to citizenship.[33] But for Grant to convince Congress to act, he was clearly swimming upstream.†

Grant's approach to administration differed little from his style in the army. As president, he delegated. During the war he had turned the Army of the Tennessee over to Sherman, the Army of the Cumberland to George Thomas, and the Army of the Potomac to George Meade. Grant provided overall direction, closer in Meade's case than the others, but he did not micromanage. So too as president. Economic policy was Boutwell's responsibility, foreign affairs fell to Fish, and Indian matters became the province

---

* *Cherokee Nation v. Georgia,* 5 Peters 1 (1831). The issue was whether the Cherokee nation was a "foreign nation" and thus entitled to bring suit in federal court. Marshall held that it was not. His reluctance is evident from his dicta:

> If Courts were permitted to indulge their sympathies, a case better calculated to excite them cannot be imagined. A people once numerous, powerful, and truly independent, found by our ancestors in the quiet and uncontrolled possession of an ample domain, gradually sinking beneath our superior policy, our arts and our arms, have yielded their lands by successive treaties, each of which contains a solemn guarantee of the residue, until they retain no more of their formerly extensive domain than is deemed necessary to their comfortable subsistence.

Subsequently, in *Worcester v. Georgia,* 6 Peters 515 (1832), the Supreme Court, speaking again through Marshall, held that the Constitution delegated to the federal government broad legislative authority over Indian matters, and that the treaties made with the Cherokee nation reserved to the Cherokees tribal self-government within Cherokee territory free of interference from the state. The decision in Worcester remains one of the five most frequently cited Supreme Court cases of the pre–Civil War era.
† It was not until June 4, 1924, that Congress adopted legislation granting citizenship to the Indians. Even then, some states, such as New Mexico, continued to prohibit Indians from voting in state elections. 43 *United States Statutes at Large* 253 (1924).

of Jacob D. Cox, the secretary of the interior, and Ely S. Parker, commissioner of Indian affairs.*

Cox had been Grant's candidate to succeed Stanton as secretary of war during the 1868 impeachment crisis. A former major general of volunteers and a law professor at the University of Cincinnati, Cox was an administrator of remarkable ability. He was also a man of contradiction and paradox. A staunch advocate of civil service reform, he immediately put the merit system into operation in his department, much to the dismay of Republican office seekers. An article he published in the *North American Review* did as much as any publication of the period to mobilize sentiment for the establishment of a classified civil service.[34] But alone among Grant's cabinet, Cox carried in his baggage a deep hostility to black equality. As governor of Ohio he opposed Negro suffrage in the state, and in a message to his abolitionist alma mater, Oberlin College, he advocated government-enforced segregation, with African-Americans placed on a reservation in the deep South.[35]

Grant's principal adviser on Indian affairs was Ely Parker, his former military secretary. Parker personified Grant's ideal of Indian assimilation. A chief of the Senecas and grand sachem of the Iroquois Confederacy, Parker was an accomplished engineer, lawyer, and soldier. As an aide, he had proved himself invaluable. At Appomattox, when other staff members were overcome with emotion, it was Parker to whom Grant turned to write out the official copy of the surrender terms he had given Lee. And it was Parker whom Grant used as his eyes and ears to keep tabs on frontier conditions after the war.

The name Parker derived from that of a British officer who had lived among the Iroquois.[36] Ely's parents resided on the Tonawanda reservation

---

* Grant's military style of delegation, the essence of the modern presidency, drew mixed reviews. Rutherford B. Hayes, a former major general of volunteers, was enthusiastic. By delegating broadly and holding cabinet officers accountable, he said, "Grant's leadership and rule is beyond question." 3 *The Diary and Letters of Rutherford Birchard Hayes* 59, Charles R. Williams, ed. (Columbus: Ohio Historical Society, 1922).

The more traditional view was put forward by Senator John Sherman. Like most at the time, Sherman believed cabinet officers were primarily responsible to Congress, not the president. He lamented that Grant "regarded these heads of departments as mere subordinates" and attributed it to his failure to understand "the true theory of our government." In Senator Sherman's view, which later critics of the Grant administration rushed to adopt, the former general in chief lacked experience "in the complicated problems of our form of government. . . . The limitation of the power of the President [over cabinet members] is one that an army officer, accustomed to give or receive orders, finds difficult to understand and to observe when elected President." John Sherman, 1 *Recollections of Forty Years in the House, Senate, and Cabinet* 449 (Chicago: Werner, 1893).

Grant's innovation, in making his cabinet officers responsible to him but not to Congress, was ultimately sustained in the magisterial decision of Chief Justice (and former president) William Howard Taft, speaking for the Supreme Court in *Myers v. United States,* 272 U.S. 52 (1926).

in upstate New York, and his father was among the 700 or so Indian warriors who fought alongside the United States during the War of 1812. Ely, who was born in 1828, was also known as Ha Sa No An Da and Donehogawa. He was educated at the Tonawanda mission school and Cayuga Academy, and as a schoolboy often acted as guide and interpreter to the leaders of the Iroquois on their trips to Washington. Serving as a bridge between two cultures, he became the principal source for the pioneer anthropologist Lewis Henry Morgan, who dedicated his landmark study of the Iroquois "to HA-SA-NO-AN-DA, (Ely S. Parker), a Seneca Indian."[37]

Parker worked initially as a director of work crews on the Erie Canal, served as resident engineer in charge of construction of the Chesapeake and Albemarle Canal linking Norfolk with Albemarle Sound in North Carolina, and then built lighthouses for the Treasury Department along the Great Lakes. In 1857 he was assigned to build the United States customshouse in Galena and decided to settle there. He and Grant, his fellow townsman, were well acquainted. When the Civil War came, Parker sought to join the army but it was not until 1863 that his request was approved. He was commissioned a captain on May 23 and joined Grant's staff at Vicksburg shortly thereafter.[38]

Cox and Parker administered Indian policy, but Grant set the tone. His messages to Congress and the American people pleaded the Indian cause with an intensity rarely encountered in official communications:

> Wars of extermination . . . are demoralizing and wicked. Our superiority should make us lenient toward the Indian. The wrongs inflicted upon him should be taken into account and the balance placed to his credit.[39]

> Our dealings with the Indian properly lay us open to charges of cruelty and swindling.[40]

> A system which looks to the extinction of a race is too horrible for a nation to adopt without entailing upon itself the wrath of all Christendom and engendering in the citizens a disregard for human life and the rights of others, dangerous to society.[41]

> Can not the Indian be made a useful and productive member of society? If the effort is made in good faith, we will stand better before the civilized nations of the earth and our own consciences for having made it.[42]

I do not believe our Creator ever placed the different races on this earth with a view of having the strong exert all his energies in exterminating the weaker.[43]

The first task for the Grant administration was to pry loose the Indian appropriation bill languishing in Congress. At the root of the delay was a classic turf battle between the House of Representatives and the Senate over the control of Indian policy. The Senate was setting policy through its ability to approve or disapprove of the treaties made with the tribes. The House resented playing second fiddle and was demonstrating its power by refusing to appropriate the money required by the treaties.* At issue was $4 million in appropriations for 1869–1870, and neither the House nor the Senate was prepared to compromise.[44] The big losers of course were the Indians, who were denied the funds the government had promised.

Grant took it upon himself to break the logjam. Recognizing that the House was in control, the president endeavored to find a face-saving formula by which the congressmen could vote the money without seeming to kowtow to the Senate's treaty prerogative. The answer came to Grant uninvited. In mid-March 1869, with the House and Senate at loggerheads, a delegation of prominent philanthropists, led by Philadelphia's William Welsh, requested an interview with the president and Secretary Cox to discuss Indian policy. Meeting in the White House on March 24, they urged Grant to appoint an autonomous commission to supervise the spending of federal funds on the Indians' behalf. Because of graft and bureaucratic overhead, only 25 percent of the money appropriated ever reached the tribes, they said, and "without the co-operation of Christian philanthropists the waste of money would be great and the result unsatisfactory."[45]

Grant agreed completely. After assuring his visitors of his desire "to make a radical change in the Indian policy of the government," he dispatched them to Capitol Hill to lobby for the long-delayed appropria-

---

* Although the Constitution specifies that treaties are the supreme law of the land (Article VI, Section 2), the House of Representatives is not bound thereby, and is under no obligation to appropriate the funds a treaty may specify. The definitive precedent was set during the administration of George Washington concerning the Jay Treaty with Great Britain. The Washington administration argued that since the treaty had been approved by two thirds of the Senate and had become part of the supreme law, the House was bound to obey it and vote the money required. James Madison led the opposition in the House and introduced a resolution stating, "It is the clear constitutional right and duty of the House of Representatives . . . to deliberate on the expediency or inexpediency of carrying such Treaty into effect, and to determine and act thereon, as, in their judgment, may be most conductive to the public good." Eventually a compromise was reached. Madison's resolution was attached to the appropriation bill providing the money needed, and President Washington signed the measure, thus conceding the point to the House. 2 *Writings of James Madison* 264, Gaillard Hunt, ed. (Washington, D.C.: Government Printing Office, 1906).

tions.[46] The suggestion of an independent commission to oversee expenditures broke the congressional deadlock. The House and Senate agreed that $5 million would be required for continued maintenance of the tribes, and then tacked on an additional $2 million to enable the president to secure peace. Grant was authorized to appoint ten men "eminent for their intelligence and philanthropy" to the commission, and the measure was enacted into law April 10, 1869.[47]

Grant's peace policy was off to a good start. With the aid of Welsh and George H. Stuart of Philadelphia, Grant enlisted nine men noted for their philanthropic leadership to serve on the new Board of Indian Commissioners. Among those appointed, in addition to Stuart and Welsh, were Felix R. Brunot, an industrialist from Pittsburgh, and the immensely wealthy William E. Dodge, one of the founders of Phelps, Dodge and Company. Grant could not have chosen better.[48] Like his blue-ribbon fact-finding panel to the Dominican Republic, the new Board of Indian Commissioners provided prestigious support for administration policy.* Stuart and Dodge had contributed generously to fund freedmen's schools in the South, and like their fellow appointees they saw the board as an opportunity not only to reform the corrupt administration of the Bureau of Indian Affairs, but to initiate practical measures for the education and Christianization of the Indians.[49]

The president and Cox met the new board in the White House on May 27, 1869. Grant repeated his desire to reform the Bureau of Indian Affairs and then laid out the broad outlines of his peace policy: insofar as possible, the government would deal with the Indians as individuals, not on a tribal basis; those Indians living on reservations would be protected from white settlers and taught the arts of civilization; previous government pledges to the Indians would be strictly adhered to; and clear titles would be granted to those plots of land Indian families could be induced to cultivate. Grant said he wanted the board to have "the fullest authority over the whole subject," and promised his complete support.[50]

The following week Grant issued an executive order giving the board plenary authority to inspect and report on all aspects on the nation's Indian policy. Government officials were enjoined to allow board members full access to records and accounts, pay respectful heed to their advice, and "co-operate with them in the most earnest manner . . . in the general work

---

* The annual reports issued by the Board of Indian Commissioners did much to arouse public support for the Indians. The first report, submitted by Brunot on November 23, 1869, was a caustic indictment of past policy, which it called "unjust and iniquitous beyond the power of words to express." The report damned the frontiersmen who wronged the Indians and placed the primary blame for Indian wars on them. "Paradoxical as it may seem, the white man has been the chief obstacle in the way of Indian civilization." *Report of the Board of Indian Commissioners,* 1869 7–9.

of civilizing the Indians, protecting them in their legal rights, and stimulating them to become industrious citizens."[51]

The board began work enthusiastically. Members went about their duties with tremendous goodwill, scrutinized vouchers presented for payment, verified the quality and quantity of goods provided for the Indians, and conducted rigorous inspections of conditions in the West. Advocates of reform were jubilant. *The Nation* reported "the complete overthrow of a most gigantic system of wrong, robbery, hypocrisy, greed, and cruelty" and the triumph of "right, official integrity, and administrative economy."[52] Among other things, the board recommended the concentration of the Indians on small reservations, abolition of the treaty system, and immediate citizenship for the Five Civilized Tribes in the Indian Territory (Creek, Cherokee, Choctaw, Chickasaw, and Seminole). Above all, the board recommended that Indian agents and district superintendents be selected on the basis of moral and business qualifications, without reference to political affiliation.[53]

Nothing could have pleased Grant more. The Indian agents were critical to the process of assimilation. A combination governor, teacher, supplier, and, theoretically at least, a defender of Indian interests, they were almost exclusively political appointees—ripe patronage plums that members of Congress considered an integral part of the spoils system. Not all agents were corrupt, but many were, and the opportunity for graft was enormous. Henry B. Whipple, the Episcopal bishop of Minnesota and a keen observer of Indian affairs, noted that it was "a tradition on the frontier that an Indian agent with [a salary of] $1500 a year could retire upon an ample fortune in three years."[54] Or as one prominent chief told Sherman, when his agent arrived "he bring everything in a little bag. When he go it take two steamboats to carry away his things."[55]

Grant had already moved to enlist Quakers as Indian agents. After meeting with delegations sent by the Society of Friends in January, the president-elect had instructed Parker to obtain a list of nominees he might appoint. The Quakers were initially hesitant about accepting posts on the frontier, but soon responded favorably and by the middle of June 1869 had accepted two superintendencies and fourteen agencies, covering the Indians in Kansas and Nebraska, as well as the Kiowas and Comanches in the Indian Territory. Under what became known as Grant's "Quaker Policy," the Society of Friends not only nominated superintendents and agents but also undertook to supervise their work after they had been appointed. "The Friends were appointed not because they have any monopoly on honesty or good will toward the Indians," said Secretary Cox, "but because their selection would of itself be understood by the country to indicate the policy adopted, namely, the sincere cultivation of peaceful relations with the tribes."[56]

Armed with the report of the Board of Indian Commissioners, Grant moved swiftly to replace the remaining Indian agents with army officers on active duty, men he was confident he could count on to carry out orders without reaching into the till. Grant saw no inconsistency in entrusting the peace policy to army officers. Aside from a high level of professional integrity, military officers held their position for life, and as he told Congress, they had a personal interest in establishing peace with the Indians.[57]

Public opinion reacted predictably. Reformers praised Grant down the line. "With full heart and most earnestly, we thank him," wrote Wendell Phillips in the *National Anti-Slavery Standard*.[58] Alfred H. Love, speaking to the Pennsylvania Peace Society, boasted "President Grant says amen to our wishes [for Indian rights]. Let this work be stamped upon the nineteenth century."[59] The *New York Times* praised the new policy and concluded that Congress would have "a clearer field than ever before for settling a broad Indian policy."[60] The *Boston Evening Transcript* stated there was uprightness, common sense, and common honesty in the new policy.[61] On the other hand, Democratic papers like the *New York World* took no notice of the peace policy, while most Western editors, regardless of political affiliation, were openly critical.

By the end of 1869 Grant's peace policy was in place. His appointments struck at the heart of the old Indian system—the patronage prerogatives of members of Congress. All Indian agencies were in the hands of Quakers or military officers, and a massive step had been taken to end the abuses of the past.

But Grant's luck was about to run out. Regardless of the commander in chief's determination to make peace with the Plains Indians, the army in the West followed its own bent. On the morning of January 23, 1870, elements of the 2nd Cavalry, seeking to punish renegade Piegan warriors (the Piegans were a band of the Blackfeet tribe), fell upon and destroyed a Piegan village along the banks of the Marias River in northern Montana. The troopers believed they were assaulting the lair of the villainous Mountain Chief.* Instead, the target was a defenseless tribal village, mostly women and children, many suffering the final stages of smallpox. It was another Sand Creek massacre. One hundred seventy-three Indians were killed; all

* "If the lives and property of the citizens of Montana can best be protected by striking Mountain Chief's band, I want them struck," Sheridan ordered. "Tell [Colonel Edward M.] Baker to strike them hard." Paul Andrew Hutton, *Phil Sheridan and His Army* 190 (Lincoln: University of Nebraska Press, 1985).

but fifteen were women and children. Fifty of the casualties were children under twelve, many in their parents' arms. The cavalry lost one man killed and another injured.[62]

Outrage swept the country. The *New York Times* called the attack "a sickening slaughter," and demanded an immediate congressional investigation. The *Tribune* said the affair was a "national disgrace." Lydia Maria Child, former editor of the *National Anti-Slavery Standard,* chastised Sheridan for believing that "the approved method of teaching red men not to commit murder is to slaughter their wives and children." Wendell Phillips, speaking at the inaugural meeting of the Philadelphia Reform League, said, "I only know the names of three savages upon the Plains: Colonel Baker, General Custer, and at the head of all, General Sheridan."

For Grant, however, Phillips had unstinting praise. "Thank God for a President in the White House whose first word was for the Negro and the second for the Indian; who saw protection for the Indian not in the rude and bloodthirsty policy of Sheridan and Sherman, but in the ballot, in citizenship, the great panacea that has always protected the rights of Anglo-Saxon individuals."[63]

Grant's peace policy survived the attack. Indeed, as Phillips's comments suggest, support in the East was stronger than ever. But the spoilsmen in Congress seized upon the episode to eviscerate a vital element of the policy. The army appropriation bill for 1870 was amended to prohibit military officers from holding civil appointments. The measure was aimed at those officers serving in the Bureau of Indian Affairs. By forcing army officers to resign as Indian agents, disgruntled lawmakers were reaching once more for the patronage levers Grant had taken away.[64] The Piegan massacre provided the excuse. But if that were the intent, the congressmen underestimated Grant's resolve. "Gentlemen, you have defeated my plan for Indian management," he told a delegation from Capitol Hill, "but you shall not succeed in *your* purpose, for I will divide these appointments up among the religious churches, with which you dare not contend."[65] In effect, Grant raised the stakes. Rather than give in to the spoilsmen, he turned all seventy-three Indian agencies over to church groups. Given the separation of church and state, Grant's move may have been of doubtful constitutionality. Yet it was never tested in the courts, and for the remainder of the Grant administration the Indian agencies were staffed by religious denominations.*

---

* Grant, who was a staunch advocate of the separation of church and state (see Chapter Eighteen), seems not to have considered the application of the First Amendment to Native Americans, and throughout his term of office the issue was rarely raised. After 1878 the application of the Establishment Clause was debated hotly in Congress. Legitimate concern for First Amendment principle dovetailed with the legislators' eagerness for Bureau of Indian Affairs patronage,

Grant's second annual message to Congress laid out the policy fully. No president before or since has taken responsibility for the Indians more earnestly. Said Grant:

> Reform in the management of Indian affairs has received the special attention of the Administration from its inauguration to the present day. The experiment of making it a missionary work was tried with a few agencies given to the denomination of Friends, and has been found to work most advantageously. All agencies not so disposed were given to officers of the Army. The act of Congress reducing the army renders army officers ineligible for civil positions. Indian agencies being civil offices, I determined to give all the agencies to such religious denominations as had heretofore established missionaries among the Indians. . . . The societies selected are allowed to name their own agents, subject to approval of the Executive, and are expected to watch over them and aid them. . . . I entertain the confident hope that the policy now pursued will in a few years bring all the Indians upon reservations, where they will live in houses, and have schoolhouses and churches, and will be pursuing peaceful and self-sustaining avocations.[66]

On March 29, 1870, as Grant was dealing with the fallout from the Piegan village massacre and the refusal of the Senate to move on Santo Domingo, Sherman walked into the president's office with sad news from the West Coast. The War Department telegraph office had just received a message from San Francisco. "I'm afraid Old Tom is gone," said Cump. George H. Thomas, commander of the Pacific Division, suffered a massive stroke the evening before and died instantly. Sherman was closer to Thomas than to any other officer. They had been classmates at West Point and they shared a mutual respect that transcended rank or station. Grant was thunderstruck. He had often been impatient with Thomas, but he never doubted Old Tom's ability or determination. Above all, he admired his loyalty to the Union. Thomas's heroic service during the war was a mat-

---

and the two were often difficult to distinguish. The Hayes administration, led by Secretary of the Interior Carl Schurz, moved to reduce church involvement on the reservations but, again, the motives were mixed. A more serious, and more often overlooked infringement of the First Amendment relates to the Free Exercise Clause. The enforced Christianization of the Plains Indians, which was at the heart of the peace policy, unquestionably denied to Native Americans the freedom to practice their own religion. Basically, Grant's desire for assimilation and the preservation of tribal customs and traditions were mutually exclusive. For a balanced and thorough discussion of the First Amendment issues, see Robert H. Keller, Jr. *American Protestantism and United States Indian Policy, 1869–82* 167–87 (Lincoln: University of Nebraska Press, 1983).

ter of record. What was less well known was his complete dedication to the policy of Reconstruction. As The *New York Times* noted, though Thomas was a Virginian, "he took the part of the freedmen and helped them to protect themselves. He was the shield of order and society against anarchy and chaos in the South."[67] What Grant remembered best was that when Andrew Johnson inveigled to have Thomas succeed Sheridan in Louisiana, Old Tom had refused. And when the former president dangled three stars in front of him, Thomas turned a blind eye.

George Thomas, age fifty-four, was the first of the surviving senior Union generals to pass from the scene, and the outpouring of grief was extraordinary. The train carrying his coffin east was met by throngs of citizens in every city it passed through. Veterans organizations adopted resolutions of sympathy, military salutes were fired, and church sermons throughout the country were dedicated to Thomas's military service. Arrangements were made for his body to be interred in Troy, New York, his wife's hometown. Grant attended the funeral along with Sherman, Sheridan, and George Meade. Sherman gave the eulogy.[68]

When Grant returned to Washington a message was waiting for him. Red Cloud, mighty chief of the Oglala Sioux, wanted to meet the "Great Father." In December 1866, Red Cloud, with Crazy Horse at his side, had led the massacre of Captain William Fetterman's patrol near Fort Phil Kearny in the Wyoming Territory, closing the Bozeman Trail to white settlers. Now, he told military authorities, he and other Sioux chiefs wanted to come to Washington to talk to Grant about the possibility of going to a reservation. This was unexpected good news. Coming on the heels of the Piegan massacre it provided eloquent testimony of the effectiveness of the peace policy. Red Cloud, the best known and most intransigent of the warrior chiefs, wanted to parley. Sherman opposed the visit, but Grant overruled him.[69] Parker was instructed to make the arrangements, and shortly thereafter the chiefs were on their way east. "If they can receive practical evidence of the nation's determination to keep faith instead of repudiating solemn treaties," said Secretary Cox, "we may reasonably expect good results."[70] After meeting Grant, Red Cloud never again took up arms against the United States.

Red Cloud's visit to Washington mixed high carnival with serious purpose. The delegation numbered twenty-one, including Red Cloud's archrival, Spotted Tail, chief of the Brule Sioux.[71] "Physically, a finer set of men would be difficult to find," wrote a reporter for the *New York Herald*. "All were tall, full chested, and with features decidedly those of the American Indian." Red Cloud appeared "like a statue"; Big Bear seemed "fierce."[72] Ely Parker asked one of the chiefs, Little Swan, how he had become a great chief. Was it by killing people? "Yes," replied the chief, "the same as the Great White Father in the White House."[73]

When the chiefs met with Grant, Spotted Tail said he was for peace but the government had not reciprocated. White men continued to harass the tribes. Grant acted swiftly. The following day the War Department issued orders to all military commanders in the West: "When lands are secured to the Indians by treaty against the occupation by whites, the military commander should keep intruders off by military force if necessary."[74] Red Cloud complained that his people were poor and naked, and appealed for food and clothing. "Our nation is melting away like the snow on the side of the hills where the sun is warm, while your people are like the blades of grass in the Spring when summer is coming." The chief said he trusted Grant, but Indian messages "never reached the Great Father. They are lost before they get here."[75]

Grant was moved by the chiefs' sincerity. He recognized the government's shortcomings and was painfully aware that the 1870 annuity goods promised the tribes had not yet been delivered. Once again the Indian appropriation bill had run afoul of congressional opposition. This time the fight was between supporters of Grant's peace policy and frontier representatives who were dead set against. The advocates of reform were pressing for passage, but the opposition had succeeded in keeping the bill bottled up in committee. Grant was convinced that if Congress did not act before the session ended, a renewal of hostilities was inevitable. Penning a special message to Congress, the president warned of the consequences if the money bill failed to pass. The suffering, loss of life, and vast expenditures that would be required in the event of another Indian war were awesome to contemplate, he said.[76] Grant's intervention did the trick. Over vigorous opposition from Western delegations, the House and Senate passed the Indian Appropriation Act for 1870–1871 one day before adjournment.

From Washington the Sioux chiefs traveled to New York. On June 16, 1870, the delegation made a triumphant appearance before a capacity crowd at Cooper Union. A packed auditorium heard Red Cloud deliver an eloquent indictment of past policy. "The riches we have in this world, Secretary Cox said truly, we cannot take with us to the next world. Then I wish to know why agents are sent out to us who do nothing but rob us and get the riches of this world away from us?"[77] Red Cloud's description of the wrongs suffered by the Indians held the audience spellbound. A reporter from *The Nation* noted that the emotional effect "was comparable to the public recital of a fugitive slave in former years."[78]

The sympathy generated for the Indians by the Piegan massacre, followed by Red Cloud's visit, stimulated support for Grant's peace policy.

During the summer of 1870 both the Connecticut and Pennsylvania branches of the Universal Peace Union congratulated the president, and at its next session Congress responded with the first general appropriation for Indian education.[79] "Had the Republican Party done nothing more than rescue our Indian affairs from the errors and rascality that have heretofore characterized their management," said the *St. Paul Press,* "it would deserve the gratitude of the country."[80]

Peace with Red Cloud and the Oglala Sioux was a major achievement. Elsewhere, events moved apace. In December 1870 the Five Civilized Tribes, meeting in Okmulgee, about forty miles south of Tulsa, approved a constitution and bill of rights for a territorial government and a future Indian state. Grant immediately forwarded the documents to Congress and urged quick approval. "This is the first indication of the aborigines desiring to adopt our form of government, and it is highly desirable that they become self-sustaining, self-relying, Christianized, and civilized. If successful in this first attempt at territorial government, we may hope for a gradual concentration of other Indians in the new Territory."[81]

But the Indian proposal for territorial government provided for more independence than Congress cared for. Amendments were proposed giving final authority over legislation and appointments to the government in Washington, and at that point the tribes backed away. The railroads, with a huge stake in rights-of-way across Indian land, also opposed territorial status, as did the increasing number of white settlers moving into the region. As a result, the most serious effort to extend citizenship to the tribes in Indian territory went for naught.[82]

The conciliatory effort of the Five Civilized Tribes was reflected elsewhere. Red Cloud and the Oglala Sioux, Spotted Tail and the Brule, and a host of lesser chiefs on the northern Plains moved to the Great Sioux Reservation in the early 1870s.[83] In the Southwest, Major General Oliver Otis Howard, who had done yeoman service for Grant heading the Freedmen's Bureau, rode unarmed and alone into Cochise's stronghold in the Dragoon Mountains of Arizona and convinced the legendary chief of the Chiricahua Apaches to move onto a nearby reservation.[84] Howard's bold gambit brought peace to a large portion of the Southwest, and for the first time since 1861 Cochise's warriors posed no danger to the settlers.

Oliver Otis Howard was typical of a number of senior officers in the West who supported Grant's peace policy. Known as "humanitarian generals," they shared the president's view that relations with the Indians should be based on honesty, justice, and eventual assimilation.[85] Howard, who had lost an arm leading his brigade at Fair Oaks (Seven Pines) in 1862, was deeply pious. His approach to the Indians, just as to the freedmen, reflected Christian sentiments indistinguishable from those of the most dedicated churchman. Another humanitarian general was Benjamin Grierson, who had led Grant's cavalry on a wave of destruction across Mississippi in 1863. Commanding the "Black Tenth," the famous buffalo soldiers at Fort Sill, Grierson worked closely with the Quaker agent, Lawrie Tatum, among the Kiowas and Comanches. Whenever the Indians' food ran short, Grierson simply ignored standing orders to the contrary and fed the tribes from cavalry rations.[86] John Pope, an old acquaintance who had befriended Grant at Camp Yates in 1861 and who did an exemplary job defending the rights of the freedmen in Alabama, Georgia, and Florida until relieved by Andrew Johnson, was another general who supported the peace policy enthusiastically. Pope commanded the Department of the Missouri from 1870 to 1883, and although he directed several campaigns against warring tribes, always sought to avoid conflict and to protect the Indians from rapacious white men.[87]*

Perhaps the greatest of the humanitarian generals was George Crook, who was also renowned as the army's greatest Indian fighter. A West Point classmate of Sheridan's, Crook had turned Jubal Early's flank at Fisher's Hill and later commanded a cavalry division in the Army of the Potomac. He served more than thirty years in the West and worked assiduously to make the Apaches capitalist farmers. Committed to making the Indians self-sufficient, he fought tenaciously against unscrupulous government functionaries both within the military and without. "The American Indian is the intellectual peer of most, if not all, the various nationalities we have assimilated," said Crook. "He is fully able to protect himself, if the ballot be given and the courts of law not closed to him."[88] When Crook died in 1890 he was eulogized as a tower of strength for those who worked for Indian equality. Red Cloud said, "General Crook came, and he, at least, never lied to us. His words gave people hope. He died. Despair came again."[89] All four officers, Howard, Grierson, Pope, and Crook, had stormy relations with Sheridan—who distrusted their sympathy for the Indians. But Grant, who had assigned each of them to the West, consistently supported them over Little Phil's objections. Together, they gave the president's peace policy a human face.

---

* Pope was among the first to argue that the Plains Indians were different from the tribes in the East, and should be treated differently. The nomadic tribesmen were hunters not farmers, he told Washington, and it would be as difficult to force them to undergo the daily toil of plowing, hoeing, and reaping "as it would be to force an Arab or a Tartar to adopt so artificial a mode of life." Pope said stock raising was a better bet. It was more suitable to the climate and topography of the reservations and provided a closer fit to the temperament of the Plains Indians. In 1875 Pope began using army funds to purchase cattle for the Indians, who quickly demonstrated their ability to care for the livestock. Richard N. Ellis, *General Pope and U.S. Indian Policy* 230–42 (Albuquerque: University of New Mexico Press, 1970); also see *Annual Report of the Secretary of War, 1877* 60.

Throughout 1871 Grant was under pressure from Western congressmen to take more aggressive action against the tribes on the frontier. As the election of 1872 approached, speculation grew that in order to secure the support of the Plains states Grant would back away from the peace policy. In late October, with election day approaching, George Stuart of Philadelphia wrote to ask if the rumors were true. Grant replied instantly. He had no intention of turning his back on the Indians to gain the frontier vote. The suggestion that the administration was planning to jettison the peace policy was preposterous, he told Stuart. "If any change takes place in the Indian Policy of the Government while I hold my present office," said Grant, "it will be on the humanitarian side of the question." [90]

Grant's response to Stuart was publicized widely. Alfred H. Love, president of the Universal Peace Union, read the letter to 2,000 delegates at the society's annual convention in Philadelphia. "Every sentence was loudly applauded," he told Grant.[91] From Iowa, an Indian missionary wrote the president that his letter to Stuart had "called forth fervent thanksgiving from multitudes who believe that 'God has made of one blood all the nations of the earth.' "[92] In the West, editorial response was predictably critical. Nevertheless, on November 5 Grant swept the Plains states, winning two thirds of the vote in Kansas and Nebraska, and taking almost 60 percent in the Far West. Only Texas, voting for the first time since the Civil War, went Democratic, and the contest there turned on Reconstruction, not Indian policy.[93]

Three weeks after the election, Grant's peace policy was jolted by an outbreak of fighting near Tule Lake, along the California-Oregon border. The Modoc Indians, a small band of sixty to seventy families, restless with reservation life, had attempted to return to their old home among the lake-dotted, lava-scored plateaus of southern Oregon and northern California. Homesteaders and ranchers who had moved into the region demanded protection, and a small detachment of troops was assigned to force the Indians back to the reservation. When the Modoc, led by a young chief dubbed Captain Jack because of the military trinkets he wore, defiantly refused to leave, the troops moved against them. Shots were exchanged, and the Indians took up a strong defensive position amid the lava beds. For two months the army attempted to dislodge them, but with no success.

At the end of January, with the nation's attention focused on what the press was calling the Modoc War, Grant stepped in and called a halt. He told Sherman to stop the fighting and negotiate a settlement. On January 31, 1873, the general in chief dutifully informed Major General Edward Canby, the department commander, of Grant's wishes. "Let all defensive measures proceed," said Sherman, "but order no attack on the Indians till the former orders are modified or changed by the President, who seems disposed to allow the peace men to try their hands on Captain Jack."[94]

Canby was instructed to make "amicable arrangements" for locating the Modoc on a new reservation, but the negotiations quickly bogged down. Sherman urged Canby to be patient—Grant wanted a peaceful solution—and discussions continued until April.[95] Suddenly, on Good Friday, April 11, 1873, the meeting site erupted in a fusillade of gunfire. The Modoc delegation, on a signal from Captain Jack, drew revolvers from under their clothing and began firing across the table. Canby, who was unarmed, was killed instantly, as was the Reverend Eleazar Thomas, a Methodist minister who had agreed to serve as a peace negotiator. Another negotiator, Alfred B. Meacham, the resident Indian agent, was shot five times, knifed, stripped of his clothes, and left for dead. When rescuers arrived he was still alive and recovered to describe what had occurred.[96]

The murder of General Canby and the Reverend Thomas shocked the nation. Sympathy for the Modocs, who had conducted a spirited defense against overwhelming odds, vanished instantly. Sherman wired General Alvan C. Gillem, commander of the Pacific Division, to make total war on the Modocs. "You will be fully justified in their extermination."[97] Sherman sent the wire without consulting Grant, who abhorred the term and all that it implied. After visiting the White House to discuss the episode, the general in chief sent a follow-up to the West Coast: "The President now sanctions the most severe punishment for the Modocs."[98] What Grant actually said was that he wanted the offenders punished, not as "an act of passionate revenge . . . but as an act of justice as well as protection of peaceful settlers."[99] Grant had the highest regard for Canby, and his assassination distressed the president greatly. Yet Grant did not seek revenge, and he certainly did not want a war of extermination.[100]

The army resumed the offensive, more troops were brought in, and by June Modoc resistance had been crushed. Captain Jack and his five fellow negotiators were captured, taken to Fort Klamath, and tried by court-martial for the murder of General Canby and the Reverend Thomas. All six were convicted and sentenced to hang. Grant commuted the punishment for two of the offenders, but Captain Jack and three of his companions were executed on October 3, 1873. The remainder of the tribe, 153 in number, were removed to the Quapaw Agency in the Indian Territory.[101]

Grant's peace policy had suffered a body blow. Newspapers throughout the country saw the slaying of Canby and Thomas as dramatic evidence that the Indians could not be trusted. Anti-administration journals such as New York's *Herald* and *World* and the *Boston Daily Globe* denounced Grant's Indian policy and the humanitarians associated with it.[102] The *Daily Col-*

orado Miner blamed the administration's "experiments with the noble red man" for the tragedy.[103] Sherman, never a friend of the peace policy, was outspoken as always. "Treachery is inherent in the Indian character," he told the *New York Times*. "I know of a case where the Indians murdered the man who not two hours before had given them food and clothing."[104]

Grant held firm. Always at his best when the going was hardest, he made it clear to a daily stream of visitors that the peace policy was in place to stay, and that it was in no way responsible for the Modoc troubles. "President Grant knows he is right, in his Indian policy," said Felix Brunot, chairman of the Board of Indian Commissioners. "Those who think they can move him from the right by personal denunciation, sneers at 'Quakers' and 'peace commissioners,' or flings at the 'red devils' and 'humanitarians' may as well give up."[105]

By year's end the furor had subsided. The peace policy, though badly shaken, had survived its first test. In December, Benjamin Potts, governor of the Montana Territory, wrote Washington praising the "humane policy of the President toward the Indian tribes." Since the adoption of the peace policy, he said, the "frequent incursions from hostile Indians" had virtually ceased.[106] From army headquarters in St. Louis, General John Pope reported that "with very trifling exceptions," the Department of the Missouri had experienced no difficulties with the Indians during the past year.[107] Most important, perhaps, the commissioner of Indian Affairs reported substantial progress in civilizing the Indians as well as his increasing satisfaction with the operation of the agencies by religious denominations.[108]

From all appearances, the peace policy had taken root. But it was touch and go. In 1874 the southern Plains erupted. The principal tribes of the region—Kiowa, Comanche, Cheyenne, and Arapaho—had been ensconced on reservations in the western portion of the Indian Territory since 1869. But reservation life proved confining; clothing and rations were scant; and the continued encroachment of white cattlemen, whiskey peddlers, hunters, and homesteaders was both irritating and debilitating. Particularly troubling, white buffalo hunters were gradually moving southward. In 1872 they had shipped 1.2 million hides east by rail. By the winter of 1873–1874, so many buffalo had been killed on the Plains north of the Cimarron River that new sources had to be secured. The obvious targets were the herds in the Texas panhandle, just west of the Cheyenne-Arapaho reservation, the prime buffalo hunting ground for the Indians. In the spring of 1874 white hunters swarmed into the region, and on June 27 the Indians retaliated. At first light, 300 Cheyenne and Comanche warriors struck the hunters in their base camp at Adobe Walls, on the north fork of the Canadian River. The assault was repulsed, but the hunters beat a hasty retreat north.

When informed of the attack, Kansas governor Thomas Osborn asked General Pope to rush troops to protect the hunters. Pope, committed to Grant's peace policy, refused. The hunters, he told Osborne, "have justly earned all that may befall them." Pope said the hunting camps were unlawful, and that if he sent any troops to the region "it would be to break them up, not protect them." Pope also noted the hunters were authors of their own fate. "Their continuous pursuit and wholesale slaughter of the buffalo, both summer and winter, have driven the great herds down into the Indian Reservation."[109]

Sheridan saw the matter differently.[110] The army commander in the West heartily approved of buffalo hunters, believing they were doing the country a service by depleting the Indians' indigenous food supply. The sooner the buffalo were killed, the sooner the Indians would be brought under control.* For Sheridan, the attack at Adobe Walls provided an excuse to destroy Indian resistance on the southern Plains once and for all. In what historians call the Red River War, Little Phil deployed his forces in five converging columns, isolated the hostile warriors among the breaks surrounding the headwaters of the Washita and the various forks of the Red, and pressed them relentlessly in a war of attrition. There were few clashes and little bloodshed, but gradually the exhaustion of the chase, the discomforts of weather and hunger, and the omnipresent fear of cavalrymen storming their camps at dawn wore the Indians down. By the spring of 1875 all had turned in their weapons and returned to the reservation.

With the Red River War successfully terminated, the military pressed to prevent a recurrence. The best way to accomplish that, in the view of Sherman and Sheridan, was to exile the leading warriors and war chiefs far from the southern Plains. Grant approved the recommendation on March 13, 1875, and immediately thereafter the War Department selected seventy-four men, chained and shackled them, and shipped them to the old Spanish fortress Castillo de San Marcos (rechristened Fort Marion) at St. Augustine, Florida, where they remained for three years.†

---

* In 1881, when Congress was considering legislation to protect what was left of the buffalo herd on the northern Plains, Sheridan wrote the War Department to protest. "The destruction of this herd would do more to keep Indians quiet than anything else that could happen. Since the destruction of the southern herd, which formerly roamed from Texas to the Platte, the Indians in that section have given us no trouble." Sheridan to the Adjutant General, October 13, 1881, Box 29, Sheridan Papers, Library of Congress. For a revisionist view, see Drew Isenberg, *The Destruction of Bison: An Environmental History* (New York: Cambridge University Press, 2000). Also see, *New York Times,* November 16, 1999.

† At Fort Marion the Indians were under the benign supervision of Lieutenant Richard H. Pratt, who treated them with kindness and consideration. Pratt was so taken with the experience that he soon resigned from the army and founded the Carlisle Indian Industrial School in Pennsylvania for the education of reservation youths. Carlisle became the model for the government's Indian school system, and Pratt dominated Indian education for al-

The army's hawks had gained a clear victory in the Red River War, not only over the Kiowa, Comanche, Arapaho, and Cheyenne, but also over the more outspoken proponents of the peace policy. Grant, who had held tight after the assassination of General Canby and the Reverend Thomas, now seemed willing to let Sherman and Sheridan have their way. It may well be that the president, now in his sixth year in office, no longer had the energy to pursue matters as diligently as he once did. The problems of Reconstruction and protecting the rights of the freedmen had moved to center stage in Washington, and Grant was focused on the deep South, not the Western frontier.[111]

The most serious military threat to the peace policy occurred in 1876, the last year of Grant's presidency. On the northern Plains, in the land of the Sioux, the construction of the Northern Pacific Railway brought swarms of settlers to the Dakota Territory. The 1874 discovery of gold in the Black Hills turned the influx into a tidal wave. Under the Treaty of Fort Laramie, negotiated with the Sioux in 1868, much of the land, including the Black Hills, was reserved to the Indians in perpetuity. Grant was determined to enforce the treaty, and at one point offered to purchase the Black Hills, but the Sioux declined and the surge of settlers proved unstoppable. Recognizing that a crisis was fast approaching, Grant summoned Sheridan to Washington in the late autumn of 1875 to discuss the situation. Meeting at the White House on November 3, Sheridan informed the president that the army, undermanned and stretched to the breaking point, could no longer restrain the vast multitude of miners flocking to the Black Hills. Accepting Sheridan's judgment at face value, Grant weakened. The presidential order protecting the Black Hills would not be rescinded, he said, but the army would no longer be obliged to enforce it. As Sheridan reported afterward, Grant believed that haphazard or only partial enforcement would merely increase the miners' desire and would exacerbate the troubles.[112] The fact is, however, that as a result of Grant's decision the miners could now enter the Black Hills with impunity. To minimize the risk, the president instructed Sheridan to round up the Sioux in the Yellowstone and Little Big Horn regions and force them onto the reservation where they could be controlled.[113]

In retrospect, it is clear that Grant erred on two counts. First, it is likely that the army, given a firm directive by the commander in chief, could have policed the Sioux boundary indefinitely. But Grant valued Sheridan's military opinion above all others, and he was always reluctant to second-guess a commander in the field. Second, by instructing Sheri-

---

most two decades. Philip Weeks, *Farewell My Nation: The American Indian and the United States, 1820–1890* 167–68 (Arlington Heights, Ill.: Harlan Davidson, 1990).

dan to corral the nonreservation Indians, Grant, no doubt unintentionally, was giving Little Phil a green light to launch a winter offensive to finish off the Sioux in whatever manner Sheridan saw fit.[114]

Sheridan moved quickly. The severity of the winter on the northern Plains made a winter campaign impossible. But with the melting snow Sheridan launched a three-pronged offensive against the Sioux, attempting to replicate the strategy of convergence that had proved so effective in the Red River War. In May, Major General George Crook was ordered north toward the Rosebud and the Little Big Horn from Fort Fetterman; Colonel John Gibbon headed another column, moving eastward from Fort Ellis in Montana; a third force, including the 7th Cavalry under Colonel George A. Custer, headed west from Fort Abraham Lincoln on the Missouri. On June 25, 1876, Custer's column made contact with the Sioux on the banks of the Little Big Horn. Seriously underestimating the size of the opposing Indian force, Custer launched a premature attack and he and his entire command were annihilated. Sheridan said after the slaughter, "it was an unnecessary sacrifice due to misapprehension and superabundant courage—the latter extraordinarily developed in Custer."[115] Grant, who had little regard or affection for Custer, said simply that the battle was "wholly unnecessary."[116]

The battle of the Little Big Horn shocked the nation. Grant and Sheridan notwithstanding, Custer became an instant hero. In frontier towns, citizens eagerly offered their services to avenge Custer and exterminate the Sioux. Congress responded with breathtaking speed. Senator Algernon Paddock of Nebraska introduced legislation authorizing the president to raise five volunteer regiments of Indian fighters. Similar legislation was proposed in the House.[117] In the West, "Remember Custer" became the watchword. In the East, patience seemed exhausted. The *New York Times* reported that many now thought the Indians should be exterminated "as though they were so many wild dogs."[118]

Custer's Last Stand brought Grant's peace policy to the verge of collapse. Throughout the Plains and Rocky Mountain region, newspapers denounced the gentle approach. The *Boulder* (Colorado) *News* blamed the massacre on the "false philanthropic sentiment in the East," which had spawned "the reprehensible policy of the government."[119] E. L. Godkin, whose *Nation* had consistently backed the peace policy, declared, "Our philanthropy and our hostility tend to about the same end, and this is the destruction of the Indian race." Grant's attempt to improve Indian policy had been worthy, he wrote, but now "the missionary expedient may be said to have failed."[120] Even such loyal supporters as Bishop Whipple expressed dismay. In a lengthy letter to Grant, he pointed out that although the peace policy had done more for the civilization of the Indians than any previous government efforts, it still led to massacre and war.[121]

The most serious threat to Grant's peace policy, however, came not from the military or the Indians, but from long-standing corruption, incompetence, and decay. The replacement of political appointees by church personnel did not purify the Indian Service, and in surprising numbers the incompetent and even the corrupt slipped through the screen of church associations.[122] Worse, perhaps, the government soon found itself embroiled in sectarian strife as denominations waged unchristian battles over agencies and territory. Fraud and venality, a major target of the peace policy, continued to flourish in the Department of the Interior. Having lost a battle to the spoilsmen, Jacob Cox resigned as secretary in 1870. His successor, Columbus Delano, was an old-school Ohio politician ever ready to cut a deal. He departed under grave allegations of impropriety late in Grant's second term.

Ely Parker, the president's favorite appointee, was forced out as commissioner of Indian Affairs in 1871 in a dispute with the board over apparent purchasing irregularities. A full-blown congressional investigation exonerated Parker, but he was precluded from further government service.* Parker's successors, Edward P. Smith and John Q. Smith, left office under suspicion of wrongdoing, though criminal charges were never filed. More ominous, the Indian Ring, the combination of bureaucrats, politicians, contractors, sutlers, and agents, always found ways to circumvent the most elaborate safeguards put in place by Grant, the churches, and the Board of Indian Commissioners. A possible solution would have been to transfer the bureau to the War Department. Grant tried repeatedly to do so, but the combination of interests, ranging from the most dedicated reformers to the most cynical spoilsmen, proved insurmountable.

Despite numerous setbacks and widespread public criticism, the peace policy proved to have a life of its own. The churches did not withdraw from the reservations, civilization remained the cornerstone of the nation's Indian policy, and the Board of Indian Commissioners continued in place, battling corruption and fighting for Indian rights as best it could.

---

* Parker resigned as commissioner of Indian Affairs, June 29, 1871, protesting that congressional legislation made the commissioner a mere clerk to the Board of Indian Affairs. Grant accepted his resignation with regret. "It severs official relations which have existed between us for eight consecutive years, without cause of complaint as to your entire fitness for either of the important places which you have had during that time. Your management of the Indian Bureau has been in entire harmony with my policy, which I hope will tend to the civilization of the Indian race. It has also been able and discreet. In leaving public service to pursue a more independent course of life, you take with you my sincere wishes for your prosperity and my hearty commendations to all with whom the accidents of life may bring you in business relations for integrity and ability." Grant to Parker, July 13, 1877, 22 *The Papers of Ulysses S. Grant* 71, John Y. Simon, ed. (Carbondale: Southern Illinois University Press, 1998).

In the West, Sheridan pacified the northern Plains, Custer was avenged, and the Sioux driven onto the reservation. Hard-edged, unsentimental, uncompromising, Sheridan saw himself as the instrument of Western civilization. "This was the country of the buffalo and the hostile Sioux only last year," he wrote in 1877. "There are no signs of either now, but in their places we found prospectors, emigrants, and farmers."[123] Grant identified with progress as well, but there was a deeper, more reflective streak in the president that valued the Great Plains in their pristine state. Grant believed deeply in human equality, and in his view, the Indian, no less than the former slave, deserved the government's protection. Grant changed the way the United States thought about Native Americans. His decision in 1869 to pursue peace, not war, helped to save the American Indian from extinction.

Grant's peace policy was nobly conceived. An occasional bad apple to the contrary, the churchmen made infinitely superior agents to the spoilsmen they replaced. Nevertheless, both the president and the churches thought in terms of transforming the Plains Indians into Christian citizens. Neither saw anything worth preserving in Indian culture, and as a consequence failed to build upon the social structure that existed in tribal communities. Today's citizens see that as a grave error. Yet, for the 1870s, Grant's policy was remarkably progressive and humanitarian. The president stood against the tide of public opinion, and for eight years held steadfastly to the goal of Indian assimilation.

CHAPTER EIGHTEEN

RECONSTRUCTION REVISITED

The adoption of the Fifteenth Amendment to the Constitution completes the greatest civil change, and constitutes the most important political event that has occurred, since the nation came into life.

ULYSSES S. GRANT
March 30, 1870

UNDER GRANT'S STYLE OF PRESIDENTIAL GOVERNMENT, Reconstruction fell to the attorney general and the secretary of war. Rockwood Hoar, Grant's first attorney general, was lukewarm about protecting the rights of the freedmen and was reluctant to move against white terrorists in the South.[1] His successor, Amos T. Akerman, a forty-nine-year-old Georgian, took on the task with gusto. As one historian put it, no attorney general before or since "has been more vigorous in the prosecution of cases designed to protect the lives and rights of black Americans."[2] Born in New Hampshire and educated at Phillips Exeter and Dartmouth College, Akerman moved to Georgia in 1842, practiced law in the hill country northeast of Atlanta, fought with the home guard when Sherman invaded, and, like Longstreet, accepted the finality of the war's verdict. As a delegate to the Georgia constitutional convention in 1867 he gained prominence as an advocate of Negro suffrage, and was among those who lobbied successfully for Georgia's readmission to Congress in 1868. When Grant took office, Akerman was appointed United States attorney for Georgia, and upon Hoar's resignation in June 1870, he was called to Washington—the first Southerner in Grant's cabinet.

The secretary of war was William Worth Belknap, a protégé of Sherman's who was snatched from Iowa obscurity to succeed Rawlins in 1869. Forty years old (the youngest member of the cabinet), Belknap was also a lawyer by training and a prewar Douglas Democrat. He fought with Sherman at Shiloh, led a regiment at Vicksburg, and commanded a division in the March to the Sea and the Carolina campaign. After the war he returned to Iowa and was appointed a tax collector for the region by Andrew Johnson. Grant considered him a capable officer and added him to his cabinet at Sherman's suggestion. Cump's judgment of people was often flawed, and he and Belknap were soon at loggerheads. The issues related less to policy than to the respective prerogatives of the general in chief and the secretary of war. Both wanted to command the army. Unlike Akerman, Belknap had little interest in the South and almost no sympathy for protecting the rights of the freedmen. Indeed, if African-Americans needed a friend in Washington, they were unlikely to find one in the upper reaches of the War Department.

Fortunately for Reconstruction, Grant exercised closer scrutiny over the military than he did over other departments, and Belknap had less freedom of action than other cabinet officers. As commander in chief, Grant continued to give orders to the army and Belknap became a de facto chief of staff, just as Rawlins had been, or Schofield, for that matter, in 1869. Grant was reluctant to use military force against civilians when other means were available. But he had no hesitation to deploy the army if that were the only way to combat terrorism in the South.

Initially, Grant put his trust in the ballot box. He worked mightily to secure the adoption of the Fifteenth Amendment,* believing the rights of the freedmen would be protected once they enjoyed the franchise.[3] Grant was not alone in that belief. When the amendment was adopted, abolitionist leader William Lloyd Garrison proclaimed that nothing equaled "this wonderful, quiet, sudden transformation of four million human beings from . . . the auction-block to the ballot box."[4] A similar euphoric mood gripped the American Anti-Slavery Society. Members believed its work was complete and soon disbanded.[5]

But neither Grant, the reformers, or the Republicans in Congress foresaw the virulence of white Southern opposition to Negro suffrage, or the proclivity for violence in states where respect for law and order had eroded substantially. Led by the Ku Klux Klan,† masked night riders in-

---

* The Fifteenth Amendment to the Constitution, proposed by Congress February 27, 1869, and ratified March 30, 1870, provides that "The right of citizens of the United States to vote shall not be denied or abridged by the United States or by any State on account of race, color, or previous condition of servitude." Congress was given the power to enforce the amendment by appropriate legislation, just as with the Fourteenth Amendment.

† Originally organized in June 1866 as a social club by six Confederate veterans in Pulaski, Tennessee, the name derived from the Greek word *kyklos*, meaning "circle," to which the word Klan was added for alliteration. The organization spread through the South like wildfire and quickly became a vehicle for hooded terrorism, working actively for the preservation of white supremacy. Structured into the "Invisible Empire of the South," and presided over by a grand wizard (Nathan Bedford Forrest), the Klan reached its peak membership between 1868 and

troduced a reign of terror in the South. Black schools were burned, teachers beaten, voters intimidated, and political opponents of both races kidnapped and murdered. The Klan's avowed purpose was to undermine Reconstruction, destroy the Republican party in the eleven states of the old Confederacy, and reestablish black subordination in every aspect of Southern life. As one scholar has observed, "The Klan was a military force serving the interests of the Democratic Party, the planter class, and all those who desired the restoration of white supremacy."[6]

As the Klan grew bolder and the death toll mounted, Southern Republicans desperately petitioned Washington for help. Traditionally, crimes such as murder, arson, and assault fell within the jurisdiction of state and local authorities, yet with rare exceptions law enforcement officials in the South refused to move against the Klan. The prosecution of such crimes by the national government would represent a significant departure. But if Washington did not act, the Klansmen would go unpunished. Both the Fourteenth and Fifteenth amendments appeared to authorize federal action to secure the rights of African-Americans, and so on May 31, 1870, over bitter Democratic opposition, Congress enacted the first of three Enforcement Acts to counter terrorist violence. The statute made it a federal offense to attempt to deprive anyone of his civil or political rights.[7]

Three weeks later, with violence still on the rise in the South, Grant brought Akerman to Washington to fight the Klan. At the same time, Congress voted to establish a Department of Justice on the same level as other cabinet departments. Previously, the attorney general was merely the legal adviser to the president, and the government's trial work was contracted out. Anticipating a significant increase in litigation, Congress created a permanent department staffed by in-house lawyers under the attorney general, who was also made responsible for supervising the work of the United States attorneys and federal marshals throughout the country. To assist the attorney general, Congress created the office of solicitor general, and Grant appointed Benjamin H. Bristow to the post. Bristow had distinguished himself as United States attorney in Kentucky by his energetic efforts on behalf of the freedmen. By bringing him to Washington, Grant was putting a powerful team at the helm of the Justice Department.[8] Akerman and Bristow knew at first hand what they were dealing with. Suppressing the Klan required "extraordinary means," said Akerman.

1870. George C. Rable, *But There Was No Peace: The Role of Violence in the Politics of Reconstruction* 95 (Athens: University of Georgia Press, 1984); Allen W. Trelease, *White Terror: The Klu Klux Klan Conspiracy and Southern Reconstruction* (New York: Harper and Row, 1971).

"These combinations amount to war, and cannot be effectively crushed on any other theory."[9]

Under Akerman and Bristow prosecution of the Klan began in earnest. In the North Carolina piedmont, where federal troops sent by Grant helped apprehend suspects, hundreds of men were indicted.[10] In northern Mississippi, where Klan violence was endemic, tenacious United States attorneys secured nearly 1,000 indictments in the early 1870s, and fully 55 percent of the cases resulted in conviction.[11] But in many localities Klan terrorism continued unabated, with violence peaking at election time. The autumn elections in 1870 were particularly violent. Accurate figures are difficult to come by, but in South Carolina observers listed 227 "outrages" in one county, 118 in another, and 300 in a third.[12] In North Carolina, Klan terrorism helped the Democrats recapture the state, electing five of seven congressmen. "An organized conspiracy is in existence in every County in the State, and its aim is to control the government," Governor William W. Holden wrote Grant. "Unless active measures are taken, the lives of loyal citizens are no longer safe and their liberties [will be] a thing of the past."[13] Congress responded with passage of the second Enforcement Act in early 1871 providing for federal oversight of voter registration and elections, but the session ended before more far-reaching legislation could be enacted.[14]

When the 42nd Congress convened on March 4, much of the South rested in the grip of white-sheeted terror. The persistence of violence, often directed at former Union soldiers, galvanized Grant to take action. Five days after the session began he requested special legislation that would authorize the government to suppress the Klan. Writing to House Speaker James G. Blaine, Grant said that if Congress could tackle only one measure during the current session, it should deal with the deteriorating situation in the South.[15] Prodded by the president, congressmen promptly introduced legislation, first Benjamin Butler, then Representative Samuel Shellabarger of Ohio, making it a federal crime to conspire to "overthrow or destroy by force the government of the United States" or to conspire to prevent persons from holding office, voting, or enjoying the equal protection of the laws. The bill empowered the president to use the army to enforce the measure, as well as to suspend the writ of habeas corpus in areas that he declared in a state of insurrection. Known as the Ku Klux Klan bill, the legislation represented an unprecedented peacetime extension of national authority. For the first time, private acts of violence were designated crimes punishable in federal court. "These are momentous changes," *The Nation* proclaimed. "They not only increase the power of the central government, but they arm it with jurisdiction over a class of cases of which it has never hitherto had, and never pretended to have, any jurisdiction whatever."[16]

The legislation mired down under its own weight. Democrats, arguing states' rights, insisted local self-government would perish if the federal government assumed responsibility for punishing criminal offenses. A number of Republicans were also alarmed. The most outspoken was Senator Lyman Trumbull of Illinois. The states, he insisted, remained "the depositories of the rights of the individual." If Congress could enact a general criminal code and punish offenses like assault and murder, "what is the need for State governments?"[17] By mid-March it was apparent the Ku Klux Klan bill was headed for defeat. The North had lost interest in "the Negro question," public support for the bill failed to materialize, and the constitutional issue of states' rights provided cover for an extraordinary array of political bedfellows, ranging from unabashed white supremacists, to civil libertarians, to Grant-haters of every variety.[18]

Confronted with what appeared to be certain defeat, Grant took the offensive. For the commander in chief, the Ku Klux Klan was attempting to reverse the decision at Appomattox. On March 23, with his entire cabinet in attendance, Grant made a rare visit to Capitol Hill to rally his forces.[19] Meeting first with Southern Republicans, then the party leadership, he laid out the necessity for the legislation. His listeners were wary. Reconstruction had lost its electoral appeal. Members said that unless the president put himself out in front and made it a matter of personal support, the congressional troops could not be whipped into line. Grant did not hesitate. Without discussing the matter further he took a sheet of paper and began to write: "A condition of affairs now exists in some of the States of the Union rendering life and property insecure, and the carrying of the mails, and the collection of the revenue dangerous." By referring to the mails and the revenue Grant was giving lawmakers an additional hook on which to hang federal intervention. He went on to say that the evils in the South were beyond the control of state authorities, and that in his view the executive branch could not act without additional authorization. "Therefore, I urgently recommend such legislation, as in the judgment of Congress, shall effectually secure life, liberty, and property, and the enforcement of law, in all parts of the United States." Just to be sure the lawmakers got the point, Grant added that there was "no other subject on which I would recommend legislation during the current session."[20]

With political cover provided by the president, Congress enacted the Ku Klux Klan bill on April 20, 1871.[21] Grant immediately issued a proclamation urging voluntary compliance with the law and asking the people of the South to help suppress the Klan. He said he would not take action unless the violence continued; if it did, he would act promptly and decisively to protect "citizens of every race and color" in the "peaceful enjoyment of the rights guaranteed to them by the Constitution."[22]

Grant meant what he said. After a series of incidents in early May, the president ordered troops in the South to take the field and help federal officials "arrest and break up bands of disguised night marauders."[23] In October, when Akerman reported the situation in South Carolina out of control, Grant proclaimed "a condition of lawlessness" in nine upland counties, suspended the writ of habeas corpus, and rushed reinforcements to the state.[24] With Akerman directing operations on the spot, United States marshals, assisted by squads of soldiers, made hundreds of arrests, forced an estimated 2,000 Klansmen to flee the state, and restored a semblance of order to the region. "Though rejoiced at the suppression of Kukluxery even in one neighborhood," Akerman wrote, "I feel greatly saddened by this business. It has revealed a perversion of moral sentiment among the southern whites which bodes ill to that part of the country for this generation."[25]

The efforts of Akerman and the Department of Justice paid quick dividends. Throughout the South the Klan was put on the defensive. Federal grand juries returned more than 3,000 indictments in 1871. The attorney general allowed those who confessed and identified the organization's leaders to escape without punishment, while bringing the worst offenders to trial. About 600 were later convicted. Most received fines or light jail sentences, but sixty-five were imprisoned for up to five years at the federal penitentiary in Albany, New York.[26] By 1872 Grant's willingness to bring the full legal and military authority of the government to bear had broken the Klan's back and produced a dramatic decline in violence throughout the South.[27] Akerman gave full credit to the president. No one, he told a friend, was "better" or "stronger" than Grant when it came to enforcing anti-terrorist measures.[28]

The election of 1872 went off without a hitch. African-Americans voted in record numbers, with federal officials standing watch. As one scholar noted, the 1872 vote was "the fairest and most democratic presidential election in the South until 1968."[29] Grant's renomination had been inevitable. Throughout the country, mainstream Republicans voiced support for the president. "There has never been a leader in the White House who has been more uniformly fair to all races and classes of men," declared the *National Republican*.[30] More important, party leaders recognized that Grant's popularity would carry the entire ticket over the top. California Republicans reported that "if Grant is the nominee we will carry the state by a hard fight. With any other [candidate] we lose." From battle-scarred South Carolina came the assurance that Grant could carry the state by 25,000. Kansas promised a 20,000-vote majority for the ticket if the president ran. Pennsylvania looked like a toss-up, but with Grant the party would win. The Indiana Republican leadership reported they were behind but were confident Grant could prevail. North Carolina, West Virginia, and New Jersey echoed the warning that only Grant could carry the state.[31] Reformers jumped on the bandwagon. Henry Ward Beecher told an audience in Brooklyn there "had never been a president more sensitive to the wants of the people." Frederick Douglass said, "We will not find a candidate equal to General Grant. . . . We must take him or take division, weakness and defeat."[32]

Grant's opponents in the party saw the handwriting on the wall. Men like Charles Sumner, Jacob D. Cox, and Carl Schurz—self-styled "liberals" who had broken with the president—bolted the party and organized a rump convention in Cincinnati in May 1872. Calling themselves Liberal Republicans, the assemblage comprised a heterogeneous collection of free traders, disillusioned reformers, and civil libertarians, plus a considerable number of politicians who had lost factional struggles in the party and who expected to benefit from Grant's defeat.[33] They were joined by a fluttering of East Coast intellectuals who had tired of cigar smoke in the White House: Edwin L. Godkin of *The Nation,* William Cullen Bryant of the *Evening Post,* James Russell Lowell and David A. Wells of the *North American Review,* and a covey of Adamses. The aim of the gathering, as Carl Schurz phrased it in his keynote address, was to elect an administration "which the best people of this country can be proud of."[34]

The Liberal Republican image of reform tarnished quickly. Following three days of backroom maneuvering that would have made a Tammany Democrat envious, the convention nominated *New York Tribune* publisher Horace Greeley. Greeley was unquestionably the nation's most influential newsman. But his credibility as a candidate for high office was doubtful. During his forty years as a journalist he had taken vigorous stands on opposite sides of most major issues. After supporting peaceful secession in 1861, he became a staunch advocate of total war; he demanded a tough Reconstruction policy for the South combined with complete forgiveness for the rebels; he was hostile to free trade and indifferent to government reform, yet resolute in his support for a variety of unorthodox causes including vegetarianism, spiritualism, and human-manure scientific farming.[35] "No two men could look each other in the face and say 'Greeley' without laughing," commented one newspaper. A more sober assessment was offered by party founder Jacob Cox: "I have only to complain that we have fallen among thieves," he wrote Congressman James Garfield. "The Cincinnati Convention that was to have been the beginning of great and good things is now the most powerful force opposing . . . the friends of reform."[36]

The one issue that united Liberal Republicans, aside from antipathy to Grant, was a new policy for the South. And on this question, Greeley's credentials were impeccable. Touting universal amnesty and reconciliation with the gentlemen of the South (Greeley had been among those who provided the bond that freed Jefferson Davis from prison), the *Tribune* publisher had become increasingly critical of the freedmen. "They are an easy, worthless race, taking no thought for the morrow," he wrote in 1870. In Greeley's view, African-Americans no longer deserved government support. His harsh injunction was "Root, hog, or die." [37] The Liberal Republican platform, taking its cue from the candidate, demanded amnesty for all former Confederates, called for "local self-government" (a euphemism for white rule in the South), and condemned Grant's use of "arbitrary measures." [38]

The Democrats, meeting in Baltimore, were equally determined to restore white supremacy. After adopting the Liberal platform in toto, the party fell in behind Greeley without a whimper. "Anything to beat Grant," became the party's rallying cry. Liberals and Democrats set up fusion tickets at the state level, and in the early stages of the campaign the Greeley candidacy, propelled by the Liberal-Democratic tie, looked formidable. Worried about the outcome, George William Childs, Republican editor of the *Philadelphia Public Ledger,* journeyed to Washington to warn Grant. While Greeley was barnstorming across the country, said Childs, the president was sitting in the White House doing nothing. Childs feared Grant was not focused on the campaign. As Childs remembered, "The general said nothing, but sent for a map of the United States. He laid the map on the table, went over it with a pencil and said, 'We will carry this state, that state, that state,' and so on. When the election came, the result was that Grant carried every state that he had said he would." [39]

Republican campaign chairman William Chandler shared Childs's concerns. But Grant would have none of it. He would not campaign. "It has been done, so far as I remember, but by two presidential candidates heretofore [Stephen A. Douglas and Horatio Seymour]. Both of them were public speakers and both were beaten. I am no public speaker and I don't want to be beaten." [40]

Grant's treatment of the South became the central issue of the campaign.* Greeley chose it, the Democrats insisted on it, yet the Republicans

---

* The Republican convention met in Philadelphia on June 5, 1872. The rhetoric, brief as it was, concentrated on the problem of racial equality in the South. Grant was renominated unanimously on the first ballot. With the president's approval, Schuyler Colfax was dumped as vice president and replaced by the junior senator from Massachusetts, Henry Wilson. An old antislavery veteran and one of the founders of the Republican party, Wilson was an able campaigner with strong labor support. His selection helped to minimize defections to the Liberal Republicans in New England and also represented a rebuff to Sumner, the Bay State's senior senator.

(*continued on next page*)

benefited most. As Greeley and his supporters railed at "bayonet rule" and proclaimed the need to restore "local self-government," it became apparent that most Northern voters were not yet ready to trust the white South or the Democrats. The same was true for most blacks. In July, Sumner addressed an open letter to African-American voters urging them to repudiate Grant. This drew a sharp retort from Sumner's onetime abolitionist ally, Lydia Maria Child. "If the Devil himself were at the helm of the ship of state," wrote Child, "my conscience would not allow me to aid in removing him to make room for the Democratic party."[41] Another of Sumner's old colleagues in the anti-slavery movement, William Lloyd Garrison, assailed the Liberals' demand for local self-government in the South as "a blow aimed at the exercise of the power entrusted to the President by the Congress for the . . . protection of the southern freedmen and loyalists against robbery, assassination, and lynch-law barbarities."[42] Frederick Douglass, who once hailed Sumner as abolition's "mind and voice for a quarter of a century," said that if Grant had not acted to crush the Klan, the Negro would have been remanded to a condition worse than that from which the Civil War had delivered him. Douglass's famous aphorism, "The Republican party is the ship and all else is the sea," became the watchword for most African-Americans.[43]

Early election returns brought the bad news to Greeley. North Carolina voted for state and local offices in August and the Democrats hoped for a sweep. Instead, the Republicans held on to the governorship and all other statewide positions. In September, when state elections were held in Maine and Vermont, the Republicans received larger majorities than usual. The "October States," Indiana, Ohio, and Pennsylvania, always closely contested, went down the line for the Republican ticket. After Ohio reported, James Garfield, who had flirted briefly with the Liberals, carried the news excitedly to the White House. Grant, who rarely enjoyed making a visitor squirm, could not resist in the case of Garfield.* The Lib-

---

In contrast to that of the Democrats and Liberals, the Republican platform declared that the Fourteenth and Fifteenth amendments should be vigorously enforced; liberty and civil equality maintained throughout the Union; and discrimination based on "race, creed, color, or previous condition of servitude" prohibited. The Republicans also pledged a "wise and humane policy toward the Indians" and a fair deal for women. "Their admission to wider fields of usefulness is viewed with satisfaction, and the honest demand of any class of citizens for additional rights should be treated with respectful consideration." The Liberal-Democratic platform was silent concerning Indians and said nothing about women. For texts of the party platforms see William Gillette, "Election of 1872," in Arthur M. Schlesinger, Jr., ed., 2 *History of American Presidential Elections* 1331–37 (New York: McGraw-Hill, 1971).
* There was little love lost between Grant and Garfield, and their relations were always guarded. Garfield had been chief of staff to Rosecrans at Chattanooga and never forgave Grant for replacing him with George Thomas as commander of the Army of the Cumberland. Grant was aware of Garfield's feelings but took it as a normal reaction. If the president held anything against Garfield, it was his role chairing the congressional investigation of

eral Republicans, the president said pointedly, were like the howling prairie wolves he had once encountered when serving with Zachary Taylor in Texas. He had estimated he was listening to at least a hundred only to discover that all of the noise came from but two animals.[44]

The presidential election on November 5 was a Republican landslide. "The Almighty did not abstain," declared New York diarist George Templeton Strong.[45] When the ballots were counted, Grant won 56 percent of the popular vote, the highest proportion of any candidate between Andrew Jackson in 1828 and Theodore Roosevelt in 1904. Despite liberal defections, the president polled 600,000 more votes than in 1868. Conversely, the Democrats, aligned with the Liberal Republicans, had their worst showing of the nineteenth century. Grant took every state north of the Mason-Dixon line and eight of the eleven states of the old Confederacy. Greeley carried only three ex-Confederate states (Georgia, Tennessee, and Texas), along with Kentucky, Maryland, and Missouri. The Republicans regained a two-thirds majority in the House of Representatives, preserved a similar majority in the Senate, and recaptured control of the legislature in Alabama, the only instance during Reconstruction in which Republicans regained control of a state previously "redeemed" by the Democrats.

For Grant, the results were a vindication. "I have been the subject of abuse and slander scarcely ever equaled in political history," said the president. "Today, I feel I can disregard [that criticism]."[46] For Greeley, the election was not only a crushing political defeat, but a personal tragedy. A week before the election, his wife died. The week after the election, he lost control of the *Tribune* because of declining circulation. Exhausted from the campaign, despondent over the result, grieving for his wife, and now without a livelihood, Greeley fell ill. His death at the end of November touched the nation. The bitterness of the campaign was forgotten. Grant, bareheaded and riding in an open carriage, led the mourners from the funeral at the Church of the Divine Paternity at 45th Street and Fifth Avenue to Hamilton Ferry at the tip of Manhattan, and then to Greeley's final resting place at Greenwood Cemetery in Brooklyn.*

Black Friday, which probed deeply into Julia's connection with Abel Corbin and Jay Gould, but eventually exonerated her.
* Grant's attendance at Greeley's funeral marked a heartfelt moment of national reconciliation. The president was accompanied by his entire cabinet, Chief Justice Chase, Roscoe Conkling, Elihu Washburne, and General Sheridan. "We forget all our differences over his bier," said Henry Ward Beecher in his eulogy. "The Government itself stands still on his demise, and the honored representative and Chief Magistrate of this great people bows his head in infinite sympathy in the presence of the dead." The following week the *New York Tribune* suggested that Greeley's 66 electors cast their votes for Grant and "lift the Administration out of partisanship," but the anti-Grant forces in the Liberal-Democratic coalition declined to make the gesture. *New York Times,* December 3, 5, 1872; *New York Tribune,* December 10, 1872.

The election of 1872 marked the high point of Grant's presidency. The Democratic opposition had been crushed, the Liberal Republican mutiny put down, and the Reconstruction policy of the administration had received a powerful endorsement. The Republican party was in the hands of organization regulars, and Grant's political popularity was at a peak. But in victory lay the seeds of defeat. Without liberal critics in Congress, political discretion collapsed. As happened with Franklin Roosevelt after his landslide win in 1936 and Ronald Reagan during his second term, hubris led to mistakes, and mistakes to poor administration, corruption, and scandal. FDR in the heady days of victory attempted to pack the Supreme Court; Reagan permitted Iran-contra to be launched; and Grant sat back benignly while administration officials shamelessly exploited their positions for personal gain.

Already dark clouds were forming. In the South, though the Ku Klux Klan was vanquished, the seeds of white supremacy continued to sprout amid the bitterness of defeat. In Washington, the specter of corruption loomed on the horizon. During the closing days of the campaign, the *New York Sun* broke the story of the Crédit Mobilier payoff. And on the final day of the session (March 3, 1873), the 42nd Congress passed an appropriations bill raising senior government salaries substantially and providing two years' back pay for members of Congress. Neither scandal involved Grant in any way. But since they were symbolic of the era, traditional historiography has placed both at the president's door.

The Crédit Mobilier affair involved efforts by directors of the Union Pacific Railroad to pirate the company's treasury and curry favor with Congress in the process. Crédit Mobilier was a dummy Pennsylvania corporation acquired by the directors of the Union Pacific as a corporate shield. In their capacity as directors they contracted with themselves as owners of Crédit Mobilier for the railroad's construction, paid themselves lavishly, and drained the capital of the Union Pacific into their own pockets. In the autumn of 1867, well before Grant was a candidate for president, the directors decided to short-circuit a possible congressional investigation by distributing shares of Crédit Mobilier to key members of the House and Senate. Rumors of the transaction had circulated in Washington for years, but it was not until 1872 that the details were published. A subsequent congressional investigation found that Representative Oakes Ames of Massachusetts, a director of Crédit Mobilier, had indeed distributed stock among his colleagues, but it exonerated those most prominently mentioned. James G. Blaine, Senator Roscoe Conkling, and then Congressman George S. Boutwell were found to have refused the bribes, while evidence against Speaker Schuyler Colfax and James Garfield, though incriminating, was not conclusive. In the end, the House censured

Ames and Representative James Brooks of New York, a government-appointed director of the Union Pacific, and the Senate voted to expel James W. Patterson of New Hampshire. The revelations added disrepute to Washington politics, but all of the transactions occurred before Grant was elected president.[47]

The "back-pay grab" was a sordid episode in which there were no heroes. A bill to raise the salaries of the president, vice president, cabinet officers, and Supreme Court justices had been introduced early in the session but languished in committee until the closing days when it was brought forward with an additional provision to increase congressional salaries from $5,000 to $7,500. The proposal had merit; congressional salaries had not been increased since 1852, but the bill contained a retroactive clause that made the increase effective at the beginning of the 42nd Congress, two years earlier. In effect, the congressmen and senators were giving themselves a $5,000 back-pay bonus.* The measure met with little congressional opposition. Democrats were as enthusiastic about the salary grab as Republicans. The pay-raise proposal was inserted into the government's general appropriation bill and enacted just prior to adjournment. Grant could not refuse to sign the measure without depriving all government departments of their operating money for the next fiscal year. That would have required him to call the newly elected 43rd Congress into special session to deal with the crisis. Perhaps Grant should have done so. It would have been a powerful statement on behalf of good government and would have solidified public support. But the president took the easy way out. He signed the bill and then urged the next Congress to enact a line-item veto provision that would permit the president to strike out individual items in an appropriations bill without having to reject the entire measure.[48]

Public reaction to the back-pay grab was immediate. An avalanche of criticism descended on Washington. When the 43rd Congress convened in December, its first order of business was to repeal the congressional pay raise, leaving intact the increases for the president and the justices of the Supreme Court. The shadow of the back-pay grab lay over Congress for the next thirty years. Not until 1904 did members feel sufficiently secure to once again consider a pay raise for themselves.†

Grant's second term began with a cabinet much weaker than his team

---

* The founding fathers were prescient. The Twenty-Seventh Amendment to the Constitution, originally proposed in 1789 but not ratified until 1992, prohibits Congress from raising its own salary "until an election of Representatives shall have intervened."
† This was not as much of a hardship as it might appear. The last quarter of the nineteenth century was a period of considerable deflation. A salary based on 1870 dollars actually went further in 1904 than it had originally.

for the first term. Of his original appointees, only Fish and Postmaster General John Creswell remained. Boutwell had been elected to the Senate by the Massachusetts legislature to replace Vice President Henry Wilson. His place at Treasury was taken by Assistant Secretary William A. Richardson, a weak administrator who brought little insight to the cabinet and who resigned under a cloud of scandal in little over a year.[49] Akerman was gone at Justice, replaced by former Senator George H. Williams of Oregon, a dim legal light whose extravagant wife would soon scuttle his political career. Williams did nothing that was illegal at the time, but his use of Justice Department funds to support lavish household expenses was surely indiscreet. At Navy, George Robeson, a New Jersey lawyer, had replaced Adoph Borie. Both were successful businessmen whose company Grant enjoyed, and both were content to leave naval matters in the hands of the admirals. Robeson later came under fire for contract improprieties, but congressional investigators found no evidence of illicit payments to the secretary. War and the Interior, where tough management was most needed, were in the hands of the two weakest of Grant's appointees. William Belknap, at the War Department, would be impeached for bribery in 1876, and Columbus Delano at Interior, would soon be forced to resign for concealing an elaborate featherbedding scheme involving his son and the so-called Indian Ring. Belknap and Delano betrayed their public trust, profiting at the expense of those who most needed government assistance: the Native American.

Grant's loyalty to his appointees went beyond prudence. Badeau, who knew the general as well as anyone, said "he was the most steadfast man imaginable when his friends were assailed. . . . His political career was blighted by those he sustained; his Presidency was less brilliant than it might have been because of the mistakes and misdeeds of others."[50]

Grant was particularly solicitous toward those who had done him kindnesses in the past. It was partly gratitude, and partly pride in not being ignoble or forgetful. Old friends from St. Louis were especially welcome at the White House. Once, Grant offered an appointment to a man who had befriended him when he was down and out. When the man pointed out he was a Democrat, the president brushed it aside. "Just before the Civil War, when I was standing on a street corner in St. Louis by a wagon loaded with wood, you approached and said: 'Captain, haven't you been able to sell your wood?' I answered: 'No.' Then you said: 'I'll buy it; and whenever you haul a load of wood to the city and can't sell it, just take it around to my residence and throw it over the fence and I'll pay you for it.' I haven't forgotten it."[51]

Another time a delegation of Tennesseeans, headed by At-Large Congressman Horace Maynard, called on Grant to urge an appointment to the

Nashville post office. The rival applicant was a former St. Louis butcher. "Gentlemen," said the president, "when I was a very poor man in St. Louis, just before the war, this German butcher furnished meat to my family on credit. And when I needed a loan of ten or fifteen or twenty dollars he was my banker without security and without charge of interest. Now I intend to appoint this German butcher postmaster of Nashville if it bursts the Republican party."[52]

There was an upside to Grant's St. Louis cronyism. On a late September morning in 1873, the president was visited by another old friend from his former home, engineer-industrialist James Buchanan Eads. In 1861, using his own money initially, Eads had pioneered construction of the fleet of ironclad, shallow-draft gunboats that supported Grant's conquest of the Mississippi. The victory at Fort Henry was entirely attributable to Eads's vessels; his boats provided fire support at Donelson and Shiloh; and Grant could not have descended below Vicksburg and moved his army across the Mississippi without the gunboats. Eads often came to the front to check on his craft, and he and Grant became warm friends. A lifelong Democrat, Eads had publicly supported Horace Greeley for president, but that made no difference to Grant.[53]

Eads was in trouble and needed the president's help. The problem was the army's Corps of Engineers: specifically, the chief of engineers, Major General Andrew A. Humphreys. In 1866 Eads had won congressional authorization to construct a steel arch bridge across the Mississippi. His proposal was revolutionary: a center arch 520 feet wide resting on piers sunk to bedrock, and two side arches 502 feet wide. The bridge would span the Mississippi *below* the mouth of the Missouri, after that river's tremendous volume joined the Father of Waters. No bridge in existence crossed a comparable flow of water; no arch was as long as those Eads proposed; and there was no steel bridge anywhere in the world. Indeed, the British explicitly forbade the use of steel in bridges. To top it off, Eads had never built a bridge before. Missouri senator Benjamin Gratz Brown said the only reason Congress voted authorization (over vigorous ferry and steamboat opposition) was that Eads's proposal was considered impossible.[54]

Eads was undaunted. No man knew the Mississippi better than he, and his Civil War experience with ironclads and naval artillery gave him a thorough respect for steel—then an experimental new metal. He quickly raised $6 million for construction (soon $9 million), and by the late 1860s had nearly 2,000 men swarming about on twenty-four large derrick-equipped barges and scaffolding as the steel and masonry took shape. By 1873 the arches spanned the river, with completion of the roadbed in sight. At that point, and without warning, the Corps of Engineers issued a finding holding the bridge "a serious obstacle to navigation." Congress had given the Corps control over navigation of the nation's waterways, and that control was absolute. On September 2, 1873, an army board in St. Louis, prodded by competing steamboat interests, found that the smokestacks on some boats were too high to fit under the bridge. Rather than order the stacks hinged, a common practice, the army engineers instructed Eads to construct a canal behind the east abutment of the bridge so the steamboats could go around it. The Corps's instructions left no wiggle room. If Eads did not build the canal, it would order the bridge demolished. Only the president, or an act of Congress, could stay the Corps's hand.*

Eads had been in Europe raising money when the order from the Corps arrived. He returned to New York, picked up William Taussig, chairman of the bridge company, and took the train to Washington. The pair walked into the White House with trepidation. In 1859 Taussig, then a member of the board of supervisors of St. Louis county, had blocked the hiring of the then struggling Grant as county engineer. When the president greeted Taussig as "Judge," his title when he rejected Grant's application, the visitors froze. Grant laughed. He bore no grudges, the president said, "since I prefer my present position to that one." [55]

They sat in Grant's office while a steward served coffee. Eads reported what had happened, along with technical details of the bridge and the friction with Humphreys. Grant listened intently. He knew Humphreys well: first as Meade's chief of staff in the Army of the Potomac, then as Hancock's replacement commanding 2nd Corps. [56] The president respected Humphreys's ability, but he also knew his innate conservatism. And he realized what the chief of engineers was doing made no sense. "Get Belknap," the president told his secretary. Runners were sent scurrying and within moments the secretary of war appeared.

Grant wasted no time with pleasantries. Did Eads's bridge conform to the congressional legislation? Had it not been approved by Rawlins in

* Eads's problem with the Corps was an outcropping of a larger struggle for primacy on the Mississippi. In early 1873, Eads addressed the perennial problem of the sandbar at the mouth of the Mississippi. The situation had become worse in recent years with the bar often blocking the entry and egress of larger ships from New Orleans. Eads proposed constructing two parallel piers (or jetties) far out into the Gulf. This would narrow the river and increase its current. Eads believed the concentrated current would cut its own channel through the bar. The Corps of Engineers took the position that the sandbar at the mouth of the river was a permanent, immovable barrier. The solution was to outflank it by building a canal to link New Orleans with the Gulf. General Humphreys was lobbying Congress for the funds, and resented Eads's intrusion into the matter. "We must get ready for combat at the next session of Congress," Humphreys told a subordinate. "The contest must be sharp and merciless." Eads was proved right. With Grant's continuing support he built the jetties and they worked. John M. Berry, *Rising Tide: The Great Mississippi Flood of 1927 and How It Changed America* 61–63 (New York: Simon & Schuster, 1997).

1869? Belknap reddened and conceded both points. The secretary, a law partner of several steamboat operators opposed to the bridge, was surprisingly familiar with the issue. Whether he had a financial stake in the outcome is unclear. Had the president read the Corps's report, he asked? "I do not care to look at the papers," Grant replied. "You cannot overturn this project on your own judgment. I think you and Humphreys better drop this."[57]

Belknap bowed and beat a hasty retreat. Humphreys was called off. Several weeks later Grant was in St. Louis and visited Eads at the bridge. The massive arches towered above them, connected only with narrow planks where the roadway would be. It was a cold November day. Holding to guide wires, Eads and Grant took a walk, single file, along the planks with the wind blowing and the white-capped river far below. On the other side they retired to a work shed where Eads broke open a bottle of brandy. Grant was in good spirits. They smoked cigars, played cards, and talked about the past.[58]*

The president's interest in civil engineering carried over into architecture. No other chief executive has given his name to the buildings of an era. "General Grant style" is a term of common usage among architectural historians.[59] It denotes a distinct American form adapted from the opulent designs of Second Empire France, the best example of which is the old State, War, and Navy Building (now the Executive Office Building) next to the White House. "Grant saw public buildings as a means of consolidating the Union," said art historian Douglas Richardson, "and he sprinkled monumental court houses and post offices all over the country."[60]

Grant had never been to France, but his eye for architecture had been sharpened in the studio of Robert Walter Weir at West Point. Grant knew what he liked, and he liked the mansarded structures of Paris, rich in classical details, with numerous columns and pilasters, elaborate pediments above decorative windows, and wide projecting cornices. Made of granite and marble, the buildings had the solidity of the man who calmly ordered the Army of the Potomac to move south after two days of unremitting slaughter in the Wilderness. Many of the stones for the State, War, and Navy Building, for example, weighed as much as twenty tons, the foundation walls were eight feet thick, and exterior walls more than four feet thick.[61]

Grant's supervising architect was Alfred Bult Mullett, a thirty-five-

* Despite Grant's order, Humphreys did not back off completely. In January 1874 the Corps issued a new report calling the bridge a "badly designed monster. . . . Justice demands that the bridge must come down." Eads ignored the order, and the bridge opened on schedule, July 4, 1874. It is not only still standing, but still carrying traffic.

year-old Englishman who had been reared in Cincinnati and apprenticed to his profession in his teens. Mullett had no college training but had traveled extensively in Europe and had become thoroughly conversant with the style of the Second Empire. Appointed supervising architect in 1866, he designed forty-two buildings for the government during Grant's tenure.[62] In addition to the monumental State, War, and Navy Building, his structures included massive federal buildings in Boston, New York, St. Louis, Philadelphia, and Cincinnati, as well as numerous customshouses, post offices, branch mints, and courthouses.[63] Unlike cookie-cutter federal architecture both before and after, Mullett rejected the premise that all post offices should look alike. "The repetition of style and design so common heretofore . . . has retarded the cultivation of correct taste and a love of art, without effecting the slightest saving, except in the labors of the designer." With Grant's approval, Mullett sought to design each building according "to the materials adopted; the wants of the officers and the public; the peculiarities of soil and climate, and the necessities of various localities."[64] Though they were monumental architectural statements, the sad fact is that more than half of the federal buildings of the Grant era have been demolished, the elegant courthouse and post office in Des Moines torn down to make way for a parking ramp. Of the major structures, only the State, War, and Navy Building in Washington and the St. Louis customshouse survive.[65]

Civil engineering and architecture were sidebars; the business of government was ongoing. Federal appointments consumed a great deal of Grant's time, and in the year following the election he was given the opportunity to fill two more vacancies on the Supreme Court. In November 1872 Justice Samuel Nelson, an old Jacksonian Democrat from New York, resigned after twenty-seven years on the bench. A firm believer in judicial restraint, Nelson had no difficulty sustaining the Reconstruction Acts passed by Congress. Speaking for the Court in *Georgia v. Stanton,* he dismissed efforts by the state of Georgia to enjoin enforcement of the measures, holding that the case presented a political question that was not justiciable.[66] Grant later asked Nelson to join the United States delegation to the Joint High Commission that settled the country's outstanding problems with Great Britain, and his departure from the Court, necessitated by ill health, was a grievous blow to the administration.*

* To replace Nelson, Grant nominated Ward Hunt of New York. A close friend of Senator Roscoe Conkling's, Hunt was a judge on the New York Court of Appeals. Conkling steered his nomination through the Senate, and Hunt was confirmed without opposition the week after Grant sent his name forward. Like Nelson, Hunt voted to uphold the Reconstruction measures passed by Congress, but he did not pull the heavy oar on the Court that Nelson did. Hunt suffered a debilitating stroke in 1878, but did not resign until 1882 when Congress voted a special pension bill for him.

Grant's second appointment came in May 1873 when Chief Justice Salmon P. Chase suffered a fatal stroke. Chase had been in poor health, yet his death (at the age of sixty-five) was unexpected. The Court had just adjourned and the 43rd Congress would not convene until December. Disregarding the advice of those who urged him to move quickly, Grant held his cards close to his chest. The president said he would not reveal his choice until Congress returned to Washington. His reason was that he did not want his nominee raked over the coals before the Senate convened. "I thought a Chief Justice should never be subjected to the mortification of a rejection," Grant wrote.[67]

On November 8 Grant offered the position to Senator Roscoe Conkling of New York. "When the Chief Justiceship became vacant I necessarily looked with anxiety to someone whose appointment would be recognized as entirely fitting," he wrote Conkling. "I now wish to state to you that my first convictions on the subject of who should be Judge Chase's successor have received confirmation by time; and I tender the nomination to you, to be made on the meeting of Congress, in the hope that you will accept."[68]

Historians and biographers have been uniformly critical of Grant for seeking to name a politician rather than a jurist as chief justice. The same criticism could be leveled at John Adams, Andrew Jackson, and Dwight Eisenhower. John Marshall, Roger Brooke Taney, and Earl Warren, three of the greatest chief justices, were themselves leading politicians of their era and were devoid of judicial experience when appointed. What sort of chief justice Conkling would have made is impossible to say. He was loved by few people in Washington, but as his biographer notes, everyone took him seriously.[69] First elected to the Senate in 1866, he was by 1873 the most powerful administration voice on Capitol Hill and the undisputed leader of the Republican party in New York. But to the surprise of observers everywhere, Conkling declined the appointment. Fiercely partisan, and at forty-five still ambitious for higher office, he wrote Grant asking him to appoint someone else. "I could not take the place," Conkling told friends, "for I would be forever gnawing at my chains."[70]*

* Conkling resigned from the Senate in 1881 and entered the practice of law in New York City. His clients included Jay Gould and railroad tycoon Collis P. Huntington, and he quickly made a fortune. Arguing the landmark case of *San Mateo County v. Southern Pacific Railroad Company* before the Supreme Court in 1882 (116 U.S. 138), Conkling succeeded in bringing corporations under the protection of the due process clause of the Fourteenth Amendment. Conkling's argument, citing original intent, of which he claimed personal knowledge, was crucial to the Court's development of the doctrine of "substantive due process" and introduced a prolonged period of judicial activism. Whether Conkling embroidered the evidence has long been disputed by scholars, but as Justice Samuel F. Miller said, "for the discussion of the law and the facts of the case Mr. Conkling is the best lawyer who comes into our court." George S. Boutwell, 2 *Reminiscences of Sixty Years in Public Af-*

Grant had not anticipated Conkling's refusal. And having waited for Congress to convene, he now had to act quickly. After a cabinet meeting at the White House on November 30, 1873, he took Fish aside and asked him to accept the post.[71] The scene is reminiscent of a similar White House conversation in 1801. John Jay had just declined Adams's offer of the chief justiceship. Jay's letter was brought to the president by Secretary of State John Marshall. Pressed for time before his term expired, Adams turned to Marshall and said, "I believe I must nominate you."[72] Marshall was stunned by the offer. So too was Fish. Unlike Marshall, however, Fish declined the appointment.

Frustrated in his first two choices, Grant lost his touch. At Benjamin Butler's suggestion he briefly considered naming Caleb Cushing of Massachusetts. Cushing was a lifelong Democrat with a fine legal mind who had represented the United States in the *Alabama* claims arbitration in Geneva. But he was seventy-three years old. Grant was attracted to him because Butler had suggested that the appointment be "temporary": that Cushing agree to resign before the president's term expired. That would give Grant time to find a proper appointment. But the cabinet was skeptical. Fish told Grant that while Cushing was certainly fit for the job, he doubted the propriety of appointing a chief justice for a provisional period. Grant saw the problem and backed away.[73]

The Supreme Court would convene in January and the time for the president to act was growing short. Instinctively, Grant turned to his attorney general. George Williams's name was sent to the Senate on December 5, 1873, along with the president's fifth annual message to Congress. By week's end it was apparent Grant had made a mistake. Williams's reputation as a lawyer rested in rural Oregon. Whenever tested as attorney general he had failed dismally. After the Crédit Mobilier investigation, for example, Congress had ordered suits against the company, which had manifestly defrauded the government of millions. The evidence was clearcut yet Williams mismanaged the case so badly that the government lost.[74] "The country should be ashamed and disgraced by the nomination of such a man," said the *Cincinnati Commercial*. The *Louisville Courier Journal* called it "the worst appointment yet."[75] In the Senate, attention quickly focused on Williams's use of Justice Department contingency funds to cover his personal expenses. Mrs. Williams had purchased the most expensive carriage in Washington and equipped it with a liveried coachman and footman, all paid for by the government. Williams had also commingled his personal accounts with those of the department, paying personal checks

---

fairs 265 (New York: McClure, Phillips, 1902). For Conkling's argument, see 536 *Transcript of Records* 1–64, U.S. Supreme Court (1882). Compare, Andrew C. McLaughlin, "The Court, the Corporation, and Conkling," 46 *American Historical Review* 55 (1940).

with government funds, although he repaid the money. Conkling and Senator Frederick T. Frelinghuysen of New Jersey told Grant that while Williams had not committed an indictable offense, it was doubtful he could be confirmed.[76]

Grant refused to back down. "The pressure from the White House is tremendous," Assistant Attorney General C. H. Hill of Massachusetts wrote Benjamin Bristow. "The President makes it a matter of party fealty."[77] The chain was finally pulled by Senator George Edmunds of Vermont, chairman of the Judiciary Committee. If the committee had to act on the nomination, Grant was told, they would unanimously advise rejection. The best course would be for the president to step back.[78] Grant bowed to the inevitable. On January 8, 1874, Williams recognized he was beaten and requested that his name be withdrawn. Grant did so the following day. Despite evidence suggesting malfeasance, he did not ask for Williams's resignation as attorney general. This was a black mark for the president. By winking at Williams's indiscretions Grant was setting a tone from which the administration never recovered. The best that can be said for Grant is that the president was angry and refused to acknowledge that the Senate might have been correct.[79]

At this point Fish urged Grant to nominate Rockwood Hoar, who had just been elected to the House of Representatives. Had Grant done so he might have salvaged the situation. But the Senate had once rejected Hoar and the president told Fish he was afraid it would do so again.[80] A precedent to the contrary would have been Roger Brooke Taney. Andrew Jackson nominated Taney to succeed Gabriel Duval as associate justice in 1835 and the Senate rejected him. Eleven months later he sent Taney's name forward to be chief justice and he was confirmed. Grant chose not to follow Jackson's example.

The president was floundering. Why not go back to Cushing, he asked his cabinet. Fish reports that "everyone assented," and if that was the case, Grant's advisers shared responsibility for another debacle. The elderly Cushing proved even less popular on Capitol Hill than Williams. Caleb Cushing ranked high among a small group of truly eminent lawyers in the United States, but he had been active in politics for over thirty years and had made enemies on every side. Most damning to his nomination was discovery of a friendly letter Cushing had written to Jefferson Davis in March 1861 recommending a former associate for possible employment with the Confederate government.[81] The letter itself was harmless, but Cushing's timing, writing just a few days before Beauregard fired on Fort Sumter, could not have been worse. When the letter became public Cushing immediately wrote Grant to ask that his nomination be withdrawn.

It was now the middle of January 1874. Eight months had elapsed since

Chase's death and the position of Chief Justice of the United States was still vacant. Grant's first two choices declined the post; two more men failed to pass Senate scrutiny. Grant made another attempt to entice Conkling to accept the appointment. When the New York senator refused, the president, at the urging of his cabinet, nominated Morrison R. Waite, a relatively obscure attorney living in Toledo, Ohio.[82] As one observer noted, it could fairly be said of Morrison Remick Waite that he stood in the front rank of the legion of second-class lawyers in the country.[83] Primarily an Ohio practitioner, Waite had served as associate counsel with Cushing in the Geneva arbitration. He stood high with the Ohio bar, and had just been chosen to chair the upcoming Ohio constitutional convention. In Washington, his principal sponsor was Interior Secretary Columbus Delano, an old hand at Ohio politics, who had known Waite for years. Delano evidently convinced his colleagues that his friend could be confirmed. Grant sent Waite's name to the Senate on January 19, 1874, and indeed he was approved unanimously two days later. His appointment inspired mixed feelings. No one suggested Waite was the best man for the post, but his character was unassailable, his exposure to partisan politics in Washington had been minimal, and he was an experienced lawyer, if not a brilliant one. "The President," wrote *The Nation,* "has, with remarkable skill, avoided choosing any first rate man. . . . But considering what he might have done, we ought to be thankful."[84]

The Supreme Court would soon play a crucial role in determining federal policy toward the South. Grant had four appointees on the bench: Strong, Bradley, Hunt, and Chief Justice Waite. Yet only Hunt voted to sustain government efforts to protect the freedmen. Two of the most egregious decisions were written by Waite. In *United States v. Reese,* a voting rights case arising in Kentucky,[85] the Court invalidated the operative sections of the Enforcement Act of 1870, holding that the Fifteenth Amendment did not confer the right of suffrage in state and local elections.* The same day that *Reese* was handed down, the Court also gutted enforcement of the Ku Klux Klan Act. Speaking once more for his colleagues, this time in *United States v. Cruikshank,*[86] Waite said the Fourteenth and Fifteenth amendments applied only to action by the states, not by individuals. "The power of Congress to legislate [to enforce the amendments] does not extend to the passage of laws for the suppression of ordinary crimes within

---

* The Court's reasoning in Reese, reflecting a determined effort to restrict the scope of national authority, rested in part on the limited view of citizenship developed by Waite the year before in *Minor v. Heppersett* 21 Wallace 162, denying women the right to vote. "Citizenship," said the Court, "did not necessarily confer the right of suffrage" (at 177). As Waite saw it, and he spoke for all of his colleagues, citizenship conveyed "the idea of membership of a nation, nothing more" (166). The effect of the Court's decision was implicitly overturned with ratification of the Nineteenth Amendment, April 18, 1920.

the States. That duty was originally assumed by the States; and it still remains there." The decisions in *Reese* and *Cruikshank* were important benchmarks in the nation's retreat from Reconstruction. Justice Hunt, the sole dissenter, noted somberly that the Court had brought to "an impotent conclusion the vigorous Amendments on the subject of slavery."[87]*

Of the two decisions, *Cruikshank* had the greater impact. The case stemmed from efforts by the Grant administration to punish perpetrators of the Colfax Massacre in Louisiana, the bloodiest act of racial violence in all of Reconstruction.[88] Louisiana never rested easy under Reconstruction. Statewide elections in 1872 further polarized the state, with Republican and Democratic candidates both claiming to have won the governorship. Eventually a federal judge ruled in favor of the Republicans, and Grant ordered troops to enforce the judgment. Louisiana whites refused to accept the verdict and formed a rival government supported by armed paramilitary units known as White Leagues. The state became an armed camp. The Leagues controlled numerous rural parishes and launched attacks on Republicans and blacks to gain control of others. The worst violence occurred in the Red River town of Colfax, in the central part of the state. Colfax was the county seat of Grant Parish.† Racial hostility in the parish was of long standing, with the African-American faction in control. Militia and freedmen loyal to the official government guarded the courthouse to protect county officers. On Easter Sunday, 1873, they were attacked and eventually overpowered by whites armed with rifles and light artillery. When the sun set, well over a hundred blacks were dead, many shot in cold blood after they had surrendered. Two white men also died.[89] A federal

---

* Grant was swimming against the tide. The American legal community had lost interest in the freedmen. Under the aegis of the Supreme Court, the Constitution ceased to be a bulwark protecting the rights of African-Americans. In 1883 the Court struck down the Civil Rights Act, which prohibited racial segregation in inns, public conveyances, and places of public amusement. In 1896, in *Plessy v. Ferguson*, 163 U.S. 537, it promulgated the doctrine of "separate but equal," giving constitutional sanction to segregation. But *Reese* and *Cruikshank* were the pivotal cases and provided the judicial rationale. Harvard legal historian Charles Warren, writing about the two cases in 1922, restated the prevailing consensus: "Viewed in historical perspective . . . there can be no question that the decisions in these cases were most fortunate. They largely eliminated from National politics the Negro question which had so long embittered Congressional debates; they relegated the burden and duty of protecting the negro to the States, to whom they properly belonged; and they served to restore confidence in the National Court in the Southern States." Charles Warren, 2 *The Supreme Court in United States History* 608 (Boston: Little, Brown, 1922). A notable exception to judicial unanimity was Justice John Marshall Harlan of Kentucky, who, like Grant, believed the Constitution was color-blind.

† The Louisiana legislature established the parish in 1868, naming it for the president-elect and designating the county seat in honor of Vice President–Elect Schuyler Colfax. The parish contained two distinct areas: a rich river valley of plantations inhabited mostly by blacks and a hardscrabble hill country populated primarily by white farmers. This was a combustible mix under the best of circumstances. Rable, *But There Was No Peace* 126–129.

grand jury indicted seventy-two whites for their part in the massacre, nine were tried, and three were convicted. When the Supreme Court overturned those convictions in *Cruikshank,* it doomed the Grant administration's legal efforts to protect the freedmen.

Meanwhile, the situation in Louisiana had gone from worse to much worse. Grant sized it up as well as anyone: "The muddle down there is almost beyond my fathoming."[90] The 1874 election campaign was the most violent to date. In Coushatta, near Shreveport, the local White League murdered six Republican officeholders. In New Orleans, on September 14, police and black militia commanded by General Longstreet fought a pitched battle with 3,500 White Leaguers intent on seizing the statehouse (the old St. Louis Hotel) and overturning the government. Longstreet, who was wounded in the fighting, lost eleven killed and sixty wounded.* The Crescent City White League suffered twenty-one dead and nineteen wounded, but succeeded in storming the state offices. A rival Democratic government was installed and the Republican officeholders took refuge in the United States customshouse. White Louisianians evidently believed the putsch would go uncontested. "This is the happiest city in the universe," proclaimed the *New Orleans Bulletin.* White League supporters from neighboring parishes poured into the city to join the festivities. Louisiana State University president David F. Boggs wrote his old friend William Tecumseh Sherman that the White League meant no harm to the United States and that if the administration would leave the state alone, there would be no further trouble. The new governor promised to keep the peace, protect blacks, and guard federal property.[91]

If Grant had been looking for an easy way out, or if his eyes were fixed on the November elections (support for the freedmen was decidedly unpopular in 1874), he would have accepted the New Orleans coup d'etat. Instead, he moved swiftly to suppress the revolt. On September 15, 1874, the day after the battle, Grant issued a presidential proclamation calling on the rebellious citizens to disperse within five days and submit to the duly elected state government.[92] Five thousand troops and three gunboats were dispatched to New Orleans, resistance crumbled, and by September 17 the insurgency had been crushed.

Republicans paid heavily for Grant's intervention. The *New York Tribune* called the president's action an outrage. "General Grant has van-

---

* Longstreet's role in the fighting on September 14 resulted in widespread denunciation and vilification in the white South. He led mostly black troops against former Confederate soldiers, which to many below the Mason-Dixon line was another indication of his betrayal of the Cause. A White League officer claimed later that "it was with greatest difficulty that I prevented the men from firing particularly at Longstreet." Jeffry D. Wert, *General James Longstreet: The Confederacy's Most Controversial Soldier* 416 (New York: Simon & Schuster, 1993).

quished the people of Louisiana again."[93] Other Northern papers took up the cry. In November, the Democrats captured control of the House of Representatives for the first time since the election of 1856 and gained ten seats in the Senate. In Louisiana, Democrats won four of six congressional districts and the statehouse was evenly divided: fifty-three Democrats, fifty-three Republicans, and five places undecided. In his annual message to Congress, Grant took on his critics. So long as he was president, he said, the Constitution and the laws of Congress would be rigorously enforced. As for the South, "Under existing conditions, the negro votes the Republican ticket because he knows his friends are of that party. Many a good citizen votes the opposite, not because he agrees with the great principles of state which separate parties, but because he is opposed to negro rule. This is a most delusive cry. Treat the negro as a citizen and as a voter, as he is and must remain, and soon parties will be divided, not on the color line, but on principle. Then we shall have no complaint of sectional interference."[94]

The election in Louisiana had been marred by enormous irregularities, with fraud and intimidation prevalent on both sides. With five legislative seats still undecided, Grant decided to head off any future violence. As in the Shenandoah in 1864, where the Union had been victim of an unending string of disasters, he turned to Sheridan. As Grant saw it, if anyone could restore order in the Bayou State, it was Little Phil. The fact that the frontier was aflame was of little consequence. On Christmas Eve 1874 the president sent a private wire to Sheridan in Chicago instructing him to undertake an immediate inspection of Louisiana and Mississippi (neither of which were in his division) and "ascertain the true condition of affairs." The order was not to be entered in official records unless "action is taken under it," but Sheridan was given what amounted to a military blank check. He was authorized to issue orders on the spot, and if he deemed it necessary, to assume command of the Division of the South, or any part of it. Neither Sherman nor Major General Irvin McDowell, the division commander, was informed of Sheridan's mission. Grant's wire instructed the nation's three-star general to report directly to the secretary of war and to use cipher when doing so. In effect, Grant was assuming personal responsibility for Louisiana; Sheridan would be his deputy.[95]

The Louisiana legislature was set to convene January 4, 1875. Sheridan, ostensibly a tourist bound for Havana, arrived a few days before and immediately met with the area commander, Major General William H. Emory. Emory and Sheridan were old comrades, the former commanding a corps under Little Phil in the Shenandoah Valley. But Emory had aged. Sheridan found him "a very weak old man, entirely unfitted for this place." Either he should be forced to retire, or at the very least relieved of his command.[96] This was exactly the type of hard-hitting report Grant expected from Sheridan (it was Sheridan, after all, who had relieved Gouverneur Warren as 5th Corps commander at Five Forks in 1865). Little Phil asked that Colonel Ranald S. Mackenzie be assigned to New Orleans, but Mackenzie, commanding the 4th Cavalry at Fort Concho, had his hands full winding down the Red River War and was unavailable. Accordingly, Sheridan advised Grant that if there was trouble when the legislature met, he would annex the Department of the Gulf (Louisiana, Alabama, Mississippi, and Arkansas) to his division and assume command himself.[97]

As Sheridan anticipated, trouble arrived on the double. When the legislature convened on January 4, the Democrats forcibly seized control of the House and proceeded to seat the five Democratic claimants to the contested seats. In response, the Republican governor requested the army to evict the five Democrats, none of whom possessed the proper election credentials.[98] With Sheridan's "advice," Emory dispatched a detail of troops to clear the House chamber of all persons who could not produce election certificates. The five newly seated Democrats were forcibly ejected, at which point the remainder of the Democrats stalked out in protest. The Republicans then organized the House and elected a speaker. That evening, after reporting what had occurred to Washington, Sheridan assumed command in New Orleans.[99]

Little Phil wasted no time before taking the offensive. On January 5 he wired Belknap recommending that the leadership of the White Leagues be arrested and tried by courts-martial. "If the president would issue a proclamation declaring them banditti, no further action need be taken except that which would devolve upon me."[100]* Grant was delighted. Sheridan was taking command as he always did. The president was not ready to issue the proclamation the general requested, but Belknap replied: "The President and all of us have full confidence and thoroughly approve your course."[101]

Sheridan's wire found its way to the press almost instantly. Most Republicans rallied to the administration's support. The White Leagues deserved no quarter, said the radical press. "Crush them utterly, remorselessly. Better military rule for forty years than the South be given over to lawlessness and blood for one day."[102] But Democrats and Liberal Republicans converted Sheridan's message into a cause célèbre. Senator Thomas Bayard of Delaware accused Sheridan of "riding rough-shod over the Bill of Rights." Carl Schurz branded Sheridan's banditti proposal as "so appalling that every American citizen who loves liberty stands aghast."

---

* There was precedent for the proclamation Sheridan requested. In 1871 Grant had suspended the writ of habeas corpus in nine South Carolina counties to combat the Klan. In 1873 the six Modoc chiefs charged with the murder of General Canby were tried in military court at the president's order, as were the Indian leaders in the Red River War. For Sheridan's view, see Paul Andrew Hutton, *Phil Sheridan and His Army* 266–67 (Lincoln: University of Nebraska Press, 1973).

William Cullen Bryant, speaking before a mass meeting in New York, said Sheridan should "tear off his epaulets and break his sword and fling the fragments into the Potomac."[103]

The firestorm raged for a week. In New Orleans, Sheridan was threatened with assassination.[104] To show his contempt, Little Phil made a point of taking his meals in the public dining room of the St. Charles Hotel and moving about the city without escort. In Washington, the Senate requested details of the situation. Grant replied on January 13 with a blistering report detailing the atrocities in Louisiana and strongly defending Sheridan's actions. "The spirit of hatred and violence is stronger than law" in the Bayou State, said the president. "Lieutenant-General Sheridan was requested by me to go to Louisiana to observe and report. No party motives nor prejudices can reasonably be imputed to him; but honestly convinced by what he has seen and heard there, he has characterized the leaders of the White Leagues in severe terms and suggested summary modes of procedure against them, which . . . if legal, would soon put an end to the troubles and disorders in that State."

To reassure the Senate, Grant added that he had no desire to have United States troops interfere in the domestic concerns of Louisiana or any other state. "I have repeatedly and earnestly entreated the people of the South to live together in peace and obey the laws. . . . I regret to say that this state of things does not exist, nor does its existence seem to be desired in some localities." It was a tough message, and Grant did not give an inch. "To the extent that Congress has conferred power upon me to prevent it, neither Ku Klux Klans, White Leagues, nor any other associations using arms and violence can be permitted to govern any part of this country."[105]

The message to Louisiana was clear. Grant was not bluffing, and neither was Sheridan. Little Phil's presence in the Crescent City in and of itself was sufficient to cow even the most aggressive White Leaguers. New Orleans had felt Sheridan's iron hand in 1866; no one doubted that any act of violence would be dealt with swiftly and harshly. In less than a week Sheridan felt sufficiently confident to wire Belknap: "The dog is dead. White Leaguers here are trying to make arrangements to surrender to the civil authorities fearing to come under my jurisdiction."[106]

With calm restored, a congressional committee chaired by George F. Hoar of Massachusetts, brother of Rockwood Hoar, undertook a firsthand investigation of the situation in Louisiana, remained for three weeks, and issued a devastating report detailing an imposing list of White League depredations and defending Sheridan's use of troops on January 4. The forceful military presence, said the committee, had prevented bloodshed that most certainly would have occurred otherwise.[107] The committee also succeeded in fashioning a temporary truce in the turbulent affairs in

Louisiana. The Democrats were awarded control of the lower house of the legislature, the senate went to the Republicans, and the Democrats agreed to allow the Republican governor to serve out the remaining two years of his term.[108] Sheridan left New Orleans at the end of March. He retained control of the Department of the Gulf, replaced Emory with Major General Christopher C. Augur ("Augur and myself have always worked together as one man," Sheridan told Belknap), and turned his attention to more pressing matters: the courtship of twenty-two-year-old Irene Rucker, the winsome daughter of his quartermaster general.[109] Sheridan had done what Grant had asked (which helps explain why the president usually did not second-guess him in the West). Louisiana, at least for the time being, was quiescent. "When I first reached here the common topic of conversation was about killing people," Sheridan informed the president. "It is not so now."[110]

Grant paid dearly for putting down the White League insurrection in Louisiana. As one scholar has written, Louisiana became the Republican party's albatross.[111] Northern voters had turned away from the Negro. Except for the Radical Republicans, the Northern commitment to black equality had never been very deep. Emancipation, civil rights, and Negro suffrage were wartime by-products: they reflected Union policy, not considered social purpose.[112] And as the war receded, support for the rights of African-Americans diminished. "The truth is, our people are tired out with this worn out cry of 'Southern outrages,'" wrote one Republican politician. "Hard times and heavy taxes make them wish the 'nigger,' 'everlasting nigger,' were in _____ or Africa."[113] In 1876 the nation repudiated Grant's policy. Under Rutherford B. Hayes, the South was turned over to Southern whites and the Democrats. The rights of African-Americans were sacrificed at the altar of national reconciliation. Grant's reputation suffered severely. White supremacist historians, the dominant school of American historiography from the 1880s to the 1950s, savaged his efforts to protect the freedmen, just as many in the West ridiculed his peace policy toward Native Americans.[114]

A third area in which Grant defended principle involved the separation of church and state. The issue had two dimensions: public funding for sectarian education, and religious exercises in public schools. The question pitted Protestants against Catholics, and Grant stepped squarely in between. Originally, with the exception of Maryland, the United States had been overwhelmingly Protestant. But in the middle of the nineteenth century increased immigration from Ireland, Bavaria, and the Rhineland swelled the nation's Catholic population. By the end of the Civil War, Catholics constituted a majority in several Northern cities and church leaders began petitioning state legislatures for government support of parochial education. Protestants responded by calling for legislation prohibiting the diversion of public funds to religious institutions. The dispute escalated. Catholics challenged the Protestant overtones of public school education (hymn singing, praying, and Bible reading), and in the 1870s won school board support in Cincinnati, Chicago, New York, Buffalo, Rochester, and several other cities for the exclusion of such exercises.[115] Fearful of the trend, Evangelical Protestants joined with nativists who were convinced of the pernicious designs of the Catholic Church to seek a constitutional amendment that affirmed the existence of God, confessed Christ as savior, and acknowledged true religion as the sole basis for civil government. By 1875 the school question, Protestant versus Catholic, had become a burning national issue.

Why Grant waded into the dispute has never been adequately explained.[116] But on September 30, 1875, without warning or preliminary buildup, the president of the United States gave both Protestants and Catholics a stern lecture on religious tolerance and the separation of church and state. Grant crystallized the issue, captured the public's attention, and redirected the debate. Speaking to the veterans of the Army of the Tennessee, a setting in which he thrived, Grant made the most emotional speech of his career. He reminded the old soldiers of the hardships and sacrifices of war. "We believed then and we believe now that we have a government worth fighting for, worth dying for." He spoke to the South of reunion: "We will not deny to any of those who fought against us any privilege under the government which we claim for ourselves." And he appealed for peace. "In this sentiment no class of people can more heartily join than the soldier who submitted to the dangers, trials, and hardships of the camp and battlefield, on whichever side he fought."

Grant's introduction was remarkable, not only for its unaccustomed rhetoric, but for the hand he extended to the veterans in gray. In effect, he was marshaling his forces for a new battle. "If we are to have another contest in the near future of our national existence, I predict that the dividing line will not be Mason and Dixon's, but between patriotism and intelligence on the one side, and superstition, ambition, and ignorance on the other." In heartfelt words, Grant asked his countrymen to defend the guarantees of "free thought, free speech, a free press, pure morals unfettered by religious sentiments, and of equal rights and privileges to all men, irrespective of nationality, color, or religion."

Grant warmed to his subject. For the president, free public education lay at the root of the nation's liberty, and with remarkable evenhandedness he belted Protestants and Catholics alike: provide no aid for parochial education, but keep religion out of the classroom. "Resolve that neither the State nor the nation shall support institutions of learning other than those sufficient to afford to every child the opportunity of a good common-school education, unmixed with sectarian, pagan, or atheistic dogmas. Leave the matter of religion to the family altar, the church, and the private school supported entirely by private contributions. Keep the church and state forever separate." [117]

Grant's unexpected intervention in the school question reverberated across the country. The *New York Times* and the *New York Tribune* joined in praising the wisdom of the president's words. The *Chicago Tribune* said the speech "set the nation agog." *The Index*, a free-thought journal, called the speech "great" in spite of Grant's negative reference to atheism. [118] Most important, perhaps, the president's demand for the separation of church and state took the wind from militant Protestants advocating a pro-religion amendment to the Constitution. [119]

Grant stayed on the offensive. In his seventh annual message to Congress, December 7, 1875, he asked for the adoption of his own version of a constitutional amendment making it the duty of each state to establish and maintain free public schools for the education of all children irrespective of sex, color, birthplace, or religion. As Grant saw it, the schools should be entirely secular: the teaching of religion would be banned, and public aid to sectarian schools would be forbidden. [120]

To emphasize the separation of church and state, Grant also recommended that church property be taxed. He estimated the value of that property at $1 billion, and said that if untaxed the figure would triple by the end of the century. "So vast a sum, receiving all the protection and benefits of government without bearing its proportion of the burden and expenses of the same, will not be looked upon acquiescently by those who have to pay the taxes." Grant recommended that all property be taxed equally, "exempting only the last resting place of the dead and possibly, with proper restrictions, church edifices." [121]

Grant struck a responsive chord. The *New York Times* called the message "at once courageous and prudent." Grant had demonstrated once again, said the *Times*, "his possession of the qualities most essential to the head of a National Administration." *Harper's Weekly* said the speech showed "a clear perception of what the people wish." The *Chicago Tribune* stated, "There seems to be nothing lacking in his suggestion, and it will be a boon to the country if the Democratic Congress shall develop sufficient patriotism to act upon it in the same spirit in which it is offered." The only negative comment came from the *Catholic World*, which criticized Grant's proposal to tax church property. [122]

Grant's intervention in the school question caused each side to draw back. His emphasis on free public education galvanized the movement for education reform. His emphasis on separation of church and state moderated the debate. The Catholic press hailed his proposed constitutional amendment as an effort "to take the religious issue out of politics."[123] The week after Grant's message, Congressman James G. Blaine introduced an amendment that would prohibit the use of tax money for parochial education. Blaine's motives were partisan, and the Blaine Amendment ignored Grant's two principal points: the requirement that each state establish a free school system for all children, and the banning of religious exercises in public schools.[124]

For the last two years of his administration, Grant stood watch over the South almost alone. His cabinet was uninterested, Sherman was dubious, the Supreme Court had eviscerated the Fourteenth and Fifteenth amendments, and the public was more interested in reconciliation than Reconstruction. Shortly after he left the presidency, Grant reflected on the postwar period.

> Looking back, over the whole policy of reconstruction, it seems to me that the wisest thing would have been to have continued for some time the military rule. That would have enabled the Southern people to pull themselves together and repair material losses. Military rule would have been just to all: the negro who wanted freedom, the white man who wanted protection, the Northern man who wanted Union. As state after state showed a willingness to come into the Union, not on their terms but upon ours, I would have admitted them. The trouble about the military rule in the South was that our people did not like it. It was not in accordance with our institutions. I am clear now that it would have been better to have postponed suffrage, reconstruction, State governments, for ten years, and held the South in a territorial condition. But we made our scheme, and must do what we can with it. Suffrage once given can never be taken away, and all that remains now is to make good that gift by protecting those that received it.

As Grant saw it, the problem with the South was that the old Bourbon leadership, men who had learned nothing and forgotten nothing, had returned to power.

> If the Southern people would only put aside the madness of their leaders, they would see that they were richer now than before the war. Money is not held in as few hands as before the war, and the people, *per capita,* are richer. And that, after all, is what we want to see in a republic. Take cotton. Before the war a crop of two-and-a-half million or three million bales at six cents a pound was

an immense result. Now we have crops of five million bales at ten cents a pound. In this you see the success of the negro as a laborer. He has worked steadily during all this time of excitement. While his old masters have been declaiming upon their misfortunes, their ruin, their oppression, he has given the South a material prosperity that it never knew before the war. What a commentary that is upon the old story that the negro could only work under the lash![125]

CHAPTER NINETEEN

THE

GILDED AGE

*He comes up to the mark so grandly on great occasions, that I wish
he were more careful of appearances in smaller matters.*

ROCKWOOD HOAR
January 25, 1877

GRANT HAD COME TO FEEL very much at home in the White House. His
family, including aides and secretaries, was an extended one, and as pater
familias he relished the warmth and companionship that buffered affairs of
state. In the spring of 1874, his sixth year in the executive mansion, he was
called on, like the fathers of his era, to give his daughter in marriage. As the
resplendent marine band sounded the strains of Mendelssohn's *Wedding
March,* the eighteenth president of the United States escorted Nellie, his
favorite child, down the aisle of the East Room to an improvised altar,
mounted under a garland of white camellias. Waiting for them stood the
groom, a young Englishman, Algernon Sartoris (pronounced Sar-tress),
joined by his best man, Lieutenant Fred Grant, and the Reverend O. H.
Tiffany, pastor of the first family's Methodist church. Before 200 guests,
Nellie and Algernon were joined in marriage. Grant had mixed feelings.
He was pleased for Nellie, but despondent she was leaving. Newsmen reported that during the ceremony the president "looked steadfastly at the
floor" and wept.[1]

Nellie—Ellen Wrenshall Grant—had grown to maturity in the White
House. She was only thirteen when Grant was inaugurated, and she soon
became the center of the capital's teenage set. Her father doted on her and
her mother secretly delighted in all the attention she received.[2] Conservative matrons were horrified at press reports that the president's young
daughter had danced all night at a society ball, yet Grant offered no objection. But in the spring of 1873, when half-grown admirers began courting

Nellie in earnest, Julia thought it best for her to go abroad. The Adolph Bories, Grant's old friends from Philadelphia, were sailing for England, and said they would be delighted to have her accompany them. The Grants and the Bories anticipated a quiet sojourn that would take Nellie away from the limelight. But they failed to take the diplomats into account. In England, General Robert C. Schenck, the American minister, was determined that the daughter of the president be treated with respect according to English rules. Nellie's arrival was officially announced, she was graciously received by Queen Victoria, and conducted through a round of social engagements that dwarfed anything she had known in Washington. Adam Badeau, who was then consul general in London, gave a garden party for her and was delighted with her ease and self-possession. "She stood by my side and smiled with democratic grace on duchesses and marchionesses as they made the same curtsy they made to royalty; for the higher their own rank the more profound the prostration they performed."[3]

Nellie was treated as an American princess, and on her return voyage to Philadelphia she met and fell in love with Algernon Sartoris, a handsome, stylish, fast-living Englishman ten years her senior. Algernon's mother, Adelaide Kemble, had been a brilliantly successful opera singer. A daughter of the great actor Charles Kemble and the sister of the famous Fanny Kemble, Adelaide was at the top of her career when she married and left the operatic stage. In London, she was a renowned hostess, "her dinners were perfection," and she was regarded as "one of the best leaders of talk" in the country. As more than one biographer noted, Adelaide Kemble was a woman of substance; but her husband was not, and neither was her son.[4]

When their ship landed, Algernon followed Nellie to Washington and was soon invited to dinner at the White House. After dinner Grant led the way to the billiard room and offered him a cigar. As Sartoris recalled, "I waited and hoped the president would help me, but not a word did he say. He sat silent, looking at me. I hesitated, and fidgeted, and coughed, and thought I should sink through the floor. Finally, I exclaimed in desperation, 'Mr. President, I want to marry your daughter.' " Nellie had warned her parents, and Grant gave his reluctant consent.[5]

After the wedding the couple moved in with Algernon's mother in England. They had four children, but the marriage proved an unhappy one. Family tradition depicts Algernon as a womanizer and a heavy drinker. Nellie returned frequently to the United States for brief visits, and was with Grant when he died. After the funeral the *New York World* reported, "Mrs. Sartoris is in correspondence with her family in England to have her children brought over here. If they consent . . . she will remain this winter with her mother." Algernon did not consent, and Nellie returned to England for another five years, at which point she filed for divorce.[6]

Nellie's White House wedding took place amid financial panic and depression. The great boom that followed the Civil War had ended. In its place came hardship and despair. Initially, people called the Panic of 1873 "a Wall Street affair" and let it go at that. It soon became evident, however, that its roots tapped deep in the national economy. Overexpansion in industry, too rapid growth of rail lines, heavy losses in the Chicago and Boston fires in 1871 and 1872, respectively, and above all the effects of the American Civil War and the Franco-Prussian War, were among the principal causes of the crisis. In both Europe and the United States an insatiable demand for money had spawned a speculative boom that skyrocketed out of control. Banks had lent money recklessly and brokerage houses had marketed securities that were often worthless.

In mid-September 1873 Wall Street financial institutions began to fall like dominoes. The New York Warehouse & Security Company, unable to meet its obligations, suspended payment on September 8; Kenyon, Cox & Co. failed on the 13th. On the 18th, Jay Cooke & Co., the Gibraltar of American finance, went down. Cooke had kept the Union afloat during the Civil War and was currently underwriting construction of the Northern Pacific Railroad. Its failure started an avalanche. The panic was so great that on September 20 the New York Stock Exchange halted trading for ten days. Bankruptcies became commonplace, factories and mills shut down, railway construction ground to a halt, and commerce dried up. On the heels of the panic came depression. Farmers lost their farms, unemployment spread, and poverty stalked the land.

Grant was in the eye of the storm. In mid-September the president had taken his son Jesse to enroll in the Cheltenham Academy, a private school just outside Philadelphia. Visiting with friends before returning to the capital, he stayed the night of the 17th with Jay Cooke at Ogontz, the financier's palatial estate. Early on the 18th messages began to arrive for Cooke warning of impending disaster. The coffers of the Northern Pacific had run dry and its bonds were dropping by the minute. If a cash bailout could not be arranged that morning, the railroad was going belly-up and would take Jay Cooke & Co. with it. Ever a gentleman, Cooke did not breathe a word of the crisis to Grant. Shortly before noon, he bade the president farewell and went into the city facing imminent bankruptcy. Grant returned to Washington completely unaware that he had slept in a doomed house.[7]

When he arrived in the capital shortly after 4 P.M., Grant learned that Cooke's banking house had failed and that a full-blown panic was in the offing. The president knew little about finance, and George Boutwell, his longtime secretary of the treasury, was now sitting in the Senate and unavailable to manage the crisis. In Boutwell's place was William A. Richardson, an untried, stop-gap appointee with little experience and virtually no political clout. For better or worse, the mantle of leadership fell directly on Grant, and he did not hesitate to assume it.

Even before the extent of the crisis was known, Grant came under pressure from Washington politicians to inflate the currency. Constituents were hurting, and the country's legislators, particularly those from the West, saw quick salvation if the president would simply pump more greenbacks into the economy. Grant, a fiscal conservative by instinct, was not convinced. On Sunday, September 21, he journeyed to New York to consult the nation's leading businessmen and bankers. Their advice was mixed. Brokers, industrialists, and men of commerce were virtually unanimous in urging the president to relieve the pressure on money markets by releasing the Treasury's greenback reserve.* Bankers were equally adamant against adding to the volume of unredeemable currency in circulation. Grant went with the bankers. Treasury Secretary Richardson announced that the government would not issue more greenbacks. Instead, the Treasury would increase liquidity by redeeming several series of outstanding bonds. There would be no stampede to the printing presses. The banks responded to the administration's tight-money stance by issuing short-term clearinghouse certificates usable as cash and by October 1, the net addition to the nation's currency was estimated at $50 million. The liquidity crunch had been temporarily overcome without undermining the value of the dollar.[8]

Press response was overwhelmingly favorable. "The proverbial obstinacy of General Grant has never found a better field of display," proclaimed the *New Haven Palladium*.[9] Secretary Fish, one of the few hard-currency men with the president's ear, immediately wrote Richardson congratulating him for holding the line. "Nothing the President has ever done," wrote Fish, gives "more satisfaction than the decision which he and you reached on Sunday last. I hear from everyone, except those interested in speculation in stocks and bonds, one universal approval of the 'heroic action' of the President."[10]

Grant's conservative course stanched the bleeding on Wall Street, but

---

* "Reserve" was the term commonly used to describe the $44 million in retired greenbacks sitting in the Treasury's vaults. By statute, Congress had authorized the temporary circulation of $400 million in greenbacks, while admonishing the Treasury to reduce the amount whenever possible, thus hastening the return to specie-backed currency. By 1873 various secretaries of the treasury had succeeded in retiring a total of $44 million in unsecured greenbacks, leaving $356 million in circulation. To call the $44 million a "reserve" was inspired spin control, but scarcely accurate.

across the country the depression deepened. In his annual message to Congress in December, the president struck a middle course. He asked Congress to improve the "elasticity" of the currency without triggering an inflation that would postpone the resumption of specie payment. Among other things, Grant suggested that a federal clearinghouse—a precursor of the Federal Reserve Board—be established to facilitate the movement of currency from one region of the country to another.[11]

In Congress, agitation to inflate the currency intensified. Within two weeks of Grant's message more than sixty bills had been introduced on Capitol Hill, virtually all of which aimed to put more money into circulation.[12] By March, legislative opinion solidified behind what became known as the inflation bill (S.617). The measure would increase the amount of greenbacks in circulation to $400 million and raise the circulation of specie-backed currency to a similar figure. Overall, this would add $100 million to the nation's money supply. The conference report reconciling the House and Senate versions passed each chamber by wide margins and went to the president April 14, 1874.

Grant was torn. Having suffered severely in the Panic of 1857–that was the Christmas the president had pawned his gold watch to buy presents for his family—he sympathized with the nation's farmers and small businessmen. Grant knew what it meant to be poor, to try to make a crop, to have a business fail, to be out of a job, and as a last resort to peddle firewood on a St. Louis street corner. His heart was responsive to those who wanted to pump more money into the economy, yet as president he felt his responsibility was to the nation's future. Cheap paper money might look like a panacea, but inflation was never a friend to stable government. The United States would be driven further from the world standard, the return to specie-backed currency would be set back, property values would be unsettled, and speculation rekindled. If Congress could simply print unredeemable paper money to appease popular demand, the nation was in peril.

By now Grant's habits were well set. In times of crisis he kept his own counsel. Talking with Fish the day after the inflation bill passed, Grant said he was in no hurry to sign the measure. Under the Constitution he had ten days in which to act, and he wished to give the matter ample reflection. Fish thought Grant was inclined to sign the bill, though the president's concern to forestall inflation was apparent.[13]

While Grant was contemplating his decision, the first real scandal of his administration broke, effectively immobilizing his secretary of the treasury. This placed the decision on the inflation bill even more squarely on the president's shoulders. The problem at Treasury arose from a time-honored but long discredited moiety system of collecting delinquent tax accounts. To maximize collections, informers who reported evasions of federal taxes were rewarded with half the money collected. The system was a fertile source of abuse and in 1872 the administration abandoned it. But Congressman Benjamin Butler of Massachusetts managed to insert an exception into an appropriations bill that year. Under that exception, Secretary Richardson had signed a moiety contract with John D. Sanborn, a Massachusetts ally of Butler's, to collect taxes evaded by railroads, distillers, and other high-cash businesses. It was a license to steal. In 1874 the House Ways and Means Committee investigated Sanborn's work. They found that Treasury officials had informed revenue agents not to press delinquent accounts so that Sanborn might have more to collect, and that most of the $427,000 he retrieved would have come to the government in due course anyway. Worse still, Sanborn testified that of the $213,500 due him, he had paid $156,000 in "expenses" to unnamed associates. The implication was that these were bribes to public officials, but the committee could find no paper trail and Sanborn steadfastly refused to provide the names. Richardson and Butler were believed to have benefited but there was no hard evidence. Grant, loyal to a fault, declined to ask for Richardson's resignation, but his usefulness to the administration had clearly ended. In May, following severe condemnation by the Ways and Means Committee, Richardson resigned from the cabinet before the House could vote censure.

Meanwhile, the inflation bill lay on the president's desk. Press speculation suggested Grant intended to sign the measure.[14] When the cabinet discussed the bill on April 17, only Fish and Postmaster General Creswell were opposed. Grant heard everyone out, but retained a sphinxlike silence. Four days later the cabinet met again, and Grant announced his decision. He said he had stayed up late the night before studying the bill. He decided to approve the measure and wrote a message to Congress marshaling the arguments in favor of it. But the more he wrote, the more convinced he became that the bill was a bad one. Grant said when he completed writing, he reread what he had written and decided the reasoning was fallacious. He tore up the message and wrote another one vetoing the bill. As the cabinet sat agog, Grant picked up the paper and began to read: "Herewith I return Senate bill No. 617 . . . without my approval. In doing so I must express my regret at not being able to give my assent to a measure which has received the sanction of a majority of the legislators chosen by the people to make laws for their guidance, and I have studiously sought to find sufficient arguments to justify such assent, but unsuccessfully."

Grant said that by adding $100 million in paper money to the economy the measure was clearly inflationary. And if the first $100 million was

insufficient to restore prosperity, the sponsors of the measure would undoubtedly seek to print another $100 million. Such procedure, said Grant,
"is a departure from the principles of finance, national interest, the nation's
obligations to creditors, Congressional promises, party pledges (on the part
of both political parties), and of personal views and promises made by me in
every annual message sent to Congress and in each inaugural address."[15]

The cabinet was stunned. Fish and Creswell immediately expressed
their gratification, while the inflationists girded for battle. Delano,
Williams, Belknap, and Robeson let fly a barrage of arguments to convince Grant the measure was not inflationary. The president was unimpressed. No chief executive was ever better than Grant at listening to a
case he disagreed with and making no comment whatever. It was a habit
acquired on the battlefield. Subordinates should speak their mind, but the
general in chief would make his own decision. When it became apparent
that Grant was impervious to arguments on the merits, the four dissenters
retreated to expediency. The remarkable cabinet exchange was recorded
by Fish:

> DELANO: Mr. President, you ought to remember that the use
> of the veto power is not popular except when exercised on the
> ground of the unconstitutionality of a bill.*
>
> FISH: Whether that is so or not, the good faith of the nation is
> above the Constitution.
>
> GRANT: That is true, and I shall stand by my veto. I wish to
> send it in today and have done with it.
>
> ROBESON: It seems to me, Mr. President, that it is always wise
> to lay a paper aside after writing it to think it over. And like
> Secretary Delano, I wish to raise the political effect of a veto.
> The Congressional elections are just ahead.

---

* The presidential veto power, patterned on the "royal assent" exercised by the British
crown, was originally conceived as a constitutional check on legislative authority, not a policy check. Washington vetoed only two bills, Jefferson and the two Adamses did not veto
any, and Monroe only one. It was Andrew Jackson who converted the veto into a policy instrument, and the precedent he set involved congressional legislation rechartering the Second Bank of the United States. In 1819, Chief Justice John Marshall, speaking for a
unanimous Supreme Court in *McCulloch v. Maryland*, 4 Wheaton 316, had held the bank to
be constitutional. Accordingly, supporters of the bank bill believed it was veto-proof. Jackson disagreed. Despite the Court decision to the contrary he vetoed the bill on July 10, 1832,
and his veto was sustained. Jackson's veto message, drafted by Roger Brooke Taney, is an important benchmark in the expansion of executive authority. When Congress failed to override, the precedent of using the veto for policy purposes was established. *Presidential Vetoes,*
1789–1988, Senate Publication 102–12 (Washington, D.C.: Government Printing Office,
1992). For Jackson's 1832 veto message, see 2 *Messages and Papers of the Presidents* 581–83,
James D. Richardson, ed. (Washington, D.C.: Bureau of National Literature and Art, 1896).

Belknap, Williams, and Delano, more or less in chorus, repeated the refrain that a veto would hurt the party in November. Grant was immovable. "I dare say the first result will be a storm of denunciation. But I am confident that the final judgment of the country will approve my veto."[16]

Grant's veto message hit the Senate on Saturday, April 22. The following week administration forces led by Conkling and John Sherman of Ohio beat back the inflationists' efforts to override by a vote of 34–30, well short of the necessary two thirds.[17]

Grant's unexpected veto of the inflation bill won widespread approval from the nation's financial community. "*Vivat* Grant!" wrote George Templeton Strong. "This veto will rank in his record with Vicksburg and Appomattox."[18] From New York, attorney Edwards Pierrepont wrote friends in Washington, "You can hardly believe what a perilous load is lifted from the hearts of sober men in this city. No braver battle did the President ever fight and no victory did he ever gain which history will record as more illustrious."[19] James Garfield, not always in Grant's corner, was overjoyed. "For twenty years no president has had an opportunity to do the country so much service by a veto message as Grant has, and he has met the issue manfully."[20]

Press response was equally laudatory. "Once more General Grant has deserved well of the country," said the Liberal Republican *New York Tribune.* The *New York Times, Harper's Weekly,* and *The Nation* were predictably enthusiastic.[21] Secretary Fish, who had watched Grant at close quarters for six years, offered the most intimate appraisal. "You must give the President the undivided credit for what he did," Fish wrote to a former colleague in New York. "Never did a man more conscientiously reach his conclusions than he did in the matter of the bill, and this in the face of the very strongest and most persistent influences brought to bear upon him." By 1874 Fish knew Grant better than almost anyone. "He has a wonderful amount of good sense, and when left alone is very apt to follow it, and to 'fight it out on that line.' He did so in this recent matter, and astounded some who thought they had captured him."[22]

Years later, Grant reflected on his veto of the inflation bill in a conversation with John Russell Young:

> The only time I ever deliberately resolved to do an expedient thing for party reasons, against my own judgment, was on the occasion of the inflation bill. I was never so pressed in my life to do anything as to sign that bill—never. It was represented to me that a veto would destroy the Republican Party in the West. Morton [Senator Oliver P. Morton of Indiana], Logan [Senator John A. "Black Jack" Logan of Illinois], and other men, friends

whom I respected, were eloquent in presenting this view. I thought at last I would try and save the party, and at the same time the credit of the nation from the evils of the bill. I resolved to write a message . . . to show that the bill need not mean inflation and that it need not affect the country's credit. I wrote the message with great care and put in every argument I could call up to show that the bill was harmless. When I finished my wonderful message, I read it over and said to myself, "What is the good of all this? You do not believe it. You know it is not true." Throwing it aside I resolved to do what I believed to be right, veto the bill! I could not stand my own arguments.[23]

Grant's 1874 veto of the inflation bill is a seminal event in American history. The nation moved away from Civil War soft money and took a massive step toward the resumption of specie payment. The veto message made it clear that Grant was fundamentally opposed to unredeemable paper currency. When the Senate sustained that veto, the days of the greenback were numbered. In his sixth annual message to Congress in December, Grant boldly pressed the case for the resumption of specie payment. "I believe firmly that there can be no prosperous and permanent revival of business and industries until a policy is adopted—with legislation to carry it out—looking to a return to specie basis." Grant said the issuance of paper money had been necessary to fight the war. But its continued circulation had produced an inflated dollar that was impossible to keep on a par with foreign currencies. As a consequence, American money had become "a subject of speculation within itself." The value of the dollar fluctuated constantly, commerce suffered, and the good faith of the government was called into question. As Grant saw it, the first step toward economic recovery involved the adoption of a stable currency. "I believe it is in the power of Congress at this session to devise such legislation as will renew confidence, revive all the industries, start us on a career of prosperity to last many years, and to save the credit of the nation and the people."[24]

Grant had the political wind at his back. Contrary to the dire predictions of his cabinet, the president's veto of the inflation bill attracted widespread support. The desire for sound money and a stable currency swept the country like wildfire.[25] Congress reacted accordingly. The Senate's Republican leadership, working under the chairmanship of John Sherman, drafted a remarkable piece of consensus legislation providing for the resumption of specie payment on January 1, 1879.* The bill was reported out

---

* Contemporary economic orthodoxy holds that depression is best fought by expanding the money supply, not contracting it. This assumes the existence of a relatively stable cur-

of the Finance Committee on December 21, 1874, and approved by the full Senate the day after. The House passed the bill unchanged during the first week in January, and Grant signed the Resumption Act into law on January 14, 1875. The president was so pleased that he took the unusual step of sending a special message to Congress announcing his approval of the measure.[26]

To the end of his life Grant viewed his veto of the inflation bill, together with passage of the Resumption Act, as the most important accomplishment of his administration. The introduction of a stable currency paved the way for the enormous growth of the American economy in the last quarter of the nineteenth century—just as currency reform in Germany and Japan precipitated their extraordinary economic revival after World War II. Inflation was tamed, speculation reined in, and the credit of the government firmly reestablished. By the century's end, the American dollar had become the international symbol of financial stability. Grant's veto of the inflation bill also established a political benchmark. From 1874 onward, the Republican party became the party of economic conservatism, fiscal restraint, and a sound dollar. The Resumption Act was not only a pivotal event in restoring the American economy, it also marked a fundamental redefinition of the nation's political parties. Grant imparted to the Grand Old Party a commercial, pro-capitalist stance that replaced emancipation as the party's raison d'être.

The nation's return to solvency was aided considerably by Grant's new secretary of the treasury, Benjamin H. Bristow. The first solicitor general of the United States (1870–1872), Bristow had acquired a well-deserved reputation as an energetic prosecutor for his pursuit of the Ku Klux Klan. When Amos Akerman stepped down as attorney general, Bristow had hoped to succeed him. Grant appointed George Williams instead and Bristow returned to private practice in Kentucky. Nevertheless, Grant retained a high regard for Bristow. The Kentuckian had a winning personality, was a forceful administrator, a distinguished lawyer, and one of the few men in public life (Logan was another) who could say he had fought with Grant at Donelson and Shiloh. In December 1873 when Williams was nominated to be chief justice, Grant notified Bristow that he was to be the next attorney general.[27] That, of course, did not happen.

Richardson's abrupt resignation from the cabinet in the spring of 1874

---

rency plus a regulatory mechanism such as the Federal Reserve Board to apply the brakes when the economy overheats. In 1874 there was no such mechanism. Without a standard of value (i.e., gold), Congress was free to expand the money supply ad infinitum. The lesson of the Weimar Republic's politically inspired hyperinflation of the early 1920s provides a textbook example of what unchecked inflation can do to a country. With the advantage of that example, it is difficult to fault Grant's insistence on a stable currency, despite the difficult transition and the temporary hardships it engendered.

caught Grant unprepared. The secretary of the treasury was the first member of Grant's official family to leave under a cloud, and the president sought to repair the damage as quickly as possible. Interior Secretary Delano badly wanted the Treasury, but his preference for soft money made him unacceptable.[28] With the wolves baying at the administration's door, Grant first turned to his old Washington mentor, Elihu Washburne. In 1868 Washburne had beseeched Grant to become secretary of the treasury, and it was possible he still wanted the post. His appointment would have brought a seasoned political hand to the cabinet and there was no question of Washburne's support for a sound dollar. On May 5, 1874, Fish wired the offer to him in Paris, but the reply was negative. The minister pleaded poor health. It is also unlikely Washburne wished to leave the French capital, where he was dean of the diplomatic corps, lionized for his heroic stance during the siege and later during the Commune.[29]

When Washburne declined, Grant turned to Bristow. The appointment was one of Grant's best. As a Kentuckian, the former solicitor general added a Western dimension to the cabinet; his reputation for probity was immaculate, and he was committed to a stable currency. "Grant knows his men pretty well," exclaimed Marshall Jewell, America's minister in St. Petersburg, "and I will bet on this being a good appointment."[30] Indeed, no sooner was Bristow installed than he began to refinance the country's debt, replacing Civil War 6 percent bonds with a new 5 percent issue. Bankers snapped up the offering, recognizing that the administration was committed to deflation and hard currency.

Bristow brought a reforming zeal to the Grant administration, reinforced by a heady dose of ambition that was not out of place for a man in his early forties. The new secretary promptly went to work cleaning up the Treasury Department—"It certainly needed it badly," said Grant's private secretary. Between 700 and 800 people were dismissed, civil service rules were established for new employees, and the Treasury became a businesslike branch of government instead of a sinecure for political favorites and old soldiers.[31]

Bristow's next target was the collection of revenue. For well over a decade rumors had circulated that the liquor industry was swindling the government out of a vast amount of federal taxes. By the time Grant was inaugurated, tax evasion had become an art form. Distillers and bottlers routinely bribed low-salaried revenue agents to ignore the mismeasurement of bottled spirits or to supply tax stamps in excess of the amount paid for them. Estimates varied, but it was reported that from 12 to 15 million gallons of whiskey escaped tax annually.[32] The collusion between revenue agents and distillers often extended to the upper echelon of district collectors and, rumor had it, to the head offices of the Internal

Revenue Service and the Treasury Department. The situation in St. Louis was the most notorious. The St. Louis revenue district included Missouri, Kansas, Arkansas, Louisiana, Indian Territory, Texas, and New Mexico. At its head was General John A. McDonald, a rough-and-ready volunteer officer appointed by Grant in 1870. An eyeball comparison of production statistics published by the St. Louis Merchants Exchange with government tax receipts indicated that two thirds of the whiskey manufactured in the Gateway City paid no taxes.

In early 1875 Bristow took aim at the Whiskey Ring. Using a small team of incorruptible investigators, he audited all railway and steamboat bills of lading in St. Louis and other key cities to obtain accurate figures on the shipment of liquor. On May 7 he took the information to Grant, laid out the magnitude of the fraud, and stressed the need for swift prosecution. The president did not hesitate. Bristow was given an immediate go-ahead. Grant told the secretary to move relentlessly against anyone who was culpable.[33] Three days later Bristow struck. Treasury agents swooped down on distilleries and bottling plants in St. Louis, Chicago, Milwaukee, and half a dozen other Midwest cities. Thirty-two installations were seized, and all Internal Revenue offices placed under Treasury custody. Ledgers and files were impounded, books and records sealed, tax receipts put under lock and key. The evidence was overwhelming. Federal grand juries returned more than 350 indictments. In Milwaukee, the trail of corruption led directly to the Wisconsin patronage boss of the Republican party. In Chicago, evidence suggested that almost every Republican officeholder had benefited from illegal distilling. As suspected, the seat of corruption was in St. Louis. Documents seized indicated that during the previous ten months, the ring had evaded $1,650,000 in taxes; over the past two years the figure exceeded $4 million.[34]

The Grant administration's crackdown on the Whiskey Ring was part of a general housecleaning. Two weeks before Bristow's agents struck, Grant asked for and received the resignation of Attorney General George Williams. The president's mistake had been to keep Williams in the cabinet after the Senate balked at his nomination to be chief justice. In 1873 the problem had been Williams's slack administration of the Department of Justice. By 1875 laxity had become corruption. Rumors swirled in Washington that the attorney general had dropped litigation against the New York mercantile house of Pratt & Boyd following a $30,000 payoff to Mrs. Williams.[35] Pratt & Boyd was accused of fraudulent customshouse entries; large sums were involved, and the evidence was clear and convincing. The Senate Judiciary Committee stumbled onto the facts, Conkling informed Grant, and Grant asked Williams to step down.[36]

To succeed Williams, Grant turned to Edwards Pierrepont, former United States attorney for the Southern District of New York. Five years Grant's senior, Pierrepont occupied a high position at the bar and an unassailable reputation for straight dealing. In 1870 he played a prominent role on the Committee of Seventy, which broke the Tweed Ring in New York City, and his prosecutorial skills were well honed. Paired with Bristow, he gave the Grant administration a formidable reformist team to root out corruption and pursue the miscreants in the Whiskey Ring.*

Grant's veto of the inflation bill and the passage of the Resumption Act, combined with the Treasury Department's well-publicized raids against the Whiskey Ring and the appointment of Pierrepont, lifted the president's prestige to new heights. Mainstream Republicans, eager to latch on to the president's coattails, began to lobby the White House for Grant to seek a third term. Throughout the country the press was inundated with stories touting the president's electoral clout and speculating on his availability. The president's staff and even Julia were caught up in the frenzy, the first lady finding that four more years in the executive mansion would be entirely to her liking.[37] Grant said nothing. Indeed, his silence increased speculation that he too might like a third term.[38] On May 27, 1875, the Pennsylvania Republican party, meeting in convention, went on record formally endorsing the president for a third term. The bandwagon had begun to roll.

Two days later Grant struck preemptively. Adjourning to his study after Sunday dinner, he composed a message that removed all doubt as to his intentions. Cabinet members were sent for surreptitiously, and quietly filed into the White House. Julia had no inkling of what was in store and was surprised at their arrival. "Is there any news? Why is it you have all happened to call?" Fish assured the first lady it was merely a coincidence. At that moment Grant entered the reception room and Julia retired, "seeing they were about to enjoy cigars." Grant read his statement to the cabinet but did not ask for comments. He was doing the members the courtesy of informing them beforehand, not asking for their advice. As the cabinet was leaving, Julia returned to the room. "I want to know what is happening. I feel sure there is something and I must know."

"Yes," said Grant, "I will explain as soon as I light my cigar." The pres-

---

* It is a rare political appointment that is without cost. In Pierrepont's case, his crusading zeal was offset by almost total indifference to the plight of the freedmen in the South. When racial violence erupted in Mississippi in 1875, Pierrepont maneuvered to avoid federal intervention, Grant's instructions to the contrary notwithstanding. As a consequence, the Democrats swept back into power in Mississippi in one of the most fraudulent elections in the postwar South. Vernon Lane Warton, *The Negro in Mississippi, 1865–1890* 181–98 (New York: W. W. Norton, 1965); Frank J. Scaturro, *President Grant Reconsidered* 88–91 (Lanham, Md.: University Press of America, 1998).

ident stepped out of the room, drew an envelope from his coat pocket, and gave it to a waiting messenger. Then he returned to Julia. "You know what a to-do the papers have been making about the third term," said Grant. "Well, until now I have never had an opportunity to answer." The president explained to Julia the resolution adopted by the Pennsylvania Republicans. "This gives me the much wished for opportunity of announcing that I do not wish a third term, and I have written a letter to that effect."

"And why did you not read it to me?"

"Oh, I know you too well," laughed Grant. "It would never have gone if I had read it to you."

"Will you bring it to me and read it now?"

"No," the president replied. "It is already posted. That is why I lingered in the hall to light my cigar, so the letter would be beyond recall."[39]

The following day the *New York Times* printed the text of Grant's letter on page one. Addressed to the chairman of the Pennsylvania Republican Party, the president disclaimed any interest in a third term. Grant said he did not feel it was proper for him to comment until the matter had been raised officially, but since the Pennsylvania convention had considered the question, "I deem it not improper that I should speak." Grant said he had never sought the office of president. He enjoyed the position of general of the army and would have been content to have retained it until he retired. "But I was made to believe that the public good called me to make the sacrifice." Grant said he had not sought a second term either, but had been renominated unanimously by the Republican party. "I cannot say I was not pleased at this, and at the overwhelming endorsement of that action at the election following." Once more Grant said he had not sought the office. As for a third term, Grant said he did not want it any more than he had the first. There was no waffling: "I am not, nor have I ever been, a candidate for renomination. I would not accept a nomination if it were tendered, unless it should come under such circumstances as to make it an imperative duty—circumstances not likely to arise."[40]

No sooner had Grant taken himself out of the presidential race than another scandal erupted. This time it was the Department of the Interior and Columbus Delano. There was no evidence that Delano was personally corrupt. But he had turned a blind eye to land frauds brazenly perpetrated by Interior employees and appeared to be knowledgeable of efforts by his son to shake down the Office of the Surveyor General– a bureau that reported to the secretary. It seems young Delano was being given partnerships in surveying contracts awarded by the surveyor general for which he rendered no cartographical service. The *New York Tribune* broke the story, asserting categorically that "corruption has at last been traced within the bosom of the Secretary's family."[41] Other newspapers picked up the charge, Congress began to investigate, and Fish called on Grant to urge Delano's dismissal. Grant refused. "If Delano were now to resign," he told Fish, "it would be retreating under fire and be an admission of the charges."[42]

The president's blind spot was never more evident. Rather than defend the integrity of government service, Grant sided with the individual accused. One writer called it the "chivalry of friendship." Throughout his life Grant's sympathy went out to those he thought the victims of injustice. They might be at fault, but his instinct was to shield them from attack.[43] The president's support of Delano was also a reflection of military discipline. Loyalty from the bottom up required loyalty from the top down. In some respects, Grant's forbearance was commendable. The reputation of his administration might suffer, but he would not sacrifice a subordinate unless the evidence was compelling.

By the summer of 1875 Delano's position had become untenable. The cloud of innuendo made his continuance in office impossible. He submitted his resignation in the middle of August, to take effect October 1. Grant had not asked Delano to step down and the president left it to the secretary to select his own time and method of announcing his departure. To replace Delano, Grant turned to former Michigan senator Zachariah Chandler. It was not one of Grant's strongest appointments, yet it worked better than expected. Chandler was an old friend from the president's time with the 4th Infantry in Detroit. He had been defeated for reelection in 1874 and, as one of the richest men who had served in the Senate, he was above temptation. He was also well versed in the ways of Washington politics. More important, Grant felt comfortable with Chandler. He was loyal to the president, and as one scholar observed, he could carry out reforms without moral cant and without bidding for the applause of the audience.[44]

That was Grant's style. The president believed deeply in reform, but he was not sanctimonious about it. "The most troublesome men in public life," he once said, "are those over-righteous people who see no motives in other people's actions but evil motives, who believe all public life is corrupt, and nothing is well done unless they do it themselves. They are narrow-headed men, their two eyes so close together that they can look out of the same gimlet hole without winking."[45]

Civil service reform is a case in point. Grant was the first president to recommend a professional civil service, pressed the initial legislation through Congress, and appointed the first Civil Service Commission. Yet unlike many reformers, he did not confuse patronage with corruption. "The impression is given by some advocates of civil service reform that most executive appointments are made out of the penitentiary," he said jokingly. "The fact is the president very rarely appoints, he merely registers the appointments of members of Congress. In a country as vast as ours the advice of congressmen as to persons to be appointed is useful, and generally in the best interests of the country."[46]

Grant was a pragmatist. His military success reflected his willingness to make do with what he had. So too in politics. Patronage was a fixture on the Washington scene. Rather than reject it, Grant sought to minimize its pernicious effects. "Civil service reform rests entirely with Congress," he often said. "If members will give up claiming patronage, that will be a step gained. But there is an immense amount of human nature in the members of Congress, and it is human nature to seek power and use it to help friends. You cannot call it corruption—it is a condition of our representative form of government."[47]

The movement for civil service reform was an outgrowth of the enormous expansion of the national government during the Civil War and reflected two distinct objectives: to eliminate the inefficiencies in a nonprofessional bureaucracy, and to check the power of Andrew Johnson. Reformers stressed the former, partisan Republicans rallied around the latter. Legislation introduced in 1866 by Representative Thomas A. Jenckes of Rhode Island (the "Father of Civil Service Reform") aimed at both. Competitive examinations would be required for appointment and promotion, and the tenure of employees would be protected. This would not only recognize merit, it would also limit Johnson's power to name and remove federal officeholders.[48] But the Jenckes bill failed passage. As the *New York Times* noted, it was "too good and too much in advance of our civilization to pass as yet."[49]

Grant's election in 1868 changed the calculus. Reformers looked to the president to ram through civil service reform, while machine-minded Republicans now shied away. George William Curtis, reformist editor of *Harper's Weekly,* predicted imminent success. "At last, thank God, we have got a President whom trading politicians did not elect, and who is no more afraid of them than he was of rebels." Julius Bing, a prolific writer on behalf of civil service reform, thought the prospects "brighter now than at any previous time." Newspapers throughout the country joined the chorus, as did leaders of the business community. The Boston Board of Trade and the New York Union League Club adopted unanimous resolutions favoring competitive examinations in the civil service.[50]

In contrast, Republican leaders in Congress had second thoughts. Competitive examinations under Andrew Johnson were one thing, but with their own man at the patronage spigot in the White House, enthusiasm for professionalism waned. Black Jack Logan, a stalwart supporter of civil service reform under Johnson, denounced any alteration of the spoils system as undemocratic, anti-republican, and aristocratic. "He who does not unite with the administration," said Logan, "should not be trusted with its employment."[51]

Grant came down on the side of the reformers. Patronage, he said, was the bane of his existence.[52] In his second annual message to Congress he denounced the spoils system as "an abuse of long standing" that he said should be remedied as soon as possible. To the consternation of party regulars, Grant recommended a merit system for federal employees that would not only guarantee tenure but would also govern appointments and promotions. "The present system does not secure the best men, and often not even fit men, for public place," said the president.[53]

Prodded by Grant, Congress enacted legislation in March 1871 establishing a commission to devise rules and regulations for reforming the civil service. The resolution was attached as a rider to the civil appropriations bill, and the vote in the Senate was close. A motion to table offered by Matthew H. Carpenter of Wisconsin lost by one vote (25–26).[54] Grant appointed *Harper's* George William Curtis to chair the commission, with Joseph Medill of the *Chicago Tribune* as vice chairman, thus guaranteeing the support of two of the nation's most influential journals. The commission reported the following year. Appointments and promotions were to be by examination, and each department would have its own board of examiners. Most shattering to party officials, no political assessments were to be levied on federal jobholders. Grant informed Congress the rules would go into effect on January 1, 1872, and he asked for legislation making the rules binding on his successors.[55] Grant told Joseph Medill that a professional civil service was long overdue. "The great defect in past custom is that executive patronage had come to be regarded as the property of the party in power. The choice of Federal officers has come to be limited to those seeking office. A true reform will let the office seek the man."[56]

Congress did not see it that way. Appropriations for the Civil Service Commission were allowed to lapse, and the nation's legislators proved unwilling to pass the laws necessary to put the commission on a permanent footing. Although Grant deplored Congress's stance, he accepted it. In his annual message in 1874 he commended the commission for its efforts and said he was mortified that its work was to be discarded. "But it is impossible to carry this system to a successful conclusion without legislation to support it. If Congress adjourns without positive action on the subject of civil service reform I will regard it as a disapproval of the system and will abandon it."[57] When Congress failed to act, Grant reluctantly dissolved the commission. The matter remained dormant until 1883 when reform pressure, combined with reaction to the assassination of President James A. Garfield, forced passage of the Pendleton Act, incorporating the rules that had been drafted by Grant's Civil Service Commission.[58]

The epitaph for civil service reform in the Grant administration was rendered by George Curtis:

> General Grant, elected by a spontaneous patriotic impulse, and new to politics and politicians, saw the reason and necessity for reform. . . . Congress, good-naturedly tolerating what it considered his whim of inexperience, granted money to try the experiment. The adverse pressure was tremendous. [Grant] was driven by unknown and incalculable currents. He was enveloped in whirlwinds of sophistry, scorn, and incredulity. . . . It was indeed a surrender, but it was the surrender of a champion who had honestly mistaken both the nature and strength of the adversary and his own power of endurance.[59]

While civil service reform was being tested, the Grant administration's pursuit of the Whiskey Ring continued full tilt. Bristow found tentacles of the conspiracy penetrating deep into his own department, the Internal Revenue Service, and the White House. William Avery, chief clerk of the Treasury, was indicted and convicted, as were General John McDonald and John A. Joyce, collector and deputy collector of taxes in St. Louis. Most embarrassing, both to the Republican party and Grant himself, the evidence amassed by Bristow suggested that Brevet Brigadier General Orville Babcock, principal secretary to the president, was part of the ring.

Grant was initially alerted to Babcock's possible complicity in July 1875 when he received a letter from St. Louis banker W. D. W. Barnard, a distant relative of Julia's. Barnard warned Grant that federal prosecutors in St. Louis were hoping to embarrass the administration and that Babcock had become a target. Grant was shocked that his aide might be involved. He immediately passed the letter to Bristow with the following endorsement: "I forward this for information and to the end that if it throws any light upon new parties to summon as witnesses they may be brought out. *Let no guilty man escape if it can be avoided.* Be especially vigilant—or instruct those engaged in the prosecution of fraud to be—against all who insinuate that they have high influence to protect—or to protect them. No personal consideration should stand in the way of performing a public duty."[60] Shortly thereafter Grant told Attorney General Pierrepont that "if Babcock is guilty, there is no man who wants him so proven guilty as I do, for it is the greatest piece of traitorism to me that a man could possibly practice."[61]

As it turned out, the evidence against Babcock was circumstantial. The prosecution's case rested on Babcock's friendship with McDonald, his occasional visits to St. Louis, and two cryptic telegrams the president's secretary sent to the general. Bristow believed the messages were code to inform the St. Louis ring of the status of the Treasury crackdown. The first, dated December 10, 1874, stated—"I have succeeded. They will not go. I will write you." It was signed "Sylph." The second, sent on February 3, 1875, read: "We have official information that the enemy weakens. Push things. Sylph."[62]

Babcock maintained the messages were for Eads and described the status of the Corps of Engineers' efforts to scuttle the bridge in St. Louis. At the time, Grant trusted General McDonald fully, and it is quite possible the president was using him to funnel information to Eads. When Grant heard Babcock's explanation, he was satisfied the telegrams were harmless.[63]

A second difficulty for the prosecution was Babcock's lifestyle. Unlike former Attorney General Williams, the president's secretary lived modestly within his income. He was not a free-spender, his bank account showed no questionable deposits, and his wife was known for her frugality. His one hobby was raising fine dahlias, which he would share with his neighbors, including the Frederick Douglasses.[64]

By late autumn 1875, Grant had become convinced that Babcock was the victim of a witch hunt. The evidence against him was flimsy, but Bristow would not let go. When Senator John Logan, a powerful voice in GOP councils (and whose reputation for probity was as pure as that of any politician of that era) reported he was the target of a Treasury investigation in Illinois,[65] Grant concluded Bristow was pursuing a personal agenda. By attempting to discredit Babcock and Logan, Bristow was striking at Grant himself, a move that would appeal to party dissidents and perhaps pave the way for the secretary of the treasury to capture the Republican nomination for president.[66]

On December 2, 1875, Babcock took the initiative and requested a military court of inquiry to clear his name. Grant presented the request to his cabinet, Secretary of War Belknap voiced approval, and the cabinet agreed. The following day Grant named Sheridan, Winfield Scott Hancock, and Major General Alfred H. Terry to investigate the accusations. Reformist historians have characterized Grant's appointment of the board as an attempt to whitewash Babcock.[67] Given the lack of hard evidence against the president's secretary, that seems a rush to judgment. Equally serious, it demeans the integrity of the general officers involved. Sheridan has been justly accused of many things, yet his worst enemies never suggested he was corrupt. Hancock, a committed Democrat who was estranged from Grant, was as unlikely to kowtow to the president as any officer on active duty, and General Terry, with thirty years' service, was widely regarded as a model of professional virtue. The issue of Babcock's complicity in the Whiskey Ring never came to judgment. Prosecutors in St. Louis declined to surrender their files, and the board adjourned without rendering a verdict. The following week, a federal grand jury in St. Louis, working closely with Treasury prosecutors, indicted Babcock "for conspiring to defraud the revenue."

Babcock's case went to trial in February 1876. Grant, who was convinced of his secretary's innocence, asked to testify. Dissuaded by the cabinet from appearing in person, the president offered to provide a deposition. On February 12, 1876, Grant's testimony was taken at the White House in a five-hour session presided over by Chief Justice Waite. In the presence of Attorney General Pierrepont and Secretary Bristow, Grant responded to questions put to him by attorneys for Babcock and the prosecution. He swore he had never seen anything in Babcock's conduct that would link him with the Whiskey Ring; that Babcock consistently displayed fidelity to the public interest, and that he performed his duties as principal secretary to the president "to my entire satisfaction." When asked by the prosecution about illicit fund-raising, the president said, "I never had any information. from Babcock or anyone else indicating in any manner, directly or indirectly, that any funds for political purposes were being raised by any improper methods." Grant swore Babcock never spoke to him about the charges against the Whiskey Ring and had not sought to influence him in any way. He described in detail his support for the Treasury investigation and said that if Babcock had been guilty of misconduct he would have known it.[68]

Grant's testimony silenced all but the most rancorous critics of the administration. The unprecedented spectacle of the president of the United States coming forward voluntarily to defend his secretary, combined with Grant's unblemished reputation for personal honesty, had an enormous impact. Hamilton Fish, one of the most honest men in public life, once said, "I do not think it would have been possible for Grant to have told a lie, even if he had composed it and written it down."[69]* The prosecution continued to present what little evidence it had against Babcock, but it was unconvincing and the general was speedily acquitted.

The verdict in St. Louis was widely applauded. The *New York Tribune,* which up to that moment had been vitriolic in its criticism of the Grant administration, led the press in expressing its approval. "The indictment has been submitted to the severest legal tests. No one can complain that the court was biased in General Babcock's favor, or that the prosecution was

---

* Former Attorney General Rockwood Hoar, who was not an altogether sympathetic admirer of Grant's second term, was asked by friends whether he thought any money might have stuck to the president's fingers. "I would as soon think St. Paul had got some of the thirty pieces of silver," replied Hoar. James Ford Rhodes, 7 *History of the United States* 188 (New York: Macmillan, 1906).

inefficient, or that the jury was prepossessed." The Whiskey Ring scandal, said the *Tribune,* "had been met at the entrance of the White House and turned back."[70] A modern-day audience, schooled in due process and fearful of guilt by association, might also approve the refusal of the St. Louis jury to convict a high administration official in the absence of adequate proof.

After his acquittal Babcock returned to Washington, but not to the White House. Grant continued to believe his secretary was innocent, but he no longer had confidence in his discretion. The job of confidential secretary to the president was assumed by Grant's sons, Fred and Ulysses, Jr., (known as Buck), and Babcock, after a brief stint as superintendent of public works, was appointed inspector of lighthouses—a job that would take him away from Washington politics. Babcock later drowned in the performance of duty at Mosquito Inlet, Florida, on July 14, 1884.

Congressional Democrats, looking for a campaign issue, called Bristow to testify before a select House committee investigating the whiskey frauds. Bristow declined, citing executive privilege, yet by so doing he left the impression the administration had something to hide. Grant moved immediately to repair the damage. Administration records were thrown open and Bristow was instructed to testify: "I beg to relieve you from all obligation of secrecy on this subject, and desire not only that you may answer all questions relating to it, but that all members of my Cabinet and ex-members of my Cabinet may also be called to testify in regard to the same matter."[71] By acting quickly and embracing full disclosure, Grant kept the focus of the investigation on the Whiskey Ring conspirators, not the White House or his former secretary.

The Babcock case was a red herring. Not so the charges against Secretary of War William Belknap. No sooner had the Babcock affair been put to rest than House investigators uncovered evidence of gross malfeasance by Rawlins's successor at the War Department. The Belknaps were socially ambitious and the women of the family were extravagant. The secretary was not independently wealthy, and his Washington salary was $8,000 a year. Feeling the pinch, the secretary's wife, Carrie Belknap, discovered that military trading posts were let through private contracts awarded by her husband's office. These concessions provided generous rewards to those who held them. In the summer of 1870 Carrie managed to secure the trading post at Fort Sill for a New York friend, Caleb P. Marsh, and share in the profits. The Fort Sill operation, the principal supply point for the Southern Cheyenne, Comanches, and Kiowas, was one of the most lucrative, and the incumbent contract holder, John S. Evans, was reluctant to surrender it. Using his leverage with Mrs. Belknap, Marsh extorted an arrangement with Evans whereby Evans would retain the Fort Sill franchise in return for a fee of $3,000 paid quarterly to Marsh. Marsh would then pass half the proceeds to Carrie Belknap.

As it turned out, Mrs. Belknap died within the year and the money was then paid directly to the secretary. When Belknap married his sister-in-law in December 1873, the money from Marsh was still coming although reduced by half due to the declining profitability of the Fort Sill operation. By 1876, Belknap had pocketed $20,000 from the arrangement.[72] The scandal broke on March 2, one week after Babcock's acquittal. In the early morning hours, Congressman Lyman K. Bass of Buffalo informed Treasury Secretary Bristow that the House committee on which he served had irrefutable evidence of Belknap's guilt and would report to the House at noon, recommending impeachment. Bristow was stunned. The Belknaps and the Bristows were close friends, attended the same Bible class, and entertained each other regularly. Bristow hurried to see Fish, caught the secretary of state still in bed, and placed the matter before him. Like Bristow, Fish was shocked. He told his friend from Kentucky to go to the White House immediately and warn Grant.[73] Bristow did as he was advised, and met with Grant just as he finished breakfast. The president was due at Henry Ulke's studio to sit for his portrait, and was in a hurry to leave. Bristow quickly explained the charges against Belknap and urged Grant to meet Congressman Bass immediately to learn the full particulars. Grant dashed off a note to Bass inviting him to the White House at noon.[74] Bristow took his leave and Grant departed for his appointment.

As the president hurried out to the front piazza, a steward informed him that Belknap and Interior Secretary Zachariah Chandler were in the Red Drawing Room and begged to see him. "I cannot now," said Grant, "but I will see them when I return."

"Oh, Mr. President, do see him before you go," said the steward. "He is in some trouble and looks very ill."

Grant went to the Red Room and found a pale and distraught Belknap and a somewhat more composed Chandler. As soon as the president entered, Belknap, on the verge of tears, blurted out that he had come to resign. He gave Grant a freshly written statement. "Accept it at once, Mr. President. For God's sake, do not hesitate."[75]

"Certainly," said Grant, "if you wish it." The president sent for his son Buck and instructed him to write a letter accepting Belknap's resignation. Grant read it over, decided it was too curt, and wrote his own. "Your tender of resignation as Secretary of War, with the request to have it accepted immediately, is received and the same is hereby accepted with great regret."[76] Still distressed, but visibly relieved, Belknap told the president how grateful he was, and quickly left the room. Grant once more made his way to the front door but was intercepted again, this time by Senators Lot Morrill and Oliver Morton, who had come to warn him against accepting Belknap's resignation. It was too late.[77] That afternoon the House of Representatives voted unanimously to impeach Belknap. Though the secretary had already resigned, Senate Democrats, sensing an important campaign issue, chose to proceed with an impeachment trial. Throughout the spring and early summer the details of Belknap's malfeasance filled the press. Seats in the Senate gallery were at a premium as House managers unfolded the tawdry case against the former secretary of war. On August 1, the Senate voted to acquit. Few thought Belknap was innocent, but those voting against conviction established the fact that the Senate lacked the jurisdiction over an individual who was no longer in office. As Roscoe Conkling noted, "In this country, by the Constitution, private citizens are not impeachable."[78]*

Grant exhibited an unruffled calm throughout. After learning the details of the case against Belknap, he walked leisurely to Henry Ulke's studio and sat before the artist for an hour and ten minutes. Congressman James Garfield asked the president if the painter found anything unusual in his expression. "I think not," Grant replied. Garfield then asked if he was himself conscious of an unusual agitation. "Oh no," said Grant, clearly surprised at the question. Garfield noted the awesome quality of composure that distinguished Grant. "I told him I did not believe there was another man on the continent who could have said the same under such circumstances." Later, Garfield wrote candidly in his diary: "His imperturbability is amazing. I am in doubt whether to call it greatness or stupidity."[79]

Grant was more outspoken with the cabinet. Sadly he remarked on his long association with Belknap in the army, the affection he and Julia had for the family, and how he had served with Belknap's father in Mexico, "one of the finest officers of the old army."[80] Nevertheless, the president's duty was to ensure that the laws were faithfully enforced. Grant instructed Attorney General Pierrepont to launch an immediate investigation to determine whether criminal charges could be brought against Belknap. After reviewing the evidence, Pierrepont concluded it was insufficient to sustain an indictment. The former secretary spent the remainder of his life in Washington eking out a living as a lawyer with a past. For Belknap's replacement, Grant turned to Judge Alphonso Taft of Cincinnati, an appointment widely applauded for its rectitude.[81]

* According to Article I, Section 3, Clause 7 of the Constitution: "Judgment in Cases of Impeachment shall not extend further than removal from Office, and disqualification to hold any Office of honor, Trust or Profit under the United States; but the Party convicted shall nevertheless be liable and subject to Indictment, Trial, Judgment and Punishment, according to Law."

The Republican convention met in Cincinnati on June 14, 1876. Former House Speaker James G. Blaine was the front-runner, followed by Senators Conkling and Morton, with Elihu Washburne on the outside. All four were Grant men, and each hoped for the president's endorsement. Of the favorite sons, Governor Rutherford B. Hayes of Ohio stood out as a sound-money man who had led the fight against inflation in his state, while Treasury Secretary Bristow was the candidate of the reformers. Grant stood on the sidelines and said nothing. He thought the convention would deadlock and turn to a dark horse. His candidate was Fish. Grant wrote a sealed letter to the convention endorsing Fish, to be used if needed, but the time never came.[82]

On the first ballot, Blaine led with 285 votes, Morton had 124, Bristow 113, Conkling 99, Hayes 61, and the remainder scattered among favorite sons. Blaine was 94 votes short of the 379 required to nominate. On the next three ballots there was little change. Michigan swung to Hayes on the fifth ballot as Morton's strength began to erode. On the sixth ballot Blaine was still in the lead with 308 votes, with Hayes rising to 113. At that point the convention hunkered down to stop Blaine. Hayes, who had been away from Washington for several years, emerged as the common denominator. Kentucky led the shift. When the state was called on the seventh ballot, John Marshall Harlan, Bristow's manager and former law partner, released the secretary's delegates to Hayes. The stampede followed.[83] The final count showed Hayes with 384 to Blaine's 351. The nomination was made unanimous, and Congressman William A. Wheeler of New York was chosen to run for vice president.*

As soon as the balloting was over, Grant wired his congratulations to Hayes, stating he felt "the greatest assurance that you will occupy my present position from the fourth of March next."[84] The next day Grant accepted Bristow's resignation at Treasury. Legend has it the secretary arrived at the White House just as Grant was preparing to enter his carriage for a drive. Bristow handed him an envelope, Grant put it in his pocket and drove off without comment.[85] On June 19 Grant replied. "Permit me to hope that our personal relations may continue as heretofore, and that you may find that peace in private life denied to anyone occupying your pres-

---

* John Marshall Harlan was rewarded by Hayes in October 1877 when he was appointed to succeed David Davis on the Supreme Court. Davis, for his part, had been Lincoln's campaign manager in 1860 and was appointed to the Court in 1862. John Marshall Harlan served on the bench for thirty-four years, a distinguished career made especially notable by his blistering dissents in the *Civil Rights Cases,* 109 U.S. 3 (1883); *Plessy v. Ferguson,* 163 U.S. 537 (1896); *Pollack v. Farmers' Loan and Trust,* 157 U.S. 429 (1895); and *Lochner v. New York,* 198 U.S. 45 (1905). In all four instances, the position Harlan took has become the law of the land.

THE GILDED AGE 597

ent official position."[86] To succeed Bristow, Grant chose Senator Lot M. Morrill of Maine. A longtime advocate of sound money, Morrill, if not a reformer, was both efficient and honest. His appointment to the cabinet also freed a Maine Senate seat for Blaine.

The Democrats met in St. Louis on June 27 and nominated Samuel J. Tilden on the second ballot. The sixty-year-old governor of New York had played a prominent role in the overthrow of the Tweed Ring and came into the lists with a reputation as a reformer. The Democratic platform predictably denounced Grant, targeted corruption, promised an end to Reconstruction, and declared for easy money and repeal of the Resumption Act. Campaign rhetoric aside, Hayes and Tilden were cautious, middle-of-the-road candidates. "There is very little to choose between them," wrote James Russell Lowell.[87] Grant's sympathy was for Hayes, but he remained above the battle. Zachariah Chandler, secretary of the interior, ably managed Hayes's campaign and most cabinet members took to the stump to support the ticket. Fish was the exception. Like Grant, the secretary of state stayed in Washington quietly tending his portfolio.[88]

The campaign was relatively free of violence, except for South Carolina, where a minor Fourth of July fracas in the village of Hamburg escalated into a racial massacre leaving five black men dead and scores wounded. Grant characterized the assault as "cruel, bloodthirsty, wanton, unprovoked, and uncalled for." When Governor Daniel H. Chamberlain inquired whether the president would provide troops if additional disorders broke out, Grant told him to stand firm. "I will give every aid for which I can find law or constitutional argument."[89]

The outrages continued. As election day approached, white South Carolinians formed rifle clubs and paraded ostentatiously, intimidating blacks and making no secret of their intention to "redeem" the Palmetto State. Chamberlain ordered the clubs to disband and called for federal troops to prevent violence at the polls. On October 17 Grant responded forcefully. He issued a presidential proclamation declaring a state of insurrection in South Carolina and ordering "all persons engaged in unlawful and insurrectionary proceedings to disperse and retire peacefully." Sherman was instructed to send all available forces in the Atlantic Division to General Thomas H. Ruger at Columbia.[90] Grant's timely show of force kept the peace. South Carolinians received the troops good-humoredly; Ruger promised they would maintain order with an even hand; and their presence calmed both sides. The press approved Grant's action, almost without exception. William Cullen Bryant, whose *Evening Post* had long opposed military action in the South, supported the president's proclamation, this time convinced there was enough evidence of violence to render it necessary.[91]

Election day on November 7 passed quietly.* Early returns indicated Tilden as good as elected. With 185 electoral votes required, the Democratic candidate was certain of 184. Hayes had 166, with three Southern states, Florida, Louisiana, and South Carolina, in dispute. To win, Hayes needed all three. "Gentlemen, it looks to me as if Mr. Tilden is elected," said Grant that evening.[92] His immediate concern was to preserve order and ensure a fair count. Before retiring for the night he ordered Ruger to proceed immediately to Florida with whatever troops were at his disposal. The next morning Grant wired Sherman to take precautions. "Instruct General Augur in Louisiana and General Ruger in Florida to be vigilant with the force at their command to preserve peace and good order, and to see that the proper and legal boards of canvassers are unmolested in the performance of their duties. Should there be any grounds of suspicion of a fraudulent count on either side it should be reported and denounced at once. No man worthy of the office of President should be willing to hold it if counted in or placed there by fraud. Either party can afford to be disappointed by the result. The country cannot afford to have the result tainted by the suspicion of illegal or false returns."[93]

On the face of the returns, Tilden had carried Florida and Louisiana, while Hayes clung to a narrow lead in South Carolina. But accusations of fraud rendered the results questionable. In all three states the existing Republican administrations controlled the returning boards responsible for certifying the vote. Politically, it was a saw-off. The Democrats used threats and violence to keep African-Americans from the polls; the Republicans used their control of the election machinery to massage the count. In Florida, the Board of State Canvassers converted a Tilden majority of eighty-six into a Hayes majority of 922. In South Carolina, the board ratified Hayes's victory and threw out enough Democratic votes to reelect Chamberlain as governor and return a Republican legislature.[94] The real contest was in Louisiana. Final returns showed Tilden ahead by 6,400 votes. Since the New York governor needed only one more electoral vote and Louisiana had eight, it looked as though victory was assured.[95] But the Louisiana returning board, which had the final word, was the same board that had fabricated results in 1874 and had already been condemned by two congressional committees.

Grant discussed the matter at a cabinet meeting on November 14. Chandler, Taft, and James D. Cameron, who had succeeded Taft at the War

---

* Professor James M. McPherson estimates that despite the lack of violence at the polls, intimidation and assaults elsewhere kept an estimated 250,000 Republicans from voting in the Southern states in 1876. *Ordeal by Fire* 588, 2nd ed. (New York: McGraw-Hill, 1992).

Department when the judge shifted to Justice,* urged immediate military intervention in Louisiana to secure a GOP victory. Fish urged caution and objectivity, and Grant agreed.[96] Instead of sending troops, the president invited a blue-ribbon panel of Republicans, including Senator John Sherman and Representative James A. Garfield, to go to New Orleans as "reliable witnesses" to ensure a fair count.[97] The Democrats named an equal number of prominent scrutineers to watch the Louisiana canvassing board, and there was some hope that an honest tabulation might be possible.

Whether the final count was honest or not has long been debated. Republican observers focused on the outrages against African-Americans in delta parishes; Democrats reported all was quiet.[98] Turnout figures support the Republicans. In one parish, 1,688 voted Republican in 1874. In 1876, only one Republican vote was tallied.[99] Writing from the besieged parish, Senator Sherman told Hayes, "It seems more like the history of hell than of civilized and Christian communities. . . . That you would have received at a fair election a large majority in Louisiana, no honest man can question."[100]

The Louisiana canvassing board reported on December 6. It rejected 13,250 Democratic votes and 2,042 Republican. What had been a 6,400 majority for Tilden was certified as a 4,807-vote victory for Hayes. The Ohio governor had taken all three disputed states, finishing with 185 electoral votes to Tilden's 184. Not since John Quincy Adams's come-from-behind win against Andrew Jackson in 1824 had an upset been so stunning.†

But the contest was not over. When the electors met in their respective state capitals on the first Wednesday in December to cast their ballots, Democratic electors in the three disputed states convened separately and recorded their votes for Tilden. The nation was thus confronted with two sets of returns from Florida, Louisiana, and South Carolina, with nineteen electoral votes hanging in the balance.

Which slate of electors was to be counted? Had both branches of Congress been Republican, the contest would have been over. But the

---

* In early 1876 Grant recalled General Robert C. Schenck from his post as minister to Great Britain following disclosure of Schenck's efforts to manipulate Utah mining stock. The president first nominated Richard Henry Dana, Jr. (*Two Years Before the Mast*), to the post, but the Senate refused confirmation. Grant then turned to Attorney General Edwards Pierrepont. That left a vacancy at Justice. Taft thereupon was named attorney general, and Cameron, the son of Senator Simon Cameron of Pennsylvania, was appointed secretary of war. Pierrepont, Taft, and Cameron were confirmed unanimously by the Senate.

† In 1824 Jackson led decisively in both popular vote and in the electoral college, but (in a four-man race) lacked the majority necessary to elect. The election was thrown into the House of Representatives. With twenty-four states in the Union, the votes of thirteen were needed to win. Jackson had the solid support of eleven and needed but two. Adams had seven and needed all six that were undecided. When the dust settled and the final tally was taken, Adams won 13–11.

Senate, with a Republican majority, was offset by a Democratic House of Representatives. The Constitution was of little help. It provided that the president of the Senate (normally the vice president of the United States) should open the ballots before a joint session of Congress.* But who was to determine which set of ballots to open? Republicans maintained it was up to the vice president to make the call; Democrats insisted the decision rested with Congress. And if the two Houses could not agree, no one would be elected and the decision would be thrown into the House of Representatives, where Tilden would prevail.[101]

While Congress grappled with the problem, political passion rose to the danger level. Rumors circulated that Democratic rifle clubs planned to march on Washington and inaugurate Tilden by force if necessary. Talk of civil war abounded. Colonel John Mosby, the Confederate cavalry leader, who like Longstreet supported Grant, reported from Virginia that "the language of the Democrats is more desperate and more threatening than that of Southerners on the election of Lincoln in 1860." The president's life was in danger, said Mosby.[102] Grant remained calm. His stance was resolutely nonpartisan. The president's task, as he saw it, was to guide the nation through the crisis, not to intervene on behalf of the Republicans. When the governor of South Carolina once again requested troops, this time to oust Democrats from the legislature, Grant refused. "Federal troops are in Columbia to maintain order, not to act on the orders of [Governor] Chamberlain," he told his cabinet. "The Executive of South Carolina occupies the same position in Columbia that the Executive does in Washington, and the organization of the legislature is a question for the State to settle, not the national government."[103] So too in Louisiana. Despite pressure from congressional Republicans to deploy troops to assist party officials in New Orleans, Grant steered a neutral course. The final outcome would be determined in the Bayou State, and the president, rejecting cabinet advice, chose to keep hands off.† Grant's unflinching resolve steadied the nation. "He comes up to the mark so grandly on great occasions," wrote Rockwood Hoar, "that I wish he were more careful of appearances in smaller matters."[104]

---

* The Twelfth Amendment, adopted after the Jefferson-Burr stalemate in 1801, said merely that "The President of the Senate shall, in the presence of the Senate and House of Representatives, open all of the certificates and the votes should then be counted."

† "I have abstained from bringing the [Louisiana] question up for more Cabinet discussion," Grant told Fish in confidence. "I believe there would be about six members against me and one for me."

Three times during November and December, Grant reined in Secretary of War Cameron, who wanted to send troops to the South. "When could the government intervene?" asked Cameron. "Not until there is actual resistance or conflict," said Grant. Fish Diary, in Allan Nevins, 2 *Hamilton Fish: The Inner History of the Grant Administration* 851–55, 2nd ed. (New York: Frederick Ungar, 1957).

In Washington, discussion between the parties as to how to handle the vote count had reached a stalemate. With a constitutional crisis imminent, Grant stepped in to break the deadlock. Four days after the electors voted, he invited New York Congressman Abram S. Hewitt, national chairman of the Tilden campaign, to the White House to review the situation. The two men were old friends. Hewitt, a noted engineer and manufacturer, had introduced the first open-hearth furnace to the United States in 1862 and produced the first American-made steel in 1870. He had managed the Cooper Union for the Advancement of Science and Art for many years, an institution Grant fervently supported.

The president greeted Hewitt cordially. Would he like a cigar? After coffee was served, Grant got to the point. First, he assured the Democratic chairman he would not use troops to install Hayes as president. As Grant saw it, Florida and South Carolina had gone for Hayes, but Louisiana was rightfully Tilden's. That meant the next president would be a Democrat.[105] The problem was to establish a mechanism for counting the electoral vote: something both parties and the public would accept as legitimate. Grant suggested Congress strike a joint committee, equally balanced between Democrats and Republicans, to devise a procedure. Hewitt was greatly relieved by Grant's assurances and agreed almost instantly. On December 14 the House appointed seven members to meet with a similar number from the Senate to draft a law for the emergency.[106] After sorting through dozens of proposals, the committee fixed on a plan for a special electoral commission to arbitrate the disputed returns. In constitutional terms the commission would be advisory to Congress, but unless *both* Houses agreed to overrule a decision, the findings of the commission would be binding. According to the agreement, the commission would contain fifteen members: five from the House (three Democrats and two Republicans), five from the Senate (party ratio reversed), and five justices from the Supreme Court. Four of the justices, two Democrats and two Republicans,* were named in the bill, and those four justices were to choose a fifth. It was assumed that he would be David Davis, Lincoln's old campaign manager, who had become an anti-Grant Liberal Republican in 1872 and was now an Independent.

Adoption of the joint committee report was touch and go. Democrats believed Davis would side with Tilden and they supported the measure almost down the line. For the same reason most Republicans were

---

* The justices named were Nathan Clifford and Stephen J. Field (Democrats); Samuel F. Miller and William Strong (Republicans). The House members of the commission were Josiah Abbot (D., Mass.); James Garfield (R., Ohio); George Frisbie Hoar (R., Mass.); Eppa Hunton (D., Va.); Henry B. Payne (D., Ohio). From the Senate, Thomas Bayard (D., Del.); George Edmunds (R., Vt.); Frederick Frelinghuysen (R., N.J.); Oliver P. Morton (R., Ind.); and Allen G. Thurman (D., Ohio).

opposed. Again Grant waded in to secure the bill's passage. Working through Speaker Samuel Jackson Randall, an old war Democrat who had fought with Meade at Gettysburg, the president was confident the House of Representatives would go along. The Republican-controlled Senate was doubtful. This time Grant relied on Conkling. "If you wish the Commission carried, I can do it," said New York's senior senator. "I wish it done," said Grant, ending the conversation.[107]

Conkling was true to his word. On January 23 and 24 he held the Senate spellbound as he demolished Republican arguments against the commission. Conkling, to the dismay of old friends like Morton and John Sherman, was going down the line for the president. As his biographer records, "It was probably Roscoe Conkling's finest moment."[108] When the votes were tallied the following day, the commission passed handily. In the Senate, the vote was 47–17, slightly more than half of the Republicans voting in favor. In the House, where the Democratic majority ensured approval, the vote was 191–86, with two thirds of the Republicans voting against.[109] Grant signed the measure into law January 29, 1877. To emphasize his approval, the president sent a special message to Congress congratulating the lawmakers for "providing in advance a constitutional, orderly, and just method of executing the Constitution in this most interesting and critical of its provisions."[110]

Suddenly all bets were off. No sooner had Grant signed the measure than the Illinois legislature, deadlocked over a second senatorial term for John Logan, turned to Justice David Davis as a compromise. To everyone's surprise Davis accepted. He stepped down from the Supreme Court to take the Senate seat and declined to serve on the commission. The remaining members of the Court were all Republican, and from them the four justices agreed on Joseph Bradley, the most independent of their colleagues, who became the swing vote.

The electoral count, alphabetical by states, commenced on February 1. Under the statute that had been adopted, only cases in which there was more than one set of returns would go before the commission. The first was Florida. Meeting in the Supreme Court chamber in the Capitol, the commission heard arguments for almost a week. It then went into secret session. On February 9 the decision was announced: the official returns signed by Florida's Republican governor would be accepted. The Hayes electors would be counted. The commission divided 7–7 along party lines with Justice Bradley casting the deciding vote.* The Florida decision set

---

* Justice Bradley applied a formula the Supreme Court had followed at least since *Fletcher v. Peck*, 6 Cranch 87 (1810), when Chief Justice John Marshall declined to look behind an act of the Georgia legislature if it was facially correct. Said Bradley, "The two Houses of Congress, in proceeding with the count, are bound to recognize the determination of the State Board

the course. On February 16 the commission ruled in favor of the certified Hayes slate in Louisiana, and on February 28 it did the same with South Carolina. Rutherford B. Hayes would become the nineteenth president of the United Sates. He had defeated Tilden in the electoral college 185–184.

Throughout February Grant's calm visage in the White House reassured the nation. His reputation for firmness, his evenhandedness during the crisis, his personal honesty and respect for the law, plus his known determination to maintain the peace, contributed to a lessening of tension. Grant said later he was prepared for any contingency. "Any outbreak would have been suddenly and summarily stopped. If Tilden was declared elected, I intended to hand him over the reins, and see him peacefully installed. I should have treated him as cordially as I did Hayes, for the question of the Presidency was neither personal nor political, but national. I tried to act with the utmost impartiality between the two. I would not have raised my finger to have put Hayes in, if in so doing I did Tilden the slightest injustice. All I wanted was for the legal powers to declare a President, to keep the machine running, to allay the passions of the canvass, and allow the country peace." [111]

The Democrats accepted the outcome with remarkable good grace. "We have just emerged from one civil war," said Governor Tilden, "and it will not do to engage in another." [112] Several dozen House Democrats, mostly from the North and West, launched an anemic filibuster to delay the final count until after March 4, but Southerners disavowed the scheme and Speaker Randall broke the resistance in the early morning hours of March 2. The Southerners' acceptance of Hayes can be easily explained. They, more than any, had suffered from the war and did not wish to see the nation unravel. After the Florida decision was announced, forty-two Southern Democrats "solemnly pledged themselves to each other upon their sacred honor to oppose all attempts to frustrate the counting of the votes for President." [113] That declaration led to a series of informal conversations between Southern moderates and Hayes men, culminating in an evening meeting on February 26 at the Wormley Hotel in Washington. Led by Senator John B. Gordon of Georgia and Congressman Lucius Quintus Cincinnatus Lamar of Mississippi,* the men from the South ar-

---

of Canvassers as the act of the State and as the most authentic evidence of the appointment made by the State; and that while they may go behind the Governor's certificate, if necessary, they can only do so for the purpose of ascertaining whether he has truly certified the results to which the board arrived. They cannot sit as a court of appeals on the action of that board." Louis A. Coolidge, *Ulysses S. Grant* 514 (Boston: Houghton Mifflin, 1917).
* In April 1874, L. Q. C. Lamar led the South to take a massive step toward reconciliation. At the invitation of the Massachusetts congressional delegation, Lamar, who had drafted Mississippi's ordinance of secession and served as a general in the Confederate army, gave the of-

rived at an understanding with Senator John Sherman, Garfield, and other friends of Hayes's. Nothing was written. There was no formal agreement. But it was accepted that Hayes would withdraw the army from the South, withhold support from the carpetbag governments in Louisiana and South Carolina, and allow the Democrats to resume control of those states. As one historian has written, the Hayes men "surrendered the Negro to the Southern ruling class, and abandoned the idealism of Reconstruction, in return for the peaceable inauguration of their president." [114] Grant played no part in the agreement. Having wrestled with the South for sixteen years, he recognized his obligation to leave the matter to his successor. Whether the deal concluded by Sherman and Gordon was necessary is open to doubt. As their pledge after the Florida decision indicated, Southern Democrats were fully prepared to accept the election results. But in the tense last days of February, with inauguration less than a week away and no candidate as yet proclaimed, the Hayes men needed every assurance they could muster.

As soon as the official count was announced on March 2, Grant invited Hayes to the White House. The president-elect arrived that afternoon. According to the *New York Herald,* the governor appeared stunned. "Grasping President Grant's hand in both of his, and looking in the President's eyes, [Hayes] seemed for a moment too overcome for expression." Grant said simply, "Governor Hayes, I am glad to welcome you." [115] The president invited the Hayeses to stay at the executive mansion but Hayes, respectful of the Grants' last days in the White House, graciously declined. After meeting Grant's cabinet, the governor and Mrs. Hayes went to the K Street home of John Sherman, where they resided until the inauguration.

The next day, Saturday, March 3, Grant called on Hayes to pay his respects. That evening there was a gala dinner for the president-elect at the White House. Just before the guests took their seats, Grant led Hayes, Fish, Navy Secretary Robeson, and Chief Justice Waite into the Red Drawing Room. By statute the president's term ended at noon, March 4. In 1877, that was a Sunday, and Hayes's inauguration was not scheduled

ficial eulogy to Charles Sumner in the House of Representatives. Lamar's elegant tribute, praising Sumner's "instinctive love of freedom," captivated the House and was reprinted verbatim in virtually every newspaper in the country. "Bound to each other by a common constitution, destined to live together under a common government, forming unitedly but a single member of the great family of nations, shall we not now at last endeavor to grow toward each other once more in heart, as we are already indissolubly linked to each other in fortunes." Lamar, elected to the Senate in 1877, later served as Grover Cleveland's secretary of the interior, and was appointed by Cleveland to the Supreme Court in 1888, the first Southerner appointed to the bench since the Civil War. Lamar's eulogy to Sumner was chronicled in *Profiles in Courage* by John F. Kennedy. Also see Wirt Armistead Cate, *Lucius Q. C. Lamar: Secession and Reunion* 1–7, 156–63 (Chapel Hill: University of North Carolina Press, 1935).

until Monday. To ensure there would be no interregnum, Waite secretly administered the oath of office to Hayes, to be repeated at the public ceremony. Similarly, the members of Grant's cabinet, breaking with tradition, submitted their resignations to Hayes on March 5, not to Grant on the 4th.[116]

On Monday, Grant joined Hayes for the ceremonial ride to the Capitol. After the formal oath of office and the new president had delivered his address, they returned for a luncheon at the White House. Julia presided for the last time as hostess. Close to dark, the Grants took their leave. "Mrs. Hayes, I hope you will be as happy here as I have been for the last eight years," said Julia.[117] Grant, for his part, was relieved. The transition had been peacefully accomplished. "We had peace, and order, and observance of law, and the world had a new illustration of the dignity and efficiency of the Republic."[118] Later, Grant told John Russell Young that he was never happier than the day he left the White House. "I felt like a boy getting out of school."[119]

Watching the Grants depart, James Garfield spoke for the nation. "No American has carried greater fame out of the White House than this silent man who leaves it today."[120]

CHAPTER TWENTY

TAPS

Now that he is untrammeled by the personal contests of partisans, all men look upon him as THE General Grant, who had the courage, with Lee at his front and Washington at his rear, to undertake to command the Army of the Potomac in 1864, to guide, direct, and push it through sunshine and storm, through praise and denunciation, steadily, surely, and finally to victory and peace; and afterwards, though unused to the ways and machinery of civil government, to risk all in undertaking to maintain that peace by the Constitution and civil forms of government.

WILLIAM TECUMSEH SHERMAN
June 27, 1877

AFTER LEAVING THE WHITE HOUSE, Grant spent the next several days resting at the Washington home of Secretary Fish. From there he briefly visited his childhood home in Georgetown, Ohio, stopped to check on things at his farm outside St. Louis, and went for several weeks to Galena. Wherever he went he was thronged by crowds of well-wishers, making the trip more of a ceremonial procession than a quiet visit of an ex-president to the heartland. "Commodore Ammen and I visited the scenes of our boyhood," Grant wrote Fish from Cincinnati. "The people seemed glad to see us, and realized no doubt more fully than we did the changes that had taken place with us." Grant said he and Julia were thinking of making Washington their home. "Had you accepted the office of Chief Justice, I would have hoped to have you for a neighbor, as I now hope to have you for a friend." [1]

From Galena, Grant went to Philadelphia, before departing for London. Before leaving the White House he and Julia had decided to travel to Europe, and perhaps around the world. Grant had his share of vices: cigars, horses, liquor in earlier years, and above all, an insatiable desire to travel. As president he logged so many miles away from Washington that the Democratic House of Representatives once launched an investigation into his peregrinations. [2] Badeau called him "the greatest traveler that ever lived," [3] and with good reason. For two and a half years Grant circumnavigated the globe. He left Philadelphia May 17, 1877, heading east. He returned to his starting point, still heading east, December 16, 1879. He visited more countries and saw more people, from kings to commoners, than anyone before. James Russell Lowell, whom Hayes had appointed minister to Spain, noted that what Grant liked best "is to escape and wander about the streets. After being here two days I think he knew Madrid better than I did. He seemed to be very single-minded, honest, and sensible. . . . He is perfectly natural, naively puzzled to find himself a personage, and going through the ceremonies to which he is condemned with a dogged imperturbability."[4]

Grant paid for the trip himself, first with $25,000 derived from what may have been his only successful investment,* then, when he decided to expand his itinerary, with $60,000 his son Buck had made by investing money on his father's behalf. Grant and Julia were accompanied by their younger son, Jesse, a maid, a man-servant, and, for the latter half of the journey, Adolph Borie, Grant's first secretary of the Navy, and Borie's nephew, who was a doctor. Last but not least was John Russell Young, a seasoned reporter for James Gordon Bennett's *New York Herald*. Bennett's nose for news had made the *Herald* the most popular newspaper in the country and Grant, in office or out, was front-page copy. Six years earlier Bennett had sent Henry M. Stanley, the *Herald*'s Mediterranean correspondent, looking for the famous African explorer and missionary Dr. David Livingston. When Stanley found Livingston at the remote village of Ujiji on Lake Tanganyika in 1871 the circulation boost had been enormous, and Bennett hoped to repeat the coup with detailed coverage of Grant's travels.

Young and Grant hit it off instantly, the former president treating the thirty-seven-year old journalist as he might have treated a member of his wartime staff, someone like Porter, or Parker, or Babcock. Young was a gifted writer, most famous for his graphic account of the Union defeat at Bull Run in 1861. He subsequently joined Horace Greeley's publishing em-

---

* Throughout the nineteenth century, White House expenses were considered personal expenses of the president, and Grant's salary, first $25,000, then $50,000, was barely enough to pay the bills. When his father died, leaving an estate of $150,000, Grant renounced his share, and income from the money he received as testimonials at the close of the war was mostly spent or given away. Hamilton Fish was astonished at Grant's generosity. "He gave to all who asked of him, giving from five to ten times the amounts that the applicants could have reasonably or probably expected."

Grant's one successful investment involved twenty-five shares of Consolidated Virginia Mining which he purchased shortly after the war for a few dollars. The company was prospecting for silver in the vicinity of Virginia City, Nevada, and in 1873 struck what became known as the Comstock Lode. Grant's twenty-five shares, which he sold, were worth more than a thousand dollars apiece in 1877.

Hamilton Fish, interview, *The Independent,* July 30, 1885; Ulysses S. Grant, Jr., interview, Hamlin Garland Papers; John Russell Young, 1 *Around the World with General Grant* 202 (New York: American News, 1879).

pire, rising to become managing editor of the *New York Tribune* in the late 1860s. He left the *Tribune* to found his own newspaper, which quickly folded, and in 1872 joined Bennett's team at the *Herald*. Young worked assiduously at his task. In addition to chronicling a detailed account of where Grant went and whom he saw, Young became the president's companion. On shipboard he drew Grant into long reminiscences about the Civil War, the personalities involved, their accomplishments and shortcomings. Grant's reflections on politics were equally candid. These were fed to an eager American public almost daily, keeping Grant's name alive while reaping a sales bonanza for the *Herald*.[5]

People throughout the world opened their hearts and their doors to "General Grant." He was received not as an ex-president but as the Hero of Appomattox, the victor of the world's greatest war since the fall of Napoleon. To heads of state and the public alike he was the most famous soldier of the era, personifying the marvel of a modern industrial power. For their part, Grant and Julia were exemplars of American simplicity and American democracy. Thanks to eight years of solid progress and the fine diplomatic hand of Hamilton Fish, the United States had become an actor on the world stage. Its diplomatic representatives still did not merit the rank of ambassador,* but Grant was accorded every honor imaginable. In England, he and Julia were Queen Victoria's houseguests at Windsor Castle. In France, Marshal MacMahon, president of the Third Republic, spent days at Grant's side. In Italy, he talked with Leo XIII, the reformist pope, and dined with King Umberto. In Russia, Czar Alexander, whom Grant found remarkably well informed, discussed the future of the Plains Indians at length with the ex-president and placed the imperial yacht at his disposal. "Since the foundation of your Government," said the czar, "relations between Russia and America have been of the friendliest character, and as long as I live nothing shall be spared to continue this friendship." Grant conceded the two forms of government were opposite in character, but "the great majority of the American people are in sympathy with Russia, which I hope will long continue."[6] Everywhere Grant went he was invited to military reviews, which he declined whenever possible. "The truth is I am more of a farmer than a soldier," he confessed to Bismarck. "I take no interest in military affairs, and, although I entered the army thirty-five years ago and have been in two wars, in Mexico as a young lieutenant, and

---

* Before World War I, diplomacy was rigidly structured. Only the five great powers of Europe, Britain, France, Prussia, Russia, and Austria-Hungary, exchanged ambassadors. The representatives of all other countries held the rank of minister. Thus, Britain's representative in Paris was an "ambassador," while Her Majesty's representative in Washington ranked only as a "minister." All United States representatives, even to the great powers, held the rank of minister.

later, I never went into the army without regret and never retired without pleasure."[7]

Grant was awed by the natural wonders of Europe and entranced by its architectural masterpieces, but it was the art galleries and museums that especially interested him. In Paris, he spent days in the Louvre admiring the works of Raphael, Correggio, Van Dyck, and Murillo. In Rome, Grant visited the museums of antiquity, browsed the Vatican library, and spent long sessions in the Sistine Chapel admiring the frescoes of Michaelangelo, the *Coronation of the Virgin* by Raphael, and the religious paintings of Domenichino and Guido Reni. In Florence, his first stop was the Uffizi Gallery, where he spent a full day. Young reported that "the General, who has no tire in him," devoted the following day to the Pitti Palace, taking in the beauty of more priceless paintings by Tintoretto, Rubens, Raphael, Titian, and Veronese.[8] In Berlin, it was Museum Island on the Spree, the famous Egyptian collection at the Altes Museum, and another of the world's great collections of old masters at the Gemäldegalerie.

It was in Berlin that Grant was drawn once more onto the world stage. The Congress of Berlin, that great conclave of European powers called by Bismarck, was meeting when he arrived, and the former president, much to his embarrassment, found himself the center of attention. Disraeli, Prince Gortschakoff of Russia, the French and Austrian foreign ministers, and Mehemet Ali, the German-born Turkish general who had commanded the sultan's army in the recent war with Russia, called on and exchanged visits with Grant. But it was Bismarck who led the way. No sooner had Grant arrived than the Iron Chancellor sent his card. The former president immediately returned the courtesy and a meeting was arranged for four o'clock that afternoon. Shortly before four, Grant left his apartment in the Kaiserhof, walked out the front door of the hotel, lit a cigar, and like any ordinary tourist, strolled a few blocks down Friedrichstrasse to the Radziwill Palace, taking in the sights as he went. Promptly at four he sauntered nonchalantly into the courtyard, tossed his half-smoked cigar away, and walked toward the front door as if he were going to knock to see if anyone was home. Startled sentries quickly came to present arms, Grant returned the salute, and two liveried servants threw open the palace's massive door to welcome him. Immediately, Grant's visit became the talk of Berlin. The ex-president of the United States had quietly walked over to see the chancellor of Germany. No coach. No team of prancing horses. No outriders, bodyguards, or military escort. It was all very unEuropean. But for iconoclastic Berliners, Grant was the hero of the hour.

Bismarck, in duty uniform, greeted his guest warmly, speaking slow but impeccable English. Within minutes the two men were talking as though they had known each other for years. Bismarck asked first about Sheridan, whom Grant had sent to observe the Franco-Prussian War. At the chancellor's invitation, Sheridan had traveled with the Prussian command group, and he and Bismarck became warm friends. Grant reported the general was well; Bismarck praised Sheridan's professionalism, and both agreed he was an officer of rare ability. For an hour or so the conversation wandered over numerous subjects, but never far from affairs of state. Bismarck, eleven years Grant's senior, led the dialogue and eventually turned to the question of war. Already the chancellor was consumed by the nightmare of hostile coalitions. "You are so happily placed in America that you need fear no wars," said Bismarck. "What always seemed so sad to me about your last great war was that you were fighting your own people. That is always so terrible in wars, so very hard."

"But it had to be done," Grant replied.

"Yes, you had to save the Union, just as we had to save Germany."

"Not only to save the Union," said Grant, "but destroy slavery."

"I supposed, however, the Union was real sentiment, the dominant sentiment," said Bismarck.

"In the beginning, yes," Grant answered. "But as soon as slavery fired upon the flag it was felt, we all felt, even those who did not object to slaves, that slavery must be destroyed. We felt that it was a stain on the Union that men should be bought and sold like cattle."

Bismarck suggested that if the Union had a large standing army in 1861, the war would have been shortened considerably. "We might have had no war at all," said Grant.

"Our war had many strange features—there were many things which seemed odd enough at the time, but which now seem Providential. If we had had a large regular army, as it was then constituted, it might have gone with the South. In fact, Southern feeling in the army among high officers was so strong that when the war broke out the army dissolved. We had no army. Then we had to organize one. A great commander like Sherman or Sheridan even then might have organized an army and put down the rebellion in six months or a year, or at the farthest, two years. But that would have saved slavery, perhaps, and slavery meant the germs of a new rebellion. There had to be an end of slavery. Then we were fighting an enemy with whom we could not make a peace. We had to destroy him. No convention, no treaty, was possible—only destruction."

"It was a long war," Bismarck noted. "And a great work well done—and I supposed it means a long peace."

"I believe so," said Grant.[9]

It was evening when the two men said goodbye. Bismarck accompanied Grant to the door, shook hands, and the general passed into the courtyard. The guard presented arms, Grant lit a fresh cigar, and slowly strolled back to his hotel.

The next day Bismarck called on Grant at the Kaiserhof, an unprecedented courtesy, and later hosted a gala dinner for the general and Julia at the Radziwill Palace, which was also the meeting place for the Congress of Berlin.[10] Julia was enchanted. "Nothing could exceed the cordiality of our reception by this great and most distinguished man," she reported later.[11] After dinner Bismarck escorted Julia to the salon where the Congress was meeting. Did she know what the sessions were about? inquired the chancellor. "Yes," Julia replied, "they are about Russia and Turkey. But what has Germany to do with that?"

Bismarck laughed heartily. "Well, to tell the truth," said the elderly count, "Russia has eaten too much Turkey, and we are trying to help her digest it."[12]

From Germany, the Grants went to Scandinavia, then to Russia, back to France, and on to the Iberian Peninsula. Egypt and the pyramids, the Holy Land, Constantinople, and Athens required another several months. Everywhere Grant was greeted with the pomp and pageantry of a conquering hero. In Turkey, Sultan Abdul Hamid II, well aware of the general's fondness for horses, invited him to visit the royal stables, select any two horses and take them to America. Grant could not resist such an offer. For several hours he studied the magnificent Arabian stallions and then made his choice. "Any other two," said the Sultan. Grant chuckled and picked the two next best. They were shipped to the United States, christened Leopard and Linden Tree, and became the foundation sires for the Arabian breed in North America.*

From the Mediterranean Grant sailed through the Suez canal to the Red Sea, India, and the Orient. The long sea passage gave Young an even greater opportunity to observe the general at close hand. Young found him to be not only a good talker, "but a remarkably good one. His manner is clear and terse. He narrates a story as clearly as he would demonstrate a problem in geometry. His mind is accurate and perspicacious." Young said

---

* Arabian horses were first imported into North America in the eighteenth century. In 1733, the first son of the Godolphin Arabian arrived in the colonies, and in 1747 Lord Lonsdale's Monkey came to Virginia. The first purebred Arabian to arrive was Ranger, who stood in Connecticut. George Washington, noting the superiority of Connecticut cavalry, purchased Ranger and took him to Virginia. But the progeny of these sires were not purebreds. The first purebred Arabian breeding program in the United States traces to Grant's imports, Leopard and Linden Tree. Leopard was given to Randolph Huntington, who imported two purebred Arabian mares in 1888, thus establishing the purebred strain. *Arabian Horse Registry Newsletter,* 1975. *The Arabian Horse in America* 173 (New York: A. S. Barnes, 1972).

that he had known Grant during the war, and that if anything, the good opinion he had formed had been strengthened during the long journey. "The impression General Grant makes upon you is that he has immense resources in reserve. He has in eminent degree that 'two o'clock in the morning courage' that Napoleon said he alone possessed among his marshals and generals. You are also impressed with his good feeling and magnanimity in speaking of comrades and rivals in the war. In some cases—especially in the cases of Sherman and Sheridan, McPherson and Lincoln—it becomes an enthusiasm quite beautiful to witness." [13]

Grant was enchanted with the Far East. China intrigued him, and he was especially taken with Li Hung-Chang, the great viceroy of the Middle Kingdom, whom Grant compared to Bismarck and Disraeli. But he noted and deplored the overbearing attitude of Westerners living in China. "The course of the average minister, consul, and merchant in this country towards the native is much like the course of the former slave owner towards the freedman when the latter attempts to think for himself in matters of choice of candidates." [14] Grant saw China mired in the past, with change coming slowly but inevitably. "When it does come," he wrote Badeau, "China will rapidly become a powerful and rich nation. Her territory is vast and full of resources. The population is industrious and frugal, intelligent and quick to learn. They must, however, have the protection of a better and more honest government to succeed." [15]

Of all the countries he visited, the Land of the Rising Sun was Grant's favorite. "My visit to Japan has been the most pleasant of all my travels," he wrote from Tokyo at the beginning of August 1879. "The country is beautifully cultivated, the scenery is grand, and the people, from the highest to the lowest, the most kindly and the most cleanly in the world." A month later he informed Badeau he was coming home, still enthusiastic about Japan, but most of all, about the Japanese. "The progress they have made in the last twelve years is almost incredible. They have now Military and Naval Academies, Colleges, Engineering schools, schools of science and free schools, for male and female, as thoroughly organized, and on as high a basis of instruction, as any country in the world. Travel in the interior is as safe for an unarmed, unprotected foreigner as it is in the New England States. Much safer from extortion. This is marvelous when the treatment their people—and all eastern peoples—receive at the hands of the average foreigner residing among them is considered. I have never been so struck with the heartlessness of Nations as well as individuals as since coming to the East. But the day of retribution is sure to come." [16]*

---

* Grant performed a valuable peacemaking role in the Orient. Japan and China were on the verge of war over the Ryukyu Islands (Loo-choo), over which the Japanese had recently as-

Grant sailed for San Francisco on the *City of Tokio,* September 3, 1879. He had been in Japan three months, and his leave-taking was poignant. The imperial cavalry escorted him to the palace, where Emperor Mutsuhito and the empress were waiting to say goodbye. Throughout his career, both as general in chief and president, and in all the countries visited, Grant had always spoken extemporaneously on such occasions. This time he wrote out his remarks beforehand, so concerned was he to say the right thing. The emperor, as he had done at their first meeting, advanced to meet the general, an equally unprecedented gesture. Grant recognized that although he was not an official representative of the government, he was nevertheless speaking for the United States. The brief address, one of Grant's finest, stressed the importance of an independent and vigorous Japan, free of foreign domination.[17]

Grant's send-off in Yokohama provided a storybook ending for the wanderings of this modern Ulysses. The route from Tokyo was lined with cheering multitudes waving American and Japanese flags. At the Admiralty Wharf, Grant was greeted by the Japanese naval command, the fleet riding at anchor in the distance. A navy band broke into "Hail Columbia," fireworks lit the sky, and the Admiralty barge, festooned with color, moved out into the harbor, carrying the general to his steamer. After another round of goodbyes, the *City of Tokio,* the largest steamer on the Pacific run, got underway, convoyed to the open seas by a Japanese man-of-war, the imperial cabinet drawn up on deck. One by one, as Grant's vessel passed, the naval ships in the harbor bellowed a twenty-one-gun salute, cheering crewmen aloft in the rigging and manning the yards. As Mount Fujiyama faded in the distance, the accompanying Japanese man-of-war turned homeward and fired a final salvo in salute. Grant, with heavy heart, was going home.

The departure from Yokohama was duplicated by a tumultuous greeting in San Francisco. Everywhere Grant went the reception was similar. As he made his way across the country, cities and towns outdid them-

---

serted sovereignty. When he was in China, Grant was asked by Li Hung-Chang to mediate the dispute, and was given a message for the Japanese government. Grant discussed the matter on several occasions with the emperor, as well as with General Saigo, the war minister. In essence, the former president told the Japanese that no one would benefit from a war between Japan and China except the Western powers, and he urged his hosts to make peace. At Grant's suggestion, the two powers withdrew the harsh notes they had exchanged and appointed commissioners to meet and negotiate. Following protracted discussions, the Chinese acquiesced in Japanese control of the islands. Because the issue had been resolved without bloodshed or foreign intervention, Grant received the thanks of both nations. John Russell Young, 2 *Around the World with General Grant* 558–61 (New York: American News Cy, 1879); Payson J. Trent, 2 *Diplomatic Relations Between the United States and Japan 1853–1895,* 98–181 (New York: Macmillan, 1932); Richard T. Chang, "General Grant's 1879 Visit to Japan," 24 *Monumenta Nipponica* 379–83 (1969).

selves with massive demonstrations to welcome the returning hero. In San Francisco, a delegation from the Chinese community sought to present Grant with a memorial scroll. California's white establishment objected vehemently. Grant overruled them. "The kindness I received in China was so marked, I would only be too happy to return it by any courtesy I might show to Chinamen in America." [18]

It was inevitable that Grant's name would be put forward for the Republican nomination. Young's articles from abroad had kept the general's name before the public, and the Republicans desperately needed a candidate to turn back the rising tide of Democracy. In the midterm elections in 1878 the Democrats had taken the Senate for the first time in twenty years, and increased their majority in the House to nineteen. Hayes had proved to be a milk-toast disappointment. When he received the nomination in 1876, he announced he would not seek a second term, and GOP leaders were happy to take him at his word. As Robert G. Ingersoll of Illinois bluntly put it, Hayes "couldn't be elected if no one ran against him." [19]

Grant was different. "A man of iron" to take the place of "a man of straw," crowed the *St. Louis Globe Democrat*. Another journalist wrote that the movement to draft Grant was "the natural reaction of the Republican Party against the insipidity and imbecility of the present Administration." [20] As Babcock wrote Badeau, "You cannot realize how deep the Grant sentiment has sunk into the minds of the people of the North." [21] The Grant boom was entirely spontaneous. But it was quickly taken in hand by party stalwarts who had been frozen out by Hayes. Those most prominently mentioned were old friends of Grant's: Roscoe Conkling of New York, James Donald Cameron of Pennsylvania, and John Logan of Illinois. This triumvirate was the hard core of the GOP, old-school practitioners of patronage and machine politics who ruled the party in the states like princely fiefdoms.

Grant let events take their course. "I am not a candidate for any office," he told friends, "nor would I hold one that required any maneuvering or sacrifice to obtain." [22] On the other hand, he made no effort to take himself out of the race. Grant made no statement, as he had in 1876, that he would not accept the nomination if it were offered, and he appears to have kept a quiet but eager eye on the proceedings. Badeau thought the general's exposure to events abroad had motivated him to run. "He had seen other countries, met the peoples and the rulers; his views were widened, and his whole character changed. In the East he had obtained knowledge of China and Japan, and conceived an Oriental policy for this country which he believed so important that a desire to achieve it was certainly one reason why he was so anxious to return to power." [23] His friends and family also pushed him to run. Julia was particularly insistent that he allow his name to be placed in nomination.[24] Finally, Grant was well rested. The fatigue of the long years in Washington had passed, he was a vigorous fifty-eight, and he was eager for new challenges.

Grant's most serious problem was that he had returned to the United States too early. The tidal wave of popular affection crested well before the convention. Other candidates entered the lists, hostile critics sprouted in every creek bottom, and the bugaboo of a third term began to erode the general's support. John Sherman, Hayes's secretary of the treasury, threw his hat into the ring in the late autumn of 1879. James G. Blaine, the perennial candidate from the state of Maine, jumped into the race shortly after New Year's. Senators George Edmunds of Vermont and William Windom of Minnesota were not far behind. Most disturbing to the Grant forces, Elihu Washburne, the general's original sponsor, announced his candidacy for the nomination shortly thereafter.

The national convention was scheduled to open in Chicago, June 2. As always, Pennsylvania was first off the mark. Republicans in the Keystone State met in Harrisburg to select delegates on February 4. Cameron marshaled his troops and the convention voted to require the Pennsylvania delegation to vote as a unit for General Grant. New York met in Utica three weeks later and it was another clean sweep. The delegates were instructed "to use their most earnest and united efforts to secure the nomination of Ulysses S. Grant."[25] The Illinois Republican party did not meet until May and by then the groundswell for Grant had dissipated. Logan bulled through the unit rule, but the vote was uncomfortably close, and fractious delegates chaffed under the restraint.[26]

Grant spent the late spring in Galena closely following the selection of delegates. Badeau visited him and thought his former commander "manifested as much anxiety as I ever saw him display on his own account." Julia was even more concerned. "How can I describe that week of suspense for me?" According to Badeau, Grant "calculated the chances, he counted the delegates, considered how every movement would affect the result, and was pleased or indignant at the conversion of enemies or the defection of friends, just as any other human being would have been."[27]

On the eve of the convention, Grant's supporters sniffed victory. Marching behind the big battalions of Pennsylvania, New York, and Illinois, rank-and-file delegates backing the general looked to win on the first ballot. The *New York Times* called Grant's nomination "certain," and reported that Roscoe Conkling was going to Chicago to take personal charge of the convention. A little less sanguine, Logan said, "General Grant is in the hands of his friends, and they will not withdraw him until he is beaten, no matter how many ballots are taken."[28]

The Chicago convention was Conkling's first, and he badly misread the delegates. Instead of building a coalition with those who might back Grant as their second choice, he tried to steamroll the opposition. As a result, delegates were quickly thrust into one of two camps: they were either for Grant or against him. That premature polarization ultimately cost Grant the nomination.

The first test of strength came on the unit rule. The rules committee, chaired by James A. Garfield, recommended that it be disallowed. If the committee report were adopted, it would free sixty or so votes in the New York, Pennsylvania, and Illinois delegations. Grant could ill afford that if he was going to win on the first ballot. Conkling's overconfidence did him in. When the question was put on Saturday afternoon, June 5, the anti-Grant forces coalesced and the unit rule went down 449–306.

In the hands of friends like Conkling, Grant did not need many enemies. On Monday, June 7, the New York senator further alienated the convention when he insisted that the delegates take a pledge to support the nominee. It was a motherhood resolution that carried 716–3, the three negative votes cast by West Virginia. Rather than let well enough alone, Conkling moved that the three West Virginians be expelled. The convention turned on a dime. Delegate after delegate rose to support the right of the West Virginians to choose for themselves. So vehement was the opposition that Conkling was forced to withdraw his motion, amid a chorus of catcalls and guffaws from the floor. Twice in two days Conkling had overplayed his hand, and it was now evident that Grant was vulnerable.

While the convention was thrashing Conkling on Monday, Grant passed through Chicago on his way to address the annual gathering of the Grand Army of the Republic, meeting in Milwaukee. Julia urged him to go to the convention and appear on the floor. She knew how he could ignite a crowd, and the resulting pandemonium might well stampede the delegates to vote for Grant. The general would have no part of it. "I would rather cut off my right arm," he told Julia. Don't you want to win, his wife asked. "Yes, of course," Grant replied. "Since my name is up, I would rather be nominated. But I will do nothing to further that end."[29]

The voting began Wednesday. As the clerk made his way through the alphabet of states, it was apparent Grant was in trouble. With the unit rule jettisoned, eighteen Illinois delegates deserted to vote for other candidates, nineteen did so in New York, and twenty-six in Pennsylvania. In Tennessee, Virginia, and Kentucky, nominally for Grant, another sixteen delegates jumped ship. When the roll call was complete, Grant led with 304; Blaine was second with 284; John Sherman had 93; and another 75 votes were split by Edmunds, Washburne, and Windom. Three hundred and seventy-nine votes, a majority of the convention, were required to nominate. Had the defectors been bound by the unit rule, Grant would have been over the top with 383.[30]

The convention was deadlocked. The delegates voted throughout the day, with little change in the tally. After the twenty-eighth roll call the convention recessed for the night. Grant led with 307 votes; Blaine had 279, and Sherman 91.

When the balloting resumed the next day, the stalemate continued. On the first ballot of the day, and the twenty-ninth of the convention, some of the Edmunds and Windom delegates shifted to Sherman, pushing the treasury secretary up to 116, but the hoped for breakthrough did not materialize. The battle lines held firm and the balloting continued. At the end of the thirty-fourth ballot there was shuffling on the floor. Wisconsin dropped Washburne and switched sixteen votes to Garfield, the unofficial leader of the anti-Grant coalition. Garfield protested he was not a candidate, but few took him seriously. On the next ballot Grant rose to 313, but the shift to Garfield had begun. The man from Mentor, Ohio, now had fifty. As the thirty-sixth ballot began, Conkling stood in the aisle encouraging the Grant delegates: "Keep steady, boys. Grant is going to win on this ballot."[31] But the Garfield vote climbed steadily. When the clerk called Maine, Blaine's state, the rout began. The Pine Tree State cast all fourteen of its votes for Garfield. Delegation after delegation followed Maine's lead. The avalanche proved unstoppable. At the end of the roll call, Garfield had 399 to Grant's 306. All but fifty of the anti-Grant delegates had fallen in behind the congressman from Ohio. Grant had lost. What seems remarkable is that the stalwarts backing the former president stayed with him, as Logan had prophesied, to the bitter end.

When the result was announced, Logan rose to make Garfield's nomination unanimous. "In union and harmony there is strength. The men who stood by Grant's banners will be seen in the front of this contest on every field."[32] The party rift was papered over, Grant called on Garfield to pledge his support, and the 306 stalwarts who stood by the general for thirty-six ballots were immortalized in Republican mythology. Badges were printed, commemorative Grant medals were struck, and Thomas C. Platt, Conkling's fellow senator from New York, listed in his *Autobiography* the names of all 306 men who voted for Grant on the final ballot.[33]

Grant was at loose ends, and he returned to Galena reluctantly. Former presidents received no pensions,* and Galena was the one place he

---

* It was not until after Harry Truman left office in 1953 that Congress voted pension, Secret Service, and office support for former presidents. Unlike Herbert Hoover, the only other living ex-president, Truman was not independently wealthy. Except for a minuscule veteran's pension and Social Security, he had no means of support. He was rescued at the insistence of

could afford.[34] Succor came once again from wealthy well-wishers who quietly organized yet another trust fund on the general's behalf. Led by George Jones of the *New York Times,* the Wall Street crowd raised $250,000 for Grant, enough to allow him to live modestly but comfortably in New York.[35] Another twenty men, headed by George Childs, Anthony Drexel, and J. Pierpont Morgan, added an additional $100,000, permitting Grant and Julia to purchase a handsome new brownstone at 3 East 66th Street, just off Fifth Avenue. The house was so crammed with Grant's memorabilia, including a 5,000-book library, that it looked like a museum. "It was a much larger and a more expensive house than we had intended," wrote Julia, "but it was so new and sweet and large that this quite outweighed our more prudential scruples."[36]

The former president adjusted poorly to private life. He pressed policy on Garfield, sided with Conkling in patronage disputes, and muttered publicly about the Ohioan's lack of judgment. "Garfield has shown that he is not possessed of the backbone of an angleworm," Grant disgustedly wrote Badeau two months after the president's inauguration.[37] Following Garfield's assassination, Grant leaned heavily on Chester Arthur. He badgered the former customs collector on appointments and sulked when his nominees were not selected. He refused to accept that Arthur wanted to be president in his own right. For Grant, loyalty to friends and benefactors was the pole around which his universe revolved, and he could not comprehend why Arthur, whose political career he had furthered, did not respond favorably to his suggestions.[38]

Grant's quest for a livelihood was soon answered. In November 1880 his old friend Matías Romero, Mexico's former minister in Washington, visited New York for the purpose of interesting American investors in the development of Mexican railroads. Romero sought to organize a company that would construct a line linking Mexico City with Guatemala, with branches to the Pacific and the Gulf of Mexico.[39] On November 11 he hosted a lavish dinner at Delmonico's for a who's who of American railroad moguls, including Jay Gould and Collis P. Huntington. Grant was the guest of honor. The railroad men were taken with Romero's scheme, the New York legislature was prevailed upon to charter the Mexican Southern Railroad, and Grant was made president of the line. Grenville Dodge, who had run Grant's railroads during the war and was now chief engineer for the Union Pacific, was added as vice president, and Russell Sage, a Gould ally, became treasurer. A New York office for the railroad

---

Speaker Sam Rayburn and Senate Majority Leader Lyndon Johnson, who, with the support of President Eisenhower, rammed through legislation providing support for former presidents. David McCullough, *Truman* 963–64 (New York: Simon & Schuster, 1992).

was established at 2 Wall Street, to which Grant went daily. Gould provided most of the initial capital. Although it paid Grant's salary and the New York office expenses, little track was laid and the line never became operational. Grant's responsibility was confined to negotiating concessions with the Mexican government, which he accomplished successfully. The railroad provided Grant a means of keeping busy while maintaining a foothold in the Wall Street financial world.

The daily exposure to the nation's titans of finance whetted Grant's acquisitive instincts. For the former president, life in New York in the 1880s was the Pacific Northwest of the 1850s redux. His son Buck (Ulysses Jr.), who seemed to have a knack for investing, was making money hand over fist on Wall Street. Buck suggested to his father that he try investment banking. Buck was in partnership with another young man, Ferdinand Ward, widely touted as the Young Napoleon of the financial world. The firm, Grant & Ward, also had its offices at 2 Wall Street, and Buck suggested his father join the company as a silent partner. Buck said he would provide the initial capital, and he and Grant could divide their share of the profits. Grant declined to accept his son's generosity, but after discussing his offer with Julia, he agreed to join the firm, investing $100,000 of his own funds and sharing responsibilities, and presumably profits, as an equal partner.[40] Ward was delighted. The general's prestige was a bankable commodity, and the ambiguity of the firm's name allowed investors to assume the former president had been the founder.

When Grant came on board, the firm recapitalized. Buck, Ward, and the former president each put in $100,000, and a fourth partner, James D. Fish, president of the Marine Bank, added another $100,000.[41] Ward continued as the managing partner, with Buck and Grant playing passive roles. Fish, however, was an active collaborator, providing an ever ready supply of cash at the Marine Bank for Ward's investments.

Between 1881 and 1884 the firm of Grant & Ward flourished. Investors reaped enormous rewards, with dividends running as high as 40 percent annually. Bradstreet rated the firm "gilt edged." Money flowed in, capitalization rose to $15 million, and Grant believed himself to be a millionaire. Neither he nor Buck paid any attention to the details, content to allow Ward to exercise his talents and enjoy the benefits.[42]

It was a fool's paradise. Ward was kiting the firm's assets, pledging the same securities as collateral against multiple loans, and using the proceeds to pay the dividends investors expected. The loans, naturally, were made by the Marine Bank. Conservative financiers suspected that the assets of Grant & Ward were unethically inflated, but Grant seemed not to care. He knew scores of men on Wall Street who had amassed fortunes quickly, and he assumed Ward had the ability to do likewise.[43] Horace Porter, Grant's former aide, who was now president of the Pullman Car Company, recognized that the profits Grant & Ward were generating could not have been made honestly, and he called at 66th Street to warn the general. As they were talking, Ward came in brimming with confidence. Porter observed the enthusiasm with which Grant welcomed him and decided to remain silent. Perhaps Grant knew the situation better than he did, and why spread suspicion if it was unfounded.[44]

In early 1884 the bubble burst. Ward could not cover his loans, payments were due, and there was no money in the till. Sunday evening, May 4, Ward called on Grant to play a final gambit. The Marine Bank was in dire straits, he announced, and needed an immediate infusion of cash. As Ward concocted the tale, the city of New York had drawn heavily on the bank Saturday, leaving it no reserves to transact business on Monday. Unless $400,000 could be raised at once, the bank would not be able to open.

"Why are you concerned about the Marine Bank?" asked Grant.

"We have $660,000 on deposit there, and it would embarrass us very much if the bank should close its doors." Ward told Grant that he had been able to find $250,000, but Grant must raise the rest. As president of the United States, Grant had wound down government spending, reduced the federal deficit, broken the gold conspiracy on Black Friday, and weaned the country away from greenback inflation onto specie payment and a sound dollar. Yet in his personal affairs he was still as gullible as when he served at Fort Vancouver in 1853. Without questioning Ward further, he went out into the night to raise the money.[45]

Grant was not immediately successful. After calling on several men who were sympathetic but unable to help, he drove to the home of William H. Vanderbilt, the guiding force behind the New York Central Railroad. Vanderbilt received the former president graciously. Grant explained that the money was not for him, but for the Marine Bank.

"I care nothing about the Marine Bank," Vanderbilt responded. "To tell the truth, I care very little about Grant & Ward. But to accommodate you personally, I will draw my check for the amount you ask. I consider it a personal loan to you, and not to any other party."[46] Vanderbilt wrote out a check for $150,000, did not ask for collateral, and gave it to Grant—an exceptional testament to his affection for the general.

Grant went home to 66th Street, where Ward was waiting. The young man took the check, thanked the former president profusely, and then deposited the money into his personal account. Late Monday, the Marine Bank announced it would no longer honor the checks of Grant & Ward. On Tuesday, the bank closed its doors, carrying the investment firm with it. Ward and Fish had been keeping two sets of books, and the public set, which listed the firm's capitalization at $15 million, was pure fiction.

Ward was indicted in state court for grand larceny, convicted, and sentenced to ten years' imprisonment at Sing Sing. Fish was tried in United States court, convicted, and sentenced to seven years in a federal penitentiary for bank embezzlement. It took the court-appointed receiver two and a half years to unravel the tangled affairs of Grant & Ward. His conclusion was that Ward had carried on the business virtually alone, commingled the firm's accounts with his own, dummied bookkeeping entries, rehypothecated securities held as collateral, and deposited loan proceeds into his private account. The liabilities of Grant & Ward exceeded $16 million. Assets totaled $57,000.[47]

Grant had been blindsided. Not since Shiloh had be been caught so unprepared. He had come into the office late Tuesday morning confident that his money worries were a thing of the distant past. "Well, Buck, how is it?" he asked cheerily.

His son, who was equally stunned, answered directly. "Grant & Ward has failed, and Ward has fled." Grant's expression did not change. He turned slowly, and without saying a word walked to his office. At five o'clock he sent for the firm's cashier, a young man named Spencer. When the cashier entered the office, he found Grant seated close to his desk, both hands tightly gripping the arms of the chair. His face twitched. "Spencer, how is it that man has deceived us all in this way?" Grant rambled on for several minutes and then became silent. The anguish of failure was upon him. "I have made it the rule of my life to trust a man long after other people gave him up. But I don't see how I can ever trust any human being again."[48]

Grant was destitute. His entire fortune had been tied into Grant & Ward. When he went home that evening he had $80 in his pocket. Julia had another $130. Bank accounts had been seized and there was no money to pay for ordinary household expenses. To make matters worse, the $250,000 trust fund that had been established for Grant in 1881 had been invested primarily in bonds of the Wabash Railroad. In 1884 the railroad defaulted, depriving Grant of that income as well.[49] "We were literally without means," Julia recalled. "A man from Lansingburg, N.Y. sent the general five hundred dollars, saying, 'General, I owe you this for Appomattox.' The General acknowledged the money and the gentleman, who was a stranger to us, then sent a cheque for one thousand dollars, telling the General to consider it a loan to be repaid at his convenience." Matías Romero, who was visiting New York, stopped to see the general, and as he was leaving, dropped a check for $1,000 on the hall table. The $2,500 tided the family over until Julia could sell two small houses she owned. Bridge builder James Eads offered to make his bank account available to Grant, but the general declined, the immediate urgency having passed with the sale of Julia's houses.[50]

William Vanderbilt also responded generously. He offered to waive Grant's debt of $150,000, but the general refused. To protect what he could of Grant's assets, the financier took title to the house on 66th Street as well as the furnishings and military memorabilia. Grant and Julia continued to live in the house just as though it were theirs, and the memorabilia was given in trust to the government, the former president to retain possession so long as he lived.

In Congress, Grant's friends sought to help by restoring him to his rank as general of the army and retiring him at full pay. In 1881 former Confederate General Joseph E. Johnston, representing Virginia's third congressional district as a Democrat, had introduced such a bill but it encountered bitter opposition and failed passage. Senate Republicans now took up the quest. President Arthur, jealous of his authority to appoint officers in the military, insisted he would veto the measure if it mentioned Grant by name, but the Senate, led by George Edmunds of Vermont, pressed on.[51]

Grant and Julia spent the summer of 1884 at their Long Branch cottage on the New Jersey shore. Grant had bought the cottage while president, and the family summered there regularly. It was at Long Branch that Grant undertook to write two articles for *Century* magazine, one about Shiloh, the other describing the capture of Vicksburg. Before Grant & Ward went under, the general had been approached by Robert U. Johnson, an editor at *Century,* to write several articles about his experiences during the war. The magazine was planning a series of articles on the Civil War by major participants, and Grant would make an obvious contributor.* At that time Grant was not interested. "It's all in Badeau," he told Johnson, referring to Adam Badeau's three-volume *Military History of U.S. Grant,* which had recently been published. "Grant's declination was so decisive, that it left us without hope," Johnson recalled.[52] But the failure of Grant & Ward caused the general to reconsider. He arrived at Long Branch almost penniless. With no income and few prospects, he dashed off a quick note to the editors asking if they were still interested. Johnson immediately visited Grant at Long Branch and it was agreed that the general would prepare four articles, beginning with Shiloh and Vicksburg, for which he would receive $500 each.[53]

Grant had little confidence in his ability as a writer, but he set to work with the same intense concentration that had allowed him to write hundreds of crystal-clear military orders in the field under the most trying con-

* Published individually, the articles were subsequently collected and republished as the authoritative *Battles and Leaders of the Civil War,* Robert U. Johnson and Clarence C. Buel, eds., 4 vols. (New York: Century, 1887–88).

ditions. The first draft of "Shiloh" was finished on July 1. It was essentially a rehash of Grant's official report of the battle and offered little of the insight the publishers were seeking. Johnson encouraged the general to rewrite the piece to reflect his personal appreciation of the fighting. Grant did so, and the article appeared in the February 1885 issue. During July he wrote "Vicksburg," writing four hours a day, seven days a week. The groove Grant settled into, and the clarity of his prose, caused Johnson and his associates to consider urging the general to write a book on his experiences during the war. By the end of the summer negotiations were underway to publish Grant's memoirs. *Century* was prepared to offer the standard 10 percent royalty, with no advance and no guarantee. Grant had discovered that he liked to write, and he desperately needed the money. He was on the verge of signing with *Century* when his old friend Samuel Clemens came to see him. Clemens had heard that Grant was writing his memoirs, and he asked him about his publishing plans. The general read the *Century* contract aloud to him. "I didn't know whether to laugh or cry," Clemens wrote later. The magazine was offering Grant the same royalty "which they would have offered to any unknown Comanche Indian whose book they thought might sell 3,000 or 4,000 copies."[54] Clemens told Grant the offer was absurd. He said the general should receive either 20 percent of the retail price of the book, or 70 percent of the profits. Clemens said he had just established his own publishing firm, Charles L. Webster & Co., and was about to bring out *The Adventures of Huckleberry Finn*.[55] If Grant would agree, he would like to publish his book next, at the figures he had just stated. "I wanted the general's book, and I wanted it very much, but I had very little expectation of getting it. I supposed that he would lay these new propositions before the *Century* people, that they would accept immediately, and that the matter would end."[56]

As Twain saw it, *Century* was exploiting Grant. After the general's first article appeared, the magazine immediately gained 50,000 new subscribers and the number of advertising pages doubled. Twain calculated that Grant had earned $100,000 for *Century,* but he was receiving only $500 per article. Strangest of all, Grant felt under great obligation to the magazine for rescuing him from poverty. Twain called him lovingly "the most simple-hearted of all men."

Eventually, Twain's message sank in and in February 1885 he and Grant came to terms. While the contract was being drawn up, Grant asked which proposition would be best: 20 percent of sales or 70 percent of profits? Twain told him to take 20 percent of sales. "It was the surest, the simplest, the easiest to keep track of, and better still, would pay him a trifle more." But Grant chose to take 70 percent of profits. He didn't want to make any money if the publisher didn't make any. "This was just like General Grant," said Twain. "It was absolutely impossible for him to entertain for a moment any proposition which might prosper him at the risk of any other man."[57]

Already Grant's health was failing. Twain was shocked at how thin and weak he had become. The previous summer at Long Branch, as Julia recalled, Grant picked up a peach from the table and bit into it. Suddenly he rose from the table complaining that the peach had hurt his throat. "He seemed to be suffering acutely. He walked up and down the room and out to the piazza, and rinsed his throat again and again. He was in great pain and said the water hurt him like liquid fire."[58] Grant did not seek medical attention until late in the summer when Dr. Jacob M. DaCosta, an eminent Philadelphia physician, visited Long Branch. DaCosta told Grant to see a throat specialist immediately. Again Grant delayed, and it was not until late October that he consulted Dr. John H. Douglas, the leading specialist in New York. Douglas had served with the United States Sanitary Commission during the war and had met Grant shortly after Donelson. His admiration for the general was unbounded, and his examination was exceedingly thorough. "Is it cancer?" asked Grant. Without using the word, Douglas indicated that it probably was. "General, the disease is serious, epithelial in character, and sometimes capable of being cured."[59]

Later in the week, Julia and Colonel Fred Grant visited Dr. Douglas. He told them the disease would take its course. "I learned the dreadful truth," said Julia, "but still could not believe the malady was a fatal one."[60] In December Grant seemed to improve. But in January his condition worsened and he was confined to the house on 66th Street. All the while he worked steadily on his memoirs. In February a battery of specialists examined him. According to the *New York Times*, "It was agreed that the trouble from which the General was suffering was cancer, and the only difference of opinion was as to the rapidity of its development." Newspapers throughout the country announced his condition: "Sinking into the Grave." "General Grant's Friends Give Up Hope."[61]

In Washington, the movement to restore Grant's rank took on added urgency. Edmunds's bill sailed through the Senate and was pending in the House. But since Arthur had announced he would veto it, Edmunds introduced another bill creating the rank but leaving the incumbent unnamed. That also sailed through the Senate, but it was hung up in the House. Democrats were inclined to favor Edmunds's original bill, seeking to force Arthur's hand on the threatened veto. Time literally was running out. The 48th Congress would adjourn sine die at noon on March 4, and the new Congress would not convene until December. Arthur's term also ended at noon that day, and Grover Cleveland would take the oath of office at that time. If Congress were going to pass the bill, it would have to act before twelve o'clock.

The initiative in the House of Representatives was taken by the Democratic leader, Samuel Randall of Pennsylvania, the former speaker who had fought for the Union at Gettysburg. At 11:40 on March 4, Randall asked unanimous consent to suspend the rules and call the Grant bill to the floor. A contested election case in Iowa still had to be dealt with, and the member in charge of the case declined to give his consent. At that point, with President-elect Cleveland expected momentarily, "Tama Jim" Wilson, the member from Iowa whose seat was at stake, jumped on top of his chair demanding recognition. "In order that this Congress shall do justice to the hero of Donelson and Appomattox, I yield to the gentleman from Pennsylvania." It cost Wilson his seat and his salary,* but with rebel yells echoing through the chamber, the House passed the Grant relief bill by acclamation.[62] The measure was rushed to President Arthur, waiting in the President's Room, who signed it immediately and, with less than ten minutes remaining in his term, nominated Grant to the post. The Senate chamber was just down the corridor from the President's Room. At 11:54 Senator Edmunds, President pro tempore of the Senate, announced a special message from the president. All other business was suspended, and Grant's nomination was confirmed unanimously amid tumultuous applause. Arthur had nominated Grant as the last act of his administration; Cleveland, as the first act of his, signed Grant's commission as general of the army.[63]

Grant followed the events in Washington closely, but doubted the relief bill would pass. "It can't be done in the confusion of the last day of the session," he told Mark Twain on March 4. As Grant was speaking a telegram arrived announcing that the bill had passed. Grant seemed quietly satisfied but showed no outward emotion. Twain was struck by the iron self-control the general exhibited. But the intensity of Grant's feeling was apparent. Later, Twain telegraphed his wife that "The effect upon him was like raising the dead."[64]

In the weeks ahead, Grant devoted himself to finishing his memoirs. As Twain recalled, Grant was determined that what he wrote should be *absolutely correct*. "His memory was superb, and nearly any other man with such a memory would have been satisfied to trust it. Not so the general.

---

* Tama Jim Wilson returned to Iowa, became director of the agricultural experimental station at Ames, and served as secretary of agriculture in the cabinets of Presidents McKinley, Roosevelt, and Taft, March 5, 1897, to March 3, 1913, the longest tenure of any cabinet officer in American history.

No matter how sure he was of the fact or the date, he would never let go until he had verified it with the official records. This constant and painstaking searching of the records cost a great deal of time, but it was not wasted. Everything stated as a fact in General Grant's book may be accepted with entire confidence as being thoroughly trustworthy."[65]

As the weather warmed that spring, Grant and Julia accepted the invitation of Joseph Drexel, president of Drexel, Morgan & Co., to summer at the Drexel country estate in the Adirondacks. Located at Mount McGregor, eleven miles north of Saratoga, the Drexel cottage was a large, rambling frame structure, built in a style that might be called "Adirondacks Queen Anne," two stories high, with a wide piazza extending around three sides. As the *New York Times* reported, "Mr. Drexel's idea was to have the cottage comfortable without making it luxurious."[66] To ease the burden of the trip, William Vanderbilt placed his private New York Central car at Grant's disposal. On June 16 Colonel Fred Grant reported that his father had borne the trip much better than anyone had anticipated. But Dr. Douglas warned newsmen that nothing more than a temporary improvement could be expected. "The decay of vitality is slowly but steadily progressing."[67]

Grant was dying. Old friends came to pay their respects—Rufus Ingalls and Sherman; Edward Beale and Sheridan; Logan and Conkling; and from the South, Simon Bolivar Buckner and Longstreet. Winfield Scott Hancock, still on active duty, having narrowly lost the presidency to Garfield in 1880, came to make peace with the general, as did Benjamin Bristow. Grant was deeply affected. Of all the visitors, Buckner stayed longest. He wanted to assure Grant that the Southern people appreciated his magnanimity at Appomattox, and also thanked Grant for preventing the Johnson administration from violating the terms of surrender. Grant could no longer speak and wrote his answers on a pad. "I have witnessed since my sickness just what I wished to see ever since the war: harmony and good feeling between the sections. . . . I believe myself that the war was worth all it cost us, fearful as that was. Since it was over, I have visited every state in Europe and a number in the East. I know as I did not before the value of our inheritance."[68]

Buckner, a widower, had just remarried and Grant asked whether his wife was with him. He wished to meet her. Mrs. Buckner was brought into the sickroom and introduced to the general. "I knew your husband long before you did," Grant wrote. "We were at West Point together and served together in the Mexican War. I was with him on a visit to the top of Popocatepetl. Your husband wrote an account of that trip for publication at the time. I have just written my account, which will be published in my forthcoming book." Buckner and his wife stayed with the former president until he tired. The Kentuckian then took Grant's hands into his. They parted. "Grant." "Buckner." [69]

Twain paid a final visit in early July. Grant, near death, was continuing to make revisions in the text of his *Memoirs,* but the manuscript was largely finished. The first volume was in page proof and advance sales for the two-volume set already exceeded 100,000. By September they would total 250,000 (500,000 single copies). One year later Twain presented Julia with a check for $200,000, the largest royalty check ever written. All told, *The Personal Memoirs of U.S. Grant* sold well over 300,000 sets and earned $450,000 for the general's impoverished family. [70]

The work was not only a financial success but a literary one as well. Twain called it "the most remarkable work of its kind since the *Commentaries of Julius Caesar.*" Edmund Wilson compared it to Thoreau's *Walden* or Walt Whitman's *Leaves of Grass*—"a unique expression of national character." Gertrude Stein, like Wilson a stern critic, considered it one of the finest books ever written by an American, and admired Grant's capacity "for watching in silence and commanding without excitement." [71]

For Grant, it had been a race against time. His determination to finish the *Memoirs* and provide for his family attracted almost as much attention as his military campaigns twenty years earlier. Both were examples of that indomitable will that brooked no failure. As Professor James McPherson noted, the elegant simplicity of Grant's prose made a difficult job look easy. "To read the *Personal Memoirs* with a knowledge of the circumstances under which Grant wrote them is to gain insight into the reasons for his military success." [72]

In extreme pain and often groggy from medication, Grant wrote 275,000 words in less than a year. The thoughts flowed steadily from his mind to the paper. The prose is lean and elegant. Action verbs predominate: "move . . . engage . . . start . . . attack." Grant is generous with praise and sparing with criticism. He admits mistakes: "I have always regretted that last attack at Cold Harbor was made. . . . No advantage whatever was gained to compensate for the heavy loss we sustained." [73]

The *Memoirs* deal with the war. Grant's early life is treated briefly, and though he describes lovingly his time in Mexico, the passages are clipped. His career after the Civil War is not mentioned. The theme is victory. Victory in war; victory over death.

Grant grew weaker as each day passed. The end came at eight minutes past eight on the morning of July 23, 1885. "Life passed away so quietly, so peacefully," said Dr. Douglas, "that we had to wait a minute to be sure it had terminated." [74]

Eulogies were heartfelt. Grant, with characteristic modesty, may have said it best. To a final visitor he wrote:

It seems that man's destiny in this world is quite as much a mystery as it is likely to be in the next. I never thought of acquiring rank in the profession I was educated for; yet it came with two grades higher prefixed to the rank of General officer for me. I certainly never had either ambition or taste for political life; yet I was twice President of the United States. If anyone had suggested the idea of my becoming an author, as they frequently did, I was not sure whether they were making sport of me or not. I have now written a book which is in the hands of the manufacturers. I ask you to keep these notes very private lest I become an authority on the treatment of diseases. I have already too many trades to be proficient at any.[75]

Notes

Preface

1. *Personal Memoirs of U.S. Grant,* 2 vols. (New York: Charles L. Webster, 1885).
2. G. P. Gooch, *History and Historians in the Nineteenth Century* xxxvi (London: Longmans, 1913).
3. William B. Hesseltine, *Ulysses S. Grant: Politician* vii (New York: Dodd, Mead, 1935).
4. David Herbert Donald, in "Overrated and Underrated Americans," 39 *American Heritage* 48–63 (1988). Donald won the Pulitzer Prize for biography in 1961 for *Charles Sumner and the Coming of the Civil War* (New York: Alfred A. Knopf, 1960) and again in 1988 for *Look Homeward: A Life of Thomas Wolfe* (Boston: Little, Brown, 1987).
5. See especially, William S. McFeely, *Grant: A Biography* (New York: W. W. Norton, 1981).
6. As Princeton historian James M. McPherson points out, "Even in the fighting from the Wilderness to Petersburg during the spring of 1864...Grant's casualties were proportionately no higher than Lee's even though Grant was fighting on the offensive and Lee's soldiers stood mainly on the defensive behind elaborate entrenchments. Lee had lost as many men in Pickett's assault at Gettysburg (and proportionately four times as many) as Grant did in the equally ill-fated June 3 Assault at Cold Harbor," 27 *Civil War History* 365 (1981). Also see Richard N. Current, "Grant Without Greatness," 9 *Reviews in American History* 507 (1981); John Y. Simon, untitled book review, 65 *Wisconsin Magazine of History* 220–21 (1982); and Brooks D. Simpson, "Butcher? Racist? An Examination of William S. McFeely's Grant," 33 *Civil War History* 63–83 (1987).
7. 2 *Personal Memoirs of Philip Henry Sheridan* 204 (New York: Charles L. Webster, 1888).
8. Lloyd Lewis, *Sherman: Fighting Prophet* 639 (New York: Harcourt, Brace, 1932).
9. James Longstreet, *From Manassas to Appomattox* 17 (Philadelphia: J. B. Lippincott, 1896).
10. T. Harry Williams, *McClellan, Sherman and Grant* 105 (New Brunswick, N.J.: Rutgers University Press, 1962).
11. Grant, 1 *Memoirs* 38–40.
12. Ibid. 248–50.
13. Ibid. 570.
14. Grant, 2 *Memoirs* 493.
15. Gen. Edward F. Beale interview, *Washington Post,* July 24, 1885.
16. *New York Times,* August 9, 1885.

CHAPTER ONE: THE EARLY YEARS

1. Ulysses S. Grant, 1 *Personal Memoirs of U.S. Grant* 18–19 (New York: Charles L. Webster, 1885); *cf.,* William S. McFeely, *Grant: A Biography* 4–5 (New York: W. W. Norton, 1981).
2. Admiral Daniel Ammen, "Recollections and Letters of Grant," 141 *North American Review* 361 (1885).
3. Hamlin Garland, *Ulysses S. Grant: His Life and Character* 3, 2nd ed. (New York: Macmillan, 1920).
4. Grant paid homage to his mother's fierce partisanship in his *Memoirs.* "Until her memory failed her, a few years ago, she thought the country ruined beyond recovery when the Democratic party lost control in 1860." Her son's success as the Republican standard-bearer in 1868 and 1872 did not moderate her stance. During the eight years Grant was president, Hannah never visited the White House. Grant, 1 *Memoirs* 23.

5. Ibid. 25.

6. Ibid. 24–25.

7. Lloyd Lewis, *Captain Sam Grant* 22 (Boston: Little, Brown, 1950).

8. Grant, 1 *Memoirs* 26–31.

9. Garland, Grant 13–15; also see Bruce Catton, *U.S. Grant and the American Military Tradition* 11–12 (Boston: Little, Brown, 1954); Lewis, *Captain Sam Grant* 31–34. Garland won the Pulitzer Prize in 1922 for *A Daughter of the Middle Border* (New York: Macmillan, 1921).

10. Ibid. 50–51. Henry Clay, Jr., commanded a regiment of Kentucky volunteers during the Mexican War and was killed rallying his men at the battle of Buena Vista.

11. Grant, 1 *Memoirs* 32. Emphasis in original.

12. Lewis, *Captain Sam Grant* 57.

13. Hamer to Sec. of War, March 4, 1839, National Archives. Also see 1 *The Papers of Ulysses S. Grant* 22 note, John Y. Simon, ed. (Carbondale: Southern Illinois University Press, 1967).

14. "Descriptive Book of Candidates," manuscript, USMA. A photo of Grant's oath of enlistment, signed "U.S. Grant," appears facing page thirty-two in Garland, Grant. Grant never acknowledged the middle name Simpson, and simply used "S." as his middle initial. His acquiescence to his name change speaks volumes about his attitude toward life. He attempted three times to call the army's attention to the mistake, but when that failed he simply accepted the situation.

15. Grant, 1 *Memoirs* 34–35.

16. Grant to R. McKinstry Griffith, Sept. 22, 1839, 1 *Grant Papers* 4–5. Emphasis in original.

17. Ibid. 7.

18. Lewis, *Captain Sam Grant* 69.

19. William Tecumseh Sherman interview, *New York Herald,* July 24, 1885.

20. The comments are those of General Lucius Clay, quoted in Jean Edward Smith, *Lucius D. Clay: An American Life* 35 (New York: Henry Holt, 1990).

21. Lewis, *Captain Sam Grant* 81. For Grant's comments on Lyon, see John Russell Young, 2 *Around the World with General Grant* 468 (New York: American News, 1879).

22. Jeffry D. Wert, *General James Longstreet: The Confederacy's Most Controversial Soldier* 31–32 (New York: Simon and Schuster, 1993); James Longstreet interview, *New York Times,* July 24, 1885.

23. Longstreet interview, ibid.

24. Reflections of General D. M. Frost, quoted in Garland, *Grant* 43.

25. Grant, 1 *Memoirs* 38–39. Grant's reference is to the nine historical novels of Bulwer-Lytton, James Fenimore Cooper, the naval adventure stories of Frederick Marryat, and the exuberant novels of Charles Lever. In the spring of his last year at the academy Grant wrote twice to Lever's American publisher for copies of *Charles O'Malley and Harry Lorrequer.* 1 *Grant Papers* 11.

26. In his senior year, Grant was elected president of the Dialectic Society, the academy's only literary club. Winfield Scott Hancock was secretary. For membership certificates signed by Grant and Hancock, see ibid. 21.

27. Weir's large mural, *The Embarkation of the Pilgrims,* painted during Grant's stay at West Point, adorns the rotunda of the United States Capitol.

28. McFeely, *Grant* 18.

29. Grant, 1 *Memoirs* 53.

30. Ibid. 39.

31. James B. Fry, "An Acquaintance with Grant," 141 *North American Review* 540 (1885).

32. "That horse will kill you some day," a classmate, Charles S. Hamilton, told Grant. "Well, I can only die once," Grant was quoted as replying. Albert Deane Richardson, *A Personal History of Ulysses S. Grant* 92–93 (Hartford, Conn.: American Publishing, 1868).

33. Fry, "An Acquaintance with Grant" 540.

34. Richardson cites the record at "over six feet." *A Personal History of Ulysses S. Grant* 92; cf., Garland, *Grant* 51.

35. Lewis, *Captain Sam Grant* 94.

36. Grant, 1 *Memoirs* 42–43.

37. Ibid. 43.

38. Ibid. 44.

39. For Kearny generally, see Dwight L. Clarke, *Stephen Watts Kearny* (Norman: University of Oklahoma Press, 1961).

40. Grant, 1 *Memoirs* 45–46.

41. Ibid.

42. Ibid.

43. Julia Dent Grant, *The Personal Memoirs of Julia Dent Grant* 47, John Y. Simon, ed. (New York: G. P. Putnam's Sons, 1975).

NOTES   631

44. Longstreet interview, *New York Times*, July 24, 1885.
45. Lewis, *Captain Sam Grant* 104. Cf., McFeely, *Grant* 22–23; Harry Wright Newman, *The Maryland Dents* 70 (Richmond: Dietz Press, 1963).
46. Longstreet became engaged to Maria Louisa Garland, daughter of the 4th Infantry's commander, Lieutenant Colonel John Garland, in May 1844. They were married March 8, 1848, the war with Mexico having intervened. Wert, *Longstreet* 36–49.
47. Emmy Dent Casey, "When Grant Went a Courtin'," typewritten manuscript, quoted in Lewis, *Captain Sam Grant* 105. Also see the remarks of Mary Robinson, a Dent family friend, in the *St. Louis Republican*, July 24, 1885.
48. P. Mauro and his daughters, the Misses Mauro, operated an Academy for Young Ladies at Fifth and Market streets, St. Louis. The course of study was advertised in the *Missouri Republican*, July 2, 1839.
49. Lewis, *Captain Sam Grant* 105; Julia Dent Grant, *Personal Memoirs* 47–48.
50. Mrs. Grant related the story to Longstreet long afterward. Longstreet interview, *New York Times*, July 24, 1885.
51. Julia Dent Grant, *Personal Memoirs* 48–49.
52. Ibid.
53. Ibid.
54. Grant, 1 *Memoirs* 48.
55. Ibid. 47.
56. Grant had great respect for Ewell, and went far out of his way in his *Memoirs* to commend him. "He was a man much esteemed, and deservedly so, in the old Army, and proved himself a gallant and efficient officer in two wars—both in my estimation unholy." Ibid. 49.
57. Ibid. 50.
58. Julia Dent Grant, *Personal Memoirs* 50.
59. Grant to Julia Dent, July 28, 1844, 1 *Grant Papers* 29–33.

CHAPTER TWO: MEXICO

General Porfirio Díaz was president of Mexico from 1876 to 1880 and 1884 to 1911. The quotation is commonly attributed to him. John S. D. Eisenhower, *So Far from God* xv (New York: Random House, 1989).

1. Richard Henry Dana, *Two Years Before the Mast: A Personal Narrative of a Life at Sea* (New York: Harper, 1840). Lieutenant John C. Frémont's *Report of the Exploring Expedition to...Oregon and North California*, the first detailed survey of the region, was not published until the autumn of 1845.
2. In 1830 the Mexican Congress, alarmed at increasing American emigration, enacted a new colonization law designed to cut off further American settlement. However, it was not implemented effectively and migration continued as before. Frederick Merk, *Manifest Destiny and Mission in American History* 20–21 (New York: Alfred A. Knopf, 1963).
3. Ulysses S. Grant, 1 *Personal Memoirs of U.S. Grant* 53 (New York: Charles L. Webster, 1885).
4. Ibid. 54–55.
5. Ibid. 56.
6. According to figures provided by the Department of Defense, American wartime casualties were as follows:

	NUMBER SERVING	DEATHS	RATE
Mexican War	78,718	13,283	16.9%
Civil War (Union)	2,213,363	364,511	16.4%
World War I	4,743,826	116,708	2.4%
World War II	16,353,659	407,316	2.5%
Vietnam War	8,744,000	58,168	0.7%

7. Grant to Mrs. George B. Bailey, June 6, 1844, 1 *The Papers of Ulysses S. Grant* 28, John Y. Simon, ed. (Carbondale: Southern Illinois University Press, 1967).
8. Grant, 1 *Memoirs* 57–58.
9. Some students of the game believe brag was the earliest example of poker. See David Parlett, *The Oxford Guide to Card Games* 101 (New York: Oxford University Press, 1990). The game itself is a

three-card form of non–draw poker, similar to 21 or three-card monte, except the hands are dealt face down with each player turning up his last card. Any player may brag he holds the best hand, and the betting begins at that point. Hoyle described it in 1751, and the 1835 edition of *Hoyle's Games,* edited by G.H____, Esq., holds that while the game is "not near so much in vogue as formerly, [it] is at present much patronized at the Oriental Club, in Hanover Square" (pages 240–42). (London: Longman, Rees, 1835). For commentary on Hoyle's "Treatise on Brag," see Allen Dowling, *The Great American Pastime* 23–40 (New York: A. S. Barnes, 1970).

10. James Longstreet interview, *New York Times,* July 24, 1885.
11. Grant to Julia, July 28, 1844, 1 *Grant Papers* 31.
12. Grant to Julia, August 31, 1844, ibid. 36.
13. Polk received 170 electoral votes to Clay's 105, with New York's 36 providing the margin of victory. If New York had gone for Clay, he would have won 141–134. Polk's popular vote total in New York was 237,588; Clay received 232,482, and Birney 15,812. Congressional Quarterly, *Guide to U.S. Elections* 267 (Washington, D.C.: Congressional Quarterly, 1975).
14. 9 *United States Statutes at Large* 108. The constitutionality of admitting Texas by joint resolution rather than treaty was briefly contested, but the text of the Constitution supported Tyler's approach. According to Article IV, Section 3, "New States may be admitted by the Congress into this Union...." The method is not specified, which would seem to leave the determination to Congress. In *United States v. Texas,* 143 U.S. 621, 634 (1892), Justice John Marshall Harlan, speaking for the Court, simply assumed the method was constitutional when he said Texas "was admitted into the Union on an equal footing with the original States in all respects whatever."
15. In his *Memoirs* Grant stated his leave commenced May 1, 1845. War Department records indicate that his leave was from April 1 to May 6. Grant, 1 *Memoirs* 35; Regimental Records, Camp Salubrity, National Archives.
16. Emma Dent Casey, "When Grant Went a Courtin'," unpublished manuscript, quoted in Lloyd Lewis, *Captain Sam Grant* 122 (Boston: Little, Brown, 1950).
17. Bancroft to Taylor, June 29, 1845, U.S. Congress, House, Executive Document No. 60, 30th Cong., 1st sess., *Messages of the President of the United States with the Correspondence Therewith Communicated, Between the Secretary of War and Other Officers of the Government on the Subject of the Mexican War* 79–81 (Washington, D.C.: Wendell and Van Benthuysen, 1848), hereinafter cited as *Mex. War Corres.*; K. Jack Bauer, *Zachary Taylor: Soldier, Planter, Statesman of the Old Southwest* 115 note 17 (Baton Rouge: Louisiana State University Press, 1985).
18. Bauer, *Zachary Taylor.* 116. Taylor was a staunch Whig, and according to Lieutenant George Meade, he was "opposed *in toto* to the Texas annexation." 1 *Life and Letters of General George Gordon Meade* 26, George Meade, ed. (New York: Charles Scribner's Sons, 1913).
19. Grant, 1 *Memoirs* 62–63.
20. In 1845 the United States had four regiments of artillery. Each regiment contained eight batteries, seven of which were equipped with heavy guns designed for stationary emplacement. Only one battery per regiment was mobile field artillery. These batteries were equipped with four howitzers each, and all four batteries were assigned to Taylor at Corpus Christi.
21. Eisenhower, *So Far from God* 35.
22. Grant, 1 *Memoirs* 168.
23. Ibid. 138, 100.
24. Ibid. 100.
25. Ibid. 139.
26. Ibid. 100.
27. Meade to his wife, April 24, 1864, 2 *Life and Letters of General George Gordon Meade* 191.
28. Lafayette McLaws interview, *New York Times,* July 24, 1885.
29. Only five of Grant's thirty-eight classmates were promoted before him. Lewis, *Captain Sam Grant* 128.
30. E. Kirby Smith to his wife, August 28, 1845, in E. Kirby Smith, *To Mexico with Scott: Letters of Ephrim Kirby Smith to His Wife* 43 (Cambridge: Harvard University Press, 1917).
31. Meade to his wife, November 3, 1845, 1 *Life and Letters of General George Gordon Meade* 35–36.
32. Grant, 1 *Memoirs* 64–65.
33. Ibid. 77–78. Emphasis in original.
34. Ibid. 87.
35. Ibid. 70.
36. Longstreet interview, *New York Times,* July 24, 1885.
37. Grant to Julia, September 14, 1845, 1 *Grant Papers* 54.
38. Grant to Julia, from Corpus Christi, October, 1845, ibid. 59.
39. Grant to Julia, February 5, 1846, ibid. 71.

40. Grant to Julia, February 7, 1846, ibid. 73. Also see Grant's letter to Julia, March 3, 1846, ibid. 74–75.
41. Grant to Julia, March 3, 1846, ibid.
42. Army of Occupation Order 30, March 8, 1846, *Mex. War Corres.* 119–120.
43. Grant, 1 *Memoirs* 85.
44. 1 *Life and Letters of General George Gordon Meade* 56.
45. Grant, 1 *Memoirs* 86.
46. Ibid. 88.
47. Grant to Julia, March 29, 1846, 1 *Grant Papers* 78.
48. E. Kirby Smith to his wife, letter written in increments beginning March 17, 1846, in Eisenhower, *So Far from God* 53–54.
49. Ibid. For Taylor's laconic report of the crossing, see his dispatch to the adjutant general, March 25, 1846, *Mex. War Corres.* 129.
50. To ease the aches of the men working on the fortifications, Taylor ordered an extra gill of whiskey be issued to them each day. Army of Occupation Order 39, Special Orders No. 45, Record Group 94, National Archives, April 6, 1846.
51. 1 *Life and Letters of General George Gordon Meade* 58–59.
52. Ampudia to Taylor, April 12, 1846, *Mex. War. Corres.* 140.
53. Ibid. 139–40.
54. Taylor to the adjutant general (TAG), April 26, 1846, ibid. 141.
55. President Polk's message to Congress, May 11, 1846, ibid. 8.
56. Grant to John W. Lowe, June 26, 1846, 1 *Grant Papers* 95.
57. Grant, 1 *Memoirs* 92.
58. Army of Occupation Order No. 58, May 7, 1846, *Mex. War Corres.* 487.
59. 1 *Life and Letters of General George Gordon Meade* 83.
60. Grant, 1 *Memoirs* 94.
61. The verse is from Rudyard Kipling's "Gunga Din," *Barrack-room Ballads and Other Verses* 23–30 (London: Methuen, 1892).
62. Grant, 1 *Memoirs* 94.
63. Ibid. 95.
64. Major Samuel Ringgold, Taylor's senior artillery officer. Ringgold is credited with developing the field artillery arm prior to the Mexican War. He was mortally wounded at Palo Alto and died several days later at Point Isabel.
65. Grant to Julia, May 11, 1846, 1 *Grant Papers* 85.
66. Ibid. Captain John Page and Lieutenant Henry D. Wallen were friends of the Dents in St. Louis. Page died of his wounds, July 12, 1846.
67. Grant to Lowe, June 26, 1846, ibid. 96.
68. Grant to Julia, May 11, 1846, ibid. 85.
69. Although the Mexican army deployed three times as many artillery pieces at Palo Alto as did Taylor, the American guns got off some 3,000 rounds to the enemy's 750. Russell F. Weigley, *History of the United States Army* 184 (New York: Macmillan, 1967).
70. 1 *Life and Letters of General George Gordon Meade* 80.
71. Grant to Lowe, June 26, 1846, 1 *Grant Papers* 96.
72. 1 *Life and Letters of General George Gordon Meade* 83.
73. Grant, 1 *Memoirs* 97–98.
74. Ibid.
75. 1 *Life and Letters of General George Gordon Meade* 81–83.
76. Taylor to adjutant general, May 12, 1846, *Mex. War Corres.* 297.
77. Grant to Julia, May 11, 1846, 1 *Grant Papers* 86.
78. Grant to Lowe, June 26, 1846, ibid. 97.
79. Bauer, *Zachary Taylor* 164–65, and the sources cited therein.
80. Grant to Lowe, June 26, 1846, 1 *Grant Papers* 97.
81. 1 *Life and Letters of General George Gordon Meade* 105, 94, 121.
82. Ibid. 121.
83. Hamlin Garland, *Ulysses S. Grant* 74, 2nd ed. (New York: Macmillan, 1920).
84. Taylor advised the War Department his prime concern was to draw volunteers from "as many states as possible." In fact, he chose the units least depleted by disease: three regiments of Texans; the Mississippi Rifles (commanded by Taylor's former son-in-law, Colonel Jefferson Finis Davis); the Tennessee Regiment; the 1st Ohio; and the Baltimore-Washington Battalion. Taylor to adjutant general, September 3, 1846, *Mex. War Corres.* 417.
85. Lewis, *Captain Sam Grant,* 167–68.

86. Ibid. 168–69.

87. Grant, 1 *Memoirs* 105–6.

88. The comment was made by Grant's friend, Alexander Hays, later General Hays, who was killed leading his brigade against Confederate forces in the Wilderness. Lewis, *Captain Sam Grant* 172.

89. Justin Smith, 1 *The War with Mexico* 230–38 (New York: Macmillan, 1919).

90. Worth's division consisted of the 5th, 7th, and 8th infantry regiments, two battalions of dismounted artillerymen, the Texas cavalry, and two howitzer batteries. *Mex. War Corres.* 102.

91. Grant, 1 *Memoirs* 110–11.

92. Ibid. 111.

93. Ibid. 112.

94. Robert McNutt McElroy, 1 *Jefferson Davis: The Unreal and the Real* 83 (New York: Harper and Brothers, 1937).

95. John R. Kenly, *Memoirs of a Maryland Volunteer* 119 (Philadelphia: J. B. Lippincott, 1873).

96. Charles P. Roland, *Albert Sidney Johnston: Soldier of Three Republics* 136 (Austin: University of Texas Press, 1964).

97. 1 *Life and Letters of General George Gordon Meade* 135.

98. John W. Emerson, "Grant's Life in the West and his Mississippi Valley Campaigns," *Midland Monthly* 40 (January 1897).

99. 1 *Life and Letters of General George Gordon Meade* 136.

100. Grant, 1 *Memoirs* 115–16.

101. The comments are those of Mary Robinson, who heard Grant tell the story at White Haven in 1848. *St. Louis Republican,* July 24, 1885.

102. Taylor's orders, sent to him by General Winfield Scott, June 12, 1846, were ambiguous: "Should continued success attend your operations, you may sometime before be met by the proposition to treat for peace, with an intermediate armistice. No such proposition will be entertained by you, without your first being satisfied that it is made in good faith on the part of the enemy. Being satisfied on that point, you may conclude an armistice for a limited time, and refer the proposition to treat for peace to the government here." Ampudia told Taylor that was the intent of the Mexican government, and Taylor was satisfied. Eisenhower, *So Far from God* 148–49.

103. James K. Polk, entry of October 11, 1846, *Polk: The Diary of a President, 1845–1849,* 155, Allan Nevins, ed. (London: Longmans Green, 1929).

104. 1 *Life and Letters of General George Gordon Meade* 138–39.

105. Ibid. 151. Emphasis in original.

106. Grant, 1 *Memoirs* 117.

107. Taylor to adjutant general, September 28, 1846, *Mex. War Corres.* 424.

108. Grant to Julia, October 3, 1846, 1 *Grant Papers* 113.

109. Ibid.

110. Grant, 1 *Memoirs* 138.

111. Ibid. 138–39.

112. Eisenhower, *So Far from God* 173.

113. Diary of Private Joshua E. Jackson, Illinois State Historical Library.

114. 1 *Life and Letters of General George Gordon Meade* 182.

115. For the role of the Mississippi Rifles at Buena Vista, see Joseph E. Chance, *Jefferson Davis's Mexican War Regiment* 81–103 (Jackson: University Press of Mississippi, 1991).

116. It was on this occasion Taylor allegedly said, "A little more grape, Captain Bragg." What Taylor actually called out was: "What are you using, Captain, grape or canister?"

    "Canister, General."

    "Single or double?"

    "Single."

    "Well, double-shot your guns and give 'em hell."

    See Grady McWhiney, *Braxton Bragg and Confederate Defeat* 90–93 (New York: Columbia University Press, 1969).

117. Smith, 1 *War with Mexico* 395.

118. Grant, 1 *Memoirs* 124.

119. Daniel H. Hill, "The Real Stonewall Jackson," 47 *Century Magazine* 624 (November 1893–April 1894).

120. *Mex. War Corres.* 230–37; Douglas Southhall Freeman, 1 *R.E. Lee* 225–35 (New York: Charles Scribner's Sons, 1934); Charles W. Eliot, *Winfield Scott: The Soldier and the Man* 461–62 (New York: Macmillan, 1937).

121. Grant to John W. Lowe, May 3, 1847, 1 *Grant Papers* 135–37.

122. Ibid.

123. *Mex. War Corres.* 1089–90; Winfield Scott, 2 *The Memoirs of Lieut-Gen Winfield Scott* 445–51 (New York: Sheldon, 1864).

124. Grant, 1 *Memoirs* 134.

125. Ibid. 132.

126. Eisenhower, *So Far from God* 297, 303.

127. Smith, 2 *War with Mexico* 89.

128. Grant, 1 *Memoirs* 137.

129. R. Ernest Dupuy and Trevor N. Dupuy, *Military Heritage of America* 160–61 (New York: McGraw-Hill, 1956).

130. The 1,053 American casualties included 137 killed, 878 wounded, and 38 missing. 30th Congress, 2nd session, House Executive Document 1, *Message of the President of the United States...With Accompanying Documents* 313–14 (Washington, D.C.: Wendall and Van Benthuysen, 1848).

131. Smith, 2 *War with Mexico* 118; K. Jack Bauer, *The Mexican War* 305 note 38 (New York: Macmillan, 1974).

132. Scott, 2 *Memoirs* 481–82.

133. Grant, 1 *Memoirs* 145–46.

134. Eisenhower, *So Far from God* 330–31; Bauer, *Mexican War* 306–7.

135. Grant, 1 *Memoirs* 148.

136. See, for example, Smith, 2 *War with Mexico* 127–39; Bauer, *Mexican War* 307–8; Lewis, *Captain Sam Grant* 237.

137. Lewis, ibid.

138. Ibid. 153.

139. Ethan Allen Hitchcock, *Fifty Years in Camp and Field: Diary of Major-General Ethan Allen Hitchcock* 297–98, W. A. Crofutt, ed. (New York: G. P. Putnam's Sons, 1909).

140. John Sedgwick, 1 *Correspondence of John Sedgwick, Major General* 113, 138 (New York: DeVinne, 1902).

141. Grant, 1 *Memoirs* 154.

142. Dupuy and Dupuy, *Military Heritage* 166.

143. Bauer, *Mexican War* 318.

144. Grant, 1 *Memoirs* 158.

145. Ibid. 159.

146. Dupuy and Dupuy, *Military Heritage* 166.

147. Bauer, *Mexican War* 326.

148. Grant, 1 *Memoirs* 164.

149. Ibid. 165–66.

150. Ibid. 168–69.

151. Grant to Julia, September 1847, 1 *Grant Papers* 146–48.

CHAPTER THREE: RESIGNATION

1. For the text of the Treaty of Guadalupe Hidalgo, see 5 *Treaties and Other International Acts of the United States* 207–36, David Hunter Miller, ed. (Washington, D.C.: Government Printing Office, 1937). Also see Robert W. Drexler, *Guilty of Making Peace: A Biography of Nicholas P. Trist* 120ff. (Lanham, Md.: University Press of America, 1991).

2. The Senate's advice and consent was a near-run thing. Democratic senators from the South, led by Sam Houston and Jefferson Davis, opposed the treaty because it did not incorporate northern Mexico into the United States, while the Whigs, led by Daniel Webster, opposed it because it took anything other than Texas. Ultimately the Democrats fell into line and the treaty was approved by a vote of 38–14, four more than the required two-thirds majority. See especially Richard Griswold del Castillo, *The Treaty of Guadalupe Hidalgo: A Legacy of Conflict* 43–51 (Norman: University of Oklahoma Press, 1990).

3. Grant to Julia, September, 1847, 1 *The Papers of Ulysses S. Grant* 146–47, John Y. Simon, ed. (Carbondale: Southern Illinois University Press, 1967).

4. Grant to Julia, January 9, 1848, ibid. 148–49.

5. Ulysses S. Grant, 1 *Personal Memoirs of U.S. Grant* 162–63 (New York: Charles L. Webster, 1885).

6. Sixty-eight were killed in battle; 218 died of wounds, disease, and accidents. *Niles Weekly Register,* November 15, 1848.

7. For McClellan's reaction to West Point and the Mexican War, see Stephen W. Sears, *George B. McClellan: The Young Napoleon* 5–27 (New York: Ticknor and Fields, 1988), as well as *The Mexican*

War Diary of General George B. McClellan, 16–21, William Starr Myers, ed. (Princeton: Princeton University Press, 1917). For Halleck, see Stephen E. Ambrose, *Halleck: Lincoln's Chief of Staff* 7 (Baton Rouge: Louisiana State University Press, 1962). Also see *Recollections of General Henry W. Halleck in 1847–49,* Doyce B. Nunis, ed. (Los Angeles: Dawson's Book Shop, 1977).

8. The comment is that of Joseph E. Johnston, quoted in A. C. Avery, "Life and Character of Lieutenant-General D. H. Hill," 21 *Southern Historical Society Papers* 115 (1893).

9. Joseph Hooker, address to the fifth reunion of the Society of the Army of the Cumberland, 1871 (Cincinnati: no publisher, 1872).

10. 30 *War of the Rebellion: A Compilation of the Official Records of the Union and Confederate Armies* 358 (Washington, D.C.: Government Printing Office, 1890).

11. Grant, 1 *Memoirs* 191–92.

12. Ibid. 180.

13. For Grant's affidavit and supporting documents concerning the theft, see 1 *Grant Papers* 162–63.

14. Grant, 1 *Memoirs* 175–78.

15. Grant to Julia, September 1847, 1 *Grant Papers* 146.

16. Grant to Julia, January 9, 1848, ibid. 148–49.

17. Grant to Julia, February 14, 1848, ibid. 150–52.

18. Grant to Julia, March 22, 1848, ibid. 153–54.

19. Grant to Julia, May 7, 1848, ibid. 155–57.

20. Cadmus Marcellus Wilcox, *History of the Mexican War* 551–52, Mary Rachel Wilcox, ed. (Washington, D.C.: Church News Publishing, 1892).

21. 1 *Grant Papers* 164, note; cf. Grant, 1 *Memoirs* 193.

22. Julia Dent Grant, *The Personal Memoirs of Julia Dent Grant: Mrs. Ulysses S. Grant* 54–55, John Y. Simon, ed. (New York: G. P. Putnam's Sons, 1975); Emma Dent Casey, "When Grant Went a Courtin',"quoted in Lloyd Lewis, *Captain Sam Grant* 283 (Boston: Little, Brown, 1950).

23. Julia Dent Grant, *Personal Memoirs* 55.

24. Ibid. 56.

25. See Grant to Maj. O. F. Winship, Ass't. Adjt. Gen., February 23, 1849, 1 *Grant Papers* 175–77.

26. Julia Dent Grant, *Personal Memoirs* 59.

27. Lee to Quartermaster General, December 2, 1848, 1 *Grant Papers* 169.

28. For the history of Madison Barracks, including a description of the battle of Sackets Harbor, May 29, 1813, see Gordon G. Heiner, *From Saints to Red Legs: Madison Barracks, the History of a Border Post* 18 (Watertown, N.Y.: A. W. Munk, n.d.).

29. Lee to the adjutant general (TAG), January 16, 1849, 1 *Grant Papers* 381.

30. Grant to the Ass't Adjt. Gen., February 23, 1849, ibid. 175–77.

31. Lee to TAG, January 29, 1849, ibid. 381.

32. Eastern Division Special Orders No. 18, March 2, 1849, cited ibid. 181, note.

33. Julia Dent Grant, *Personal Memoirs* 61–62.

34. From Julia's description of social life in Detroit, see ibid. 65–68.

35. Grant, 1 *Memoirs* 233.

36. Albert Deane Richardson, *A Personal History of Ulysses S. Grant* 138 (Hartford, Conn.: American Publishing, 1868).

37. Grant to Julia, June 4, 1851, 1 *Grant Papers* 204–5.

38. Julia Dent Grant, *Personal Memoirs* 69–71. Also see Grant to Julia, June 29 and August 3, 1851, 1 *Grant Papers* 214, 223.

39. Grant's commission as brevet captain carried the date of rank as May 27, 1851. It is reproduced in William H. Allen, *The American Civil War Book and Grant Album* 82 (Boston: W. H. Allen, 1894).

40. Julia Dent Grant, *Personal Memoirs* 71.

41. Grant, 1 *Memoirs* 194.

42. Grant to Julia, June 24, 1852, 1 *Grant Papers* 237–39.

43. At Grant's request, General Worth convened a board of inquiry in Mexico. Chaired by Colonel Francis Lee of the 4th Infantry, it concluded "no blame can attach to Lt. U.S. Grant, that he took every means to secure the Money, and that the place he deposited it was the most secure in camp." Mary A. Benjamin, "Grant and the Lost $1,000," 69 *The Collector* 17–20 (1956).

44. The statement of fact is provided by John S. Gallagher, third auditor of the Treasury, in a letter to Thomas Corwin, Secretary of the Treasury, February 12, 1852. It is quoted in 1 *Grant Papers* 244 note 1.

45. Grant to Julia, July 4, 1852, ibid. 245–46. Grant's effort to clear the record began in 1849 when at his request Representative David Fisher of Ohio introduced a private bill "The Memorial of U.S. Grant, of the United States Army, praying to be released from further payment to the government, of public moneys which were stolen from him near Jalapa, in Mexico." 30th Cong., 2d sess.,

House Journal 345. The same petition was reintroduced in the next Congress by Representative Jonathan Morris of Ohio. 31st Cong., 1st sess., *House Journal* 1073.

46. "Reminiscences of Delia B. Sheffield" 50, William S. Lewis, ed., 15 *Washington Historical Quarterly* (Summer 1924).

47. John Haskell Kemble, *The Panama Route* 239 (Berkeley: University of California Press, 1943).

48. Grant to Julia, July 15, 1852, 1 *Grant Papers* 247–49.

49. Grant, 1 *Memoirs* 195–97; 1 *Grant Papers* 249–50, 261–62. One survivor wrote "the most laborious part [of the trip] fell to the lot of our quartermaster, Captain Grant, [whose] services were of the greatest importance....His kindliness and thoughtfulness were not confined to his own command, but he assisted many [civilian] passengers in getting across the Isthmus." [Lieutenant] Henry C. Hodges to William Conant Church, July 7, 1897, Church Papers, Library of Congress.

50. Sheffield, "Reminiscences" 56.

51. Hamlin Garland, *Ulysses S. Grant* 119 (New York: Macmillan, 1920); Frank A. Burr, *General U.S. Grant* 114 (Boston: Little, Brown, 1885).

52. Grant to Julia, August 9, 1852, 1 *Grant Papers* 251–53.

53. Grant to Julia, February 15, 1853, ibid. 287–90.

54. Hodges to Church, July 7, 1897, Church Papers.

55. Grant told Congress "The subject of an interocean canal to connect the Atlantic and Pacific oceans through the Isthmus of Darien is one in which commerce is greatly interested. Instructions have been given to our minister to the Republic of Columbia [sic] to endeavor to obtain authority for a survey by this Government, in order to determine the practicability of such an undertaking, and a charter for the right of way to build, by private enterprise, such a work, if the survey proves it to be practicable." 7 *Messages and Papers of the Presidents, 1789–1897* 33, James D. Richardson, ed. (Washington, D.C.: Bureau of National Literature and Art, 1898).

56. Charles G. Ellington, *The Trial of U.S. Grant: The Pacific Coast Years, 1852–1854* 64 (Glendale, California: Arthur H. Clarke, 1987).

57. *Panama Herald,* July 27, 1852.

58. Major O. Cross to Quartermaster General, August 31, 1852, *House Executive Document No. 1* 89 (Serial No. 674), 32nd Cong., 1st sess.

59. Grant to Julia, August 9, 1852, 1 *Grant Papers* 253. Grant's subsequent statement to the board of survey placed responsibility on the local contractor's failure to provide prompt transportation across the isthmus. Ibid. 261–62.

60. Bureau of the Census, *A Century of Population Growth, 1790–1900* 222–23 (Washington, D.C.: Government Printing Office, 1909); Joann Levy, *They Saw the Elephant: Women in the California Gold Rush* xv (Hamden, Conn.: Anchor, 1990).

61. Grant to Julia, September 19, 1852, 1 *Grant Papers* 265–67.

62. Grant, 1 *Memoirs* 200.

63. Hodges to Church, July 7, 1897, Church Papers.

64. Grant to Julia, August 20, 1852, 1 *Grant Papers* 256–58.

65. Grant, 1 *Memoirs* 201.

66. Grant to Julia, August 30, 1852, 1 *Grant Papers* 258–60.

67. Arthur S. Morton, *A History of the Canadian West to 1870–71* 2nd ed., Lewis G. Thomas, ed. (Toronto: University of Toronto Press, 1973). Also see Richard I. Ruggles, *A Country So Interesting: The Hudson's Bay Company and Two Centuries of Mapping* 175–77 (Montreal: McGill-Queen's University Press, 1991).

68. Grant to Julia, October 7, 1852, 1 *Grant Papers* 267–69.

69. Julia Dent Grant, *Personal Memoirs* 72. Grant's veiled account of the episode is lightly touched on in his letters to Julia of February 15, March 31, and June 15, 1853, 1 *Grant Papers* 289, 297, 301.

70. Frank A. Burr, *General U.S. Grant* 116 (Boston: Little Brown, 1885).

71. Ibid.

72. Grant to Julia, February 15, 1853, 1 *Grant Papers* 287–90.

73. Grant to Julia, March 4, 1853, ibid. 290–93.

74. Grant to Julia, March 31, 1853, ibid. 296–98.

75. Grant to Julia, March 19, 1853, ibid. 294–96.

76. Grant to Julia, June 15, 1853, ibid. 301–3.

77. The episode was related by Delia Sheffield, whose husband had been recruited by Grant to buy the chickens. Sheffield, "Reminiscences" 61.

78. 2 *Historical Magazine* 179, 2nd Series, September 1867.

79. Burr, *General Grant* 116. It was typical of Grant's sense of honor that on June 28, 1855, when he was struggling to make a living as a farmer in Missouri, he wrote Wallen a promise to pay $300 be-

cause of "our unfortunate San Francisco speculations." Ten years later, on December 29, 1865, General Grant sent Wallen a check canceling the debt.

80. Grant to Julia, October 26, 1852, 1 *Grant Papers* 269–70.
81. Grant to Julia, December 3, 1852, ibid. 274–76.
82. Grant to Julia, December 19, 1852, ibid. 277–79.
83. Grant to Julia, March 4, 1853, ibid. 290–93.
84. Grant to Julia, March 31, 1853, ibid. 296–98.
85. Grant to Julia, June 15, 1853, ibid. 301–3.
86. Ibid.
87. Second Lieutenant George Crook, who joined the 4th Infantry in San Francisco in 1852, remembered that all of the officers he met were drunk at least once a day, "and mostly until the wee hours of the morning. I never had seen such gambling and carousing before or since.

    "My first duty after reporting was a file closer to the funeral escort of major [Albert S.] Miller, who had just died from the effects of strong drink. Major Hannibal Day commanded the escort, and when all of us officers had assembled in the room where the corpse was lying, he said, 'Well, fellows, Old Miller is dead and he can't drink, so let's us all take a drink.' I was never more horrified in my life." *General George Crook: His Autobiography* 7, Martin F. Schmitt, ed. (Norman: University of Oklahoma Press, 1946).
88. The testimony is that of Commissary General Robert McFeely, then a second lieutenant in the 4th Infantry, who served with Grant from 1851 to 1853. Ellington, *Trial of U.S. Grant* 167.
89. Hodges to Church, January 5, 1897, Church Papers.
90. McClellan was a perfectionist even then. His plans called for a party of 61 persons, 200 horses and pack mules, three months' rations, plus an infantry escort of 29 soldiers from Fort Vancouver. Two weeks out McClellan realized he had overprepared. He cut everything by half and sent the infantry escort back. Sears, *George B. McClellan* 38. For Grant's comments on the expedition, see his letters to Julia, June 15 and June 28, 1853, and to the chief quartermaster of the Pacific Division, July 25, 1853. 1 *Grant Papers* 301–5, 308–10.
91. Hodge to Church, January 5, 1897, Church Papers. Also see Sears, *George B. McClellan* 38, 73.
92. Grant to Commissary General, September 8, 1853, 1 *Grant Papers* 312–13.
93. For Grant's intent, see his letters to Julia, January 29 and February 15, 1853, ibid. 285–90.
94. Ibid. 311 note.
95. Quartermaster General to Grant, December 2, 1853, ibid. note. The commissary general's office also replied negatively, December 17, 1853, ibid. 313 note.
96. Lloyd Lewis states Grant received notification on September 20, 1853. The vacancy occurred upon the death of Brevet Lieutenant Colonel William W. S. Bliss, the longtime aide to General Taylor, August 5, 1853. Bliss had been carried on the rolls of the 4th Infantry for nineteen years, although except for a few months after his graduation from West Point in 1834, he had not served with the regiment. Lewis, *Captain Sam Grant* 320, 322.
97. Davis's letter to Grant was dated August 9, 1853, although President Pierce did not sign his commission until February 9, 1854. 1 *Grant Papers* 312 note. The War Department was often behind in its paperwork and there was nothing unusual in the delay.
98. Sheffield, "Reminiscences" 61.
99. Lewis, *Captain Sam Grant* 323. Lieutenant George Crook, who served with Buchanan at Fort Humboldt, thought he was "particularly elated with his own importance and lost no opportunity to impress upon all of us...how far we fell short of what he expected." Crook was appointed Buchanan's adjutant and as he reports, "I soon became familiar with his idiosyncrasies, and I avoided him whenever it was possible, for I never believed in that mode of discipline which consists in trying to break down men's self respect and make a mere machine of them instead of appealing to their better feelings and judgment.

    "Colonel Buchanan's principle was to allow no subordinate to make suggestions unasked, and told me, on one occasion, never to take the suggestions of a non-commissioned officer but go ahead and do it my own way, even if I knew I was wrong. It was clear he must have followed this principle, judging from the number of mistakes he made."

    Crook wrote with an acid pen. His view of Buchanan is benign compared with his appreciation of Philip H. Sheridan, his former West Point roommate, with whom he served at Cedar Creek. "The adulations heaped on him by a grateful nation for his supposed genius turned his head, which, added to his natural disposition, caused him to bloat his little carcass with debauchery and dissipation, which carried him off prematurely." Crook, *Autobiography* 9–10, 134 note.
100. J. C. Ropes, *The Army Under Pope* 140 (New York: Charles Scribner's Sons, 1882).
101. The inspector general's report was rendered by Colonel Joseph Mansfield, later Major General Mansfield, who was killed leading his division of the Army of the Potomac at Antietam. *Joseph K.*

F. Mansfield on the Conditions of the Western Forts, 1853–1854 119–20, 162–63, Robert W. Frazer, ed. (Norman: University of Oklahoma Press, 1963).

102. Grant to Julia, July 13, 1853, 1 *Grant Papers* 305–7.
103. Grant to Julia, January 18, 1854, ibid. 315.
104. Grant to Julia, February 2, 1854, ibid. 316–18.
105. W. I. Reed to William C. Church, August 25, 1909, Church Papers.
106. Grant to Julia, February 6, 1854, 1 *Grant Papers* 320–22.
107. Ibid. 322 note 2.
108. Grant to Julia, March 6, 1854, ibid. 322–24. Emphasis in original.
109. Ibid.
110. Grant to Julia, April 3, 1854. Grant began the letter on March 25, was interrupted after writing a few lines, and continued on April 3. Ibid. 326–28.
111. Grant to the adjutant general (TAG), April 11, 1854, ibid. 329.
112. Hodges to Church, January 5, 1897, Church Papers.
113. Garland, Grant 127.
114. Grant, 1 *Memoirs* 210.
115. John Eaton and Ethel O. Mason, *Grant, Lincoln, and the Freedmen: Reminiscences of the Civil War with Special Reference for the Work of the Contrabands and Freedmen of the Mississippi Valley* 100 (New York: Longmans, Green, 1907).
116. The regimental commander to whom Buchanan spoke was Thomas Anderson, who afterward commanded Fort Vancouver and became a general officer during the Philippine Insurrection. Thomas Anderson to Hamlin Garland, August 15, 1896, Garland Papers.
117. Julia Dent Grant, *Personal Memoirs* 75.
118. Grant to Julia, May 2, 1854, 1 *Grant Papers* 332.
119. War Department Special Orders No. 87, June 3, 1854.
120. 1 *Grant Papers* 330.
121. Ibid.
122. Ibid. 330–31.
123. Ibid. 331.
124. *New York Daily Times,* June 26, 1854. For details of Grant's voyage home, see Ellington, *Trial of U.S. Grant* 191–98.
125. Garland, *Grant* 128–29; Lewis, *Captain Sam Grant* 336–37.
126. Buckner interview with Hamlin Garland, Garland Papers.
127. Ibid. Also see Arndt M. Stickles, *Simon Bolivar Buckner: Borderland Knight* 34 (Chapel Hill: University of North Carolina Press, 1940).
128. Julia Dent Grant, *Personal Memoirs* 72.
129. William S. McFeely, *Grant: A Biography* 57 (New York: W. W. Norton, 1981).
130. Grant, 1 *Memoirs* 210–11.
131. Julia Dent Grant, *Personal Memoirs* 79.
132. The team of horses was provided on easy terms by Charles Ford, manager of the United States Express at St. Louis, an old friend of Grant's from Sackets Harbor. Grant never forgot Ford's assistance. Hamlin Garland, "Grant's Life in Missouri," 8 *McClure's Magazine* 516 (1897).
133. Grant to Jesse Grant, December 28, 1856, 1 *Grant Papers* 334–35.
134. Grant to Jesse Grant, February 1857, ibid. 336–37.
135. *Washington Post,* July 24, 1885.
136. Lewis, *Captain Sam Grant* 346–47.
137. Garland, *Grant* 137–38. After leaving the presidency in 1877, whenever Grant visited Washington he stayed with General Beale, and it was Beale to whom he gave the two Arabian stallions presented to him by the sultan of Turkey. Beale later sold one of the stallions, Leopard, to Randolph Huntington, who began the first purebred Arabian breeding program in the United States. See Chapter 20. For Beale on Grant, see *Washington Post,* July 24, 1885.
138. Church, *Grant* 57.
139. Ibid.
140. Grant to his sister Mary, August 22, 1857, 1 *Grant Papers* 338–39.
141. Grant received $22 from J. S. Freligh of St. Louis. Whether he redeemed the watch is unknown. Ibid. 339–40.
142. Grant to Mary Grant, March 21, 1858, ibid. 340–41; Julia Dent Grant, *Personal Memoirs* 80.
143. James Longstreet interview, *New York Times,* July 24, 1885.
144. Grant to Mary Grant, September 7, 1858, 1 *Grant Papers* 343.
145. Garland, "Grant's Life in Missouri" 518.
146. Ibid. 518–19.

147. The figures were compiled from the *St. Louis Republican,* 1856–58.
148. Lewis, *Captain Sam Grant* 363.
149. 1 *Grant Papers* 353 note 1.
150. Ibid. 347. After describing William Jones's appearance, Grant certified that he did "hereby manumit, emancipate and set free said William from slavery forever."
151. The text of Reynolds's letter, with Frost's endorsement, is ibid. 348–49. Reynolds later served as a major general of volunteers and was Thomas's chief of staff in the Army of the Cumberland. Frost became a brigadier general in the Confederate army.
152. Grant to Jesse Root Grant, September 23, 1859, ibid. 351–53. *Cf.,* Garland, "Grant's Life in Missouri" 517–18.
153. In his *Memoirs,* Grant attributed his 1856 vote to his fear of war and disunion. "Under these circumstances I preferred the success of a candidate whose election would prevent or postpone secession, to seeing the country plunged into a war the end of which no man could foretell. With a Democrat elected by the unanimous vote of the Slave States, there could be no pretext for secession for four years. I very much hoped that the passions of the people would subside in that time, and the catastrophe be averted altogether; if it was not, I believed the country would be better prepared to receive the shock and resist it. I therefore voted for James Buchanan for President." Grant, 1 *Memoirs* 215.
154. John Russell Young, 2 *Around the World with General Grant* 268 (New York: American News, 1879).
155. Lewis, *Captain Sam Grant* 370.
156. The comment is by George W. Fishback, publisher of the *Missouri Democrat,* written expressly for *McClure's Magazine.* Garland, "Grant's Life in Missouri" 520.
157. Julia Dent Grant, *Personal Memoirs* 82.
158. Lewis, *Captain Sam Grant* 371.
159. Grant to Julia, March 14, 1860, 1 *Grant Papers* 355–56.
160. Bruce Catton, *U.S. Grant and the American Military Tradition* 53 (Boston: Little, Brown, 1954).
161. Lewis, *Captain Sam Grant* 373.
162. Hamlin Garland, "Grant at the Outbreak of the War," 9 *McClure's Magazine* 601 (1897).
163. Jesse has been quoted as saying Grant "took hold of the business with his accustomed industry and was a very good salesman." The comment was made after the war and warrants skepticism. James Grant Wilson, *The Life and Public Services of Ulysses Simpson Grant* 16 (New York: R. M. DeWitt, 1885).
164. Lewis, *Captain Sam Grant* 377.
165. 1 *Grant Papers* 359.
166. Richardson, *A Personal History of Ulysses S. Grant* 172, 175.
167. Richardson, 5 *Messages and Papers of the Presidents* 3206–13.
168. "I am ordered by the Government of the Confederate States to demand the evacuation of Fort Sumter," wrote Beauregard. "All proper facilities will be afforded for the removal of yourself and command...to any post in the United States which you may select. The flag which you have upheld so long and with so much fortitude, under the most trying circumstances, may be saluted by you on taking it down." 1 *War of the Rebellion.*
169. "General," wrote Anderson, "I have the honor to acknowledge the receipt of your communication demanding the evacuation of this fort, and to say, in reply thereto, that it is a demand with which I regret that my sense of honor, and of my obligations to my Government, prevent my compliance. Thanking you for the fair, manly, and courteous terms proposed, and for the high compliment paid me, I am, general, very respectfully your obedient servant, Robert Anderson, Major, First Artillery, Commanding." Ibid.
170. Anderson's forces held Fort Sumter for a day and a half under sustained fire from Confederate shore batteries. Not until his provisions were exhausted did he strike his colors. As a result of his heroic defense, Anderson became an immediate Union hero. Lincoln promoted him to brigadier general and dispatched him to his native Kentucky to keep that state in the Union. Ill health forced Anderson to retire from the army late in 1861, but he was recalled to active duty briefly in April 1865 and presided over the ceremony on April 12 that raised his shot and tattered battle flag above Fort Sumter once more.

CHAPTER FOUR: WAR

Chaplain Crane's epigraph quotation is from his article, "Grant As a Colonel: Conversation Between Grant and His Chaplain," 7 *McClure's Magazine* 40 (June 1896).

1. David Herbert Donald suggests Lincoln's newness in Washington, his inexperience as an administrator, and his preference to react to events rather than take the initiative help explain his inaction during his first six weeks in office. *Lincoln* 292–93, 645 (New York: Simon and Schuster, 1995). For additional discussion of Lincoln's motives, see James M. McPherson, *Battle Cry of Freedom* 272 note 78 (New York: Oxford University Press, 1988); James G. Randall, *Lincoln the Liberal Statesman* 88–117 (New York: Dodd, Mead, 1947); Richard N. Current, *Lincoln and the First Shot* 194–99 (Philadelphia: J. B. Lippincott, 1963); John Shipley Tilley, *Lincoln Takes Command* 172–75, 179–89 (Chapel Hill: University of North Carolina Press, 1941); Charles W. Ramsdell, "Lincoln and Fort Sumter," 3 *Journal of Southern History* 259–88 (1937); Kenneth Stampp, "Lincoln and the Strategy of Defense in the Crisis of 1861," 11 ibid. 297–32 (1945).

2. On April 9, 1861, Davis, with the consent of his cabinet, and fearing Lincoln was about to reinforce the beleaguered Charleston garrison, instructed Beauregard to "at once demand [Fort Sumter's] evacuation, and, if this is refused, proceed in such manner as you may determine to reduce it." Quoted in Shelby Foote, 1 *The Civil War* 48 (New York: Random House, 1958).

3. The quotation is from T. Harry Williams, *P. G. T. Beauregard: Napoleon in Gray* 50 (Baton Rouge: Louisiana State University Press, 1954).

4. Orville Hickman Browning, entry of July 3, 1861, 1 *The Diary of Orville Hickman Browning* 477, Theodore C. Pease and James G. Randall, eds. (Springfield: Illinois State Historical Library, 1925).

5. George Ticknor, 2 *Life, Letters, and Journals of George Ticknor* 433–34, Anna Ticknor and George S. Hillard, eds. (Boston: J. R. Osgood, 1877).

6. *New York Times,* April 15, 1861.

7. *New York Tribune,* April 17, 1861.

8. *Chicago Tribune,* April 15, 1861.

9. Robert W. Johannsen, *Stephen A. Douglas* 868 (New York: Oxford University Press, 1973).

10. Allan Nevins, 1 *The War for the Union* 93 (New York: Charles Scribner's Sons, 1959).

11. *New York Evening Post,* April 23, 1861.

12. John B. Gordon, *Reminiscences of the Civil War* 10 (New York: Charles Scribner's Sons, 1904).

13. Henry T. Shanks, *The Secession Movement in Virginia, 1847–1861* 268 (Richmond, Va.: Garrett and Massie, 1934).

14. William Howard Russell, *My Diary North and South* 52, Fletcher Pratt, ed. (New York: Harper, 1954).

15. James D. Richardson, ed., 6 *Messages and Papers of the Presidents, 1789–1897* 13–14 (Washington, D.C.: Bureau of National Literature and Art, 1897).

16. The Virginia convention adopted an ordinance of secession (88–55) on April 17; Arkansas on May 6 (65–5); Tennessee on May 7 (59–22); and North Carolina on May 20 (unanimous). Ralph A. Wooster, *The Secession Conventions in the South,* 151ff. (Princeton: Princeton University Press, 1962).

17. Ulysses S. Grant, 1 *The Personal Memoirs of U.S. Grant* 231 (New York: Charles L. Webster, 1885).

18. Grant to Frederick Dent, April 19, 1861, 2 *The Papers of Ulysses S. Grant* 3–4, John Y. Simon, ed. (Carbondale: Southern Illinois University Press, 1969).

19. Ibid.

20. Augustus Louis Chetlain interview with Hamlin Garland, Hamlin Garland Papers, University of Southern California.

21. Hamlin Garland, "Grant at the Outbreak of the War," 9 *McClure's Magazine* 605 (May 1897).

22. The Galena company styled itself the Jo Daviess Guards, Galena being the county seat of Jo Daviess County. The county was named for Jo Hamilton Daviess, a prominent Kentucky lawyer and Indian fighter. A brother-in-law of Chief Justice John Marshall, Daviess was killed leading a charge at the battle of Tippecanoe in November 1811.

The uniform Grant prescribed was similar to the regular army infantry: blue frock coats and dark gray pants with a blue cord down the side of the trousers. Money to buy the cloth was advanced by the Galena bank, N. Corwith & Co. Local tailors volunteered their services to cut the cloth, and the ladies of Galena made them up. Grant, 1 *Memoirs* 231–32; 2 *Grant Papers* 8 note 3.

23. Grant to Jesse Root Grant, April 21, 1861, 2 *Grant Papers* 6–7. Grant had little reason for concern. Jesse Grant lived unmolested in Kentucky throughout the war. Jesse also anticipated his son's desire to return to the service. The day after Lincoln's call for volunteers Jesse had written to General Winfield Scott asking that Grant be recalled to active duty. On April 25, 1861, after receiving Grant's letter, Jesse wrote to his friend, Attorney General Edward Bates, requesting him to "see General Scott & if necessary the Pres & let me know soon if they can restore him to the Reg Army." 2 ibid., note 2.

24. Lloyd Lewis, *Captain Sam Grant* 410 (Boston: Little, Brown, 1950).

25. Grant to Julia, April 27, 1861, 2 *Grant Papers* 9–11.

26. Wallace J. Schutz and Walter N. Trenerry, *Abandoned By Lincoln: A Military Biography of General John Pope* 62–64 (Urbana: University of Illinois Press, 1990).

27. Van Dorn resigned from the United States army on January 3, 1861, six days before his native state of Mississippi seceded. When Jefferson Davis was elected president of the Confederacy, Van Dorn succeeded him as major general of the Mississippi militia. Robert G. Hartje, *Van Dorn: The Life and Times of a Confederate General* 77 (Nashville: Vanderbilt University Press, 1967). Longstreet offered his services to the state of Alabama at about the same time. Jeffry D. Wert, *General James Longstreet* 52–55 (New York: Simon and Schuster, 1993). Kirby Smith to his mother, March 3, 1861, Kirby Smith Papers, University of North Carolina. Also see Joseph Howard Parks, *General Edmund Kirby Smith, C.S.A.* 119 (Baton Rouge: Louisiana State University Press, 1954).

28. Craig L. Symonds, *Joseph E. Johnston: A Civil War Biography* 96–97 (New York: W. W. Norton, 1992).

29. Michael B. Ballard, *Pemberton: A Biography* 84–87 (Jackson: University Press of Mississippi, 1991).

30. Freeman Cleves, *Rock of Chickamauga: The Life of General George H. Thomas* 67–68 (Norman: University of Oklahoma Press, 1948). Thomas's three maiden sisters, living at the family homestead in Spotswood, Virginia, responded by turning George's picture to the wall and never spoke or wrote to him again. Insofar as they were concerned, George Thomas died April 17, 1861.

31. Charles P. Roland, *Albert Sidney Johnston: Soldier of Three Republics* 252 (Austin: University of Texas Press, 1964).

32. Foote, 1 *Civil War* 59.

33. Walter H. Hebert, *Fighting Joe Hooker* 49–51 (Indianapolis: Bobbs-Merrill, 1944).

34. Stephen W. Sears, *George B. McClellan: The Young Napoleon* 64–70 (New York: Ticknor and Fields, 1988).

35. Stephen E. Ambrose, *Halleck: Lincoln's Chief of Staff* 8–11 (Baton Rouge: Louisiana State University Press, 1962).

36. Arndt M. Stickles, *Simon Bolivar Buckner: Borderland Knight* 52–79 (Chapel Hill: University of North Carolina Press, 1940).

37. Franklin Buchanan commanded the Chesapeake Bay Squadron of the Confederate navy with the *Merrimack* (C.S.S. *Virginia*) as his flagship. Later he commanded Confederate forces in the battle of Mobile Bay, the greatest naval engagement of the war. Charles Lee Lewis, *Admiral Franklin Buchanan: Fearless Man of Action* (Baltimore: Norman, Remington, 1929).

38. Russell F. Weigley, *History of the United States Army* 199–200 (New York: Macmillan, 1967).

39. Schutz and Trenerry, *Abandoned By Lincoln* 60. Also see Clark Ezra Carr, *The Illini: A Story of the Prairies* 364 (Chicago: A. C. McClung, 1905).

40. Grant, 1 *Memoirs* 239.

41. Grant to Jesse Root Grant, May 6, 1861, 2 *Grant Papers* 20–22.

42. Grant to Julia, April 27, 1861, ibid. 9.

43. During the period between Lincoln's election in November 1860 and the inauguration in March, Washburne served as the president-elect's informal representative in Washington. It was to Washburne that Lincoln sent a statement of his no-compromise policy. He asked him to tell General Winfield Scott to be ready to defend Federal forts in the South, and even had him make hotel arrangements in Washington. When Lincoln departed from his schedule and entered Washington surreptitiously, only Washburne greeted him on the station platform. John Y. Simon, "From Galena to Appomattox: Grant and Washburne," 58 *Journal of the Illinois State Historical Society* 165–70 (1965).

44. *Cincinnati Commercial,* November 16, 1868.

45. Albert Deane Richardson, *A Personal History of Ulysses S. Grant,* 182–183 (Hartford, Conn.: American Publishing Co., 1868).

46. The voluminous Washburne Papers at the Library of Congress contain no reference to Washburne's intervention; by 1885, when Grant published his memoirs, he and Washburne had fallen out politically and he barely mentioned his long association with the congressman. But see the essay on Washburne in W. C. King and W. P. Derby, *Campfire Sketches and Battle-Field Echoes of the Rebellion* 119 (Springfield, Mass.: W. C. King, 1887); Richardson, *Personal History of Ulysses S. Grant* 181–82; Augustus L. Chetlain, "Recollections of General U.S. Grant," 1 *Military Essays and Recollections* 13 (Chicago: Military Order of the Loyal Legion of the United States, 1891).

47. Simon, "From Galena to Appomattox," 187–89.

48. R.H. McClellan, Galena's delegate in the Illinois legislature, reports that Grant told him, "I'm going home. The politicians have got everything here; there's no chance for me. I came down [to Springfield] because I felt it my duty. The government educated me, and I felt I ought to offer my services again. I have applied, to no result. I can't afford to stay here longer, and I am going home." Garland, "Grant at the Outbreak" 605.

49. Grant, 1 *Memoirs* 232–33.
50. Grant to Mary Grant, April 29, 1861, 2 *Grant Papers* 13–14.
51. Hamlin Garland, *Life of Ulysses S. Grant* 164 (New York: Macmillan, 1898).
52. Grant to Governor Richard Yates, April 29, 1861, 2 *Grant Papers* 12–13.
53. Garland, *Grant* 164.
54. Lewis, *Captain Sam Grant* 418–19.
55. Garland, *Grant* 164–65.
56. Illinois General Orders No. 52, May 8, 1861, 2 *Grant Papers* 25 note.
57. Illinois numbered its Civil War regiments beginning with the number seven, out of deference to the six regiments of volunteers that served in the Mexican War.
58. Garland, "Grant at the Outbreak," 607.
59. Grant's pay voucher, dated May 22, 1861, is reprinted in Garland, *Grant* 166.
60. "Tell Orvil that he need not be surprised if I should have to draw again for some money," Grant wrote Julia. "Paying for my meals and tobacco (I have not spent a dollar otherwise and have gone without my dinner sometimes to save four bits) takes a good deal. It will all be made up to me [by the state] when I return home." Grant to Julia, May 10, 1861, 2 *Grant Papers* 26–27.
61. The comments are those of Colonel (later Major General) John M. Palmer, quoted in Garland, *Grant* 166–68.
62. Garland, "Grant at the Outbreak," 608.
63. Grant to Lorenzo Thomas, TAG, May 24, 1861, 2 *Grant Papers* 35–36. Many years later Grant wrote he "felt some hesitation in suggesting rank as high as the colonelcy of a regiment....But I had seen nearly every colonel who had been mustered in from the State of Illinois, and some from Indiana, and felt that if they could command a regiment properly, and with credit, I could also." 1 *Memoirs* 240–41.
64. Grant to Jesse Root Grant, May 30, 1851, 2 *Grant Papers* 37.
65. Grant to Julia, June 6, 10, ibid. 37–39.
66. Grant, 1 *Memoirs* 241.
67. John Russell Young, 2 *Around the World with General Grant* 214–15 (New York: American News, 1879). McClellan's recollection of the episode differs, but as his most recent biographer notes, "One officer he did not seek for his staff was Ulysses S. Grant....Grant was known in the old army as a drinker and McClellan would not have forgotten his spree at Fort Vancouver during the Pacific railroad survey in 1853, and he no doubt considered this reason enough to avoid the interview." Sears, *George B. McClellan* 73. Cf., George B. McClellan, *McClellan's Own Story* 47, W. C. Prime, ed. (New York: Charles L. Webster, 1887).
68. John Luther Ringwalt, *Anecdotes of General Ulysses S. Grant* 25 (Philadelphia: J. B. Lippincott, 1886).
69. Lewis, *Captain Sam Grant* 426.
70. *New York Herald Tribune,* September 27, 1885; 2 *Grant Papers* 44 note 1.
71. Garland, "Grant at the Outbreak," 609; Lewis, *Captain Sam Grant* 427.
72. Jesse R. Grant, "The Early Life of General Grant," *New York Ledger,* March 21, 1868; Young, 2 *Around the World* 215. For documentation relating to Yates's order, see 2 Grant Papers 43 note 1.
73. Grant to Julia, June 17, 1861, 2 *Grant Papers* 42–43; Orders No. 7, June 18, 1861, ibid. 45–46.
74. Lewis, *Captain Sam Grant* 427.
75. Major J. W. Wham interview, *New York Tribune,* September 27, 1885.
76. Regimental Order Book, 21st Illinois, June 16, 1861, RG 94, National Archives.
77. Crane, "Grant As a Colonel," 7.
78. Orders No. 7, 21st Ill., June 18, 1861, *Grant Papers* 45–46.
79. I am indebted to Bruce Catton for this insight into Grant's assumption of command. *Grant Moves South* 6–7 (Boston: Little, Brown, 1960).
80. Private Aaron Elliott, in *St. Louis Republican,* August 22, 1885.
81. Orders No. 8, 21st Illinois, June 19, 1861, 2 *Grant Papers* 46.
82. Wham interview, *New York Tribune,* September 27, 1885.
83. Orders No. 9, 21st Illinois, June 19, 1861, 2 *Grant Papers* 47.
84. Crane, "Grant As a Colonel," 40.
85. 2 *Grant Papers* 44–45, note 4. Also see Lewis, *Captain Sam Grant* 428.
86. Special Orders No. 13, 21st Illinois, June 26, 1861, 2 *Grant Papers* 49.
87. Special Orders No. 14, 21st Illinois, June 26, 1861, ibid.
88. Grant, 1 *Memoirs* 243.
89. Garland, "Grant at the Outbreak," 610.
90. Crane, "Grant As a Colonel," 9.
91. Grant, 1 *Memoirs* 246.

92. Garland, "Grant at the Outbreak," 610.
93. Grant, 1 *Memoirs* 246–247; Garland, "Grant at the Outbreak" 610; Bruce Catton, *U.S. Grant and the American Military Tradition* 58–59 (Boston: Little, Brown, 1954).
94. Garland, "Grant at the Outbreak." 610. Also see Grant's instructions to his company commanders specifying the items to be requisitioned and packed. Special Orders No. 17, 21st Illinois, June 28, 1861, 2 *Grant Papers* 55. For an eyewitness account of the march, see Ensley Moore, "Grant's First March," *Transactions of the Illinois State Historical Society for 1910* 55–62 (Springfield: ISHS, 1912).
95. Catton, *U.S. Grant* 59. "Promptness," said Chaplain Crane, "was one of Grant's characteristics, and is one of the causes of his success. A general behind time with his division or corps and the day is lost." "Grant As a Colonel," 41.
96. Grant to Julia, July 7, 1861, 2 *Grant Papers* 59–60.
97. The order to Grant has not been located, but see McClellan to Lt. Col. Charles Harding, July 5, 1861, and follow-up telegrams, 3 *The War of the Rebellion: Official Records* 390–91, 399–401 (Washington, D.C.: Government Printing Office, 1880).
98. Orders No. 23, 21st Illinois, July 9, 1861, 2 *Grant Papers* 61.
99. General Orders No. 24, July 9, 1861, ibid. 62–64.
100. Pope to Grant, July 10, 1861, ibid. 64–65, note. On July 13, 1861, Grant wrote to his father that his regiment performed as effectively as veteran troops might have done. "At the Illinois River, I received a dispatch at eleven o'clock at night that a train of cars would arrive at half past eleven to move my regiment. All the men were of course asleep, but I had the drum beaten, and in forty minutes every tent and all the baggage was at the water's edge ready to put on aboard the ferry to cross the river." Ibid. 66–67.
101. Grant, 1 *Memoirs* 252; General Orders No. 1, July 25, 1861, 2 *Grant Papers* 74–75. When the 21st was relieved of constabulary duty on the Hannibal & St. Joseph Line, Brigadier General Stephen A. Hurlbut wrote Grant: "In taking leave of the Regt which now probably leaves his command, [the commanding general] desires to render his thanks for orderly and Soldierlike deportment which has given the Regiment a most desirable reputation—no complaint has been made to any Citizen against the 21st Regt. and their Obedience to all Orders and promptness of movement are the best evidence of the attention of the Officers." Hurlbut to Grant, July 19, 1861, 2 *War of the Rebellion* 188.
102. Grant to Jesse Root Grant, August 3, 1861, 2 *Grant Papers* 80–81.
103. Grant, 1 *Memoirs* 252–53.
104. Crane, "Grant As a Colonel," 43.
105. Act of July 22, 1861, 12 Stat. 279.
106. Lincoln submitted Grant's name to the Senate on July 31, 1861. *New York Times,* August 1, 1861. For Grant's relative ranking, see *Register of the United States Army, September 1861* (Washington, D.C.: Government Printing Office, 1861). Also see Simon, "From Galena to Appomattox," 171–72.
107. Frémont assumed command of the Western Department, July 25, 1861. Grant was nominated brigadier general by Lincoln on July 31, and confirmed by the Senate on August 5. 8 *The Collected Works of Abraham Lincoln* 593, Roy P. Basler, Marion Delores Pratt, and Lloyd A. Dunlap, eds. (New Brunswick, N.J.: Rutgers University Press, 1967).
108. Frémont manuscript memoirs, Bancroft Library, Berkeley, California. Quoted in Allan Nevins, 2 *Frémont: The West's Greatest Adventurer* 536 (New York: Harper and Brothers, 1928).
109. Thomas L. Snead, *The Fight for Missouri from the Election of Lincoln to the Death of Lyon* 199–200 (New York: Charles Scribner's Sons, 1886).
110. Quoted in Foote, 1 *The Civil War* 87.
111. Grant, 1 *Memoirs* 253.
112. Schutz and Trenerry, *Abandoned by Lincoln* 63.
113. The phrase is that of Missouri railroad superintendent Edward H. Castle. Castle to Frémont, August 8, 1861, 2 *Grant Papers* 87 note. Castle added, "Genl Grant I am pleased with. He will do to lead."
114. General Orders No. 9, August 9, 1861, ibid. 88–89. Grant said "Hereafter the strictest discipline is expected to be maintained...and the General Commanding will hold responsible for this all officers, and the degree of responsibility will be in direct ratio with the rank of the officer."
115. Grant to Capt. John C. Kelton, Ass't. Adj. Genl., August 9, 1861, ibid. 89–90.
116. At Wilson's Creek, Lyon's present for duty strength was 5,400, of whom 258 were killed, 873 wounded, and 183 were missing, total casualties amounting to 1,314, or 24 percent of those engaged. Confederate losses totaled 279 killed and 951 wounded of 11,000 men engaged. In percentage terms, total casualties were double that at Bull Run.
117. Frémont to Grant, August 19, 1861, National Archives, Record Group 393, Western Department, Letters Sent. For Grant's intention to return to Galena, see his letters to Julia, August 10 and August 25, 1861, 2 *Grant Papers* 96–97, 140–41.

118. Grant to Capt. Speed Butler, Ass't. Adj. Gen., August 22, 1861, ibid. 128–29.

119. Grant to Butler, August 23, 1861, ibid. 131–32.

120. Grant to Julia, August 26, 1861, ibid. 140–41.

121. Frémont wrote Grant, "Colonel Jefferson C. Davis will relieve you in command at Jefferson City and you are directed to report yourself forthwith to these Head Quarters for special orders." Ibid. 150–51 note 1.

122. The decision was partially personal. Most West Pointers bore ill-concealed animosity toward Frémont (who was not an academy graduate) for his insubordination in the old army, his quarrel with General Stephen Watts Kearny in California, his subsequent court-martial and popular vindication. Pope, in particular, talked and wrote in the most reckless fashion about his superior, including letters to the Illinois congressional delegation suggesting that he, Pope, rightfully should be the major general commanding the Western Department. Grant on the other hand was delighted just to be back on active duty and did not complain. Long after the war he admitted Frémont had been a puzzle to him. "He sat in a room in full uniform, with his maps before him. When you went in he would point to one line or another in a mysterious manner, never asking you to take a seat. You left without the least idea of what he meant or what he wanted you to do." Young, 2 *Around the World* 215. Also see Allan Nevins, 1 *The War for the Union* 321–322 (New York: Charles Scribner's Sons, 1959).

123. Grant had given his colonel's uniform away and claimed he had not had a chance to have a general's uniform tailored. Grant to Mary Grant, August 12, 1861; Grant to Julia, August 15, 1861, 2 *Grant Papers* 105–6, 115–17.

124. Frémont manuscript memoirs, quoted in Nevins, 2 Frémont 591–92.

125. Frémont to W. A. Croffet in Ringwalt, *Anecdotes of Grant* 34.

126. Frémont to Grant, August 28, 1861, 2 *Grant Papers* 151.

127. Frémont manuscript memoirs, Bancroft Library.

128. General Orders No. 1, August 30, 1861, 2 *Grant Papers* 153–54. Also see Grant to Captain John C. Kelton, August 30, 1861, ibid. 154–55.

129. Grant to Julia, August 29, 1861, ibid. 148–49.

130. Grant to Jesse Root Grant, August 31, 1861, ibid. 158–59.

131. Foote, 1 *The Civil War* 88.

132. Edward Conrad Smith, *The Borderland in the Civil War* 301 (New York: Macmillan, 1927). Following the action by the legislature, Governor Beriah Magoffin and Senator John C. Breckinridge resigned and cast their lot with the Confederacy. Other Kentuckians followed. On November 18, 1861, a rump convention meeting at Russellville passed an ordinance of secession and formed a provisional government, which the congress at Richmond admitted as the thirteenth state in the Confederacy on December 10 (Missouri had been admitted on November 28, 1861).

133. Grant's initial September 5 telegram to Frémont has been lost. But the substance is set forth in 2 *Grant Papers* 191–92 note, and in Grant's subsequent messages that day. Also see Grant, 1 *Memoirs* 264–65.

134. Grant to the Speaker of the House and President of the Senate, September 5, 1861, published in 1 *Journal of the House of Representatives of the Commonwealth of Kentucky* 49 (Frankfort: Hunter and Beaumont, 1861).

135. Grant to Frémont, September 5, 1861, 2 *Grant Papers* 193.

136. Grant to Frémont, September 6, 1861, ibid. 196–97.

137. Grant, 1 *Memoirs* 265–66.

138. Grant to Frémont, September 6, 1861, 2 *Grant Papers* 196.

139. Grant to Brig. Gen. Eleazer A. Paine, September 6, 1861, ibid. 195.

140. Frémont to Grant, September 5, 1861, ibid. 189 note.

141. Major Joseph H. Eaton [military secretary to Frémont] to Grant, September 6, 1861, ibid. 189 note.

142. Frémont to Grant, September 6, 1861, ibid. 198 note.

143. Looking back on his cadet years, Grant wrote that he regarded General Winfield Scott, the army's commanding general, and "Captain C.F. Smith, the Commandant of Cadets, as the two men most to be envied in the nation." Grant, 1 *Memoirs* 33.

144. Ibid. 221.

145. In his communications with Smith, Grant invariably signed himself, "Very Respectfully, Your Obedient Servant, U.S. Grant," a closing he rarely used when writing to Frémont, or later to Halleck. For Grant's comment, see Military Order of the Loyal Legion, 1 *Military Essays and Reflections: Papers Read Before the Commandery of the State of Illinois* 22–25.

146. Louis A. Coolidge, *Ulysses S. Grant* 82 (Boston: Houghton Mifflin, 1917).

147. Lew Wallace, 1 *Lew Wallace: An Autobiography* 338–45 (New York: Harper and Brothers, 1906).
148. Grant to Frémont, September 10, 1861, 2 *Grant Papers* 224–25.
149. Grant to Frémont, September 12, 1861, ibid. 241–42.
150. Frémont to Grant, September 26, 1841, ibid. 301 note.
151. Catton, *Grant Moves South* 59. Also see 3 *War of the Rebellion* 494.
152. 2 *Grant Papers* 240 note.
153. 3 *War of the Rebellion,* 732 ff.
154. Ibid. 712, 730.
155. Grant to Captain Chauncey McKeever, Ass't. Adj. Gen., Western Department, 3 *Grant Papers,* 24.
156. Grant to McKeever, October 27, 1861, ibid. 78–79.
157. Grant to Benson J. Lossing, printed in William W. Belknap, *History of the 15th Regiment Iowa Veteran Volunteer Infantry* 422 (Keokuk, Iowa: R. B. Ogden and Son, 1887). The special agent, Absalom H. Markland, had been a classmate of Grant's in Maysville Seminary in Kentucky. For details of the arrangement, see 4 *Grant Papers* 204–5 note.
158. Grant to McKeever, 3 *Grant Papers* 78.
159. Testimony of U.S. Grant before the House Select Committee on Government Contracts, October 31, 1861, 3 ibid. 90, 94–95.
160. Ibid. 90–98.
161. Washburne to Chase, October 31, 1861, 2 *Annual Report of the American Historical Association for the Year 1902* 507–8 (Washington, D.C.: Government Printing Office, 1903).
162. McKeever to Grant, November 1, 1861, 3 *Grant Papers* 143–44.
163. McKeever to Grant, November 2, 1861, ibid. 144.
164. Grant to Plummer, November 4, 1861, ibid. 111–12.
165. Grant to Oglesby, November 3, 1861, ibid. 108–9.
166. Grant to Smith, November 5, 1861, ibid. 114–15. Emphasis added.
167. Grant to Col. C. Carroll Marsh, Birds Point, Mo., November 5, 1861. Similar instructions were sent to Col. Henry Dougherty and Brig. Gen. John A. McClernand. Ibid. 113–15.
168. The most extensive description of the battle of Belmont is provided in Nathaniel C. Hughes, Jr., *The Battle of Belmont: Grant Strikes South* (Chapel Hill: University of North Carolina Press, 1991). Grant's preparations are described, 45–56.
169. Smith's troops were organized in two columns: the 9th, 12th, 40th, and 41st Illinois (about 2,000 men) under Brig. Gen. Eleazer Paine moved in the direction of Columbus via Melvin, while the 23rd Indiana (800 men) advanced to the railhead at Plumley's Station. Smith to Grant, November 6, 1861, 3 *Grant Papers* 114–15.
170. Grant to Colonel John Cook, November 6, 1861, ibid. 121.
171. 1 *Medical and Surgical History of the Rebellion, 1861–1865,* Appendix, 19 (Washington, D.C.: Government Printing Office, 1870).
172. Grant to Oglesby, November 6, 1861, 3 *Grant Papers* 123–24.
173. Grant to William H. L. Wallace, November 6, 1861, ibid. 124–25; Oglesby to Grant, November 7, 1861, ibid. 124 note.
174. Grant to Smith, ibid. 120.
175. Grant to Julia, September 22, 1861, 2 ibid. 299–300. Also see Grant to Julia, September 25, 1861, ibid. 311–12.
176. Adam Badeau, 1 *Military History of U.S. Grant* 20–21 (New York: D. Appleton, 1881).
177. Porter to Foote, November 15, 1861, 22 *Official Records of the Union and Confederate Navies in the War of the Rebellion* 430 (Washington, D.C.: Government Printing Office, 1894).
178. Ibid. 397. Foote was on station in St. Louis and requested Grant to inform him by telegram when action was to be taken. Grant agreed but either forgot, or decided it was too risky to telegraph St. Louis lest department headquarters countermand him. Grant said later he forgot. As Foote informed navy secretary Gideon Welles, "General Grant, on my arrival this morning [November 9, 1861], called upon me and expressed his regret that he had not telegraphed as he had promised, assigned as the cause that he had forgotten it...until it was too late." Ibid. 399–400.
179. Wallace, 1 *Autobiography* 341, 351–353.
180. Ibid. 355–56.
181. News dispatches from Springfield dated November 4, 1861, were printed in all major newspapers the following day. See, for example, the *New York Times,* November 5, 1861. Rumors of Frémont's impending dismissal were carried November 3 and 4, 1861. Also see John Y. Simon, "Grant at Belmont," 45 *Military Affairs* 163 (1981).
182. Special Orders, On Board Steamer *Belle Memphis,* November 7, 1861, 3 *Grant Papers* 125.
183. John H. Brinton, *Personal Memoirs,* 73 (New York: Neale, 1914).

184. Grant to Jesse Root Grant, November 8, 1861, 3 *Grant Papers* 136–38. Emphasis in original.
185. Hughes, *Battle of Belmont* 78–177.
186. Grant, 1 *Memoirs* 274.
187. Cheatham took command of all the forces on the riverbank. The regiments that accompanied him were the 13th Arkansas, 2nd Tennessee, and 13th Tennessee. Timothy D. Johnson, "Benjamin Franklin Cheatham at Belmont," 81 *Missouri Historical Review* 159, 167 (1987).
188. Brinton, *Memoirs* 77.
189. Grant, 1 *Memoirs* 276.
190. Brinton, *Memoirs* 78.
191. Patrick H. White, "Civil War Diary of Patrick H. White," J. E. Boos, ed., 15 *Journal of the Illinois State Historical Society* 640, 647 (1922–23).
192. Grant, 1 *Memoirs* 276.
193. White, "Civil War Diary," 647.
194. Byron Andrews, *A Biography of General John A. Logan* 397 (New York: H. S. Goodspeed, 1884); 3 *War of the Rebellion* 289.
195. Lt. Charles James Johnson to Lou Johnson, November 8, 1861, Johnson Letters, Louisiana State University. Southerners refer to what the Union calls Bull Run as Manassas. Manassas is the closest town; Bull Run is the creek nearby.
196. Brinton, *Memoirs* 92; Hughes, *Battle of Belmont* 158. Also see Grant to Jesse Root Grant, November 27, 1861, 3 *Grant Papers* 227.
197. The incident was related to Grant by a member of Polk's staff. Grant, 1 *Memoirs* 281.
198. Ibid. 278–79.
199. The precise number of casualties at Belmont is difficult to determine, largely because of the inaccurate after-battle reports filed by both Grant and Polk. The most detailed revised figures indicate that the Union lost 120 killed, 383 wounded, and 104 captured or missing. Confederate losses are put at 105 killed, 419 wounded, and 117 missing or captured. The 7th Iowa, with 512 men present for duty, lost 31 killed, 77 wounded, and 114 missing, for a total of 43 percent. The 22nd Illinois, with 562 present, lost 146, or 26 percent. Dr. William M. Polk, "General Polk and the Battle of Belmont," in 1 *Battles and Leaders of the Civil War* 355–56 note, Robert Underwood Johnson and Clarence Clough Buel, eds. (New York: Century, 1887); Hughes, *Battle of Belmont* 184–185; 3 *War of the Rebellion* 310.
200. John Seaton, "The Battle of Belmont," in *War Talks in Kansas* 316 (Kansas City: Military Order of the Loyal Legion of the United States, 1906).
201. 3 *Grant Papers* 148. Grant's instructions were oral, but the gist is revealed in the subsequent report of Colonel Nicholas Perczel of the 10th Iowa, who quotes Oglesby as saying, "Our friends [Grant's forces] had engaged the enemy at Belmont and...had been routed." 3 *War of the Rebellion* 257.
202. Grant to Smith, November 6, 1861, 3 *Grant Papers* 129.
203. Grant to McKeever, November 6, 1861, ibid. 128.
204. On April 27, 1864, Grant's chief of staff, Brig. Gen. John Rawlins, wrote his wife "Colonel [Theodore S.] Bowers and myself finished yesterday General Grant's report on the battle of Belmont." The revised report was sent forward to Secretary of War Stanton, June 26, 1865. James Harrison Wilson, *The Life of John A. Rawlins* 425 (New York: Neale, 1916).
205. For the text of Grant's revised report, see 3 *Grant Papers* 143–49.
206. In his revised report Grant claimed to have received a telegram from department headquarters in St. Louis on November 5, 1861, instructing him to move immediately to prevent a linkup between Polk and General Price. He also reported that at 2 A.M. on the morning of November 7, while his ships lay at anchor along the Kentucky shore, he received a message from Colonel W. H. L. Wallace warning him of major Confederate troop movements from Columbus to Belmont for the purpose of following after and cutting off the forces under Colonel Oglesby. According to Grant, "Such a move on [Polk's] part seemed to me more than probable, and gave at once a two-fold importance to my demonstration against the enemy, namely: the prevention of reinforcement to General Price, and the cutting off of the two small columns that I had sent...in pursuit of Jeff Thompson. *This information determined me to attack vigorously at Belmont.*"

   Neither the telegram from St. Louis nor the message from Wallace can be authenticated. John Y. Simon, editor of the *Grant Papers*, reports the telegram cannot be found and that it may have been "extrapolated by Grant's staff." Frémont had already been relieved of command and General Hunter, his replacement, had no staff in St. Louis. Given the changeover, "it is unlikely that St. Louis hd. qrs. would have issued orders for an offensive on Nov. 5." In Simon's opinion, "It is more than odd that this telegram was not officially mentioned until 1865, four years after the battle....[I]t is almost surely nonexistent." More to the point perhaps, Captain Chauncey Mc-

Keever, Frémont's adjutant general, stated explicitly on November 9, 1861 (two days after the battle), that "General Grant did not follow his instructions. No orders were given to attack Belmont or Columbus."

The message from Wallace is equally suspect. According to Simon: "No mention of the 2 A.M. message from Wallace appears in any USG account written soon after the battle; no contemporary documentary record has been found; and it is not listed in USG's register of letters received. [Confederate records] clearly indicate that there had been no movement from Columbus to Belmont or against Oglesby; additional troops were sent to Belmont only when Maj. Gen. Leonidas Polk learned of USG's approach." Like McKeever, Colonel Wallace is also on record contrary to Grant. Writing to his wife immediately after Belmont, Wallace said the report of Polk's troops crossing into Missouri was just Grant blowing smoke.

For Grant's revised report, see 3 *War of the Rebellion* 267–272, emphasis added. For Simon's comments see 3 *Grant Papers* 149–52; John Y. Simon, "Grant at Belmont," 45 *Military Affairs* 161–65 (1981). Also see McKeever to Frémont, November 9, 1861, 53 *War of the Rebellion* 507, and Isabel Wallace, *Life and Letters of W. H. L. Wallace* 141 (Chicago: R. R. Donnelley, 1909).

207. Grant, 1 *Memoirs* 271.
208. For a summary of criticism from the St. Louis, Missouri, *Weekly Democrat,* the *Chicago Tribune,* the *Louisville Daily Journal,* and the *Illinois State Journal,* see Hughes, *Battle of Belmont* 195.
209. *Cincinnati Gazette,* November 9, 1861.
210. *Chicago Journal,* November 11, 1861.
211. *National Intelligencer,* November 11, 1861; *Philadelphia Daily Ledger,* November 11, 1861.
212. *New York Times,* November 11, 1861.
213. *St. Louis Republican,* November 11, 1861.
214. *New York Herald,* November 19, 1861.
215. Simon, "Grant at Belmont," 165; *Chicago Tribune,* November 9, 1861.
216. *The Living Lincoln* 444, Paul M. Angle and Earl Schenck Miers, eds. (New Brunswick, N.J.: Rutgers University Press, 1955).
217. McPherson, *Battle Cry of Freedom* 396.

CHAPTER FIVE: "UNCONDITIONAL SURRENDER"

The epigraph is from Grant's message to Halleck pertaining to the situation in southeastern Missouri. 3 *The Papers of Ulysses S. Grant* 211–12, John Y. Simon, ed. (Carbondale: Southern Illinois University Press, 1970).

1. Polk to Davis, November 8, 1861, 3 *The War of the Rebellion: A Compilation of the Official Records of the Union and Confederate Armies* 304 (Washington: Government Printing Office, 1881).
2. Polk to Gen. A. S. Johnston, November 10, 1861, ibid. 306–10.
3. Joseph C. Benson, "Belmont Quick Step," Nashville: C. D. Benson, 1861; Augustine J. Signaigo, "Battle of Belmont," in *War Songs and Poems of the Southern Confederacy, 1861–1865,* H. M. Wharton, ed. (Philadelphia: John C. Winston, 1904).
4. 3 *War of the Rebellion* 312.
5. Halleck's command was designated the Department of the Missouri, and consisted of Missouri, Iowa, Minnesota, Wisconsin, Illinois, Arkansas, and Kentucky west of the Cumberland River. Frank J. Welcher, 2 *The Union Army, 1861–1865* 88 (Bloomington: Indiana University Press, 1993).
6. Buell's central theater was titled the Department of the Ohio. On November 9, 1861 (the same day Halleck's department was delineated), it was reorganized to include Ohio, Michigan, Indiana, Tennessee, and Kentucky east of the Cumberland. Ibid. 127.
7. Shelby Foote, 1 *The Civil War* 169 (New York: Random House, 1958).
8. Ibid. 173.
9. See especially Stephen D. Engle, "Don Carlos Buell: Military Philosophy and Command Problems in the West," 41 *Civil War History* 89–115 (1995).
10. 7 *War of the Rebellion* 532.
11. For details of the battle at Mill Springs, see R. M. Kelly, "Holding Kentucky for the Union," 1 *Battles and Leaders of the Civil War* 373–392, R. U. Johnston and C. C. Buel, eds. (New York: Century, 1887); Freeman Cleaves, *Rock of Chickamauga: The Life of General George H. Thomas* 81–100 (Norman: University of Oklahoma Press, 1948); and especially Gerald J. Prokopowicz, "All for the Regiment: Unit Cohesion and Tactical Stalemate in the Army of the Ohio, 1861–1862" (unpublished Ph.D. dissertation, Harvard University, 1994), Chapter 3.
12. Halleck was a pedant at heart and could not resist lecturing Lincoln on military strategy. What the

president had suggested, he said, is "condemned by every military authority I have ever read." Halleck to Lincoln, January 6, 1862, 7 *War of the Rebellion* 532–33. "It is exceedingly discouraging," Lincoln noted at the foot of Halleck's letter. "As everywhere else, nothing can be done." Ibid.

13. McClellan's instructions to Halleck are reprinted in Adam Badeau, 1 *Military History of Ulysses S. Grant* 583–84 (New York: D. Appleton, 1881).

14. Halleck to Grant, ibid. 537–38; 4 *Grant Papers* 4 note.

15. For a vivid description of conditions on the approach to Columbus in January 1861, see Benjamin F. Cooling, *Forts Henry and Donelson: Key to the Confederate Heartland* 70–71 (Knoxville: University of Tennessee Press, 1987).

16. Grant to Halleck, January 20, 1862, 4 *Grant Papers* 74–75.

17. John Emerson, "Grant's Life in the West and His Mississippi Valley Campaign," *Midland Monthly Magazine* (May 1897).

18. Smith to Grant, January 21, 1862, 7 *War of the Rebellion* 561; 4 *Grant Papers* 90–91 note.

19. Grant to Halleck, January 20, 1862, ibid. 74–75; also see Ulysses S. Grant, 1 *Personal Memoirs of U.S. Grant* 286–87 (New York: Charles L. Webster, 1885).

20. Halleck to Grant, January 22, 1861, 7 *War of Rebellion* 561–62; 4 *Grant Papers* 75 note 2. Twice before, on November 20, 1861, and January 6, 1862, Grant asked permission to come to headquarters but Halleck said no. "You will send reports in writing," he told Grant, and emphasized there was no reason for him to be in St. Louis. 3 ibid. 202 note. Halleck's sudden change of heart is best explained by his concern over Thomas's triumph at Mill Springs.

21. Grant to Mary Grant, January 23, 1862, 4 ibid. 96–97.

22. Grant, 1 *Memoirs* 287.

23. Stephen E. Ambrose, *Halleck: Lincoln's Chief of Staff* 21 (Baton Rouge: Louisiana State University Press, 1962); William S. McFeely, *Grant: A Biography* 96–97 (New York: W. W. Norton, 1981).

24. Bruce Catton, *Grant Moves South* 97 (Boston: Little, Brown, 1960); A. L. Conger, *The Rise of U.S. Grant* 128–29 (New York: Century, 1931).

25. Special Orders No. 78, Department of the Missouri, December 20, 1861. 3 *Grant Papers* 330–32.

26. Conger, *Rise of Grant* 128–29.

27. See Grant to Washburne, July 22, 1862, 5 *Grant Papers* 225.

28. Grant, 1 *Memoirs* 287. Also see Ambrose, *Halleck* 24; Catton, *Grant Moves South* 123–24; *cf.* Conger, *Rise of Grant* 151–53.

29. 5 *The Collected Works of Abraham Lincoln* 111–12, Roy P. Basler, ed. (New Brunswick, N.J.: Rutgers University Press, 1953).

30. David Herbert Donald, *Lincoln* 334–35 (New York: Simon & Schuster, 1995).

31. Grant to Halleck, January 28, 1862, 4 *Grant Papers* 99.

32. Foote to Halleck, January 28, 1862, 7 *War of the Rebellion* 120.

33. Grant to Halleck, January 29, 1862, 4 *Grant Papers* 103–4.

34. Ibid.

35. Halleck to McClellan, January 20, 1862, 8 *War of the Rebellion* 508–11.

36. Halleck to Grant, January 30, 1862, 7 ibid. 121.

37. Halleck to Grant, January 30, 1862, ibid. 121–22.

38. Grant to Halleck, February 3, 1862, 4 *Grant Papers* 145.

39. Foote's flotilla consisted of the ironclads *Cincinnati, Essex, Carondelet,* and *St. Louis,* plus three wooden gunboats—*Conestoga, Tyler,* and *Lexington.*

40. Halleck to Buell, February 7, 1862, 7 *War of the Rebellion* 593. Pursuant to General Halleck's instructions of January 30, Grant left eight regiments at Cairo (plus supporting cavalry and artillery) to guard against a possible northern thrust by Polk from Columbus. 4 *Grant Papers* 141.

41. Emerson, "Grant's Life in the West," *Midland Monthly* (June 1898).

42. Ambrose, *Halleck* 26.

43. Halleck to Buell, February 3, 1862, 7 *War of the Rebellion* 583; Halleck to McClellan, February 3, 1862, ibid.

44. Ambrose, *Halleck* 38.

45. Halleck to Cullum, February 7, 1862. 4 *Grant Papers* 172–73 note. Also see Cooling, *Forts Henry and Donelson* 119–20.

46. Cullum to C. F. Smith, February 1, 1862, Smith Papers, Glenbrook, Conn.

47. Brinton, *Memoirs* 130–31.

48. Cooling, *Forts Henry and Donelson* 93.

49. Grant, 1 *Memoirs* 290.

50. Fort Henry was named for Gustavus A. Henry, the senior Confederate senator and a native of nearby Montgomery County. Cooling, *Forts Henry and Donelson* 14.

51. Foote, 1 *Civil War* 180.

52. For an eyewitness description of Fort Henry's shortcomings, see Captain Jesse Taylor, C.S.A., "The Defense of Fort Henry," in 1 *Battles and Leaders* 368–72.

53. Ibid. 369.

54. Foote, 1 *Civil War* 185. In a letter to Julia, written on the eve of battle, Grant estimated Confederate strength at "probably 10,000 men." February 5, 1862, 4 *Grant Papers* 153.

55. Field Orders No. 1, Camp in the field, near Fort Henry, Tenn., February 5, 1862, ibid. 150–51.

56. Taylor, "Defense of Fort Henry," 369.

57. Grant to Julia, February 5, 1862, 4 *Grant Papers* 153.

58. James Mason Hopping, *Life of Andrew Hull Foote: Rear-Admiral United States Navy* 20–26 (New York: Harper & Brothers, 1874).

59. Foote's report on the storming of the barrier forts is reprinted ibid. 113–21. The incident occurred during the so-called Arrow War, pitting Britain and France against China. The United States remained neutral, but in the Treaty of Tientsin, which ended the conflict in 1858, the United States and Russia, along with France and Great Britain, gained valuable trade concessions from the Manchu dynasty. See Edward D. Graham, *American Ideas of a Special Relationship with China* 134–39 (New York: Garland, 1988).

60. Foote, 1 *Civil War* 184–85.

61. 7 *War of the Rebellion* 858–59. Tilghman was so confident he could hold Fort Henry that he turned down Leonidas Polk's offer of cavalry support, "I'd rather have disciplined infantry," and he was picky even about that. "I don't want new troops who are just organized; they are in my way." Tilghman to Polk, ibid. 580–87.

62. Taylor, "Defense of Fort Henry" 170.

63. Rear Admiral Henry Walke, "Gunboats at Belmont and Fort Henry," 1 *Battles and Leaders* 364–65.

64. Taylor, "Defense of Fort Henry" 170.

65. Grant to Halleck, February 6, 1862, 7 *War of the Rebellion* 124.

66. Grant to Julia, February 6, 1862, 4 *Grant Papers* 163.

67. General McClernand, in his report to Grant on February 6, stated the rebel fortifications were "far beyond expectations and the haste with which they were abandoned proves the efficiency of the cannonade and their apprehension of being cut off from retreat by my command." 4 *Grant Papers* 159 note. The best evidence of the panicked flight from Fort Henry, however, is in the contemporaneous reports filed by newsmen accompanying McClernand's division. According to the correspondent of the *Cincinnati Gazette and Commercial,* "We found that the rebel infantry, encamped outside the fort, had cut and run, leaving the rebel artillery company in command of the fort....The infantry left everything in their flight. A vast amount of trophies have fallen into our hands."

The correspondent of the *New York Herald,* who reached the Confederate trench line while the rebel flag still flew over Fort Henry, reported it was deserted. "Not a solitary rebel remained. They had taken alarm, and fled precipitately, leaving all their effects except their arms and the clothing they wore."

The *Herald*'s reporter noted the defensive position was well prepared and "would have presented almost insurmountable obstacles to the approach of cavalry or artillery, had the rifle pits been filled with men. But despite their much vaunted determination to 'die in the last ditch,' the Rebels had run away with marvellous celerity, equaled only by John Phenix's [*sic*] hero, who 'was compelled by the prejudices of the inhabitants to leave home in such haste that he took nothing with him except a single shirt, which he happened to have about him at the time.' [The reference is to George Horatio Derby, who wrote under the pseudonym John Phoenix and whose principal work, *Phoenixiana; or Sketches and Burlesques,* published in New York by D. Appleton in 1856, was in wide circulation.]

"Crossing the rifle pit we were in the enemy camp, but there was no enemy to be seen. Here were the wall tents of a regiment, all standing in complete order, with the camp-fires still blazing, the copper pots of stew for dinner boiling over them, and half-made biscuits in the pans beside them. Inside the tents everything was just as they had left it—pistols, shot-guns, muskets, bowie-knives, books, clothing, tables partially set for dinner, letters half-opened, cards thrown down in the middle of a game, overcoats, blankets, trunks, carpet sacks, and so on through all the articles of camp life. It looked as though the men were out at guard mounting, expecting to return in ten minutes....

"One Inhabitant of the Camp Who Didn't Run

"Standing in front of one of the dwellings, we encountered the first occupant of the Rebel camp we had met, in the form of an old negress, who was rubbing her hands with glee.

" 'You seem to have had hot work here, aunty?'

" 'Lord, yes, mess'r, we did; just dat. De big balls, dey come whizzing and tearing 'bout, and I thought de las' judgment was cum, sure?'

" 'Where are all your soldiers?'

" 'Lord a'mighty knows. Dey jus' runned away like turkeys—nebber fired a gun.'

" 'How many were there?'

" 'Dere was one Arkansas regiment over dere, where you see de tents, a Mississippi regiment dere, another dere, two Tennessee regiments here, and lots more over de river.'

" 'Why didn't you run with them?'

" 'I was sick, you see [she could only speak in a whisper]; besides, *I* wasn't afraid—only ob de shots. I jus' thought if dey didn't kill me I was all right.'"

This dispatch was dated Fort Henry, February 7, 1862, and was printed in the *New York Herald,* February 14, 1862. Also see *Cincinnati Gazette and Commercial,* February 8, 1862, reprinted in the *National Intelligencer* (Washington, D.C.), February 10, 1862. For additional documentation of the garrison's panic, see A. L. Conger, comp., *Donelson Campaign Sources; Supplementing Vol. VII of the Official Records* (Fort Leavenworth: Army Service Schools, 1912). Also see A. L. C. [Conger], "Fort Donelson," 1 *The Military Historian and Economist* 33, 40–41 (1916); Frank Moore, *The Rebel Record* 4, 69 (New York: G. P. Putnam, 1862); Cooling, *Forts Henry and Donelson* 109–10, and the original diary sources cited therein.

68. Grant, 1 *Memoirs* 292.

69. Taylor, "Defense of Fort Henry," 372.

70. *New York Tribune,* February 8, 1862.

71. Ibid.

72. *New York Times,* February 8, 1862.

73. *New York Herald Tribune,* February 8, 1862.

74. The gunboats were commanded by Lieutenant S. T. Phelps, captain of the *Conestoga.* His report of the mission is reprinted in Hopping, *Life of Andrew Hull Foote* 211–15.

75. Alfred D. Roman, 1 *The Military Operations of General Beauregard in the War Between the States* 221–23 (New York: Harper, 1883); T. Harry Williams, *P. G. T. Beauregard* 151–54 (Baton Rouge: Louisiana State University Press, 1954); Cooling, *Forts Henry and Donelson* 123–25.

76. Foote, 1 *Civil War* 191.

77. The validity of Johnston's strategy is attested by the subsequent reunion of the two wings at Corinth and the battle of Shiloh. Had the men lost at Donelson been present at Shiloh, the course of the war might have been different.

78. Like other Civil War historians, Johnston's biographer is at a loss to explain Johnston's change of heart. See Charles P. Roland, *Albert Sidney Johnston: Soldier of Three Republics* 289–91 (Austin: University of Texas Press, 1964).

79. J. F. C. Fuller, *The Generalship of Ulysses S. Grant* 85–86 (London: John Murray, 1929).

80. Johnston to Davis, March 17, 1862, Roland, *Albert Sidney Johnston* 291.

81. Grant to McClernand, February 7, 1862, 4 *Grant Papers* 165–66.

82. Grant to Mary Grant, February 9, 1862, ibid. 179–80.

83. Halleck to Grant, February 8, 1862, ibid. 193–94 note.

84. Ambrose, *Halleck* 28.

85. McClellan to Halleck, February 7, 1862, 7 *War of the Rebellion* 591.

86. Richey Kamm, *The Civil War Career of Thomas A. Scott* 105 (Philadelphia: University of Pennsylvania Press, 1940).

87. Halleck to Stanton, February 8, 1862, 7 *War of the Rebellion* 594. Stanton immediately agreed to Halleck's proposal. See Stanton to Halleck, February 8, 1862, 3 ibid. 208. On February 5, 1862, General Winfield Scott, retired but still in Washington, informed Hitchcock he would be recalled to replace Grant on the Cumberland and Tennessee. Hitchcock's appointment as a major general was confirmed by the Senate on February 10, 1862. 12 *Senate Executive Journal* 115.

88. Halleck to Cullum, February 9, 1862, 7 *War of the Rebellion* 597–98. Halleck told Cullum that Hitchcock was coming to take charge of the overall operation between the rivers and that he should prepare to assume command of the column on the Cumberland.

89. Halleck to Buell, February 13, 1862, ibid. 609. Also see Halleck's telegrams to Buell, February 11 and February 12, 1862, ibid. 605, 607.

90. Grant, 1 *Memoirs* 315; John F. Marszalek, *Sherman: A Soldier's Passion for Order* 169–73 (New York: Free Press, 1993).

91. Grant to Halleck, February 11, 1862, 4 *Grant Papers* 193. In his *Memoirs,* Grant said he received Halleck's instructions to fortify Fort Henry when he was already in the field in front of Fort Donelson. His message to Halleck of February 11 suggests otherwise. Cf., Grant, 1 *Memoirs* 296.

92. General Field Orders No. 12, February 11, 1862, ibid. 191–92.

93. John Russell Young, 2 *Around the World with General Grant* 213 (New York: American News, 1879).

94. Grant, 1 *Memoirs* 297–98.

95. John H. Brinton, *Personal Memoirs* 115 (New York: Neale, 1914).

96. Grant, 1 *Memoirs* 299.

97. *New York Tribune,* February 22, 1862.

98. Grant, 1 *Memoirs* 302. Grant's air of confidence was reported by a newsman on the scene. Cooling, *Forts Henry and Donelson* 153.

99. Rear Admiral Henry Walke, "The Western Flotilla," 1 *Battles and Leaders* 433.

100. Foote to Secretary of the Navy Gideon Welles, February 15, 1862, in Hopping, *Life of Andrew Hull Foote* 226.

101. Cooling, *Forts Henry and Donelson* 157.

102. Walke, "Western Flotilla," 433–36.

103. Foote, 1 *Civil War* 205.

104. Grant to Cullum, February 14, 1862, 4 *Grant Papers* 209.

105. Grant to Julia, February 14, 1862, 4 ibid. 211.

106. 7 *War of the Rebellion* 800–801.

107. Roy P. Stonesifer, Jr. "Gideon J. Pillow: A Study in Egotism," 25 *Tennessee Historical Quarterly* 344 (1966).

108. Cooling, *Forts Henry and Donelson* 162–65, and the sources cited therein.

109. Grant, 1 *Memoirs* 304–5.

110. *Harper's Magazine* 697 (April 1862).

111. 7 *War of the Rebellion* 163.

112. Catton, *Grant Moves South* 163–64.

113. Grant, 1 *Memoirs* 307.

114. Ibid. 307–8.

115. Lew Wallace, "The Capture of Fort Donelson," 1 *Battles and Leaders* 422.

116. Grant to Foote, February 15, 1862, 4 *Grant Papers* 214. Foote had already departed for Cairo when Grant's message arrived, but Commander Benjamin J. Dove promptly took *St. Louis* and *Louisville* upstream and spent the late afternoon lobbing shells at Donelson. 22 *War of the Rebellion* 588.

117. Benjamin Franklin Cooling, in his thorough study of the fighting at Donelson, lays out the considerations that might have precipitated the Southern decision, but concludes, "What really caused this turn of events will never be known for sure." Cooling, *Forts Henry and Donelson* 181–83.

118. Wallace, "Capture of Fort Donelson," 422.

119. Corporal Voltaire P. Twombley of Co. F, 2nd Iowa, "took the colors after three of the color guard had fallen…and although almost instantly knocked down by a spent ball, immediately rose and bore the colors to the end of the engagement." On March 17, 1897, he would be awarded the Medal of Honor for the deed at Donelson. V. P. Twombley, *The Second Iowa Infantry at Fort Donelson, February 15, 1862* 27 (Des Moines: Plain Talk Printing House, 1901).

120. Wallace, "Capture of Fort Donelson," 423; Brinton, *Personal Memoirs* 120–21.

121. Cooling, *Forts Henry and Donelson* 185.

122. Emerson, "Grant's Life in the West."

123. Ibid. The lines are from Burns's "Man Was Made to Mourn," stanza 7.

124. McPherson, *Battle Cry of Freedom* 401.

125. Wallace, "Capture of Fort Donelson," 429 note; Cooling, *Forts Henry and Donelson* 201.

126. 7 *War of the Rebellion* 273, 287–88, 295–97, 334, 385–86.

127. Nathaniel C. Hughes., Jr., and Roy P. Stonesifer, Jr., *The Life and Wars of Gideon J. Pillow* 233–39 (Chapel Hill: University of North Carolina Press, 1993).

128. Ibid. 288.

129. Ibid.

130. Catton, *Grant Moves South* 174.

131. Brinton, *Personal Memoirs* 129.

132. 4 *Grant Papers* 218. Grant's letter to Buckner is preserved in the Smithsonian Institution, Washington, D.C.

133. Ibid.

134. Grant, 1 *Memoirs* 313. Earlier, Buckner told Smith his charge had carried the day. "I simply obeyed orders, nothing more, sir," Smith replied. 5 *Grant Papers* 82 note.

135. Cooling, *Forts Henry and Donelson* 212.

136. Brinton, *Personal Memoirs* 133.

137. Grant to Halleck, February 16, 1862, 7 *War of the Rebellion* 625.

138. Grant to Cullum, February 16, 1862, ibid. 159–60.

139. *New York Tribune,* February 18, 1862.

140. 7 *War of the Rebellion* 627–28, 641–42.

141. "Was it not funny to see a certain military hero [McClellan] in the telegraph office at Washington last Sunday organizing victory and by sublime military combinations capturing Fort Donelson *six hours after* Grant and Smith had taken it...! It would be a picture worthy of *Punch*." Stanton to Charles A. Dana, in Dana, *Recollections of the Civil War* 10–14 (New York: D. Appleton, 1899). Emphasis in original.

142. Helen Nicolay, *Lincoln's Secretary: A Biography of John G. Nicolay* 131–32 (New York: Longmans, Green, 1949).

143. Grant to Julia, February 16, 1862, 4 *Grant Papers* 229.

144. Buckner Papers, quoted in Arndt Stickles, *Simon Bolivar Buckner: Borderland Knight* 173 (Chapel Hill: University of North Carolina Press, 1940).

145. Grant to Cullum, February 17, 1862, 4 *Grant Papers* 235.

146. M. B. Morton interview with Gen. Buckner, 1909, *Nashville Banner,* December 11, 1909.

147. Fuller, *Generalship of Grant* 93–94.

148. On March 11, 1862, James Mason, the Confederacy's agent in London, informed Richmond that "the late reverses at Fort Henry and Fort Donelson have had an unfortunate effect upon the minds of our friends here." From Paris, John Slidell filed a similar report with the Confederate secretary of state on March 26. Virginia Mason, *The Public Life and Diplomatic Correspondence of James M. Mason* 264 (New York: Neale, 1906); James D. Richardson, ed. 2 *Messages and Papers of the Confederacy* 207 (Washington, D.C.: United States Publishing Co., 1905).

149. Catton, *Grant Moves South* 181.

150. Foote, 1 *Civil War* 214.

151. Cullum to Grant, February 20, 1862, 4 *Grant Papers* 235–36 note.

152. On February 19, Halleck's assistant adjutant general issued General Orders No. 43: "The major-general commanding the department congratulates Flag-Officer Foote, Brigadier-General Grant, and the brave officers and men under their commands, on the recent brilliant victories on the Tennessee and Cumberland." 7 *War of the Rebellion* 638–39. Halleck did not write to Grant, although on February 17 he told Assistant Secretary of War Scott (who was in St. Louis) that he thought Grant should be promoted. Scott to Stanton, February 17, 1862, 4 *Grant Papers* 272–73 note.

CHAPTER SIX: SHILOH

1. Grant to Cullum, February 19, 1862, 4 *The Papers of Ulysses S. Grant* 245–46, John Y. Simon, ed. (Carbondale: Southern Illinois University Press, 1972).

2. Grant to Brig. Gen. Stephen A. Hurlburt, February 20, 1862, ibid. 252.

3. General Orders No. 6, February 21, 1862, ibid. 253–54.

4. Grant to Cullum, February 21, 1862, ibid. 257.

5. Halleck to Grant, February 18, 1862, ibid. 260 note. The telegram was sent to Sherman at Paducah, who forwarded it to Grant. Grant did not receive it until the 21st.

6. Foote to Cullum, 7 *War of the Rebellion: A Compilation of the Official Records* 648 (Washington: Government Printing Office, 1881).

7. Stephen E. Ambrose, *Halleck: Lincoln's Chief of Staff* 33 (Baton Rouge: Louisiana State University Press, 1962); A. L. Conger, *The Rise of U.S. Grant* 201 (New York: Century, 1931).

8. Halleck to McClellan, February 20, 1862, 7 *War of the Rebellion* 641.

9. Foote to Grant, February 22, 1862, 22 *Official Records of the Union and Confederate Navies in the War of the Rebellion* 624 (Washington, D.C.: Government Printing Office, 1894).

10. Halleck to McClellan, February 17, 1862, 7 *War of the Rebellion* 628 (see Chapter 5).

11. 22 *War of the Rebellion (Navy)* 626.

12. Grant to Julia, February 24, 1862, 4 *Grant Papers* 284. In December 1861, Congress established a joint seven-member committee to keep tabs on the conduct of the war. On January 10, 1862, the committee began taking testimony pertaining to John C. Frémont's conduct of the war in the Western Department, and that may be what Grant was alluding to. See William Whatley Pierson, Jr., "The Committee on the Conduct of the Civil War," 23 *American Historical Review* 550–76 (1918).

13. Ulysses S. Grant, 1 *Personal Memoirs of U.S. Grant* 317–18 (New York: Charles L. Webster, 1885).

14. Commander Benjamin M. Dove to Grant, February 23, 1862, 4 *Grant Papers* 279–80 note. Grant received a similar message from C. F. Smith at Clarksville.

15. Grant to Cullum, February 24, 1862, ibid. 278–79.

16. Grant to Nelson, February 24, 1862, ibid. 282. For Grant's meeting with Nelson, see John H. Brinton, *Personal Memoirs* 139–43 (New York: Neale, 1914).

17. Nelson to Grant, February 23, 1862, ibid. 282–83 note.

18. Stephen D. Engle, "Don Carlos Buell: Military Philosophy and Command Problems in the West," 41 *Civil War History* 101 (1995).

19. For Buell's order to C. F. Smith, February 25, 1862, see 7 *War of the Rebellion* 944–45.

20. Grant, 1 *Memoirs* 320.

21. William B. Shanks, *Personal Recollections of Distinguished Generals* 252 (New York: Harper and Brothers, 1866).

22. Buell to McClellan, December 10, 1862, Buell Papers, Huntington Library, San Marino, California.

23. Lincoln later told Halleck "a McClellan in the army was lamentable, but a combination of McClellan and Buell was deplorable." Ambrose, *Halleck* 88. There is as yet no biography of Buell, but see James R. Chumney, "Don Carlos Buell: Gentleman General," Ph.D. diss., Rice University, 1964.

24. Charles P. Roland, *Albert Sidney Johnston: Soldier of Three Republics* 298–303 (Austin: University of Texas Press, 1964).

25. Grant to Cullum, February 25, 1862, 4 *Grant Papers* 286–87.

26. Grant to Julia, February 26, 1862, ibid. 292.

27. On March 1 Buell wrote he finally had enough men in the city "to feel secure." 7 *War of the Rebellion* 675.

28. *New York Herald Tribune,* March 6, 1862; Isabel Wallace, ed., *Life and Letters of General W. H. L. Wallace* 171 (Chicago: R. R. Donnelley, 1909); *New York Times,* March 5, 1862; *Chicago Tribune,* March 8, 12, 1862; Walter T. Durham, *Nashville: The Occupied City* 52 (Nashville: Tennessee Historical Society, 1985).

29. Brinton, *Personal Memoirs* 139.

30. Grant, 1 *Memoirs* 321.

31. Grant to Buell, February 27, 1862, 4 *Grant Papers* 293–94. It was not until March 1 that Buell felt sufficiently secure in Nashville to return Smith's division to Clarksville. Buell to Halleck, March 1, 1862, 7 *War of the Rebellion* 675.

32. Halleck to McClellan, March 3, 1862, 7 ibid. 679–80.

33. McClellan to Halleck, March 3, 1862, ibid. 680.

34. Halleck to McClellan, March 4, 1862, ibid. 682.

35. See McPherson to Grant, February 21, 1862, 4 *Grant Papers* 222–23 note.

36. Halleck to Cullum, February 25, 1862, 7 *War of the Rebellion* 677.

37. Grant to Cullum, February 24, 25, 28, 1862; Grant to Kelton, February 28, March 1, 1862; Grant to Halleck, March 1, 1862, 4 *Grant Papers* 278–305.

38. Grant, 1 *Memoirs* 325. Compare Conger, *Rise of U.S. Grant* 211 note.

39. Halleck to Grant, March 1, 1862, 7 *War of the Rebellion* 674.

40. Halleck to Grant, March 4, 1862, 4 *Grant Papers* 319–20 note 1.

41. Grant, 1 *Memoirs* 326.

42. Grant to Julia, March 1, 1862, 4 *Grant Papers* 305–6.

43. Grant to Halleck, March 5, 1862, ibid. 317–19.

44. Ibid.

45. Grant, 1 *Memoirs* 328.

46. Brinton, *Personal Memoirs* 150.

47. Grant, 1 *Memoirs* 328.

48. William Tecumseh Sherman, 1 *Memoirs of General William T. Sherman* 245 (New York: Library of America, 1990).

49. Halleck to Grant, March 6, 1862, 4 *Grant Papers* 331 note.

50. Grant to Halleck, March 7, 1862, ibid. 331.

51. Copies of Halleck's telegram of March 6, 1862, and Grant's reply can be found in the Washburne Papers, Library of Congress.

52. Halleck to Grant, March 8, 1862, 7 *War of the Rebellion* 21.

53. Grant to Halleck, March 9, 1862, 4 *Grant Papers* 334.

54. Grant to Halleck, March 9, 1862, ibid. 334–35 note.

55. Halleck to Grant, March 9, 1862, 10 *War of the Rebellion* (Part 2) 22. Emphasis added.

56. Grant to Smith, March 11, 1862, 4 *Grant Papers* 343.

57. Smith to Grant, March 14, 1862, 10 *War of the Rebellion* (Part 2) 29.

58. Smith to an unidentified person, March 17, 1862, 4 *Grant Papers* 344 note.

59. Lorenzo Thomas, TAG, to Halleck, March 10, 1862, 7 *War of the Rebellion* 683.

60. Halleck to Thomas, March 15, 1862, ibid. 683–84.

61. "The want of order and discipline and the numerous irregularities in your command since the capture of Fort Donelson," wrote Halleck, "are matters of general notoriety, and have at-

tracted the serious attention of the authorities in Washington. Unless these things are immediately corrected I am directed to relieve you of the command." Halleck to Grant, March 6, 1862, 11 ibid. 13.

62. Grant to Halleck, March 13, 1862, 4 *Grant Papers* 353.
63. Halleck to Grant, March 13, 1862, 10 *War of the Rebellion* (Part 2) 32.
64. Grant to Halleck, March 14, 1862, 4 *Grant Papers* 358–59.
65. Grant, 1 *Memoirs* 327. By the time Grant wrote his *Memoirs,* he was aware of Halleck's correspondence with McClellan about his drinking, and he never forgave him.
66. General Orders No. 21, March 15, 1862, 4 *Grant Papers* 364.
67. Grant to Julia, March 15, 1862, ibid. 375.
68. Halleck to Grant, March 16, 1862, 10 *War of the Rebellion* (Part 2) 42.
69. Bruce Catton, *Grant Moves South* 213 (Boston: Little, Brown, 1960).
70. Shelby Foote, 1 *The Civil War* 321 (New York: Random House, 1958).
71. Grant to Capt. N. H. McLean, Ass't. A.G., St. Louis, March 17, 1862, 4 *Grant Papers* 378–79; Grant, 1 *Memoirs* 331.
72. Sherman to Rawlins [Grant], March 17, 1862, 10 *War of the Rebellion* (Part 1) 27.
73. Larry Daniel, *Shiloh: The Battle That Changed the Civil War* 102 (New York: Simon and Schuster, 1997). Also see Stacey D. Allen, "Shiloh! The Campaign and First Day's Battle" 14 *Blue and Gray* 16 (1997).
74. Owl Creek flowed into Snake Creek before reaching the Tennessee, but since the latter did not figure in the fighting at Shiloh, I have used the designation Owl Creek throughout.
75. Halleck to Grant, March 18, 1862, 10 *War of the Rebellion* (Part 2) 46.
76. Grant to Smith, March 20, 1862, 4 *Grant Papers* 398.
77. Grant to Halleck (via Cairo), March 20, 1862, ibid. 391–92. Grant followed up his telegram with a letter to headquarters in St. Louis stating that he intended to lead the expedition to Corinth in person unless he received orders to the contrary. Grant said he hoped to leave on the 22nd, but delays in bringing the 1st and 2nd divisions forward set him back a day or two. "I will take no risk at Corinth under the instructions I now have. If a battle on anything like equal terms seems to be inevitable I shall find it out in time to make a movement on some other point of the railroad, or at least seem to fill the object of the expedition without a battle and thus save the demoralizing effect of a retreat upon the troops." Grant to McLean, May 20, 1862, 4 *Grant Papers* 396–97.
78. Halleck to Grant, March 20, 1862, 10 *War of the Rebellion* (Part 2) 50–51.
79. Grant to Halleck, March 21, 1862, 4 *Grant Papers* 400–401.
80. Ibid.
81. Grant to Smith, March 23, 1862, ibid. 411.
82. Halleck to Buell, 10 *War of the Rebellion* (Part 2) 42. As a historian sympathetic to Buell has noted, " 'As rapidly as possible' might have implied, 'haste,' but to Buell it essentially meant whenever he was ready for his army to march in full—again exercising his own judgment." Stephen D. Engle, "Don Carlos Buell: Military Philosophy and Command Problems in the West," 41 *Civil War History* 102 (1995).
83. Logistical support during the first year of the war was often a comedy of errors. After reaching Columbia, Buell wired Halleck that he had ordered pontoons shipped from Nashville to assist Grant crossing the Tennessee. Grant, however, was already across the Tennessee, while the Army of the Ohio sat idle for lack of pontoons. Ibid. 82, 86. Also see Kenneth P. Williams, 3 *Lincoln Finds a General* 326 (New York: Macmillan, 1952).
84. In March 1862 the Army of the Ohio numbered well over 65,000 men, but they were scattered hither and yon. Buell left a garrison of 18,000 to guard his supply base in Nashville; a division of 8,000 was dispatched to Murfreesboro to protect the army's flank; and another division sent to defend the Cumberland Gap. That left Buell with a field force of approximately 37,000 men organized into five divisions. These were commanded (in march order) by Alexander McCook (2nd); Bull Nelson (4th); Thomas Crittenden (5th); Thomas Wood (6th); and George Thomas (1st).
85. 10 *War of the Rebellion* (Part 2) 70; Engle, "Don Carlos Buell" 103.
86. On March 26 Grant wired Halleck that Buell's army was "yet on the east side of Duck river detained in bridge building," but he expressed no alarm. The following day he wrote St. Louis, "I have no news yet of any portion of Gen. Buell's command being this side of Columbia." Again he expressed no alarm. 4 *Grant Papers* 424–28.
87. Daniel, *Shiloh* 114.
88. Grant, 1 *Memoirs* 333.
89. Edwin C. Bearss, "General Nelson Saves the Day at Shiloh," 63 *Register of the Kentucky Historical Society* 45 (1965).

90. 10 *War of the Rebellion* (Part 1) 329–30. Ordinarily the privilege of leading an army's advance fell to the senior division commander, who in this case was Brigadier General Alexander McCook commanding the 2nd division.

91. Bearss, "General Nelson Saves the Day" 50.

92. Daniel, *Shiloh* 94–95.

93. Johnston to "Soldiers of the Army of the Mississippi," M. J. Solomon Papers, Duke University. Bragg called the army "a heterogeneous mass in which there was more enthusiasm than discipline, more capacity than knowledge, more valor than instruction." Braxton Bragg, "General Albert Sidney Johnston and the Battle of Shiloh," Johnston Papers, Tulane University.

94. Allen, "Shiloh!" 18.

95. Foote, 1 *Civil War* 329.

96. Bragg, "General Albert Sidney Johnston at Shiloh."

97. Charles P. Roland, *Albert Sidney Johnston: Soldier of Three Republics* 325 (Austin: University of Texas Press, 1964).

98. Allen, "Shiloh!" 18.

99. 11 *War of the Rebellion* 93–94.

100. John K. Duke, *History of the 53rd Ohio Volunteer Infantry* 41 (Portsmouth, Ohio: Blade Printing Company, 1900).

101. Grant to Halleck, April 5, 1862, 5 *Grant Papers* 13–14. After the battle, Grant told the *Cincinnati Commercial* that although some skirmishing had occurred on April 4–5, "I did not believe [the Confederates] intended to make a determined attack but were simply making a reconnaissance in force." Reprinted in the *New York Herald,* May 3, 1862.

102. Daniel, *Shiloh* 130.

103. Franklin Bailey (12th Michigan) to his parents, March 27, 1862, Franklin Bailey Letters, Michigan Historical Society.

104. Lt. Seymour D. Thompson, *Recollections with the Third Iowa Regiment* 62 (Cincinnati: privately published, 1864).

105. Payton Shumway (52nd Illinois) to his wife, March 19, 1862, Shumway Letters, Illinois State Library.

106. Mary Ann Anderson, ed., *The Civil War Diary of Allen Morgan Greer* 23–24 (New York: Appleman, 1977).

107. William Skinner (71st Ohio) to his brother and sister, March 27, 1862, Shiloh National Military Park Collection.

108. Foote, 1 *Civil War* 323.

109. Sherman, 1 *Memoirs* 249.

110. Grant, 1 *Memoirs* 332–33. Grant was confident, in retrospect overconfident, that he would have to carry the attack to Johnston. On April 3 he wrote Julia he hoped to move forward soon. "When I do there will probably be the greatest battle of the War. I do not feel that there is the slightest doubt about the result and therefore, individually, feel as unconcerned about it as if nothing more than a review was to take place. Knowing however that a terrible sacrifice of life must take place I feel concerned for my army and their friends at home." 5 *Grant Papers* 7.

111. Grant, 1 *Memoirs* 335.

112. E. Hannaford, *The Story of a Regiment* 237–38 (Cincinnati: Hannaford, 1868).

113. 10 *War of the Rebellion* (Part 1) 330–31.

114. Ibid. (Part 2) 387; Alfred D. Roman, 1 *The Military Operations of General Beauregard in the War Between the States* 271 (New York: Harper, 1884); T. Harry Williams, *P. G. T. Beauregard: Napoleon in Gray* 126 (Baton Rouge: Louisiana State University Press, 1959). Also see James L. Morrison, Jr., "Educating Civil War Generals: West Point, 1833–1861" 38 *Military Affairs* 108, 109 (1974).

115. Allen, "Shiloh!" 19–20.

116. Charles A. Morton, "A Boy at Shiloh" 59–60 *Military Order of the Loyal Legion of the United States* (1907).

117. Edwin L. Hobart, *The Truth About Shiloh* 12 (Springfield, Ill., 1909).

118. Allen, "Shiloh!" 21.

119. Catton, *Grant Moves South* 223.

120. Grant to Nelson, April 6, 1862, 5 *Grant Papers* 18 note.

121. Grant to Wood, April 6, 1862, ibid. 18–19 note.

122. Grant to Buell, April 6, 1862, ibid. On April 4 Buell had written Grant, "I shall be in Savannah myself tomorrow with one perhaps two divisions. Can I meet you there? Have you any information for me that should affect my movements? What of your enemy, and your relative positions?" Grant had replied on April 5 that the enemy was still "at and near Corinth and probably from 60 to 80 thousand." Ibid. 16–17 note.

123. Grant, 1 *Memoirs* 336; Foote, 1 *Civil War* 335; Catton, *Grant Moves South* 224–25.
124. 10 *War of the Rebellion* (Part 1) 181.
125. Ibid. 179, 185. Baxter was a quartermaster on Grant's staff.
126. Grant to Nelson, April 6, 1862, in Adam Badeau, 1 *Military History of Ulysses S. Grant* 77 (New York: D. Appleton, 1881).
127. Allen, "Shiloh!" 21.
128. Ibid.
129. John F. Marzalek, *Sherman: A Soldier's Passion for Order* 178 (New York: Free Press, 1993).
130. Sherman, *Memoirs* 266.
131. Grant, 1 *Memoirs* 343.
132. 10 *War of the Rebellion* (Part 1) 278.
133. Thompson, *Recollections with the Third Iowa* 214.
134. Allen, "Shiloh!" 27.
135. Ibid. 48.
136. Grant to Commanding Officer Advance Forces [Buell's army], near Pittsburg, April 6, 1862, 5 *Grant Papers* 18.
137. Grant, 1 *Memoirs* 342.
138. Foote, 1 *Civil War* 338. Also see Daniel, *Shiloh* 209.
139. Don Carlos Buell, "Shiloh Reviewed," 1 Battles and Leaders of the Civil War 487–95 (New York: Century, 1887).
140. Badeau, 1 *Military History of Ulysses S. Grant* 82. *Cf.* Buell, "Shiloh Reviewed" 493–94 note.
141. Allen, "Shiloh!" 52–53.
142. Grant, 1 *Memoirs* 342.
143. Ibid. 337.
144. Daniel, *Shiloh* 260–61. For Wallace's account, see "The March of Lew Wallace's Division to Shiloh," 1 *Battles and Leaders of the Civil War* 609.
145. Badeau, 1 *Military History of Ulysses S. Grant* 81 note, citing a letter from Grant to the War Department, April 13, 1863.
146. Grant, 1 *Memoirs*.
147. Allen, "Shiloh!" 53.
148. Grant, 1 *Memoirs* 356.
149. Foote, 1 *Civil War* 341.
150. Bearss, "General Nelson Saves the Day" 57.
151. Allen, "Shiloh!" 62.
152. Catton, *Grant Moves South* 239.
153. Daniel, *Shiloh* 255.
154. Ibid.
155. Ibid.
156. Allen, "Shiloh!" 63.
157. Charles F. Hubert, *History of the 50th Regiment of Illinois Volunteer Infantry* 93 (Kansas City: Western Veteran Publishing Company, 1894).
158. Whitelaw Reid, reported in the *Chicago Tribune,* November 21, 1880.
159. Grant, 1 *Memoirs* 348.
160. Sherman, 1 *Memoirs* 266.
161. Catton, *Grant Moves South* 240–41.
162. Sherman interview in the *Washington Post,* quoted in the *Army and Navy Journal,* December 30, 1893.
163. Allen, "Shiloh!" 64.
164. 10 *War of the Rebellion* (Part 1) 384.
165. The report was from Colonel Benjamin H. Helm, whose scouts observed the division of General Ormsby Mitchell marching toward Alabama and assumed that the entire Army of the Ohio was following. Roman, 1 *Military Operations of General Beauregard* 531–32.
166. Thomas Jordan and Roger Pryor, *The Campaigns of Lieut.-Gen. Nathan Bedford Forrest* 136–37 (New Orleans: Blelock, 1868).
167. 10 *War of the Rebellion* (Part 1) 518.
168. Daniel, *Shiloh* 262–63.
169. Lew Wallace, 2 *Autobiography* 544–45.
170. Allen, "Shiloh!" 17.
171. Ibid.
172. Thomas Jordan, "Notes of a Confederate Staff Officer at Shiloh," 1 *Battles and Leaders of the Civil War* 603.

173. Grant, 1 *Memoirs* 354–55. When he left the field that evening, Grant wrote Buell he intended "to occupy the most advanced position possible for the night...and follow up our success with cavalry and fresh troops. The great fatigue of our men...would preclude the idea of making any advance at night without the arrival of the expected reinforcements. My plan therefore will be to feel on in the morning with all the troops on our outer lines, until our Cavalry can be organized and a sufficient Artillery and Infantry support to follow them are ready for a move." Grant said his instructions from Halleck precluded moving beyond Pea Ridge, Tennessee, about five miles away.

174. Grant, 1 *Memoirs* 368–69.

175. Wellington to Thomas Creevey, 1 *The Creevey Papers* 237, Sir Herbert Maxwell, ed. (London: John Murray, 1904).

176. *New York Herald,* April 9, 1862.

177. *New York Times,* April 9, 1862; *New York Herald,* April 9, 1862.

178. Alexander K. McClure, *Abraham Lincoln and Men of War Times* 193–96 (Philadelphia: Times Publishing, 1892).

CHAPTER SEVEN: VICKSBURG

The epigraph is attributed to Sherman by T. Harry Williams, *McClellan, Sherman, and Grant* 46 (New Brunswick, N.J.: Rutgers University Press, 1962).

1. Halleck to Grant, April 9, 1862, 10 *The War of the Rebellion: A Compilation of the Official Records of the Union and Confederate Armies* (Part 2) 99 (Washington, D.C.: Government Printing Office, 1884).

2. Even Grant was reluctant to push on without reinforcements. In his *Memoirs* Grant argued that Beauregard should have been pursued aggressively and "the arrival of Pope should not have been awaited." But in a letter to Halleck three days after Shiloh, Grant wrote: "I do not like to suggest but it appears to me that it would be demoralizing upon our troops here to be forced to retire upon the opposite bank of the river and unsafe to remain on this, many weeks, without large reinforcements." *Cf.,* Ulysses S. Grant, 1 *Personal Memoirs of U.S. Grant* 374 (New York: Charles L. Webster, 1885) and 5 *The Papers of Ulysses S. Grant* 31, John Y. Simon, ed. (Carbondale: Southern Illinois University Press, 1973).

3. Bragg to Beauregard, 10 *War of the Rebellion* (Part 2) 398–99.

4. Ibid. (Part 1) 400.

5. An Impressed New Yorker, *Thirteen Months in the Confederate Army* (New York: Barnes and Burr, 1862).

6. Stephen E. Ambrose, *Halleck: Lincoln's Chief of Staff* 47 (Baton Rouge: Louisiana State University Press, 1962).

7. Halleck to Grant, April 14, 1862, 10 *War of the Rebellion* (Part 2) 105–06.

8. General Orders No. 16, April 13, 1862, ibid. 105. Halleck told Grant, "Your army is not now in condition to resist an attack. It must be made so without delay."

9. Halleck to Grant, April 14, 1862, ibid. 106. Emphasis added.

10. William Tecumseh Sherman, 1 *Memoirs of W. T. Sherman* 270 (New York: D. Appleton, 1875).

11. Henry Wager Halleck, *Elements of Military Art and Science* 132 (New York: D. Appleton, 1846).

12. Ambrose, *Halleck* 46–47. Writing years later, Grant ridiculed Halleck's places theory, arguing it was unclear "how the mere occupation of places was to close the war while large and effective rebel armies existed." 1 *Memoirs* 381.

13. Stanton to Halleck, April 23, 1862, 10 *War of the Rebellion* (Part 1) 98–99.

14. Halleck to Stanton, April 24, 1862, ibid. 99. On June 15, 1862, after reviewing all of the battle reports from Shiloh, Halleck wrote a follow-up to Stanton exonerating Grant. "The impression which at one time seems to have been received by the Department that our forces were surprised in the morning of [April] 6th is erroneous. I am satisfied from a patient and careful inquiry and investigation that all our troops were notified of the enemy's approach some time before the battle commenced." Halleck to Stanton, June 15, 1862, ibid.

15. Grant to Julia. April 30, 1862, 5 *Grant Papers* 102.

16. Two days before his death, General Smith wrote Grant to express his admiration and affection. It was the last letter Smith would write. Grant was deeply touched and passed the message to Julia. "I want the letter saved. Gen. Smith was my old Commandant whilst a Cadet and a better soldier or truer man does not live." Grant to Julia, April 25, 1862, 5 ibid. 72. Also see Grant to Julia, May 4, 1862, ibid. 110–11.

17. Grant to Mrs. Charles F. Smith, April 26, 1862, ibid. 83. Years later, when Grant was writing his *Memoirs,* he looked back on his days at West Point: "I regarded General [Winfield] Scott and Captain C. F. Smith, the Commandant of Cadets, as the two men most to be envied in the nation. I retained a high regard for both up to the day of their death." 1 *Memoirs* 42.

18. Sherman to R. W. Scott, September 6, 1885, Sherman Papers, Library of Congress.

19. General Orders No. 21, April 25, 1862.

20. Stanton's announcement is reprinted in the *New York Times,* April 28, 1862.

21. *Philadelphia Inquirer,* April 28, 1862.

22. Special Field Orders No. 31, April 28, 1862, 10 *War of the Rebellion* (Part 2) 138–39.

23. Special Orders No. 35, April 30, 1862, ibid. 144. Also see Halleck to Grant, April 30, 1862, 52 ibid. (Part 1) 245.

24. I am indebted to Colonel Arthur L. Conger for these observations. *The Rise of U.S. Grant* 272–73 (New York: Century, 1931).

25. Grant, 1 *Memoirs* 376.

26. Sherman, 1 *Memoirs* 274.

27. Allan Nevins, 2 *The War for the Union* 112 (New York: Charles Scribner's Sons, 1960).

28. Grant to Julia, April 30, May 11, May 13, 1862, 5 *Grant Papers* 101–2, 115–16, 117–18.

29. Grant to Halleck, May 11, 1862, ibid. 114.

30. Halleck to Grant, May 12, 1862, 10 *War of the Rebellion* (Part 2) 182–83.

31. Grant to Julia, May 16, 1862, 5 *Grant Papers* 123–24.

32. Grant to Julia, May 20, 1862, ibid. 127–28.

33. Grant to Julia, May 24, 1862, ibid. 130.

34. Ambrose, *Halleck* 52.

35. Grant, 1 *Memoirs* 379. Colonel John Webster, Grant's chief of staff, said that Halleck rejected the proposal "in the most insulting and indignant manner." It was one of the very few times, said Webster, he ever saw Grant struggle to keep his temper. Afterward, Grant was depressed for hours. *New York Times* interview with Webster, reprinted in the *Cincinnati Commercial,* October 26, 1867.

36. 10 *War of the Rebellion* (Part 2) 223, 225.

37. Ibid. 228.

38. Ambrose, *Halleck* 53.

39. Grant, 1 *Memoirs* 380–81.

40. Lew Wallace, 2 *Lew Wallace: An Autobiography* 581 (New York: Harper and Brothers, 1906).

41. Kenneth P. Williams, 3 *Lincoln Finds a General* 417 (New York: Macmillan, 1952).

42. Lieutenant Seymour D. Thompson, *Recollections with the Third Iowa Regiment* 275 (Cincinnati: privately published, 1864).

43. Shelby Foote, 1 *The Civil War* 387–88 (New York: Random House, 1958).

44. 10 *War of the Rebellion* (Part 1) 668.

45. Grant, 1 *Memoirs* 381. Grant was more outspoken writing to Julia. "The rebels will turn up some where and have to be whipped yet," he wrote on May 31. 5 *Grant Papers* 134–35.

46. Sherman, 1 *Memoirs* 275–76.

47. In his *Memoirs,* Grant wrote he had "obtained permission to leave the department, but General Sherman happened to call on me as I was about starting and urged me so strongly not to think of going, that I concluded to remain." 1 *Memoirs* 385.

48. Sherman, 1 *Memoirs* 276.

49. Grant to Julia, June 3, 1862, 5 *Grant Papers* 137–38.

50. Sherman to Grant, June 6, 1862, Sherman, 1 *Memoirs* 276.

51. I am indebted to William S. McFeely for this observation. *Grant: A Biography* 119 (New York: W. W. Norton, 1981).

52. 17 *War of the Rebellion* (Part 2) 5; 10 ibid. (Part 2) 254.

53. Special Field Orders No. 90, June 10, 1862, ibid. 288.

54. Foote, 1 *Civil War* 543.

55. Grant, 1 *Memoirs* 388–90.

56. Grant to Halleck, June 24, 1862, 5 *Grant Papers* 149–50.

57. Hillyer [Grant] to Hurlbut, June 24, 1862, 17 *War of the Rebellion* (Part 2) 30. Emphasis in original.

58. Halleck to Grant, June 29, 1862, ibid. 46. For Grant's original message, see Grant to Halleck, June 29, 1862, 5 *Grant Papers* 167.

59. Grant to Halleck, June 29, 1862, ibid. 168–69.

60. Halleck to Grant, July 3, 1862, 17 *War of the Rebellion* (Part 2) 67–68. Emphasis in original.

61. Three weeks later Grant wrote Congressman Washburne that if President Lincoln intended to make Halleck general in chief "a better selection could not be made. He is a man of gigantic intel-

lect and well studied in the profession of arms. He and I have had several little spats but I like and respect him nevertheless." Grant to Washburne, July 22, 1862, 5 *Grant Papers* 225–26.

62. Foote, 1 *Civil War* 567.

63. David Herbert Donald, *Lincoln* 361 (New York: Simon and Schuster, 1995); Gideon Welles, 1 *Diary of Gideon Welles* 119 (Boston: Little, Brown, 1909). Also see Ambrose, *Halleck* 60–62.

64. Halleck to Lincoln, July 11, 1862, 17 *War of the Rebellion* (Part 2) 90.

65. Halleck to Grant, July 11, 1862, ibid.

66. Grant to Halleck, July 11, 1862, 5 *Grant Papers* 207 note.

67. Halleck to Grant, July 11, 1862, ibid.

68. Grant, 1 *Memoirs* 393.

69. Some writers, taking their cue from Adam Badeau, have suggested Halleck was unwilling to entrust the command at Corinth to Grant. Badeau (who despised Halleck) based the assertion on a personal letter he received from Colonel Robert Allen, a quartermaster officer, in 1866. Allen claimed Halleck offered command of the Army of the Tennessee to him, and he turned it down. Aside from Allen's letter there is no evidence to support that wild assertion and a great deal of evidence, beginning with Halleck's July 11, 1862, telegram to Lincoln, to the contrary. *Cf.,* Badeau, 1 *Military History of Grant* 107–8; Bruce Catton, *Grant Moves South* 287–88 (Boston: Little, Brown, 1960); Geoffrey Perret, *Ulysses S. Grant: Soldier and President* 214 (New York: Random House, 1996).

70. 17 *War of the Rebellion* (Part 2) 101.

71. See Grant to Maj. Gen. Samuel R. Curtis, August 7, 1862, 5 *Grant Papers* 270–71.

72. Grant, 1 *Memoirs* 395.

73. Beauregard and Bragg remained on surprisingly good terms after Bragg took command, a fact that is especially surprising given Bragg's reputation for being quarrelsome. Beauregard was quoting Danton's famous speech to the French Legislative Assembly in 1792. Beauregard told Bragg "I have no doubt that with anything like equal numbers you will meet with success." Foote, 1 *Civil War* 573.

74. Grant to Halleck, July 30, August 1, 1862, 5 *Grant Papers* 254–55, 257.

75. Halleck to Grant, July 31, 1862, 17 *War of the Rebellion* (Part 2) 142.

76. Grant to Rosecrans, August 17, 1862, 5 *Grant Papers* 305.

77. Foote, 1 *Civil War* 583.

78. Grant, 1 *Memoirs* 410.

79. Foote, 1 *Civil War* 722.

80. Ibid. 724.

81. Ibid. 738.

82. Bragg's abrupt decision to withdraw has been often criticized. Yet as he wrote his wife, "With the whole southwest in the enemy's possession, my crime would have been unpardonable had I kept my noble little army to be ice-bound in a northern clime, without tents or shoes, and obliged to forage daily for bread, etc." Ibid. 739.

83. Roy P. Basler, ed., 5 *The Collected Works of Abraham Lincoln* 433–36 (New Brunswick, N.J.: Rutgers University Press, 1953).

84. Message to Congress in Special Session, July 4, 1861, 4 ibid. 429–31. Lincoln's emphasis.

85. Grant to Halleck, October 26, 1862, 6 *Grant Papers* 199–201.

86. Grant to Halleck, November 2, 1862, ibid. 243.

87. Halleck to Grant, November 3, 1862, ibid. note.

88. Ambrose, *Halleck* 92.

89. Grant to Halleck, December 8, 1862; Grant to Sherman, December 8, 1862, 6 *Grant Papers* 403–5. Also, Grant to Sherman, December 8, 1862, ibid. 406–7. *Cf.,* Grant, 1 *Memoirs* 431.

90. Catton, *Grant Moves South* 460.

91. McClernand to Stanton, October 21, 1862; Foote, 1 *Civil War* 763.

92. Ambrose, *Halleck* 111.

93. Halleck met with Elihu Washburne in early December and expressed unlimited confidence in Grant. Grant acknowledged the accolade December 14, 1862. Grant to Halleck, 7 *Grant Papers* 32.

94. Halleck to Grant, November 9, 1862, 17 *War of the Rebellion* (Part I) 468.

95. Grant to Halleck, November 10, 1862, 6 *Grant Papers* 288.

96. Halleck to Grant, November 11, 1862, 17 *War of the Rebellion* (Part I) 469.

97. Grant, 1 *Memoirs* 430–31.

98. Grant to Sherman, December 8, 1862, ibid. 429.

99. Grant to Halleck, December 9, 1862, 7 *Grant Papers* 6. Sherman's task force, loaded on more than a hundred steamers, did not depart Memphis until December 20. But for Grant and Halleck, the kidnap operation was accomplished when Grant ordered Sherman to take command.

100. Ambrose, *Halleck* 115.
101. Grant to Halleck, December 14, 1862, 7 *Grant Papers* 28–29.
102. Grant, 1 *Memoirs* 430–31.
103. Foote, 2 *Civil War* 65; Grant, 11 *Memoirs* 108. Also see Jerry O'Neil Potter, "The First West Tennessee Raid of General Nathan Bedford Forrest," 28 *West Tennessee Historical Society Papers* 55–74 (1974).
104. J. G. Deupree, "The Capture of Holly Springs, Mississippi, December 20, 1862," 4 *Publications of the Mississippi Historical Society* 49–61 (1901).
105. Grant, 1 *Memoirs* 435.
106. Sherman to Rawlins, December 19, 1862, 17 *War of the Rebellion* (Part I) 603–4.
107. Foote, 2 *Civil War* 77.
108. Tyler Anbinder, "Ulysses S. Grant, Nativist," 43 *Civil War History* 120 (1997).
109. Charles A. Dana to Edwin M. Stanton, January 21, 1863, 52 *War of the Rebellion* (Part 1) 331.
110. See Anbinder, "Ulysses S. Grant, Nativist" 122.
111. James McPherson, *Battle Cry of Freedom* 622 (New York: Oxford University Press, 1988).
112. Grant to Hurlbut, November 9, 1862, 6 *Grant Papers* 283
113. Grant to Webster, November 10, 1862, ibid.
114. Grant to Sherman, December 5, 1862, ibid. 394.
115. 7 *Grant Papers* 50.
116. Simon Wolf, *The Presidents I Have Known from 1860–1918* 70–71 (Washington, D.C.: Press of B. S. Adams, 1918).
117. See Bertram Wallace Korn, *American Jewry and the Civil War* 140–44 (Philadelphia: Jewish Publication Society of America, 1951).
118. McPherson, *Battle Cry of Freedom* 622 note.
119. James H. Wilson, *The Life of John A. Rawlins* 96 (New York: Neale, 1916); Albert Deane Richardson, *A Personal History of Ulysses S. Grant* 277 (Hartford, Conn.: American Publishing, 1868).
120. 7 *Grant Papers* 51 note; *cf.* Korn, *American Jewry* 142.
121. For an extensive analysis of Grant's nativism, see Anbinder, "Ulysses S. Grant, Nativist" 117–41.
122. Stephen V. Ash, "Civil War Exodus: The Jews and Grant's General Orders No. 11," 44 *The Historian* 509 (1982).
123. *New York Times,* January 18, 1863.
124. Halleck to Grant, January 4, 1863, 7 *Grant Papers* 53 note. Emphasis added.
125. Halleck to Grant, January 21, 1863, ibid. 54 note. Emphasis added.
126. *Congressional Globe,* 37th Congress, 3rd session, 184, 222, 245–46.
127. 7 *Grant Papers* 54 note.
128. Grant to Halleck, January 11, 1863, 7 *Grant Papers* 209.
129. Halleck to Grant, January 12, 1862, 17 *War of the Rebellion* (Part 2) 555.
130. Grant to McPherson, January 13, 1862, 7 *Grant Papers* 220.
131. Grant to Halleck, January 20, 1863, ibid. 233–35.
132. Grant, 1 *Memoirs* 441.
133. 24 *War of the Rebellion* (Part I) 11.
134. McClernand to Grant, January 30, 1863, ibid. (Part 3) 18–19.
135. Grant to McClernand, January 31, 1863, 7 *Grant Papers* 264.
136. McClernand to Grant, February 1, 1863, 24 *War of the Rebellion* (Part I) 13–14.
137. Grant to Halleck, February 1, 1863, 7 *Grant Papers* 274.
138. Lincoln to McClernand, January 22, 1863, 6 *Collected Works of Lincoln* 71.
139. J. F. C. Fuller, *The Generalship of Ulysses S. Grant* 135 (London: John Murray, 1929).
140. Grant, 1 *Memoirs* 443.
141. Ibid. 446.
142. Foote, 2 *Civil War* 192.
143. Grant, 1 *Memoirs* 449.
144. Samuel Carter III, *The Final Fortress: The Campaign for Vicksburg, 1862–1863* 147 (New York: St. Martin's, 1980).
145. Grant to Julia, February 11, 1863, 7 *Grant Papers* 311.
146. Cadwallader Washburn to Elihu Washburne, March 28, 1863. Washburne Papers, Library of Congress.
147. *New York World,* March 12, 1863.
148. Medill to Elihu Washburne, January 16, 1863, in Catton, *Grant Moves South* 369.
149. Halstead's letter, February 19, 1863, was printed in the *Chicago Tribune,* September 28, 1885.
150. Foote, 2 *Civil War* 217.
151. John Eaton, *Grant, Lincoln, and the Freedmen* 64 (New York: Longmans, Green, 1907).

152. Eyewitness reports of Grant's drinking are numerous. In addition to those cited below in the text, see the comments of Brigadier General Charles S. Hamilton quoted in Catton, *Grant Moves South* 395, and of journalist Sylvanus Cadwallader, *Three Years with Grant* 103–19 (reprint, Lincoln: University of Nebraska Press, 1996).

153. Lyle W Dorsett, "The Problem of Grant's Drinking During the Civil War, 4 *Hayes Historical Journal* 45–46 (1983).

154. *New York Sun,* January 28, 1887; Harry J. Maihafer, "Mr. Grant and Mr. Dana," 35 *American History* 24–32 (2000).

155. Foote, 2 *Civil War* 417.

156. 8 *Grant Papers* 322–23 note.

157. Cadwallader, *Three Years with Grant* 118–19.

158. *New York World,* February 20, 1863.

159. A. O. Marshall, *Army Life: From a Soldier's Journal* 274–76 (Joliet, Ill.: privately published, 1884).

160. Foote, 2 *The Civil War* 218–19.

161. Interview with Dr. E. A. Duncan, in the *National Republican,* August 9, 1886.

162. Sherman interview, *New York Tribune,* August 2, 1885.

163. Marshall, *Army Life* 275.

164. Eaton, *Grant, Lincoln, and the Freedmen* 89–90.

165. Foote, 2 *Civil War* 218.

166. Charles A. Dana, *Recollections of the Civil War* 61–62 (New York: D. Appleton, 1902).

167. Grant, 1 *Memoirs* 459–60.

168. Donald, *Lincoln* 435.

169. Halleck to Grant, March 20, 1863, 24 *War of the Rebellion* (Part 1) 22.

170. Grant to Porter, April 2, 1863, 8 *Grant Papers* 3–4.

171. Grant to Halleck, April 2, 1863, ibid. 5 note.

172. Grant to Halleck, January 18, 1863, 7 ibid. 231.

173. Richardson, *Personal History of Ulysses S. Grant* 295.

174. Grant to Halleck, April 4, 1863, 8 *Grant Papers* 11–12.

175. Grant, 1 *Memoirs* 542–43 note.

176. David D. Porter, *Incidents and Anecdotes of the Civil War* 175 (New York: D. Appleton, 1886).

177. 24 *War of the Rebellion,* (Part 3) 179–80. Also see Sherman, 1 *Memoirs* 342–45. Badeau, 1 *History of Grant* 184–85.

178. Grant, 1 *Memoirs* 543 note.

179. Halleck to Grant, April 9, 1863, 24 *War of the Rebellion,* (Part 1) 27–28.

180. James R. Arnold, *Grant Wins the War: Decision at Vicksburg* 76 (New York: Wiley, 1997).

181. Grant, 1 *Memoirs* 464.

182. Pemberton to Cooper, April 11, 1863, 24 *War of the Rebellion* (Part 3) 733.

183. Pemberton to Chalmers, April 18, 1863, ibid. 765.

184. Lee to Jefferson Davis, April 27, 1863, 25 ibid. (Part 2) 752–53.

185. Ira Blanchard, *I Marched with Sherman: Civil War Memoirs of the Twentieth Illinois* 82 (San Francisco: J. D. Haff, 1992).

186. Grant to Halleck, April 21, 1863, 8 *Grant Papers* 102.

187. Porter to Welles, April 24, 1863, 24 *War of the Rebellion (Navy)* 607.

188. Porter to Fox, April 25, 1863, in Gustavus Fox, 2 *Confidential Correspondence of Gustavus Fox, Assistant Secretary of the Navy* 125 (New York: De Vinne, 1919).

189. Arnold, *Grant Wins the War* 93.

190. Grant to Halleck, April 29, 1863, 8 *Grant Papers* 133.

191. Foote, 2 *Civil War* 342–43.

192. Grant, 1 *Memoirs* 480–81. Emphasis added.

193. Grant to Sherman, April 27, 1863, 8 *Grant Papers* 130.

194. Sherman to Grant, April 28, 1863, 24 *War of the Rebellion* (Part 3) 242–44.

195. Foote, 2 *Civil War* 332.

196. Sherman to Grant, May 1, 1863, 24 *War of the Rebellion* (Part 1) 576–77.

197. Foote, 2 *Civil War* 334.

198. Grant to Halleck, May 3, 1863, 8 *Grant Papers* 144.

199. Foote, 2 *Civil War* 345.

200. Grant to Halleck, May 3, 1863, 8 *Grant Papers* 145–48.

201. Grant to Sherman, May 3, 1863, ibid. 151–52. Emphasis in original.

202. Mary Ann Anderson, ed., *The Civil War Diary of Allen Morgan Greer* 99 (Tappan, N.Y.: Cosmos, 1977).

203. Arnold, *Grant Wins the War* 120.

204. Foote, 2 *Civil War* 350.

205. Grant, 1 *Memoirs* 490–91.
206. Grant to Halleck, May 3, 1863, 8 *Grant Papers* 148.
207. Grant to Julia, May 3, 1863, ibid. 155.
208. Grant, 1 *Memoirs* 492–93.
209. Joseph Orville Jackson, ed., *Some of the Boys: The Civil War Letters of Isaac Jackson, 1862–1865* 90 (Carbondale: Southern Illinois University Press, 1960).
210. Grant, 1 *Memoirs* 483.
211. Grant to Halleck, May 6, 1863, 8 *Grant Papers* 169.
212. Sherman to Grant, May 9, 1863, 24 *War of the Rebellion* (Part 3) 284–85.
213. Grant to Sherman, May 9, 1863, 8 *Grant Papers* 183–84.
214. Grant to Hillyer, May 9, 1863, ibid. 187.
215. Ibid. 186.
216. Osborn H. Oldroyd, *A Soldier's Story of the Seige of Vicksburg* 11–12 (Springfield, Ill.: privately published, 1885).
217. Grant to Halleck, May 11, 1863, 8 *Grant Papers* 196. Emphasis added.
218. Grant, 1 *Memoirs* 492.
219. Grant to McClernand, May 11, 1863, 8 *Grant Papers* 197.
220. Grant to McPherson, May 11, 1863, ibid. 200.
221. Pemberton to Gregg, May 12, 1863, 24 *War of the Rebellion* (Part 3) 862.
222. Grant, 1 *Memoirs* 500.
223. Grant to Halleck, May 14, 1863, 8 *Grant Papers* 213. Grant's message arrived in Washington on May 18.
224. Johnston to [Secretary of War James A.] Seddon, May 13, 1863, 24 *War of the Rebellion* (Part 1) 215.
225. Johnston to Pemberson, May 14, 1863, Grant, 1 *Memoirs* 465.
226. Ibid. 507.
227. Foote, 2 *Civil War* 363.
228. Grant, 1 *Memoirs* 508.
229. Grant to McClernand, May 14, 1863, 8 *Grant Papers* 215.
230. Grant to McPherson, May 14, 1863, ibid. 226.
231. Arnold, *Grant Wins the War* 145.
232. Grant, 1 *Memoirs* 512.
233. Grant to McClernand, 5:40 A.M., May 16, 1863, 8 *Grant Papers* 224.
234. Grant, 1 *Memoirs* 513.
235. Arnold, *Grant Wins the War* 151. Bowen was promoted to major general after the battle of Port Gibson.
236. Carter, *The Final Fortress*.
237. John B. Sanborn, *The Crisis at Champion's Hill: The Decisive Battle of the Civil War* 14 (St. Paul, Minn.: n.p., 1903).
238. S. H. M. Byers, "Some Recollections of Grant," in *Annals of the War Written by Leading Participants North and South* 346–56 (Edison, N.J.: Blue and Grey Press, 1996). Reprint.
239. Report of Brigadier General Alvin P. Hovey, May 25, 1863, 24 *War of the Rebellion* (Part 2) 44.
240. I am indebted to James R. Arnold for this reference. *Grant Wins the War* 199.
241. Grant, 1 *Memoirs* 519–20.
242. Ibid. 522.
243. Grant, 1 *Memoirs* 524–25. *Cf.*, Catton, *Grant Moves South* 447–48.
244. Cadwallader, *Three Years with Grant* 83.
245. Dora [Miller] Richards, "War Diary of a Union Woman in the South," 38 *Century Magazine* 931–46 (October 1889).
246. Samuel Lockett, "The Defense of Vicksburg," 3 *Battles and Leaders of the Civil War* 488.
247. Grant, 1 *Memoirs* 528. "I do not claim to quote Sherman's language," Grant wrote, "but the substance only."
248. Lincoln to Arnold, May 26, 1863, *Collected Works* 270.
249. Special Field Orders No. 134, May 19, 1863, 8 *Grant Papers* 237.
250. Foote, 2 *Civil War* 384.
251. Ibid. 386.
252. Grant to Halleck, May 24, 1863, 8 *Grant Papers* 260–62.
253. Grant, 1 *Memoirs* 531.
254. Foote, 2 *The Civil War* 387.
255. Carter, *Final Fortress* 241.
256. A. A. Hochling, *Vicksburg* 92 (Englewood Cliffs, N.J.: Prentice Hall, 1969).
257. McPherson, *Battle Cry of Freedom* 635.

258. Foote, 2 *Civil War* 414.
259. Ibid.
260. Grant told Sherman that "should Johnston come, we want to whip him if the Siege has to be raised to do it." Grant to Sherman, June 23, 1863, 8 *Grant Papers* 410–11.
261. Foote, 2 *Civil War* 414.
262. Grant, 1 *Memoirs* 549.
263. Foote, 2 *Civil War* 425.
264. Ibid. 426.
265. Grant, 1 *Memoirs* 556–57.
266. Ibid. 557–58.
267. Grant, 1 *Memoirs* 558.
268. Grant to Pemberton, July 3, 1863, 8 *Grant Papers* 457–58.
269. Jackson, *Some of the Boys* 112.
270. Richards, "War Diary of a Union Woman" 775.
271. Willie H. Tunnard, *A Southern Record* 272 (Baton Rouge: privately published, 1866).
272. Porter, *Incidents and Anecdotes* 201.
273. Lincoln to Grant, July 13, 1863, 6 *Collected Works* 326.

CHAPTER EIGHT: CHATTANOOGA

The epigraph is from B. H. Liddell Hart, *Sherman: Soldier, Realist, American* 196 (New York: Dodd, Mead, 1929).

1. Grant to Sherman, July 4, 1863, 24 *War of the Rebellion* (Part 3), 473.
2. Lincoln to James C. Conkling, August 26, 1863, 6 *The Collected Works of Abraham Lincoln* 409, Roy P. Basler, ed., (New Brunswick, N.J.: Rutgers University Press, 1967).
3. James M. McPherson, *Battle Cry of Freedom* 638 (New York: Oxford University Press, 1988).
4. T. Harry Williams, *Lincoln and His Generals* 272 (New York: Alfred A. Knopf, 1952).
5. Lincoln to Burnside, July 27, 1863, 6 *Collected Works* 350.
6. Williams, *Lincoln and His Generals* 262.
7. Ulysses S. Grant, 1 *Personal Memoirs of U.S. Grant* 99–100 (New York: Charles L. Webster, 1885).
8. Shelby Foote, 2 *The Civil War* 638 (New York: Random House, 1963).
9. Lincoln to Meade, July 14, 1863 (not sent), 6 *Works of Lincoln* 327–28.
10. Grant to Dana, August 5, 1863.
11. Grant to Halleck, July 18 and July 24, 1863, 9 *Grant Papers* 186.
12. Halleck to Grant, August 6 and August 9, 1863, 24 *War of the Rebellion* (Part 3) 558.
13. Halleck to Grant, July 30, 1863, ibid. 562.
14. Lincoln to Grant, August 9, 1863, ibid. 584.
15. Halleck to Grant, September 17, 1863, ibid. 538–62.
16. Sherman to Halleck, ibid. 695–97.
17. 24 *War of the Rebellion* (Part 3) 562.
18. 30 ibid. 732.
19. Bruce Catton, *Grant Takes Command* 20–21 (Boston: Little, Brown, 1968).
20. Henry Coppee, *Life and Services of General U.S. Grant* 206–7 (Chicago: Charles B. Richardson, 1868).
21. 9 *Grant Papers* 222 note.
22. Foote, 2 *Civil War* 774.
23. Grant, 1 *Memoirs* 581–82.
24. So out of touch was Union intelligence that on September 11, 1863, when Longstreet's corps had been underway to join Bragg for three days, Halleck telegraphed Rosecrans that according to Union intelligence reports Bragg was sending men north to reinforce Lee! 30 *War of the Rebellion* (Part 1) 34.
25. Foote, 2 *Civil War* 748.
26. Ibid. 768.
27. Dana to Stanton, October 13, 1863, in Freeman Cleaves, *Rock of Chickamauga: The Life of General George H. Thomas* 180 (Norman: University of Oklahoma Press, 1948).
28. Tyler Dennett, ed., *Lincoln and the Civil War in the Diaries and Letters of John Hay* 106 (New York: Dodd, Mead, 1939).
29. Grant, 1 *Memoirs* 583–84.
30. Ibid.
31. 30 *War of the Rebellion* (Part 4) 404.

32. Grant, 2 *Memoirs* 17–18.
33. 9 *Grant Papers* 281 note.
34. Grant, 2 *Memoirs* 19.
35. Grant to Rosecrans, October 19, 1863, 9 *Grant Papers* 286.
36. Grant to Thomas, October 19, 1863, ibid. 287.
37. Thomas to Grant, October 19, 1863, 30 *War of the Rebellion* (Part 4) 479.
38. Grant, 2 *Memoirs* 26–27.
39. Harvey Reid to Sarah Reid, Reid Papers, October 21, 1863, Huntington Library.
40. John Russell Young, 2 *Around the World with General Grant* 288 (New York: American News, 1879).
41. Grant, 2 *Memoirs* 28.
42. Rawlins to Mary Emma Hurlbut, November 16, 1863, Rawlins Papers, Chicago Historical Society.
43. Horace Porter, *Campaigning with Grant* 2 (New York: Century, 1897).
44. Ibid. 4.
45. Catton, *Grant Takes Command* 40. After the war, Reynolds said there was never any bad feeling between Thomas and Grant. "They were both big men. The only thing Grant ever had against Thomas was that Thomas was slow. And it's the God of Mighty's truth he was slow."
46. Grant, 2 *Memoirs* 29.
47. Porter, *Campaigning with Grant* 4–5, 8.
48. Grant, 2 *Memoirs* 31.
49. Ibid. 38–39.
50. Grant to Halleck, October 29, 1863, 9 *Grant Papers* 295.
51. Ibid.
52. Catton, *Grant Takes Command* 56.
53. Grant to Julia, October 27, 1883, 9 *Grant Papers* 288.
54. Porter, *Campaigning with Grant* 14–16.
55. Charles Francis Adams, Jr., quoted in T. Harry Williams *McClellan, Sherman, and Grant* 82–83 (New Brunswick, N.J.: Rutgers University Press, 1962).
56. Allan Nevins, 3 *The War for the Union, 1863–1864* 184 (New York: Charles Scribner's Sons, 1947).
57. Catton, *Grant Takes Command* 42–43.
58. Grant, 2 *Memoirs* 42–43.
59. Young, 2 *Around the World* 295.
60. Grant, 2 *Memoirs* 50.
61. 9 *Grant Papers* 315.
62. Grant to Julia, November 14, 1863, ibid. 317.
63. "Grant to Chattanooga," in Frederick D. Grant, 1 *Personal Reflections of the War of the Rebellion* 244–257 (New York: Charles Scribner's Sons, 1907).
64. Ibid.
65. William Tecumseh Sherman, 1 *Memoirs of General W. T. Sherman* 387 (New York: Literary Classics, 1990). Reprint.
66. Cleaves, *Rock of Chickamauga* 192.
67. Foote, 2 *Civil War* 845.
68. Catton, *Grant Takes Command* 72.
69. Grant, 2 *Memoirs* 64.
70. *Richmond Dispatch*, quoted in Catton, *Grant Takes Command* 72.
71. Grant, 2 *Memoirs* 72.
72. Grant to Halleck, November 24, 1863, 9 *Grant Papers* 439–40.
73. Lincoln to Grant, November 25, 1863, 7 *Works of Lincoln* 30.
74. Halleck to Grant, November 25, 1863, 9 *Grant Papers* 440 note.
75. Rawlins (Grant) to Sherman, November 24 [25] 1863, 31 *War of the Rebellion* (Part 2) 43–44.
76. Grant to Hooker, November 25, 1863, 55 Ibid. 44.
77. Grant to Thomas, November 24 [25] 1863, 9 *Grant Papers* 443.
78. 31 *War of the Rebellion* (Part 2) 116.
79. Irving Buck, *Cleburne and His Command* 167 (Jackson, Tenn.: McCowat-Mercur, 1959).
80. Grant's orders to Thomas have been subject to varying interpretations, some historians insisting that Grant did not mean for the Army of the Cumberland to move beyond the rifle pits. The *Official Record* suggests otherwise. Grant saw the taking of the rebel first line as a preliminary to attacking the ridge itself, but he assumed that Thomas's men would halt at the pits and re-form before proceeding against the heights. The most useful analysis is by J. F. C. Fuller in *The Generalship of Ulysses S. Grant* 176–77. Also see 55 *War of the Rebellion* 508 and Appendix II; 9 *Grant Papers* 447 note.

81. Foote, 2 *Civil War* 853.
82. Catton, *Grant Takes Command* 80.
83. 31 *War of the Rebellion* (Part 2) 78–79.
84. Grant, 2 *Memoirs* 79.
85. James A. Connolly, *Three Years in the Army of the Cumberland* 158, Paul M. Angle, ed. (Blooming-ton: Indiana University Press, 1959).
86. Joseph S. Fullerton, "The Army of the Cumberland at Chattanooga," 3 *Battles and Leaders of the Civil War* 725.
87. Douglas MacArthur, *Reminiscences* 8–9 (New York: Random House, 1964). Arthur MacArthur, the father of Douglas MacArthur, best known for his role in suppressing the Philippine Insurrec-tion, was the senior general in the army from 1902 to 1909, but was never chief of staff. The Medal of Honor for his role on Missionary Ridge was awarded in 1890.
88. Foote, 2 *Civil War* 858.
89. 31 *War of the Rebellion* (Part 2) 666.
90. Ulysses S. Grant, "Chattanooga," 3 *Battles and Leaders of the Civil War* 693 note.
91. Grant, 2 *Memoirs* 86.
92. Ibid. 87.
93. Williams, *McClellan, Sherman, and Grant* 100.
94. 31 *War of the Rebellion* (Part 3) 402.
95. William S. McFeely, *Grant: A Biography* 139 (New York: W. W. Norton, 1981).
96. Longstreet to Maj. Gen. LaFayette McLaws, November 29, 1863, 31 *War of the Rebellion* (Part 1) 494.
97. Grant to McPherson, December 1, 1863, 9 *Grant Papers* 480–81.
98. Grant to Halleck, December 7, 1863, ibid. 500–501.
99. Halleck to Grant, December 21, 1863, 31 *War of the Rebellion* (Part 1) 458.
100. Lincoln to Grant, December 8, 1863, 7 *Works of Lincoln* 35, 53.

CHAPTER NINE: GENERAL IN CHIEF

The epigraph is Lincoln's comment to his secretary, John Hay, during the battle of the Wilderness. *Lincoln and the Civil War in the Diaries and Letters of John Hay* 180, Tyler Dennett, ed. (New York: Dodd, Mead, 1939).

1. *New York Herald,* December 8, 1863.
2. Washington held the rank of lieutenant general for eight months during the naval war with France in 1798. Winfield Scott was brevetted to rank on a temporary basis in 1855.
3. Shelby Foote, 2 *The Civil War* 918–19 (New York: Random House, 1963).
4. Editorials in the *New York Herald,* December 15, 18, 1863.
5. Barnabus Burns to Grant, December 7, 1863, 9 *The Papers of Ulysses S. Grant* 542 note, John Y. Simon, ed. (Carbondale: Southern Illinois University Press, 1979).
6. Grant to Burns, December 17, 1863, ibid. 541.
7. Grant to Rear Admiral Daniel Ammen, February 16, 1864, 10 *Grant Papers* 132–33; Grant to Brigadier General Frank Blair, February 28, 1864, ibid. 166–67; Grant to Rear Admiral Daniel Porter, ibid. note.
8. Grant to Jesse Root Grant, February 20, 1864, ibid. 148–149.
9. Grant to I. N. Morris, January 20, 1864, ibid. 52–53.
10. Quoted in Bruce Catton, *Grant Takes Command* 110 (Boston: Little, Brown, 1968).
11. Albert Deane Richardson, *A Personal History of Ulysses S. Grant* 380–81 (Hartford, Conn.: American Publishing, 1868).
12. Ida M. Tarbell, interview with J. Russell Jones, 2 *The Life of President Lincoln* 188 (New York: McClure, 1900). Also see 9 *Grant Papers* 543 note.
13. Jones interview, *Life of President Lincoln,* 186–88.
14. Catton, *Grant Takes Command* 112.
15. Opposition to the bill was led by radical Republican Thaddeus Stevens of Pennsylvania and former brigadier general James A. Garfield of Ohio. Stevens, who suspected Grant's views on slavery, argued that "Saints are not canonized until after death," suggesting that the promotion should be held until the war was won. Garfield, who had been Rosecrans's chief of staff, took the same line in addition to being deeply resentful of Grant's decision to relieve Rosecrans. (Never an admirer of Grant, Garfield would eventually wrest the Republican presidential nomination from him in 1880.)
16. Halleck to Grant, March 3, 1864, 32 *Offical Records of the War of the Rebellion* (Part 3) 13.

17. Halleck to Grant, March 6, 1864, 10 *Grant Papers* 189 note.

18. Hay, *Lincoln and the Civil War* 164.

19. Halleck to Sherman, December 14, 1863, 32 *War of the Rebellion* (Part 2) 408.

20. Halleck to Francis Lieber, March 7, 1864, Lieber Collection, Huntington Library.

21. Grant to Sherman, March 4, 1864, 10 *Grant Papers* 189 note. Also see Ulysses S. Grant, 2 *Personal Memoirs of U.S. Grant* 116 (New York: Charles L. Webster, 1886).

22. Grant to Sherman, March 4, 1864, 10 *Grant Papers* 186–87.

23. Sherman to Grant, March 10, 1864, quoted in Adam Badeau, 1 *Military History of Ulysses S. Grant* 373–74 (New York: D. Appleton, 1881).

24. Shelby Foote, 3 *The Civil War* 5 (New York: Random House, 1974).

25. Horace Porter, *Campaigning with Grant* 19 (New York: Da Capo, 1986). Reprint.

26. Ibid. 20–21.

27. Foote, 3 *Civil War* 6.

28. 10 *Grant Papers* 195.

29. Grant, 2 *Memoirs* 122.

30. Hamlin Garland, *Ulysses S. Grant: His Life and Character* 266 (New York: Doubleday, 1920).

31. Badeau, 2 *Military History of Ulysses S. Grant* 16.

32. Dana to Grant, December 21, 1863, 9 *Grant Papers* 502 note.

33. Meade to Mrs. Meade, March 8, 1864, in George Meade, 2 *The Life and Letters of General George Gordon Meade* 176 (New York: Charles Scribner's Sons, 1913).

34. Porter, *Campaigning with Grant* 83.

35. John Russell Young, 2 *Around the World with General Grant* 181 (New York: American News, 1879).

36. 2 *Life and Letters of General George Gordon Meade* 189.

37. Grant, 2 *Memoirs* 117.

38. Catton, *Grant Moves South* 129.

39. 2 *Life and Letters of General George Gordon Meade* 191.

40. Grant, 2 *Memoirs* 117–18.

41. 32 *War of the Rebellion* (Part 3) 58.

42. Foote, 3 *Civil War* 12.

43. Garland, *Grant* 260–61.

44. Foote, 3 *Civil War* 13.

45. Meade to Mrs. Meade, April 24, 1864, 2 *Life and Letters of General George Gordon Meade* 191.

46. Garland, *Grant* 262.

47. Catton, *Grant Takes Command* 137.

48. Richardson, *Grant* 386.

49. Badeau, 2 *Military History of Ulysses S. Grant* 21.

50. Speech of General Grenville Dodge before the Society of the Army of the Potomac in 1898, reprinted in the Society's report of its twenty-ninth reunion.

51. William Tecumseh Sherman, 1 *Memoirs of General W. T. Sherman* 430 (New York: Literary Classics of the United States, 1990). Reprint. For the text of Grant's speech, see 10 *Grant Papers* 214.

52. Dodge speech. See note 50.

53. Foote, 3 *Civil War* 13.

54. Catton, *Grant Takes Command* 139.

55. Grant to Halleck, March 30, 1864, 10 *Grant Papers* 240.

56. Badeau, 2 *Military History of Ulysses S. Grant* 29–32.

57. William Conant Church, *Ulysses S. Grant and the Period of National Preservation and Reconstruction* 248–49 (New York: G. P. Putnam's Sons, 1897).

58. Grant, 2 *Memoirs* 127, 129–30.

59. Badeau, 2 *Military History of Ulysses S. Grant* 34.

60. Grant, 2 *Memoirs* 128.

61. Grant to Meade, April 9, 1864, ibid. 134–35 note.

62. Grant to Sherman, April 4, 1864, ibid. 130–32 note.

63. J. F. C. Fuller, *The Generalship of Ulysses S. Grant* 214 (London: John Murray, 1929).

64. Grant to Sherman, April 4, 1864, Grant 2 *Memoirs* 130.

65. Grant to Meade, April 9, 1864, ibid. 135.

66. Grant to Sherman, April 4, 1864, ibid. 132.

67. Foote, 3 *Civil War* 19. At the 1860 Democratic convention, Butler had voted to nominate Jefferson Davis as president of the United States on fifty-seven consecutive ballots.

68. Grant, 2 *Memoirs* 133–34; 10 *Grant Papers* 217 note; Philip H. Sheridan, 1 *Personal Memoirs of P. H. Sheridan* 339 (New York: Charles L. Webster, 1895).

69. Foote, 3 *Civil War* 136.
70. Porter, *Campaigning with Grant* 26.
71. Badeau, 2 *Military History of Ulysses S. Grant* 9–10.
72. Grant, 2 *Memoirs* 142–43.
73. Grant to Sherman, April 4, 1864, ibid. 130–32 note.
74. Hay, *Lincoln and the Civil War* 178.
75. Letters of Richard Henry Dana, April 21, May 4, 1864, Dana Papers, Massachusetts Historical Society; Foote, 3 *Civil War* 4–5; James M. McPherson, *Battle Cry of Freedom* 221 (New York: Oxford University Press, 1988); G. T. Strong, *The Diary of George Templeton Strong: The Civil War, 1860–1865* 416, Allan Nevins and Milton Halsey Thomas, eds. (New York: Macmillan, 1952).
76. Foote, 3 *Civil War* 123.
77. Porter, *Campaigning with Grant* 46–47.
78. The army's total strength on May 1, 1864, was 662,345, but the operative figure is "present for duty, equipped." Badeau, 2 *Military History of Ulysses S. Grant* 32.
79. Porter, *Campaigning with Grant* 45–46.
80. John Keegan, *The Mask of Command* 204 (New York: Viking, 1987).
81. Bruce Catton, *A Stillness at Appomattox* 38 (Garden City, N.Y.: Doubleday, 1956).
82. Frederick Dent Grant, quoted in "War Horses," 4 *Photographic History of the Civil War* 292–98, Francis Trevelyan Miller, ed. (New York: Review of Reviews, 1911).
83. Ibid.
84. Badeau, 2 *Military History of Ulysses S. Grant* 34.
85. John Russell Young interview with Grant, *New York Herald,* July 24, 1878.
86. Ibid.
87. Foote, 3 *Civil War* 134–35.
88. Grant to Meade, April 9, 1864, 10 *Grant Papers* 273–75.
89. Grant to Sherman, April 19, 1864, ibid. 331–32.
90. Grant to Smith, April 26, 1864, ibid. 356–57.
91. Foote, 3 *Civil War* 132.
92. Letter of Selden Connor, April 16, 1864, Brown University Library.
93. Morris Schaff, *The Battle of the Wilderness* (Boston: Little, Brown, 1910).
94. Stanton P. Allen, *Down in Dixie: Life in a Cavalry Regiment in the War Days* 187–88 (Boston: D. Lothrop, 1892).
95. Foote, 3 *Civil War* 132.
96. Ibid.
97. Statement of Sergeant John D. Reed, in John L. Parker and Robert G. Carter, *History of the Twenty-second Massachusetts Infantry* 81 (Boston: Rand Avery, 1887).
98. William O. Stoddard, Jr., *William O. Stoddard: Lincoln's Third Secretary* 197–98 (New York: Exposition Press, 1955).
99. For Grant's instructions, see Grant to Hunter, April 17, 1864, 10 *Grant Papers* 305–7. Hunter's reports are dated April 28 and May 2, 1864, ibid. 308 note.
100. Grant to Halleck, April 25, April 28, 1864, ibid. 351, 363–64.
101. Grant to Halleck, April 19, 1864, ibid. 369–70. For Halleck's reply see Halleck to Grant, May 2, 1864, ibid. 375 note. A fine summary of the Red River fiasco is contained in Badeau, 2 *Military History of Ulysses S. Grant* 82ff.
102. Lee to Davis, April 5, 1864, 33 *War of the Rebellion* 1273.
103. Lee to Davis, April 8, 1864, ibid. 1267–69, 1290–91.
104. Lee to Davis, April 15, 1864, ibid. 1144, 1282–83.
105. Lee to Davis, April 30, 1864, ibid. 1320–21.
106. Grant to Meade, April 27, 1864, 10 *Grant Papers* 344 note.
107. Badeau, 2 *Military History of Ulysses S. Grant* 88–89.
108. Foote, 3 *Civil War* 136.
109. Grant to Sherman, April 28, 1864, 10 *Grant Papers* 354 note.
110. Grant to Butler, April 28, 1864, ibid. 364.
111. Grant to Sigel, April 24, April 28, 1864, ibid. 313–14 note.
112. Grant to Halleck, April 29, 1864, ibid. 370–71.
113. Lincoln to Grant, April 30, 1864, Abraham Lincoln 7 *The Collected Works of Abraham Lincoln,* Roy P. Basler, ed. (New Brunswick: Rutgers University Press, 1953).
114. Grant to Lincoln, May 1, 1864, 10 *Grant Papers* 380.
115. Grant to Sherman, May 2, 1864, 10 *Grant Papers* 355 note.
116. Grant to Butler, May 2, 1964, ibid. 366 note.
117. Grant to Burnside, May 2, 1864, ibid. 388–89.

118. Grant to Halleck, May 3, 1864, ibid. 395. On the eve of battle, Grant cleared the deck. He told Halleck to handle affairs in the trans-Mississippi in the best way he could, "but I do think it is a waste of struggle to trust General Banks with a large command or an important mission."
119. Douglas Southall Freeman, 3 *R. E. Lee: A Biography* 273 (New York: Charles Scribner's Sons, 1935).
120. Ibid. 269–70; 36 *War of the Rebellion* (Part 1) 1081.
121. Grant, 2 *Memoirs* 183.
122. Grant to Halleck, May 4, 1864, 10 *Grant Papers* 397.

CHAPTER TEN: THE WILDERNESS

The epigraph is from Herman Melville's "The Armies of the Wilderness," in *Battle-Pieces and Aspects of the War* 99, Sidney Kaplan, ed. (Gainesville: University of Florida Press, 1960).

1. Horace Porter, *Campaigning with Grant* 41–41 (New York: Da Capo, 1986). Reprint.
2. Adam Badeau, 2 *Military History of Ulysses S. Grant* 109 (New York: D. Appleton, 1881).
3. Theodore Lyman, *Meade's Headquarters, 1863–1865: Letters of Colonel Theodore Lyman from the Wilderness to Appomattox* 87, George R. Agassiz, ed. (Boston: Little, Brown, 1922).
4. Sylvanus Cadwallader, *Three Years with Grant* 174–75 (Lincoln: University of Nebraska Press, 1996). Reprint.
5. Charles A. Page, *Letters of a War Correspondent* 48 (Boston: L. C. Page, 1899).
6. Brig. Gen. Rufus Ingalls, Report, 36 *War of the Rebellion: A Compilation of the Official Records* (Part 1) 276–78 (Washington: Government Printing Office, 1884).
7. Cadwallader, *Three Years with Grant* 43.
8. Porter, *Campaigning with Grant* 44.
9. Grant to Burnside, May 4, 1864, 10 *The Papers of Ulysses S. Grant* 397 note, John Y. Simon, ed. (Carbondale: Southern Illinois University Press, 1982).
10. For the Army of the Potomac's march plan, drafted by Meade's chief of staff, Major General A. A. Humphreys, see 36 *War of the Rebellion* (Part 2) 331–34.
11. Gordon L. Rhea, *The Battle of the Wilderness: May 5–6, 1864* 57 (Baton Rouge: Louisiana State University Press, 1994).
12. 36 *War of the Rebellion* (Part 2) 948.
13. William G. Bean, *The Liberty Hall Volunteers: Stonewall's College Boys* 185 (Charlottesville: University Press of Virginia, 1964).
14. William M. Dame, *From the Rapidan to Richmond and the Spotsylvania Campaign* 71–72 (Baltimore: Green-Lucas, 1920).
15. Grant 2 *Memoirs* 192; Badeau, 2 *Military History of Ulysses S. Grant* 102–3.
16. Andrew A. Humphreys, *The Virginia Campaign of '64 and '65* 56 (New York: Charles Scribner's Sons, 1883).
17. Porter, *Campaigning with Grant* 45.
18. Richard S. Ewell's report, 36 *War of the Rebellion* (Part 1), 1070.
19. Warren to Humphreys, May 5, 1864, ibid. (Part 2) 413.
20. Meade to Warren, May 5, 1864, ibid. (Part 1) 189. Also see Page, *Letters of a War Correspondent* 47.
21. Meade to Grant, May 5, 1864, 10 *Grant Papers* 399 note.
22. Grant to Meade, May 5, 1864, ibid., 399.
23. Grant, 2 *Memoirs* 193.
24. Meade to Grant, May 5, 1864, 10 *Grant Papers* 399 note.
25. Joseph Ward Keifer, 2 *Slavery and Four Years of War* 78 (New York: G. P. Putnam's Sons, 1900).
26. Rhea, *Battle of the Wilderness* 132.
27. Thomas W. Hyde, *Following the Greek Cross; or, Memories of the Sixth Army Corps* 183 (Boston: Houghton Mifflin, 1894).
28. Porter, *Campaigning with Grant* 50.
29. Robert G. Scott, *Into the Wilderness with the Army of the Potomac* 41 (Bloomington: Indiana University Press, 1992).
30. Brig. Gen. Hazard Stevens, Getty's chief of staff, said that he did not know of "a single emergency where he [Getty] failed to act precisely as he should have acted." Hazard Stevens, "The Sixth Corps in the Wilderness," 4 *Papers of the Military Historical Society of Massachusetts* 180 (1918).
31. Ibid. 189–190; Getty's report, 36 *War of the Rebellion* (Part 1) 676.
32. Rhea, *Battle of the Wilderness* 137–41; Bruce Catton, *Grant Takes Command* 187–88 (Boston: Little, Brown, 1968).

33. The statement was attributed to Meade by Warren in a letter written ten years later. Rhea, *Battle of the Wilderness* 141.
34. Ibid. 129.
35. Catton, *Grant Takes Command* 189.
36. Rhea, *Battle of the Wilderness* 246.
37. Morris Schaff, *The Battle of the Wilderness* 201 (Boston: Houghton Mifflin, 1910).
38. Henry Heth, *The Memoirs of Henry Heth* 182–83, James L. Morrison, ed. (Westport, Conn.: Greenwood, 1974).
39. Grant, 2 *Memoirs* 539–40.
40. 36 *War of the Rebellion* (Part 1) 219.
41. Porter, *Campaigning with Grant* 52–53.
42. Survivors' Association, *121st Regiment Pennsylvania Volunteers* 403 (Philadelphia: Catholic Standard and Times, 1906).
43. Henry E. Wing, *When Lincoln Kissed Me* 10 (New York: Abingdon, 1913). Meade was the victim of a bad press. When he learned of the false report, he protested to Grant, who denounced the rumor. See Porter, *Campaigning with Grant* 190–91.
44. Porter, *Campaigning with Grant* 53.
45. Rhea, *Battle of the Wilderness* 271.
46. Humphreys, *Virginia Campaign* 30–31.
47. Porter, *Campaigning with Grant* 53–54.
48. Schaff, *Battle of the Wilderness* 225–27.
49. "After conversing with my corps commanders," wrote Meade, "I am led to believe that it will be difficult, owing to the dense thicket in which their commands are located, the fatigued condition of the men rendering it difficult to rouse them early enough, and the necessity of some daylight, to properly put in reinforcements." Meade to Grant, May 5, 1864, 36 *War of the Rebellion* (Part 2) 404–5.
50. Grant to Meade, May 5, 1864, 10 *Grant Papers* 400.
51. John Daniel McDowell, "Recollections of the War," quoted in Rhea, *Battle of the Wilderness* 297.
52. J. F. J. Caldwell, *The History of a Brigade of South Carolinians* 132–33 (Philadelphia: King and Baird, 1866).
53. Charles D. Page, *History of the Fourteenth Regiment, Connecticut* 242 (Meridan, Conn.: Horton, 1906); Thomas Chamberlin, *History of the One Hundred and Fiftieth Regiment Pennsylvania Volunteers* 215 (Philadelphia: F. McManus, Jr., 1905); George R. Agassiz, ed., *Meade's Headquarters, 1863–1865* 93–94 (Boston: Houghton Mifflin, 1913).
54. Agassiz, *Meade's Headquarters* 94.
55. Joseph B. Polley, *Hood's Texas Brigade: Its Marches, Its Battles, Its Achievements* 230 (New York: Neale, 1910).
56. Samuel Finley Harper, quoted in Rhea, *Battle of the Wilderness* 295.
57. Jennings C. Wise, 2 *The Long Arm of Lee; or, The History of the Artillery of the Army of Northern Virginia* 767 (Lynchburg, Va.: J. P. Bell, 1915).
58. Dame, *From the Rapidan to Richmond* 85.
59. Evander M. Law, "From the Wilderness to Cold Harbor," 4 *Battles and Leaders of the Civil War* 124.
60. R.C., "Texans Always Move Them," 5 *The Land We Love* 482.
61. Foote, 3 *The Civil War* 170.
62. Moxley Sorrel to Longstreet, July 21, 1879, quoted in Jeffry D. Wert, *General James Longstreet: The Confederacy's Most Controversial Soldier* 384 (New York: Simon and Schuster, 1993).
63. Foote, 3 *Civil War* 171.
64. Porter, *Campaigning with Grant* 63.
65. Ibid. 59.
66. Charles S. Venable, quoted in Rhea, *Battle of the Wilderness* 298–99.
67. G. Moxley Sorrel, *Recollections of a Southern Staff Officer* 241–42 (New York: Neale, 1905).
68. Foote, 3 *Civil War* 176–77.
69. Wyman diary, May 6, 1864; Henry T. Waltz diary, May 6, 1864, quoted in Rhea, *Battle of the Wilderness* 325.
70. James Longstreet, *From Manassas to Appomattox* 568 (Bloomington: Indiana University Press, 1960). Reprint.
71. Foote, 3 *Civil War* 179.
72. Francis W. Dawson, *Reminiscences of Confederate Service* 116, Bell Wiley, ed. (Baton Rouge: Louisiana State University Press, 1980).
73. Warren Cudworth, *History of the First Regiment Massachusetts Infantry* 462–63 (Boston: Walker, Fuller, 1886); Page, *Letters of a War Correspondent* 55.

74. Hancock to Meade, May 6, 1864, 36 *War of the Rebellion* (Part 1) 445–46.
75. Edward Porter Alexander, *Military Memoirs of a Confederate* 363 (Bloomington: Indiana University Press, 1962). Reprint.
76. John B. Gordon, *Reminiscences of the Civil War* 258. (New York: Charles Scribner's Sons, 1902). Whether Lee visited the Confederate army's left flank on May 6 is a subject of controversy. For a splendid reconstruction of the argument, see Rhea, *Battle of the Wilderness* 412–16.
77. Rhea, ibid.
78. George W. Nichols, *A Soldier's Story of His Regiment* 148–49 (Jessup, Ga.: Continental Book, 1898).
79. Agassiz, *Meade's Headquarters* 98; Page, *Letters of a War Correspondent* 57.
80. Porter, *Campaigning with Grant* 69–70.
81. Ibid. 63.
82. Ibid. 67.
83. Ibid. 70.
84. "Return of Casualties in the Union Forces," 36 *War of the Rebellion* (Part 1), 119–37.
85. Grant to Halleck, May 7, 1864, 10 *Grant Papers* 405.
86. Wing, *When Lincoln Kissed Me* 12–13.
87. Porter, *Campaigning with Grant* 65–66, 76.
88. Cadwallader, *Three Years with Grant* 181–182.
89. Douglas Southall Freeman, 3 *R. E. Lee* 298 (New York: Charles Scribner's Sons, 1949).
90. Benjamin Justice to his family, May 7, 1864, Justice Papers, Emory University.
91. William Pendleton to his wife, May 7, 1864, William Pendleton Collection, University of North Carolina.
92. Foote, 3 *Civil War* 187–88.
93. Schaff, *Battle of the Wilderness* 326.
94. Foote, 3 *Civil War* 190–91.
95. Grant to Meade, May 7, 1864, 10 *Grant Papers* 408–9.
96. Quoted in Foote, 3 *Civil War* 191.
97. Porter, *Campaigning with Grant* 79.
98. William T. Sherman, 4 *Battles and Leaders of the Civil War* 248.
99. Porter, *Campaigning with Grant* 85.

CHAPTER ELEVEN: GRANT AND LEE

1. Douglas Southall Freeman, 1 *R. E. Lee: A Biography* 24–28 (New York: Charles Scribner's Sons, 1934).
2. Ibid. 38–44.
3. Ibid. 360.
4. James M. McPherson, *Battle Cry of Freedom* 281 (New York: Oxford University Press, 1988).
5. Lee to Reverdy Johnson, February 25, 1868, in Freeman, 1 *Lee* 437.
6. In April 1861, a friend gave Lee two bottles of whiskey, which he carried in his headquarters wagon for medicinal use. At the end of the war they had still not been opened. Freeman, 3 *R. E. Lee* 377 note.
7. Ibid. 450–53.
8. Shelby Foote, 1 *The Civil War* 130–31 (New York: Random House, 1958).
9. Stephen W. Sears, *George B. McClellan: The Young Napoleon* 180 (New York: Ticknor and Fields, 1988).
10. Gordon C. Rhea, *The Battle of the Wilderness: May 5–6, 1864* 403 (Baton Rouge: Louisiana State University Press, 1994).
11. See, in particular, Alan T. Nolan, *Lee Considered: Robert E. Lee and the Civil War* (Chapel Hill: University of North Carolina Press, 1991); Thomas Z. Connelly, *The Marble Man: Robert E. Lee and His Image in American Society* (New York: Alfred A. Knopf, 1997); and John D. McKenzie, *Uncertain Glory: Lee's Generalship Re-Examined* (New York: Hippocrene, 1997). Cf., James M. McPherson, "How Noble Was Robert E. Lee?," *New York Review of Books* 10–14 (November 7, 1991).
12. John Keegan, *The Mask of Command* 200 (New York: Viking, 1987).
13. Ulysses S. Grant, 2 *Personal Memoirs of U. S. Grant* 218 (New York: Charles L. Webster, 1885).
14. A. A. Humphreys, *The Virginia Campaign of '64 and '65* 75–76 (New York: Charles Scribner's Sons, 1883).

15. Freeman, 3 *Lee* 308–9.
16. Foote, 3 Civil War 202.
17. Theodore Lyman journal, May 8, 1864, quoted in Gordon C. Rhea, *The Battles for Spotsylvania Court House and the Road to Yellow Tavern* 68 (Baton Rouge: Louisiana State University Press, 1997).
18. Horace Porter, *Campaigning with Grant* 84 (New York: Century, 1897).
19. Bruce Catton, *Grant Takes Command* 216 (Boston: Little, Brown, 1968).
20. Philip H. Sheridan, 1 *Personal Memoirs* 386–87 (New York: Charles L. Webster, 1888).
21. Hancock to Humphreys, May 10, 1864, 36 *War of the Rebellion* (Part 2) 599.
22. Porter, *Campaigning with Grant* 90.
23. Grant to Halleck, May 9, 1864, 10 *The Papers of Ulysses S. Grant,* John Y. Simon, ed. (Carbondale: Southern Illinois University Press, 1982).
24. Grant to Halleck, May 10, 1864, ibid. 418–19.
25. Rhea, *Battles for Spotsylvania* 181.
26. Ibid. 163.
27. Porter, *Campaigning with Grant* 96–97.
28. Rhea, *Battles for Spotsylvania* 176–77.
29. Grant, 2 *Memoirs* 550.
30. Grant to Meade, May 11, 1864, 10 *Grant Papers* 427.
31. Porter, *Campaigning with Grant* 97.
32. Ibid. 98.
33. Grant to Halleck, May 11, 1864, 10 *Grant Papers* 422–23. Also see Grant to Stanton, May 11, 1864, ibid. 422.
34. Foote, 3 *Civil War* 214–15.
35. George A. Bruce, *The Twentieth Regiment of Massachusetts Infantry,* 1861–1865 374 (Boston: Houghton Mifflin, 1906).
36. William G. Mitchell, quoted in Rhea, *Battles for Spotsylvania* 225.
37. Ibid. 229.
38. Samuel Dunham, "Spotsylvania: A 63rd Pennsylvania Comrade Tells About the Fight," *National Tribune,* June 10, 1886.
39. St. Claire Augustine Mulholland, *The Story of the 116th Regiment Pennsylvania Volunteers in the War of the Rebellion* 197 (Philadelphia: F. McManus, 1899).
40. Albert Marsh, 64th New York Infantry, quoted in Rhea, *Battles for Spotsylvania* 235.
41. William J. Seymour, *The Civil War Memoirs of Captain William J. Seymour: Reminiscences of a Louisiana Tiger* 123–24 (Baton Rouge: Louisiana State University Press, 1991).
42. McHenry Howard, *Recollections of a Maryland Confederate Staff Soldier and Officer Under Johnston, Jackson, and Lee* 294–95 (Baltimore: Williams and Wilkins, 1914).
43. Hancock to Meade, May 12, 1864, 36 *War of the Rebellion* (Part 2) 657.
44. Hancock to Humphreys, May 12, 1864, ibid.
45. Porter, *Campaigning with Grant* 102.
46. Grant to Burnside, May 12, 1864, 10 *Grant Papers* 431 note.
47. Porter, *Campaigning with Grant* 103–5.
48. Grant to Burnside, May 12, 1864, 10 *Grant Papers* 431 note.
49. Rhea, *Battles for Spotsylvania* 246.
50. M. S. Stringfellow, "Letter to the *Richmond Times,*" February 20, 1893, in 21 *Southern Historical Society Papers* 244–51.
51. Foote, 3 *Civil War* 218.
52. John B. Gordon, *Reminiscences of the Civil War* 280 (New York: Charles Scribner's Sons, 1903).
53. Eugene M. Ott, Jr., "The Civil War Diary of James J. Kirkpatrick, Sixteenth Mississippi Infantry, C.S.A." M.A. thesis, Texas A&M University, 1984.
54. Rhea, *Battles for Spotsylvania* 273.
55. Joseph P. Cullen, *Where a Hundred Thousand Fell: The Battles of Fredericksburg, Chancellorsville, the Wilderness, and Spotsylvania Court House* 52–53 (Washington, D.C.: National Park Service, 1966).
56. Brig. Gen. Lewis A. Grant, quoted in "Bloody Angle" (Washington, D.C.: National Park Service, 1998).
57. Catton, *Grant Takes Command* 228.
58. G. Norton Galloway, "Hand to Hand Fighting at Spotsylvania," 4 *Battles and Leaders of the Civil War* 174.
59. Foote, 3 *Civil War* 223.
60. McPherson, *Battle Cry of Freedom* 732.
61. Grant to Halleck, May 12, 1864, 10 *Grant Papers* 428.
62. Grant to Julia, May 13, 1864, ibid. 443–44.

63. Grant to Stanton, May 13, 1864, ibid. 434. Grant also recommended the promotion of Hancock to be a brigadier general in the regular army. The following day Stanton assured Grant that the promotion would be made. Also see Halleck to Grant, May 16, 1864: "After your splendid victories almost anything you ask for will be granted. The case may be different if you meet with reverses. I therefore ask that you urge them now." Ibid. 436 note.

64. Humphreys, *Virginia Campaign* 83 note.

65. Porter, *Campaigning with Grant* 114–15.

66. Ibid.

67. George Gordon Meade, 2 *The Life and Letters of General George Gordon Meade* 197–98, George Meade, ed. (New York: Charles Scribner's Sons, 1913).

68. Rhea, *Battles for Spotsylvania,* 302–3, 317.

69. Adam Badeau, 2 *Military History of General Ulysses S. Grant* 184 (New York: D. Appleton, 1881).

70. Journal of Theodore Lyman, May 8, 1864, Massachusetts Historical Society.

71. Grant, 2 *Memoirs* 445.

72. Grant to Meade, May 12, 1864, 10 *Grant Papers* 433.

73. Oliver Wendell Holmes, Jr., *Touched with Fire: Civil War Letters and Diary of Oliver Wendell Holmes, Jr.* 116, Mark DeWolfe Howe, ed. (Cambridge: Harvard University Press, 1946).

74. Peter S. Michie, *The Life and Letters of Emory Upton* 108–9 (New York: D. Appleton, 1885).

75. Grant to Halleck, May 14, 1864, 10 *Grant Papers* 445.

76. Meade to Mrs. Meade, May 19, 1864, 2 *Life and Letters of General George Gordon Meade* 197.

77. Halleck to Grant, May 17, 1864, 10 *Grant Papers* 460 note.

78. 36 *War of the Rebellion* (Part 1) 20. Grant borrowed the expression from his chief engineer, General John Bernard, who said the Confederates had Butler bottled up. In Bernard's words, the enemy had corked the bottle and with a small force could hold it in place.

79. Grant to Halleck, May 22, May 25, 1864, 10 *Grant Papers* 477, 487–88. As Grant continued to move to his left, Smith was ordered to debark at White House on the Pamunkey and join the army at Cold Harbor. Grant to Smith, May 30, 1864, ibid. 498.

80. Grant, 2 *Memoirs* 243.

81. Freeman, 3 *R. E. Lee* 359.

82. Grant to Halleck, May 26, 1864, *Grant Papers* 490–91.

83. Grant to Halleck, May 30, 1864, ibid. 495–96.

84. 36 *War of the Rebellion* (Part 3) 820.

85. Foote, 3 *Civil War* 282.

86. McPherson, *Battle Cry of Freedom* 733.

87. Holmes, *Touched with Fire* 149–50.

88. Foote, 3 *Civil War* 288.

89. Badeau, 2 *Military History of Ulysses S. Grant* 281–82.

90. Porter, *Campaigning with Grant* 174–75.

91. Foote, 3 *Civil War* 290.

92. Freeman, 3 *R. E. Lee* 391.

93. Foote, 3 *Civil War* 292–93.

94. Porter, *Campaigning with Grant* 176.

95. Ibid. 179. Also see Grant, 2 *Memoirs* 276–78.

96. Meade, 2 *Life and Letters of General George Gordon Meade* 200–201.

97. Badeau, 2 *Military History of Ulysses S. Grant* 318.

98. Freeman, 3 *R. E. Lee* 389.

99. Badeau, 2 *Military History of Ulysses S. Grant* 317–18.

100. Horace Porter to Mrs. Porter, June 4, 1864, Porter Papers, Library of Congress.

101. Adams to R. H. Davis, Jr., June 5, 1864, Davis Papers, Massachusetts Historical Society.

102. Letter of James Keleher, 3rd New York, June 8, 1864, Huntington Library.

103. Letter of George Murray, 11th Infantry, Chicago, Ill.

104. David Herbert Donald, *Lincoln* 515 (New York: Simon & Schuster, 1996).

105. Grant to Halleck, June 5, 1864, 11 *Grant Papers* 19–20.

CHAPTER TWELVE: APPOMATTOX

1. Of Patton's maneuver, R. Ernest Dupuy and Trevor N. Dupuy wrote: "This shift from an offensive across the Saar on a west–east axis to a general attack on a north–south axis in southern Luxembourg was no simple 'squads left' evolution. It meant new road nets, filled with moving troops, cutting across the old at right angles....This was a brilliant military accomplishment, in-

volving corps and army staff work of the highest order." *Military Heritage of America* 551 (New York: McGraw-Hill, 1956).

2. When the movement of pontoons was initially reported, Lee assumed it was preparatory to crossing the Chickahominy and an assault on Richmond from the same direction from which McClellan came in 1862. Douglas Southall Freeman, 3 *R. E. Lee* 399–400 (New York: Charles Scribner's Sons, 1935).

3. Ibid. 398.

4. 11 *The Papers of Ulysses S. Grant* 45, John Y. Simon, ed. (Carbondale: Southern Illinois University Press, 1984).

5. Several times Halleck warned Grant against crossing the James, but his views are most crisply stated in an "I told you so" personal letter to Sherman, written on July 16 after the initial Union assault on Petersburg had failed. Halleck wrote: *"Entre nous,* I fear Grant has made a fatal mistake in putting himself south of James river. He cannot now reach Richmond without taking Petersburg, which is strongly fortified, crossing the Appomattox and recrossing the James. Moreover, by placing his army south of Richmond he opens the capital and the whole North to rebel raids. Lee can at any time detach 30,000 or 40,000 men without our knowing it till we are actually threatened. I hope we may yet have full success, but I find that many of Grant's general officers think the campaign already a failure." 38 *War of the Rebellion: A Compilation of the Official Records* (Part 5) 151 (Washington, D.C.: Government Printing Office, 1884).

6. 7 *The Collected Works of Abraham Lincoln* 393, Roy P. Basler, et al., eds. (New Brunswick, N.J.: Rutgers University Press, 1955).

7. Grant interview, *Chicago Tribune,* April 22, 1880.

8. Brig. Gen. Edward Porter Alexander, chief of artillery of the Confederate 1st Corps, wrote afterward that when the Army of Northern Virginia failed to pursue Grant during his withdrawal from Cold Harbor, "the last, and perhaps the best, chances of Confederate success, were not lost in the repulse of Gettysburg, nor in any combat of arms. They were lost during the three days of lying in camp, believing that Grant was hemmed in by the broad part of the James below City Point, and had nowhere to go but to come and attack us. The entire credit for this strategy belongs, I believe, to Grant." *Military Memoirs of a Confederate* 547 (Bloomington: Indiana University Press, 1962). Reprint.

9. Ulysses S. Grant, 2 *Personal Memoirs of U.S. Grant* 293 (New York: Charles L. Webster, 1885).

10. Adam Badeau, 2 *Military History of Ulysses S. Grant* 359 (New York: D. Appleton, 1881); 36 *War of the Rebellion* (Part 1) 25.

11. P. G. T. Beauregard, "Four Days of Battle at Petersburg," 4 *Battles and Leaders of the Civil War* 541, Clarence C. Buel and Robert U. Johnson, eds. (New York: Century, 1888).

12. Badeau, 2 *Military History of Ulysses S. Grant* 361.

13. Grant, 2 *Memoirs* 293–94.

14. Beauregard to Cadmus Wilcox, 5 *Papers of the Military Historical Society of Massachusetts* 121.

15. Grant to Meade, June 18, 1864, 11 *Grant Papers* 78.

16. Shelby Foote, 3 *Civil War* 441 (New York: Random House, 1974).

17. Bruce Catton, *Grant Takes Command* 292 (Boston: Little, Brown, 1968).

18. J. F. C. Fuller, *The Generalship of Ulysses S. Grant* 293 (London: John Murray, 1929).

19. James M. McPherson, *Battle Cry of Freedom* 743 (New York: Oxford University Press, 1988).

20. Lincoln, 7 *Collected Works* 394–95.

21. Horace Porter to Mrs. Porter, June 24, 1864, Horace Porter Papers, Library of Congress. *Cf.,* Horace Porter, *Campaigning with Grant* 216–24 (New York: Century, 1897).

22. Foote, 3 *Civil War* 443.

23. Porter, *Campaigning with Grant* 223.

24. Gideon Welles, 2 *Diary of Gideon Welles* 58, Howard K. Beale, ed. (New York: W. W. Norton, 1960).

25. Lincoln to Grant, July 10, 1864, Lincoln, 7 *Collected Works* 437.

26. Grant to Lincoln, July 10, 1864, 11 *Grant Papers* 203.

27. Lincoln to Grant, July 11, 1864, 7 *Collected Works* 438.

28. Dana to Grant, July 11, 1864, 37 *War of the Rebellion* (Part 2) 192–94.

29. McPherson, *Battle Cry of Freedom* 757.

30. London *Times,* quoted in Foote, 3 *Civil War* 461.

31. George Templeton Strong, *Diary* 467, 474.

32. Grant to Halleck, August 1, 1864, 11 *Grant Papers* 358–59.

33. Lincoln to Grant, August 3, 1864, 7 *Collected Works* 476.

34. Catton, *Grant Takes Command* 343. Also see note 5, above.

35. Grant's colorful phraseology was in a letter to Halleck, July 14, 1864, but as he had a way of repeating himself it is likely he used the same metaphor speaking to Sheridan. His written instruc-

tion to Sheridan stated: "Take [from the valley] all provisions, forage and stock wanted for the use of your command. Such as cannot be consumed, destroy." Grant to Halleck, July 14, 1864, 11 *Grant Papers* 242–43; Grant to [Sheridan] August 5, 1864, ibid. 377–78.

36. Philip H. Sheridan, 1 *Personal Memoirs of P.H. Sheridan* 465 (New York: Charles L. Webster, 1888); Theodore S. Bowers to William R. Rowley, August 9, 1864, Rowley Papers, Illinois State Historical Society.

37. Grant to Sheridan, August 7, 1864, 11 *Grant Papers* 381.

38. Catton, *Grant Takes Command* 348.

39. Bowers to Rawlins, August 10, 1864, in James H. Wilson, *The Life of John A. Rawlins* 257 (New York: Neale, 1916).

40. Grant to Sherman, August 7, 1864, 11 *Grant Papers* 381.

41. Grant to Julia, August 5 and August 8, 1864, ibid. 372, 384. Grant's aide Colonel Horace Porter attended Princeton prior to West Point and undertook to find a house there for Julia.

42. Catton, *Grant Takes Command* 322.

43. Grant to Halleck, August 1, 1864, 11 *Grant Papers* 361–62.

44. Halleck to Grant, August 11, 1864, ibid. 424–25 note.

45. Grant to Halleck, August 15, 1864, ibid. 424.

46. Lincoln to Grant, August 17, 1864, Lincoln, 7 *Collected Works* 499.

47. Porter, *Campaigning with Grant* 279.

48. Grant to Washburne, August 16, 1864, 12 *Grant Papers,* 16–17.

49. Grant to Ammen, August 18, 1864, ibid. 35–36.

50. In his acceptance letter McClellan backed away from the platform pledge. Nevertheless, the election of 1864 came as close to being a referendum on the war as the 1844 contest between Polk and Clay offered a choice concerning the annexation of Texas.

51. Slocum to War Department, September 2, 1864, 38 *War of the Rebellion* (Part 5) 763; Sherman to War Department, September 3, 1864, quoted in McPherson, *Battle Cry of Freedom* 774.

52. Grant to Sherman, 12 *Grant Papers,* 154–55.

53. *St. Paul Dispatch,* September 4, 1864.

54. Lee to Seddon, August 23, 1864, quoted in Catton, *Grant Takes Command* 353.

55. Lee to Jefferson Davis, September 2, 1864, *Wartime Papers of R. E. Lee* 847–48, Clifford Dowdey, ed. (Boston: Little, Brown, 1961).

56. Lee to Seddon, August 23, 1864, quoted in Catton, *Grant Takes Command* 353

57. Grant to Sheridan, August 26, 1864, 12 *Grant Papers* 96–97.

58. Lincoln to Grant, September 12, 1864, Lincoln, 7 *Collected Works* 548.

59. Grant to Lincoln, September 13, 1864, 12 *Grant Papers* 163 note.

60. Catton, *Grant Takes Command* 363.

61. Grant, 2 *Memoirs* 328.

62. Grant to Stanton, September 20, 1864; Stanton to Grant, September 20, 1864; Grant to Sheridan, September 20, 1864, 12 *Grant Papers* 175 note, 177.

63. Grant to Sheridan, September 22, 1864, ibid. 191.

64. Sheridan to Grant, October 1, 1864, ibid. 268–69 note.

65. Sheridan to Grant, October 7, 1864, ibid. 269–70 note.

66. Bruce Catton, *A Stillness at Appomattox* 314 (Garden City, N.Y.: Doubleday, 1956).

67. Lincoln, 7 *Collected Works* page 586; Meade, 2 *Life and Letters* 235–36.

68. Lee to Davis, November 2, 1864, *Wartime Papers of R. E. Lee* 818.

69. Lee to Grant, October 1, 1864; Grant to Lee, October 2, 1864; Lee to Grant, October 3, 1864; Grant to Lee, October 3, 1864. 12 *Grant Papers* 258, 263.

70. Grant to Stanton, November 10, 1864, 12 *Grant Papers* 398.

71. Grant to Jones, November 13, 1864, ibid. 415–16.

72. Grant to Julia, November 9, 1864, ibid. 397–98.

73. Jefferson Davis, 6 *Jefferson Davis, Constitutionalist: His Letters, Papers, and Speeches* 341–42, Dunbar Rowland, ed. (Jackson: Mississippi Department of Archives and History, 1923); Porter, *Campaigning with Grant* 313.

74. 12 *Grant Papers* 157 note.

75. Ibid. 290–91 note.

76. Grant to Sherman, October 12, 1864, ibid. 298.

77. Lincoln wrote that he was "*anxious,* if not fearful" of Sherman's plan, and in the draft of his annual message to Congress included the observation that "our cause could, if need be, survive the loss of the whole detached force." Lincoln deleted the phrase before transmitting the message, believing it too pessimistic. Lincoln, 8 *Collected Works* 181.

78. Grant to Stanton, October 13, 1864, ibid. 302–3. Stanton's reservations were partially fueled by

Grant's adjutant, John Rawlins, who went out of channels to urge the secretary of war to quash Sherman's scheme. Grant did not discover Rawlins's intervention until years later, and was bitter at what he considered a betrayal by his chief of staff. Grant, 8 *Memoirs* 326.

79. 44 *War of the Rebellion* 783. Lincoln received the message on Christmas Eve.
80. Grant to Halleck, December 8, 1864, 13 *Grant Papers* 83.
81. Thomas to Grant, December 8, 1864, ibid. 88 note.
82. Grant to Thomas, December 9, 1864, ibid. 97.
83. Grant to Thomas, December 11, 1864; Thomas to Grant, December 11, 1864, ibid. 107.
84. McPherson, *Battle Cry of Freedom* 815.
85. *Mary Chesnut's Civil War* 694, C. Vann Woodward, ed. (New Haven: Yale Univeristy Press, 1981).
86. 46 *War of the Rebellion* (Part 2) 1258.
87. Sherman to Grant, January 21, 1865. 13 *Grant Papers* 350–51 note.
88. Grant to Sherman, February 1, 1865, ibid. 349–51.
89. Lee to Grant, March 2, 1865, 46 *War of the Rebellion* (Part 2) 824. Lee told Jefferson Davis he was not sanguine about the prospects because Grant would undoubtedly demand a return to the Union. "Whether this will be acceptable to our people *yet awhile* I cannot say," Freeman, 4 *R. E. Lee* 6. Emphasis added.
90. Lincoln, 8 *Collected Works* 330–31.
91. Grant to Sheridan, February 20, 1865, 13 *Grant Papers* 457–58.
92. Grant, 2 *Memoirs* 424–25.
93. Freeman, 4 *R. E. Lee* 7.
94. Porter, *Campaigning with Grant* 402–3.
95. Foote, 3 *Civil War* 845.
96. David Herbert Donald, *Lincoln* 572 (New York: Simon and Schuster, 1995).
97. Admiral David D. Porter, *Incidents and Anecdotes of the Civil War* 313–17 (New York: D. Appleton, 1885); Donald, *Lincoln* 574.
98. Foote, 3 *Civil War* 857.
99. William Tecumseh Sherman, 2 *Memoirs of General W. T. Sherman* 327 (New York: Century, 1893).
100. Catton, *Grant Takes Command* 440.
101. Grant to Sheridan, March 29, 1865, 14 *Grant Papers* 253–54.
102. Grant, 2 *Memoirs* 440.
103. Lee to John C. Breckenridge, April 2, 1865, *Wartime Papers of Lee* 924–25.
104. Foote, 3 *Civil War* 913–14.
105. Ibid. 914.
106. Ibid. 909.
107. Sheridan to Grant, April 5, 1865, 14 *Grant Papers* 345 note.
108. Foote, 3 *Civil War* 915.
109. Sheridan to Grant, April 6, 1865, 14 *Grant Papers* 358 note.
110. Lincoln to Grant, April 7, 1865, Lincoln, 8 *Collected Works* 388.
111. Catton, *Grant Takes Command* 456.
112. Grant to Lee, April 7, 1865, 14 *Grant Papers* 361.
113. Lee to Grant, April 7, 1865, *Wartime Papers of Lee* 931–32.
114. Grant to Lee, April 8, 1865, 14 *Grant Papers* 367.
115. Lee to Grant, April 8, 1865, *Wartime Papers of Lee* 932.
116. Catton, *Grant Takes Command* 439–60; Foote, 3 *Civil War* 936.
117. Sheridan to Grant, April 8, 1865, 14 *Grant Papers* 369 note.
118. Grant to Lee, April 9, 1865, ibid. 371.
119. Freeman, 4 *R. E. Lee* 123.
120. Ibid. 126.
121. Lee to Grant, April 9, 1865, *Wartime Papers of Lee* 932.
122. Lee to Grant, April 9, 1865, ibid. 933.
123. Grant, 2 *Memoirs* 485.
124. Grant to Lee, April 9, 1865, 14 *Grant Papers* 372–73; Catton, *Grant Takes Command* 462.
125. Freeman, 4 *R. E. Lee* 131.
126. Colonel Charles Marshall, *An Aide-de-Camp of Lee* 268–69 (Boston: Little Brown, 1927).
127. Catton, *Grant Takes Command* 464.
128. Grant, 2 *Memoirs* 489.
129. Freeman, 4 *R. E. Lee* 135.
130. The details of the surrender at Appomattox, including the texts of the documents, are drawn primarily from Grant's memoirs and Douglas Southall Freeman's biography of Lee. Grant, 2 *Memoirs* 483–95; Freeman, *R. E. Lee* 134–143.

131. Catton, *Grant Takes Command* 468.
132. Grant to Stanton, April 9, 1865, 14 *Grant Papers* 375 note.
133. Joshua L. Chamberlain, *The Passing of the Armies* 260–66 (Dayton, Ohio: Morningside Bookshop, 1991), reprint; McPherson, *Battle Cry of Freedom* 850.

CHAPTER THIRTEEN: RECONSTRUCTION

1. Edward Porter Alexander, *Fighting for the Confederacy* 540 (Chapel Hill: University of North Carolina Press, 1989). Reprint.
2. John B. Gordon, *Reminiscences of the Civil War* 231 (New York: Charles Scribner's Sons, 1904).
3. Longstreet interview, *New York Times,* July 25, 1885. In a fitting tribute to his old friend, Longstreet said that Grant's renown as a fighter was unsurpassed, "but the biggest part of him was his heart." Horace Porter, *Campaigning with Grant* 515–16 (New York: Century, 1897).
4. Abraham Lincoln, 8 *The Collected Works of Abraham Lincoln* 393 Roy P. Basler, ed. (New Brunswick: Rutgers University Press, 1967).
5. Julia Dent Grant, *The Personal Memoirs of Julia Dent Grant* 153, John Y. Simon, ed. (New York: Putnam, 1975).
6. Edward Pollard, *The Lost Cause* 712 (New York: Treat, Morrow, 1867).
7. Adam Badeau, *Grant in Peace* 21 (Hartford, Conn.: Scranton, 1887).
8. John Russell Young, 2 *Around the World with General Grant* 356 (New York: American News, 1879). Historians have assumed that Julia did not wish to spend the evening in Mrs. Lincoln's company.
9. 14 *The Papers of Ulysses S. Grant* 390 note, John Y. Simon, ed. (Carbondale: Southern Illinois University Press, 1989).
10. Young, 2 *Around the World* 354.
11. Julia Dent Grant, *Personal Memoirs* 156.
12. Shelby Foote, 3 *The Civil War: A Narrative* 977 (New York: Random House, 1974); Young, 2 *Around the World* 355; Brooks D. Simpson, *Let Us Have Peace* 92 (Chapel Hill: University of North Carolina Press, 1991).
13. Geoffrey Perret, *Ulysses S. Grant: Soldier and President* 362 (New York: Random House, 1997).
14. Grant to Ord, April 15, 1865, 14 *Grant Papers* 391.
15. Ord to Grant, April 15, 1865, ibid., 391–92 note.
16. Grant to Ord, April 15, 1865, ibid.
17. Grant to Julia, April 16, 1865, ibid. 396–97.
18. Ewell to Grant, 46 *War of the Rebellion: A Compilation of the Official Records* (Part 3) 787 (Washington, D.C.: Government Printing Office, 1884).
19. Noah Brooks, *Washington in Lincoln's Time* 233–34 (New York: Century, 1896).
20. Young, 2 *Around the World* 354, 357.
21. Sherman to Grant, April 17, 1865, 14 *Grant Papers* 419 note.
22. Sherman to Grant, April 15, 1865, ibid. 418 note; also see Sherman to Grant, April 12, 1865, ibid. 375 note.
23. Grant, 2 *Memoirs* 754–55.
24. Sherman to Grant, April 18, 1865, 14 *Grant Papers* 419–20 note. Sherman went on to say that the surrender document "is an absolute submission of the Enemy to the lawful authority of the United States, and disperses his Armies absolutely."
25. For the text of the Sherman-Johnston accord, see 47 *War of the Rebellion* (Part 3) 243–44.
26. Grant to Stanton, April 21, 1865, 14 *Grant Papers* 423.
27. The cabinet meeting on April 21, 1865, is best described by Navy Secretary Gideon Welles. 2 *Diary of Gideon Welles* 294–95, Howard K. Beale, ed. (New York: Norton, Alfred A. Knopf, 1960). Also see Benjamin T. Thomas and Harold Hyman, Stanton: *The Life and Times of Lincoln's Secretary of War* 405–7 (New York: Alfred A. Knopf, 1962); Porter, *Campaigning with Grant* 503–4.
28. Grant to Julia, April 21, 1865, 14 *Grant Papers* 428–29.
29. Grant to Stanton, April 24, 1865, ibid. 431–32.
30. For text, see 47 *War of the Rebellion* (Part 3) 313.
31. Grant to Julia, April 25, 1865, 14 *Grant Papers* 433.
32. Badeau, *Grant in Peace* 120.
33. Sherman to Grant, April 28, 1865, reprinted in William Tecumseh Sherman, *Memoirs of General William T. Sherman* 856 (New York: Library of America, 1990). Reprint.
34. Badeau, *Grant in Peace* 90; Philip H. Sheridan, *The Personal Memoirs of P. H. Sheridan* 402 (New York: Charles L. Webster, 1888).

35. Grant to Sheridan, May 3, 1865, 14 *Grant Papers* 439 note; Grant to Sheridan, May 17, 1865, 15 ibid. 43–44; Sheridan, *Memoirs* 399–411.

36. In total, there were twelve excluded categories. Simpson, *Let Us Have Peace* 101.

37. The text of President Johnson's proclamation is in 8 *War of the Rebellion*, 2nd Series, 578–80.

38. Grant to Halleck, May 6, 1865, 15 *Grant Papers* 11.

39. Lee to Beauregard, October 3, 1865, quoted in Douglas Southall Freeman, 4 *R. E. Lee* 202 (New York: Charles Scribner's Sons, 1935).

40. *New York Times,* April 19, 26, June 4, 17, 1865; Butler to Johnson, April 25, 1865, 7 *The Papers of Andrew Johnson* 234–37, Paul H. Bergeron, ed. (Knoxville: University of Tennessee Press, 1992).

41. Freeman, 4 *R. E. Lee* 202–3.

42. Badeau, *Grant in Peace* 25.

43. Lee to Grant, June 13, 1865, 15 *Grant Papers* 150 note.

44. Grant to Stanton, June 16, 1865, ibid. 149.

45. Ibid., 150 note.

46. Quoted in Hamlin Garland, *Ulysses S. Grant: His Life and Character* 332–333 (New York: Doubleday & McClure, 1898). Emphasis added. Also see 2 *The Diary of Orville Browning* 32, James G. Randall and Theodore C. Pease, eds. (Springfield: Illinois Historical Library, 1933); and Young, 2 *Around the World* 460–61.

In 1867, the House Judiciary Committee, holding hearings pertaining to the possible impeachment of President Johnson, interrogated Grant extensively about General Lee's petition for pardon and Grant's discussion with the president. Grant's replies do not differ from the account I have reported. See 17 *Grant Papers* 213–32.

47. Grant to Lee, June 20, 1865, 15 ibid. 210–11.

48. Garland, *Grant* 338.

49. Grant to Washburne, May 21, 1865, 15 *Grant Papers* 88.

50. Grant to William Coffin, November 3, 1865, ibid. 388, 389 note; Grant to J. Russell Jones, March 27, 1866, 16 ibid. 136–37.

51. Grant to Charles W. Ford, October 28, 1865, 15 ibid. 372.

52. Both Grant and Julia were aware of Butterfield's efforts. Butterfield to Washburne, December 8, 1865, 16 *Grant Papers* 75 note. General Butterfield had a distinguished war record, winning the Medal of Honor for his actions at Gaines Mill in 1862. He served briefly as chief of staff of the Army of the Potomac under Hooker and then followed Hooker to Chattanooga. Butterfield spent his spare time composing bugle calls and is the author of "Taps."

53. When discharged, the mortgage on 205 I Street amounted to $30,437.50. Grant put $54,725 in bonds and took $19,837.50 in cash. Julia Dent Grant, *Personal Memoirs* 167 note 12. Also see Grant to J. Russell Jones, March 17, 1866, 16 *Grant Papers* 136–37.

54. Grant to Butterfield, February 17, 1866, ibid. 74.

55. For an example of Corbin's duplicity, see his letter to Andrew Johnson, June 25, 1866, urging the president to bypass Grant's supporters when making appointments. "If we treat Grant well, without recognizing distinctive 'Grant men,' he will not be a candidate [for president in 1868]; he is too poor and can't afford so soon to give up his present valuable position." 10 *Johnson Papers* 622–24.

56. Grant to Johnson, December 18, 1865, 15 *Grant Papers* 434–37. Also see William S. McFeely, *Yankee Stepfather: General O. O. Howard and the Freedmen* 25ff. (New Haven: Yale University Press, 1970).

57. *Cincinnati Enquirer,* September 30, 1865, quoted in Eric L. McKitrick, *Andrew Johnson and Reconstruction* 184 (Chicago: University of Chicago Press, 1960). Also see Eric Foner, *Reconstruction: America's Unfinished Revolution* 180 (New York: Harper and Row, 1988).

58. Under Article I of the Constitution, slaves were counted as three fifths of a person in calculating congressional representation. Emancipation counted as a legislative windfall for the South, since African-Americans would now be counted as whole persons. The intent of Section 2 of the Fourteenth Amendment was to give Southerners a choice. They could let blacks vote and have them counted in congressional apportionment, or they could disenfranchise them and suffer a reduction in their numbers in Congress.

59. *New York Times*, April 7, 1866.

60. Badeau, *Grant in Peace* 37.

61. Rutherford B. Hayes, 3 *Diary and Letters of Rutherford B. Hayes* 22, Charles R. Williams, ed. (Columbus: Ohio Historical Society, 1922).

62. William S. McFeely, *Grant: A Biography* 246 (New York: W. W. Norton, 1981).

63. For background, see Bobby L. Lovett, "Memphis Riots: White Reaction to Blacks in Memphis, May 1865–July 1866," 38 *Tennessee Historical Quarterly* 9–33 (1979).

64. Grant to Stanton, July 7, 1866, 16 *Grant Papers* 233–34. Grant wrote Stanton after receiving the official report of the riot from General Thomas. His earlier correspondence with military officials in Memphis, beginning immediately after the riot, is reprinted in the notes, 16 *Grant Papers* 234–36.

65. Speed to Johnson, July 13, 1866, ibid. 234–35 note.

66. *New York Times*, May 24, 1866.

67. Grant to Thomas, July 6, 1866, 16 *Grant Papers* 230–31.

68. Ibid. 228.

69. Sheridan to Grant, August 2, 1866, 16 ibid. 289 note.

70. Grant to Sheridan, August 12, 1866, ibid. 292. Grant was concerned that Sheridan's telegram be published in full because the White House, in releasing the message, omitted the paragraph quoted above. The failure of the White House to print Sheridan's message in full figured prominently in the House of Representatives' impeachment investigation of President Johnson. *House Reports,* 40th Cong., 1st sess., No. 7, "Impeachment Investigation" 535–40, 635–43. For comments of the *Times* reporter who was given the censored version of Sheridan's message by the White House, see McKitrick, *Andrew Johnson and Reconstruction* 426–27 note.

71. Horace Porter reported that "General Grant, at first regarding [Johnson's request] merely as an invitation, endeavored to decline it as politely as possible, but it was put in the form of an order, and he had to obey." *Chicago Inter-Ocean,* October 24, 1885. Also see Badeau, *Grant in Peace* 38–39.

72. *New York Times,* August 31, 1866.

73. *New York Herald,* August 31, 1866. When Julia read of the race she wrote to rebuke Grant. His reply was Clintonesque: "The race you saw reported is almost without foundation." 16 *Grant Papers* 307.

74. Johnson's speech is reprinted in 11 *Johnson Papers* 192–201. For the swing around the circle, see McKitrick, *Andrew Johnson and Reconstruction* 428–38. For the itinerary, see 11 *Johnson Papers,* Appendix III.

75. Grant to Julia, September 9, 1866, 16 *Grant Papers* 308. Also see *New York Herald,* September 6, 1866; McKitrick, *Andrew Johnson and Reconstruction* 248–49 note.

76. Badeau, *Grant in Peace* 39; Louis A. Coolidge, *Ulysses S. Grant* 239 (Boston: Houghton Mifflin, 1917).

77. Grant to William S. Hillyer, September 19, 1866, 16 *Grant Papers* 310. Grant sent a copy of the letter to the Republican opposition in Indiana and authorized them to use it as they saw fit. Ibid. note.

78. Sherman to Ellen Ewing Sherman, October 26, 1866, 16 *Grant Papers* 339–40 note.

79. For Johnson's inquiry, see Welles, 2 *Diary* 625–26. Also see the Baltimore *American and Commercial Advertiser,* October 10, 11, 1866.

80. Ulysses S. Grant III, *Ulysses S. Grant: Warrior and Statesman* 279, 292 (New York: William Morrow, 1969).

81. Grant to Brig. Gen. Alexander B. Dyer, chief of ordnance, September 22, 1866, 16 *Grant Papers* 331–32 note. Grant also opposed providing weapons for newly organized militia in the Southern states. Grant to Johnson, August 22 and November 9, 1866. Ibid. 302–4, 376.

82. Grant to Sheridan, October 12, 1866, ibid. 330–31. Emphasis in original.

83. Grant to Washburne, October 23, 1866, ibid. 349.

84. On October 21 Grant had written to Johnson asking to be excused from the mission. "It is a diplomatic service for which I am not fitted, either by education or taste. It has necessarily to be conducted under the State Department with which my duties do not connect me. Again then I most urgently but respectfully repeat my request to be excused, from the performance of a duty entirely out of my sphere, and one which can be so much better performed by others." 16 *Grant Papers* 346–47.

85. Badeau, *Grant in Peace* 53.

86. Sherman immediately accepted the assignment. "My mission is already ended," he told Captain Alden as his ship, the *Susquehanna,* departed New York harbor. "By substituting myself I have prevented a serious quarrel between the Administration and Grant." Badeau, *Grant in Peace* 54–55. Also see Grant to Stanton, October 27, 1866, 16 *Grant Papers* 357–58.

87. Johnson to Stanton, October 25, 1866, 11 *Johnson Papers* 386. For background, see Jean H. Baker, *The Politics of Continuity: Maryland Political Parties From 1858 to 1870* 143–64 (Baltimore: Johns Hopkins University Press, 1973).

88. Grant to Johnson, October 24, 1866, 16 *Grant Papers* 352–53 note. Emphasis in original. Also see Grant to Stanton, October 27, 1866, ibid.

89. *Baltimore Sun,* November 3, 4, 5, 6, 1866; Johnson to Swann, November 6, 1866, 11 *Johnson Papers* 424–25; Simpson, *Let Us Have Peace* 160–61.

90. McKitrick, *Andrew Johnson and Reconstruction* 447.
91. See Grant to Ord, December 6, 1866, urging Arkansas to ratify the Fourteenth Amendment. 16 *Grant Papers* 405–6.
92. Grant to Richard Taylor, November 15, 1868. With Joseph E. Johnston and James Longstreet, Taylor was one of the early advocates of Southern compliance with Reconstruction legislation. Ibid. 394–95.
93. Baltimore, *American and Commercial Advertiser,* November 2, 1866.

CHAPTER FOURTEEN: LET US HAVE PEACE

The first three stanzas of O'Reilly's verse were run by the *New York Tribune* on its front page every morning for the two months preceding the 1868 election.

1. For Johnson's formal protest concerning the rider, see his message to the House of Representatives, March 2, 1867, 12 *The Papers of Andrew Johnson* 77–78, Paul H. Bergeron, ed. (Knoxville: University of Tennessee Press, 1995). Also see *The Diary of Orville Hickman Browning* 134, James G. Randall and Theodore C. Pease, eds. (Springfield: Illinois State Historical Society, 1933).
2. Johnson's veto message is reprinted, 11 *Johnson Papers* 577–88.
3. Hans L. Trefousse, *Andrew Johnson: A Biography* 276 (New York: W. W. Norton, 1989).
4. Johnson's veto message, drafted by Seward, is a tightly written constitutional brief that is difficult to fault. The position Johnson argued was later affirmed by Chief Justice Taft, speaking for the Court in *Myers v. United States,* 272 U.S. 52 (1926). For Johnson's message, see 12 *Johnson Papers* 95–101.
5. Eric Foner, *A Short History of Reconstruction* 122 (New York: Harper and Row, 1990).
6. George S. Boutwell, 2 *Reminiscences of Sixty Years in Public Affairs* 107–8 (New York: McClure, Phillips, 1902); Trefousse, *Andrew Johnson* 277.
7. Grant to Stanton, January 29, 1867, *The Papers of Ulysses S. Grant* 38, John Y. Simon, ed. (Carbondale: Southern Illinois University Press, 1985).
8. At Grant's suggestion, the House version, which authorized him to appoint the district commanders, was changed to allow the president to make that choice. Louis A. Coolidge, *Ulysses S. Grant* 249 (Boston: Houghton Mifflin, 1917). Also see Brooks D. Simpson, *Let Us Have Peace* 173–74 (Chapel Hill: University of North Carolina Press, 1991).
9. *New York Independent,* March 7, 1867.
10. Cyrus B. Comstock Papers, Library of Congress.
11. Henry Latham, *Black and White: A Journal of a Three Months' Tour of the United States* 63 (London: Macmillan, 1867).
12. Grant to Washburne, March 4, 1867, 17 *Grant Papers* 76–77.
13. Grant to Sherman, January 13, 1867, ibid. 13–14.
14. Sherman to Grant, January 17, 1867, ibid. 14 note.
15. Colonel Ely S. Parker, Grant's longtime aide, was a full-blooded Seneca Indian from Galena, Illinois. He conducted an unofficial, on-site investigation of the incident for the general in chief in March 1867. Parker concluded that Fetterman, contrary to orders, had strayed into hostile Indian territory; that his troops were poorly disciplined; and that the garrison at Fort Kearny was remiss in not rushing to his aid. Parker's report convinced Grant that army authorities at Fort Phil Kearny were negligent. He ordered an immediate change in command, but otherwise took no further action. Ibid. 57–60 note.
16. Grant to Stanton, January 15, 1867, ibid. 21–22.
17. Grant to Sherman, January 15, 1867, ibid. 23–24.
18. Grant to Stanton, February 1, 1867, ibid. 40–41.
19. Grant to Stanton, March 9, 1867, ibid. 78.
20. Grant to Ford, March 24, 1867, ibid. 90.
21. Grant to Morris, March 27, 1867, ibid. 91.
22. Adam Badeau, *Grant in Peace* 75–76 (Hartford, Conn.: Scranton, 1887).
23. Grant to Washburne, April 5, 1867, 17 *Grant Papers* 98.
24. Sarah Woolfolk Wiggins, "The 'Pig-Iron' Kelley Riot in Mobile" 23 *Alabama Review* 1 (1970). Pope's correspondence with Grant concerning the incident is at 17 *Grant Papers* 442–45.
25. For a survey of actions by the five district commanders, see James E. Sefton, *The United States Army and Reconstruction, 1865–1877* 118–27 (Baton Rouge: Louisiana State University Press, 1967).
26. Grant to Pope, April 21, 1867, 17 *Grant Papers* 117–18.
27. Grant to Sheridan, March 29, 1876, ibid. 91–92. Emphasis in original. Longstreet was one of the

few former Confederate commanders to provide public support for Reconstruction. On March 19 and April 7, Old Pete published open letters in the *New Orleans Times* calling upon his fellow Southerners for compliance. "No one has worked more for the South than I, nor lost more. I think the time has come for peace and I am not willing to lose more blood....If there are any in the country inclined to fight the question, I hope not to be included in that number." Grant appreciated Longstreet's support. "These ideas freely expressed by one who occupies a position like yours, have to exercise a beneficial influence." Grant to Longstreet, April 16, 1867, 17 *Grant Papers* 115–16. Also see, Jeffry D. Wert, *General James Longstreet* 410–13 (New York: Simon and Schuster, 1993).

28. Grant to Sheridan, April 5, 1867, 17 *Grant Papers* 95–96. Two weeks later Grant advised Sheridan that the attorney general had not reported, and that in the interim any civil officer who obstructed the law should be suspended and tried by a military commission. "This right certainly does exist on the part of District Commanders, and I have no doubt of their power to remove arbitrarily." April 21, 1867, ibid. 122–23.

29. For the text of Stanbery's opinion, see 12 *Johnson Papers* 320–32. For a preliminary opinion, issued May 24, 1867, see ibid. 289–90.

30. Sheridan to Grant, June 22, 1867, 17 *Grant Papers* 198 note.

31. To have issued the attorney general's opinion as an executive order would have given it the force of law. Gideon Welles, 3 *Diary of Gideon Welles,* John T. Morse, ed. 109–14. (June 14, 1867); Martin E. Mantell, *Johnson, Grant, and the Politics of Reconstruction* 32–33 (New York: Columbia University Press, 1923).

32. Grant to Ord, June 23, 1867, 17 *Grant Papers* 192.

33. Grant to Pope, June 28, 1867, ibid. 204.

34. Grant to Sheridan, June 24, 1867, ibid. 195–96.

35. Badeau, *Grant in Peace* 71.

36. For Johnson's veto message, see 12 *Johnson Papers* 415–23.

37. *New York Times,* July 24, 1867.

38. Badeau, *Grant in Peace* 88; Trefousse, *Andrew Johnson* 293–94.

39. Grant to Johnson, August 1, 1867, 17 *Grant Papers* 250–52.

40. A useful summary of the Grant-Stanton relationship is provided by Badeau, *Grant in Peace* 77–83. Also see, John M. Schofield, *Forty-six Years in the Army* 412–13 (New York: Century, 1897); Fletcher Pratt, *Stanton: Lincoln's Secretary of War* 340–43, 352–53 (New York: W. W. Norton, 1953).

41. Welles, 3 *Diary* 140; Mantell, *Johnson, Grant, and the Politics of Reconstruction* 36.

42. Johnson to Stanton, August 5, 1867, 12 *Johnson Papers* 461.

43. Stanton to Johnson, August 5, 1867, ibid.

44. Badeau, *Grant in Peace* 90; Pratt, *Stanton* 450.

45. Trefousse, *Andrew Johnson* 295. Grant told Julia that he accepted the position because he thought it "most important that someone should be there who cannot be used." *The Personal Memoirs of Julia Dent Grant* 165, John Y. Simon, ed. (New York: G. P. Putnam's Sons, 1975).

46. Johnson to Stanton, 12 *Johnson Papers* 476–77.

47. Stanton to Johnson, ibid. 477.

48. Grant to Stanton, August 12, 1867, 17 *Grant Papers* 268. "I have no alternative but to submit, under protest, to the superior force of the President," Stanton replied. "You will please accept my acknowledgment of the kind terms in which you have notified me of your acceptance of the president's appointment, and my cordial reciprocation of the sentiments expressed." Stanton to Grant, August 12, 1867, ibid. 269 note.

49. *New York Independent,* August 29, 1867.

50. Schurz to his wife, August 20, 1867, *Intimate Letters of Carl Schurz* 388, Joseph Schafer, ed. (Madison: University of Wisconsin Press, 1928).

51. Henry D. Cooke to John Sherman, August 19, 1867, John Sherman Papers, Library of Congress. Emphasis in original.

52. For the text of Johnson's orders, see 17 *Grant Papers* 279 note.

53. Grant to Johnson, ibid. 277–78.

54. Johnson to Grant, August 19, 1867, 12 *Grant Papers* 493–96. Also see Mantell, *Johnson, Grant, and the Politics of Reconstruction* 36; Edward McPherson, *The Political History of the United States During the Period of Reconstruction* 307 (Washington: Philip and Solomons, 1871).

55. Thomas to Grant, August 22, 1867, 17 *Grant Papers* 282–83 note.

56. Lt. Col. Alexander B. Hasson to Grant, August 21, 1867, ibid. 282 note.

57. Johnson to Grant, August 24, 1867, ibid. 296 note. Also see Grant to Sickles, August 24, 1867, ibid. 294–94; Sefton, *United States Army and Reconstruction* 158–64; Max L. Heyman, Jr., *Prudent Soldier: A Biography of Major General E. R. S. Canby, 1817–1873* 303–10 (Glendale, Calif.: A. H. Clark, 1959).

58. Grant to Johnson, August 26, 1867, 17 *Grant Papers* 301–2.
59. For text, see ibid. 304 note.
60. *Army and Navy Journal, Philadelphia North American, Hartford Courant,* August 31, 1867.
61. Badeau, *Grant in Peace* 107–8.
62. Grant to Ord, September 22, 1867, 17 *Grant Papers* 354.
63. Trefousse, *Andrew Johnson* 299.
64. Andrew Johnson, Third Annual Message to Congress, December 3, 1867, 13 *Johnson Papers* 280–306. The quotation is at page 289.
65. Ibid. 137 note. Also see Trefousse, *Andrew Johnson* 298; Robert G. Athearn, *William Tecumseh Sherman and the Settlement of the West* 183 (Norman: University of Oklahoma Press, 1956).
66. Sherman to Grant, October 3, 1867, 17 *Grant Papers* 347 note. On October 2, 1867, Johnson wired Sherman to come to Washington. "The President desires to confer with you upon matters of public interest, and requests you to report to him in person for that purpose." Sherman attempted to decline ("I prefer to confine myself to matters purely Military") but said that if the president insisted, "I will start for Washington on your repeating your order." After another exchange of telegrams, Sherman left St. Louis for Washington by train on October 4. 13 *Johnson Papers* 131, 136–37.
67. *Washington Evening Star,* October 7, 9, 10, 11, 1867.
68. Sherman to Ellen Ewing Sherman, October 7, 1867, *Home Letters of General Sherman* 361, Mark A. DeWolfe Howe, ed. (New York: Charles Scribner's Sons, 1909).
69. Welles, 3 *Diary* 234–35 (October 19, 23, 1867). One week after calling on Grant, Johnson formally raised at a cabinet meeting the issue of his possible suspension during an impeachment trial. The cabinet agreed unanimously that such action would be unconstitutional. Cabinet minutes, November 30, 1867, 13 *Johnson Papers* 269–71.
70. Act of March 2, 1867, 14 *U. S. Statutes at Large* 430.
71. Message to the Senate, December 12, 1867, 13 *Johnson Papers* 313–19.
72. Special Orders No. 40, March 19, 1867. For text, see *American Annual Cyclopedia* (1867) 463.
73. Grant authorized Hancock to revoke or sustain orders issued after Sheridan's departure (November 10, 1867), but none before that date. Grant to Hancock, November 29, 1867, 18 *Grant Papers* 39. Johnson's message to Congress, December 18, 1867, is at 13 *Johnson Papers* 349–50.
74. 40 Cong., 2nd sess. *Congressional Globe* 264, 322. *Washington Daily Chronicle,* December 21, 1867. Johnson's proposal was tabled by the House; the Senate ignored it.
75. General Orders, December 28, 1867, 18 *Grant Papers* 87–88. Meade, a Pennsylvanian like Hancock, was thought by the press and many in Congress to be hostile to Reconstruction. But as a soldier, Meade did not let his personal views intrude. He enforced the law just as Pope did, and when in doubt he instinctively turned to Grant for advice. Gillem was more of a problem, but his appointment was only temporary awaiting the arrival of Irvin McDowell from California. McDowell proved to be indistinguishable from Ord when it came to enforcing the Reconstruction Acts. Mantell, *Johnson, Grant, and the Politics of Reconstruction* 75–79.
76. William Hall to Garfield, January 4, 1868, Garfield Papers, Library of Congress. Early in 1868, Johnson removed Brigadier Generals Wager Swayne and Joseph Mower, the heads of the Freedmen's Bureau in Alabama and Louisiana. Richard H. Abbott, *The Republican Party in the South* 104 (Chapel Hill: University of North Carolina Press, 1986).
77. James L. Dunning to Charles Sumner, December 17, 1867, Sumner Papers, Harvard University; Foster Blodgett to William Pitt Fessenden, December 30, 1867, Fessenden Papers, Library of Congress; Frank Bird to Sumner, January 1, 1868, Sumner Papers.
78. Johnson had already told his private secretary that Grant had "served the purpose for which he had been selected" and that it would be desirable to replace him. "Notes of Colonel W. G. Moore: Private Secretary to President Johnson, 1866–68" 115, St. George L. Sioussat, ed., 19 *American Historical Review* 98–132 (1913).
79. Eric L. McKitrick, *Andrew Johnson and Reconstruction* 500–501 (Chicago: University of Chicago Press, 1960); Trefousse, *Andrew Johnson* 306.
80. Sherman's account of the January 11 meeting in Grant's office is contained in a letter Sherman wrote to the general in chief, January 27, 1868. 17 *Grant Papers* 106 note. Also see Sherman's recollection (which does not differ) in his *Memoirs* at pp. 910–11 (American Library reprint edition).
81. Grant to Johnson, January 28, 1868, 17 *Grant Papers* 116–18.
82. Johnson to Grant, January 31, 1868, 17 *Johnson Papers* 508–12. Also see McKitrick, *Andrew Johnson and Reconstruction* 501.
83. Eric McKitrick, in his exhaustive work on Johnson and Reconstruction, gives Grant the benefit of the doubt. Grant's case, he writes, "rests mainly on the emphasis with which he expressed his desire to Johnson, in their interview of January 11, to leave the War Office. Johnson's side depends on the clarity with which it was understood that Grant would remain pending further develop-

ments. Badeau, who saw Grant before and after this interview, says that the General was adamant and that Johnson, who 'pleaded and argued,' was the indecisive one. This is 'indirect' evidence, but then so is everything that followed." McKitrick, *Andrew Johnson and Reconstruction* 503 note. Also see William B. Hesseltine, *Ulysses S. Grant: Politician* 104. (New York: Dodd, Mead, 1935).

84. Sherman to Grant, January 27, 1868, 18 *Grant Papers* 107 note.
85. Ibid.
86. Trefousse, *Andrew Johnson* 307; "Notes of Colonel Moore" 114–15.
87. Adam Badeau believed the president was simply indecisive. "Johnson was indeed always slow in arriving at a decision. He did not positively decline to nominate Cox; he delayed on Sunday, and on Monday; but the Senate acted, and then Grant did exactly what he said he would do. He gave up the office, and Stanton at once took possession." *Grant in Peace* 112.
88. Julia Dent Grant, *Personal Memoirs* 166.
89. Badeau, *Grant in Peace* 111–12.
90. Grant to Johnson, January 14, 1868, 18 *Grant Papers* 102–3.
91. Sherman to Grant, January 27, 1864, ibid 108 note.
92. Simpson, *Let Us Have Peace* 229.
93. Badeau, *Grant in Peace* 112. Also see Grant to Johnson, January 28, 1868, 18 *Grant Papers* 116–18.
94. Grant to U.S. Representative John A. Bingham of Ohio, February 12, 1868, ibid. 149 note.
95. Trefousse, *Johnson* 307.
96. Sherman to Grant, January 27, 1868, *Grant Papers* 108 note.
97. Ibid. Also see Sherman, *Memoirs* 912–13 (reprint edition). After the meeting Johnson had his secretary clip the article in the *Intelligencer* and paste it in his scrapbook. The president read it approvingly to his cabinet at its next meeting, and insisted that Grant "had not been true to his understanding." After listening to Johnson's version, all but Seward agreed. 13 *Johnson Papers* 512.
98. *New York Tribune,* January 17, 1868.
99. *New York World,* January 16, 1868; *New York Tribune,* January 20, 1868; *New York Times,* January 21, 1868.
100. Grant to Johnson, January 24, 1868, 18 *Grant Papers* 121–22 note.
101. Sherman to Johnson, January 27, 1868, 13 *Johnson Papers* 497.
102. Grant to Johnson, January 28, 1868, 18 *Grant Papers* 116–18.
103. Sherman to Johnson, January 31, 1868, 13 *Johnson Papers* 512–13.
104. Johnson to Grant, January 31, 1868, ibid. 508–12.
105. Grant to Johnson, February 3, 1868, 18 *Grant Papers* 124–26.
106. *New York Independent,* January 13, 1868; *New York Times,* January 21, 1868.
107. *Philadelphia Ledger,* February 10, 1868.
108. Samuel Galloway to Washburne, February 6, 1868, Washburne Papers; *National Anti-Slavery Standard,* February 8, 1868; *New York Times,* February 6, 1868.
109. Badeau, *Grant in Peace* 114.
110. Sherman to Grant, February 14, 1868, 18 *Grant Papers* 139–40 note.
111. Sherman to Johnson, February 14, 1868, 13 *Johnson Papers* 559–60. Senator John Sherman followed through and introduced a resolution holding that the Senate should not consider additional brevet nominations. *New York Tribune,* February 17, 1868.
112. George Thomas to Johnson, February 22, 1868, 13 *Johnson Papers* 586.
113. Johnson to Stanton, February 21, 1868; Johnson to Lorenzo Thomas, February 21, 1868, 13 *Johnson Papers* 577.
114. Trefousse, *Andrew Johnson* 312.
115. For the text of the Senate resolution and Johnson's reply, 13 *Johnson Papers* 579–86.
116. The Articles of Impeachment are reprinted, ibid. 619–28; the president's response, March 23, 1868, is at pages 664–89.
117. For Grant's testimony, see 18 *Grant Papers* 185–89.
118. Grant to Sheridan, March 31, 1868, 18 *Grant Papers* 212. Earlier Grant told Sherman, "This constant jarring is getting very tedious to us who can be nothing other than victims." March 18, 1868, ibid. 204.
119. Grant to Ford, March 18, 1868, ibid. 205.
120. *New York Tribune,* April 3, 1868. Also see *New York Times,* April 4, 1868.
121. John B. Henderson, "Reflections on Public Life," *Century Magazine* 202–14 (December 1912).
122. Trefousse, *Andrew Johnson* 323. Just prior to the vote, Senator Ross suggested that it would have a salutary effect if the president would transmit to Congress the radical constitutions of South Carolina and Arkansas without delay. Johnson promptly complied. George P. Brockway, *Political Deals That Saved Andrew Johnson* 12–15 (New York: Coalition of Publishers for Employment, 1977).
123. See Schofield to Grant, April 18, 1868, 18 *Grant Papers* 221–24 note.

124. At the last minute Grant had a change of heart and wired Schofield not to accept the position. "I regret exceedingly that your advice comes too late," Schofield replied. "You are aware that I do not want that office; yet, under existing circumstances, if the Senate should wish me to serve I could not decline." Grant to Schofield, April 25, 1868; Schofield to Grant, April 25, 1868, ibid. 235. Also see Schofield, *Forty-six Years* 413–18. Following Johnson's acquittal, Schofield was confirmed (May 29, 1868).

125. Badeau, *Grant in Peace* 142–43.

126. Ibid. 144.

127. John Sherman to Grant, June 28, 1868, 18 *Grant Papers* 294–95.

128. Badeau copied down Grant's words as he spoke. The quoted passage constituted the entirety of the general's remarks. *Grant in Peace* 144.

129. Grant to Hawley, May 29, 1868, 18 *Grant Papers* 263–64.

CHAPTER FIFTEEN: GRANT IN THE WHITE HOUSE

The epigraph is from *The Personal Memoirs of Julia Dent Grant* 182, John Y. Simon, ed. (New York: G. P. Putnam's Sons, 1975).

1. John Hope Franklin, "Election of 1868," in 2 *History of American Presidential Elections* 1279, Arthur M. Schlesinger, Jr., ed. (New York: Chelsea House, 1971).

2. As Secretary of State Seward noted, the Democrats "could have nominated no candidate who would have taken away fewer Republican votes." Quoted in Eric Foner, *A Short History of Reconstruction* 145 (New York: Harper and Row, 1990).

3. Grant to Julia, July 17, 1868. Also see his letter to Julia from Denver, July 21, 1868, 19 *The Papers of Ulysses S. Grant* 9–10, John Y. Simon, ed. (Carbondale: Southern Illinois University Press, 1995).

4. Adam Badeau, *Grant in Peace* 145–46 (Hartford, Conn.: Scranton, 1887).

5. Grant to Badeau, August 18, 1868, 19 *Grant Papers* 24.

6. For a sampling of Badeau's correspondence with the Jewish community, see Badeau to Simon Wolf, April 22, 1868, ibid. 17–18 note; Simon Wolf, *The Presidents I Have Known from 1860–1918* 66 (Washington, D.C.: B. S. Adams, 1918).

7. Grant to Morris, September 14, 1868, 19 *Grant Papers* 37.

8. Badeau, *Grant in Peace* 148.

9. Grant to Washburne, September 23, 1868, 19 *Grant Papers* 42.

10. Grant to Schofield, September 25, 1868, ibid. 43–44.

11. "To all who apply to me," Sherman wrote, "I say you will be elected, and ought to be elected, and that I would rather trust to your being just & fair, yea even moderate to the South, than Seymour and Blair [Democratic vice presidential nominee Francis P. Blair, Jr., of Missouri]....To talk of such men and *principle,* is like trusting convicts with property." Sherman to Grant, September 28, 1868, ibid. 46 note.

12. Badeau, *Grant in Peace* 148.

13. *Galena Gazette,* November 5, 1868.

14. Badeau, *Grant in Peace* 149.

15. *New York Tribune,* November 12, 1868; Sherman to Grant, November 18, 1868, 19 *Grant Papers* 82 note.

16. Badeau, *Grant in Peace* 150–51.

17. *Personal Memoirs of W. T. Sherman,* 930 (New York: D. Appleton, 1875).

18. Grant to Sherman, January 5, 1869, 19 *Grant Papers* 103. Also see Grant to Ellen Sherman, February 2, 1869; Grant to Sherman, February 12, 1869; Sherman to Grant, February 21, 1869; Sherman to Senator John Sherman, February 21, 1869; Grant to William H. Aspinwall, February 25, 1869, ibid. 122–23, 128–29, 133.

19. The figure $65,000 included most of the furnishings. For Ellen Sherman's caustic appraisal of the furniture the Grants left, see her letter to WTS, June 21, 1876, quoted in Stanley P. Hirshson, *The White Tecumseh* 360 (New York: Wiley, 1997). Also see Sherman to Senator John Sherman, January 15, 1869, 19 *Grant Papers* 103 note. The donors, in addition to Stewart, included Hamilton Fish, William H. Aspinwall, and Daniel Butterfield. Three of the four were subsequently appointed by Grant to significant positions. Ibid. 123 note.

20. Badeau to Matías Romero, September 13, 1868, 19 *Grant Papers* 282.

21. Matías Romero to Grant, November 9, 1868, ibid. 69 note. Grant replaced Rosecrans with Thomas H. Nelson of Indiana, former United States minister to Chile, April 12, 1869.

22. For a general view of the *Alabama* claims, see Maureen M. Robson, "The *Alabama* Claims and the Anglo-American Reconciliation, 1865–1871," 43 *Canadian Historical Review* 11ff. (March 1961).

23. Badeau, *Grant in Peace* 153–54.

24. Samuel Flagg Bemis, *A Diplomatic History of the United States* 406 (New York: Holt, Rinehart and Winston, 1955).

25. Henry Adams, *The Education of Henry Adams: An Autobiography* 260 (Boston: Houghton Mifflin, 1918).

26. 1 *Letters of James Russell Lowell* 7, Charles Elliot Norton, ed. (New York: Harper and Brothers, 1894).

27. Quoted in Allan Nevins, 1 *Hamilton Fish: The Inner History of the Grant Administration* 107–8 (New York: Frederick Ungar, 1936).

28. *New York Times,* July 11, 1868, in Paxton Hibben, *Henry Ward Beecher: An American Portrait* 221 (New York: Doran, 1927).

29. E. L. Godkin, "The Men Inside Politics," *The Nation,* March 4, 1869.

30. Badeau, *Grant in Peace* 156, 410.

31. Ibid. 156–57.

32. For the text of Grant's inaugural address, along with his initial draft, see 19 *Grant Papers* 136–42.

33. *New York Times,* March 5, 1869.

34. *The Nation,* March 11, 1869.

35. *Harper's Weekly,* April 3, 1869.

36. For a sampling of a Southern comment, see Hamlin Garland, *Ulysses S. Grant: His Life and Character* 389 (New York: Doubleday and McClure, 1898).

37. *New York Times,* March 5, 1869.

38. Grant to Thomas L. Tullock, January 20, 1869. "If any choice is left to me," wrote Grant, "I would be pleased to see it dispensed with. I do not wish to disarrange any plans…but it will be agreeable to me if your committee should agree that the ball is unnecessary." 19 *Grant Papers* 111.

39. *New York Times,* March 5, 1869.

40. Garland, *Grant* 388–89.

41. *New York Times, New York Tribune, New York Herald,* March 6, 1869.

42. Nevins, 1 *Hamilton Fish* 110.

43. Robert V. Friendenberg, "John A. J. Creswell of Maryland: Reformer in the Post Office," 64 *Maryland Historical Magazine* 133–43 (1969). Also see Hesseltine, *Grant* 160; William S. McFeely, *Grant: A Biography* 302 (New York: W. W. Norton, 1981).

44. Hoar was the center of his circle of friends in Concord. James Russell Lowell related in the *Bigelow Papers* how he would spend a long morning in conversation

> Along the Jedge, who covers with his hat
> More wit, an' gumption, an' shrewd Yankee sense,
> Than there is mosses on an ole stone fence.

45. Emory Washburn to Elihu Washburn, March 8, 1969, Washburne Papers, Library of Congress.

46. *New York Times,* March 8, 1869.

47. *New York Tribune,* March 6, 1869.

48. *Harper's Weekly,* April 3, 1869.

49. 15 *U.S. Statutes at Large* 644 (September 2, 1869).

50. Message to the Senate, March 6, 1869, 19 *Grant Papers* 147–48.

51. David M. Jordan, *Roscoe Conkling of New York: Voice in the Senate* 120 (Ithaca, N.Y.: Cornell University Press, 1971). Grant withdrew his request for congressional dispensation, March 9, 1869. 19 *Grant Papers* 148 note.

52. A sampling of letters to Grant, is ibid. 148–49 note.

53. Badeau, *Grant in Peace* 161–62. Also see Gaillard Hunt, *Israel, Elihu, and Cadwallader Washburn: A Chapter in American Biography* 243–45 (New York: Macmillan, 1925).

54. Washburne to Grant, March 10, 1869, 19 *Grant Papers* 151 note. George Boutwell believed that Washburne was removed to make way for Fish after Stewart resigned, but he cites no evidence. 2 *Reminiscences of Sixty Years in Public Affairs* 213 (New York: McClure, Phillips, 1902).

55. James H. Wilson, *The Life of John A. Rawlins* 351–52 (New York: Neale, 1916). Rawlins died September 6, 1869, less than six months after his confirmation as secretary of war.

56. Badeau, *Grant in Peace* 167.

57. Grant to Fish, March 11, 1869, 19 *Grant Papers* 151–52.

58. Nevins, 1 *Hamilton Fish* 114; *New York Times,* March 12, 1869.

59. *New York Tribune,* March 12, 1869.

60. Ibid.

61. *New York Times,* March 15, 1869.

62. *New York Herald,* March 12, 1869.

63. On February 15, 1869, Parker wrote to the secretary of the Society of Friends, "General Grant, the President elect, desirous of inaugurating some policy to protect the Indians in their just rights and enforce integrity in the administration of their affairs, as well as to improve their general condi-

tion...directs me to request that you will send him a list of names, members of your society, whom your society will endorse, as suitable persons for Indian agents." 19 *Grant Papers* 193 note.

64. "Indian wars have grown out of mismanagement of the bureau," Grant wrote Sheridan, and he said he intended to correct that. Grant to Sheridan, December 24, 1868, ibid. 99–100.

65. Geoffrey Perret, *Ulysses S. Grant* 401 (New York: Random House, 1997).

66. Badeau, *Grant in Peace*, 243.

67. Daniel Ammen, *The Old Navy and the New* 503 (Philadelphia: J. B. Lippincott, 1891).

68. Jesse R. Grant, *In the Days of My Father: General Grant* 57, 153 (New York: Harper and Brothers, 1925).

69. Ibid. 76–77; Ben Perley Poore and O. H. Tiffany, *Life of Grant* 49–50 (Philadelphia: Hubbard Brothers, 1895).

70. William H. Crook, *Through Five Administrations* 154–56 (New York: Harper and Brothers, 1910).

71. The first volume of Badeau's three-volume work, *Military History of Ulysses S. Grant, April, 1861, to April, 1865* was published in 1869 by D. Appleton and Company.

72. Adams, *Education of Henry Adams* 265–66.

73. Edmund Wilson, *Patriotic Gore* 160–61 (New York: Oxford University Press, 1962). Worthington Chauncey Ford, 2 *Cycle of Adams Letters, 1861–1865* 243 (Boston: Houghton Mifflin, 1920).

74. Sherman, *Memoirs* 931; Hirshson, *White Tecumseh* 389; John F. Marszalek, *Sherman: A Soldier's Passion for Order* 383–85 (New York: Free Press, 1993).

75. War Department General Orders No. 11, March 5, 1869, 19 *Grant Papers* 143 note. Also see Schofield, *Forty-six Years in the Army* 421.

76. Wilson, *Life of John A. Rawlins* 366.

77. Ibid. 365–67.

78. Sherman to Schofield, March 29, 1869, 19 *Grant Papers* 144 note; Sherman, *Memoirs* 932–33; Manning F. Force, *General Sherman* 325–26 (New York: D. Appleton, 1899).

79. Sherman to Grant, March 26, 1969, 19 *Grant Papers* 144 note. Sherman reminded Grant that the order had been long contemplated and was working well. "There has not been a particle of confusion or difficulty with its execution....If you want to define more clearly what class of business the Secretary should have exclusive control of, it is easily done....I am perfectly willing Genl Rawlins should pick out his own business, only leaving me a clear field of command."

80. War Department General Orders No. 28, March 26, 1869, ibid.

81. "General Sherman's Opinion of General Grant," *Century Magazine* 31 (March 1879).

82. *Congressional Globe*, 40th Cong., 3rd sess. 1415.

83. Jordan, *Roscoe Conkling* 124–25.

84. Hesseltine, *Ulysses S. Grant* 166.

85. 19 *Grant Papers* 140. Emphasis in original. The term specie is the ablative form of the Latin word *specie*, meaning solid. The frequent phrase, "to be paid in specie," meant to be paid in solid currency, i.e., gold or silver.

86. *New York Times*, March 19, 1869.

87. *New York Tribune*, March 19, 1869; *New York Commercial and Financial Chronicle*, March 27, 1869. The value $130 was per $100 gold coin, each of which weighed one ounce.

88. *New York Tribune*, September 2, 1869; *New York Times*, July 14, 1869.

89. Grant to Badeau, July 14, 1869, 19 *Grant Papers* 212–13.

90. Kenneth D. Ackerman, *The Gold Ring: Jim Fisk, Jay Gould, and Black Friday, 1869* 93 (New York: Dodd, Mead, 1988).

91. Allan Nevins, *The Emergence of Modern America* 194–99 (New York: Macmillan, 1927); Hesseltine, *Ulysses S. Grant* 169–70.

92. Ackerman, *Gold Ring* 58–59. *Gold Panic Investigation* 243, House of Representatives, Report No. 31, 44th Cong., 2nd sess. (1870).

93. 93. Ackerman, *Gold Ring* 76–77.

94. Porter's unrebutted sworn testimony before the House committee investigating the debacle quotes Gould as saying that he knew when gold was going up or down on the market. "You had better let me get you some gold; gold is going to rise before long, and suppose I purchase some for you." Porter was appalled. "I have neither the inclination nor the means of purchasing gold; and if I had, I am an officer of the Government, and cannot enter into anything that looks like speculation. It may be perfectly proper for you to do it, but it would be manifestly improper for me." House Report 31 at 447.

95. Ibid. 445–46. "I have not authorized any purchase of gold, and request that none be made on my account," Porter wired Gould. "I am unable to enter into any speculation whatever." 19 *Grant Papers* 245 note.

96. Corbin testimony, House Report 31, at 270–71.

97. William Marcy "Boss" Tweed (and the judges beholden to him) played a crucial role in Gould's takeover of the Erie Railway. "Tweed's a man I can do business with," Fisk told Gould after the Erie

deal had been struck. When Tweed was arrested on 204 counts of fraud in 1871, Gould posted Tweed's unprecedented $1 million bail bond. For Tweed generally, including his relationship with Gould, see Leo Hershkowitz, *Tweed's New York: Another Look* (Garden City, N.Y.: Doubleday, 1977); Denis Tilden Lynch, *"Boss" Tweed: The Story of a Grim Generation* (New York: Boni and Liveright, 1927).

98. Bank examiner testimony, House Report 31 at 84–85, 88, 410–11.
99. Grant interview, *New York Sun,* October 4, 1969.
100. Ackerman, *Gold Ring* 74*ff.*
101. House Report 31 at 163.
102. Grant to Boutwell, September 12, 1869, 19 *Grant Papers* 242–43. Boutwell received the message on September 15, 1869.
103. The text of Corbin's letter has been lost. For Gould's recollection see House Report 31 at 155.
104. Hesseltine, *Ulysses S. Grant* 176–77; Ackerman, *Gold Ring* 136–46. The testimony of Gould's messenger, William O. Chapin, is at House Report 31, 230–31.
105. Ackerman, *Gold Ring* 144.
106. Julia Dent Grant, *Personal Memoirs of Julia Dent Grant* 182, John Y. Simon, ed. (New York: G. P. Putnam's Sons, 1975). Mrs. Grant omitted the names of Gould and Fisk in her memoirs. They are supplied by Dr. Simon, 198 note 11.
107. House Report 31 at 8, 211.
108. Ackerman, *Gold Ring* 151.
109. Corbin testimony, House Report 31 at 251–56; Ackerman, *Gold Ring* 155–57.
110. *New York Tribune,* September 24, 1869.
111. *New York Times,* September 24, 1869.
112. Boutwell, 2 *Reminiscences* 174.
113. Boutwell testimony, House Report 31 at 344–46. In testimony before the House committee investigating Black Friday, as the next day's trading came to be known, Gould and Fisk endeavored to implicate Grant in their scheme and to suggest that he had instructed Boutwell in early September to slow or even halt gold sales. Some historians and biographers have accepted Gould's testimony as true and have rendered their accounts accordingly. Secretary Boutwell explicitly refuted Gould's assertion, but his statement has often been overlooked. In Boutwell's words: "As far as I know, the effort [of Gould and Fisk] had been directed chiefly to the support of a *false* theory that the President was opposed to the sale of gold....They even went so far as to allege that the President had ordered the Secretary of the Treasury to suspend the sale of gold during the month of September, *for which there is no foundation whatever.* Indeed, up to the 22nd of September, when I introduced the subject of the price of gold to the President, he had neither said nor done anything, except to write a letter from New York City under date of September 12, 1869." (Boutwell then quotes Grant's letter in full. That letter instructs the secretary to continue his existing policy. [See above.]) Boutwell, 2 *Reminiscences* 169. Emphasis added.
114. *New York Times,* September 25, 1869.
115. *New York Sun,* September 25, 1869.
116. Benedict testimony, House Report 31 at 56–57.
117. Fahnestock to Boutwell with copy to Jay Cooke, September 24, 1869. Cooke Papers, Historical Society of Pennsylvania.
118. Boutwell, 2 *Reminiscences* 177.
119. Ibid. 175.
120. House Report 31 at 330, 346.
121. Corbin testimony, ibid. at 266.
122. David Dudley Field was the brother of United States Supreme Court Justice Stephen J. Field; Albert Cardozo was the father of United States Supreme Court Justice Benjamin Cardozo.

CHAPTER SIXTEEN: DIPLOMACY

The epigraph is from Grant's first annual message to Congress, December 4, 1869, 20 *The Papers of Ulysses S. Grant* 30–31, John Y. Simon, ed. (Carbondale: Southern Illinois University Press, 1992).

1. John Jay to Fish, March 12, 1869, Fish Papers, Library of Congress. Jay (grandson of the founding father) was soon appointed by Grant to be United States minister to Vienna.
2. Adam Badeau, *Grant in Peace* 232–33 (Hartford, Conn.: Scranton, 1887).
3. Allan Nevins, 1 *Hamilton Fish: The Inner History of the Grant Administration* 182 (New York: Frederick Ungar, 1937).
4. Fish diary, April 6, 1869. For Hoar's views see Moorfield Storey and Edward W. Emerson, *Ebenezer Rockwood Hoar: A Memoir* 179–80 (Boston: Houghton Mifflin, 1911).

5. Badeau, *Grant In Peace* 233; *New York Tribune,* April 30, 1869; Nevins, 1 *Hamilton Fish* 183–84.
6. In 1869 the Cuban exile committee distributed bonds lavishly among senators, congressmen, editors, and lobbyists. Spanish intelligence services compiled a list of the recipients, and Madrid's minister in Washington, López Roberts, showed the list to Secretary of State Fish. Fish, it appears, was skeptical and made no further inquiry. But in 1875 Grant told Fish and Secretary of the Navy George M. Robeson the story of Rawlins's bonds, how he had ordered them destroyed, and how they were still in existence. As Fish recorded in his diary, "The President seemed in doubt as to what should be done with the bonds. Robeson suggested they be sold. I thought it would not do for the President, even as executor, to be selling such bonds, in which opinion he agreed. I then informed him that prior to Rawlins's death I had been told of the bonds. I further stated that Mr. Roberts had, more than once, produced a list of persons holding Cuban bonds...I said that I had been shown names in the list, but had never been shown the whole list." Fish diary, November 5, 1875.

  After Rawlins's death the Cuban exile committee contributed $20,000 in bonds to the Rawlins family fund. This gift was open and aboveboard, and was not the gift to which Grant referred. Nevins, 2 *Hamilton Fish* 921; *New York Tribune,* September 16, October 11, 1869.
7. Commander E. B. Lansing, New York Department, G.A.R., to Bancroft Davis, November 12, 1869. Davis Papers, Library of Congress.
8. Nevins, 1 *Hamilton Fish* 191–92.
9. Fish's original memorandum is among his papers in the Library of Congress. It is reprinted, ibid. 193.
10. Sickles to Fish, August 1, 1869, Fish Papers.
11. Grant to Fish, August 14, 1869, 19 *The Papers of Ulysses S. Grant* 234–36, John Y. Simon, ed. (Carbondale: Southern Illinois University Press, 1995).
12. Sickles to Fish, August 15, 16, 1869, Fish Papers.
13. Porter to Fish, August 20, 1869, 19 *Grant Papers* 236 note.
14. *New York Sun,* August 30, 1869.
15. Nevins, 1 *Fish* 244.
16. 19 *Grant Papers* 238.
17. On his deathbed, Rawlins cried out to Postmaster General Creswell, "There is Cuba, poor, struggling Cuba. I want you to stand by the Cubans. Cuba must be free. Her tyrannical enemy must be crushed. Cuba must not only be free, but all her sister-islands." Nevins, 1 *Fish* 247. Contrary to traditional interpretations of the Grant administration, Professor Nevins is highly critical of Rawlins's role as secretary of war. "Actually, he was the most dangerous member of the original Cabinet, and his death, so frequently described as a disaster to Grant, was rather a blessing. He had often said that he hoped to see 'the aegis of our power spread over this continent'...and had talked of freeing the Western Hemisphere from 'the influence and dangers of monarchism.' While he stayed at Grant's right hand the peril of war with England and Spain would remain great." Ibid.
18. Annual Message, December 6, 1869, 19 *Grant Papers* 20, 25.
19. John Bassett Moore, the dean of American international law scholars, called Grant's speech the "classic exposition of the juridical conception of belligerency." *Digest of International Law* 194–96 (Washington, D.C.: Government Printing Office, 1906). Also see Thomas A. Bailey, *A Diplomatic History of the American People* 380 (New York: Appleton-Century-Crofts, 1964); Samuel Flagg Bemis, *A Diplomatic History of the United States* 435 note (New York: Holt, Rinehart, and Winston, 1963); Alexander DeConde, *A History of American Foreign Policy* 287 (New York: Charles Scribner's Sons, 1963).
20. James D. Richardson, ed., 7 *A Compilation of the Messages and Papers of the Presidents, 1789–1897* 64–69 (Washington, D.C.: Bureau of National Literature and Art, 1897).
21. *New York Herald, New York Tribune,* June 15, 1869.
22. Fish diary, June 17, 1869.
23. Grant to Fish, July 10, 1869, 19 *Grant Papers* 169 note.
24. Bemis, *A Diplomatic History* 400.
25. On March 28, 1867, the House of Representatives served notice that it would not appropriate money for the Danish purchase, even if the Senate gave its advice and consent to the treaty. By a vote of 93–43, the House resolved "That in the present financial condition of the country, any further purchases of territory are inexpedient, and this House will hold itself under no obligation to vote money to pay for such purchases unless there is greater present necessity for the same than now exists."

  American interest in Samaná Bay first developed in 1846 when Secretary of State John C. Calhoun dispatched a young naval officer, Lieutenant David D. Porter, to inspect the bay as a possible base. In 1854 Secretary of State William L. Marcy attempted to acquire the bay, but was foiled by British and French intervention. See Charles Callan Tansill, *The United States and Santo Domingo, 1798–1873* 182–204 (Baltimore: Johns Hopkins University Press, 1938); William Javier Nelson, *Almost A Territory: America's Attempt to Annex the Dominican Republic* 48 (Newark: University of Delaware Press, 1990).

26. "I am satisfied that the time has arrived," said Johnson, "when even so direct a proceeding as a proposition for an annexation of the two Republics on the island of Santo Domingo would not only receive the consent of the people interested, but would also give satisfaction to all other foreign nations." Emphasis added. Unlike the Dominicans, the Haitians had made no overture to the United States. Johnson to Congress, December 9, 1868, 13 *The Papers of Andrew Johnson* 213–14, Paul H. Bergeron, ed. (Knoxville: University of Tennessee Press, 1996).

27. Fish diary, April 5, 1869.

28. Ibid. April 6, 1869.

29. Nevins, 1 *Hamilton Fish* 263.

30. In late May 1869, Grant expressed his views to E. D. Bassett, the new minister to the United States from Haiti. According to Bassett, "The President was very emphatic, and at the same time very cautious in expressing himself about the policy of annexation. He said his own views were in favor of such a policy, but that he thought in all cases the people of a country to be annexed should first show themselves anxious for union with us." *New York Herald,* June 1, 1869.

31. Fish to Hunt, June 2, 1869, 2 *Special Missions,* MS, Department of State.

32. Nevins, 1 *Hamilton Fish* 264. Also see J. D. Cox, "How Judge Hoar Ceased to Be Attorney-General," *Atlantic Monthly,* August 1895.

33. It was Babcock whom Grant sent in 1864 to appraise how Sherman was doing in Georgia, and who frequently carried Grant's confidential messages to Stanton.

34. Grant to Báez, July 13, 1869, 19 *Grant Papers* 209.

35. Nevins, 1 *Hamilton Fish* 269–72. Writing twenty-five years afterward, Interior Secretary Cox, who had broken with Grant, wrote a jaundiced account of the cabinet session in the *Atlantic* ("How Judge Hoar Ceased to Be Attorney General"). Historians Allan Nevins and Charles Tansill both dismiss Cox's often quoted version as prejudiced and full of errors. Ibid. 272; Tansill, *The United States and Santo Domingo* 366–70.

36. Tansill, *The United States and Santo Domingo* 463–64. Also see Professor Tansill's "War Powers of the President of the United States with Special Reference to the Beginning of Hostilities," 45 *Political Science Quarterly* 41ff. (1930), which is critical of Grant's decision.

37. George S. Boutwell, 2 *Reminiscences of Sixty Years in Public Affairs* 215 (New York: McClure, Phillips, 1902).

38. 2 *Letters of Charles Eliot Norton* 43, Sara Norton and M. A. DeWolfe Howe, eds. (Boston: Houghton Mifflin, 1931).

39. 2 *Letters of James Russell Lowell* 233, Charles Eliot Norton, ed. (New York: Harper and Brothers, 1894).

40. David Herbert Donald, 2 *Charles Sumner* 338–339, 368–373 (New York: Knopf, 1970).

41. Bancroft Davis to George Bancroft (in Berlin), July 11, 1870, Bancroft Collection, Massachusetts Historical Society.

42. Donald, 2 *Charles Sumner* 435.

43. Letter of Ben: Perley Poore to the *Boston Journal,* October 21, 1877 (published October 24, 1877).

44. Donald, 2 *Charles Sumner* 437.

45. Fish to George Bancroft, February 9, 1870, in Nevins, 1 *Hamilton Fish* 313.

46. Carl Schurz, 6 *Speeches, Correspondence, and Political Papers of Carl Schurz* 282 (New York: G. P. Putnam's Sons, 1913). There is peripheral evidence to suggest that Sumner held his fire, hoping that Grant would retain the Massachusetts senator's friend James M. Ashley as governor of the Montana Territory. When Grant replaced Ashley, Sumner went into opposition. See the correspondence between Wisconsin Senator Timothy O. Howe and Fish, November 8, 1877, reprinted in Nevins, 1 *Hamilton Fish* 322.

47. Because the Senate was in closed session, Sumner's speech was not recorded. The reconstructed summary of his remarks is drawn from reports in the *New York Times, New York Herald,* and *New York Tribune,* March 25, 1870, and the *Boston Advertiser,* March 26, 1870.

48. Nevins, 1 *Hamilton Fish* 317.

49. Tansill, *The United States and Santo Domingo* 414–15.

50. U.S. Grant, Second Annual Message, December 5, 1870, Richardson, 7 *Messages and Papers of the Presidents* 101.

51. *Congressional Globe,* 41st Cong., 3rd sess., 271 (December 22, 1870); 416 (January 9, 1871). The Senate vote was 32–9. The House, before final passage, attached a rider introduced by Representative Jacob A. Ambler stating that the resolution "shall not be held, understood, or construed as com-

mitting Congress to the policy of annexing the territory of said republic of Dominica." The final vote in the House was 123–63. The Senate concurred with the amended resolution, 57–0.

52. Nevins, 2 *Hamilton Fish* 497–98.

53. "Report of the Commission of Inquiry to Santo Domingo," Senate Executive Document No. 9, 42nd Cong., 1st sess. (1871).

54. Presidential message, April 5, 1871, 21 *Grant Papers* 292–95.

55. 12 *Statutes at Large* 794 (March 3, 1868). The ostensible reason for increasing the size of the Court during the war was to provide a new 10th Circuit comprising California and the West Coast. Stephen J. Field of California was appointed to the new seat on March 8, 1863, and was confirmed by the Senate on March 16.

56. Act of July 23, 1866.

57. Passage of the 1866 act followed immediately upon the 5–4 decision of the Court in *Ex Parte Milligan,* 4 Wallace 2 (1866), holding that the president had no power to institute trial by military tribunal in localities where the civil courts were open. Congressional Republicans saw the decision as a threat to the use of the military in carrying out Reconstruction. The problem would be especially severe if Johnson were able to make additional appointments to the Court. There was already one vacancy (caused by the death of Justice John Catron) and the president had nominated Attorney General Henry Stanbery to fill it. Rather than vote on Stanbery's nomination, Congress chose to decrease the size of the Court.

58. Justice James M. Wayne of Georgia died July 5, 1867. Like Catron, he was not replaced.

59. Act of April 10, 1869.

60. *New York Times,* December 16, 1869.

61. *Washington Chronicle,* December 22, 1869; *The Nation,* December 23, 1869; *Chicago Republican,* December 22, 1896; *New York World,* December 21, 1869.

62. Charles Warren, 2 *The Supreme Court in United States History* 501–7 (Boston: Little, Brown, 1926); 20 *Grant Papers* 52–55; Storey and Emerson, *Ebenezer Rockwood Hoar* 189–98; Nevins, 1 *Hamilton Fish* 303–5.

63. Nevins, 1 *Hamilton Fish* 305.

64. Storey and Emerson, *Ebenezer Rockwood Hoar* 198–202; Warren, 2 *Supreme Court* 516–19. Also see Charles Fairman, "Mr. Justice Bradley's Appointment to the Supreme Court and the Legal Tender Cases," 54 *Harvard Law Review* 998 (1940); Sidney Ratner, "Was the Supreme Court Packed by President Grant?," 50 *Political Science Quarterly* 343–58 (1935).

65. Sumner, 13 *Works* 76–88; Donald, *Charles Sumner* 375–76.

66. Nevins, 1 *Hamilton Fish* 156–73.

67. 20 *Grant Papers* 30–31.

68. Nevins, 2 *Hamilton Fish* 459–63.

69. Gladstone to Granville, October 14, 1870, Gladstone Papers. In 1869 Fish had made a similar suggestion to Sir Edward Thornton, the British minister in Washington, but the Foreign Office was uninterested. Nevins, 1 *Hamilton Fish* 423–425.

70. Ibid. 436.

71. 21 *Grant Papers* 175–76. At the time the commission met, Hoar had resigned as attorney general and was replaced by Senator Williams.

72. Nevins, 1 *Hamilton Fish* 447.

73. Newspapers quoted in 2 Ibid. 470–74.

74. Fish diary, May 8, 1871, reprinted ibid. 490–91.

75. Second Hague Conference, Convention Number XIII, Articles VI, VII, and VIII. Also see John Bassett Moore, 1 *International Arbitrations* 666–70 (Washington, D.C.: Government Printing Office, 1898).

76. Treaty of Washington, Article VI. The United States and Great Britain further agreed "to observe these rules between themselves in the future and to bring the knowledge of other maritime Powers, and to invite them to accede to them."

77. Many historians and most analysts of the Treaty of Washington believe that to achieve an accord with Washington, Great Britain was prepared to sell Canada short, even to the point of abandonment.

78. Northcote to Macdonald, May 15, 1871, quoted in Nevins, 2 *Hamilton Fish* 479.

79. George Bancroft, one of America's premier historians, was on close terms with Bismarck and the emperor, and his scholarship was widely respected in Berlin. Unlike the British, who submitted their arbitration brief in English, Bancroft wrote the American submission in flawless German, as well as the United States rejoinder to the British argument. Bancroft to Fish, February 16, 1872, in Nevins, 2 *Hamilton Fish* 536.

80. Republicans voting no were William Sprague of Rhode Island, Morgan G. Hamilton of Texas,

and Francis P. Blair of Missouri. Democrats Thomas F. Bayard of Delaware and William T. Hamilton of Maryland voted yes.

81. Edward L. Pierce, ed., 4 *Memoir and the Letters of Charles Sumner* 489 (Boston: Roberts Brothers, 1894).

82. Nevins, 2 *Hamilton Fish* 564. The cashed check for $15.5 million has been framed and hangs in 10 Downing Street as a lesson to future British governments.

83. Draft Message to Congress, December 4, 1871, 22 *Grant Papers* 254–55.

84. John Bassett Moore, quoted in Robert H. Ferrell, *American Diplomacy* 291 (New York: W.W. Norton, 1975).

CHAPTER SEVENTEEN: GREAT WHITE FATHER

The first epigraph quotation was apparently made by Sheridan in January 1869 at Fort Cobb in Indian Territory. Captain Charles Nordstrom, 10th Cavalry, who was present, claimed Sheridan made the famous statement after the Comanche leader, Toch-a-way, striking his chest, declared, "Me, Toch-a-way; me good Injun." To which Sheridan replied, "The only good Indians I ever saw were dead Indians." Sheridan repeatedly denied making the statement. The second quotation is from Sheridan's annual report in 1878. See Paul Hutton, *Phil Sheridan and His Army* 180 (Lincoln: University of Nebraska Press, 1973); *Annual Report of the Secretary of War for the Year 1878* 36 (Washington, D.C.: Government Printing Office, 1878).

1. In a remarkably candid conversation, Grant expressed his empathy to his friend George Stuart. The president said that "as a young lieutenant he had been much thrown among the Indians, and had seen the unjust treatment they had received at the hands of white men." George H. Stuart, *The Life of George H. Stuart* 239, Robert E. Thompson, ed. (Philadelphia: J. M. Stoddart, 1890).

2. Robert M. Utley, "The Celebrated Peace Policy of General Grant," 20 *North Dakota History* 122 (1953).

3. Max Farrand, "The Indian Boundary Line," 10 *American Historical Review* 782–91 (1905).

4. *British Royal Proclamations Relating to America: 1603–1783* 212, 215–16, Clarence Saunders Brigham, ed. (Worcester, Mass.: American Antiquarian Society, 1911).

5. 8 *Works of Thomas Jefferson* 241–49, Paul Leicester Ford, ed. (New York: G. P. Putnam's Sons, 1905); Anthony F. C. Wallace, *Jefferson and the Indians: The Tragic Fate of the First Americans* 222–26 (Cambridge: Harvard University Press, 1999); Robert Wooster, *The Military and United States Indian Policy* 6–11 (New Haven: Yale University Press, 1988).

6. 2 *Messages and Papers of the Presidents* 261, James D. Richardson, ed. (Washington, D.C.: Bureau of National Literature and Art, 1908).

7. 4 *United States Statutes at Large* 409 (1830).

8. The rationale for Indian removal was stated by Jackson in his farewell address, March 3, 1837: "The States which had so long been retarded in their improvement by the Indian tribes residing in the midst of them are at length relieved of the evil, and this unhappy race—the original dwellers in our land—are now placed in a situation where we may well hope that they will share in the blessings of civilization." 2 *Messages and Papers of the Presidents* 418.

9. Elsie M. Rushmore, *The Indian Policy During Grant's Administration* 12 (Jamaica, N.Y.: Marion Press, 1914).

10. In 1859 Indian agent William Bent estimated the number of settlers crossing the Plains at 60,000 each season. "The trains of vehicles and cattle are frequent....Post lines and private expresses are in constant motion. The explorations of this season have established the existence of precious metals in absolutely infinite abundance....A concourse of whites is, therefore, constantly swelling an incapability of control or restraint by the government." *Annual Report of the Commissioner of Indian Affairs for the Year 1859* 137–38, Sen. Exec. Doc. No. 1, 36th Cong., 1st sess.

11. For an objective narrative, see Kenneth Carley, *The Sioux Uprising of 1862* (St. Paul: Minnesota Historical Society, 1961). Also see the fine study by Francis Paul Prucha, *American Indian Policy in Crisis: Christian Reformers and the Indian, 1865–1900* 7–14 (Norman: University of Oklahoma Press, 1976), as well as William Watts Folwell, 2 *A History of Minnesota* 109–301 (St. Paul: Minnesota Historical Society, 1921).

12. William H. Leckie, *The Military Conquest of the Southern Plains* 19–24 (Norman: University of Oklahoma Press, 1963). Also see Stan Hoig, *The Sand Creek Massacre* (Norman: University of Oklahoma Press, 1961); Donald J. Berthrong, *The Southern Cheyennes* (Norman: University of Oklahoma Press, 1963); Raymond G. Carey, "The Puzzle of Sand Creek," 41 *Colorado Magazine* 279–98 (1964).

13. Chivington to Evans, 41 *War of the Rebellion* (Part 4) 797. Chivington's estimate of casualties is open to question. See Leckie, *Military Conquest* 23–24.

14. The most critical report was that issued by the congressional Joint Committee on the Conduct of the War. It spoke of the "fiendish malignity of the officers who had plotted the massacre" and said the Colorado soldiers "indulged in acts of barbarity of the most revolting character, such as never before disgraced the acts of men claiming to be civilized." A second congressional inquiry led by Senator James Doolittle reached similar conclusions, as did the official military investigation presided over by Samuel F. Tappan. "Massacre of the Cheyenne Indians," *Report of the Joint Committee on the Conduct of the War,* Senate Report No. 142, 38th Cong., 2nd sess. (1865); "The Chivington Massacre," in *Condition of the Indian Tribes: Report of the Joint Special Committee,* Senate Report No. 156, 39th Cong., 2nd sess. (1867); "Proceedings of a Military Commission in the Case of Colonel J. M. Chivington, First Colorado Cavalry," Senate Executive Document No. 26, 39th Cong., 2nd sess. (1867).

15. "Conditions of the Indian Tribes: Report of the Joint Special Committee" 3–10, *Senate Report No. 156,* 39th Cong., 2nd sess. (1867).

16. Ibid.

17. Chaired by Nathaniel G. Taylor, Commissioner of Indian Affairs, the commission included Senator John B. Henderson of Missouri, Samuel F. Tappan, John B. Sanborn, Sherman, Brigadier General Alfred H. Terry, and Brigadier General William S. Harney.

18. "Report of the Indian Peace Commissioners," *House Exec. Doc. No. 97* 17–18, 40th Cong., 3rd sess. (1868).

19. Leckie, *Military Conquest* 63–87.

20. Sherman to Sheridan, November 1, 1868, Sheridan Papers, Library of Congress.

21. Sherman to John Sherman, September 23, 1868, Sherman Papers, Library of Congress. Quoted in Robert G. Athearn, *William Tecumseh Sherman and the Conquest of the West* 223 (Norman: University of Oklahoma Press, 1956). Sherman's attitude toward the Indians was not unlike his all-or-nothing view of war in the South. "Either the Indians must give way," he wrote Samuel F. Tappan, "or we must abandon all west of the Missouri River and confess...forty millions of whites are cowed by a few thousand savages." September 24, 1868, Sherman Papers, Library of Congress.

22. "Report of the Commissioner of Indian Affairs" 5–11, *House Exec. Doc. No. 240,* 41st Cong., 2nd. sess. (1868). Samuel F. Tappan, a member of the Peace Commission, added his voice to the protest and urged an "immediate and unconditional abandonment of the present war policy." Reverend Henry B. Whipple, the Episcopal bishop of Minnesota, said, "This shameless disregard for justice has been the most foolhardy course we could have pursued." Ibid.

23. Ibid. 166. Also see Paul Andrew Hutton, *Phil Sheridan and His Army* 69, 97 (Lincoln: University of Nebraska Press, 1973).

24. Robert M. Utley, *The Indian Frontier of the American West, 1846–1890* 129 (Albuquerque: University of New Mexico Press, 1984).

25. In 1868 Texas had not been readmitted to the Union and consequently did not vote. Overall, Grant's percentage of the popular vote was 52.7. But he carried the frontier states of Kansas with 62 percent, Nebraska by 64 percent, and Minnesota by 61 percent. *Congressional Quarterly Guide of U.S. Elections* 337, 2nd ed. (Washington; D.C.: Congressional Quarterly, 1985).

26. Grant to Julia, March 19, 1853, 1 *Grant Papers* 294–96. At the same time, to a brother officer in San Francisco, Grant wrote that "this poor remnant of a once powerful tribe is fast wasting away before those blessings of 'civilization,' whiskey and small pox." Lloyd Lewis, *Captain Sam Grant* 313 (Boston: Little, Brown, 1950).

27. Grant to Sherman, May 19, 1868, 18 *Grant Papers* 257–58.

28. Grant to Sheridan, December 24, 1868, 19 ibid. 99–100.

29. Inaugural Address, March 4, 1869, ibid. 139–42. Reformers such as Wendell Phillips responded enthusiastically to Grant's citizenship suggestion. "Let [Grant] cover the Indian with this shield and give him...a Department in the Cabinet which shall watch his rights," Phillips told the *New York Times.* Phillips suggested revising the text of the Fourteenth Amendment, which did not include Indians, to provide for equal rights for all human beings. *New York Times,* March 11, 1869.

30. Athearn, *William Tecumseh Sherman* 249–50; Philip Weeks, *Farewell My Nation: The American Indian and the United States, 1820–1890* 154 (Arlington Heights, Ill.: Harlan Davidson, 1990).

31. *Cherokee Nation v. Georgia,* 5 Peters 1 (1831).

32. *Elk v. Wilkins,* 112 U.S. 94, 99 (1884); *United States v. Wong Kim Ark,* 169 U.S. 649, 680–82 (1898). Also see the Report of Senate Judiciary Committee, "The Effect of the Fourteenth Amendment on the Indian Tribes," 41st Cong., 3rd sess. (1870–1871).

33. Article I, Section 8 of the Constitution gives Congress the authority "To establish an uniform Rule of Naturalization." That authority is exclusive.

NOTES 693

34. Jacob D. Cox, "The Civil Service Reform," 112 *North American Review* 81–113 (1871).
35. Cox to Oberlin College, "Reconstruction and the Relations of the Races in the United States," July 25, 1865, Jacob Delson Cox Papers, Oberlin University. Cox's letter was printed by the Ohio State Journal Steam Press (1865).
36. William H. Armstrong, *Warrior in Two Camps: Ely S. Parker, Union General and Seneca Chief* 7–8 (Syracuse, N.Y.: Syracuse University Press, 1978).
37. Lewis Henry Morgan, *League of the HO-DE-NO-SAU-NEE, Iroquois* (Rochester, N.Y.: Dodd, Mead, 1851).
38. Grant, who was well aware of the deficiencies of his staff, intervened directly with the adjutant general to secure Parker's appointment. "I am personally acquainted with Mr. Parker and I think him eminently qualified for the position. He is a full blooded Indian but highly educated and very accomplished. He is a Civil Engineer of considerable eminence and served the Government some years in supervising the building of Marine Hospitals and Customs Houses on the upper Mississippi river." Grant to Lorenzo Thomas, June 25, 1863. 8 *Grant Papers* 434–35.
39. First Annual Message to Congress, December 6, 1869, Richardson, 7 *Messages and Papers* 38.
40. *Boston Daily Advertiser,* January 2, 1869.
41. Richardson, 7 *Messages and Papers* 38.
42. Second Inaugural, March 4, 1873, ibid. 222.
43. Grant to George H. Stuart, October 26, 1872, 23 *Grant Papers* 270.
44. Rushmore, *Indian Policy* 20.
45. After the meeting Welsh wrote Bishop Henry B. Whipple, "I told the Secretary [Cox] that altho' the community had perfect confidence in him that unless there was a commission to free him from the thraldom of party politics, philanthropists would not rally to his support, for *his* department had always been prey of the most thievist party politicians and what had always been, might be again." Welsh to Whipple, March 26, 1869, Whipple Papers, quoted in Prucha, *American Indian Policy* 35. Also see Rushmore, *Indian Policy* 19; Weeks, *Farewell, My Nation* 156; Henry E. Fritz, *The Movement for Indian Assimilation, 1860–1890* 74–75 (Westport, Conn.: Greenwood, 1963).
46. *New York Herald,* March 25, 1869; 19 *Grant Papers* 193 note; Robert H. Keller, Jr. *American Protestantism and United States Indian Policy, 1869–82* 25 (Lincoln: University of Nebraska Press, 1983); 72–89; Fritz, *Movement for Indian Assimilation* 75.
47. Utley, *Indian Frontier* 132; Rushmore, *Indian Policy* 20; Fritz, *Movement for Indian Assimilation* 75–83. Originally authorized for one year only, the board continued until 1934.
48. "It was in every way a representative body of men," wrote one biographer, "being carefully chosen from different Christian denominations and from different political parties." Charles Lewis Slattery, *Felix Reville Brunot* 143 (New York: Longmans, Green, 1901). In addition to William Welsh, who was elected chairman, and Felix R. Brunot and William E. Dodge, the board included George H. Stuart, John V. Farwell, Edward S. Tobey, Henry S. Lane, Vincent Colyer, and Nathan Bishop.
49. William E. Dodge to Felix R. Brunot, June 25, 1869, quoted in Robert Winston Mardock, *Reformers and the American Indian* 59 (Columbia: University of Missouri Press, 1971).
50. Minutes, May 27, 1869, Records of the Board of Indian Commissioners, National Archives.
51. Executive Order, June 3, 1869, 19 *Grant Papers* 191–93.
52. 13 *The Nation* 100–101 (August 17, 1871).
53. *Report of the Board of Indian Commissioners, 1869* 9–11.
54. Rushmore, *Indian Policy* 26.
55. Slattery, *Felix Reville Brunot* 145.
56. *Report of the Secretary of the Interior, 1869* x.
57. First Message to Congress, December 6, 1869, 19 *Grant Papers* 39.
58. *New York Times,* March 11, 1869.
59. Mardock, *Reformers and the American Indian* 54–55.
60. *New York Times,* September 30, 1869.
61. *Boston Evening Transcript,* March 20, 1869.
62. Report of Vincent Colyer, secretary of the Board of Indian Commissioners, to the House of Representatives, February 25, 1870, *Congressional Globe,* 41st Cong., 2nd sess., Part 2, 1576.
63. *New York Times,* February 24, 1870; *New York Tribune,* March 15, 1870; Lydia Maria Child, "The Indians," 1 *The Standard* 1 (May 1870); *National Anti-Slavery Standard* April 16, 1870.
64. *Congressional Globe,* 41st Cong., 2nd. sess., Part 6, 5402.
65. 2 *Memoirs of General William T. Sherman* 436, 2nd ed. (New York: Charles L. Webster, 1891).
66. Second Message to Congress, December 5, 1870, Richardson, 7 *Messages and Papers* 109–10. Of the seventy-four agencies assigned, the Quakers were awarded seventeen (24,322 Indians);

Methodists fourteen (54,473 Indians); Presbyterians nine (38,069); Espicopalians eight (26,929); Catholics seven (17,856); Baptists five (40,800); Reformed Dutch five (8,118); Congregationalists three (14,476); Christians two (8,287); Unitarians two (3,800); Lutherans one (273); Board of Foreign Missions one (1,496). For a breakdown by tribe, see Keller, *American Protestantism and Indian Policy* 226–28; Fritz, *Movement for Indian Assimilation* 76–79.

67. *New York Times*, March 30, 1870. "I yield to no one in my admiration of Thomas," Grant told John Russell Young. "As a commander, he was slow. We used to say laughingly, 'Thomas is too slow to move, and too brave to run away.' The success of his campaign [in front of Nashville] will be his vindication even against my criticisms. That success, and all the fame that came with it belong to Thomas." John Russell Young, 2 *Around the World with General Grant* 295 (New York: American News, 1879).

68. No member of Thomas's Virginia family was present. Freeman Cleaves, *Rock of Chickamauga* 306–7 (Westport, Conn.: Greenwood, 1974).

69. "I do not think it worthwhile to bring these Indians here," Sherman wrote a Western subordinate. "[It is] a mere concession to the popular sympathy felt in the East for the oppressed Indian." Sherman to Brig. Gen. Christopher C. Augur, June 9, 1870, quoted in Athearn, *William Tecumseh Sherman* 286–87. Also see James C. Olson, *Red Cloud and the Sioux Problem* 93–95 (Lincoln: University of Nebraska Press, 1965).

70. *New York Times*, May 19, 1870.

71. Utley, *Indian Frontier* 148.

72. *New York Herald*, June 2, 1870.

73. The best accounts of Red Cloud's visits are in the *New York Times*, June 4, 5, 8,10, and 11, 1870.

74. Ibid. June 8, 1870.

75. Ibid. June 11, 1870.

76. For Grant's special message to Congress, July 15, 1870, see Richardson, 7 *Messages and Papers* 79.

77. *New York Times*, June 17, 1870.

78. *The Nation*, June 23, 1870.

79. 16 *United States Statues at Large* 359.

80. *St. Paul Press*, December 6, 1870.

81. Grant to Congress, July 30, 1871, 21 *Grant Papers* 152–53.

82. See Allen G. Applen, "An Attempted Indian State Government: The Okmulgee Constitution in Indian Territory," 3 *Kansas Quarterly* 89–99 (Fall 1971).

83. The Red Cloud Agency and the Spotted Tail Agency were located in the northwest corner of Nebraska, just outside the boundary of the Great Sioux Reservation in the Dakota Territory. See Utley, *Indian Frontier* 150–51.

84. In March 1871, Grant authorized Ely Parker to invite Cochise to Washington for talks similar to those held with Red Cloud. The invitation was dispatched on March 18, 1871, Cochise was located, and the invitation delivered in late June, but the chief declined, noting his distrust of military officers with whom he might come in contact. It is unquestionably a tribute to Howard that he won Cochise's confidence. See 22 *Grant Papers* 66–67 notes. For Howard's report of his foray, see *My Life and Experience Among Our Hostile Indians* 186–225 (Hartford, Conn.: A. D. Wothington, 1907); *Annual Report of the Commissioner of Indian Affairs, 1872* 175–78. Also see John Ford's *Rio Grande*, the third of Ford's cavalry trilogy, in which John Wayne, as Colonel Kirby Yorke, performs a similar feat.

85. See especially Richard N. Ellis, "The Humanitarian Generals," 3 *Western Historical Quarterly* 169–78 (April 1972), as well as his earlier "The Humanitarian Soldiers," 10 *Journal of Arizona History* 53–66 (Summer 1969).

86. Hutton, *Phil Sheridan* 230. Also see Wilbur S. Nye, *Carbine and Lance: The Story of Old Fort Sill* 111 (Norman: University of Oklahoma Press, 1937).

87. Richard N. Ellis, *General Pope and U.S. Indian Policy* (Albuquerque: University of New Mexico Press, 1970).

88. Crook to Herbert Welsh, July 3, 1885, quoted in Prucha, *American Indian Policy* 100. Also see James T. King, "George Crook: Indian Fighter and Humanitarian," *Arizona and the West* 333–48 (Winter 1967).

89. Hutton, *Phil Sheridan* 129.

90. Grant to George H. Stuart, October 26, 1872, 23 *Grant Papers* 270.

91. Love to Grant, November 2, 1872, ibid. 271 note.

92. L. S. Williams to Grant, November 14, 1872, ibid.

93. Grant received 66.5 percent of the vote in Kansas, 70.7 percent in Nebraska, and 61.4 percent in Minnesota. In Nevada he received 57.4 percent, and 58.8 percent in Oregon. In Texas, 41.4 percent. Nationally, Grant won 55.6 percent of the popular vote to Horace Greeley's 43.8 percent.

Congressional Quarterly's Guide to U.S. Elections 274 (Washington, D.C.: Congressional Quarterly, 1975).

94. Sherman to Canby, January 31, 1873, *Official Modoc War Correspondence* 65, House Exec. Doc. No. 122, 43rd Cong., 1st sess.

95. Sherman to Canby, March 13, 1873, ibid.

96. Alfred B. Meacham, *Wigwam and Warpath* (Boston: John P. Dale, 1875).

97. Sherman to Gillem, April 12, 1873, *Modoc War Correspondence* 77.

98. Ibid.

99. *New York Times,* April 15, 1873.

100. Ibid. In his *Memoirs,* Grant, who did not bestow praise promiscuously, called Canby an officer of great merit. "His character was as pure as his talent and learning were great." 2 *Personal Memoirs of U.S. Grant* 763 (New York: Charles L. Webster, 1885).

101. The Modocs lived quietly as productive farmers in the Indian Territory until 1909, when they were allowed to return to the Klamath Reservation in southern Oregon. Prucha, *American Indian Policy* 88.

102. *New York Herald, New York World,* April 13, 14, 1873; *Boston Daily Globe,* April 14, 1873.

103. *Daily Colorado Miner,* April 22, 1873.

104. *New York Times,* April 15, 1873.

105. Ibid. April 14, 1873.

106. Slattery, *Felix Reville Brunot* 212–13.

107. *Annual Report of the Secretary of War,* 1873 42, 43rd Cong., 1st sess., House Exec. Doc. No. 1.

108. *Annual Report of the Commissioners of Indian Affairs, 1873* 3, 9 ibid.

109. James L. Harley, *The Buffalo War: The History of the Red River Indian Uprising of 1874* 101–2 (Garden City, N.Y.: Doubleday, 1976).

110. For the squabble between Sheridan and Pope, which quickly became public, see Hutton, *Phil Sheridan* 246–48; Ellis, *General Pope* 183–85.

111. Telephone coversation, JES–John Y. Simon, October 19, 1999.

112. Sheridan to Major General Alfred H. Terry, November 11, 1875; Sheridan to Sherman, November 13, 1875, Sheridan Papers, Box 39.

113. Hutton, *Phil Sheridan* 299.

114. Ibid. 308.

115. Sheridan to Sherman, July 7, 1876, ibid. 310.

116. *New York Times,* July 7, 1876.

117. *Boston Daily Advertiser,* July 8, 1876.

118. *New York Times,* July 12, 1876.

119. *Boulder News,* July 7, 1876.

120. *The Nation,* July 13, 1876.

121. Bishop Whipple to Grant, July 31, 1876, quoted in Mardock, *Reformers and the American Indian* 147–48.

122. Utley, *Indian Frontier* 154 55.

123. *Reports of Inspection Made in the Summer of 1877 by Generals P. H. Sheridan and W. T. Sherman of Country North of the Union Pacific Railroad* 5 (Washington, D.C.: Government Printing Office, 1878).

CHAPTER EIGHTEEN: RECONSTRUCTION REVISITED

The epigraph is from Grant's message to Congress upon the ratification of the Fifteenth Amendment, March 30, 1870. 20 *The Papers of Ulysses S. Grant* 130–31, John Y. Simon, ed. (Carbondale: Southern Illinois University Press, 1992).

1. William S. McFeely, *Grant: A Biography* 365–66 (New York: W. W. Norton, 1981). Also see James M. McPherson, *Ordeal by Fire* 559, 2nd ed. (New York: McGraw-Hill, 1992).

2. William S. McFeely, "Amos T. Akerman: The Lawyer for Racial Justice," in J. Morgan Kousser and James M. McPherson, eds., *Region, Race, and Reconstruction* 395 (New York: Oxford University Press, 1982).

3. On April 1, 1870, two days after ratification, Grant told a Republican audience in Washington that "there has been no event since the close of the war in which I have felt so deep an interest as that of the ratification of the Fifteenth Amendment. I have felt the greatest anxiety ever since I have been in this house to know that that was to be secured. It looked to me as the realization of the Declaration of Independence." 20 *Grant Papers* 137.

4. Eric Foner, *A Short History of Reconstruction* 193 (New York: Harper and Row, 1990).

5. James M. McPherson, *The Struggle for Equality* 429 (Princeton: Princeton University Press, 1964).

6. Foner, *Short History of Reconstruction* 184.

7. Act of May 31, 1870, 16 *United States Statutes at Large* 140–46. The act forbade state officials from discriminating among voters on the basis of race or color in the application of local election laws; outlawed force, bribery, threats, and intimidation of voters; and made it a misdemeanor to deprive a citizen of employment or occupation in order to control his vote. Most important, the law prohibited disguised groups from going "upon the public highways, or upon the premises of another" with intent to interfere with constitutional liberties.

8. Ross A. Webb, "Benjamin H. Bristow: Civil Rights Champion, 1866–1872," 15 *Civil War History* 39 (1969).

9. Akerman to Foster Blodgett, November 8, 1871, quoted in Eric Foner, *Reconstruction: America's Unfinished Revolution* 457 (New York: Macmillan, 1988).

10. On July 20, 1870, Governor William W. Holden of North Carolina wrote Grant urgently requesting federal troops to suppress the Klan. Grant instructed Belknap to dispatch six infantry companies immediately. To Holden, he wrote: "Your favor of the 20th *inst.* detailing the unsettled and threatening condition of North Carolina is just received, and I will telegraph the Sec. of War immediately, to send more troops to the State without delay. They will be used to suppress violence and to maintain the law if other means should fail." Grant [in Long Branch, New Jersey] to Holden, July 22, 1870, 20 *Grant Papers* 210.

11. Stephen Cresswell, "Enforcing the Enforcement Acts: The Department of Justice in Northern Mississippi, 1870–1890" 53 *Journal of Southern History* 423 (1987). Cresswell takes care to point out that traditional histories of the 1870s, generally written in the "William A. Dunning School" of white redemption, woefully understate the federal conviction rate in north Mississippi. Ibid. 421 note. Also see Everette Swinney, "Enforcing the Fifteenth Amendment, 1870–1877" 28 *Journal of Southern History* 203–7 (1962). Professor Dunning's principal work, *Reconstruction: Political and Economic, 1865–1877* (New York: Harper, 1907), set the tone for the dominant stream of anti-black historiography.

12. Francis Butler Simkins and Robert Hilliard Woody, *South Carolina During Reconstruction* 446ff. (Chapel Hill: University of North Carolina Press, 1934).

13. Holden to Grant, July 1, 1871, 21 *Grant Papers* 151 note.

14. Act of February 28, 1871, 16 *United States Statutes at Large* 433–40.

15. Grant to Blaine, March 9, 1871, 21 *Grant Papers* 218–19.

16. *The Nation,* March 23, 1871.

17. *Congressional Globe* 575–79, 42nd Cong., 1st sess.

18. See, for example, James A. Garfield to Jacob D. Cox, March 23, 1871, 21 *Grant Papers* 247–48 note.

19. *Philadelphia Public Ledger,* March 24, 1871.

20. Grant to Congress, March 23, 1871, 21 *Grant Papers* 246. Also see George F. Hoar, 1 *Autobiography of Seventy Years* 205–6 (New York: Charles Scribner's Sons, 1963); George S. Boutwell, 2 *Reminiscences of Sixty Years in Public Affairs* 252 (New York: McClure, Phillips, 1907).

21. Act of April 20, 1871, 17 *United States Statutes at Large* 13–15. The final Senate vote on the conference report was 36–13, Republicans voting yes, Democrats no. Twenty-one senators did not vote, including Schurz, Trumbull, and Sumner, though Sumner was paired in favor. *Congressional Globe* 836, 42nd Cong., 2nd sess. (1872).

22. Presidential Proclamation, May 3, 1871, 21 *Grant Papers* 336–37.

23. Grant to Belknap, May 13, 1871, ibid. 355.

24. Presidential Proclamation, October 17, 1871, 22 ibid. 176–78.

25. Akerman to B. Silliman, March 9, 1871, Akerman Papers, University of Virginia.

26. McPherson, *Ordeal by Fire* 560.

27. Foner, *Reconstruction: America's Unfinished Revolution* 458–59.

28. Akerman to Garnet Andrews, July 31, 1871, Akerman Papers.

29. McPherson, *Ordeal by Fire* 560.

30. *National Republican,* January 19, 1872.

31. Letters to William Chandler, secretary of the Republican National committee, from E. L. Sullivan (California) March 16, 1872; A. J. Ransier (South Carolina), March 16, 1872; D. R. Anthony (Kansas), March 25, 1872; Russell Scott (Pennsylvania), March 26, 1872; George Foster (Indiana), April 3, 1872; S. E. Phillips (North Carolina), March 23, 1872; C. W. B. Allison (West Virginia), April 3, 1872; T. B. Van Buren (New Jersey), March 29, 1872. William E. Chandler Papers, Library of Congress.

32. *New York Times,* April 11, 1872; Douglass to Cassius M. Clay, July 26, 1871, Frederick Douglass Papers, Frederick Douglass Memorial Home, Washington, D.C.

33. See, for example, Irving Katz, *August Belmont: A Political Biography* 198 (New York: Random House, 1968).
34. 2 *Speeches, Correspondence, and Political Papers of Carl Schurz* 359, Frederic Bancroft, ed. (New York: G. P. Putnam's Sons, 1913).
35. Greeley's views are detailed in a lengthy chapter entitled "Sewage" in his book, *What I Know of Farming* (New York: Tribune Association, 1871). "The application of sewage is in its infancy, since the perfect and total conversion of all that a city excretes into the most available food for plants, requires not only immense mains and reservoirs, with a costly network of distributing dykes or ditches, but novel appliances in engineering, and a large investment of time as well as money. Years must yet elapse before all the excretions of a great city like London or New York can thus be transmuted into the means of fertilizing whole counties in their vicinity" (pages 268–69).
36. William B. Hesseltine, *Ulysses S. Grant: Politician* 274 (New York: Dodd, Mead, 1935). Cox to Garfield, May 10, 1872, Garfield Papers, Library of Congress. Charles A. Dana, editor of the *New York Sun,* called Greeley "a visionary without faith, a radical without root, an extremist without persistency, a strifemaker without courage." Quoted in William Gillette, "Election of 1872," in Arthur M. Schlesinger, Jr., ed., 2 *History of American Presidential Elections* 1314 (New York: Mc-Graw-Hill, 1971).
37. Horace Greeley, *Mr. Greeley's Letters from Texas and the Lower Mississippi* 48–53 (New York: Tribune Office, 1871).
38. Gillette, "Election of 1872" 1335–36.
39. George W. Childs, *Recollections* 75 (Philadelphia: Collins Printing House, 1890).
40. Grant to Roscoe Conkling, July 15, 1872, Conkling Papers, Library of Congress.
41. For Sumner's letters, see 15 *The Works of Charles Sumner* 175–95. (Boston: Lee and Shepard, 1883). Child's reply, July 28, 1872, is among the Sumner Papers in the Library of Congress.
42. Articles by Garrison in the *Independent* January 4, April 4, 1872, quoted in James M. McPherson, "Grant or Greeley: The Abolitionist Dilemma in the Election of 1872," 71 *American Historical Review* 49 (1965).
43. Ibid. 50; Foner, *Reconstruction: America's Unfinished Revolution* 507.
44. Garfield diary, October 18, 1872, Garfield Papers.
45. Gillette, "Election of 1872" 1328.
46. Second Inaugural, March 4, 1873, 7 *Messages and Papers of the Presidents* 223, James D. Richardson, ed. (Washington, D.C.: Bureau of National Literature and Art, 1908).
47. For the reports of the investigation of the Crédit Mobilier affair, see the "Poland Report" (Representative Luke Poland of Vermont chaired the House investigation), and the "Wilson Report" (Senator J. M. Wilson of Iowa chaired the Senate inquiry), both 42nd Cong., 2nd sess.
48. Fifth Annual Message to Congress, December 1, 1873, Richardson, 7 *Messages and Papers of the Presidents* 242. Also see Louis A. Coolidge, *Ulysses S. Grant* 435–37 (Boston: Houghton Mifflin, 1917).
49. For the details surrounding Richardson's appointment, see Allan Nevins, 2 *Hamilton Fish: The Inner History of the Grant Administration* 697–99 (New York: Frederick Ungar, 1957). Fish opposed Richardson's appointment, and even Boutwell was skeptical. "I am at a loss to know who else can be named," Fish quotes Boutwell as saying. Ibid. 698.
50. Adam Badeau, *Grant in Peace* 406. (Harford, Conn.: Scranton, 1887).
51. Mrs. Archibald Dixon, *True Story of the Missouri Compromise and Its Repeal* 273–74 (Cincinnati: R. Clarke, 1903).
52. Hesseltine, *Ulysses S. Grant* 303.
53. John M. Berry, *Rising Tide: The Great Mississippi Flood of 1927 and How It Changed America* 64 (New York: Simon and Schuster, 1997).
54. Ibid. 57.
55. For details of the meeting with Grant, see William Taussig, "Personal Recollections of General Grant," 2 *Missouri Historical Society Publications* 1–13 (1903).
56. In November 1864 Hancock's Gettysburg wounds were giving him such trouble that he could no longer actively command the 2nd Corps. By order of the secretary of war he was relieved and ordered to Washington to organize and command a corps of veterans. Grant ordered Humphreys to take the 2nd Corps in Hancock's place. Ulysses S. Grant 2 *Memoirs* 631 (New York: Charles L. Webster, 1885).
57. Taussig, "Personal Recollections of General Grant."
58. Berry, *Rising Tide* 65.
59. Lawrence Wodehouse, "General Grant Architecture in Jeopardy!," 22 *Historic Preservation* 20–26 (1970). Also see Wodehouse, "Alfred B. Mullett and His French Style of Government Buildings," 31 *Journal of the Society of Architectural Historians* 22–37 (March 1972); S. Allen Chambers, John

Poppeliers, and Nancy B. Schwartz, *What Style Is It?* 23 (Washington, D.C.: Preservation Press, 1979).

60. Telephone conversation, JES—Professor Douglas Richardson, University of Toronto, November 15, 1999.

61. Donald H. Lehman, *Executive Office Building* 36–37 (Washington, D.C.: General Services Administration, 1964). "That the building was designed and constructed in the French Second Empire style in deliberate contrast to the classical style of government buildings constructed before the Civil War implied that the government of the newly reunited nation perceived itself as different from the government that had represented the young republic. In style and size, the new State, War, and Navy Building equaled and rivaled its European counterparts and expressed the ambitious aspirations of the American republic that had endured and was expanding across the continent." Elsa M. Santoyo, ed., *Creating an American Masterpiece: Architectural Drawings of the Old Executive Office Building* 5 (Washington, D.C.: Executive Office of the President, 1988).

62. Mullett resigned November 21, 1874, after a falling out with Treasury Secretary Benjamin H. Bristow concerning disbursement accounts. Mullett proved to be clean as a hound's tooth. Wodehouse, "Alfred B. Mullett" 34–36.

63. For a compilation of Mullett's works see "Alfred B. Mullett," *Macmillian Encyclopedia of Architects* 251–52, Adolph H. Placzek, ed. (New York: Free Press, 1982).

64. Annual Report of the Supervising Architect, 1868, quoted in Bates Lowry, *Building a National Image: Architectural Drawings for the American Democracy, 1789–1912* 58 (Washington, D.C.: National Building Museum, 1985).

65. Congress considers the old State, War, and Navy Building a national monument, wrote former Secretary of State Dean Acheson. "Congress does not entertain the same sentiment about those who have inhabited it." *Present at the Creation* 9 (New York: W. W. Norton, 1969). Also see Wodehouse, "General Grant Architecture in Jeopardy" 21.

66. 6 Wallace 50 (1868). Nelson also wrote the original majority opinion in *Dred Scott v. Sandford,* 19 Howard 393 (1857), disposing of the case on narrow procedural grounds. Had Nelson's opinion prevailed as the opinion of the Court, the *Dred Scott* case would be all but forgotten.

67. Grant to Conkling, November 8, 1873, quoted in David M. Jordan, *Roscoe Conkling of New York: Voice in the Senate* 199 (Ithaca, N.Y.: Cornell University Press, 1971).

68. Ibid.

69. Ibid. 145.

70. Thomas Collier Platt, *The Autobiography of Thomas Collier Platt* 67–68, Louis J. Lang, ed. (New York: B. W. Dodge, 1910).

71. Nevins, 2 *Hamilton Fish* 661.

72. John Marshall, *An Autobiographical Sketch* 30, John Stokes Adams, ed. (Ann Arbor: University of Michigan Press, 1937); also see Jean Edward Smith, *John Marshall: Definer of a Nation* 14–15 (New York: Henry Holt, 1996).

73. Nevins, 2 *Hamilton Fish* 661–62.

74. *The Nation,* December 11, 1873.

75. *New York Tribune,* December 6, 15, 1873.

76. Nevins, 2 *Hamilton Fish* 662; Jordan, *Roscoe Conkling* 202.

77. C. H. Hill to Benjamin Bristow, December 13, 19, 1873, quoted in McFeely, *Grant* 390.

78. Nevins, 2 *Hamilton Fish* 663.

79. Tom Murphy in *The Nation,* January 22, 1874.

80. Nevins, 2 *Hamilton Fish* 664.

81. Cushing's letter to Davis was found in the Confederate archives, which the government had purchased in 1872. *New York Tribune* January 10, 1874.

82. For Grant's second approach to Conkling, see Jordan, *Roscoe Conkling* 203, and the sources cited therein.

83. Nevins, 2 *Hamilton Fish* 665.

84. *The Nation* January 27, 1874, quoted in Charles Warren, 2 *The Supreme Court in United States History* 578 (Boston: Little Brown, 1922).

85. 2 Otto [92 U.S.] 214 (1876).

86. 2 Otto [92 U.S.] 542 (1876).

87. *United States v. Reese,* 2 Otto [92 U.S.] 214, 253 (1876). (Dissent).

88. Foner, *Reconstruction: America's Unfinished Revolution* 530.

89. For a concise account of the Colfax Massacre, see George C. Rable, *But There Was No Peace: The Role of Violence in the Politics of Reconstruction* 126–29 (Athens: University of Georgia Press, 1984).

90. William Gillette, *Retreat from Reconstruction: 1869–1879* 107 (Baton Rouge: Louisiana State University Press, 1979).

91. *New Orleans Bulletin,* September 16, 1874; Boyd to Sherman, September 16, 1874, Walter L. Fleming Collection, Louisiana State University.
92. Richardson, 7 *Messages and Papers of the Presidents* 276.
93. *New York Tribune,* September 18, 1874.
94. Sixth Annual Message to Congress, December 7, 1874, Richardson, 7 *Messages and Papers of the Presidents* 299.
95. *Senate Exec. Doc.* No. 17, 43rd Cong., 2nd sess. 19–20, 65–66.
96. Sheridan to Belknap, January 2, 1875, Sheridan Papers, Library of Congress. (Emory was sixty-three.)
97. Ibid.
98. Rable, *But There Was No Peace* 141.
99. Sheridan to Belknap, January 4, 1875, Division of the Missouri, Letters Sent, R.G. 393, U.S. Army, National Archives.
100. Ibid. January 5, 1875.
101. Belknap to Sheridan, January 6, 1875, Sheridan Papers.
102. James M. McPherson, *The Abolitionist Legacy: From Reconstruction to the NAACP,* 40–41 (Princeton: Princeton University Press, 1975).
103. *Congressional Record* 331, 367–71, 43rd Cong., 2nd sess; Richard O'Conner, *Sheridan the Inevitable* 330 (Indianapolis: Bobbs-Merrill, 1953).
104. "Some of the Banditti made idle threats last night that they would assassinate me," Sheridan wired Belknap on January 6. "I am not afraid and will not be stopped from informing the government that there are localities in this Department where the very air has been impregnated with assassination for some years." Sheridan Papers.
105. Message to the Senate, January 13, 1875, Richardson 7 *Messages and Papers of the Presidents* 305–14.
106. Sheridan to Belknap, January 10, 1875, Sheridan Papers.
107. *House Report* 127, 43rd Cong., 2nd sess. (1875).
108. Hoar, *Autobiography* 208ff.
109. Sheridan to Belknap, February 24, 1875, Sheridan Papers. Sheridan and Irene Rucker were married in a private ceremony in Chicago, June 3, 1875.
110. Sheridan to Orville Babcock, January 24, 1875, Sheridan Papers.
111. Rable, *But There Was No Peace* 143.
112. James C. McPherson, *Ordeal by Fire* 583.
113. T. Wilson [U.S. consul, Nuremberg] to Lucius C. Fairchild, January 17, 1875, Fairchild Papers, State Historical Society of Wisconsin Library.
114. The tone of American historiography concerning Reconstruction was set by William A. Dunning, Francis Lieber Professor of History and Political Philosophy at Columbia University. Between 1886 and 1922, Dunning directed the research of two generations of graduate students, edited the influential *Political Science Quarterly* for ten years, and was the only person to have been elected president of both the American Historical Association and the American Political Science Association.

  According to the 1930 *Dictionary of National Biography,* edited by Dumas Malone, "no one did more than Dunning to rewrite the history of the generation following the Civil War." Dunning saw Reconstruction in starkly racial terms and believed that white graduate students from the South were best qualified to write about it because of their personal experience and "empathy." Known as "the Dunning School," their works, all of which were published by Columbia University Press, include J. G. de Roulhac Hamilton's *Reconstruction in North Carolina* (1914), W. W. Davis's *The Civil War and Reconstruction in Florida* (1913), Walter L. Fleming's *The Civil War and Reconstruction in Alabama* (1905), Thomas S. Staples's *Reconstruction in Arkansas* (1923), and Charles W. Ramsdell's *Reconstruction in Texas* (1910).

  Lincoln biographer David Herbert Donald has described the work of the Dunning School as follows: "Researched from primary sources, factually accurate, and presented with an air of objectivity, these dissertations were acclaimed as triumphs of the application of the scientific method to historiography, and indeed they still provide our basic knowledge of the political history of the South during the postwar years. Yet, with every conscious desire to be fair, these students of Dunning shaped their monographs to accord with the white Southerner's view that the Negro was innately inferior....Consequently, the Dunning students generally condemned Negro participation in Southern Reconstruction governments, even while they condoned white terrorist organizations such as the Ku Klux Klan." [Donald's Introduction to Dunning's *Essays on the Civil War and Reconstruction* (Gloucester, Mass.: Peter Smith, 1969). Reprint.]

  The 1999 *American National Biography,* published under the auspices of the American Council of Learned Societies, is more critical. "Rather than seeing the abolitionists and radical Republicans as brave idealists coming to the aid of African Americans oppressed by traitorous rebels, these largely southern-born historians depicted a helpless white population tyrannized by ignorant blacks manipulated by venal northern carpetbaggers and southern scalawags."

Dunning's principal work, *Reconstruction: Political and Economic, 1865–1877* (New York: Harper, 1907), refers to "barbarous" freedmen committing "the hideous crime against white womanhood" and corrupt northern politicians willing to force opponents "of their own race...to permanent subjection to another race" (pp. 212–14). The widespread acceptance of the Dunning School's interpretation of Reconstruction reflected the prejudices of the period and the desire of most Northerners to conciliate the white South.

115. For a general review of the School Question, see Steven K. Green, "The Blaine Amendment Reconsidered," 36 *American Journal of Legal History* 38–69 (1992).

116. Sister Marie Carolyn Klinkhamer, "The Blaine Amendment of 1875: Private Motives for Political Action," 42 *Catholic Historical Review* 17 (1956). *Cf.,* Tyler Ambinder, "Ulysses S. Grant, Nativist," 43 *Civil War History* 120 (1977).

117. The text of Grant's speech to the Army of the Tennessee, Des Moines, Iowa, September 30, 1875, is reprinted in *Harper's Weekly,* October 30, 1875.

118. *New York Times, New York Tribune, Chicago Tribune,* October 1875; *The Index,* November 4, 1875.

119. Robert H. Keller, *American Protestantism and United States Indian Policy, 1869–82* 168 (Lincoln: University of Nebraska Press, 1983).

120. Richardson, 7 *Messages and Papers of the Presidents* 334.

121. Ibid. 334–35.

122. *New York Times,* December 8, 1875; *Harper's Weekly,* January 1, 1876; *Chicago Tribune,* December 8, 1875; *Catholic World* 705, February 1876.

123. *Catholic World* 434–35 (January 1876).

124. Green, "Blaine Amendment" 67–68. The text of the Blaine Amendment provided:

> No State shall make any law respecting an establishment of religion, or prohibiting the free exercise thereof; and no money raised by taxation in any State for the support of public schools, or derived from any public fund therefor, nor any public lands devoted thereto, shall ever be under the control of any religious sect or denomination; nor shall any money so raised or lands so devoted be divided between religious sects or denominations. This article shall not vest, enlarge, or diminish legislative power in the Congress.

125. John Russell Young, 2 *Around the World with General Grant* 359–65 (New York: American News, 1879).

CHAPTER NINETEEN: THE GILDED AGE

The epigraph is from a letter Hoar sent to Hamilton Fish commending Grant for his handling of the Hayes-Tilden crisis. Quoted in Allan Nevins, 2 *Hamilton Fish: The Inner History of the Grant Administration* 855 (New York: Frederick Ungar, 1937).

1. *New York Herald,* May 22, 1874.

2. William S. McFeely, *Grant: A Biography* 400–401 (New York: W. W. Norton, 1981).

3. Adam Badeau, *Grant In Peace* 411–12 (Hartford, Conn.: Scranton, 1887).

4. McFeely, *Grant* 401; Algernon Bertram Freeman-Mitford, Baron Redesdale, 2 *Memoirs* 516 (London: Hutchinson, 1915). Also see Catherine Clinton, *Fanny Kemble's Civil Wars* 130–33 (New York: Simon & Schuster, 2000).

5. William B. Hesseltine, *Ulysses S. Grant: Politician* 299 (New York: Dodd, Mead, 1935).

6. *New York World,* September 5, 1885.

7. Henrietta Melia Larson, *Jay Cooke: Private Banker* 291–95 (New York: Greenwood, 1968); *New York Times,* September 19, 1873.

8. *The Nation,* October 2, 1873.

9. Quoted in the *New York Tribune,* September 24, 1873.

10. Fish to Richardson, September 26, 1873, in Nevins, 2 *Hamilton Fish* 698.

11. Fifth Annual Message, December 1, 1873, 7 *Messages and Papers of the Presidents* 245–46, James D. Richardson, ed. (Washington, D.C.: Bureau of National Literature and Art, 1908).

12. Hesseltine, *Ulysses S. Grant* 332–33. Also see John Sherman, 1 *Recollections of Forty Years in the House, Senate, and Cabinet* 490 (New York: Werner, 1895).

13. Nevins, 2 *Hamilton Fish* 707–8.

14. *New York Tribune,* April 14, 18, 1874; *New York Times,* April 21, 1874.

15. Veto Message, April 22, 1874, 7 *Messages and Papers of the Presidents* 268–71.

16. Fish diary, April 21, 1874, in Nevins, 2 *Hamilton Fish* 712–13.

17. David M. Jordan, *Roscoe Conkling of New York* 208–9 (Ithaca, N.Y.: Cornell University Press, 1971). For the inflationist view, see James Pickett Jones, *John A. Logan: Stalwart Republican from Illinois* 76–78 (Tallahassee: University Presses of Florida, 1982). During his eight years in office, Grant vetoed ninety-three pieces of legislation. This was five more than his seventeen predecessors combined. Of the ninety-three, forty-five were regular vetoes and forty-eight were pocket vetoes. Only four of Grant's vetoes were overridden, and three of those involved private bills for the relief of particular individuals. By contrast, Andrew Johnson vetoed twenty-nine bills and was overridden fifteen times—virtually all on matters of public policy. *Presidential Vetoes, 1789–1988* 38–56, S. Pub. 102–12 (Washington, D.C.: Government Printing Office, 1992).

18. *The Diary of George Templeton Strong* 523, Allan Nevins and Milton Halsey Thomas, eds. (New York: Macmillan, 1952).

19. Pierrepont to Fish, April 23, 1874, quoted in Nevins, 2 *Hamilton Fish* 713.

20. Garfield to A. B. Hinsdale, April 23, 1874, quoted in Hesseltine, *Ulysses S. Grant* 336.

21. *New York Tribune, New York Times,* April 23, 1874; *Harper's Weekly,* April 30, 1874; *The Nation* May 5, 1874.

22. Fish to General L. Schuyler, April 25, 1874, in Nevins, 2 *Hamilton Fish* 714.

23. John Russell Young, 2 *Around the World with General Grant* 153 (New York: American News, 1879).

24. Sixth Annual Message to Congress, December 7, 1874. Richardson, 7 *Messages and Papers of the Presidents* 285–88.

25. Hesseltine, *Ulysses S. Grant* 340.

26. Special Message to the Senate, January 14, 1875, Richardson, 7 *Messages and Papers of the Presidents* 314–16.

27. McFeely, *Grant* 390. Also see Edwards Pierrepont to Bristow, December 2, 1873, Bristow Papers, Library of Congress.

28. Nevins, 2 *Hamilton Fish* 715–16.

29. Fish to Washburne, May 5, 1874; Washburne to Grant, May 7, 1874, ibid.

30. Jewell to Washburne, June 4, 1874, Washburne Papers, Library of Congress.

31. Levi P. Luckey to Washburne, July 3, 1874, ibid. Also see Nevins, 2 *Hamilton Fish* 720–21.

32. H. V. Boynton, "The Whiskey Ring," 123 *North American Review* (1876); John McDonald, *Secrets of the Great Whiskey Ring* (St. Louis: W. S. Bryan, 1880).

33. Bluford Wilson testimony in *Whiskey Frauds* 355, House Misc. Doc. 186, 44th Cong., 1st sess. Wilson, Bristow's assistant secretary, was present at the White House meeting with Grant. His version, given in sworn testimony, stands uncontradicted.

34. Nevins, 2 *Hamilton Fish* 768–69.

35. Fish diary, March 12, 1875.

36. Nevins, 2 *Hamilton Fish* 770–772.

37. *The Personal Memoirs of Julia Dent Grant* 185–86, John Y. Simon, ed. (Carbondale: Southern Illinois University Press, 1975).

38. Theodore Clark Smith, ed., 1 *The Life and Letters of James Abram Garfield* 583–84 (New Haven: Yale University Press, 1925).

39. Julia Dent Grant, *Personal Memoirs* 185–86.

40. *New York Times,* May 30, 1875.

41. *New York Tribune,* April 24, 1875.

42. Nevins, 2 *Hamilton Fish* 775.

43. Louis A. Coolidge, *Ulysses S. Grant* 474 (Boston: Houghton Mifflin, 1917).

44. Hesseltine, *Ulysses S. Grant* 377.

45. Young, 2 *Around the World* 365.

46. Ibid. 263. Accusations of corruption that attach to the Grant administration are in some measure a result of careless semantics. Much of what the reformist school of historiography has called corruption was merely the dominant mode of choosing government officials through the patronage system. "Scholars have tended to accept the judgment of the anti-Grant reformers that this system was inherently corrupt, but that is a very questionable conclusion, and reformers had ulterior, political motives for making the charge." Michael Les Benedict, "Ulysses S. Grant," in 2 *The American Presidents* 376, Frank N. Magill, ed. (Pasadena: Salem Press, 1989).

Professor Ari Hoogenboom, a leading scholar of civil service reform, concurs: "The typical historian has been too loose in applying the term 'corruption.' Specifically, he labels a partisan civil service corrupt rather than inefficient; he equates the spoils system with corruption when honest spoilsmen far outnumber dishonest ones." "Spoilsmen and Reformers: Civil Service Reform and Public Morality," in *The Gilded Age: A Reappraisal* 71, H. Wayne Morgan, ed. (Syracuse, N.Y.: Syracuse University Press, 1963).

47. Young, 2 *Around the World* 265.
48. Ari Hoogenboom, "Thomas A. Jenckes and Civil Service Reform" 47 *Mississippi Valley Historical Review* 636–42 (1966).
49. *New York Times,* January 18, 1866.
50. Coolidge, *Ulysses S. Grant* 399; Bing to Jenckes, October 27, 1868, Jenckes Papers, Library of Congress *The Nation,* December 10, 31, 1868.
51. *Congressional Globe* 212–66, 40th Cong., 3rd sess. (January 8, 1869). During the previous session Logan had introduced a bill calling for the creation of a Civil Service Bureau to examine candidates for federal employment. *Congressional Globe* 366, 806, 40th Cong., 2nd sess. (January 8, 28, 1868).
52. Young, 2 *Around the World* 265.
53. Second Annual Message, December 5, 1870, Richardson, 7 *Messages and Papers of the Presidents* 109.
54. *Congressional Globe* 1935, 41st Cong., 3rd sess. (March 3, 1871).
55. "Rules for the Civil Service," Grant to Congress, December 19, 1871, Richardson, 7 *Messages and Papers of the Presidents* 156–59.
56. Grant to Medill, February 1, 1872, 23 *Grant Papers* 3–4.
57. Sixth Annual Message, December 7, 1874, Richardson, 7 *Messages and Papers of the Presidents* 301.
58. Hoogenboom, "Thomas A. Jenckes and Civil Service Reform" 639, 658.
59. Coolidge, *Ulysses S. Grant* 403–4.
60. *Whiskey Frauds* 186, 349, 357ff; Coolidge, *Ulysses S. Grant* 479; Nevins, 2 *Hamilton Fish* 788. Emphasis added.
61. *Whiskey Frauds* 11, 30, 485; Coolidge, *Ulysses S. Grant* 483.
62. The text of the two telegrams is reprinted in Hesseltine, *Ulysses S. Grant* 788, and McFeely, *Grant* 409.
63. Hesseltine, *Ulysses S. Grant* 384–85; Coolidge, *Ulysses S. Grant* 480; Nevins, 2 *Hamilton Fish* 788–89; McFeely, *Grant* 410.
64. McFeely, *Grant* 416.
65. Jones, *John A. Logan* 87–88.
66. Hesseltine, *Ulysses S. Grant* 385; Nevins, 2 *Hamilton Fish* 797–98, 800–1; Geoffrey Perret, *Ulysses S. Grant: Soldier and President* 443–44 (New York: Random House, 1997).
67. Nevins, 2 *Hamilton Fish* 790–93; McFeely, *Grant* 411–12.
68. Deposition of the President of the United States, February 12, 1876, reprinted in full in *New York Times,* February 18, 1876. I am indebted to Sam Mok of the University of Minnesota for locating this document.
69. John Russell Young, *Men and Memories* 369 (New York: F. Tennyson Neely, 1901).
70. *New York Tribune,* February 25, 1876. The *New York Times, The Nation,* and the *Springfield Republican* were equally effusive. The *Times* went on to report "a continuance of the hearty cooperation of the President in the Secretary [of the Treasury]'s fight with the whiskey thieves." February 25, 1876.
71. Grant to Bristow, March 6, 1876, in Coolidge, *Ulysses S. Grant* 486. Inexplicably, Bristow continued his refusal to testify, despite being authorized by Grant to do so.
72. *Malfeasance of W. W. Belknap, Late Secretary of War,* 44th Cong., House Report 186, March 2, 1876. In sworn testimony before the House committee, Marsh stated, "The money was sent according to the instructions of the Secretary of War; sometimes in bank notes...I think on more than one occasion by certificates of deposit on the National Bank of America in New York. Sometimes I paid him in New York in person." Ibid. 3–4.
73. Nevins, 2 *Hamilton Fish* 805.
74. Ross A. Webb, *Benjamin Helm Bristow: Border State Politician* 223–25 (Lexington: University of Kentucky Press, 1969); Garfield 3 *Diary* 243–44, March 3, 1876.
75. Julia Dent Grant, *Personal Memoirs* 190. Compare Perret, *Ulysses S. Grant* 437.
76. Nevins, 2 *Hamilton Fish* 805.
77. Julia Dent Grant, *Personal Memoirs* 191; Hesseltine, *Ulysses S. Grant* 396.
78. *Congressional Record,* Impeachment Proceedings, 344, August 1, 1876. Also see *Report of the House Managers on the Impeachment of W. W. Belknap,* House Report 791, August 2, 1876, 44th Cong. In late May, when the issue of jurisdiction was first raised, the Senate voted 37–29 (all Democrats voting in favor) to assume jurisdiction. The impeachment vote was 37–25 to convict, twenty-three senators voting against because they believed the Senate lacked jurisdiction. Jordan, *Roscoe Conkling* 224; cf. Nevins 2 *Hamilton Fish* 809–10.
79. James A. Garfield, 3 *The Diary of James A. Garfield* 243–44, Harry J. Brown and Frederick D. Williams, eds. (East Lansing: Michigan State University Press, 1973).
80. Nevins, 2 *Hamilton Fish* 805; Julia Dent Grant, *Personal Memoirs* 190–92.

81. *New York Times, New York Herald, New York Tribune,* March 4, 1876; Nevins, 2 *Hamilton Fish* 829. Judge Taft was the father of William Howard Taft, twenty-seventh president of the United States, and tenth chief justice of the United States.
82. Young, 2 *Around the World* 273–75.
83. Webb, *Benjamin Helm Bristow* 248.
84. Grant to Hayes, June 16, 1876, Grant Papers, Carbondale, Illinois.
85. Webb, *Bristow* 251; McFeely, *Grant* 441.
86. Grant to Bristow, June 19, 1876, Grant Papers.
87. Coolidge, *Ulysses S. Grant* 499.
88. Nevins, 2 *Hamilton Fish* 840–41.
89. Grant to Chamberlain, July 26, 1876, Grant Papers.
90. Proclamation, October 17, 1876, Richardson, 7 *Messages and Papers of the Presidents* 396–97.
91. *New York Times, Evening Post,* October 18, 1876.
92. George W. Childs, *Recollections of General Grant* 10 (Philadelphia: Collins, 1885).
93. Grant to Sherman, November 8, 1876, Grant Papers.
94. Paul Leland Haworth, *The Hayes-Tilden Disputed Election of 1876* 68, 113–14 (Indianapolis: Bobbs-Merrill, 1927).
95. Nevins, 2 *Hamilton Fish* 853.
96. Ibid. 844–45.
97. Garfield, 1 *Diary* 614; Grant to Garfield, November 15, 1868, Grant Papers.
98. Coolidge, *Ulysses S. Grant* 506–7.
99. James M. McPherson, *Ordeal by Fire* 589, 2nd ed. (New York: McGraw-Hill, 1992).
100. John Sherman, 2 *Recollections of Forty Years* 558.
101. In 1865 Congress had adopted a joint rule (22) that required the concurrence of both Houses to count the electoral vote from a state. But the rule expired in 1875 and the House and Senate had not been able to agree on anything to take its place.
102. Fish diary, November 14, 1876, in Nevins, 2 *Hamilton Fish* 844.
103. Ibid. 848.
104. Hoar to Fish, January 25, 1877, Fish Papers, quoted ibid. 855.
105. Hesseltine, *Ulysses S. Grant* 418–19; Ellis Paxson Oberholtzer, 3 *A History of the United States Since the Civil War* 292–94 (New York: Macmillan, 1916); Haworth, *Hayes-Tilden Disputed Election* 122–28.
106. The House members of the joint committee were Democrats Henry Payne (Ohio), Eppa Hunton (Va.), Abram Hewitt (N.Y.), and W. M. Springer (Ill.); Republicans George McCrary (Pa.), George F. Hoar (Mass.), and George Willard (Mich.). From the Senate, Republicans George Edmunds (Vt.), Oliver P. Morton (Ind.), Frederick Frelinghuysen (N.J.), and Roscoe Conkling (N.Y.), taking the place of John Logan, who declined to serve. The Senate Democrats were Allen G. Thurman (Ohio), Thomas Bayard (Del.), and M. W. Ransom (N.C.)
107. Jordan, *Roscoe Conkling* 255, reflecting Grant's conversation with George W. Childs of Philadelphia.
108. Ibid. 257. Conkling's speech is in *Congressional Record* 825–31; 870–78, 44th Cong., 2nd sess. (1877).
109. In the House, 159 Democrats and thirty-two Republicans voted in favor; eighteen Democrats and sixty-eight Republicans voted against. In the Senate, twenty-six Democrats and twenty-one Republicans voted yes; sixteen Republicans and one Democrat voted no.
110. Message to Congress, January 29, 1877, Richardson, 7 *Messages and Papers of the Presidents* 422–24.
111. Young, 2 *Around the World* 271–72.
112. C. Vann Woodward, *Reunion and Reaction: The Compromise of 1877 and the End of Reconstruction* 23, rev. ed. (New York: Doubleday, 1956); Harry Barnard, *Rutherford B. Hayes and His America* 343 (Indianapolis: Bobbs-Merrill, 1956).
113. A Southern Democrat told Garfield they would not follow their Northern colleagues who were "invincible in peace and invisible in war." McPherson, *Ordeal by Fire* 591. Also see Coolidge, *Ulysses S. Grant* 516.
114. Hesseltine, *Ulysses S. Grant* 421. Also see Rhodes, 7 *History of the United States* 291–350; Haworth, *Hayes-Tilden Disputed Election* 162–65.
115. *New York Herald,* March 25, 1877.
116. Badeau, *Grant in Peace* 252. In 1821, March 4 also fell on a Sunday. This was the end of James Monroe's first term and the beginning of his second. With little at stake, Chief Justice Marshall recommended postponing the oath until Monday, March 5, "unless some official duty should require its being taken on Sunday." Marshall to Monroe, February 20, 1821, 9 *The Papers of John Marshall.* Charles F. Hobson, ed. (Chapel Hill: University of North Carolina Press, 1996).

117. Julia Dent Grant, *Personal Memoirs* 196.
118. *Chicago Tribune,* September 1, 1885.
119. Young, 2 *Around the World* 272.
120. Garfield, 3 *Diary* 453–54, March 5, 1877.

CHAPTER TWENTY: TAPS

The epigraph is from a letter Sherman wrote to Badeau, June 27, 1877. Adam Badeau, *Grant in Peace,* 122–23 (Hartford, Conn.: Scranton, 1887).

1. Grant to Fish, March 22, 1877, quoted in Allan Nevins, 2 *Hamilton Fish: The Inner History of the Grant Administration* 893, rev. ed. (New York: Frederick Ungar, 1957).
2. House of Representatives Resolution, April 3, 1876. For Grant's hard-edged response, May 4, 1876, including an appendix providing details of travel by his predecessors, see *Messages and Papers of the Presidents* 361–66, James D. Richardson, ed. (Washington, D.C.: Bureau of National Literature and Art, 1908).
3. Badeau, *Grant in Peace* 297.
4. Lowell to Charles Eliot Norton, in *Letters of James Russell Lowell* 233, Charles Eliot Norton, ed. (New York: Harper and Brothers, 1894).
5. Young's accounts were collected and published by the American News Company in two volumes, *Around the World with General Grant,* which appeared in 1879.
6. 1 ibid. 468. Also see Grant to Fish, August 22, 1878. "When I called [at the Summer Palace] the Emperor approached me and taking me by the hand led me to a seat, after which we had a talk of twenty minutes or more. I tell you this because we both had serious apprehensions that the case would be quite different." Nevins, 2 *Hamilton Fish* 895.
7. Young, 1 *Around the World* 416.
8. Ibid. 365–68.
9. Ibid. 416–17.
10. Most of the elder statemen attending the Congress were suffering badly from gout, and the menu of the dinner Bismarck gave for Grant suggests why:

Potage mulligatawny	Poulardes de Bruxelles
Pâtes à la financière	Salade
Turbot d'Ostende a l'Anglaise	Compotes
Quartier de boeuf a la Hosteinaise	Fonds d'artichauts a la Hollandaise
Canetons aux olives	Pain de fraises à la Chantilly
Ris de veau a la Milanaise	Glaces
Punch romain	Dessert

Young, 1 *Around the World* 420.
11. Julia Dent Grant, *The Personal Memoirs of Julia Dent Grant* 246, John Y. Simon, ed. (Carbondale: Southern Illinois University Press, 1975).
12. Ibid. The purpose of the Congress was to modify the terms of the Treaty of San Stefano, concluded by Turkey (under duress) with Russia, March 23, 1878. With the Russian army at the gates of Constantinople, Turkey conceded several Asian provinces to Russia, recognized the autonomy of Bulgaria, and granted independence to Romania and Serbia. The great powers believed the terms excessive, and intervened on the sultan's behalf.
13. Young, *Around the World* 219–20
14. Grant to Nellie Sartoris, August 10, 1879, Grant Papers, Carbondale, Illinois.
15. Grant to Badeau, July 16, 1879, reprinted in Badeau, *Grant in Peace* 516–17. Writing from Japan, Grant told Badeau that the Chinese "Liked Americans better, or rather perhaps hate them less, than any other foreigners. The reason is palpable. We are the only power that recognize their right to control their own internal affairs. My impression is that China is on the verge of a great revolution that will land her among the nations of progress." June 22, 1879, ibid. 515–16.
16. Grant to Badeau, August 1, August 25, 1879, ibid. 517–19. Grant's reference to "the last twelve years" pertains to the time from the date of the Meiji restoration in 1868.
17. The text of Grant's remarks is ibid. 603–4.
18. Ibid. 629–30.
19. Harry Barnard, *Rutherford B. Hayes and His America* 487 (Indianapolis: Bobbs-Merrill, 1954).
20. *St. Louis Globe Democrat; New York Tribune,* July 22, 1878.
21. Babcock to Badeau, undated, Babcock Papers, Chicago Historical Society.
22. Badeau, *Grant in Peace* 318.
23. Ibid. 319–21.

24. Julia Dent Grant, *Personal Memoirs* 321–22.

25. *New York Times,* February 26, 1880.

26. Logan carried the crucial procedural vote 309–304 at 2:00 A.M. on May 20. James Pickett Jones, *John A. Logan: Stalwart Republican from Illinois* 132–34 (Tallahassee: University Presses of Florida, 1982).

27. Badeau, *Grant in Peace* 320; Julia Dent Grant, *Personal Memoirs* 321.

28. *New York Times,* June 2, 1880, Logan quoted in David M. Jordan, *Roscoe Conkling of New York* 326 (Ithaca, N.Y.: Cornell University Press, 1971).

29. Julia Dent Grant, *Personal Memoirs* 321–22.

30. For a tabulation of the 1880 Republican convention votes, see *National Party Conventions 1831–1972* 137 (Washington, D.C.: Congressional Quarterly, 1976).

31. Jordan, *Roscoe Conkling* 340.

32. James, *John A. Logan* 137.

33. Thomas C. Platt, *The Autobiography of Thomas C. Platt* 120–23, Louis J. Lang, ed. (New York: B. W. Dodge, 1910). In late 1880 the stalwarts published a pamphlet called *The Roll of Honor,* which contained the names of the 306 as well as Roscoe Conkling's nominating speech. The Grant medals were struck by Chauncey I. Filley and distributed to each of the 306 delegates.

34. Grant to Mary King, January 27, 1881, Grant Papers.

35. Nevins, 2 *Hamilton Fish* 897.

36. Julia Dent Grant, *Personal Memoirs* 323–24; *New York Herald Tribune,* April 24, 1927.

37. Grant to Badeau, May 7, 1882, Badeau, *Grant in Peace* 533–34.

38. Ibid. 334–42.

39. Ibid. 395. Also see David M. Pletcher, *Rails, Mines, and Progress: Seven American Promoters in Mexico, 1867–1911* 150 (Ithaca, N.Y.: Cornell University Press, 1958).

40. Julia Dent Grant, *Personal Memoirs* 323.

41. Grant and Buck put down cash. Ward and Fish pledged securities. Hamlin Garland, *Ulysses S. Grant: His Life and Character* 490 note (New York: Macmillan, 1898).

42. Louis A. Coolidge, *Ulysses S. Grant* 555–60 (Boston: Houghton Mifflin, 1917); William B. Hesseltine, *Ulysses S. Grant: Politician* 445–47 (New York: Dodd, Mead, 1935); Thomas M. Pitkin, *The Captain Departs* 206 (Carbondale: Southern Illinois University Press, 1973).

43. Badeau, *Grant in Peace* 418–19; William S. McFeely, *Grant: A Biography* 489–92. (New York: W. W. Norton, 1981).

44. Hesseltine, *Ulysses S. Grant* 446.

45. Garland, *Ulysses S. Grant* 492.

46. Ibid.

47. *New York Times* May 8–13, 15, 21, July 8, 1884; *New York Tribune,* June 23, 1886.

48. Pitkin, *The Captain Departs* 9–10.

49. Garland, *Ulysses S. Grant* 495–99.

50. Julia Dent Grant, *Personal Memoirs* 328. Grant's letter of appreciation to Charles Wood of Lansingburg was published in the *New York Times,* August 5, 1892.

51. Badeau, *Grant in Peace* 432.

52. Robert U. Johnson, *Remembered Yesterdays* 209 (Boston: Little, Brown, 1923).

53. Pitkin, *The Captain Departs* 10–15.

54. Samuel Clemens, 1 *Mark Twain's Autobiography* 33–36 (New York: Harper and Brothers, 1924).

55. Charles L. Webster, Clemens's partner, was the husband of his niece. *Huckleberry Finn* was their first publishing venture, and was sold by subscription.

56. Clemens, 1 *Mark Twain's Autobiography* 36.

57. Ibid. 40.

58. Julia Dent Grant, *Personal Memoirs* 328–29.

59. Pitkin, *The Captain Departs* 24.

60. Julia Dent Grant, *Personal Memoirs* 329.

61. *New York Times,* March 1, 1885; *New York World,* February 20, 28, 1885.

62. L. White Busbey, *Uncle Joe Cannon* 303–6 (New York: Henry Holt, 1927); U.S. Congress, *Congressional Record,* 48th Cong., 2nd sess. 2503.

63. 48th Cong., 2nd sess. 2565–66. Also see Badeau, *Grant in Peace* 443, Hesseltine, *Ulysses S. Grant* 450–51; Garland, *Ulysses S. Grant* 508.

64. Pitkin, *The General Departs* 30.

65. Clemens, *Mark Twain's Autobiography,* 48.

66. *New York Times,* June 12, 16, 1885.

67. *New York Tribune,* June 17, 1885.

68. Julia Dent Grant, *Personal Memoirs* 330–31.

69. John R. Proctor, "A Blue and Gray Friendship," 31 *Century Magazine* 942–49 (1897); Arndt M. Stickler, *Simon Bolivar Buckner: Borderland Knight* 324–29 (Chapel Hill: University of North Carolina Press, 1940).

70. McFeely, *Grant* 501.

71. Edmund Wilson, *Patriotic Gore* 132–33, 140 (New York: Oxford University Press, 1962). In *Four in America,* Stein devoted her initial essay to Grant, before treating Wilbur Wright, Henry James, and George Washington. (New Haven: Yale University Press, 1947) 3–82.

72. James M. McPherson, "The Unheroic Hero," *New York Review of Books,* 16–19 (February 4, 1999).

73. Grant, 2 *Memoirs* 276.

74. Pitkin, *The Captain Departs* 92–93.

75. Wilson, *Patriotic Gore* 138–39.

Bibliography

Unpublished Papers and Manuscripts

Amos Akerman Papers. University of Virginia.
Andrews, Richard A. "Years of Frustration: William T. Sherman, the Army, and Reform, 1869–1883." Unpublished Ph.D. dissertation, Northwestern University, 1968.
Orville Babcock Papers. Chicago Historical Society.
Franklin Bailey Letters. Michigan Historical Society.
George Bancroft Collection. Massachusetts Historical Society.
Benjamin H. Bristow Papers. Library of Congress.
Browning, Orville H. Diary. Illinois State Historical Library.
Don Carlos Buell Papers. Huntington Library, San Marino, California.
Cadwallader, Sylvanus. "Four Years with Grant." Unpublished manuscript, Illinois State Historical Library.
Casey, Emma Dent. "When Grant Went a Courtin'." Typewritten manuscript, Missouri Historical Society.
Chumney, James R. "Don Carlos Buell: Gentleman General." Unpublished Ph.D. dissertation, Rice University, 1964.
William C. Church Papers. Library of Congress.
Cyrus D. Comstock Papers. Library of Congress.
Roscoe Conkling Papers. Library of Congress.
Letter of Selden Connor, April 16, 1864. Brown University Library.
Jacob Delson Cox Papers. Oberlin University.
Charles A. Dana Papers. Massachusetts Historical Society.
Bancroft Davis Papers. Library of Congress.
"Descriptive Book of Candidates." Unpublished manuscript, United States Military Academy.
Frederick Douglass Papers. Frederick Douglass Memorial Home, Washington, D.C.
Eidson, William G. "John Alexander Logan: Hero of the Volunteers." Ph.D. dissertation, Vanderbilt University, 1967.
Lucius C. Fairchild Papers. State Historical Society of Wisconsin Library.
Farnen, Russell F., Jr. "Ulysses S. Grant: The Soldier as Politican (1861–1868)." Unpublished Ph.D. dissertation, Syracuse University, 1963.
William Pitt Fessenden Papers. Library of Congress.
Hamilton Fish Papers. Library of Congress.
Walter L. Fleming Collection. Louisiana State University.
John C. Frémont Manuscript Memoirs. Bancroft Library.
James A. Garfield Papers. Library of Congress.
Hamlin Garland Papers. University of Southern California.
Grant, Ulysses S. "Account Book, 1839–1843". Huntington Library, San Marino, California.
——. "Headquarters Records." 62 vols. Unpublished manuscript, Library of Congress.
——. "Personal Memoirs." Unpublished manuscript, Library of Congress.
Hicken, Victor. "From Vandalia to Vicksburg: The Political and Military Career of John A. McClernand." Unpublished Ph.D. dissertation, University of Illinois at Urbana, 1955.
Holliday, Charles L. "The Military Career of General John Alexander Logan, 1861–1865." Unpublished Ph.D. dissertation, Washington University, 1948.
Jackson, Private Joshua E. Diary. Illinois State Historical Library.

Thomas A. Jenckes Papers. Library of Congress.
Lee, Jen-Wha. "The Organization and Administration of the Army of the Potomac Under General George B. McClellan." Unpublished Ph.D. dissertation, University of Maryland, 1960.
Francis Lieber Collection. Huntington Library, San Marino, California.
John A. Logan Papers. Library of Congress.
Lord, Mrs. W. W. "Journal Kept During the Siege of Vicksburg, May–July 1863." Unpublished manuscript, Library of Congress.
Journal of Theodore Lyman. Massachusetts Historical Society.
Messamore, Ford. "John A. Logan: Democrat and Republican." Unpublished Ph.D. dissertation, University of Kentucky, 1939.
Montagna, Dennis R. "Henry Merwin Shrady's Ulysses S. Grant Memorial in Washington, D.C.: A Study in Iconography, Content, and Patronage." Unpublished Ph.D. dissertation, University of Delaware, 1987.
Morrison, James L., Jr. "The United States Military Academy, 1833–1866: Years of Progress and Turmoil." Unpublished Ph.D. dissertation, Columbia University, 1970.
Ott, Eugene M., Jr. "The Civil War Diary of James J. Kirkpatrick, Sixteenth Mississippi Infantry, C.S.A." Unpublished M.A. thesis, Texas A&M University, 1984.
William Pendleton Collection. University of North Carolina.
Horace Porter Papers. Library of Congress.
Powell, William H. "History of the Organization and Movements of the Fourth Regiment of Infantry, 1871." National Archives.
Prokopowicz, Gerald J. "All for the Regiment: Unit Cohesion and Tactical Stalemate in the Army of the Ohio, 1861–1862." Unpublished Ph.D. dissertation, Harvard University, 1994.
John A. Rawlins Papers. Chicago Historical Society.
Records of the Board of Indian Commissioners. National Archives.
Regimental Order Book, 21st Illinois. National Archives.
Regimental Records, Camp Salubrity. National Archives.
Harvey Reid Papers. Huntington Library, San Marino, California.
William R. Rowley Papers. Illinois State Historical Society.
Philip H. Sheridan Papers. Library of Congress.
John Sherman Papers. Library of Congress.
William Tecumseh Sherman Papers. Library of Congress.
Shiloh National Military Park Collection.
Charles Ferguson Smith Papers. Glenbrook, Connecticut.
Smith, Everard H., III. "The General and the Valley: Union Leadership During the Threat to Washington in 1864." Unpublished Ph.D. dissertation, University of North Carolina, 1977.
E. Kirby Smith Papers. University of North Carolina.
Smith, W. W. "Diary of a Visit to General Grant's Headquarters, 1863." Unpublished manuscript, Library of Congress.
M. J. Solomon Papers. Duke University.
St. Pierre, Judith. "General O. O. Howard and Grant's Peace Policy." Unpublished Ph.D. dissertation, University of North Carolina, 1990.
Charles S. Sumner Papers. Harvard University.
Thompson, Margaret S. "The 'Spider Web': Congress and Lobbying in the Age of Grant." Unpublished Ph.D. dissertation, University of Wisconsin, 1979.
Ulrich, William J. "The Northern Military Mind in Regard to Reconstruction, 1865–1872: The Attitudes of Ten Leading Union Generals." Unpublished Ph.D. dissertation, Ohio State University, 1959.
Elihu Washburne Papers. Library of Congress.
Wooster, Robert A. "The Military and United States Indian Policy, 1865–1903." Unpublished Ph.D. dissertation, University of Texas, 1985.

Official Publications

Adjutant General's Office. *Chronological List of Actions with Indians from January 15, 1837, to January 1891.* Fort Collins, Colo.: Old Army Press, 1979.
Annual Reports of the Commissioner of Indian Affairs. 1868–1877.
Annual Reports of the Secretary of War. 1865–1877.
Bearss, Edwin C. *Decision in Mississippi.* Jackson: Mississippi Commission of the War Between the States, 1962.

Beers, Henry Putney, and Kenneth W. Munden. *Guide to Federal Archives Relating to the Civil War.* Washington, D.C.: National Archives and Records Services, General Services Administration, 1962.

Bureau of the Census. *A Century of Population Growth, 1790–1900.* Washington, D.C.: Government Printing Office, 1909.

Carter, William H. *Creation of the American General Staff.* 68th Congress, 1st session. In *Senate Documents,* vol. 2, no. 119. Serial 8254.

Cullum, George W. *Biographical Register of the Officers and Graduates of the U.S. Military Academy.* West Point: United States Military Academy, 1966.

Fiebeger, G. J. *Campaigns of the American Civil War.* West Point: United States Military Academy Printing Office, 1914.

Fourth U.S. Infantry Regiment. *Day Book of Company A: 1848–1853.*

Hansen, David, and William Woodward, eds. *Military Influences on Washington History.* Tacoma: Washington Army National Guard, 1984.

Journal of the House of Representatives of the Commonwealth of Kentucky. Frankfort: Hunter and Beaumont, 1861.

Leyden, James A. *A Historical Sketch of the Fourth Infantry.* Fort Sherman, Id.: Press of the Fourth United States Infantry, 1891.

Miller, David Hunter, ed. *Treaties and Other International Acts of the United States.* Washington, D.C.: Government Printing Office, 1937.

Moore, John Bassett. *International Arbitrations.* Washington, D.C.: Government Printing Office, 1898.

———. *International Law Digest,* vol. 1. Washington, D.C.: Government Printing Office, 1906.

Official Records of the Union and Confederate Navies in the War of the Rebellion. Washington, D.C.: Government Printing Office, 1894.

Register of the United States Army, September 1861. Washington, D.C.: Government Printing Office, 1861.

Report of the Board of Indian Commissioners, 1869.

Report of the Congressional Committee on the Conduct of the War. 5 vols. Washington, D.C.: Government Printing Office, 1863, 1865–66.

Report of the Secretary of the Interior, 1869.

Reports of Inspection Made in the Summer of 1877 by Generals P. H. Sheridan and W. T. Sherman of Country North of the Union Pacific Railroad. Washington, D.C.: Government Printing Office, 1878.

Richardson, James D., ed. *A Compilation of the Messages and Papers of the Presidents.* Washington, D.C.: Bureau of National Literature and Art, 1896.

———. *The Messages and Papers of the Confederacy, Including Diplomatic Correspondence, 1861–1865.* 2 vols. Nashville: Harper, 1905.

U.S. Congress. *Congressional Globe.*

———. *Congressional Record.*

U.S. Congress, House. *Gold Panic Investigation.* 41st Congress, 2nd session, March 1, 1870. Report No. 31.

———. *Impeachment Investigation.* 40th Congress, 1st session. Report No. 7.

———. *Malfeasance of W. W. Belknap, Late Secretary of War.* 44th Congress, March 2, 1876. H.R. 186.

———. *Official Modoc War Correspondence.* 43rd Congress, 1st session. House Exec. Doc. 122.

———. *Poland Report.* 42nd Congress, 2nd session.

———. *Report of the House Managers on the Impeachment of W. W. Belknap.* 44th Congress, August 2, 1876. H.R. 791.

———. *Report of the Indian Peace Commissioners.* 40th Congress, 3rd session, 1868. House Exec. Doc. 97.

———. *Whiskey Frauds.* 44th Congress, 1st session. House Misc. Doc. 186.

U.S. Congress, Senate. *Conditions of the Indian Tribes: Report of the Joint Special Committee.* 39th Congress, 2nd session, 1867. Report No. 156.

———. "The Effect of the Fourteenth Amendment on the Indian Tribes." *Report of Senate Judiciary Committee.* 41st Congress, 3rd session, 1870–1871.

———. "Massacre of the Cheyenne Indians." By Samuel F. Tappan. *Report of the Joint Special Committee.* 39th Congress, 2nd session, 1867. Report No. 156.

———. *Presidential Vetoes, 1789–1988.* Senate Publication 102–12. Washington, D.C.: Government Printing Office, 1992.

———. *Proceedings of a Military Commission in the Case of Colonel J. M. Chivington, First Colorado Cavalry.* 39th Congress, 2nd session, 1867. Sen. Exec. Doc. 26.

———. *Report of the Commission of Inquiry to Santo Domingo.* 42nd Congress, 1st session, 1874. Sen. Exec. Doc. 9.

——. *Report of the Secretary of War Showing the Number of . . . Killed and Wounded.* 30th Congress, 1st session. Sen. Exec. Doc. 36. Washington, D.C.: Wendell and Van Benthuysen, 1848.

——. *Wilson Report.* 42nd Congress, 2nd session.

U.S. Library of Congress, Manuscript Division. *Index to Ulysses S. Grant Papers.* Washington, D.C.: Government Printing Office, 1965.

U.S. President. *Messages of the President of the United States with Their Correspondence Therewith Communicated, Between the Secretary of War and Other Officers of Government on the Subject of the Mexican War.* 30th Congress, 1st session. House Exec. Doc. 60. Washington, D.C.: Wendell and Van Benthuysen, 1848.

Upton, Emory. *The Military Policy of the United States.* Washington, D.C.: Government Printing Office, 1917.

War of the Rebellion: A Compilation of the Official Records of the Union and Confederate Armies. 128 vols. Washington, D.C.: Government Printing Office, 1880–1901.

BOOKS

Abbott, John S. C. *The Life of General Ulysses S. Grant.* Boston: Russell, 1868.

Abbott, Richard H. *The Republican Party and the South, 1855–1877.* Chapel Hill: University of North Carolina Press, 1986.

Acheson, Dean. *Present at the Creation.* New York: W. W. Norton, 1969.

Ackerman, Kenneth D. *The Gold Ring: Jim Fisk, Jay Gould, and Black Friday, 1869.* New York: Dodd, Mead, 1988.

Adams, George Worthington. *Doctors in Blue: The Medical History of the Union Army in the Civil War.* New York: H. Schuman, 1952.

Adams, Henry. *The Education of Henry Adams: An Autobiography.* Boston: Houghton Mifflin, 1918.

Agassiz, George R., ed. *Meade's Headquarters, 1863–1865: Letters of Colonel Theodore Lyman from the Wilderness to Appomattox.* Boston: Houghton Mifflin, 1913.

Alexander, Edward Porter. *Fighting for the Confederacy.* Chapel Hill: University of North Carolina Press, 1989. Reprint.

——. *Military Memoirs of a Confederate.* New York: Charles Scribner's Sons, 1910.

Allen, Stanton P. *Down in Dixie: Life in a Cavalry Regiment in the War Days.* Boston: D. Lothrop, 1892.

Allen, William H. *The American Civil War Book and Grant Album.* Boston: W. H. Allen, 1894.

Altschuler, Glenn C. *Andrew D. White: Educator, Historian, Diplomat.* Ithaca, N.Y.: Cornell University Press, 1979.

Ambler, Charles H. *Francis H. Pierpont, Union War Governor of Virginia and Father of West Virginia.* Chapel Hill: University of North Carolina Press, 1937.

Ambrose, Stephen E. *Crazy Horse and Custer: The Parallel Lives of Two American Warriors.* Garden City, N.Y.: Doubleday, 1975.

——. *Duty, Honor, Country: A History of West Point.* Baltimore: Johns Hopkins University Press, 1966.

——. *Halleck: Lincoln's Chief of Staff.* Baton Rouge: Louisiana State University Press, 1962.

——. *Upton and the Army.* Baton Rouge: Louisiana State University Press, 1964.

Ammen, Daniel. *The Old Navy and the New . . . with an Appendix of Personal Letters from General Grant.* Philadelphia: J. B. Lippincott, 1891.

Anderson, Nancy S., and Dwight Anderson. *The Generals: Ulysses S. Grant and Robert E. Lee.* New York: Random House, 1988.

Andrews, Bryon. *A Biography of General John A. Logan: With an Account of His Public Service in Peace and War.* New York: H. S. Goodspeed, 1884.

Andrews, J. Cutler. *The North Reports the Civil War.* Pittsburgh: University of Pittsburgh Press, 1955.

Anjou, Gustave. *The Grant-Dent Family.* Privately published, 1906.

Annals of the War, Written by Leading Participants North and South. Philadelphia: Philadelphia Weekly Times, 1879.

Archer, Jules. *A House Divided: The Lives of Ulysses S. Grant and Robert E. Lee.* New York: Scholastic, 1995.

Armstrong, William H. *Warrior in Two Camps: Ely S. Parker, Union General and Seneca Chief.* Syracuse, N.Y.: Syracuse University Press, 1978.

Arnold, James R. *The Armies of U.S. Grant.* London: Arms and Armour, 1995.

——. *Chickamauga 1863: The River of Death.* London: Osprey, 1992.

——. *Grant Wins the War: Decision at Vicksburg.* New York: Wiley, 1997.

Arnold, Matthew. *Civilization in the United States: First and Last Impressions of America*. Freeport, N.Y.: Books for Libraries, 1972.
——. *General Grant with a Rejoinder by Mark Twain*. Carbondale: Southern Illinois University Press, 1966.
Athearn, Robert G. *William Tecumseh Sherman and the Settlement of the West*. Norman: University of Oklahoma Press, 1956.
Atkinson, C. F. *Grant's Campaigns of 1864 and 1865*. London: Hugh Rees, 1908.
Badeau, Adam. *Grant in Peace: From Appomattox to Mount McGregor. A Personal Memoir*. Hartford, Conn.: Scranton, 1887.
——. *Military History of Ulysses S. Grant, from April 1861 to April 1865*. 3 vols. New York: D. Appleton, 1881.
——. *The Vagabond*. New York: Rudo and Carleton, 1859.
Bailey, Thomas A. *A Diplomatic History of the American People*. New York: Appleton-Century-Crofts, 1964.
Baker, Jean H. *The Politics of Continuity: Maryland Political Parties from 1858 to 1870*. Baltimore: Johns Hopkins University Press, 1973.
Ballard, Colin R. *The Military Genius of Abraham Lincoln*. New York: Oxford University Press, 1952.
Ballard, Michael B. *Pemberton: A Biography*. Jackson: University Press of Mississippi, 1991.
Barber, James G. *U.S. Grant: The Man and the Image*. Carbonale: Southern Illinois University Press, 1986.
Barnard, Harry. *Rutherford B. Hayes and His America*. Indianapolis: Bobbs-Merrill, 1956.
Bauer, K. Jack. *The Mexican War*. New York: Macmillan, 1974.
——. *Zachary Taylor: Soldier, Planter, Statesman of the Old Southwest*. Baton Rouge: Louisiana State University Press, 1985.
Baxter, Maurice G. *Orville H. Browning: Lincoln's Friend and Critic*. Bloomington: Indiana University Press, 1957.
Bean, William G. *The Liberty Hall Volunteers: Stonewall's College Boys*. Charlottesville: University Press of Virginia, 1964.
Bearss, Edwin C. *The Campaign for Vicksburg*. 4 vols. Dayton, Ohio: Morningside, 1986.
Bearss, Edwin C., and Chris Calkins. *Battle of Five Forks*. Lynchburg, Va.: H. E. Howard, 1985.
Beaver, Robert P. *Church, State, and the American Indians: Two and a Half Centuries of Partnership in Missions Between Protestant Churches and Government*. St. Louis: Concordia Publication House, 1966.
Belfords, Clarke & Co. *General Grant Abroad*. Chicago: Belfords, Clark & Co., 1879.
Belknap, William W. *History of the 15th Regiment Iowa Veteran Volunteer Infantry*. Keokuk, Iowa: R. B. Ogden and Son, 1887.
Belz, Herman. *Reconstructing the Union: Theory and Practice During the Civil War*. Ithaca, N.Y.: Cornell University Press for the American Historical Association, 1969.
Bemis, Samuel Flagg. *A Diplomatic History of the United States*. New York: Holt, Rinehart and Winston, 1963.
Bender, Norman J. *New Hope for the Indians: The Grant Peace Policy and the Navajos in the 1870's*. Albuquerque: University of New Mexico Press, 1989.
Benedict, Michael Les. *A Compromise of Principle: Congressional Republicans and Reconstruction, 1863–1869*. New York: W. W. Norton, 1974.
——. *The Impeachment and Trial of Andrew Johnson*. New York: W. W. Norton, 1973.
Bentley, Bill. *Ulysses S. Grant*. New York: Franklin Watts, 1993.
Berry, John M. *Rising Tide: The Great Mississippi Flood of 1927 and How It Changed America*. New York: Simon and Schuster, 1997.
Berthrong, Donald J. *The Southern Cheyennes*. Norman: University of Oklahoma Press, 1963.
Bigelow, John. *The Principles of Strategy: Illustrated Mainly from American Campaigns*. Philadelphia: J. B. Lippincott, 1894.
Blaine, James G. *Twenty Years of Congress: from Lincoln to Garfield. With a Review of the Events Which Led to the Political Revolution of 1860*. 2 vols. Norwich, Conn.: Henry Bill, 1884–1886.
Blanchard, Ira. *I Marched with Sherman: Civil War Memoirs of the Twentieth Illinois*. San Francisco: J. D. Haff, 1992.
Blue, Frederick J. *Salmon P. Chase: A Life in Politics*. Kent, Ohio: Kent State University Press, 1987.
Boatner, Mark Mayo, III. *The Civil War Dictionary*. New York: David McKay, 1959.
Boothe, Norton. *Ulysses S. Grant*. Great American Generals Series. New York: Smithmark Publishers, 1990.
Boritt, Gabor S., ed. *Lincoln's General*. New York: Oxford University Press, 1994.
Boutwell, George S. *The Lawyer, the Statesman, and the Soldier*. New York: D. Appleton, 1887.
——. *Reminiscences of Sixty Years in Public Affairs*. 2 vols. New York: McClure, Phillips, 1902.

Bowers, Claude G. *The Tragic Era*. New York: Literary Guild of America, 1929.

Bowman, John. *Pictorial History of the American Presidency*. New York: Bison, 1986.

Bowman, Samuel M., and Richard Bache Irwin. *Sherman and His Campaigns: A Military Biography*. New York: Richardson, 1865.

Boyd, James P. *The Gallant Trooper, General Philip H. Sheridan*. Philadelphia: Franklin News, 1888.

——. *The Life of William T. Sherman*. Philadelphia: Publishers' Union, 1891.

——. *Military and Civil Life of Gen. Ulysses S. Grant*. Philadelphia: P. W. Ziegler, 1885.

Brandt, Nat. *The Congressman Who Got Away with Murder*. Syracuse, N.Y.: Syracuse University Press, 1991.

Brigham, Clarence Saunders, ed. *British Royal Proclamations Relating to America: 1603–1783*. Worcester, Mass.: American Antiquarian Society, 1911.

Brinton, John H. *Personal Memoirs of John H. Brinton, Major and Surgeon, 1861–1865*, Jacob D. Cox, ed. New York: Charles Scribner's Sons, 1914.

Brisbin, James S. *Campaign Lives of Ulysses S. Grant and Schuyler Colfax*. Chicago: J. S. Goodman, 1868.

Brock, William R. *The Civil War*. New York: Harper and Row, 1969.

Brockett, Linus P. *Our Great Captains: Grant, Sherman, Thomas, Sheridan, and Farragut*. New York: C. B. Richardson, 1865.

Brockway, George P. *Political Deals That Saved Andrew Johnson*. New York: Coalition of Publishers for Employment, 1977.

Brooks, Noah. *Washington in Lincoln's Time*. New York: Century, 1896.

Brooks, William E. *Grant of Appomattox: A Study of the Man*. Westport, Conn.: Greenwood, 1971.

Brown, Dee A. *Grierson's Raid*. Urbana: University of Illinois Press, 1954.

Browning, Orville Hickman. *The Diary of Orville Hickman Browning*. Theodore C. Pease and James G. Randall, eds. Springfield: Illinois State Historical Library, 1925.

Bruce, George A. *The Twentieth Regiment of Massachusetts Infantry, 1861–1865*. Boston: Houghton Mifflin, 1906.

Bruce, Robert V. *Lincoln and the Tools of War*. Indianapolis: Bobbs-Merrill, 1956.

Buck, Irving. *Cleburne and His Command*. Jackson, Tenn.: McCowat-Mercur, 1959.

Buel, Clarence C., and Robert U. Johnson, eds. *Battles and Leaders of the Civil War*. 4 vols. New York: Century, 1887–88.

Burne, Alfred H. *Lee, Grant and Sherman: A Study of Leadership in the 1864–65 Campaign*. New York: Gale and Polden, 1939.

Burr, Frank A. *The Complete Story of the Man, the Soldier, and the Statesman: An Original and Authentic Record of the Life and Deeds of General U.S. Grant*. Chicago: National Publishing, 1885.

——. *General U.S. Grant*. Boston: Little, Brown, 1885.

Busbey, L. White. *Uncle Joe Cannon*. New York: Henry Holt, 1927.

Butler, Benjamin F. *Autobiography and Personal Reminiscences of Major-General Benj. F. Butler*. Boston: A. M. Thayer, 1892.

——. *Private and Official Correspondence of Gen. Benjamin F. Butler During the Period of the Civil War*. 5 vols. Privately published, 1917.

Cadwallader, Sylvanus. *Three Years with Grant: As Recalled by War Correspondent Sylvanus Cadwallader*. Lincoln: University of Nebraska Press, 1996. Reprint.

Caldwell, J. F. J. *The History of the Brigade of South Carolinians*. Philadelphia: King and Baird, 1866.

Campbell, James H. *McClellan: A Vindication of the Military Career of General George B. McClellan: A Lawyer's Brief*. New York: Neale, 1916.

Carley, Kenneth. *The Sioux Uprising of 1862*. St. Paul: Minnesota Historical Society, 1961.

Carpenter, John A. *Sword and Olive Branch: Oliver Otis Howard*. Pittsburgh: University of Pittsburgh Press, 1964.

——. *Ulysses S. Grant*. New York: Twayne, 1970.

Carr, Clark Ezra. *The Illini: A Story of the Prairies*. Chicago: A. C. McClung, 1905.

Carter, Robert G., and John D. Reed. *History of the Twenty-second Massachusetts Infantry*. Boston: Rand Avery, 1887.

Carter, Samuel, III. *The Final Fortress: The Campaign for Vicksburg, 1862–1863*. New York: St. Martin's, 1980.

——. *The Last Cavaliers: Confederate and Union Cavalry in the Civil War*. New York: St. Martin's, 1979.

Carter, William H. *The American Army*. Indianapolis: Bobbs-Merrill, 1915.

del Castillo, Richard Griswold. *The Treaty of Guadalupe Hidalgo: A Legacy of Conflict*. Norman: University of Oklahoma Press, 1990.

Castleman, Alfred L. *The Army of the Potomac . . . A Diary of Unwritten History from the Organization of the Army to the Close of the Campaign in Virginia, About the First Day of January, 1863*. Milwaukee: Strickland, 1863.

Cate, Wirt Armistead. *Lucius Q. C. Lamar: Secession and Reunion*. Chapel Hill: University of North Carolina Press, 1935.

Catton, Bruce. *The Army of the Potomac*. Garden City, N.Y.: Doubleday, 1953.

——. *Glory Road: The Bloody Route from Fredericksburg to Gettysburg*. Vol. 2, *The Army of the Potomac*. Garden City, N.Y.: Doubleday & Co., 1952.

——. *Grant Moves South, 1861–1863*. Boston: Little, Brown, 1960.

——. *Grant Takes Command, 1863–1865*. Boston: Little, Brown, 1969.

——. *Mr. Lincoln's Army*. Vol.1, *The Army of the Potomac*. Garden City, N.Y.: Doubleday, 1951.

——. *Never Call Retreat*. Vol. 3, *The Centennial History of the Civil War*. Garden City, N.Y.: Doubleday, 1965.

——. *A Stillness at Appomattox*. Garden City: Doubleday, 1956.

——. *Terrible Swift Sword*. Vol. 2, *The Centennial History of the Civil War*. Garden City, N.Y.: Doubleday, 1963.

——. *This Hallowed Ground: The Story of the Union Side of the Civil War*. Garden City, N.Y. Doubleday, 1956.

——. *U.S. Grant and the American Military Tradition*. Boston: Little, Brown, 1954.

Chamberlain, Joshua L. *The Passing of the Armies: An Account of the Final Campaign of the Army of the Potomac*. New York: G. P. Putnam's Sons, 1915.

Chamberlin, Thomas. *History of the One Hundred and Fiftieth Regiment Pennsylvania Volunteers*. Philadelphia: F. McManus, Jr., 1905.

Chamberlin, William H., and G. A. Thayer, eds. *Sketches of War History, 1861–1865*. 5 vols. Cincinnati: Robert Clarke, 1903.

Chambers, S. Allen, John Poppeliers, and Nancy B. Schwartz. *What Style Is It?* Washington, D.C.: Preservation Press, 1979.

Chambrun, Charles Adolphe de Pineton. *Impressions of Lincoln and the Civil War*. Aldebert de Chambrun, trans. New York: Random House, 1952.

Chance, Joseph E. *Jefferson Davis's Mexican War Regiment*. Jackson: University Press of Mississippi, 1991.

Chaplin, Jeremiah. *Life of Charles Sumner*. Boston: Lothrop, 1874.

Chase, Salmon P. *Inside Lincoln's Cabinet: The Civil War Diaries of Salmon P. Chase*. David Herbert Donald, ed. New York: Longmans, Green, 1954.

Chesnut, Mary. *Mary Chesnut's Civil War*. C. Vann Woodward, ed. New Haven: Yale University Press, 1981.

Chetlain, Augustus Louis. *Recollections of Seventy Years by Augustus L. Chetlain: Brigadier and Brevet Major General U.S. Vols., Civil War, 1861–65*. Galena: Gazette, 1899.

Childs, George W. *Recollections of General Grant*. Philadelphia: Collins, 1890.

Church, William Conant. *Ulysses S. Grant and the Period of National Preservation and Reconstruction*. New York: G. P. Putnam's Sons, 1897.

Clarke, Dwight L. *Stephen Watts Kearny*. Norman: University of Oklahoma Press, 1961.

Clarke, Oliver P. *General Grant at Mount McGregor by O. P. Clarke, Custodian of the Grant Cottage*. Saratoga Springs, N.Y.: Cozzens and Waterbury, 1895.

Clemens, Samuel. *Mark Twain's Autobiography*. New York: Harper and Brothers, 1924.

Cleaves, Freeman. *Meade of Gettysburg*. Norman: University of Oklahoma Press, 1960.

——. *Rock of Chickamauga. The Life of General George H. Thomas*. Norman: University of Oklahoma Press, 1948.

Clews, Henry. *Twenty-eight Years in Wall Street*. New York: Irving, 1888.

Cole, Arthur C. *The Era of the Civil War, 1848–1870*. vol. 3, *Centennial History of Illinois*. Springfield: Illinois Centennial Commission, 1919.

Coleman, Charles. *The Election of 1868*. New York: Columbia University Press, 1933.

Collidge, Louis A. *Ulysses S. Grant*. Boston: Houghton Mifflin, 1917.

Commager, Henry S., ed. *The Blue and the Gray: The Story of the Civil War as Told by Participants*. Indianapolis: Bobbs-Merrill, 1950.

Conger, A. L. *The Rise of U.S. Grant*. New York: Century, 1931.

Conger, A. L., comp. *Donelson Campaign Sources; Supplementing Vol. VII of the Official Records*. Fort Leavenworth, Kans.: Army Service Schools, 1912.

Congressional Quarterly Guide to U.S. Elections, 2nd ed. Washington, D.C.: Congressional Quarterly, 1985.

Conn, Dr. George H. *The Arabian Horse in America*. New York: A. S. Barnes, 1972.

Connelly, Thomas Z. *The Marble Man: Robert E. Lee and His Image in American Society*. New York: Alfred A. Knopf, 1997.

Connolly, James A. *Three Years in the Army of the Cumberland.* Paul M. Angle, ed. Bloomington: Indiana University Press, 1959.

Cook, Adrian. *The Alabama Claims: American Politics and Anglo-American Relations, 1865–1872.* Ithaca, N.Y.: Cornell University Press, 1975.

Coolidge, Louis A. *Ulysses S. Grant.* Boston: Houghton Mifflin, 1917.

Cooling, Benjamin F. *Forts Henry and Donelson: The Key to the Confederate Heartland.* Knoxville: University of Tennessee Press, 1987.

Coppee, Henry. *Grant and His Campaigns: A Military Biography.* New York: Charles B. Richardson, 1866.

——. *Life and Services of General U.S. Grant.* New York: Richardson, 1868.

Cornish, Dudley T. *The Sable Arm: Black Troops in the Union Army, 1861–1865.* New York: Longmans, Green, 1956.

Cox, Jacob D. *Military Reminiscences of the Civil War.* 2 vols. New York: Charles Scribner's Sons, 1900.

Cox, Lawanda C. *Politics, Principle and Prejudice, 1865–1866: Dilemma of Reconstruction America.* New York: Atheneum, 1969.

Coy, Owen Cochran. *The Humboldt Bay Region, 1850–1875.* Los Angeles: California State Historical Association, 1929.

Cozzens, Peter. *General John Pope: A Life for the Nation.* Urbana: University of Illinois Press, 2000.

——. *This Terrible Sound: The Battle of Chickamauga.* Urbana: University of Illinois Press, 1992.

Cresap, Bernard. *Appomattox Commander. The Story of General E. O. C. Ord.* New York: A. S. Barnes, 1981.

Crook, George. *General George Crook: His Autobiography.* Martin F. Schmitt, ed. Norman: University of Oklahoma Press, 1946.

Crook, William H. *Through Five Administrations,* vol. 1. New York: Harper and Brothers, 1910.

Cross, Nelson. *The Life of General Grant, His Political Record, etc.* New York: J. S. Redfield, 1872.

Crotty, D. G. *Four Years Campaigning in the Army of the Potomac.* Grand Rapids, Mich.: Dygert Brothers, 1874.

Crummer, Wilbur C. *With Grant at Fort Donelson, Shiloh, and Vicksburg.* Oak Park, Ill.: E. C. Crummer, 1915.

Cudworth, Warren. *History of the First Regiment Massachusetts Infantry.* Boston: Walker, Fuller, 1886.

Cullen, Joseph P. *Where a Hundred Thousand Fell: The Battles of Fredericksburg, Chancellorsville, the Wilderness, and Spotsylvania Court House.* Washington, D.C.: National Park Service, 1966.

Cullum, George W. *Biographical Register of Officers and Cadets of the U.S. Military Academy at West Point, N.Y. from Its Establishment in 1802 to 1890. With the Early History of the United States Military Academy.* 3rd ed. rev. and ext. Boston: Houghton Mifflin, 1891.

Current, Richard N. *Lincoln and the First Shot.* Philadelphia: J. B. Lippincott, 1963.

Current, Richard N., and J. G. Randall. *Lincoln the President: Last Full Measure.* Urbana: University of Illinois Press, 1991.

Curtis, George T. *McClellan's Last Service to the Republic.* New York: D. Appleton, 1886.

Dame, William M. *From the Rapidan to Richmond and the Spottsylvania Campaign.* Baltimore: Harper, 1920.

Dana, Charles A., *Recollections of the Civil War.* New York: D. Appleton, 1899.

Dana, Charles A., and James H. Wilson. *The Life of Ulysses S. Grant, General of the Armies of the United States.* Springfield: Gordon Bill, 1868.

Dana, Richard Henry. *Two Years Before the Mast: A Personal Narrative of a Life at Sea.* New York: Harper, 1840.

Daniel, Larry. *Shiloh: The Battle That Changed the Civil War.* New York: Simon and Schuster, 1997.

Davis, Jefferson. *Jefferson Davis, Constitutionalist: His Letters, Papers, and Speeches.* Dunbar Roland, ed. Jackson: Mississippi Department of Archives and History, 1923.

Davis, William C. *The Battlefields of the Civil War: The Bloody Conflict of North Against South Told Through the Stories of Its Battles. Illustrated with Collections of Some of the Rarest Civil War Historical Artifacts.* Norman: University of Oklahoma Press, 1996.

——. *Death in the Trenches: Grant at Petersburg.* Alexandria, Va.: Time-Life Books, 1986.

Dawson, Francis W. *Reminiscences of Confederate Service.* Bell Wiley, ed. Baton Rouge: Louisiana State University Press, 1980.

Dawson, George F. *Life and Services of Gen. John A. Logan as Soldier and Statesman.* Chicago: T. H. Buch, 1887.

DeConde, Alexander. *A History of American Foreign Policy.* New York: Charles Scribner's Sons, 1963.

DeForest, John William. *A Volunteer's Adventures: A Union Captain's Record of the Civil War.* New Haven: Yale University Press, 1946.

Denison, C. W. *Illustrated Life, Campaigns, and Public Services of Philip Henry Sheridan.* Philadelphia: T. B. Peterson, 1865.

Dennett, Tyler, ed. *Lincoln and the Civil War in the Diaries and Letters of John Hay.* New York: Dodd Mead, 1939.

De Paris, Comte. *History of the Civil War in America.* 4 vols. Henry Coppee, ed. Philadelphia: Porter and Coates, 1875–88.

Dixon, Mrs. Archibald. *True Story of the Missouri Compromise and Its Repeal.* Cincinnati: R. Clarke, 1903.

Dodge, Grenville M. *Personal Recollections of President Abraham Lincoln, General U.S. Grant, and William T. Sherman.* Iowa: Monarch, 1902.

Donald, David Herbert. *Charles Sumner.* New York: Alfred A. Knopf, 1970.

——. *Liberty and Union.* Boston: Little, Brown, 1978.

——. *Lincoln.* New York: Simon and Schuster, 1995.

——. *Lincoln Reconsidered: Essays on the Civil War Era.* Westport, Conn.: Greenwood, 1980.

Donald, David Herbert, ed. *Why the North Won the Civil War.* Baton Rouge: Louisiana State University Press, 1960.

Doubleday, Abner. *Chancellorsville and Gettysburg: Campaigns of the Civil War.* New York: Charles Scribner's Sons, 1882.

Dowling, Allen. *The Great American Pastime.* New York: A. S. Barnes, 1970.

Downey, Fairfax. *Storming of the Gateway, Chattanooga.* New York: David McKay, 1960.

Drexler, Robert W. *Guilty of Making Peace: A Biography of Nicholas P. Trist.* Lanham, Md.: University Press of America, 1991.

Duke, John H. *History of the 53rd Ohio Volunteer Infantry.* Portsmouth, Ohio: Blade, 1900.

Dunning, William A. *Reconstruction, Political and Economic, 1865–1877.* New York: Harper, 1907.

DuPont, H. A. *The Campaign of 1864 in the Valley of Virginia and the Expedition to Lynchburg.* New York: National American Society, 1925.

Dupuy, R. Ernest. *Men of West Point: The First 150 Years of the United States Military Academy.* New York: Sloane, 1951.

Dupuy, R. Ernest, and Trevor N. Dupuy. *Military Heritage of America.* New York: McGraw-Hill, 1956.

Durham, Walter T. *Nashville: The Occupied City.* Nashville: Tennessee Historical Society, 1985.

Dye, John S. *History of the Plots and Crimes of the Great Conspiracy to Overthrow Liberty in America.* Freeport, N.Y.: Books for Libraries Press, 1969.

Dyer, Frederick A. *A Compendium of the War of the Rebellion.* 3 vols. New York: Oxford University Press, 1959.

Early, Jubal A. *Autobiographical Sketch and Narrative of the War Between the States.* Philadelphia: J. B. Lippincott, 1912.

——. *War Memoirs.* Bloomington, Ind.: Indiana University Press, 1960. Reprint.

Eaton, Herbert. *Presidential Timber: A History of Nominating Conventions, 1868–1960.* New York: Harper, 1964.

Eaton, John, and Ethel O. Mason. *Grant, Lincoln, and the Freedmen: Reminiscences of the Civil War with Special Reference to the Work of the Contrabands and Freemen of the Mississippi Valley.* New York: Longmans, Green, 1907.

Eckenrode, H. J., and Bryan Conrad. *George B. McClellan: The Man Who Saved the Union.* Chapel Hill: University of North Carolina Press, 1941.

Edgar, George P., ed. *Gems of the Campaign of 1880. By General Grant and Garfield.* Jersey City: Lincoln Association, 1881.

Edmonds, Franklin Spencer. *Ulysses S. Grant.* Philadelphia: George W. Jacobs, 1915.

Eisenhower, John S. D. *So Far from God.* New York: Random House, 1989.

Eliot, Charles W. *Winfield Scott: The Soldier and the Man.* New York: Macmillan, 1937.

Ellington, Charles G. *The Trial of U.S. Grant: The Pacific Coast Years, 1852–1854.* Glendale, Calif.: Arthur H. Clarke, 1987.

Ellis, Richard N. *General Pope and U.S. Indian Policy.* Albuquerque: University of New Mexico Press, 1970.

Evans, Clement A. *Confederate Military History.* 12 vols. Atlanta: J. B. Lippincott, 1899.

Fabens, Joseph W. *Life on the Isthmus.* New York: George P. Putnam, 1853.

Fairman, Charles. *Reconstruction and Reunion, 1864–1888.* 2 vols. New York: Macmillan, 1971.

Falkof, Lucille. *Ulysses S. Grant. 18th President of the United States.* Ada, Okla.: Garrett, 1988.

Faust, Patricia L., ed. *Historical Times Illustrated Encyclopedia of the Civil War.* New York: Harper and Row, 1986.

Fellman, Michael. *Citizen Sherman: A Life of William Tecumseh Sherman.* New York: Random House, 1995.

Ferrell, Robert H. *American Diplomacy.* New York: W. W. Norton, 1975.

Ficklen, John Rose. *History of Reconstruction in Louisiana.* Baltimore: Johns Hopkins University Press, 1910.

Fiske, John. *The Mississippi Valley in the Civil War.* Boston: Houghton Mifflin, 1901.

Fitch, Michael H. *The Chattanooga Campaign. With Special Reference to Wisconsin's Participation Therein.* Madison: Wisconsin History Commission, 1911.

Fleming, George T., ed. *Life and Letters of Alexander Hays: Brevet Colonel United States Army, Brigadier General and Brevet Major General United States Volunteers.* Edited and Arranged with Notes and Contemporary History by George Thornton Fleming from Data Compiled by Gilbert Adams Hays. Pittsburgh, 1919.

Fleming, Walter L., ed. *Documentary History of Reconstruction.* 2 vols. Gloucester, Mass.: P. Smith, 1960.

Folwell, William Watts. *A History of Minnesota.* St. Paul: Minnesota Historical Society, 1921.

Foner, Eric. *Reconstruction: America's Unfinished Revolution, 1863–1877.* New York: Macmillan, 1988.

———. *A Short History of Reconstruction.* New York: Harper and Row, 1990.

Foner, Jack D. *The United States Soldier Between Two Wars: Army Life and Reforms, 1865–1898.* New York: Humanities Press, 1970.

Foote, Shelby. *The Civil War: A Narrative.* 3 vols. New York: Random House, 1958–1974.

Forbes-Lindsay, C. H. *Panama: The Isthmus and the Canal.* Philadelphia: John C. Winston, 1906.

Force, Manning F. *From Fort Henry to Corinth.* New York: Charles Scribner's Sons, 1881.

———. *General Sherman.* New York: D. Appleton, 1899.

Ford, Paul Leicester, ed. *The Works of Thomas Jefferson.* New York: G. P. Putnam's Sons, 1905.

Ford, Worthington Chauncey, ed. *Cycle of Adams Letters, 1861–1865.* Boston: Houghton Mifflin, 1920.

Foster, G. Allen. *The Eyes and Ears of the Civil War.* New York: Criterion, 1963.

Fox, Gustavus. *Confidential Correspondence of Gustavus Fox, Assistant Secretary of the Navy.* New York: De Vinne Press, 1919.

Fox, William F. *Regimental Losses in the American Civil War, 1861–1865.* Albany, N.Y.: Harper, 1889.

Frassanito, William A. *Grant and Lee: The Virginia Campaigns, 1864–1865.* New York: Scribner's Reference, 1983.

Frazer, Robert W. *Forts of the West.* Norman: University of Oklahoma Press, 1965.

Frazer, Robert W., ed. *Joseph K. F. Mansfield on the Conditions of the Western Forts, 1853–1854.* Norman: University of Oklahoma Press, 1963.

Frederick, Maurice. *Statesmen and Soldiers of the Civil War: A Study of the Conduct of War.* New York: Charles Scribner's Sons, 1926.

Freeman, Douglas Southhall. *R. E. Lee.* 4 vols. New York: Charles Scribner's Sons, 1934.

Freeman-Mitford, Algernon Bertram, Baron Redesdale. *Memoirs.* London, 1915.

Fritz, Henry E. *The Movement for Indian Assimilation, 1860–1890.* Westport, Conn.: Greenwood, 1963.

Frost, John. *The Mexican War and Its Warriors.* New York: Harper, 1848.

Frost, Lawrence A. *U.S. Grant Album: A Pictorial Biography of Ulysses S. Grant.* Seattle: Superior, 1966.

Fry, Joseph A. *Henry S. Sanford: Diplomacy and Business in Nineteenth-Century America.* Reno: University of Nevada Press, 1982.

Fuller, J. F. C. *The Conduct of War, 1789–1961.* New Brunswick, N.J.: Rutgers University Press, 1961.

———. *The Generalship of Ulysses S. Grant.* London: John Murray, 1929.

———. *Grant and Lee: A Study in Personality and Generalship.* Bloomington, Ind.: Eyre and Spottiswoode, 1933.

Furgurson, Ernest B. *Chancellorsville 1863: The Souls of the Brave.* New York: Alfred A, Knopf, 1992.

———. *Not War But Murder: Cold Harbor 1864.* New York: Alfred A. Knopf, 2000.

Gage, Moses D. *From Vicksburg to Raleigh. A Complete History of the 12th Regiment Indiana Volunteer Infantry and the Campaign of Grant and Sherman, with an Outline of the Great Rebellion.* Chicago: Clarke, 1865.

Ganoe, William A. *The History of the United States Army.* Ashton, Md.: Eric Lundberg, 1964.

Gardner, Asa B. *Argument on Behalf of Lieut. Gen. Philip H. Sheridan.* Chicago: T. H. Buch, 1881.

Garfield, James A. *The Diary of James A. Garfield.* Harry J. Brown and Frederick D. Williams, eds. East Lansing: Michigan State University Press, 1973.

Garland, Hamlin. *A Daughter of the Middle Border.* New York: Macmillan, 1921.

———. *Ulysses S. Grant: His Life and Character.* 2 ed. New York: Macmillan, 1920.

Geer, Walter. *Campaigns of the Civil War.* New York: Brentano, 1926.

Gibbon, John. *Personal Recollections of the Civil War.* New York: G. P. Putnam's Sons, 1928.

Gilder, Richard Watson. *Letters of Richard Watson Gilder.* Rosamond Gilder, ed. London: Harrap, 1931.

Gillette, William. *Retreat from Reconstruction, 1869–1879.* Baton Rouge: Louisiana State University Press, 1979.
――. *The Right to Vote: Politics and the Passage of the Fifteenth Amendment.* Baltimore: Johns Hopkins University Press, 1965.
Goldhurst, Richard. *Many Are the Hearts: The Agony and Triumph of Ulysses S. Grant.* New York: Reader's Digest, 1975.
Gooch, G. P. *History and Historians in the Nineteenth Century.* London: Longmans, 1913.
Goodrich, Arthur. *Mr. Grant.* New York: Robert McBride, 1932–34.
Gordon, George H. *History of the Campaigns of the Army of Virginia, Under John Pope . . . from Cedar Mountain to Alexandria, 1862.* Boston: Houghton, Osgood, 1880.
――. *A War Diary of Events in the War of the Great Rebellion, 1863–1865.* Boston: J. R. Osgood, 1882.
Gordon, John B. *Reminiscences of the Civil War.* New York: Charles Scribner's Sons, 1904.
Govan, Gilbert, and James Livingwood. *General Joseph E. Johnston, C.S.A.: A Different Valor.* New York: Smithmark, 1995.
Gracie, Archibald, Jr. *The Truth About Chickamauga.* Boston: Houghton Mifflin, 1911.
Graham, Edward D. *American Ideas of a Special Relationship with China.* New York: Garland, 1988.
Grant, Arthur H. *The Grant Family: A Genealogicial History of the Descendants of Matthew Grant of Winsor, Conn. 1601–1898.* Poughkeepsie, N.Y.: A. V. Haight, 1898.
Grant, Jesse R., and Henry Francis Granger. *In the Days of My Father, General Grant.* New York: Harper and Brothers, 1925.
Grant, Julia Dent. *My Life Here and There.* New York: Harper, 1921.
――. *The Personal Memoirs of Julia Dent Grant.* John Y. Simon, ed. New York: G. P. Putnam's Sons, 1975.
Grant, Matthew G. *Ulysses S. Grant: General and President.* With illustrations by John Nelson. Mankato, Minn.: Creative Education, 1974.
Grant, Ulysses S. *General Grant's Letters to a Friend, 1861–1880.* With an introduction and notes by James Grant Wilson, ed. New York: Thomas Y. Crowell, 1897.
――. *Letters of Ulysses S. Grant to His Father and Youngest Sister.* New York: D. Appleton, 1912.
――. *Mr. Lincoln's General: U.S. Grant. An Illustrated Autobiography.* Roy Meredith, ed. New York: Dutton, 1959.
――. *Official Report of Lieut.-Gen. Ulysses S. Grant; Embracing a History of the Operations of the Armies of the Union from March 1862 to the Closing Scene of the Rebellion.* New York: Beadle, 1865.
――. *The Papers of Ulysses S. Grant.* 24 vols. John Y. Simon, ed. Carbondale: Southern Illinois University Press, 1967–2000.
――. *Personal Memoirs of U.S. Grant.* 2 vols. New York: Charles L. Webster, 1885.
――. *Report of Lieutenant-General U.S. Grant, of the Armies of the United States—1864–65.* New York: D. Appleton, 1866.
――. *Ulysses S. Grant: Conversations and Unpublished Letters.* M. J. Cramer, ed. New York: Eaton and Mains, 1897.
――. *Ulysses S. Grant, 1822–1885; Chronology, Documents, Bibliographical Aids.* Philip R. Moran, ed. Dobbs Ferry, N.Y.: Oceana, 1968.
――. *Words by Our Hero, Ulysses S. Grant.* Jeremiah Chaplin, ed. Boston: D. Lothrop, 1885.
Grant, Ulysses, III. *Ulysses S. Grant: Warrior and Statesman.* New York: William Morrow, 1969.
Greeley, Horace. *The American Conflict: A History of the Great Rebellion in the United States of America, 1860–1864.* 2 vols. Hartford, Conn.: Harper, 1865.
――. *Mr. Greeley's Letters from Texas and the Lower Mississippi.* New York: Tribune Office, 1871.
――. *What I Know of Farming.* New York: Tribune Association, 1871.
Green, Horace. *General Grant's Last Stand: A Biography.* New York: Century, 1936.
Greene, Francis Vinton. *Campaigns of the Civil War.* New York: Charles Scribner's Sons, 1884.
Greer, Allen Morgan. *The Civil War Diary of Allen Morgan Greer.* Mary Ann Anderson, ed. Tappan, N. Y.: Cosmos, 1977.
Griffith, Paddy. *Battle Tactics of the Civil War.* New Haven: Yale University Press, 1989.
Grinnell, Josiah B. *Men and Events of Forty Years: Autobiographical Reminiscences of an Active Career from 1850–1890.* Boston: Lothrop, 1891.
Hagerman, Edward. *The American Civil War and the Origins of Modern Warfare: Ideas, Organization, and Field Command.* Bloomington: Indiana University Press, 1988.
Halleck, Henry Wager. *Elements of Military Art and Science.* New York: D. Appleton, 1846.
Hamilton, James. *The Battle of Fort Donelson.* New York: Oxford University Press, 1968.
Hancock, Almira R. *Reminiscences of Winfield Scott Hancock.* New York: Charles L. Webster, 1887.
Hanly, J. Frank. *Vicksburg.* Cincinnati: Jennings and Graham, 1912.

Hanna, Ronnie. *Never Call Retreat. The Life and Times of Ulysses. S. Grant, Ulster-American Hero.* Lurgan: Ulster Society, 1991.

Hannaford, E. *The Story of a Regiment: A History of the Campaigns and Associations in the Field of the Sixth Regiment Ohio Volunteer Infantry.* Cincinnati: Hannaford, 1868.

Harley, James L. *The Buffalo War: The History of the Red River Indian Uprising of 1874.* Garden City, N.Y.: Doubleday, 1976.

Harrison, Frank. *Anecdotes and Reminiscences of General U.S. Grant.* Comp. by an Old Soldier. New York: Cheap Publishing, 1885.

Hart, Herbert M. *Old Forts of the Far West.* Seattle: Superior, 1965.

——. *Old Forts of the Northwest.* Seattle: Superior, 1963.

——. *Old Forts of the Southwest.* Seattle: Superior, 1964.

Hartje, Robert G. *Van Dorn: The Life and Times of a Confederate General.* Nashville: Vanderbilt University Press, 1967.

Harvey, George W. *Ulysses S. Grant: The Citizen, the Soldier, the Statesman.* Chicago: T. H. Bush, 1885.

Hassler, Warren W. *General George B. McClellan, Shield of the Union.* Baton Rouge: Louisiana State University Press, 1957.

Hattaway, Herman, and Archer Jones. *How the North Won: A Military History of the Civil War.* Urbana: University of Illinois Press, 1983.

Haworth, Paul Leland. *The Hayes-Tilden Disputed Election of 1876.* Indianapolis: Bobbs-Merrill, 1927.

Hay, John. *Lincoln and the Civil War in the Diaries and Letters of John Hay.* Tyler Dennett, ed. New York: Dodd, Mead, 1939.

Hayes, Rutherford B. *Diary and Letters of Rutherford B. Hayes.* Charles R. Williams, ed. Columbus: Ohio Historical Society, 1922.

Headley, Joel T. *Grant and Sherman: Their Campaigns and Generals.* New York: E. B. Treat, 1866.

——. *The Life and Travels of General Grant, from His Boyhood to the Surrender of Lee.* Philadelphia: Hubbard Brothers, 1879.

——. *The Travels of General Grant.* Philadelphia: New World, 1881.

Headley, P. C. *Facing the Enemy: The Life and Military Career of Gen. William Tecumseh Sherman.* Boston: Lee and Shepard, 1865.

——. *The Hero Boy; or, The Life and Deeds of Lieut-Gen. Grant.* New York: W. H. Appleton, 1864.

——. *The Life and Campaigns of General U.S. Grant.* New York: W. H. Appleton, 1868.

Hebert, Walter H. *Fighting Joe Hooker.* Indianapolis: Bobbs-Merrill, 1944.

Heiner, Gordon G. *From Saints to Red Legs: Madison Barracks, the History of a Border Post.* Watertown, N.Y.: A. W. Munk, n.d.

Hendrick, Burton J. *Lincoln's War Cabinet.* Boston: Little, Brown, 1946.

Hergesheimer, Joseph. *Sheridan: A Military Narrative.* Boston: Houghton Mifflin, 1931.

Hershkowitz, Leo. *Tweed's New York: Another Look.* Garden City, N.Y.: Doubleday, 1977.

Hesseltine, William B. *Lincoln and the War Governors.* New York: Alfred A. Knopf, 1948.

——. *Ulysses S. Grant: Politician.* New York: Dodd, Mead, 1935.

Heth, Henry. *The Memoirs of Henry Heth.* James L. Morrison, ed. Westport, Conn.: Greenwood, 1974.

Heyman, Max L. *Prudent Soldier: A Biography of Major General E. R. S. Canby, 1817–1873.* Glendale, Calif.: A. H. Clark, 1959.

Hibben, Paxton. *Henry Ward Beecher: An American Patriot.* New York: Doran, 1927.

Hillard, G. S. *Life and Campaigns of George B. McClellan, Major-General U.S. Army.* Philadelphia: J. B. Lippincott, 1864.

Hine, Robert F., and Savoie Lottinville. *Soldier in the West: Letters of Theodore Talbot During His Services in California, Mexico, and Oregon, 1845–53.* Norman: University of Oklahoma Press, 1972.

Hirshson, Stanley P. *Grenville M. Dodge: Soldier, Politician, Railroad Pioneer.* Bloomington: Indiana University Press, 1967.

——. *The White Tecumseh.* New York: Wiley, 1997.

Hitchcock, Ethan Allen. *Fifty Years in Camp and Field: Diary of Major-General Ethan Allen Hitchcock.* W. A. Crofutt, ed. New York: G. P. Putnam's Sons, 1909.

Hittle, Lt. Col. J. D. *Jomini and His Summary of the Art of War.* Harrisburg, Pa.: Military Service Publishing, 1947.

Hoar, George F. *Autobiography of Seventy Years.* New York: Charles Scribner's Sons, 1903.

Hobart, Edwin L. *The Truth About Shiloh.* Denver: Hicks-Fairall, 1909.

Hochling, A. A. *Vicksburg.* Englewood Cliffs, N.J.: Prentice Hall, 1969.

Hoig, Stan. *The Sand Creek Massacre.* Norman: University of Oklahoma Press, 1961.

Holmes, Oliver Wendell, Jr. *Touched with Fire: Civil War Letters and Diary of Oliver Wendell Holmes, Jr.,* Mark DeWolfe Howe, ed. Cambridge: Harvard University Press, 1946.

Holton, Bill. *From Battlefield to Bottom Line: The Leadership Lessons of Ulysses S. Grant.* Novato, Cal.: Presidio Press, 1995.

Hood, John B. *Advance and Retreat: Personal Experiences in the United States and Confederate Armies.* New Orleans: P. G. T. Beauregard for the Hood Orphan Memorial Fund, 1880.

Hopping, James Mason. *Life of Andrew Hull Foote: Rear-Admiral United States Navy.* New York: Harper and Brothers, 1874.

Horn, Stanley F. *The Decisive Battle of Nashville.* Knoxville: University of Tennessee Press, 1958.

Hosemer, James K. *Outcome of the Civil War, 1863–1865.* New York: Harper and Brothers, 1907.

Howard, McHenry. *Recollections of a Maryland Confederate Staff Soldier and Officer Under Johnston, Jackson, and Lee.* Baltimore: Williams and Wilkins, 1914.

Howard, Oliver Otis. *Autobiography of Oliver Otis Howard, Major General, United States Army.* 2 vols. New York: Baker and Taylor, 1908.

——. *My Life and Experience Among Our Hostile Indians.* Hartford, Conn.: A. D. Worthington, 1907.

Howard, Victor B. *Black Liberation in Kentucky: Emancipation and Freedom, 1862–1884.* Lexington: University Press of Kentucky, 1983.

Howell, Col. Willey. *Lieut.-General Grant's Campaign of 1864–65.* Cambridge: Harvard University Press, 1916.

Howland, Edward. *Grant As a Soldier and Statesman, Being a Succinct History of His Military and Civil Career.* Hartford, Conn.: J. B. Burr, 1868.

Hoyle, Edmund. *Hoyle's Games,* G. H. ——, Esq., ed. London: Longman, Rees, 1835.

Hubbell, John T., and James W. Geary, eds. *Biographical Dictionary of the Union: Northern Leaders of the Civil War.* Westport, Conn.: Greenwood, 1995.

Hubert, Charles F. *History of the 50th Regiment of Illinois Volunteer Infantry.* Kansas City: Western Veteran Publishing Company, 1894.

Hughes, Nathaniel C., Jr. *The Battle of Belmont: Grant Strikes South.* Chapel Hill: University of North Carolina Press, 1991.

Hughes, Nathaniel C., Jr., and Roy P. Stonesifer, Jr. *The Life and Wars of Gideon J. Pillow.* Chapel Hill: University of North Carolina Press, 1993.

Humphreys, Andrew A. *The Virginia Campaign of '64 and '65: The Army of the Potomac and the Army of the James.* New York: Charles Scribner's Sons, 1883.

Hunt, Gaillard. *Israel, Elihu, and Cadwallader Washburn: A Chapter in American Biography.* New York: Macmillan, 1925.

Hurlbert, William H. *General McClellan and the Conduct of the War.* New York: Sheldon, 1864.

Hussey, John A. *The History of Fort Vancouver.* Portland: Abbot, Kerns & Bell, 1957.

Hutton, Paul A. *Phil Sheridan and His Army.* Lincoln: University of Nebraska Press, 1973.

Hyde, Thomas W. *Following the Greek Cross; or, Memories of the Sixth Army Corps.* Boston: Houghton Mifflin, 1894.

Hyman, Harold M., and William M. Wiecek. *Equal Justice Under Law: Constitutional Development, 1835–1875.* New York: Harper and Row, 1982.

Illustrated Life, Campaigns, and Public Services of Lieutenant General Grant. Philadelphia: T. B. Peterson and Brothers, 1865.

An Impressed New Yorker. *Thirteen Months in the Confederate Army.* New York: Barnes and Burr, 1862.

Ingersoll, L. D. *A History of the War Department of the United States.* Washington, D.C.: Francis D. Mahun, 1880.

Jackson, Joseph Orville. *Some of the Boys: The Civil War Letters of Isaac Jackson, 1862–1865.* Carbondale: Southern Illinois University Press, 1960.

Jaynes, Gregory. *The Killing Ground: Wilderness to Cold Harbor.* Alexandria, Va.: Time-Life Books, 1986.

Johannsen, Robert W. *Stephen A. Douglas.* New York: Oxford University Press, 1973.

——. *The Union in Crisis, 1850–1877.* New York: Free Press, 1965.

Johnson, Andrew. *The Papers of Andrew Johnson.* 6 vols. Paul H. Bergeron, ed. Knoxville: University of Tennessee Press, 1992.

Johnson, Richard W. *Memoir of Major General George H. Thomas.* Philadelphia: J. B. Lippincott, 1881.

Johnson, Robert U. *Remembered Yesterdays.* Boston: Little, Brown, 1923.

Johnson, Robert U., and Clarence C. Buel., eds. *Battles and Leaders of the Civil War.* 4 vols. New York: Century, 1884–88.

Johnston, Joseph E. *Narrative of Military Operations, Directed During the Late War Between the States, by Joseph E. Johnston, General, C.S.A.* New York: D. Appleton, 1874.

Joinville, Prince de. *The Army of the Potomac: Its Organization, Its Commander, and Its Campaign.* New York: Anson D. F. Randolph, 1862.

Jomini, Antoine-Henri. *The Art of War.* G. H. Mendell and W. P. Craighill, trans. Novato, Calif.: Presidio Press, 1992.

Jones, Archer. *Civil War Command and Strategy: The Process of Victory and Defeat.* New York: Maxwell Macmillan, 1992.

———. *Confederate Strategy from Shiloh to Vicksburg.* Baton Rouge: Louisiana State University Press, 1961.

Jones, James Pickett. *John A. Logan: Stalwart Republican from Illinois.* Tallahassee: University Presses of Florida, 1982.

Jones, John W. *Life and Letters of Robert E. Lee: Soldier and Man.* New York: Neale, 1906.

Jordan, David M. *Roscoe Conkling of New York: Voice in the Senate.* Ithaca, N.Y.: Cornell University Press, 1971.

———. *Winfield Scott Hancock: A Soldier's Life.* Bloomington: Indiana University Press, 1988.

Jordan, Thomas, and Roger Pryor. *The Campaigns of Lieut.-Gen. Nathan Bedford Forrest.* New Orleans: Blelock, 1868.

Kamm, Richey. *The Civil War Career of Thomas A. Scott.* Philadelphia: University of Pennsylvania Press, 1940.

Kantor, MacKinlay. *Lee and Grant at Appomattox.* New York: Random House, 1964.

Katz, Irving. *August Belmont: A Political Biography.* New York: Random House, 1968.

Keegan, John. *The Mask of Command.* New York: Viking, 1987.

Keifer, Joseph Ward. *Slavery and Four Years of War.* New York: G. P. Putnam's Sons, 1900.

Keller, Robert H., Jr. *American Protestantism and United States Indian Policy, 1869–82.* Lincoln: University of Nebraska Press, 1983.

Kemble, John Haskell. *The Panama Route.* Berkeley: University of California Press, 1943.

Kenly, John R. *Memoirs of a Maryland Volunteer.* Philadelphia: J. B. Lippincott, 1873.

Kent, Zachary. *Ulysses S. Grant: Eighteenth President of the United States.* Chicago: Children Press, 1989.

Kinead, Robert. *The Simpson Grant Story.* Dungannon: Dungannon District Council, 1984.

King, Charles. *The True Ulysses S. Grant.* Philadelphia: J. B. Lippincott, 1914.

King, W. C., and W. P. Derby. *Campfire Sketches and Battle Field Echoes of the Rebellion.* Springfield, Mass.: W. C. King, 1887.

Korn, Bertram Wallace. *American Jewry and the Civil War.* Philadelphia: Jewish Publication Society of America, 1951.

Korn, Jerry. *The Fight to Chattanooga: Chickamauga to Missionary Ridge.* Alexandria, Va.: Time-Life Books, 1985.

———. *Pursuit to Appomattox: The Last Battles.* Alexandria, Va.: Time-Life Books, 1987.

———. *War on the Mississippi: Grant's Vicksburg Campaign.* Alexandria, Va.: Time-Life Books, 1985.

Larke, Julian K. *General Grant and His Campaigns: Illustrated with a Portrait, and Views of the Surrender of Fort Donelson and Vicksburg, and the Battles at Pittsburg Landing and Chattanooga.* New York: Derby, 1864.

Larke, Julian K., and J. Harris Patton. *General U.S. Grant: His Early Life and Military Career.* New York: Thomas Kelly, 1885.

Larson, Henrietta Melia. *Jay Cooke: Private Banker.* New York: Greenwood, 1968.

Latham, Henry. *Black and White: A Journal of a Three Months' Tour of the United States.* London: Macmillan, 1867.

Laubers, John. *The Inventions of Mark Twain.* New York: Hill and Wang, 1990.

Leckie, William H. *The Military Conquest of the Southern Plains.* Norman: University of Oklahoma Press, 1963.

Lee, Robert E. *Lee's Dispatches to Jefferson Davis.* Douglas Southall Freemen and Grady McWhiney, eds. New York: Harper, 1957.

———. *Papers of R. E. Lee.* Theodore Dwight, ed. Boston: Military Historical Society of Massachusetts, 1895.

———. *The Wartime Papers of R. E. Lee.* Clifford Dowdey and Louis H. Manarin, eds. Boston: Little, Brown, 1961.

Lehman, Donald H. *Executive Office Building.* Washington, D.C.: General Services Administration, 1964.

Levy, Joann. *They Saw the Elephant: Women in the California Gold Rush.* Hamden, Conn.: Anchor Books, 1990.

Lewis, Charles Lee. *Admiral Franklin Buchanan: Fearless Man of Action.* Baltimore: Norman, Remington, 1929.

Lewis, Lloyd. *Captain Sam Grant.* Boston: Little, Brown, 1950.

———. *Sherman: Fighting Prophet.* New York: Harcourt, Brace, 1932.

———. *Letters from Lloyd Lewis, Showing Steps in the Research for His Biography of U.S. Grant.* Robert Maynard Hutchins, ed. Boston: Little, Brown, 1950.

Lewis, Thomas S. W. *"To Do, to Be, to Suffer": The Memoirs of Ulysses S. Grant.* Saratoga Springs, N.Y.: Skidmore College Press, 1985.

Liddell Hart, B. H. *Sherman: Soldier, Realist, American.* New York: Praeger, 1958.

———. *Sherman: The Genius of the Civil War.* London: Benn, 1930.

———. *Strategy: The Indirect Approach.* London: Faber and Faber, 1954.

———. *Thoughts on War.* London: Faber and Faber, 1944.

Lincoln, Abraham. *The Collected Works of Abraham Lincoln.* Roy P. Basler, Marion Delores Pratt, and Lloyd A. Dunlap, eds. 10 vols. New Brunswick, N.J.: Rutgers University Press, 1954.

———. *The Collected Works of Abraham Lincoln. Second Supplement, 1848–1865.* Roy P. Basler and Christian O. Basler, eds. New Brunswick, N.J.: Rutgers University Press, 1990.

———. *The Living Lincoln.* Paul M. Angle and Earl Schenck Miers, eds. New Brunswick, N.J.: Rutgers University Press, 1955.

Lindsay, T. J. *Ohio at Shiloh: Report of the Commission.* Cincinnati: Combined Books, 1903.

Lindsley, John B., ed. *The Military Annals of Tennessee.* Nashville: Riverside, 1896.

Livermore, Thomas L. *Numbers and Losses in the Civil War in America: 1861–1865.* Bloomington: Indiana University Press, 1957.

Livermore, William R. *The Story of the Civil War: A Concise Account of the War in the United States of America Between 1861 and 1865.* New York: G. P. Putnam's Sons, 1933.

Logan, John A. *The Volunteer Soldier of America. By John A. Logan. With Memoir of the Author and Military Reminiscences from General Logan's Private Journal.* Chicago: T. H. Bush, 1887.

Long, Everette B. *The Civil War Day by Day: An Almanac, 1861–1865.* Garden City, N.Y.: Doubleday, 1971.

Longacre, Edward G. *From Union Stars to Top Hat: A Biography of the Extraordinary General James Harrison Wilson.* Harrisburg, Penn.: Stackpole, 1972.

Longstreet, James. *From Manassas to Appomattox: Memoirs of the Civil War in America.* James I. Robertson, Jr., ed. Bloomington: Indiana University Press, 1960. Reprint.

Lowe, Richard. *Republicans and Reconstruction in Virginia, 1856–1870.* Charlottesville: University Press of Virginia, 1991.

Lowell, James Russell. *Letters of James Russell Lowell.* Charles Eliot Norton, ed. New York: Harper and Brothers, 1894.

Lowry, Bates. *Building a National Image: Architectural Drawings for the American Democracy, 1789–1912.* Washington, D.C.: National Building Museum, 1985.

Lowry, Don. *Dark and Cruel War: The Decisive Months of the Civil War. September-December 1864.* New York: Hippocrene, 1993.

———. *No Turning Back: The Beginning of the End of the Civil War, March-June, 1864.* New York: Hippocrene, 1992.

———. *Towards an Indefinite Shore: The Final Months of the Civil War, December 1864–May 1865.* New York: Hippocrene, 1995.

Luthin, Reinhard H. *The Real Abraham Lincoln.* Englewood Cliffs, N.J.: Prentice Hall, 1960.

Lyman, Payson W. *With Grant and Meade from the Wilderness to Appomattox.* Lincoln: University of Nebraska Press, 1994. Reprint.

Lynch, Denis Tilden. *"Boss" Tweed: The Story of a Grim Generation.* New York: Boni and Liverwright, 1927.

MacArthur, Douglas. *Reminiscences.* New York: Random House, 1964.

Macartney, Clarence E. *Grant and His Generals.* New York: Robert M. McBride, 1953.

———. *Mr. Lincoln's Admirals.* New York: Funk and Wagnalls, 1956.

Madison, James. *Writings of James Madison.* 12 vols. Gaillard Hunt, ed. Washington, D.C., 1906.

Mantell, Martin E. *Johnson, Grant, and the Politics of Reconstruction.* New York: Columbia University Press, 1973.

Mardock, Robert Winston. *The Reformers and the American Indian.* Columbia: University of Missouri Press, 1971.

Marrin, Alber. *Unconditional Surrender: U.S. Grant and the Civil War.* New York: Maxwell Macmillan, 1994.

Marshall, A. O. *Army Life: From a Soldier's Journal.* Joliet, Ill.: privately published, 1884.

Marshall, Col. Charles. *An Aide-de-Camp of Lee.* Boston: Little, Brown, 1927.

Marshall, Edward C. *The Ancestry of General Grant, and Their Contemporaries.* New York: Sheldon, 1869.

Marshall, John. *An Autobiographical Sketch.* John Stokes Adams, ed. Ann Arbor: University of Michigan Press, 1937.

———. *The Papers of John Marshall.* 10 vols. Charles F. Hobson, ed. Chapel Hill: University of North Carolina Press, 1996.

Marshall-Cornwall, James. *Grant As Military Commander.* New York: Van Nostrand Reinhold, 1970.

Marszalek, John F. *Sherman: A Soldier's Passion for Order.* New York: Free Press, 1993.

Martin, Asa Earl. *After the White House.* State College, Penn.: Penns Valley Publishers, 1951.

Mason, Virginia. *The Public Life and Diplomatic Correspondence of James M. Mason.* New York: Neale, 1906.

Mauck, Jeffrey. *The Education of a Soldier. Ulysses S. Grant in the War with Mexico.* Steamboat Springs, Colo.: American Kestrel Press, 1996.

Maxwell, Sir Herbert, ed. *The Creevey Papers.* London: John Murray, 1904.

McClellan, Carswell. *The Personal Memoirs and Military History of U.S. Grant Versus the Record of the Army of the Potomac.* Boston: Houghton Mifflin, 1887.

McClellan, George B. *The Civil War Papers of George B. McClellan: Selected Correspondence, 1860–1865.* Stephen W. Sears, ed. New York: Ticknor and Fields, 1989.

——. *McClellan's Own Story.* W. C. Prime, ed. New York: Charles L. Webster, 1887.

McClure, Alexander K. *Abraham Lincoln and Men of War Times.* Philadelphia: Times Publishing, 1892.

McConnell, Thomas G. *Conversations with General Grant. An Informal Biography.* Annandale, Va.: Walnut Hill, 1990.

McCormick, Robert R. *Ulysses S. Grant: The Great Soldier of America.* New York: D. Appleton–Century, 1934.

——. *The War Without Grant.* New York: Bond Wheelwright, 1950.

McCulloch, Hugh. *Men and Measures of Half a Century.* New York: Charles Scribner's Sons, 1889.

McCullough, David. *The Path Between the Seas.* New York: Simon and Schuster, 1977.

——. *Truman.* New York: Simon and Schuster, 1992.

McDonald, John. *Secrets of the Great Whiskey Ring.* St. Louis: W. S. Bryan, 1880.

McDonough, James L. *Chattanooga: A Death Grip on the Confederacy.* Knoxville: University of Tennessee Press, 1984.

——. *Schofield: Union General in the Civil War and Reconstruction.* Tallahassee: Florida State University Press, 1972.

——. *Shiloh: In Hell Before Night.* Knoxville: University of Tennessee Press, 1977.

McDonough, James L., and Thomas L. Connelly. *Five Tragic Hours: The Battle of Franklin.* Knoxville: University of Tennessee Press, 1983.

McDonough, James L., and James Picket Jones. *War So Terrible: Sherman and Atlanta.* New York: W. W. Norton, 1987.

McElroy, Robert McNutt. *Jefferson Davis: The Unreal and the Real.* New York: Harper and Brothers, 1937.

McFeely, William S. *Grant: A Biography.* New York: W. W. Norton, 1981.

McHenry, Robert, ed. *Webster's American Military Biographies.* Springfield, Mass.: G. & C. Merriam, 1978.

McKenzie, John D. *Uncertain Glory: Lee's Generalship Re-Examined.* New York: Hippocrene, 1997.

McKinney, Francis F. *Education in Violence.* New York: Charles Scribner's Sons, 1961.

McKitrick, Eric L. *Andrew Johnson and Reconstruction.* Chicago: University of Chicago Press, 1960.

McMaster, John Bach. *The Life, Memoirs, Military Career, and Death of General U.S. Grant.* Philadelphia: Barclay, 1850.

McPherson, Edward. *The Political History of the United States During the Period of Reconstruction.* Washington, D.C.: Philip and Solomons, 1871.

McPherson, James M. *The Abolitionist Legacy: From Reconstruction to the NAACP.* Princeton: Princeton University Press, 1975.

——. *Battle Cry of Freedom: The Civil War Era.* New York: Oxford University Press, 1988.

——. *Ordeal by Fire.* 2nd ed. New York: McGraw-Hill, 1992.

——. *The Struggle for Equality.* Princeton: Princeton University Press, 1964.

McWhiney, Grady. *Battle in the Wilderness: Grant Meets Lee.* Fort Worth: Ryan Place, 1995.

——. *Braxton Bragg and Confederate Defeat.* New York: Columbia University Press, 1969.

McWhiney, Grady, ed. *Grant, Lee, Lincoln, and the Radicals: Essays on Civil War Leadership.* Evanston, Ill.: Northwestern University Press, 1964.

Meacham, Alfred B. *Wigwam and Warpath.* Boston: John P. Dale, 1875.

Meade, George, ed. *Life and Letters of General George Gordon Meade, Major-General United States Army.* 2 vols. New York: Charles Scribner's Sons, 1913.

Medical and Surgical History of the Rebellion, 1861–1865, vol. 1. Appendix. Washington, D.C.: Government Printing Office, 1870.

Meredith, Roy. *Mr. Lincoln's General, U.S. Grant.* New York: E. P. Dutton, 1959.

Merk, Frederick. *Manifest Destiny and Mission in American History.* New York: Alfred A. Knopf, 1963.

Meyer, Howard. *Let Us Have Peace: The Story of Ulysses S. Grant.* New York: Collier, 1966.

Michie, Peter S. *General McClellan*. New York: D. Appleton, 1901.
———. *The Life and Letters of Emory Upton*. New York: D. Appleton, 1885.
Miers, Earl S. *The General Who Marched to Hell: William Tecumseh Sherman*. New York: Alfred A. Knopf, 1951.
———. *The Great Rebellion*. New York: World, 1958.
———. *The Last Campaign. Grant Saves the Union*. Philadelphia: J. B. Lippincott, 1972.
———. *The Web of Victory: Grant at Vicksburg*. Baton Rouge: Louisiana State University Press, 1955.
Millis, Walter. *Arms and Men: A Study in American Military History*. New York: Capricorn, 1967.
Mitchell, Joseph B. *Decisive Battles of the Civil War*. New York: G. P. Putnam's Sons, 1955.
———. *Discipline and Bayonets: The Armies and Leaders in the War of the American Revolution*. New York: G. P. Putnam's Sons, 1967.
———. *Military Leaders in the Civil War*. New York: G. P. Putnam's Sons, 1972.
———. *Rebellion Record: A Diary of American Events, with Documents, Narratives, Illustrative Incidents, Poetry, etc.* 10 vols. New York: Harper, 1961–63.
———. *Twenty Decisive Battles of the World*. New York: Macmillan, 1964.
Moore, Frank. *The Rebel Record*. New York: G. P. Putnam, 1862.
Moran, P. *Ulysses S. Grant, Eighteen Twenty-two to Eighteen Eighty-five. Chronology, Document, Bibliographical Aids*. Dobbs Ferry, N.Y.: Oceana, 1968.
Morgan, Lewis Henry. *League of the HO-DE-NO-SAU-NEE, Iroquois*. Rochester, N.Y.: Dodd, Mead, 1851.
Morison, Samuel Eliot. *The Oxford History of the American People*. New York: Oxford University Press, 1965.
Morris, Roy, Jr. *Sheridan: The Life and Wars of General Phil Sheridan*. New York: Crown, 1992.
Morrison, James L., Jr. *The Best School in the World: West Point, the Pre–Civil War Years, 1833–1866*. Kent, Ohio: Kent State University Press, 1986.
Morton, Arthur S. *A History of the Canadian West to 1870–71*. Lewis G. Thomas, ed. Toronto: University of Toronto Press, 1973.
Mulholland, St. Claire Augustine. *The Story of the 116th Regiment Pennsylvania Volunteers in the War of the Rebellion*. Philadelphia: F. McManus, 1899.
Myers, William Starr, ed. *The Mexican War Diary of George B. McClellan*. Princeton: Princeton University Press, 1917.
National Party Conventions, 1831–1972. Washington, D.C.: Congressional Quarterly, 1976.
Nelson, William Javier. *Almost a Territory: America's Attempt to Annex the Dominican Republic*. Newark: University of Delaware Press, 1990.
Nevin, David. *The Road to Shiloh: Early Battles in the West*. Alexandria, Va.: Time-Life Books, 1983.
Nevins, Allan. *Civil War Books: A Critical Bibliography*. Baton Rouge: Published for the U.S. Civil War Centennial Commission by Louisiana State University, 1967–69.
———. *The Emergence of Modern America*. New York: Macmillan, 1927.
———. *Frémont: The West's Greatest Adventurer*. New York: Harper and Brothers, 1928.
———. *Hamilton Fish: The Inner History of the Grant Administration*. 2 vols. New York: Frederick Ungar, 1937.
———. *Ordeal of the Union. Selected Chapters*. With an introduction by E. B. Long, comp. New York: Charles Scribner's Sons, 1973.
———. *The War for the Union*. 6 vols. New York: Charles Scribner's Sons, 1959.
Newman, Harry Wright. *The Maryland Dents*. Richmond: Dietz Press, 1963.
Nichols, George W. *A Soldier's Story of His Regiment*. Jessup, Ga.: Continental Book, 1898.
Nicolay, Helen. *Lincoln's Secretary: A Biography of John G. Nicolay*. New York: Longmans, Green, 1949.
Nolan, Alan T. *Lee Considered: Robert E. Lee and the Civil War*. Chapel Hill: University of North Carolina Press, 1991.
Nolan, Dick. *Benjamin Franklin Butler: The Damndest Yankee*. Novato, Calif.: Presidio, 1991.
Norton, Charles Eliot. *Letters of Charles Eliot Norton*. Sarah Norton and M. A. DeWolfe Howe, eds. Boston: Houghton Mifflin, 1931.
Nunis, Doyce B., ed. *Recollections of Gen. Henry W. Halleck in 1847–49*. Los Angeles: Dawson's Book Shop, 1977.
Nye, Wilbur S. *Carbine and Lance: The Story of Old Fort Sill*. Norman: University of Oklahoma Press, 1937.
Oberholtzer, Ellis Paxson. *A History of the United States Since the Civil War*, vol. 3. New York: Macmillan, 1916.
O'Brien, Steven. *Ulysses S. Grant*. New York: Chelsea House, 1991.
O'Connor, Richard. *Sheridan the Inevitable*. Indianapolis: Bobbs-Merrill, 1953.

————. *Thomas: Rock of Chickamauga*. New York: Prentice Hall, 1948.

Okie, Howard S. *General U. S. Grant: A Defense*. New York: Vantage, 1970.

Oldroyd, Osborn H. *A Soldier's Story of the Siege of Vicksburg. From the Diary of Osborn H. Oldroyd with Confederate Accounts from Authentic Sources and an Introduction by Brevet Major-Gen. M. F. Force*. Springfield, Ill.: privately published, 1885.

Olgin, Joseph. *Ulysses S. Grant: General and President*. With illustrations by William Moyers. Boston: Houghton Mifflin, 1967.

Olson, James C. *Red Cloud and the Sioux Problem*. Lincoln: University of Nebraska Press, 1965.

Our Great Captains: Grant, Sherman, Thomas, Sheridan, and Farragut. New York: Charles B. Richardson, 1865.

Owens, Kenneth N. *Galena, Grant, and the Fortunes of War: A History of Galena, Illinois, During the Civil War*. DeKalb, Ill.: Northern Illinois University Press, 1963.

Page, Charles A. *Letters of a War Correspondent*. Boston: L. C. Page, 1899.

Page, Charles D. *History of the Fourteenth Regiment, Connecticut*. Meridan, Conn.: Horton, 1906.

Paine, Albert Bigelow. *Mark Twain, A Biography: The Personal and Literary Life of Samuel Langhorne Clemens*. 3 vols. New York: Harper and Brothers, 1912.

Palmer, Loomis T. [L. T. Remlap]. *General U.S. Grant's Tour Around the World*. Chicago: J . Fairbanks, 1885.

————. *The Life of General Grant: His Early Life, Military Achievements, and History of His Civil Administration, His Sickness and Death* Chicago: Winters and Stackhouse, 1885.

Parker, Arthur C. *The Life of General Ely S. Parker, Last Great Sachem of the Iroquois and General Grant's Military Secretary*. Buffalo: Buffalo Historical Society, 1919.

Parks, Joseph Howard. *General Edmund Kirby Smith, C.S.A*. Baton Rouge: Louisiana State University Press, 1954.

Parlett, David. *The Oxford Guide to Card Games*. New York: Oxford University Press, 1990.

Patrick, Marsena Rudolph. *Inside Lincoln's Army: The Diary of Marsena Rudolph Patrick, Provost Marshal General, Army of the Potomac*. David S. Sparks, ed. New York: Thomas Yoseloff, 1964.

Patrick, Rembert W. *The Fall of Richmond*. Baton Rouge: Louisiana State University Press, 1960.

Peltcher, David M. *Rails, Mines, and Progress: Seven American Promoters in Mexico, 1867–1911*. Ithaca, N.Y.: Cornell University Press, 1958.

Pemberton, John C. *Pemberton, Defender of Vicksburg*. Chapel Hill: University of North Carolina Press, 1944.

Pendel, Thomas F. *Thirty-six Years in the White House*. Washington: Neale, 1902.

Penniman, Major. *The Tanner-Boy and How He Became Lieutenant-General*. Boston: Roberts Brothers, 1864.

Perman, Michael. *The Road to Redemption: Southern Politics, 1869–1879*. Chapel Hill: University of North Carolina Press, 1984.

Perret, Geoffrey. *Ulysses S. Grant: Soldier and President*. New York: Random House, 1996.

Peyton, George Q. *A Civil War Record for 1864–1865*. Robert A. Hodge, ed. Fredericksburg, Va.: Oxford University Press, 1981.

Phelps, Charles A. *Life and Public Services of General Ulysses S. Grant, from his Boyhood to the Present Time*. New York: Lee and Shepard and Dillingham, 1868.

Piatt, Donn. *Memories of the Men Who Saved the Union*. New York: Belford, Clarke, 1887.

Pierce, Edward L. *Memoir and the Letters of Charles Sumner*, vol. 4. Boston: Roberts Brothers, 1894.

Pierpoint, Francis H. *Letters of Governor Pierpoint to His Excellency the President and the Honourable Congress on the Subject of the Abuse of Military Power in the Command of General Butler in Virginia and North Carolina*. Washington: McGill and Witherow, 1864.

Pitkin, Thomas M. *The Captain Departs: Ulysses S. Grant's Last Campaign*. Carbondale: Southern Illinois University Press, 1973.

————. *Grant the Soldier*. Washington: Acropolis Books, 1965.

Platt, Thomas C. *The Autobiography of Thomas Collier Platt*. Louis J. Lang, ed. New York: B. W. Dodge, 1910.

Pleasants, Henry J., Jr., and George H. Straley. *Inferno at Petersburg*. Philadelphia: J. B. Lippincott, 1961.

Polk, James K. *Polk: The Diary of a President, 1845–1849*. Allan Nevins, ed. London: Longmans Green, 1929.

Pollard, Edward A. *The First Year of the War*. Richmond, Va.: M. Gleason, 1862.

Pollard, Edward. *The Lost Cause*. New York: Treat, Marrow, 1867.

Polley, Joseph B. *Hood's Texas Brigade: Its Marches, Its Battles, Its Achievements*. New York: Neale, 1910.

Pond, George E. *The Shenandoah Valley in 1864*. New York: Charles Scribner's Sons, 1883.

Poore, Benjamin P., and O. H. Tiffany. *Life and Public Services of Ambrose E. Burnside, Soldier, Citizen, and Statesman.* With an introduction by Henry B. Anthony. Providence, R.I.: J. A. and R. A. Reid, 1882.

——. *Life and Public Services of John Sherman.* Cincinnati: Sherman Club, 1880.

——. *Life of U.S. Grant.* Philadelphia: Hubbard Brothers, 1885.

——. *The West Point Cadet: The Turns of Fortune's Wheel.* Boston: Elliott, Thomas and Talbot, 1863.

Porter, David D. *Incidents and Anecdotes of the Civil War.* New York: D. Appleton, 1885.

——. *Naval History of the Civil War.* New York: Sherman, 1885.

Porter, Horace. *Campaigning with Grant.* New York: Century, 1897.

Post, James L., ed. *Reminiscences by Personal Friends of Gen. U.S. Grant and the History of Grant's Log Cabin.* St. Louis: privately published, 1904.

Potter, David M. *The Impending Crisis, 1848–1861.* Completed by Don E. Fehrenbacher, ed. New York: Harper and Row, 1976.

Powell, William H. *A History of the Fourth Regiment of Infantry, U.S. Army from May 30, 1796 to December 31, 1870.* Washington, D.C.: M'Gill and Witherow, 1871.

Pratt, Fletcher. *Stanton: Lincoln's Secretary of War.* New York: W. W. Norton, 1953.

Prucha, Francis Paul. *American Indian Policy in Crisis: Christian Reformers and the Indian, 1865–1900.* Norman: University of Oklahoma Press, 1976.

——. *A Guide to the Military Posts of the United States, 1789–1895.* Madison: State Historical Society of Wisconsin, 1964.

Quarles, Benjamin. *Lincoln and the Negro.* New York: Oxford University Press, 1962.

——. *The Negro in the Civil War.* Boston: Little, Brown, 1953.

Rable, George C. *But There Was No Peace: The Role of Violence in the Politics of Reconstruction.* Athens: University of Georgia Press, 1984.

Rahill, Peter J. *The Catholic Indian Missions and Grant's Peace Policy, 1870–1884.* Washington, D.C.: Catholic University of America Press, 1953.

Randall, James G. *Lincoln the Liberal Statesman.* New York: Dodd, Mead, 1947.

Randall, James G., and David Donald. *The Civil War and Reconstruction.* 2nd ed. Boston: D. C. Heath, 1961.

Rawley, James A. *The Politics of Union: Northern Politics During the Civil War.* Hinsdale, Ill.: Dryden Press, 1974.

Reed, Rowena. *Combined Operations in the Civil War.* Annapolis, Md.: Naval Institute Press, 1978.

Reed, Samuel Rockwell. *The Vicksburg Campaign and the Battles About Chattanooga Under the Command of General U.S. Grant in 1862–1863: An Historical Review.* Cincinnati: R. Clarke, 1882.

Reeder, Russell P. *U.S. Grant: Horseman and Fighter.* With illustrations by Ken Wagner. Champaign, Ill.: Garrard, 1964.

Reitz, Earl F. *American Gold Mettle. A Sentient Perspective of Ulysses Grant.* Louisa, Fla.: Xenolith Press, 1994.

Remlap, L. T., ed. *The Life of General U.S. Grant.* Chicago: Charles Scribner's Sons, 1885.

Repp, Stephen. *Ulysses S. Grant: The Galena Years.* Galena, Ill.: S. Repp., 1985.

Rhea, Gordon C. *The Battle of the Wilderness, May 5–6, 1864.* Baton Rouge: Louisiana State University Press, 1994.

——. *The Battles for Spotsylvania Court House and Yellow Tavern, May 7–12, 1864.* Baton Rouge: Louisiana State University Press, 1997.

Rhodes, Elisha Hunt. *All for the Union: The Civil War Diary and Letters of Elisha Hunt Rhodes.* Robert H. Rhodes, ed. New York: Charles Scribner's Sons, 1991.

Rhodes, James Ford. *History of the United States.* New York, Macmillan, 1906.

Richardson, Albert Deane. *A Personal History of Ulysses S. Grant.* Hartford, Conn.: American Publishing, 1868.

Rickerby, Laura A. *Ulysses S. Grant and the Strategy of Victory.* Englewood Cliffs, N.J.: Silver Burdett, 1991.

Riddleberger, Patrick W. *1866: The Critical Year Revisited.* Carbonale: Southern Illinois University Press, 1979.

Ringwalt, John Luther. *Anecdotes of General Ulysses S. Grant, Illustrating His Military and Political Career and His Personal Traits.* Philadelphia: J. B. Lippincott, 1886.

Robinson, H. E. *American Ancestry of U.S. Grant.* Salem: Higginson, 1993.

Rodenbough, Theodore F., and William L. Haskin, eds. *The Army of the United States: Historical Sketches of Staff and Line with Portraits of Generals-in-Chief.* New York: Argonaut Press, 1966.

Rodick, Burleigh Cushing. *Appomattox: The Last Campaign.* New York: Philosophical Library, 1965.

Roland, Charles. *Albert Sidney Johnston: Soldier of Three Republics.* Austin: University of Texas Press, 1964.

Roman, Alfred D. *The Military Operations of General Beauregard in the War Between the States.* New York: Harper, 1883.

Ropes, J. C. *The Army Under Pope*. New York: Charles Scribner's Sons, 1882.

——. *The Story of the Civil War*. 4 vols. New York: G. P. Putnam, 1894–98.

Ross, Isabel. *The General's Wife: The Life of Mrs. Ulysses S. Grant*. New York: Dodd, Mead, 1959.

Ruggles, Richard I. *A Country So Interesting: The Hudson's Bay Company and Two Centuries of Mapping, 1670–1870*. Montreal: McGill-Queen's University Press, 1991.

Rushmore, Elsie M. *The Indian Policy During Grant's Administration*. Jamaica, N.Y.: Marion Press, 1914.

Russell, William Howard. *My Diary North and South*. Fletcher Pratt, ed. New York: Harper, 1954.

Sanborn, John B. *The Crisis at Champion's Hill: The Decisive Battle of the Civil War*. St. Paul, Minn., n.p., 1903.

Sanger, Donald B. and Thomas R. Hay. *James Longstreet*. Baton Rouge: Louisiana State University Press, 1952.

Scaturro, Frank J. *President Grant Reconsidered*. Lanham, Md.: University Press of America, 1998.

Schaff, Morris. *The Battle of the Wilderness*. Boston: Houghton Mifflin, 1910.

——. *The Sunset of the Confederacy*. Boston: John W. Luce, 1912.

Schofield, John M. *Forty-six Years in the Army*. New York: Century, 1897.

Schuckers, Jacob S. *The Life and Public Services of Salmon Portland Chase*. New York: D. Appleton, 1874.

Schurz, Carl. *Intimate Letters of Carl Schurz*. Joseph Schafer, ed. Madison: University of Wisconsin Press, 1928.

——. *Speeches, Correspondence, and Political Papers of Carl Schurz*. Frederic Bancroft, ed. New York: G. P. Putnam's Sons, 1913.

Schutz, Wallace J., and Walter N. Trenerry. *Abandoned by Lincoln: A Military Biography of General John Pope*. Urbana: University of Illinois Press, 1990.

Schwartz, Harold. *Samuel Gridley Howe: Social Reformer, 1801–1876*. Cambridge, Mass.: Harvard University Press, 1956.

Scott, Myron. *Ten Generations of Grants*. Washington, D.C.: privately published, 1971.

Scott, Robert G. *Into the Wilderness with the Army of the Potomac*. Bloomington: Indiana University Press, 1985.

Scott, Winfield. *The Memoirs of Lieut-Gen Winfield Scott*. New York: Sheldon, 1864.

Sears, Stephen W. *George B. McClellan: The Young Napoleon*. New York: Ticknor and Fields, 1988.

——. *To the Gates of Richmond: The Peninsula Campaign*. New York: Ticknor and Fields, 1983.

Sedgwick, John. *Correspondence of John Sedgwick, Major General*. New York: DeVinne Press, 1902.

Sefton, James E. *The United States Army and Reconstruction, 1865–1877*. Baton Rouge: Louisiana State University Press, 1967.

Seifert, Shirley. *Captain Grant: A Novel*. Philadelphia: J. B. Lippincott, 1946.

Seymour, William J. *The Civil War Memoirs of Captain William J. Seymour: Reminiscences of a Louisiana Tiger*. Baton Rouge: Louisiana State University Press, 1991.

Shankle, George Earlie. *State Names, Flags, Seals, Songs, Birds, Flowers, and Other Symbols*. New York: H. W. Wilson, 1941.

Shanks, Henry T. *The Secession Movement in Virginia, 1847–1861*. Richmond, Va.: Garrett and Massie, 1934.

Shanks, William B. *Personal Recollections of Distinguished Generals*. New York: Harper and Brothers, 1866.

Shannon, Fred A. *The Organization and Administration of the Union Army*. 2 vols. Cleveland: Arthur H. Clarke, 1928.

Sheridan, Philip H. *Personal Memoirs of P. H. Sheridan, General, United States Army*. 2 vols. New York: Charles L. Webster, 1888.

Sherman, John. *Recollections of Forty Years in the House, Senate, and Cabinet*. Chicago: Werner, 1893.

Sherman, William T. *Home Letters of General Sherman*. Mark A. DeWolfe Howe, ed. New York: Charles Scribner's Sons, 1909.

——. *Personal Memoirs of Gen. W. T. Sherman*. 2 vols. New York: D. Appleton, 1875.

——. *The Sherman Letters; Correspondence Between General and Senator Sherman from 1837 to 1891*. Rachel Sherman Thorndike, ed. New York: Charles Scribner's Sons, 1894.

——. *Two Letters from General William Tecumseh Sherman to General Ulysses S. Grant and William T. McPherson. In the Collection of W. K. Bixby of Saint Louis*. Boston: Merrymount Press, 1919.

Shotwell, Walter G. *Life of Charles Sumner*. New York: Thomas Y. Crowell, 1910.

Shrady, George F. *General Grant's Last Days*. New York: privately published, 1908.

Simkins, Francis Butler, and Robert Hilliard Woody. *South Carolina During Reconstruction*. Chapel Hill: University of North Carolina Press, 1934.

Simon, John Y. *Ulysses S. Grant Chronology*. Athens: Ohio Historical Society, 1963.

Simon, John Y., and David L. Wilson., ed. *Ulysses S. Grant: Essays, Documents.* Carbondale: Southern Illinois University Press, 1981.

Simpson, Brooks D. *Let Us Have Peace. Ulysses S. Grant and the Politics of War and Reconstruction, 1861–1868.* Chapel Hill: University of North Carolina Press, 1991.

Slattery, Charles Lewis. *Felix Reville Brunot.* New York: Longmans, Green, 1901.

Smith, Donald V. *Salmon P. Chase and Civil War Politics.* Columbus, Ohio: F. J. Heer, 1931.

Smith, E. Kirby. *To Mexico with Scott: Letters of Ephrim Kirby Smith to His Wife.* Cambridge: Harvard University Press, 1917.

Smith, Edward Conrad. *The Borderland in the Civil War.* New York: Macmillan, 1927.

Smith, Gene. *Lee and Grant: A Dual Biography.* New York: McGraw-Hill, 1984.

Smith, Jean Edward. *John Marshall: Definer of a Nation.* New York: Henry Holt, 1996.

———. *Lucius D. Clay: An American Life.* New York: Henry Holt, 1990.

Smith, Justin. *The War with Mexico.* New York: Macmillan, 1919.

Smith, Colonel Nicholas. *Grant, the Man of Mystery.* Milwaukee: Young Churchman Co., 1909.

Smith, Robert G. *Into the Wilderness with the Army of the Potomac.* Bloomington: Indiana University Press, 1985.

Smith, Theodore Clark, ed. *The Life and Letters of James Abram Garfield.* New Haven: Yale University Press, 1925.

Smith, William F. *From Chattanooga to Petersburg Under Generals Grant and Butler: A Contribution to the History of the War, and a Personal Vindication.* Boston: Houghton Mifflin, 1893.

Snead, Thomas L. *The Fight for Missouri from the Election of Lincoln to the Death of Lyon.* New York: Charles Scribner's Sons, 1886.

Sommers, Richard J. *Richmond Redeemed: The Siege at Petersburg.* Garden City, N.Y.: Doubleday, 1981.

Sorrel, G. Moxley. *Recollections of a Southern Staff Officer.* New York: Neale, 1905.

Sparks, David S., ed. *Inside Lincoln's Army: The Diary of Marsena Rudolph Patrick, Provost Marshal General, Army of the Potomac.* New York: Charles Scribner's Sons, 1964.

Stackpole, Edward J. *The Fredericksburg Campaign.* Harrisburg, Penn.: Stackpole, 1957.

Stampp, Kenneth M. *The Era of Reconstruction, 1865–1877.* New York: Alfred A. Knopf, 1965.

Starr, Stephen Z. *The Union Cavalry in the Civil War.* 2 vols. Baton Rouge: Louisiana State University Press, 1985.

Steele, Matthew F. *American Campaigns.* Washington, D.C.: Byron S. Adams, 1909.

Steere, Edward. *The Wilderness Campaign. The Meeting of Grant and Lee.* Introduction by Robert Krick. Mechanicsburg, Pa.: Stackpole, 1994.

Stein, Gertrude. *Four in America.* New Haven: Yale University Press, 1947.

Steins, Richard. *Lincoln, Johnson, and Grant.* Vero Beach, Fla.: Rourke, 1996.

Stephenson, Nathaniel W. *Abraham Lincoln and the Union.* New Haven: Yale University Press, 1918.

Stern, Philip Van Doren. *An End to Valor: The Last Days of the Civil War.* Boston: Houghton Mifflin, 1958.

Stevens, Walter B. *Grant in St. Louis, from Letters in the Manuscript Collection of William K. Bixby.* St. Louis: Franklin Club, 1916.

Stickles, Arndt M. *Simon Bolivar Buckner: Borderland Knight.* Chapel Hill: University of North Carolina Press, 1940.

Stoddard, William O. *William O. Stoddard: Lincoln's Third Secretary.* New York: Exposition, 1955.

Storey, Moorfield, and Edward W. Emerson. *Ebenezer Rockwood Hoar: A Memoir.* Boston: Houghton Mifflin, 1911.

Strong, George Templeton. *The Diary of George Templeton Strong: The Civil War, 1860–1865.* Allan Nevins and Milton Halsey Thomas, eds. New York: Macmillan, 1952.

Strozier, Charles B. *Unconditional Surrender and the Rhetoric of Total War: From Truman to Lincoln.* New York: Oxford University Press, 1987.

Stuart, George H. *The Life of George H. Stuart.* Philadelphia: J. H. Stoddard, 1890.

Sturgis, S. D. *The Other Side, as Viewed by Generals Grant, Sherman, and Other Distinguished Officers, Being a Defence of His Campaign into N.E. Mississippi in the Year 1864.* Washington, D.C., 1882.

Summers, Mark W. *Railroads, Reconstruction, and the Gospel of Progess: Aid Under the Radical Republicans, 1865–1877.* Princeton: Princeton University Press, 1984.

Sumner, Charles. *The Works of Charles Sumner,* vol. 13. Boston: Lee and Shepard, 1875.

Survivor's Association. *121st Regiment Pennsylvania Volunteers.* Philadelphia: Catholic Standard and Times, 1906.

Swift, John L. *About Grant.* New York: C. T. Dillingham, 1880.

Swinton, William. *Campaigns of the Army of the Potomac.* New York: Charles B. Richardson, 1866.

———. *The Twelve Decisive Battles of the War, A History of the Eastern and Western Campaigns in Relation to the Actions That Decided Their Issue.* New York: Dick and Fitzgerald, 1867.

Sword, Wiley. *Shiloh: Bloody April*. Dayton, Ohio: Morningside Bookshop, 1988.

Symonds, Craig L. *Joseph E. Johnston: A Civil War Biography*. New York: W. W. Norton, 1992.

———. *Stonewall of the West: Patrick Cleburne and the Civil War*. Lawrence: University Press of Kansas, 1997.

Taft, William Howard. *Our Chief Magistrate and His Powers*. New York: Columbia University Press, 1916.

Tansill, Charles Callan. *The United States and Santo Domingo, 1798–1873*. Baltimore: Johns Hopkins University Press, 1938.

Tatum, Lawrie. *Our Red Brothers and the Peace Policy of President Ulysses S. Grant*. Lincoln: University of Nebraska Press, 1970.

Taussig, William. *Personal Recollections of General Grant*. St. Louis: Missouri Historical Society Publications, 1903.

Taylor, Walter H. *General Lee: His Campaigns in Virginia, 1861–1865, with Personal Reminiscences*. Lincoln: University of Nebraska Press, 1906.

Tenney, William J. *Military and Naval History of the Rebellion in the United States. With Biographical Sketches of Deceased Officers*. New York: D. Appleton, 1865.

Thayer, W. M. *From Tannery to the White House: The Life of Ulysses S. Grant*. Boston: Hurst, 1885.

Thian, Raphael P. *Notes Illustrating the Military Geography of the United States, 1813–1880*. Austin: University of Texas Press, 1979.

Thomas, Benjamin P. *Abraham Lincoln: A Biography*. New York: Alfred A. Knopf, 1952.

Thomas, Benjamin P., and Harold Hyman. *Stanton: The Life and Times of Lincoln's Secretary of War*. New York: Alfred A. Knopf, 1962.

Thomas, Henry. *Ulysses S. Grant*. New York: G. P. Putnam's Sons, 1961.

Thompson, George H. *Arkansas and Reconstruction*. Port Washington, N.Y.: Harper and Row, 1976.

Thompson, Robert E., ed. *George H. Stuart: The Life of George H. Stuart*. Philadelphia: J. M. Stoddard, 1890.

Thompson, Lieutenant Seymour D. *Recollections with the Third Iowa Regiment*. Cincinnati: privately published, 1864.

Thorndike, Rachel S., ed. *The Sherman Letters: Correspondence Between General and Senator Sherman from 1837 to 1891*. New York: Charles Scribner's Sons, 1894.

Ticknor, George. *Life, Letters, and Journals of George Ticknor*. Anna Ticknor and George S. Hillard, eds. Boston: J. R. Osgood, 1877.

Tilley, John Shipley. *Lincoln Takes Command*. Chapel Hill: University of North Carolina Press, 1941.

Todd, Helen. *A Man Named Grant*. Boston: Houghton Mifflin, 1940.

Townsend, Edward D. *Anecdotes of the Civil War*. New York: Charles Scribner's Sons, 1884.

Trefousse, Hans L. *Andrew Johnson: A Biography*. New York: W. W. Norton, 1989.

———. *Ben Butler: The South Called Him BEAST!* New York: Octagon, 1974.

———. *Historical Dictionary of Reconstruction*. New York: Greenwood, 1991.

Trent, Payson J. *Diplomatic Relations Between the United States and Japan, 1853–1895*. New York: Macmillan, 1932.

Trowbridge, John T. *A Picture of the Desolated States and the Work of Restoration, 1865–1868*. Hartford, Conn.: L. Stebbins, 1868.

Trudeau, Noah A. *Bloody Roads South: The Wilderness to Cold Harbor, May–June 1864*. Boston: Little, Brown, 1989.

Tucker, Glenn. *Chickamauga: Bloody Battle in the West*. Indianapolis: Bobbs-Merrill, 1961.

———. *High Tide at Gettysburg*. Indianapolis: Bobbs-Merrill, 1958.

Tunnard, Willie H. *A Southern Record*. Baton Rouge: privately published, 1866.

Turchin, John B. *Chickamauga*. Chicago: Fergus, 1888.

Turner, George Edgar. *Victory Rode the Rails*. Indianapolis: Bobbs-Merrill, 1953.

Twain, Mark. *The Gilded Age*. New York: American, 1874.

———. *Mark Twain's Letters*. Albert Bigelow Paine, ed. 2 vols. New York: Harper and Brothers, 1917.

Twombly, V. P. *The Second Iowa Infantry at Fort Donelson, Feb. 15, 1862*. Des Moines: Plain Talk Printing House, 1901.

The Ulysses S. Grant Song Book. New York: Dawley, 1868.

Unger, Irwin. *The Greenback Era: A Social and Political History of American Finance, 1865–1879*. Princeton: Princeton University Press, 1964.

U.S. Infantry School. *Battle of Belmont*. Camp Benning, Ga.: Bobbs-Merrill, 1921.

Utley, Robert M. *Frontiersmen in Blue, The United States Army and the Indian, 1848–1865*. New York: Macmillan, 1967.

———. *The Indian Frontier of the American West, 1846–1890*. Albuquerque: University of New Mexico Press, 1984.

Vance, Wilson J. *Stone's River: The Turning-Point of the Civil War.* New York: Neale, 1914.

Van Horne, Thomas B. *The Life of General George H. Thomas.* New York: Charles Scribner's Sons, 1882.

Vetter, Charles E. *Sherman: Merchant of Terror, Advocate of Peace.* Gretna: Pelican, 1992.

Vilas, William F. *A View of the Vicksburg Campaign. A Paper Read Before the Madison Literary Club, October 14th, 1907.* Madison: Wisconsin History Commission, 1908.

Wainwright, Charles S. *A Diary of Battle: The Personal Journals of Colonel Charles S. Wainwright, 1861–1865.* Allan Nevins, ed. New York: Harcourt, Brace and World, 1962.

Walker, Francis A. *General Hancock.* New York: D. Appleton, 1895.

———. *Hancock in the War of the Rebellion.* New York: G. J. Little, 1891.

———. *History of the Second Army Corps in the Army of the Potomac.* New York: Charles Scribner's Sons, 1886.

Walker, Henry. *Naval Scenes and Reminiscences of the Civil War in the United States.* New York: Harper, 1877.

Walker, Peter F. *Vicksburg, A People at War, 1860–1865.* Chapel Hill: University of North Carolina Press, 1960.

Wallace, Ernest. *Texas in Turmoil: The Saga of Texas, 1849–1875.* New York: Garrett, 1969.

Wallace, Lew. *Lew Wallace: An Autobiography.* 2 vols. New York: Harper and Brothers, 1906.

Wallace, W. H. L. *Life and Letters of W. H. L. Wallace.* Isabel Wallace, ed. Chicago: R. R. Donnelley, 1909.

Walters, John B. *Merchant of Terror: General Sherman and Total War.* Indianapolis: Bobbs-Merrill, 1973.

Warden, Robert B. *An Account of the Private Life and Public Services of Salmon Portland Chase.* Cincinnati: Wilstach, Baldwin, 1874.

Warner, Ezra J. *Generals in Blue: Lives of the Union Commanders.* Baton Rouge: Louisiana State University Press, 1964.

———. *Generals in Gray: Lives of the Confederate Commanders.* Baton Rouge: Louisiana State University Press, 1959.

Warren, Charles. *The Supreme Court in United States History.* 2 vols. Boston: Little, Brown, 1926.

Webb, Ross A. *Benjamin Helm Bristow: Border State Politician.* Lexington: University of Kentucky Press, 1969.

———. *Kentucky in the Reconstruction Era.* Lexington: Little, Brown, 1979.

Webster, Samuel C., ed. *Mark Twain, Business Man.* Boston: Houghton Mifflin, 1946.

Weeks, Philip. *Farewell My Nation: The American Indian and the United States, 1820–1890.* Arlington Heights, Ill.: Harlan Davidson, 1990.

Weigley, Russell F. *The American Way of War: A History of United States Military Strategy and Policy.* New York: Macmillan, 1973.

———. *History of the United States Army.* New York: Macmillan, 1967.

———. *Quartermaster General of the Union Army: A Biography of M. C. Meigs.* New York: Columbia University Press, 1959.

———. *Towards an American Army: Military Thought from Washington to Marshall.* New York: Columbia University Press, 1962.

Weisberger, Bernard A. *Reporters for the Union.* Boston: Little, Brown, 1953.

Welcher, Frank J. *The Union Army, 1861–1865: Organization and Operations.* 2 vols. Bloomington: Indiana University Press, 1989–93.

Welles, Gideon. *Diary of Gideon Welles, Secretary of the Navy Under Lincoln and Johnson.* John T. Morse, ed. 3 vols. Boston: Houghton Mifflin, 1911.

Wert, Jeffry D. *General James Longstreet: The Confederacy's Most Controversial Soldier.* New York: Simon and Schuster, 1993.

West, Richard S., Jr. *Lincoln's Scapegoat General: A Life of Benjamin F. Butler, 1818–1893.* Boston: Houghton Mifflin, 1965.

Wharton, H. M., ed. *War Songs and Poems of the Southern Confederacy, 1861–1865.* Philadelphia: John C. Winston, 1904.

Wharton, Vernon L. *The Negro in Mississippi, 1865–1890.* New York: Harper and Row, 1965.

Wheeler, Richard. *Lee's Terrible Swift Sword: From Antietam to Chancellorsville, an Eyewitness History.* New York: HarperCollins, 1992.

———. *Witness to Appomattox.* New York: Harper and Row, 1989.

White, Andrew Dickson. *Autobiography of Andrew Dickson White.* New York: Century, 1905.

White, Charles T. *Grant's Tribute to Lincoln.* Brooklyn, N.Y.: Macmillan, 1932.

White, Leonard D. *The Republican Era: A Study in Administrative History, 1869–1901.* New York: Free Press, 1965.

Wilcox, Cadmus Marcellus. *History of the Mexican War.* Mary Rachel Wilcox, ed. Washington, D.C.: Church News Publishing, 1892.

Wiley, Bell I. *The Road to Appomattox.* Baton Rouge: Louisiana State University Press, 1994.

Wiley, Bell I., and Hirst D. Milhollen. *They Who Fought Here.* New York: Macmillan, 1959.

Williams, George W. *A History of the Negro Troops in the War of the Rebellion. Preceded by a Review of the Military Services of Negroes in Ancient and Modern Times.* New York: W. Y. Bergman, 1968.

Williams, Kenneth P. *Lincoln Finds a General: A Military Study of the Civil War.* 5 vols. New York: Macmillan, 1952.

Williams, T. Harry. *Lincoln and His Generals.* New York: Alfred A. Knopf, 1952.

——. *McClellan, Sherman, and Grant.* New Brunswick, N.J.: Rutgers University Press, 1962.

——. *P. G. T. Beauregard: Napoleon in Gray.* Baton Rouge: Louisiana State University Press, 1954.

Williamson, Joel. *After Slavery: The Negro in South Carolina During Reconstruction, 1861–1877.* Chapel Hill: University of North Carolina Press, 1965.

Wilson, Edmund. *Patriotic Gore: Studies in the Literature of the American Civil War.* New York: Oxford University Press, 1962.

Wilson, James Grant. *General Grant.* New York: D. Appleton, 1897.

——. *The Life and Campaigns of Ulysses Simpson Grant: General-in-Chief of the United States Army.* New York: R. M. De Witt, 1868.

——. *The Life and Letters of Fitz-Greene Halleck.* New York: D. Appleton, 1869.

——. *The Life and Public Services of Ulysses Simpson Grant: General of the United States Army and Twice President of the United States.* New York: R. M. DeWitt, 1885.

Wilson, James H. *The Campaign of Chancellorsville, April 27-May 5, 1863. A Critical Review by Major John Bigelow Jr.* Wilmington, Del.: C. L. Story, 1911.

——. *The Life of Charles A. Dana.* New York: Harper and Brothers, 1907.

——. *The Life of John A. Rawlins: Lawyer, Assistant Adjutant General, Chief of Staff, Major General of Volunteers, and Secretary of War.* New York: Neale, 1916.

——. *Under the Old Flag: Recollections of Military Operations in the War for the Union, the Spanish War, the Boxer Rebellion, etc.* 2 vols. New York: D. Appleton, 1902.

Wilson, John. *Chattanooga's Story.* Chattanooga: Chattanooga Publishing Co., 1980.

Wing, Henry E. *When Lincoln Kissed Me: A Story of the Wilderness Campaign.* New York: Abingdon, 1913.

Wirt, Armistead Cate, ed. *Two Soldiers, The Campaign Diaries of Thomas J. Key, C.S.A. and Robert J. Campbell, U.S.A.* Chapel Hill: University of North Carolina Press, 1936.

Wise, Jennings C. *The Long Arm of Lee; or, the History of the Artillery of the Army of Northern Virginia.* Lynchburg, Va: J. P. Bell, 1915.

Wister, Owen. *Ulysses S. Grant.* Boston: Small, Maynard, 1909.

Wolf, Simon. *The Presidents I Have Known from 1860–1918.* Washington, D.C.: B. S. Adams, 1918.

Wood, Walter B., and James E. Edmonds. *The Civil War in the United State with Special Reference to the Campaigns of 1864 and 1865.* London: Methuen, 1937.

Wood, William C. H. *Captains of the Civil War, A Chronicle of the Blue and Gray.* New Haven: Yale University Press, 1921.

Woodward, C. Vann. *Reunion and Reaction: The Compromise of 1877 and the End of Reconstruction,* rev. ed. New York: Doubleday, 1956.

Woodward, W. E. *Meet General Grant.* New York: Horace Liveright, 1928.

Woodworth, Stephen E. *A Deep Steady Thunder: The Battle of Chickamauga.* Fort Worth: Ryan Place Publishers, 1996.

Wooster, Ralph A. *The Secession Conventions in the South.* Princeton: Princeton University Press, 1962.

Wooster, Robert. *The Military and United States Indian Policy.* New Haven: Yale University Press, 1988.

Young, Bob. *Reluctant Warrior: Ulysses S. Grant.* New York: Julian Messner, 1971.

Young, John Russell. *Around the World with General Grant: A Narrative of the Visit of General U.S. Grant, Ex-President of the United States, to Various Countries in Europe, Asia, and Africa, in 1877, 1878, 1879.* 2 vols. New York: American News, 1879.

——. *Men and Memoirs: Personal Reminiscences.* 2 vols. May D. Russell Young, ed. New York: F. Tennyson Neely, 1901.

Zadra, Dan. *Ulysses S. Grant: General and President, 1822–1885.* Mankato, Minn.: Creative Education, 1988.

Articles

Adams, Z. Boylston. "In the Wilderness." In *Civil War Papers.* 2 vols. Boston: Houghton Mifflin Company, 1900, pp. 373–99.

Alexander, Edward P. "The Wilderness Campaign." In *Annual Report of the American Historical Association for the Year of 1908*, vol. 1. Washington, D.C., 1909, pp. 223–47.

Alexander, Thomas G. "A Conflict of Perceptions: Ulysses S. Grant and the Mormons." *Newsletter*. Carbondale, Ill.: U.S. Grant Association, 1971.

"Alfred B. Mullett." In Adolph H. Placzek, ed., *Macmillan Encyclopedia of Architects*. New York: Free Press, 1982, pp. 251–52.

Allen, Stacey D. "Shiloh! The Campaign and First Day's Battle." In *Blue and Gray*, vol. 14 (1997).

Ammen, David. "Recollections and Letters of Grant." *North American Review*, vol. 141 (July–December 1885), pp. 361–73.

Anbinder, Tyler. "Ulysses S. Grant, Nativist." *Civil War History*, vol. 43 (1997).

Andreas, Alfred T. "The 'Ifs and Buts' of Shiloh." In *Military Essays and Recollections*, vol. 1. Chicago: Belfords, Clark, 1891, pp. 528–62.

Andrews, Peter. "The Rock of Chickamauga." *American Heritage*, vol. 41, no. 2 (1990), pp. 81–91.

Applen, Allen G. "An Attempted Indian State Government: The Okmulgee Constitution in Indian Territory." *Kansas Quarterly*, vol. 3 (Fall 1971), pp. 89–99.

Armstrong, Warren B. "Union Chaplains and the Education of the Freedmen." *Journal of Negro History*, vol. 52, no. 2 (1967), pp. 104–15.

Ash, Stephen V. "Civil War Exodus: The Jews and Grant's General Orders No. 11." *The Historian*, vol. 44 (1982).

Ashcraft, Allan C., ed. "Mrs. Russell and the Battle of Raymond, Mississippi." *Journal of Mississippi History*, vol. 25, no. 1 (1963), pp. 38–40.

Athos, E. "Some Aspects of the American Civil War, 1861–1865." *Journal of the Royal United Service Institute* (Great Britain), vol. 101, no. 603 (1956), pp. 387–95.

Avery, A. C. "Life and Character of Lieutenant-Gen. D. H. Hill." In *Southern Historical Society Papers*, vol. 21 (1893), p. 115.

Babbitt, Juliette M. "Nellie Grant Sartoris and Her Children." *Midland Monthly*, vol. 7 (February 1897), pp. 99–102.

Badeau, Adam. "General Grant." *Century Magazine*, vol. 30 (October 1885), pp. 151–63.

———. "The Last Days of General Grant." *Century Magazine*, vol. 30 (October 1885), pp. 919–39.

———. "Lieut.-General Sheridan." *Century Magazine*, vol. 27 (February 1884), pp. 496–511.

———. "The Mystery of Grant." *Cosmopolitan*, vol. 20 (March 1896), pp. 483–92.

Balling, Ole Peter H. "An Artist's Close-up of Lincoln, Grant, and Sherman." *Civil War Times Illustrated*, vol. 3, no. 6 (1964), pp. 12–18.

Barnes, William Henry Linow. "Grant." Before Commandery of California, Military Order of the Loyal Legion of the United States. *War Papers*, no. 19 (December 22, 1896), pp. 22–78.

Barnwell, Robert W. "The Battle of Belmont." *Confederate Veteran*, vol. 39, pp. 370–71.

Bauer, Dan. "The Big Bender." *Civil War Times Illustrated*, vol. 27, no. 8 (1988), pp. 34–43.

Bearss, Edwin C. "Battle at Champion Hill: Sealing the Fate of Vicksburg." *Strategy and Tactics*, vol. 103 (1985), pp. 21–24.

———. "The Day at Shiloh." *Register of Kentucky Historical Society*, vol. 63, no. 1 (1965), pp. 39–69.

———. "General Nelson Saves the Day at Shiloh." *Register of the Kentucky Historical Society*, vol. 63 (1965).

———. "Misfire in Mississippi: McPherson's Canton Expedition." *Civil War History*, vol. 8, no. 4 (1962), pp. 401–16.

———. "Sherman's Demonstration Against Snyder's Bluff." *Journal of Mississippi History*, vol. 27, no. 2 (1965), pp. 168–86.

———. "Unconditional Surrender: The Fall of Fort Donelson." *Tennessee Historical Quarterly*, vol. 35 (March–June 1962), pp. 254–78.

Bearss, Edwin C., ed. "The Civil War Diary of Colonal William H. Raynor During the Vicksburg Campaign." *Louisiana Studies*, vol. 9, no. 4 (1970), pp. 243–300.

Beaver, R. Pierce. "American Missionary Efforts to Influence Government Indian Policy." *Journal of Church and State*, vol. 5, no. 1 (1963), pp. 77–94.

Becker, Carl M. "Was Grant Drinking in Mexico?" *Cincinnati Historical State Bulletin*, vol. 24, no. 1 (1966), pp. 68–71.

Bedford, M. L. "Fight Between the Batteries and Gunboats at Fort Donelson." *Southern Historical Society Papers*, vol. 13 (January–December 1885), pp. 247–98.

Bell, Patricia. "Gideon Pillow: A Personality Profile." *Civil War Times Illustrated*, vol. 6 (June 1967), pp. 12–19.

Benedict, Michael Les. "The Rout of Radicalism: Republicans and the Elections of 1867." In Robert P. Swierenga, ed., *Beyond the Civil War Synthesis: Political Essays of the Civil War Era*. Westport, Conn.: Greenwood, 1975, pp. 137–48.

———. "Ulysses S. Grant." In Frank N. Magill, ed., *The American Presidents.* Pasadena, Calif.: Salem Press, 1989.

Benjamin, Mary A. "Grant and the Lost $1,000." *The Collector,* vol. 69 (1956), pp. 17–20.

Bolles, Charles E. "General Grant and the News of Mr. Lincoln's Death." In "Memoranda on the Life of Lincoln." *Century Magazine,* vol. 40, no. 2 (June 1890), pp. 309–10.

Bond, Brian. "Appomattox: The Triumph of General Grant." *History Today* (Great Britain), vol. 15, no. 5 (1965), pp. 297–305.

Boutwell, George S. "General Grant's Administration." *McClure's Magazine,* vol. 14 (November 1899), pp. 355–62.

Bowfield, Hartwell. "Louis Riel's Letter to President Grant, 1875." *Saskatchewan Historical Review,* vol. 21, no. 2 (1968), pp. 67–75.

Boynton, H. V. "The Whiskey Ring." *North American Review* (1876).

Bradwell, Isaac G. "Battle of the Wilderness." *Confederate Veteran,* vol. 16 (1908), pp. 447–48.

———. "One Hour Saved the Union." *Confederate Veteran,* vol. 34 (1926), pp. 252–53.

———. "Second Days' Battle of the Wilderness." *Confederate Veteran,* vol. 28 (1920), pp. 20–22.

Breithaupt, John. "U.S. Grant, Writing to Meet the Emergency." *Technical Communication,* vol. 38 (February 1991), pp. 150–51.

Brock, Darla. " 'Our Hands Are at Your Service' The Story of Confederate Women in Memphis." *West Tennessee Historical Society Papers,* vol. 45 (1991), pp. 19–34.

Brooksher, William R., and David Snider. "A Visit to Holly Springs." *Civil War Times Illustrated,* vol. 14, no. 3 (1975), pp. 4–17.

Brown, D. Alexander. "Grierson's Raid, 'Most Brilliant' of the War." *Civil War Times Illustrated,* vol. 3, no. 9 (1965), pp. 4–11, 30–32.

Brown, Dee. "The Last Days of 'Sam' Grant." *American History Illustrated,* vol. 7, no. 8 (1972), pp. 4–9, 42–48.

Brown, Walter L. "Pea Ridge: Gettysburg of the West." *Arkansas Historical Quarterly,* vol. 15, no. 1 (Spring 1956), pp. 49–65.

Bruce, George A. "The Donelson Campaign." *Military Historical Society of Massachusetts,* vol. 7 (1908), pp. 257–98.

———. "General Buell's Campaign Against Chattanooga." *Military Historical Society of Massachusetts,* vol. 8 (1910), pp. 32–78.

Bryson, Thomas A. "Walter George Smith and General Grant's Memoirs." *Pennsylvania Magazine of History and Biography,* vol. 94, no. 2 (1970), pp. 233–44.

Buell, D. C. "Shiloh Reviewed." *Century Magazine,* vol. 31 (April 1886), pp. 749–81.

Burke, Albie. "Federal Regulation of Congressional Elections in Northern Cities, 1871–94." *American Journal of Legal History,* vol. 14, no. 1 (1970), pp. 17–34.

Burleigh [pseud.]. "Caesarism: General Grant for a Third Term." *Boston Journal.* New York: Hurd and Houghton, 1873.

Busbey, Hamilton. "Recollections of Abraham Lincoln and the Civil War." *Forum,* vol. 45 (March 1911), pp. 282–90.

Byers, Samuel H. M. "Some More War Letters." *North American Review,* vol. 144 (April 1887), pp. 374–80.

———. "Some Personal Recollections of General Sherman." *McClure's Magazine,* vol. 3 (August 1894), pp. 212–24.

———. "Some Recollections of Grant." In *Annals of the War Written by Leading Participants North and South.* Reprint. Edison, N.J.: Blue and Grey Press, 1996.

Campbell, John A. *Recollections of the Evacuation of Richmond, April 1865.* Pamphlet. Baltimore, 1880.

———. *Reminiscences and Documents Relating to the Civil War During the Year 1865.* Pamphlet. Baltimore, 1886.

Carey, Raymond G. "The Puzzle of Sand Creek." *Colorado Magazine,* vol. 41 (1964), pp. 279–98.

Carnes, W. W. "In the Battle of Belmont." *Confederate Veteran,* vol. 39, pp. 369–70.

Carpenter, John A. "Washington, Pennsylvania, and the Gold Conspiracy of 1869." *Western Pennsylvania Historical Magazine,* vol. 48, no. 4 (1965), pp. 345–54.

Casey, Emma Dent. "When Grant Wooed and Won Julia Dent." *Sunday Magazine,* vol. 24 (January–February 1909), pp. 178–79.

Castel, Albert. "The Road to Vicksburg: Grant's Masterpiece in the Mississippi Valley." *Strategy and Tactics,* vol. 103 (1985), pp. 14–21.

———. "William Tecumseh Sherman." *Civil War Times Illustrated.* vol. 18, no. 4 (1979), pp. 4–7.

Catton, Bruce. "Grant and the Politicans." *American Heritage,* vol. 19, no. 6 (1968), pp. 32–35, 81–87.

———. "Two Porches, Two Parades." *American Heritage,* vol. 17 (June 1966), pp. 35–38.

———. "U.S. Grant: Man of Letters." *American Heritage,* vol. 19 (June 1968), pp. 45–48.

Catton, Bruce, ed. "Grant Writes Home." *American Heritage,* vol. 24, no. 6 (October 1973), pp. 92–93.

Chamberlain, Joshua L. "Appomattox." In Military Order of the Loyal Legion of the United States, New York Commandry. *Personal Recollections of the War of Rebellion,* 3rd series. New York: Charles Scribner's Sons, 1907, pp. 260–80.

Chang, Richard T. "General Grant's 1879 Visit to Japan." *Monumenta Nipponica* (Japan), vol. 24, no. 4 (1969), pp. 373–92.

Chase, John L. "Unconditional Surrender Reconsidered." *Political Science Quarterly,* vol. 70, no. 2 (1955), pp. 258–79.

Chetlain, Augustus Louis. "Recollections of General U.S. Grant." In *Military Essays and Recollections,* vol. 1. Chicago: Military Order of the Loyal Legion of the United States, 1891.

Coates, Foster. "The Courtship of General Grant." *Ladies' Home Journal,* vol. 12 (October 1890), pp. 4–8.

Coles, Oscar. "Seward or Grant in 1868?" *New York History,* vol. 15 (April 1934), pp. 195–200.

Colling, B. F. "Campaign for Forts Henry and Donelson." *Conflict,* vol. 7 (1974), pp. 28–39.

Colton, Kenneth E., ed. "With Frémont in Missouri in 1861: Letters of Samuel Ryan Curtis." *Annals of Iowa,* vol. 24, 3rd series (1942).

Conger, A. L. "Fort Donelson." *The Military Historian and Economist,* vol. 1 (1916).

Cooling, Benjamin F. "Gideon Johnson Pillow." In Roger J. Spiller, ed., *Dictionary of American Military Biography,* vol. 3. Westport, Conn.: Harper and Row, 1985, pp. 861–65.

Cosdorf, Paul D. "West Virginia and the 1880 Republican Convention." *West Virginia History,* vol. 24, no. 2 (1963), pp. 147–55.

Cox, J. D. "The Civil Service Reform." *North American Review,* vol. 112 (1871), pp. 81–113.

———. "How Judge Hoar Ceased to Be an Attorney-General." *Atlantic Monthly* (August 1895).

Coxe, John. "Last Struggles and Successes of Lee." *Confederate Veteran,* vol. 22 (1914), pp. 356–59.

Crane, James L. "Grant As a Colonel: Conversation Between Grant and His Chaplain." *McClure's Magazine,* vol. 7 (June 1896), pp. 40–45.

———. "Grant from Galena." *Civil War Times Illustrated,* vol. 18, no. 4 (1979), pp. 26–29.

Crawford, T. C. "General Grant's Greatest Year." *McClure's Magazine,* vol. 2 (May 1894), pp. 535–43.

Creswell, Stephen. "Enforcing the Enforcement Acts: The Department of Justice in Northern Mississippi, 1870–1890." *Journal of Southern History,* vol. 53 (1987).

Crowell, Jackson. "The United States and a Central American Canal, 1869–1877." *Hispanic American Historical Review,* vol. 49, no. 1 (1969), pp. 27–52.

Cullen, Joseph P. "Battle of the Wilderness." *Civil War Times Illustrated,* vol. 10, no. 1 (1971), pp. 42–47.

———. "Encounters of Grant and Lee." *Civil War Times Illustrated,* vol. 10, no. 1 (1971), pp. 4–11.

———. "Spotsylvania." *Civil War Times Illustrated,* vol. 10, no. 2 (1971), pp. 4–9, 46–48.

———. "When Grant Faced Lee Across the North Anna." *Civil War Times Illustrated,* vol. 3, no. 10 (1965), pp. 16–23.

Current, Richard N. "Grant Without Greatness." *Reviews in American History,* vol. 9, no. 4 (1981), pp. 507–9.

———. "Let Us Have Peace: Ulysses S. Grant and the Politics of War and Reconstruction, 1861–1868." *Hayes Historical Journal,* vol. 11, no. 3 (1992), pp. 40–42.

Curtis, David. "Early Failure of a Conquering Hero." *The Pacific Historian.* vol. 19, no. 4 (Winter 1975), pp. 356–362.

Dailey, Douglass C. "The Elections of 1872 in North Carolina." *North Carolina Historical Review,* vol. 40, no. 3 (1963), pp. 338–60.

Daniel, Larry J. "Bruinsburg: Missed Opportunity or Postwar Rhetoric?" *Civil War History,* vol. 32, no. 3 (1986), pp. 256–67.

Dauphine, James G. "The Knights of the White Camellia and the Election of 1868: Louisiana's White Terrorists; A Benighting Legacy." *Louisiana History,* vol. 30, no. 2 (1989), pp. 173–90.

Davis, Theodore R. "General Sheridan's Personality." *Cosmopolitan,* vol. 13 (June 1892), pp. 209–16.

Dawes, Ephraim C. "The Battle of Shiloh." *Military Historical Society of Massachusetts,* vol. 7 (1908), pp. 201–22.

Deupree, J. G. "The Capture of Holly Springs, Mississippi, Dec. 20, 1862." *Publications of the Mississippi Historical Society* (1901), pp. 49–61.

Dick, David B. "Resurgence of the Chicago Democracy, April–November 1861." *Journal of the Illinois State Historical Society,* vol. 56, no. 2 (1963), pp. 139–49.

Dickson, John N. "The Civil War Years of John Alexander Logan." *Journal of the Illinois State Historical Society,* vol. 56, no. 2 (1963), pp. 212–32.

Dillon, Rodney E., Jr. "Don Carlos Buell and the Union Leadership." *Lincoln Herald,* vol. 82, no. 2 (1980), pp. 363–73.

Dodge, Grenville M. "Personal Recollections of General Grant and His Campaigns in the West." In

Military Order of the Loyal Legion of the United States, New York Commandry, *Personal Recollections of the War of the Rebellion,* 3rd series. New York: D. Appleton, 1907, pp. 347–72.

———. "Personal Recollections of Some of Our Great Commanders in the Civil War." In Military Order of the Loyal Legion of the United States, New York Commandry, *Personal Recollections of the War of the Rebellion,* 3rd series. New York: D. Appleton, 1907, pp. 207–27.

Donald, David Herbert. "Overrated and Underrated Americans." *American Heritage,* vol. 39 (1988), pp. 48–63.

Dorsett, Lyle W. "The Problem of Ulysses S. Grant's Drinking During the Civil War." *Hayes Historical Journal,* vol. 4, no. 2 (1983), pp. 37–48.

Dunham, Samuel. "Spotsylvania: A 63rd Pennsylvania Comrade Tells About the Fight." *National Tribune,* June 10, 1886.

Dunlap, Lloyd A. "The Grant–Lee Surrender Correspondence." *Manuscripts,* vol. 21, no. 2 (1969), pp. 79–92.

Eastman, John. "U.S. Grant Slept Here." *Civil War Times Illustrated,* vol. 25, no. 3 (1986), pp. 44–46.

Edwards, E. J. "Grant: Before He Won His Stars." *McClure's Magazine,* vol. 5 (June 1895), pp. 38–44.

Eisenschiml, Otto. "The 55th Illinois at Shiloh." *Journal of the Illinois State Historical Society,* vol. 56, no. 2 (1963), pp. 193–211.

———. "Shiloh—The Blunders and the Blame." *Civil War Times Illustrated,* vol. 2, no. 1 (1963), pp. 6–13, 30–34.

Ellis, Richard N. "Civilians, the Army, and the Indian Problem on the Northern Plains, 1862–1866." *North Dakota History,* vol. 37, no. 1 (1970), pp. 20–39.

———. "The Humanitarian Generals." *Western Historical Quarterly,* vol. 3 (April 1972), pp. 169–78.

———. "The Humanitarian Soldiers." *Journal of Arizona History,* vol. 10 (Summer 1969), pp. 53–66.

Elson, Henry W. "Shiloh—The First Grand Battle." *By Valor and Arms,* vol. 2, no. 4 (1976), pp. 54–69.

Emerson, John W. "Grant's Life in the West and His Mississippi Valley Campaigns." *Midland Monthly Magazine,* vol. 6 (July–December 1896), pp. 291–303, 387–99, 488–499; vol. 7 (January–June 1897), pp. 30–41, 138–47, 218–26, 316–29, 430–38, 497–501; vol. 8 (July–December 1897), pp. 3–9, 138–43, 206–20, 316–25, 451–60, 494–504.

Engle, Stephen D. "Don Carlos Buell: Military Philosophy and Command Problems in the West." *Civil War History,* vol. 41 (1995), pp. 89–115.

Erhardt, Joel B. "Grant's Reasons for Relieving General William F. Smith." *Century Magazine,* vol. 32 (October 1886), pp. 783–88.

Erickson, Edgar L., ed. "With Grant at Vicksburg. From the Civil War Diary of Charles E. Wilcox." *Journal of the Illinois State Historical Society,* vol. 30 (April 1937–January 1938), pp. 256–98.

Fairman, Charles. "Mr. Justice Bradley's Appointment to the Supreme Court and the Legal Tender Cases." *Harvard Law Review,* vol. 54 (1940).

Farnum, George R. "John A. Rawlins: Country Lawyer and Grant's Lieutenant." *American Bar Association Journal,* vol. 29 (November 1943), pp. 165–70.

Farrand, Max. "The Indian Boundary Line." *American Historical Review,* vol. 10 (1905), pp. 782–91.

Feis, William B. "Neutralizing the Valley: The Role of Military Intelligence in the Defeat of Jubal Early's Army of the Valley, 1864–1865." *Civil War History,* vol. 39, no. 3 (1993), pp. 199–215.

———. "A Union Military Intelligence Failure: Jubal Early's Raid, June 12–July 14, 1864." *Civil War History,* vol. 36 (September 1990), pp. 209–25.

Feller, John Q. "The China Trade and the Asiatic Squadron." *Winterthur Portfolio,* vol. 18, no. 4 (1983), pp. 291–99.

———. "Julia Dent Grant and the Mikado Porcelain." *Winterthur Portfolio,* vol. 24, no. 2–3 (1989), pp. 165–74.

———. "The White House 'Rose Medallion': Daniel Ammen and the Ulysses S. Grant Porcelain." *American Neptune,* vol. 43, no. 3 (1983), pp. 177–86.

Ferris, S. C. "Hardships of the Isthmus in '49." *Century Magazine,* vol. 46 (April 1891), pp. 53–62.

Field, Charles W. "Campaign of 1864 and 1865." *Southern Historical Society Papers,* vol. 14. Richmond: Southern Historical Society Publications, 1876–1944, pp. 542–63.

Field, Erastus. "The Visit of General Ulysses S. Grant and His Entourage to Italy in 1878." *Antiques,* vol. 136 (October 1989), pp. 627–31.

Fiorentino, Daniele. "La Politica Di Ripartizione Delle Terre Indiane Nelle Grandi Pianure Degli Stati Uniti" [The Politics of Indian Land Distribution in the Great Plains of the United States]. *Storia Contemporanea* (Italy), vol. 16, no. 1 (1985), pp. 91–112.

Fishel, Edwin C. "The Mythology of Civil War Intelligence." *Civil War History,* vol. 10, no. 4 (December 1964), pp. 344–67.

Frank, Fedora S. "Nashville Jewry During the Civil War." *Tennessee Historical Quarterly,* vol. 39, no. 3 (1980), pp. 310–22.

Franklin, John Hope. "Election of 1868." In Arthur M. Schlesinger, Jr., ed., *History of American Presidential Elections*, vol. 2. New York: McGraw-Hill, 1971.

Freeman, John C. "Address on the Civil and Military Career of General William Tecumseh Sherman." In *War Papers Read Before the Commandery of the State of Wisconsin, Military Order of the Loyal Legion of the United States*, vol. 3. Milwaukee: Burdick, Armitage, and Allen, 1903, pp. 296–316.

Freidel, Frank. "General Orders 100 and Military Government." *Mississippi Valley Historical Review*, vol. 32 (March 1946), pp. 541–56.

Friendenberg, Robert V. "John A. J. Creswell of Maryland: Reformer in the Post Office." *Maryland Historical Magazine*, vol. 64 (1969), pp. 133–43.

Fry, James B. "An Acquaintance with Grant." *North American Review*, vol. 141 (July–December 1885), pp. 540–52.

———. "McClellan and His 'Mission.'" *Century Magazine*, no. 48 (October 1894), pp. 931–46.

Fuller, Alfred M. "Grant's Horsemanship: An Incident." *McClure's Magazine*, vol. 8 (April 1897), pp. 501–3.

Fullerton, J. S. "The Army of the Cumberland at Chattanooga." *Century Magazine*, vol. 34 (October 1887), pp. 136–50.

Galbreath, C. B. "Centennial Anniversary of the Birth of Ulysses S. Grant." *Ohio Archaeological and Historical Quarterly*, vol. 21 (1922), pp. 221–88.

Gallagher, Gary W. "The Army of Northern Virginia in May 1864: A Crisis of High Command." *Civil War History*, vol. 36, no. 2 (1990), pp. 101–18.

Garland, Hamlin. "The Early Life of Ulysses Grant." *McClure's Magazine*, vol. 8 (April 1897), pp. 125–39.

———. "Grant at the Outbreak of the War." *McClure's Magazine*, vol. 9 (May 1897), pp. 601–10.

———. "Grant at West Point: The Story of His Cadet Days." *McClure's Magazine*, vol. 8 (April 1897), pp. 195–210.

———. "Grant: His First Meeting with Lincoln." *McClure's Magazine*, vol. 9 (May 1897), pp. 892–95.

———. "Grant in a Great Campaign: The Investment and Capture of Vicksburg." *McClure's Magazine*, vol. 9 (May 1897), pp. 805–11.

———. "Grant in the Mexican War." *McClure's Magazine*, vol. 8 (April 1897), pp. 366–67.

———. "Grant's First Great Work in the War." *McClure's Magazine*, vol. 9 (May 1897), pp. 721–26.

———. "Grant's Life in Missouri." *McClure's Magazine*, vol. 8 (April 1897), pp. 514–20.

———. "Grant's Quiet Years at Northern Posts." *McClure's Magazine*, vol. 8 (April 1897), pp. 402–12.

———. "A Romance of Wall Street: The Grant and Ward Failure." *McClure's Magazine*, vol. 10 (April 1898), pp. 498–505.

———. "Ulysses Grant—His Last Year." *McClure's Magazine*, vol. 11 (October 1898), pp. 86–96.

"General Sherman's Opinion of General Grant." *Century* (March 1879).

"The General's Last Victory." In *New York State and the Civil War*, vol. 2. Albany: New York Civil War Centennial Commission, August 1962, pp. 213–45.

Giberson, N. S. "Captain Grant's Old Post, Fort Humboldt." *Overland Monthly*, vol. 8, 2nd series (1886), pp. 22–25.

Gillette, William. "Election of 1872." In Arthur M. Schlesinger, Jr., ed., *History of American Presidential Elections*. New York: McGraw-Hill, 1971, pp. 1331–37.

Gluek, Alvin C., Jr. "The Riel Rebellion and Canadian-American Relations." *Canadian Historical Review*, vol. 36, no. 3 (1955), pp. 199–221.

Goda, Paul. "The Historical Background of California's Constitutional Provisions Prohibiting Aid to Sectarian Schools." *California Historical Society Quarterly*, vol. 46, no. 2 (1967), pp. 149–71.

Godkin, E. L. "The Men Inside Politics." *The Nation*, March 4, 1869.

Gold, Charles H. "Grant and Twain in Chicago: The 1879 Reunion of the Army of the Tennessee." *Chicago History*, vol. 7, no. 3 (1978), pp. 150–60.

Goss, Warren L. "McClellan at the Head of the Grand Army." *Century Magazine*, vol. 32 (October 1886), pp. 131–36.

Grant, Federick D. "A Boy's Experience at Vicksburg." In Military Order of the Loyal Legion of the United States, New York Commandry, *Personal Recollections of the War of the Rebellion*, 3rd series. New York (1907), pp. 86–100.

———. "With Grant at Vicksburg." *Outlook*, vol. 24 (July 2, 1898), pp. 167–76.

Grant, Jesse R. "The Early Life of General Grant." *New York Ledger*, March 21, 1868.

Grant, Ulysses S. "The Battle of Shiloh." *Century Magazine*, vol. 29 (February 1885), pp. 593–613.

———. "Chattanooga." *Century Magazine*, vol. 31 (April 1886), pp. 128–45.

———. "The Collection of Original Autograph Dispatches of Gen. Grant During the Wilderness Campaign, 1964–5 . . . Preserved by his Aide-de-Camp, Major George Keller Leet." Philadelphia, 1917.

——. "General Grant on the Terms of Vicksburg." *Century Magazine,* vol. 34 (October 1887), pp. 617–31.

——. "Grant and Schurz on the South. Letter of General Grant Concerning Affairs at the South, and Extracts from a Report by Carl Schurz Submitted to President Andrew Johnson, and by Him Communicated to Congress, December 19, 1865." Washington, 1872.

——. "Grant's Letters to His Missouri Farm Tenants." LeRoy H. Fischer, ed. *Agricultural History,* vol. 21 (1947), pp. 26–42.

——. "Letter to the Workmen of Lamson & Goodnow Manufacturing Company, Shelburne Falls, Massachusetts, dated November 17, 1869." With a foreword by Paul M. Angle. Shelburne Falls, Mass., 1962.

——. " 'Our Candidate—Match Him' . . . the Recorded Opinions of the Republican Candidate, General U.S. Grant." Washington, D.C., 1868.

——. "Preparing for the Campaigns of '64." In Clarence C. Buel and Robert U. Johnson, eds., *Battles and Leaders of the Civil War,* vol. 4. New York: Century, 1886. pp. 97–118.

——. "Preparing for the Wilderness Campaign." *Century Magazine,* vol. 31 (April 1886), pp. 573–82.

——. "Shiloh: General Lew Wallace and General McCook." *Century Magazine,* vol. 30 (October 1885), pp. 276–302.

——. "The Siege of Vicksburg." *Century Magazine,* vol. 30 (October 1885), pp. 752–65.

Grant, Ulysses S., III. "Civil War: Fact and Fiction." *Civil War History,* vol. 2, no. 2 (1956), pp. 29–40.

——. "Military Strategy of the Civil War." *Military Affairs,* vol. 22, no. 1 (1958), pp. 13–25.

Green, Anna Maclay. "Civil War Public Opinion of General Grant." *Journal of Illinois State History Society,* vol. 22, no. 1 (April 1929), pp. 1–64.

Green, Horace. "General Grant's Last Stand." *Harper's Magazine,* vol. 170 (April 1935), pp. 533–40.

Green, Michael S. "Picks, Spades, and Shiloh: The Entrenchment Question." *Southern Studies,* vol. 13, no. 1 (1992), pp. 45–54.

Green, Steven K. "The Blaine Amendment Reconsidered." *American Journal of Legal History,* vol. 36 (1992), pp. 38–69.

Green, William H. "From the Wilderness to Spotsylvania." In *Papers Read Before the Commandery of the State of Maine, Military Order of the Loyal Legion of the United States,* vol. 2. Portland, Maine, 1902.

Greenberg, Evelyn L. "An 1869 Petition on Behalf of Russian Jews." *American Jewish Historical Quarterly,* vol. 54, no. 3 (1965), pp. 278–95.

Grimsley, Mark. "Ulysses S. Grant: A Special Issue." *Civil War Times Illustrated,* vol. 28, no. 7 (1990), pp. 20–66.

Guback, Thomas H. "General Sherman's War on the Press." *Journalism Quarterly,* vol. 36, no. 2 (1959), pp. 171–76.

Halliday, E. M. "The Man on Horseback." *American Heritage,* vol. 15, no. 5 (1964), pp. 11–23.

Hancock, Winfield S. "Correspondence Between General Grant and Major General Hancock, Relative to the Removal of Members of the City Council." New Orleans, 1868.

Hardy, Osgood. "Ulysses S. Grant, President of the Mexican Southern Railroad." *Pacific Historical Review,* vol. 24 (1955), pp. 111–20.

Harris, Neil. "The Battle for Grant's Tomb." *American Heritage,* vol. 36, no. 5 (1985), pp. 70–79.

Hass, Paul H. "The Vicksburg Diary of Henry Clay Warmoth." *Journal of Mississippi History,* vol. 31, no. 4 (1969), pp. 334–47; vol. 32, no. 1 (1969), pp. 60–74.

Hay, Thomas R. "The Battle of Spring Hill." *Tennessee Historical Magazine,* vol. 6 (October 1920), pp. 213–65.

Heater, Jacob. "Battle of the Wilderness." *Confederate Veteran,* vol. 14 (1906), pp. 262–64.

Hiatt, Burritt. "M. James, M. Haworth, Quaker Indian Agent." *Bulletin of Friends Historical Association,* vol. 47, no. 2 (1958), pp. 80–93.

Hill, Daniel H. "The Great Battle of the West: Chickamauga." *Century Magazine,* vol. 33 (April 1887), pp. 937–62.

——. "The Real Stonewall Jackson." *Century Magazine,* vol. 47 (April 1894), pp. 623–28.

Holzman, Robert S. "Ben Butler in the Civil War." *New England Quarterly,* vol. 30, no. 3 (1957), pp. 330–45.

Hoogenboom, Ari. "Spoilsmen and Reformers: Civil Service Reform and Public Morality." In H. Wayne Morgan, ed., *The Gilded Age: A Reappraisal.* Syracuse, N.Y.: Syracuse University Press, 1963.

——. "Thomas A. Jenckes and Civil Service Reform." *Mississippi Valley Historical Review,* vol. 47 (1966), pp. 636–42.

Hooker, Joseph. "Letter on the Chancellorsville Campaign." *Century Magazine,* vol. 35 (April 1888), pp. 962–87.

Howard, Brett. "The Story of Vicksburg." *Mankind*, vol. 1, no. 2 (1967), pp. 4–19.

Howard, O. O. and Ely S. Parker. "Some Reminiscences of Grant." *McClure's Magazine*, vol. 2 (May 1894), pp. 532–35.

Hubbard, George H. "In the Battle of Belmont, Mo." *Confederate Veteran*, vol. 30, pp. 459–68.

Hunt, Henry J. "The First Day at Gettysburg." *Century Magazine*, vol. 33 (April 1887), pp. 112–33.

——. "The Second Day at Gettysburg." *Century Magazine*, vol. 33 (April 1887), pp. 278–95.

——. "The Third Day at Gettysburg." *Century Magazine*, vol. 33 (April 1887), pp. 451–63.

Huntington, James F. "In Reply to General Pleasonton." *Century Magazine*, vol. 33 (April 1887), pp. 471–72.

Huston, James A. "Logistical Support of Federal Armies in the Field." *Civil War History*, vol. 7, no. 1 (1961), pp. 36–47.

Hyman, Harold M. "Johnson, Stanton, and Grant: A Reconsideration of the Army's Role in the Events Leading to Impeachment." *American Historical Review*, vol. 66 (October 1960), pp. 85–100.

Illick, Joseph E. " 'Some of Our Best Friends Are Indians . . .': Quaker Attitudes and Actions Regarding the Western Indians During the Grant Administration." *Western Historical Quarterly*, vol. 2, no. 3 (1971), pp. 283–94.

Isaacs, Joakim. "Candidate Grant and the Jews." *American Jewish Archives*, vol. 17, no. 1 (1965), pp. 3–16.

Isham, Asa. "Through the Wilderness to Richmond." In *Sketches of War History, 1861–1865: Papers Read Before the Ohio Commandery of the Military Order of the Loyal Legion of the United States*. 2 vols. Cincinnati: D. Appleton, 1888.

Janda, Lance. "Shutting the Gates of Mercy: The American Origins of Total War, 1860–1880." *Journal of Military History*, vol. 59 (January 1995), pp. 7–26.

Jenkins, Kirk C. "A Shooting at the Galt House: The Death of General William Nelson." *Civil War History*, vol. 43 (1997), pp. 101–18.

Jensen, Dana O. "The Memoirs of Daniel M. Frost." *Bulletin of the Missouri Historical Society*, vol. 26, no. 2 (1970), pp. 89–112; vol. 26, no. 3 (1970), pp. 200–226.

Jensen, Ronald J. "The Politics of Discrimination: America, Russia and the Jewish Question, 1869–1872." *American Jewish History*, vol. 75, no. 3 (1986), pp. 280–95.

Johnson, Ludwell. "Civil War Military History: A Few Revisions in Need of Revising." In John T. Hubbell, ed., *Battles Lost and Won*. Westport, Conn.: Greenwood, 1975, pp. 3–18.

Johnson, Timothy D. "Benjamin Franklin Cheatham at Belmont." *Missouri Historical Review*, vol. 81, no. 2 (1987), pp. 159–72.

——. "Benjamin Franklin Cheatham: The Early Years." *Tennessee Historical Quarterly*, vol. 42 (Fall 1983), pp. 269–75.

Jones, Archer. "Confederate Strategy from Shiloh to Vicksburg, Baton Rouge, 1961; and the Gettysburg Decision." *Virginia Magazine of History and Biography*, vol. 56 (June 1960), pp. 21–54.

Jones, Frank H. "An Address Delivered by Frank H. Jones Before the Chicago Historical Society at the Celebration of the 100th Anniversary of the Birth of General Ulysses S. Grant, Thursday, April 27th, 1922." Chicago, 1922.

Jones, George R. "Joseph Russell Jones." *Lincoln Herald*, vol. 74, no. 1 (1972), pp. 41–52.

Jones, Idwal. "A Captain at Fort Humboldt." *Westways*, vol. 43 (January 1949), pp. 67–98.

——. "Dining with Captain Grant." *Gourmet*, vol. 12 (November 1951), pp. 121–25.

Jones, Terry L. "Grant's Canals in Northeast Louisiana." *North Louisiana Historical Association Journal*, vol. 10, no. 2 (1979), pp. 7–17.

Jorgensen, Jay A. "Scouting for Ulysses S. Grant: The 5th Ohio Cavalry in the Shiloh Campaign." *Civil War Regiments*. vol. 4, no. 1 (1994), pp. 44–77.

Joyce, Marion D. "Tactical Lessons of the War." *Civil War Times*, vol. 2, no. 10 (1964), pp. 42–47.

Kahn, David M. "The Grant Monument." *Journal of the Society of Architectural Historians*, vol. 41, no. 3 (1982), pp. 212–31.

Kaiser, Leo M., ed. "Letters from the Front." *Journal of the Illinois State Historical Society*, vol. 56, no. 2 (1963), pp. 150–63.

Kautz, August V. "Our National Military System: What the United States Army Should Be." *Century Magazine*, vol. 36 (October 1888), pp. 934–39.

Keise, Thomas J. "The St. Louis Years of Ulysses S. Grant." *Gateway Heritage*, vol. 6, no. 3 (1985–86), pp. 10–21.

Keller, Robert H., Jr. "Ulysses S. Grant: Reality and Mystique in the Far West." *Journal of the West*, vol. 31, no. 3 (1992), pp. 68–80.

King, James T. "George Crook: Indian Fighter and Humanitarian." *Arizona and the West* (Winter 1967), pp. 333–48.

Kipling, Rudyard. "Gunga Din." In *Barrack-room Ballads and Other Verses*, London: Methuen, 1892, pp. 23–30.

Kirkpatrick, R. Z. "General Grant in Panama." *The Military Engineer,* vol. 26, no. 146 (March–April 1934), pp. 154–69.

Kite, Elizabeth S. "Genius of the Civil War." *Commonweal,* vol. 27 (1938), pp. 541–43.

Klein, Frederic S. "Bottling Up Butler at Bermuda Hundred." *Civil War Times Illustrated,* vol. 6, no. 7 (1967), pp. 4–11, 45–47.

Klingelhofer, Herbert E. "The Generals Speak." *Manuscripts,* vol. 16, no. 3 (1964), pp. 3–24.

Klinkhamer, Sister Marie Carolyn. "The Blaine Amendment of 1875: Private Motives for Political Action." *Catholic Historical Review,* vol. 42 (1956), p. 17.

Klopfenstein, Carl. "The Matter of a Pencil." *Hayes Historical Journal,* vol. 6, no. 4 (1987), pp. 6–15.

Kurtz, Henry I. "The Battle of Belmont." *Civil War Times Illustrated,* vol. 3 (June 1963), pp. 18–24.

Lacy, J. Horace. "Lee at Fredericksburg." *Century Magazine,* vol. 32 (October 1886), pp. 605–8.

Lathrop, Barnes F. "A Confederate Artilleryman at Shiloh." *Civil War History,* vol. 8, no. 4 (1962), pp. 373–85.

Law, Evander M. "From the Wilderness to Cold Harbour." *Century Magazine,* vol. 34 (October 1887), pp. 277–301.

Layne, J. Gregg. "Edward Otho Cresap Ord, Soldier and Surveyor." *Historical Society of Southern California Quarterly,* vol. 17 (1935), pp. 139–42.

Lehman, Godfrey D. "Susan B. Anthony Cast Her Ballot for Ulysses S. Grant." *American Heritage,* vol. 37, no. 1 (1985), pp. 24–31.

Leiter, Kelly. "A President and One Newspaper: U.S. Grant and the Chicago 'Tribune.' " *Journalism Quarterly,* vol. 47, no. 1 (1970), pp. 71–80.

Leitman, Spencer L. "The Revival of an Image: Grant and the 1880 Republican Nominating Campaign." *Missouri Historical Society Bulletin,* vol. 30, no. 3 (1974), pp. 196–204.

Leslie, Leigh. "Grant and Galena." *Midland Monthly Magazine,* vol. 4 (September 1895), pp. 195–215.

Levine, Richard R. "Indian Fighters and Indian Reformers: Grant's Indian Peace Policy and the Conservative Consensus." *Civil War History,* vol. 31, no. 4 (1985), pp. 329–52.

Livermore, William R. "The Vicksburg Campaign." *Military Historical Society of Massachusetts,* vol. 9 (1912), pp. 538–71.

Lockett, S. H. "Controversies in Regard to Shiloh." *Century Magazine,* vol. 31 (April 1886), pp. 781–83.

Long, E. B. "Dear Julia: Two Grant Letters." *Civil War History,* vol. 1, no. 1 (1955), pp. 61–64.

———. "John A. Rawlins: Staff Officer Par Excellence." *Civil War Times Illustrated,* vol. 12, no. 9 (1974), pp. 4–9, 43–46.

———. "The Paducah Affair: Bloodless Action That Altered the Civil War in the Mississippi Valley." *Register of the Kentucky Historical Society,* vol. 70, no. 4 (1972), pp. 253–76.

———. "Ulysses S. Grant for Today." In David L. Wilson and John Y. Simpson, eds., *Ulysses S. Grant: Essays and Documents.* Carbondale, Ill.: University of Illinois Press, 1981, pp. 9–26.

Longstreet, James. "The Battle of Fredericksburg." *Century Magazine,* vol. 32 (October 1886), pp. 609–26.

———. "Lee's Invasion of Pennsylvania." *Century Magazine,* vol. 33 (April 1887), pp. 622–36.

Lovett, Bobby L. "Memphis Riots: White Reaction to Blacks in Memphis, May 1865–July 1866." *Tennessee Historical Quarterly,* vol. 38 (1979), pp. 9–33.

Lowe, Donald V. "Army Memoirs of Lucius W. Barber." *Journal of the Illinois State Historical Society,* vol. 56, no. 2 (1963), pp. 298–315.

Lowell, James R. "General McClellan's Report." *North American Review,* vol. 203 (April 1864), pp. 550–66.

Lunde, Erik S. "The Ambiguity of the National Idea: The Presidential Campaign of 1872." *Canadian Review of Studies in Nationalism* (Canada), vol. 5, no. 1 (1978), pp. 1–23.

Lyman, Theodore. "Addenda to the Paper by Brevet Lieutenant-Colonel W. W. Swan, U.S.A., on the Battle of the Wilderness." *Papers of the Military Historical Society of Massachusetts,* vol. 4. Boston: Houghton Mifflin, 1881–1918, pp. 165–73.

Mahan, D. H. "The Cadet Life of Grant and Sherman." (Letter of March 8, 1866). *Army and Navy Journal,* vol. 22 (March 31, 1866), pp. 507–9.

Maihafer, H. J. "The Partnership." *U.S. Naval Institute Press,* vol. 93, no. 5 (1967), pp. 49–57.

Majeske, Penelope K. "Johnson, Stanton, and Grant: A Reconsideration of the Events Leading to the First Reconstruction Act." *Southern Studies,* vol. 22 (Winter 1983), pp. 340–50.

Mallam, William D. "Butlerism in Massachusetts." *New England Quarterly,* vol. 33, no. 2 (1960), pp. 186–206.

———. "The Grant-Butler Relationship." *Mississippi Valley Historical Review,* vol. 41, no. 2 (1954), pp. 259–76.

Mangum, Ronald S. "The Vicksburg Campaign: A Study in Joint Operations." *Parameters,* vol. 21, no. 3 (1991), pp. 74–86.

Mann, Charles S. "The Bucks and Montgomery County Kindred of General U.S. Grant." In *Historical Sketches: A Collection of Papers Prepared for the Historical Society of Montgomery County, Pennsylvania, 1915.* Norristown, Pa., 1915, pp. 218–36.

Marshall, W. R. "Reminiscences of General U.S. Grant." In *Glimpses of the Nation's Struggle,* 1st series. St. Paul, Minn.: Harper & Co., 1887, pp. 89–106.

Mason, Edwin C. "Through the Wilderness to the Bloody Angle at Spottsylvania Court House." In *Glimpse of the Nation's Struggle: Papers Read Before the Commandery of the State of Minnesota, Military Order of the Loyal Legion of the United States,* rev. ed. St. Paul, Minn.: Harper, 1898, pp. 291–312.

Mattox, Henry E., and Robert W. Mattox. "Appomattox Court House Revisited." *Southern Historian,* vol. 8 (1987), pp. 64–73.

McClellan, Henry B. "The Wilderness Fight: Why General Lee's Expectations of Longstreet Were Not Realized." *Weekly Times,* Philadelphia, January 26, 1878.

McFeely, William S. "Amos T. Akerman: The Lawyer for Racial Justice." In J. Morgan Kousser and James M. McPherson, eds., *Region, Race, and Reconstruction.* New York: Oxford University Press, 1982.

———. "The Personal Memoirs of Ulysses S. Grant." *History Today* (Great Britain), vol. 32 (December 1982), pp. 5–10.

———. "Ulysses S. Grant." In C. Vann Woodward, ed., *Responses of the Presidents to Charges of Misconduct.* New York: Charles Scribner's Sons, 1974.

McGhee, James E. "The Neophyte General: U.S. Grant and the Belmont Campaign." *Missouri Historical Review,* vol. 67, no. 4 (1973), pp. 465–83.

McLaughlin, Andrew C. "The Court, the Corporation, and Conkling." *American Historical Review,* vol. 46 (1940).

McPherson, James M. "Coercion or Conciliation? Abolitionists Debate President Hayes's Southern Policy." *New England Quarterly,* vol. 39, no. 4 (1966), pp. 474–97.

———. "Grant or Greeley? The Abolitionist Dilemma in the Election of 1812." *American Historical Review,* vol. 71, no. 1 (1965), pp. 43–61.

———. "How Noble Was Robert E. Lee?" *New York Review of Books,* November 7, 1991, pp. 10–14.

———. "Lincoln and the Strategy of Unconditional Surrender." In Gabor S. Boritt, ed., *Lincoln the War President: The Gettysburg Lectures.* New York: Oxford University Press, 1992.

———. "Ulysses S. Grant's Final Victory." *The Quarterly Journal of Military History,* vol. 2, no. 4 (1990), pp. 96–103.

———. "The Unheroic Hero." *New York Review of Books,* 4 February 1999, pp. 16–19.

Meigs, Montgomery C. "General M. C. Meigs on the Conduct of the Civil War." *American Historical Review,* vol. 26, no. 2 (January 1921), pp. 285–303.

Melcher, Holman S. "An Experience in the Battle of the Wilderness." In *War Papers Read Before the Commandery of the State of Maine, Military Order of the Loyal Legion of the United States.* 3 vols. Portland, Maine, 1898, pp. 73–84.

Melville, Herman. "The Armies of the Wilderness." In Sidney Kaplan, ed., *Battle-Pieces and Aspects of the War.* Gainesville: University of Florida Press, 1960.

Merritt, Wesley. "Note on the Surrender of Lee." *Century Magazine,* vol. 79, no. 6 (April 1902), pp. 120–28.

Military Order of the Loyal Legion. *Military Essays and Reflections: Papers Read Before the Commandery of the State of Illinois,* vol. 1.

Miller, Robert R. "Lew Wallace and the French Intervention in Mexico." *Indiana Magazine of History,* vol. 59, no. 1 (1963), pp. 31–50.

Mills, William H. "Chancellorsville." *Magazine of American History,* vol. 15, no. 4 (April 1886).

"The Miracle on Missionary Ridge." *American Heritage,* vol. 20, no. 2 (1969), pp. 60–73.

Mitchell, Michael D. "Acculturation Problems Among the Plains Tribes of the Governmental Agencies in Western Indian Territory." *Chronicles of Oklahoma,* vol. 44, no. 3 (1966), pp. 281–89.

Moffett, Cleveland. "Grant and Lincoln in Bronze." *McClure's Magazine,* vol. 5 (June 1895), pp. 419–32.

———. "Partridge's Statute of General Grant." *McClure's Magazine,* vol. 6 (December 1895), pp. 290–92.

Moore, Ensley. "Grant's First March." *Transactions of the Illinois State Historical Society for 1910.* Springfield: Illinois State Historical Society, 1912, pp. 55–62.

Morrison, James L., Jr. "Educating Civil War Generals: West Point, 1833–1861." *Military Affairs,* vol. 38 (1974).

———. "The Memoirs of Henry Heth." *Civil War History,* vol. 8, no. 1 (1962), pp. 5–24; vol. 8, no. 3 (1962), pp. 300–326.

Morton, Charles A. "A Boy at Shiloh." *Military Order of the Loyal Legion of the United States,* 1907.

Mullen, Jay Carlton. "The Turning of Columbus." *Register of the Kentucky Historical Society*, vol. 44 (July 1966), pp. 209–55.

Murray, Donald M., and Robert M. Rodney. "Colonel Julian E. Bryant: Champion of the Negro Soldier." *Journal of the Illinois State Historical Society*, vol. 56, no. 2 (1963), pp. 257–81.

Myers, James E. "Lincoln and the Jews." *Midstream*, vol. 27, no. 2 (1981), pp. 26–29.

Nagler, Jorg. "Deutschamerikaner und das Liberal Republican Movement 1872" [German Americans and the Liberal Republican Movement of 1872]. *Amerikastudien/American Studies* (Germany), vol. 33, no. 4 (1988), pp. 415–38.

Neely, Mark E., Jr. "Was the Civil War a Total War?" *Civil War History*, vol. 37, no. 1 (1991), pp. 5–28.

Newman, John P. "The Baptism of U.S. Grant." *Life*, vol. 30 (March 26, 1951), pp. 102–4.

Northrop, Jack. "Richard Yates: A Personal Glimpse of the Illinois Soldiers' Friend." *Journal of the Illinois State Historical Society*, vol. 56, no. 2 (1963), pp. 121–38.

Northrup, L. B. "A Hill of Death." *Civil War Times Illustrated*, vol. 30, no. 2 (1991), pp. 24–26.

Nye, Wilbur S. "Grant: Genius or Fortune's Child." *Civil War Times Illustrated*, vol. 4, no. 3 (1965), pp. 4–13, 43–44.

Parks, George E. "One Story of the 109th Illinois Volunteer Infantry Regiment." *Journal of Illinois State Historical Society*, vol. 56, no. 2 (1963), pp. 282–97.

Peckham, Howard H. "I Have Been Basely Murdered." *American Heritage*, vol. 14 (1963), pp. 88–92.

Perry, William F. "Reminiscences of the Campaign of 1864 in Virginia." *Southern History Society Papers*, vol. 7. Richmond, Va.: D. Appleton, 1876–1944, pp. 49–63.

Peskin, Allan. "The 'Little Man on Horseback' and the 'Literary Fellow': Garfield's Opinions of Grant." *Mid-America*, vol. 55, no. 4 (1973), pp. 271–82.

Pierson, William Watley, Jr. "The Committee on the Conduct of the Civil War." *American Historical Review*, vol. 23 (1918), pp. 550–76.

Pirtle, John B. "Defence of Vicksburg in 1862—The Battle of Baton Rouge." *Southern Historical Society Papers*, vol. 8 (June–July 1880), pp. 78–90.

Pitre, Althea D. "The Collapse of the Warmoth Regime, 1870–72." *Louisiana Historical Review*, vol. 6, no. 2 (1965), pp. 161–87.

Pleasonton, Alfred. "The Successes and Failures of Chancellorsville." *Century Magazine*, vol. 32 (October 1886), pp. 745–61.

Polk, William M. "General Polk and the Battle of Belmont." In Clarence C. Buel and Robert Underwood Johnson, eds., *Battles and Leaders of the Civil War*, vol. 1. New York: T. Yoseloff, 1956, pp. 348–57.

———. "General Polk at Chickamauga." *Century Magazine*, vol. 33 (April 1887), p. 964.

Porter, Charles H. "Opening of the Campaign of 1864." *Papers of the Military Historical Society of Massachusetts*, vol. 4. Boston: Houghton Mifflin, 1881–1918, pp. 1–24.

Porter, Horace. "Appomattox: Grant's Last Campaign." *Century Magazine*, vol. 35 (April 1888), pp. 126–52.

———. "Lincoln and Grant." *Century Magazine*, vol. 30 (October 1885), pp. 939–47.

———. "Personal Traits of General Grant." *McClure's Magazine*, vol. 2 (May 1894), pp. 507–32.

Potter, Henry C. "General Robert B. Potter and the Assault at Petersburg Crater." *Century Magazine*, vol. 35 (April 1888), pp. 481–96.

Potter, Jerry O'Neil. "The First West Tennessee Raid of General Nathan Bedford Forrest." *West Tennessee Historical Society Papers*, vol. 28 (1974), pp. 55–74.

Pound, Roscoe. "The Military Telegraph in the Civil War." *Proceedings of the Massachusetts Historical Society* (1938), pp. 185–203.

Prentice, Sartell. "The Opening Hours in the Wilderness in 1864." In *Military Essays and Recollections: Papers Read Before the Commandery of the State of Illinois, Military Order of the Loyal Legion of the United States*. 2 vols. Chicago, 1894, pp. 99–119.

Proctor, John R. "A Blue and Gray Friendship." *Century Magazine*, vol. 31 (1897), pp. 942–49.

Prosch, Thomas W. "The United States Army in Washington Territory." *Washington Historical Quarterly*, vol. 43 (October 1907), pp. 120–35.

Railton, Arthur R. "When Grant Took the Island: President and Party Visit Martha's Vineyard in 1874." *Dukes County Intelligencer*, vol. 29, no. 1 (1987), pp. 3–25.

Ramsdell, Charles W. "Lincoln and Fort Sumter." *Journal of Southern History*, vol. 3 (1937), pp. 259–88.

Ratner, Sidney. "Was the Supreme Court Packed by President Grant?" *Political Science Quarterly*, vol. 50 (1935), pp. 343–58.

Reaves, Wendy W. "Thomas Nast and the President." *American Art Journal*, vol. 19, no. 1 (1987), pp. 60–71.

Reid, Brian H. "Another Look at Grant's Crossing of the James, 1864." *Civil War History*, vol. 39, no. 4 (1993), pp. 291–316.

Resseguie, Harry E. "Federal Conflict of Interest: The A. T. Stewart Case." *New York History,* vol. 47, no. 3 (1966), pp. 271–301.

"Reunions of Taylor's Battery, 18th Anniversary of the Battle of Fort Donelson, Feb.14, 1880, 25th Anniversary of the Battle of Belmont, Nov. 6, 1886." Chicago, 1890.

Rice, Allen Thorndike. "Sherman on Grant." *North American Review,* vol. 142 (January–June 1886), pp. 111–13.

Richards, Dora [Miller]. "War Diary of a Union Woman in the South." *Century Magazine,* vol. 38 (October 1889), pp. 931–46.

Richter, William L. "The Papers of U.S. Grant: A Review Essay." *Civil War History,* vol. 36, no. 2 (1990), pp. 149–66.

Ripley, C. Peter. "Prelude to Donelson: Grant's January 1862 March into Kentucky." *Register of the Kentucky Historical Society,* vol. 68, no. 4 (1970), pp. 311–18.

Robertson, Robert S. "From the Wilderness to Spottsylvania." In *Sketches of War History, 1861–1865: Papers Read Before the Ohio Commandery of the Military Order of the Loyal Legion of the United States.* 2 vols. Cincinnati, 1888, pp. 252–92.

——. "War Horses." In Francis T. Miller, ed., *Photographic History of the Civil War,* vol. 4. New York: Review of Reviews, 1911, pp. 289–316.

Robson, Maureen M. "The Alabama Claims and the Anglo-American Reconciliation, 1865–1871." *Canadian Historical Review,* vol. 43 (March 1961).

Rodenbaugh, Theodore F. "Sheridan's Richmond Raid." In Clarence C. Buel and Robert U. Johnson, eds., *Battles and Leaders of the Civil War,* vol. 4. New York: T. Yoseloff, 1884–88, pp. 188–94.

Rogers, William Warren, Jr. " 'The Past Is Gone,' Ulysses S. Grant Visits Mobile." *Gulf Coast Historical Review,* vol. 5, no. 1 (1989), pp. 7–20.

Roland, Charles P. "Albert Sidney Johnston and the Loss of Forts Henry and Donelson." *Journal of Southern History,* vol. 62 (February 1957), pp. 24–67.

——. "Albert Sidney Johnston and the Shiloh Campaign." *Civil War History,* vol. 54 (December 1958), pp. 56–98.

Ropes, John C. "Campaign in Virginia in 1864." *Papers of the Military Historical Society of Massachusetts.* Boston: Houghton Mifflin, 1881–1918, pp. 363–405.

Rosecrans, W. S. "The Campaign for Chattanooga." *Century Magazine,* vol. 34 (October 1887), pp. 129–35.

——. "Corinth." *Century Magazine,* vol. 32 (October 1886), pp. 901–18.

Rosser, R. W., ed. "The Battle of Belmont: Pvt. John Bell Battle's Eyewitness Account." *Confederate Chronicles of Tennessee,* vol. 2 (1987), pp. 21–54.

Roth, David E. "The Civil War at the Confluence, Where the Ohio Meets the Mississippi." *Blue and Gray Magazine,* vol. 2 (July 1985), pp. 6–20.

Rowland, Thomas J. "In the Shadows of Grant and Sherman: George B. McClellan Revisited." *Civil War History,* vol. 40, no. 3 (1994), pp. 202–25.

Russell, Henry M. W. "The Memoirs of Ulysses S. Grant: The Rhetoric of Judgement." *Virginia Quarterly Review,* vol. 66, no. 2 (1990), pp. 189–209.

Sanborn, John B. *The Crisis at Champion's Hill, the Decisive Battle of the Civil War.* Pamphlet. St. Paul, Minn., 1903.

Satterlee, Scott K. "The Political Origins of Grant's Vicksburg Campaign." *E. C. Barksdale Student Lecturers,* vol. 11 (1989–90), pp. 104–26.

Schmitz, Neil. "Doing the Fathers: Gertrude Stein on U.S. Grant in *Four in America." American Literature,* vol. 65, no. 4 (1993), pp. 751–60.

Scroggs, Jack B., and Donald E. Reynolds. "Arkansas and the Vicksburg Campaign." *Civil War History,* vol. 5, no. 4 (1959), pp. 391–401.

Seaton, John. "The Battle of Belmont." In *War Talks in Kansas.* Kansas City: Military Order of the Legion of the United States, Kansas Commandery, 1906.

Seawell, M. E. "General Grant's Premonition." *Century Magazine,* vol. 30 (October 1885), p. 958.

Seematter, Mary E. "The St. Louis Whiskey Ring." *Gateway Heritage,* vol. 8, no. 4 (1988), pp. 32–42.

Sehlinger, Peter J. " 'At the Moment of Victory . . . ' The Battle of Shiloh and General A. S. Johnston's Death as Recounted in William Preston's Diary." *Filson Club History Quarterly,* vol. 61, no. 3 (1987), pp. 315–45.

Sellery, George Clarke. "Lincoln's Suspension of *Habeas Corpus* as Viewed by Congress." *Bulletin of the University of Wisconsin,* vol. 1 (1907).

Shanks, W. F. G. "Chattanooga and How We Held It." *Harper's New Monthly Magazine,* vol. 36 (January 1868), pp. 137–49.

——. "How We Get Our News." *Harper's New Monthly Magazine,* vol. 34 (March 1867), pp. 511–22.

——. "Recollections of General Sherman." *Harper's New Monthly Magazine,* vol. 30 (April 1865), pp. 640–46.

——. "Recollections of General Thomas." *Harper's New Monthly Magazine,* vol. 30 (April 1865), pp. 754–59.

Sharp, Thomas. "Colonel Dent of Whitehaven: The Father-in-Law of General Grant." *McClure's Magazine,* vol. 9 (May 1897), p. 667.

Sheffield, Delia B. "Reminiscences of Delia B. Sheffield." William Lewis, ed. *Washington Historical Quarterly,* vol. 15 (Summer 1924).

Sheridan, Philip H. "The Last Days of the Rebellion." *North American Review,* vol. 305 (August 1890), pp. 121–45.

Sherman, Hoyt. "Personal Recollections of General Grant." *Midland Monthly,* vol. 9 (April 1898), pp. 325–27.

Sherman, William T. "An Address on Grant." In *Military Order of the Loyal Legion of the United States. New York Commandery, First Series.* New York: 1891, pp. 108–12.

——. "The Grand Strategy of the Last Year of the War." In Clarence C. Buel and Robert U. Johnson, eds., *Battles and Leaders of the Civil War,* vol. 4. New York: Century, 1886, pp. 247–59.

——. "The Grand Strategy of the War of the Rebellion." *Century Magazine,* vol. 35 (April 1888), pp. 582–98.

——. "A Reminiscence of the War." In Thomas B. Reed, ed., *Modern Eloquence.* Philadelphia: J. D. Morris, 1900.

——. "Sherman's Estimate of Grant." *Century Magazine,* vol. 70 (May 1905), pp. 316–18.

Shields, Clara M. George. "General Grant at Fort Humboldt in the Early Days." *Humboldt Times,* vol. 35 (November 10, 1912), pp. 25–32.

Shrady, George F. "General Grant's Last Days." *Century Magazine,* vol. 76 (July 1908), pp. 78–92.

——. "The Surgical and Pathological Aspects of General Grant's Case." *New York Tribune* (July 31, 1885).

Simon, John Y. "From Galena to Appomattox: Grant and Washburne." *Journal of the Illinois State Historical Society,* vol. 58 (Summer 1965), pp. 165–89.

——. "Grant at Belmont." *Military Affairs,* vol. 45 (December 1981), pp. 161–66.

——. "Grant at Hardscrabble." *Missouri Historical Bulletin,* vol. 35 (July 1979), pp. 191–201.

——. "John Alexander McClernand." In Patricia L. Faust, ed., *Historical Times Illustrated Encyclopedia of the Civil War.* New York: Charles Scribner's Sons, 1986, pp. 456–57.

——. "The Paradox of Ulysses S. Grant." *Register of the Kentucky Historical Society,* vol. 81, no. 4 (1983), pp. 366–82.

——. "The Rediscovery of Ulysses S. Grant." *Inland: The Magazine of the Middle West,* vol. 98 (January 1974), pp. 26–45.

——. "The Road to Appomattox: The Generalship of Ulysses S. Grant." *Timeline,* vol. 8, no. 4 (1991), pp. 2–19.

——. "That Obnoxious Order." *Civil War Times Illustrated,* vol. 23, no. 6, pp. 12–17.

——. "Ulysses S. Grant and Civil Service." *Hayes Historical Journal,* vol. 4, no. 3 (1984), pp. 8–15.

——. "Ulysses S. Grant One Hundred Years Later." *Illinois Historical Journal,* vol. 79, no. 4 (1986), pp. 245–56.

Simplot, Alex. "General Grant and the Incident at Dover." *Wisconsin Magazine of History,* vol. 44 (Winter 1960–61), pp. 83–84.

Simpson, Brooks D. " 'All I Want is to Advance': Ulysses S. Grant's Early Civil War Career." *Gateway Heritage,* vol. 15, no. 1 (1994), pp. 4–19.

——. "Another Look at the Grant Presidency." *Proceedings of the South Carolina Historical Association* (1990), pp. 7–16.

——. "Butcher? Racist? An Examination of William S. McFeely's *Grant: A Biography.*" *Civil War History,* vol. 33, no. 1 (1987), pp. 63–83.

——. "Carnage, Consequences, and Character." *Reviews in American History,* vol. 14, no. 3 (1986), pp. 368–76.

——. "The Doom of Slavery: Ulysses S. Grant, War Aims, and Emancipation, 1861–1863." *Civil War History,* vol. 36 (March 1990), pp. 36–56.

——. "Grant's Tour of the South Revisited." *Journal of Southern History,* vol. 54 (August 1988), pp. 425–48.

——. "Henry Adams and the Age of Grant." *Hayes Historical Journal,* vol. 8, no. 3 (1989), pp. 5–23.

——. "Ulysses S. Grant and the Electoral Crisis of 1876–1877." *Hayes Historical Journal,* vol. 11, no. 2 (1992), pp. 5–22.

——. "Ulysses S. Grant and the Failure of Reconciliation." *Illinois Historical Journal,* vol. 81 (Winter 1988), pp. 269–82.

——. "Ulysses S. Grant and the Fruits of Victory." *Essays in History,* vol. 23 (1979), pp. 23–36.

Singletary, Don. "The Battle of Belmont." *Confederate Veteran*, vol. 23, pp. 506–7.

——. "The Day of the Battle of Belmont." *Hickman County Gazette*, September 30, 1971.

Smith, Joe. "U.S. Grant, Black Bart, and the Covered Bridges." *Ford Times*, vol. 62 (September 1958), pp. 328–34.

Smith, John Corson. "Grant: An Address Delivered at the 23rd Annual Reunion of the Old Soldiers' and Sailors' Association of Jo Daviess County, Turner Hall, Galena, Ill., August 15, 1905." Chicago, 1905.

——. "Personal Recollections of General Ulysses S. Grant; Before U.S. Grant Post, No.28, G.A.R., Department of Illinois, Grand Army of the Republic . . . February 11, 1904." Chicago, 1904.

Smith, William F. "Chattanooga: Was It Fought as Planned?" *Century Magazine*, vol. 31 (April 1886), pp. 146–47.

——. "In Reply to General Grant." *Century Magazine*, vol. 32 (October 1886), pp. 153–59.

——. "Shiloh." *Magazine of American History*, vol. 39 (April 1886), pp. 567–89.

Smith, William W. "Holocaust Holiday: Vacationing at Chattanooga, 1863." *Civil War Times Illustrated*, vol. 18, no. 6 (1979), pp. 28–40.

Stampp, Kenneth. "Lincoln and the Strategy of Defense in the Crisis of 1861." *Journal of Southern History*, vol. 11 (1945), pp. 297–332.

Stern, Norton B. "Los Angeles Jewish Voters During Grant's First Presidential Race." *Western States Jewish Historical Quarterly*, vol. 13, no. 2 (1981), pp. 179–85.

Stevens, Brigadier General Hazard. "The Sixth Corps in the Wilderness." *Papers of the Military Historical Society of Massachusetts*, vol. 4. 1918.

Stone, Henry. "The Battle of Shiloh." *Papers of the Military Historical Society of Massachusetts*, vol. 7 (1908), pp. 223–56.

Stonesifer, Roy P., Jr. "Gideon J. Pillow: A Study in Egotism." *Tennessee Historical Quarterly*, vol. 25 (1966).

Stouffer, Allen P. "Avoiding a 'Great Calamity': Canada's Pursuit of Reciprocity, 1864–1870." *Upper Midwest History*, vol. 4 (1984), pp. 39–55.

Sullivan, Charles F. "A Crimson Fury—But Not in Vain: U.S. Grant at Cold Harbor." *E. C. Barksdale Student Lectures*, vol. 9 (1985–86), pp. 114–37.

Sullivan, Gordon R. "Ulysses S. Grant and America's Power-Projection Army." *Military Review*, vol. 74, no. 1 (1994), pp. 5–14.

Summers, Mark W. "The Press Gang: Corruption and the Independent Press in the Grant Era." *Congress and the Presidency*, vol. 17, no. 1 (1990), pp. 29–44.

Sutherland, Daniel E. "Abraham Lincoln, John Pope, and the Origins of Total War." *Journal of Military History*, vol. 56, no. 4 (1992), pp. 567–86.

——. "Edwin Deleon and Liberal Republicanism in Georgia: Horace Greeley's Campaign for President in a Southern State." *Historian*, vol. 47, no. 1 (1984), pp. 38–57.

Swan, William W. "Battle of the Wilderness." *Papers of the Military Historical Society of Massachusetts*, vol. 4. Boston: Houghton Mifflin, 1881–1918, pp. 117–63.

Swift, Lester L. "The Preacher Regiment at Chickamauga and Missionary Ridge." *Lincoln Herald* (Summer 1970), pp. 51–60.

Swinney, Everette. "Enforcing the Fifteenth Amendment, 1870–1877." *Journal of Southern History*, vol. 28, no. 2 (1962), pp. 202–18.

Tansill, Charles Callan. "War Powers of the President of the United States with Special Reference to the Beginning of Hostilities." *Political Science Quarterly*, vol. 45 (1930).

Taussig, William. "Personal Recollections of General Grant." *Missouri Historical Society Publications*, vol. 2 (1903), pp. 1–13.

Taylor, William. "About the Battle of Belmont." *Confederate Veteran*, vol. 16, pp. 345–46.

Temple, Wayne C. "U.S. Grant in Military Service for the State of Illinois." *Lincoln Herald*, vol. 83, no. 3 (1981), pp. 705–8.

Temple, Wayne C., ed. "A Signal Officer with Grant: The Letters of Captain Charles L. Davis." *Civil War History*, vol. 7, no. 4 (1961), pp. 428–37.

Thayer, John M. "Grant at Pilot Knob." *McClure's Magazine*, vol. 5 (June 1895), pp. 433–37.

Thomas, Henry G. "The Colored Troops at Petersburg." *Century Magazine*, vol. 34 (October 1887), pp. 777–82.

"Thomas Nast in the Age of Grant." *Hayes Historical Journal*, vol. 8, no. 3 (1989), pp. 52–60.

Thompson, Joseph D. "The Battle of Shiloh." *Tennessee Historical Quarterly*, vol. 17, no. 3 (September 1958), pp. 345–67.

Tobin, Richard L. "The Great Petersburg Mine." *Mankind*, vol. 1, no. 5 (1968), pp. 26–33, 57–60.

Trefousse, Hans L. "Civil Warriors in Memory and Memoir: Grant and Sherman Remember." *Georgia Historical Quarterly*, vol. 75, no. 3 (1991), pp. 542–56.

Treichel, James A. "Lew Wallace at Fort Donelson." *Indiana Magazine of History,* vol. 59, no. 1, pp. 3–18.

Tucker, Glenn. "The Battle of Chickamauga." *Civil War Times Illustrated* (May 1969), pp. 5–46.

——. "The Battles for Chattanooga." *Civil War Times Illustrated,* (September 1971), pp. 4–44.

Twain, Mark. "The Private History of a Campaign That Failed." *Century Magazine,* vol. 31 (April 1886), pp. 193–204.

"Ulysses S. Grant Visits Japan, 1879." *American History Illustrated,* vol. 16, no. 3 (1981), pp. 36–45.

Utley, Robert M. "The Celebrated Peace Policy of General Grant." *North Dakota History,* vol. 20 (July 1953), pp. 121–42.

Van Arsdol, Ted. "History of the 14th Infantry." *Clark County History,* vol. 56 (1971), pp. 12–26.

Vaughn, William P. "Separate and Unequal: The Civil Rights Act of 1875 and Defeat of the School Integration Clause." *Southwestern Social Science Quarterly,* vol. 48, no. 2 (1967), pp. 146–54.

Venable, Charles S. "The Campaign from the Wilderness to Petersburg." *Southern Historical Society Papers,* vol. 14. Richmond: D. Appleton, 1876–1944, pp. 522–42.

——. "General Lee in the Wilderness Campaign." In Clarence C. Buel and Robert U. Johnson, eds., *Battles and Leaders of the Civil War,* vol. 4. New York: Century, 1888. pp. 240–46.

Vincent, John H. "The Inner Life of Ulysses S. Grant." *The Chautauquan; a Weekly Newsmagazine,* vol. 30 (October 1899–March 1900), pp. 634–38.

Walke, Henry. "The Gun-boats at Belmont and Fort Henry." In Clarence C. Buel and Robert Underwood Johnson, eds., *Battles and Leaders of the Civil War,* vol. 1. New York: Century, 1888, pp. 358–67.

Walker, Peter F. "Command Failure: The Fall of Forts Henry and Donelson." *Tennessee Historical Quarterly,* vol. 16, no. 4 (December 1957), pp. 258–79.

Walker, Robert S. "Pyramids at Chickamauga." *Chattanooga Times,* September 13, 1936.

Wallace, Harold L. "Lew Wallace's March to Shiloh Revisited." *Indiana Magazine of History,* vol. 59, no. 1 (1963), pp. 19–30.

Wallace, Lew. "The Capture of Ft. Donelson." In Clarence C. Buel and Robert Underwood Johnson, eds., *Battles and Leaders of the Civil War.* New York: T. Yoseloff, 1956. vol. 1. pp. 398–428.

Waltmann, Henry G. "Circumstantial Reformer: President Grant and the Indian Problem." *Arizona and the West,* vol. 13, no. 4 (1971), pp. 323–42.

Warren, James R. "Ulysses S. Grant's Experiences in the West: The Review of a New Book by a Bellevue Author." *Portage,* vol. 8, no. 3 (1987), pp. 19–20.

Watrous, A. E. "Grant as His Son Saw Him. An Interview with Colonel Frederick D. Grant About His Father." *McClure's Magazine,* vol. 2 (May 1894), pp. 515–42.

Webb, Alexander S. "Through the Wilderness." In Clarence C. Buel and Robert U. Johnson, eds., *Battles and Leaders of the Civil War,* vol. 4. New York: T. Yoseloff, 1956, pp. 152–69.

Weber, F. A. "The U.S. Grant Cabin." (Letter). *Missouri Historical Review,* vol. 15 (1920–21), pp. 413–15.

Weigley, Russell F. "Philip H. Sheridan: A Personality Profile." *Civil War Times Illustrated,* vol. 7 (July 1968), pp. 4–11.

Well, E. T. "The Campaign and Battle of Chickamauga." *United Service Magazine,* vol. 16, new series (September 1896), pp. 205–33.

Welles, Gideon. "Lincoln's Triumph in 1864." *Atlantic Monthly,* vol. 41 (March 1878), pp. 90–106.

Wert, Jeffrey D. "One Great Regret: Cold Harbor." *Civil War Times Illustrated,* vol. 17, no. 10 (1979), pp. 23–35.

West, Elliott. "Jerome B. Chaffee and the Mc Cook-Elbert Fight." *Colorado Magazine,* (1969), pp. 145–65.

West, Richard S., Jr. "Gunboats in the Swamps: The Yazoo Pass Expedition." *Civil War History,* vol. 9, no. 2 (1963), pp. 157–66.

Westwood, Howard C. "Ben Butler Takes on a Chaplain." *Civil War History,* vol. 35, no. 3 (1989), pp. 225–38.

——. "Grant's Role in Beginning Black Soldiery." *Illinois Historical Journal,* vol. 79, no. 3 (1986), pp. 197–212.

——. "The Singing Wire Conspiracy: Manipulation of Men and Messages for Peace." *Civil War Times Illustrated,* vol. 19, no. 8 (1980), pp. 30–35.

——. "Ulysses S. Grant and Benjamin Butler in the Appomattox Campaign." *Illinois Historical Journal,* vol. 84, no. 1 (1991), pp. 39–54.

——. "The Vicksburg Campaign: The Raiment of the Gods of War, May 13–14, 1863." *Journal of Mississippi History,* vol. 44, no. 3 (1982), pp. 193–216.

——. "The Vicksburg/Port Hudson Gap—The Pincers Never Pinched." *Military Affairs,* vol. 46, no. 3 (1982), pp. 113–19.

White, Patrick H. "Civil War Diary of Patrick H. White." J. E. Boos, ed. *Journal of the Illinois State Historical Society,* vol. 15 (1922–23), pp. 640–47.

Whitner, Robert L. "Grant's Peace Policy on the Yakima Reservation." *Pacific Northwest Quarterly*, vol. 50, no. 4 (1959), pp. 135–43.

Whitsell, Robert D. "Military and Naval Activity Between Cairo and Columbus." *Register of the Kentucky Historical Society*, vol. 61, no. 2 (1963), pp. 107–21.

Wiener, Frederick B. "Decline of a Leader, the Case of General Meade." *Infantry Journal*, vol. 45 (November–December 1938), pp. 535–42.

Wiggins, Sarah Woolfolk. "The 'Pig-Iron' Kelley Riot in Mobile." *Alabama Review*, vol. 23 (1970).

Wilcox, Cadmus. "Lee and Grant in the Wilderness." *Annals of the War Written by Leading Participants North and South*. Issued by *Philadelphia Weekly Times*, 1879.

Wilds, George B. "Battle of Belmont, Mo." *Confederate Veteran*, vol. 32, pp. 485–86.

Wilkin, Jacob W. "Personal Recollections of General U.S. Grant." *Transactions of the Illinois State Historical Society for the Year 1907*, vol. 12. Springfield: Illinois State Historical Society, 1908.

Wilson, James Grant. "Washington—Lincoln and Grant. An Address by General James Grant Wilson Delivered Before the New York Society of the Order of the Founders and Patriots of America, April 6, 1903." New York: New York Society, 1903.

Wilson, James H. "Reminiscences of General Grant." *Century Magazine*, vol. 30 (October 1885), pp. 947–54.

Wilson, Ronald G. "Meeting at the McLean House." *American History Illustrated*, vol. 22, no. 5 (1987), pp. 46–49.

Wilson, Thomas. "Feeding a Great Army." *Civil War Times Illustrated*, vol. 4, no. 10 (1966), pp. 28–35.

Winschel, Terrence J. "The Guns at Champion Hill (Part II)." *Journal of Confederate History*, vol. 6 (1990), pp. 94–105.

Wister, Owen. "Ulysses S. Grant." In M. A. DeWolfe Howe, ed., *Beacon Biographies of Eminent Americans*. Boston: Houghton Mifflin, 1911.

Wodehouse, Lawrence. "Alfred B. Mullett and His French Style of Government Buildings." *Journal of the Society of Architectural Historians*, vol. 31 (March 1972), pp. 22–37.

——. "General Grant Architecture in Jeopardy." *Historic Preservation*, vol. 22 (1970), pp. 20–26.

Woodward, C. Vann. "The Lowest Ebb." *American Heritage*, vol. 8, no. 3 (1957), pp. 52–57, 106–9.

Woodworth, Charles Louis. *A Commemorative Discourse on the Work and Character of Ulysses Simpson Grant*. Pamphlet. Boston, 1885.

Wright, A. O. *General Grant's Military Service*. Pamphlet.

Wright, Marcus Joseph. "The Battle of Belmont." *Southern Historical Society Papers*, vol. 16, pp. 69–82.

——. "Personal Recollections of General Grant." *Confederate Veteran*, vol. 17, pp. 400–2.

Wynn, B. L. "Lee Watched Grant at Locust Grove." *Confederate Veteran*, vol. 21 (1913), pp. 68–73.

Zilversmit, Arthur. "Grant and the Freedmen." In Robert H. Abzug and Stephen E. Maizlish, eds., *New Perspectives on Race and Slavery in America: Essays in Honour of Kenneth M. Stampp*. Lexington: University Press of Kentucky, 1986, pp. 128–45.

Zornow, William F. "When the Czar and Grant Were Friends." *Mid-American*, vol. 43, no. 3 (1961), pp. 164–81.

Acknowledgments

Many people have helped to make this book possible. My greatest debts are to Professor James McPherson of Princeton and Professor John Simon, editor of the Grant Papers. When I began to write *Grant,* I did not know either. Yet when I approached them, both unhesitatingly gave generously of their time and expertise. Without their assistance, the book could scarcely have been written.

I am also indebted to the three institutions where this book was written: the University of Toronto, Princeton University, and Marshall University. The support and encouragement I received from colleagues and students was invaluable.

Because I write in longhand, I am eternally grateful to those who can read my scribbling and convert it into typescript. My special debt is to Cora Curtis and Beth Tappan of Marshall University; Pamela Long of Princeton; and Hyla Levy of the University of Toronto.

To those who have read the manuscript, I am indebted beyond measure. Their comments have improved the book enormously, and I thank them for the time and effort they generously granted. They include: William Beaney, Thomas Bergquist, David Bronskill, George Carter, Paul Ehrlich, Joanne Feld, Alan Gould, Sanford Lakoff, Tara Lambert, Sam Mok, William Nelson, John Seaman, Jeannie Sears, Monica Shin, and Jenny Weber. The bibliography was prepared by Joanne Wong and David Jenkins. The copy editing was done by Frederick Chase. Philip Metcalf supervised the production editing.

To Robert Bender, my editor at Simon & Schuster, and to his assistant, Johanna Li, I am indebted beyond measure. Finally, as always, I am grateful to Elizabeth Kaplan, my agent at the Ellen Levine Agency. Elizabeth and Bob have seen the work since its inception, and have never hesitated to offer advice and encouragement.

Index